T0180452

Information Systems Development

Information Systems Development

Towards a Service Provision Society

Edited by

GEORGE A. PAPADOPOULOS
University of Cyprus
Nicosia, Cyprus

GREGORY WOJTKOWSKI
Boise State University
Boise, ID, USA

WITA WOJTKOWSKI
Boise State University
Boise, ID, USA

STANISLAW WRYCZA
University of Gdansk
Sopot, Poland

JOZE ZUPANCIC
University of Maribor
Kranj, Slovenia

 Springer

Editors

George A. Papadopoulos
Department of Computer Science
University of Cyprus
Nicosia 1678, Cyprus
george@cs.ucy.ac.cy

Gregory Wojtkowski
Department of Information Technology
College of Business and Economics
Boise State University
Boise, ID 83725-1615, USA
gwojtkow@boisestate.edu

Wita Wojtkowski
Department of Information Technology
College of Business and Economics
Boise State University
Boise, ID 83725-1615, USA
riswoj2t@cobfac.boise.state.edu
riswojt2@cobfac.idbsu.edu

Stanislaw Wrycza
Department of Information
  Systems
University of Gdansk
Krajowej 119121, Poland
swrycza@univ.gda.pl

Joze Zupancic
University of Maribor
Kranj SI-4000, Slovenia
joze.zupancic@fov.uni-mb.si

ISBN 978-1-4899-7757-1   e-ISBN 978-0-387-84810-5
DOI 10.1007/b137171
Springer New York Dordrecht Heidelberg London

Springer is part of Springer Science + Business Media (www.springer.com)

Preface

This two-volume book is the published proceedings of the 17th International Conference on Information Systems Development (ISD2008) that was hosted by the Department of Computer Science of the University of Cyprus at the Annabelle Hotel, Paphos, Cyprus, from 25–27 August 2008. The theme of the conference was "Towards a Service Provision Society".

In total, 131 delegates from 34 different countries registered for the conference, making it a truly international event. Papers presented at the conference strongly reflected the conference theme. Of 165 papers submitted, 99 were presented at the conference, representing an acceptance rate of approximately 60%. All papers were peer reviewed by 3 or 4 referees (a total of 543 review reports were submitted, corresponding to an average of 3.29 reviews per paper).

Over the course of 3 days, 28 paper sessions were held, covering a range of areas such as "Information Systems Engineering & Management", "Business Systems Analysis & Design", "Intelligent Information Systems", "Agile and High-Speed Systems Development Methods", "Enterprise Systems Development & Adoption", "Public Information Systems Development", "Information Systems Development Education", "Information Systems Development in Developing Nations", "Legal and Administrative Aspects of Information Systems Development", "Information Systems Research Methodologies", "Service-Oriented Analysis and Design of Information Systems", "IT Service Management", "Philosophical and Theoretical Issues in Information Systems Development", "Model-driven Engineering in ISD", "Human Computer Interaction (HCI) in Information Systems Development". The book is organised by order of the conference sessions.

While all the presented papers were of high quality, we have selected two of them to share the *Best Paper Award*. The first one is "Modeling the contribution of enterprise architecture practice to the achievement of business goals" by Marlies van Steenbergen and Sjaak Brinkkemper. The second one is "Why can't we bet on ISD Outcomes?: ISD 'Form' as a Predictor of Success" by Mike Newman, Shan L Pan and Gary Pan. Furthermore, to acknowledge the quality of the reviews he completed, the quality of the paper he submitted, his role as a track and session chair, and his general participation in the conference, we have awarded an *Overall Contribution Award* to Michael Lang of the National University of Ireland, Galway. Details of these awards can be found on the conference Web site at http://isd2008.cs.ucy.ac.cy.

Our gratitude is extended first to all those who attended and authored work for the conference. The contribution of the International Program Committee was invaluable in identifying track chairs and reviewers to commit to doing vital work. While volunteering to host a conference is a highly personal undertaking, without support it would be impossible. Thus, we wish to thank our sponsors for their financial support and other aid.

The ISD conference community has developed over the years a real sense of collegiality and friendliness, perhaps unusually so for a conference. At the same time it has been a stimulating forum where a free exchange of views and perspectives is encouraged. Perhaps what brings the community together is a belief that the process of systems development is important; whether it is systematic or structured or improvised or spontaneous, there is something about the process and the outcomes that excites us. We form a spectrum of thought from those who see the activity as somewhat scientific to others that see it as wholly sociological; we span a divide between abstract and conceptual, to hard code and artefacts – somewhere in-between lies the truth. If our work is to make a meaningful contribution to both practice (by teaching students) and research (by sharing our experiences and studies with others), then hopefully this conference will have done a little of the former and much for the latter.

George A. Papadopoulos
Gregory Wojtkowski
Wita Wojtkowski
Stanislaw Wrycza
Joze Zupancic

</div>

Contents

4. Improving Knowledge Management in the Health Service: Re-Engineering Approach Towards Successful Implementation

Regina Gyampoh-Vidogah and Robert Moreton

5. Accounting, Charging and Billing for Dynamic Service Composition Chains

F.J. Rumph, G.H. Kruithof and G.B. Huitema

6. Web Service Execution and Monitoring in Integrated Applications in Support of Business Communities

Rares M. Chiriacescu, Alexandru Szőke, Sorin Portase and Monica Florea

7. Scrutinizing UML Activity Diagrams

Sabah Al-Fedaghi

8. Integration of Weakly Heterogeneous Semistructured Data

George Feuerlicht, Jaroslav Pokorný, Karel Richta and Narongdech Ruttananontsatean

9. Investigating the Applicability of Structural Analysis Techniques in Distributed Systems

Karen Hamber, Graham Low and Greg Stephens

10. Web-Based Systems Development: Analysis and Comparison of Practices in Croatia and Ireland

Michael Lang and Dijana Plantak Vukovac

11. The Solution Space Organization: Linking Information Systems Architecture and Reuse

Salem Ben Dhaou Dakhli

12. Designing Cognition-Adaptive Human–Computer Interface for Mission-Critical Systems

Yu Shi, Eric Choi, Ronnie Taib and Fang Chen

13. Conceptual Web Users' Actions Prediction for Ontology-Based Browsing Recommendations

Tarmo Robal and Ahto Kalja

14. Web Portal Design: Employment of a Range of Assessment Methods

Andrina Granić, Ivica Mitrović and Nikola Marangunić

15. A Proposed Extension of the CODAM Model for Human Attention

Kleanthis C. Neokleous, Marios N. Avraamides, Andreas A. Ioannides, Costas K. Neocleous and Christos N. Schizas

16. Aligning Service Requirements with Business Strategy: A Proposed Stakeholder Value Model for SOA

H. Luthria, A. Aurum, G.C. Low and F.A. Rabhi

25. Specification and Verification of an Agent-Based Auction Service

Amelia Badica and Costin Badica

26. A Practical Environment to Apply Model-Driven Web Engineering

Maria Jose Escalona, J.J. Gutiérrez, F. Morero, C.L. Parra, J. Nieto, F. Pérez, F. Martín and A. Llergo

27. An Approach to Generating Program Code in Quickly Evolving Environments

Linas Ablonskis

28. Devising a New Model-Driven Framework for Developing GUI for Enterprise Applications

Pierre Akiki

29. Model-Driven Development of Decision Support Systems: Tackling the Variability Problem

María Eugenia Cabello and Isidro Ramos

30. Foundations on Generation of Relationships Between Classes Based on Initial Business Knowledge

Oksana Nikiforova and Natalya Pavlova

31. Expert Systems Development Through Software Product Lines Techniques

María Eugenia Cabello and Isidro Ramos

32. Framework for Using Patterns in Model-Driven Development

Picek Ruben and Strahonja Vjeran

33. Ontology of Domain Analysis Concepts in Software System Design Domain

Robertas Damaševičius

34. An Anonymity Revocation Technology for Anonymous Communication

Giannakis Antoniou, Lynn Batten and Udaya Parampalli

47. Design Patterns Application in the ERP Systems Improvements

Bojan Jovičić and Siniša Vlajić

48. Determinants of Open Source Software Adoption – An Application of TOE Framework

Tomasz Przechlewski and Krystyna Strzała

49. Hybridization of Architectural Styles for Integrated Enterprise Information Systems

Lina Bagusyte and Audrone Lupeikiene

50. Proposing a Formalised Model for *Mindful* Information Systems Offshoring

Gabriel J. Costello, Chris Coughlan, Brian Donnellan and Andreas Gadatsch

51. Negotiating a Systems Development Method

Fredrik Karlsson and Karin Hedström

56. Current Trends in Testing XMLMSs

Irena Mlynkova

57. Service-Oriented Software Development Value Chain and Process

Yuan Rao, Shumin Lu and ZhiXiong Yang

58. A Content Markup Language for Data Services

Noviello C., Acampa P. and Mango Furnari M.

59. Organizational Learning Literature Visited – Fresh Lenses to Study Practices in ISD Organizations?

Pasi Juvonen and Päivi Ovaska

60. Contract Negotiations Supported Through Risk Analysis

Sérgio A. Rodrigues, Marco A. Vaz and Jano M. Souza

61. Instantiating Software Processes: An Industry Approach

Peter Killisperger, Georg Peters, Markus Stumptner and Thomas Stückl

62. A Language for Modelling Trust in Information Systems

Kamaljit Kaur Bimrah, Haralambos Mouratidis and David Preston

67. Method Engineering: A Formal Description

Ali Sunyaev, Matthias Hansen and Helmut Krcmar

68. A Methodological Framework for Enterprise Information System Requirements Derivation

Albertas Caplinskas and Lina Paškevičiūtė

69. Measuring Communication Heterogeneity Between Multiple Web-Based Agents

Maricela Bravo and Martha Coronel

70. Requirements Modeling with Agent Programming

Aniruddha Dasgupta, Aneesh Krishna and Aditya K. Ghose

71. BPMN, Toolsets, and Methodology: A Case Study of Business Process Management in Higher Education

Balbir S. Barn and Samia Oussena

72. Incorporating Spatial Data into Enterprise Applications

Pierre Akiki and Hoda Maalouf

73. The Development of Mobile Services – The Impact of Actor Groups in the Standardization Process

Endre Grøtnes and Steinar Kristoffersen

74. Reducing Health Cost: Health Informatics and Knowledge Management as a Business and Communication Tool

Regina Gyampoh-Vidogah, Robert Moreton and David Sallah

75. The Information Architecture of E-Commerce: An Experimental Study on User Performance and Preference

Wan Abdul Rahim Wan Mohd Isa, Nor Laila Md Noor and Shafie Mehad

76. Computer Literacy of Population 50+ – A Case from Slovenia

Barbara Vogrinec

77. A Taxonomy of E-Health Standards to Assist System Developers

Emma Chávez, Padmanabhan Krishnan and Gavin Finnie

78. Mobile Location-Based Services for Trusted Information in Disaster Management

Lemonia Ragia, Michel Deriaz and Jean-Marc Seigneur

79. Resolution of Complexity in ISD Projects

Jill Owen and Henry Linger

84. Exploring the Role of Method Rationale in the Context of Teaching Information Systems Development Methods

Kai Wistrand, Fredrik Karlsson and Pär J. Ågerfalk

85. Four Levels of Moral Conflict in ISD

Tero Vartiainen

93. IS Degrees – Sociotechnical or Technosocial?

Jenny Coady and Rob Pooley

94. Teaching Medium-Sized ERP Systems – A Problem-Based Learning Approach

Axel Winkelmann and Martin Matzner

95. Statistical Analysis for Supporting Inter-Institutional Knowledge Flows in the Context of Educational System

Renate Strazdina, Julija Stecjuka, Ilze Andersone and Marite Kirikova

96. Using Agile Methods? – Expected Effects

Stefan Cronholm

97. Finding Categories and Keywords in Web Services

Christian Kop, Doris Gälle and Heinrich C. Mayr

98. MEDNET: Telemedicine via Satellite Combining Improved Access to Health-Care Services with Enhanced Social Cohesion in Rural Peru

Dimitrios Panopoulos, Ilias Sachpazidis, Despoina Rizou, Wayne Menary, Jose Cardenas and John Psarras

99. Why Can't We Bet on ISD Outcomes: ISD "Form" as a Predictor of Success

Mike Newman, Shan L. Pan and Gary Pan

Conference Organisation

The 17th International Conference on Information Systems Development was hosted by the Department of Computer Science of the University of Cyprus at the Annabelle Hotel, Paphos, 25–27 August from 2008. The organization and management of such a major international conference requires the collaboration and dedication of very many people. We are especially grateful to our international programme committee who voluntarily gave their time to review the submissions. The excellent standard of papers contained within this volume bears testimony to the diligence and rigour of the peer review process. We are also very appreciative of the efforts of all the conference officers and the tremendous support provided by the local organizing committee.

Programme Chair

George A. Papadopoulos, University of Cyprus, Nicosia, Cyprus

Organising Chair

George A. Papadopoulos, University of Cyprus, Nicosia, Cyprus

International Advisory Committee

Gregory Wojtkowski	Boise State University	USA
Wita Wojtkowski	Boise State University	USA
Stanislaw Wrycza	University of Gdansk	Poland
Joze Zupancic	University of Maribor	Slovenia

Local Organising Committee

Pyrros Bratskas	University of Cyprus	Cyprus
Pericles Cheng	University of Cyprus	Cyprus
Constantinos Kakousis	University of Cyprus	Cyprus
Nearchos Paspallis	University of Cyprus	Cyprus

Track Chairs
Information Systems Engineering & Management

Andreas Andreou	University of Cyprus	Cyprus

Business Systems Analysis & Design

Michael Lang   National University of Ireland, Galway   Ireland

Intelligent Information Systems

Spyridon Likothanassis   University of Patras   Greece
Efstratios Georgopoulos   Technological Educational Institute of Kalamata   Greece
Adam Adamopoulos   Demokritus University of Thrace   Greece

Agile and High-Speed Systems Development Methods

Outi Salo   VTT Technical Research Centre of Finland   Finland
Geir Hanssen   SINTEF   Norway

Enterprise Systems Development & Adoption

Angelika I. Kokkinaki   University of Nicosia (formerly Intercollege)   Cyprus

Public Information Systems Development

George A. Papadopoulos   University of Cyprus   Cyprus
Yannis Charalabidis   National Technical University of Athens   Greece
Costas Kalaboukas   Singular-Logic   Greece

Information Systems Development Education

Aimilia Tzanavari   University of Cyprus   Cyprus

Information Systems Development in Developing Nations

John Traxler   University of Wolverhampton   UK

Legal and Administrative Aspects of Information Systems Development

Rónán Kennedy   National University of Ireland, Galway   Ireland

Information Systems Research Methodologies

Malgorzata Pankowska   University of Economics in Katowice   Poland

Service-Oriented Analysis and Design of Information Systems

Remigijus Gustas	Karlstad University	Sweden
William Song	University of Durham	UK
Stefanos Mavromoustakos	European University	Cyprus

IT Service Management

Vjeran Strahonja	University of Zagreb	Croatia

Philosophical and Theoretical Issues in Information Systems Development

Björn Niehaves	University of Münster	Germany
Karlheinz Kautz	Copenhagen Business School	Denmark

Model-driven Engineering in ISD

Maria Jose Escalona	University of Sevilla	Spain

Human Computer Interaction (HCI) in Information Systems Development

Andrina Granic	University of Split	Croatia

International Programme Committee

Witold Abramowicz	Economic University	USA
Par Agerfalk	University of Limerick	Sweden
Aiste Aleksandraviciene	Kaunas University of Technology	Lithuania
Patricia Alexander	Department of Informatics	South Africa
Alla Anohina	Riga Technical University	Latvia
Dace Apshvalka	Riga Technical University	Latvia
David Avison	ESSEC Business School	France
Per Backlund	University of Skovde	Sweden
Akhilesh Bajaj	The University of Tulsa	USA
Michal Barla	Slovak University of Technologies	Slovakia
Balbir Barn	Thames Valley Univesity	UK
Chris Barry	National University of Ireland	Galway
Rabih Bashroush	Queen's University of Belfast	UK
Richard Baskerville	Georgia State University	USA
Dragana Becejski-Vujaklija	Faculty of Organizational Sciences	Serbia
Peter Bellström	Karlstad University	Sweden
Paul Beynon-Davies	Cardiff Business School	UK

El Hassan Bezzazi	University de Lille 2	France
Juris Borzovs	Information Technology Institute	Latvia
Alena Buchalcevová	University of Economics	Chzech Rep
Dumitru Burdescu	University of Craiova	Romania
Frada Burstein	Monash University	Australia
Dave Bustard	University of Ulster	UK
Rimantas Butleris	Kaunas University of Technology	Lithuania
Albertas Caplinskas	Institute of Mathematics and Informatics	Lithuania
Sven Carlsson	Lund University	Sweden
Michael Cavanagh	Balmoral Consulting	UK
Dubravka Cecez-Kecmanovic	University of New South Wales	Australia
Antanas Cenys	Semiconductor Physics Institute	Lithuania
Jenny Coady	Heriot-Watt University	UK
Gerry Coleman	Dundalk Institute of Technology	Ireland
Andy Connor	Auckland University of Technology	New Zealand
Alfredo Cuzzocrea	University of Calabria	Italy
Darren Dalcher	Middlesex University	UK
Gert-Jan de Vreede	University of Nebraska at Omaha	USA
Jack Downey	LERO	Ireland
Xiaofeng Du	Durham University	UK
Jim Duggan	University of Alabama	USA
Sean Duignan	Galway-Mayo Institute of Technology	Ireland
Dale Dzemydiene	Law University	Lithuania
Erki Eessaar	Tallinn University of Technology	Estonia
Owen Eriksson	Dalarna University College	Sweden
Chris Exton	University of Limerick	Ireland
George Feuerlicht	University of Technology	Australia
Gavin Finnie	Bond University	Australia
Marko Forsell	SESCA Technologies	Finland
Odd Fredriksson	Karlstad University	Sweden
Andreas Gadatsch	FH Bonn-Rhein-Sieg	Germany
Prima Gustiene	Karlstad University	Sweden
Javier Jesús Gutiérrez Rodríguez	University of Sevilla	Spain
Samer Hanna	Durham University	UK
G Harindranath	University of London	UK
Igor Hawryszkiewycz	University of Technology Sydney	Australia
Jonas Hedman	Copenhagen Business School	Sweden
Kevin Heffernan	Galway-Mayo Institute of Technology	Ireland
Markus Helfert	Dublin City University	Ireland
Ola Henfriddson	Viktoria Institute	Sweden
Alan Hevner	University of South Florida	USA
Val Hobbs	Murdoch University	Australia
Mairéad Hogan	National University of Ireland	Galway
Jesper Holck	Copenhagen Business School	Denmark
Helena Holmstrom	University of Limerick	Ireland

Magda Huisman	North-West University	South Africa
Sergey Ivanov	George Washington University	USA
Mirjana Ivanovic	University of Novi Sad	Serbia
Letizia Jaccheri	Norwegian University of Science and Technology	Norway
Christian Janiesch	SAP Australia Pty Ltd	Australia
Arek Januszewski	University of Technology and Agriculture	Poland
Björn Johansson	Copenhagen Business School	Danmark
Pasi Juvonen	South Carelia Polytechnic	Finland
Roland Kaschek	Massey University	New Zealand
Marite Kirikova	Riga Technical University	Latvia
Gabor Knapp	Budapest Univ of Technology & Economics	Hungary
Christian Kop	Alpen-Adria Universitaet Klagenfurt	Austria
John Krogstie	Norwegian University of Science and Technology	Norway
Gert Kruithof	TNO Information and Communication Techno	Netherlands
Marian Kuras	Cracow Academy of Economics	Poland
Rein Kuusik	Economic University	Estonia
Sergei Kuznetsov	Institute for System Programming of Russia	Russia
Vitus Lam	The University of Hong Kong	Hong Kong
John Lannon	University of Limerick	Ireland
Przemyslaw Lech	University of Gdansk	Poland
Mauri Leppänen	University of Jyvaskyla	Finland
Mikael Lind	University of Boras	Sweden
Henry Linger	Monash University	Australia
Graham Low	University of New South Wales	Australia
Audrone Lupeikiene	Institute of Mathematics and Informatics	Lithuania
Kalle Lyytinen	Case Western Reserve University	USA
Dear Leszek A. Maciaszek	Macquarie University	Australia
Brenda Mallinson	Rhodes University	South Africa
Yannis Manolopoulos	Aristotle University Greece	Greece
Dorina Marghescu	Turku Centre for Computer Science/ Åbo A	Finland
Lars Mathiassen	Georgia State University	USA
John McAvoy	University College Cork	Ireland
Orla McHugh	National University of Ireland	Galway
Anna Medve	University of Pannonia Veszprem	Hungary
Regis Meissonier	Management School Montpellier	France
Ulf Melin	Linkoping University	Sweden
Elisabeth Metais	CNAM University	France
Peter Middleton	Queen's University of Belfast	UK
Owen Molloy	National University of Ireland	Galway
Robert Moreton	University of Wolverhampton	UK
Haris Mouratidis	University of East London	UK
Malcolm Munro	Durham University	UK
Anatoli Nachev	National University of Ireland	Galway
Pavol Navrat	Slovak University of Technology	Slovakia
Géza Németh	Budapest University of Technology and Economics	Hungary

Lina Nemuraite	Kaunas Technical University	Lithuania
Edephone Nfuka	Stockholm University	Sweden
Peter Axel Nielsen	Aalborg University	Denmark
Anders G. Nilsson	Karlstads University	Sweden
Ovidiu Noran	Griffith University	Australia
Jacob Norbjerg	Copenhagen Business School	Denmark
Gerard o'Donovan	Cork Institute of Technology	Ireland
Päivi Ovaska	South Carelia Polytechnic	Finland
Jill Owen	University College Canberra	Australia
Caroline Pade	Rhodes University	South Africa
Oscar Pastor	University of Valencia	Spain
Natalja Pavlova	Riga Technical University	Latvia
Anne Persson	University of Skoevde	Sweden
John Soren Pettersson	Karlstad University	Sweden
George Philip	The Queen's University of Belfast	UK
Maritta Pirhonen	University of Jyvaskyla	Finland
Alain Pirotte	University of Louvain	Belgium
Dijana Plantak Vukovac	University of Zagreb	Croatia
Tomasz Plata-Przechlewski	Gdansk University	Poland
Jaroslav Pokorny	Charles University	Czech Rep.
Norah Power	University of Limerick	Ireland
Adam Przybylek	Gdansk University	Poland
Boris Rachev	Technical University of Varna	Bulgaria
Isidro Ramos Salavert	Universitat Politecnica de Valencia	Spain
Birger Rapp	Linkoping University	Sweden
Vaclav Repa	Prague University of Economics	Czech Rep
Karel Richta	Czech Technical University	Czech Rep
Peter Rittgen	University College of Boras	Sweden
Tarmo Robal	Tallinn University of Technology	Estonia
Kamel Rouibah	Kuwait University	Kuwait
Alice Rupe	AR IT Solutions	USA
Adriana Schiopiu Burlea	University of Craiova	Romania
Dirk Schreiber	FH Bonn-Rhein-Sieg	Germany
Maha Shaikh	London School of Economics	UK
Peretz Shoval	Ben-Gurion University	Israel
Keng Siau	University of Nebraska – Lincoln	USA
Klaas Sikkel	University of Twente	Netherlands
Rok Skrinjar	University of Ljubljana	Slovenia
Piotr Soja	Cracow University of Economics	Poland
Tor Stalhane	Norwegian University of Science and Technology	Norway
Ioannis Stamelos	Aristotle University	Greece
Larry Stapleton	Waterford Institute of Technology	Ireland
Odd Steen	Lund University	Sweden
Darijus Strasunskas	NTNU	Norway
Uldis Sukovskis	Riga Technical University	Latvia

Bo Sundgren	Mid Sweden University	Sweden
Janis Tenteris	Riga Technical University	Latvia
Domonkos Tikk	Budapest University of Technology and Economics	Hungary
Anna Trifonova	Norwegian University of Science and Technology	Norway
Tuure Tuunanen	The University of Auckland	New Zealand
Tero Vartiainen	Turku School of Economics	Finland
Olegas Vasilecas	Vilnius Gediminas Technical University	Lithuania
Damjan Vavpotic	University of Ljubljana	Slovenia
Anna Vindere	Latvia University of Agriculture	Latvia
Jiri Vorisek	Prague University of Economics	Czech Rep
Gottfried Vossen	University of Munster	Germany
Taujanskas Vytautas	Kaunas University of Technology	Lithuania
Hongbing Wang	Southeast University	China
Leoni Warne	Defence Science and Technology Organisation	Australia
Dave Wastell	University of Salford	UK
Christine Welch	University of Portsmouth	UK
Wita Wojtkowski	Boise State University	USA
Carson C. Woo	University of British Columbia	Canada
Stanislaw Wrycza	University of Gdansk	Poland
Heitor Augustus Xavier Costa	Universidade Federal de Lavras	Brazil
Chia-Hui Yen	Wu-Feng Institute of Technology	Taiwan
Gian Piero Zarri	Universite Paris 4/Sorbonne	France
Jozef Zurada	University of Louisville	USA

Contributors

Linas Ablonskis
Department of Information Systems
Kaunas University of Technology
Kaunas, Lithuania

P. Acampa
Istituto di Cibernetica "E. Caianiello"
Consiglio Nazionale delle Ricerche, Italy

Adam V. Adamopoulos
Pattern Recognition Laboratory
Department of Computer Engineering and Informatics
and
University of Patras Artificial Intelligence Research Center
   (U.P.A.I.R.C.)
University of Patras
Patras, Greece
and
Medical Physics Laboratory
Department of Medicine
Democritus University of Thrace
Alexandroupolis, Greece

Pär J. Ågerfalk
Department of Information Science,
Uppsala University, Uppsala, Sweden
and
Lero – The Irish Software Engineering Research Centre
Limerick, Ireland

Pierre Akiki
Department of Computer Science
Notre Dame University
Zouk Mosbeh, Lebanon

Sabah Al-Fedaghi
Computer Engineering Department
Kuwait University
Kuwait

Christos Nikolaos Anagnostopoulos
Cultural Technology and Communication Department
University of the Aegean
Aegean, Greece

Ilze Andersone
Department of Systems Theory and Design
Riga Technical University
Riga, Latvia

Alla Anohina
Department of Systems Theory and Design
Riga Technical University
Riga, Latvia

Giannakis Antoniou
The University of Melbourne
Victoria, Australia

Nicolas Arni-Bloch
University of Geneva
Geneva, Switzerland

Aybüke Aurum
School of Information Systems, Technology and Management
The Australian School of Business
University of New South Wales
Sydney, Australia

Jan Helge Austbø
Department of Information Systems
University of Agder
Kristiansand, Norway

Marios N. Avraamides
Department of Psychology
University of Cyprus
Nicosia, Cyprus

Amelia Badica
Department of Business Information Systems
University of Craiova
Craiova, Romania

Costin Badica
Department of Software Engineering
University of Craiova
Craiova, Romania

Lina Bagusyte
Software Engineering Department
Institute of Mathematics and Informatics
Vilnius, Lithuania

Balbir S. Barn
Middlesex University
London, UK

Hamish T. Barney
School of Information Systems Technology and Management
The University of New South Wales
Sydney, Australia

R. Bashroush
ECIT
Queen's University of Belfast
Belfast, UK

Lynn Batten
Deakin University
Victoria, Australia

Jörg Becker
European Research Center for Information Systems
University of Münster
Münster, Germany

Peter M. Bednar
School of Computing
University of Portsmouth
Portsmouth, UK
and
Department of Informatics
Lund University
Lund, Sweden

Peter Bellström
Department of Information Systems
Karlstad University
Karlstad, Sweden

Yolande Berbers
University of Leuven
Leuven, Belgium

Solvita Bērziša
Faculty of Computer Science and Information Technology
Riga Technical University
Riga, Latvia

Kamaljit Kaur Bimrah
Innovative Informatics, School of Computing and Technology
University of East London
London, UK

Pyrros Bratskas
Department of Computer Science
University of Cyprus
Nicosia, Cyprus

Maricela Bravo
Informatique Department
Morelos State Polytechnic University
México

Ramunas Brazinskas
Department of Informatics
Klaipeda University
Klaipeda, Lithuania

Sjaak Brinkkemper
Institute of Information and Computer Sciences
University of Utrecht
Utrecht, The Netherlands

Dumitru Dan Burdescu
Department of Software Engineering
University of Craiova
Craiova, Romania

María Eugenia Cabello
Polytechnic University of Valencia
Valencia, Spain

Albertas Caplinskas
Software Engineering Department
Institute of Mathematics and Informatics
Vilnius, Lithuania

Jose Cardenas
Department of Informatics
DIRESA Junin
Peru

Yannis Charalabidis
Decision Support Systems Laboratory
National Technical University of Athens
Athens, Greece

Karel Charvat
Czech Centre for Science and Society
Praha, Czech Republic

Deren Chen
College of Computer Science
Zhejiang University
Zhejiang, China

Fang Chen
National Information and Communication Technology
Australia (NICTA) Australian
Technology Park
Sydney, Australia

Rares M. Chiriacescu
SIVECO Romania
Bucharest, Romania

Eric Choi
National Information and Communication Technology
Australia (NICTA) Australian
Technology Park
Sydney, Australia

Emma Chávez
School of Information Technology
Bond University
Australia
and
Departamento de Ing. Informática
Universidad Católica de la Ssma Concepción
Chile

Jenny Coady
Department of Computer Science
Heriot Watt University
Edinburgh, Scotland

Martha Coronel
Informatique Department
Morelos State Polytechnic University
México

Gabriel J. Costello
Galway-Mayo Institute of Technology
Galway, Ireland
and
Centre for Innovation and Structural Change
National University of Ireland
Galway, Ireland

Fanny Coudert
Interdisciplinary Centre for Law and ICT
K.U. Leuven
Leuven, Belgium

Chris Coughlan
Hewlett-Packard Galway Limited
Ireland

Stefan Cronholm
Department of Management and Engineering
Linköping University
Linköping, Sweden

Stephen Cummins
Department of Computer Science
Durham University
Durham, UK

Salem Ben Dhaou Dakhli
CERIA Laboratory
Paris-Dauphine University
France

Robertas Damaševičius
Software Engineering Department
Kaunas University of Technology
Kaunas, Lithuania

Aniruddha Dasgupta
Decision System Laboratory
School of Computer Science and Software Engineering
University of Wollongong
Wollongong, NSW, Australia

E. de-Miguel
Lingüística General
Facultad de Filología
Universidad Complutense de Madrid
Madrid, Spain

Michel Deriaz
Advanced Systems Group
Centre Universitaire d'Informatique
University of Geneva
Geneva, Switzerland

Yun Ding
European Media Laboratory GmbH
Heidelberg, Germany

Brian Donnellan
National University of Ireland
Galway, Ireland

Xiaofeng Du
Computer Science Department
University of Durham
Durham, North Carolina
USA

M.J. Escalona
University of Seville
Seville, Spain

A. Fernández-Pampillón
Lingüística General
Facultad de Filología
Universidad Complutense de Madrid
Madrid, Spain

George Feuerlicht
University of Technology
Sydney
Australia
and
University of Economics
Prague, Czech Republic

Gavin Finnie
School of Information Technology
Bond University
Australia

Monica Florea
SIVECO Romania
Bucharest, Romania

Andreas Gadatsch
Bonn-Rhein Sieg University of Applied Science
Sankt Augustin, Germany

Joe Geldart
Department of Computer Science
Durham University
Durham, UK

Efstratios F. Georgopoulos
Pattern Recognition Laboratory
Department of Computer Engineering and Informatics
and
University of Patras Artificial Intelligence
    Research Center (U.P.A.I.R.C.),
University of Patras
Patras, Greece
and
Technological Educational Institute of Kalamata
Kalamata, Greece

Aditya K. Ghose
Decision System Laboratory
School of Computer Science and
    Software Engineering
University of Wollongong
Wollongong, NSW
Australia

Jānis Grabis
Faculty of Computer Science and
    Information Technology
Riga Technical University
Riga, Latvia

Andrina Granić
Faculty of Science
University of Split
Split, Croatia

Janis Grundspenkis
Department of Systems Theory and Design
Riga Technical University
Riga, Latvia

Endre Grøtnes
Department of Informatics
University of Oslo
Oslo, Norway

Remigijus Gustas
Department of Information Systems
Karlstad University
Karlstad, Sweden

Prima Gustiene
Department of Information Systems
Karlstad University
Karlstad, Sweden

J.J. Gutiérrez
University of Seville
Seville, Spain

Regina Gyampoh-Vidogah
Care Services Improvement Partnership
Department of Health
London, UK

Doris Gälle
Institute of Applied Informatics
Alpen-Adria-Universität Klagenfurt
Austria

Karen Hamber
School of Information Systems, Technology and Management
University of New South Wales
Sydney, Australia

Matthias Hansen
Department of Informatics
Technische Universität München
München, Germany

Karin Hedström
MELAB
Swedish Business School
Örebro University
Örebro, Sweden

Petr Horak
Wirelessinfo
Litovel, Czech Republic

Xiaoming Hu
European Media Laboratory GmbH
Heidelberg, Germany

Mats-Åke Hugoson
Department of Informatics
Jönköping International Business School
Jönköping, Sweden

G.B. Huitema
TNO Information and Communication Technology
Groningen, The Netherlands

Andreas A. Ioannides
Laboratory for Human Brain Dynamics
Brain Science Institute
Saitama, Japan

V. Iordan
Computer Science Department
West University of Timisoara
Timisoara, Romania

Björn Johansson
Copenhagen Business School
Center for Applied Information and Communication
    Technology
Frederiksberg, Denmark

Bojan Jovičić
Delta Sport
Belgrade, Serbia

Darius Jurkevicius
Department of Information Systems
Faculty of Fundamental Sciences
Vilnius Gediminas Technical University
Vilnius, Lithuania

Pasi Juvonen
South Karealia University of Applied Sciences
Imatra, Finland

Judith Kabeli-Shani
Department of Industrial and Management Engineering
Shenkar College of Engineering and Design
Ramat-Gan, Israel

Konstantinos Kakousis
Department of Computer Science
University of Cyprus
Nicosia, Cyprus

Ahto Kalja
Department of Computer Engineering
Tallinn University of Technology
Estonia

Fredrik Karlsson
MELAB
Swedish Business School
Örebro University
Örebro, Sweden

Nina Kilbrink
Department of Information Systems
Karlstad University
Karlstad, Sweden

Peter Killisperger
Competence Center Information Systems
University of Applied Sciences – München
Germany
and
Advanced Computing Research Centre
University of South Australia
Adelaide, Australia

Marite Kirikova
Department of Systems Theory and Design
Riga Technical University
Riga, Latvia

Christian Kop
Research Group Application Engineering
Institute for Applied Informatics
Alpen-Adria-Universität Klagenfurt
Austria

V. Koufi
Department of Digital Systems
University of Piraeus
Piraeus, Greece

Helmut Krcmar
Department of Informatics
Technische Universität München
München, Germany

Aneesh Krishna
Decision System Laboratory
School of Computer Science and Software Engineering
University of Wollongong
Wollongong, NSW, Australia

Padmanabhan Krishnan
School of Information Technology
Bond University
Australia

Steinar Kristoffersen
Faculty of Computer Science
Østfold University College
Halden, Norway

G.H. Kruithof
TNO Information and Communication Technology
Groningen, The Netherlands

Fenareti Lampathaki
Decision Support Systems Laboratory
National Technical University of Athens
Athens, Greece

Michael Lang
Business Information Systems Group
Cairnes School of Business and Economics
National University of Ireland
Galway, Ireland

Mauri Leppänen
University of Jyväskylä
Computer Science and Information Systems
Jyväskylä, Finland

Spiridon D. Likothanassis
Pattern Recognition Laboratory
Department of Computer
    Engineering and Informatics
and
University of Patras Artificial Intelligence Research Center
    (U.P.A.I.R.C.)
University of Patras
Patras, Greece

Henry Linger
Faculty of Information Technology
Monash University
Melbourne, Australia

A. Llergo
Servicio Andaluz de Salud
Seville, Spain

Bogdan Logofatu
CREDIS Department
University of Bucharest
Bucharest, Romania

Graham C. Low
Information Systems, Technology and Management
The Australian School of Business
University of New South Wales
Sydney, Australia

Shumin Lu
The Key Lab of Electronic-Commerce
Xi'an Jiaotong University
China

Audrone Lupeikiene
Software Engineering Department
Institute of Mathematics and Informatics
Vilnius, Lithuania

H. Luthria
Information Systems, Technology and Management
The Australian School of Business
University of New South Wales
Sydney, Australia

C. López-Alonso
Lingüística General
Facultad de Filología
Universidad Complutense de Madrid
Madrid, Spain

Hoda Maalouf
Department of Computer Science
Notre Dame University
Zouk Mosbeh
Lebanon

F. Malamateniou
Department of Digital Systems
University of Piraeus
Piraeus, Greece

M. Mango Furnari
Istituto di Cibernetica "E. Caianiello"
Consiglio Nazionale delle Ricerche
Italy

F. Martín
Servicio Andaluz de Salud
Seville, Spain

Nikola Marangunić
Faculty of Science
University of Split
Split, Croatia

Martin Matzner
European Research Center
    for Information Systems
University of Muenster
Münster, Germany

Heinrich C. Mayr
Institute of Applied Informatics
Alpen-Adria-Universität Klagenfurt, Austria

Wayne Menary
GeoPac
Coventry, UK

Marian Cristian Mihaescu
Department of Software Engineering
University of Craiova
Craiova, Romania

Ivica Mitrović
Arts Academy
University of Split
Split, Croatia

Irena Mlynkova
Department of Software Engineering
Charles University
Prague, Czech Republic

F. Morero
Sun Microsystems
Madrid, Spain

Robert Moreton
School of Computing and IT
University of Wolverhampton
Wolverhampton, UK

Haralambos Mouratidis
Innovative Informatics, School
   of Computing and Technology
University of East London
London, UK

Malcolm Munro
Computer Science Department
University of Durham
Durham, North Carolina
USA

Oliver Müller
European Research Center for Information Systems
University of Münster
Münster, Germany

Costas K. Neocleous
Department of Mechanical Engineering
Cyprus University of Technology
Lemesos, Cyprus

Kleanthis C. Neokleous
Department of Computer Science
University of Cyprus
Nicosia, Cyprus

Mike Newman
Manchester Business School
The University of Manchester
Manchester, UK
and
Copenhagen Business School
Copenhagen, Denmark

J. Nieto
Servicio Andaluz de Salud
Seville, Spain

Oksana Nikiforova
Department of Applied Computer Science
Riga Technical University
Riga, Latvia

Evita Nikitenko
Department of Systems Theory and Design
Riga Technical University
Riga, Latvia

Anders G. Nilsson
Department of Information Systems
Karlstad University
Karlstad, Sweden

Ovidiu Noran
School of ICT
Griffith University Australia
Australia

Md Noor Nor Laila
Department of System Science
Universiti Teknologi MARA
Malaysia

C. Noviello
Istituto di Cibernetica "E. Caianiello"
Consiglio Nazionale delle Ricerche
Italy

Samia Oussena
Thames Valley University
London, UK

Päivi Ovaska
South Karealia University of Applied Sciences
Imatra, Finland

Jill Owen
School of Business, Australian
   Defence Force Academy
University of New South Wales
Sydney, Australia

Tero Päivärinta
Department of Information Systems
University of Agder
Kristiansand, Norway

Gary Pan
Singapore Management University
Singapore

Shan L. Pan
Department of Information Systems
National University of Singapore
Singapore

Malgorzata Pankowska
University of Economics
Katowice, Poland

Dimitrios Panopoulos
Decision Support Systems Laboratory
National Technical University of Athens
Athens, Greece

George A. Papadopoulos
Department of Computer Science
University of Cyprus
Nicosia, Cyprus

D. Papakonstantinou
Department of Digital Systems
University of Piraeus
Piraeus, Greece

Udaya Parampalli
The University of Melbourne
Victoria, Australia

C.L. Parra
Servicio Andaluz de Salud
Seville, Spain

Lina Paškevičiūtė
Software Engineering Department
Institute of Mathematics and Informatics
Vilnius, Lithuania

Nearchos Paspallis
Department of Computer Science
University of Cyprus
Nicosia, Cyprus

Natalya Pavlova
Department of Applied Computer Science
Riga Technical University
Riga, Latvia

F. Pérez
Servicio Andaluz de Salud
Seville, Spain

D. Petcu
Institute e-Austria Timisoara
Timisoara, Romania
and
Computer Science Department
West University of Timisoara
Timisoara, Romania

Georg Peters
Department of Computer
  Science and Mathematics
University of Applied Sciences – München
München, Germany

Manuele Kirsch Pinheiro
University of Leuven
Leuven, Belgium

G. Pita
Lingüística General
Facultad de Filología
Universidad Complutense de Madrid
Madrid, Spain

Dijana Plantak Vukovac
Department of Information Systems Development
Faculty of Organization and Informatics
University of Zagreb
Varazdin, Croatia

Jaroslav Pokorný
Charles University of Prague
Prague, Czech Republic

Rob Pooley
Department of Computer Science
Heriot Watt University
Edinburgh, Scotland

Sorin Portase
SIVECO Romania
Bucharest, Romania

David Preston
Innovative Informatics, School
  of Computing and Technology
University of East London
London, UK

Tomasz Przechlewski
Katedra Informatyki Ekonomicznej
Uniwersytet Gdański
Piaskowa, Poland

John Psarras
Decision Support Systems Laboratory
National Technical University of Athens
Athens, Greece

F.A. Rabhi
Information Systems,
Technology and Management
The Australian School of Business
University of New South Wales
Sydney, Australia

Lemonia Ragia
Advanced Systems Group
Centre Universitaire d'Informatique
University of Geneva
Geneva, Switzerland

Jolita Ralyté
University of Geneva
Geneva, Switzerland

Isidro Ramos
Polytechnic University of Valencia
Valencia, Spain

Yuan Rao
College of Software Engineer
Xi'an Jiaotong University
China

Karel Richta
Charles University of Prague
Prague, Czech Republic

Despoina Rizou
Department Cognitive Computing
   and Medical Imaging
Fraunhofer IGD
Darmstadt, Germany

Tarmo Robal
Department of Computer Engineering
Tallinn University of Technology
Estonia

Sérgio A. Rodrigues
COPPE/UFRJ – Computer Science Department
Graduate School of Engineering
Federal University of Rio de Janeiro
Brazil

Picek Ruben
Department of Information System Development
Faculty of Organization and Informatics
University of Zagreb
Varaždin, Croatia

F.J. Rumph
TNO Information and Communication Technology
Groningen, The Netherlands

Narongdech Ruttananontsatean
Kanchanaburi Rajabhat University
Thailand

Øystein Sæbø
Department of Information Systems
University of Agder
Kristiansand, Norway

Ilias Sachpazidis
Department Cognitive Computing
   and Medical Imaging
Fraunhofer IGD
Darmstadt, Germany

Tomas Salamon
Department of Information Technologies
University of Economics
Prague, Czech Republic

David Sallah
University of Wolverhampton
Wolverhampton, UK

Demetrios Sarantis
Decision Support Systems Laboratory
National Technical University of Athens
Athens, Greece

Svein Sundfør Scheie
The Norwegian Post and Telecommunications
   Authority
Norway

Christos N. Schizas
Department of Computer Science
University of Cyprus
Nicosia, Cyprus

Ulf Seigerroth
Department of Informatics
Jönköping International Business School
Jönköping, Sweden

Jean-Marc Seigneur
Advanced Systems Group
Centre Universitaire d'Informatique
University of Geneva
Geneva, Switzerland

Mehad Shafie
Department of System Science
Universiti Teknologi MARA
Malaysia

Yu Shi
National Information and Communication Technology Australia
   (NICTA) Australian
Technology Park
Sydney, Australia

Peretz Shoval
Department of Information Systems Engineering
Ben-Gurion University
Beer-Sheva, Israel

Aidas Smaizys
Department of Informatics
Klaipeda University
Klaipeda, Lithuania

Darja Solodovnikova
University of Latvia
Riga, Latvia

William Song
Computer Science Department
University of Durham
Durham, North Carolina
USA

Jano M. Souza
COPPE/UFRJ – Computer Science Department
Graduate School of Engineering
Federal University of Rio de Janeiro
Brazil
and
DCC-IM/UFRJ – Computer Science Department
Mathematics Institute
Federal University of Rio de Janeiro
Brazil

I. Spence
ECIT
Queen's University of Belfast
Belfast, UK

Julija Stecjuka
Department of Systems Theory and Design
Riga Technical University
Riga, Latvia

Greg Stephens
School of Information Systems, Technology and Management
University of New South Wales
Sydney, Australia

Renate Strazdina
Department of Systems Theory and Design
Riga Technical University
Riga, Latvia

Krystyna Strzała
Katedra Ekonometrii
Uniwersytet Gdański
Poland

Markus Stumptner
Advanced Computing Research Centre, University of South
    Australia
Adelaide, Australia

Thomas Stückl
Siemens Corporate Technology, Software and System Processes
Munich, Germany

Ali Sunyaev
Department of Informatics
Technische Universität München
München, Germany

Alexandru Szőke
SIVECO Romania
Bucharest, Romania

Ronnie Taib
National Information and Communication Technology
    Australia (NICTA) Australian
Technology Park
Sydney, Australia

Christos Tsiakaliaris
Planet
Athens, Greece

Katariina Valtonen
University of Jyväskylä
Computer Science and Information Systems
Jyväskylä, Finland

Yves Vanrompay
University of Leuven
Leuven, Belgium

Marlies van Steenbergen
Architecture and Business Solutions
Sogeti Netherlands B.V
The Netherlands

Tero Vartiainen
Pori Unit
Turku School of Economics
Turku, Finland

Olegas Vasilecas
Department of Informatics
Klaipeda University
Klaipeda, Lithuania
and
Department of Information Systems
Faculty of Fundamental Sciences
Vilnius Gediminas Technical University
Vilnius, Lithuania

G. Vassilacopoulos
Department of Digital Systems
University of Piraeus
Piraeus, Greece

Marco A. Vaz
COPPE/UFRJ – Computer Science Department
Graduate School of Engineering
Federal University of Rio de Janeiro
Brazil

Strahonja Vjeran
Department of Information System Development
Faculty of Organization and Informatics
University of Zagreb
Varaždin, Croatia

Siniša Vlajić
Faculty of Organizational Sciences
University of Belgrade
Belgrade, Serbia

Martin Vlk
Help Forest
Sumperk, Czech Republic

Barbara Vogrinec
CPZ-International
Centre for Knowledge Promotion
Ljubljana, Slovenia

Eftichia Vovoli
Cultural Technology and Communication Department
University of the Aegean
Aegean, Greece

Jürgen Vöhringer
Research Group Application Engineering
Institute for Applied Informatics
University of Klagenfurt
Austria

Wan Mohd Isa Wan Abdul Rahim
Department of System Science
Universiti Teknologi MARA
Malaysia

Christine Welch
Department of Strategy and Business Systems
University of Portsmouth Business School
Portsmouth, UK

Evi Werkers
Interdisciplinary Centre for Law and ICT
K.U. Leuven
Leuven, Belgium

Axel Winkelmann
European Research Center for Information Systems
University of Muenster
Münster, Germany

Kai Wistrand
MELAB
Swedish Business School
Örebro University
Örebro, Sweden

ZhiXiong Yang
Zhongguancun Haidian High-Technique Park Postdoc
    Workstation-UFIDA Substation
Beijing, China

Gian Piero Zarri
Virthualis
Politecnico di Milano
Milano, Italia

1

Designing Class Methods from Dataflow Diagrams

Peretz Shoval and Judith Kabeli-Shani

Abstract

A method for designing the class methods of an information system is described. The method is part of FOOM – Functional and Object-Oriented Methodology. In the analysis phase of FOOM, two models defining the users' requirements are created: a conceptual data model – an initial class diagram; and a functional model – hierarchical OO-DFDs (object-oriented dataflow diagrams). Based on these models, a well-defined process of methods design is applied. First, the OO-DFDs are converted into transactions, i.e., system processes that supports user task. The components and the process logic of each transaction are described in detail, using pseudocode. Then, each transaction is decomposed, according to well-defined rules, into class methods of various types: basic methods, application-specific methods and main transaction (control) methods. Each method is attached to a proper class; messages between methods express the process logic of each transaction. The methods are defined using pseudocode or message charts.

Keywords Information systems design · System development methodology · Object-oriented development · Class diagram · Dataflow diagram · Transactions · Methods

1. Introduction

In early information systems development (ISD) methodologies, e.g., DeMarco [2], the emphasis of analysis was on describing the functional requirements by conducting top-down functional decomposition of the system using dataflow diagrams (DFDs) or similar techniques. In the early 1990s, with the emergence of the object-oriented (OO) approach to ISD, methodologies such as Coad and Yourdon [1] and Shlaer and Mellor [7] suggested a different analysis concept: object-driven; that is, the analysis phase emphasized on finding the domain objects, while the design phase concentrated on identifying the services (functions) which these objects provide. Aiming at solving problems raised by the vast amount of methods developed during the OO era, UML (unified modeling language) was adopted by OMG as its standard for modeling OO systems [5]. UML consists of a set of models and notations for describing various products of the OO system's lifecycle.

UML's main tool for describing the user/functional requirements is use cases. A use case is presented as an interaction between the system and an entity external to it called "actor," for the purpose of achieving the actor's goal. Many methodologies that use UML prescribe functional modeling via use case diagrams. Methodologies that adopt use cases as the requirements description tool are called "use case-driven" meaning that the development process is derived by describing, realizing, and developing use case scenarios. Use cases are usually used to develop sequence diagrams (or some semantically equivalent diagram). A sequence diagram illustrates the objects that participate in a use case and the messages that pass between them over time. A message sent to an object, possibly with parameters, is assumed to invoke a certain

Peretz Shoval · Department of Information Systems Engineering, Ben-Gurion University, Beer-Sheva 84105, Israel   **Judith Kabeli-Shani** · Department of Industrial and Management Engineering, Shenkar College of Engineering and Design, Ramat-Gan 2526, Israel

G.A. Papadopoulos et al. (eds.), *Information Systems Development*, DOI 10.1007/b137171_1,
© Springer Science+Business Media, LLC 2009

method that performs a certain task. Hence, the design of the class methods begins with use cases, from which sequence diagrams are developed, which in turn "give birth" to methods that are attached to class objects.

Evidently, use cases replaced DFDs as a tool for defining the user/functional requirements. Without going into the pros and cons of each of these techniques, we only mention that DFDs emphasize a top-down, functional decomposition process. Contrarily, in the use case-driven approach, decomposition is almost completely absent; use cases are treated just one at a time. Many researchers question the effectiveness of use cases as a functional modeling tool. For example, Dobing and Parsons [3] identified several problems with both the application of use cases and their theoretical underpinnings. In their opinion, the roles and values of use cases are unclear and debatable, and the process of moving forward from use cases to classes does not appear to be clearly defined or articulated. Similarly, Irwin and Turk [4] claimed that it is unclear whether or to what extent use cases provide a good basis from which to move forward to other conceptual models. They say that use case modeling grammar is deficient with respect to representing system structure and system decomposition, and hypothesize that analysts using use case will have difficulty mapping them to classes, relationships, and/or behaviors. Jeyaray and Sauter [6] compared DFDs and use case diagrams in an experimental setting. They found out that for users trained in methodologies, DFDs were more effective than use case diagrams for requirements verification, and that overall, DFD seems to be superior to use cases as an analysis tool, since DFDs provide more information. With DFDs, users are more likely to identify a misunderstanding in the current process or a misspecification of user requirements in the proposed system. Moreover, DFD allow better verification of the models.

FOOM is an ISD methodology that combines the functional and OO approaches [9, 10]. As opposed to UML-based methodologies, it utilizes DFDs as a tool for functional modeling, thus enabling a top-down functional decomposition process. At the analysis phase of FOOM, user requirements are defined by two complementing modeling activities: (a) conceptual data modeling, producing an *initial class diagram* - a class diagram consisting of data classes, attributes, and relationships, but not methods (yet); (b) functional modeling producing object-oriented DFDs (OO-DFDs), i.e., hierarchical DFDs that instead of data stores as in traditional DFDs, include data classes, which are already defined in the initial class diagram. These two products synchronize, i.e., it is verified that every class appearing in the class diagram also appear in the OO-DFDs and vice versa.

The products of the analysis phase are used to design the system. The products of the design phase include: (a) a complete class diagram, which includes additional classes, and all the classes' methods; (b) detailed descriptions of the methods; (c) the user interface – a menus tree; (d) the input/output screens and reports.

This chapter concentrates on one part of the design phase – design of the class methods. It describes how the class methods of an application, which express the "behavior" of a system, are defined and designed systematically, beginning from the users' requirements expressed in OO-DFDs.

The rest of this chapter is structured as follows: Section 2 provides an overview of the design phase of FOOM. Section 3 defines transactions and describes how they are derived from OO-DFDs and their top-level description. Section 4 shows how the description of each transaction is detailed and then decomposed into various class methods and messages. Section 5 summarizes this chapter.

2. Overview of the Design Phase of FOOM

At the end of the design phase, the following products are obtained: (a) A complete class diagram, which includes, in addition to the data classes already defined in the analysis phase, the Menus, Forms (inputs), and Reports (outputs) classes. Each class includes, in addition to its attributes and various relationships to other classes, a list of its methods. (b) Detailed descriptions of the class methods. The methods are described using pseudocode or message charts. (c) The user interface in the form of a menus tree. (d) The input and output screens/reports. These products enable programming of the system in an object-oriented environment. In order to create these products, the design phase is carried out in the following stages:

(a) Identification of the transactions of the system and creation of their top-level descriptions.
(b) Design of user interface – a menus tree – and addition of the Menus class.
(c) Design of the input and output screen/reports and addition of the Forms and Reports classes.
(d) Detailed design of transactions and their decomposition into class methods.

3. Transactions and Their Descriptions

3.1. What is a Transaction?

A transaction is an independent system process that performs a task for a user in order to assist her in the completion of a business process. The concept "transaction" is taken from Shoval's *ADISSA* methodology [8]. (Note: "transaction" in FOOM and ADISSA is not a database transaction but rather a broader concept, more similar to a business transaction. One may find similarity between "transaction" and "use case," but unlike use case, a transaction includes not only functions but also data classes and various external/user entities, and their interactions.) A transaction may include a series of activities/functions performed by the system in support of a user's task. All transactions taken together express the functionality of the system. Transactions will eventually become application programs, which are built of class methods. In a business/organizational information system, most of the transactions are activated (run) by users who interact with the system using the menus interface. But some transactions may be activated "automatically" by the system, at certain points of time or time intervals, or as a result of real-time events.

The first task in the design of transactions is to "extract" them from the functional model, i.e., the OO-DFDs, identify their components, and describe their general (top-level) process logic. Later on, each top-level description will be detailed and then decomposed into various methods that will be attached to proper classes.

In terms of OO-DFD components, a transaction consists of one or more elementary (i.e., non-decomposable) functions which are connected directly to each other by dataflows. It also includes the classes and external entities that are connected to those functions. A transaction must include at least one external entity, which signifies that it can be activated. An external entity can be a user-entity (U), a time-entity (T), or a real-time entity (R).

The existence of a user-entity in a transaction means that the transaction will be activated by a user; it is called *user transaction* and is the most common type of transaction in information systems. The existence of a time-entity means that the transaction will be activated "automatically" on a certain point of time or time interval, as indicated on the triggering dataflow; this type of transaction is called *time transaction*. The existence of a real-time entity means that the transaction will be activated by a certain device that senses the environment and sends messages to the transaction which interprets the messages in real time and reacts accordingly; this type is called *real-time transaction*. Real-time transactions are rare in business-oriented information systems. Some transactions may be "mixed"; for example, a transaction that includes both a user entity and a time entity indicating that it can be activated both by a user who interacts with the system and "automatically" on predefined time intervals.

Figure 1.1 shows an example of one OO-DFD of an application (the *Apartments Building* System). This diagram includes functions dealing with payment of fees – sub-functions of the general function "Payment of Fees" that is included in the root DFD of this system. (More OO-DFDs are not shown due to space limit.)

The OO-DFD in Fig. 1.1 includes five transactions: one consists of function 1.1 (add/update tenant) and the elements connected to it, i.e., user-entity U1 (Tenant) and class C1 (Apartment); another transaction consists of functions 1.2 and 1.3; the third consists of functions 1.4 and 1.5; the fourth consists of function 1.6; and the fifth consists of functions 1.7 and 1.8. Note that each of the transactions includes not only the functions but also the classes and external entities connected to those functions.

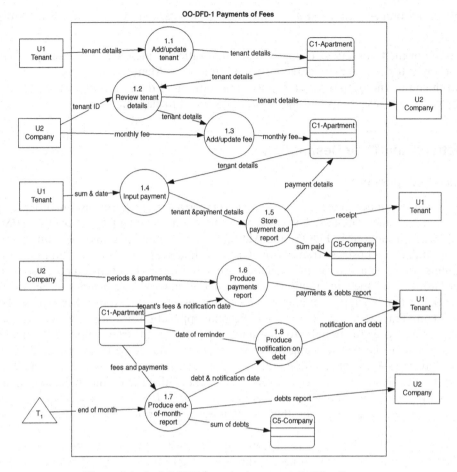

Figure 1.1. An OO-DFD from the Apartments Building System.

The diagram of one of the transactions is presented separately in Fig. 1.2. The meaning of this transaction can be interpreted as follows (at this stage the description is "informal"): it will be activated, possibly by an authorized officer/clerk of the company, to enable input and storage of a (possibly monthly) payment obtained from a tenant. Once activated, function 1.4 will present an input screen to enable the user/operator input an apartment ID or family name; this is signified by the dataflow from U1 to function

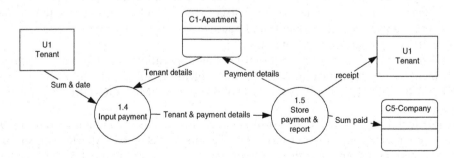

Figure 1.2. A Transaction extracted from the OO-DFD.

1.4. Based on that, the function will find the object of that tenant in the Apartments class C1. Consequently, the input screen will enable the user input the payment details (e.g., amount paid, date, and payment method). Then function 1.4 will trigger function 1.5 and pass to it these details. Function 1.5 will update the Apartment object with the payment details; then it will update the total payments received in the Company object (in this example, Company is a singular class), and finally it will produce a receipt to be delivered/sent to the tenant.

3.2. Top-Level Descriptions of Transactions

Note that a transaction diagram only details its components and the possible flows of data to and from its functions, but it does not necessarily prescribe specific process logic. Sometimes, the meaning of a transaction may be interpreted in different ways. The analyst, in cooperation with the user, should determine and define the specific process logic of each transaction. Various techniques can be used to define process logic; we opt to use pseudocode. In this stage we only create a general, top-level description of each transaction; later on, this description will be more detailed, and eventually it will be decomposed into proper class methods.

A top-level description of a transaction describes the transaction in general terms. The description consists of two types of commands: (a) commands defining the main activities that the transaction performs; (b) commands defining the process logic according to which the activities are performed.

The commands that define the main activities of a transaction are based on its functions and the other components as follows:

- Each function of the transaction translates to a command "execute function..." followed by the function number and name.
- Each dataflow from a user entity to a function translates to a command "input from U..." followed by the entity number and name and dataflow name.
- Each dataflow from a function to a user entity translates to a command "output to U..." followed by the entity number and name and dataflow name.
- Each dataflow from a class to a function translates to a command "read from C..." followed by the class number and name and the dataflow name.
- Each dataflow from a function to a class translates to a command "write to C..." followed by the class number and name and dataflow name.
- Each dataflow from a function to the next function translates to a command "move to F..." followed by the function number and dataflow name.

As said, the process logic of the transaction is defined using the "standard" structured-programming patterns, i.e., sequence, condition (branch), and iteration (loop). Here is an example of top-level descriptions of the above transaction:

Begin transaction 1.4/5 *(the transaction number is arbitrary; it is simply a concatenation of its function numbers)*
Input from U1-Tenant: Apartment number or family name
Read from C1-Apartments: tenant details *(the function finds and retrieves the apartment object)*
If not found then present error message and ask user to input again apartment ID
Else input from U1-Tenant: payment details *(the exact details are specified in the data dictionary)*
    Execute F1.4 Input payment *(actually, this function does the previous activities; it is brought here just for the completeness of the description)*
    Move to F1.5: tenant and payment details
    Execute F1.5: Store payment and report *(actually, this function does the following activities; again, it is brought just for the completeness of the description)*
    Write to C1-Apartment: payment details
    Write to C5-Company: sum paid
    Output to U1-Tenant: receipt
End transaction.

4. Detailed Design of Transactions and Class Methods

4.1. Steps in the Design of Transaction and Class Methods

In the first step, we convert the top-level description of each transaction into a *detailed description*. A detailed description of a transaction is expressed in pseudocode, and it details the various procedures performed by the transaction, as derived from the process logic of its elementary functions and the dataflows between the functions and the external entities and classes.

In the second step, the detailed description of each transaction is "decomposed" into various procedures; some of these procedures are defined as methods, which are removed from the main transaction description, attached to proper classes, and replaced by messages to those methods. The remaining parts of the transaction are defined as the "main" method of the transaction; this method is attached to a "control" class named Transactions. Eventually, each transaction of the system consists of a "main" method, which includes messages to other methods that are attached to proper classes.

When a user works with a system, he actually browses the menus; once he selects a bottom-level menu item, actually a message will be sent to the Transactions class, which will activate the desired Transaction method. That method will execute according to its internal process logic; during the execution, it may send a message to a certain method of certain class; that method will execute its "share" of the transaction, and may possibly send messages to other class methods, and so on – till the execution of the transaction ends.

4.2. From Top-Level to Detailed Transaction Descriptions

The transition from a top-level description of a transaction to its detailed description is based on the commands included in the initial description: every command is being either elaborated or replaced by specific commands as follows:

- Every "execute function..." command is replaced by a detailed description of the function, according to its internal process logic. The amount of detail may vary from function to function; in some cases an elementary function may be very simple and easy to describe; in other cases it may be more complex and involve various activities, conditions, loops, etc.
- Every "input from U..." command is replaced by a reference to an input screen or a different input device, as defined for that input. Similarly, every "output to U..." command is replaced by a reference to an output screen or a different output device. Note that at this stage, all input and output screens and reports of the transactions have already been designed and possibly prototyped. More details on how this is done can be found in [9].
- Every "read from C..." is replaced by a more detailed command that includes conditions for retrieval (if any). For example, which objects and which of their attributes to retrieve. Similarly, every "write to C..." command is replaced by a more detailed command which specifies the type of the update (add, change, or delete) and its conditions, if any. (Note that the data elements (attributes) to be retrieved or updated have already been defined in a data dictionary, which specifies the data elements that are included in each dataflow.)

Here is an example of the transition from a top-level description of a transaction to its detailed description. Assume that for the "input" command included in this transaction we have already designed an input screen entitled "Payment Form," and that for the output command included in this transaction we have already designed a report "Payment Receipt." Assume that the input screen includes a scroll window displaying the apartment numbers and family names, from which the user can choose a specific apartment or family using the mouse device. This means that the entire list of apartments and families is first retrieved from the Apartments class, so that the user can choose one of them. Consequently, the rest of the input fields will "open," to enable keying in the payment details.

Begin transaction 1.4/5
Do while "update" not chosen:
Read C1-Apartments – Retrieve all apartment objects from the class and save their *apartment number* and *family name* attributes. *(Assume that thesedetails are saved in memory variables.)*
Input from U1-Tenant – Use Input "Payment Form." *(At this point only the apartment number and family name scroll window is "open," displaying apartment numbers and family names. The user chooses a number or name using the mouse device. (Note that the command "Execute F1.4..." is not detailed here; it is actually performed using the above input screen. As a result of the user's choice, the remaining windows on the screen become active; the user keys in the payment details; afterward, the user would press the "update" button.)*
End while *(the loop terminates once "update" is pressed)*
(Note also that the command "Move to F1.5..." is redundant because all data retrieved from C1 and input U1 is available within the procedure. (Similarly, "Execute F1.5..." is redundant because the update is performed by the next command "Write to C1....")
Write to C1-Apartments – Update the apartment object by adding the payment details to its respective attributes.
Write to C5-Company – Update the singular class with the paid amount. The sum is added to attribute *total annual payments from tenants.*
Output to U1-Tenant – Use Output "Payment Receipt."
End transaction.

4.3. From Detailed Descriptions of Transaction to Class Methods

In this stage, the detailed description of each transaction is "decomposed" into methods which are attached to proper classes. Before elaborating on this, let us make a distinction between two major types of methods:

- **Basic methods** enable performing the four basic operations: create, read, update, and delete (CRUD). It is assumed that every data class has basic methods.
- **Application-specific methods** are defined according to the specific needs of the application. Such methods may perform various specific tasks, beyond those which are performed by basic methods. It is possible/ reasonable that a specific method includes messages to basic methods.

Generally, the detailed description of each transaction is decomposed into methods and messages according to the following guidelines:

- A command "Input from User..." is translated into a message to the Display method of class **Forms** (whose objects are the various forms); the message will include an ID of a specific Form object. The Display method will enable feeding in the input data and will return an object containing the input values.
- A command "Output to User..." is translated into a message to the Display method of the class *Reports*; the message will include an ID of the specific Reports object and the output values. The display method will enable the display/production of the output, according to its design.
- A command "Read from Class..." is translated into a message to a *basic* method of that class that will retrieve one or more objects, according to conditions defined in the transaction. Therefore, the message will include the class name, name of the Read method, and search conditions, if any.
- A command "Write to Class..." is translated into a message to a *basic* method of that class that will perform the specific Write command, according to the transaction description. Recall that Write may mean add, update, or delete one or more objects. Hence, the message will include the class name, the name of the specific Create/Delete/Update method, and the conditions, if any.
- A detailed description of a transaction may include commands which describe a certain procedure, possibly derived from an "Execute function..." command. We need to review the procedure and

determine if it can be defined as a *specific method* that can be detached from the "main" part of the transaction and attached to one of the classes involved in the transaction. This may be a class which is used by that procedure (i.e., which the procedure retrieves from or updates). For example, assume that a certain transaction includes a procedure which updates the average grade of a student as a result of reporting a new course grade. It makes sense to define this procedure as a specific method to be attached to class *Student*.

If a procedure cannot be assigned to any class, for example, because it involves several classes, or involves no classes – just some general calculations, it remains in the transaction. The remaining parts of the transaction are, as said, defined as the "main" *method* of the transaction; this method is attached to the *Transactions* class.

The following example shows the mapping of the detailed description of the transaction into methods and messages. The example shows only the Transaction method; other methods can be described similarly. The description is brought in pseudocode; it is important to point out that this description is not as "formal" as a programming language; its aim is to provide guidelines to programmer who will program the method. Therefore, the description should also include explanations.

Begin Transaction.Method-1.4/5
Do while "update" not chosen:
    apart-numbers & family-names = Apartments.GetObjects (All)
    payment-details = Forms.Payment-Form.Display (apart-numbers & family-names)
End while
Apartments.Add payment (payment-details)
Company.Change (Add, total annual payments from tenants, sum paid)
Reports.Payment Receipt.Display
End.

Here are a few explanations:

1. The above describes the main Transaction method 1.4/5 only. As can be seen, the body of the method includes messages to other class methods.
2. The method performs a loop as long as the user does not press the "update" button of the Payments Form, i.e., - did not complete keying in the input.
3. Within the loop, a message is sent to class *Apartments* to its method *GetObjects*. The parameter "All" means that the method retrieves all apartment objects, but only their apartment numbers and family names are kept in respective memory variables. (This is not a "standard" way to define messages and parameters; as said, this notation is not formal and is mainly aimed to direct the programmers who will eventually write the programs.)
4. A message is sent to the Display method of class *Forms* in order to display its object Payment Form. The parameters apartment numbers and family names pass these data so that the receiving method can display them in the respective windows. Then the user chooses an apartment number or a family name. As result, the other input fields of the form are opened, and the user can key in the rest of the payment details. The method returns the payment details, which are kept in variables named payment details. (Note again, this is not a "formal" way to define variables; this will be done later by the programmer.)
6. After the payment data has been received, a message is sent to class *Apartments* to its method *Add payment*, with the parameter payment details. *Add payment* is assumed to be a *specific method* that has to be defined (but is not described here); its task is to add the details of the new payment to the apartment object; specifically to its attribute named *set payments*.
7. Following that, a message is sent to the Change method of *Company*. The method's parameters include type of change (Add), applicable attribute (*total annual payments from tenants*), and the sum to be added (*sum paid*).

8. Finally, a message is sent to the Display method of the Reports class in order to produce the payment receipt.

4.4. Message Charts

A message chart provides a visual presentation of a method – equivalent to a description in pseudocode. It can be viewed as a variation of a "traditional" program flowchart as it employs the same process logic patterns and the same symbols; only the class symbol is added. It signifies the class receiving a message to activate one of its methods. The midpart of the class symbol contains the name of the specific class object on which the method is to be activated; an object name is specified only if the method acts on a specific object. The lower part contains the name of activated method, its parameters, and the return value. Figure 1.3 presents a message chart of the above Transaction method.

A complete description of a complex transaction may include several massage charts: a "main" chart for the Transaction method and sub-charts for the specific methods. Being semantically equivalent, the two techniques for describing methods – pseudocode and message charts – may be used interchangeably.

5. Summary

We presented the steps of the FOOM methodology for designing and describing class methods of an application. The design of methods actually starts in the early stage of system analysis, where a conceptual data model is created in the form of an initial class diagram, and functional model is created in the form of a hierarchy of OO-DFDs. From the OO-DFDs, the transactions of the system are extracted and defined. In well-defined steps, each transaction is first described in a diagram and a top-level description; then it is

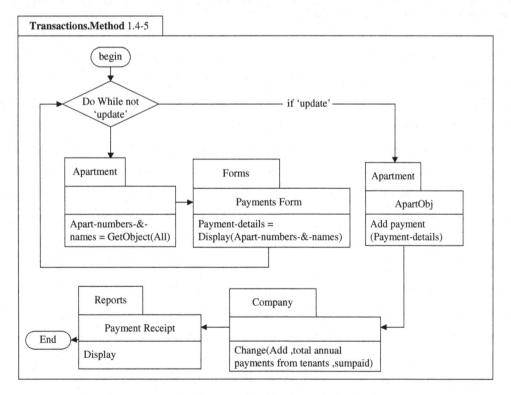

Figure 1.3. Message chart of the Transaction method.

further described in more detail, including details of the process logic, the inputs and outputs, and the reads and writes/updates of class objects. Eventually, the transaction description is decomposed into basic methods, application-specific methods, and a main Transaction method. Each method is described in pseudocode or message chart.

The FOOM methodology is easy to learn and apply. It involves three main techniques (notations) only: class diagram, dataflow diagram and pseudocode (while massage chart is an option, as it is equivalent to pseudocode). The methodology provides well-structured rules and guidelines of how to move from one stage and product to the next one. The end products of the design phase are very detailed and can be easily used to program the system in an object-oriented development environment.

References

1. Coad, O. and Yourdon, E. (1991). *Object-Oriented Design*. Prentice Hall, Englewood Cliffs, NJ.
2. DeMarco, T. (1978). *Structured Analysis and System Specifications*. Prentice-Hall, Englewood Cliffs, NJ Yourdon Press.
3. Dobing, B. and Parsons, J. (2000). Understanding the Role of Use Cases in UML: A Review and Research Agenda. *Journal of Database Management* 11(4), 28–36.
4. Irwin, G. and Turk, D. (2005). Ontological Analysis of Use Case Modeling Grammar. *Journal of the Association of Information Systems* 6(1), 1–36.
5. Jacobson, I., Booch, G. and Rumbaugh, L. (1999). *The Unified Software Development Process*. Addison-Wesley.
6. Jeyaraj, A. and Sauter, V.L. (2007). An Empirical Investigation of the Effectiveness of Systems Modeling and Verification Tools. *Communications of the ACM* 50(6), 63–67.
7. Shlaer, S. and Mellor, S.J. (1992). Modeling the World with States. Prentice Hall, Englewood Cliffs, NJ.
8. Shoval, P. (1988). ADISSA: Architectural Design of Information Systems based on Structured Analysis. *Information Systems* 13(2), pp. 193–210.
9. Shoval, P. (2007). *Functional and Object-Oriented Analysis and Design – An Integrated Methodology*. IGI Global (IDEA Group), Hershey, PA.
10. Shoval, P. and Kabeli, J. (2001). FOOM: Functional- and Object-Oriented Analysis and Design of Information Systems – an Integrated Methodology. *Journal of Database Management* 12(1), 15–25.

2

On The Human, Organizational, and Technical Aspects of Software Development and Analysis

Robertas Damaševičius

Abstract

Information systems are designed, constructed, and used by people. Therefore, a software design process is not purely a technical task, but a complex psycho-socio-technical process embedded within organizational, cultural, and social structures. These structures influence the behavior and products of the programmer's work such as source code and documentation. This chapter (1) discusses the non-technical (organizational, social, cultural, and psychological) aspects of software development reflected in program source code; (2) presents a taxonomy of the social disciplines of computer science; and (3) discusses the socio-technical software analysis methods for discovering the human, organizational, and technical aspects embedded within software development artifacts.

Keywords Socio-technical software analysis · Program comprehension · Information system development

1. Introduction

Software engineering (SE) is primarily concerned with developing software that satisfies functional and non-functional requirements, internal and external constraints, and other requirements for usability, compatibility, portability, reusability, documentation, etc. Such requirements reflect social and organizational expectations of how, where, when, and why a software system may be used. However, software developers are not influenced just by given requirements and constraints. The quality, structure, and other characteristics of the developed software systems also depend upon education of software designers and programmers, their work experience, problem-solving strategies [56], organizational structure and social relations, shared mental models [22], cultural traditions and nationality [6], worldview, religion (Eleutheros), and even such minor aspects whether a coffee machine is installed in their workplace [27]. The importance of non-technical factors in information systems development (ISD) is underscored by a survey [17], which claims that 90% of ISD project failures can be attributed to non-technical (social, organizational, etc.) factors. Therefore, a software design process is not purely a technical task, but also a social process embedded within organizational and cultural structures. These structures influence and govern the work behavior of programmers and their final products, such as source code and documentation.

The socio-technical relationships between programmers and their developed software are very complex to register and study and they cannot be replicated experimentally or described using formal models. The actions and environment of software designers are rarely directly available for study. In many cases the only available material for analysis is program source code. The knowledge gained from source code analysis despite its likely partiality and ambiguity can tell us about software design processes, its

Robertas Damaševičius • Software Engineering Department, Kaunas University of Technology, Kaunas, Lithuania

G.A. Papadopoulos et al. (eds.), *Information Systems Development*, DOI 10.1007/b137171_2,
© Springer Science+Business Media, LLC 2009

development history, and provides us with some information about its author. Comprehension of source code may allow us to understand what the original programmer had comprehended [18].

From the socio-technical perspective, the structure of software systems can be described in terms of technical relationships between software units (components, classes, units, etc.) and social relationships between software developers and their environment. By analyzing such relationships and dependencies, we can uncover and comprehend not just the links between programmers and their code, but also the relations between programmers through their code. Socio-technical software analysis [62, 63, 16, 28] tries to uncover these socio-technical dependencies by analyzing artifacts of software design processes.

The aims of this chapter are (1) to overview the psycho-socio-technical aspects of software design reflected in program source code; (2) to discuss the social disciplines of computer sciences; and (3) to focus on socio-technical software analysis methods for discovering psycho-socio-technical aspects embedded within it.

2. Non-Technical Aspects of Software Development

2.1. Social Aspects

ISD is a socio-technical process [45, 57], which is affected by personal [13] and group [68] factors. Sawyer and Guinan [58] even claim that social processes had more influence on software quality than design methodologies or automation. There is considerable evidence that software design processes are influenced by social and psychological factors [30, 4, 27, 47, 7, 19, 10, 57]. The social nature of software development and use suggests the applicability of social psychology to understanding aspects of SE.

Programmers do not exist in isolation. They usually communicate about technical aspects of their work. Several studies [25, 62] suggest that technical dependencies among software components create "social dependencies" or "networks" among software developers implementing these components. For example, when developers are working to implement a software system within the same team, the developers responsible for developing each part of the system need to interact and coordinate to guarantee a smooth flow of work [65]. Inevitably, during such coordination and communication, the designers are influenced by each others' domain knowledge, programming techniques, and styles. Such influence can be uncovered in software repositories and found in the structure of the software artifact itself [63]. Therefore, software development (certainly at a large-scale) can be considered as a fundamental social process embedded within organizational and cultural structures. These social structures enable, constrain, and shape the behavior, knowledge, programming techniques, and styles of software developers [27].

2.2. Organizational Aspects

Other socio-technical aspects that influence the work of software designer are organizational aspects (e.g., structure of organization, management strategy, business model). Such dependence is often formulated as Conway's Law: "organizations which design systems are constrained to produce designs which are copies of the communication structures of these organizations" [11]. There are numerous interpretations of Conway's Law [29, 2]. In general, Conway's Law states that any piece of software reflects the organizational structure that produced it. For example, two software components A and B cannot interface correctly with each other unless the designer of component A communicates with the designer of component B. Thus the interface structure of a software system will match the structure of the organization that has developed it.

Parnas further clarified how the relationship between organization and its product occurs during software development process. He defined a software module as "a responsibility assignment" [53], which means that the divisions of a software system correspond to a division of labor. This division of labor among different software developers creates the need to discuss and coordinate their design efforts [29]. Therefore, the analysis of software architectures can allow us to make conclusions about the organizational structure and social climate of the software designer's team.

2.3. Psychological Aspects

Software design decisions are often based on psychological rationale, rather than purely computational or physical factors [69]. Software developers frequently think about the behavior of a program in mental or anthropomorphic terms, e.g., what a component "knows" or is "trying to do," rather than formal, logical, mathematical, or physical ones [68]. About 70% of software representations are metaphorical [19], representing system behavior as physical movement of objects, as perceptual processes, or anthropomorphically by ascribing beliefs and desires to the system [30].

Software architecture is commonly considered as a structure of a software system. However, software architecture can also be analyzed as a mental model shared among software developers [51, 8, 33]. Mental models are high-level knowledge concepts of a designer that reflect both domain system structure and functions, software goals, design tasks, implementation strategies together with social, organizational, and psychological aspects that influenced the development of this system [31]. Uncovering and analyzing a mental model of a program is as important as analyzing formal or abstract models, and contributes toward a more comprehensive understanding of software development processes [44].

2.4. Cultural Aspects

To fully understand the relationship between software and programmers' thoughts and actions, we need to understand the relationships between software and programmer culture [52]. The improvement of software design processes requires understanding of cultural context, practices, and sensitivities that these processes may relate to [60]. For example, although the need of transition to a new technology to improve the process of developing quality software products is well understood, new technologies are often adopted as a "silver bullet" without any convincing evidence that they will be effective, yet other technologies are ignored despite the published data that they will be useful [70]. Cultural concepts such as *postmodernism* [50] migrate to computer science and affect software development methodologies (e.g., claiming that there are no longer correct algorithms, but only contextual decisions), emphasizing code reuse, glue programming, and scripting languages.

For a long times the adaptation of software to a different culture has been only focused on the user interface (software internationalization). However, there is a growing trend that not only software, but also its development processes and methodologies need to be adapted [40]. Methods that were thought to be "best practices" for some cultural groups turn out to be ineffective or very difficult to implement for software developers from other cultural groups [6]. Nationality also has the influence. For example, one study [6] shows that American teams are culturally well suited for iterative development and prototyping. The same study asserts that American teams seem to enjoy the chaos, often to the detriment of project progress, whereas Japanese software project teams are more suited toward waterfall development styles.

3. Social Disciplines of Computer Science

The interdisciplinary nature of aspects related to software design has led to the arrival of social branches of computer science. The taxonomy of such branches is proposed in Table 2.1. The main object of research in these disciplines is the virtual world of software and its relationship with the real world of designers and users. These disciplines reflect a multitude of diverse views toward software as an object of creativity, medium of communication and idea sharing, and an evolving entity with its own life cycle and habitat.

When people program they express a philosophy about what operations are important in the world [21]. Common propositions such as "The best way to develop software is to use object-oriented design methodology" and "GOTO statements are harmful" relate as much to SE methodologies and programming language semantics as to philosophy and epistemology. *Software epistemology* [32, 38], which analyzes forms and manifestations of knowledge in software, examines the truthfulness of these and other propositions based on authority (expert's opinion), reason (using rules of deductive logic), and

Table 2.1. Taxonomy of social disciplines of computer science.

Discipline	Object of research	Aims
Social informatics (software sociology)	Uses and consequences of IT that takes into account their interaction with institutional and cultural contexts	To understand the relationship of technological systems to social systems
Software archeology	Legacy software or software versions	To recover, analyze, and interpret legacy software artifacts including source code, documentation, and specifications
Software axiology	Value and quality of software	To analyze formal methods for evaluating software value (formal software axiology), to analyze principles of visual beauty and appeal of software (software aesthetics), and to propose elegant programming methods and techniques
Software ecology	Software environment	To analyze methods for prevention of software pollution
Software epistemology	Forms and manifestations of knowledge in software	To analyze interaction between belief, intention, justification, and action that occurs in complex software systems
Software anthropology	Practices of software engineering	To analyze the day-to-day work of software engineers in the field
Software gerontology	Software aging processes	To analyze software aging, its causes, and prevention
Software morphology	Forms and shapes of software representations	To analyze the relationships between various parts of software
Software ontology	Kinds and structures of the objects, properties, and relations in software	To analyze structure and relationships between software elements, models, and meta-models
Software psychology	Human factors in computer systems	To study, model, and measure human behavior in creating or using software systems

experience (anecdotal and experimental). Neither of these methods produces absolute truth, but rather a probable truth that depends upon human opinion or prejudice. *Software ontology* is another philosophy-oriented discipline that analyzes kinds and structures of the software objects, properties, and relations (the reader should not confuse software ontology with the ontologies, i.e., data models).

Postmodern computer languages, such as Perl, put the focus not so much onto the problem to be solved, but rather onto the person trying to solve the problem [67]. The way humans interact with software and the effect software structures and systems have on human behavior become a factor that influences software development methodologies and even the syntax of programming languages [61]. Such a human behavior in creating or using software systems is studied by *software psychology* [14, 23].

Software axiology analyzes the value and quality of software based on formal as well as aesthetic criteria (based on visual attractiveness of a software system or source code) [64]. The example of the latter can be literate programming [12], a problem which is totally irrelevant for computers, yet very important for programmers. *Software aesthetics* also has a practical level: often an elegant code runs faster, compiles better, and is more resource efficient and less prone to software bugs. Therefore, aesthetics and elegance in programming are often equivalent to good design [46].

Software archeology (or *software paleontology*) presents another view to software as a historical and material artifact and aims at the excavation of essential details about a software system sufficient to reason about it [3, 36, 34]. Archeology is a useful metaphor, because researchers try to understand what was in the minds of other software developers using only the artifacts they have left behind [41].

According to Minsky [48], computer programs are societies. The study of such societies and their relationship to human societies is a subject of *software sociology* or *social informatics* [26, 59]. Social informatics envisions information systems in general and software in particular as a web-like arrangement of technological artifacts, people, social norms, practices, and rules. As a result, the technological artifact and the social context are inseparable [42]. All stages of software's life cycle are shaped by the social context [59]. *Software anthropology* (*ethnography*) uses field study techniques in industrial software settings to study the work practices of individuals and teams during SE activities, and their material artifacts such as the tools used and the products of those tools (documentation, source code, etc.) [35, 5, 66].

Large software systems follow the same distribution laws as social systems [1, 39]. OO programs have fractal-like properties [55] similar to natural, biologic, or social systems. These observations lead to software morphology, a discipline that studies forms of shapes of software, its parts (components, objects), and their representations. *Software gerontology* continues this view toward software as living entities, which grow, mature, and age [54]. *Software ecology* [43] becomes important, where sustainable software development and prevention of software pollution (i.e., harm to environments and users) are the main issues.

4. Socio-Technical Software Analysis

4.1. Concept, Context, and Aims of Socio-Technical Software Analysis

Analysis of a domain is the essential activity in SE, or more generally, in domain engineering. The aim of domain analysis (DA) is to recognize a domain by identifying its scope and boundaries, common and variable parts, which are then used to produce domain models at different levels of abstraction (such as feature models, UML models, source code). Though the objects of socio-technical analysis (STA) are artifacts of SE process in general, STA focuses on real world rather than on a particular domain problem. That is, the objects of study are the influence of used design methods, techniques, styles, programming practices, tool usage patterns, and the designer himself, his behavior, mental models, rationale and relationship with other designers, the organizational structure of a design team and business models on developed systems, and their quality and impact on other systems.

The new emerging discipline of STA should be viewed within the context of meta-engineering and meta-design. Meta-design [24, 15] extends the traditional system design beyond the development of a specific system to include the end-user-oriented design for change, modification, and reuse. A particular emphasis is given to increasing participation of users in system design process, and evolutionary development of systems during their use time when dealing with future uses and problems unanticipated at domain analysis and system design stages. A fundamental objective of meta-design is to create socio-technical environments that empower users to engage actively in the continuous development of systems rather than use of existing systems. Rather than presenting users with closed systems, meta-design provides them with opportunities, tools, and social structures to extend the system to fit their needs. Other approaches that argue for a more active user participation in IS and software design are ETHICS [49], soft system methodology [9].

STA includes the application of other empirical methods for studying complex socio-technical relationships between designers, software systems and their environment, including the social, organizational, psychological, and technological aspects. The ultimate aim of STA is the evaluation of design methodologies, the discovery of design principles, the formalization of mental models of designers, which precede design meta-models, comparison of design metrics, comparison of design subjects (actors, designers) rather than design objects (programs), discovery and analysis of design strategies, patterns and meta-patterns, and analysis of external factors that affect software design.

4.2. Socio-Technical Software Analysis vs. Traditional Domain Analysis

The following is a result of author's observations on differences between socio-technical analysis (STA) of software systems and domain analysis (DA).

In general, analysis is the procedure by which we break down an intellectual or substantial system into parts or components. DA is a part of SE that deals with the analysis of existing complex, large-scale software systems, and other relevant information in a domain (interactions within those systems, their development history, etc.) aiming to fill a gap in the business framework where a newly designed software system should exist. DA results in the development of domain models, which are further used for developing required software system(s).

The STA methods attempt to uncover information about software engineers by looking at their produced output (source code, comments, documentation, reports) and by-products (tool usage logs, program traces, events). It deals with the analysis of models and meta-models behind these systems and their application domain rooted in the mental models of system designers and social (organizational) structure of the environment. STA aims to understand complexity, interconnectedness, and wholeness of components of systems in specific relationship to each other.

DA focuses on separation and isolation of smaller constituent parts of a system, and analyzes their interaction and relationship. STA aims at expanding its view and including other related systems and domains in order to take into account larger number of interactions involved with an object of study. It adopts a holistic approach and focuses on the interaction of the study object with other objects and its environment, including other systems, domains, and the designer himself.

Traditional DA tends to involve linear cause and effect relationships. STA aims to include the whole complex of bidirectional relationships. Instead of analyzing a problem in terms of an input and an output, e.g., we look at the whole system of inputs, processes, outputs, feedback controls, and interaction with its environment. This larger picture can typically provide more useful results than traditional DA.

Traditional DA focuses on the behavior and functionality of designed domain systems (components, entities). The result is the data that characterize domain systems (e.g., its features, aspects, characteristics, and metrics). STA continues the DA further by analyzing data and content yielded during previous analysis stages using mathematical, statistical, and/or socio-technical methods. The aim is to obtain data about data (or meta-data) that help to reveal deeper properties of software systems that are usually buried in its source code or documentation.

STA does not replace the traditional DA methods, but rather extends them for deeper analysis and domain knowledge. The results of STA (*meta-knowledge*) can be used for increasing quality of software products, improving software design processes, providing recommendations for better management of design organizations, raising the level of education, spreading good design practices and programming styles, improving workplace conditions, etc.

5. Discussion and Conclusions

Software design processes and their artifacts have many perspectives: technological, social, cultural, and psychological. The psycho-socio-technical perspectives of software and IS development provide deeper insight into the relationship among methods, techniques, tools and their usage habits, software development environment and organizational structures, and allow to highlight the analytic distinction between how people work and the technologies they use. These perspectives can be traced to program source code analyzed and uncovered using social disciplines of computer science and the socio-technical software analysis methods.

The main object of research in the social disciplines of computer science is the virtual world of software and its relationship with the real world of designers and users. These disciplines reflect diverse views toward software as an environment (software ecology), imprints of the programmer's psyche (software psychology), artifacts of past information systems (software archeology), form of knowledge (software epistemology), growing and aging entities (software gerontology) that have their own form and shape (software morphology), and entities that interact with institutional and cultural contexts (software sociology).

Socio-technical analysis (STA) can be used for a number of problems, including program comprehension, plagiarism detection, design space exploration, and pattern mining. However, in practice it is very difficult to disentangle social aspects from purely technological aspects of software design, because they are mutually interdependent. The application of the STA methods may provide valuable insights into software development processes, the structure of the development team, the relationship of the software developers with their environments, understanding of programmer communication knowledge sharing, cognitive and mental processes of the developers and what influence it has on the quality and other characteristics of the produced software product. The results of STA can be used for improving programmer education, spreading good programming practices and styles, improving the management structure of the development team and the quality of its environment, and improving the performance of software design processes and quality of design artifacts (source code, documentation, etc.).

References

1. Adamic, L.A., Lukose, R.M., Puniyani, A.R. and Huberman, B.A. (2001) Search in Power-Law Networks. *Physical Review E*, 64, 046135.
2. Amrit C., Hillegersberg, J. and Kumar, K. (2004) A Social Network Perspective of Conway's Law. In *CSCW'04 Workshop on Social Networks*, Chicago.
3. Antón, A.I. and Potts, C. (2003) Functional Paleontology: The Evolution of User-Visible System Services. *IEEE Transactions on Software Engineering* 29(2), 151–166.
4. Bannon, L. (2001) Developing Software as a Human, Social and Organizational Activity. In *13th Workshop on Psychology of Programming (PPIG'2001)*, Bournemouth University, UK.
5. Beynon-Davies, P. (1997) Ethnography and Information Systems Development: Ethnography of, for and Within is Development. *Information and Software Technology* 39, 531–540.
6. Borchers, G. (2003) The Software Engineering Impacts of Cultural Factors on Multi-cultural Software Development Teams. In *Proc. of the 25th Int. Conf. on Software Engineering*, May 3–10, 2003, Portland, Oregon, USA, 540–547.
7. Bryant, S. (2004) XP: Taking the Psychology of Programming to the eXtreme. In *16th Workshop on Psychology of Programming (PPIG'2004)*, Carlow, Ireland.
8. Cannon-Bowers, J.E., Salas, E. and Converse, S. (1993) Shared Mental Models in Expert Team Decision-Making. In Castellan, J. (Ed.), *Individual and Group Decision-Making: Current Issues*. Lawrence Earlbaum and Associates, Inc., Mahwah, NJ, 221.
9. Checkland, P.B. (1999) *Soft Systems Methodology in Action*. John Wiley and Sons Ltd., New York
10. Chong, J., Plummer, R., Leifer, L., Klemmer, S.R., Eris, O. and Toye, G. (2005) Pair Programming: When and Why it Works. In *Proc. of Workshop on Psychology of Programming (PPIG 2005)*, University of Sussex, Brighton, UK.
11. Conway, M.E. (1968) How Do Committees Invent. *Datamation* 14(4), 28–31.
12. Cordes, D. and Brown, M. (1991) The Literate-Programming Paradigm. *Computer* 24(6), 52–61.
13. Curtis, B. (1988) The Impact of Individual Differences in Programmers. In van der Veer, G.C. (Ed.), *Working with Computers: Theory Versus Outcome*. Academic Press, New York, 279–294.
14. Curtis, B., Soloway, E.M., Brooks, R.E., Black, J.B., Ehrlich, K. and Ramsey, H.R. (1986) Software Psychology: The Need for an Inter-Disciplinary Program. In *Proceedings of the IEEE* 74(8), 1092–1106.
15. Damašević, R. (2006) On the Application of Meta-Design Techniques in Hardware Design Domain. *International Journal of Computer Science (IJCS)*, 1(1), 67–77.
16. Damašević, R. (2007) Analysis of Software Design Artifacts for Socio-Technical Aspects. *INFOCOMP Journal of Computer Science*, 6(4), 7–16.
17. Doherty, N.F. and King, M. (1998) The Importance of Organisational Issues in Systems Development. *Information Technology and People* 11(2), 104–123.
18. Douce, C. (2001) Long Term Comprehension of Software Systems: A Methodology for Study. In *13th Workshop on Psychology of Programming (PPIG'2001)*, Bournemouth, UK.
19. Douce, C. (2004) Metaphors We Program by. In *16th Annual Workshop on Psychology of Programming (PPIG'2004)*, Carlow, Ireland.
20. Eleutheros Manifesto. http://www.eleutheros.it/documenti/Manifesto
21. Eno, B. (1996) *A Year with Swollen Appendices*. Faber and Faber.
22. Espinosa, J., Slaughter, S. and Herbsleb, J. (2002) Shared Mental Models, Familiarity and Coordination: A Multi-Method Study of Distributed Software Teams. In *Proc. of 23rd Int. Conf. on Information Systems*, Barcelona, Spain, 425–433.
23. Finholt, T. (2004) Toward a Social Psychology of Software Engineering, Perspectives Workshop: Empirical Theory and the Science of Software Engineering, Dagstuhl Seminar 04051.
24. Fischer, G., Giaccardi, E., Ye, Y., Sutcliffe, A.G. and Mehandjiev, N. (2004) Meta-Design: A Manifesto for End-User Development. *Communications of ACM* 47(9), 33–37.

25. Grinter, R.E. (2003) Recomposition: Coordinating a Web of Software Dependencies. *Computer Supported Cooperative Work* 12(3), 297–327. Springer.
26. Halavais, A. (2005) Social Informatics: Beyond Emergence. *Bulletin of the American Society for Information Science and Technology* 31(5), 13.
27. Hales, D. and Douce, C. (2002) Modelling Software Organisations, In Kuljis, J., Baldwin, L. and Scoble, R. (Eds.). *Proceedings of PPIG 2002,* Brunel University, UK, 140–149.
28. Hall, J.G. and Silva, A. (2003) A Requirements-Based Framework for the Analysis of Socio-Technical System Behaviour. In *Proc. of 9th Int. Workshop on Requirements Engineering: Foundations of Software Quality (REFSQ03),* 117–120.
29. Herbsleb, J.D. and Grinter, R.E. (1999) Splitting the Organization and Integrating the Code: Conway's Law Revisited. In *Proc. of Int. Conf. on Software Engineering,* Los Angeles, CA, 85–95.
30. Herbsleb, J.D. (1999) Metaphorical Representation in Collaborative Software Engineering. In *Proc. of Joint Conf. on Work Activities, Coordination*and*Collaboration,* San Francisco, CA, 117–125.
31. Hoc, J.M. and Nguyen-Xuan, A. (1990) Language Semantics, Mental Models and Analogy. In Hoc, J.M., Green, T.R.G., Samuray, R. and Gilmore D.J. (Eds.), *Psychology of Programming,* London: Academic Press, 139–156..
32. Holloway, C.M. (1995) Software Engineering and Epistemology. *Software Engineering Notes,* 20(2), 20–21.
33. Holt, R.C. (2002) Software Architecture as a Shared Mental Model. In *ASERC Workshop on Software Architecture,* Alberta, Canada.
34. Hsi, I., Potts, C. and Moore, M. (2003) Ontological Excavation: Unearthing the Core Concepts of the Application. In van Deursen, A., Stroulia, E. and Storey, M.-A. D. (Eds.), *Proc. of 10th Working Conference on Reverse Engineering (WCRE 2003),* 13–16 November 2003, Victoria, Canada, 345–352.
35. Hughes, J.A., Somerville, I., Bentley, R. and Randall, D. (1993) Designing with Ethnography: Making Work Visible. *Interacting with Computers* 5(2), 239–253.
36. Hunt, A. and Thomas, D. (2002) Software Archaeology. *IEEE Software,* 19(2), 20–22.
37. Hvatum, L. and Kelly, A. (2005) What Do I Think About Conway's Law Now? *Conclusions of EuroPLoP2005 Focus Group.*
38. Iannacci, F. (2005) *The Social Epistemology of Open Source Software Development: the Linux Case Study.* PhD. Thesis, Department of Information Systems, London School of Economics and Political Science, London, UK.
39. Jing, L., Keqing, H., Yutao, M. and Rong, P. (2006) Scale Free in Software Metrics. In *Proc. of the 30th Annual Int. Conf. on Computer Software and Applications, COMPSAC 2006,*1, 229–235.
40. Kersten, G.E., Kersten, M.A. and Rakowski, W.M. (2001) Application Software and Culture: Beyond the Surface of Software Interface. InterNeg Research Paper INR01/01.
41. Kerth, N.L. (2001) On Creating a Disciplined and Ethical Practice of Software Archeology. In *OOPSLA01 Workshop Software Archeology: Understanding Large Systems,* Tampa Bay, FL.
42. Kling, R., Rosenbaum, H. and Sawyer, S. (2005) *Understanding and Communicating Social Informatics: A Framework for Studying and Teaching the Human Contexts of Information and Communications Technologies.* Information Today, Inc.
43. Lanzara, F.G. and Morner, M. (2003) The Knowledge Ecology of Open-Source Software Projects. In *19th EGOS Colloquium,* Copenhagen, Denmark.
44. Letovsky, S. (1986) Cognitive Processes in Program Comprehension. In Soloway, E. and Iyengar, S. (ed.), *Empirical Studies of Programmers,* Ablex Publishing Company, New York, 58–79.
45. Luna-Reyes, L.F., Zhang, J., Gil-Garcia, J.R. and Cresswell, A.M. (2005) Information Systems Development as Emergent Socio-Technical Change: A Practice Approach. *European Journal of Information Systems* 14, 93–105.
46. MacLennan, B.J. (1997) Who Cares About Elegance? The Role of Aesthetics in Programming Language Design. *SIGPLAN Notices* 32(3): 33–37.
47. Marshall, L. and Webber, J. (2002) The Misplaced Comma: Programmers' Tales and Traditions. In *Proc. of PPIG 2002,* Brunel University, UK, 150–155.
48. Minsky, M. (1986) Introduction to LogoWorks. In Solomon, C., Minsky, M. and Harvey, B. (Eds.), *LogoWorks: Challenging Programs in Logo.* McGraw-Hill.
49. Mumford, E. (1995) *Effective Systems Design and Requirements Analysis: The ETHICS Approach to Computer Systems Design.* Macmillan, London.
50. Noble, J. and Biddle, R. (2004) Notes on Notes on Postmodern Programming. *SIGPLAN Notices* 39(12), 40–56.
51. Norman, D.A. (1986) Cognitive Engineering. In Norman, D.A. and Draper, S.W. (Eds.), *User Centred System Design.* LEA Associates, NJ.
52. Ørstavik, I.T.B. (2006) How Programming Language Can Shape Interaction and Culture. *Int. European Conf. on Computing and Philosophy, ECAP 2006,* June 22–24, Trondheim, Norway.
53. Parnas D.L. (1972) On the Criteria to Be Used in Decomposing Systems into Modules. *Commun. of the ACM* 15(12), 1053–1058.
54. Parnas, D.L. (1994) Software aging. In *Proc. of the 16th Int. Conf. on Software Engineering,* Sorrento, Italy, 279–287.
55. Potanin, A., Noble, J., Frean, M. and Biddle, R. (2005) Scale-Free. Geometry in OO Programs. *Commun. of the ACM,* 48(5), 99–103.
56. Robles, G., González-Barahona, J.M. and Guervós, J.J.M. (2006) Beyond Source Code: The Importance of Other Artifacts in Software Development (A Case Study). *Journal of Systems and Software* 79(9), 1233–1248.
57. Rosen, C.C.H. (2005) The Influence of Intra-Team Relationships on the Systems Development Process: A Theoretical Framework of Intra-Group Dynamics. In *Proceedings of Workshop on Psychology of Programming (PPIG 17),* Brighton, UK, 30–42.

58. Sawyer, S. and Guinan, P.J. (1988) Software Development: Processes and Performance. *IBM Systems Jounal* 37(4), 553–569.

59. Sawyer, S. and Tyworth, M. (2006) Social Informatics: Principles, Theory and Practice. In *7th Int. Conf. 'Human Choice and Computers', IFIP-TC9 'Relationship between Computers and Society',* Maribor, Slovenia.

60. Sharp, H.C., Woodman, M., Hovenden, F. and Robinson, H. (1999) The Role of Culture in Successful Software Process Improvement. In *Proc. of 25th Euromicro Conf.,* 8–10 September 1999, Milan, Italy, 170–176.

61. Shneiderman, B. (1980) *Software Psychology: Human Factors in Computer and Information Systems.* Winthrop.

62. Souza, de C., Dourish, P., Redmiles, D., Quirk, S. and Trainer, E. (2004) From Technical Dependencies to Social Dependencies. In *Social Networks Workshop at CSCW Conf.,* Chicago, IL.

63. Souza, de C., Froehlich, J. and Dourish, P. (2005) Seeking the Source: Software Source Code as a Social and Technical Artifact. In *Proc. of Int. ACM SIGGROUP Conf. on Supporting Group Work, GROUP 2005,* Sanibel Island, FL, 197–206.

64. Tractinsky, N. (2004) Toward the Study of Aesthetics in Information Technology. In *Proc. of the Int. Conf. on Information Systems,* ICIS 2004, December 12–15, 2004, Washington, DC, USA, 771–780.

65. Trainer, E., Quirk, S., de Souza, C. and Redmiles, D.F. (2005) Bridging the Gap Between Technical and Social Dependencies with Ariadne. In *Proc. of the 2005 OOPSLA Workshop on Eclipse Technology eXchange (eTX),* San Diego, CA, 26–30.

66. Viller, S. and Sommerville, I. (1999) Coherence: An Approach to Representing Ethnographic Analyses in Systems Design. *Human-Computer Interaction* 14(1,2), 9–41.

67. Wall, L. (1999) Perl, The First Postmodern Computer Language. Speech at *Linux World.*

68. Watt, S.N.K. (1998) Syntonicity and the Psychology of Programming. In *Proc. of 10th Workshop for the Psychology of Programming Interest Group (PPIG),* Open University, UK, 75–86.

69. Weinberg, M.W. (1971) *The Psychology of Computer Programming.* Van Nostrand Reinhold, New York.

70. Zelkowitz, M.V., Wallace, D. and Binkley, D. (1998) Culture Conflicts in Software Engineering Technology Transfer. In *NASA Goddard Software Engineering Workshop,* Greenbelt, MD, USA, February 12, 1998.

3

Toward Modeling Language-Independent Integration of Dynamic Schemata

Peter Bellström, Jürgen Vöhringer and Christian Kop

Abstract

In the early phases of the software development process we generally deal with systems requirements that are gathered from various sources. These requirements can be represented in the form of structural and behavioral schemata. But heterogeneous system requirements frequently contain conflicts and overlap. Requirements schema integration is therefore essential for successful further system development. The complex integration of dynamic schemata in particular cannot be fully automated and even partial automation is not a trivial task. In this chapter we demonstrate a partially automated, guideline based, modeling language-independent integration approach for dynamic schemata. We also show how our guidelines can be applied during the typical steps of an integration process.

Keywords Schema integration · Behavioral/dynamic system requirements

1. Introduction

View and schema integration has been a research area for quite a long time now and was described by Batini et al. [2] as "[...] the process of merging several conceptual schemas into a *global conceptual schema* that represents all the requirements of the application." (p. 119). In the early phases of the software development process we deal with heterogeneous systems requirements from various sources. These requirements can be represented in the form of structural and behavioral schemata illustrating the services the future information system is going to provide. Following all these requirements is not always possible as conflicts and overlaps can occur between several requirements. An integration of the requirements schemata is therefore essential for further systems development.

A lot of effort has been put into the integration of static schemata while the integration of dynamic schemata has been neglected until recently. Our previous research [5] produced valuable insights into structure integration in the early phase of software engineering and its advantages. Currently we put focus on applying these insights on the integration of dynamic schemata. Henceforward our use of the word "schema" implies both views and schemata.

Our goal is to develop a computer aided semi-automatic integration approach that supports designers and domain experts during the integration process. An important feature of our proposed strategy is its modeling language independence. The relevance of a language-independent strategy is easily illustrated: Imagine two companies that are merged or that start cooperating closely, as is very common in our global society. Both companies keep their original staff and strategies, but they must consolidate and assimilate some of their processes or at least define common interfaces of services that they are providing.

Peter Bellström • Department of Information Systems, Karlstad University, Karlstad, Sweden. **Jürgen Vöhringer and Christian Kop** • Research Group Application Engineering, Institute for Applied Informatics, University of Klagenfurt, Austria.

G.A. Papadopoulos et al. (eds.), *Information Systems Development*, DOI 10.1007/b137171_3,
© Springer Science+Business Media, LLC 2009

Our method supports the integration of business processes even if the source schema languages are different. The integrated schema could be provided in one or both of the source model languages or even in a different third one that is understood by both parties.

In [6] we described a number of generic guidelines that can help achieving successful integration of dynamic schemata. Because of their language independence, these guidelines support the integration of arbitrary dynamic schemata like UML activity diagrams, business process models, etc. In this chapter we demonstrate our integration method with a specific example and show how the guidelines can be used to facilitate the integration process.

This chapter is structured as follows: In Section 2 we present some examples of related work and distinguish it from our own approach. In Section 3 our integration strategy is described in deeper detail. We also position our previously presented guidelines (see [6]) within the common four-step integration process. Section 4 deals with an exemplary application of our integration strategy. We use this example to illustrate our resolution techniques for conflict recognition and resolution in dynamic schemata. Finally, the chapter closes with an outlook to future work.

2. Related Work

While the problem of integration of dynamic schemata is far from being solved, some strategies have been described and reported. One approach focusing on state chart integration was described by Frank and Eder (see [9]). They distinguish five relationship classes between the involved state charts: *parallel*, *disjoint*, *consecutive*, *alternative*, and *mixed*. A description of each type is given in Table 3.1.

Table 3.1.   State chart relationship types [9].

Relationship	Description
Parallel	An object of the integrated type has to pass both state charts in parallel
Disjoint	An object of the integrated type has to pass either the first or the second state
Consecutive	An object of the integrated type has to pass first the one and second the other
Alternative	An object of the integrated type has to pass the state charts alternatively
Mixed	An object of the integrated type has to pass a "mixture" of both state charts

While it is possible to develop straightforward resolution techniques for the first four relationship types, the *mixed* relationship type poses more severe problems and challenges. Mixed relationships mean that the compared schemata have some common parts and some different parts, which implies its complexity. Even though the relationship types were defined on a level closer to design and implementation than ours we find them applicable for a first classification of relationships between the compared schemata.

Examples of other approaches for integration of behavioral schemata are given in [13] and [15]. In [13] the authors propose to use generalization for similar objects and specialization for equal objects of classes. In [15] the authors identified four subcases of the integration problem, where objects are integrated mainly by discriminated generalization (see [11]).

The authors in [15] criticized the approach given in [9] for not dealing with loosely coupled systems and for ignoring concurrency aspects. This criticism confirms our belief that integration should be done as early as possible in the information systems development process (see [4] and [16]). A high level of abstraction means that we can ignore implementation and design details like loose or tight coupling and instead put focus on modeling and integrating contents. While details like concurrency can be described in pre-design schemata if they are explicitly demanded, these issues are by default postponed for later phases of the design process. We therefore propagate an approach where the modeling and integration of the systems' functionality comes first and only in later phases specializations in regard to the implementation are made.

Finally, to our knowledge no general frameworks or in-depth analysis and descriptions exist yet that deal with integration of dynamic schemata on a level both independent of design and implementation issues. From that we conclude that our approach is rather unique. It should interest researchers and practitioners alike since we are trying to resolve problems as early as possible in the information systems development process and the information systems life cycle, instead of postponing conflicts until later design phases.

3. Guidelines for Language Independent Schema Integration

In [6] we introduced and described the following guidelines for modeling language-independent integration of schemata:

(1) *Performing schema integration on the pre-design level.* Integration takes place very early in information systems development on a high level of abstraction. Therefore we do not deal with detailed design and implementation issues; hence, fewer conflicts might occur.
(2) *Standardizing concept notions and utilizing them during integration.* Concept notions are standardized in a way that facilitates the integration process for both the human participants (the concept notions are easily readable) and the integration tool (the concept notions are easier to compare).
(3) *Using domain repositories for supporting the integration process.* We use the term domain repository for different meta-sources such as ontologies, taxonomies, and lexicons. Repositories are used to facilitate the integration process since they not only store concept notions but also semantic relationships between them.
(4) *Neighborhood-based conflict recognition.* During conflicts identification we not only compare concepts but also their neighborhoods. In that way synonym and homonym conflicts can be identified that might otherwise stay unnoticed.
(5) *Pattern-based resolution of integration conflicts.* We use relationship patterns listed in Table 3.1 (see [9]) for a first classification of schema relationships.
(6) *Computer-supported integration with utilizing user feedback.* Computer-based applications can and should support conflict recognition and resolution. However, since full automation is not possible we also recommend user verifications to ensure correct integration.

In this section we discuss not only how the guidelines can be applied during the integration process but also the benefits of various guidelines. In [1] the authors concluded that most methodologies for integration of static schemata include at least four phases. Regarding integration of dynamic schemata we have identified similar standard phases in the literature. In [10] the authors give a proposal for the state chart integration process phases: *schema analysis*, *schema transformation*, *schema merging*, and finally *schema restructuring*. For our own integration method we propose the following four sub-phases:

Phase 1: *Preparation of source schemata*
Phase 2: *Recognition of conflicts and commonalities between source schemata*
Phase 3: *Resolution of conflicts and commonalities between source schemata*
Phase 4: *Merging the source schemata and restructuring the global schema*
In the following we map our integration guidelines to these integration phases.

3.1. Phase 1 – Preparation of Source Schemata

The first phase in our integration process is *preparation of source schemata*. In this phase guidelines 1 and 2 should be applied. According to guideline 1 we suggest performing integration very early in the conceptual design (pre-design), because we do not need to deal with detailed design and implementation issues. Therefore we deal with fewer structural conflicts during integration. Moreover, pre-design schemata are less complex and easier to interpret for domain experts and designers alike. This makes external involvement in the integration process easier. While some languages explicitly support pre-design modeling [7, 12], any modeling language can be stripped down to its basic modeling concepts. It was argued in [6] that *conditions* and *process types* are the minimal concepts for dynamic modeling.

Also during schema preparation we follow guideline 2: we provide a number of naming guidelines, which can be used to evaluate whether concept names follow our proposed structure. The naming guidelines describe a controlled subset of the natural language, which concept names in dynamic schemata should follow. Our goal is to ensure that meta information about the described concept (e.g., the actor of a process step or the process step's parameters) is made explicit via the concept name. The structured concept notions are more easily interpretable by users and since a certain format is adhered they are also easier to process automatically.

In the first integration phase we also try to identify and resolve intra-schema conflicts such as synonymous or homonymous schema concepts. Applying guidelines 3–6 to the single source schema achieve this. Homonym and synonym conflicts are usually solved by standardizing one or both of the compared concepts. However, standardization of concept notions is not the same as renaming the concept names, because the original concept names are still kept although with more precise notions. If renaming is used, the original concept names are often lost which results in concept name compression and semantic loss [3]. The process of identifying and resolving homonyms and synonyms will be described in more detail in the context of the phases 2 and 3 of the integration process, where such conflicts will be identified and resolved between two schemata.

3.2. Phase 2 – Recognition of Conflicts and Commonalities Between Source Schemata

The second phase of the integration process deals with the *recognition of conflicts and commonalities between source schemata*. Guidelines 3 and 4 are relevant for this phase. We choose the binary integration order (see [1, 2]): two schemata are compared to identify conflicts and commonalities. In guideline 3, we suggest using domain repositories such as ontologies, taxonomies, and lexicons for facilitating computer-supported schema matching. Ontologies have the advantage of not only storing hypernym–hyponym relationships like taxonomies, but also providing additional semantic relationships like antonym–, synonym– and holonym–meronym relationships. Domain repositories are particularly helpful for concept disambiguation during the schema integration. Furthermore we suggest that the integrated static schema should be presupposed for the integration of dynamic schemata (see [4, 16]), since it can be used for complementing the repository data.

Following the schema matching strategy classification of [14], the schema matching is not based alone on the linguistic comparison of concept notions and on looking up concept relationships in a repository. Through structural comparisons we also try to identify additional homonym and synonym conflicts that are not yet described in the domain repositories. This goal is achieved by comparing the concepts' neighborhoods, i.e., their context (see guideline 4). Concepts with synonymous or equal names but different neighborhoods could hint at a homonym conflict, while concepts with unrelated names but equal or similar neighborhoods could hint at synonym conflicts. In dynamic schemata concepts like *processes* or *conditions* often are compounds of different linguistic fragments. We propose to deconstruct such notions before comparing the fragments. This is made much easier when the notions follow the naming guidelines described in guideline 2.

3.3. Phases 3 and 4: Conflict Resolution and Schema Merging

The schema integration process deals with the *resolution of conflicts and commonalities between source schemata* in its third phase. During this phase, guidelines 5 and 6 are of particular interest. After identifying possible conflicts in phase 2 of the integration process, we can use the *relationship types* described by Frank and Eder (see Table 3.1) as a first method for classifying schema relationship patterns. If the relationships between schemata correspond to such a pattern, we follow Frank and Eder's [8] integration advices, as described in our integration guideline 5. In practice, schema relationships rarely correspond to just one of the proposed types; instead parts of the compared schemata are connected by different relationship types. In such mixed relationships the danger of overlapping conflicts is high. Frank and Eder mentioned overlapping conflicts first in the context of *state overlapping*, i.e., a state within a state chart corresponds partially to a state within another state chart. Such overlapping conflicts are not restricted to state chart integration; similar conflicts were identified in the general integration of behavioral schemata [6], where they were called *process type overlapping* and *condition overlapping*, respectively.

Although our method aims to automate the integration process as far as possible, full automation is not realistic (see [15]): ultimately we need user verifications to ensure semantic correct integration. Guideline 6 responds to this by underlining the importance of user feedback during integration. With our approach we present the expert users automated integration suggestions, which were derived during the preceding phases. The user is free to accept or decline these suggestions.

Particularly overlapping conflicts as described above are a reason for bad integration suggestions. In these cases a domain expert's knowledge is needed to resolve the complex conflicts. After developing the integration suggestions and collecting optional user feedback in phase 3, the source schemata are merged and the global integrated schema is constructed in phase 4: *merging the source schemata and restructuring the global schema*.

4. Applying the Guidelines – A Motivating Example

In this section we demonstrate how our guidelines for the integration of dynamic schemata can be utilized for partially automating the integration process. Our example deals with a project aiming to introduce a new common library system for a school center that consists of several school types. The school center also houses two school libraries for the different school types, which are a business school (BS) and a technical school (TS). Both libraries have their own distinct information system.

External software developers are assigned to develop a new information system that would be used by both libraries. The new system is required to provide all the features of the previous systems but also facilitate the borrowing process. Naturally the first step in the project consists of requirements elicitation and analysis, which in this case must start with an examination of the two existing systems.

In order to minimize personal meetings of all stakeholders the designers are expected to propose a first suggestion for the new system based on documentation of the existing system and on schemata showing the expected future behavior. Qualified contact persons from the different schools (so-called "domain experts") have prepared these schemata independently from each other, which must now be integrated with regard to the new common library system, i.e., the conflicts between them must be identified and resolved.

4.1. The Applied Modeling Languages

We assume that KCPM (Klagenfurt Conceptual Pre-Design Model) [7] and EM (Karlstad Enterprise Modeling approach) [12], respectively, were chosen as modeling languages for the example. In [5] we showed that these languages work on a higher level of abstraction compared with traditional modeling languages, which makes them particularly useful for our integration approach. In order to improve the *readability* of the example in Section 4.2, Table 3.2 provides an overview of the most central concepts of KCPM and EM dynamic schemata and how they are graphically represented.

Organizations frequently commit to specific modeling languages that their employees are familiar with. In this case we assume that while one domain expert prefers KCPM, the one is an EM supporter. The involved parties eventually agree to use a neutral common modeling language for the integrated schema, which is understood by all involved parties. In our example, the project parties agree on the business process modeling language Adonis (see http://www.cso.net/boc/english/index.htm). While our school library example does not comprise processes with economic added value, they can still be interpreted as business processes, as they describe a servicing process. Table 3.3 explains Adonis concepts and how to interpret them.

Table 3.2. Most important KCPM and EM dynamic concepts.

Language	Concept name	Graphical Representation	Description
KCPM	Operation-type		Processes that are executed in the system (usually have actors and parameters assigned to them)
KCPM	Cooperation-type		Groups processes (operations) with the same pre-conditions (but possibly different actors) that can be performed concurrently
KCPM	Pre- and post-conditions		Conditions that hold true before/after certain process groups (cooperations) are executed. Logical operators can join several conditions
EM	Action		Processes that are executed in the system (usually have actors assigned to them, which can be visualized in the dynamic schema together with the parameters)
EM	State		Illustrates a state or condition of a concept/object and corresponds to pre- and post-conditions that hold true before/after certain processes (actions) are executed

Table 3.3. Most important Adonis concepts.

Concept name/description	Graphical representation	Concept name/ description	Graphical representation
Business process start		Decision (= pre- and post-conditions)	
Activity (= process)		Split/join (of parts of the business process)	
Succeeder (joins process steps)		Business process end	

4.2. Integrating Language-Independent Source Schemata

Figure 3.1 shows the EM- (*left*) and KCPM-schemata (*right*) developed by the domain experts. The next project goal is identifying the commonalities and conflicts between these two schemata and integrating them. We follow the four typical integration phases described in Section 3.

According to guideline 1 from integration phase 1 we follow the pre-design approach and remove all modeling elements besides conditions and processes. Table 3.2 lists the essential modeling concepts for dynamic KCPM and EM models. This guideline leaves the KCPM schema unchanged (since it only consists of concepts equivalent to processes and conditions) but removes actors, flows, and references to static concepts from the EM schema leaving only expressions (e.g., "Ed. Book Reserved").

According to guideline 2, we then check whether the concept names in the schemata follow our naming guidelines. This is not the case in any of the two schemata, since process step names must, for instance, contain a subject (which identifies the actor of the process step) and, if available, objects (which identify parameters of the process step). The missing information in the concept name can however be automatically generated from meta-data about the source schemata. This information is made explicit not by using additional modeling concepts but by updating the concept names. The results are lean dynamic schemata that are easily interpreted by human readers and that still can be easily processed automatically.

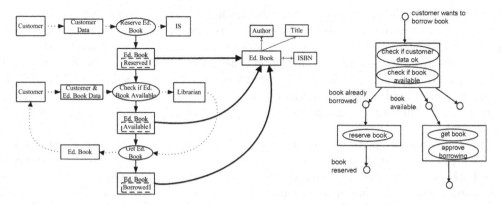

Figure 3.1. Original EM and KCPM source schemata.

In phase 2 of the integration process, guideline 3 is used for disambiguating concept notions with the help of domain repositories. Both compared schemata use similar words like "Customer" and "Reserve" in their concept notions. However, while the KCPM schema consistently uses the word "book", the EM schema uses "Ed. book" (i.e., educational book) instead. As proposed in guideline 3, the integration of static schemata has already been performed before the integration of dynamic schemata and the static concepts involved in the process steps and conditions have therefore already been disambiguated. In the integration of static schemata it was concluded that "Book" and "Ed. Book" are synonymous concepts in the given domain. Any other kind of book would have to be referenced by its full notion, e.g., "novel". Figure 3.2 shows the EM and KCPM source schemata after applying guidelines 1, 2, and 3.

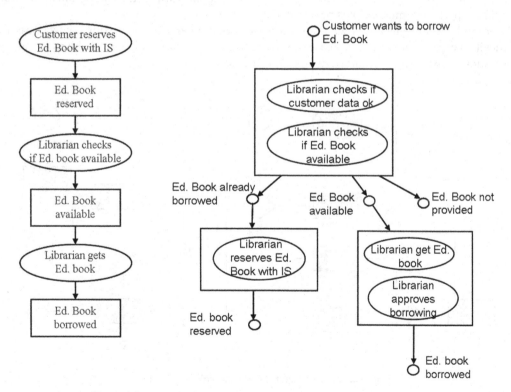

Figure 3.2. EM and KCPM source schemata after applying guidelines 1–3.

Also in phase 2 of the integration process, the neighborhood of concepts is compared in order to identify homonym and synonym conflicts. While this is specifically important during integration of the structure, it can also be applied when comparing actions. For instance, the actions "Customer reserves Ed. Book with IS" from the EM schema and "Librarian reserves Ed. Book with IS" from the KCPM schema have similar names. The adjacent pre-conditions of the process steps do not match however and comparing more than just the direct neighbors, we notice that the context of the process steps is completely different. Thus we are warned that the compared process steps in the schemata might have different semantics.

In the third process phase, automated integration suggestions are developed. For mixed schemata, we provide suggestions on the concept level based on the similarity of concepts and their neighborhood. If process steps are perceived as equal or synonymous, the suggestion is to merge them (but keep the original process names in an ontology), while we suggest introducing both of them to the integrated schema if they are perceived as different. If possible homonym or synonym conflicts are identified, the expert user is asked to confirm or discard the conflict, and a fitting integration strategy is then automatically proposed. When two process steps are identified as equal, the integration of differing pre- and post-conditions can be hard to solve the problem, since the conditions could be interpreted as logical AND-, OR-, or XOR-conjunctions. Here again user feedback is needed to resolve the problem, else some default suggestions are made.

In our example, the process steps "Customer reserves Ed. Book with IS" and "Librarian reserves Ed. Book with IS" were identified as probably different based on the neighborhoods of the process steps. The domain expert feedback would lead us to the conclusion that both kinds of reservations are actually different, since when customers reserve books online (as described in the EM schema) they actually have to check first whether the book is even provided by the library. In the KCPM schema, the checking whether the book is provided by the library was already done during the step "Librarian checks if book is available." This means that the two different reservation activities are actually different: they contain an overlapping conflict. The expert users must help us resolving the conflict.

After applying our guidelines we receive a list of final integration suggestions, which are used to automatically merge the schemata in phase 4 of the integration process. Figure 3.3 shows the integrated common Adonis schema for the university library example.

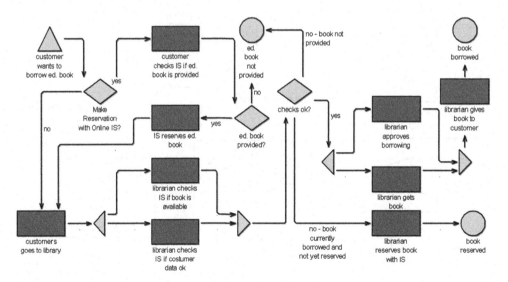

Figure 3.3. Final integrated schema described with Adonis.

5. Summary and Conclusion

In [6] we presented a number of generic guidelines for integration of dynamic schemata on the pre-design level. We argued that integration in an early phase of the software development process has a number of advantages, i.e., the source schemata tend to be less complex and less structural conflicts occur.

This chapter builds on previous research by demonstrating the integration of dynamic schemata based on the guidelines discussed in [6] and introducing a process model for business process integration. We showed that the integration process is very similar for different modeling languages and that the resolution of overlapping conflicts still depends largely on expert user feedback.

Future research will deal with the conduction and evaluation of scientific studies regarding the success of our integration guidelines. We plan improving our automatically derived integration suggestions and facilitating the user feedback cycles during integration. We also plan to progress with our work on concept notion standardization and its role for the integration process.

References

1. Batini, C., Lenzerini, M. and Navathe, S.B. (1986) A Comparative Analysis of Methodologies for Database Schema Integration, *ACM Computing Surveys*, 18(4): 323–363.
2. Batini, C., Ceri, S. and Navathe, S.B. (1992) *Conceptual Database Design an Entity-Relationship Approach*, The Benjamin/Cummings Publishing Company, Inc.
3. Bellström, P. (2009) On the Problem of Semantic Loss in View Integration, In Barry, C. et al. (eds), *Information Systems Development: Challenges in Practice, Theory, and Education*, Vol. 2, Springer Science, New York, pp. 963–974.
4. Bellström, P. and Jakobsson, L. (2006) Towards a Generic and Integrated Enterprise Modeling Approach to Designing Databases and Software Components, In Nilsson. A.G. et al. (eds), *Advances in Information Systems Development: Bridging the Gap between Academia and Industry*, Springer, New York, pp. 635–646.
5. Bellström P., Vöhringer J. and Salbrechter A. (2007) Recognition and Resolution of Linguistic Conflicts: The Core to a Successful View and Schema Integration, In Magyar, G. et al. (eds), *ISD New Methods and Practices for the Networked Society*, Springer, New York, pp. 77–87.
6. Bellström, P., Vöhringer, J. and Kop, C. (2008) Guidelines for Modeling Language Inde-pendent Dynamic Schema Integration, In Pahl, C. (ed), *Proceedings of The IASTED In-ternational Conference on Software Engineering*, ACTA Press, New York, pp. 112–117.
7. Fliedl, G., Kop, C., Mayr, H.C., Mayerthaler, W. and Winkler, C. (2000) Linguistically based requirements engineering – The NIBA project, *Data and Knowledge Engineering*, 35: 111–120.
8. Frank, H. and Eder J. (1997) Integration of Behaviour Models. In: *ER'97 Workshop on Behavioural Models and Design Transformations* pp. 4(1)–4(16).
9. Frank, H. and Eder, J. (1998) Integration of Statecharts, *Proceedings of the 3rd COOPIS Conference*, pp. 364–372.
10. Frank, H. and Eder, K. (1999) Towards an Automatic Integration of Statecharts, In Akoka, J. et al. (eds), *Proceedings of ER'99*, Springer, New York, pp. 430–445.
11. García-Solaco, M., Saltor, F. and Castellanos, M. (1995) A semantic discriminated approach to integration of federated databases, *Proceedings of COOPIS*, pp. 19–31.
12. Gustas, R. and Gustiené, P. (2009) Service-Oriented Foundation and Analysis Patterns for Conceptual Modeling of Information, In Barry, C. et al. (eds), *Information Systems Development: Challenges in Practice, Theory, and Education*, Vol. 1, Springer Science, New York, pp. 249–265.
13. Preuner, G., Conrad, S. and Schrefl, M. (2001) View integration of behaviour in object-oriented databases, *Data and Knowledge Engineering*, 36: 153–183.
14. Rahm, E. and Bernstein, P.A. (2001) A survey of approaches to automatic schema matching, *VLDB Journal*, 10: 334–350.
15. Stumptner, M., Schrefl, M. and Grossmann, G. (2004) On the Road to Behavior-Based Integration, *Proc. of the 1st Asia-Pacific Conference on Conceptual Modelling*, pp. 15–22.
16. Vöhringer, J. and Mayr, H.C. (2006) Integration of Schemas on the Pre-Design Level Using the KCPM-Approach. In Nilsson, A.G. et al. (eds), *Advances in Information Systems Development: Bridging the Gap between Academia and Industry*, Springer, New York, pp. 623–634.

4

Improving Knowledge Management in the Health Service: Re-Engineering Approach Towards Successful Implementation

Regina Gyampoh-Vidogah and Robert Moreton

Abstract

Changes to business practices involve risks. There has always been an attempt to develop various concepts for successful restructuring of business processes to enable technology adoption. This is due to the fact that the success of any business depends as much on how it is structured, as well as its ability to adopt new technology. As a consequence, the great success stories of the global economy emanate from those organisations most capable of adopting new technology, which invariably includes information technology (IT). This chapter examines how business process re-engineering (BPR) can be used to improve knowledge management (KM) in health services by (i) assessing the effectiveness and usefulness of BPR; (ii) present a critical review of approaches to BPR; and (iii) describe a framework for using BPR for KM based on empirical research. The aim is to provide a sound strategic and tactical management approach for successful implementation of knowledge management systems (KMS) to improve health-care service project administration.

Keywords Knowledge management systems · Business process re-engineering · Health services information technology · Health informatics · Information systems

1. Introduction

The success of any business depends as much on how it is structured, as well as its ability to adopt new technology. The great success stories of the global economy emanate from those organisations most capable of adopting new technology. In this context, such technology predominantly includes information technology (IT) [1]. Since change in business practices involves risks, there has always been an attempt to develop various concepts for successful restructuring of business processes to enable technology adoption. One concept which has been widely used (in various guises) to achieve an efficient business structure is business process re-engineering (BPR). Over the past decade, IT has been an essential element of BPR [2].

Given the benefits that other sectors of industry have made, it is noticeable that practical examples of business process re-engineering (BPR) application in the health service are much less common or non-existent [3]. The lack of conviction to apply BPR can be explained partly by the fact that the health service is partly project oriented. This means that in general, short term rather than long-term financial considerations influences management decisions. As a result proponents for implementing [4] fundamental changes to health service business activities have to contend with three important factors; (i) the absence of a model

Regina Gyampoh-Vidogah • Care Services Improvement Partnership, Department of Health, London, UK
Robert Moreton • School of Computing and IT, University of Wolverhampton, Wolverhampton, UK

G.A. Papadopoulos et al. (eds.), *Information Systems Development*, DOI 10.1007/b137171_4,
© Springer Science+Business Media, LLC 2009

for evaluating IT projects; (ii) lack of financial resources; and (iii) the long payback periods associated with most IT projects. Under these circumstances winning new bids to shore up the short-term financial standing takes precedence to change implementation to adopt technology [5]. However, other researchers have argued that alternatives for re-engineering the health-care process are needed [6, 7]. Other researchers [3, 8, 9] among others propose concepts such as concurrent engineering as vehicles for increasing productivity to improve efficiency and reduce cost.

Perhaps the real reason for the lack of process re-engineering take-up in the health-care service can be traced to the services perception of process re-engineering [7]. A report has been proposed [10, 11] to benchmark the health-care process. Other researchers identified the need to re-engineer health processes taking a functional and task-oriented view. To emphasise this point, the researcher [12] went to great lengths to explain how re-engineering can offer industry the best opportunity to improve productivity and competitiveness.

In today's environment the key technology is IT. For example, BPR concept has been applied by some blue-chip companies (including Ford Motors and IBM) to gain business benefits [13]. Ford, for example, improved their procurement process with the help of IT, while IBM Credit Corporation re-engineered their application processes, leading to a significant increase in the number of credit requests processed by the same number of staff. These views are supported by practitioners who considered BPR as the key enabler for successful IT/information systems (IS) implementation. The use of IT to challenge assumptions inherent in current work processes, which were established before the advent of modern computer and communication technologies, has been suggested [15]. A broader view of both IT and business activities and the relationships between them have also been proved [16]. It was suggested that IT should be viewed as more than an automating or mechanising force, but rather, as a means to fundamentally reshape the way that business is performed. In other words, the integrated project process envisaged by proponent of improving KM is achievable using the benefits of IT to challenge current practices. This being the case, one wonders why despite the great advances in IT, the health service does not have an enviable record of accomplishment of using IT in this way.

In this chapter, BPR is defined and various elements and tools used in BPR are adapted with specific focus on how KMS can be implemented to improve health informatics (HI) systems in general. The goal is to encourage lower cost and greater productivity and improved services. The added benefit is engaging service users, stakeholders, partners and employees using IT as an advantage to support its users. In order to effectively apply the BPR for KMS implementation, the project environment had to be understood. Consequently, the model used in reported prototypes do closely match actual information exchange during project cycle. In many ways, this lack of success is not surprising, because conventional wisdom suggests BPR should be used to re-engineer the existing business processes in order to successfully implement IT/IS in general [17, 18, 19].

2. Business Process Re-Engineering (BPR)

BPR is derived from the key words, "business process" and "re-engineering". Business process (BP) is defined as "a set of logically related tasks performed to achieve a defined business outcome" or "a structured, measured set of activities designed to produce a specified output for a particular customer or market [20]. This implies a strong emphasis on how work is done within an organisation." An effective BP can be said to be a collection of activities that takes one or more kinds of inputs and creates an output that is of value to the customer [21].

Various techniques and methods exist for identifying an effective BP. One such technique is the value chain method [22]. Another is the strengths, weaknesses, opportunities and threats (SWOT) analysis [23]. Although this technique can be used at the strategic level, this technique was used to evaluate the impact that each possible strategic opportunity might have on the business and its use of IT during implementation stage. This does not exclude other techniques for identifying BP such as PEST analysis, portfolio analysis [24], stakeholder analysis and user needs survey.

Taken together, BPR for NHS could be defined as "fundamental rethinking and radical redesign of health processes to achieve dramatic improvements in critical, contemporary measures of performance such as cost, quality, service and speed" [21]. BPR is therefore a technique that reviews all business activities in such a way that enables their redefinition. This facilitates changes to organisational structures and the adoption of IT. It is, in essence, a conscious reshaping of an organisation behind a new corporate vision, designed to meet the needs of the business environment (the market place) and the needs/aspirations of the business's client(s). Researchers and practitioners have suggested that the implementation of BPR concepts have generally been beneficial. However, [18] reported that the use of BPR is not without its stories of failure but it is mainly due to the simple fact that IT systems were not then capable of truly automating working process as required. It was indicated [25, 1] that in recent times, organisations that prospered during the recession were those that had undertaken a major re-engineering exercise. They suggested that reaping the benefits has involved the following:

- The abrogation of traditional (vertical, top-down) management hierarchies.
- Emphasis on establishing clear objectives for project or teams and understanding the culture of group processes by all parties within the business.
- Establishing clear links between the company's mission statement, business objectives and the goals of group processes that would allow the company to become client driven.
- Understanding the core business processes and what they are designed to achieve.
- Ensuring that all staff belong to one or more groups of teams dedicated to a specific project or processes.
- Setting up teams for the duration of a project life cycle.
- Implementing IT/IS systems to allow access to databases and share document libraries.
- Managing project documentation as a corporate resource with the IT/IS systems.
- Ensuring that where participants are geographically distributed IT/IS systems are in place to aid communication.
- Ensuring participants depend on GroupWare to streamline administration and increase the quality of teamwork.

However, in order to put into effective BPR processes, knowledge management (KM) system is required.

3. Knowledge Management (KM)

"Knowledge is not a radically different concept than information and data" [26]. Knowledge is required for the creation of information and data, just as the creation of knowledge often requires information or data [27, 28]. Knowledge management is therefore the management, communication and different interpretation of data. This also refers to the degree of IT utilisation in everyday work [29] with emphasis on the learning techniques and knowledge-transferring mechanisms by experts.

KM has the potential to radically improve the way processes are managed. Experience has shown that simply deploying new IT/IS systems without careful examination of the specific functions and problems they produce can lead to failure [18]. To avoid this especially for a system intended to replace the traditional way of managing information each step of the planning and implementation process needs to be systematically tackled as suggested [30]. This is because knowledge can be considered as the ultimate competitive advantage only if it was understood from an action-oriented perspective, which is achieved by translating information and decisions into actionable value propositions.

4. The Case Study

A simple study was conducted to (i) examine the current problems with information and exchange among users and stakeholders; (ii) investigate the current information process and preparation at each functional level; (iii) review how information is accessed, response times and the availability of information; (iv) estimate the management overheads associated with knowledge management; (v) assess the current usage of IT and software; (vi) identify IT strategic issues that are affecting users and stakeholders; and (vii) find out how project participants and employees interact and how it affects information exchange.

This study focused on a case in the mental health of the National Health Service in the United Kingdom. The purpose is to redesign the roles and functions of information and knowledge management as a unit and its alignment to the health service. A team was set up to steer the planning and implementation of this work and an interim project plan has been agreed with a subgroup. The team reviewed initial proposed aims, roles and functions of the redesigned work and approved further development of this work. It also underlined the need to address the issues of roles and accountability due to duplication, which is being taken forward alongside the developing functions. However, because of past experience of IT, the prime concern was how to avoid past failures in IT/IS project implementation in order to achieve implementation objectives. The central problems identified are as follows:

- The current knowledge portal is not sending the appropriate messages regarding the programme and its activities.
- An editorial group was not in place to edit contents centrally.
- Internal communications strategy was not properly put in place to support the information needs.
- Plan of work on how to gather new information relating to contents was not in place.
- Search for all relevant national mental health information is not a priority and there are no links to some of the relevant remote locations.
- There were some technical challenges regarding enterprise or professional software to develop other areas.
- Financial constraints to support implementation.
- Resistance to change in using new technology.

In view of the potential of KM/BPR and the findings of the case study, it became apparent to the researchers that the department could benefit from the application of BPR as the basis for implementing a KM system. This is because the central problems can be matched to key BPR activities adapted [5] based on the value chain [22] shown in Table 4.1.

Table 4.1. BPR activities.

Problem	BPR value chain process	Adapted process
The current knowledge portal is not sending the appropriate messages regarding the programme and its activities	Process capture	KM capture
An editorial group was not in place to edit contents centrally	Goal setting	KM analysis
Internal communications strategy was not properly put in place to support its information needs	Goal setting	KM analysis
Plan of work on how to gather new information relating to contents was not in place	Operations	KM re-design
Search for all relevant national mental health information is not a priority and there are no links to some of the relevant remote locations	Process support	KM support
There were some technical challenges regarding enterprise or professional software to develop other areas	Process support	KM support
Financial constraints to support implementation	Goal Setting	KM support
Resistance to change in using new technology	Communication process	KM analysis

5. BPR Processes and Activities

To resolve the key issues raised by the case study in an organised manner, the researchers mapped the key activities or stages for successful implementation of knowledge management using BPR (Fig. 4.1, Table 4.1). This is particularly important if the potential offered by KM is to be realised.

The key activities are to (i) set business goals and objectives; (ii) review the programme and its activities; (iii) identify communication strategy and information exchanged during the project cycle; (iv) estimate costs of the system; (v) examine the technical challenges; (vi) redesign the health-care process; (vii) evaluate change management issues affecting KM; and (viii) implement systems. These activities are depicted in Fig. 4.1 and each are briefly described now.

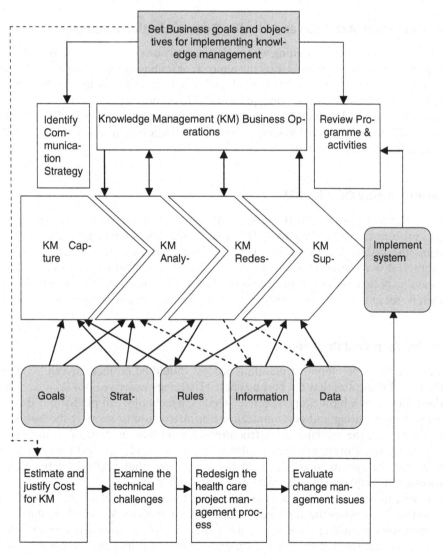

Figure 4.1. Redesigning concepts for knowledge management implementation. Adapted from Porter 1985.

5.1. Set Business Goals and Objectives for Implementing KM

Goals are defined [32] as broad statements what the organisation intends to accomplish in order to fulfil its mission, whilst objectives are more specific, measurable elements of a goal. Setting the goals and objectives for implementing KMS depends on what the organisation wants to achieve. However, one fundamental issue is that the "system designers" need to fully understand what is *actually achievable*. This is because an under-designed system will not be optimal whilst an over-designed system might not be achievable. Mapping key activities and relationships to business processes as shown in Fig. 4.1 can do this.

The figure shows that knowledge management system (KMS) goals should relate to cost reductions, improving interaction with users and stakeholders, corporate IT/IS strategy, available technology, implication for employees (people) and the external business environment. Knowledge Managers have to state clearly what impact the implementation of KMS will have on these aspects of the business. With goals established, a detailed review of programme activities and identification of communication strategy can be carried out.

5.2. Review Programme, Activities and Identify Communication Strategies

This review can be aided by examining what value each process adds to the final product. One way of achieving more effective business systems is by the removal or minimisation of non-value-adding processes or activities. It is therefore recommended that a "chain" of activities such as knowledge capture, analysis, redesign, support that add value to the services proposed [22] can be adapted for this part of exercise. Using the value chain in this way helps to clearly identify areas where strategies for KMS implementation can focus. In this way, KMS can be applied to specific business activities on the chain that are likely to increase productivity and efficiency for the health service.

5.3. Estimate and Justify Cost for KM

To assist in the cost justification process, a full appraisal of the existing system is required. Any shortcomings or problems inherent therein need to be identified. This enables the organisation to determine which cost items the system has to address before actual implementation begins. In simple terms, a cost–benefit appraisal is required to identify whether the effects of any proposed system will lead to improvements and expected savings to justify the cost of implementation. Also a criterion for minimum savings can then be set in terms of value for person hours for the project management process.

5.4. Examine the Technical Challenges

Every strategic IT/IS development planning process should be business driven [33] not technology driven [34]. Figure 4.2 illustrates that the best business IT strategy is derived not because of technological innovation alone, but from a business perspective. That is, a technological platform is designed solely to provide the required computing and communications infrastructure to support the business. For KMS implementation purposes, the available infrastructure will determine the type of operational and specialised databases (including information sites, analytical databases and archives) that will be needed. This review is needed for the system to be designed to support essential health-care functions and cross-functional processes. A simple conceptual platform is depicted in Fig. 4.2.

The review reveals health-specified data loaded on the technological platform, which then authorised by KM expertise that also queries the knowledge repository for analysis. Various hospitals can then access the local KM repository regarding data types such as demographic, treatment, clinical and a lot more. Statisticians to query statistical data using a unique subject identifier access the central health data integrator. These important outcomes can then be related to the health-care goals and objectives for the system (Fig. 4.2).

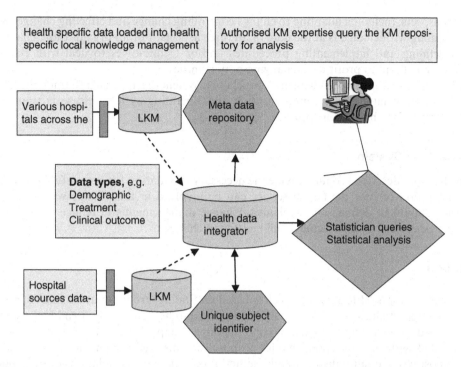

Figure 4.2. Knowledge management process model. Adapted from: Kucza, (2001) Technical Research Centre of Finland.

5.5. ReDesign the Health-Care Project Management Process

A clear understanding of the information flows within an organisation is a necessary part of the redesign process. This stage involves the determination of current physical flow to provide an overview of the processes. This results in a checklist for organisations that can potentially interact with the system. For the health-care service, stakeholders, service providers, service users, employees, consultants and government authorities to name but a few.

5.5.1. Re-Engineer Towards IT Infrastructure

The rationalisation of this flow will form the basis on which the basic functionality and infrastructure of the required KM will be established. Based on Fig. 4.2, the system needs to interface with different types of sectors within the health service. Undertaking this exercise will allow the rationalisation of information exchanged with other participants. The key difference between this model and perhaps previous models is that, the goal here is to produce an actual physical representation.

5.5.2. Consideration of KMS

Once the redesign process has been completed, enough information will be available to formulate specific requirements for introducing new technical developments. The aim is to enrich the functionality available for KMS and reduce implementation costs.

5.6. Evaluate Change Management Issues

Change management is a systematic approach to dealing with change, both from the perspective of an organisation and on the individual level. A somewhat ambiguous term, change management has at least three different aspects, including adapting to change controlling change and effecting change. A proactive approach to dealing with change is at the core of all three aspects. For an organisation, change management means defining and implementing procedures and/or technologies to deal with changes in the business environment and to profit from changing opportunities.

In KM environment, change management refers to a systematic approach to track the details of the system (for example what project, communication and operating system release is running on each computer and which fixes have been applied).

5.7. Implement the System

The BPR stages described so far provide the necessary foundation for successful implementation of KMS. An illustration of how the health service can be involved in this change with respect to KMS implementation should be defined and explained. Change management will reduce the risk and cost of change and provides clear plans to achieve full benefits of change.

6. Limitations

This research adopts BPR analysis which is based on findings from literature study supported for a case study. The research draws complementary work of researchers such as [32] and hence complements previous work by demonstrating how existing concepts can be adapted. For future work, a new assessment method associated with the conceptual model proposed in this study might be studied and used, for example, as a positivistic quantitative research methodology where the correlations of the model components might be examined on similar case organisations, so that the results could be compared with the findings of this research.

7. Summary and Recommendations

Success in adopting information technology (IT), at least as a concept for improving the efficiency of health care, is seen as a goal to be fully realised. Experience from other industries suggests that the application of BPR has been an important factor in their success. This chapter has described how using BPR the health service can be used to successfully implement the various stages of BPR processes by considering the following:

- More empirical details on information systems management within heath-care environments where they are heavily influenced by a plethora of socio-technical factors that are often indirect in nature.
- More discussions on prevailing technologies and their application theories of health service and health-care change development.
- What methodologies and tools are needed from both management and information systems perspective to identify cases of success or impact of management information systems on health service.
- The concepts should be further tested for usefulness and applicability in the health service.
- Researchers and research managers must engage with electronic record initiatives to realise these benefits by establishing adequate information governance arrangements within the above ethical framework.

8. Conclusion

A critical review of a number of approaches of evaluation related with BPR effectiveness has been presented. The BPR effectiveness assessment framework has been described. The empirical work where the proposed BPR effectiveness assessment framework is applied to KM is described. Finally, the contributions and limitations of the research in both academic and practical terms are summarised. Based on these, issues for the utilisation of the research contributions in terms of potential future research topics have been addressed.

Acknowledgement

The authors wish to thank and acknowledge Melba Wilson, Director, Delivering Race Equality (DRE) Programme, Care Services Improvement Partnership for allowing them to use the simple study to promote the work of DRE.Accounting, Charging and Billing for Dynamic Service Composition Chains.

References

1. Gyampoh-Vidogah, R. and Moreton, R. (2003) New Framework for Strategic Information Systems Planning in Construction. *International Conference, Innovation in Architecture, Engineering and Construction (AEC). Innovative Developments in Architecture, Engineering and Construction.* Proceedings of the 2nd International Conference in Innovation Architecture, Engineering and Construction. Loughborough, UK, pp. 581–594.
2. Gupta, A. (2008) Application of BPR in healthcare. http://www. expresshealthcaremgmt.com/20020515/focus2.shtml (Retrieved April, 2008).
3. Bliemel, M. and Hassanein, K. (2005) E-health: applying business process reengineering principles to healthcare in Canada. *International Journal of Electronic Business*, 2(6): 6 February 2005, pp. 625–643 (19).
4. Jacobson, I. Ericsson, I.M. and Jacobson, A. (2007) *The Object Advantage: Business Process Reengineering With Object Technology*. ACM Press, New York.
5. Gyampoh-Vidogah, R (2002) Improving project Administration in the construction industry using EDMS: An integrated IS/IT solution. PhD Thesis, University of Wolverhampton, UK
6. O'Hara, K. and Stevens, D. (2006) Democracy, Ideology and Process Re-Engineering: Realising the Benefits of e-Government in Singapore. In: Workshop on e-Government: Barriers and Opportunities. (Available at http://eprints.ecs.soton.ac.uk /12474/1/ ohara_stevens.pdf)
7. Khoumbati, K. Marinos, T. and Irani, Z. (2006) Application of fuzzy simulation for evaluating enterprise application integration in healthcare organisations. *European and Mediterranean Conference on Information Systems (EMCIS)* 2006, July 6–7 2006, Costa Blanca, Alicante, Spain.
8. Irani, Z. Sharif, A.P.L. and Kahraman, C. (2002) Applying concepts of fuzzy cognitive mapping to model: The IT/IS investment evaluation process. *International Journal of Production Economics*, 75(1–2), 199–211.
9. Koskela, L. (1997) Lean Production in construction. In Alarrcon L (Eds). *Lean Construction*. AA Balkema, Rotterdam, pp. 2–9.
10. Min, H., Mitra, A. and Oswald S. (1997) Competitive benchmarking of health care quality using the analytic hierarchy process: an example from Korean cancer clinics. *Socio-Economic Planning Sciences* 31(2): 147–159 (13).
11. Department of Health (2001) The Essence of Care: Patient-focused benchmarking for health care practitioners. (Available at tttp://www.dh.gov.uk/en/Publicationsandstatistics/Publications/)
12. Traintafillou P. (2007) Benchmarking in the public sector: a critical conceptual framework. *Public Administration* 85(3): 829–846.
13. O'Brien, J. (1997) *Management Information Systems: Managing Information Technology in the Networked Enterprise*. International student Eds. p. 277.
14. Chang, J.F. (2005) *Business Process Management Systems: Strategy and Implementation*. Auerback Publications, Taylor and Francis Group ISBN 0-8493-2310-x.
15. Hammer, M. (1990) *Re-Engineering Work: Don't Automate, Obligate*. Harvard Business Review 68(4): 104–112.
16. Liebowitz, J. and Megbolugbe, I. (2003) A set of frameworks to aid the project manager in conceptualising and implementing knowledge management initiatives. *International Journal of Project Management* 21(3): 189–198.
17. Riva, A., Mandl, K.D., Oh, D.H., Szolovits, P. and Kohane IS. The personal Internet worked notary and guardian. *International Journal Medical Information*.
18. Mainwaring J. (1999). *Evolution! Not Revolution. Manufacturing Computer Solutions*. September, pp. 44–47
19. Mandl, K.D., Szolovits, P. and Kohane, I.S. (2001) Public standards and patients' control: how to keep electronic medical records accessible but private. *Information in Practice. BMJ* 322(3): 283–287.
20. Bolinger, A. and Smith, R. (2001) Managing organizational knowledge as strategic asset. *Journal of Knowledge Management*. MCB University Press 1(5): 8–18.
21. Gunter, T.D and Terry, N.P. (2005) The emergence of national electronic health record architectures in the United States and Australia: models, costs, and questions. *Journal of Medical Internet Research* 1(14): 7
22. Porter, M.E. and Miller, V.E. (1985). How Information gives you competitive advantage. *Harvard Business Review* 63(4): 149–160
23. Myers, M.D. (1997) Qualitative research in information systems. *MIS Quarterly* 21(2), June 1997: 241–242. MISQ Discovery, archival version, June 1997,
24. McFalan, F.W. (1991) The Expert Opinion. *Information Resources Management Journal*, Fall 1991.
25. Dale, M. (1997) The re-engineering route to business transformation. In Hussey D. and Wiley J. (Eds). *Innovation Challenge* pp. 4–15.
26. Tsai, J and Bond, G. (2008) A comparison of electronic records to paper records in mental health centres. *International Journal of Quality Health Care* 20(2): 136–143.

27. Beveren, J.V. (2002) A model of knowledge acquisition that refocuses knowledge management. *Journal of Knowledge Management* 6(1): 18–22.

28. Adler, K.G. (2006) Web portals in primary care: an evaluation of patient readiness and willingness to pay for online services. *Journal of Medical Internet.* 8(4): 26

29. Özkan, S. (2006) Process based information systems success model: assessment of the information technology function in three healthcare organizations. *European and Mediterranean Conference on Information Systems (EMCIS)* 2006, July 6–7 2006, Costa Blanca, Alicante, Spain.

30. Hahn, J and Subramani, M. (2000) A framework of knowledge management systems: issues and challenges for theory and practice. *21st International Conference on Information Systems (ICIS 2000)* Brisbane, Australia.

31. Shortliffe, E.H. (1998) Health care and the next generation internet [editorial]. *Annals of Internal Medicine* 129: 138–140.

32. Özkan, S and Bilgen, S. (2005) Merging information technology process quality frameworks with other business process measurement frameworks in proceedings of the *12th European Conference on Information Technology Evaluation,* ECITE 2005.

33. Fitzgerald, B. (1997) The use of systems development methodologies in practice: a field study. *Information Systems Journal* 7(3): 201–212.

34. Earl, M.J. (1995) Experiences in strategic information systems planning. *MIS Quarterly,* 2–3

35. Kucza, T. (2001) Knowledge Management Process Model. Technical Research Centre of Finland, ESPOO Technical Report. (Available at http://www.vtt.fi/inf/pdf/publications/2001/P455.pdf)

5

Accounting, Charging and Billing for Dynamic Service Composition Chains

F.J. Rumph, G.H. Kruithof and G.B. Huitema

Abstract

Services delivered to an end user can be composed of numerous subservices and form chains of composed services. These service composition chains traditionally consist of a static set of business entities. However, in order to increase business agility, dynamic service composition chains can be used by leveraging techniques of service publishing and discovery, and consist of more short-lived relations between the various business entities. This chapter focuses on issues concerning accounting, charging and billing of such dynamic service composition chains. In this type of service delivery, several traditional settlement models are not applicable since existing architectures lack support of automated negotiation of settlement parameters. Examples of such parameters are what the service consumer will be charged for and how much, how and when the consumer will be billed. In this chapter, the requirements that have to be fulfilled with respect to accounting, charging and billing in dynamic service composition chains are explored. Based on these requirements, a framework architecture for accounting charging and billing is described.

Keywords Accounting · Charging · Billing · Service delivery · Dynamic business relationships

1. Introduction

The software industry is currently in a transition from the traditional business model in which software is deployed as components on the hardware of their customers towards software that is deployed as a service that can be accessed remotely. In this chapter, we take the concept of software as a service (SAAS) as example of a service delivery environment, but the concepts described in this chapter are also likely to be applied in other areas, such as multimedia or telecommunication services. SAAS can be defined as "time and location independent online access to a remotely managed server application, that permits concurrent utilization of the same application installation by a large number of independent users (customers), offers an attractive payment logic compared to the customer value received, and makes a continuous flow of new and innovative software possible" [6]. Although SAAS can be deployed as a new technology within old business models, new business models also become available to the software industry [1, 5] in which software products are no longer charged on a license basis, but on their actual usage. However, the change from the license-based revenue models towards usage-based revenues requires accounting, charging and billing (ACB) in SAAS applications. Billing can be defined as the process of collecting and collating, accurately, all the transaction data in order to present customers an invoice for the goods (services/goods) delivered to them. In a typical SAAS application

F.J. Rumph, G.H. Kruithof and G.B. Huitema • TNO Information and Communication Technology, P.O. Box 1416, 9701, BK Groningen, The Netherlands

G.A. Papadopoulos et al. (eds.), *Information Systems Development*, DOI 10.1007/b137171_5,
© Springer Science+Business Media, LLC 2009

- accounting information is generated dynamically;
- tariffs may depend on the combination of services consumed, the duration of consumption, the time of consumption and the quality of service (QoS);
- accounting information may be generated by a number of physical locations; and
- in a business-to-business context, billing may also require adaptation of the charges due to SLA violation.

The SAAS concept, however, also enables new business models that add substantial complexity to the billing processes. First of all, SAAS allows the relationship between the application provider and the consumer to last for a single transaction only. This implies that accounting, charging and billing have to be fulfilled within the duration of that transaction. Secondly, the composition of the application of individual services can be performed dynamically. This in turn leads to a service composition chain which is also dynamic. An example of such a dynamic service composition chain is a SAAS application that requires a language translation service. For language translation, multiple services may be available provided by third parties. The service which is actually used can be negotiated dynamically on the basis of price or quality. Another example of a dynamic service supply chain is the usage of sensor services in an application for the agricultural sector. Commercial application of dynamic service composition chains requires that the accounting, charging and billing functions of all links in the chain are aligned and standardized to a degree which enables dynamic composition.

In the software industry, billing processes as for instance described in the enhanced Telecom Operations Map [4] increase in complexity as we move from traditional hosted software towards software that is deployed as a service. Cusumano has investigated the shift in revenue models from traditional licensing towards other forms [3]. Although a trend is visible that revenue models shift from the traditional license model towards more innovative, web-based business models, the application of pay per use is still limited. Stiller et al. investigated new pricing models for Internet Service Providers (ISPs) and propose an architecture that includes metering, accounting, charging and billing [7]. Bhushan et al. also investigated usage-based pricing for Internet, but focused on the interconnection of multiple ISPs which requires federated accounting [2].

In the context of SAAS, we do not only require usage-based charging on the level of connection services but also on the level of software services. Taylor et al. have performed an initial investigation with respect to charging and accounting issues in service-oriented computing [8]. In the context of SAAS, accounting, charging and billing have to be extended to include not only the services transport layer and the services technology layer, but also the service layer in which applications are created on demand from smaller services [9]. Furthermore, the complexity of the service composition chain itself has to be taken into account since the diversity of services on the SAAS level and the associated number of business relationships are unlimited.

This chapter mainly focuses on the ACB of dynamic service composition chains. For this, we first describe and compare the structure of static and dynamic service supply chains in Section 2. Here the approach is followed that service composition chains can be thought of as a repetition of simple provider–consumer relationships. Furthermore, we describe the regular ACB aspects of static service composition chains and the impact of dynamic business relationships on these aspects. From the conclusions of this section, a framework for an ACB architecture for dynamic service composition chains is developed (Section 3). Finally, the conclusions and contributions of this chapter are presented (Section 4).

2. ACB in Service Composition Chains

In this section static service composition chains are described and a high-level view on the ACB functions for such composition chains is given. Next dynamic service composition chains and the difference with static service composition chains are described and also the impact on ACB.

2.1. ACB in Static Service Composition Chains

In this section we describe static service composition chains and related ACB aspects.

2.1.1. Static Business Relationships

In a static business relationship, a service is consumed and paid for by a service consumer under a certain long-lived contract with a service provider, as is illustrated in Fig. 5.1. The contract governs various aspects of the usage of one or more services and the payment thereof, such as tariff, quality of service and performance.

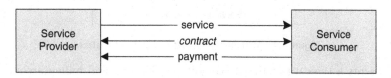

Figure 5.1. Static business relationship.

Figure 5.2 shows how the consumer perceives the business activity in a static business relationship. During the lifetime of a contract the service is consumed multiple times and that service usage is paid for multiple times.

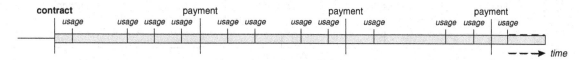

Figure 5.2. Consumer view on static business activity.

2.1.2. Static Service Composition Chains

A service composition chain consists of multiple business parties which either provide a basic service, a composite service or adds value to a service acquired elsewhere. A service provider providing a composite service is both provider and consumer. A static service composition chain may be considered as a concatenation of static business relationships as is illustrated in Figure 5.3.

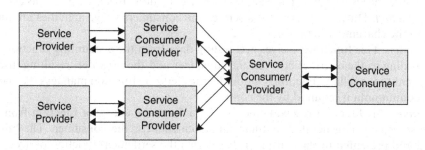

Figure 5.3. Static service composition chain.

2.1.3. ACB in Static Service Composition Chains

Figure 5.4 shows the context of the ACB operations and management for a provider and consumer in a service composition chain. It must be noted that in many cases the ACB management and operations layers are not present in the case of a service consumer.

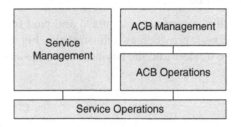

Figure 5.4. ACB operations and management context.

Figure 5.5 presents a typical functional accounting, charging and billing architecture required to deliver a service which is to be monetized. Since accounting, charging and billing cannot be addressed separately the scope is broadened with authentication, authorization and settlement functionality.

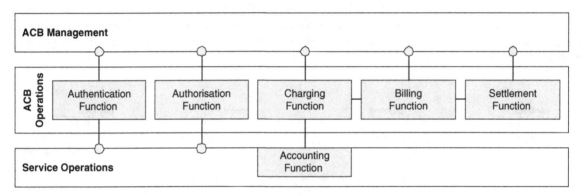

Figure 5.5. Example of ACB architecture.

The functions in the presented ACB architecture are explained below. It must be noted that the ACB management layer is not described in detail since the management of ACB functions is most commonly a manual process and is performed through the (graphical) user interfaces of the ACB functions.

Authentication Function. When a consumer makes a service request, the consumer is authenticated (i.e. the user's identity is asserted to be correct). The authentication function contains functionality and has data with which the consumer can be authenticated.

Authorization Function. When the consumer is authenticated, the authorization for the consumer to consume the service is checked. This can, for instance, be done by checking an access control list.

Accounting Function. During the usage of a service the consumers usage activities are monitored and reported to the charging function.

Charging Function. This function receives accounting data from the accounting function and rates the usage according to the contract between the consumer and the provider, resulting in charging data which are sent to the billing function. Optionally the charging function manages the account balance and or account quota if required by the contract.

Billing Function. This function receives charging data from the charging function from which a bill requiring settlement is generated or financial statements for the consumer. The bill can be then formatted and presented to the consumer. It informs the settlement function of accounts requiring settlement.

Settlement Function. This function maintains accounts receivables and payables. It can also reconsolidate incoming payments or make payments.

2.2. ACB in Dynamic Service Composition Chains

This section describes dynamic service composition chains and the impact on ACB.

2.2.1. Dynamic Business Relationships

Dynamic service composition chains are regarded in this chapter as service composition chains where the parties providing a service to consumers and their business relationship can vary very quickly, e.g. on a per transaction frequency. This requires an automated service contract negotiation process to be added. For example, in order to establish a service contract, one or more negotiation rounds are performed to mutually agree on the aspects of the contract, such as tariff, quality of service and performance. This is shown in Fig. 5.6.

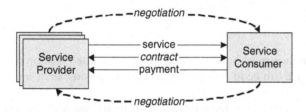

Figure 5.6. Dynamic business relationship.

Figure 5.7 shows how the consumer perceives the business activity in a dynamic business relationship. The provider and consumer negotiate a service contract and during the lifetime of that contract the service is consumed only once and is paid for immediately after the usage. It must be noted that this is a postpaid scenario and that it is also possible that the service provider requires prepayment.

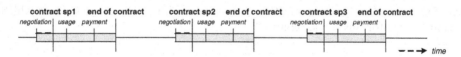

Figure 5.7. Consumer view on dynamic business activity.

2.2.2. Dynamic Service Composition Chains

A dynamic service composition chain consists of several dynamic business relationships as is shown in Fig. 5.6. The parties providing the services and composite services can frequently vary over time. Service providers can be selected based on a number of criteria, such as tariff, quality of service, performance and service-specific criteria. Figure 5.8 illustrates a dynamic service composition chain.

2.2.3. Impact on ACB in Dynamic Service Composition Chains

In this section the impact on accounting, charging, billing and closely related functions are analysed.

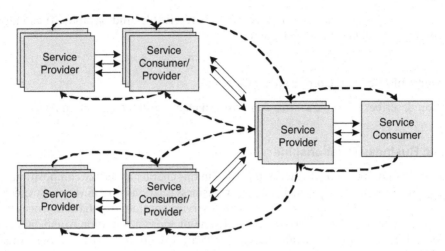

Figure 5.8. Dynamic service composition chain.

Authentication. This function must be provisioned in an automated fashion with information with which a consumer of a service can be identified. This could be, for instance, a certificate or user credential information.

Authorization. If the contract negotiated contains limits on the usage of the service by the consumer, this must be provisioned to an authorization system in an automated fashion. This functionality may be partially included in the charging function, for instance, for quota and credit limits.

Accounting. This function must be provisioned with information on how to recognized chargeable events for which accounting data are to be generated and which format to use for the accounting data.

Charging. The charging function must be provisioned with the pricing formulas to be applied when rating accounting data received from the accounting function.

Billing. Billing in dynamic service composition chains might be performed in a traditional paper bill, but it might also use electronic bill presentment technologies to send bills to the consumer. This information must be provisioned to the billing function after a service contract is negotiated.

Settlement. The settlement function must be provisioned with information such as which payment model is to be used for this service contract.

3. Dynamic Service Composition ACB Framework

This section presents a framework architecture which addresses the described impact on accounting, charging, billing and closely related functionality.

3.1. Dynamic Service Composition Architecture

Figure 5.9 shows a high-level overview of an architecture for dynamic SAAS. In respect to the architecture presented in Section 2.1.3 it is extended with a Service Advertisement & Discovery responsible for the automated advertisement (e.g. registration in a service directory) and discovery of services and a negotiation layer which is responsible for the negotiation and creation of a service contract between provider and consumer. Also the ACB management layer is elaborated since it requires automated configuration capabilities.

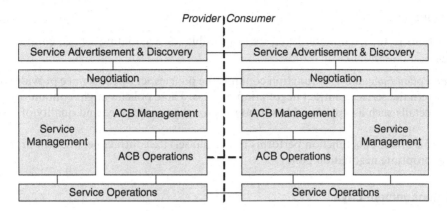

Figure 5.9. Dynamic SAAS architecture.

3.2. Framework Function Descriptions

Figure 5.10 provides a detailed view on the ACB in the dynamic SAAS architecture.

The following sections explain the various functions of the ACB management and negotiation layers of the dynamic SAAS ACB architecture. The working of the other ACB functions is explained in Section 2.1.3.

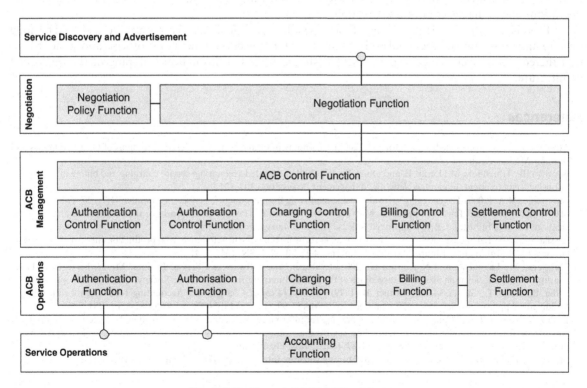

Figure 5.10. Dynamic SAAS ACB architecture.

3.2.1. Negotiation Layer

The functions in the negotiation layer are responsible for negotiating service contracts in an automated fashion.

Negotiation Policy Function. This function contains the policies set by the service provider or consumer which govern the service contract negotiation process. These policies might contain rules concerning financial details such as upper and lower bounds for the service price and quality of service-related preferences and rules.

Negotiation Function. This function performs the actual service contract negotiation process governed by the appropriate negotiation policy.

3.2.2. ACB Management Layer

The ACB management layer consists of a number of control functions per operation function in the ACB operations layer and a governing ACB control function layer. These control functions translate service contracts into policies specific for the function in the ACB operations layer.

4. Conclusion

In this chapter we have made the first steps in discovering the impact of dynamic business relationships on the management and operation of accounting, charging and billing in service composition chains. Most notably dynamic service composition chains create the requirement for automation of the service advertisement and discovery, negotiation processes and also in the management of accounting, charging and billing functions. This chapter shows that dynamic service composition chains and dynamic business relationships in general cannot be realized without addressing accounting, charging and billing and the operations and management of these functions.

This chapter should be regarded as a first step in the research of this area. Future work should be done on detailing the proposed functional architecture for ACB, the development of protocols and standardization thereof. Moreover, the concepts presented should be tested through prototyping of the functional architecture.

References

1. Altmann, J., Bany Mohammed, A. and Ion, M. (2007) Taxonomy of Grid Business Models, Proceedings of Grid Economics and Business Models, Rennes, France.
2. Bhushan, B., Tshichholz, M., Leray, E. and Donnelly, W. (2001) Federated accounting: service charging and billing in a business-to-business environment. Integrated Network Management Proceedings 107–121.
3. Cusumano, M.A. (2008) The changing software business: moving from products to services. Computer 41(1), 20–27.
4. eTOM (2003) enhanced Telecom Operations Map (eTOM), The Business Process Framework for the Information and Communications Services Industry. GB 921 Approved Release 7.0, TeleManagement Forum.
5. Lassila, A. (2006) Taking a service-oriented perspective on software business: how to move from product business to online service business IADIS International Journal on WWW/Internet 4(1), 70–82, ISSN: 1645–7641
6. Sääksjärvi, M., Lassila, A. and Nordström H. (2005) Evaluating the Software as a Service Business Model: From CPU Time-Sharing to Online Innovation Sharing. Proceedings of the IADIS International Conference e-Society, Qawra, Malta, pp. 177–186.
7. Stiller, B., Braun, T., Günter, M. and Plattner, B. (1999) The CATI Project: Charging and Accounting Technology for the Internet Multimedia Applications, Services and Techniques — ECMAST'99, (LNCS) ISBN 978-3-540-66082-8, pp. 281–296.
8. Taylor, K., Austin, T. and Cameron, M. (2005) Charging for information services in Service-Oriented Architectures. In Proceedings of the IEEE Eee05 international Workshop on Business Services Networks (Hong Kong, March 29–29, 2005). ACM International Conference Proceeding Series, Vol. 87. IEEE Press, Piscataway, NJ, 16–16.
9. Turner M., Budgen D. and Brereton O.P. (2003) Turning software into a service. IEEE Computer 36(10), 38–44.

6

Web Service Execution and Monitoring in Integrated Applications in Support of Business Communities

Rares M. Chiriacescu, Alexandru Szőke, Sorin Portase and Monica Florea

Abstract

Emerging technology is one of the key factors that drive the business world to faster adaptation, reaction and shorter communication path. Building upon such technologies, business communities emerge, geared toward high flexibility in their offerings and collaboration: business-to-customer and business-to-business collaborations. Adapting to the market requirements, companies must address several technical challenges that arise from the main requirements of the system they have to introduce: a high degree of flexibility, heterogeneous system collaboration and security of the transferred data.

Industry experience shows that many companies and public institutions have to address these kinds of challenges when introducing systems in support of business communities. In this chapter we present a general solution to facilitate the introduction of a universal platform for the execution and monitoring of web services, as part of complex business processes.

Keywords Design patterns · Service oriented architecture · Web services · Business processes

1. Introduction

In order to remain competitive in the market, business providers focus on their core products and services. Hence, adjacent activities are either outsourced to or contracted from business partners specialized in carrying out these activities. This business transition brings along a high demand for collaboration in business communities (as presented in [1]). For instance, offering eGovernment services, public institutions typically collaborate with private companies in realizing complex business scenarios. These scenarios involve the interaction of several subsystems hosted by different parties. In consequence, a solution has to be developed to address the problem of integration and wiring of the software components provided by the different parties to build up coherent, complex business logic. This procedure typically involves a high amount of money spent for the problem analysis, design and implementation of a new custom-made software platform customized to solve a concrete business case.

Based on our industry experience, we argue that the problem briefly described above is rather general and that numerous companies and public institutions are confronted with it. Therefore, in this chapter, we present a pattern that addresses the depicted challenges, proposing a technical solution in terms of a software platform.

In Section 2, we introduce a general business scenario that motivates the problem we address in this chapter. Subsequently, in Section 3, we describe the conceptual architecture of the software platform (the

Rares M. Chiriacescu, Alexandru Szőke, Sorin Portase and Monica Florea • SIVECO Romania, Victoria Park, 73–81, Bucuresti-Ploiesti Drive, Building C4, District 1, 013685, Bucharest, Romania

G.A. Papadopoulos et al. (eds.), *Information Systems Development*, DOI 10.1007/b137171_6,
© Springer Science+Business Media, LLC 2009

pattern) we propose to address the challenges implied by the presented business scenario. In Section 4, aspects regarding the implementation of the system will be discussed. Summarizing, we conclude the chapter in Section 5.

2. Basic Business Scenario

For a better understanding of the solution presented in the upcoming chapters, we proceed with a detailed discussion of the problem that is addressed in this chapter. Technology is driven by business requirements. Therefore we introduce a representative usage scenario that is to be supported by the presented system. This scenario is technology independent in the sense that it does not delve into any realization details.

For realizing an eGovernment system that provides access to complex public processes to citizens, a public institution (*PI*) has to collaborate with several other public institutions or companies (*BP 1..n*) that offer certain specialized services. The kind of service provided by PI is complex, in that it integrates (uses) other atomic services exposed by BPs in conjunction with own private functionality.

In Fig. 6.1, the business partners BP1 and BP2 provide their services to the public by exposing certain Web Services [2], which in turn implement several operations (e.g., the validation of bank account details of citizens). All operations provided by a Web Service are annotated with meta-information regarding the functionality they provide, the business partner that offers this functionality, quality-of-service details, and other relevant information. Among other operations, BP2 offers a similar operation to the *bank account validation* exposed by BP1, though having different meta-information. For instance, the operation exposed by BP2 is much more expensive to access but the response time of its execution is much shorter.

For the functionality exposed by business partners to be accessed, it has to be made somehow public and stored in a global service registry which serves as a lookup service for PI. Additionally, this lookup service should manage the semantic descriptions of the registered services using ontology concepts, in support of a high degree of automation (as discussed in [3]). Having access to such a semantic repository for

Figure 6.1. Basic business scenario.

service information, the public institution PI could compose more complex services depending on the user's preferences (e.g., cheapest one or the ones that execute fastest).

Besides using functionality provided by external business partners, PI utilizes own private application modules that realize a certain specialized functionality. This functionality should be somehow integrated with the services provided by BPs as part of the offered complex services. However, the private PI's application modules are not exposed as Web Services, but implemented as simple Java applications.

As presented above, the problem faced by PI is rather complex, not because of a difficult system processing logic (e.g., complicate algorithms, high computational effort) but for the high effort that is necessary to integrate all the different external and internal services into a coherent system. Such a system should not only allow the execution of complex services but also provide other adjacent functionality like monitoring, so that the users know the state of the service execution (e.g., in progress, faulted, successfully terminated) and have additional feedback in this regard. Designing a system to address scenarios similar to the one presented in this section would necessitate a high software engineering effort, bringing along a high expenditure of money. In the next sections we present an enterprise integration pattern proposed to address the scenario presented above.

3. Conceptual Architecture

Logically, the system components that build up the pattern proposed in this chapter can be grouped in three layers providing distinct functionalities. Figure 6.2 presents the logical layers in which our platform is structured. The interaction between these layers is rather unidirectional in that bottom layers provide their functionality to the layers on top of them. Secondary, bottom layers do not know about the existence of any top layer. In the following, we present each platform layer individually.

The *Integration Tools* layer provides application integration support for private internal application and/or external services. Typically, this layer provides an Enterprise Service Bus [4], Message Queues [5], and other integration applications. Using the tools offered by this layer, software engineers can integrate heterogeneous applications and expose them as standard Web Services in order to be used by the upper layer.

The *Component Execution* layer can be characterized as the platform's engine. It comprises applications for the registration, management, and execution of standardized services, in terms of Web Services and BPEL [6] business processes. This layer provides a Service Registry, a Web Service Execution Engine, and a Workflow engine. The registry uses ontology concepts to manage the semantic information regarding the Web Services that can either be directly invoked by system users or used in business processes choreographies expressed in BPEL. These choreographies can then be executed by the workflow engine included in this layer.

As aforementioned, using integration applications provided by the Integration Tools layer, a software engineer could expose certain private application modules (e.g., simple Java applications) as Web Services so that they can be choreographed and composed to business processes.

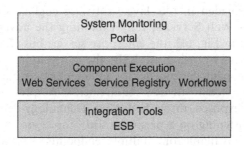

Figure 6.2. Logical platform layers.

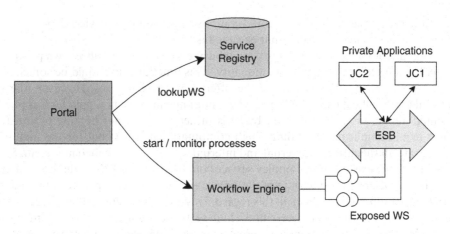

Figure 6.3. Fine-grained platform architecture.

The *System Monitoring* layer bundles applications used to manage and monitor the services and business processes used in the layer beneath. All the platform management functionality is centralized, provided by a *Portal* application. This portal provides core management and monitoring functionality like *Web Service registration and semantic annotation (meta-data)* [3], *Web Service deployment, execution and monitoring*, and *business process execution and monitoring*. We delve into the benefits of using a portal for interfacing with our platform in one of the following subsections.

Figure 6.3 presents a fine-grained view of the presented platform, depicting the main system components along with their belonging to the previously discussed platform layers. This architecture can easily address the scenario presented in the previous section. For instance, the public institution, *PI*, may use the enterprise service bus (*ESB*) from the Integration Tools layer to expose its private simple Java applications (*JC1* and *JC2*) as Web Services. These services are then used within BPEL business processes which are executed by the *Workflow Engine*.

Additionally, the private Java applications exposed as Web Services can be registered to the *Service Registry* so that they can be used for dynamic service discovery (as discussed in [7]) as an alternative to other services publicly exposed by business partners. The whole platform can be manipulated through the *Portal* application which provides user access to the service meta-data (stored in the Service Registry), control of Web Service, and business process execution and monitoring.

In the following subsections, we provide you an insight of the platform, by delving into the details of the system, layer by layer.

3.1. Integration Tools

By using components provided in this layer, software engineers can easily integrate custom applications exposing them as Web Services, fully exploiting the advantages that are provided by Integration Tools. As depicted in Fig. 6.3, the enterprise service bus (*ESB*) is the central component of this layer. In the first place, by using an ESB, the integration time and effort is drastically reduced. Using an ESB, component dependency or interaction is rather wired than hard-coded, it can be easily modified and adapted to fit new requirements. As presented in [4], by simple config-uration, components can be exposed through various technology-dependent endpoints like Web Services, Event-driven Beans listening on a particular JMS topic, etc. Actually, the same component can be configured and made available on multiple endpoints, so that it can be accessed using different mechanisms simultaneously.

Additionally, heterogeneous components based on different technologies can be used without requiring any modifications (reimplementation or wrapper applications). More value to the component integration is added by using *message transformers*. These implement the transformation logic for messages sent by one component and received by another. This way, message transformation logic is deflected from the application to dedicated objects managed by the ESB.

Another great benefit of using an ESB in the platform is the fact that it brings along support for reliable messaging, enabling asynchronous component communication. Typically, in this regard, an ESB is used in conjunction with a JMS messaging system which serves as message broker.

3.2. Component Execution

The first step toward component execution considers the actions that service providers have to make in order to register their services in a service registry. The service registry entries are made in accordance to a reference ontology which guides the service provider through the process of *service annotation* (as discussed in [3]). The annotations can be considered as descriptions of the provided service from different points of view. The general aim of this process is to facilitate the steps of discovery, selection, and input generation, while asking the provider to describe general functionality and concrete operations of the exposed services.

Regarding the matter of component execution, we need to wire appropriate Web Services in our workflows. Given a business service, the first step is to see what kinds of activities are able to fulfill the service request. These activities are extracted from the *business service ontology* [8], in accordance to which the search and discovery engine can find properly annotated *Web Services*, in order to complete an activity. *Search and discovery* relies on the reference ontology in the way that it tries to obtain relevant services from the registry, given an abstract business scenario.

Now it is up to the user to decide which Web Services will be used for each activity. He may consider time boundaries; cost boundaries, personal preferences regarding the provider or any other information that is provided. After completing the selection stage we are looking at the final configuration for our workflow in terms that the activity sequence and service endpoints are defined.

In a next step, process input is collected and the main process request is generated. Each service endpoint has associated specific input/output data which the system has to provide/administer. In the matter of input data management, each service specifies the type and description of each parameter as annotations in the service registry. The system gathers all parameters from the registry and matches those which correspond to similar reference-ontology entries obtaining a unique set of input data that are presented within a generated form. After collecting the input, the system can instantiate the concrete process and proceed to its execution. Each workflow's activity will correspond to a concrete discovered service and will have a fixed role in the business service structure.

The *generic business process* is used as a model to generate instances that correspond to the selected configuration. Therefore, one can model the process' start message to contain all the relevant execution data, since this data are available. The generic process is made up of a BPEL *flow* activity which contains a pre-condition for the service execution, the service invocation, and a post-condition. These conditions' purpose is to control and manage dependencies together with testing if the service has been executed properly. The service invocation uses dynamic endpoints according to the selected Web Service (as previously discussed). In this manner not just the client will be dynamically generated but the whole request.

The main benefits of the presented generic workflow structure are that it requires a single *BPEL process*, given the fact that the set of input data defines a concrete instance which may involve different *Web Services*. Another benefit is that in this way, processes may be embedded into other processes in order to fulfill a more complex business service. The presented structure can also support human tasks in the way that the services that compose the workflow can be substituted by human task activities.

3.3. System Monitoring

Representing the *System Monitoring* layer, an enterprise portal [9], also known as an Enterprise Information Portal (EIP) or Corporate Portal, is a framework for integrating information [10], people, and processes across organizational boundaries.

Because enterprises often use heterogeneous solutions to run their business, this results in a decrease in user productivity. Users must now remember multiple logins, one for each application, and must become conversant with different platforms. The solution comes in the form of *Single Sign-On* (SSO) [11] which is one of the core services provided by an enterprise portal. With SSO, users log in once to access multiple applications. This also comes in hand when user authentication and authorization is necessary in order to access secured services (working with sensitive data) provided by different business partners.

Being specifically designed to act as the single source of interaction with corporate information and the focal point for conducting day-to-day business, portals are also becoming a key component of any business process management (BPM), enterprise application integration (EAI), and business activity monitoring (BAM) initiative, as they represent the easiest way to present people with intelligent, relevant, and personalized information [12].

Most of today's portal implementations provide a component model that allows plugging in components referred to as *portlets* [13] into the portal infrastructure. Portlets are user-facing, interactive web application components rendering markup fragments to be aggregated and displayed by the portal. They can act like small, independent applications dedicated to a specific task (e.g., workflow monitoring). This gives the portal the flexibility much needed when integrating heterogeneous and distributed components. The portlets can be developed by the service providers and then seamlessly deployed inside the service consumer's portal.

In the proposed architecture, the portal is used mainly for system monitoring. Special portlets use the *workflow administration and monitoring API* discussed below, in order to allow users to get relevant information on the running processes and alter their behavior if required (start a process instance, end the execution of a running process instance, etc.). Another problem that often occurs during workflow execution and can be successfully addressed by portlets is the human interaction in business processes (*human activities*) [14]. In this regard, human tasks are displayed by specialized portlets so that users can claim and process them. From the user's point of view, processing a human task that may or may not be part of a business process is filling up a markup form (e.g., HTML form) corresponding to the claimed task. After the task-form is filled up by the user, the portlet submits the data associated with the task to the workflow engine, using the administration and monitoring API.

Figure 6.4 presents the interaction between the Portal (Presentation layer) and the Component Execution layer. In order to improve the flexibility of the system regarding the business process interaction, portlets can be developed that are capable of generating markup supported by mobile devices [15] and to customize the themes of the enterprise portal. This way, the monitoring system can be accessed from virtually anywhere a GSM or any kind of mobile network is available.

Process monitoring is a key feature that has to be provided by the Portal at runtime. Since we have decided to integrate our services in a more complex structure, we have to be able to get feedback regarding possible changes in state of the executed process instances. Our main concern is to be able to offer information about each activity (i.e., start time, end time, result, etc.) and provide a global view of the process state.

In order to achieve the needed monitoring functionality, we developed a custom Java API that provides methods for gathering information about processes directly from the workflow engine. As depicted in Fig. 6.4, the main subscriber to the API is our Portal, which accesses information related to the business processes in order to present it in an appropriate manner to the user. We discuss the implementation of the workflow system's API in greater detail in the next section.

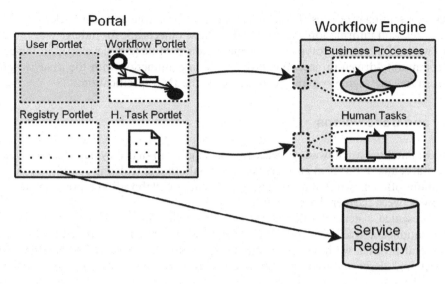

Figure 6.4. System monitoring.

4. Implementation Aspects

After having discussed the platform architecture, describing each system component in detail, we now focus on several implementation aspects that should contribute to the understanding of the overall system.

We envisage providing the presented platform in terms of an open, free system based on popular products that are developed by a wide community of developers. This way, the risk of not driving the development of the products used in the presented platform further is much lower. Additionally, using popular products, the user community is wide enough so that one can find support and instructions for free, for most of the problems that may occur. All the components of the platform presented in this chapter are implemented in Java, as the platform is aimed to support and integrate Java-based application components. The prototypical implementation we used for the evaluation of the platform is mainly based on the community-driven JBoss Application Server [16]. JBoss is used to host most of the components of the *Component Execution* and *System Monitoring Layer* discussed in the previous section. For instance, we have used the JBoss jBPM-BPEL Workflow engine [17] to run our BPEL business process. This workflow engine is deployed within the JBoss server. Additionally, we have used JBoss to deploy and execute internal Web Services. Another system component that is run within JBoss is the Portal application (JBoss Portal [18]). Having most of the components running within the same application server, we achieve a better system performance (e.g., a smaller memory footprint and faster response times) and a better integration of all components into a coherent platform.

Besides the configuration work that has to be performed when setting up the platform, some modules had to be implemented from scratch. Most of the implementation work that had to be done provides a basis for the Web Service and business process monitoring. Besides the presentation logic implemented as a part of the Portal (as a dedicated portlet), an API was developed to provide access to the business processes and human tasks managed by the Workflow engine. This API is used by all workflow engine clients (in this case the Workflow and Human Task Portlet from Fig. 6.4). Technically, the API has been developed as a stateless Session Bean Facade [19] and deployed on JBoss, together with JBoss jBPM–BPEL. It provides access to processes and human tasks in terms of Java objects. As shown in Fig. 6.4, when accessing a business process, the Portal invokes some methods of the API bean which operate on the engine's internal data structures representing processes. These objects are then serialized and sent back to the Portal, which presents the user-relevant information encapsulated by these objects appropriately.

The ESB we used in our prototypical implementation is Mule [20], developed in the context of an open source, community-driven project. We have used it in conjunction with the *Apache ActiveMQ* [21] message broker, a free messaging system that implements the JMS specification.

5. Summary and Conclusions

Business communities are nowadays geared toward agility in that they have to adapt fast to market and environmental changes. Business partners have to collaborate in realizing complex services composed of simple operations offered by different parties. Such business collaboration represents the integration of information flow between partners based on information systems.

We have presented a general solution that addresses the challenges of business integration and collaboration mentioned above by introducing a high-level system pattern. Based on the experience we gained from several projects we have participated in ([22] and [23]), we claim that the basic scenario presented in Section 2 describes a common problem that many public institutions and companies are confronted with. Therefore, the purpose of the system pattern presented in this chapter is to provide a solution for a common problem that fits into the presented scenario.

In Section 3 we have presented the components that build up the platform, grouping them logically in three layers (Integration Tools, Component Execution, and System Monitoring) having distinct functionality. Basically, each layer provides its functionality to the layer on top of it.

As mentioned in Section 4, the system prototype is not intended to end up in a product. Its primary purpose is in providing a subject for the system evaluation, so that the qualification of the platform as a high-level system pattern can be demonstrated. The products we have chosen to use within the platform prototype are all implemented in Java. They are popular, free, and have a large user community.

The implementation of the prototype is part of an ongoing project, so that not all areas presented in Section 3 have been covered yet. For example, the semantic-based service registry presented above has not been integrated yet, as we are still in search of a project implementing an open service registry that addresses the requirements presented in this chapter [10]. Additionally, work has to be carried out in the area of business process monitoring, in providing the user with an appropriate dynamic view of the business processes that are executed.

Another area that requires a detailed research is the offline processing of human tasks that are part of business processes. With offline task processing we mean working on human tasks without being connected to the workflow system (e.g., during a flight). At first glance, besides the technical problem of connecting to the workflow system and synchronizing business processes and task from the client application to the workflow system, the conceptual problem of a suitable task representation on various devices has to be analyzed.

References

1. Frank L. and Dieter R.: Production Workflow: Concepts and Techniques. Prentice Hall International, Upper Saddle River, NJ, 1999.
2. Web Services Activity. World Wide Web Consortium, January 2007. Internet: http://www.w3.org/2002/ws
3. Moulin, C. and Sbodio, M.: Using ontological concepts for Web service composition. Proceedings of the IEEE/WIC/ACM International Conference, Sept 2005. http://www.w3.org/Submission/OWL-S/
4. Chappel, D.: ESB Integration Patterns, An insider's look into SOA's implementation backbone. Internet: http://webservices.syscon.com/read/46170.htm
5. Java Message Service (JMS) Specification v. 1.0.2, November 1999. Internet: http://dlc.sun.com/pdf/816-5904-10/816-5904-10.pdf
6. Business Process Execution Language for Web Services Specification, version 2.0, April 2007. Internet: http://www.oasis-open.org/committees/tc_home.php?wg_abbrev=wsbpel
7. Hicks J., Govindaraju M. and Meng W.: Search Algorithms for Discovery of Web Services. ICWS 2007. IEEE International Conference, July 2007.

8. Baolin W., Li L. and Yun Y.: Ontological Approach Towards E-business Process Automation. Proceedings of the IEEE International Conference, Oct. 2006.
9. Paul Y.: What is a Portal, January 2007. Internet: http://www.governmentict.qld.gov.au/02_infostand/downloads/What_Is_a_-Portal-White_Paper.pdf
10. Colasuonno, F., Coppi, S., Ragone, A., Scorcia, L.L.: SisInf Lab, Politecnico di Ban. jUDDI+: A SemanticWeb Services Registry enabling Semantic Discovery and Composition. Proceeding of the E-Commerce Technology, 2006.
11. Abhinav Gattani, Sue Vickers: How to Integrate Enterprise Applications into Your Portal, December 2004. http://www.oracle.com/technology/products/ias/portal/pdf/oow_10gr2_1335_gattani_vickers.pdf
12. Colin W.: Business Integration: Enterprise Portal Evolution. Internet:http://www.b-eye-network.com/view/1762
13. Stefan H.: JSR 168 Java Portlet Specification compared to the IBM Portlet API, June 2004. Internet: http://download.boulder.ibm.com/ibmdl/pub/software/dw/wes/pdf/0406_hepper-Whitepaper-JSR168-WP5PortletAPI-comparison.pdf
14. Microsoft patterns & practices Developer Center: Portal Integration. Internet: http://msdn2.microsoft.com/en-us/library/ms978585.aspx
15. Peter F., Stephan H., Thomas S.: Understanding the Portlet Component Model in IBM WebSphere Portal,July 2003. Internet: ftp://ftp.software.ibm.com/software/dw/wes/pdf/WebSpherePortalandPortlets.pdf
16. JBoss Application Server, May 2008. Internet: http://www.jboss.org
17. JBoss JBPM workflow system. Internet: http://www.jboss.org/jbossjbpm/
18. JBoss Portal, May 2008. Internet: http://www.jboss.org/jbossportal
19. Session Facade. Sun Design Patterns, May 2008. Internet: http://java.sun.com/blueprints/patterns/SessionFacade.html
20. Mule Open Source Enterprise Service Bus. Intenet: http://mule.mulesource.org/display/MULE/Home
21. Apache ActiveMq Message Broker v. 4.1.1, April 2007. Internet: http://activemq.apache.org/activemq-411-release.html
22. Local Development Cooperation Actions Enabled by Semantic Technology (LD-CAST), EU Project (FP6-2004-IST-4-26919). Internet: http://www.ldcastproject.com/
23. Semantic-based Integration of Public Services in Support of Business Communities (SEM-A2B), Romanian National Project. Internet: http://www.ici.ro/sema2b/
24. Mark E., Jenny A., Ali A., Sook C., Philippe C., Pal K., Min L., and Tony N.: Patterns: Service Oriented Architecture and WebServices. IBM Redbook, 2004.
25. Web Service Definition Language (WSDL). World Wide Web Consortium, January 2007. Internet: http://www.w3.org/TR/wsdl20
26. Chiriacescu R., Szőke A., Florea M., Dobrică L., Kamara L., Pitt J., Neville B., Ramirez-Cano D.: Regulatory Compliance And Alternative Dispute Resolution In E-Societies. Proceedings of the IADIS International Conference, e-Society 2008.

7

Scrutinizing UML Activity Diagrams

Sabah Al-Fedaghi

Abstract

Building an information system involves two processes: conceptual modeling of the "real world domain" and designing the software system. Object-oriented methods and languages (e.g., UML) are typically used for describing the software system. For the system analysis process that produces the conceptual description, object-oriented techniques or semantics extensions are utilized. Specifically, UML activity diagrams are the "flow charts" of object-oriented conceptualization tools. This chapter proposes an alternative to UML activity diagrams through the development of a conceptual modeling methodology based on the notion of flow.

Keywords UML · Conceptual modeling · Activity diagrams · Flow model

1. Introduction

An information system (IS) represents a real business establishment. It should reflect the reality of the organization and its operations. Consequently, building an IS begins by drawing a picture of the business establishment as a part of the real world domain. This conceptual model is a picture that describes this real world domain that does not include any information technology aspects. It serves as a guide for the subsequent information systems design phase that involves the description of the software system under development.

Object-oriented methods and languages (e.g., UML) are typically used to describe the software system. Researchers have examined and proposed extending the use of object-oriented software design languages such as UML in order to apply them at the conceptual level (e.g.,[6]). According to Evermann [5], "UML is suitable for conceptual modelling but the modeller must take special care not to confuse software aspects with aspects of the real world being modelled."

In this chapter, we concentrate on a specific UML structure, activity diagrams, as a conceptualization tool. UML activity diagrams are described as the "flow charts" of object-oriented methodology. The problem with extending object-oriented models and languages is "that such languages [e.g., UML] possess no real-world business or organizational meaning; i.e., it is unclear what the constructs of such languages mean in terms of the business" [5]. The object-oriented IS design domain deals with objects and attributes, while the real world domain deals with things and properties. According to Storrle and Hausmann [7], in UML, "activity diagrams have always been poorly integrated, lacked expressiveness, and did not have an adequate semantics in UML." With the development of UML 2.0, "several new concepts and notations have been introduced, e.g., exceptions, collection values, streams, loops, and so on" [7].

This chapter argues that enhancing UML to incorporate semantics necessary for conceptual modeling will not satisfy conceptual modeling needs. Instead, we present a new conceptual model called the flow

Sabah Al-Fedaghi • Computer Engineering Department, Kuwait University, Kuwait.

G.A. Papadopoulos et al. (eds.), *Information Systems Development*, DOI 10.1007/b137171_7,
© Springer Science+Business Media, LLC 2009

model (FM) that provides a more suitable description. While work in developing FM is still in progress, it is possible to integrate the important features of UML in FM or vice versa. The purpose of this chapter is to raise interest in the new FM approach and the possibility of integrating it with UML.

2. The Flow Model

The flow model (FM) was first introduced by Al-Fedaghi [2], and it has been used since then in several applications such as software requirements [1]. This section provides a review of the basic model as it has been described in other publications. It includes new illustrations of the model.

A flow model is a uniform method to represent things that "flow," i.e., things that are exchanged, processed, created, transferred, and communicated. "Things that flow" include information, materials (e.g., manufacturing), money, etc. To simplify the review of FM, we introduce a method of describing *information* flow. The first five states of information flow are the main stages of the stream as illustrated in Fig. 7.1.

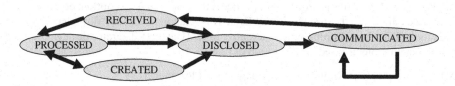

Figure 7.1. Transition states of things that flow.

To follow the information as it moves along different paths, we can start at any point in the stream. Suppose that information enters the processing stage, where it is subjected to some process. The following are ultimate possibilities:

1. It is stored.
2. It is destroyed.
3. It is disclosed and transferred to another sphere.
4. It is processed in such a way that it generates implied information.
5. It is processed in such a way that it generates new information.
6. It is used to generate some action.

The *storage* and *uses/actions* sub-stages (called gateways) can be found in any of the five stages; however, in the release and transfer stages, information is not usually subject to these substages, so we apply these substages only to the receiving, processing, and creation stages without loss of generality. To illustrate the "gateway" substage, consider that a person in Barcelona uses the Internet to ask a person in New York whether it is raining in there. First, the query flows to the receiving stage of the person in New York. The New Yorker's reception of the query triggers an *action* such as physical movement to look outside to check whether it is currently raining. The gateway in his/her information system transforms the information flow to an action flow.

3. Some FM Features

In FM, the sphere is described by using a five-stage schema. The five-stage schema is reusable because a copy of it is assigned to each entity. An entity may have multiple subspheres, each with its own flow schemata. A "schema" in FM here indicates a system or subsystem that represents the flow of something.

Consider the notion of intrinsic and extrinsic properties. In semantics, a *property* is the components of a word's meaning. For example, "young" is a semantic property of baby, kitten, colt, etc. The intrinsic property of a thing is an attribute that is essential to the thing's identity. It is used to define a class. In modeling, it is often said that some properties such as *color* and *length* are common to all classes of objects. Some objects have specific properties that distinguish them from others. In UML, an "object property" may be modeled as a binary association between classes. In semantic Web languages, such as RDF and OWL, a property is a *binary* relation; that is, it links two individuals or an individual and a value. In FM, a property is a thing that flows in the system (i.e., schema). An attribute such as *Name* is a stage-less schema that can flow (belong) to several spheres as shown in Fig. 7.2. An attribute can also be internal to the sphere as in *Grade* and *Salary*.

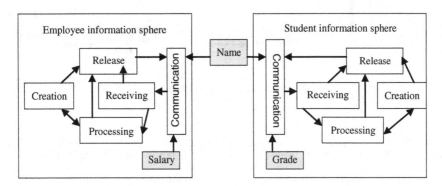

Figure 7.2. Attributes in FM are stage-less schemata that can be external or internal to the sphere of entities.

Name is something that circulates in the informational sphere of Student. Ideally, each type of flowing thing has its own circulation system; however, from the practical point of view, it is suitable to mix these flows as shown in Fig. 7.2. Things that flow in an entity characterize it, just as whiteness "flows" in cotton, "youngness" in babies, and voltage in computers, robots, etc.

FM is a model of things that flow. To use a neutral term, we will use the term *flowthing* to denote these things that flow. In addition to the fundamental characteristic of flow in FM, the following types of possible operations exist in different stages:

- *Copying*: Copy is an operation such that *flowthing* f $\Rightarrow$ f.
- *Erasure*: Erasure is an operation such that *flowthing* f $\Rightarrow \emptyset$, where $\emptyset$ denotes the *empty flowthing*.
- *Canceling*: *Anti-flowthing* f̄ (f superscripted with -) is a flowthing such that (f̄ + f) $\Rightarrow \emptyset$, where $\emptyset$ denotes the empty flowthing, and + denotes the presence of f̄ and f simultaneously.

4. Comparison of Some FM Features with UML

According to Ambler [3, Chapter 9], "In many ways UML activity diagrams are the object-oriented equivalent of flow charts and data flow diagrams (DFDs) from structured development." It is interesting to examine the type of "flow" in these activity diagrams. Ambler introduces Fig. 7.3 as a UML activity diagram for the *Distribute Schedules* use case. Parts of Ambler's description of the figure are copied here, but emphasis and some other indications are inserted in his explanation.

The activity starts when the *Schedule Printed signal* is received. This signal would be sent from one or more other activity diagrams, and it is April 1st (or later). The hourglass symbol represents *time*. The circle on the flow indicates a transformation, in this case the people on the mailing list are sorted by zip code, and then each individual is listed so that a mailing label can be printed for each individual.

According to Ambler [3, Chapter 9] "The *Labeled Schedule* box is an example of an object being passed between activities". He stated, "I rarely show objects in this manner as I feel this notation is a little bit goofy. You can usually read between the lines and determine what is flowing between activities. For example, it is clear that labels are being passed from the *Print Mailing Label* activity to the *Attach Labels to Schedules* activity."

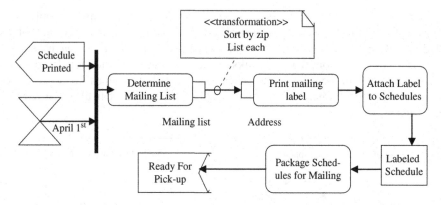

Figure 7.3. Distributing schedules.

The UML diagram merges many flows, like those listed below, into a single "flow."

- *Schedule printed signal,* which seems to be a type of information;
- *Time,* which seems to be an electronic indication flow;
- *Mailing list,* which is information;
- *Labels,* which are physical cards;
- *Schedule,* which is a physical booklet;
- *Package,* which includes a labeled schedule.

We can see here how a heterogeneous flow is indicated by solid arrows. Conceptually, this is just like representing the flows of water, electrical current, and air as one connected line of arrows. Additionally, the flow in Fig. 7.3 moves through several spheres (ontological worlds) – a human being who triggers the process, time, information, labels, schedules, and packages – without a clear indication of movement from one ontological sphere to another. The diagram lacks uniformity with its many types of representative shapes and connections.

Figure 7.4 shows the FM description that corresponds to Fig. 7.3. First, *Administrator* is used to designate the entity that triggers *Schedule Printed*. Schedule Printed seems to denote a process. Conceptually, a process usually comes from somewhere or it is in the context of something. Such a move fixes conceptual inaccuracy in Fig. 7.3. An arrow that comes out of *Schedule Printed* and goes into the command *Determine Mailing List* is like an arrow from *Pizza Prepared* to *Determine Grocery List*. *Pizza Prepared* may be the title, but it does not flow into *Determine Grocery List*. The administrator in Fig. 7.4 is the entity in an information sphere that initiates an *order* that flows (circle 1) to the printing schedule. We can draw the interior of Administrator, show how he/she *creates* an order to print a schedule and communicates this order to the system. To keep FM as close as possible to Fig. 7.3, we draw the Administrator as a stage-less schema that initiates order flow to Mailing address.

Time also can be modeled as triggering flow (circle 2 – dotted line because time flow is different from information flow) to mailing address. It is appropriate to model the Time sphere inside the Mailing Addresses sphere as it is something that automatically triggers Mailing address; however, we draw it outside to keep the FM and UML descriptions closer to each other.

In Fig. 7.4, the flow in *Mailing address* starts because of two signals from Administrator and Time. The address list is stored in the sphere of the Mailing address. We assume that it is in the storage of the processing stage. However, the location of the store in a five-stage schema may be conceptually significant. Store in the receiving stage indicates "raw data" (with respect to the sphere) that is imported from outside the sphere (e.g., collected from students). Store in the processing stage indicates addresses that are processed locally. Store in the creation stage indicates addresses that are produced by some type of

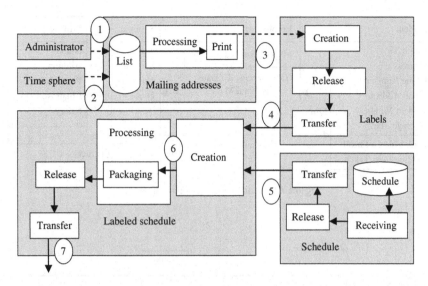

Figure 7.4. FM description that corresponds to Fig. 7.3.

deduction (e.g., important in spheres such as police departments). It is possible that addresses are a mixture of these types.

FM embeds all of these potential semantics. For example, the Mailing address sphere in Fig. 7.4 could include a receiving stage to indicate where the list has come from: e.g., collected by the sphere itself which is a part (module) of the information system of the registration department of the university.

Print in the processing stage of the Mailing address triggers (dotted line – circle 3) the physical process of printing the (physical) labels that flow to Labeled schedule (circle 4). Simultaneously, in the schedule sphere, physical schedules are withdrawn from store and flow to Labeled schedule (circle 5). In the Labeled schedule sphere, the labels and schedule are used to makeup a package (circle 6) and then released to the outside.

FM description presents a uniform and clear account of all flows involved in the process described in Fig. 7.4. It is like storytelling: The hero creates something that flows to another world and processes something that triggers the creation of. Thus, it is suitable for non-technicians, and it can be used as a communication tool between developers and system analysts.

5. Conceptual Class Diagrams

For a further comparison of UML with FM, it is important to examine the notion of class in UML. According to Ambler [4, Chapter 8], "UML 2 class diagrams are the mainstay of object-oriented analysis and design." Class diagrams are used for both conceptual/domain modeling and detailed design modeling. Figure 7.5 shows a version of a UML-based conceptual model for a university developed by Ambler [4, Chapter 8]. Classes include both an attribute and a method box in the class. Again, we observe the conceptual fogginess of UML.

The *Student* flows (labeled as *enrolled*) to a class Enrollment that flows (labeled as *in*) to Seminar. Then *Professor* is connected (directionless arrow) to the Seminar. The semantics is supposed to express the meaning that the student enrolled in a seminar that is associated with a professor. However, *enrolled* is a label to an arrow, and somehow it is connected with *Enrollment,* which is connected to *Seminar* with an arrow labeled *in*. An *arrow-enrolled* is supposed to be the same kind as the *arrow-in*. The FM description that corresponds to Fig. 7.5 is shown in Fig. 7.6.

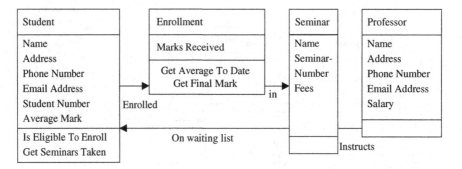

Figure 7.5. Initial conceptual class diagram.

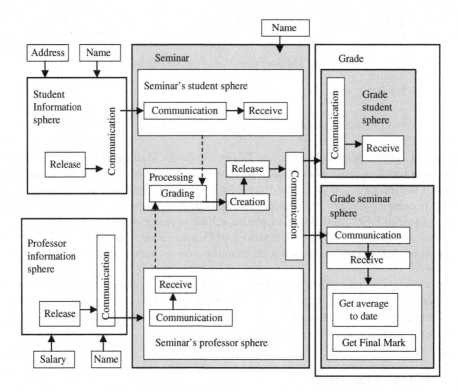

Figure 7.6. FM description that corresponds to Fig. 7.5.

The *seminar* intuitively includes student and professor plus information about the seminar itself. For sake of simplicity only one of the seminar attributes, Name, is shown. Similarly, the attributes of two students and the professor are shown. Unused stages are also removed. The seminar receives information about students and information about professors.

For example, the seminar "Introduction to Software Engineering" includes students' data and a professor's data. It has its own schema, as the figure shows (in the middle of the dark box) the processing, creation, release, and communication stages in the global schema of the seminar. Any seminar includes a process called grading that causes the creation of grades. This process is triggered by a student and a professor. Conceptually, this means that a student and a professor in a seminar produce a grade. The triggering (dotted arrows) here denotes that two schemata trigger the start of a flow in another schema. It is triggering – not flow – because the flow in the Seminar's student sphere is flow of *information* about the student, while the flow in the Seminar's professor sphere is flow of *information* about the professor, and the *grade* that has been decided is a different type of flow.

Triggered grades flow into the Grade sphere that includes two subspheres: students and seminar spheres. That is, in the sphere of grade, there are two different (parallel) spheres: students and seminar. A grade, say it is a "C," plays two roles (contexts): (1) a grade of a certain student, say "John Smith" and (2) one of the grades of the seminar "Introduction to Software Engineering" that is counted in such processes as averaging grades in the seminar.

The interesting aspect of FM description is the repeated application of the same generic stages for entities, sub-entities, and spheres. Notice how the grade fits in the student, seminar, and professor spheres. The flow is created by their interactions with each other in this context.

In contrast, the UML description leads to conceptual confusion. Ambler [4, Chapter 8] reconsidered the *Student* class modeled in Fig. 7.7, which has an attribute called *Address*.

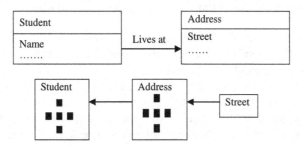

Figure 7.7. Student-Address UML description (*upper diagram*) and FM description (*lower diagram*). In FM, Street is a stage-less schema that flows in Address, which flows in Student.

According to Ambler [4, Chapter 8], "Addresses have complex data, containing street and city information, for example, and they potentially have behavior. An arguably better way to model this is depicted in Fig. 7.7 (upper diagram). When the *Address* class is introduced, the *Student* class becomes more cohesive. It no longer contains logic (such as validation) that is pertinent to addresses. The *Address* class could now be reused in other places, such as the *Professor* class, reducing overall development costs."

Hence, an attribute has been elevated to the status of an entity. This makes the semantics more difficult. Using linguistic description does not improve the semantics in UML. For example, "lives in" in Fig. 7.7 (upper diagram) implies that Address is where a person lives. Nevertheless, this is not necessarily so, since giving a post office box number as an address does not mean that the person lives in that box. By contrast, flow in FM reflects structural semantics.

In FM, all concepts are treated in a similar way: schemata have things that flow inside them. The address flows in the entity *student* just as any other attributes of a student do, such as being blond or having an age, as described previously. This flow means that it characterizes the student or part of the description of the student. Similarly, the stage-less street flows (part of) in address.

6. Example of FM Capabilities: Exceptions in UML 2.0

UML version 2.0 was developed to improve expressiveness and semantic modeling, particularly evident in activity diagrams, which acquired a completely new metamodel and semantic foundation. According to Storrle and Hausmann [7], "One of the most prominent additions in UML 2.0 Activities are exceptions." Possible semantics for UML exceptions provide an opportunity to contrast FM with UML. Storrle and Hausmann [7] give the example (adapted from the standard) shown in Fig. 7.8. According to Storrle and Hausmann, it is supposed to be interpreted as follows: While processing the part of the activity that is enclosed by the dashed line (a so-called "InterruptibleActivityRegion"), the

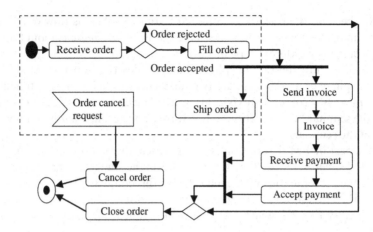

Figure 7.8. Example of UML 2.0 Activity (from Storrle and Hausmann [7]).

reception of an "Order cancel request" event triggers the preemptive abortion of this part of the activity and continues execution with the "Cancel Order" – Action.

According to Storrle and Hausmann [7], "There are a couple of problems with this interpretation that require substantial semantic clarification.... But there is also another, more fundamental question: Exceptions are a prime example of non-local behavior." Figure 7.9 shows the corresponding FM diagram.

In FM, the semantics are clear: simply canceling an order means initiating the *anti-flowthing* of the order. First, we identify flowthings in the spheres as follows:

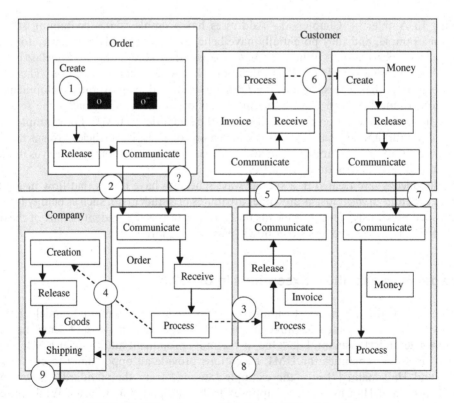

Figure 7.9. FM mechanism of flowthing and its anti-flowthing.

- Customer: Order, Invoice, and Money
- Company: Order, Invoice, Money

Thus, there are seven schemata as shown in Fig. 7.9. An order (o in the black box) is created (circle 1) by the customer that flows (circle 2) to the order schema of the company. This schema triggers the creation of an invoice in the invoice schema (circle 3) and the creation of "shipping goods" in the goods schema (circle 4). The invoice flows from the company's invoice schema to the customer's invoice schema (circle 5). It crosses over to the customer money schema (circle 6), causing the creation of a payment (e.g., money order) that flows to the company (circle 7), then to the goods schema (circle 8) to finalize shipping (circle 9).

If the customer creates an anti-order (indicated by o¯in the black box), it flows to the company's order schema (circle 10). It spreads in that schema and causes the creation of anti-"shipping goods" in the goods schema and an anti-invoice in the invoice schema. These anti-flowthings cause the "killing" of the transaction. It is possible to tie-up the example by putting the invoice and money schemas of the company in one department. The FM solution is conceptually very pleasing since it uses the same flow mechanism as the original order.

7. Conclusion

We have shown that FM presents a more suitable conceptual description than certain UML constructs. The aim is to raise interest of others to go beyond the mere presentation of the model.

References

1. Al-Fedaghi, S. (2008) Software engineering interpretation of information processing regulations. *IEEE 32nd Annual Computer Software and Applications Conference*, Turku, Finland.
2. Al-Fedaghi, S. (2006) Some aspects of personal information theory. *7th Annual IEEE Information Assurance Workshop*, USA Military Academy, West Point, New York.
3. Ambler, W. (2006a) UML 2 activity diagrams. Agile Modeling. http://www.agilemodeling.com/artifacts/activityDiagram.htm. Accessed March, 2008.
4. Ambler, W. (2006b) UML 2 class diagrams. Agile Modeling. UML 2. http://www.agilemodeling.com/artifacts/classDiagram.htm
5. Evermann, J. (2005) Thinking ontologically: Conceptual versus design models in UML. In: Rosemann, M. and Green, P. (eds.) *Ontologies and Business Analysis*. Idea Group Publishing. http://www.mcs.vuw.ac.nz/~jevermann/EvermannChapter05.pdf.
6. Evermann, J. and Wand, Y. (2001) Towards ontologically based semantics for UML constructs. In: Kunii, H., Jajodia, S. and Solvberg, A. (eds.) *Proceedings of the 20th International Conference on Conceptual Modeling*. Yokohama, Japan.http://www.mcs.vuw.ac.nz/ ~jevermann/EvermannWandER01.pdf.
7. Storrle, H. and Hausmann, J. H. (2005) Towards a formal semantics of UML 2.0 activities. *German Software Engineering Conference*. http://wwwcs.uni-paderborn.de/cs/ag-engels/Papers/2005/SE2005-Stoerrle-Hausmann-ActivityDiagrams.pdf. Accessed March 2008.

Integration of Weakly Heterogeneous Semistructured Data

George Feuerlicht, Jaroslav Pokorný, Karel Richta
and Narongdech Ruttananontsatean

Abstract

While most business applications typically operate on structured data that can be effectively managed using relational databases, some applications use more complex semistructured data that lacks a stable schema. XML techniques are available for the management of semistructured data, but such techniques tend to be ineffective when applied to large amounts of heterogeneous data, in particular in applications with complex query requirements. We describe an approach that relies on the mapping of multiple semistructured data sets to object-relational structures and uses an object-relational database to support complex query requirements. As an example we use weakly heterogeneous oceanographic data.

Keywords Weakly heterogeneous data · Semistructured data · Data integration

1. Introduction

Many organizations are facing the challenge of managing large amounts of complex information stored in different databases and files across multiple computer systems. This situation is particularly difficult to address in environments where traditional, structured data are combined with *semistructured* data, as such data are irregular and often incomplete making them difficult to manage using traditional database technology. While data management solutions exist for each particular type of data (i.e. structured, unstructured, and semistructured) in practice it is difficult to manage such data in an integrated way [5].

Semistructured data are commonly encountered in various business applications including document processing systems, web-based applications, and in scientific data-intensive environments. Because of the lack of uniformity (each data set tends to have a slightly different structure) it is not possible to describe semistructured data using a database schema and consequently self-describing formats are widely used to manage this type of information. XML [19] is now being used almost universally as a standard formatting language for the description of semistructured data.

However, the lack of the uniformity across different data sets and the heterogeneity of storage formats and data models (i.e. relational databases, XML files, etc.) make the data difficult to manage. Addressing this problem by embedding schema information within the data records using a markup language does not, in itself, provide a mechanism for managing large amounts of heterogeneous, semi-structured data in an efficient manner. Because of the increasing importance of semistructured data to

George Feuerlicht • University of Technology, Sydney, Australia; University of Economics, Prague, Czech Republic
Jaroslav Pokorný • Charles University of Prague, Prague, Czech Republic   Karel Richta • Charles University of Prague, Prague, Czech Republic   Narongdech Ruttananontsatean • Kanchanaburi Rajabhat University, Thailand

G.A. Papadopoulos et al. (eds.), *Information Systems Development*, DOI 10.1007/b137171_8,

many organizations today, extensive research is being conducted to devise efficient methods to manage such data [14].

In this chapter we focus on a particular type of semistructured data that we call *weakly heterogeneous*. Weakly heterogeneous data are characterized by relatively small variations in the structure between individual records, caused, for example, by changes in the data collection method (e.g. collecting additional attributes during patient follow-up visits). This type of data is common in many business and scientific applications, for example, in business portals and health-care applications, where individual records have slightly different data structure that may include additional data elements, and possibly omit some existing data elements.

The main contribution of this chapter is to describe a technique for the integration of weakly heterogeneous XML data sets that are suitable for the analysis of business and scientific information. The approach is based on the type apparatus of objects in an object-relational database and there is no requirement on existence of a schema for semistructured data to be integrated. We illustrate our approach using an example of oceanographic data and introduce the concept of a *disposable* data warehouse – a segment of the data stored temporally in an object-relational database and structured for the purposes of the analysis. The data warehouse supports repeated queries over a specific segment of weakly heterogeneous data and is discarded once the analysis is complete.

The rest of the chapter is organized as follows. In Section 2 we discuss the challenges of managing weakly heterogeneous data using an illustrative example of oceanographic information. In Section 3 we review related research, and in Section 4 we describe our approach to integrating weakly heterogeneous data sets. In the final section (Section 5), we give our conclusions and briefly outline future work.

2. Oceanographic Data Example

To illustrate the challenges of managing weakly heterogeneous data, consider an oceanographic data scenario. Organizations that are responsible for the collection and management of oceanographic data such as the Australian Oceanographic Data Center (AODC: http://www.aodc.gov.au/) have to deal with a large collection of scientific data stored in a variety of different formats. In addition to data collected in Australia, AODC exchanges data sets with other organizations such as the U.K. National Oceanography Centre (http://www.noc.soton.ac.uk/). The primary function of AODC is to collect oceanographic data from local and international sources and deliver oceanographic information to organizations that request various subsets of the data for research purposes. In order to service such requests AODC needs to provide an effective query support across a large and complex collection of oceanographic data. What makes this particularly challenging is the nature of oceanographic information. Oceanographic data are characterized by:

(i) Very large data volumes collected over a long period of time; the total size of active data is measured in terabytes.

(ii) Complexity of the data structures; the data sets typically contain series of measurements (e.g. water temperature and salinity) measured at a given location and point in time (i.e. data has spatial and time coordinates).

(iii) Data sets are irregular as a result of data being acquired using different instrumentation and measuring techniques over a period of time; new measuring techniques and instrumentation typically result in additional data items.

(iv) Data are *sparse*, i.e. measurements only exist for some spatial coordinates and points in time.

(v) Data are heterogeneous; i.e. data are stored in a multitude of data formats and databases, potentially associated with different semantics of the information.

Furthermore, new instrumentation typically produces better quality measurements, so that the accuracy of data varies over time.

Figure 8.1 shows a typical example of oceanographic temperature profile data. The data contain a range of measured parameters, including the ocean water temperature at various levels of depths. Each temperature profile record consists of information that describes the context of the measurement, including

```
<?xml version="1.0"?>
<marineData>
<marineRecord id="24" ver="1" cavCode="0">
<obsHeader>
  <obsID>689</obsID>
  <srcAgency>AODC</srcAgency>      ...
  <obsDate year="2000" month="6" day="23" hour="9"min="14"/>
  <latitude deg="12" min="11" sec="42" hem="S">-12.195</latitude>
  <longitude deg="130" min="11" sec="42"
             hem="E">130.195</longitude> ...
</obsHeader>
<ancillaryObservations>
  <ancObs aid="1" . . . unitsCode="DEGC" QCF="0">24.5</ancObs>
  <ancObs aid="2" . . . unitsCode="METR" QCF="0">72.0</ancObs>
</ancillaryObservations>
<obsData>
  <profile pid="1">
    <profileHeader>
      <dataType>TEMP</dataType> ...
      <obsUnits>DEGC</obsUnits><numObs>705</numObs>.
    </profileHeader>
    <profileFlags><pFlag z="46.72">1</pFlag></profileFlags>
    <profileData><param ID="0" z="0.66" QCF="0">25.9</param> ...
  </profile>
</obsData>
</marineRecord>
              ...
</marineData>
```

Figure 8.1. Example of oceanographic temperature profile data (marineData.xml).

the geographic position and the date of measurement, the instruments used, surface conditions, and a series of the temperature observations. Measurements can be taken from a stationary or moving platform (e.g. a ship), using various types of instruments. While all temperature profile data sets record essentially the same information (i.e. water temperature at various levels of depth), there are significant differences in the measured parameters, the number of observations collected, the accuracy of the measured values, and other attributes associated with the measurements. Although there are attempts to standardize oceanographic data, see, for example, [9], most existing data sets exhibit variations in data structures and can be characterized as weakly heterogeneous data.

2.1. Querying Weakly Heterogeneous Data

Existing XML query languages such as XQuery [3] can be used to query the temperature profile data. For example, the query (Q1) "*List temperature records for latitude between -15 and 3*", can be written in XQuery as shown in Fig. 8.2, with the corresponding result fragment shown in Fig. 8.3:

```
<marineData>
  { FOR $m IN doc('marinedata.xml')/marineData/marineRecord
    LET $n := $m//param
    WHERE $m//latitude > -15 and $m//latitude < 3
    RETURN <temperature>{data($n)}</temperature> }
</marineData>
```

Figure 8.2. Example query Q1 using XQuery.

Figure 8.3 shows the corresponding result set:

```
<marineData>
    <temperature>25.9</temperature>
    <temperature>25.82</temperature> ...
</marineData>
```

Figure 8.3. Q1 result fragment in XML.

However, because of the large amounts and complexity of such data, XML query techniques cannot support user requirements in an effective manner. Consider, for example, another typical query (Q2) "*Find the maximum temperature for latitudes between -15 and 3, longitudes between 100 and 140, at the depth between 100 and 200 meters, for the month of June, during the period of 2000–2007*". Evaluating this type of query requires spatial query support and typically involves combining several temperature profile data sets with potentially different data structure (e.g. the level of depths at which temperature is measured can vary between records).

An important aspect of the operation of an oceanographic data center is the delivery of data sets to clients (on-demand) for further analysis. This type of analysis typically involves repeated queries over a pre-specified segment of the data, for example, Australian temperature profile data collected between 2000 and 2007. While the extraction of this data set will typically involve the integration of a number of weakly heterogeneous data records (i.e. individual temperature profiles), and is best done using XML query techniques (e.g. XQuery), the subsequent analysis of the data that involves repeated queries over this data set needs to be supported with a database management systems with sophisticated query capabilities that include spatial query support.

Our proposal is to re-structure the extracted data segment integrating individual data sets, and store the data in an object-relational database in a form suitable for analysis. The resulting data warehouse of oceanographic information is made available to the users who can execute repeated queries over this data set using the full capabilities of an ORDBMS (object-relational database management system). This solution involves a combination of XML and object-relational database techniques. We first generate an object-relational schema by traversing XML data from multiple temperature profile data sets and store the resulting data segment in an object-relational database (Oracle 10g). The users can then execute repeated queries against an SQL 2003 compatible object-relational database. Results of the queries are returned as XML documents or in another specified format (e.g. HTML).

3. Related Research

XML data formats are widely used in applications such as Web portals and other document-intensive environments to store, interchange, and manage semistructured data. These activities are made difficult by the issues discussed in the previous section that include multiple data formats and lack of metadata standardization. Using XML-based systems to manage this kind of information provides a number of advantages such as dynamic and flexible presentation and enhanced search capabilities [18]. There is also a trend toward industry-wide standardization of XML formats based on industry-specific markup language standards such as the geography markup language [13], addressing the problem of data heterogeneity.

There are many different storage options for XML data with corresponding query capabilities. Depending on the application constraints one may choose a file system, a native storage system, see, for example, [7], [8], or a XML-enabled ORDBMS [12].

Native XML databases provide storage for XML documents in their native format together with support for the search and retrieval of these documents (see [4] for a list of available commercial products). Object-relational DBMSs such as Oracle 10g provide a repository functionality called XML native type to store XML documents in the database without any conversion and support updates, indexing, search, and multiple views on this data type [11]. As an alternative to storing data in the native XML format, XML data can be *shredded* (i.e. converted) into relational (or object-relational) tables [2].

Other studies [17] propose alternative ways of efficiently constructing fully materialized XML views of the data using SQL extended with element constructors to allow mapping to XML, and at the same time supporting XML query translation to SQL. Both approaches, i.e. native XML and conversion to object-relational structures, have advantages and drawbacks. Querying semistructured data directly in the native XML format has the advantage of avoiding the need for conversion, but does not have the benefits of query optimization and advanced query capabilities (e.g. spatial query support) available in ORDBMSs, and may require introduction of additional features such as numbering schemes.

Surprisingly, most XML-enabled approaches do not use type apparatus of objects, or assume an existence of a schema of semistructured data expressed in DTD or XML Schema language; see, for example, [15], [1].

The above-reviewed approaches typically address the management of semistructured data in general without paying specific attention to the type and extent of data heterogeneity, and may not be suitable in situations where intensive analysis of a specific segment of the data derived from multiple heterogeneous data sets is required. Our approach, described in the next section, combines the use of an XML query language for the integration of multiple weakly heterogeneous XML data sets and the capabilities of object-relational databases following the transformation of the XML data into an object-relational form. Another benefit of this approach is that the semistructured data can now be combined with other data held in the object-relational database.

4. Proposed Approach

Commercially available object-relational technology provides a comprehensive solution for the management of XML data. This allows the storage of XML data in the database, either fully or partially. A combination of storing XML data externally and internally within the database may be appropriate in situations where the data volumes are very large and access to the entire set of data at the same time is not required, as is the case in the previously described AODC environment. In order to address the requirements of applications that use weakly heterogeneous data (i.e. data sets with slightly varying structure) several steps are required:

(i)   integration of weakly heterogeneous XML data sets;
(ii) extraction of object-relational schema from XML data to be integrated; and
(iii) transformation of XML data and its storage in the ORDBMS.

4.1. Query System Architecture

Figure 8.4 describes the proposed system architecture and the steps required to generate the data warehouse to support repeated queries over a selected data segment. First, given the user data requirements specified via the user interface a selected data segment, e.g. Australian temperature profiles for the period 2000–2007, is extracted from the corresponding XML data sets (step 1).

The system extracts this data by identifying the relevant XML files (individual temperature profiles, in this example) using the XML Repository. The XML Repository holds information such as the date and the position where the experiment was conducted. The identified XML files are then processed and using XQuery, aggregating the results into a single XML document (step 2). The corresponding object-relational schema is then generated (step 3) and the XML data are mapped into object-relational structures and stored in the ORDBMS (step 4). At this point the data warehouse constructed from weakly heterogeneous XML data sets is ready to support user queries.

The Query Composer is used to rewrite user queries presented via a graphical interface into SQL and the query is executed against the ORDBMS (step 5). The query results can be published as an XML document or transformed (step 6) into another presentation format (e.g. plain text, HTML), as required by the user.

This system architecture and the implementation of a proof-of-concept prototype are described in detail elsewhere [16]. In this chapter we focus on extracting object-relational schema from XML data sets (i.e. step 3 in Fig. 8.4).

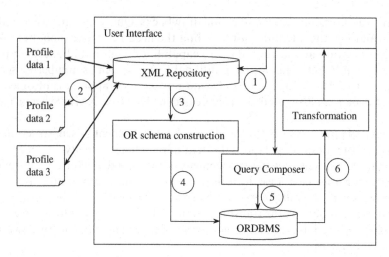

Figure 8.4. Query system architecture

4.2. Mapping Schema

The oceanographic data sets that we use to illustrate our approach are characterized by deeply nested data structures that make the data unsuitable for mapping into *flat* relational tables. We use object-relational mapping that supports nested structures and fits well with this type of data. We note here that there is no direct unique mapping between XML structures and an object-relational schema. There are a number of alternative methods that can be used to perform the mapping. One approach, for example, is to create an object-relational view over the target schema, and to make the view the new query target. Another possibility is to use XSLT [6] to transform the XML document (i.e. to transform XML attributes to elements, etc.). We use the latter approach to *normalize* the original XML document so that it can be mapped to object-relational structures. We apply a well-known principle for the transformation – an element:

```
<E attr₁=a₁ attr₂=a₂ ...attrₖ=aₖ>E-content</E>
```

is transformed to:

```
<E>
   <attr₁>a₁</attr₁>
   <attr₂>a₂</attr₂>
      ...
   <attrₖ>aₖ</attrₖ>
   <value>E-content</value>
</E>
```

in a situation where E is a leaf element. Otherwise, E-content replaces the value element. Figure 8.5 shows a general XSLT template for transforming the temperature profile data into a new temperature profile data (XML format).

Applying the template in Fig 8.5 to the temperature profile data shown in Fig 8.1 produces the transformation shown in Fig 8.6. We now proceed to devise an algorithm to generate an object-relational schema that conforms to the SQL standard [10] from the normalized data sets.

```
<xsl:stylesheet xmlns:xsl="http://www.w3.org/1999/XSL/Transform">
  <xsl:template match="*">
    <xsl:copy><xsl:for-each select="@*">
      <xsl:element name="{name()}">
        <xsl:value-of select="."/></xsl:element></xsl:for-each>
      <xsl:apply-templates select="./*"/>
      <xsl:choose><xsl:when test="count(@*) > 0">
        <xsl:element name="value"><xsl:value-of select="."/>
        </xsl:element></xsl:when>
        <xsl:otherwise><xsl:if test="string-length(text())> 0">
        <xsl:value-of select="."/></xsl:if></xsl:otherwise>
      </xsl:choose>
    </xsl:copy>
  </xsl:template>
</xsl:stylesheet>
```

Figure 8.5. XSLT template (skeleton).

The transformation algorithm generates user-defined types, more specifically structured types. Structured types that we need to use for this purpose have an internal structure composed from other structured types and include collections (i.e. ARRAYs, MULTISETs). The definitions of the basic data types have to be added manually. We use the Oracle SQL syntax for our examples (we note that Oracle implements a subset of the SQL 2003 standard).

The algorithm assumes a DOM version of a normalized XML document D. The associated tree is traversed in a depth-first manner to extract information about elements and their structure. Due to normalization of XML data we will not consider the order of elements. Consequently, the order of attributes of a structured type T is not relevant, and we consider T to be a set of attributes, and denote it as A_T. The key principle of our transformation is to assign an SQL structured type to each element of XML data in the repository. Text nodes will become attributes of a basic type, repeating subelements of an element will compose a collection (e.g. ARRAY, MULTISET).

Formally, we consider a structured type $T(T_1, \ldots, T_n)$ whose construction depends on recognized occurrences of elements in the traversal and uses the following rules for generating the types:

```
<?xml version="1.0"?>
<marineData>
 <marineRecord>
   <id>24</id> ...
   <obsHeader> ...
     <latitude>
       <deg>12</deg>
       <min>11</min>
       <sec>42</sec>
       <hem>0</hem>
       <value>-12.195</value>
     </latitude>
     <longitude> ...
       <hem>0</hem>
     <value>130.195</value>
     </longitude>        ...
   </obsHeader>
   <ancillaryObservations>
     <ancObs>
       <aid>1</aid> ...
     <unitsCode>DEGC</unitsCode>
       <value>24.5</value>
     </ancObs>
     <ancObs>
       <aid>2</aid>    ...
 </marineRecord>
     ...
</marineData>
```

Figure 8.6. Temperature profile data.

```
1.  IF E is the element associated with the first visit a node in
    the traversal and T is its associated type to be generated
    THEN A_T := Ø;
2.  IF E_i is a direct subelement of E and T_i its associated type.
    THEN IF T_i ∈ A_T
         THEN generate collection type T_Ti whose members are of
              type T_i;
              A_T := (A_T - T_i) ∪ T_Ti
         ELSE IF T_Ti ∉ A_T THEN A_T := A_T ∪ T_i;
3.  IF no further E_i exists and A_T ≠ Ø THEN generate T;
```

Since the XML data appear as a collection of specific records, we can stop generating types before the last generated collection type T_{Ti}. Then the database objects can be defined by CREATE TABLE DB-T_i OF T_i statement.

A problem can arise when type T that was already generated earlier during the traversal appears again with potentially different semantics. This may require user intervention to align the semantics of the generated types. A comprehensive discussion of the resolution of such semantic conflicts can be found in [16] and will not be considered further in this chapter.

In our implementation we generate names of types for each tag tag as tagType. This avoids problems with missing elements as all elements have to be mapped to nullable columns – the default for every nonprime attribute of a relation. Figure 8.7 shows a fragment of database schema in Oracle 10 g syntax generated for data in Figure 8.6.

```
CREATE TYPE ancObsType AS OBJECT
(          aid           NUMBER,
           paramCode     VARCHAR2(30),
           unitsCode     VARCHAR2(30),
           QCF           NUMBER,
           value         NUMBER(20,10) );
CREATE TYPE ancillaryObservationsType
AS VARRAY(1000) OF ancObsType; …
CREATE TYPE marineRecordType AS OBJECT
(          id            NUMBER,
           ver           NUMBER,
           cavCode       NUMBER,
           obsHeader     obsHeaderType, …
           obsData           obsDataType);
CREATE TABLE marineRecord OF marineRecordType;
```

Figure 8.7. Object-Relational Schema (a fragment).

One potential improvement of the algorithm concerns the case when two structured types are differentiated only by name (i.e. are synonymous). Then the set of attributes can be aggregated into one type as shown in Fig 8.8. The name of such type can be generated or determined manually.

The example database uses a single table of oceanographic data with richly structured rows.

```
CREATE coordinateType AS OBJECT
(          deg NUMBER,
           min NUMBER,
           sec NUMBER,
           hem VARCHAR2(30),
           value NUMBER(20,10) );
CREATE obsHeaderType AS OBJECT
(          obsID   NUMBER,
           …
           latitude   coordinateType,
           longitude  coordinateType, …);
```

Figure 8.8. Object-Relational Schema (a fragment).

5. Conclusions and Future Work

In this chapter we describe an approach suitable for supporting complex query requirements of applications that use semistructured data. We have described the overall system architecture and focused on the transformation of weakly heterogeneous data sets into the corresponding object-relational structures. We have illustrated our approach using weakly heterogeneous oceanographic data sets that exhibit complex multi-dimensional data. We note, however, that such weakly heterogeneous data are common in many business applications (e.g. Web portals), data warehousing applications, and in application domains such as health care. Frequently, such data need to be subject to intensive analysis and often involve multi-dimensional data that require the support of object-relational database management system, making the proposed approach of general interest.

Further work is needed to address the various semantic issues that typically arise in environments that use heterogeneous semistructured data to assist the users in semiautomatic resolution of semantic conflicts.

Acknowledgments

This research has been partially supported by the National Program of Research, Information Society Project No. 1ET100300419 and also by the grants of GACR No. GA201/09/0990, GA201/06/0175, and GA201/06/0648.

References

1. Amornsinlaphachai, P., Rossiter, N. and Ali, M.A. (2006) Storing Linked XML Documents in Object-Relational DBMS. *Journal of Computing and Information Technology (CIT)* 14(3), 225–241.
2. Beyer, K., Cochrane, R.J., Josifovski, V., Kleewein, J., Lapis, G., Lohman, G., Lyle, B., Ozcan, F., Pirahesh, H., Seemann, N., Truong, T., Van der Linden, B., Vickery, B. and Zhang1, Ch. (2005): *System RX: One Part Relational, One Part XML.* In *Proc. of the 2005 ACM SIGMOD Int. Conf. on Management of Data, Baltimore*, Maryland, USA, ACM Press, pp. 347–358.
3. Boag, S., Chamberlin, D., Fernández, M.F., Florescu, D., Robie, J. and Siméon, J. (2005) XQuery 1.0: An XML Query Language, W3C Working Draft, 04 April 2005. Retrieved July 4, 2008 from: http://www.w3.org/TR/xquery/
4. Bourret, R. (2007) XML Database Products. Retrieved July 4, 2008 from: http://www.rpbourret.com/xml/XMLDatabaseProds.htm
5. Buneman, P. (1997) *Semistructured Data.* In *Proc. of 1997 Symposium on Principles of Database Systems (PODS97)*, Tucson, Arizona, pp.117–121.
6. Clark, J. (1999): XSL Transformations (XSLT) Version 1.0. W3C Recomm. Nov 16, 1999.
7. Fiebig, T., Helmer, S., Kanne, C.-C., Moerkotte, G., Neumann, J., Schiele, R. and Westmann, T. (2002): Anatomy of a native XML base management system. *VLDB Journal*, 11(4), 292–314.
8. Harold, E.R. (2005) Managing XML data: Native XML databases. Retrieved July 4, 2008 from: http://www.ibm.com/developer-works/xml/library/x-mxd4.html
9. Isenor, A.W. and Keeley, J.R (2005) Modeling Generic Oceanographic Data Objects in XML. *Computing in Science and Engineering*, July/August, 58–65.
10. ISO/IEC 9075:2003 (2003) Information Technology, Database Languages, SQL. Part 2: Foundations.
11. Liu, Z.H., Krishnaprasad, M. and Arora, V. (2005): *Native XQuery Processing in Oracle XMLDB.* In *Proc. of the ACM SIGMOD Int. Conf. on Management of Data.* Baltimore, MD, pp. 828–833.
12. Mlýnková, I. and Pokorný, J. (2005) XML in the World of (Object-)Relational Database Systems. In Vasilecas, O., et al. (Eds.), *Information Systems Development Advances in Theory, Practice, and Education 2004.* Springer Science + Business Media, Inc., pp. 63–76.
13. OCG (2008) Geography Markup Language. Retrieved July 4, 2008 from: http://www.opengeospatial.org/standards/gml
14. Rahayu, J.W., Pardede, E. and Taniar, D. (2007) XML Databases: Trends, Issues, and Future Research. In *The 9th Int. Conf. on Information Integration and Web-based Applications and Services (iiWAS 2007)*, ACS, 229, 9–10, Jakarta, Indonesia. http://www.ocg.at/publikationen/books/volumes/sr229.html
15. Runapongsa, K. and Patel, J.M. (2002) Storing and Querying XML Data in Object-Relational DBMSs. In *XML-Based Data Management and Multimedia Engineering.* EDBT 2002 Workshops, LNCS 2490/2002.
16. Ruttananontsatean, N. (2007) An Investigation of Query Techniques for Semistructured Data, PhD Thesis, Faculty of Information Technology, University of Technology, Sydney, Australia, November 2007.

17. Shanmugasundaram, J., Shekita, E., Barr, R., Carey, M., Lindsay, B., Pirahesh H. and Reinwald B. (2001) Efficiently Publishing Relational Data as XML Documents. *VLDB Journal* 10(2–3), 133–154.

18. Suresh, R., Shukla, P. and Schwenke G. (2000) XML-Based Data Systems for Earth Science Applications. In *Proc. of Geoscience and Remote Sensing Symposiun (IGARSS)*, *IEEE* 2000 Int., 3, 1214–1216.

19. W3C (2004): Extensible Markup Language (XML) 1.1. (Second Edition), W3C Recommendation 16 August 2004. Retrieved July 4, 2008 from: http://www.w3.org/TR/xml11/

9

Investigating the Applicability of Structural Analysis Techniques in Distributed Systems

Karen Hamber, Graham Low and Greg Stephens

Abstract

An object-oriented system is comprised of a number of objects that work together to achieve a common goal. In a distributed system, these objects are distributed around a computer network to improve the overall performance or reliability of the system. However, care must be taken in the placement of the components because inappropriate assignment onto processors or subsystems can substantially degrade the performance of the system. The distribution process can be broken up into two stages, partitioning and allocation. Partitioning is the process of dividing the system into tasks; these tasks are then assigned to the system's various processors in the allocation stage. This chapter describes a new approach to the distribution process and investigates the use of structural analysis as developed for social network analysis for making distribution process decisions.

Keywords Allocation · Distributed systems · Partitioning · Systems design

1. Introduction

In a distributed application system, objects are distributed around a computer network so as to improve the overall performance or reliability of the system. There are many advantages to distributing a system; however, these advantages come at a cost of increased complexity in development. Furthermore, random assignment of tasks or modules onto processors or subsystems can substantially degrade the performance of the entire distributed system [1].

The distribution process is broken up into two important stages, partitioning and allocation. Partitioning refers to the process of dividing the system into tasks that are then assigned to the system's various processors in the allocation stage [2, 3]. Partitioning decisions are made by considering communication and the potential concurrency between the components of the system. Once the partitions are assigned to processors, there are a number of metrics to determine the quality of the assignment, viz., inter-processor communication and execution costs. The optimal solution is one that minimizes the overall cost to the system.

A number of techniques are available based on the proposed approaches (e.g., [2–7]). These techniques have not generally been incorporated into distributed systems design in practice. One reason for this may be the manual nature of the proposals and the multitude of steps involved. Techniques developed for social network analysis may offer alternative approaches that may be more easily adopted, as well as being potentially automated.

Karen Hamber, Graham Low and Greg Stephens • School of Information Systems, Technology and Management, University of New South Wales, Australia

G.A. Papadopoulos et al. (eds.), *Information Systems Development*, DOI 10.1007/b137171_9,
© Springer Science+Business Media, LLC 2009

Social network analysis is a research perspective within the social and behavioral sciences. It is based on an assumption of the importance of relationships among interacting units. Social network analysis is made up of a number of concepts, notations, and definitions that are used to model the social network; thus allowing operations and calculations to be performed on the network in order to analyze it.

One of the major concerns of social network analysis is the identification of cohesive subgroups of actors within a network. Such groups are subsets of actors among whom there are relatively strong, direct, intense, frequent or positive ties [8]. Similarly, one of the major concerns when distributing a system, both in the partitioning and allocation stages, is co-locating those parts of the system between which there is a large amount of communication. Furthermore, there are a number of other similarities between social and computer networks. This chapter reports an investigation into the applicability of social network methods for the partitioning process.

2. Structural Analysis Techniques

One of the major concerns of social network analysis, which uses structural analysis techniques, is the identification of cohesive subgroups of actors within a network. Cohesive subgroups are subsets of actors among whom there are relatively strong, direct, intense, frequent, or positive ties [9]. There are a number of different ways to conceptualize subgroups. The following four properties provide the basis upon which the social network concepts of a cohesive subgroup were developed.

- The mutuality of ties.
- The closeness or reachability of subgroup members.
- The frequency of ties among members.
- The relative frequency of ties among subgroup members compared to non-members.

By considering each of the above properties, network analysis methods were formalized into definitions and descriptions about the structural properties of the actors or groups.

The "foundational idea" for studying cohesive subgroups in social networks is the clique. A clique is defined as a maximally complete subgraph of three or more nodes. It is based on the mutuality of ties defining a subset of nodes, all of which are adjacent to each other. The clique is a very strict definition with the absence of a single line preventing a subgraph from meeting the criteria. The second and third properties take the clique as a starting point and use different structural properties to generalize the idea.

Closeness or reachability of subgroup members assumes that "important social processes occur through intermediaries" [9]. Under this assumption, subgroups are considered to be cohesive as long as the distance among the members is small. Three definitions were created under this reachability notion: n-cliques, n-clans, and n-clubs.

An n-clique is a maximal subgroup in which the largest distance between any two nodes is no greater than n. That is, we can specify a cutoff value, n, which is the largest distance between any two nodes. When $n = 1$, the n-clique is really a clique, as all nodes in the subgraph must be directly connected to every other node. A value of $n = 2$ has been identified as a useful cutoff value. 2-cliques are subgraphs in which every member need not be adjacent; however, they must be reachable through at most one intermediary [9].

Two problems result from the definition of an n-clique, both arising because it is possible that one or more of the intermediaries is not actually a member of the n-clique. The first problem is that the diameter, the length of the longest path between the nodes in the subgraph, may be more than n. This problem is addressed by the creation of an n-clan, an n-clique where the nodes within the subgraph must have a path of n or less. The second problem is that an n-clique may not even be connected. That is, two nodes may have no path between them that consists of only n-clique members and consequently the n-clique is disconnected. n-clubs were designed to cater to this problem and are subgraphs where the distance between all the nodes within the diameter can be no more than n. All n-clans are both n-cliques and n-clubs, however, n-clubs are not necessarily n-cliques or n-clans.

2.1. Support from Structural Analysis Techniques

The concepts of actors and relational ties from social networking are of particular interest to the distributed systems domain. To map between the two disciplines we can consider the actors in a social network as the objects in a system. Relational ties, in social network data, relate to specific kinds of linkages between the actors. Similarly, in distributed systems, these ties relate to the different types of links between the objects in the system, namely, communication and/or dependency. By focusing on each of these different types of links we are able to group the objects in the system. We examine their application to two key concepts in the partitioning process: concurrency and communications.

Concurrency: When partitioning objects we are concerned with placing those objects that are not related (i.e., those objects that can run concurrently) into separate partitions. Low and Rasmussen [2] take account of different levels of concurrency in their method. They first create an adjacency matrix of the system and then apply Warshall's algorithm to it. The resulting matrix is the transitive closure matrix for the system and is used to show which objects can operate concurrently with each other.

From a social network perspective, A may be able to "reach" C by using B as an intermediary. This is referred to as a walk of length 2 or a 2-chain; a → b, b → c. The number of 2-chains between i and j can be determined by squaring the sociomatrix, X [10].

$$X_{ij}^2 = \sum_{k=1}^{\varepsilon} X_{ik} X_{kj}$$

When applied in distributed systems, the → can be described as "is dependent on". When determining the transitivity in a distributed system, we are concerned with chains of length 2. Consequently, we can square the adjacency matrix and if the value x_{ij} in the resulting matrix is greater than 0, then nodes i and j are transitively dependent. We now have two matrices of interest, X and X^2. The matrix X shows the original dependencies within the system. X^2 shows the transitive dependencies within the system. Binary addition of these two matrices will result in a matrix containing all the dependencies within the system. (We are not interested in the actual number of 2-chains between nodes, only whether or not they exist. Binary addition will ensure that the resulting matrix is in dichotomous form.)

Communication: When partitioning a system we are interested in grouping those objects between which there are "high" levels of communication. Similarly, one of the major concerns of social network analysis is the identification of cohesive subgroups. "Cohesive subgroups are subsets of actors among whom there are relatively strong, direct, intense, frequent or positive ties" [9]. When the strength or intensity of ties between actors is being examined valued relations are used. Cohesive subgroups in such relations focus not just on whether ties between actors are present, but on subsets of actors among whom ties are strong or frequent. When partitioning a system we must consider the different levels of communication between the objects. Clearly, there are strong parallels between these two objectives. The question then becomes how to detect the cohesive subgroups in such relations.

There are a number of different ways to conceptualize and detect subgroups. Some of the techniques (cliques, n-cliques and n-clubs) to identify these subgroups were introduced above. We can now extend these notions and apply them to valued relations where the value of the tie is considered, not just whether it exists or not. A threshold value c is introduced and actors are only considered members of the subgroup if they have ties of at least c. Specifically, a clique at level c can be defined where the ties between all actors in the clique must have a value of at least c. By increasing (or decreasing) this threshold value we can detect subgroups that are more (or less) cohesive.

From a distributed system perspective, a clique is a group of objects, each of which communicates with every other object in the group. In a clique at level c, the communication cost/amount between each of the objects must be greater than c. Ideally we want to partition a system based on clique analysis. The straight clique definition is, however, very strict with the absence of one communication link between objects preventing a group from being identified. As described in the literature review we can generalize the clique definition slightly and determine the 2-cliques within the system. This method will still determine strict cliques, but also allows for the absence of some links.

We can further validate this approach by revisiting the notion of dependency. We described a situation where a → b, b → c and hence a → c, where → refers to "is dependent on". We determine the dependencies by analyzing a class diagram of the system. If a and b communicate in a synchronous manner, that is, if a must wait for a reply from b before proceeding, then we can say that a is dependent on b. We can now view the relationships as a and b communicating, b and c communicating and a transitively dependent on c. This situation would not be identified as a clique, however, it would be identified by a 2-clique analysis because there is a 2-chain between a and c. Consequently we would place all a, b, and c in the same partition. There is no processing benefit by placing a and c in separate partitions because they cannot run in parallel as they are dependent on one another. Furthermore there are communication minimization benefits in placing a, b and c in the same partition. Hence, the 2-clique analysis has combined the notions of communication and dependency. It is noted that it is possible for two cliques to share members and hence overlap. Consider Fig. 9.1, object C is a member of two cliques, {A, B, C} and {C, D, E}.

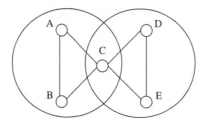

Figure 9.1. Overlapping cliques.

3. Application to Distributed Systems

In this section we discuss an approach to the design of distributed systems using structural analysis techniques.

3.1. Proposed Technique

Concurrency Analysis: To determine the groups of objects that are dependent on each other we use the trace tables and class diagrams of the system to create a dependency matrix. This matrix is similar to that in Low and Rasmussen [2], however, it should only reflect the synchronous communication. This is because when communication is synchronous, the sender must wait for a response from the receiver before continuing processing and hence the sender is "dependent" on a response from the receiver. When communication is asynchronous the sender need not wait for a reply from the receiver and hence is not "dependent" on the receiver object even though they communicate. We therefore do not include asynchronous communication when creating the original dependency matrix. We can square this matrix to determine the transitive dependencies within the system (as described above). The original synchronous dependencies plus the transitive dependencies will give us an overall dependency matrix. A clique analysis on this matrix will determine which objects are dependent on each other.

By removing any objects that overlap from the cliques, we are left with a number of distinct groups. We can now re-introduce any objects that communicate asynchronously, creating a new group for each. Each of the members within a group will be dependent on the other members from their group, but not on the members of other groups. Hence we now have a list of groups that can run concurrently with each other. We will use this list to help determine where to place objects when investigating communication.

Communication Analysis: Whilst investigating communication, Low and Rasmussen [2] create a matrix showing the communication levels between the different objects/classes by collating the information in the trace tables for the system. It is with this communication matrix that we begin our investigations into mapping the cohesive subgroup methods used within social network analysis to the distributed computing domain. It is noted that communication between objects/classes can be measured in a number of different ways: number of messages sent, the frequency of messages sent and the size of messages sent. This study is not concerned with which communication metric is used and takes the completed communication matrix as a starting point.

When grouping objects/classes based on their communication costs it becomes irrelevant which direction the information is flowing. Instead, we are interested in the total amount of communication between the two objects/classes. Consequently we can recode the communication matrix by adding the value of x_{ij} to the value of x_{ji}. The resulting matrix will be symmetrical with $x_{ij} = x_{ji}$.

We are interested in grouping objects/classes between which there are large communication levels. Following on from Tamhankar and Ram [1], three levels of communication are introduced – low, medium and high. As Tamhankar and Ram state, the basis for classification should be related to a percentage of the total cost. We follow the suggestions made by Tamhankar and Ram and determine the cost levels are as follows:

1. arrange the communication amounts in ascending order of costs;
2. calculate the total cost;
3. assign the costs at the top, comprising 10% of the overall communication cost, as LO;
4. assign the costs at the next higher group, comprising 20% of the overall communication cost, as MD; and
5. assign the remaining costs, comprising 70% of the overall communication cost, as HI.

Three new matrices have now been created, one for each of the different communication levels – LO, MD and HI. For example, in the HI communication matrix, there will be a value of 1 in x_{ij} ($=x_{ji}$) where there is a HI communication cost between object i and object j. A clique and 2-clique analysis can now be run on each of these matrices. The results of these analyses will fall into one, or a combination, of the following categories:

1. no cliques;
2. a number of mutually exclusive cliques; and
3. a number of overlapping cliques.

If no clique is found when analyzing a HI or MD communication level, then we can turn to the results of the analysis of a lower communication level. If no cliques are found in any of the communication levels then we move to the 2-clique analysis. Ideally we would want the results to fall into the second category from above – a number of mutually exclusive cliques. In this case we could place each clique in its own partition. However, realistically the results are more likely to fall into the third category – a number of overlapping cliques (or a combination of the second and third category). This is due to the fact that cliques can share members.

There are a number of issues that need to be taken into consideration when determining how to choose which clique. If the cliques contain different numbers of members, then the overlapping object should remain in the clique with more members. However, if each of the cliques contains exactly the same number of members then each of the groups is just as cohesive as the other. In this case, the communication level that we are examining should be taken into account. If we are analyzing the HI communication then it would make sense to put all of the objects in the one partition because separating them would result in a high inter-process communication cost. If we are investigating LO or MD communication then we would examine the size of each of the partitions already created from analysis of higher communication levels. In the allocation stage it is easier to allocate a larger number of small partitions rather than a small number of large partitions. For example, assume we have a system with four processors. We will have more flexibility in assigning 10 small partitions rather than five large partitions.

A 2-clique analysis will follow the same process as a clique analysis. We note that a 2-clique is a generalization of a clique; therefore, any cliques will be contained within the results obtained from a 2-clique analysis.

Combining Concurrency and Communication: When analyzing communication we start with the high communication, then the medium and finally the low. For each of these communication levels we examine 1-clique and 2-clique. For the HI communication it is proposed that we place objects in order to minimize communication costs. For the MD communication we aim to minimize communication costs, while considering the size of the partitions created so that flexibility in the allocation stage is maintained. When considering the LO communication it is proposed that we also consider the concurrency.

A real-world computer system will be comprised of hundreds of objects. The results of LO communication clique analysis (both 1-clique and 2-clique) may be a large number of groups of objects. Some of these groups may contain objects that have already been placed into existing groups (as a result of the HI and MD communication). In determining whether to place the objects discovered in the LO communication analysis with these existing groups we must consider the group size. For example, consider a group of three objects resulting from a LO communication analysis: a, b, and c. If object a is already located in a large existing group then, in the interest of limiting the size of processes, we would not locate objects b and c with this object. There are now two options as to where to place the remaining group members: create a new group or place the members in an existing group so as to exploit concurrency.

Recall that the result of our concurrency analysis is a number of groups of objects that can run concurrently with each other. Each of the members within these groups is dependent on the other members. There may be no direct communication benefit of placing objects together in the one group; however, they may be dependent on other members of the group. Therefore, by placing the object with this group, as opposed to a group where it has no dependencies with members, we are utilizing the potential concurrency. (Once again, the size of the group that we are wishing to place the object into should be taken into account.)

3.2. Application of Proposed Technique

The technique developed above will be applied to the airline ticket system taken from [11]. Figures 9.2 and 9.3 provides the communications matrix and currency identification matrix for the system. The comparison of the results will help determine the efficacy of the social network approach.

- Determine an overall dependencies matrix (original dependencies + transitive dependencies).

	1	2	3	4	5	6	7	8	9	10
1	-	75.600	248,400	14,803,440	510,560	20,600	5,670,000	0	0	121,600
2		-	0	0	0	0	0	0	0	0
3			-	0	0	0	0	0	0	0
4				-	0	63,792,000	842,280	9,420	0	0
5					-	2,208,000	29,440	0	0	0
6						-	49,500	36,000	0	40,500
7							-	0	0	0
8								-	1,400	2,000
9										27,000
10										

Figure 9.2. Communication matrix (taken from Barney [11]).

Original Dependency Matrix

	1	2	3	4	5	6	7	8	9	10
1		1	1				1			1
2	1									
3	1									
4							1			
5							1			
6							1			1
7	1			1	1	1	1			
8										
9										1
10	1						1			1

Transitive Dependency Matrix

	1	2	3	4	5	6	7	8	9	10
1	1			1	1	1	1		1	
2		1	1				1			1
3		1	1				1			1
4	1			1	1	1	1			
5	1			1	1	1	1			
6	1			1	1	1	1		1	
7		1	1				1			1
8										
9	1					1			1	
10		1	1				1			1

Overall Dependency Matrix

	1	2	3	4	5	6	7	8	9	10
1	1	1	1	1	1	1	1	1	1	1
2	1	1	1	1			1			1
3	1	1	1	1			1			1
4	1			1	1	1	1	1		
5	1			1	1	1	1	1		
6	1			1	1	1	1	1	1	1
7	1	1	1	1	1	1	1	1		1
8										
9	1					1			1	1
10	1	1	1	1		1	1		1	1

Figure 9.3. Concurrency identification matrix (taken from Barney [11]) concurrency analysis.

The communication matrix above (Fig. 9.2) shows all the communication between objects in the system. To determine whether the communication is synchronous or asynchronous we consider the concurrency matrix, provided the "B" entries refer to asynchronous communication.

	1	2	3	4	5	6	7	8	9	10
1	X	X	X	B	B	B	X	X	X	X
2	A	X	A	A	A	A	A	A	A	A
3	A	A	X	A	A	A	A	A	A	A
4	A	A	A	X	A	B	X	A	A	X
5	A	A	A	A	X	B	X	A	A	A
6	A	A	A	A	A	X	X	A	A	A
7	A	A	A	A	A	A	X	A	A	A
8	A	A	A	B	A	B	X	X	B	B
9	A	A	A	A	A	A	A	A	X	A
10	A	A	A	A	A	A	A	X	X	X

Figure 9.4. Original, transitive, and overall dependency matrices.

```
CLIQUES
-------------------------------------------------------------------------

Minimum Set Size:        3
Input dataset:           oveall_dep

4 cliques found.

    1:   1 4 5 6 7
    2:   1 6 7 10
    3:   1 2 3 7 10
    4:   1 6 9 10
```

Figure 9.5. Dependency clique analysis.

- Run clique analysis on the dependencies [12].
- Remove the overlapping objects and re-introduce any missing objects that communicate asynchronously.

Overlapping objects: 1 6 7 10. Missing Objects: 8. By removing the overlap from the groups and re-introducing the missing object as a new group we determine four groupings that exhibit concurrency.

Communication Analysis

- Recode the communication matrix to show the sum of the communication costs between each pair of objects. The communication matrix is already given in a "sum" format, see Fig. 9.2.
- Determine LO, MD, and HI communication levels – see in Fig. 9.6 above.
- Create new communication matrices for each of the different communication levels; LO, MD, and HI – Fig. 9.7.
- Run clique analysis on communication matrices. Output obtained using UCINET [12]. 2-clique (Fig. 9.8); 1-clique (Fig. 9.9).

HI Communication: One 2-clique was detected, between objects 4 and 6. We place these together in a group. [Group 1: 4 6]

COST	% of Cost	% of Cumulative Cost	Communication Level
0	0	0	–
1400	0.00	0.00	LO
2000	0.00	0.00	LO
9420	0.01	0.01	LO
20600	0.02	0.04	LO
27000	0.03	0.07	LO
29440	0.03	0.10	LO
36000	0.04	0.14	LO
40500	0.05	0.19	LO
49500	0.06	0.24	LO
75600	0.09	0.33	LO
121600	0.14	0.47	LO
248400	0.28	0.75	LO
510560	0.58	1.32	LO
842280	0.95	2.28	LO
2208000	2.50	4.77	LO
5670000	6.41	11.18	MD
14803440	16.79	27.91	MD
63792000	72.09	100.00	HI
88487740	100	100	

Figure 9.6. LO, MD, HI communication levels.

HI Communication

	1	2	3	4	5	6	7	8	9	10
1							1			
2										
3										
4						1				
5										
6										
7				1						
8										
9										
10										

MD Communication

	1	2	3	4	5	6	7	8	9	10
1				1			1			
2										
3										
4	1									
5										
6										
7	1									
8										
9										
10										

LO Communication

	1	2	3	4	5	6	7	8	9	10
1		1	1		1	1				1
2	1									
3	1									
4							1	1		
5	1					1	1			
6	1				1		1	1		1
7				1	1	1				
8				1		1			1	1
9								1		1
10	1					1		1	1	

Figure 9.7. LO, MD, HI communication matrices.

```
N-CLIQUES
--------------------------------------------------------------------
Max Distance (n-):          2
Minimum Set Size:           2
Input dataset:              comm_HI

1 2-cliques found.

   1:  4 6
--------------------------------------------------------------------
Max Distance (n-):          2
Minimum Set Size:           2
Input dataset:              comm_MD

1 2-cliques found.

   1:  1 4 7
--------------------------------------------------------------------
Max Distance (n-):          2
Minimum Set Size:           2
Input dataset:              comm_HO

5 2-cliques found.

   1:  1 2 3 5 6 10
   2:  1 5 6 7 8 10
   3:  4 5 6 7 8 10
   4:  1 6 8 9 10
   5:  4 6 8 9 10
```

Figure 9.8. Comunication *n*-clique analysis.

```
CLIQUES
--------------------------------------------------------------------
Minimum Set Size:           3
Input dataset:              comm_HI

0 cliques found.
--------------------------------------------------------------------
Minimum Set Size:           3
Input dataset:              comm_MD

0 cliques found.
--------------------------------------------------------------------
Minimum Set Size:           3
Input dataset:              comm_LO

5 cliques found.

   1:  1 5 6
   2:  1 6 10
   3:  5 6 7
   4:  8 9 10
   5:  6 8 10
```

Figure 9.9. Communication clique analysis.

MD Communication: One 2-clique was determined, containing objects 1, 4, and 7. Object 4 is already in an existing group (after HI communication analysis). Since the communication level is MD and the existing group has a small amount of objects in it (i.e., only two) we place objects 1 and 7 in this existing group. [Group 1: 1 4 6 7]

LO Communication: Five cliques were identified. Of these, the clique containing {8 9 10} is the only group which contains members not already placed into existing groups. The other cliques contain at least object 6 which has already been placed into an existing partition. Hence we can make a second group containing [8, 9 and 10] in addition to [Group 1: 1 4 6 7].

A 2-clique analysis also detected five cliques. Removing the overlap and objects already assigned to partitions, we are only left with the group [2 3 5].

We now combine dependency and communication analysis to determine where to place these objects.

Combine concurrency and communication analysis results

The concurrency analysis determined that objects 2 and 3 are dependent on one another, but that there is potential concurrency between these objects and object 5. Hence, we sacrifice the potential communication benefit of placing them in the same partition, since it is LO, and maximize the potential concurrency by placing them in different partitions. The resulting partitioning solution is

[Group 1: 1 4 6 7]; [Group 2: 8 9 10]; [Group 3: 2 3]; [Group 4: 5]

4. Conclusion

This chapter aimed to investigate a new approach to distributing the objects in a system by examining the similarities between social and computer networks. By modeling the objects in a system as actors in a network the research was able to detect cohesive groups and clique-like structures within the system and thus distribute the objects around the network.

The proposed method conducted a number of clique analyses. These analyses could return one, or a combination, of the following results: no cliques; a number of mutually exclusive cliques; and/or a number of overlapping cliques. Overlapping cliques occur when two cliques share an object. It is believed that additional research into this overlap may indicate which objects should be replicated and where they should exist.

Further investigation is continuing to compare the proposed technique with existing techniques in the literature (e.g., [2, 4–7]), which method provides the most efficient and/or effective solution. This will require the assessment of the solutions provided and investigation of the inter- and intra-node communications under various load and processing patterns. Of the tools available the structural analysis methods developed for social network analysis provide an iterative approach that has the potential to be more readily automated. The ability to easily map the solutions into a three-dimensional space may also assist designers in fine tuning the final solution.

References

1. Tamhankar, A.M., Ram, S.: Database fragmentation and allocation: an integrated technique and case study. IEEE Transactions on Systems, Man, and Cybernetics **28** (1998) 288–305
2. Low, G.C., Rasmussen, G.: Partitioning and allocation of objects in distributed application development. Journal of Research and Practice on Information Technology, **32** (2000) 75–106
3. Shatz, S.M., and Yau, S.S.: A partitioning algorithm for distributed software system design. Information Sciences **38** (1986) 15
4. Chang, W.T., Tseng, C.C.: Clustering approach to grouping objects in message-passing systems. Journal of Object Orientated Programming **7** (1995) 42–43, 46–50
5. Huang, J.L., Chang C.K.: Supporting the partitioning of distributed systems with Function-Class Decomposition. The 24th Annual International Computer Software and Applications Conference (COMPSAC 2000) (2000) 351–356
6. Yua, S.S., Bae, D.H., Pour, G.: A Partitioning Approach for Object-Oriented Software Development for Parallel Processing Systems. Proc. 16th Ann. Int'l Computer Software and Applications Conf., Sept 1992 (1992) 5
7. Huang, J.L., Chang, C.K.: Supporting the partitioning of distributed systems with Function-Class Decomposition. The 24th Annual International Computer Software and Applications Conference (COMPSAC 2000), Oxford (2000) 351–356
8. Scott, J.: Social Network Analysis: A Handbook. Newbury Park, CA: Sage Publications (1991)
9. Wasserman, S., Fuast, K.: Social Network Analysis: Methods and Applications. Cambridge: Cambridge University Press (1994)

10. Luce, R.D., Perry, A.D.: A method of matrix analysis of group structure. Psychometrika **14** (1949) 21
11. Barney, H.: Object Replication: A methodology for improving the performance of object oriented distributed systems. Submitted for Honors thesis, UNSW (2003)
12. Borgatti, S.P., Everett, M.G., Freeman, L.C.: Ucinet for Windows: Software for Social Network Analysis. Harvard: Analytic Technologies (2002)

Web-Based Systems Development: Analysis and Comparison of Practices in Croatia and Ireland

Michael Lang and Dijana Plantak Vukovac

Abstract

The "dot.com" hysteria which sparked fears of a "Web crisis" a decade ago has long subsided and firms established in the 1990s now have mature development processes in place. This chapter presents a timely re-assessment of the state of Web development practices, comparing data gathered in Croatia and Ireland. Given the growth in popularity of "agile" methods in the past few years, a secondary objective of this research was to analyse the extent to which Web development practices are guided by or otherwise consistent with the underlying principles of agile development.

Keywords IS development methods · Web design · Agile methods · Project management

1. Introduction

A decade ago, the sudden and frenetic growth of the newborn World Wide Web caused considerable apprehension within academia. Murugesan et al. [20] spoke of "a pressing need for disciplined approaches and *new* methods and tools", while Oinas-Kukkonen et al. [22] claimed that "systematic analysis and design methodologies for developing Web information systems are necessary and urgently needed among practitioners". Thus began a flurry of academic activity that became known as the "Web Engineering" movement, and many methods and techniques specific to Web/hypermedia design were proposed (see [19]).

During the peak years of the Web Engineering movement (circa 1998–2002), a substantial number of empirical studies of Web-based systems development were published in the academic literature. However, very few studies of commercial Web design practices have since appeared. After the abatement of the pre-Y2K "dot.com" hysteria, there ensued an industry shake-up whereby many of the firms engaging in shoddy or casual practices were found wanting and did not survive. Development technologies have advanced substantially in recent times, and many Web development firms originally established in the mid- to late-1990s have at this stage attained process maturity. It is therefore a timely juncture to once again look at the state of Web development practices a few years on.

Within systems development in general, there has been a shift of attention in recent years to the new wave of "agile methods", a loosely related family of development approaches which are underpinned by the values and principles of the "Agile Manifesto" (www.agilemanifesto.org). Unlike the aforementioned Web/hypermedia methods, these agile approaches originated not from academia but rather from professional communities of practice. They emerged as a reaction to the inflexibility of the so-called "plan-driven" or "document-driven" development approaches which came to prominence in the "methodologies era" of the

Michael Lang • Business Information Systems Group, Cairnes School of Business & Economics, National University of Ireland, Galway. **Dijana Plantak Vukovac** • Department of Information Systems Development, Faculty of Organization and Informatics, University of Zagreb, Varazdin, Croatia.

G.A. Papadopoulos et al. (eds.), *Information Systems Development*, DOI 10.1007/b137171_10,

1970s and 1980s. While the rate of adoption of "pure" agile methods in industry is still relatively low [3, 24], we suspect that many Web developers are using their own in-house hybrid approaches which, even if not directly informed by the principles of the Agile Manifesto, share similarities with methods such as eXtreme Programming, Scrum, or DSDM. With regard to general software development practices, such was indeed the finding of Hansson et al. [14]. One of the objectives of this chapter is therefore to review Web development practices and developers' attitudes and assess how they correspond with the "agile" philosophy.

2. The Software Industry in Croatia and Ireland

Since the inception of the ISD international conference series in 1988, one of its primary aims has been the exchange of scholarly knowledge between the western and eastern nations of Europe. Consistent with this tradition, this chapter compares Web development practices in Croatia against those of Ireland. Apart from the literature on globally distributed software development (e.g. [10, 21]), there are relatively few studies which compare and contrast systems development practices in different countries. Cusumano et al. [9] performed an interesting analysis of general software development practices across various geographic regions, but specifically in the area of Web development we know of only two studies that compare experiences between different nations [2, 13].

Croatia and Ireland are both small European countries with similar populations (4.4 and 4.2 million, respectively). Both nations experienced turmoil in the process of gaining independence, but in Croatia the consequent period of recovery was much more recent with the result that, as yet, Croatia lies behind Ireland in terms of key economic/ICT indicators (Table 10.1). As a result of judicious targeting of foreign investment from the mid-1980s onwards, most of the world-leading ICT companies established plants in Ireland and it developed into a major centre for software development [5]. Ireland's "Celtic Tiger" economy spawned hundreds of indigenous software companies in the 1990s leading to comparisons with California's "Silicon Valley" [7]. The Irish ICT sector had a turnover of 63.5 billion in 2005, representing 22% of national turnover in industry and services [8]. The Croatian ICT industry is newer than in Ireland but is growing at a rate of 18% per annum supported by strong inward investment. There are now over 1,400 companies in the sector with about 23,000 employees (compared to 82,000 in Ireland). Overall, the Croatian ICT sector contributes 5% to national GDP. Though there is not yet the same presence of foreign multinationals as in Ireland, this is increasing, with companies such as Microsoft, IBM, Hewlett-Packard, Oracle, SAP and Ericsson now having bases in Croatia [1, 15]. Croatia can therefore be regarded as a progressive but as yet developing nation in terms of its ICT sector, so it is interesting to compare Croatian Web development practices against those of Ireland.

Table 10.1.   Global Information Technology Report 2007/2008: head-to-head.

Variable	Croatia	Ireland
High-tech exports (% of total exports)	3.65%	20.75%
Secure Internet servers (per 1 million inhabitants)	48	420
Personal computers (per 100 inhabitants)	19.42	52.99
Internet bandwidth (mB/s per 10,000 inhabitants)	10.37	59.97

Source: http://www.insead.edu/v1/gitr/wef/main/analysis/headtoheadint.cfm

3. Research Method

This research sets out to answer the questions:

- RQ1. What processes and methods are used by Web developers in practice?
- RQ2. What if any essential differences exist between Web development practices in Croatia and Ireland?
- RQ3. How do Web development practices correspond with the general principles of "agile" methods?

In Ireland, a dual-mode (postal and Web-based) questionnaire was initially distributed to a purposefully selected sample of 438 organisations. Follow-up qualitative interviews were then conducted with Web developers in 13 organisations. Meanwhile in Croatia, an extended Web-based adaptation of the Irish questionnaire was circulated to 418 companies.

Conducting surveys across different countries presents a number of methodological challenges [18]. As Webster [26] explains, "a bias or error inherent in any given [research] method may interact with differential factors in each country so that the results will not be comparable". Both surveys used a similar research design. In neither country did a readily available register of Web development companies exist, so the respective samples were compiled by searching various business directories. The Web sites of all organisations were then visited to ascertain if they were likely to be involved in the types of development activities we interested in. The Irish sample excluded all companies which appeared to be engaged mainly in the production of simple "brochureware" Web sites (see [19]). The Croatian sample was not as restrictive in its selection, though care was taken only to include legitimate registered businesses (further reported in [23]). Both the Irish and Croatian surveys had comparable item response rates. No discernable differences in response tendencies were evident, except where one open-ended question on the Irish questionnaire was substituted by a drop-down list on the Croatian questionnaire.

Though problems with linguistic equivalence are always prone to occur in international surveys, the fact that the second author, who is fluent in Croatian and English, personally translated the questionnaire means that the likelihood that any such errors arose is greatly reduced. Coverage error was not an issue either in Ireland or Croatia because multiple sources were used to compile the sample, and all survey participants had access to the distribution channels. While the Irish software industry arguably has a headstart on Croatia, the significance of the timelag factor (i.e. "temporal equivalence") is moderated here because the Croatian survey was conducted almost 4 years after the initial stage of the Irish study.

The SPSS data sets from both studies were re-coded into a combined data file, with a total of 268 usable responses (167 from Ireland, 101 from Croatia). Mann–Whitney tests were then run to compare the two data sets. Significant differences were revealed for organisation size ($p < 0.001$), respondent experience ($p < 0.01$), and background discipline ($p < 0.05$). As can be seen in Table 10.2, there was a higher concentration of large organisations in the Irish sample than in Croatia (most of these were multinational IT or financial services companies). On the whole, the Croatian respondents had a few years more experience than the Irish respondents, but this can be explained by the timelag between the execution of the two studies. The Croatian sample had a higher proportion of visual designers, whereas the Irish sample had a larger number of "miscellaneous" respondents who could not be clearly placed into either the "software development" or "visual design" camps.

Table 10.2. Profile of survey respondents.

	Croatia	Ireland
Organisation size	$N = 101$	$N = 167$
1–10 employees	81 (80.2%)	95 (56.9%)
11–50 employees	12 (11.9%)	33 (19.8%)
51–250 employees	7 (6.9%)	9 (5.4%)
> 250 employees	1 (1.0%)	30 (18.0%)
Respondent background	$N = 101$	$N = 167$
Software development	36 (35.6%)	55 (32.9%)
Visual / graphic design	36 (35.6%)	44 (26.3%)
Miscellaneous	29 (28.7%)	68 (40.7%)
Respondent experience	$N = 99$ Mean: 7.1; median: 7.0	$N = 161$ Mean: 6.1; median: 5.0
Less than 2 years	3 (3.0%)	2 (1.2%)
2–4 years	12 (12.1%)	54 (33.5%)
5 years or more	84 (84.9%)	105 (65.3%)

4. Findings and Discussion

4.1. Small Development Teams and Collective Knowledge

Both in Ireland in Croatia, it was found that most Web design teams are small, typically comprising five or less members (Table 10.3), with Croatian teams tending to be slightly smaller (p < 0.01). Where teams consist of just a few co-located close-knit workers, intra-group communication problems are lessened and can be more easily resolved [17]. Not surprisingly, both groups therefore responded that communication within design teams caused few problems. It should be noted that in the Croatian sample, most of the companies are small (80% had 10 or less employees) so development teams were therefore also bound to be small. However, in the Irish sample, where there are many large companies, it would seem that teams are actually kept small on purpose. As one Irish respondent remarked, "project management skills are the most lacking; keeping a team small is the best way to control the chaos".

Table 10.3. Size of development teams.

	Croatia	Ireland
Size of development teams *	$N = 87$	$N = 166$
	Mean: 3.4; median: 3	
1 developer	12 (13.8%)	9 (5.4%)
2–4 developers	57 (65.5%)	96 (57.8%)
5–10 developers	15 (17.2%)	51 (30.7%)
> 10 developers	3 (3.4%)	10 (6.0%)

* Mann–Whitney $p < 0.01$

Small teams also have the advantage that they can share knowledge and expertise more readily, which are key factors in high-speed development environments because they contribute to greater productivity and better decision-making. As later elaborated, it was found (Table 10.6) that the development processes of many organisations, though clear, are not explicitly articulated. The question therefore arises as to how new recruits acquire a sense of "the way we do things around here". The obvious explanation is that, because Web development teams are generally small, shared understandings are easier to build and team members can more readily learn by virtue of working in close proximity to each other. Indeed, when asked to rate the level of usefulness of different sources of design knowledge, both the Croatian and Irish developers indicated that "observing or consulting experienced colleagues" is most useful. The literature suggests that as teams become larger, there is a greater need for formalised processes and procedures. Conversely, "lighter" methods may be better suited to small teams because traditional "heavyweight" methods are unduly cumbersome [6, 25]. Our findings uphold this generalisation: in both countries it was found that as team size increased, there was a greater propensity to use documented guidelines and procedures.

4.2. Project Management and Requirements Management

Most projects (Croatia 80.6%; Ireland 62.8%) are delivered in 15 weeks or less with a typical delivery time being of the order of 3 months (Table 5). It therefore seems that the so-called "3 × 3" profile [12] typifies Web-based systems development in both Ireland and Croatia – teams of about three developers working to deliver a project in about 3 months. In spite of these short release cycles, we found that "Web time" development pressures are regarded as a major problem by very few respondents (Croatia 2.3%; Ireland 4.3%), and that mostly there are no or only minor problems in controlling project tasks and managing team collaboration (Croatia 69.9%; Ireland 76.2%). The most acute problem for the Irish respondents was the old classic: controlling project scope/feature creep. This was not quite as much an issue for the Croatian developers, whose stand-out biggest problem was "coping with volatile and changing requirements" (Table 10.4). A difference ($p < 0.001$) was revealed here between the two groups, suggesting that the Irish cohort are better at managing requirements changes. One explanation for this emerged from interviews where it was found that phase "sign-offs" is a very common practice in Ireland, whereby a detailed requirements specification is produced and "frozen" before commencing full scale production. If requirements subsequently change the client must bear the cost, thus forcing them to prioritise requirements according to value-added. In contrast, the use of requirements specifications is not as common in Croatia (Tables 10.5 and 10.6), a difference that is significant ($p < 0.001$).

Table 10.4. Problematic issues in project management and requirements management.

Issue/Extent of problems experienced		None (%)	Minor (%)	Moderate (%)	Major (%)
Coping with volatile and changing requirements **	Croatia $N = 93$	1.1	10.7	43.0	45.1
	Ireland $N = 164$	1.8	38.4	46.4	13.4
Preparing accurate time and cost estimates *	Croatia $N = 93$	11.8	25.8	46.3	16.2
	Ireland $N = 156$	3.8	43.6	45.5	7.0
Controlling project scope / feature creep	Croatia $N = 87$	11.5	25.3	52.9	10.3
	Ireland $N = 161$	1.2	39.1	42.8	16.8
Controlling and coordinating project tasks	Croatia $N = 93$	26.9	43.0	26.9	3.3
	Ireland $N = 164$	11.6	64.6	20.7	3.0
Coping with speed of Web development cycles	Croatia $N = 84$	25.0	39.3	33.3	2.4
	Ireland $N = 140$	13.6	55.7	26.5	4.3

* Mann–Whitney $p < 0.05$; ** Mann–Whitney $p < 0.001$

Table 10.5. Comparison of project management metrics.

	Croatia	Ireland
**Project duration (weeks) **	$N = 72$ 5% trimmed mean: 10.8 median: 6.0	$N = 140$ 5% trimmed mean: 14.3 median: 10.5
Variance in project duration *(actual – planned)*	$N = 66$ 5% trimmed mean: 33% over median: 25% over	$N = 137$ 5% trimmed mean: 27% over median: 21% over
Variance in project costs *(actual – planned)*	$N = 32$ 5% trimmed mean: 2% over median: 0% (on target)	$N = 76$ 5% trimmed mean: 4% over median: 0% (on target)
**Use of requirements spec. ** Yes	$N = 87$ 48 (55.2%)	$N = 163$ 143 (87.7%)
**Size of requirements spec. ** *(number of pages)*	$N = 47$ 5% trimmed mean = 12.9	$N = 124$ 5% trimmed mean = 40.7

** Mann–Whitney $p < 0.001$

Given their difficulties managing volatile requirements, it is not surprising that the Croatian respondents also had significantly ($p < 0.05$) greater problems preparing accurate time and cost estimates. Nevertheless, project managers in both countries seem to be faring reasonably well in this regard. It was found that most projects (Croatia 68.8%; Ireland 65.9%) are delivered within the agreed budget and though only about, one-third of projects (Croatia 39.3%; Ireland 32.2%) are actually delivered on time time or cost over-runs of more than 50% are relatively few (Croatia 22.7% and 12.6%, respectively; Ireland 16.8% and 2.6%, respectively).

Table 10.6. Formality of development practices

	Croatia	Ireland
Development process *	$N = 101$	$N = 165$
Clear process, explicit	23 (22.8%)	69 (41.8%)
Clear process, but not explicit	63 (62.4%)	69 (41.8%)
No clear process, not a problem	7 (6.9%)	14 (8.5%)
No clear process, is a problem	8 (7.9%)	13 (7.9%)
Use of guidelines and procedures	$N = 94$	$N = 167$
Yes **	35 (37.2%)	114 (68.3%)

* Mann–Whitney $p < 0.05$; ** Mann–Whitney $p < 0.001$

4.3. Development Processes and Procedures

Both groups overwhelmingly responded that they have clear development processes (Croatia 85.2%; Ireland 83.6%), but the extent to which the process is explicitly documented differs with a significantly ($p < 0.05$) greater proportion of the Irish sample having a written-down process. Similarly, a substantially higher percentage of Irish Web developers use documented guidelines and procedures (Croatia 37.2%; Ireland 68.3%). The percentages of respondents who indicated that they used guidelines and procedures for the following purposes are as follows requirements documentation (Croatia 22.8%; Ireland 63.5%), technical design (Croatia 22.8%; Ireland 49.7%), project planning (Croatia 24.8%; Ireland 62.9%), system testing (Croatia 19.8%; Ireland 39.5%), interface design/usability (Croatia 26.7%; Ireland 50.9%) and coding practices (Croatia 23.8%; Ireland 34.7%). The existence of documented procedures and guidelines may suggest a certain degree of formality, but we found that in most organisations that have them in place, they are loose or moderately prescriptive rather than stringent. The role of procedures and guidelines therefore seems not to be an attempt to codify design knowledge but rather to serve as a checklist or high-level road map. This interpretation is held up by an analysis of the additional qualitative data we gathered. In general, though process documentation in many cases is rather comprehensive in so far as there are guidelines to cover most aspects of development, our findings indicate that this documentation is typically lean and of the form of "how-to" pages.

In the Irish questionnaire, survey participants were presented with an open-ended question that invited them to outline whatever Web development methods and approaches they had used. The responses were then coded into the categories shown in Table 10.7. On the Croatian questionnaire, this question was not open-ended, but rather a list of drop-down items seeking the extent of usage of the same re-coded method categories as had been revealed by the Irish survey. This difference in questionnaire format may in part explain the observed variation in response patterns between the two samples. In particular, the level of reported usage of Web/hypermedia methods (e.g. WSDM, WebML) is surprisingly high in Croatia compared to Ireland. We acknowledge that there is a margin for error with this particular question, owing to the known differences in response tendencies for list items as opposed to open-ended questions [11]. Nevertheless, the response category "Hybrid or customised in-house approach" has a clear lead ahead of all the others both in Croatia and in Ireland. Our qualitative data provided evidence to suggest that these in-house work practices have evolved out of reflective evaluations of recurrent challenges and constraints encountered within previous projects. The interpretation that in-house methods and approaches are the outcome of reflective practice and continuous process improvement is further supported by the finding, in response to a separate question, that "Learning-by-doing on real projects" is regarded as one of the most useful sources of design knowledge by both Irish and Croatian respondents.

Table 10.7. Use of development methods and approaches.

Type of method/approach	Croatia $N = 101$	Ireland $N = 78$	Overall $N = 179$
Hybrid or customised in-house method	53 (52.5%)	18 (23.1%)	71 (39.7%)
Object-oriented development approaches	37 (36.6%)	6 (7.7%)	43 (24.0%)
Rapid or agile development methods	29 (28.7%)	13 (16.7%)	42 (23.5%)
HCI / Human Factors Engineering methods	27 (26.7%)	6 (7.7%)	33 (18.4%)
Traditional "legacy" software development methods and approaches, or variant	16 (15.8%)	17 (21.8%)	33 (18.4%)
Incremental or evolutionary approaches	17 (16.8%)	10 (12.8%)	27 (15.1%)
Project management methods (e.g. PRINCE2)	20 (19.8%)	4 (5.1%)	24 (13.4%)
Approaches focused on software quality *e.g. ISO9001, CMM*	18 (17.8%)	3 (3.8%)	21 (11.7%)
Web/hypermedia methods *e.g. RMM, OOHDM, WSDM, WebML*	12 (11.9%)	4 (5.1%)	16 (8.9%)

4.4. Attitudes Towards Documented Plans

In both samples (Table 10.8), nearly all respondents (Croatia 96.8%; Ireland 92.7%) agreed that "to combat system complexity and time pressure, plans are essential". However, in a separate question that measured the level of agreement with the statement that "plans and working methods should be explicitly documented" (Croatia 61.9%; Ireland 79.4%), it was revealed the Croatian developers are significantly less convinced about the need for *documented* plans than the Irish contingent ($p < 0.001$). A similar disparity of opinion was found in reaction to the statement that "ad hoc improvised methods generally result in systems of poor quality", with a significantly greater proportion of the Croatian respondents disagreeing with this assertion. Of the Croatian and Irish respondents who disagreed with this statement, 24 (68.6%) and 17 (48.6%) of them, respectively, had earlier indicated that their organisation has a clear though not explicit development process. This suggests that in some cases developers are engaging in the sort of behaviour which Ciborra [4] calls "smart improvisation" – situated problem-solving based on knowledge and competencies.

Table 10.8. Opinions about Web-based systems development.

Issue		Disagree(%)	Neutral(%)	Agree(%)
To combat system complexity and time pressure, plans are essential	Croatia $N = 94$	1.1	2.1	96.8
	Ireland $N = 165$	1.2	6.1	92.7
To ensure effective teamwork, plans should be documented **	Croatia $N = 92$	17.4	20.7	61.9
	Ireland $N = 165$	7.3	13.3	79.4
Ad hoc improvised methods generally result in systems of poor quality **	Croatia $N = 93$	37.6	21.5	40.8
	Ireland $N = 153$	23.5	7.8	68.6

** Mann–Whitney $p < 0.001$

5. Conclusions

Overall, the findings of our research indicate that, in general, Web development practices in Croatia and Ireland are systematic and guided by purposefully designed processes and procedures. It is notable that, regarding our RQ1, the most popular development approach is to use customised/hybrid methods, whereby Web developers assemble fragments of textbook methods and distill the most useful elements into a home-cooked approach which is then tailored to the needs of each project. The analysis of our qualitative data (further reported in [19] and [23]) revealed that these in-house methods typically blend together the phases of the classical waterfall model with aspects of newer rapid/agile approaches and influences derived from graphic design, marketing and industrial design/HCI. While 23.5% of respondents made direct reference to their use of "agile" methods, our suspicion that many more organisations are using approaches founded on values and principles similar to those of the Agile Manifesto was confirmed by data gathered in the two surveys and the Irish interviews. Evidence of the manifestation of "agile" principles in common Web development practices provides the answers to RQ3 and can be summarised as follows:

- *Deliver working software frequently:* Web development is characterised by short project cycles and the use of rapid development tools.
- *Emphasis on valuable software:* In Ireland, it is common practice to insist that clients sign-off on a prioritised list of requirements. Subsequent change requests are separately costed, which forces clients to consider value-added.
- *Emphasis on "light" documentation:* We found that development guidelines and written-down processes are often in place, but they generally take the form of loosely prescriptive "how to's" rather than step-by-step procedures.
- *Most effective communication is face-to-face conversation:* Web development is characterised by small teams working in close proximity. The most useful source of knowledge is learning from colleagues.
- *Sustainable pace and concern for employee morale/welfare:* Streamlined processes, reliable project estimation techniques and standardised ways of working together not only minimise waste but also reduce the need for overtime and facilitate the equitable division of workload.
- *Collective code ownership:* In both countries, but more so in Ireland, we found evidence of the use of coding standards and an emphasis on simplicity and reusability, the rationale being that if a team member is unavailable or if there is a requirement to re-use part of a previous project, anybody should be able to pick up a colleague's work and easily "key into it".
- *Reflective evaluation of practices:* Substantial evidence was found of evolutionary process improvement whereby developers regularly reflect on their own experiences and accordingly refine their practices.

We accept that, on the face of it, most of these practices are not new or original. Rather, for the most part they have long been recognised as standard best practice and as such are not essentially "agile". Indeed, a criticism that has been made of agile methods is that they can be argued to be "old wine in new bottles" [16]. The counterpoint is that, in practice, very many in-house approaches combine elements of "agile" and "plan-driven", mixing the tried-and-trusted benefits of the old with the more radical and innovative elements of the new.

Regarding the comparability of the two surveys, care must be taken in interpreting the findings because the fact that the Croatian sample contained a greater concentration of small companies and graphic designers may have biased the results somewhat. That said, the findings of the two studies are more alike than different, which suggests that for the most part they can be broadly generalised across similar European nations. The most notable difference between the two samples is that Croatian Web developers seem much less inclined to use explicit, written-down plans, processes and requirements specifications than Irish Web developers. This, we suggest, is a contributory factor to the greater level of difficulty experienced by the Croatian developers as regards the management of changing requirements and the preparation of accurate project estimates. In both of these regards, Irish Web development firms appear to be ahead of their Croatian counterparts in terms of process maturity, so in light to provide answer to RQ2, here is one area where lessons can possibly be learned. First steps have already been taken by introducing the students in Croatia to the state-of-theory in Web/hypermedia methods and current web development practices as well as the differences between Ireland and Croatia.

The limitations of survey research are well known, not least of which being that a survey reflects a situation at a snapshot in time and by the stage the findings are produced that situation may well have changed considerably. Nevertheless, we submit that this chapter makes an interesting contribution to the existing body of knowledge in the field, especially because comparatively few empirical surveys of Web-based systems development practices have appeared in recent years. Lessons learnt during analysis of the Irish and Croatian research results enabled us to focus our activities in two areas: first, to enhance/renew academic course curricula with contemporary and practical information, and second, to explore the issues uncovered by the surveys. Further research is ongoing, involving closer follow-up interviews and case studies that investigate more deeply the use of agile or agile-like methods in Web-based system development.

References

1. APIU (2007) *IT and Software Development in Croatia*. Republic of Croatia, Trade and Investment Promotion Agency, Zagreb. Retrieved April 29, 2008 from: http://tinyurl.com/4844L7
2. Baskerville, R. and Pries-Heje, J. (2004) Short Cycle Time Systems Development. *Information Systems Journal*, 14(3): 237–264
3. Buchalcevova, A. (2008) Research of the Use of Agile Methodologies in the Czech Republic. In Barry, C. et al. (eds) *Proceedings of ISD2007 Conference, Galway, Ireland, August 29–31*
4. Ciborra, C. U. (1999) A Theory of Information Systems Based on Improvisation. In Currie, W. L. and Galliers, B. (eds) *Rethinking Management Information Systems*, Oxford: OUP, pp. 136–155
5. Coe, N. (1997) US Transnationals and the Irish Software Industry. *European Urban and Regional Studies*, 4(3): 211–230
6. Cockburn, A. (2000) Selecting a Project's Methodology, *IEEE Software*, 17(4): 64–71
7. Crone, M. (2004) Celtic Tiger Cubs: Ireland 's VC-Funded Software Start-ups. Presented at *Institute for Small Business Affairs Conference*. Newcastle-Gateshead, UK, November 2–4. Retrieved April 29, 2008 from http://tinyurl.com/4L5h3u
8. CSO (2008) *Information Society and Telecommunications 2007*, Irish Central Statistics Office, Retrieved April 29, 2008 from: http://tinyurl.com/3n5x3e
9. Cusumano, M., MacCormack, A., Kemerer, C.F. and Crandall, B. (2003) Software development worldwide: the state of the practice, *IEEE Software*, 20(6): 28–34
10. Damian, D.E. and Zowghi, D. (2003) An insight into the interplay between culture, conflict and distance in globally distributed requirements negotiations. In *Proceedings of 36th Annual Hawaii International Conference on System Sciences (HICSS)*, January 6–9
11. Dillman, D. A. (2000) *Mail and Internet Surveys: The Tailored Design Method*, 2nd edition. New York: Wiley.
12. Glass, R. (2001) Who's Right in the Web Development Debate?, *Cutter IT Journal*, 14(7): 6–10
13. Greenbaum, J. and Stuedahl, D. (2000) Deadlines and Work Practices in New Media Development: Its About Time. In Cherkasky, T. et al. (eds), *Proceedings of PDC 2000 Participatory Design Conference*, New York, USA, November 28 – December 1, pp. 70–77.
14. Hansson, C., Dittrich, Y., Gustafsson, B. and Zarnak, S. (2006) How agile are industrial software development practices? *Journal of Systems and Software*, 79: 1295–1311
15. HGK (2004) *Croatian ICT Sector*. Croatian Chamber of Economy, Information System and Statistics Department, Zagreb. Retrieved April 29, 2008 from: http://tinyurl.com/4xwecz
16. Hilkka, M.-R., Tuure, T. and Matti, R. (2005) Is Extreme Programming Just Old Wine in New Bottles: A Comparison of Two Cases. *Journal of Database Management*, 16(4): 41–61
17. Kraut, R. E. and Streeter, L. A. (1995) Coordination in Software Development, *Communications of the ACM*, 38(3): 69–81
18. Lang, M. (2002) *The Use of Web-based International Surveys in Information Systems Research*. In Remenyi, D. (ed), *Proceedings of European Conference on Research Methodology for Business and Management (ECRM)*, Reading, UK, Apr 29–30, pp. 187–196.
19. Lang, M. and Fitzgerald, B. (2006) New Branches, Old Roots: A Study of Methods and Techniques in Web/Hypermedia Systems Design. *Information Systems Management*, 23(3): 62–74.
20. Murugesan, S., Deshpande, Y., Hansen, S. and Ginige, A. (1999) Web Engineering: A New Discipline for Development of Web-Based Systems. In *Proceedings of 1st ICSE Workshop on Web Engineering*, Los Angeles, California, USA, May 16–17, pp. 1–9. ACM Press.
21. Nicholson, B. and Sahay, S. (2001) Some political and cultural issues in the globalisation of software development: case experience from Britain and India. *Information and Organization*, 11: 25–43.
22. Oinas-Kukkonen, H., Alatalo, T., Kaasila, J., Kivelä, H. and Sivunen, S. (2001) Requirements for Web Engineering Methodologies. In Rossi, M. and Siau, K. (eds), *Information Modeling in the New Millennium*, pp. 360–382. Hershey, PA: Idea Group Publishing.

23. Plantak Vukovac, D. and Kliček, B. (2007) Web and Multimedia Systems Development State of the Practice. In Aurer, B. and Bača, M. (eds), *Proceedings of CECIIS Conference*, September, 12–14, Varazdin, Croatia, pp. 396–403 (available at http://tinyurl.com/3zarrr)
24. Schwaber, C. and Fichera, R. (2005) *Corporate IT Leads the Second Wave of Agile Adoption*, Forrester Research Inc.
25. Taylor, M.J., Moynihan, E., and Wood-Harper, A. T. (1996) The Use of Systems Development Methodologies in Small I.T. Departments. *Systemist*, 18(1): 33–40
26. Webster, L.L. (1966) Comparability in Multi-Country Surveys. *Journal of Advertising Research*, December, 14–18.

11

The Solution Space Organization: Linking Information Systems Architecture and Reuse

Salem Ben Dhaou Dakhli

Abstract

Nowadays, improvement of software development productivity is among the main strategies proposed by academics and practitioners to deal with the chronic software crisis. As stressed by many authors during the last two decades, reuse of software artifacts provides efficient instruments to implement this strategy. Nevertheless, despite organizations high investments in defining software reuse plans, implementation of such plans has often failed. We think that the identification and description of the relationships between the areas of information systems architecture and software reuse are required to define a successful reuse approach which takes into account all the dimensions of information systems. In this chapter, we propose a structural and architecture-oriented description of the solution space associated with information systems development. We use such a description to build a reuse approach compliant with all the dimensions of information systems including the organizational, economic, and human dimensions.

Keywords Project space · Software solution · Architecture · Organizational actor · Business process · Business function · Business entity · Software component · Reuse

1. Introduction

The term software crisis was coined since 1968 to describe the considerable portion of software projects missing schedules, exceeding their budgets, and delivering software with poor quality and even wrong functionality [10, 20, 21]. The software crisis results in an ever-increasing burden and in user resistance to change related to the frustration that software development, maintenance, and use generate [11, 30]. Two categories of remedies have been proposed in order to solve the software crisis. The first category is composed of development methods and approaches like the spiral model [4], the formal development methods, the object-oriented paradigm, the component-based software engineering (CBSE), and the model-driven development process. The second category is composed of development tools and techniques like computer-aided software engineering (CASE) and automatic testing tools. Nevertheless, as stressed by [5], there is no silver bullet. In particular, the success of the proposed methods, tools, and techniques is limited by many factors related to their immaturity and inappropriate use, unsatisfactory training, and organizational resistance to change. In addition to these factors, many authors have noted that software is complex, uncertain, and risky to develop and maintain in particular because it supports complex operational and decision-making processes within organizations [5, 27]. The complexity, the uncertainty, and the risk inherent in software engineering have become more extreme due to the increasing role of Internet-based software systems in organizations. Indeed, as noticed by [2], the development of such software products involves rapid requirement changes and unpredictable product complexity. Nowadays,

Salem Ben Dhaou Dakhli · CERIA Laboratory, Paris-Dauphine University, France

G.A. Papadopoulos et al. (eds.), *Information Systems Development*, DOI 10.1007/b137171_11,
© Springer Science+Business Media, LLC 2009

improvement of software development productivity is among the main strategies proposed by academics and practitioners in order to deal with the chronic software crisis. As stressed by many authors during the last two decades, reuse of software artifacts provides efficient instruments to implement this strategy [31]. Nevertheless, despite organizations' high investments in defining software reuse plans, implementation of such plans has often failed. The lack of reusable artifacts and the weaknesses of the architecture models that facilitate putting them together are among the most difficult problems encountered by software reuse. Another problem of the software reuse based on component-based software development results from the lack of traceability between software components and stakeholders' requirements. We think that the identification and description of the relationships between the areas of information systems architecture and software reuse are required to define a successful reuse approach which takes into account all the dimensions of information systems. In this chapter, we propose a structural and architecture-oriented description of the solution space associated with information systems development. We use such a description to build a reuse approach compliant with all the dimensions of information systems including the organizational, economic, and human dimensions [27]. Our chapter is organized as follows. In Section 2, we present a literature review of software reuse paradigm. Section 3 provides a synthetic description of the software global model [29]. In Section 4, we present the solution space structure based on information systems architecture and describe our reuse approach. We conclude our chapter in Section 6 by listing lessons learned from experimentation and future research directions.

2. The Software Reuse Paradigm: A Literature Review

Although software reuse has been defined at the end of the 1960s, this topic depends strongly on the component-based development paradigm which describes how to integrate reuse in the software development process [1, 3, 6, 13, 15]. In this chapter, by the expression software reuse we mean the reuse of software artifacts that include subroutines in library, commercial-off-the-shelf (COTS) assets, open source software (OSS) assets, architecture models, or software product-lines [1, 3, 26]. In this section, we review the most important contributions to software reuse.

As noticed by [19], software reuse is an umbrella concept, encompassing a variety of approaches and situations. These authors define software reuse as the systematic practice of developing software from a stock of building blocks, so that similarities in requirements and/or architecture between applications can be exploited to achieve substantial benefits in productivity, quality, and business performance. Frakes and Fox [9] consider that software reuse is the use of existing software knowledge or artifacts to build new software artifacts. Mili et al. [18] analyze the reusability of software artifacts from two perspectives: usability and usefulness. According to these authors, usability is the extent to which a software artifact is packaged for reuse while usefulness is the extent to which a software artifact is needed. Usefulness means generality and is often in conflict with short-term usability without customization of software artifacts. Therefore, to be effective, software reuse has to be supported by a decision-making process including a trade-off activity between these two perspectives. Griss [12] emphasizes the role of management support, domain stability, and experience for successful reuse strategies. Mili et al. [18] provide a deep analysis of technological, organizational, and management or control aspects of software reuse while Morisio et al. [19] and Rine and Sonnemann [24] identify the main success factors of reuse strategies. For large-scale software reuse, Jacobson et al. [14] propose a reuse-driven software engineering approach which links business processes, organization, and software architecture and splits the component-based development process into three sub-processes: component system engineering, application system engineering, and application family engineering. Because of its dependence on the component-based development paradigm, software reuse effectiveness is impacted by problems inherent in componentbased software engineering in particular those problems related to the lack of traceability between software components and stakeholders' requirements. Indeed, software components reflect the structure of a software solution while stakeholders' requirements describe the behavior of a software solution. Therefore, a successful reuse strategy must propose a solution to the traceability gap between software components and stakeholders' requirements.

3. The Software Global Model

The software global model is a framework proposed by Toffolon and Dakhli [29] in order to improve software engineering processes. It is based on four project spaces (the problem space, the solution space, the construction space, and the operation space) which represent the businesses of four categories of actors involved in software artifacts development, maintenance, and use. A role played by a project's actor in one of the four spaces is either principal or secondary. The software global model is illustrated by a tetrahedron (USAD) where each face represents one space and each vertex represents a type of actor (Fig. 11.1). Each line of the tetrahedron (USAD) shows the interaction between two project actors belonging to the same space and each space is designated by a three-letter acronym where the second letter corresponds to the project's actor playing the principal role in this space. According to this schema,

1. The problem space (USA) represents the stakeholder/customer's business and specifies the customers' and users' problems and their organizational solutions. In this space, the stakeholder/customer (S) plays the principal role while the user (U) and the architect (A) play secondary roles.
2. The solution or architectural space (SAD) represents the architect's business and specifies the computer solutions of the customer/user's problems. In this space, the architect (A) plays the principal role while the stakeholder/customer (S) and the developer (D) play secondary roles.
3. The construction space (ADU) represents the developer's business and constitutes the environment where the computer solutions of the customer/user's problems are implemented. In this space, the principal role is played by the developer (D) and the secondary roles are played by the architect (A) and the end user (U).
4. The operation space (DUS) represents the end user's business and constitutes the environment where the software contribution to the organization's competitiveness and its usability from the user's perspective are evaluated. In this space, the principal role is played by the user (U) and the secondary roles are played by the developer (D) and the stakeholder/customer (S).

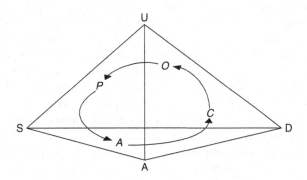

Figure 11.1. The four project spaces and associated actors.

The transition between the four spaces is based on the iterative software development meta-lifecycle, designated by the acronym (**PACO**) (Problem-Architecture-Construction-Operation): the definition of a computer solution of an organizational problem permits the transition from the problem space to the solution space; the implementation of this solution expresses the transition from the solution space to the construction space; the installation of the software artifacts built in the construction space results in the transition from this space to the operation space; and the description of problems and needs generated by the use of the software installed permits the transition from the operation space to the problem space.

Prior to the description of the structure of the solution space, the software global model is improved by defining its links with organization strategy and technical infrastructure. The traceability between software components and stakeholders' requirements is based on information provided by these links.

The modifications of the software global model consist on the one hand, in describing the role of organizations strategy and technology in computerization and on the other hand, in identifying the organizational processes involved in software solution definition. In the rest of this section, we present synthetically the modified software global model.

As noticed above, the software global model describes how to move from an organizational solution of an organizational problem to a software system which implements a software solution supporting this organizational solution. However, the software global model does not describe the origin of organizational problems and how an organizational solution to an organizational problem is defined. Moreover, the software global model does not provide any information about the software solution lifecycle. Finally, this model does not refer to the technical infrastructure required to the operational use of software solutions.

According to the Leavitt model of organization [16, 25], we conclude that organizational problems are generated by the economic, social, legal, political, and technical constraints of environment on an organization. These constraints disturb the equilibrium defining the role of an organization and its relationships with the environment. The role of organization strategy is to define organizational solutions to organizational problems in order to take into account the environment constraints. An organizational solution consists either in creating new processes or in modifying existing processes within an organization. In this chapter we focus on those processes – called business processes – which create value for the organization's customers and for the organization itself. The amount of value a business process brings to customers and organization depends on the effectiveness of support and decision-making processes. A support process is a nexus of activities which provides resources to business processes in compliance with optimal rules defined within an organization. The business process activities are accomplished by the actors who play the principal role in the problem and operation spaces. In the problem space, the customer plays the principal role by carrying out management and monitoring activities related to the organization business processes. In the operation space, the end user plays the principal role by accomplishing the operational activities of the organization business processes in order to produce goods and services for customers. Organizational problems are detected in the operation and the problem spaces and reported to the strategic level which defines organizational solutions in terms of creation or modification of business processes. The implementation of a software solution defined in the solution space results in a software system delivered to the end user and validated by the customer. However, to be used effectively in the operation space, a software system depends on the organization technical infrastructure composed of hardware, operating system tools, and network which play an important role in each space. In particular, what is really delivered to the end user is a computer system composed of a software system and a technical infrastructure. Moreover, the definition of a software solution and its implementation rely on the organization technical resources. Consequently, the software global model may be enhanced by

1. adding two layers – the technical infrastructure layer and the strategic layer – which interact with the project spaces;
2. describing how organizational problems and solutions are generated; and
3. describing the structure of the solution space.

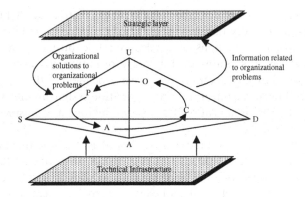

Figure 11.2. The enhanced software global model.

Figure 11.2 illustrates the enhanced software global model.

4. The Solution Space Structure

In this section, we propose a layered description of the solution space structure before presenting a synthetic reuse approach based on this structure. The solution space structure provides information related to a software solution lifecycle.

4.1. A Layered Description of the Solution Space

The solution space structure rests on three layers: the functional architecture (information system architecture) layer, the applicative architecture layer, and the software architecture layer (Fig. 11.3).

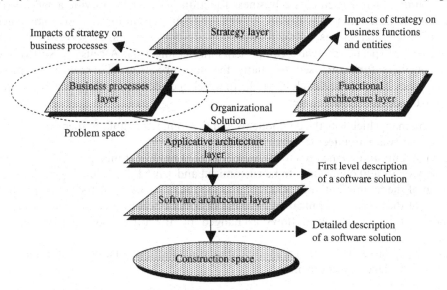

Figure 11.3. The structure of the solution space.

The functional architecture layer describes the information system architecture as a nexus of business entities and functions. A business entity is a set of information chunks which define a concept used by the organizational actors while carrying out a business process. A business function is an action which uses and transforms at least one business entity. A business process manipulates business entities through the use of business functions. Business entities are described in a business dictionary. A business function may be considered as an aggregation on many business subfunctions. Business functions may be used by many business processes. Such business functions are called reusable business functions. Business entities manipulated by many business processes are called shared information. Because of the invariant and stable nature of business entities and business functions, they are independent of the organizational structure and the roles played by actors within an organization. An information system architecture of an organization is defined as a model describing the organization's business functions and business entities as well as the relationships between these concepts.

The applicative layer provides a map which describes the organization's applications and information flows they exchange. An application is a set of software systems which computerize at least partly a business process. So, an application provides a software support to the value creation behavior of organizational actors. This behavior consists in carrying out business processes activities which manipulate business information by using business functions. An application may be considered as a dynamic conjunction of a set of business process activities with business entities and business functions in order to contribute to goods and services production. The applicative layer results from the interaction between the functional layer and the business process layer which supports the problem and operation spaces. The applicative layer delivers a first-level description of a software solution as a new or enhanced application which interacts with existing and future applications.

The software layer describes each software solution as a set of software components and connectors distributed according to a software architecture model (e.g., MVC). A software solution is either the architecture of a new application which supports at least partly a new business process or the architecture of an existing application which is enhanced in order to take into account the modifications of an existing business process. Despite the richness of the existing definitions of the software component concept, we propose in this chapter a definition of this concept which refers to business functions. Our definition states that a software component is an autonomous and homogeneous logical unit which implements a business function in order to provide a service either to end users or to other logical units. A software connector is an autonomous and homogeneous logical unit which facilitates interactions between two software components. A software solution is composed of reusable and specific software components and connectors. A reusable software component implements a business function used by many business processes. To realize the principal-agent contract which links him to the developer [29], the architect delivers – for each software solution – the following artifacts to the developer:

- An architecture map which lists the components and the connectors linking them and their distribution according to a software architecture model.
- A list of components and connectors to be reused without modifications.
- A list of components and connectors to be customized and reused.
- A description of the required modifications of existing reusable components and connectors.
- A description of the detailed technical architecture of specific software components and connectors.
- A description of the information flows exchanged by the future software system and existing applications.
- Information about the repositories of reusable components and a set of architecture rules and standards to respected by the development teams.

Generally, in order to respect the architecture and quality constraints, the customization of components and connectors is carried out by software technical architects who cooperate with the development team [28]. In the construction space, the role of the developer is to implement the software solution in order to build a software system. In addition to coding and testing tasks, implementation activities include the design of the software system as a composition of use cases in order to meet the stakeholders' requirements.

4.2. The Reuse Approach

The reuse approach proposed in this chapter emphasizes the development for reuse aspect of the computer-based software development paradigm [1, 3, 28, 30]. The presentation of the development by reuse activities [1, 3, 28, 30] is beyond the scope of this chapter. Since software connectors are nowadays based on standard protocols (SOAP, RPC, etc.) and available in the software products market, our approach focuses on the development of reusable business software components. We think that the failure of reuse approaches defined within organizations is due to three important problems: conceptual, organizational, and technical. Firstly, it is difficult to identify the reusable business software components to be developed. Secondly, there are few organizational models which contribute to improve the management of reusable components (Who does what? Where? When?) [28]. Finally, even if reusable components are stored in repositories, retrieval methods and techniques permitting to find a reusable component are generally inefficient or difficult to use [7, 8, 17, 22, 23, 32]. The reuse approach presented in this chapter proposes a solution to the first problem.

As noticed above, business processes and business functions are orthogonal. So, a business function may be used by many business processes. For instance, assessing a student's homework is a business function used by all the teaching business processes in a university. As we stressed above, a reusable business software component is a component which implements a business function used by many business processes.

Figure 11.4 illustrates the relationships between business processes and business functions: the business function 3 is used by four business processes, the business function 1 is used by three business processes, and the business function 2 is used by two business processes while only one business process uses the business function 4. Besides, the business functions 3, 1, and 2 may be implemented by two reusable business software components.

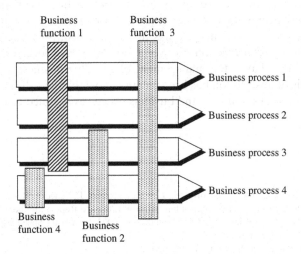

Figure 11.4. Business processes and business functions.

On the other hand, because of the high costs and important delays necessary to develop high-quality reusable components, the development for reuse process is associated with a decision-making process which permits making trade-off between business functions that are candidates to be implemented by reusable components. This process selects those business functions which have the highest priority according to the organization constraints. The priority degree of a business function takes into account many factors, in particular, the most important software dimensions [27] and the business function reuse coordinates (m,n) where m is the number of business processes using this function and n is the sum of the number of times this function is used by each business process. For each business function, the first coordinate m is the vertical intensity of reuse while the second coordinate n is its horizontal intensity of reuse. Finally, the reuse approach presented in this chapter includes three main activities:

1. identify the business functions' intensities of reuse;
2. select the business functions to be implemented by reusable components; and
3. develop the reusable components.

5. Conclusion and Future Research Directions

In this chapter, we have presented the structure of the solution space where software architects build software solutions which support organizational solutions. Moreover, we have explained that organizational solutions are built in the problem space as implementations of the organization strategy which materializes how an organization faces problems generated by the environment constraints. The presentation of the solution space structure as a layered framework has three main advantages. Firstly, the gap between the software components and the stakeholders' requirements is filled by explaining the links between the strategy layer, the functional architecture layer, and the organization business processes. Secondly, a macroscopic lifecycle of a software solution may be defined on the basis of the solution space layered structure. Indeed, building a software solution may be considered as a sequence of models linked by abstraction and specialization relationships, where each model is issued from a layer of the solution space structure. Finally, the description of the software solution structure permits identifying the business software components which are candidates to be developed as high quality and generic reusable components.

The validation of the solution space structure and the reuse approach presented in this chapter have taken place within a French insurance company and permit identifying many research issues to be addressed as well as the practical work to be accomplished for successful use of this framework. On the one hand, a software solution detailed lifecycle has to be described. Such lifecycle is aimed to provide guidelines to software solution construction given a set of business processes, business functions, and business entities. On the other hand, the management of reusable business software components in a repository with many levels of abstraction has been recommended by the validation team. This repository linking business functions, business entities, and business processes is aimed to help architects in defining software solutions.

References

1. Bachmann, F., Bass, L., Buhman, C., Comella-Dorda, S., Long, F., Robert, J., Seacord, R. and Wallnau, K. (2000) *Technical Concepts of Component-Based Software Engineering*, Volume II, SEI Technical Report number CMU/SEI-2000-TR-008.
2. Baskerville, R., Ramesh, B., Levine, L., Pries-Heje, J. and Slaughter S. (2003) Is Internet-Speed Software Development Different?. *IEEE Software*, 15(6), November/December, pp. 70–77.
3. Bass, L., Buhman, C., Comella-Dorda, S., Long, F., Robert, J., Seacord, R. and Wallnau K. (2001) *Market Assessment of Component-based Software Engineering*, Volume I, SEI Technical Report number CMU/SEI-2001-TN-007.
4. Boehm, B.W. (1988) A Spiral Model of Software Development and Enhancement, *IEEE Computer*, 21(5), May, pp. 61–72.
5. Brooks Jr., F.P (1987) No Silver Bullet-Essence and Accidents of Software Engineering, *Computer*, 20(4), April, pp. 10–19.
6. Crnkovic, I. and Larsen, M. (2002) *Building Reliable Component-Based Software Systems*, *Artech* House Publishers.
7. Drummond, C.G., Ionescu, D. and Holte R.C. (2000) A Learning Agent that Assists the Browsing of Software Libraries, *IEEE Transactions on Software Engineering*, 26(12), December.
8. Frakes, W.B. and Baeza-Yates R.A. (eds.) (1992) *Information Retrieval: Data Structures and Algorithms*, Prentice-Hall, Upper Saddle River, NJ.
9. Frakes, W.B. and Fox, C.J. (1995) Sixteen Questions About Software Reuse, *Communications of the ACM*, 38(6), June, pp. 75–87.
10. Gibbs, W. (1994) Software's Chronic Crisis, *Scientific American*, September, pp. 72–81.
11. Griss, M.L. and Wosser, M. (1995) Making Reuse Work in Hewlett-Packard, *IEEE Software*, 12(1), January, pp. 105–107.
12. Griss, M.L. (1993) Software Reuse: From Library to Factory, *IBM Systems Journal*, 32(4), November–December, pp. 548–566.
13. Heineman, G.T. and Councill, W. T. (2001) *Component-Based Software Engineering: Putting Pieces Together*, Addison-Wesley.

14. Jacobson, I., Griss, M. and Jonsson, P. (1997) *Software Reuse: Architecture, Process and Organization for Business Success*, Addison-Wesley, New York.

15. Karlsson, E.A. (Ed.) (1995) *Software Reuse: a Holistic Approach*, John Wiley & Sons, New York.

16. Leavitt, H.J. (ed.) (1963) *The Social Science of Organizations, Four Perspectives*, Prentice-Hall, Englewood Cliffs, NJ.

17. Maarek, Y.S., Berry, D.M. and Kaiser, G.E. (1991) An Information Retrieval Approach for Automatically Constructing Software Libraries, *IEEE Transactions on Software Engineering*, 17(8), August.

18. Mili, H., Mili, A., Yacoub, S. and Addy, E. (2002) *Reuse-based Software Engineering. Techniques, Organizations, and Controls*, John-Wiley & Sons, New York.

19. Morisio, M., Ezran, M. and Tully, C. (2002) Success and Failures in Software Reuse, *IEEE Transactions on Software Engineering*, 28(4), April, pp. 340–357.

20. Neumann, P.G. (1995) *Computer Related Risks*, ACM Press, New York.

21. Pressman, R.S. (2004) *Software Engineering: A Practitioner's Approach*, McGraw-Hill Series in Computer Science, 6th Edition.

22. Prieto-Diaz, R. (1987) Classifying Software for Reusability, *IEEE Software* 4(1).

23. Prieto-Diaz, R. (1991) Implementing Faceted Classification for Software Reuse, *Communications of the ACM*, 34(5), May.

24. Rine, D.C. and Sonnemann R.M. (1998) Investments in Reusable Software: A Study of Software Reuse Investment Success Factors, *The Journal of Systems and Software*, 41, pp. 17–32.

25. Stohr, E.A. and Konsynski, B.R. (1992) *Information Systems and Decision Processes*, IEEE Computer Society Press, 1992.

26. Szyperski, C., Gruntz, D. and Murer, S. (2002) *Component Software: Beyond Object-Oriented Programming*, 2nd edition, Addison Wesley, New York.

27. Toffolon, C. (1999) The Software Dimensions Theory, In Joaquim F. (ed.), *Enterprise Information Systems, Selected Papers Book*, Kluwer Academic Publishers, Dordrecht.

28. Toffolon, C. and Dakhli, S. (1998) Software Artifacts Reuse and Maintenance: An Organizational Framework, in *Proceedings of the Euromicro Conference on Software Maintenance and Reengineering (CSMR'98)*, Florence, Italy, March 9–11.

29. Toffolon, C. and Dakhli, S. (2002) The Software Engineering Global Model, in *Proceedings of the COMPSAC'2002 Conference*, August 26–28, Oxford, United Kingdom.

30. Toffolon, C. (1996) L'Incidence du Prototypage dans une Démarche d'Informatisation, Thèse de doctorat, Université de Paris-IX Dauphine, Paris, Décembre.

31. Vitharana, P., Jain, P. and Zahedi, F (2004) Strategy-Based Design of Reusable Business Components, *IEEE Transactions on Systems, Man and Cybernetics—Part C Applications and Reviews*, 4(34), April, pp. 460–475.

32. Ye, Y. and Fischer, G. (2005) Reuse-Conducive Development Environments, *Automated Software Engineering*, 12(2), Kluwer Academic Publishers, Hingham.

12

Designing Cognition-Adaptive Human–Computer Interface for Mission-Critical Systems

Yu Shi, Eric Choi, Ronnie Taib and Fang Chen

Abstract

With applications of new information and communication technologies, computer-based information systems are becoming more and more sophisticated and complex. This is particularly true in large incident and emergency management systems. The increasing complexity creates significant challenges to the design of user interfaces (UIs). One of the fundamental goals of UI design is to provide users with intuitive and effective interaction channels to/from the computer system so that tasks are completed more efficiently and user's cognitive work load or stress is minimized. To achieve this goal, UI and information system designers should understand human cognitive process and its implications, and incorporate this knowledge into task design and interface design. In this chapter we present the design of CAMI, a cognition-adaptive multimodal interface, for a large metropolitan traffic incident and emergency management system. The novelty of our design resides in combining complementary concepts and tools from cognitive system engineering and from cognitive load theory. Also presented in this chapter is our work on several key components of CAMI such as real-time cognitive load analysis and multimodal interfaces.

Keywords Human–computer interaction · Cognitive load theory · Cognitive system engineering · Multimodal interfaces · Decision support

1. Introduction

Computer-based information systems are becoming more and more sophisticated and complex. This is particularly true for information systems in mission-critical applications, such as traffic incident management systems and natural disaster response systems. The increasing complexity is partly due to introduction of new technologies such as new sensors for incident detection and new communication channels, and also due to effort to meet ever higher performance requirements for these systems. All this often place users of these systems under high mental workload. The increasing complexity of the information systems for mission-critical applications and the necessity of addressing high user cognitive load create significant challenges to the design of user interface (UI) for these systems. An important objective of UI design is to provide users with intuitive and effective interaction channels to/from the computer system so that user tasks are completed more efficiently and at the same time user's cognitive workload or stress is minimized, especially when complicated and emergency tasks are performed.

In our work for a major metropolitan Traffic Control Centre in Australia we are given the task of designing a new human–computer interface for their traffic incident management (TIM) system. The TIM system is deployed in a control room and is composed of about 20 different computer programs,

Yu Shi, Eric Choi, Ronnie Taib and Fang Chen · National Information and Communication Technology Australia (NICTA) Australian Technology Park, Sydney, Australia.

G.A. Papadopoulos et al. (eds.), *Information Systems Development*, DOI 10.1007/b137171_12,
© Springer Science+Business Media, LLC 2009

applications, and devices used for incident detection, verification, response, and recovery. The TIM system is operated by Traffic Control Officers (TCOs) on a 24/7 basis to manage all road traffic incidents and emergencies. One of the most important requirements for the design of the new interface put forward by the centre is the ability to reduce operator cognitive load during stressful situations so that human errors and mistakes can be reduced to minimum. Our approach to the design of the new interface centered on the question of how to detect and model human cognitive state and cognitive load, and how to incorporate this knowledge into the design of dynamic and adaptive interfaces, so that they achieve the objective of joint human–machine optimization by maximizing system performance and at the same time minimizing human cognitive load.

In this chapter, we present our use-inspired research in the design and development of CAMI, a cognition-adaptive multimodal interface, for TIM applications. We describe our novel approach to the design of CAMI by combining complementary concepts and tools from cognitive system engineering and cognitive load theory. The focus of this chapter is on the high-level system design of CAMI. We also present our work in developing several key components of CAMI, such as real-time cognitive load analysis based on user behavior analysis through speech and galvanic skin response and multimodal interfaces. Although CAMI is designed for a specific application in transport domain, its core technologies apply to a wide range of intelligent information systems, such as intelligent decision support systems, information systems for education, and so on.

2. Literature Review

Researchers have long since recognized the importance of understanding human cognitive process to the design of effective and efficient human–computer interfaces (HCI). All user interfaces make cognitive demands on users. Users must master special rules of system use, learn new concepts, and retain information in memory. They must create and refine a mental model of how the system works and how they should use it [1]. Researches from cognitive science, cognitive psychology, and cognitive ergonomics have contributed to create new theories and frameworks to help HCI designers to apply knowledge of human cognitive processes to the creation of user interfaces based on the awareness of human cognitive process and cognitive resources. Among these new theories and frameworks, we are particularly interested in cognitive load theory and cognitive system engineering framework.

Cognitive load theory, or CLT, was originated in the 1980s and it underwent significant development and expansion in the 1990s by researchers all over the world [2]. John Sweller and others proposed the CLT as a way to describe human cognitive architecture and to deal with the interaction between information and cognitive structures and with the implications of that interaction for instruction [3]. The concept of cognitive load is central to the CLT and is defined as the total amount of mental activity imposed on working memory at an instance in time. Working memory is inherently limited and is a critical cognitive resource for learning, reasoning, problem-solving, and decision making. CLT proposes an instructional design framework to help manage the amount of information that a user is to handle at a time, to stimulate user attention but also to avoid split-attention, and to control the conditions of learning. For example, they proposed the use of mixed auditory and visual presentation modes to increase effective working memory [4]. Clearly, cognitive load of a user represents an important factor for adaptive human–computer interfaces, especially under high intensity work conditions and complex tasks. CLT differentiates three different types of cognitive load which are additive [5]: intrinsic cognitive load, which is determined by an interaction between the nature of the material being learned and the expertise of the learners; extraneous cognitive load, which is the extra load beyond intrinsic load resulting from mainly poorly designed interface, instruction, and tasks; and germane cognitive load, which is the load related to processes that contribute to the construction and automation of schemas. While interface designs should aim to induce low user intrinsic load and low extraneous load, they should seek to promote germane load in appropriate ways so as to make better use of users' cognitive resource and stimulate active information processing by users.

While minimizing user's overall cognitive load is a clear goal of the instructional design framework promoted by CLT, how to measure cognitive load has been a challenging research topic. Traditional cognitive load measurement methods proposed by previous research rely either on subjective ranking of load, requiring user introspection, on task performance analysis, or on some physiological psycho-physiological measurements [6]. The subjective ranking method has been largely used and is believed to be consistent over time, it requires users to interrupt their current task and complete questionnaires or respond to interview questions, and cannot realistically be used as a real-time control indicator. While task performance method is more objective than subjective ranking, it does not provide reliable indication or measurement of instantaneous load, peak load, and accumulated load. Physiological sensors on the other hand seem to be ideal in providing real-time control indications of experienced cognitive load, despite their level of intrusiveness. They can help uncover smaller variations that may occur as the subject completes the task, indicating fluctuating levels of cognitive load experienced. Some of the physiological and psycho-physiological measurements that have been used to measure cognitive load include EEG, ECG, and EKG which measure arousal, stress, and attention; fNIR (functional near infrared) which measures brain blood flow volume and oxygenation indicates potential working memory bottlenecks; blood pressure; heart rate; electro-dermal activity such as galvanic skin response (GSR) [7]. Recently a new cognitive load assessment technique is emerging which is based on the analysis of user behaviors during interaction, for example, analysis of eye gaze movement and changes in pupil dilation, user's voice and speech analysis [8], and user's combined multimodal integration patterns [9]. These works provided important guidance to our work on CAMI.

Cognitive System Engineering The idea of cognitive engineering can be traced back to early 1980s when Norman, Hollnagel, and Woods proposed a new discipline to emphasize the application of knowledge and techniques from cognitive psychology to the design of joint human–machine systems, from both cognitive science and computer system engineering point of views [10]. Cognitive system engineering (CSE) is a variant of cognitive engineering concept that emerged at about the same time. CSE offers a broader, systems perspective to the analysis and design of joint cognitive system involving both humans and computers or machines [10]. The focus of CSE is on how humans can cope with and master the complexity of processes and technological environments, initially in work contexts, but increasingly also in every other aspect of daily life [11].

Since the acceptance of CSE by researchers and designers as one of the guiding principles for the building of complex information systems, various scientific approaches and engineering techniques have been developed to form a CSE research framework. These approaches and techniques include [10]

- Cognitive task analysis, which aims to decompose a complex task into either rule-based or knowledge-based subtasks, and the description and design of each and all of them, so as to approach joint optimization of task performance on one hand, and user's cognitive performance and user satisfaction on the other.
- Cognitive work analysis (or ecological interface design), which emphasizes the importance of carrying out information system and user interface design based on ecological psychology and cognitive ergonomics. The idea is to avoid automation-centered approach, but to help system users to perform their tasks better by providing an appropriate working environment that are cognitive resource friendly.
- Context awareness (or situation awareness), which focuses on examining how users develop and maintain accurate and up-to-date mental representations of the systems they operate through user interface and the world in which they and their systems operate, as well as designing systems that support that critical construct. A user interface with context awareness is critical to supporting human decision-making for mission-critical applications.
- Knowledge-driven system design, which seeks to apply artificial intelligence tools to design interfaces and tasks that help users to carry out complex tasks that are context-sensitive and knowledge-driven, and that cannot be easily be described using nested rules or cases.

- Dynamic tools to augment user cognitive ability, which include in-task cognitive state estimation, real-time user cognitive strategy analysis, user cognitive profile analysis, cognitive aids such as memory aid, strategy aid, and interaction aid.

CLT and CSE are two of the most useful and powerful tools to support the design and development of cognition-adaptive information systems and their user interfaces. CLT and CSE are similar in their acknowledgment of the importance of the understanding and knowledge of human cognitive process to the design of user interfaces and information systems, and of the importance of helping users to manage their cognitive resources and of providing tools to augment users' cognitive ability. On the other hand, the close linkages between CLT and cognitive psychology and between CSE and control system have led to some significant but complementary differences between CLT and CSE. Some of the differences between CLT and CSE are as follows:

- CLT is mainly founded on the mental construct of cognitive load in the form of short-term working memory and attention. CSE, on the other hand, seems to avoid low-level mental construct and focus more on macro-level cognitive constructs such as situation awareness and cognitive task analysis.
- For CLT, minimizing user or learner cognitive load is a grand goal of interface design. For CSE, optimization of joint human–machine system is the ultimate goal, which covers both task performance, system performance, and human performance and experience.
- A range of techniques and methods have been developed for CLT to detect and measure cognitive load. These methods provide significant support to the design and evaluation of user interfaces for information systems. CSE, on the other hand, provides designers with tools for and beyond interface design, such as task analysis, situation awareness, dynamic cognitive aids.
- CLT has been primarily applied to educational applications such as teaching, training, and recently the development of multimodal user interfaces. CSE has been applied to a wider range of applications, especially in large-scale and complex types of applications such as interfaces and decision support systems for mission-critical applications (e.g., air traffic control).

Understanding the strengths and weak points of both CLT and CSE has allowed us to take advantages of both methods in our work on CAMI.

3. Design of Cognition-Adaptive Multimodal Interface (CAMI)

3.1. Motivation and Objectives

In this section we describe our work in the design and development of a cognition-adaptive multimodal interface (CAMI), which is inspired from and for a real-world traffic incident management system. CAMI is motivated by these factors:

- While the idea of cognition-adaptive user interfaces has been around for a long time, there has not been many case studies or design examples reported in the literature, especially for large-scale mission-critical applications.
- Our industry partner has provided us with an interface design task which is technically challenging and economically significant, and at the same time they provide us with an ideal research and development platform.
- We aim to combine concepts and methods from both CLT (cognitive load theory) and CSE (cognitive system engineering) and develop a new type of design methodology based on the complementary nature of both.
- We intend to apply our prior experiences and expertise in the area of multimodal user interfaces to the development of CAMI.

The system objective of CAMI is to create an interface that is able to support the work of traffic control officers so that their cognitive work load is reduced, their use of existing technical and business resources is "cognitively" facilitated, and their task performance is improved (e.g., total incident handling time is reduced). The research objective of CAMI is to combine expertise from CLT, CSE, and multimodal interfaces to create a new design methodology for cognition-adaptive information systems and their user interfaces.

3.2. CAMI Design and Analysis

Figure 12.1 shows the simplified traffic incident management system (TIM) used by traffic control officers (TCOs) without CAMI. Basically, TIM operations consist of incident detection, incident verification, and incident response. At the Traffic Management Centre (TCC) with which we collaborate, TCOs use more than 15 different programs, software, and devices to perform TIM operations on a 24/7 basis. Many of these programs and device controllers have different user interfaces. TCOs' cognitive workload can become very high when emergency incidents occur during peak hours everyday. CAMI project aims to significantly simplify the TIM operations and provide TCOs with a new user interface that can sense TCOs cognitive workload and provide cognitive support adaptively. CAMI will not touch heavy back-end system of detection, verification, response, field device, and personnel shown on the left-hand side of the dotted line in Fig. 12.1. CAMI will add in a decision-supporting middleware layer between these components and the new multimodal user interface as shown in Fig. 12.2.

CAMI has four main parts: a multimodal interface which facilitates user's input to the system and detection of user's cognitive state; an input and context analyzer (input analyzer, cognitive load analyzer, user model, and context model) which analyzes user's intention and cognitive load level; an output and support part (cognitive aids, adaptive content presentation, incident response plans, retrieval support) which provides user with information display and tools based on user needs and context; and finally an incident management engine which connects TIM back-end, user input, and output modules. A detailed description of these components and modules are provided below. The term "user" is used interchangeably to mean traffic control officer (TCO).

A multimodal user interface (MMUI) is an emerging technology that allows a user to interact with a computer by using his or her natural communication modalities, such as speech, pen, touch, gestures, eye gaze, and facial expression. An MMUI consists of devices and sensors, in addition to conventional keyboard and mouse, to facilitate user's intuitive input to the system. In CAMI, the MMUI includes a microphone to capture user's speech and voice during phone calls and oral reports, which will be used for the detection and assessment of user cognitive load levels. Speech can be used as an input mode for users to quickly find a location or another piece of information which may be difficult to do using key presses or mouse clicks on the on-screen electronic forms. We also plan to include a video camera into the MMUI

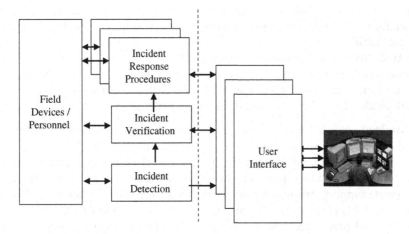

Figure 12.1. Simplified TIM system at the TCC without CAMI.

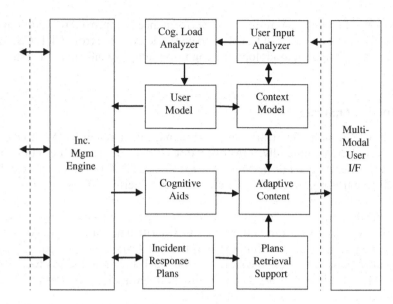

Figure 12.2. CAMI consists of a multimodal user interface and a decision-supporting middleware that sits between the interface and the back-end TIM system (between the two dotted lines).

which can analyze user's eye-gaze movement and changes to user's pupil diameter, both of which can also provide indication of user cognitive load levels. Touch-screen and digital pen can also be part of the MMUI that provides users with more direct and intuitive input modes.

For the output part, apart from LCD monitors for information display, speakers and alarm devices are included in the MMUI to provide users with combined audio–visual information delivery.

The user input analyzer (UIA) receives all user inputs including key presses, mouse clicks, mouse movement, speech, and voice. It can also include user eye-gaze movement and pupil diameter changes. It also keeps track of time and consults context model for context and task-related information. The main functionality of the UIA includes

- Filtering and passing user commands and communication (key presses, mouse clicks, phone calls, etc.) to the TIM system, as if CAMI does not exist.
- Analyzing user's intention: What is he or she trying to achieve at the moment? What is user's strategy to solve a problem? The UIA does this by consulting context model (CM) and the TIM task model in CM. The idea is that for rule-based tasks (e.g., a reported incident has to be verified before any response actions are taken; if there is casualty in an incident, ambulance must be called immediately) the CM and TM can predict and enforce (if necessary) compulsory actions. A task model for current task is built and compared to the "ideal" task model.
- Extracting features from user's speech and voice signals for cognitive load analysis purpose.
- Calculating time a user has spent in current task or subtask. The time information can then be correlated with the CM data and user's past performance for similar task or subtask. This information can also provide indication about whether user is in difficulty or needs help.

The cognitive load analyzer (CLA) is one of the core modules of CAMI. Features extracted from user's speech and voice signals are analyzed and user's cognitive load levels are estimated. User's task timing information will also be used to aid cognitive load level estimation. The results from CLA will provide vital information to incident management engine to decide when and how to provide users with timely and appropriate support through cognitive aids, incident response plans, etc.

The user model (UM) contains user's current cognitive state (input from CLA), cognitive profile, performance history, and preferences. At the Traffic Control Centre (TCC), the traffic control officers (TCOs) are divided into at least four categories: junior TCO, TCO, senior TCO, and chief TCO. Different

TCOs have different skill set and experiences. They also have different responsibility boundaries. These data are useful for CAMI to provide timely and appropriate support to the users.

The context model (CM) is the instantiation of CAMI's ability to maintain situation awareness during the life cycle of an incident or emergency. The CM keeps track of all important events that have happened since the start of an incident. These events may be outcomes of user's interventions or results of actions by other entities (e.g., weather changes, ambulance delays). The CM also provides context information to cognitive aids and plans retrieval support modules (links not shown in Fig. 12.2) to keep users aware of latest and important developments.

An important component of the CM is task models (TMs), which are developed off-line using Cognitive Work Analysis and Cognitive Task Analysis methods. The idea is to identify tasks or subtasks that are rules based or knowledge driven and be used online to compare with user's task sequence or problem-solving strategy.

Cognitive aids (CAs) are tools that provide users with memory support (user's working memory is inherently limited, which is the source of cognitive or information overload), strategy support, and interaction support. They also include simple tools such as automatic phone dialing, automatic message or e-mail composition, reminders, alarms, prompts, and links to handy resources.

Incident response plans (IRP) is a list of recommended actions to be taken, either in sequence or in a prioritized order, so that incident response actions can be implemented in a logical, complete, and speedy fashion. The IRPs are important decision support mechanism that provides significant help to users when dealing with large-scale incidents or emergencies. The IRPs are developed off-line based on past user experience, knowledge drawn from historical incident databases (through data mining), and business logic and rules. The IRPs can play essential roles in reducing total incident handling time and user cognitive workload. However, usually the real-world situation is different from the one under which an IRP was developed. So the plan retrieval support (PRS) module needs to allow and empower users to modify an existing IRP to suit situation at hand.

The adaptive content presentation (ACP) is the planning and management module which determines when and what information should be delivered to a user in which way. Depending on user cognitive state, user preference, and context, the ACP may deliver information to user through visual or audio channel, or both channels combined.

The incident management engine (IME) is the information and command hub between CAMI and underlining TIM system. The IME takes care of complex interfacing with various TIM back-end components so that the other CAMI modules can focus on providing core functionality of delivering productivity increase and cognitive workload reduction.

4. Multimodal Interface Development and Cognitive Task Analysis

We have successfully developed several multimodal user interfaces for our industry partner, the TCC, in the past several years. One interface allows traffic controllers to request information and issue commands using speech and handwriting on tablet monitor, facilitating fast incident data input, and eliminating tedious form filling and paper scratch pad [12]. Another interface supports speech and handgesture-based interaction and facilitates traffic controllers' work in handling incident response and developing response plans [13]. The two pictures in Fig. 12.3 show user studies we conducted on these two novel interfaces. Analyses on task performance and on measurements of galvanic skin response (GSR) from users have shown that these multimodal interfaces provided reduction in user cognitive workload and improved task performance, compared against unimodal and conventional GUI interfaces. These results correlated well with users' subjective rating of their experienced cognitive load.

Cognitive task analysis and design was involved in every user study we carried out. We used several independent control variables to induce different levels of intrinsic cognitive load and extraneous cognitive load from the users, such as incident complexity, dual tasks, time pressure, and number of interactions required.

Figure 12.3. User studies on two multimodal interfaces for traffic incident management applications. *Left* picture shows a user working on a speech and pen-based interface; *right* picture shows a user working on a speech and hand gesture-based interface.

5. Cognitive Load Analysis and Measurement

Cognitive load detection and measurement is a core module for CAMI. We have carried out research in using speech, user multimodal integration patterns (e.g., the way a user combines speech and gesture together to deliver a message), and user GSR measurements as indices to indicate cognitive load in real time [13, 14, 15].

Using speech to measure cognitive load is a new and challenging task requiring expertise in speech analysis and behavioral psychology. We found that speech features such as spectrum features, and prosodic features, and pause rate can be utilized to index and classify cognitive load levels. In one user study, we designed a speech-based multimodal interface to solicit natural user speech at three different levels of cognitive load. Some of the speech data produced were used to train a number of models to automatically detect cognitive load. We then applied an in-house built classifier to the rest of speech data so that the three load levels were automatically classified and output as discrete level ranges. The final system achieved a 71.1% accuracy for three levels of classification in a speaker-independent setting [15].

GSR or skin conductance is a psycho-physiological signal that has long been linked to human affective arousal and cognitive activity [6]. GSR is highly sensitive to changes in arousal and can be obtained in high frame rate using affordable measurement kit. We developed a GSR analysis framework for cognitive load, assessment and interface usability evaluation purposes. It allows us to record and plot user GSR in real time at high frame rate, and to calculate user's peak load, accumulated load, average load and normalized load, which can be correlated with user subjective ranking of task complexity and experienced cognitive load [13]. Besides speech and GSR-based cognitive load analysis, we also use user's task time correlated with historical data to complement cognitive load measurement so that false alarm can be reduced and adaptive cognitive support be provided.

6. Conclusions and Future Work

We are working with a large metropolitan traffic control centre in Australia to design and develop a new user interface for their incident management system. The novel functionality of the new interface, called CAMI or cognition-adaptive multimodal interface, is its awareness of and adaptability to user's cognitive process and changes in user's cognitive workload. We conducted extensive literature review and drew inspiration from the advances in cognitive load theory and cognitive system engineering. The architecture and functionality design of CAMI has been completed and described in this chapter. Our research on cognitive load measurement, a core module in CAMI, has yielded promising outcome and validated the feasibility of CAMI. We also presented our original work in developing multimodal interfaces for traffic incident management applications. At the moment, we are working on the software architecture of CAMI and the development of other key modules shown in Fig. 12.2.

References

1. Balogh, J., Cohen, M., Giangola. (2004) Voice User Interface Design: Minimizing Cognitive Load. Addison Wesley Professional.
2. Paas, F., Renkl, A., Sweller, J. (2003) Cognitive Load Theory ad Instructional Design: recent Developments. Educational Psychologist 2003, 38(1), 1–4.
3. Sweller, J., van Merriënboer, J., Paas, F. (1998) Cognitive Architecture and instructional design. Educational Psychology Review 1998, 10, 251–296.
4. Mousavi, S.Y., Low, R., Sweller, J. (1995) Reducing Cognitive Load by Mixing Auditory and Visual Modes. Journal of Educational Psychology 1995, 87, 319–334.
5. Paas, F., Tuovinen, J.E., Tabbers, H., Van Gerven, P.W.M. (2003) Cognitive Load Measurement as a Means to Advance Cognitive Load Theory. Educational Psychologist, 38(1), 63–71.
6. Lin, T., Hu, W., Omata, M., Imamiya, A. (2005) Do Physiological Data relate To Traditional Usability Indexes? Proceedings of ozCHI 2005. Nov. 23–25, 2005. Canberra, Australia.
7. Reeves, L.M., Schmorrow, D.D., Stanney, K.M. (2007) Augmented Cognition and Cognitive State Assessment Technology. Proceedings of HCII 2007, LNAI 4565, pp. 220–228, 2007.
8. Jameson, A., Kiefer, J., Muller, C. (2006): Assessment of a User's Time Pressure and Cognitive Load on the Basis of Features of Speech. Journal of Computer Science and technology 2006.
9. Oviatt, S., Coulston, R., Lunsford, R. (2004) When Do We Interact Multimodally? Cognitive Load and Multimodal Communication Patterns. In Proc. Int. Conf. on Multimodal Interfaces.
10. Endsley, M.R., Hoffman, R., Kaber, D., Roth, E. (2007): Cognitive Engineering and Decision Making: An Overview and Future Course. Journal of Cognitive Engineering and Decision Making 1(1), Spring 2007, 1–27.
11. Hollnagel, E. and Woods, D.D. (2005) Joint Cognitive Systems: Foundations of Cognitive Systems Engineering. Boca Raton, Florida. CRC Press. 2005.
12. Ruiz, N., Taib, R., Shi, Y., Choi, E. Chen, F., "Using Pen Input Features as Indices of Cognitive Load" Proc. 9th International Conference on Multimodal Interfaces (ICMI'07), Nagoya, Japan, Nov. 2007, pp. 315–318.
13. Shi, Y., Ruiz, N., Taib, R., Choi, E. Chen, F., "Galvanic Skin Response (GSR) as an Index of Cognitive Load", Proc. SIGCHI Conference on Human Factors in Computing Systems (CHI'07), San Jose, April/May 2007, pp. 2651–2656.
14. Ruiz, N., Taib, R. and Chen, F., "Examining the Redundancy of Multimodal Input", Proc. Annual Conference of the Australian Computer-Human Interaction Special Interest Group (OzCHI'06), Sydney, Nov. 2006, pp. 389–392.
15. Yin, B., Ruiz, N., Chen, F. and Khawaja, M.A., "Automatic Cognitive Load Detection from Speech Features", Proc. Australasian Computer-Human Interaction Conference 2007 (OzCHI'07), Adelaide, Nov. 2007, pp. 249–255.

13

Conceptual Web Users' Actions Prediction for Ontology-Based Browsing Recommendations

Tarmo Robal and Ahto Kalja

Abstract

The Internet consists of thousands of web sites with different kinds of structures. However, users are browsing the web according to their informational expectations towards the web site searched, having an implicit conceptual model of the domain in their minds. Nevertheless, people tend to repeat themselves and have partially shared conceptual views while surfing the web, finding some areas of web sites more interesting than others. Herein, we take advantage of the latter and provide a model and a study on predicting users' actions based on the web ontology concepts and their relations.

Keywords Web usage mining · Domain ontology modelling · Web users conceptual profiling · User behaviour prediction

1. Introduction

The Internet has become a part of our everyday lives, providing an enormous source of information. Daily, people use the Internet to search for information, read news and communicate with friends and colleagues. While browsing web sites, users follow certain patterns of behaviour, dependent on their approach to the subject area and driven by the informational needs and expectations. Factors such as visual experience and site attractiveness, logical organisation of navigation, placement of objects, colour schema and page loading time [1–4] also have an effect on the users, browsing behaviour, producing the first impression of the site and attitude towards it. In the real world users are able to explicitly state what they are searching for and how they want to do it. Still, in the web world the real intentions of users at that particular moment they were clicking some link to see some page remain veiled. Nevertheless, we can learn from users' actions by logging their operations and use this accumulated knowledge for predicting their future actions, to be employed in providing a kind of personalisation service as customised views to web pages or dynamically discovered (personalised) recommendations, thereby assisting users in finding needed information. The latter is the interest of our research.

In this chapter, we provide an approach to predict web users' actions on the basis of their conceptual interest on the web site. As users are browsing the web according to a conceptual model of the domain in their minds, the pages they view must be conceptually related. Moreover, users tend to repeat themselves as the understanding of the domain knowledge is largely shared. We exploit this for modelling users' actions prediction. Utilizing a fully automated log system, data about users' preferences and behaviour are collected and processed. Based on original log data mining procedure, users' preferences are found and concepts corresponding to their interest are derived from the mining result and web ontology. This forms

Tarmo Robal and Ahto Kalja • Department of Computer Engineering, Tallinn University of Technology, Estonia.

G.A. Papadopoulos et al. (eds.), *Information Systems Development*, DOI 10.1007/b137171_13,

the basis for the conceptual model and prediction engine (PE) resulting in an ability to implement a personalisation service, where recommendations rely on the learnt users' interest model, predefined user profiles and web ontology. The PE proposed and implemented herein is a part of a recommender engine under development.

The research is based on the usage data collected from the web site of the Department of Computer Engineering (DCE) at Tallinn University of Technology, which is a dynamic web site run by the systems kernel developed at our lab. In addition to providing information to general public, the web site serves as an experimental environment for research and development.

The rest of the chapter is organised as follows. Section 2 reviews the related research by other authors as well as presents an overview of our previous work. In Section 3, we discuss the mining of users' conceptual interest. Section 4 discusses predictions on sequential and conceptual model, coupled with the results from the empirical study on a real web site.

2. Related Works

The works related to this study mainly fall into three categories: web mining, adaptive web sites and recommender systems and web personalisation. The majority of research is tightly connected with web mining and its techniques, being explored by many researchers [5,6,7]. Web personalisation based on usage mining and conceptual relationships between web documents has been explored in [8], and data processing and mining for such processes in [9]. Several methods for improving web mining techniques by using ontologies have been explored. Lim and Sun [10] proposed to define web pages as concept instances and apply ontology-based structure mining to derive linkage patterns among concepts from web pages. They analysed user historical data, clustering previously visited pages based on content similarities in order to recommend users similar pages. In our approach, the key factor is in the locality model, which follows the paths users take while browsing. Several recommender systems based on web mining with ontological approach to help users to find information easily have been developed [11,12]. However, in none of the works the approach of our locality model is present, though, clustering of actions and weighting algorithms are being generally used.

The methods for data collection vary from implicit to explicit, where active participation of users is needed. Yet, researchers have not come to a common understanding of which method is the best to be used. Explicit data collection methods deliver the opinions and ideas of users. Still, Sarwar et al. concluded in [13] that even though explicit rating, provided by the users is precise, users are not willing to rate each page they visit; thus explicit rating cannot be as efficient as expected. Moreover, explicit rating is claimed to disturb users' browsing activities and greatly affect their browsing behaviour [14,15]. Implicit techniques, being transparent to the users, help to overcome these disadvantages and provide good accuracy. The techniques of implicit data collection usually involve data collection from server, proxy or client level using either web server logs, customised web browsers or special log systems [5]. The problem with HTTP traffic logs is that they appear to be flawed [16] and suffer from difficulties due to data incompleteness [5,17], one of which is the inability to identify visitor sessions [18].

Our previous research has concentrated on extracting user profiles from the web usage data for providing recommendations for online user based on his/her active profile discovery [19]. In [20] we proposed a new method for learning users' domain models in order to provide personalisation services, giving conceptual meaning to web usage mining results by using ontologies and automatic classification of concepts to ontologies via ontology reasoning as a part of the system. The provided approach allows to specify rather general user profile concepts according to mined user preferences giving as a result a definition of domain ontology of users. As a result of our web mining studies, we have developed and put into operation a model for users' action prediction based on sequential locality profiles [21]. The latter is also the basis for our studies herein. The work described in this chapter is tightly connected to our previous research, providing the logical continuation towards ontology-based personalisation service.

3. Mining of Users' Interest Concepts for Predictions

Automated and implicit data gathering methods allow to monitor pages users visit, navigational paths they follow while browsing, and to discover the usage patterns and user profiles. Collecting users' interaction data during their web sessions, analysing it further and applying techniques of web mining are crucial for discovering and understanding users' behaviour for predicting their future actions.

Herein, we applied implicit data collection methods to capture web usage data, mainly for the reasons outlined in Section 2. In particular, we employed a special log system [22], as web server logs contain all the accesses to objects on that server and are developed for general purposes, e.g. error tracking. Evidently, they are not designed for the purpose of specific studies of users' web behaviour.

The log system was developed in 2003 based on an earlier log system. The major improvement towards the new system was the ability to capture distinct and recurring user sessions, which is also the basis for users' navigational paths construction. Presently, the log system is an extension to the web systems kernel delivering the web site of DCE and providing sufficient basis for the studies discussed here. From the data captured by the log system, we have used the following attributes to model and extract users' interest concepts: (1) requested page identifier, (2) user identifier (session based ID), (3) set of operations performed during a session, (4) timestamps for operations and (5) recurrent visit identifier (if available).

3.1. Web Ontology

To extract the users' interest concepts, a web ontology describing the concepts of the site is needed. Typically semantic portals rely on domain ontologies to structure knowledge provided on the web site. Still, according to our view, web ontology should be created based on the informational needs of potential users, defining the concepts captured by the web site and the relationships between them. An expert of the domain may create this ontology.

The DCE web ontology used herein is a simple university department web site ontology describing the concepts on that web site. The ontology was created and modelled using the Protégé 3.3 ontology editor [23] and also used in [20]. An excerpt of the web site ontology is shown Fig. 13.1. As we can see, there are classes describing information provided for students, information provided about the department and so forth, covering the information concepts introduced on the DCE web site. Each of those classes can have subclasses, e.g. class InformationForStudents has subclasses for subjects, course schedule, etc. in a is-a hierarchy. Pages, where the concept is present, are added as class individuals, making the web site conceptual description finite. This allows to acquire the concept of where a particular page belongs to and vice versa.

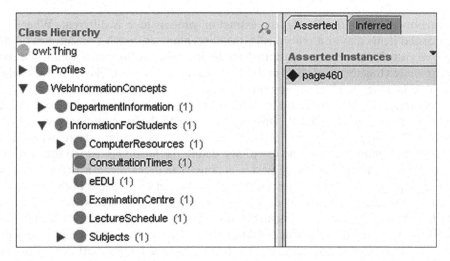

Figure 13.1. An excerpt of the DCE web site web ontology modelled in the Protégé ontology editor.

3.2. Extraction of Users' Interest Concepts into Prediction Model

The raw access data in the log need to be cleaned from noise and filtered before it can be used for user navigational paths extraction. This was done by our log system and analyser. As a result, we derived from the log 87,953 navigational paths as series of unique numerical identifiers set for each page in the web site management system in the order and occurrence of visited pages. A fair 37.5% of sessions presenting the derived navigational paths were classified as recurrent. Thus, the training set for the prediction engine contains more than one-third of sessions of returning users. The navigational paths describe the user behaviour while browsing the web site and were further processed for extracting users' conceptual interest as described in Fig. 13.2.

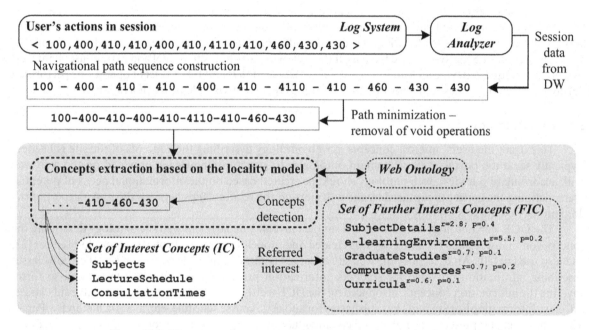

Figure 13.2. The process of user conceptual interest mining from navigational paths.

In comparison to our earlier study, the extraction process here is different. Whereas in [21] the sequence of accessed items played a crucial role, the conceptual approach concentrates on the concepts behind the pages visited. Hence, the conceptual model is based on the presumption that conceptually related pages are viewed together regardless of the sequence they are visited. The locality model is applied in both cases for attaining the users' latest browsing history.

The locality model [19–21] is based on the belief that if a large number of users frequently access a set of pages, then these pages must be related. This also conforms to the presumption that users access pages that are conceptually related, according to the domain model in their minds. Here, we have adapted the model onto concepts behind the pages accessed. We define the locality L as the user's nearest activity history on web site in a sliding window of past w actions. The user session is defined as a sequence of accessed pages $s = <p_i, p_{i+1}, \ldots, p_n>$, where $p \in P$ and P is the set of all pages in the web system. As the model is adapted onto concepts, represented by one or more pages in the web system, we are now dealing with localities L consisting of those concepts such that $L = \{c_1, c_2, \ldots, c_m\}$, where $c_i \in C$ and C is the set of the concepts in web ontology; and the following condition holds: $\forall(p_i \in P) \exists (c_j \in C) \mid <p_i, c_j> \in \varphi \ \& \ \varphi \subset P \times C$. For the extraction of users' interest concepts, we applied a function $L = \text{ExtractInterestConcepts}(s_i, w)$ on each $s_i \in S$.

The result of the extraction process is a set of interest concepts (IC) referring to a set of further interest concepts (FIC).

During the process, we extracted 897,579 interest patterns (IP) from the navigational paths of sizes 2–6 with an average pattern length 4.1 from the DCE web site access log. For each of the IP, corresponding concepts of the web ontology were detected and annotated with concepts users also found interesting while having paid attention to the ones in the interest pattern. Based on the interest patterns, we derived 177,621 ICs referring to 313,910 FICs. For each FIC rank (Eq. 13.1) and probability (Eq. 13.2) was calculated as follows:

$$\text{Rank} = p_r \sum_{i=1}^{n} \frac{\text{Interest value}(i)}{\text{Age}(i)} \tag{13.1}$$

$$p = \sum_{i=1}^{n} \frac{\text{FIC rate}(i)}{\text{IC rate}(i)} \tag{13.2}$$

In Eq. (13.1), Age (i) represents the time period into past (e.g., days, weeks, months), Interest value (i) the number of hits for a page during Age (i), p_r a probability value between 0 and 1 and can be predefined for adjustment purposes. In our experiments, for simplicity $p_r = 1$ was used. Thus, only the nearest past will play a crucial role in ranking. We applied the period of 1 month for Age as a reasonable time for changes to occur in users' behaviour trends.

4. Predictions on Sequential and Conceptual Models

Having extracted the interest concepts (IC) and corresponding further interest concepts (FIC) into the conceptual model, one is now able to predict users' actions. We studied the prediction generation for the purpose of providing enhanced user experience by producing recommendations as a kind of personalisation service [19,20]. According to our view, the prediction engine is a part of the recommendation engine used to provide (semi-) personalised browsing experience.

The predictions for current user online are generated based on the user's latest browsing history defined by the locality window size w and kept in the operations track updated with every operation. In [14] we determined $w = 3$ to perform the best for the DCE web site. The predictions can be generated as soon as the user has made at least $q = \min(w) = 2$ operations. Obviously, there can be multiple concepts predicted with different or equal rank and probability, and a selection has to be made. This is up to the algorithm used for the prediction. The prediction provided in web time thus needs to have a short response time.

Previously in [21] we have described and implemented a model for users' actions prediction based on locality profiles. This model differs from the one proposed herein by concentrating on the order in which the pages are accessed (see Section 3.2), making it a sequential access model. For the purpose of evaluating the sequential model proposed previously and the conceptual approach described herein, we implemented a prediction engine (PE), which was integrated into the department's web site to produce prognosis while users were browsing the site in real time. The paths followed by users, their nearest browsing history for the time of prediction making and results of various algorithms were collected into database for further analyses. For both of the prediction models, equal conditions were applied, enabling us to compare the results. We used the same algorithms as in our previous work for the conceptual model, adding an additional algorithm P, based on the distance D between the concepts in the web ontology taxonomy (see Section 4.1). The algorithms used for action prediction are described in Table 13.1.

Up to the day of analysis, the PE had produced 43,285 predictions for 5,714 user sessions during 335 days. The operations track containing the nearest browsing history of users was implemented based on cookies. On an average, 4.66 predictions were made per session. Please note that the prediction engine was only invoked if and only if user had performed $q = 2$ operations. During the study period, the web site structure remained unchanged, whereas minor updates were made to the content. This provides a good basis for a long-period comparison analyses. Experiments on a medium-size web site with an average access

Table 13.1. Algorithms used for prediction in sequential and conceptual models.

Algorithm	Sequential model	Conceptual model
A1	Locality profiles, $w = 2$	IC in locality profiles, $w = 2$
A2	Locality profiles, $w = 3$	IC in locality profiles, $w = 3$
A3	Combined locality profiles, $w = 2$ and $w = 3$	IC in locality profiles, $w = 2$ and $w = 3$
A4	Algorithm A1, where an ordered set of three prognosis is calculated	
A5	Algorithm A2, where an ordered set of three prognosis is calculated	
A6	Algorithm A3, where an ordered set of four prognosis is calculated	
P	n/a	IC in locality profiles with inverse relationship to D

rate enables us to observe the prediction engine behaviour. Rapid changes on pages would probably have an effect also on the engine and its predictions, especially on its accuracy.

4.1. Conceptual Distance Between Pages Accessed

When users are browsing the web, they have a certain conceptual model in their minds which they apply. Also, the content presented on a web site is organised according to some kind of a conceptual model. The conceptual prediction model proposed here is based on the belief that users are interested in conceptually close items. A study into the users' actions confirmed this.

We define the conceptual distance D as the number of relationships between two concepts, c_i and c_j, in a is-a hierarchy in the web ontology. While studying the users' behaviour, we discovered that pages are accessed with an average conceptual distance $D = 1.9$. In case of the prediction mismatch, users had searched for items averagely on the distance of $D = 2.0$. Thus, in both cases, users had concentrated on the neighbouring items, where the presented information had been conceptually related. This led to a development of the algorithm P, where the prediction is calculated based on the rank, probability, and the distance between the last accessed concept and the ones being predicted.

The proposed prediction algorithm P for conceptual prognosis performed the best in sense of the average deviation from the actually viewed concept, having $D = 2.0$ and $D_{\text{diff}} = 0.1$ in case of prediction mismatch. Other algorithms provided predicted web items from the average distance, $D = 2.5$, with deviation from the actual viewed page concept $D_{\text{diff}} = 0.6$. Thus, the range from which the FIC was provided was wider than exploited by the algorithm P. Over all the sessions the average deviation, however, remained in the range of $D_{\text{diff}} = 0.3$.

4.2. Empirical Study of the Prediction Models

The empirical study of the previously proposed sequential prediction model [21] and the conceptual prediction model described herein showed that overall, the conceptual model provides stable performance with good results.

We compared the prognosis based on the sequential locality model and conceptual model made for the DCE web site in real time. The study lasted for the period of 11 months, during which the conceptual model for the prediction engine performed better in sense of error rate – situations where no predictions were made because the model was unable to provide it. The average error rate for sequential approach was 32%, whereas for the conceptual model only 21%, thus providing 11% more predictions. Figure 13.3 describes the prediction error rate and accuracy during the period of the empirical study. The results are provided in three categories: over all the algorithms (A1–A6) for both prediction models and for newly introduced algorithm P in the conceptual model.

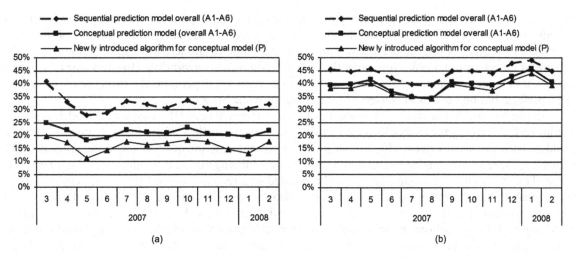

Figure 13.3. Prediction analyses. Comparison of the sequential and conceptual models (**a**) error rate; (**b**) prediction accuracy when a prediction was available.

Despite the good coverage for predictions, the accuracy of available prognosis was in favour of the sequential model. The average accuracy of the sequential model was 44% and for the conceptual prediction model 39%, making the difference of 4.6%, which we consider not to be a major one. Also, the higher accuracy rate of the sequential model is decreased, when taking into account the error rate (Fig. 13.4). We believe that by modifying the algorithms in the conceptual model, the accuracy can be increased. However, for the purpose of the comparative study, we limited the algorithms here to A1–A6 and P. The accuracy for algorithm P was 39%. One should note that the accuracy mainly depends on the amount of choices the prediction engine has to choose from, thus, training. Evidently, the more options there are, the vaguer the accuracy can be. The average number of pages to be predicted for each locality profile using the sequential model was 1.4, whereas for the conceptual model the average number of FIC was 1.8.

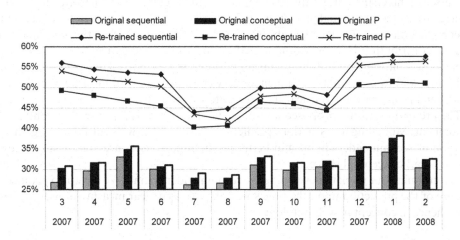

Figure 13.4. Overall performance of the PE for sequential and conceptual models: real web access and simulation with re-trained engine.

The small accuracy difference with the two aforementioned approaches, however, shows a slightly dropping effect over time, as the boost obtained from the freshly trained sequential model settles down. In that sense, the experiment did not provide very good results as there were no major changes on the web site, neither in the content nor in the structure. However, the development plan for the DCE web site contains the launch of the new web site soon and then it would be interesting to analyse the difference of these two approaches in sense of the model performance and reaction to moderate changes. Presumably, the sequential model accuracy will drop when these modifications are introduced. However, the conceptual model should remain at almost same level, as this model does not depend on the sequence of operations users perform but on the concepts users are searching for while browsing.

In conclusion, for our study, the conceptual model performed better than sequential model, as shown in Fig. 13.4, describing the successfully performed prognosis, regardless of whether the prognosis engine could provide the result or not. The lines in Fig. 13.4 present experiment results with the re-trained PE. Clearly, as the re-trained engine has all the data which were missing during the empirical study, it performs better. Thus, the prediction engine data are to be updated on a regular basis; otherwise the performance of the sequential PE will drop, especially when modifications occur. The analysis revealed regularly updated and fresh sequential model to have a boost which for a while guarantees better performance, as it is trained according to the users' actions in the nearest past. From that point of view, the conceptual model is safer, providing more stable prognosis and better coverage for making the predictions, however, on the small cost of prediction accuracy. Nevertheless, in our opinion, it is better to have the PE to produce a sort of prediction for the recommendation engine than producing nothing.

5. Conclusions

Recently, the importance of the Internet and applications based on it has rapidly increased in our lives. While browsing the web, users follow certain patterns of behaviour according to the conceptual model of the subject domain in their minds. Nonetheless, users tend to repeat patterns as the understanding of the domain knowledge is largely shared. In this chapter, we have provided an approach to exploit this shared knowledge for producing users' actions predictions based on the users' interest concepts. A fully automated log system was exploited and data about users' preferences were collected and processed based on original log data mining procedure and web ontology. This formed the basis for the conceptual interest model and prediction engine.

As discussed in this chapter, users are searching conceptually close items. The long-term empirical study conducted here proved the conceptual prediction model to perform better compared to the sequential model, having better prediction coverage and being able to provide prognosis even when the sequential model failed.

Our main contribution is in providing a method for attaining a conceptual model for predicting users' actions based on the web ontology and users' interest concepts. This is a part of our ongoing research with the goal to develop a recommender service to provide a kind of personalisation service, where recommendations rely on the learnt users' interest model, predefined user profiles and web ontology. The prediction engine proposed and implemented herein is a part of a recommender engine under development. Modelling users' actions predictions based on the web ontology, we gain a successful implementation of recommender engine and better prediction, as users are mainly staying during their searches in the small conceptual space.

We are continuing our work in developing the recommender engine. We have also planned to explore the dependence of the prediction upon the time spent on page as a clear measure of user interest towards page content; hence, a concept in web ontology.

References

1. Bernard, M. L. (2001) User expectations for the location of web objects. In *Proceedings of CHI '01 Conference: Human Factors in Computing Systems*, Seattle, WA, USA, March 31 – April 5, pp. 171–172.
2. Geissler, G., Zinkhan, G., and Watson, R. (2001) Web Home Page Complexity and Communication Effectiveness, *Journal of the Association for Information Systems*, 2(2): 1–48.

3. Bernard, M. L., and Chaparro, B. S. (2000) Searching within websites: A comparison of three types of sitemap menu structures. In *Proceedings of The Human Factors and Ergonomics Society 44th Annual Meeting in San Diego*, pp. 441–444. (available at http://psychology.wichita.edu/hci/projects/sitemap.pdf).

4. Lee, A.T. (1999) Web usability: a review of the research, *ACM SIGCHI Bulletin*, 31(1): 38–40.

5. Srivastava, J. Cooley, R., Deshpande, M., and Tan, P-T. (2000) Web Usage Mining: Discovery and Applications of Usage Patterns from Web Data, *SIGKDD Explorations*, 1(2): 12–23.

6. Kolari, P., and Joshi, A. (2004) Web Mining – Research and Practice, *IEEE Computing in Science and Engineering – Web Engineering Special Issue*, 6(4): 49–53.

7. Berendt, B., Hotho, A., Mladenic, D., Someren, M., Spiliopoulou, M., and Stumme, G. (2004) A roadmap for web mining: From web to semantic web. In Berendt, B., Hotho, A., Mladenic, D., Someren, M., Spiliopoulou, M., and Stumme, G. (eds), *First European Web Mining Forum, EWMF 2003*, LNCS 3209, pp. 1–22, Springer, Heidelberg.

8. Eirinaki, M., Lampos, C., Paulakis, S., and Vazirgiannis, M. (2004) Web personalization integrating content semantics and navigational patterns. In *WIDM '04: Proceedings of the 6th Annual ACM International Workshop on Web Information and Data Management*, November 12–13, Washington DC, USA, pp. 72–79.

9. Baglioni, M., Ferrara, U., Romei, A., Ruggieri, S., and Turini, F. (2003) Preprocessing and mining web log data for web personalization. In Cappelli, A., and Turini, F. (eds), *Proceedings of the 8th Congress of the Italian Association for Artificial Intelligence (AI*IA)*, Lecture Notes in Computer Science, 2829, Springer-Verlag, Berlin, 2003, pp. 237–249.

10. Lim, E-P., and Sun, A. (2005) Web mining – the ontology approach. In *The International Advanced Digital Library Conference (IADLC'2005)*, August 25–26, Nagoya, Japan, (available at http://iadlc.nul.nagoya-u.ac.jp/archives/IADLC2005/Ee-Peng.pdf).

11. Middleton, S., De Roure, D, and Shadbolt, N. (2001) Capturing knowledge of user preferences: ontologies in recommender systems. In *Proceedings of the 1st International Conference on Knowledge Capture (K-CAP 2001)*, October 21–23, Victoria, BC, Canada, pp. 100–107.

12. Li, Y., and Zhong, N. (2006) Mining ontology for automatically acquiring web user information needs. *IEEE Transactions on Knowledge and Data Engineering*, 18(4): 554–568.

13. Sarwar, B., Konstan, J., Borchers, A., Herlocker, J., Miller, B., and Reidl, J. (1998) Using filtering agents to improve prediction quality in the grouplens research collaborative filtering system. In *Proceedings of ACM Conference on Computer Supported Collaborative Work (CSCW)*, November 14–18, Seattle, Washington, USA, pp. 345–354.

14. Middleton, S. E., Shadbolt, N. R., and De Roure, D. C. (2003). Capturing interest through inference and visualization: ontological user profiling in recommender systems. In *Proceedings of the 2nd International Conference on Knowledge Capture*, October 23–25, Sanibel Island, FL, USA, pp. 62–69.

15. Shapira, B., Taieb-Maimon, M., and Moskowitz, A. (2006) Study of usefulness of known and new implicit indicators and their optimal combination for accurate inference of users interest. In *Proc. of the 2006 ACM Symposium on Applied Computing (SAC '06)*, April 23–27, Dijon, France, pp. 1118–1119.

16. Davison, B. (1999) Web traffic logs: an imperfect resource for evaluation. In *Proceedings of Ninth Annual Conference of the Internet Society (INET '99)*, June 22–25, San Jose, CA, (available at http://www.isoc.org/inet99/proceedings/4n/4n_1.htm).

17. Mobasher, B., Cooley, R., and Srivastava. J. (2000) Automatic personalization based on web usage mining. *Communications of the ACM*, 43(8): 142–151.

18. Kimball, R., and Margy, R. (2002) *The Data Warehouse Toolkit: The Complete Guide to Dimensional Modelling*. John Wiley & Sons, New York, 2nd ed., 464p.

19. Robal, T., and Kalja, A. (2007) Applying user profile ontology for mining web site adaptation recommendations. In Ioannidis, Y., Novikov, B. and Rachev, B. (eds) *11th East-European Conference on Advances in Databases and Information Systems (ADBIS 2007)*, September 29 – October 03, Varna, Bulgaria., pp. 126–135.

20. Robal, T., Haav, H-M., and Kalja, A. (2007) Making web users' domain models explicit by applying ontologies. In Hainaut, J.-L., et al. (eds) *Advances in Conceptual Modeling – Foundations and Applications: ER 2007 Workshops CMLSA, FP-UML,ONISW, QoIS, RIGiM, SeCoGIS*, November 5–9, Auckland, New Zealand, Berlin: Springer, (LNCS), pp. 170–179.

21. Robal, T., and Kalja, A. (2008) A model for users' action prediction based on locality profiles. In Lang,M., Wojtkowski, W., Wojtkowski, G., Wrycza, S., and Zupancic, J. (eds). *The Inter-Networked World: ISD Theory, Practice, and Education*, Springer-Verlag, New York, ISBN 978-0387304038, to appear.

22. Robal, T., Kalja, A., and Põld, J. (2006) Analysing the web log to determine the efficiency of web systems. In Vasilecas, O., Eder, J., and Caplinskas, A. (eds) *Proceedings of the 7th International Baltic Conference on Databases and Information Systems (DB&IS'2006), Communications*, July 03–06, Vilnius, Lithuania, pp. 264–275.

23. The Protégé Ontology Editor and Knowledge Acquisition System, (available at http://protege.stanford.edu/)

14

Web Portal Design: Employment of a Range of Assessment Methods

Andrina Granić, Ivica Mitrović and Nikola Marangunić

Abstract

This chapter reports on the experience regarding usability evaluation of web portals. The study is placed in Croatian web sphere where the most visited portals are the broad-reach web ones. Consequently, such a research may be of interest to the communities with comparable user population and market characteristics. The evaluation methodology advocates a number of usability test methods along with specialists' inspection. The results of the first study indicated that the chosen research instruments, measures and methods for usability testing were consistent. Conversely, the results of the second study, which employs the guideline-based inspection, did not agree with those obtained through the end-user testing. Although showing significant potential, the methodology needs to be improved.

Keywords Usability evaluation · Web portals · Guideline inspection · User testing · Discount approach

1. Introduction

Usability evaluation plays a fundamental role in a human-centered design process, because it enables and facilitates design according to usability engineering principles. It is related to ease of use and ease of learning. As usability is defined as a relationship between task, user and system purpose, there is no simple definition or meaningful single measure of usability. Most assessment methods are grouped into two usability test methods, namely, user-based methods which involve end users or usability inspection methods engaging usability experts. Recent research has tended to bring together these two basic approaches, cf. [7]. When considering usability of a web portal, a site that functions as a point of access to information on the www, it should be noted that current usability evaluation research is mostly concerned with focused, domain-specific portals. This is the result of a global trend of portal specialization which has made it difficult to find studies related to assessments of broad-reach web portals.

This chapter reports on our experience with the design of a "discount evaluation approach" to web portal usability assessment. The main motivation for undertaking this research initiative came from reports stating that the most visited Croatian web sites are broad-reach web portals. In order to evaluate how easy to use and efficient those portals are, we conducted an experiment employing a range of assessment methods, both empirical and analytic. A major strength of such an approach is the chance to supplement results from both the guideline evaluation and the empirical end user-based one, enhanced by users' feedback on their comfort while working with the web portal. The complementing usability test methods employed in the first study proved to be consistent. Conversely, results of the guideline-based evaluation from the second study were not in agreement with the ones obtained from the usability testing, raising some

Andrina Granić · Faculty of Science, University of Split, Split, Croatia   **Ivica Mitrović** · Arts Academy, University of Split, Split, Croatia   **Nikola Marangunić** · Faculty of Science, University of Split, Split, Croatia

G.A. Papadopoulos et al. (eds.), *Information Systems Development*, DOI 10.1007/b137171_14,
© Springer Science+Business Media, LLC 2009

concerns which will be addressed in our future work. The results support the assertion that we should not rely on isolated evaluations. Instead, usability assessment methods should be combined, giving rise to different kinds of usability improvement suggestions.

The chapter is organized as follows. Section 2 briefly introduces some background to the research, addressing web portals and web usability. Section 3 presents the experimental study for web portal usability testing, while an approach which advocates guideline inspection is offered in Section 4. Section 5 concludes the chapter and in addition provides some directions for future research.

2. Background to the Research

A *web portal* can be defined as a personalized, single point of access to information, resources and services covering a wide range of topics [21]. As an Internet-based application, a portal typically uses more advanced technologies that go beyond the simple interface used for the solely information-based, standard web page. Through the blend of information, services and collaboration among users, a portal's primary objective is to create a working environment that users can easily navigate through. *Broad-reach web portals*, also called "general" or "generic" portals, as gateways to the web, represent starting points in user browsing and may serve as users' anchor sites. They offer a collection of services such as search engines, online shopping, e-mail, news, forums, maps, event guides, employment, travel and other kinds of information. Nowadays portals have evolved from monolithic systems to loosely coupled compounds that glue together different application [12]. Furthermore, information presented in each page addresses a very large user group with highly diverse needs and interests, and portal design has to reflect this.

Market research findings related to the Croatian web sphere, and which was undertaken in the last few years, report that broad-reach portals are the most visited web sites, cf. [5]. This is the basic distinction between Croatia and the countries with high levels of Internet literacy, where more *specialized web portals* are seen as gateways to varieties of web information related to specific contexts [15].

In the context of the global trend of web portal specialization, recent research related to *usability evaluation* is mostly connected with focused portals, often called "vertical" or "domain specific", such as enterprise portals [1], travel portals [4], news portals [19], library web portals [2], tourist portals [10], health-care portals [16] and similar. Apparently, while there are a number of studies related to the evaluation of specialized portals, some of which also taking into account the particular cultural context, e.g. [16, 19] there is very little research dealing with broad-reach portal assessment. Taking into consideration outcomes of prior research related to web portals and usually employed usability assessment methods, the aim of the study is to design a methodology for usability evaluation of web portals. The study is placed in the Croatian web sphere where broad-reach portals are much more popular and accepted than specific ones, thus implying that they would be familiar to end users and designers. For that reason such a research may be helpful to other countries/communities with similar context.

3. Study 1: Usability Testing

We conducted a controlled experiment which advocates scenario-guided user evaluations involving a number of usability testing methods, cf. [14], used to collect both quantitative data and qualitative "remarks" (refer to [6] too). The study involved 30 participants with basic computer literacy skills. According to their practical experience in web design, they were classified into two different groups composed of 15 participants: (i) the "practitioner" group was composed of three independent subgroups of randomly chosen participants including computer science experts, marketing experts familiar with Internet issues and students of web design, and (ii) the "non-practitioner" group was composed of three independent subgroups of randomly chosen young, middle aged and elderly participants.

End user testing was based on criteria expressed in terms of two types of measures [9]: (i) objective performance measurement of effectiveness and efficiency, and (ii) subjective users' assessment. The System Usability Scale (SUS), a simple, standard, 10-item attitude questionnaire with a five-point Likert scale [3],

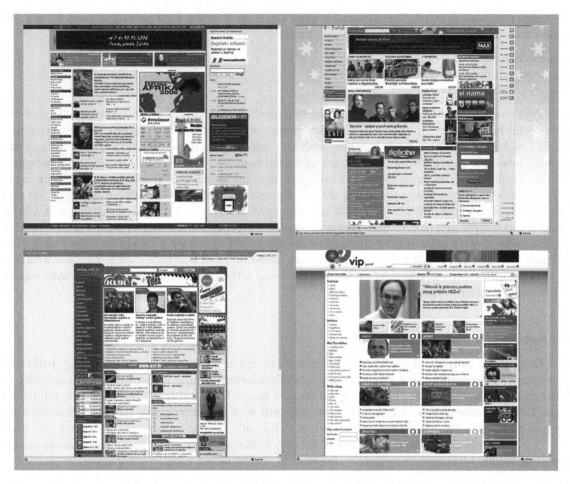

Figure 14.1. User interface screenshots of evaluated portals (clockwise, starting from *top left*: Index portal, Net portal, Vip portal and T-Portal).

was used for the subjective evaluation. As additional subjective feedback, answers to the semi-structured interview were collected.

We included four broad-reach web portals in our experiment, the most visited and also the first-established ones, see Fig. 14.1: Index portal (www.index.hr), Net portal (www.net.hr), Vip portal (www.vip.hr) and T-Portal (www.tportal.hr).

3.1. Research Design and Methodology

In order to understand the effect of web portal design in a sample work situation, we described a work scenario, a sequence of typical tasks and user actions. To test assigned tasks and time interval, clarity and unambiguity of measuring instruments for subjective assessment and adequacy of hardware and software support, pilot testing was performed. We chose several typical tasks whose structure and location on the portals had not changed over time. The tasks covered different topics, offering diverse groups of participants a similar opportunity for finding task-related information. For each portal selected, the tasks undertaken were the same and the probability of their completion was similar.

The evaluation procedure was carried out individually with each test user, using a personal computer with Internet access in addition to software and hardware support for tracing and recording users' actions and navigation. Within each evaluation session all the portals were assessed, with the order of their evaluation randomly selected. The allocated session's average time for each participant was 45 min. An evaluation procedure consisted of the following steps:

- task-based end user testing,
- usability satisfaction questionnaire and
- semi-structured interview.

Task-based end user testing involved a scenario-guided user assessment with tasks selected to show the basic portal functionality. It enabled us to determine user efficiency (time on task) and effectiveness (percent of task completed) while working with the web portal. A user's objective accomplishment measure, labeled as *fulfillment*, was calculated as the average time spent on all allocated tasks weighted with successfulness of task completion. For each user, the time limit for all assigned tasks was 15 min per portal. A *usability satisfaction questionnaire* enabled the assessment of the users' subjective satisfaction with diverse types of interaction. We used the SUS questionnaire, as it is argued that this yields the most reliable results across sample sizes [20]. Its questions address different aspects of the user's reaction to the portal as a whole, providing an indication of the level of statement agreement on a five-point Likert scale. The feedback was augmented with the users' answers in a *semi-structured interview*. In this interview we asked the participants to rate and comment on the portal's visual attractiveness as well. In the following section we present experimental results and findings.

3.2. Results and Discussion of Findings

Descriptive statistics of the objective accomplishment measure fulfillment, including arithmetic means, standard deviations and significance levels (Kolmogorov-Smirnov coefficient) for normality of distribution are shown in Table 14.1. We noted that the results for the distribution of measure fulfillment on the T-Portal differs significantly from normal distribution (K-S = 0.008). Accordingly, Friedman's test as a non-parametrical procedure was performed. A statistically significant value of chi square ($\chi^2 = 49.4$, df = 3, $p < 0.01$) indicates the existence of differences in the objective accomplishment measure among portals (see Table 14.1).

Table 14.1. Objective performance achievement (the lower *M* score indicates a better result).

Fulfillment	*M*	SD	K-S	M Rank	df	χ^2	*p*
Index portal	59.77	38.726	0.292	1.57	3	49.4	<0.01
Net portal	108.40	46.300	0.720	2.93			
Vip portal	62.13	17.211	0.656	1.87			
T-Portal portal	171.64	168.143	0.008	3.63			

Descriptive statistics of results acquired for subjective satisfaction, measuring the SUS for each and every participant on every web portal, are shown in Table 14.2.

Table 14.2. Subjective assessment (the higher M score indicates a better result).

SUS	*M*	SD	K-S	df	*F*	*p*
Index portal	75.33	18.820	0.819	29	746.94	<0.01
Net portal	56.00	25.194	0.902			
Vip portal	77.83	15.821	0.319			
T-Portal portal	51.75	23.836	0.961			

No statistical difference in the distribution of the results from the expected normal distribution was found (K-S1,2,3,4 > 0.05). In order to test the difference among portals, the analysis of variance as a parametric procedure was applied. Significant F-ratio ($F = 746.94$, df $= 29$, $p < 0.01$) indicates the existence of differences among the portals in the results related to the obtained subjective measure.

We also considered all completed experimental results related to the two groups of participants – the practitioner group and the non-practitioner group. The differences in the user's objective achievement and subjective satisfaction measures between the two groups were tested with t-tests for small independent samples. A statistically significant difference between the groups was found for results of the fulfillment measure ($t = 2.95$, $p < 0.01$). The group of practitioners showed better results on mean values (mean $=$ 308.4, SD $= 57.217$) than the non-practitioners group (mean $= 495.46$, SD $= 238.479$). In contrast, a statistically significant difference was not found for the results related to the subjective satisfaction measure SUS ($t = 1.95$, $p = 0.062$) between the practitioner group (mean $= 243.17$, SD $= 51.317$) and the non-practitioner group (mean $= 278.67$, SD $= 48.531$). Pearson's correlation coefficients for the participants' results in the achieved usability objective and subjective measures showed no significant correlation between overall SUS and overall fulfillment ($r = 0.14$). But, significant correlation was found between overall SUS and the overall visual attractiveness ($r = 0.41$).

The results of the task-based end user testing showed statistically significant differences among the portals according to the measure of user's objective achievement. This suggests that portals could be ranked by mean values. The results of the subjective satisfaction measure also showed differences among portals and their ranking by mean values. The measures of user's objective achievement and her/his subjective satisfaction were not significantly correlated. This is in accordance with the results of the meta-analytic research report on correlations among usability measures calculated from the raw data of 73 studies [8].

The overall results achieved could be further related to the most frequent statements from the interviews. Participants felt especially pleased and comfortable working with the portals where their objective achievement was high. They considered them as sites with good quality of information structure, respectable layout and straightforward navigation. A correlation between overall SUS results and overall visual attractiveness indicates that a pleasant appearance influences the subjective perception of portal usability. The interview statements support this finding. Such an assumption is in line with related studies which, along with the related HCI issues, also address aesthetic aspects of design, cf. [18].

The results of the objective accomplishment measure revealed expected differences between non-practitioners and practitioners, the latter being faster and more successful in the tasks' achievement. This indicates that the selected tasks and the objective accomplishment measure were consistent. Conversely, the measure of subjective satisfaction did not show any statistically significant difference between these two groups. Such findings indicate that the questionnaire itself and its translation into Croatian could be considered to be an appropriate instrument for subjective assessment by users. Moreover, our experience suggests that the choice of sample size, in addition to the "profile" of engaged users, is also in line with the outcomes of related studies, cf. [8]. However, we analysed several randomly chosen samples extracted from the original one. A reduced sample of 20 participants shows no or very little difference, whilst a sample with less than 10 participants skews original variable relations completely. Therefore, in future research a sample of 13–16 participants will be considered, thus being in line with the overall objective of the conducted research – the design of a "discount evaluation approach" to web portal usability assessment.

4. Study 2: Guideline-Based Inspection

In addition, user-based testing was supplemented with less strict heuristic evaluation [13], i.e. *guideline inspection*. This particular procedure was conducted with a group of 10 "instant" specialists from the HCI field. With the intention of overcoming the problem of not having enough usability experts who could be involved in the web portal evaluation process, we had the guideline inspection performed by "instant experts" [23]. These were web design practitioners who learnt the principles of good, user-centered design and provided usability expert assessment. *An evaluation form* consisting of a set of principles/guidelines augmented with auxiliary guidelines as additional explanations related to web portals was prepared. Individual expert's *marks* and *comments* concerning the assessed portals were collected. The score for every portal was calculated as an average mark on a seven-point Likert scale. Additional *observations* concerning the inspection procedure could be provided as well. The same four *broad-reach web portals* were included in the study: Index portal, Net portal, Vip portal and T-Portal portal.

4.1. Assessment Procedure

A document containing detailed instructions and an evaluation form was sent to chosen experts. Aiming to discover possible problems in the interface design, they had to mentally simulate the tasks to be performed on portals, mark and comment on the evaluation form, following the instructions and the provided guidelines along with the auxiliary ones. Thus, in order to supply all necessary information, the evaluation form had to be very detailed and self-explanatory. Nielsen's usability heuristics as a set of 10 key principles [13] were explained and adjusted to portal usage. In addition, as additional explanation to the guideline, a series of auxiliary guidelines concerning portal design were also provided, cf. [22; 11].

Experts had (i) to specify a level of their conformity with a principle/guideline and related set of auxiliary guidelines on a seven-point Likert scale and (ii) to provide a comment to justify the mark they assigned since they were encouraged to offer additional notes related to advantages and disadvantages of assessed portals. Furthermore, observations and remarks concerning the overall guideline assessment procedure were welcomed.

4.2. Results and Analysis

Comprehensive analysis of data obtained by means of 10 evaluation forms was performed. The result of usability inspection achieved did not conform to those obtained through applied usability testing. The highest ranked web portal in the end user testing scored as the lowest one in the "instant expert" evaluation. There are two possible reasons for such an outcome – the design of the evaluation form or the selection of usability specialists. The experimental results and findings acquired through guideline inspection are addressed in what follows. Arithmetic means of marks from a seven-point Likert scale provided by 10 specialists according to 10 usability guidelines show that the highest mark was given to Vip portal (mean = 5.38), followed by Net portal (mean = 4.85), T-Portal portal (mean = 4.64) and Index portal (mean = 4.01).

Overall results could be further related to experts' comments obtained by means of the form. Vip portal experts emphasized the well-adjusted and consistent layout, simple navigation and feeling of control. This portal scored the best for guidelines 8 and 2. The Net portal obtained its highest scores for guidelines 2 and 4, and lowest for 10. It was described as consistent with well-structured information, but with poor and old fashion visual appearance. T-Portal complied very well with guideline 5, but conversely did not comply at all with guideline 8. Identified problems were related to overly diverse types of navigation and an initial page that was too lengthy. Lack of consistency and aggressive "visual noise" were the main reasons why Index portal got mostly bad marks. The worst marks were obtained for guideline 4. Identified problems included an ambiguous home page, lack of consistency and navigation overload. The evaluation form analysis included the assessment of the adapted guidelines themselves and a judgment of the quality of the experts' evaluations. Qualitative analysis criteria were expressed in terms of mark span and value of comments (see columns *Mark Span* and *Info* in Table 14.3).

The guidelines were "horizontally" examined through expert's comments and observations, assigning low (L), medium (M) and high (H) values according to the quantity and the level of details of comments provided (Info column). The range of marks expresses the lowest and highest marks given by the experts (Mark span column). "Vertical" analysis comprised an inspection of the specialist's answers to the

Table 14.3. Analysis of the adapted guidelines.

Portals	Index portal		Vip portal		Net portal		T-Portal portal	
Guidelines	Mark span	Info	Mark span	Info	Mark span	Info	Mark span	Info
1. Portal actively informs the user about its processes (information about what is going on is always present)	4–6 (2–7)	L	2–6 (2–7)	L	3–6 (2–6)	L	2–6 (2–6)	L
2. Concept of portal is well adjusted to the user context	5–6 (4–6)	M	5–7 (3–7)	M	5–6 (3–7)	L	2–6 (1–6)	M
3. While working with portal users have a feeling of control, safety and navigation freedom	3–6 (2–7)	H	4–7 (4–7)	M	2–6 (2–7)	H	2–6 (1–7)	H
4. Portal respects media standards and usual practice/usage/ routine	1–4 (1–4)	H	5–7 (4–7)	M	4–6 (3-6)	M	2–7 (1–7)	M
5. Portal prevents possible user errors	2–6 (1–6)	L	3–7 (3–7)	L	3–7 (2-7)	L	2–7 (2–7)	L
6. User gets information intuitively on the portal, i.e. user does not have to remember the information path but recognize it	4–5 (1–7)	M	4–7 (4–7)	L	3–6 (2–7)	M	2–6 (1–7)	L
7. Portal is adjusted for efficient use by novice users as well as by experts	3–5 (2–6)	H	4–6 (3–7)	M	3–6 (2–6)	H	2–6 (1–7)	M
8. Portals' design is clear, understandable and transparent, i.e. the most needed information is at the same time most visible	2–5 (1–7)	M	5–7 (4–7)	M	4–6 (4–7)	M	2–6 (2–7)	L
9. Portal enables the user to recognize and help recover from errors	2–6 (1–7)	L	3–7 (2–7)	L	2–7 (2–7)	L	3–7 (2–7)	L
10. Portal offers help while working on it.	2–5 (1–5)	M	3–6 (3–7)	M	3–6 (2–6)	M	2–7 (2–7)	M

guideline compliance related to assessed portals (see Table 14.4). The same information quality criteria were used while analyzing experts' work: number, percentage and quality of comments provided and number of additional observations.

The quality of information obtained through individual expert's comments was categorized as low, medium and high. For instance, remarks like "there is no mistake" or "not good at all" represent comments of low information quality. Conversely, detailed ones which listed specific observations related to page layout, fonts, navigation/links and graphics were classified in the medium and high information quality

Table 14.4. Analysis of the experts' feedback.

Expert ID	Number of comments	Percentage of comments	Quality of comments	Additional observations
1	None	0%	None	None
2	29	73%	Medium	5
3	None	0%	None	None
4	40	100%	High	5
5	38	95%	High	1
6	34	85%	Medium	1
7	29	73%	Medium	None
8	8	20%	Low	2
9	40	100%	High	5
10	40	100%	Medium	4

categories. Analyses of the marks and comments for each guideline obtained from the evaluation form indicate that some provide extremely poor information. Those guidelines have a wide mark span, which could imply limitations in their understanding or their vague formulation. Furthermore, because they do not evoke sufficient portal analysis from experts, they offer minimal amount of comments as well. Moreover, additional information regarding problems and possible solutions in portal design is not offered. According to the above discussion, our results suggest that a good guideline is one which (i) is characterized by a narrow mark span and (ii) "provokes" high quality comments, criticisms which identify user interface design problems and at the same time offers solutions (for example see guidelines no. 2, no. 3 and no. 7).

Regarding the choice of usability "instant experts", significant differences in acquired information suggest that the group was non-homogeneous concerning their HCI knowledge and usability expertise. This problem was difficult to avoid due to an inadequate number of resident HCI specialists and the high costs of engaging foreign experts.

5. Conclusion and Future Steps

The objective of the research is the design of a "discount evaluation approach" to web portal assessment. Aiming to achieve this goal, the design of the most visited Croatian web portals was assessed both through a number of usability test methods and the usability inspection method. The main motivation for considering broad-reach web portals was that reports indicate that they are the most visited Croatian web sites, implying that they would be familiar to end users and designers. The evaluation methodology, thus being significant to the communities with comparable level of web literacy too, as an approach which advocates specialists' assessment with scenario-guided user evaluations was used to collect both quantitative data and qualitative remarks and provided comprehensive valuation feedback. The experience reported in this chapter indicates that the chosen research instruments, measures and methods for user-based evaluation were consistent. However, assessments could be improved by employing a faster and less expensive procedure involving fewer test users. Still, the results of the inspection method were not in agreement with the ones obtained from the user test methods. The guideline-based evaluation, although showing considerable potential, raised a number of concerns.

Quantitative and qualitative analyses of the evaluation form showed that it needs significant revision. Some of principles adapted from Nielsen showed poor applicability in web portal context. The derived guidelines did not provide information which is useful for improving portals' usability. As a result, a number of guidelines should be clarified, auxiliary guidelines need to be revised and redundant ones excluded. We will prepare a new set of guidelines which is not so strictly based on Nielsen's heuristics but more suitable for a portal context. The issue of "instant" specialists should be carefully considered although it cannot be avoided due to the inadequate number of resident HCI experts and the high cost of engaging foreign specialists. Diversity in quality and quantity of acquired information suggests the non-homogeneous group of "instant experts" concerning their HCI expertise. Moreover, our future work will be focused on specialized web portals in general and news portals in particular. Concerning their structure and media specificities, news portals are very similar to the broad-reach ones. They are designed as sites that function as single points of access to information on the web [21] and are typically based on more advanced technologies that go beyond the simple interface of basic, information-based, standard web pages. It has been argued that major Croatian broad-reach portals are reminiscent of the web sites of broadsheet newspapers or public service broadcasters [17]. Additionally, they organize services such as e-mail, news, forums, search engines, maps and the like, delivering information to a diversity of users having different needs, motivations and goals, which the portal design has to reflect.

As discussed above, it seems valuable to perform a usability assessment of specialized Croatian web portals, evaluating at the same time the designed methodology. Accordingly, first the applied inspection method will be upgraded: (i) the experts selection will include only five specialists' but with higher HCI expertise; (ii) the evaluation form will be revised and a new set of guidelines less dependent on Nielsen's heuristics will be prepared; (iii) the number of test users will be reduced to 15 and (iv) the redesigned methods will be applied in assessing specialized Croatian web portals (for example news portals). Second, to improve the applicability of the methodology to practice and to achieve its broad generalization, the inclusion of a cross-cultural sample will be considered.

Acknowledgements

This chapter describes the results of research being carried out within the project 177-0361994-1998 *Usability and Adaptivity of Interfaces for Intelligent Authoring Shells* funded by the Ministry of Science and Technology of the Republic of Croatia. The experiment was conducted at the Department of Visual Communication Design, Arts Academy.

References

1. Boye, J. (2006) Improving portal usability. *CMS Watch*. http://www.cmswatch.com/Feature/151-Portal-Usability.
2. Brantley, S., Armstrong, A. and Lewis, K.M. (2006) Usability testing of a customizable library web portal. *College & Research Libraries* 67, 2.
3. Brooke, J. (1996) SUS: a "quick and dirty" usability scale. In Jordan, P.W., Thomas, B., Weerdmeester, B.A., McClelland, A.L. (Eds.): *Usability Evaluation in Industry*. Taylor and Francis, London.
4. Carstens, D.S. and Patterson, P. (2005) Usability Study of travel websites. *Journal of Usability Studies* 1, 1.
5. GemiusAudience, (2007). http://www.cati.hr/GemiusAudience-ozujak.pdf.
6. Granić, A., Mitrović, I. and Marangunić, N. (2008) Experience with usability testing of web portals. In Cordeiro, J., Filipe, J., Hammoudi, S. (Eds). *Proceedings of the Fourth International Conference on Web Information Systems and Technologies: WEBIST 2008; Vol. 2: Web Interfaces and Applications*. INSTICC Press, Portugal, pp.161–167.
7. Hornbæk, K. (2006) Current practice in measuring usability: Challenges to usability studies and research. *International Journal of Man-Machine Studies* 64, 2.
8. Hornbæk, K. and Law, E.L-C. (2007) Meta-Analysis of Correlations Among Usability Measures. *CHI 2007 Proceedings*, April 28–May 3, San Jose, California, USA.
9. ISO/IEC 25062:2006 (2006) Software engineering – Software product Quality Req. and Evaluation (SQuaRE) – Common Industry Format (CIF) for usability test reports.
10. Klausegger, C. (2006). Evaluating internet portals – an empirical study of acceptance measurement based on the austrian national tourist office's service portal. *Journal of Quality Assurance in Hospitality & Tourism* 6, 3–4.
11. MIT Usability Guidelines (2004) http://web.mit.edu/is/usability/selected.guidelines.pdf.
12. Moraga, M., Calero, C., Piattini, M., and Diaz, O. (2007) Improving a Portlet Usability Model. *Software Quality Journal* 15, 2
13. Nielsen, J. (1994) Heuristic evaluation. In Nielsen, J., Mack, R. (Eds.): *Usability Inspection Methods*. John Wiley and Sons Inc., New York.
14. Shackel, B. (1991) Usability – context, framework, design and evaluation. In Shackel, B., Richardson, S. (eds.): *Human Factors for Informatics Usability*, Cambridge University Press, Cambridge, 21–38.
15. Tatnall, A. (Ed.), (2005) Web Portals: The New Gateways to Internet Information and Services. Idea Group Publishing, Hershey.
16. Theng, Y.L. and Soh, E.S. (2005) An Asian Study of Healthcare Web Portals: Implications for Healthcare Digital Libraries. *Proc. of 8th Int. Conf. on Asian Digital Libraries*, ICADL. Bangkok.
17. Tomić-Koludrović, I., Petrić, M., (2004) Identities on the Net: Gender and National Stereotypes on Croatian Broad-Reach Portals. *Društvena istraživanja* 13, 4–5.
18. Tractinsky, N., Katz, A. and Ikar, D. (2000) What is beautiful is usable. *Interacting with Computers* 13, 2.
19. Tsui, W.C., Paynter, J., (2004) Cultural usability in the globalisation of news portal. In Masoodian, M., Jones, S., and Rogers, B. (Eds.): *Computer Human Interaction, Proceedings of the 6th Asia Pacific Conference, APCHI*. Lecture Notes in Computer Science 3101. Springer.
20. Tullis, T.S. and Stetson, J.N. (2004) A Comparison of Questionnaires for Assessing Website Usability. *Proc. of UPA Conf.* Minneapolis. http://home.comcast.net/~tomtullis/publications/ UPA2004TullisStetson.pdf.
21. Waloszek, G. (2001) Portal Usability – Is There Such A Thing?. *SAP Design Guild*, Edition 3. http://www.sapdesignguild.org/editions/edition3/overview_edition3.asp.
22. Wood, J. (2004) Usability Heuristics Explained, *iQ Content*. http://www.iqcontent.com/publications/features/article_32.
23. Wright, P. and Monk, A. (1991) A cost-effective evaluation method for use by designers. *International Journal of Man-Machine Studies* 35(6), 891–912.

15

A Proposed Extension of the CODAM Model for Human Attention

Kleanthis C. Neokleous, Marios N. Avraamides, Andreas A. Ioannides, Costas K. Neocleous and Christos N. Schizas

Abstract

A new computational model of visual attention is proposed on a theoretical basis, based on the CODAM model (Taylor, 2002, [25], 2006). Also a more general mechanism is proposed for an attention model of two or more senses working concurrently. The additional mechanism is mainly based on the interaction of the attention mechanism in the brain with working memory.

Keywords Attention · Adaptive neural networks · Computational model · Control theory

1. Introduction

In the last few years there is an increasing research interest in the general area of human–computer interaction. Within this research area, it is of great importance to develop new computational models of human behavior. More specifically there is a lot of interest and concentration toward the development of systems capable of reasoning about a user's attention and how this could be effectively guided to certain desired applications. In addition, good understanding of the human attention can be proved to be very important in computer vision, in cases of transferring compressed data, for focusing on important information of a scene and many other applications.

Several definitions have been proposed to describe the nature of visual attention. It has been described as "a bottleneck through which a limited amount of information can be filtered" [1], as "a limited capacity for information processing" [2], as a "spotlight with a moving fixed size of a focus diameter" [21], as "a glue that binds together features of things that are being processed" [27], as "a multimodal process in which different processing modes are implicated at different stages" [20], and many others.

Many computational models of human visual attention are based on psychological and neuro-biological findings. The development of computational models started with the feature-integration theory of Treisman and Gelade [26]. Following that, the theory was extended and developed with the use of a neural architecture by Koch and Ullman [17] and more recently by Itti et al. [12]. These proposed models are mainly based on the theory of saliency map, according to which, an image is initially analyzed in a group

Kleanthis C. Neokleous • Department of Computer Science, University of Cyprus, 75 Kallipoleos, 1678, POBox 20537, Nicosia, Cyprus. **Marios N. Avraamides** • Department of Psychology, University of Cyprus, 75 Kallipoleos, 1678, POBox 20537, Nicosia, Cyprus. **Andreas A. Ioannides** • Laboratory for Human Brain Dynamics, Brain Science Institute, RIKEN, 2-1 Hirosawa, Wako-shi, 351-0198, Saitama, Japan. **Costas K. Neocleous** • Department of Mechanical Engineering, Cyprus University of Technology, Lemesos, Cyprus. **Christos N. Schizas** • Department of Computer Science, University of Cyprus, 75 Kallipoleos, 1678, PO Box 20537, Nicosia, Cyprus.

G.A. Papadopoulos et al. (eds.), *Information Systems Development*, DOI 10.1007/b137171_15,
© Springer Science+Business Media, LLC 2009

of different characteristics maps and then processed by specific operants inspired by the functionality of the brain. The overall process is completed in the saliency map and a winner-take-all neural network selects the area of the image to turn the attention to. In the next section, a more recent and important computational model of attention will be described which is based on control theory combined with information measured by brain imaging data. This model will be the basis on which we build the proposed modified model.

2. Control Theory Approach for Computational Modeling of Attention

Numerous experiments on human attention, using modern brain imaging techniques, have demonstrated that there exists a network of cortical modules involved in the development of attention [11]. Moreover, it has been observed that there is continuous communication between these modules during the attention process, something that suggests the existence of some sort of mechanism in the form of a dynamical system that is responsible for this special behavior of the human brain. In addition to that, considerable progress has lately been done in using brain imaging that has shown convincingly that there are two regions of brain tissue involved in attention. Specifically, a region that receives information on where to produce the neural activity that will be attended and another area that creates the actual signal that gives this information [3]. Based on some recent results on attention of brain imaging experiments (Kanwisher and Wojciulik, 2000; [4] it may be supposed that it is appropriate to employ control engineering techniques for dynamical systems to model attention and enable an investigator to effectively understand the complexity of operations in a network of modules as they function in a collaborative manner during human attention.

One of the best attempts to model attention, based on ideas from control engineering, is the CODAM (corollary discharge of attention movement) model proposed by John Taylor and his co-researchers (Taylor et al., 2002, 2003, 2006).

This model has been based on experimental data and tested with good simulation results on several behavioral experiments (Frangopanagos et al, 2007).

In Fig. 15.1 a block diagram of the CODAM model is shown, indicating its various modules. Each module is used to model a particular function, and it is primarily based on experimental observations through brain imaging data. In this chapter, an emphasis will be given on the timing and connectivity between the modules as well as more specifically on the interaction of the goals and the working memory (WM) modules as specified in the CODAM model. As has previously been stated, there is good experimental evidence that attention acts in a control manner since it has been observed that several regions in the brain are dynamically involved.

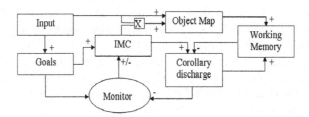

Figure 15.1. The CODAM model of attention.

3. Brief Description of the CODAM Model

In the CODAM model, the plant being controlled is considered to be composed of early sensory or more general motor cortices and it is identified as the *Object Map* in Fig 15.1. It is now accepted that attention in the brain is manifested through a mechanism of desired neural activity amplification of the objective that we actually want to turn our attention to, as well as on inhibition of distracting elements in the neural representations of the same cortical sites. The Object Map can be seen as the place where the information is registered and waits for the signal from the controller to amplify the selected neural activity. For example, while we are talking to a person, a fly passes behind the other person's head. If our attention does not change toward the fly, then it will not be observed. However, in the Object Map it would be possible to "see" neural activation that comes from the visual input and is related to the fly. So, in order to turn our attention to a specific object or event, a signal needs to come and amplify the relevant neural activity in the Object Map. This signal is considered to be the signal from the controller where, based on experimental data, its creation is assumed to be initiated in parietal and frontal lobes. In the CODAM model this assumption is presented by the *inverse model controller* (IMC) for attention movement, as shown in Fig. 15.1. An important question that arises is on how IMC is activated. In the CODAM model it is suggested that a goal module exists, which is needed to process where the attention should be drawn by biasing the controller. The *goal module* can be separated in the two subcomponents. The exogenous goals that basically process sudden external stimulations and the endogenous goals that are internally generated goals for attention to be directed to. More specifically, this separation of the goals module can direct to two relevant attention networks that have been noted to be very similar [5]. Namely, the top-down (endogenous) which is guided by the long-term goals possibly held in prefrontal cortex and are set up when a specific psychological task is requested to be carried out by a subject as, for instance, the GO/NOGO task and an exogenous attention. The exogenous or bottom-up attention is created by external stimulations. This can be seen as some kind of threshold that if these stimulations exceed, then the direction of attention is changed toward the new source of stimulation. The direction of the focus of attention by amplification of the relevant neural activity in the posterior cortices (in the visual system) can be described by the so-called "bias competition model" suggested by Desimone and Duncan [8].

The next component of the CODAM model is the *Corollary Discharge module* which can be seen as a forward model or a predictor of the direction of the focus of attention. In general, this is a very important and common component in modern control theory, the only difference being that in the CODAM model the estimation is on the attended lower level activity rather than on the state of the system. Such a control component was used to give an early boost to the buffer working memory activity which arises from the neural representative activity that is attended. This mode of operation of the corollary discharge was used in a successful simulation of the phenomenon of attentional blink [10].

Finally, the *Monitor* is needed for calculating the error in the goal and the feedback result either from the prediction of the corollary discharge module or as actual sensory feedback from working memory.

4. Some Important Issues and Questions on Specific Characteristics of Attention

As has been previously stated, the basic mechanism of human attention can be seen as a dynamical control system with communication between various components presented in different cortical networks of the brain. However, there are some questions that involve special characteristics of the human attention that arise by observing this mechanism in a more general aspect. These questions are as follows:

- Is attention adaptive to different situations based on the current state of the person or the external environment?
- Is attention somehow modified with learning?
- Are the inputs of the system that arise externally or internally correlated?

We propose that the answer to these questions is yes, as can be seen from our daily life observations, as well as from specific experiments such as the change blindness and inattentional blindness [23].

The adaptation of attention can be simulated by the error module in the CODAM model, since a feedback error-learning signal from the monitor, proportional to the error, can be used to train both the IMC and the goals. To obtain the learning chunks in the attention mechanism, a recurrent architecture between different cortical areas is possibly needed. Most probably, these cortical areas involve the frontal cortex and it has been simulated with attention agents [14,15]. Furthermore, it has been proposed by Taylor et al. (2006) to extend the CODAM by including value maps and a reward error prediction delta as well as with the addition of cerebellum to act as an error learner by combining chunked sequences together.

5. Proposed Modifications on the Attention Model

Despite the previously proposed modifications/solutions and possible extensions of the model, there are still some issues that could be approached in a different manner. Firstly, the adaptation proposed by the monitor in the CODAM model can provide corrections in possible "wrong" directions of the focus of attention, but it cannot change the significance of the goals so that they adapt to the current situation, unless a feedback signal from the monitor is used to influence the goals module. Also, one very important aspect of human attention concerns the relation with working memory (WM). It is widely accepted now that the working memory has limited capacity. This is the main reason why we cannot have our attention on many different things at the same time, but only on a few that we select. To this end, we propose that there should be an earlier mechanism, such as an adaptive neural network, to work as a pre-controller that "decides" how much of the working memory capacity can and will be used by a specific attended neural activity and additionally to be able to include the previously mentioned characteristics of human attention. The adaptive neural network should be able to give different WM usages on specific neural activity based on the importance of the external stimulation or internal goal that will bias the controller. The weights of the goals are most probably affected by previously attended activity, by emotions and in the case of the general model of attention for multiple senses, by correlation between them. This can be better understood with an example. Let us consider two persons talking to each other. In this case both persons have increased attention in both senses visual and auditory, since what they see and hear is very much related. However, if one person was looking at the other but trying to hear somebody else talking, then one of the two senses will have reduced attention. In an analogous manner, the adaptive neural network can be applied as a pre-controller for the CODAM model for the visual control system but instead of weighting related activity of different sensory systems, if compares different stimulations in the visual system as will be explained in the next section.

Some important issues that need to be taken into consideration about the addition of the adaptive neural network is the justification based on behavioral experiments as well as the confirmation from brain imaging data.

As for the behavioral justification, various experiments have been performed that examine the relationship between attention and working memory. More specifically, for the case of visual stimuli one of the first studies by De Fockert et al. [7] has shown how working memory could modulate attention and affect the processing of relevant and irrelevant stimuli, since significant difference was observed in the relative reaction time. This gives us the indication that a different kind of processing has been done during the mechanism of attention in the brain, or more specifically it directs us to the assumption that a different "weight" was assigned to the goals so that they produced stronger and faster activations of the controller in the case of relative stimulation.

As for the temporal analysis from brain imaging data, what is generally accepted and presented in the CODAM model is that the different signals from the components that form the control system of visual attention are activated in the range of 150–600 ms post-stimulus. The reason for that is because the first electrophysiological signal that is assumed to be related with attention is the P1/N1 and is observed around 150 ms after the stimulation. There are also early signals in cortex before the first 150 ms following stimulus presentation. However, until now these activations have been known to be independent of attention. A critic that one could put forward is that if the proposed adaptive neural network behaves as a pre-controller, it means that its operation and functionality must be prior to the 150 ms in the temporal flow activity in the cortex. Nevertheless, new recent brain imaging data [19] have suggested an early attentional activity in the primary visual cortex within the 100 ms after stimulation, which basically confirms our assumption of the existence of a pre-controller. In the following section the suggested additional mechanisms will be shown in the modified CODAM model and be described. This will be done first for the visual control system and then for a possible way of extending it to two (or more) senses.

In Fig. 15.2, the proposed modified CODAM model is shown. It is noted that a major addition is the adaptive neural network as a pre-controller.

The adaptation of the weights of the neural network will be influenced by the feedback of the error module. The inputs of the neural network will be influenced by the endogenous goals in the way that if one person is looking for something internally, for example, a face or a specific letter in a psychological task such as the attentional blink [22], then the weight that corresponds to that specific goal should be increased. This means that if the endogenous goal is recognized, more weight in the form of bias will activate the controller and thus the neural activity that corresponds to the specific goal will be amplified with additional weight in order to have access to more working memory "space." Similarly, the external inputs that correspond to external visual stimulations should be compared with the actual neural activity that the attention is focused to. This can be explained by considering that if a person's attention is toward some specific point of a visual scene, then any new external stimulation that rises from near that neighborhood of the attended area will have more chances to be noticed (to be attended) than if the same stimulation was in a different area. Finally, the output of the neural network selectively changes the influence of each goal so that the corresponding neural activity will have access to more or less working memory which eventually leads to stronger or weaker attention.

Furthermore, an extension of the model of Fig. 15.2 is proposed for a general system of two or more senses. One important difference from the single-sense model is that the extended model should have a correlation check in the inputs between the attended neural activities of one sense compared with the external stimulations of the other as can be seen in Fig. 15.3. The importance of the correlation check between the two senses arises from the example mentioned earlier about two persons talking and watching each other. If the information coming from the auditory sensor has strong correlation with the attended visual neural activity, then the corresponding auditory external stimulation will have an increased weight in the goals module so that it can earn space of the working memory's capacity.

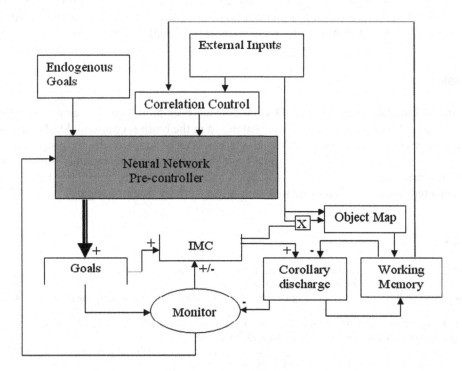

Figure 15.2. An adaptive neural network as a pre-controller for the visual attention system.

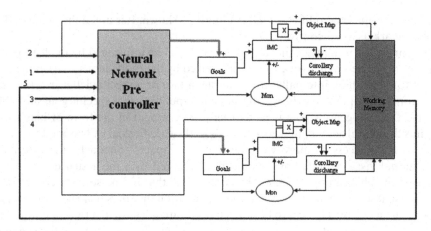

Figure 15.3. Extended modified control model for two senses.
Inputs:
1: Endogenous information from visual sense
2: External visual stimulations
3: Endogenous information from auditory sense
4: External auditory stimulations
5: Previous attended information

One more important difference of the proposed general model, as compared to the visual control model of Fig. 15.2, concerns the endogenous inputs. In the visual system, the endogenous inputs can be related with specific visual recognition desires, like, for example, the desire to recognize a face in the crowd. In the proposed general model, the endogenous inputs have an additional contribution since in the case that the two senses are processing information of the same nature, there is a competition between them about who will access the WM. So, if an endogenous desire is to recognize a specific face in the crowd, this means that more weight has to be applied initially to the goals of the visual system in general.

6. Discussion

In summary a modification of the CODAM model has been presented. The modified model includes an adaptive neural network as a pre-controller. Attention in the brain is considered to be one of the most complicated systems. However, some specific characteristics can be adapted with the proposed mechanism. Nevertheless, there is a great need for additional brain imaging experiments mainly focused on the early neural activation prior the 150 ms in order to support and confirm this assumption. The proposed model will be implemented, simulated, and evaluated with respect to real attentional data.

References

1. Broadbent D.E. (1958). Perception and Communication. London: Pergamon.
2. Broadbent D.E. (1971). Decision and Stress. London: Academic Press.
3. Corbetta M., Shulman G.L. (2002). Control of goal-directed and stimulus-driven attention in the brain. *Nat. Rev. Neurosci.* 3, 201–215.
4. Corbetta M., Tansy A.P., Stanley C.M., Astafiev SV., Snyder A.Z., Shulman G.L. (2005). A functional MRI study of preparatory signals for spatial location and objects. *Neuropsychologia* 43, 2041–2056.
5. Coull J.T., Nobre A.C. (1998). Where and when to pay attention: the neural systems for directing attention to spatial locations and to time intervals as revealed to both PET and fMRI. *J. Neurosci.* 2, 7426–7735.
6. Cowan N. (2001). The magical number 4 in short-term memory: a reconsideration of mental storage capacity. *Behav. Brain Sci.* 24(1), 87–114.

7. De Fockert JW, Rees G, Frith CD, Lavie N (2001). The role of working memory in visual selective attention. *Science* 291, 1803–1806

8. Desimone R., Duncan J. (1995). Neural mechanics of selective visual attention. *Annu. Rev. Neurosci.* 18, 193–222.

9. Fragopanagos N., Taylor J.G. (2007). Resolving some confusions over attention and consciousness. *Neural Netw.* 20, 993–1003

10. Fragopanagos N., Kockelkoren S., Taylor J.G. (2005). A neurodynamic model of the attentional blink. *Brain Res. Cogn. Brain Res.* 24, 568–586.

11. Hopfinger J.B., Buonocore M.H., Mangun G.R. (2000). The neural mechanisms of top-down attentional control. *Nat. Neurosci.* 3, 284–291.

12. Itti L., Koch C., Niebur E., (1998). A model of saliency-based visual attention for rapid scene analysis. *IEEE Trans. on Pattern Anal. Mach. Intell.* 20(11), 1254–1259.

13. Itti L., Koch C., (2000). A saliency-based search mechanism for overt and covert shifts of visual attention. *Vision Res.* 40, 1489–1506.

14. Kasderidis S., Taylor J.G. (2005). Combining attention and value maps. *Proc. ICANN.*

15. Kasderidis S., Taylor J.G. (2004). Attentional agents and robot control. *Int. J. Knowledge-based Intell. Syst.* 8, 69–89.

16. Kastner S., Ungerleider L.G. (2000). Mechanisms of visual attention in the human cortex. *Annu. Rev. Neurosci.* 23, 315–341.

17. Koch C., Ullman S. (1985). Shifts in selective visual attention: towards the underlying neural circuitry. *Human Neurobiol.* 4, 219–227.

18. Korsten N.H., Fragopanagos N., Hartley M., Taylor N., Taylor J.G. (2006). Attention as a controller. *Neural Netw.* 19(9), 1408–1421.

19. Okazaki Y., Abrahamyan A., Stevens C.J., Ioannides A.A. (2008). The timing of the face selectivity and attentional modulation in visual processing. *Neuroscience* 152, 1130–1144.

20. Pashler H., Johnstone J.C., Ruthruff E. (2001). Attention and performance. *Ann. Rev.Psycho.* 52, 629–651.

21. Posner, M.I. (1980). Orienting of attention. *Q. J. Exp. Psychol.* 32, 3–25

22. Raymond J.E., Shapiro K.L., Arnell K.M. (1992). Temporary suppression of visual processing in an RSVP task: an attentional blink?. *J. Exp. Psychol. Hum. Percept. Perform.* 18 (3): 849–60.

23. Reason, J. (1990). Human Error. Cambridge, UK: Cambridge University Press.

24. Taylor J.G., Rogers M. (2002). A control model of the movement of attention. *Neural Netw.* 15, 309–326.

25. Taylor J.G. (2003) Paying attention to consciousness. *Prog. in Neurobiol.* 71, 305–335.

26. Treisman A., Gelade G. (1980). A feature integration theory of attention. *Cogn. Psychol.* 12(1), 97–136.

27. Treisman, A. (1986). Features and objects in visual processing. *Sci. Am.* 254, 114–124.

16

Aligning Service Requirements with Business Strategy: A Proposed Stakeholder Value Model for SOA

H. Luthria, A. Aurum, G.C. Low and F.A. Rabhi

Abstract

Value-based requirements engineering plays a critical role in software development because it seeks to align requirements with the organizational strategy that drives business value. This chapter discusses the value proposition of service-oriented architectures and proposes a value-based decision mechanism for requirements engineering for service-oriented systems. In doing so, it lays the groundwork for future research into the important but relatively unexplored area of service-oriented requirements engineering.

Keywords Service-oriented computing · Value engineering · SOA · SORE

1. Introduction

The paradigm of service-oriented computing (SOC) has emerged as an architectural approach to flexibility and agility, not only in systems development but also in business process management. This modular approach to defining business flows as technology-independent services has gained popularity among end-users and technology vendors.

Service orientation promotes the reorganization of enterprise information resources as independent, reusable services, creating a new kind of business model [24], and consequently, earlier development methodologies cannot be applied to this new service-based model [12, 22, 26]. What is needed is the use of methodologies that include not only techniques and tools for analysis, design, deployment, and support of the services, but also a set of principles and guidelines that allow for the evaluation and modification of existing business processes and relationships [22]. Most major software vendors and some researchers have proposed methodologies for the development and management of services [12, 23]. Generally built on the proven concepts of component and object orientation, these methodologies identify the basic phases of development and operational management of the service lifecycle. Some studies even propose capability maturity models to assess and improve the service lifecycle [2, 20]. However, these models and methodologies do not consider how stakeholders select requirements [12].

Software developers rank requirements specification and management of customer requirements as the most complex task in the development process [16]. Despite a strong correlation between managing customer requirements and a system's marketability [16], there is minimal research into the requirements engineering task – the methodical discovering, identifying, and defining of software and system

H. Luthria, A. Aurum, G.C. Low and F.A. Rabhi • Information Systems, Technology & Management, The Australian School of Business, University of New South Wales, Sydney, Australia.

G.A. Papadopoulos et al. (eds.), *Information Systems Development*, DOI 10.1007/b137171_16,

requirements – in the context of service-based systems [17]. There exists then, arguably, a strong need to identify workable approaches to developing service requirements.

This chapter proposes a value-based approach to requirements engineering for service-oriented systems, laying the groundwork for future research in aligning service requirements with business strategy. Section 2 provides some background on key concepts discussed in this chapter and reviews the service-oriented requirements engineering literature. Section 3, then (i) elicits potential business drivers for SOA from empirical cross-firm data, (ii) examines the value attributes of SOA from existing literature, and (iii) proposes a stakeholder-based value model using empirical data to categorize the value attributes of SOA. The proposed stakeholder value model allows for the value-based appraisal of requirements for service-oriented development, pulling together key concepts from the research in value-based requirements engineering and service-oriented computing. Section 4 summarizes the contribution of this chapter and outlines future research options.

2. Service-Oriented Requirements Engineering – A Review

A service is a business function implemented in software, wrapped with a formal documented interface that is well known and can be found not only by agents who designed the service but also by agents who do not know about how the service has been designed and yet want to access and use it [21]. While services manifest business functionality in the service-based computing model, a service-oriented architecture (SOA) provides a framework for an infrastructure to facilitate the interactions and communications between services [21]. SOAs require service providers to advertise their services independent of the underlying technologies, and with associated service-level agreements (SLAs) in registries that can be discovered, accessed, and used by clients [21].

The focus of most studies that have attempted to explore service-oriented requirements engineering (SORE) has been to view the definition of a service's requirements in the context of service level agreements (SLAs) between service consumers and service providers [17, 25–27]. Others have examined approaches to tuning the modularity of services to optimize and balance the requirements of service consumers and providers [7] or even suggested goal-based service creation by identifying broad categories of industry goals and associated service patterns [29].

Van Eck and Wieringa [26, 27] discuss the need to separate requirements engineering activities for service consumers and service providers. Consumers look to meet a specific business goal, while providers look for economies of scale by capturing requirements from the various consumers serviced. The authors suggest that service providers create a service blueprint that identifies how consumers can use their service, the inputs and outputs of the services, and the workflow associated with the use of the service.

Treinikens et al. [25] note that the SLA creation is not a one-time process but a continuously evolving process between consumer and provider. They identify the role of service processes or workflows associated with the use of the services (as distinct from the services) and stress the need to parametrically manage quality characteristics (availability, performance, etc.) of both the service object and service process.

Lichtenstein et al. [17] review the literature on SORE and note that past studies have addressed the process of creating SLAs in a sterile environment, eschewing the practical issues of the communication between service consumers and providers. They address the socio-technical aspects of SORE and in the context of a case study identify five key categories of issues to be considered when creating and managing SLAs between service consumers and providers: (a) service roles, responsibilities, and accountability; (b) service performance metrics; (c) resolution of conflicting stakeholder service requirements; (d) customer acceptance of change; and (e) service provider team structure. These, they argue, are critical aspects to consider for a successful requirements engineering approach to service-oriented systems.

Gu and Lago [12] define a stakeholder model based on three stakeholders – service consumers, providers, and brokers. They examine the activities associated with design time, run time, and change time of the service lifecycle, and the associated activities for each stakeholder. As part of this analysis, requirements engineering is identified as a design time activity for service consumers and providers. Similar to other studies, this chapter also highlights the differing interests of service consumers and service providers when it comes to requirements definition.

Bohmann and Krcmar [7] address the dichotomy of contrasting requirements of service consumers and providers by recommending the use of modular service architectures. The authors identify three broad categories of service: those that execute business logic; those that execute application or infrastructure tasks; and lastly those that manage supporting requirements (what Trienikens et al. refer to as quality characteristics). They advocate that providers allow customization requirements for quality attributes as inputs to the service but do not address business and infrastructure services.

Zlatev et al. [29] examine requirements engineering in the context of business alignment. The authors identify the generic functionality of an e-intermediary (an entity that performs, for example, the business function of mediation between transactional partners, auctioneering, or price-searching). They then construct a goal tree for an e-intermediary, the leaves of the tree being the sub-goals that roll up iteratively to the main business goals. The authors then map these sub-goals to service patterns in a typical e-business environment, in this case a trading system, thus providing a means to ensure that the services developed are aligned with the goals of the business.

Although these studies have made significant contributions, there is much more work to be done to align service requirements with business strategy. With the exception of the Zlatev et al. study, few of the published papers have specifically addressed the alignment of requirements and business strategy. The value-based requirements engineering approach described in the next section is one possible approach to achieving this alignment.

3. Applying a Value-Based Approach to Service Requirements

Requirements engineering approaches generally neglect the value proposition of information systems, despite an understanding that this is critical to the development of e-commerce applications [11]. Using a value-based approach could offer a means to map service requirements to the potential value of services, thus aligning service requirements with the business strategy.

Value-based requirements engineering (VBRE) attempts to incorporate economic value into requirements engineering activities [5]. It is difficult, however, to define the concept of value in software engineering, as the development process involves many stakeholders, each defining value from their own point of view. Each stakeholder group's perception of value is different. They are often incompatible and must be reconciled [6]. Interestingly stakeholders are not always aware of their own value propositions, which can often only be elicited through experience in the problem domain [1]. In fact, only a limited number of companies in the software business are able to define or measure value from their customers' perspectives despite many describing the achievement of this as having "never been more important" [1].

Analytical literature indicates that the value is of services stems from their inherent attributes of modularity, loose coupling, technology neutrality, and location transparency. There is little empirical evidence of what criteria businesses actually are using to assess the potential value of SOA. To address this gap, qualitative data was collected across several firms in an attempt to understand the business drivers for the move to SOA.

3.1. An Empirical Understanding of the Business Drivers for SOA

Semi-structured interviews were conducted with enterprise architects and CIOs/CTOs of 10 firms – a mix of both financial service institutions in the banking and insurance sectors and software service providers that supported them. These firms were in various stages of implementing SOA, some of them already having migrated targeted business functions to a service-based deployment. Others, while committed to SOA, were yet to identify discrete business functions to transform. The firms that had implemented SOA to varying degrees were able to provide some insight into the observed benefits of the migration to a service-oriented approach. The product and software service providers were able to provide an insight not only into the business drivers for their product offerings but also their perception of the business drivers for their clients. Table 16.1 outlines the profile of the firms interviewed and the designation of the interviewees.

Table 16.1. A summary of the firms interviewed.

Firm	Sector	Interviewee	Profile
1	Bank	Head of strategy	Large Australian bank
2	Bank	Business development executive Technical architect	Large UK-based bank
3	Bank	Business development executive	Large Europe-based bank
4	Bank	CIO	India's second largest private bank
5	Insurance	Technology manager / architect	Mid-sized Indian private general insurance firm
6	Insurance	CTO	Large Indian public sector general insurance firm
7	Product and services	CTO VP of strategic accounts	Small India-based software solutions firm
8	Product and services	Technical architect	Large European software solutions firm
9	Product and services	Technical architect	Large US-based software and services firm
10	Services	Technical architect / product manager	Large India-based software services and consulting firm

A broad set of questions focused on organizational and business drivers for IT infrastructure was used to guide the interviews. Wherever possible, the interview data were augmented by documents provided by the interviewees. The intended outcome of these interviews was to understand, among other SOA-related issues, what these firms and their clients considered to be their business drivers for adopting SOA and the anticipated benefits. Business drivers were extracted from the transcribed interview data using a two-pass coding process and categorized into strategic, tactical, and operational drivers.

From a strategic perspective, a business requirement that was common across most of the firms (firms 1–6, 8) interviewed was the delivery of a standardized set of products, both internal and those provided by strategic partners, over a unified *service delivery platform*. Firms envisage a seamless customer experience across all of their offerings. The tactical business drivers according to firms 2, 4, and 6–10 appear to be the need for process and infrastructure *agility*. Firms are looking for the ability to integrate new products and third-party services into their product offerings for increased customer value – a flexible plug-and-play approach to facilitate the use of best-of-breed products transparently over their service delivery platform. At an operational level, firms are pursuing opportunities for *efficiency gains*, looking to optimize their business processes and reduce costs, as indicated by firms 1, 7, 9, and 10.

Existing literature indicates that SOAs can potentially offer corporations increased business value. This literature is now examined to understand how SOA may satisfy the strategic, tactical, and operational business drivers identified from the analysis of the cross-firm data.

3.2. The Value Proposition of SOA

3.2.1. Strategic Value Proposition

The ability to integrate external resources from strategic partners and internal resources, including legacy systems, seamlessly enables a single *service delivery platform*, while the reuse of existing assets promotes standardization [14, 18].

Strategic partnerships: The transformation of an enterprise's business processes to services, along with standards-based communication protocols, opens up new avenues of strategic partnerships with suppliers, partners, and customers beyond traditional organizational boundaries [22]. This causes the emergence of a new business model – a re-bundling of intra- and inter-enterprise business processes as seamless services [13].

Leveraging legacy systems: Moving to a service-based approach also allows existing and proven legacy system functions on a diverse set of hardware and software platforms to be encapsulated as services on a new standards-based integration platform [8-10].

Seamless Integration: The location transparency and technology neutrality of services allow businesses to include services from third-party providers or business partners into their own processes as value-added service offerings [18]. Firms can take advantage of this seamless integration of internal and external resources and pull together disparate best-of-breed products and services to create a single service delivery platform, independent of the physical implementations of each individual component.

Reuse: The reuse of existing components, while enabling rapid product development and cost efficiencies, allows for a standardized implementation of business functionality and consequently, a more consistent customer experience across product offerings [14].

3.2.2. Tactical Value Proposition

Service-oriented systems enable *agility* in business processes by virtue of modularity and loose coupling, and allow for a flexible plug-and-play approach to business and infrastructure functions by abstracting the underlying service implementations [18].

Process flexibility: Effective SOAs tend to be well-defined process-centric architectures facilitating better process visibility and process knowledge resulting in easier design, automation, monitoring, and most significantly, modification of business processes i.e., resulting in improved process flexibility [8, 14, 19].

Portability across infrastructures: As the service paradigm permeates organizations, the services themselves can be virtualized from the underlying hardware platform. The underlying technology platform can be potentially substituted with ease, allowing for the best choice of platform for the services. This allows the business to focus on the core services while the infrastructure used to run the services become more of a commodity, to be leased or purchased from the provider of choice [8, 13, 24]. Organizations can focus on the efficient orchestration of services to form a product and shed the burden of owning resources [8].

Phased adoption: SOA's modular approach also means that companies need not plan to take on a high-risk all-or-nothing approach to its implementation [13]. They can adopt a phased migration to service-orientation and leverage this approach to focus initially on opportunities that meet immediate customer requirements.

3.2.3. Operational Value Proposition

SOAs can potentially offer corporations the opportunity to realize process and development *efficiency gains* while mitigating the overall change and technology-related risks of the corporation.

Process improvement: Existing architecture frameworks tend to be program-centric with business flow or process knowledge often spread across individual system components. This hampers the consolidation of information relevant to clearly understanding business flows. Well-designed service architectures allow for better process knowledge and facilitate the potential for continuous process improvement [8, 14, 19, 24].

Process visibility: Service orientation enables monitoring of services from a business perspective rather than systems perspective, allowing for better process visibility [8, 14, 19, 24]. Business services that are the core competence of the organization can be clearly identified, and the non-core services can then be candidates for substitution by those provided by vendors with the relevant expertise [13].

Additional revenue streams: In addition to improving the existing business models, service-based architectures provide a framework for corporations to offer their core competencies as services to other companies [13, 14, 18], focusing on areas of comparative advantage while buying or leasing services in which they lack superior expertise from other service providers [9]. SOA, thus, potentially allows for the creation of new products generating additional revenue streams.

Reduced costs: The reuse of existing components, while providing potential savings in operational costs could also reduce risk in more ways than one [8, 10]. The enhanced business process incurs no new potential points of failure, and the maintenance of the supporting infrastructure continues to remain unaltered. In addition to the reduction in development and testing costs brought about by modularity and re-usability of service modules [15], the learning curve of the development or assembly team could potentially reduce over time due to familiarity with existing services [8, 14, 15, 18, 19, 28]. Gains may also be realized in terms of development and maintenance cost savings by purchasing services from reliable providers with a comparative advantage in developing the services [13].

Rapid product development: Over time, the developed services become a core asset of the organization – a library of tested, ready to use, compatible components [8]. This promotes rapid product development, reducing the time to pull together well-design tested functionality to meet new and changing market needs [14, 18].

3.3. Proposing a Stakeholder Value Model for SOA

Aurum and Wohlin [4] argue that the value of software products can be determined by three main stakeholders and their value perspectives. Product/sales managers focus on the *organizational perspective*, associating value with product sales. Developers focus on the *product perspective* which elicits value from customer and market requirements. Project managers are more concerned with the *project perspective*, associating value with project budget, delivery, and timing. Value creation in software development may then be achieved by aligning these differing value perspectives with organizational, product, and project level decisions made during the software development process [3]. Aurum and Wohlin posit a framework that uses this taxonomy to place requirements engineering (RE) decisions in the context not only of organizational, product, and project perspectives, but also decisions made across three management levels: strategic, tactical, and operational. This framework appears to provide a potential decision mechanism for service requirements to be aligned with the relevant stakeholders' definition of value and consequently with the business strategy.

In order to apply this framework to service requirements, we need to first understand the value proposition of SOA for the concerned stakeholders from the perspectives of the organization, product, and project. The value attributes of SOA categorized in Section 3.2 along the dimensions of strategic, tactical, and operational business drivers may now be classified orthogonally along organizational, product, and project perspectives using the cross-firm interview data as a guide.

The resulting framework (Table 16.2) represents the stakeholder value model for SOA, incorporating value perceptions of key stakeholders across strategic, tactical, and operational business drivers. Aligning the requirements decisions with this value model may provide a means to prioritize the service requirements according to business objectives.

Table 16.2. Proposed stakeholder value model for SOA.

	Strategic service delivery platform	Tactical agility	Operational efficiency gains
Organization sales	Strategic partnerships Seamless integration	Phased migration Portability across infrastructures	Additional revenue
Product customer and market requirements	Leverage legacy systems	Process flexibility	Process visibility Process improvement Rapid product development
Project delivery	Reuse of existing assets	Portability across infrastructures	Reduced development and testing costs

The focus of perceived value from an *organization perspective* in the RE decisions framework is on product sales. Firms 1, 4, and 10 emphasized the importance of *strategic partnerships* to their bottom line, while firms 4, 5, and 6 also indicated that the *seamless integration* of resources was critical. Firm 8 indicated that a service-based approach allowed them to market individual modules as services enabling a *phased migration* of products into customer environments. This provides value for both customers from a risk mitigation perspective and providers by getting a foot in the door by marketing smaller, and potentially more manageable, services. Firm 7 was also able to expand its client base by virtue of the *portability* of its services across infrastructures. Exploring avenues of new business value, firm 4 indicated that their internal business functions could be marketed as industry-specific common services allowing for possible *additional revenue*.

From a *product perspective*, firms 1, 4, and 8 indicated the need to *leverage legacy systems*, integrating proven business functionality into new product offerings to meet customer requirements. Firms 1, 2, 6, 9, and 10 indicated the need for process agility – i.e., better *process visibility, modification, and generally flexibility* – to meet changing market needs, while firm 5 was able to see benefits in terms of *rapid product development* as a direct result of migrating core customer functions to a service infrastructure.

Delivery is critical from a *project perspective*, and firm 5 was able to realize *reduction in development and testing costs* by the *reuse of existing services*. They were able to deploy a quote generating service offered on their web site as a new point-of-sale product offering 60% faster than the time it took to develop the original web-based service, down to 4 days compared to 10 days for the original service. Project delivery could also be sped up by virtue of the *portability* of services according to firm 7. Services may be installed on smaller servers initially to realize immediate benefits, and then migrated to a more robust infrastructure once the functionality is proven with the organizational environment.

4. Contributions and Future Research

Service lifecycle methodologies highlight the identification of business functions to be converted to services as a critical phase in the service lifecycle, but offer little guidance on how to prioritize these functions. The RE decisions framework [3] provides a means to align RE decisions with stakeholder value models, thus aligning RE activities with the business strategy. In order to use this framework to align service requirements with the business strategy, the value perspectives of the stakeholders in the context of SOA need to be understood.

Empirical evidence from semi-structured interviews across 10 firms was first used to identify the potential strategic, tactical, and operational business drivers for SOA adoption. Existing literature was then parsed to understand the value proposition of SOA, and the value attributes of SOA that align with these business drivers. These value attributes were further classified orthogonally along organization, product, and project perspectives using the empirical cross-firm data as a guide. The resulting grid of SOA value attributes (Table 16.2) represents the proposed stakeholder value model for SOA, aligning key stakeholder value perspectives. This stakeholder value framework can now allow for service requirements decisions at the organization, product, and project levels to be aligned.

In addressing the issue of defining a stakeholder value model for services, this chapter adds to the service orientation literature (a) an empirical understanding of the business drivers of SOA along strategic, tactical, and operational dimensions; (b) an analysis of the existing literature related to the value proposition of SOA along strategic, tactical, and operational dimensions; (c) a critical analysis of these value attributes of SOA aligned along organizational, product, and project perspectives based on empirical data; and (d) a mechanism to allow for the alignment of service requirements with the business objectives and strategy, using the value proposition of SOA to extend a proven value-based requirements engineering decisions framework.

The proposed stakeholder value model for SOA represented by Table 16.2 is the first step toward a value-based decision mechanism for RE activities in the service context. Future research directions include extending this model to identify and evaluate the RE decisions for SOA corresponding to the stakeholder perspectives described in the SOA stakeholder value model, and subsequently testing the model empirically to understand the definition and prioritization of SOA requirements along these stakeholder value perspectives.

References

1. Anderson, J.C. and J.A. Narus, *Business Marketing: Understand What Customers Value*. Harvard Business Review, 1998, **76**(6): 58–65.
2. Arsanjani, A. and K. Holley, *Increase flexibility with the Service Integration Maturity Model (SIMM)*. 2005, Technical report, IBM Whitepaper. (Cited on page 42.).
3. Aurum, A. and C. Wohlin, *Aligning Requirements with Business Objectives: A Framework for Requirements Engineering Decisions*. Proceedings of Requirements Engineering Decision Support Workshop, 2005.
4. Aurum, A. and C. Wohlin, *Requirements Engineering: Setting the Context*. Engineering and Managing Software Requirements, A. Aurum and C. Wohlin, Eds., 2005, pp. 1–15.
5. Biffl, S., et al., *Value-Based Software Engineering*. 2005, Springer-Verlag New York, Inc. Secaucus, NJ, USA.
6. Boehm, B., *Value-Based Software Engineering: Seven Key Elements and Ethical Considerations* in *Value-based Software Engineering* S. Biffl, et al., Eds. 2005, Springer, Berlin, Heidelberg, New York.
7. Bohmann, T., M. Junginger, and H. Krcmar, *Modular Service Architectures: A Concept and Method for Engineering IT Services*. System Sciences, 2003, Proceedings of the 36th Annual Hawaii International Conference on, 2003: p. 10.
8. Channabasavaiah, K., K. Holley, and E.M.J. Tuggle, *Migrating to a Service-Oriented Architecture*, in On Demand Operating Environment Solutions. 2004, IBM.
9. Curbera, F., et al., *The Next Step in Web Services*. Communications of the ACM, 2003, **46**(10): 29–34.
10. Datz, T., *What You Need to Know About Service-Priented Architecture*, in CIO Magazine. 2004.
11. Gordijn, J. and J.M. Akkermans, *Value-Based Requirements Engineering: Exploring Innovative E-Commerce Ideas*. Requirements Engineering, 2003, **8**(2): 114–134.
12. Gu, Q. and P. Lago, *A Stakeholder-Driven Service Life Cycle Model for SOA*. Foundations of Software Engineering, 2007, pp. 1–7.
13. Hagel, J.I. and J.S. Brown, *Your Next IT Strategy*. Harvard Business Review, 2001, pp. 105–113.
14. Huang, D.C. and Q. Hu, *Integrating Web Services with Competitive Strategies: The Balanced Scorecard Approach*. Communications of the Association of Information Systems, 2004, **13**.
15. Huhns, M.N. and M.P. Singh, *Service-Oriented Computing: Key Concepts and Principles*. IEEE Internet Computing, 2005, **9**(1): 75–81.
16. Ibanez, M. and H. Rempp, *European User Survey Analysis*, in ESPITI project report, February. 1996.
17. Lichtenstein, S., L. Nguyen, and A. Hunter, *Issues in IT Service-Oriented Requirements Engineering*. Australasian Journal of Information Systems, 2004, **13**.
18. Luthria, H., F. Rabhi, and M. Briers, *Investigating the Potential of Service Oriented Architectures to Realize Dynamic Capabilities*. Asia-Pacific Service Computing Conference, The 2nd IEEE, 2007: 390–397.
19. Natis, Y.V., *Service-Oriented Architecture Scenario*, in Gartner, 2003, Gartner, Inc.
20. Niessink, F. and H. Vliet, *Towards Mature IT Services*. Software Process: Improvement and Practice, 1998, **4**(2): 55–71.
21. Papazoglou, M.P. *Service-Oriented Computing: Concepts, Characteristics and Directions*. in Fourth International Conference on Web information Systems Engineering (WISE). 2003.
22. Papazoglou, M.P. and W.J. Van Den Heuvel, *Service-oriented design and development methodology*. International Journal of Web Engineering and Technology, 2006, **2**(4): 412–442.
23. Ramollari, E., D. Dranidis, and A.J.H. Simons, *A Survey of Service Oriented Development Methodologies*. The 2nd European Young Researchers Workshop on Service Oriented Computing, 2007.
24. Sprott, D., *The Business Case for Service Oriented Architecture*. CBDI Journal, 2004.
25. Trienekens, J.J.M., J.J. Bouman, and M. van der Zwan, *Specification of Service Level Agreements: Problems, Principles and Practices*. Software Quality Journal, 2004, **12**(1): 43–57.
26. van Eck, P. and R. Wieringa, *Requirements Engineering for Service-Oriented Computing: A Position Paper*. Workshop, ICEC 03, Pittsburgh, USA, 2003.
27. van Eck, P. and R. Wieringa, *Web Services as Product Experience Augmenters and the Implications for Requirements Engineering: A Position Paper*. Proceedings of the International Workshop in Service-oriented Requirements Engineering, Kyoto, Japan, September, 2004, **6**.
28. Zhang, J., J.-Y. Chung, and C.K. Chang. *Migration to Web Service Oriented Architecture*. in *SAC'04*. 2004, Nicosia, Cyprus: ACM.
29. Zlatev, Z., et al., *Goal-Oriented RE for E-Services*. International Workshop on Service-oriented Requirements Engineering workshop at RE, 2004, **4**.

17

A New Method for Conceptual Modelling of Information Systems

Remigijus Gustas and Prima Gustiene

Abstract

Service architecture is not necessarily bound to the technical aspects of information system development. It can be defined by using conceptual models that are independent of any implementation technology. Unfortunately, the conventional information system analysis and design methods cover just a part of required modelling notations for engineering of service architectures. They do not provide effective support to maintain semantic integrity between business processes and data. Service orientation is a paradigm that can be applied for conceptual modelling of information systems. The concept of service is rather well understood in different domains. It can be applied equally well for conceptualization of organizational and technical information system components. This chapter concentrates on analysis of the differences between service-oriented modelling and object-oriented modelling. Service-oriented method is used for semantic integration of information system static and dynamic aspects.

Keywords Service-oriented modelling · Integrity of statics and dynamics · Conceptualization of events · Rules · Constraints

1. Introduction

Information systems can be structurally visualized as evolving conceptualizations of service architectures. Service orientation promotes autonomy, flexibility and interoperability of enterprise system components. The changes of enterprise architecture (EA) can be enabled by creation, removal or replacement of loosely coupled information system components. Traditionally, graphical representations of EA are built fragment by fragment and when all is done, then typically the business design is not aligned with the information system design. It is very difficult to maintain semantic integrity of multiple EA specification fragments. Service architectures are intrinsically complex engineering products [5] that can be defined on different levels of abstraction and represented by using several dimensions. One of the reasons why the traditional information system engineering methods do not provide effective support is that service architectures are difficult to visualize across disparate modelling dimensions such as the "why", "what", "who", "where", "when" and "how" [23]. Another problem is that the same implementation specific artefacts, which are less comprehensible for business experts, are used in both system analysis and design phases.

Service-oriented method consists of models and associated techniques. Computation-specific techniques include the object-oriented (OO) design point of view [2] adopted by rational unified process (RUP) with an additional component-oriented layer above it [24]. It is illustrated in Fig. 17.1.

Remigijus Gustas and Prima Gustiene · Department of Information Systems, Karlstad University, Karlstad, Sweden.

G.A. Papadopoulos et al. (eds.), *Information Systems Development*, DOI 10.1007/b137171_17,

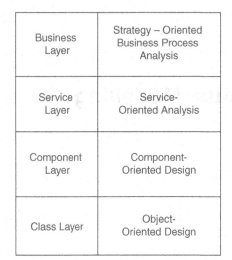 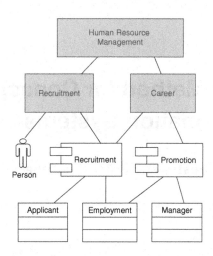

Figure 17.1. Service-oriented analysis and design layers.

The computation-specific techniques are more comprehensible for software designers, but not readily accessible and understandable for business consultants and managers. Computation-specific design is based on the idea of dividing the conceptual representations into three major parts that are known as data architecture, application architecture and technology architecture. Although there are some advantages in separation of different types of system specifications, unfortunately the conventional methods are not provided by techniques that help to control semantic integrity between the static and dynamic aspects of EA.

Service-oriented models represent only computation neutral aspects. Graphical representations of the service layer are less complex and can be successfully used by non-technicians who play a key role in system integration. It is recognized that UML support for such a task is quite vague, because semantic integration principles of different diagram types are still lacking [12]. The concept of service is not used explicitly in the conventional information system methodologies. That is a major reason why system designers are not able to separate concerns and distinguish clearly among semantic details of specifications that belong to different enterprise system components. Service-oriented analysis can be used for motivation of various technical system components [7] and for validation of the overall business process. One of the main objectives of the strategy-oriented analysis is to produce a pragmatic description [9]. Pragmatics [19] provides motivation for various configurations of service architectures and defines the "*why*" aspect [23]. Service-oriented models should be able to integrate the static and dynamic structures of business process fragments across organizational and technical system boundaries. Class and component layers define the technical details of a specific application. Business process layer motivates and prescribes the service layer details, which are defined in terms of the basic service-oriented constructs.

2. Intersubjective and Objective View in System Analysis

There are two significant qualities that characterize information system development traditions: intersubjectivity and objectivity. The methods, which put into foreground modelling of the external behaviour, can be classified as intersubjective [4]. From the intersubjective point of view a service is a unit of functionality that is exposed to environment. An external behaviour of service component helps to analyze it as a 'black box' in a usage perspective. The dynamics of intersubjectivity is expressed by interaction dependencies [8], which represent physical, information or a decision flow between two kinds of actors involved. Service providers are actors that typically receive service requests, over which they have

Figure 17.2. Service as an interaction loop.

no direct control, and transform them into responses that are sent to service requesters. Each *Service Response* is a function of a *Service Request*. This idea is illustrated graphically in Fig. 17.2.

The intersubjective bias is especially obvious in the enterprise modelling language Archimate [16]. Archimate approach can be used to analyze business processes that are defined through actor cooperation. It is typically supported by interacting technical and organizational components. A similar type of actor link that is called strategic dependency was introduced in i* framework [22]. In our method, the strategic dependency is considered to be an interaction flow and action. Service requester initiates an action in order to achieve his goal.

The intersubjective view can be expressed in OO methods by combining use case, sequence and activity diagrams, which altogether constitute an interaction model [1]. Both interaction and state models are necessary to fully define a process. State changes are typically specified by using a finite state machine. It describes the sequences of operations that occur in response to events. State changes define the objective view, which is complementary to intersubjective view. Service architecture is capable of expressing both views together [8] that are integrated in one diagram type. Most OO diagrams are relevant for definition of the internal behaviour of objects. The objective bias is very strong in the conventional information system modelling approaches. Internal changes of services [14] are typically represented by the state transition links. Transitions are triggered by operations, which specify the permissible ways for changes to occur in different classes of objects. Graphical example of a state transition diagram is represented in Fig. 17.3.

Figure 17.3. State-transition diagram.

A state can be defined as a collection of associations an object has with other types of objects and its attribute values [18]. There are six types of events in OO analysis: creation, termination, classification, declassification, connection and disconnection of an association between objects, which can be represented in a variety of ways. For instance, creation and termination operations are represented by transitions from an initial state and to final state. Connection and disconnection events may correspond to an update operation that is associated with the state transition. Classification and declassification events can be implemented by using a sequence of object creation and termination operations.

Another alternative for representation of object manipulation events is by using the object flow diagrams. Object flows are capable of expressing the dynamic relationship between an operation and its input/output objects that are represented as arguments. Object flows are typically used together with the UML activity diagrams. A diagram showing operations and object flows with states has most of the advantages of an activity diagram without most of their disadvantages [1]. It integrates moving data and control flow in the same diagram type. An input arrow to an operation or output arrow from an operation represents a control flow. Termination event can be expressed by using removal operation, which consumes an input object in the final state. It is represented in Fig. 17.4.

Figure 17.4. Graphical representation of termination and creation.

The object flow can be created by an access operation. A creation event is defined by using creation operation, which produces an output object in an initial state. To perform a state change, an object needs to be accessed. Semantics of a state change can be defined as a reconnection operation, which is realized as an update of one or more references to other classes of objects or/and attribute values. An object flow diagram is able to define an object progression from one state to another. A reconnection event pattern is represented in Fig. 17.5.

Figure 17.5. Graphical representation of reconnection.

Reconnection pattern, which is defined by object flow diagram, is not unique. It cannot be visually recognized by a system designer. The same pattern can be used for representation of other types of object manipulations. A state change can be interpreted as a reconnection event, which is represented by a sequence of one disconnection and one connection event. The sequence of such two events requires an intermediate state, which makes no sense for a person, who has no or even little expertise in the area of object-oriented design. Such artificial states are implementation-oriented details, which add complexity. An intermediate state is redundant and it cannot be justified by a business analysis expert.

Object-oriented approaches are not supporting the dynamic reclassification. Termination and creation operations are used for implementation of a declassification and classification. Reclassification is a compound event that should be viewed as a simultaneous declassification and classification. Semantics of reclassification is quite comprehensible for business experts. Nevertheless, reclassification event has no easily recognizable counterpart in object-oriented models. The method of reclassification, declassification and classification from class 1 to class 2 can be shortly characterized as follows:

- Creation of an object in class 2 by copying all attribute values from class 1 to a newly created object in class 2,
- Disconnection of all associations pointing to the old object and connection of them to the new one in class 2,
- Removal of the old object in class 1.

The described sequence of operations artificially adds complexity by multiplying a number of states, which cannot be justified from the system analysis point of view. The conclusion is quite obvious: UML notation is inconvenient for integrated analysis of interplay between business data and processes. Usage of implementation-dependent constructs increases system specification complexity. It creates diffi culties in the process of validation and verification of diagrams by design experts.

3. Integration of Static and Dynamic Aspects

The starting point of service-oriented modelling is definition of interaction flows between actors, which play the role of service requester and service provider. From the objective standpoint, a request and response action is changing business data from one consistent state to another. Quite often service outputs depend not only on inputs, but also on availability of stored data that result from other services. Such data are supposed to constrain service responses to the present or future inputs. For instance, if and only if the reservation of trip is created, then it can be paid by using a trip payment service. Moving flows together with request and response actions, which create or remove objects of various classes, are crucial to understand the semantic aspects of services. The precondition object and the input flow should be sufficient for determining a service output flow and a post-condition object. Information system can be defined as a set of interacting loosely coupled components, which are able to perform the specific services on request. This idea is illustrated by Fig. 17.6.

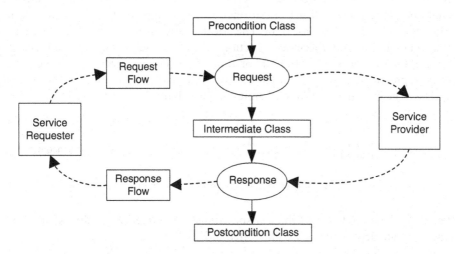

Figure 17.6. Representation of internal and external behaviour.

Service requesters and providers are enterprise system components, which can be viewed as dynamic subsystems, because their outputs depend not only on inputs, but also on the associated object internal states. Properties of objects restrict service responses to the present and future inputs. There are just two basic events in our service-oriented approach: creation and termination [8]. They are fundamental for the definition of reclassification event that can be understood as a communication action [3]. A communication action between two actors (agent and recipient) indicates that one actor depends on another actor. An instance of actor can be an individual, a group of people, an organization, a machine, a software or hardware component, etc. The actor dependency (⋯▶) is usually viewed as a physical, information or a decision flow between two parties involved. Graphical notation of the reclassification is shown in Fig. 17.7.

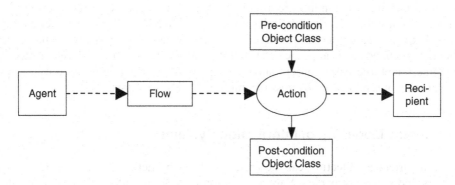

Figure 17.7. Construct for representation of reclassification.

Communication action is able to express semantics of all types of the object-oriented events [18]. It additionally specifies precondition and postcondition object class associations, which are sufficient to visually recognize and understand the details of disconnection and connection events. An action is defined as a transition (⟶) from the precondition object class to the postcondition object class. Fundamentally, two kinds of changes occur during any transition: removal of an object from a precondition class and creation of an object in a postcondition class. Sometimes, objects are passing several classes and then are destroyed. It should be noted that either precondition or postcondition class may be missing.

The internal changes of services are defined by using transition links. For instance, a request action is supposed to remove an object from a precondition class and to create an object in an intermediate class. It is necessary for initiation of response action by performer, which is supposed to remove the intermediate data values and to create a postcondition class data. The effect of any response or request is a reclassification, removal or creation of an object. Otherwise, an action is not purposeful. These three types of actions are used for the conceptualization of a continuous or finite life cycle of objects. The noteworthy semantic difference can be represented by a set of attributes or state that is associated to the precondition and postcondition class. The graphical notation of states and attributes is represented in Fig. 17.8.

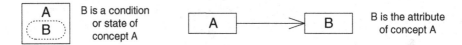

Figure 17.8. Attributes and states of concepts.

Semantics of various kinds of attribute associations are defined by multiplicities. Three ways of representing the attribute dependencies are illustrated in Fig. 17.9.

Figure 17.9. Graphical notation of the attribute dependencies.

In examples of this chapter, we use a classical way (see notation in the middle) for representing associations without mapping names in two opposite directions.

Service-oriented representations are built by conceptualizing interactions among organizational and technical components, which are viewed as various types of enterprise actors. Any two concepts can be linked by inheritance, composition, classification and interaction dependencies. Inheritance is often promoted as a core link to connect a specific concept to more general one. The similarities between concepts can be shared by extracting and attaching common links to a more general concept. In such a way, various dependencies can be inherited. Composition is a conceptual dependency used to relate a whole to other concepts that are viewed as parts. The composition that is used in service-oriented diagrams is more restrictive as compared to a composition that is defined in OO approaches [17]. It should be noted that the service-oriented method and resulting diagrams follow the basic conceptualization principle [6] in representing only computationally neutral aspects that are not influenced by possible implementation solutions.

4. Service-Oriented Modelling of Information Systems

Information system architecture can be conceptualized by defining mutual interactions between service requesters and service providers. Superimposition of different interaction loops result into more complex conceptual representations, which express sequence, branching or synchronization of actions [8].

Various combinations of the static and dynamic dependencies are capable of specifying the main workflow control patterns [21]. By matching the actor dependencies from service requesters to recipients, one can explore opportunities, rights and responsibilities that are predefined to different types of actors. We shall illustrate interplay of two interaction loops, which can be initiated by user's action *Switch on Clock*. Superimposition of the interaction loops is illustrated in Fig. 17.10.

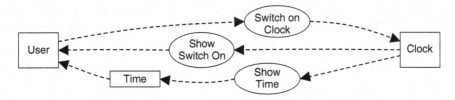

Figure 17.10. Illustration of two interaction loops.

This diagram illustrates effects of a *Switch on Clock* event, which can be represented by using two simple triggering rules [1]. The rules can be defined by using the following expression: *Event [Condition]/ Action*. The event specifies the signal that triggers the invocation of the rule. If the condition is evaluated to be true, then the action is carried out. The condition item is not mandatory. The action performs update on data. Two interaction loops of the presented diagram correspond to the following rules:

(1) SwitchOnClock/ShowSwitchOn(),
(2) SwitchOnClock/ShowTime(Time)

Parameter list of an action can be represented within the parentheses. Such rules are often used for representation of triggering effects on transition links in the UML state diagram, which is essentially a Harel statechart [13]. The effects resulting from actions, which are related to static aspects, are not captured by the triggering rules. Nevertheless, such effects are crucial for complete definition of the interaction loop dynamics. That is why the consequences of actions are difficult to trace by using object-oriented approaches. The difficulty resides in failures to recognize the noteworthy changes that are caused by various events. It makes overall enterprise architecture prone to mistakes, which are introduced by inconsistencies, discontinuities and ambiguities. Since service-oriented diagrams provide integration of the static and dynamic aspects, they do not suffer from the above-mentioned drawbacks. The process and data views can be merged into one diagram, which is represented in Fig. 17.11.

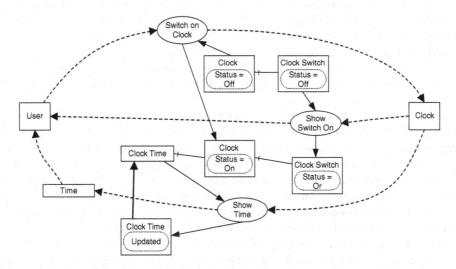

Figure 17.11. Statics and dynamics of two interaction loops.

This service-oriented diagram represents not just actions, but additionally defines conditions on classes of objects, which must hold for triggering of these actions. For instance, complete expressions of the first rule must include a condition related to a clock switch status. It must be in state *Off* for *Show Switch On* action to take place. The complete definition of the triggering rule would be as follows:

SwitchOnClock [Clock.Switch.Status = Off]/ShowSwitchOn().

Unfortunately, this rule defines a very small portion of semantic details that is prescribed by the presented service-oriented diagram. These complementary constraints do not fit easily into the conventional event/action rule [20] formats, because they are dealing with the intersubjective and objective views at the same time. For instance, our example prescribes the following additional constraints:

(1) If *Show Switch On* action is successful, then the switch status must be *On* (see the postcondition Clock.Switch.Status = On),
(2) The condition for the clock switch status to become *On* is the Clock Status must be equal to *On* as well.
(3) Any Clock in state On must have exactly one Clock Time value (it cannot be missing value at the time Clock is On).
(4) Time flow is created by Clock (*Show Time* action) after Clock Switch Status is changed to *On*. From this moment, a clock time value is iteratively updated by Clock (see inheritance link). Removal of a clock object or failure to satisfy a Clock condition (Status = On) would stop reiteration of *Show Time* action.
(5) The condition for initiation of the *Switch on Clock* action by User is the clock status value equal to *Off*.

Information flows of service-oriented diagrams are reminiscent of arrows in the data flow diagrams [15]. Data flows represent moving data between enterprise system components, which may be interpreted as data sources and sinks. If a system is implemented without any computer support, then information flows may be understood as moving documents' pre-post-condition classes define semantic details of an enterprise system data at rest. Service-oriented diagrams are not prescribing any implementation-specific details. The implementation-specific solutions can be introduced during the technical design phase [7, 10, 11]. Service-oriented paradigm helps us to distinguish clearly between system analysis and system design phase.

5. Concluding Remarks

Enterprise models traditionally define how business, data, software application and technology architecture is perceived by various stakeholders. Since different modelling views and dimensions are highly intertwined, it is crucial to maintain integrity, continuity and consistency across multiple diagrams on various levels of abstraction. Traceability of changes from one diagram type to another is a bottleneck in the conventional information system modelling approaches. Service-orientated method, which is presented in this chapter, can be applied for validation and verification of system development decisions. Intersubjective and objective views are distinguished to conceptualize the organizational as well as technical parts of information system.

UML diagrams are projecting the interaction and state-transition aspects into totally different types of models. Coherence of both aspects is crucial in order to facilitate reasoning and to define the holistic understanding of enterprise architecture. State changes represent structural changes of objects, which cannot be analyzed in isolation from the interactions. UML individual diagram types are clear enough, but integrated semantics among models is missing. The diagrams alone are difficult to apply for semantic integrity control and for consistent business logic alignment with the system design for making both organizational and technical system parts more effective. A mechanism of semantic integrity control of static and dynamic aspects is not clear in object-oriented approaches. That is why object-oriented diagrams are difficult to apply for conceptual modelling of service architectures.

The intersubjective semantics of services are captured by interaction loops, which are able to express the main workflow patterns such as sequence, selection, synchronization and iteration [8]. The objective tradition can be effectively used for defining the internal behaviour of objects. An object lifecycle in service-oriented diagrams is represented by using initial, intermediate and final classes, which are analyzed in the context of interactions between organizational and technical system components. Semantics of object changes is expressed by using three types of actions: reclassification, creation and termination.

The understanding of enterprise system architecture relies on knowing how different subsystems are interconnected. Interactions among enterprise system components are used to conceptualize semantics of information system data and processes. Interplay of intersubjective and objective views in one service-oriented diagram facilitates better semantic integrity control between the static and dynamic aspects. It is not reasonable to duplicate the same concepts many times in different diagrams just because such separation is required from a technical design point of view. For systematic analysis of service architectures, it is crucial to maintain a holistic representation, where external and internal views are visualized together.

Conceptual models of enterprise system architecture can be defined as a set of loosely coupled components. Service orientation has the potential for organizations to reduce system architecture evolution complexity and to improve learning capacity. A new service-oriented method for system analysis and design should bring significant benefits, including improved ability for organizations to maintain strategic knowledge in a systematic way, reduced costs for a systematic analysis of new IT solutions before they are implemented, and improved integrity and traceability of knowledge within companies by providing comprehensible service architecture descriptions. Our experience in analysing system specifications demonstrates that service-oriented method is more comprehensible for personnel without a technical background. Service-oriented diagrams have no implementation bias and therefore they can be used for bridging a communication gap among system designers and business analysis experts.

References

1. Blaha, M. and Rumbaugh, J. (2005) *Object-Oriented Modelling and Design with UML*, Pearson, London.
2. Booch, G., Rumbaugh, J. and Jacobsson, I. (1999) *The Unified Modelling Language User Guide*, Addison Wesley Longman, Inc., Massachusetts.
3. Dietz J.L.G. (2001) DEMO: Towards a Discipline of Organisation Engineering, *European Journal of Operational Research (128)*, Elsevier Science, 351–363.
4. Dietz J.L. G. (2006) Enterprise Ontology: Theory and Methodology, Springer, Berlin.
5. Erl, T. (2005) Service-Oriented Architecture: Concepts, Technology, and Design, Pearson Prentice Hall, Crawfordsville, Indiana.
6. van Griethuisen, J.J. (1982) Concepts and Terminology for the Conceptual Schema and Information Base, Report ISO TC97/SC5/WG5, No 695.
7. Gustas, R. and Gustiene, P. (2004) Towards the Enterprise Engineering Approach for Information System Modelling across Organisational and Technical Boundaries, *Enterprise Information Systems V,* Kluwer Academic Publisher, Netherlands, pp. 204–215.
8. Gustas, R. and Gustiene, P. (2007) Service-Oriented Foundation and Analysis Patterns for Conceptual Modelling of Information Systems, *International Conference on Information System Development*, Springer.
9. Gustas R. and Gustiene P, (2008) Pragmatic – Driven Approach for Service-Oriented Analysis and Design, *Information Systems Engineering - from Data Analysis to Process Networks*, IGI Global, USA.
10. Gustas, R. and Jakobsson, L. (2004) Enterprise Modelling of Component Oriented Information System Architectures, *New Trends in Software Methodologies, Tools and Techniques*, IOS Press, pp. 88–102.
11. Gustiene, P., and Gustas, R. (2008) Introducing Service Orientation into System Analysis and Design, *International Conference on Enterprise Information Systems*, June 12–16, Barcelona, Spain.
12. Harel, D. and Rumpe, B. (2004) Meaningful Modeling: What's the Semantics of 'Semantics'?, *IEEE Computer*, October, pp. 64–72.
13. Harel, D. (1987) Statecharts: A Visual Formalism for Complex Systems, Science of Computer Programming 8, North-Holland, pp. 231–274.
14. Hull, R., Christophides, V. and Su, J. (2003) E-services: A look Behind the Curtain, *ACM PODS*, San Diego, CA.
15. Hoffer, J.A., George, J.F. and Valacich J.S. (2004) *Modern System Analysis and Design*, Pearson Prentice Hall, New Jersey.
16. Lankhorst, M. et al. (2005) *Enterprise Architecture at Work*, Springer, Berlin.
17. Maciaszek, L.A. (2001) *Requirements Analysis and System Design*, Addison Wesley, New York.
18. Martin, J., Odell, J.J. (1998), *Object-Oriented Methods: A Foundation (UML edition)*, Prentice-Hall, Englewood Cliffs, New Jersey.

19. de Moor, A. (2005) Patterns for the Pragmatic Web, *Proc. of the 13th International Conference on Conceptual Structures*, Kassel, Germany, LNAI, Springer, Berlin, pp. 1–18.
20. Paton, N.W. and Diaz, O. (1999) Active Database Systems, *ACM Computing Surveys*, 31(1), 63–103.
21. Russell, N., Hofstede, A.H.M., Aalst W.M.P. and Mulyar, N. (2006) Workflow Control-Flow Patterns: A Revised View, *BPM Center Report,* BPM-06-22, BPMcenter.org
22. Yu, E. and Mylopoulos, J. (1994) From E-R to 'A-R' – Modelling Strategic Actor Relationships for Business Process Reengineering, *13th International Conference on the Entity - Relationship Approach*, Manchester.
23. Zachman, J.A. (1996) "Enterprise Architecture: The Issue of the Century", *Database Programming and Design Magazine*.
24. Zimmerman, O., Krogdahl, P. and Gee, C. (2004) Elements of Service-Oriented Analysis and Design, www-128.ibm.com/developerworks/library/ws-soad1/

18

Using ESB and BPEL for Evolving Healthcare Systems Towards Pervasive, Grid-Enabled SOA

V. Koufi, F. Malamateniou, D. Papakonstantinou and G. Vassilacopoulos

Abstract

Healthcare organizations often face the challenge of integrating diverse and geographically disparate information technology systems to respond to changing requirements and to exploit the capabilities of modern technologies. Hence, systems evolution, through modification and extension of the existing information technology infrastructure, becomes a necessity. Moreover, the availability of these systems at the point of care when needed is a vital issue for the quality of healthcare provided to patients. This chapter takes a process perspective of healthcare delivery within and across organizational boundaries and presents a disciplined approach for evolving healthcare systems towards a pervasive, grid-enabled service-oriented architecture using the enterprise system bus middleware technology for resolving integration issues, the business process execution language for supporting collaboration requirements and grid middleware technology for both addressing common SOA scalability requirements and complementing existing system functionality. In such an environment, appropriate security mechanisms must ensure authorized access to integrated healthcare services and data. To this end, a security framework addressing security aspects such as authorization and access control is also presented.

Keywords Evolution · Healthcare systems · SOA · ESB · BPEL · Standards · EMR, grid technology · Pervasive access · Context-aware access control

1. Introduction

Healthcare organizations often invest significant resources in the development of large and complex information systems that must be modified and extended to respond to changing requirements, in addition to capitalizing on modern technologies [1]. Technologically innovative efforts of the past have often resulted in the development of disparate, incompatible and heterogeneous systems based on the traditional transaction processing paradigm rather than on supporting business processes. Thus, the integration of diverse and disparate information systems with emphasis on secure communication and collaboration is a challenge often faced by healthcare organizations [1, 2]. To meet this challenge, a systems evolution process must be designed and implemented with the objective to achieve interoperability among diverse systems that may have been developed at different times and with different technologies, and to support a process view of the healthcare delivery context. As healthcare domain imposes strict security requirements on all transactions involved in each healthcare delivery situation, security must be one of the most important criteria to be taken under consideration while designing the systems evolution process.

V. Koufi, F. Malamateniou, D. Papakonstantinou and G. Vassilacopoulos · Department of Digital Systems, University of Piraeus, Piraeus 185 34, Greece.

G.A. Papadopoulos et al. (eds.), *Information Systems Development*, DOI 10.1007/b137171_18,
© Springer Science+Business Media, LLC 2009

System evolution is an iterative and incremental process directed towards long-term user needs and operating on legacy or existing systems [3]. Having a certain direction, evolution differs from an unconstrained series of small modifications that may have little direction over long term. It also differs from systems development that has a specific direction or unifying intent but can start from scratch. Thus, the complexity and volatility of requirements for large-scale healthcare systems and the large in-place investments make evolution a necessity.

In most cases, the decision for system evolution hinges on whether the existing system architecture and functions fit current and anticipated requirements of the problem domain. Thus, in evolving existing systems, most weight must be placed upon the need to explore the systems operating context, develop this context where necessary and make the target system serve it. When this context is described in terms of its constituent business processes and interactions among them, as is often the case, the evolution process focuses on designing a system in terms of how it supports business processes and how these processes can be made available to authorized users in a pervasive and ubiquitous manner.

When a pervasive, integrated, process-oriented healthcare system is envisaged, developers are required to first solve communication-level integration issues, ensuring that existing systems using different transport protocols and data formats can exchange information, then to decide how existing systems can interact to support business processes [4], and finally to design an entry point (e.g. a portal) whereby this integrated system can be made accessible by authorized users when and where needed through wireless devices and according to context information [19]. Along these lines, this chapter presents a healthcare systems evolution process that is directed towards the Service-Oriented Architecture (SOA) philosophy using the Enterprise Service Bus (ESB) middleware to resolve integration issues, the Business Process Execution Language (BPEL) to support systems integration and collaboration and the grid middleware technology to address common SOA scalability requirements (service-level grid enablement) and complement existing system functionality (resource-level grid enablement). A security framework, which addresses access control in the context of a pervasive process-based healthcare system build on a grid infrastructure, is also presented.

2. A System Evolution Process

The drive in healthcare to contain cost and improve quality has called for a transition from the institution-centered to consumer-centered care, requiring increased cooperation and collaboration among functional units. This creates an impetus for healthcare organizations to evolve their existing systems so that to enable integrated access to patient information irrespective of the location it resides. SOA, as a set of guidelines for integrating disparate systems, represents a view as to how business and technology architectures can be integrated and how composite application functionality is delivered to a portal or Web browser. Hence, SOA constitutes a promising evolution intent for healthcare systems since technological heterogeneity is more a rule than the exception in most healthcare organizations [1, 2, 3].

SOA is a concept that enables end-to-end application integration across and among healthcare providers, and provides a flexible model that permits the healthcare organizations to respond to environmental changes quickly and efficiently. It constructs applications from the ground up, taking one or more services and connecting them to form a complete, cross-functional, end-to-end healthcare process such as "medical order". This architectural style is dependent on the Internet and is a combination of business architecture, application architecture and software architecture. In addition, it allows users to rapidly build, reuse and reconfigure automated workflow processes (services) as healthcare priorities, regulatory requirements or environmental conditions change [5]. Hence, SOA responds to the need of exchanging medical information between diverse healthcare systems on the web and can form an ideal architectural basis for evolving existing healthcare systems [6, 7, 8].

SOA is mostly realized through the use of web services technology platform which is based on open standards such as XML, WSDL, UDDI and SOAP [9]. However, in the last few years, it has become clear that there is considerable overlap between the goals of grid computing and the benefits of an SOA based on Web services; the rapid advances in Web services technology and standards have thus provided an evolutionary path from the "stovepipe" architecture of current grids to the standardized, service-oriented, enterprise-class grid of the future [10]. Thus, SOA may be underpinned by both web services and grid technologies. Web services technology can support exposure of legacy system functionality as well as development of applications from scratch in order to provide additional system functionality. grid technology not only provides additional system functionality by means of grid service applications but also supports building out high performance SOA implementations through service-level grid enablement which helps addressing common SOA scalability requirements, such as mid-tier caching, load-balancing and high availability [11].

A SOA environment needs a robust and secure infrastructure that can easily combine and re-assemble services to meet changing requirements without disruption and can span new service-enabled applications as well as existing ones [12]. ESB meets the connectivity needs of applications and services, by matching and routing messages between them, and makes services available for broad access and reuse [12, 13]. An ESB operates as a bus that connects the various resources, ensures that services are exposed over standards-based protocols (e.g. SOAP, HTTP and JMS), enabling any client to contact them directly and to perform transformation and routing of service requests. ESB increases system performance, thus enabling the development of virtual healthcare applications as a connected, process-based set of independent services that exist inside or outside the healthcare organization. Thus, ESB facilitates cross-platform interoperability, unifies message oriented, event driven and service-oriented approaches for integrating applications and services, and hence provides a technological basis for evolving existing healthcare systems into an integrated district-wide environment [12, 13].

In a federated healthcare environment (i.e. one in which services cross organizational boundaries) or in a distributed healthcare environment (i.e. one in which service communications bridge geographic boundaries) it is critical that data, events and replies are directed to the right place at the right time according to certain security policies without management overhead. To this end, an ESB, besides resolving integration issues, provides the capability of orchestrating healthcare activities into processes, typically via BPEL [4]. BPEL provides a standard, XML-based platform that expresses a business process' event sequence and collaboration logic, whereas the underlying web/grid services provide the process functionality. Hence, in a SOA approach that aims at supporting healthcare processes, BPEL, enriched with suitable access control mechanisms, can be used to implement intra- and interprocess collaboration.

Based on the above, a system evolution process towards a process-based SOA consists of the following stages:

1. Develop a process description of the healthcare organization, or part of the organization, under review and specify process support requirements, including collaboration and cooperation requirements. To this end, generate a graphical representation of how and in what order process activities are executed as part of a human workflow.
2. Map existing system applications onto the process models developed to compare "what is available" with "what is needed". From this comparison, identify which applications to keep, which to modify or upgrade, which to create or develop and which to discontinue so that the target system meets the requirements. Then, develop old and new applications as web and/or grid services that are deployed to the relevant grid nodes of the underlying grid infrastructure and are assigned to process activities. The development of applications using grid services may involve grid-enabling the existing databases (i.e. expose them to the grid by generating the relevant grid database services).
3. Describe services into the BPEL engine that generates an XML file which tells the message router (service bus) the rules associated with each service, and use ESB as a message router and rules engine that performs validations on messages, transformations on data and ensures message delivery from one system to the next, and eventually the delivery of information to the user's portal or browser on his Personal Digital Assistant (PDA). Thus, a message is simply the packet of data requested by any service.

4. Determine the security risks, especially with regard to authorization and access control, arising during workflow enactment and web/grid service invocation. Then, design and develop suitable mechanisms for addressing these risks efficiently.

The above approach suggests an evolution direction where a pervasive, grid-enabled SOA implemented on an ESB/BPEL software infrastructure becomes a vital issue in providing quality healthcare at the point of care when needed by means of supporting relationships such as those which exist between the healthcare systems and their operating context, relationships between roles at work and relationships between parts of the systems which are expressed as services. This chapter focuses on the third and fourth stages.

3. Motivating Scenario

To illustrate the technical aspects of the above approach to systems evolution, a sample integration project is described which is concerned with the automation of cross-organizational healthcare processes spanning a health district. Typically, a health district consists of one district general hospital and a number of peripheral hospitals and health centers. As patient referrals are usually made among various healthcare providers within a district, there is a need to ensure that access to integrated patient information by authorized users is enabled when and where needed. Thus, the sample process considered here is concerned with patient referrals from health centers to hospitals and it involves four separate systems based on different technologies:

- *Radiology Order System (ROS)*: a system that handles medical order processing among healthcare organizations and is already exposed as a web service.
- *Radiology Report System (RRS)*: a system that uses a Java Message Service (JMS) queuing system for communication.
- *Electronic Medical Record (EMR)*: a customized system implemented in Corba.
- *Medical Image Processing System (MIPS)*: a system that performs medical image processing and is already exposed as a grid service.

Suppose a healthcare process that begins with a health centre's physician request for a radiological procedure on one of his/her patients and ends with issuing a radiological report by a radiologist. In this process two functional units are involved: the health centre and the radiology department of a hospital and the roles participating in the healthcare process are physician and radiologist.

On performing the radiological procedure requested, the radiologist accesses the relevant part of the patient record and issues a radiological report, incorporating both the radiological images and the associated assessment, which is sent to the requesting physician. The radiologist, before issuing a radiological report, may need to process the radiological images. Figure 18.1 shows a high-level view of the healthcare process concerned with radiology orders.

From an architectural perspective, the healthcare process of Fig. 18.1 surfaces several requirements with regard to collaboration among the aforementioned systems:

- *Exposure of legacy systems*
  Generation of the web services that encapsulate legacy application logic.
- *Grid enablement of web services exposing diverse systems*
  The web services that encapsulate both legacy and new application logic become grid-enabled by being deployed on the grid nodes of the underlying grid infrastructure. Each healthcare organization within a health district is considered as a grid node.
- *System integration*
  Integration of legacy and new service-enabled systems via ESB/BPEL software.

From an authorization perspective, the healthcare process of Fig. 18.1 surfaces a requirement with regard to task execution, namely *restricted task execution*. According to this, in certain circumstances the

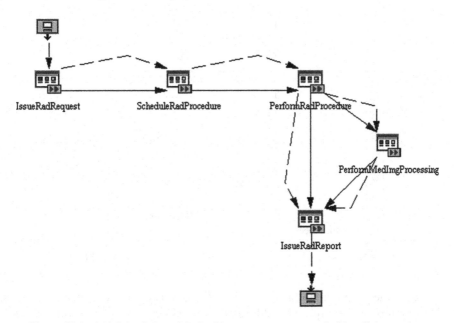

Figure 18.1. A high-level view of the healthcare process concerned with radiology orders.

candidates for a task instance execution should be dynamically determined and be either a subgroup of the authorized users or only one specific authorized user. For example, a request for performing a radiological procedure on a patient (e.g. CT or MRI), issued by a physician, should be routed only to the subgroup of on-duty radiologists who hold the relevant subspecialty and the radiological report, issued by the radiologist, should be routed only to the requesting physician.

The above requirement suggests that certain permissions of the healthcare process participants depend on the process execution context. In particular, contextual information available at access time, such as proximity, location and time, can influence the authorization decision that allows a user to perform a task. This enables a more flexible and precise access control policy specification that satisfies the least privilege principle.

4. System Architecture

The system architecture described here delineates the intent of an evolution process directed towards a SOA implementation on an ESB/BPEL software infrastructure to enable authorized access to integrated patient information during the execution of healthcare processes spanning a health district. To this end, the sample applications mentioned in the previous section are synthesized within a SOA so that they serve as a unified whole.

Uniting these applications into business processes involves solving various integration issues by exposing each application as a web service, and then using BPEL to combine these services into business processes. Figure 18.2 shows a schematic view of the architecture's five main components: the existing IT infrastructure (legacy systems); the ESB which includes adapters to expose existing systems and provide transport connectivity; the BPEL engine that is capable of interpreting and executing business processes described in BPEL by orchestrating existing services; the web/grid services developed or created from the existing systems and deployed on the relevant grid nodes of the underlying grid infrastructure; and the authorization server that manages who, in terms of role, can perform the various BPEL activities, such as invoking a service or assigning a new value in an XML document.

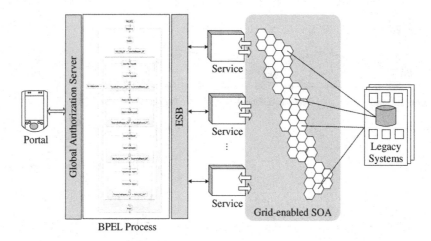

Figure 18.2. A service-oriented architecture implemented on ESB and BPEL.

In the context of the proposed architecture, the ROS is already implemented as a web service and, hence, no further development is required. Additional work is required for exposing the RRS and EMR systems as services. Specifically, an ESB allows clients to access the services through HTTP (or other protocols) and forwards client requests to the RRS via JMS. In this context, new message formats are defined using a CDA-based XML Schema and transformation rules are created to convert to the existing application's format. This results in a new ESB-based web service for RRS, which receives requests and transforms them before placing them in the JMS queue and communicates with other web services via BPEL. Figure 18.3 shows the BPEL constructs that were added to WSDL files for this purpose. The PartnerLinkType defines the role of each partner in a healthcare process and ties it to a given PortType (i.e. the WSDL term for interfaces). In this example, the presence of a single role implies a client–server relationship. The figure also shows the RadProcCd property definition and a property alias that describes how to extract that property's value from the authentication message.

The Corba-based EMR must be addressed and to this end an ESB wizard can be used to automatically create the web service by designing the interface in WSDL and create the web service from there. The service implementation acts as a client to the Corba system directly or though an ESB-generated web service interface.

Finally, the MIPS has been implemented as a grid service (a set of web services deployed in the nodes of a grid infrastructure). This system is based on Open Grid Services Architecture – Data Access and Integration (OGSA-DAI), an extension to the OGSA framework which allows access and integration of medical image data held in heterogeneous data resources.

```
<plnk:PartnerLinkType name="RRSLinkType">
  <plnk:role name="serviceProvider">
    <plnk:PortType name="tns:RRS "/>
  </plnk:role>
</plnk:partnerLinkType>
<bpws:property name="RadProcCd" type="xsd:string" />
<bpws:propertyAlias messageType="tns:authenticate" part="request"
propertyName="tns:RadProcCd "
 query="/xsd1:EMRDetails/RadProcCd" />
```

Figure 18.3. Example of BPEL's WSDL extensions.

The web services exposing ROS, RRS and EMR must then become grid-enabled by being deployed to the relevant grid nodes (computing elements residing at healthcare settings) comprising the underlying Grid infrastructure. Thus, common SOA scalability requirements, such as mid-tier caching, load-balancing and high availability, can be dealt with more efficiency.

This architecture is compatible with the EN 12967 "Health Informatics Service Architecture" (HISA) standard, which aims at providing a reference model for healthcare IT services, facilitating the building and purchasing of interoperable systems [14]. Thus, healthcare information is clearly separated from the applications and can be made available where and when needed to the various modules of the information system.

In order to validate the proposed architecture, an experimental, proof-of-concept system has been developed. This system is essentially a simplified version of the architecture and provides part of the functionality presented in the motivating scenario of Section 3. Hence, it is currently being used for validating the efficiency of the proposed approach and architecture.

5. Security Framework

The proposed system architecture requires enhanced security mechanisms which are mainly concerned with authorization and access control over the tasks comprising the BPEL processes and, hence, over the web/grid services invoked by them since each task invokes exactly one web/grid service. Such security aspects are being addressed in the proposed security framework, consisting of a global access control service, residing on a server at the DGH site and one local access control service, residing at each healthcare organization within the health district.

5.1. Access Control Mechanism

In the proposed architecture, access control needs to be provided at the BPEL task level via a global authorization server. It is assumed that local authorization servers have been incorporated into the legacy systems. Thus, the authorization rules of the global authorization server are designed so that they are compatible with the authorization rules of the local authorization servers.

The proposed access control mechanism is middleware-based as it is employed to mediate between subjects (healthcare professionals) and objects (BPEL tasks) and to decide whether access of a given subject to given object should be permitted or denied by taking into account the current context. In particular, this mechanism will consist of an external to the BPEL engine access control service that will regulate user access to tasks and can be implemented by using Java Authentication and Authorization Service (JAAS) [15].

The access control mechanism can rely on Grid Security Infrastructure (GSI). In particular, it can use Community Authorization Service (CAS) certificates issued to healthcare professionals by a CAS server residing at the DGH site. These certificates specify user-to-role assignments in the form of security assertions, expressed in Security Assertion Markup Language (SAML) [16]. CAS certificates will accompany every request for task execution. The roles used in the certificates will be functional and, hence, they will remain unchanged until the certificate expires as they are independent of the constraints held at the time of attempted access.

The mapping of the aforementioned roles to the relevant permissions will be performed by means of access control policies expressed by using the RBAC profile of eXtensible Access Control Markup Language (XACML). These policies will be specified at the site where the target object (task) resides (tasks are hosted on the BPEL engine at the DGH site) and will assist in the derivation of the exact permissions a subject should acquire for performing a task. In particular, on issuing a request for a task execution, the roles contained in the CAS certificate accompanying the request will be extracted and their relevant permissions regarding access to BPEL tasks will be specified using a file storing the XACML policies [17]. This file will reside on the same server of the DGH site with the BPEL engine. Then, during task execution, a request for invocation of the underlying web service will be issued.

In the case that additional system functionality is provided by means of grid database services (generated by OGSA–DAI), an, external to OGSA–DAI, access control service is required that enhances its mechanism by adding context-awareness features. This mechanism will lie in each healthcare setting (i.e. grid node) and will be triggered during task execution. More specifically, when a request for invocation of the underlying grid database services will be issued, it will be accompanied by the same CAS certificate as the request for the execution of the task invoking it. The roles extracted from this certificate will be used in order to specify the relevant permissions regarding grid database services using XACML policies stored in one file at each grid node (i.e. healthcare organization) providing the portion of medical information requested.

In both access control services (managing access to BPEL tasks and grid database services, respectively), permissions will be dynamically adapted by the constraints imposed by the current context.

5.2. Context Information Management

In the proposed architecture, the contextual information is determined by a pre-defined set of attributes related to the user (e.g. user certificate, user/patient relationship), to the environment (e.g. client location and time of attempted access) and to the data resource provider hosting them, namely to the healthcare organization (e.g. local security policy). For example, the permissions of a physician requesting a radiological procedure through his PDA are adapted depending on his/her identity (included in the CAS certificate), location and time of access as well as the security policy of each healthcare organization where a portion of the requested information is stored.

Context information will be collected by a Context Manager, which can be implemented as a multi-agent system, in JADE [18]. Thus, the Context Manager may consist of two kinds of agents:

– *Wireless client agent:* it will be hosted on each PDA and manages user and environmental context.
– *Service integration agent*: it will be hosted on a server at the DGH site and manages user permissions on BPEL tasks.

In the case that grid database services are used to provide additional system functionality, a third kind of agent is required. This will be hosted on a server at the site of each healthcare organization participating in a healthcare process and will manage user permissions on grid database services.

Each agent will use middleware context collection services to monitor context and will interact with a state machine that maintains the permission subset of each role. The state machine consists of variables that encode state (permissions of each role) and events that transform its state. At the time of an attempted access to a task, the relevant agent will generate an event to trigger a transition of the state machine. Changes in user and environment context will be sensed by all agents.

6. Concluding Remarks

Healthcare organizations are faced with the challenge to improve healthcare quality, preventing medical errors, reducing healthcare costs, improving administrative efficiencies, reducing paper work and increasing access to affordable healthcare. To these ends, innovative health information technologies are often used in order to shift focus from traditional transaction processing into communication and collaboration. This chapter describes an approach to evolving existing systems towards a certain direction, namely, a SOA-based solution which is based on the ESB middleware technology to resolve integration issues and BPEL to orchestrate individual healthcare activities into healthcare processes. The proposed architecture is pervasive and grid-enabled as it uses wireless technology to provide access to integrated healthcare services at the point of care when needed and grid middleware technology to both address common SOA scalability requirements and complement existing system functionality. Thus, through the evolution process presented in this chapter, communication-level integration issues are solved first to ensure that all partial systems (existing and new) using different transport protocols and data formats can exchange information and, once these issues are resolved, the various IT systems are made to interact to support healthcare processes. Hence, the result of evolution is a grid-enabled interoperable process and service-oriented healthcare information system that can be accessible via a portal intended for use with PDAs. In this system, security aspects, such as authorization and access control, can be addressed via an appropriate security mechanism which is also presented in this chapter.

An implementation of the proposed approach and architecture in a wider spectrum of healthcare processes is certainly needed to reveal their potential strengths and weaknesses. This is a task to be undertaken in the near future.

References

1. Lenz R. and Kuhn KA. Towards a continuous evolution and adaptation of information systems in healthcare. Intl J of Med Inf 2004; 73:75–89.
2. Huizen Van G. and Backman AJ. SOA: First Principles. SONIC software, 2005.
3. Ferrara FM. The CEN healthcare information systems architecture standard and the DHE middleware – A practical support to the integration and evolution of healthcare systems. Intl J of Med Inf 1998; 48:173–182.
4. Pasley J. How BPEL and SOA are changing web services development. IEEE Int Comp 2005; 9(3) 60–67.
5. Erl T. Service-Oriented Architecture (SOA): Concepts, Technology, and Design. The Prentice Hall Service-Oriented Computing Series from Thomas Erl 2005.
6. Bloomberg J. Service-Oriented Architecture: why and how?. Zapthink Whitepaper, 2003.
7. Fisher M. and Jendrock E. Chapter 1: Introduction to web services. Java Web Services Tutorial. Sun Microsystems, 2002.
8. Schulte R. SOA is changing software. Gartner Research, 2002.
9. Kapova L. and Hnetynka P. Model-driven Development of Service Oriented Architectures. WDS'07 Proceedings of Contributed Papers, Part I, 72–77, 2007.
10. Srinivasan L. and Treadwell J. An Overview of Service-oriented Architecture, Web Services and Grid Computing. White Paper, 2005.
11. Chappell D. and Berry D. SOA – Ready for Primetime: The Next-Generation, Grid-Enabled Service-Oriented Architecture. The SOA Magazine, Issue X: September 2007.
12. Davidsen L. Building an ESB without limits. IBM Software Workgroup, 2007.
13. Balani N. Model and build ESB SOA frameworks – Adapt service-oriented architectures for easy application integration. IBM DeveloperWorks, 2005.
14. Bott OJ. European Standards for the Electronic Health Record. eHealth benchmarking 2006. http://www.ehealth-benchmarking. org/2006/images/stories/10_bott_european_standards.pdf
15. Java Authentication and Authorization Service, http://java.sun.com/javase/6/docs/technotes/guides/security/jaas/ JAASRefGuide.html
16. Pearlman L., Welch V., Foster I., Kesselman C. and Tuecke S. A Community Authorization Service for Group Collaboration. Proceedings of the 3rd IEEE International Workshop on Policies for Distributed Systems and Networks, 2002.
17. OASIS Standards, http://www.oasis-open.org/
18. Java Agent Development Framework, http://jade.tilab.com/
19. Stanford V. Pervasive Health Care Applications Face Tough Security Challenges. Pervasive Computing, 2002.

MISS: A Metamodel of Information System Service

Nicolas Arni-Bloch and Jolita Ralyté

Abstract

Integration of different components that compose enterprise information systems (IS) represents a big challenge in the IS development. However, this integration is indispensable in order to avoid IS fragmentation and redundancy between different IS applications. In this work we apply service-oriented development principles to information systems. We define the concept of information system service (ISS) and propose a metamodel of ISS (MISS). We claim that it is not sufficient to consider an ISS as a black box and it is essential to include in the ISS specification the information about service structure, processes and rules shared with other services and thus to make the service transparent. Therefore we define the MISS using three informational spaces (static, dynamic and rule).

Keywords Information system service · Service modelling · Service integration · Service metamodel

1. Introduction

Enterprise information systems (IS) are generally composed of applications and data that represent enterprise legacy. Due to constant changes and evolution that an enterprise undergoes, like organization restructuring or merging with a group of partners, business process reengineering and innovation, as well as evolution of information technologies, the enterprise legacy became heterogeneous and specialized by trade, department, service etc. Besides, new applications are constantly added to the legacy ones. This situation leads to fragmented IS and therefore to the redundancy between different IS parts which introduces the need for a permanent validation of data, process and rules consistency. The common part of different IS components represents the interoperability area of the enterprise IS. If no integration is done between these IS components, the interoperability challenge is left to the human using this IS, i.e. the human has to validate "by hand" the consistency between different IS components. Such a human intervention generates extra cost and leads to a poor data quality. In this work we confront the problems of IS fragmentation and interoperability of different IS components and, in general, the challenge of sustainable IS development from the method engineering perspective. We aim to define a method supporting IS components construction and integration. For this purpose, we consider the main principles of the SOA (service oriented architecture) [9, 10] approach that are the modularity, autonomy, reusability and evolution [6, 7]:

- *Modularity and autonomy*: SOA is based on the notion of service that represents a system functionality encapsulated into a more or less autonomous system component. In this work we consider that an IS is composed of a collection of interrelated and autonomous components – services – that allow to avoid chaotic IS fragmentation. Therefore, we define the notion of a specific service that we call information system service (ISS).

Nicolas Arni-Bloch and Jolita Ralyté • University of Geneva, CUI, 24 rue General Dufour, CH-1204, Geneva, Switzerland.

G.A. Papadopoulos et al. (eds.), *Information Systems Development*, DOI 10.1007/b137171_19,
© Springer Science+Business Media, LLC 2009

- *Reusability*: The reuse of a service can be considered from two perspectives: composition and integration. The SOA approach is based on service composition – the capabilities of a service are reused by other services. The interaction between the consumer of a capability and the provider of a service is governed by the notion of contract [9] which defines, among other things, the information to be provided as input and the information to be obtained as output. To be composed, a service has to be published in the registry of services. In case of IS development, an ISS has to be deployed in the IS. We name the process of ISS publication – the integration of ISS into the IS. Indeed, by integrating a new ISS into an IS we extend the IS with new capabilities, i.e. the domain of the IS is extended. When an ISS is developed from scratch, the integration process is relatively simple because the new service is designed by considering the existing services. On the contrary, when an ISS is developed independently, the integration process demands to take into account the overlap that this service could have with other services of the IS. Handling this overlap is not a simple task and can lead to several situations. In [2] we propose a situation-driven process model supporting new ISS integration into a legacy IS.
- *Evolution*: In SOA a service can be easily replaced by a new one. In the IS development this principle allows to extend legacy IS with new services. Integration of a new ISS implies evolution of the ISS itself as well as evolution of the existing IS. This evolution has to be mastered and the integration process has to guarantee the autonomy of services and to limit the coupling between services.

In this work we define the concept of information system service (ISS) that adapts traditional service definition to the service-oriented IS engineering and we propose a metamodel of ISS (MISS) which aims to support ISS engineering and integration. From the integration perspective, we claim that it is not sufficient to consider an ISS as a black box with only interface part available for its integration and we argue that it is essential to include in the ISS specification the information about service structure, processes and rules shared with other services and thus to make the service transparent. Therefore, the MISS extends service description with its informational knowledge:

1. service data structure and semantics;
2. service behaviour in terms of actions that can be executed by the service and
3. rules (data integrity and process rules) to be respected when realizing the service.

This chapter is organized as follows. In Section 2 we define the notion of ISS and present the MISS. Section 3 illustrates MISS with two services while Section 4 discusses the modularity and autonomy of ISS and proposes rules validating ISS completeness. Finally, Section 5 concludes the paper.

2. Information System Service

Traditional object-oriented methods propose two categories of models, static and dynamic, to specify software and information systems. Static models deal with data structure and system architecture definition while dynamic models define system functionalities, activities, states and behaviour. In our opinion, these two modelling perspectives are not sufficient to completely specify an IS. We agree with Turki and Leonard [12] that there is a need for a third perspective, specific to the IS engineering, allowing to specify the rules governing the IS and ensuring the integrity of its data. Therefore, from the conceptual point of view the specification of an IS is a triplet <static space, dynamic space, rules space> [13]. The static space represents the structure of the information, the dynamic space captures the manipulations that the information can undergo and finally the rules space represents the constraints that the static space must satisfy.

Following the same reasoning, we define an information system service (ISS) as an autonomous coherent and interoperable component of an information system. Therefore, an ISS is also considered through the same three spaces: static, dynamic and rules. Figure 19.1 represents our metamodel of information system service (MISS), more exactly the informational part of a service.

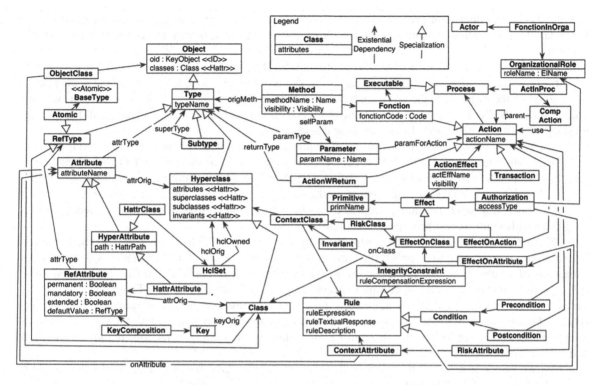

Figure 19.1. Metamodel of the informational part of an ISS.

Similarly, Andrikopoulos et al. [1] propose an abstract service definition model based on three layers – structural, behavioural and regulatory – to deal with web service evolution. In our work, MISS is mainly dedicated to the ISS integration. In the following we use the word "service" as a synonym to "ISS".

An *ISS* is a component of an information system that offers capabilities and owns resources to realize these capabilities. These resources can be technical (hardware or software), informational (classes, actions and rules as defined in the metamodel shown in Fig. 19.1) and organizational (actors). Formally, at the informational level an ISS ς is a set of objects: $\varsigma^{**} = \{O_1, \cdots O_n\}$ because in the MISS model everything is an object. In fact, in MISS a class is a clabject [3], i.e. a class and object. An ISS is expressed by a triplet $<sSs, sDs, sRs>$ where

- sSs is the static space of the ISS, i.e. the set of classes of the ISS;
- sDs is the dynamic space of the ISS; it is composed of a set of actions (sDs_{action}) and a set of effects (sDs_{effect}) that the ISS actions are allowed to produce;
- sRs is the rule space of the ISS, i.e. the set of rules of the ISS.

An information system is built of a collection of services: ξ represents the set of all services of the IS: $\xi = \{\varsigma_1, \ldots, \varsigma_n\}$. ξ^{**} represents the objects of the IS: the union of the objects of all services, $\xi^{**} = \varsigma^{**}_1 \cup \ldots \cup \varsigma^{**}_n$.

2.1. Static Space

The static space of the MISS represents the data structure of an ISS. This structure is expressed with an object-oriented model called Binex [13]. The particularity of the Binex model is that classes are linked only via existential dependencies. An existential dependency is materialized via an attribute with mandatory and permanent constraints. The use of only existential dependencies simplifies the ISS static model and therefore the integration process. To better represent the domain of a service, we use the notion of *hyperclass* [12] that allows to put together a set of classes and in this way to represent more complex concepts.

An *object* is a concretization of a concept in a service. It belongs to a context – the service defining the conditions of its execution and its persistence. An object is defined by a tuple o = <oid, cxt> where cxt is the *context* of the object, i.e. the service which owns the object, and oid is the object identifier, which is unique within the IS. An object belongs to one or several classes and represents an instance of these classes; it takes values for its attributes defined in these classes.

The *context* allows to define the notion of redundancy. An object (or class) is *redundant* if there are two objects with the same oid in the ISS. An object o is redundant if $\exists$ o', oid(o) = oid(o') and cxt(o)$\neq$cxt(o') with o, o' $\in \xi^{**}$. A *class* is an object that defines the common informational structure of a set of other objects. This informational structure is based on the static part (attributes and their types), behaviour part (methods) and rules part (invariants). Dependencies between classes are specified through their attributes. As a class is also an object it belongs to a context.

The notion of *hyperclass* was first introduced by Turki et al. in [12] to better represent the domain of information systems and to support their evolution and integration. "A Hyperclass is a large class, composed of a subset of conceptual classes of the IS schema, forming a unit with a precise semantic" [12]. It represents the structure of complex objects composed of several classes. These complex objects, called *hyperobjects*, are particularly adapted to represent responsibility area and parameters of complex actions. The notion of hyperclass allows to represent the semantic area of a class. This area is represented as a set of classes (*sCl*) needed for the structural representation (attributes), behaviour definition (method) and rules validation (invariant).

An *attribute* is a property that defines static structure of a class. It has origin, i.e. the hyperclass to which it belongs, and defines the type of its value. We distinguish two kinds of attributes: *Hyperattribute* and *RefAttribute*. A RefAttribute is a class attribute that offers a storage or memory space for a value and defines reference between objects. A Hyperattribute is a calculated property of a hyperclass.

2.2. Dynamic Space

There are several ways to express the dynamic specifications of an ISS. For example, it can be done with state diagrams, object life cycles described with state-charts (UML), Petri nets or bipartite nets. We use a bipartite net where one type of nodes represents classes and the other type represents actions [13]. We adapt it for representing the context of a service and we extend it with the notion of effect. The main concepts of the dynamic space are *action* and *effect*.

An *action* is an object that defines a behaviour having an effect on other objects. An action is defined by the following set <*name, {parameter}, {precondition}, {action}, {effect}, process, {postcondition}*>. *Parameters* denote objects to be given to the action for its execution. An action can use other *actions* during its execution. These actions can be either method calls on objects passed through parameters or action instantiations during the process. An action is described by a *process* to be executed and produces one or more *effects* that specify the type of its result. The process can be *executable* (a function), i.e. expressed as an algorithm, or *enactable*, i.e. realized trough interactions with IS actors. An action with an executable process can be atomic, also called a primitive action, or composed. A transaction is an action with transactional properties. A method is an action that is linked to a class. Finally, the execution/ enactment of an action is constrained by a set of preconditions and a set of postconditions.

An *effect* is a tuple <primitive, target> where *primitive* defines the kind of effect (Table 19.1) and *target* is a class, a class and a set of attributes or a action in the case of the *call* primitive. The set of attributes is used with the *update* and *read* primitive to refine the attributes that are updated or read. If no attribute are defined, it is assumed that all attributes of the class are concerned with the effect. Associated to an action an effect has a *name* and a *visibility*. The visibility (public or private) of the effect defines if it is visible outside the service or not. It is used in a composition perspective to define the effects that are part of the action interface.

Table 19.1. The six types of primitives that describe effects of an action.

Primitive	Description
Create	The *create* primitive characterizes creation of a new object in a class. $|cl^{**}_{before}| = |cl^{**}_{after}|-1$ and $|\varsigma^{**}_{before}| = |\varsigma^{**}_{after}|-1$ where cl^{**} represents the set of objects of cl.
Enter	The *enter* primitive characterizes the addition of an existing object to a class. $|cl^{**}_{before}| = |cl^{**}_{after}|-1$ and $|\varsigma^{**}_{before}| = |\varsigma^{**}_{after}|$
Exit	The *exit* primitive characterizes the deletion of an object from a class. $|cl^{**}_{before}| = |cl^{**}_{after}|+1$ and $|\varsigma^{**}_{before}| = |\varsigma^{**}_{after}|$. Note that if cl = Object then the object will exit the root class; it is equivalent to the delete effect. In this case $|\varsigma^{**}_{before}| = |\varsigma^{**}_{after}| + 1$
List	The *list* primitive characterizes the access to the set or subset of objects of a class.
Return	The *return* primitive characterizes an action that sends back a result. The return primitive is always a public effect.
Update	The *update* primitive characterizes the change of the values of class attributes.
Read	The *read* primitive characterizes the access to the attributes of an object.
Call	The *call* primitive characterizes the sending of a message to an action. Therefore the use of a capability, i.e. the public effects of the called action.

2.3. Rule Space

The objective of this space is to preserve the coherence, correctness and consistency of an ISS during its exploitation. The main type of rules to be considered here is the integrity rules [12], the role of which is to ensure the integrity of the ISS data.

A *rule* is an expression/algorithm that returns a Boolean value when evaluated. The rule is *valid* if the evaluation result is *true* and it is *invalid* if the result is *false*. The classes and attributes that participate in the validation of the rule define its validation *context*. Rules are used as a basis for the specification of *integrity constraints* and *conditions*. An integrity constraint (IC) is a rule that has to be verified in each state of the services or at each modification of it. An IC has a *scope* which represents the effects that could transgress the rule. This effect is called a *risk* of the IC. Thanks to the context of IC, we can identify invariants of a class as integrity constraints that have to be validated. The matching between action effects and IC risk identifies the actions that can transgress the IC.

A *condition* is a rule that has to be valid at some point of process execution. In particular, it can be a precondition to be validated before the execution of a process or a postcondition to be validated at the end of the process.

The last type of rule is the *authorization*. An authorization links an organizational role to an effect and defines the information that can be accessed, modified or deleted and the action that can be called by this role. An organizational role is an element of an organization to which management level associate, and that has responsibilities in achieving activities to reach a common objective of the organization.

3. Examples of ISS

In order to illustrate the MISS we propose the following example: the IS of a university (simplified version) providing a service for diploma management *DiplomaManagementService (DMS)* has to be extended with a new service supporting online registration of students to the university *URegistration-Service (URS)*.

The *DMS* is a legacy service (Fig. 19.2) that offers capabilities to manage several diplomas of the university. It allows to create the curriculum of each diploma by defining courses and linking them to their teachers. It also supports the management of students that follow different diplomas by providing actions for their inscription to the courses as well as their examination.

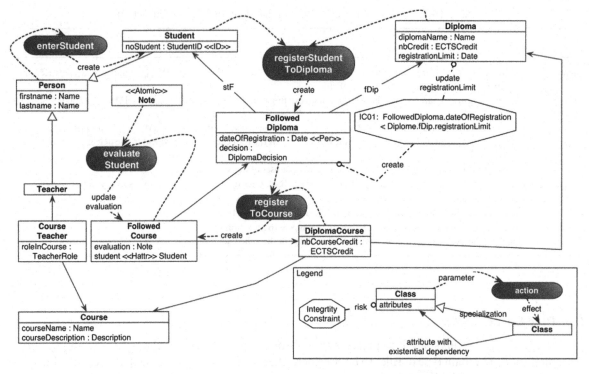

Figure 19.2. Partial specification of the DiplomaManagement Service (DMS).

The new service *URS* offers capabilities for students' online registration to the university. It is composed of a set of classes and actions defined in Fig. 19.3. This service publishes two actions as public methods: *OnlineRegistration* and *RegisterToUniversity*. The first action allows to create a *University Registration-Request* on the web. It is a complex process (not detailed here) that builds the registration including different required documents, according to the integrity constraints defined in the *UniversityRegistrationRequest*.

This example illustrates several overlap situations between the two services, the legacy one and the new one. In fact, we can see that there is a static overlap between classes *Person*, *Student*, *Diploma* and *FollowedDiploma* as well as a dynamic overlap between actions *registerStudentToDiploma*. As mentioned before, if an object, class or action belongs to several services that has to be integrated in the same IS, this introduces information redundancy that has to be managed. Moreover, it is not only a question of redundancy; it is also a question of responsibility: "Which service is responsible for the common objects, classes and actions?" The integration of services consists in defining if the responsibility is shared or delegate to one of the services. In the case where a new service is integrated into a legacy IS, all responsibilities have to be delegated to the legacy ISS in order to preserve the integrity of existing data and processes.

For example, as the class *Student* already exists in the IS the creation of a new *student* must be the responsibility of the *DMS*. Therefore, the *URS* delegates the management of the student information and its persistence to the *DMS*. The same reasoning can be applied for the delegation of the *registerStudentTo-Diploma* action by the *URS*. Other integration strategies can be defined but will require the evolution of the IS which is a costly process. To help the engineer in identifying overlap situations, analysing integration choices and integrating services, a specific methodological support is necessary. The process model for ISS integration is introduced in [2].

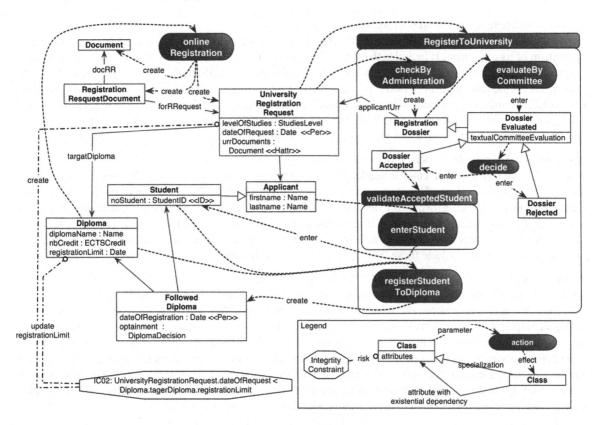

Figure 19.3. Partial specification of the URegistrationService (URS).

4. Modularity and Autonomy of ISS

The definition of an ISS is based on the principle of modularity which offers a way to group a set of elements together in order to crate a semantic unit. In this way capabilities are grouped to form a service. This grouping can be defined explicitly or constrained by the coherence rules. The explicit definition of service boundaries can be reached by analysing the application domain in which this service is relevant. However, some rules have to be validated to guarantee the autonomy of the service. This autonomy aims to guarantee that the service owns the required resources to support its capabilities. In this work we focus our attention on the informational resources (required data, processes and rules), and we define the following completeness rules in order to reach the autonomy of a service:

Class completeness: $\forall cl \in sSs(\varsigma), sCl(cl) \subset sSs(\varsigma)$

where $sCl(cl)$ is a set of classes necessary for the structural representation (attributes), behaviour definition (method) and rules validation (invariant) of the class cl. The class completeness ensures that an ISS is defined on the static space (sSs) that offers all the information needed by its classes. For example, the class *UniversityRegistrationRequest* (Fig. 19.3) is existentially dependant on the classes *Diploma* and *Applicant*. In addition, the hyperattribute *urrDocuments* associates the *UniversityRegistrationRequest* to the class *Document* that represents the exam reports and others files needed during the registration process. Therefore, $sCl(UniversityRegistrationRequest)$ is equal to {Diploma, Applicant, Document, RegistrationRequestDiploma} and the service that includes this class has to be build on the static space that also includes $sCl(UniversityRegistrationRequest)$.

Action completeness: $\forall act \in sDs(\varsigma), sCl(act) \subset sSs(\varsigma)$

where $sCl(act)$ is a set of classes needed for the realization of the process of the action *act* and for the validation of its condition. It includes the type of action parameters, the classes concerned by its effect and the context of its conditions. The action completeness ensures that an ISS is defined on the static space (sSs) that offers all the information required by its actions. For example, the action *RegisterStudentToDiploma* (Fig. 19.2) requires as parameters the classes *Student* and *Diploma* and has an effect to create a *Followed-Diploma*. Therefore, sCl(*RegisterStudentToDiploma*) includes these three classes. The action completeness rule requires that the static space of the service includes also these classes.

Rule completeness: $\forall rule \in sRs(\varsigma), sCl(rule) \subset sSs(\varsigma)$

where $sCl(rule)$ is a set of classes needed for the evaluation of the rule, i.e. the context of the rule $(sCl(rule) = context(rule))$. The rule completeness ensures that the ISS is defined on the static space (sSs) that offers all the information needed by its rules. For example, the *IC02* constraint (Fig. 19.3) needs the *Diploma* and *UniversityRegistrationRequest* classes for its validation. As a consequence, these classes are in the context of the rule and in sCl(*IC02*). Therefore, a service that includes this integrity constraint will have to include these two classes, in order to be able to validate the rule.

Process completeness: $\forall act \in sDs(\varsigma), sCl^+(actions(act)) \subset sSs(\varsigma)$

where sCl^+ represents a set of classes needed for the realization of the public part of the ISS process. It includes the type of the action parameter, the classes concerned by its public effect and the context of its conditions. The process completeness ensures that the service includes at least the classes needed for the interaction with the subactions. [1] This rule is used in a composition perspective. If a service uses an action from other services in one of its processes, only classes from the public effects of this action have to be included in the static space of the service. In the case of the action *RegisterToUniversity*, only the classes *UniversityRegistrationRequest*, *Student* and *Applicant* are part of sCl$^+$. If other services reuse this action, they have to include only these three classes and not all the other classes (i.e. classes needed for the *Dossier* life cycle).

Responsibility coherence: $\forall act \in sDs_{action}(\varsigma), effects(act) \subset sDs_{effect}(\varsigma)$

The responsibility coherence ensures that the actions of a service produce effect included in the service responsibility space, i.e. the service has the right to produce this effect.

5. Positioning and Future Work

According to several reference models for SOA [6, 7, 10], SOA aims to provide support for the reuse of system engineering principles with the help of the service *description* concept. Indeed, the concept of service description is used to define the reuse context of a service as well as the contracts between services. A service description includes two models: the *information model* representing its structure and semantics and the *behaviour model* describing its actions and processes. These two models constitute *service interface* which defines the possible ways to interact with services and to compose them. At the technical level, this interaction is generally realized using the concept of message that plays a key role in allowing communication between services. However, several authors [4, 5, 11] recognize the need to extend the service definition beyond its technical dimension. Quartel et al. [11] focus their attention on the interaction between services. They define a formalism to model the common results of cooperation between service provider and user by using description logic and define orchestration for service composition by using causality relations. Similarly to our proposal, Dubray [4] extends the definition of a service with the notion of *resource* which allows to specify objects managed by the service and therefore to better represent the internal part of the service. Viewing services as black boxes is key from the composition point of view, but it is problematic from the integration point of view. In this second perspective, it is crucial to have the opportunity to identify common data and processes of different services. Without this knowledge, it is difficult to guarantee the coherence and consistency of the IS.

---

[1] In fact, from the composition point of view, sCl^+ represents the static part of the contract.

MISS offers a way to express the knowledge necessary for service composition but also for service integration. This integration is fundamental if we do not want to leave the validation of the data and process to the actors of the IS. However, this is a complex task that can lead to several situations and requires methods and tools to help in the integration process. Due to the diversity of integration situations, the corresponding method should be flexible and modular. In [2] we have presented the process model for integrating a new ISS into an existing IS following chunk-driven situational method engineering approach [8] and based on MISS. This process mainly consists in resolving the information overlap situations between the ISS and the legacy IS. To make our method operational we need to define various method chunks supporting different process activities. First, we need to define a set of service evolution and integration operations. Second, we have to specify the rules to be satisfied during the integration process; we already defined some of them, e.g. the completeness rules. Finally, we have to elaborate metrics allowing to evaluate the impact of the integration on the informational coupling, the level of complexity and the involved service capabilities.

6. Conclusion

In this chapter we look at IS development from the perspective of sustainability and evolution and we propose to consider principles of the SOA approach in order to develop service-oriented IS and to avoid chaotic IS fragmentation and problems of IS interoperability.

Before publishing an information system service to be reused in some composition, the validation of data consistency, soundness of rules and compatibility of processes has to be guaranteed. This is a complex task that needs models representing different information spaces of service definition and methods to help engineers for taking the right choices during the integration process. In this perspective we see the following contributions of this chapter:

- We define the notion of information system service (ISS) and propose a metamodel of ISS (MISS) representing the static, dynamic and rule space of a service. The notions *action effect*, *rule context* and *risk* provide a ground for identifying the overlap between different ISSs during their integration process.
- Thanks to the notion of *effect visibility*, the overlap between services can be analysed in the public part but also in the private part of the service. This allows to consider services as white boxes and offers a way to improve the coherence and consistency of an IS made of services.
- Finally, we specify a set of completeness rules to ensure the autonomy of ISS at the end of their integration process. These rules allow us to ensure the quality of the integration.

Currently, we focus our effort on identifying and evaluating other situations that can occur in the ISS integration process, defining method chunks satisfying these situations and evaluating them with a set of metrics. A tool support is also under development to help in the integration process.

References

1. Andrikopoulos, V., Benbernou, S. and Papazoglou, M.P. (2008) Managing the Evolution of Service Specifications. Proceedings of the 20th International Conference on Advanced Information Systems Engineering (CAiSE'08), LNCS 5074, Springer, pp. 359–374.
2. Arni-Bloch, N. and Ralyté, J. (2008) Service-oriented information systems engineering: A situation-driven approach for service integration. Proceedings of the 20th International Conference on Advanced Information Systems Engineering (CAiSE'08), LNCS 5074, Springer, pp. 140–143.
3. Atkinson, C. and Kühne, T. (2000) Meta-level independent modeling. In *Int. Workshop on Model Engineering (in conjunction with ECOOP'2000)*. Cannes, France, June 2000.
4. Dubray, J.-J. (2007) Wsper an abstract SOA framework, http://www.wsper.org/primer.html.
5. Erickson, J. and Siau, K. (2008) Web services, service-oriented computing, and service-oriented architecture: Separating hype from reality. *Journal of the Database Management* 19(3):42–54.
6. Erl, T. (2005) Service-Oriented Architecture (SOA): Concepts, Technology, and Design. Prentice Hall PTR.
7. Krafzig, D., Banke, K. and Slama, D. (2004) Enterprise SOA: Service-Oriented Architecture Best Practices. Prentice Hall PTR.

8. Mirbel, I. and Ralyté, J. (2006) Situational Method Engineering: Combining Assembly-Based and Roadmap-Driven Approaches. *Requirements Engineering*, 11(1):58–78.

9. OASIS (2006) Reference model for service oriented architecture 1.0. *Technical Report.*

10. Papazoglou, M.P., et al. (2006) Service-Oriented Computing Research Roadmap. http://ftp.cordis.europa.eu/pub/ist/docs/directorate_d/st-ds/services-research-roadmap_en.pdf

11. Quartel, D.A.C., Steen, M.W.A., Pokraev, S. and van Sinderen, M. (2007) Cosmo: A conceptual framework for service modelling and refinement. *Information Systems Frontiers* 9(2–3):225–244.

12. Turki, S. and Léonard, M. (2002) Hyperclasses: towards a new kind of independence of the methods from the schema. *Proc. of ICEIS'2002* 2:788–794, ISBN: 972-98050-6-7.

13. Turki, S., Léonard, M. and Arni-Bloch, N. (2003) From Hyperclasses to IS Components. *Proc. of the 10th Int. Conference on Concurrent Engineering* (CE'2003), Madeira, Portugal. R. Jardim-Goncalves, H. Cha, A. Steiger-Garcao (eds.), Balkema Publishers, The Netherlands, pp. 235–242.

20

An Examination on Service Science: A View from e-Service

William Song and Deren Chen

Abstract

Since it was proposed in 2003, service science has become a keen topic in the communities of web services, semantic web, and e-businesses. According to a recent proposal by IBM, it covers service science, service management, and service engineering (SSME). Although there have been many discussions and reports on this topic, it is still quite unclear these debates would contribute to the establishment of service science as a research subject. This chapter intends to address this issue by comparing related studies on service science or SSME, discussing interrelationships among the components of service science (SSME), outlining its evolutionary process in terms of the enterprise modeling approach, and illustrating a number of possible research subtopics.

Keywords Service science · Web services · e-Services · Service architecture

1. Introduction

Recently, the term service science has emerged as a response to the convergence of various service-related topics such as web services, grid services, e-services, and services-oriented science. More generally, service science is considered to be an interdisciplinary effort, called service science, management and engineering (SSME), aiming to "understand how an organization can invest effectively to create service innovations and to realize more predictable outcomes" [16]. Existing efforts have previously been put in and focused on web-based information technology support facilitating services on the web, where many service-related standards such as WSDL, OWL-S, and OGSA, have been the main research practice. SSME, as is proposed as a science of service systems, is believed to "provide theory and practice around service innovation" [16]. In the Fig. 20.1 we explain these parts that make up service science.

Each part in service science receives contributions from its associated discipline. Based on what discipline it is associated to, we name the parts service science (SS), service management (SM), service engineering (SE), respectively. These three parts cannot be separated and more often than not they work together. The activities and tasks of these parts are intertwisted and the results are integrated to produce and improve the generated service systems. These three parts can be briefly described as follows:

- Service science consists of fundamental theories and research methodologies that deal with basic service structure, service data analysis and management, service modeling, and service processes.

William Song · Computer Science Department, Durham University, Durham, UK. **Deren Chen** · College of Computer Science, Zhejiang University, Zhejiang, China.

G.A. Papadopoulos et al. (eds.), *Information Systems Development*, DOI 10.1007/b137171_20,
© Springer Science+Business Media, LLC 2009

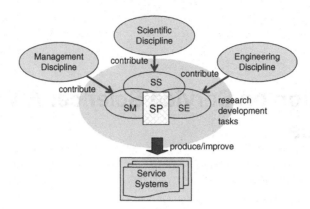

Figure 20.1. Service science, an interdisciplinary topic, aims to produce and improve service systems through research and development tasks carried on inside it.

- Service management focuses on connections of services with external actors, such as service end users, using management and organizational methodologies including psychology, industrial management, finance and economics, and administration.
- Service engineering aims at research and development of services realizations and applications using systematic and engineering approaches together with information and communication technologies (ICT).

Although SSME emphasizes on its association with the three general disciplines, we maintain that service practice should naturally be a part of it. Therefore, in addition to the above three parts, we propose to service science a fourth part called service practice (SP) which aims at testing and practicing the theories and methodologies produced from the rest three parts. The fourth part is defined as follows:

- Service practice defines processes or activities that are carried on for the purposes of prototyping, testing, and practicing the methods and models proposed from other parts.

Note that the outcomes that SSME produces or improves are general-purposed services including those only served by human beings. Next we try to shift our focus from such general services to web-based e-services in order to explore what the existing web-based service research and development contributes to this new discipline service science and what novel research areas there remained for further exploration.

The advance of the web technologies is the main reason to arouse the huge research wave on services. There have been many existing research activities and fruitful results that greatly contribute to service science. However, most of them are closely related to or based on the web technology. Typical topics include service-oriented architecture, web services, grid services, service-oriented science, and e-services.

Web services are "web-based applications composed of coarse-grained business functions accessed through the Internet" [6]. Grid services are considered as encapsulations of resources and their operations remotely performed to serve an assigned task [7]. e-Services emerge as a new paradigm to bring to distributed computation and services the flexibility that the web has brought to the sharing of e-documents. It aims at building a collection of web-based services accessible via standard protocols, whose functionality can be automatically discovered and integrated into applications or composed from more complex services [11].

These service-related topics address a variety of aspects of the problems and applications in the context of service science (SSME):

- The service-oriented architecture provides a range of communications and protocols from high-level business, services, down to low level messaging.
- Semantic web/grid provides a kind of methodologies for service description and interaction.
- e-Services can be viewed to be a working environment in which web services are maintained, discovered, and performed.
- Web services provide a practical and workable communication layer for service description and interaction.

Together with various resources from the web, be they data or applications, e-services are composed to form a great variety of service systems.

These four parts (SSME)[1] are themselves interlinked to each other and as a whole related to service providers and service consumers, which are regarded as external agents. However, each of them has its own focus and plays different roles in service science: the service engineering part is more closely related to the external agents than the other parts, whereas the service science part focuses on the theoretical and intrinsic nature of services, the service management part aims at the strategic and managerial problems of services, and the service practice part deals with the practical and development methods of services. In this chapter we intend to discuss that, in the environment of e-services, how these parts work and their interrelationships, and how this discipline connects to its outside world. In the following, first we make a close observation on the service science parts and propose a lattice structure to describe their interrelationships (Section 3).

Second, although the service science discipline has been proposed and is believed to receive an increasing attention, what to be included in or excluded from its research and development area as a discipline is not clear. Therefore, incorporated with the authors' experiences, we would propose and discuss some contextual topics, including business process and integration (BPI), interoperability, and quality of services (QoS). We believe they are closely related to and contribute to the establishment of service science (Section 4).

The rest of this chapter is organized as follows. In the next section, by proposing a lattice structure to describe service science, we consider two layers in which each part and the relationships among the parts can be better described and illustrated. In Section 3, we focus on the contextual issues and address some such as service interoperability, QoS, and SLA. Finally we conclude this chapter in Section 4 by discussing some related work which has strong impact on service science and proposing our future work.

2. A Structure for Service Science

A lattice structure. Service science consists of four parts or subconcepts, each addressing different aspects of problems. Table 20.1 is a list of goals and tasks for these four parts. Here, we can observe that these four parts not only contribute to the entire service science discipline, but suggest inter-aspect links as well. As a whole, a lattice structure can be used to describe service science and its inter-component links, see Fig. 20.2.

Table 20.1. The goals and tasks for service science, management, engineering, and practice.

Subject	Goal	Major tasks
Service science	Provides a fundamental and theoretical study on its intrinsic structures of services	Include service structure, service nature, inter- and intra-service relationships, and service anatomic analysis
Service engineering	Focuses on how a service system is developed and its activities	Include service requirements analysis, service processes analysis, service design, and service evaluation
Service management	Focuses on service managerial aspects	Include service policy and strategy making, service level agreement, service planning and controls, and service agent management, as well as quality of services (QoS)
Service practice	Offers support in concrete service realization and practical activities	Include service standards exercises, system prototyping, business and service case analysis, demonstration, and test model

---

[1] Without causing any misunderstanding, we will use the term service science and its short form SSME interchangeably.

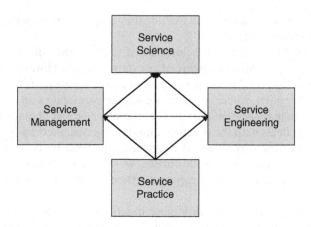

Figure 20.2. The structure of service science where the four parts are interlinked together forms a lattice, where the fundamental theory converges to the service science part and the practical activities subsume to the service practice part.

The overall structure and interconnections of service science embody a converging trend that the concepts defined at the lower-level nodes are subsumed to the concepts defined at the high-level nodes. More precisely, the practices at the lower nodes support and manifest the upper nodes and the upper nodes direct and constrain the lower nodes. In other words, from top-down: concepts become more concrete and from bottom-up: concepts becomes more accurate.

2.1. Representative Concepts

In this section, we discuss two main research problems: service description and service scheduling, which will lead to the construction of three main parts of service science: service science, engineering, and management.

Service description. Many research papers have tried to give a full description of a (web) service. We only summarize them as follows.

A service can be described by its metadata, for example, its name, its textual description, its identity, and its synonyms. A service can be described by its attributes such as inputs, outputs, preconditions, and effects (IOPE we borrowed from OWL-S). The service inputs and outputs have a name and a type to provide further semantic meanings. The preconditions and effects may require a rule system to describe them. We also use a service name and description in natural language to represent the concept of the service. Using the service concepts we build a service ontology. The service ontology can be used for conceptual description and search for services.

The above-mentioned service description does not reveal the relationships between two services. Of course, the relationships between services do provide semantic descriptive information about services. An internal structure of a service exposes the relationship between a service and its subservices (composite services). An external structure of a service demonstrates its relationship with other services in its super-service pattern (as a composite service).

Now we can redefine an atomic service as a service that contains no internal structure. Also we redefine service composition as two services that can be composed into a composite service if (1) the IOPE of the first service is compatible to the IOPE of the second service, (2) the composed service fits a service pattern (i.e., meeting a business requirement), and/or (3) the two services have a common ancestor service in the service ontology.

Service scheduling. The concept of scheduling of services refers to the mechanism of ensuring reliable service processing in terms of monitoring and controlling the service operations. Service requestors can ask for a desired service to be put into the operation chain. On the other hand, the service scheduler, which keeps a record of the service selection and execution sequence according to the requirement and decomposition, manages the whole service procedure.

Each atomic service can only respond to a single request and realize a single function. These fundamental services need to be integrated in order to fulfill complex tasks. Different ways of allocating services provide different functions and the styles of scheduling services play an important role in service composition and flow control. There a number of manners for service scheduling, such as sequential one and parallel one.

Sequential services indicate the chronological order of services in terms of the time sequence of being operated. In this case, each service can only be "active" when its predecessor finishes operation. According to scheduling session, previous services inform the admin and the admin invokes the following service. Each and every service is implemented as on an assembly line. However, parallel services need to be implemented concurrently rather than sequentially in order to perform certain tasks.

Services organized in a scheduled process are invoked in certain order, either sequential or parallel. It is also possible that two services run individually with no relation between them. The invocation of some later-scheduled service may rely on the result of previous ones. Therefore, this kind of services has to wait for the completion of its predecessors. This dependent relationship between services is referred as a critical point in service scheduling.

Service scheduling leads to a key issue: how to determine and manage a service schedule. We will address this issue in terms of service agreement and quality in Section 3.3.

2.2. Four Subtopics from the Four Parts

Now in the light of the previous discussion, we address the concepts or subtopics representing the four parts of service science, i.e., atomic services, service composition, service scheduling, and WSDL/SaaS. The four representatives attempt to reveal the above-proposed lattice structure and inter-aspect links. These concepts are defined as follows:

Atomic services – an atomic service is a service that cannot be further decomposed, links directly to its physical resources, and meets the basic service characteristics.

Furthermore, from this definition, it is not difficult to notice at least three meanings: (1) an atomic service is a service which can perform a function or realize a method, just like all other services; (2) it can meet a requirement which is uniquely corresponded to; (3) it is not decomposable, which means it does not contain any subservices.

Service composition – following a set of composition rules and satisfying a set of users requirements, a number of candidate services are put together to form a new, composite service using a matchmaking algorithm to meet a given requirement.

Service scheduling – based on a business process or workflow, from service pool (e.g., a UDDI service registry), services are selected, compared with each other, and formed a reasonable, executable service sequence.

Service practice standards (WSDL) – a web service standard used to describe physical properties such as number of inputs and outputs, and messaging channels such as message ports.

The above-defined four concepts can be viewed as four representative topics for the four aspects of service science on one hand, and on the other hand, they can be four different foci of one aspect as well. These four subtopics also form a lattice structure which follows the properties we discussed previously. Other than the general interaspect relationships, there are a number of specific relationships we can define between these concepts as in next section.

2.3. Interdependencies Among the Four Parts

In the following, we explore three interrelations between these parts' representatives to illustrate how the relationships follow the lattice structure of service science, see Fig. 20.3.

First, according to a formal definition given in [14], a service consists of a substructure, a concept node in the service ontology, a set of inputs, and an output among other items. If a service contains an empty substructure and its concept node in the ontology tree is a leaf, we call it an atomic service.

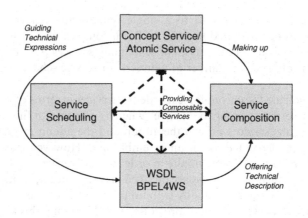

Figure 20.3. Four representative concepts for the four parts of service science and their interdependent relationships.

A composed service is a service composite, consisting of a number of subservices (called a service substructure). Obviously an atomic service is the most elementary service that makes up a service composite.

Second, two services S1 and S2 are considered to be composable, i.e., formed a service composite S1—S2 if they meet some conditions, e.g., the output of S1 is compatible with one of the inputs of S2. In contrast, service scheduling is a more complicated process. Service scheduling focuses more on the principles and rules for selection of services that meet quality, requirements, and goals set by the end users. Various interservice dependencies, such as input—output dependency, time dependency, contextual dependency, and semantic dependency, may play a crucial role in service scheduling. Composable relationships between services provide a functional possibility for scheduling, and inversely, a scheduled chain of services may require investigation of functional composability of the services in question.

Third, a web service standard is prepared for describing web services. Such description should be precisely and effectively based on the core concepts of the domain of study, i.e., atomic service here. As an essential concept, atomic services reflect most fundamental characteristics of service study and use and therefore become a basic guideline to service standards. There may be a number of web service standards, such as WSDL and OWL-S, focusing on different aspects and emphases. It is evident that these service standards attempt to describe the most fundamental elements required by atomic services. Some standards during development lack reflection of expressions required by service science. For example, service composition was not expressed in WSDL. However, OWL-S improves this and provides expression for service composition.

The above example also illustrates that, as a service practice, service standards offer technical support to service composition as a part of service engineering.

3. Context of Service Science

Previously, our main focus was on service science per se, discussing its educational and research elements as a new discipline. Now let us discuss service science from its perspective. In this section we consider the contexts in which how service science is related to other areas. We will focus on the following aspects: service interoperability, service management including service agreement SLA, and quality control (QoS).

3.1. Service Interoperability

As stated in [9], "creating a service involves describing the operations that the service supports; defining the protocols used to invoke these operations; operating a server to process requests". Here a number of significant issues are raised, including service interoperability, scalability, service management, and quality control. In the following, we focus on the issues of service interoperability with business processes and with software resources.

Businesses and their requirements have always been considered to be a driving force to service science. There are three layers that should be identified here: business processes, service structures, and software resources. The link between the business processes and the service structures is identified as "web based applications composed of coarse-grained business functions accessed through the Internet" [6]. The interoperability represented in this link is to be facilitated using semantic description of businesses, their processes and requirements, and finer workflows. BPEL4WS can be seen as a standard seeking to bridge businesses and services.

Considering the link between the services and software resources (systems), it is useful to refer to [5] where the authors have offered these four "essential characteristics of a service (or object): being used rather than owned, conforming to a document-style interface, being stateless, and providing a contractual interface". Further exploring these characteristics, we see that there is a functional transfer from software to services in which lies the interoperability between services and software components. Such interoperability exists in the relation between services and software users and between the interfaces of services.

3.2. Service Management and Quality Control

Service management is indispensable when many valuable services are available and require coordination. We also need "to control who uses the services and for what purposes" [9], which contributes to how to meet external users' requirements and business objectives. Concerning service systems, it maintains the viewpoint of "understanding service system improvements and failures to improve is important to a theory of service systems, as it would enable effective management of service systems." [11] Here a distinction for service management and quality control is between the level of service systems and the level of services.

Undoubtedly, service management involves in actors (human beings and software agents) heavily. A widely discussed issue in this regard is a service level agreement (SLA), as "the part of a contract between the client and provider of a service that defines the parties' obligations with respect to the qualities of the services, usually taken to mean its performance and reliability" [13]. Obviously, this service measurement in its performance and reliability among others requires various methods quality of services (QoS). For example, in selecting a sequence of services (determined through a service scheduling process) to meet a set of requirements, the total cost the service sequence (composition) depends on the cost of every single service participating in the sequence. Situations quickly become complicated when a huge number of services are required to sort out to satisfy a huge number of clients' requirements.

Usually, a web service is determined only according to a customer's demand, and the QoS objective functions and QoS constraints are defined to represent the customer's requirements. However, in the real world, a web service composition process is also (if not only) relied on a service provider's demands. In this case, to determine a QoS value of one service is also dependent on other services (and their QoS values). In [18], this situation is called a context-sensitive QoS model for web service composition. The authors propose this context-sensitive QoS-based model to extend the traditional context-free QoS model for service composition.

4. Conclusion

In this chapter, we intend to take a further examination on service science as a new discipline from two angles: a structural analysis inside it and a contextual view. The origin of service science, from which it develops and the context in which it plays role, is critical to understanding of service science as a new discipline. In this section, we discuss related work and research activities in web services in particular, as well as our next steps for further exploration of service science.

In [1], Abe made a relatively complete discussion of various issues around service science and compared current states of development in different regions. After carefully defining the terms of services, businesses, service science and its evolution, he states that "in essence, service science focuses on those services that handle multiple providers and clients (i.e. service systems) are conducted in multi-phase business processes, and necessitate the frequent use of IT".

By its name service science is close to service-oriented science but the latter focuses more on services in the context of the web and grid. In [9], Foster addressed research problems in it. The term "Service-oriented science" refers to scientific research enabled by distributed networks of interoperating services. The author's definition of service-oriented science is closely associated with and derived from the terms service-oriented architecture and information encapsulation services. Grid technologies can accelerate the development and adoption of service-oriented science. Here it is mainly emphasized that what functionalities and capabilities are researched in the service science, such as service interoperability.

Many service or service-related researches have been based on the areas of the web technologies, the semantic web technologies and the grid technologies. In [3] the authors discuss the further development of OGSA to the emerging grid web services standards to capture generic middleware components in a form to facilitate migration and interoperability.

How to schedule web services and model the scheduling still remains a critical and not-yet-well-solved problem. In [10], this problem is presented as how to design service systems of asynchronous web services. This problem is also significant to service management in general. The authors in [2] analyze the policies and mechanisms for both scheduling and allocating Web Services that constitute a plan, in order to generate an intelligent execution. A number of methods are discussed to provide a suitable selection of the plans of services.

Software as a service (SaaS) is a concept proposed to define the architecture of web services in terms of software structures, reuse models, and development approaches [17]. Probably, a most important contribution of SaaS to service science lies in building a bridge between software engineering and service engineering in terms of service reusability, service encapsulation, and service quality.

In [12] the author identified QoS issues in web services as "a combination of several qualities or properties of a service", such as availability, security, response time, and throughput. He argues that web services users that observe the QoS measure "are not human beings but programs that send requests for services to Web service providers" and provide a model of further analysis of QoS from both service provider perspective and service user perspective.

The study of service science as a new discipline is just at its infant stage. Although these four parts: service science, management, engineering, and practice are suggested to make up service science, what they are and how they connect to each other and work together remains a first question. The second question will be an exploration and examination of each part. This chapter has tried to provide some partial answers to its internal construction and interpart relationships, as well as contextual factors affecting the discipline. However, many more unsolved problems require further investigation. For example, human interaction with services is undoubtedly an essential question to not only service management, but also to other parts, as to scrutinizing interoperability as one of the fundamental properties of services and its impact on human behavior management, real-time service access control, and service standard evolution.

Currently we focus our study on service science in the following two steps. The first is to continue close examination and analysis of essential properties of services of atomic services to build up an atomic service theory. As an earlier research result we proposed a contextual semantic description framework for web services [8] where basic properties of services have been extracted.

Our second step is to introduce the Enterprise Modeling (EM) technology [4] to make an insight study on service science. The EM technology provides us an analysis tool with which we can place our concerns on various aspects and different layers of services, from business objectives model, agent and actor model, process and flow model, to concept and subject matter model, and functional and non-functional model.

References

1. T. Abe (2005) What is Service Science? *Research Report No. 246, Fujitsu Research Institute, Dec. 2005.*
2. E. Alwagait and S. Ghandeharizadeh (2004) A Comparison of Alternative Web Service Allocation and Scheduling Policies, in Proc. of International Conference on Service Computing 2004.
3. M. Atkinson et al. (2005) Web Service Grids: an Evolutionary Approach, *in Concurrency and Computation: Practice and Experience* 17, pp. 377–389.
4. J. A. Bubenko, C. Rolland, P. Loucopoulos, and V. De Antonelli (1994) Facilitating "Fuzzy to Formal" Requirements Modelling, in *Proc. of IEEE International Conference on Requirements Engineering.*
5. D. Budgen, P. Prereton, and M. Turner (2007), Experiences with Using a Software Service Architecture, Software: Practice and Experience (JSPE), pp.
6. J. Chung, K. Lin, and R. Mathieu (2003) Web Services Computing: Advancing Software Interoperability. *IEEE Computer* 36, pp. 35–37, October 2003.
7. D. De Roure (2005) The Semantic Grid: Past, Present and Future, in *Proc. of European Semantic Web Conference (ESWC 2005),* pp. 726–726.
8. X. Du, W. Song, and M. Munro (2007) Semantic Service Description Framework for Addressing Imprecise Service Requirements, in *Proc. of the 17th International Conference on ISD.* Sept. 2007, Galway, Ireland.
9. I. Foster (2005) Service Oriented Science. *Science* 308, May 2005, pp. 814–817.
10. J. Henderson and J. Yang (2004) Reusable Web Services, in *Proc. of the 8th International Conference on Software Reuse* (ICSR2004), pp. 185–194.
11. R. Hull et al. (2003) E-Services: A Look behind the Curtain, in *Proc. of PODS 2003.* June, San Diego, CA.
12. D. Menasce (2002) QoS Issues in Web Services. *IEEE Internet Computing* Nov.–Dec. 2002
13. J. Skene and W. Emmerich (2004) Generating a Contract Checker for an SLA Language, in *Proc. of the International Conference EDOC workshop on Contract Architecture and Language.* Monterey, CA.
14. W. Song (2006) A Semantic Modeling Approach to Automatic Services Analysis and Composition, in *Proc. of the International Conference on Web Technologies, Applications and Services* (WTAS2006), July 2006, Calgery, Canada
15. W. Song (2006) Business Process and Integration Model: An Approach to Guide Constructing Service Flows, in *Proc. of the International Conference on Web Technologies, Applications and Services* (WTAS2006), July 2006, Calgery, Canada
16. J. Spohrer et al. (2007) Steps Toward a Science of Service Systems. *IEEE Computer*, Jan. 2007, pp. 71–77.
17. M. Turner, D. Budgen, and P. Brereton, Turning Software into a Service. *IEEE Computer*, October 2003, Vol. 36(10).
18. T. Zhou et al. (2008) Context-Sensitive QoS Model: a Rule Based Approach to Service Composition, in *Proc. of WWW2008 Poster.* Beijing, China, April 2008.

21

Mapping SOA Artefacts onto an Enterprise Reference Architecture Framework

Ovidiu Noran

Abstract

Currently, there is still no common agreement on the service-Oriented architecture (SOA) definition, or the types and meaning of the artefacts involved in the creation and maintenance of an SOA. Furthermore, the SOA image shift from an infrastructure solution to a business-wide change project may have promoted a perception that SOA is a parallel initiative, a competitor and perhaps a successor of enterprise architecture (EA). This chapter attempts to map several typical SOA artefacts onto an enterprise reference framework commonly used in EA. This is done in order to show that the EA framework can express and structure most of the SOA artefacts and therefore, a framework for SOA could in fact be derived from an EA framework with the ensuing SOA–EA integration benefits.

Keywords Service-oriented architecture · Enterprise architecture · ISO15704 · GERAM · SOA integration

1. Introduction

Although several definitions for service-oriented architecture (SOA) exist, the prevalent view appears to be that SOA is in essence an architectural style promoting the concepts of service (packaged business functions with all necessary information) and service consumer as a basis to structure the functionality of an entire business. Although the SOA concept originates in the modular, object-oriented and component-based software development paradigms, the lack of adequate supporting and realisation infrastructure have hindered its early adoption [1]. According to the Gartner Group, after the typical wave of vendor hype and unrealistic expectations, SOA appears to be now finally heading towards the plateau of productivity [2]. Even though standardisation attempts are underway, currently there is still no common agreement on a rigorous SOA definition, or the types and meaning of the artefacts that should be involved in the creation and maintenance of an SOA [3]. Furthermore, the realisation that building an SOA involves significant costs and changes to the entire business has contributed to SOA being seen in some circles as a separate approach, a competitor and (aided by vendor hype) perhaps a potential successor of enterprise architecture (EA).

This chapter attempts to advocate the benefits of using a reference framework in finding common, agreed-upon meanings and actual coverage of the various artefacts involved in an SOA effort. More importantly however, it attempts to show that SOA is potentially a style and component of EA rather than an alternative. These aims are pursued by mapping several typical artefacts described in SOA literature against a reference architecture framework (AF), obtained by combining a number of mainstream enterprise AFs and validated against several others. Note that a comprehensive mapping of all SOA artefacts currently identified is beyond the scope and space available for this chapter; the aim is to prove the concept and promote constructive debate. In addition, the scope of this chapter is limited to 'top-down' SOA.

Ovidiu Noran • School of ICT, Griffith University Australia, Australia.

G.A. Papadopoulos et al. (eds.), *Information Systems Development*, DOI 10.1007/b137171_21,
© Springer Science+Business Media, LLC 2009

2. The Reference Framework

The need to establish a framework early in an SOA project appears to be generally accepted [5–7]. The assumption made in this chapter is that if SOA-specific artefacts can be mapped onto an enterprise reference AF in a meaningful way, then the required 'SOA framework' could in fact be specialised from that enterprise reference AF, thus facilitating synergy and integration of SOA and EA.

The reference framework proposed is described in Annex C of ISO15704:2000/ Amd1:2005 and it is called the generalised enterprise reference architecture and methodology, or GERAM [4] (see Fig. 21.1). ISO15704:2000 sets requirements for reference architectures and methodologies (without prescribing any specific artefacts) and GERAM is provided as an example of a generalised enterprise AF that satisfies these requirements. As such, GERAM can be used to assess particular AFs, or to establish selections of AF components to be used in a specific EA project since often, one single AF does not have all the elements required. Several mainstream AFs have been mapped against GERAM [8–10] and a 'Structured Repository' (knowledge base-like) of mainstream AF elements is being built using GERAM as a decomposition and structuring tool [11]. GERAM is one of the most complete reference AFs; in addition, as part of ISO15704:2000, it is regularly reviewed so as to harmonize it with other standardisation efforts, such as ISO/IEC 42010:2007 [12].

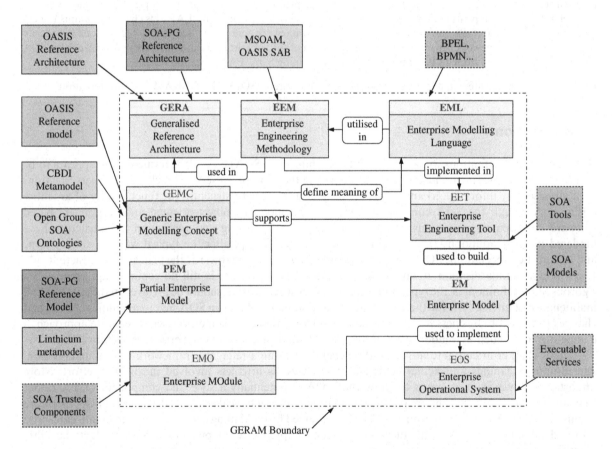

Figure 21.1. Sample mapping of SOA artefacts on GERAM [4] (*dashed outline boxes* show possible and/or generic SOA elements).

The generalised enterprise reference architecture (GERA) component of GERAM contains the multi-dimensional modelling framework (MF) and other essential concepts such as life history and enterprise entity. The GERA MF (see Fig. 21.2) contains a multitude of aspects that may be required in modelling an EA project/product in the context of the project/product's life cycle. The GERA MF also features the genericity dimension, which allows representing the metamodels and ontological theories underlying languages used to build partial and particular models. Thus, the GERA MF contains place-holders for models describing the components shown in the GERAM structure depicted in Fig. 21.1. Full descriptions of GERAM, GERA and GERA MF are beyond the scope of and space available for this chapter. The keen reader can find all the details in [4].

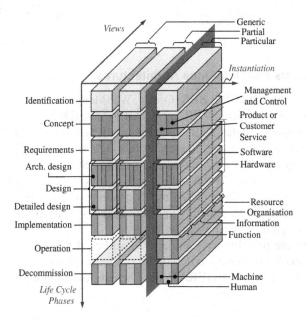

Figure 21.2. GERA MF [4].

3. Mapping Typical SOA Artefacts on the Reference Framework

The following section attempts to map several SOA artefacts currently offered by vendors and/or described in SOA literature deemed of interest to the scope of this chapter. The selection does not imply endorsement of any specific artefacts.

3.1. SOA Ontologies

The SOA Working Group (WG) of The Open Group aims to provide ontologies for SOA so as to promote 'common understanding of SOA in order to facilitate alignment between the business and information technology communities' [13]. In GERAM, ontological theories are a kind of generic enter-prise model, describing the most general aspects of enterprise-related concepts and defining the semantics of the modelling languages used. The Open Group Ontology document currently contains definitions for contract, visibility, registry' etc. Due to its structure and contents it does abide by the GERAM definition and it maps onto the generic concepts area of GERAM (see Fig. 21.1) and the generic area of GERA MF (detailed mapping not shown due to space limitations).

3.2. SOA Metamodels

In GERAM, a metamodel describes the properties and relationships of concepts used in the model-ling effort, as well as some basic constraints, such as cardinality [4]. Thus, an SOA metamodel should unambiguously define relationships between SOA components, elicit rules for building relevant models and define terminology in a consistent and unambiguous manner.

Linthicum [14] proposes an artefact called an SOA metamodel. However, according to the definitions above, the artefact is rather a high-level reference model since it describes an SOA model at the architectural level life-cycle phase (see the mapping in Fig. 21.1).

Another metamodel proposition is offered by Everware-CBDI [15]. This artefact appears to fulfil the requirements of a metamodel by GERAM (although admittedly it lacks some SOA principles such as loose coupling, autonomy, mediation) and thus can be mapped on the generic concepts area of GERAM. In addition, the various artefacts depicted in the metamodel can be mapped onto the aspects present at the generic level of the GERA MF.

3.3. SOA Reference Models and Reference Architectures

Many vendors and consultants (IBM, BEA, Oracle, WebMethods, etc.) offer what they call 'reference models' (RMs) and 'reference architectures' (RAs). In GERAM, RMs are seen as blueprints describing features common to specific types of enterprises, while RAs are RMs created at the architectural design level.

The OASIS RM [16] in its current version is closer to a metamodel than to an RM from the GERAM perspective since it does not appear to express a blueprint for SOA implementation. OASIS RAs and patterns do however match the GERAM RA definition since they are RMs for particular SOA systems expressed at the architectural design level. The OASIS concrete architecture is in EA the architectural design level model of a particular SOA system – and thus maps on the particular level within the GERA MF, at the architectural design life-cycle phase.

The RA described in the practitioner's guide (PG) authored by Durvasula et al. [17] specifies the structure and the functionality of model components and thus appears to be a proper RM at the architectural level, i.e. a RA within the GERA MF. The proposed mappings of the two artefacts are shown in Figs. 21.1 and 21.3.

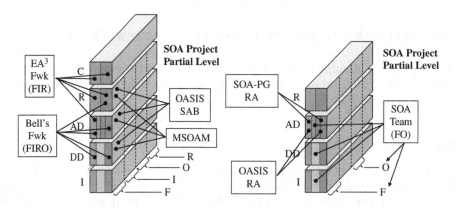

Figure 21.3. Sample mappings of MF and methodologies (*left*) and human aspect of SOA projects (*right*) on simplified GERA MF (aspects/levels irrelevant to specific mapping omitted).

3.4. SOA Modelling/Documentation Framework

An MF according to ISO15704:2000 is a structure that holds models describing all necessary aspects of enterprises and/or EA projects during their entire life.

The EA documentation framework (DF) is described by Bernard [6] as one of the main components of any EA endeavour. Similarly, in the SOA domain McGovern [5] emphasizes the importance of having a framework guiding the SOA initiative. It appears that the general meaning given to a DF is in fact that of MF. Knippel [18] describes the SOA DF as a new product, however, he suggests investigating whether the SOA and EA frameworks could have common areas and even be merged. This supports the SOA–EA integration proposition of this chapter.

The SOA MF described by Bell [19] provides conceptual, analysis and logical life-cycle phases that can map onto the requirements, architectural and detailed design phases of GERA; however, the MF appears to lack several other aspects. For example, the human aspect and the management/service distinction are not explicitly represented. Therefore, if such aspects are deemed necessary for the SOA project at hand, elements of other frameworks may need to be employed.

As another example, the EA³ framework described by Bernard [6] as expressed in its graphical form (which may not completely reflect the written content) appears to map on the partial Level, at concept and architectural design levels (life-cycle phases), and cover Function, information and resource aspects (see Fig. 21.3, *left*).

3.5. SOA Life Cycle and Service Life Cycle

The SOA PG [17] describes a set of life-cycle phases for SOA projects. On mapping onto GERA, a possible interpretation is that the requirements life-cycle phase has been omitted from the model, and so have the phases beyond detailed design (see Fig. 21.4, right). This may be due to the intended scope of the SOA PG; however, when managing an SOA project, the practitioner should be aware of the issue and if necessary seek to complement or replace this life-cycle model with one that provides all necessary phases.

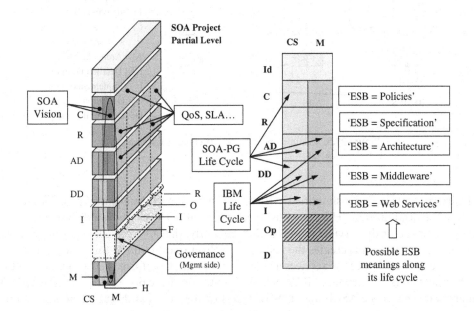

Figure 21.4. Life-cycle models, reference architectures and enterprise service bus mappings on simplified GERA MF (aspects irrelevant to specific mapping omitted).

Another life-cycle model is proposed by IBM [20, 21]. Again, it appears that some life-cycle phases are not covered – notably concept and requirements. It is interesting to note that this model distinguishes between the management and service/production aspects of the SOA project; this subdivision exists in the GERA MF and the mapping reflects this situation (see Fig. 21.4, *right*).

It should be noted that the IBM model also distinguishes between the SOA project life cycle and the service life cycle. The distinction between a project and the product(s) of the project figures prominently in EA best practice and is also reflected in GERAM – which allows for the representation of the business, project, product and any other relevant EA artefacts' life cycles as illustrated in Fig. 21.5.

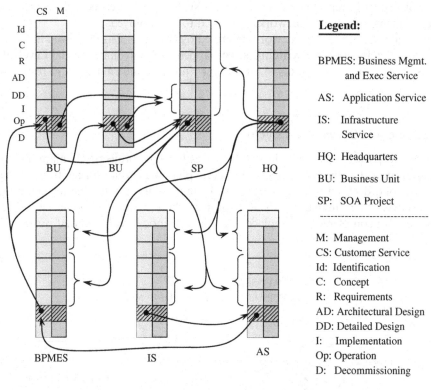

Figure 21.5. Relation project/product/services (based on [22]).

The figure presents (using a simplified GERA MF modelling formalism) a possible SOA initiative scenario, where the headquarters (HQ) of a business sets up an SOA project but also sets the mission and high-level requirements for the services required. Subsequently, the SOA project starts operating and with assistance from all business units creates the rest of the deliverables required for the business, application and infrastructure services. Once the services are operational, they perform their primary function, i.e. to support the business units' operation. In EA, such representations have proven to be effective in achieving a common understanding of the AS-IS and TO-BE states of the business. Figure 21.4 shows how an EA-specific representation can be used to describe an SOA-specific scenario.

3.6. SOA Vision

Articulating a coherent and easy-to-communicate vision is identified by Knippel [18] as paramount to any successful SOA initiative and it is no different in any EA project. The vision maps onto the concept development life-cycle activity of GERA, where the stakeholders decide if and how to satisfy the need(s) present in the identification life-cycle phase.

3.7. SOA Governance

In the mainstream literature it is often argued that an SOA initiative would not succeed without a proper cross-departmental governance approach. Governance should be present at all SOA project life-cycle phases and a governance model should also make clear which business units influences which area of the SOA project, the authority of the SOA/EA team, how services will affect the business units etc. Thus, SOA governance maps onto the management part of the GERA MF and should cover all relevant aspects and life-cycle phases of the SOA project, similar to the area occupied by the SOA team; however, it must include the non-human area of the management side as well. Depending on the specific details of the SOA project, various extents of the project's life-cycle phases may be managed by the business headquarters (HQ) as shown in Fig. 21.5. Representing the location and extent of governance on the GERA framework allows HQ and the SOA team to unambiguously represent their position/authority and to specify governance deliverables needed in each area for each life-cycle phase of the SOA project.

3.8. The SOA Team

The SOA team in GERA terms the human aspect of the SOA project processes. We subscribe to Knippel's [18] view that a dedicated SOA team can be detrimental if an EA team exists and has (or can acquire) the necessary SOA skills. The SOA/EA team must also have sufficient authority and management support. Such aspects can be detailed in the functional and organisational aspect (Fig. 21.3, *right*).

3.9. SOA Methodologies

In GERAM terms, EA methodologies (called enterprise engineering methodologies – EEMs) aim to assist in the (re)engineering and in the management of on-going change within a business. Typically, models of an AS-IS (present) state and one or several TO-BE (desired future) state(s) are created, with the methodology providing a set of process descriptions required to reach the chosen TO-BE from the AS-IS. An important issue in EA is achieving a common stakeholder understanding of the AS-IS and potential TO-BE states. Similarly, in an SOA adoption/on-going project, understanding the AS-IS is paramount, e.g. in order to determine what might constitute a service and what services may be needed in the TO-BE state.

Many EA methodology models (such as proposed by Spewak [23]) include guidelines reflecting principles that cut across business units, e.g. cultural change and politics. Such principles applied to SOA, e.g. promoting a culture of sharing and reuse and obtaining enterprise-wide support are at the heart of a successful outcome.

Noran [24] describes a set of steps that can be used to produce a methodology for a specific EA project (a 'meta-methodology') involving several businesses. This concept can be readily applied to an SOA project if the participating businesses are replaced with units of the same or other business, business HQ etc. and the end products are deemed to be the SOA project and its deliverables/artefacts.

Sample dedicated SOA methodologies are the OASIS SOA adoption blueprints (SAB) [25] and Erl's mainstream SOA methodology (MSOAM) [26]. These methodologies in GERA terms reference models of processes and as such they map onto the functional aspect at the partial level of GERA (see Fig. 21.3, left) at the requirements and architectural and detailed design life-cycle phases. Further mapping details are available, however, have not been shown here due to space limitations.

3.10. SOA Quality of Service and Quality Control

Quality of service (QoS) is an essential aspect in SOA acceptance. QoS monitoring can be partially automated; however, underlying requirements must be specified, e.g. in service level agreements (SLAs) that would map onto the functional aspects at the requirements life-cycle phase in the GERA MF. Quality control aspects such as version control, reuse policies, service document rules, security models and policies and test procedures are also typically expressed in specification documents. Depending on the detail level, they could be mapped onto the functional aspect of the concept, requirements and/or architectural life-cycle phases in the GERA MF (Fig. 21.4, *left*).

3.11. Enterprise Service Bus and Policies

The current definition of an enterprise service bus (ESB) according to various sources (vendors, practitioners, academics etc.) appears to be inconsistent: service integration architecture, integration middleware product, web services-capable infrastructure and others.

It may be that in fact all these views are correct and that they are simply expressing the same concept materialised at different life-cycle phases of the ESB. Thus, using a life cycle-enabled perspective (such as provided by a 'type 2' architecture described in the GERAM specification), the ESB policies can reside in the concept area; the ESB as architecture can be an RM in the architectural design life-cycle phase and ESB as middleware and possibly part of the infrastructure could then reside in the detailed design life-cycle phases. Therefore, various stakeholders can describe the ESB differently depending on the life-cycle phase context (see Fig. 21.4, *right*).

4. Conclusions and Further Work

In this chapter, we have argued that the use of an enterprise reference AF is suitable and beneficial in an effort to assess and select suitable artefacts for specific SOA initiatives. The mappings shown are by no means comprehensive, nor are they an attempt to criticise valuable work in the SOA domain, but rather aim to exemplify how a common reference can help business management and the EA/SOA team work out areas that can be covered by the various artefacts on offer and also point out potential gaps and overlaps. Making sense of the myriad of SOA artefacts created by interest groups, academics, vendors, etc. appears to be a crucial early step when attempting to gather support for an imminent SOA initiative.

The chosen generalised enterprise AF was able to represent the SOA entities artefacts identified (detailed mappings may make the object of further publication due to space restrictions). A lot more mapping work needs to be accomplished; however, this early result appears to support the idea that an SOA framework could be derived from an EA reference framework. This course of action would promote SOA–EA integration rather than rivalry and be highly beneficial to the organisation. Thus, EA can help an SOA initiative get off the ground by more accurately identifying and predicting required business and supporting services, and then sustain it by a cross-departmental approach. EA can also help achieve a cultural change promoting reuse – e.g. by a system of values that rewards business units who share services that become frequently reused.

References

1. Schönherr, M. Connecting EAI-Domains via SOA – Central vs. Distributed Approaches to Establish Flexible Architectures, in Knowledge Sharing in the Integrated Enterprise: Interoperability Strategies for the Enterprise Architect, P. Bernus, M. Fox, and J.B.M. Goossenaerts, Editors. 2004, Kluwer Academic Publishers: Toronto/Canada. pp. 111–113.
2. Fenn, J., A. Linden, and D. Cearley. Hype Cycle for Emerging Technologies, 2005Gartner Group. Retrieved June 5, 2008 from http://www.gartner.com/teleconferences/attributes/attr_129930_115.pdf
3. Erickson, J. and K. Siau. Web Services, Service Oriented Computing and Service Oriented Architecture: Separating Hype from Reality. Journal of Database management, 2008, 19(3): pp. 42–54.
4. ISO/IEC. Annex C: GERAM, in ISO/IS 15704:2000/Amd1:2005: Industrial automation systems – Requirements for Enterprise-Reference Architectures and Methodologies. 2005.
5. McGovern, J. Service Oriented Architecture, in A Practical Guide to Enterprise Architecture, J. McGovern, et al. Editors. 2003, Prentice Hall PTR: Upper Saddle River, NJ. pp. 63–89.
6. Bernard, S.A. An Introduction To Enterprise Architecture. 2005, Bloomington, IN: AuthorHouse.
7. Sprott, D. and L. Wilkes. Enterprise Framework for SOA. Component based Development and Integration Journal, 2005.

8. Noran, O. An Analysis of the Zachman Framework for Enterprise Architecture from the GERAM perspective. IFAC Annual Reviews in Control, 2003. Special Edition on Enterprise Integration and Networking 27: pp. 163–183.

9. Noran, O. An Analytical Mapping of the C4ISR Architecture Framework onto ISO15704 Annex A (GERAM). Computers in Industry, 2005, 56(5): pp. 407–427.

10. Saha, P. A Synergistic Assessment of the Federal Enterprise Architecture Framework Against GERAM (ISO15704:2000 Annex A), in *Enterprise Systems Architecture in Practice*, P. Saha, Editor. 2007, IDEA Group: Hershey, USA. pp. 1–17.

11. Noran, O. Discovering and modelling Enterprise Engineering Project Processes, in *Enterprise Systems Architecture in Practice*, P. Saha, Editor. 2007, IDEA Group: Hershey, USA.

12. ISO/IEC, ISO/IEC 42010:2007: Recommended Practice for Architecture Description of Software-Intensive Systems. 2007.

13. SOA WG. Open SOA Ontology The Open Group,. Retrieved June 23, 2008 from http://www.opengroup.org/projects/soa-ontology/uploads/40/12153/soa-ont-06.pdf

14. Linthicum, D.S. SOA Meta-Model, (PDF). Linthicum Group. Retrieved June 12, 2008 from http://www.linthicumgroup.com/paperspresentations.html

15. CBDI. CBDI-SAE™ Meta Model for SOA Version 2 Retrieved from http://www.cbdiforum.com/public/meta_model_v2.php

16. OASIS SOA Reference Model TC. OASIS Reference Model for Service Oriented Architecture V 1.0OASIS Group. Retrieved June 20, 2008 from http://www.oasis-open.org/committees/download.php/19679/soa-rm-cs.pdf

17. Durvasula, S., et al. SOA Practitioner's Guide. BEA Systems, Inc. Retrieved 2008 from http://dev2dev.bea.com/pub/a/2006/09/soa-practitioners-guide.html

18. Knippel, R. Service Oriented Enterprise Architecture (Doctoral Thesis), in *IT*. 2005, IT-University of Copenhagen: Copenhagen. pp. 125.

19. Bell, M. Introduction to Service-Oriented Modeling, in Service-Oriented Modeling (SOA): Service Analysis, Design, and Architecture. 2008, Wiley & Sons.

20. IBM. SOA Governance and LifeCycle Management Retrieved April 12, 2008 from http://download.boulder.ibm.com/ibmdl/pub/software/au/solutions/businessflexibility/soahighway/pdf/SOA_Gov_SLM_Brochure.pdf

21. IBM. The Role of SOA Quality Management in SOA Service Lifecycle Management, (PDF Document). Retrieved March 10, 2008 from http://www.ibm.com/developeworks/rational/library/mar07/mcbride/

22. Bernus, P. How To Implement SOA For The Whole Of Business. in *Service Oriented Architecture 2008 – Implementing And Measuring SOA Projects To Drive Business Value*. 2008. Syndey: IQPC.

23. Spewak, S.H. Enterprise Architecture Planning: Developing a Blueprint for Data, Applications, and Technology. 1993, Wiley: New York.

24. Noran, O. Refining a Meta-methodology for Collaborative Networked Organisations: A Case Study. International Journal of Networking and Virtual Organisations, 2006, 3(4): pp. 359–377.

25. OASIS SOA Adoption TC. SOA Adoption Blueprint – 'Generico'. OASIS Group. Retrieved June 20, 2008 from http://www.oasis-open.org/committees/download.php/17616/06-04-00002.000.doc

26. Erl, T. Appendix B: Process Descriptions, in SOA: Principles of Service Design. 2007. Prentice Hall PTR: Upper Saddle River, NJ.

22

Comparing Architectural Styles for Service-Oriented Architectures – a REST vs. SOAP Case Study

Jörg Becker, Martin Matzner and Oliver Müller

Abstract

Two architectural styles are currently heavily discussed regarding the design of service-oriented architectures (SOA). Within this chapter we have compared those two alternative styles – the SOAP-style with procedural designs similar to remote procedure calls and the REST-style with loosely coupled services similar to resources of the World Wide Web. We introduce the case of a business network consisting of manufacturers and service providers of the electronics industry for deriving a set of requirements towards a specific SOA implementation. For each architectural style we present a concrete SOA design and evaluate it against the defined set of requirements.

Keywords Service-oriented architecture · REST · SOAP

1. Motivation and Outline

A software architecture is an abstraction of the run-time elements of a software system [5][8]. It is defined by the configuration of its elements – components, connectors, and data – constrained in their function and relationships in order to achieve a desired set of architectural properties (e.g., reliability, scalability, extensibility, reusability). A coordinated set of such architectural constraints is called an architectural style.

> A good architecture is not created in a vacuum. All design decisions at the architectural level should be made within the context of the functional, behavioral, and social requirements of the system being designed, which is a principle that applies equally to both software architecture and the traditional field of building architecture. The guideline that "form follows function" comes from hundreds of years of experience with failed building projects, but is often ignored by software practitioners. FIELDING [5].

Currently, two architectural styles are heavily discussed in the context of SOA [13]: On the one hand, styles based on SOAP and related standards (e.g., WSDL) with procedural designs similar to remote procedure calls. And on the other hand, styles based on REST with loosely coupled designs similar to resources of the World Wide Web.

While the REST vs. SOAP debate is largely ignored in academia, the SOA community is fighting a spirited battle about the pros and cons of each style [9, 13] . Following these – sometimes not very objective – discussions on numerous blogs and mailing lists two research questions arise:

- RQ1: How does the design of a SOA differ depending on the chosen architectural style?
- RQ2: Which architectural style is appropriate for a given use case?

Jörg Becker, Martin Matzner and Oliver Müller • European Research Center for Information Systems, University of Münster, Münster, Germany.

G.A. Papadopoulos et al. (eds.), *Information Systems Development*, DOI 10.1007/b137171_22,
© Springer Science+Business Media, LLC 2009

Most existing work on the REST vs. SOAP debate focuses on technical issues and draws on rather simplified examples. In this chapter we try to tackle this issue from a more business centered than technical perspective. We use an exploratory case study [12] to find first answers to the above-named questions. We address RQ1 by describing and comparing a SOAP-style and a REST-style SOA for one and the same real-life use case. Furthermore, based on the lessons learned from this case and an accompanying literature review, we want to give first guidelines addressing RQ2.

The remainder of this chapter is structured as follows: First, we introduce the case study from a business point of view and derive requirements for an underlying SOA. The identification of requirements was guided by the frameworks of architectural properties and quality attributes presented in [1] and [5]. Next, we present two concrete physical SOA designs – one in SOAP style and one in REST style – which we have derived from the case. We conclude with the evaluation of the resulting designs and an outlook for further research.

2. Case Study

Many industries are currently facing a transition from a goods-dominant to a service-dominant business model [11]. Instead of offering goods solely, manufacturers strive to provide tailored solutions composed of physical products and related services as integrated value propositions to their customers. As today's highly specialized companies seldom possess all necessary resources for the efficient provisioning of such integrated value propositions, they often form or engage in business networks to offer customer-specific product-service bundles.

The analyzed case study is an example of such a business network consisting of OEMs (original equipment manufacturers) and various service providers of the electronics industry. The primary subject of analysis is Hellmann Process Management GmbH & Co. KG (HPM), a provider of end-of-life solutions. In cooperation with its partners, HPM offers logistics and recycling services for electronic products which have reached the end of their life cycle. By the commencement of the European Union WEEE (waste electrical and electronic equipment) directive, the demand for recycling and related after-use services has dramatically grown. WEEE establishes rules for the collection, treatment, recycling, and recovery of electronic waste in the EU. Since August 2005 all OEMs and importers are committed to collect and dispose their products according to specified standards and at their own costs [4]. For monitoring purposes, OEMs have to report the realized input and output (into and out of the WEEE system) quantities to their national registers, which control all recycling activities.

→ **Req.1 (Simplicity):** Since participation in the WEEE system is mandatory for all industry members – regardless of size and financial strength – and not associated with any financial incentives, simplicity is desirable to allow for a low entry barrier.

Typically, OEMs outsource WEEE-related business processes to specialized service providers such as HPM. Due to the dynamics of the electronics industry (rapid innovation, short product life cycles, high product diversity, and large number of OEMs, distributors, and retailers) the institutionalization of the resulting business network is subject to constant change: To realize economies of scale service providers handle returns for various and changing OEMs. The rapid innovation rates of the industry forces them to constantly adapt their processes and resources. On the other hand, OEMs team up with multiple service providers to realize location economies, to reduce dependencies which could be exploited opportunistically and last but not least because the often small- and medium-sized service providers can serve only a limited product portfolio or geographical region. Furthermore it is planned to expand the directive to other product groups (e.g., medical equipments, machinery) in the near future.

→ **Req.2 (Scalability):** As the business network comprises thousands of members and will substantially grow in the near future the architecture should be highly scalable.

OEMs sell new electronic products to private consumers and have to regularly report the corresponding quantities to the national registers – either directly or via their service provider (see Fig. 22.1). Those

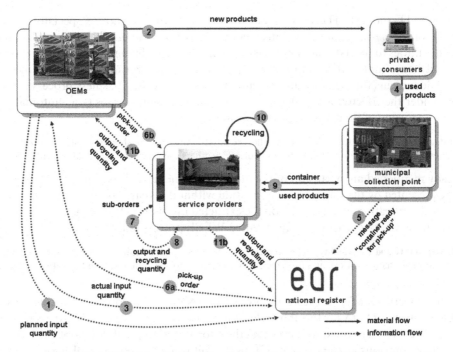

Figure 22.1. Material and information flows emerging from the WEEE directive.

reports comprise the planned input of products (into the WEEE system) for the upcoming year, which is certainly confidential information, as well as the actual input for the past month.

→ **Req.3 (Security):** As confidential information is exchanged through the system there must be security mechanisms protecting communication and providing authorization that attests the identity of the interacting business partners.

Private consumers return their end-of-life products at municipal collection points for free. As soon as a collection box is full, the municipal collection point notifies the national register. Based on the already realized input and output quantities, the national register determines which OEM is responsible for the disposal of the current container and issues a pick-up order. The OEM forwards the pick-up order to its service provider. Within 48 h the service provider has to pick up the full container and leave an empty one at the collection point. Beforehand he has to contact the collection point to find out about the container owner and to clarify the conditions regarding a container use or exchange. Due to time and capacity bottlenecks and the geographical distribution of the municipal collection points service providers frequently assign suborders for this task.

→ **Req.4 (Distributed and Decentralized):** The WEEE system comprises many distributed partners such as OEMs, service providers, national registers, and municipal collection points. For reasons of performance and reliability, the architecture should therefore support bilateral communication between members, independent from a central system.

Failing the 48 h deadline can result in various logistic problems at the municipal collecting points, which are limited in their capacities. Furthermore service providers rely on the timeliness of announced orders as they highly optimize their business processes and resources. Consequently, violating deadlines is punished by noticeable fines.

→ **Req.5 (Reliability):** Due to the short time frames for order fulfillment the architecture should allow for warranting that messages are delivered on time.

After having conducted the pick up and recycling operations, the service provider reports the output quantity (amount of products picked up at the collection point) and recycling quantity (amount of products reused, recycled, or disposed) to the OEM and the national register. Currently, this process suffers from poor IT support. There exists hardly any standard software. Especially, a standardized message format for the exchange of the various quantity reports is lacking. The reporting of input, output, and recycling quantities to the national register is only possible via a dialog-based web client or fax. Hence, most parties rely on simple office applications (e.g., word and spreadsheet processing, e-mail) and semistructured documents for planning and execution of WEEE-related business processes. The resulting media breaks hinder the effective and efficient automation of these processes (e.g., automated extraction and subsequent reporting of input quantities out of invoices).

→ **Req.6 (Standardization and Configurability):** The exchanged information should be standardized in terms of semantics. However, different data formats are desirable as members use very heterogeneous information systems.

As already mentioned an expansion of the affected product groups is planned. A respective draft is expected to be presented by the European Commission within this year. Those changes can also comprise extended reporting obligations (e.g., reports on the extracted raw materials). Furthermore, there are trends to align the so far very heterogeneously implemented WEEE process in the several member states.

→ **Req.7 (Extensibility and Evolvability):** The architecture should allow for adding and changing functionality (e.g., new messages to be exchanged or existing messages to be extended) to the system without negatively affecting other components.

Within the government-funded research project FlexNet, we developed various designs and proto-typical implementations of SOA for the above-described case and other cases of business networks. In the course of the project we therefore developed a method for the conceptual design of SOA which we have published in several previous articles, cf. e.g., [3]. In the following sections we will show two SOA designs for the above-described scenario – one following the SOAP style and one following the REST style.

3. SOAP-Style architecture

We use the term SOAP style to characterize web services or SOA which are based on SOAP (simple object access protocol) for messaging and related standards such as WSDL (web service description language) for addressing and interface description. The SOAP/WSDL pair is currently the most popular basis for SOA and is heavily promoted by major software vendors (e.g., SAP, Microsoft). The SOAP style draws largely on the remote procedure call (RPC) technique. It is intended to allow for calling procedures on remote systems as if they were local. As SOAP is a transport protocol it contains little constraints regarding interface design. Thus every SOAP-style service has its own specific interface and can contain an arbitrary number of operations (in contrast to objects, services do not represent types of entities but are merely a more or less arbitrary collection of operations). On the one hand, this gives developers lots of freedom making capabilities of software available remotely. On the other hand, this flexibility typically results in tightly coupled designs as providers and potential service consumers need to share a common understanding of the syntax and semantics of services and their specific operations.

Figure 22.2 shows the services of our case study in SOAP style. As one can see there are relatively few services, but each with its own specific interface and operations:

- The PickUpOrderService encapsulates all capabilities required for the management and reporting of pick-up orders from and to the national register. Besides the typical CRUD (create, read, update, delete) operations it allows for forwarding orders to subcontractors and extracting output quantities from single or multiple orders.
- The RecyclingOrderService comprises all functionalities for the management and reporting of recycling orders between service providers. Besides CRUD it allows to send shipping notification to recyclers and provides operations for the extraction of the realized recycling quantities.
- The ReportingService bundles all functionalities required to report planned and realized input, output, and recycling (reuse, material recycling, and other recycling) quantities to the national register. The

Service	Operation	Input	Output
PickUpOrderService	createPickUpOrder	PickUpOrderHeader, PickUpOrderBody	PickUpOrderID, Status
	readPickUpOrder	PickUpOrderID	PickUpOrderHeader, PickUpOrderBody
	changePickUpOrder	PickUpOrderID, PickUpOrderHeader, PickUpOrderBody	PickUpOrderID, Status
	cancelPickUpOrder	PickUpOrderID	PickUpOrderID, Status
	getListOfPickUpOrders	Filter	PickUpOrderIDs, PickUpOrderHeaders
	forwardPickUpOrder	PickUpOrderID, PartnerID	PickUpOrderID, Status
	getOutputQuantity	PickUpOrderID	ProductGroup, Quantity, Weight
RecyclingOrderService	createRecyclingOrder	RecyclingOrderHeader, RecyclingOrderBody	RecyclingOrderID, Status
	readRecyclingOrder	RecyclingOrderID	RecyclingOrderHeader, RecyclingOrderBody
	changeRecyclingOrder	RecyclingOrderID, RecyclingOrderHeader, RecyclingOrderBody	RecyclingOrderID, Status
	cancelRecyclingOrder	RecyclingOrderID	RecyclingOrderID, Status
	getListOfRecyclingOrder	Filter	RecyclingOrderIDs, RecyclingOrderHeaders
	forwardRecyclingOrder	RecyclingOrderID, PartnerID	RecyclingOrderID, Status
	sendShippingNotification	RecyclingOrderID, PartnerID, Location, Date, Time	ShippingNotificationID, Status
	getReuseQuantity	RecyclingOrderID	ProductGroup, Quantity, Weight
	getMaterialRecyclingQuantity	RecyclingOrderID	ProductGroup, Quantity, Weight
	getOtherRecyclingQuantity	RecyclingOrderID	ProductGroup, Quantity, Weight
ReportingService	reportPlannedInputQuantityNextYear	PartnerID, ProductGroup, Quantity, Weight	ReportID, Status
	reportInputQuantityLastMonth	PartnerID, ProductGroup, Quantity, Weight	ReportID, Status
	reportOutputQuantityLastMonth	PartnerID, ProductGroup, Weight	ReportID, Status
	reportReuseQuantityLastYear	PartnerID, ProductGroup, Quantity, Weight	ReportID, Status
	reportMaterialRecyclingQuantityLastYear	PartnerID, ProductGroup, Quantity, Weight	ReportID, Status
	reportOtherRecyclingQuantityLastYear	PartnerID, ProductGroup, Quantity, Weight	ReportID, Status
AdministrationService	getListOfServiceProviders	Filter	PartnerIDs, PartnerNames
	getDetailsOfServiceProvider	PartnerID	PartnerMasterData
	getContainerOwner	ContainerID	PartnerID

Figure 22.2. SOAP-style SOA.

service can use operations of the PickUpOrderService and RecyclingOrderService to automatically determine the output and recycling quantities.

- The AdministrationService comprises operations that allow service providers to search for registered subcontractors and to find out about the owner of a to be picked up container.

4. REST-Style Architecture

Analogue to the preceding reasoning on SOAP, we use the term REST style to characterize web services or SOA which makes use of the architectural style called representational state transfer (REST). REST is the model on which the HTTP protocol – and hence the World Wide Web itself – is built. REST addresses four main goals [5, 9]:

- scalability of component interactions;
- generality of interfaces;

- independent deployment of components; and
- intermediary components to reduce interaction latency, enforce security, and encapsulate legacy systems.

REST achieves these goals by implementing the following principles [7, 9]. Here, we do make use of the labels introduced by Richardson and Ruby [10] in their proposal for a REST-oriented architecture, which are

- Addressability,
- Uniform Interface,
- Statelessness,
- Connectedness.

In REST everything which can be addressed uniquely is a resource. A resource is typically an exposed object instance (e.g., .../Manufacturer/4711 – returns data about manufacturer with the ID 4711) or the result of an algorithm (e.g., /Manufacturer/4711/PickUpOrders – returns a list of all current pick-up orders of manufacturer 4711). The concept of *Addressability* makes use of the Internet's URI (uniform resource identifier). Thus, it is possible to address a resource through a global scheme of unique identifiers [2]. "This identifier can be bookmarked, passed around between applications or used as a stand-in for the actual resource" [10]. Every resource possesses a representation – i.e., data about the current state of the resource. This data can be presented in different representation formats, e.g., one and the same order can be presented as a PDF-, DOC-, HTML-, or XML-document. The client can simply specify the MIME-type of the desired format in the HTTP-header of the resource request. The concept of the *Uniform Interface* explicates that all communication between client and the server is conducted using the fixed operation set provided by HTTP: GET, PUT, POST, DELETE [6]. A GET method transfers the current representation of the requested resource from the server to the client. The client can change the state of the resource by modifying its representation and transferring it back to the server via a PUT method. The POST method along with its payload is used to initially create a resource on the server. DELETE removes a resource from the server.

The concept of *Statelessness* means that the server never stores any application state, which represents the client's operating context. In contrast, each client request has to be fully self-descriptive, is considered in isolation, and is interpreted only in context of the current resource state [10]. Application state is maintained by the clients. The concept of *Connectedness* allows for linking resources and performing application state transitions by following these links. For example, an order representation could contain a link to the representation of its status (e.g., new, released, or closed) which can be modified via a PUT method by the client.

Figure 22.3 shows the services of our case study in REST style. As one can see there are many services, but they all share a common interface and operations. Every service can be addressed by an URI and services are explicitly linked to each other to allow clients to perform application state transitions. In contrast to the SOAP-style services, the input and output parameters within one service do not differ but are merely mirrored.

The services *Manufacturers* and *ServiceProviders* mark a natural entry point to the scenario. Their implementation would deliver a list of all manufacturers/service providers registered at the national register. The answer to a GET request to those services would comprise a list of all URIs, representing all registered manufacturers/service providers. The delivered URIs allow for proceeding to the next activity and for calling services, which are assigned to one specific network member. Assume that the national register tries to put a pick-up order to a certain manufacturer. It would use the retrieved manufacturer URI and send a POST statement to the manufacturers PickUpOrder resource. The manufacturer itself can now enlist registered service providers, retreive the associated URIs, and forward an recycling order to a service provider sending a POST containing the before-received information to the RecyclingOrder service.

Service	Operation	Input	Output
/Manufacturers	GET	-	PartnerIDs, Names
	POST	PartnerID, Name	HTTP Status Code
/Manufacturers/{id}	GET	-	PartnerMasterData
	PUT	PartnerMasterData	HTTP Status Code
	DELETE	-	HTTP Status Code
/Manufacturers/{id}/PlannedInputQuantity/{year}	GET	-	ProductGroup, Quantity, Weight
	PUT	ProductGroup, Quantity, Weight	HTTP Status Code
/Manufacturers/{id}/InputQuantity/{month}	GET	-	ProductGroup, Quantity, Weight
	PUT	ProductGroup, Quantity, Weight	HTTP Status Code
/Manufacturers/{id}/OuputQuantity/{month}	GET	-	ProductGroup, Quantity, Weight
	PUT	ProductGroup, Quantity, Weight	HTTP Status Code
/Manufacturers/{id}/ReuseQuantity/{year}	GET	-	ProductGroup, Quantity, Weight
	PUT	ProductGroup, Quantity, Weight	HTTP Status Code
/Manufacturers/{id}/MaterialRecyclingQuantity/{year}	GET	-	ProductGroup, Quantity, Weight
	PUT	ProductGroup, Quantity, Weight	HTTP Status Code
/Manufacturers/{id}/OtherRecyclingQuantity/{year}	GET	-	ProductGroup, Quantity, Weight
	PUT	ProductGroup, Quantity, Weight	HTTP Status Code
/Manufacturers/{id}/PickUpOrders	GET	-	PickUpOrderIDs PickUpOrderHeaders
	POST	PickUpOrderHeader	HTTP Status Code
/Manufacturers/{id}/PickUpOrders/{id}	GET	-	PickUpOrderHeader, PickUpOrderBody
	PUT	PickUpOrderHeader, PickUpOrderBody	HTTP Status Code
	DELETE	-	HTTP Status Code
/Manufacturers/{id}/PickUpOrders/{id}/OutputQuantity	GET	-	ProductGroup, Quantity, Weight
	PUT	ProductGroup, Quantity, Weight	HTTP Status Code
/Manufacturers/{id}/PickUpOrders/{id}/ContainerOwner	GET	-	PartnerID
	PUT	PartnerID	HTTP Status Code
/ServiceProviders	GET	-	PartnerIDs, Names
	POST	PartnerID, Name	HTTP Status Code
/ServiceProviders/{id}	GET	-	PartnerMasterData
	PUT	PartnerMasterData	HTTP Status Code
	DELETE	-	HTTP Status Code
/ServiceProviders/{id}/RecyclingOrders	GET	-	RecyclingOrderIDs, RecyclingOrderHeaders
	POST	RecyclingOrderID, RecyclingOrderHeader	HTTP Status Code
/ServiceProviders/{id}/RecyclingOrders/{id}	GET	-	RecyclingOrderHeader, RecyclingOrderBody
	PUT	RecyclingOrderHeader, RecyclingOrderBody	HTTP Status Code
	DELETE	-	HTTP Status Code
/ServiceProviders/{id}/RecyclingOrders/{id}/ShippingNotification	GET	-	PartnerID, Location, Date, Time
	PUT	PartnerID, Location, Date, Time	HTTP Status Code
/ServiceProviders/{id}/RecyclingOrders/{id}/ReuseQuantity	GET	-	ProductGroup, Quantity, Weight
	PUT	ProductGroup, Quantity, Weight	HTTP Status Code
/ServiceProviders/{id}/RecyclingOrders/{id}/MaterialRecyclingQuantity	GET	-	ProductGroup, Quantity, Weight
	PUT	ProductGroup, Quantity, Weight	HTTP Status Code
/ServiceProviders/{id}/RecyclingOrders/{id}/OtherRecyclingQuantity	GET	-	ProductGroup, Quantity, Weight
	PUT	ProductGroup, Quantity, Weight	HTTP Status Code

Figure 22.3. REST-style SOA.

5. Evaluation and Outlook

We have presented two alternative styles for the design of SOA – the SOAP style with procedural designs similar to remote procedure calls and the REST style with loosely coupled designs similar to resources of the World Wide Web. We described a case study introducing a real-life example of a network of manufacturers and service providers. From this case we derived a set of requirements toward a SOA representing the information flows of the case study. For each architectural style we presented a concrete SOA design. We evaluated each design against the defined set of requirements. The results are summarized in Table 22.1.

Referring to research question 1, we argue that the two resulting SOA designs differ substantially. The SOAP-style design comprises only few services, which look promising at first sight. However, the

Table 22.1.   Evaluation of SOAP-style and REST-style SOA designs.

Requirement	SOAP-style design	REST-style design
Req.1 Simplicity	The overhead of SOAP and the expressiveness and variety of related WS-* standards lead to a great deal of complexity. However, good tool support is provided by major software vendors	REST leverages well-known W3C standards (esp. HTTP, URI). Infrastructure as well as client and server applications are on hand. The principle of uniform interface positively impacts simplicity
Req.2 Scalability	Specificity of interfaces requires detailed knowledge about service operations (method names, procedural structure, addressing model) and/or an enterprise service bus (ESB). Both aspects hinder scalability	Addressability, generality of interfaces, and statelessness allow for anarchic scalability [5]. Side-effect-free GET commands are cacheable
Req.3 Security	Can be provided via related standards such as HTTPS and WS-security	Can be provided via HTTPS
Req.4 Distributed and decentralized	Lack of addressability and need for ESB hinder decentralization and bi-lateral ad hoc communication	Can be accomplished due to addressability and connectedness
Req.5 Reliability	Can be provided via related standards such as WS-reliability	Only possible via HTTP status response headers. Messages can be resend if they got lost due to idempotency of GET, PUT, and DELETE
Req.6 Standardization and configurability	Standardization can be provided via XML-schema. Configurability cannot be achieved	Can be provided via schema definition. Multiple formats for one and the same representation allow for configurability of messages
Req.7 Extensibility and evolvability	Cohesion of services (as seen in the SOAP-style design) is often low as software development kits are often misused to convert existing software components into services. Low cohesion leads to tight coupling and hence to limited extensibility and evolvability	The constraint of generality of interface forces developers to build services with high cohesion and low coupling which favors extensibility and evolvability

services possess a low cohesion (i.e., low similarity between provided capabilities) and represent a more or less random collection of custom operations. The REST style comprises many services (or better resources) which are explicitly linked to each other. This might look complicated and overwhelming in the beginning, but due to the uniform and fixed interfaces of each service it leads to a much looser coupling in the end.

Considering research question 2, we conclude that while the SOAP-style architecture due to the family of related WS-* standards nicely covers the primarily technical requirements such as security and reliability, the REST-style architecture has its strengths in the more business-driven requirements such as scalability, extensibility and evolvability, and simplicity.

We presented an application scenario, consisting of a multitude of only loosely coupled partners. Transactions between the business partners are mainly reduced to exchanging messages. Here, REST-style design might compete the SOAP version due to its strengths regarding simplicity. We found out that bilateral interaction between single business partners is hard to realize in the SOAP-style implementation, which basically relies on a central instance, e.g., an enterprise service bus for transporting messages between those partners, whereas REST with its concept of addressability suits better as it, e.g., allows passing of URIs between business partners.

SOAP in contrast is more likely to be used in closely tied relationships of few business partners, which actually allows for a more tied fixture of implementation details. This includes adaptation of interfaces and their implementation in business software. So finally, if introducing SOAP as a "new protocol" into the landscape there is a debt to be discharged at creditor's domicile, which we could not find within the scenario. Categorically, a multiplicity of protocols is not desirable and there have to be strong reasons for reverting to them in our application context. That finally led us to the decision to make use of the REST-style architectural design.

Acknowledgments

This chapter was written within the context of the research projects FlexNet and ServPay, funded by the German Federal Ministry of Education and Research (BMBF), promotional references 01FD0629 and 02PG1010.

References

1. Bass, L., Clements, P. and Kazman, R. (2003) *Software Architecture in Practice*. Addison Wesley, Reading.
2. Berners-Lee, T., Fiedling, R.T. and Masinter, L. (2005) Uniform Resource Identifier (Uri): Generic Syntax, *ITEF FC 3986*.
3. Beverungen, D., Knackstedt, R. and Müller, O. (2008) Developing Service Oriented Architectures for Product-Service Systems. *Wirtschaftsinformatik* 50(3), 220–234.
4. EU (2002) *Directive 2002/96/Ec of the European Parliament and of the Council of 27 January 2003 on Waste Electrical and Electronic Equipment (Weee)*, European Parliament.
5. Fiedling, R.T. (2000) *Architectural Styles and the Design of Network-Based Software Architectures*. University of California, Irvine.
6. Fielding, R., Irvine, U.C., Gettys, J., Mogul, J., Frystyk Nielsen, H., Masinter, L., Leach, P. and Berners-Lee, T. (1999) [Rfc2616] *Hypertext Transfer Protocol – Http/1.1*.
7. Pautasso, C., Zimmermann, O. and Leymann, F. (2008) Restful Web Services Vs. "Big" Web Services: Making the Right Architectural Decision. *Proceedings of the 17th International World Wide Web Conference*. Bejing, China (to appear).
8. Perry, D.E. and Wolf, A.L. (1992) Foundations for the Study of Software Architecture. *Software Engineering Notes* 17(4), 40–52.
9. Prescod, P. (2002) Roots of the Rest/Soap Debate. *Proceedings of the Extreme Markup Languages 2002 Conferences*. Quebec, Canada.
10. Richardson, L. and Ruby, S. (2007) *Restful Web Services*. O'Reilly, Sebastopol, CA.
11. Vargo, S.L. and Lusch, R.F. (2008) Service-Dominant Logic: Continuing the Evolution. *Journal of the Academy of Marketing Science* 36(1), 1–10.
12. Yin, R.K. (2003) *Case Study Research – Design and Methods*. SAGE Publications, Thousands Oaks, London, New Delhi.
13. zur Muehlen, M., Nickerson, J.V. and Swenson, K.D. (2005) Developing Web Services Choreography Standards – the Case of Rest Vs. Soap. *Decision Support Systems* 40, 9–29.

23

A Method for Transforming Existing Web Service Descriptions into an Enhanced Semantic Web Service Framework

Xiaofeng Du, William Song and Malcolm Munro

Abstract

Web Services as a new distributed system technology has been widely adopted by industries in the areas, such as enterprise application integration (EAI), business process management (BPM), and virtual organisation (VO). However, lack of semantics in the current Web Service standards has been a major barrier in service discovery and composition. In this chapter, we propose an enhanced context-based semantic service description framework (CbSSDF+) that tackles the problem and improves the flexibility of service discovery and the correctness of generated composite services. We also provide an agile transformation method to demonstrate how the various formats of Web Service descriptions on the Web can be managed and renovated step by step into CbSSDF+ based service description without large amount of engineering work. At the end of the chapter, we evaluate the applicability of the transformation method and the effectiveness of CbSSDF+ through a series of experiments.

Keywords Web Services · Semantic Web Services · Service description · Service context

1. Introduction

In the last decade, Web Services has become an important research topic in the fields of service-oriented architecture (SOA) [8] and grid computing [7]. Web Services as a new distributed system technology has been widely adopted by industries in the areas, such as enterprise application integration (EAI), business process management (BPM), and virtual organisations (VO). With an exponential increase of services available on the Web, it has is becoming an extremely difficult task than ever to timely find a service that fits well to a user's requirements without automating the process of service discovery and composition. The problem of automation is twofold: a formal representation for services such that service comparison and matching could be done more precisely and efficiently and a powerful expressiveness of a service description framework such that richer semantic description for services is introduced and less semantic loss occurs during service construction and organisation. To overcome the problem, an emerging research area, Semantic Web Services, has gained considerable attention as a most promising way towards achieving automatic service discovery and composition. Semantic Web Services combine the Semantic Web and Web Service technologies to make a service description understandable not only by humans but also by computer software [12].

Enormous research efforts on Semantic Web Services have been spent on, from service description [11, 2, 6], service discovery [10, 13, 14], to service composition [1, 4]. In our previous work [5], we proposed a

Xiaofeng Du, William Song and Malcolm Munro • Computer Science Department, University of Durham, Durham, NC, USA.

G.A. Papadopoulos et al. (eds.), *Information Systems Development*, DOI 10.1007/b137171_23,

context-based semantic service description framework (CbSSDF) and a two-step service discovery mechanism to improve the flexibility of service discovery and the correctness of generated composite services. In this chapter, we propose an enhanced CbSSDF (CbSSDF+) that can address more sufficient context information in service descriptions. The context addressed in CbSSDF+ is the information that can help to understand the usage of a service and the relationships with other services. We call it service usage context. Two levels of service usage context have been addressed in CbSSDF+: the conceptual service usage context and the instance service usage context. Through these two levels of service usage context, service discovery can be flexibly carried out based on not only precisely defined technical requirements but also imprecisely described business scenarios, and the service composition process can be more effective and efficient.

However, no matter how good a new service description framework is and how well it can solve the problems of Web Services, if it does not provide a sound method to manage the existing services and their descriptions, its applicability will be limited. Currently, most of the enterprises and organisations have their own Web Services already in use and those services have been described using WSDL or other description methods. It is unrealistic to convert the existing service descriptions into a new framework manually because an overwhelming engineering work would greatly hinder use of a new service description framework. In this chapter, we provide an agile transformation method to demonstrate how the various formats of Web Service descriptions on the Web can be managed and renovated step by step into CbSSDF+ based description without large amount of engineering work. We run a series of experiments to examine the applicability of the proposed transformation method on different formats of Web Service descriptions and the effectiveness of CbSSDF+ through comparison with OWL-S.

The rest of this chapter is organised as follows: in Section 2, we give an overview of CbSSDF+. In Section 3, we give a detailed discussion on the transformation method. In Section 4, we evaluate our work through a series of experiments to examine the applicability of the transformation method and the effectiveness of CbSSDF+. Finally, the summary and future work are given in Section 5.

2. Enhanced CbSSDF (CbSSDF+)

To fully describe a service, we must address how a service interacts with the outside world. In our work, such relationships (interactions) between a service and the outside world, called service usage context (SUC), are defined at two levels. At the conceptual level, SUC defines the conceptual relationships between a service concept and other service concepts and business entities, such as users, service providers and other business-application-related concepts. At the instance level, SUC defines the interactions between a service and other services at runtime, i.e. the composability between services. The reason to define the SUC is that each service is not only a self-contained functional component, itself but also other services are often linked together to form a complex, composite service to fulfil complex requirements. Such potential relationships between services at the conceptual level represent the potential scenarios that services can participate, which can help service discovery to be more flexible and effective. When end users are looking for services, more often than not, they already have some usage scenarios in their mind for the required services, but not their technical details, such as input or output data types. If the conceptual relationships between services are addressed in each service's description, a service search engine can locate services approximately using end users' usage scenarios rather than directly asking for providing technical details of required services. The technical details of required services can be provided later to refine the service discovery result. On the other hand, the instantial relationships between services are represented by service composability. Such service composability information can reduce a service composition engine's candidate services for planning a composite service and, therefore, improve the efficiency of service composition process.

Based on the idea of service usage context discussed above and our previous work [5], we propose an enhanced context-based semantic service description framework (CbSSDF+) to bridge between service requirements and technical service descriptions and improve the flexibility and efficiency of service discovery and composition. CbSSDF+ contains two main components that are building up virtually two layers in a service description.

The component in the higher layer is a set of service conceptual graphs (S-CGs) that describes the conceptual relationships between services. Each S-CG can be considered as a formally defined scenario in which a service or a group of services participate. S-CGs are represented using the conceptual graphs formalism [15]. Because S-CGs are conceptual descriptions of service usage scenarios, they can be used to interpret end users' service usage scenarios and approximately locate relevant services. The set of S-CGs is a realisation of the conceptual level SUC. Let T be an ontology and $\Re$ be a set of relations between the concepts in T; and S-CG is an extended simple conceptual graph [15], defined as follows:

Definition 1. An S-CG is a 5-tuple (T_c, C, R, E, ID), where

- T_1: A set of concepts in T,
- $C = \{c_1, c_2, \ldots, c_n\}$: A set of concept nodes that are related to the described services and their interactive business entities (for a concept node $c_1, c_i \in c$, type $(c_i) \in T_1$, where $type()$ is a function that returns the concept of c_i),
- $-R = \{r_1, r_2, \ldots, r_n\}$: A set of relation nodes that represent the conceptual relations between concept nodes in an S-CG (for a relation node r_i, $r_i \in R$, $type(r_i) \in \Re$, where $type()$ is a function that returns the relation of a relation node),
- E: A set of directed arcs that connect the relation nodes and the concept nodes in an S-CG,
- ID: A set of service IDs that identify the corresponding Web Services to an S-CG.

A single S-CG may not be able to address a complex scenario, however, the joinable feature of S-CGs enable them to be able to join together to form complex scenarios to match with complex user requirements. Once an S-CG or a joined S-CG is matched with a user's scenario, then the S-CG's corresponding Web Services are the relevant services to the scenario. An S-CG example represented using the graphical notation of the conceptual graphs [15] is given in Fig. 23.1. It demonstrates a usage scenario that involves a "Parcel Delivery" service and an "Address Lookup" service.

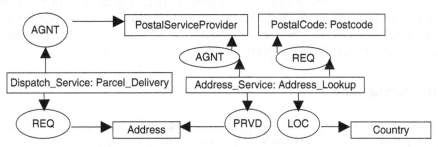

Figure 23.1. An S-CG example.

The component in the lower layer is called semantic service description model (SSDM) that provides enriched semantic description of a service's capabilities. The information of a service provided in SSDM includes input and output data types and concepts, pre- and post-conditions, service internal structure, service concept, service metadata, and binding information. Furthermore, an important part of SSDM is a set of common usage pattern (CUPs) that is used to realise the instance level SUC. A CUP defines a way that a service can be used through a given set of services that can directly interact with the service to achieve a potential task or a part of a potential task. The direct interaction means that a service provides input data required by the described service or consumes output data from the described service. A set of CUPs associated with a service collectively represents the composability of the service with other services. As CUPs only consider the composability between services, not the meaning of the compositions, the potential task that a CUP tries to achieve may or may not exist in real business. However, no matter the potential task is real or not, the information provided in CUPs can help a service composition engine to efficiently construct composite services by reducing the number of candidate service in planning processes.

The composability between two services is represented by a service link. A service link is a directed relation that links a service input with a service output. The establishment of a service link is depending on a set of basic attributes of services. The service basic attributes that are essential for composing services are input parameters (*in*), output parameters (*out*), pre-conditions (*p*), and effects (*e*). Formally, a service link is defined as follows:

Definition 2. Let s_i, and s_j be two services. A service link between s_i and s_j is a directed relation that links one of s_i's output, $s_i.out_i$, to one of s_j's input, $s_j.in_i$, denoted as l $(s_i, s_j, s_i.out_i, s_j.in_i)$, and it satisfies the following conditions:

– $Sim(s_i.out_i, s_j.in_i) > 0$, where $Sim()$ is a semantic similarity function to compute the semantic distance between $s_i.out_i$ and $s_j.in_i$. The returned value of it is within range [0, 1] to indicate the similarity degree.
– $Comp(s_i.out_i, s_j.in_i) > 0$, where $Comp()$ is a compatibility function to determine whether $s_i.out_i$ and $s_j.in_i$ are data type compatible. The returned value of it is within range [0, 1] to indicate the compatibility degree.
– $Satisfy(s_i.e, s_j.p) = true$, where $Satisfy()$ is a Boolean function that determines whether $s_j.p$ can be satisfied by $s_i.e$.

By having the definition of service link, a CUP can be defined as below.

Definition 3. For a given service s, its CUP is a binary $(S, £)$, where:

– S: A set of services that can directly interact with s.
– $\mathcal{L}$: A set of service links that describes how the services in S are linked with s.

The number of services $|S|$ in a CUP is not greater than the summation of the number of inputs and the number of outputs of s. If $s \in S$, it means that s can be invoked by itself. A CUP only describes the relationships between a service and its direct interacting services. However, the indirect relationships can be derived from other services' CUPs. A CUP can be considered as a segment of a business process. Service composition is to construct suitable business process. Assembling segments of business process in the service composition process is much more efficient than assembling individual services. CUPs of a service also tell a service composition engine which services can interact with the service. Therefore, the engine does not need to consider the services that are not addressed in CUPs.

3. Transformation Method

Web Services as a new distributed computing technology has been around for a long while. Many enterprises and organisations have adopted Web Services as one of their crucial technologies in enterprise application integration, business intelligence, and data integration, etc. The existing services have been described differently using the available frameworks, for example, WSDL and OWL-S. To allow an enterprise or organisation using a newly proposed service description framework without affecting their existing service operations, a sound transformation method is needed. In this section, we propose an agile method that transforms the existing Web Service descriptions into CbSSDF+ based service descriptions. This method uses a bottom-up approach that gradually collects and fills the information of a service required by CbSSDF+. The method has three steps: (1) the ontology-based service classifying step, (2) the CUPs generating step, and (3) the S-CGs generating step.

3.1. Step One: Ontology-Based Service Classification

Suppose we have a service ontology $\mathcal{O}$ that contains all the concepts that are relevant to a specific business domain's services, the classification process can be performed based on $\mathcal{O}$. Each concept in $\mathcal{O}$ has a set of data properties that are corresponding to some of the information addressed in SSDM, such as inputs, outputs, and metadata. Each data property has a set of keywords that are used to match with the information contained in a Web Service's current description to classify the service. For example, for a weather service concept, its name property may contain keywords, such as "weather", "weather forecast", and "weather report". Several vector-based methods proposed in the literatures [3, 9, 17] can be applied here for similarity measurement and ontology-based classification. Once a service is associated to a service concept, the best matched keywords in each data property of the concept will remain as a part of the SSDM description of the service. The classification process obeys the "least concept first" rule, which means that if a service is associated to both a service concept and its super-concept, then the super-concept association will be removed.

How much information can be acquired for existing service descriptions is heavily depending on the type of the descriptions. A WSDL-based description can provide some basic information, such as service name, inputs and outputs data types and concepts, through some meaningfully defined tags, for example, "<*wsdl*:operation name = "GetLatestWeather">". If a service's WSDL document is accompanied with a natural language description, more information can be gained. Nowadays, as the Semantic Web Service technologies are becoming mature, some organisations provide semantically annotated Web Service descriptions, such as MINDSWAP,[1] which provides a list of Web Services described using OWL-S. The semantically annotated service descriptions can make the classification more accurate.

3.2. Step Two: CUPs generation

Let $S = \{s_1, s_2, \ldots, s_n\}$ be a set of services that have been classified using $\mathcal{O}$. According to the service link definition, a set of graphs can be generated by linking services using service links. These graphs represent the composability between the services in S. We call them instance services graphs. Formally, an instance services graph is defined as follows:

Definition 4. An instance services graph is a directed graph denoted as $G = <V, E>$, where

- $V = \{s_1, s_2, \ldots, s_m\}$: is a set of instance services, $V \subseteq S$.
- $E = \{l\,(s_1, s_2, s_1.out_i, s_2.in_i), l\,(s_2, s_3, s_2.out_i, s_3.in_i), \ldots, l\,(s_i, s_j, s_i.out_i, s_j.in_i)\}$: is a set of service links.
- Loops in E are allowed, e.g. $l\,(s_i, s_i, s_i\,out_i, s_i\,in_i)$ means that s_i is repeatedly invoked until the desired condition is met.

The smallest instance services graph can be just one vertex, it means that the service in the graph cannot be composed with other services, but works individually.

After the services in S are connected into instance services graphs, the CUPs of each service in these graphs can be generated based on the service links in the graphs. Let s_i be a service in an instance services graph. Its CUP candidate services are the services that have service links with s_i. The CUPs of s_i can be a combination of the services that are connected to each of the inputs and outputs of s_i. Let N_{in} be the number of the inputs of s_i, N_{out} be the number of the outputs of s_i, the number of CUPs of s_i is

$$N_{CUP} = \prod_{k=1}^{N_{in}} I_k \prod_{h=1}^{N_{out}} O_h$$

where I_k is the number of services connected to the kth input of s_i, and O_h is the number of services connected to the hth output of s_i.

3.3. Step Three: S-CGs Generation

To generate S-CGs, we first replace the instance services in the instance services graphs with their associated service concepts that are allocated in step one. If two services s_i and s_j in an instance services

---

[1] http://www.mindswap.org/2004/owl-s/services.shtml

graph have been replaced with the same service concept, we say these two services are equivalent services, written as $s_i = s_j$. Let s_k be another service in the same instance services graph, if $s_i = s_j$, then $l\,(s_i, s_k)$ and $l\,(s_j, s_k)$ are equivalent service links. Here, we ignore which input or output of s_k, s_i, and s_j are actually connected to because it does not affect the conceptual relationship between services. Now, if we merge all the vertexes with the same service concepts and all the edges with the equivalent service links in all the instance services graphs, we can get a set of service concepts graphs. However, in a service concepts graph, the edges between nodes are not service links anymore. They are the conceptual relationships between service concepts. Service conceptual relationships are depending on individual business domain. Suppose, we have a set of pre-defined service conceptual relations $\mathcal{R}$ for a specific business domain, a labelling function $\mathcal{R}()$ can be defined to label the edges in a service concepts graph with conceptual relations by giving a pair of service concepts, i.e. $\mathcal{R}(sc_i, sc_j) \in \mathcal{R}$. Finally, to get S-CGs, we need to replace $\mathcal{R}(sc_i, sc_j)$ with relation nodes that can be generated based on $\mathcal{R}(sc_i, sc_j)$. Some extra concept nodes may also be generated according to $\mathcal{R}(sc_i, sc_j)$ and the participated services' inputs and outputs.

By converting instance services graphs into S-CGs, we can see that the composability between instance services has a significant impact on the relationships between service concepts. In other words, the low-level instance services determine which kind of business services that an enterprise can provide. If there are mismatches between instance service links and their corresponding service conceptual relations, it means that either the enterprise has proposed some business services that cannot be achieved by their instance services or the enterprise has the potential to provide more business services than what they have already provided.

3.4. An Illustrative Example

Suppose we have four services: an "Address Lookup" service, an "Address Finder" service, a "Route Planner" service, and a "Delivery" service, that are described using WSDL plus natural language descriptions. The reason for choosing WSDL plus natural language-described services as examples is that WSDL plus natural language is the most popular approach to describe Web Services at moment. After analysing "<wsdl: types>", "<wsdl: message>", "<wsdl: operation>", and "<wsdl: service>" tags in the example services' WSDL documents and applying the ontology-based classification methods [3, 9, 17], we can get the following information shown in Table 23.1.

As WSDL-based service descriptions do not provide pre- and post-condition information, we need to analyse the natural language descriptions of each example service to find relevant information. For

Table 23.1. Acquired information from WSDL and ontology-based classification.

Web Services	Service concept	Inputs	Outputs
Address Lookup (s_1)	Address_Service	Input1: Data Type: String Concept: ZipCode	Output1: Data Type: String Concept: Address
Address Finder (s_2)	Address_Service	Input1: Data Type: String Concept: Postcode	Output1: Data Type: String Concept: Address
Route Planner (s_3)	Travel_Helper	Input1: Data Type: String Concept: Address Input2: Data Type: String Concept: Address	Output1: Data Type: String Concept: Route Plan
Delivery (s_4)	Dispatch_Service	Input1: Data Type: String Concept: Address	Output1: Data Type: Boolean Concept: Delivery Status

example, a part of the "Delivery" service's description is "only delivers to a UK address". Based on this information, a pre-condition for the "Delivery" service is *Address.Country* = UK. All these four services have no internal structures because they are atomic services.

The second step is to generate CUPs. First, we need to determine service links between services based on the services' inputs, outputs, pre-conditions, and post-conditions. In our example, five service links are established: $l(s_2, s_4, s_2.out_1, s_4.in_1), l(s_1, s_3, s_1.out_1, s_3.in_1), l(s_1, s_3, s_1.out_1, s_3.in_2), l(s_2, s_3, s_2.out_1, s_3.in_1)$, and $l(s_2, s_3, s_2.out_1, s_3.in_2)$. The services are then connected into an instance services graph, which is shown below:

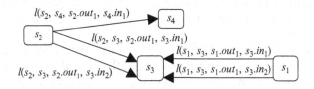

Figure. 23.2. The generated instance services graph.

From the instance services graph, we obtain the CUPs of each service through the service links of each service. For example, s_2's CUPs are $<\{s4\}, \{ l (s_2, s_4, s_2.out_1, s_4.in_1)\}>$, $<\{s3\}, \{ l (s_2, s_3, s_2.out_1, s_3.in_1)\}>$, and $<\{s3\}, \{ l (s_2, s_3, s_2.out_1, s_3.in_2)\}>$.

The last step is to convert the instance services graph into S-CG. We first replace the services with their service concepts in the graph and merge the same service concepts and the equivalent service links, then label the edges with domain-specific conceptual relations to get a service concepts graph, see Fig. 23.3.

Figure 23.3. The generated service concepts graph.

Finally, based on the labels of the service concepts graph and semantics of participated services' inputs and outputs, an S-CG can be generated as below:

Figure 23.4. The generated S-CG.

4. Evaluation

To evaluate our work, we perform two series of experiments. The first series of experiments is to examine the applicability of the transformation method on different types of service description (in our experiments, we apply our method on service descriptions in WSDL, WSDL with additional natural language, and OWL-S). The second series of experiments is to evaluate the accuracy and performance of the CbSSDF+ based service discovery.

In the first series of experiments, we choose three groups of services that are described differently using WSDL, WSDL with additional natural language, and OWL-S. Each group has 500 sample services. The metrics of the experiments is the average percentage of how much the information required by CbSSDF+ can be filled in by performing the transformation method from different types of service descriptions. The results show that the WSDL-based description only provides, averagely, one-third of the required information through the transformation method, and the WSDL with additional natural language provides nearly 60%, whereas the OWL-S-based description doubles that of the WSLD-based description by reaching nearly 75% of the required information. The proposed CbSSDF+ is a semantic richer service description framework and this is no existing service description that provides 100% of the required information. The results indicate that the transformation method is applicable to different types of service descriptions, although some types of service descriptions may need more manual manipulation after the transformation method.

In the second series of experiments, we select OWL-S as the existing service description framework to compare with CbSSDF+ in order to examine the CbSSDF+ based service discovery's accuracy and performance. We have created 2000 Web Services and deployed on a server. Among these 2000 services, a half of them are described in OWL-S, and the other half is described in CbSSDF+. The WSDL2OWL-S tool [16] is used to generate the OWL-S-based service descriptions and the OWL-S/UDDI Matchmaker and Client API [16] is used to implement a simple service searching interface. We also developed an experimental prototype that implements the two-step service discovery mechanism [5], called Service-Comp, for service discovery and composition.

We first evaluate the accuracy of the service discovery by comparing the results returned from the *ServiceComp* and the OWL-S-based service searching interface. The accuracy of the result is measured by precision and recall. Precision is used to measure the retrieved services that are relevant to a user's need. Recall is used to measure the services that are relevant to the query and that are successfully retrieved. Let A be a set of relevant services in the service repository, B be a set of retrieved services from the service repository, the precision and recall can be calculated as below:

$$Precision = \frac{|A \cap B|}{|B|}, Recall = \frac{|A \cap B|}{|A|}$$

The precision–recall curves in Fig. 23.5 shows that the CbSSDF+ based approach significantly improves the accuracy of the search result in comparison with the OWL-S-based approach. During the experiments, we observed that a large number of attribute fields provided in the OWL-S-based search interface remained empty by the participated users because they have no idea how to fill in them. This is one of the reasons that the OWL-S approach offers lower accuracy because the search engine lacks sufficient information to precisely locate services. By using the two-step service

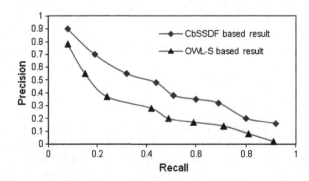

Figure 23.5. Precision-Recall curves.

discovery mechanism, the users can provide more detailed information. The CbSSDF+ based approach can produce better result is also because CbSSDF+ provides richer service description, especially considering the service usage context, so that the search engine can have more evidence to identify services.

The performance of the system is evaluated based on the time for returning search results. We compare the first-step search, the second-step search, and the overall search result returning time of the two-step service discovery mechanism with the OWL-S-based approach, see Fig. 23.6. The figure illustrates that the speed of the first-step search and the overall search is slower than the OWL-S-based approach. This is due to the complexity of the graph matching algorithm. However, the second step is much faster than the OWL-S-based approach because after the first step, only the relevant services are passed to the second step, thus the search space is relatively small. Although the overall performance of our approach is slower than OWL-S-based approach, it is compensated by high accuracy service discovery results.

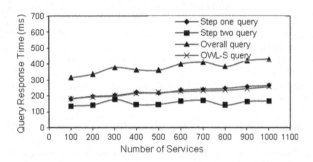

Figure 23.6. Query response time for performing on the centralised service repository.

5. Conclusion

As Web Service technology has been adopted widely and the number of Web Services is increasing exponentially, it is no more feasible for people to search and manage services manually without any automation. Due to lack of semantics, the current Web Service standards have limited the realisation of automatic service discovery and composition. To overcome the problem, an emerging research area, so called Semantic Web Services, has gained considerable attention. A number of Semantic Web Service frameworks have been proposed, such as WSDL-S [2] and OWL-S. In this chapter, based on service usage context (SUC) and our previous work, we propose an enhanced context-based semantic service description framework (CbSSDF+) that addresses not only richer semantics of services but also the interrelationships between services, which can help to generate accurate service discovery result and improve service composition efficiency.

We also propose a transformation method that can gradually transform existing Web Service descriptions into CbSSDF+ based descriptions without large amount of engineering work. The evaluation results show that the transformation method is applicable to majority of current service description frameworks and the CbSSDF+ based approach can significantly improve service discovery accuracy in comparison with OWL-S. The performance of our approach is not ideal; however, it is compensated by the accurate service discovery results.

Our work is only implemented by an experimental prototype. In our future work, we are going to fully implement the framework and the transformation method and propose a comprehensive evaluation model to evaluate our work.

References

1. Agarwal, S., Handschuh, S., and Staab, S. (2005) Annotation, Composition and Invocation of Semantic Web Services. Journal of Web Semantics 2(1).
2. Akkiraju, R., Farrell, J., Miller, J., Nagarajan, M., Schmidt, M., Sheth, A., and Verma, K. (2005) Web Service Semantics – WSDL-S, A joint UGA-IBM Tchnical Note, version 1.2, Appril 18, 2005, http://lsdis.cs.uga.edu/projects/METEOR-S/WSDL-S
3. Berry, M. W., Drmac, Z., and Jessup, E. R. (1999) Matrices, Vector Spaces, and Information Retrieval. SIAM Review 41(2), (Jun. , 1999), 335–362.
4. Du, X., Song, W., and Munro, M. (2006) Using Common Process Patterns for Semantic Web Services Composition, to appear in *Proc.* of 15th International Conference on Information System Development (ISD2006), Budapest, Hungary, Aug. 31 – Sept. 2, 2006
5. Du, X., Song, W., and Munro M. (2007) Semantic Service Description Framework for Addressing Imprecise Service Requirements, in Proc. of 16th International Conference on Information System Development (ISD2007), Galway, Ireland, Aug. 29–31, 2007.
6. Fensel, D. and Bussler, C. (2002) The Web Service Modeling Framework WSMF. Electronic Commerce Research and Applications 1(2), Summer 2002, 113–137.
7. Foster, I., Kesselman, C., and uecke, S. (2001) The Anatomy of the Grid: Enabling Scalable Virtual Organizations. International J. Supercomputer Applications 15(3).
8. Huhns, M. N. and Singh, M. P. (2005) Service Oriented Computing: Key Concepts and Principles. IEEE Intelligent System January–February 2005, 75–81.
9. Joachims, T. (1998) Text Categorization with Support Vector Machines: Learning with Many Relevant Features. European Conf. Mach. Learning, ECML98, Apr. 1998.
10. Ludwig, S. and Reyhani, S. (2005) Semantic Approach to Service Discovery in a Grid Environment. Journal of Web Semantics 3(4).
11. Martin, D., Burstein, M., Hobbs, J., Lassila, O., McDermott, D., Mcllraith, S., Narayanan, S., Paolucci, M., Parsia, B., Payne, T., Sirin, E., Srinivasan, N., and Sycara, K. (2004) OWL-S: Semantic Mark-up for Web Services, http://www.daml.org/services/owl-s/1.0/owl-s.html
12. McIlraith, S., Son, T.C., and Zeng, H. (2001) Semantic Web Services. IEEE Intelligent System Special Issue Semantic Web 16(2), 46–53.
13. Paolucci, M., Sycara, K., and Kawamuwa, T. (2003) Delivering Semantic Web Services, in Proceedings of WWW2003, pp. 829–836, May 20–24, 2003, Budapest, Hungary.
14. Song, W. and Li, X. (2005) A Conceptual Modeling Approach to Virtual Organizations in the Grid to appear in Proceedings of GCC2005. Zhuge, H. and Fox, G.C. (eds.) Springer LNCS 3795, pp. 382–393.
15. Sowa, J. F. (1984) Conceptual Structures: Information Processing in Mind and Machine, Addison-Wesley, Canada.
16. Srinivasan, N., Paolucci, M., and Sycara, K. (2006) Semantic Web Service Discovery in the OWL-S IDE. Proceedings of the 39th Annual Hawaii International Conference on System Sciences. Hawaii, 2006.
17. Xu, B., Wang, Y., Zhang, P., and Li, J. (2005) Proceedings of the 2005 IEEE International Workshop on Service-Oriented System Engineering (SOSE'05).

24

An Extensible ADL for Service-Oriented Architectures

R. Bashroush and I. Spence

Abstract

While architecture description languages (ADLs) have gained wide acceptance in the research community as a means of describing system designs, the uptake within the service-oriented architecture (SOA) domain has been slower than might have been expected. A contributory cause may be the perceived lack of flexibility and, as yet, the limited tool support. This chapter describes ALI, a new ADL that aims to address these deficiencies by providing a rich, extensible and flexible syntax for describing component and service interface types and the use of patterns and meta-information. These enhanced capabilities are intended to encourage more widespread ADL usage.

Keywords Architecture description languages · Service-oriented architectures

1. Introduction

In recent years, architecture description languages (ADL) have emerged as potential tools for formally describing system architectures at a reasonably high level which enables better intellectual control over the system [1]. ADLs model not only system structure, but also address component behavior specification as well as communication protocols. While some ADLs provide graphical notations (e.g. boxes and lines), others also provide textual notations.

Architecture descriptions can also be used as a communication vehicle among the different stakeholders. With the formality introduced by ADLs to the architecture description, more architectural analysis of qualities such as consistency, modifiability and performance can be carried out on the system at an early stage. Although it is not clear yet what aspects of the architecture should be included or excluded from the architecture description (e.g. behavior, structure, interfaces), it is widely agreed within the ADL community that software architecture is a set of components (or services) and the connections among them conforming to a set of constraints.

Although some ADLs have been put to industrial use [2], the majority of ADLs have not scaled up and remain confined to small-scale case studies. Yet, little adoption of ADLs has been witnessed within the SOA domain. A number of potential limitations demonstrated by current ADLs were identified in previous work [3]. Among these limitations are over constraining syntax, single view presentation of the architecture and lack of tool support. The ALI ADL has been designed to address these limitations. The rationale behind the ALI notation was discussed in [3]. Among the main concepts driving the ALI notation are flexible interface description, architectural pattern description, formal syntax for capturing meta-information and linking the feature and architecture spaces. ALI built on our experience with the ADLARS [4]

R. Bashroush and I. Spence • ECIT, Queen's University of Belfast, Belfast, UK.

G.A. Papadopoulos et al. (eds.), *Information Systems Development*, DOI 10.1007/b137171_24,

ADL and adopted many of the solution space provided by ADLARS such as its support for software product lines.

In this chapter, we introduce the different parts of the ALI notation to show how the goals of [3] are realized in the language. ALI comprises seven parts:

1. *meta types*, which provides a notation for capturing meta-information
2. *interface types*, which provides a notation for creating types of interfaces
3. *connector types*, where architectural connectors are defined
4. *component types*, where architectural components are defined
5. *pattern templates*, where design patterns are defined
6. *features*, where the system features are catalogued
7. *system*, where the system architecture is described

In the following sections, the different parts of the ALI notation are discussed. Section 9 concludes with a discussion.

2. Meta Types

Meta types provide a formal syntax for capturing (meta-)information related to the architecture. A meta type is defined by the information it contains. The information is captured within fields, where each field has a data type (text, number, etc.) and a name (*tag*). Consider the example below for defining a meta type called *MyMetaType1*:

```
meta type MyMetaType1 {
    tag creator, description: text;
    tag cost, version: number;
    tag edited* : date; }
```

In this example, the keyword "`meta type`" is used to start a meta type definition. `MyMetaType1` is the name of the meta type being specified. Each meta type contains a number of tags which can be either textual, numeral or date (if needed, the tag types could be extended to include enumeration, character, etc.). In the example above, five tags are defined: two textual, two numeral and one date. The date tag "*edited*" is marked with an asterisk "*" to indicate an optional tag.

Once meta types are specified, *meta objects* conforming to these types can then be created throughout the architecture. These meta objects are attached to architectural elements (e.g. components, connectors) to provide a corner for appending additional information related to these elements. Below is an example meta object that conforms to the meta type given in the example above.

```
meta: MyMetaType1 {
    creator: "John Smith";
    cost: 5,000;
    version: 1;
    edited: 12-02-2006;
    description: "A GUI component ... "; }
```

A meta object could also conform to more than one meta type. It is also possible to create meta objects that do not conform to any meta type. This enhances the language flexibility. However, little automated analysis can be done over such informally provided information.

The formal specification of meta-information would considerably enhance the development of CASE tool support that could harness these meta objects and conduct automated analysis on the data (e.g., cost/

benefit analysis, project timing/scheduling, based on what meta-information is available). Other meta-information might include design decisions, component compatibility, etc., which, when extracted and formatted using proper CASE tools, allow automated architecture documentation to be achieved on the fly.

In general, it is expected that the meta types will be created once and used repeatedly within different systems developed by the same enterprise. A standard set of information required (tags) may be first identified by the project management team (or any other stakeholder), and then provided to architects to conform to. This insures that critical information is always provided within an architecture description. The flexible syntax also allows the architects to augment this information with fields (tags) that they may need temporarily or internally within the architecture team.

3. Interface Types

Interface types have been introduced to ALI to allow for the usage of multiple interfaces within a system description. The practice would be to create a set of common interface types needed within an application domain once (e.g., WSDL, IDL, Invocation), and then use these interfaces in the design of components and systems.

The interface type definition is divided into two sections:

- *Syntax definition*, where the syntax of the interface description is specified using a subset of the JavaCC [5] notation.
- *Constraints*, where the interface binding (connectivity) constraints are specified. These include
  - *Should match*: Here the terms (identified in the syntax definition section using the JavaCC notation) that should match between two interfaces to be considered compatible (allowed to bind) are identified. For example, in a functional interface, for two interfaces to be compatible, the function names and argument types should match.
  - *Protocols supported*: A list of the protocols that this interface type can support for communication is provided, e.g., IIOP, HTTP, method invocation.
  - *Allow multiple bindings*: This is a Boolean value that states whether multiple binding is allowed on this interface. For example, this property is set to true on a server socket interface to allow for binding multiple client socket interfaces. On the other hand, it is set to false on the client socket interface.
  - *Factory*: This is a Boolean value that states whether the interface is a factory. A factory interface means that when a connection request is received on this interface, a new connection dedicated interface is created to handle that particular request while the main interface continues to listen to new incoming requests. For example, server socket interfaces in java are factories. On the other hand, C++ sockets are not. In C++, the factory functionality is to be implemented by the programmer if needed.
  - *Persistent*: This is a Boolean value which when set to true indicates a persistent interface (the internal data of the interface component are kept unchanged after the current connection has ended) and when set to false indicates a transient interface (internal data are reset to initial values when the current connection is terminated).

Below is an example for defining an interface type *functional*:

```
interface type functional {
  syntax definition:    {
    "Provided" ":"    "{"
      [ "function"    <PROV_FUNCTION_NAME>
          "{"
              "impLanguage"    ":"
```

```
                              <PROV_LANGUAGE_NAME> ";"

                "innvocation"  ":"
                              <PROV_INVOCATION> ";"
                "paramterlist" ":"
                  "("[  <PROV_PARAMETER_TYPE> [","
                   <PROV_PARAMETER_TYPE:]* ]? ")" ";"
             "return type"  ":"
                      <PROV_RETURN_TYPE> ";"
          "}"]*    "}"
          // Required:  etc.
      }
  constraints:  {
     should match: {
     PROV_INVOCATION_NAME,
     PROV_PARAMETER_TYPE
             }
     protocols supported: {  RMI-IIOP, JRMP }
     allow multiple bindings: false;
     factory: false;
     persistent: false;
   }
 }
```

For further details about the notation used for specifying the interface syntax, please refer to JavaCC [5].

It is important to emphasize here that the interface type definition is not meant to be read by humans, but rather created once and then read by CASE tools that would verify the interface descriptions and bindings made throughout the architecture definition.

4. Connector Types

As in Acme [6] and other ADLs, connectors are considered first-class citizens in ALI.

Below is a simple example of a connector type definition:

```
connector type SOAP/HTTP {
    interfaces {
        a, b of type WSDL;
    }
    layout {
        if (supported(FULL_DUPLEX_FEATURE))
            connect a and b;
        else
            connect a to b;
    }
}
```

The connector type definition consists of two parts:

- *interfaces*: Where the connector interfaces are defined. These resemble the input/output terminals of the connector. A connector must have at least two interfaces (for input/output) while theoretically there is no restriction on the maximum number of interfaces allowed. For example, a bus connector would need to have a number of bi-directional interfaces to serve all components connected to the bus. On the other hand, a simple connector like the one in the example above has only two interfaces (of type WSDL, where WSDL is an interface type that should be defined in the interface type section).

- *layout*: The layout section describes the internal configuration of the connector. It shows how the connector interfaces are connected internally, that is, how the traffic travels internally from one interface to another. There are two types of configurations allowed between connector interfaces:
  - *unidirectional connections (to)*: Which specify that the data/requests received on one interface to be output on another interface. This is done using the keywords: "connect" and "to". For example, connect a to b; outputs the data/requests received on the *a* interface to the *b* interface.
  - *bi-directional connection (and)*: Which specify that the data/requests received on one interface be output on another interface and vice versa. This is done using the keywords: "connect" and "and". For example, connect a and b; outputs the data/requests received on the *a* interface to the *b* interface and vice versa. The keyword "all" can be used to connect a connector interface to all other interfaces of the connector using a bi-directional or unidirectional communication as described above. For example, connect a to all makes the input on interface *a* available as output on all other interfaces of the connector. In contrast, connect a and all makes the input on *a* available on all other interfaces and the input on all other interfaces available on *a*. The statement: connect all to all can be used to create bi-directional connections among all ports (connect all and all is not defined).

As with interface types and meta types, a set of connector types can be defined per domain which can then be reused across multiple projects within that domain.

In the example given above, the connector definition is linked to the system feature model to allow for connector customization based on features selected. This is done using the if /else structure and the keywords "supported /unsupported." So, in the example above, if the system supports the FULL_ DUPLEX_FEATURE, interfaces *a* and *b* are connected as bi-directional (using "and"); otherwise, they are connected as unidirectional (using "to"). This syntax introduces a high level of configurability to the connector definition which provides better support for defining configurable and product line architectures.

Meta objects can be attached to connector types by simply defining the meta object (as explained in Section 2) inside the connector type definition (anywhere between the start and end brackets).

5. Component Types

Component type definition forms a crucial part of the ALI notation. In this section, a very brief description is given due to space limitation.

The component type definition consists of two sections:

- *interfaces*: which specifies the different component interfaces. These interfaces are described conforming to defined interface types (included in the interface type section). A component can have one or more interfaces of different types.
- *subsystem*: Where the internal structure (subsystem) of the component is described. The subsystem section is divided into three sections:
  - *Components*: where the different subcomponents included within the component are defined.
  - *Connectors*: where the different connectors to be used in connecting subcomponents are defined.
  - *Configuration*: where the way in which subcomponents are connected is described. Three methods can be used to connect components:
    a. *Using connectors*: where a connector mediates the connection between two or more components.
    b. *Direct connection*: where component interfaces are bound directly without the use of a connector.

c. *Using patterns*: where predefined connection patterns can be used to connect a set of components according to a selected architectural pattern. More details on architectural patterns are
given in the next section.

Below is an example of a component type definition:

```
component type MyComponentType1
{
//a meta object attached to the component type
 meta: MyMetaType1 {
  description: "this is an example component";
  cost: 20,000;
}
 interfaces:    {
  // specifying a functional interface
  myInterface1 of type functional {
      Provided: {
            function myAddFunction
    {
      impLanguage: "Java";
      invocation: "add";
      parameterlist: ( "int" );
      return: "void";
      } // etc.
       }
       Required: { }
    //no required functions specified
   }
  if(supported(Provide_WSDL_Interface_Feature))
  {
      myInterface2 of type WSDL {
        // WSDL interface description
      }
  }
}
sub-system: {
  components {
   comp1  <custom_feature_set1>: ComponentType1;
    if( supported(Some_Feature_A))
     comp4  <custom_feature_set4>:
                                ComponentType3;
    else
     comp4  <custom_feature_set5>:
                                ComponentType3;
    //etc.
  }
  connectors {
   conn1  <custom_feature_set1>: ConnectorType1;
   // etc.
  }
  configuration {
```

```
//1 - connecting components using connectors
  connect comp1.interface1 with conn1.a;
  connect comp2.interface1 with conn1.b;
//2 - connecting components without connectors
  bind comp3.interface1 with comp1.interface2;
//3 - connecting components using patterns
  if( supported(Some_Feature_B) ){

   Client_Server(ServerComponent1.interface1,
     [ ClientComponent1.interface1,
        ClientComponent2.interface1,
        ClientComponent3.interface2]
       );
  } } }
```

In the example above, we begin the component description using the keyword 'component type' followed by the component type name, MyComponent1 in this example.

The first section of the component definition contains a meta object which conforms to meta type MyMetaType1.

The second section is the component interfaces section where two interfaces are defined: myInterface1

of type *functional* (an interface type that was defined as an example in Section 3) and myInterface2 of type WSDL that only exists if the feature Provide_WSDL_Interface_Feature is supported by the system.

We could define as many interfaces as we wish, where we could link the existence of interfaces to the support /unsupport of system features. We could also attach meta objects to interfaces simply by defining them within the scope of the interface definition (somewhere between the two curly brackets of the interface definition).

It is recommended that interface definitions conform to defined interface types as per the example above (*functional* and *WSDL* types). However, to allow for maximum flexibility, it is possible to define interfaces that do not conform to any predefined interface type, in which case, no analysis or automated tool support can be enabled over that interface definition or any connection made over it (similar to the concept of creating arbitrary meta objects that do not adhere to any meta type definition). This is done by dropping the interface type name that follows the interface name in the interface definition. For example, one could define a port-like interface without having an interface type readily available:

```
myPortInterface3 :
{
input in1, in2, in3;
output out1, out2, out3;
}
```

However, it will not be possible to verify whether the connection between this interface and any other interface within the system is valid or not (as the interface syntax and constraints are not formally defined). This could be practical at early design stages when the exact interface type specification is not clear. When the interface type matures enough throughout the design process, an interface type is defined for this type of interface, and then the interface type name is appended to the interface definition above to allow for verification, and perhaps automated analysis with the aid of appropriate CASE tool support.

The third section in the component definition is the description of the sub-system. In the example above, three components are defined in the components section, each customized with a different feature set. Also, a component of type ComponentType3 is defined; however, its customization is dependent on the existence of the feature Some _Feature _A.

Similarly, a number of connectors are defined in the connectors section within the subsystem description.

The configuration section shows how the components and connectors defined in the subsystem section are configured (connected). As explained earlier, there are three ways in which components can be connected and these are demonstrated in this example.

6. Pattern Templates

The ALI notation allows for the definition and usage of architectural patterns. This is done using *pattern templates*. Pattern templates are first defined and then used throughout the architecture with a simple call to the pattern template needed. Pattern templates take as an argument the interfaces to be connected according to the pattern template definition.

Pattern templates are defined in similar way to the definition of functions (methods) in programming languages. A pattern template definition contains

- *Pattern name*: a unique pattern name.
- *Arguments*: the set of interfaces to be connected. Single interface and/or arrays of interfaces can be passed as arguments. In the case of arrays of interfaces as arguments, the minimum and maximum number of interfaces passed can be specified.
- *Definition*: the specification of how the interfaces are to be connected (the pattern). The syntax used for defining patterns is very simple and provides support for
  - *connecting interfaces*: using the same syntax used in the connections section of the connector type definition (discussed in Section 4).
  - *defining loops*: to allow for connecting arrays of interfaces. The syntax used here is the same syntax used in C for creating *for* loops. Note here that the arrays of interfaces start at index 1 and not at 0 (like in C).

Below is an example that defines a Client /Server pattern:

```
pattern templates:
{
   Client_Server( server : InterfaceType1,
              clients [1..N] : IntefaceType1 ) {
          for( i = 1 ; i    <= N ; i++)
              connect clients[i] and server;
       } }
```

In this example, the Client _Server pattern takes as an argument one interface called server of type InterfaceType1, and an array of interfaces called clients (with [1..N] meaning a minimum of one client interface) of type InterfaceType1. The pattern is defined as for all N clients, create a bi-directional connection with the server interface (refer to Section 4 for more details on the use of the keywords: "connect ", "and ", and "to " for connecting interfaces).

An example of how to invoke the Client /Server pattern template to connect a number of component interfaces was given within the example in Section 5.

7. Features

The feature description section provides a catalogue of the features used within the system. The feature definition consists of

- *Alternative names*: In many cases, different groups within the development process refer to the same feature using different names. This part of the feature definition keeps track of the different names (if any) that are used to reference the same feature (within the different design and development groups involved in the project).
- *Feature parameters*: A feature can carry a number of parameters (textual, numerical, etc.). For example, if the feature is "Manual Gearbox", the parameter would be the "number of gears" available (a numerical value).

Below is an example of how features are defined in ALI:

```
features {
    featureA {
        alternative names: {
            Developer.X, Evaluator.F112
        }
        parameters: {
            (windowTitle: text),
            (windowWidth,windowHeight: number)
        }
    }
    // etc.
}
```

In the example above, featureA was defined showing that it is referred to as "X" by the development team and as "F112" by the evaluation team. The feature encompasses three parameters: one textual and two numerical.

The features defined in this section are usually extracted from the feature model of the system. This is carried out at a prior stage of embarking on the architecture design. CASE tools could be used to read feature models and populate this section (work on this aspect is ongoing in our group). This is an important part of the notation as it makes ALI independent of any particular feature modeling technique.

8. System

Finally, the system section is where the overall product (or product line) architecture is specified. The syntax used in this section is the same as the syntax used in the subsystem section (described in component types, Section 5) with the major difference that the system section is not contained within any component definition but rather provides the description of the overall system architecture (rather than a subsystem of a component). As a result, the keyword "external" can be used in the system description section to reference interfaces of external systems (when needed) providing a means of capturing the system interaction with its environment (operating system, other systems, etc.).

Below is an example of the overall structure of the system section showing how the external keyword could be used to reference external interfaces (parts similar to the example given in Section 5 are replaced with "..." due to space limitation):

```
system {
    components { ... }
    connectors   { ...}
    configuration {  ...
        bind comp1.interface with external.windowHandleAPI;
    }
}
```

9. Discussion

Potential limitations within existing ADLs which could be discouraging their use within the SOA domain and restricting their application to small-scale case studies were discussed in [3]. Restrictive syntax/ structure, lack of tool support and single view presentation are among the limitations identified. In this chapter we have presented the different parts of the ALI notation which were designed to address the identified limitations. ALI built on our experience with ADLARS [4] and introduced a blend between flexibility and formalism. While flexibility gives freedom for the architect during the design process, formalism allows for architecture analysis and potential automation using proper CASE tool support (e.g. on-the-fly architecture documentation, code generation).

Among the new concepts in ALI, the notation provides no predefined interface types. Instead, ALI introduces a sublanguage that gives users the flexibility to define their own interface types. Also, the notation focuses on capturing architectural meta-information and introduces formal syntax (*meta types* and *meta objects*) for this purpose.

Continuing the theme of flexibility, ALI permits the user significant scope for defining architectural patterns. In essence, patterns may be defined and instantiated in similar fashion to function calls in programming languages.

Among the successful concepts adopted from ADLARS, ALI supports the relationship between components, connectors, patterns etc. in an architecture description and features in the feature model using first-order logic. This direct link between the architectural structure and the feature model [7] allows the capture of complex relationships that might arise between the two spaces in real-life systems.

The textual notation described in this chapter serves as a central knowledgebase for the architecture description. CASE tools may then be used to extract the necessary information from this knowledgebase to be presented as different views of the architecture. The centralized approach would help alleviate multiple architectural views mismatch when the different views are maintained separately [8].

As for future work, two items top the list for the work on the ALI project. The first is to develop a CASE toolset for the notation. The toolset will benefit from the experience gained with designing the *ADLARS Development Studio* [9, 10]. And the second is to explore the potential for providing *round-trip* to code. The ability to go from architecture to code and back seems to be attracting more interest and momentum in industry (e.g. the work on model-driven architecture, MDA[11]).

References

1. P. Clements, R. Kazman, and M. Klein, *Evaluating Software Architecture: Methods and Case Studies*: SEI series in software engineering. Addison-Wesley, 2002.
2. R. v. Ommering, F. v. d. Linden, J. Kramer, and J. Magee, "The Koala Component Model for Consumer Electronics Software." *IEEE Computer*, pp. 78–85, March 2000.
3. R. Bashroush, I. Spence, P. Kilpatrick, and T. Brown, "Towards More Flexible Architecture Description Languages for Industrial Applications." V. Gruhn and F. Oquendo (Eds.). *EWSA 2006, Lecture Notes in Computer Science*. Vol. (4344), pp. 212–219, September 2006.
4. R. Bashroush, T. J. Brown, I. Spence, and P. Kilpatrick, "ADLARS: An Architecture Description Language for Software Product Lines." *In proceedings of the 29th Annual IEEE/NASA Software Engineering Workshop*, Greenbelt, Maryland, USA, April 2005. pp. 163–173.
5. "The Java Compiler Compiler [tm] (JavaCC [tm]) – The Java Parser Generator.," https://javacc.dev.java.net/.
6. D. Garlan, R. Monroe, and D. Wile, "Acme: Architectural Description of Component-Based Systems." In *Foundations of Component-Based Systems*, G. T. Leavens and M. Sitaraman (Eds.) Cambridge University Press, 2000, pp. 47–68.
7. T. Brown, R. Gawley, R. Bashroush, I. Spence, P. Kilpatrick, and C. Gillan, "Weaving Behavior into Feature Models for Embedded System Families." *In proceedings of the 10th International Software Product Line Conference SPLC 2006*, Baltimore, Maryland, USA, August 2006. pp. 52–64.
8. J. Muskens, R. Bril, and M. Chaudron, "Generalizing Consistency Checking Between Software Views." *In Proceedings of the 5th International Working Conference on Software Architecture, WICSA-05*, Pittsburgh, PA, November 2005. pp. 169–180.

9. R. Bashroush, I. Spence, P. Kilpatrick, and T. J. Brown, "Deriving Product Architectures from an ADLARS Described Reference Architecture using Leopard." *ACM SIGSOFT Foundations of Software Engineering FSE-12*, October 2004.

10. R. Bashroush, I. Spence, P. Kilpatrick, and T. J. Brown, "Towards an Automated Evaluation Process for Software Architectures." *In Proceedings of the IASTED International Conference on Software Engineering SE 2004*, Innsbruck, Austria, February 2004. pp. 54–58.

11. OMG, "Model Driven Architecture," http://www.omg.org/mda/

25

Specification and Verification of an Agent-Based Auction Service

Amelia Badica and Costin Badica

Abstract

In this chapter we propose a rigorous modelling and analysis of complex interactions occurring between providers and users of an agent-based English auction service. In our model several auctions initiated by different seller agents are carried out in parallel. Buyer agents can dynamically decide to register for participation in auctions that match their goals. Our approach is based on conceptualising these interactions by formal specification using FSP process algebra and formal verification using FLTL temporal logic.

Keywords Formal methods · Auctions · Software agents

1. Introduction

E-commerce is a key service of modern information society. Negotiations (and auctions in particular) are complex activities frequently encountered in modern e-commerce processes. Their understanding, especially when negotiations are automated using software agents [13], requires a careful study and analysis, usually supported by appropriate formal modelling frameworks.

Our recent work in the area of agent-based automated auctions was mainly focused on two aspects: (i) software development for agent-based auctions that combines service orientation with rule-based representation of the auction mechanism [2, 1, 6, 7]; (ii) formal modelling of an agent-based English auction [4].

The development of formal frameworks for modelling agent interactions, including those encountered in negotiations and auctions, generated a lot of interest during the last years [5, 9, 10, 17–19]. Many of these approaches utilize process algebras as foundational formalisms [11, 16, 14].

Following the trend, in this chapter we present a formal specification and verification of agent interactions in an agent-based English auction service. This work builds on our initial results reported in [4] and extends them along the following directions: (i) the ability of the service to handle multiple parallel auctions and thus allowing the construction and study of more complex models; (ii) the possibility of specification and verification of more complex properties by means of *fluent linear temporal logic* – FLTL [14]. The modelling discussed here utilizes the formal framework based on *finite state process algebra* – FSP proposed in [3].

Amelia Badica • Department of Business Information Systems, University of Craiova, Romania.
Costin Badica • Department of Software Engineering, University of Craiova, Romania.

G.A. Papadopoulos et al. (eds.), *Information Systems Development*, DOI 10.1007/b137171_25,
© Springer Science+Business Media, LLC 2009

We start in Section 2 with an overview of our negotiation model. We follow in Section 3 with an overview of the FSP language and with details of our FSP model of the agent-based English auction service. In Section 4 we present the FLTL-based framework for property specification and verification. Section 5 presents conclusions and proposed future work.

2. Agent Negotiation Model

We understand automated negotiations as a process by which a group of software agents communicate with each other to reach a mutually acceptable agreement on some matter [13]. In this chapter we focus our attention on *auctions* – a particular form of negotiation where resource allocations and prices are determined by bids exchanged between participants according to a given set of rules [15].

In automated negotiations (including auctions) it is important to distinguish between *protocols* (or *mechanisms*) and *strategies*. The protocol comprises public "rules of encounter" between negotiation participants by specifying the requirements that enable them to interact and negotiate. The strategy defines the private behaviour of participants aiming at achieving their desired outcome [20].

We consider an environment that provides one or more types of auction services. Each service is providing one type of auction. Trading partners represented by buyer and seller agents can discover auction services that match their requirements and use them in order to achieve their goals of buying and/or selling goods.

Using a service-oriented approach, our e-commerce environment can be conceptualised as providing one or more *Auction Services* (*AS*) [6]. An *AS* (see Fig. 25.1) implements a specific type of auction and has two important functions: (i) management of active auctions including activities like auction creation and auction termination; (ii) coordination of auction participants, including activities like offer and counter-

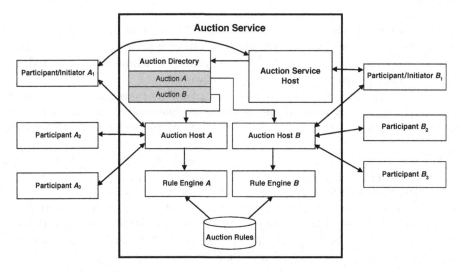

Figure 25.1. Architecture of an auction service.

offer submission (bidding) and clearing (agreement formation), for each active auction within the service. Each *AS* includes a collection of agents that collaborate to support the *AS* to achieve its functions.

An *AS* contains a local directory of active auctions – the *Auction Directory* or *AD*. An active auction, also known as *auction instance* (*AI*), is a process that coordinates behaviours of participants that are registered with that particular auction. An *AS* is managed by a specialized agent known as *Auction Service Host* or *ASH*. *ASH* serves as *AS* entry point and she is also in charge with creation, deletion and management of *AI*s.

An agent, usually a buyer or seller agent that registered to participate in an auction hosted by an *AS*, is called *Auction Participant* or *AP*. Additionally, an auction is initiated by a specialized *AP* called *Auction Initiator Participant* – *AIP*. Initiation of an *AI* determines the creation, internal registration and starting of its associated process. For each active *AI* inside an *AS*, there is an associated entry in *AD* that contains the identifier of the corresponding *AH* together with an appropriate description of the *AI*. Creation and deletion of *AH*s together with their registration and respectively deregistration with the *AD* are handled by the *ASH* agent.

Figure 25.1 shows an *AS* – let us suppose it is a service that provides English auctions. The service is currently running two *AI*s, i.e. *Auction A* and *Auction B*. Both *Auction A* and *Auction B* are in fact English auctions governed by similar auction mechanisms, but possibly characterized by different parameters – i.e. different auctioned product, different starting time and ending time, different minimum bid increment, different sets of auction participants, and others Three participants are shown to be registered to *Auction A* – *Participant/Initiator A_1*, *Participant A_2*, and *Participant A_3*. Note that *Participant/Initiator A_1* is also the initiator of *Auction A*.

We have conceptualised an *AI* using the negotiation model inspired from [5] and [1]. This framework comprises (1) negotiation infrastructure, (2) generic negotiation protocol and (3) taxonomy of declarative rules.

The *negotiation infrastructure* defines roles of negotiation participants (e.g. *Buyer* or *Seller* in an English auction) and of a negotiation host. Within our model the negotiation host agent is known as the *Auction Host (AH)*. An *AH* is responsible for coordinating the behaviour of agents participating to a single *AI*.

The *generic negotiation protocol* controls how messages are exchanged by the host and participants by facilitating the following negotiation activities: (1) *Admission to negotiation*. This activity starts when a new participant requests admission to the host. The host grants (or not) participant admission by responding with accept or reject message. In particular, the first admission request (always submitted by a seller participant in an English auction) initiates the negotiation; (2) *Bid submission*. Participants can start submitting bids after they were admitted to negotiation by sending a bidding message. The participant will be notified by the host if her proposal was either accepted or rejected; (3) *Informing participants*. There are situations where negotiation participants must be informed about changes of the negotiation state and/ or generation of intermediate information like price quotes, identity of participants, transaction history, negotiation stage or round. Usually this situation happens after a new bid was admitted or a given interval of time elapsed. The negotiation protocol requires that participants will always be notified about any new state of the negotiation; (4) *Agreement formation* can be triggered at any time during negotiation. When agreement formation rules signal that an agreement was reached, the protocol states that participants involved in the agreement will be notified by the host and (5) *Negotiation termination* can be triggered at any time during negotiation. When negotiation termination rules signal that the negotiation process reached its final state, the protocol states that all participants will be notified by the host.

Negotiation rules deal with the semantic constraints of a particular negotiation mechanism (e.g. English auctions). Rules are used for checking validity of proposals and sequences of exchanged messages, updating of negotiation status and informing participants, and controlling agreement formation and negotiation termination. An *AH* incorporates a rule engine that checks the rules for that auction type. Note that, as we assumed that an *ASH* provides a certain and unique type of auction – e.g. English, Dutch, Vickrey and others, we have a single set of rules for each *ASH*. However, for each active *AH* within the *ASH* we have a separate rule engine that is initialised with the set of rules corresponding to that auction type.

In this chapter we consider the modelling of an agent-based English auction service, therefore we now briefly overview English auctions. Technically, English auctions are single-item, first-price, open-cry, ascending auctions [12, 20]. In an English auction there is a single item sold by a single seller and many buyers bidding for buying the item until the auction terminates. Usually, there is a time limit for ending the auction (either a total time limit or a certain inactivity period), a seller reservation price that must be met by the winning bid for the item to be sold and a minimum value of the bid increment. A new bid must be higher than the currently highest bid plus the bid increment in order to be accepted. All the bids are visible to all the auction participants, while seller reservation price is not disclosed to buyers.

3. FSP Model of Agent Negotiation

We briefly overview FSP and then we show how the FSP model of an English auction introduced in [4] can be extended to handle multiple parallel auctions.

3.1. Overview of the Modelling Approach

FSP is an algebraic specification technique of concurrent and cooperating computational processes as {finite} state-labeled transition systems (LTS hereafter). FSP allows a more compact and easy to manage description of a LTS, rather than directly describing it as a list of states and transitions between states.

A FSP model consists of a finite set of sequential and/or composite process definitions. Additionally, a sequential process definition consists of a sequence of one or more definitions of local processes. A process definition consists of a process name associated to a process term. FSP uses a rich set of constructs for process terms (see [14] for details). For the purpose of this chapter we are using the following constructs: action prefix ($a \rightarrow P$), non-deterministic choice ($P \mid Q$) and process alphabet extension ($P + \{a_1, \ldots, a_n\}$) for sequential process terms and parallel composition ($P \parallel Q$) and re-labeling ($P/\{new_1/old_1, \ldots, new_k/old_k\}$) for composite process terms. FSP has an operational semantics given via a LTS (see [14]).

The proposed modeling follows the general guidelines outlined in [3]: (i) agents are modelled as FSP processes and an agent system is modelled as a parallel composition of processes; (ii) sets B of buyers and S of sellers are initially given; (iii) agent requests and replies are indexed with buyer and/or seller identifiers.

Our models define the following FSP processes: (i) *AuctionServiceHost* process that represents the *AS* and manages all the active *AI*s within the *AS*; (ii) *AuctionHost* to orchestrate an auction instance and coordinate participants by employing the general negotiation protocol. Note that there is a separate *AuctionHost* for each active auction in the system and all the active hosts are managed by a *Auction-ServiceHost* process; (iii) *Buyer* and *Seller* processes, as usually these are the roles defined by an auction. Interactions between these processes within an *AS* during and before initiation/after termination of an *AI* are illustrated in Figs. 25.2 and 25.3.

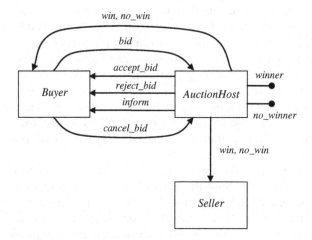

Figure 25.2. Roles interaction during negotiation.

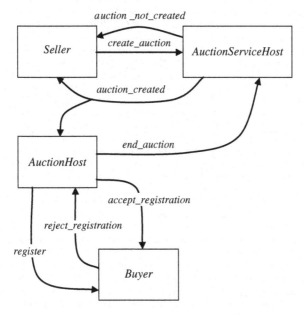

Figure 25.3. Roles interaction before and after negotiation.

3.2. Auction Host

An *AuctionHost* handles a single *AI* at a certain time. An *AI* consists of a series of stages that, in what follows, are particularized for the case of an English auction:

- *Initiation* – an auction is initiated by a seller using the *init_auction* action; initiation acts also as a registration of the seller agent participant; initiation is either accepted (action *accept_init*) or rejected (action *reject_init*) by the host;
- *Buyer registration* – each buyer agent must register with the negotiation using *register* action before she is allowed to submit bids; registration is granted (action *accept_registration*) or not (action *reject_registraton*) by the auction host;
- *Bids submission* – each registered buyer is allowed to submit bids using *bid* action; bids are either accepted (action *accept_bid*) or not (action *reject_bid*) by the host; when a certain bid is accepted, the other registered buyer participants are notified accordingly by the host (action *inform*).
- *Agreement formation* – when the host observes a certain period of bidding inactivity, it triggers auction termination via action *no_bid*. This event subsequently triggers agreement formation. In this stage the host checks if an agreement can be generated or not – *winner* and *no_winner* actions. If agreement cannot be made then notification *no_win* is sent to all registered participants (buyers and the seller). However if the host decides that there is a winner then notification *win* is sent to all registered participants.

Negotiation host behaviour is described as the *AuctionHost* process (see Fig. 25.4). Note that message contents (i.e. bid value or submission time), excepting buyer identities, are ignored in this model. The main difference from the model introduced in [4] is that there the decision of accepting the initiation of a new negotiation was taken by the *AuctionHost*, while in this model the decision is taken by the *AuctionServiceHost* process (see Fig. 25.5).

Note that *AuctionHost* process has a cyclic behavior and thus it runs infinitely, being able to handle an infinite sequence of auctions, one auction at a time.

In a real setting, participants are created and destroyed dynamically. In our model we assume that there is a given set of buyers as well as a given set of sellers that are created when the system is started. Buyers are able to dynamically register to auctions while sellers are able to dynamically initiate auctions.

$$
\begin{aligned}
AuctionHost &= (init\_auction \rightarrow ServerBid(\perp,\emptyset)),\\
ServerBid(chb,Bs) &= (bid(b \in Bs) \rightarrow AnswerBid(b,chb,Bs)|\\
&\quad register(b' \notin Bs) \rightarrow AnswerReg(b',chb,Bs)|\\
&\quad no\_bid \rightarrow ServerAgree(chb,Bs)),\\
AnswerReg(b',chb,Bs) &= (accept\_registration(b') \rightarrow ServerBid(chb,Bs \cup \{b'\})|\\
&\quad reject\_registration(b') \rightarrow ServerBid(chb,Bs)),\\
AnswerBid(b,chb,Bs) &= (accept\_bid(b) \rightarrow InformBuyers(b,Bs)|\\
&\quad reject\_bid(b) \rightarrow ServerBid(chb,Bs)),\\
InformBuyers(b,Bs) &= (inform(b_1) \rightarrow inform(b_2) \rightarrow \ldots \rightarrow inform(b_k) \rightarrow ServerBid(b,Bs)),\\
ServerAgree(chb,Bs) &= (while\ chb \neq \perp\ winner(chb) \rightarrow ServerAgreeWinner(chb,Bs)|\\
&\quad no\_winner(chb) \rightarrow ServerAgreeNoWinner(chb,Bs)),\\
ServerAgreeWinner(chb,Bs) &= (win(chb,b_1) \rightarrow win(chb,b_2) \rightarrow \ldots \rightarrow win(chb,b_k) \rightarrow\\
&\quad win(chb) \rightarrow AuctionHost),\\
ServerAgreeNoWinner(chb,Bs) &= (no\_win(chb,b_1) \rightarrow no\_win(chb,b_2) \rightarrow \ldots \rightarrow no\_win(chb,b_k) \rightarrow\\
&\quad no\_win(chb) \rightarrow AuctionHost),\\
AuctionHost(s \in S) &= AuctionHost/\{auction\_created(s)/init\_auction,end\_auction(s)/no\_bid,\\
&\quad win(s)/win,no\_win(s)/no\_win,register(s,b \in \mathcal{B})/register(b),\\
&\quad inform(s,b \in \mathcal{B})/inform(b),accept\_registration(s,b \in \mathcal{B})/accept\_registration(b),\\
&\quad reject\_registration(s,b \in \mathcal{B})/reject\_registration(b),\\
&\quad winner(s)/winner,no\_winner(s)/no\_winner,\\
&\quad reject\_bid(s,b \in \mathcal{B})/reject\_bid(s),accept\_bid(s,b \in \mathcal{B})/accept\_bid(s)\}.\\[6pt]
Auctions &= ||_{s \in S} AuctionHost(s)
\end{aligned}
$$

Figure 25.4. *AuctionHost* that describes the negotiation host role for controlling a single negotiation.

$$
\begin{aligned}
AuctionServiceHost &= ServerHost(\emptyset),\\
ServerHost(S) &= (end\_auction(s \in S) \rightarrow ServerHost(S \setminus \{s\})|\\
&\quad create\_auction(s \notin S) \rightarrow ServiceHost(s,S)),\\
ServerHost(s,S) &= (auction\_not\_created(s) \rightarrow ServerHost(S)|\\
&\quad auction\_created(s) \rightarrow ServerHost(S \cup \{s\})).
\end{aligned}
$$

Figure 25.5. *AuctionServiceHost* process.

Assuming each buyer agent has a unique name, let $\mathcal{B}$ be the set of all names of buyer agents and let S be the set of all names of seller agents that were created when the system was initiated. Let $\perp$ be a name not in $\mathcal{B}$. Definition of the *AuctionHost* process is using several indexed families of local processes:

- *ServerBid(b,B)* such that $b \in B \cup \{\perp\}$, $B \subseteq \mathcal{B}$. Here b records the buyer associated with currently highest bid and B denotes the set of registered buyers. The condition $b \in B \cup \{\perp\}$ means that neither buyer agent has submitted a bid in the current negotiation ($b = \perp$) or the buyer agent that submitted the currently highest bid must have already registered with the negotiation before the submission $b \in B$.

- *AnswerReg(b_1,b_2,B)* such that $b_1 \in \mathcal{B} \setminus B$, $b_2 \in B \cup \{\perp\}$, $B \subseteq \mathcal{B}$. Here b_1 denotes the buyer that requested registration with the current negotiation, b_2 denotes the buyer associated with currently highest bid and B denotes the set of registered buyers. The fact that $b_1 \in \mathcal{B} \setminus B$ means that the registration request comes from a buyer that is not yet registered with the negotiation. The fact that $b_2 \in B \cup \{\perp\}$ means that either the currently highest bid has not been submitted yet ($b_2 = \perp$) or it was submitted by a registered buyer ($b_2 \in B$).

- *InformBuyers(b,B)* such that $b \in B$, $B \subseteq \mathcal{B}$. Here b denotes the buyer that submitted an accepted bid and B denotes the set of registered buyers. The fact that $b \in B$ means that the bid that was accepted comes from a buyer that has registered with the negotiation.

- *ServerAgreementWinner(b,B)*, *ServerAgreementNoWinner(b,B)* and *ServerAgreement(b,B)* such that $b \in B \cup \{\perp\}$ and $B \subseteq \mathcal{B}$. Here b denotes the buyer that submitted the currently highest bid, if any and B denotes the set of registered buyers. *ServerAgreement* process models the host decision if there is or not an auction winner and *ServerAgreementWinner* and *ServerAgreementNoWinner* are responsible with sending the appropriate notifications to auction participants – *win(b,b')*, *no_win(b,b')* to registered buyers for all $b' \in B$ and *win(b)*, *no_win(b)* to the seller.

3.3. Auction Service Host

AuctionServiceHost manages all the active *AI*s at a given time. Whenever a new auction is created, it is registered with the *AuctionServiceHost*. Whenever an auction is terminated it is deregistered with the *AuctionServiceHost*. The decision of accepting or not the creation of a new auction belongs to the *AuctionServiceHost*.

3.4. Buyer and Seller Roles

The *Buyer* selects a convenient active auction initiated by one seller $s \in S$ and then registers to the auction before starting to submit bids. If registration is granted then she can start bidding according to her private strategy – action *bid*. We chose a very simple strategy: each *Buyer* submits a first bid immediately after it is granted admission to the negotiation and subsequently, whenever it gets a notification that another participant issued a bid that was accepted by the host. Additionally, each *Buyer* has its own valuation of the negotiated product. If the current value that the buyer decided to bid exceeds her private valuation, i.e. product became "too expensive" then the *Buyer* has the option to decide to stay silent and not to bid. Note that after a *Buyer* submitted a bid that was accepted, she will enter a state waiting for a notification that either another successful bid was submitted or that she eventually was the last submitter of a successful bid in the current auction (a potentially winning bid, depending if that bid value was higher than the seller reservation price) – action *end*.

The seller agent initiates the auction – action *init* and then, assuming initiation was successful, waits for the auction to terminate – action *end*, before issuing a new initiation request.

$$
\begin{aligned}
Buyer &= (register(s \in S) \rightarrow BuyerRegister(s)), \\
BuyerRegister(s \in S) &= (accept\_registration(s) \rightarrow BuyerBid(s)|reject\_registration(s) \rightarrow Buyer), \\
BuyerBid(s \in S) &= (bid(s) \rightarrow WaitBid(s)|inform(s) \rightarrow BuyerBid(s)|end(s) \rightarrow Buyer), \\
WaitBid(s \in S) &= (accept\_bid(s) \rightarrow Wait(s)|reject\_bid(s) \rightarrow BuyerBid(s)|inform(s) \rightarrow BuyerBid(s)), \\
Wait(s \in S) &= (inform(s) \rightarrow BuyerBid(s)|end(s) \rightarrow Buyer). \\
\\
Seller &= (init \rightarrow WaitInit), \\
WaitInit &= (accept\_init \rightarrow WaitEnd|reject\_init \rightarrow Seller), \\
WaitEnd &= (end \rightarrow Seller).
\end{aligned}
$$

Figure 25.6. *Buyer* and *Seller* processes.

3.5. System with Buyers, Sellers and an Auction Service

Buyer and seller agents are created by instantiating *Buyer* and *Seller* roles. Instantiation of *Buyer* roles assumes also indexing of actions *bid*, *reject_bid*, *accept_bid*, *inform*, *register*, *accept_registration*, *reject_registration* with buyer's name and also renaming action *end* with an indexed set of actions {*win*, *no_win*}. Similarly, instantiation of *Seller* role assumes renaming action *end* with a set of actions denoting various ways the auction may terminate: (i) without a winner assuming no buyer submitted an accepted bid – *no_win*, with or without a winner assuming at least one buyer submitted an accepted bid – indexed set of actions {*win*, *no_win*}.

Finally the system is defined as parallel composition of auction service host, auctions, sellers and buyers processes – see Fig. 25.7.

$$
\begin{aligned}
BuyerAgent(b \in \mathcal{B}) &= Buyer/\{bid(s \in \mathcal{S}, b)/bid(s), reject\_bid(s \in \mathcal{S}, b)/reject\_bid(s), \\
&\quad accept\_bid(s \in \mathcal{S}, b)/accept\_bid(s), inform(s \in \mathcal{S}, b)/inform(s), \\
&\quad \{win(s, b' \in \mathcal{B}), no\_win(s, b' \in \mathcal{B} \cup \{\bot\}, b)\}/end(s), \\
&\quad register(s \in \mathcal{S}, b)/register(s), accept\_registration(s \in \mathcal{S}, b)/accept\_registration(s), \\
&\quad reject\_registration(s \in \mathcal{S}, b)/reject\_registration(s)\}. \\
SellerAgent(s \in \mathcal{S}) &= Seller/\{\{win(s, b \in \mathcal{B}), no\_win(s, b \in \mathcal{B} \cup \{\bot\})\}/end, \\
&\quad create\_auction(s)/init, auction\_created(s)/accept\_init, \\
&\quad auction\_not\_created(s)/reject\_init\}. \\
\\
Buyers &= \|_{b \in \mathcal{B}} BuyerAgent(b) \\
\\
Sellers &= \|_{s \in \mathcal{S}} SellerAgent(s) \\
\\
System &= (AuctionServiceHost\|Auctions\|Sellers\|Buyers).
\end{aligned}
$$

Figure 25.7. *System* process as parallel composition of auction service host, auctions, buyers and sellers processes.

We have determined the LTS of a sample negotiation system with three buyers and two sellers using LTSA tool ([14]). The analysis performed revealed that the system has 16,238 states and 43,700 transitions and it is free of deadlocks. After minimization the number of states was reduced to 4523.

4. Modelling System Properties

Formal modelling of agent systems has the advantage that models can be systematically checked against user-defined properties. A property is defined by a statement that is true for all the possible execution paths of the system. A property is used to describe a desirable feature of the system behaviour. Definition of properties of systems has the advantage that it enables a formal and concise, rather than informal and speculative analysis of the system behaviour.

Properties are usually expressed as formulas in a temporal logic language. A property holds if the associated formula is true for all the possible executions of the system, as it is described by the model of the system. For system models captured using FSP it has been argued that a very convenient temporal logic for property expression is *fluent temporal logic* – FLTL ([14]).

In FLTL primitive properties are expressed using *fluents*. A fluent is a property whose truth is triggered by an initiating event and that holds until the signaling of a terminating event. In FSP it is natural to model initiating and terminating events by execution of specific actions. Following [14], a fluent is defined as a triple:

fluent $F = \langle \{i_1, \ldots, i_m\}, \{t_1, \ldots, t_n\} \rangle$ **initially** B

where (i) $\{i_1, \ldots, i_m\}$ and $\{t_1, \ldots, t_n\}$ are disjoint sets of *initiating events* and *terminating events* and (ii) B is true or false and represents the initial value of F. When any of the initiating actions is observed, F becomes true and stays true until any of the terminating actions is observed. When the initial value of the fluent is not given it is assumed to be false.

Every action a defines a singleton fluent $F(a)$ having a as the single initiating action and the rest of all actions as terminating actions, as follows:

fluent $F(a) = \langle \{a\}, A \setminus \{a\} \rangle$ **initially false**

A singleton fluent $F(a)$ is usually written as a in FLTL formulas.

For our auctioning system we can define two fluents (that will be useful later): (i) a fluent that starts to hold when the *AuctionServiceHost* registers a *Buyer* with a given auction and ceases to hold when the *Buyer* is notified that the auction terminated; (ii) a fluent that starts to hold when an auction is created and ceases to hold when that auction is terminated.

fluent $BIDDING(b \in \mathcal{B}, s \in S) =$
$\langle \{accept\_registration(s,b)\}, \{win(s,b' \in \mathcal{B},b), no\_win(s,b' \in \mathcal{B} \cup \{\bot\},b)\} \rangle$

fluent $AUCTION\_ACTIVE(s \in S) = \langle \{auction\_created(s)\}, \{end\_auction(s)\} \rangle$

FLTL formulas are built over fluent propositions (including singleton fluents) using the usual logical operators $\wedge, \vee, \rightarrow, \neg$ and temporal operators **X** (next), **U** (until), **W** (weak until), **F** (eventually) and **G** (always) (see [14]). A property P is specified using an FLTL formula Φ as follows:

assert $P = \Phi$

Property specification was recognized as a very difficult task requiring expert knowledge in formal methods, especially in temporal logic. However, according to the rigorous analysis performed in [8], it has been observed that most of the specifications usually fall into a category of specification patterns. Therefore in our work we have initially looked into the application of property specification patterns to the verification of the auctioning system.

In this chapter we applied the following four specification patterns for the verification of our system: (i) *absence* – a given situation does not occur; (ii) *existence* – a given situation must occur; (iii) *precedence* – a given situation must always be preceded by another situation; (iv) *response* – a given situation must always be followed by another situation. Note that each pattern has a given scope that describes the portion of the system execution over which the pattern applies [8].

Examples of *absence* pattern for the auctioning system are (i) "A *Buyer* cannot bid in an auction to which she was not registered yet"; (ii) "A *Buyer* cannot simultaneously bid in two different auctions" and (iii) "A *Buyer* cannot register to an auction that was not created before".

assert $CANNOT\_BID = \wedge_{b \in \mathcal{B}, s \in S} (\mathbf{F} \; accept\_registration(s,b) \rightarrow$
$(\neg \; bid(s,b) \; \mathbf{U} \; accept\_registration(s,b)))$

assert $CANNOT\_BID\_MULTIPLY(s_1 \neq s_2 \in S) =$
$\wedge_{b \in \mathcal{B}} \mathbf{G}(\neg (BIDDING(b,s_1) \wedge BIDDING(b,s_2)))$
assert $CANNOT\_REGISTER = \wedge_{b \in \mathcal{B}, s \in S} (\mathbf{F} \; auction\_created(s) \rightarrow$
$(\neg register(s,b) \mathbf{U} \; auction\_created(s)))$

An example of the *existence* pattern for the auctioning system is "Each *Seller* can initiate an auction".

assert $AUCTION\_ACTIVATED = \wedge_{s \in S} \mathbf{G} \; AUCTION\_ACTIVE(s)$

An example of the *precedence* pattern for the auctioning system is "During an auction a *Buyer* must first request the accept to bid before she is granted this accept by the *AuctionHost*".

assert $REQUEST\_REG = \wedge_{b \in \mathcal{B}, s \in S} \mathbf{F} \; ((accept\_created(s) \wedge \mathbf{F} \; end\_auction(s))$
$\rightarrow (\neg \; accept\_registration(s,b) \mathbf{U} \; (register(s,b) \vee end\_auction(s))))$

An example of the *response* pattern for the auctioning system is "During an auction if the bid submitted by a *Buyer* was accepted then all the other registered *Buyers* will be notified accordingly".

assert $INFORM(b \in \mathcal{B}) = \wedge_{b' \in \mathcal{B}/ \{b\}, s \in S} (\mathbf{F} \; end\_auction(s) \rightarrow ((BIDDING(b,s)$
$\wedge \; accept\_bid(s,b') \rightarrow (\neg \; end\_auction(s) \mathbf{U} \; (inform(s,b) \wedge \neg \; end\_auction(s))))$
$\mathbf{U} \; end\_auction(s)))$

We conducted a series of experiments with the FSP model of the auctioning system. The main goal was to check the correctness of agent interactions in the system against the properties introduced in this section. We expressed our FSP models using the FSP language supported by LTSA tool [14] by applying the techniques described in [3] that were updated for mapping of FLTL formulas.[1]

5. Conclusions and Future Work

In this chapter we applied a formal framework based on FSP process algebra for modelling a system that contains multiple *Seller* and *Buyer* agents engaged in English auctions. We checked the resulting model with the help of LTSA analysis tool against sample qualitative properties expressed in FLTL. As future work we intend to (i) model more complex systems containing other types of auctions and possibly other e-commerce activities (matchmaking, brokerage or recommendation); (ii) develop a more complete framework for specification and verification of qualitative properties of agents engaged in e-business services.

References

1. Badica, C., Ganzha, M. and Paprzycki, M. (2007) Implementing Rule-Based Automated Price Negotiation in an Agent System. *Journal of Universal Computer Science*, 13(2): 244–266.
2. Badica, C., Giurca, A. and Wagner, G. (2007) Using Rules and R2ML for Modeling Negotiation Mechanisms in E-commerce Agent Systems. In *Proceedings of the 1st Int. Conf. Trends in Enterprise Application Architecture, TEAA 2006*, pp. 84–99. Lecture Notes in Computer Science 4473, Springer.
3. Badica, A., Badica, C. and Litoiu, L. (2007) Middle-Agents Interactions as Finite State Processes: Overview and Example. In *Proc. 16th IEEE International Workshops on Enabling Technologies: Infrastructure for Collaborative Enterprises (WETICE 2007)*, pp. 12–17, IEEE Computer Society Press.
4. Badica, C. and Badica, A. (2008) Formalizing Agent-Based English Auctions Using Finite State Process Algebra. *Journal of Universal Computer Science*, 14(7): 1118–1135.
5. Bartolini, C., Preist, C. and Jennings, N.R. (2005) A Software Framework for Automated Negotiation. In: *Proc. SELMAS'2004*, pp. 213–235 Lecture Notes in Computer Science 3390, Springer.
6. Dobriceanu, A., Biscu, L., Badica, C. and Popescu, E. (2008) Considerations on the design and implementation of an agent-based auction service. In *Advances in Intelligent and Distributed Computing, Proc.IDC 2007*, pp.75–84. Studies in Computational Intelligence, 78, Springer.
7. Dobriceanu, A., Biscu, L. and Badica, C. (2007) Adding a declarative representation of negotiation mechanisms to an agent-based negotiation service. In *Proceedings of WI/IAT 2007 Workshops*, pp. 471–474. IEEE Computer Society Press.
8. Dwyer, M.B., Avrunin, G.S. and Corbett, J.C. (1999) Patterns in property specifications for finite-state verification. In *ICSE'99: Proceedings of the 21st International Conference on Software Engineering*, pp. 411–420. IEEE Computer Society Press.

---

[1] FSP and FLTL models developed for our experiments are available for download at http://software.ucv.ro/~badica_costin/fsp/isd08_model.zip.

9. Esterline, A., Rorie, T. and Homaifar, A..(2006) A Process-Algebraic Agent Abstraction. In Rouff, C.A., Hinchey, M., Rash, J., Truszkowski, W. and Gordon-Spears, D. (eds.) *Agent Technology from a Formal Perspective*, pp. 88–137. NASA Monographs in Systems and Software Engineering, Springer.

10. Hillston, J. and Kloul, L. (2001) Performance investigation of an on-line auction system. *Concurrency and Computation: Practice and Experience*, 13(1): 23– 41.

11. Hoare, C.A.R. (1985) *Communicating Sequential Processes*. Prentice Hall International Series in Computer Science, Hemel Hempstead.

12. Laudon, K.C. and Traver, C.G. (2004) *E-Commerce, Business, Technology, Society* (2nd ed.), Pearson Addison-Wesley, New York.

13. Lomuscio, A.R., Wooldridge, M. and Jennings, N.R. (2002) A classification scheme for negotiation in electronic commerce. In Dignum, F. and Sierra, C. (eds.), *Agent Mediated Electronic Commerce: The European AgentLink Perspective*, pp. 19–33. Lecture Notes in Computer Science 1991, Springer.

14. Magee, J. and Kramer, J. (2006) *Concurrency. State Models and Java Programs* (2nd ed.), John Wiley & Sons, New York.

15. McAfee, R.P. and McMillan, J. (1987) Auctions and bidding. *Journal of Economic Literature*, 25(2): 699–738

16. Milner, R. (1999) *Communicating and Mobile Systems: The π-calculus*. Cambridge University Press, Cambridge.

17. Podorozhny, R. M., Khurshid, S., Perry, D. E. and Zhang, X. (2007) Verification of Multi-agent Negotiations Using the Alloy Analyzer. In *Proc. 6th Int. Conf on Integrated Formal Methods, IFM 2007, Oxford, UK*, pp. 501–517. Lecture Notes in Comp. Sc. 4591, Springer.

18. Rouff, C., Rash, J., Hinchey, M. and Truszkowski, W. (2006) Formal Methods at NASA Goddard Space Flight Center. In Rouff, C.A., Hinchey, M., Rash, J., Truszkowski, W. and Gordon-Spears, D. (eds.) *Agent Technology from a Formal Perspective*, pp. 287–309. NASA Monographs in Systems and Software Engineering, Springer

26

A Practical Environment to Apply Model-Driven Web Engineering

Maria Jose Escalona, J.J. Gutiérrez, F. Morero, C.L. Parra, J. Nieto, F. Pérez, F. Martín and A. Llergo

Abstract

The application of a model-driven paradigm in the development of Web Systems has yielded very good research results. Several research groups are defining metamodels, transformations, and tools which offer a suitable environment, known as model-driven Web engineering (MDWE). However, there are very few practical experiences in real Web system developments using real development teams. This chapter presents a practical environment of MDWE based on the use of NDT (navigational development techniques) and Java Web systems, and it provides a practical evaluation of its application within a real project: specialized Diraya.

Keywords Model-driven engineering · Web engineering

1. Introduction

Web engineering [5] and the new paradigm of model-driven engineering [16] have been defined as suitable solutions for companies and Web development in the research environment [17]. New techniques for Web system developments introduced by Web engineering and the application of model-driven engineering in this area offer very interesting solutions of high quality and reduced cost.

However, although these ideas have been widely accepted by the research community, few practical applications can be obtained in the literature. In fact, during 2005 and 2006 we interviewed a group of 30 software companies in Andalusia, Spain. More than 50 project managers and 70 analysts were interviewed. These companies represent local, national, and international companies and thereby offer a very representative sample. One of our questions was whether the company knew anything about Web engineering. In big and medium-sized companies (more than 50 employees), 25% knew something about Web engineering, while in small companies, only 10% had heard about it. Overall, only 1% knew about Web engineering and applied it in projects. These results are very representative since, although the interviews indicate that Web engineering could be very useful, it is not currently in use.

One of the most important aspects relevant for the practical application of software engineering in general, and in Web engineering in particular, is the use of suitable tools that guarantee that the application of these techniques is profitable [6]. In comparative studies of Web engineering, one of the most important gaps detected is the lack of tools to support the application of Web approaches [4, 11]. Only some

Maria Jose Escalona • Department of Computer Languages and Systems, University of Seville, ETS Ingenieria Informática. Av. Reina Mercedes S/N. Seville, Spain. **J.J. Gutiérrez** • University of Seville, Seville, Spain. **F. Morero** • Sun Microsystems, Madrid, Spain. **C.L. Parra, J. Nieto, F. Pérez, F. Martín and A. Llergo** • Servicio Andaluz de Salud, Seville, Spain.

G.A. Papadopoulos et al. (eds.), *Information Systems Development*, DOI 10.1007/b137171_26,
© Springer Science+Business Media, LLC 2009

methodologies, such as UWE (UML Web engineering) [11] that offers ArgoUWE[1], or WebML [3] that offers WebRatio[2], introduce suitable solution tools.

This chapter presents a practical solution in the application of model-driven Web engineering. In the chapter, the Web methodology NDT (navigational development techniques) [9] is presented as a practical solution for Web developments. NDT is an approach to define and analyze Web systems and capture their requirements. The practical version of this approach is oriented to offer a suitable methodological environment for Web development. The chapter is structured as follows. In Section 2, the methodological solution is presented. This solution is oriented in the area of public administration in Andalusia in the south of Spain. In this environment, a methodology, named Métrica v3,[3] is used to develop software systems in public administration. Métrica v3 is a widely used methodology but is too ambiguous in some cases and offers no special treatment of Web characteristics. The methodological solution is composed of a fusion between Métrica and NDT. In Section 3, the set of tools to support this environment is presented: tools to support the methodology and tools to guarantee the results. In Section 4, a practical example of the application of this solution is given. In the Diraya project [8], this methodological environment is currently being applied with very good results. And, finally, in Section 5, conclusions are drawn and future work is proposed.

2. The Methodology

The methodological environment proposed in this chapter is based on the model-driven paradigm. This environment is a fusion between Métrica v3 and NDT, a model-driven Web methodology.

In this section, a comprehensive vision of this environment is shown and a presentation of the overall approach is put forward.

2.1. Métrica v3

Métrica is a methodological environment developed by the Spanish Ministry of Public Administration. In the latest version of Métrica v3, the object-oriented paradigm is included as a development option, and Métrica proposes the use of UML [14] to model different aspects in the life cycle.

Métrica v3 is the reference frame for the development of software in public organisms in Spain. Every software project developed for any government in Spain has to follow Métrica rules.

The fact that Métrica is obligatory for public organisms has provoked most software providers to use this methodology in their software projects. It has therefore become a widely used methodology in Spain. The life cycle of Métrica v3 is presented in Fig. 26.1.

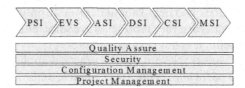

Figure 26.1. Life cycle of Métrica v3.

---

[1] http://www.pst.informatik.uni-muenchen.de /projekte/argouwe

[2] http://www.webratio.com

[3] http://www.map.es

This life cycle starts with the information system planning (PSI) where the organization is studied and the development environment for new systems in the organization is defined. PSI must be applied every 4 years in order to define the reference environment for the organization.

When the PSI defines the necessity of a new system, a viability study must be developed (EVS). EVS is normally an optional phase although it is mandatory in large and complex developments.

The next phases are obligatory for each system. The first phase, the analysis phase (ASI), must detect system requirements and then analyze them in order to define the scope of the system. After the analysis, the design phase must be tackled (DSI). The next phase is the construction of the system (CSI), where the system is translated into the selected programming language. And, finally, the maintenance phase must be applied (MSI).

In parallel to this life cycle, Métrica proposes four interfaces in order to control development.

- The quality assurance interface that applies quality techniques to control quality of the results.
- The security interface to control the security aspects of the systems.
- The configuration management interface to manage the structure and the organization's construction rules.
- The project management interface to control the management of the project throughout the life cycle.

For each phase, Métrica defines tasks and objectives that must be covered. Furthermore, Métrica offers a technique guide that can be applied in each task.

Métrica is a very complex and extensive approach. It offers a wide life cycle with a great number of techniques and tasks. However, for companies, it is sometimes very complex to identify which part of Métrica must be used or what products must be generated. This problem is very relevant in the treatment of requirements since, in Métrica, only use case diagram technique [14] is proposed for this phase. Use cases, mainly in complex environments, are very ambiguous and must be complemented with some description in order to solve this ambiguity [10, 18]. Moreover, use cases are insufficient for the extraction of the necessary information to attain analysis models. Furthermore, in the Web environment, Métrica does not offer special techniques or models to deal with the most critical characteristics of the Web: navigation, critical interface, multiple unknown final users, etc.

2.2. NDT – Navigational Development Techniques

NDT is a Web methodological process focused on both the requirement and the analysis phases. NDT offers a systematic way to deal with the special characteristics of the Web environment. NDT is based on the definition of formal metamodels [9] that allow derivation relations to be created between models. NDT takes this theoretic base and enriches it with the elements necessary for the definition of a methodology: techniques, models, methodological process, etc., in order to offer a suitable context for application in real projects.

In Fig. 26.2, the life cycle of NDT is presented. NDT only covers the requirement and the analysis phases. In the requirement phase, it involves the capture, definition, and validation of requirements. To this end, NDT proposes the division of requirements into different groups depending on their nature: storage information requirements, functional requirements, actors' requirements, interaction requirements, and non-functional requirements. In order to deal with each kind of requirement, NDT proposes the use of special patterns and UML techniques, such as the use case techniques. Requirements in NDT are formally presented in a requirement metamodel, where some constraints and relations are defined.

The life cycle then passes to the analysis phase. NDT proposes three models in this phase: the conceptual model, the navigational model, and the abstract interface model. The conceptual model of NDT is represented in the methodology using the class diagram of UML, and the other two models are represented using UWE notation [12].

The class diagram of UML and the navigational and the abstract interface of UWE have their own metamodels. From among the requirement metamodels and analysis metamodels, NDT defines a set of QVT transformations that are represented in the figure with the *QVT Transformation* stereotype. Thus, the

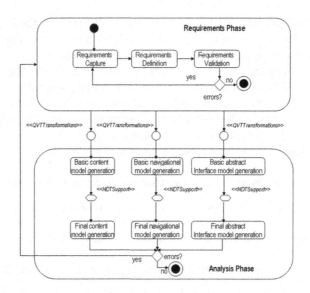

Figure 26.2. Life cycle of NDT.

shift from requirements to analysis in NDT is a systematic method based on these formal transformations. The direct application of these transformations generates a set of analysis models known in NDT as the basic analysis models. After the systematic generation, the analyst group can change these basic models by adding new relations, attributes, etc., that improve the models. This step depends on the analyst knowledge and is presented in the figure with the stereotype *NDTSupport*. This improvement generates the final analysis models. This second step is not systematic. However, NDT has to ensure that agreement between requirement and analysis models is maintained. Hence, this step is controlled by a set of rules and heuristics defined in NDT.

After the analysis model has been created, the development process can continue with another methodology, such as UWE or OOHDM [15], in order to obtain the code.

NDT offers a suitable environment for the development of Web systems. It offers specific techniques to deal with critical aspects in the Web environment. If a correlation with MDA (model-driven architecture) [13] is made, NDT presents a CIM (computational-independent model) in the requirements phase; a set of PIMs (platform-independent models), in the analysis phase; and a set of formal transformations between them.

NDT has been widely applied in practical environment and has achieved very good results, since it reduces the development time with the application of transformations and ensures agreement between requirements and analysis. In [7] the practical evolution of NDT is presented together with some of the most important practical applications.

2.3. A Practical Combination Between Métrica v3 and NDT

As stated in [7], Métrica and NDT can be easily merged to offer a suitable environment for Web development.

Métrica, in its object-oriented version, is based on UML models which are formally defined as extensions of NDT. Thus, the incorporation of NDT ideas in Métrica is, basically, the incorporation of its UML extensions.

As a practical solution, the research group of NDT has developed an approach which merges these two methodologies. This fusion is put forward in [7] and it follows the life cycle of Métrica presented in Fig. 26.1 albeit with some modifications. The ASI phase is divided into two parts: the requirement phase and the analysis phase. Both are developed using the life cycle of NDT. Thus, a navigational model and an abstract interface model are developed. Furthermore, metamodels, techniques, and transformations of NDT are applied. The DSI phase is also enriched with some specific concepts of Web engineering. Therefore, a design navigational model has to be defined.

This practical solution has been widely accepted in Andalusia. In this area, the software development in public administration is big business for consultants and software companies.

However, the application of this approach without a set of suitable tools to support the development is impossible. For this reason, a set of tools for supporting this fusion between Métrica and NDT is presented in the next section.

3. Tool Support

In order to support this practical approach, a set of tools were defined to help development teams apply this approach. The set of tools is composed of two main tools that support the development process. The first one, NDT-Profile, is oriented toward the first phases of the life cycle: requirements, analysis, and design and also includes artifacts for the test phase. The second one is CADI, a tool to ensure the traceability between design and code.

In this section, both tools are introduced. After the tool presentations, a global vision of the practical solution and the connection between the two tools is described.

3.1. NDT-Profile

As mentioned earlier, NDT is a methodology based on the extension of UML with special artifacts to deal with the special Web characteristics. NDT has an associated tool, named NDT-Tool [9], which supports its complete life cycle and that permits the application of all its transformations. However, there are several areas where NDT-Tool has yet to be applied in real projects.

The first one is the life cycle. NDT-Tool, as NDT, only covers requirements and analysis and, in real projects, design, implementation, and testing are necessary phases. Furthermore, NDT-Tool is completely based on NDT and no changes, modifications, or adaptations of the methodology to real necessities are permitted. For instance, NDT-Tool only works with patterns and use case diagrams in requirements. Other suitable diagrams such as activity or sequence diagrams are not supported. NDT-Tool was, therefore, not a suitable solution for the practical application of NDT and for its fusion with Métrica.

For this reason, a new solution was defined. This solution was named NDT-Profile. NDT-Profile is the definition of NDT metamodels and rules in a commercial tool called Enterprise Architect.[4] Enterprise Architect is a tool to support development with UML and it permits the definition of formal extensions of UML. The profile of NDT for the requirement phase in Enterprise Architect is shown in Fig. 26.3, In this profile, all the specific artifacts of NDT can be observed. For instance, AC is an NDT actor and is defined as a formal extension of UML actors. In www.iwt2.org a complete definition of NDT-Profile can be obtained.

In NDT-Profile, other profiles are defined: the analysis profile, a profile for design obtained from the fusion with Métrica, and a test profile also obtained from our fusion with Métrica. In Enterprise Architect when a profile is defined, it can be exported as an xmi file. When this file is included in a project, the set of artifacts defined in the profile are included in the set of tools of Enterprise Architect and can be used easily. Thus, in our practical collaborations, companies include the NDT-Profile in their projects, and NDT artifacts can be used as classic UML elements.

---

[4] www.sparxsystems.com

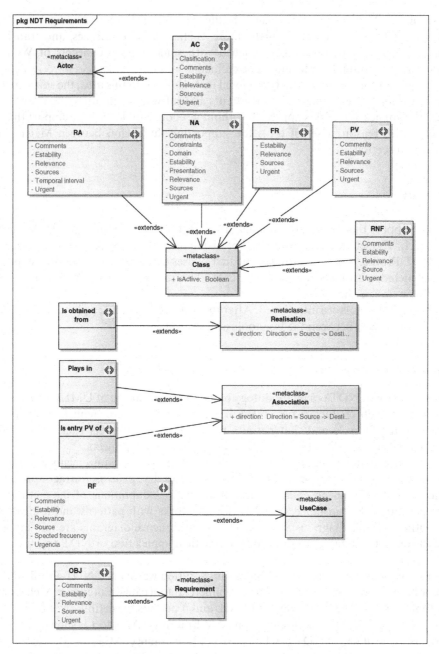

Figure 26.3. The NDT-Profile in enterprise architect for requirements.

3.2. CADI

NDT-Profile covers from the requirement to the design phase as well as the test phase, leaving a gap between them: implementation. CADI plays its role in this phase. Ever since UML reverse engineering tools appeared,[5] the common way to achieve traceability between the design and implementation phases was based on a human approach: the UML class diagrams created by the design team were manually

---

[5] http://uml.netbeans.org/

compared with those obtained from source code via reverse engineering. This approach has two main disadvantages. It is a highly time-consuming task which is also extremely error prone. Therefore, an automatic solution is needed. As always, there are several solutions for the automatization of this traceability task, each with its own advantages and disadvantages. The solution chosen by CADI is perhaps a very theoretical one, but is undoubtedly very effective and flexible: it is based on the ASTs (Abstract Syntax Trees) which underpin the theory of compilers.

ASTs [2] are well known in the theory of compilers and widely used [1]. Their main advantage for the purpose of this tool resides in the point that they do not make a direct but a symbolic representation of the code, thereby eliminating any inherent ambiguity in the codification process. ASTs allow all kinds of analysis to be carried out (syntactical, grammatical, and semantic) against the code; and these can be performed separately. ASTs create a clean interface between the code and the later phases that has to be accomplished. In this way, the process of traceability from the design phase to that of implementation is reduced (from a simplistic perspective) to the comparison of two ASTs, the one from design and the one from implementation. The latter is obtained directly, provided by the development team, and the former can be easily obtained by a feature that most software similar to Enterprise Architect offers: to generate source code from UML class diagrams.

These are the theoretical principles behind CADI. And even if CADI is implemented in Java, it is clear that the same procedures could be used with other computing languages. Moreover, CADI works with Java grammar although it is language neutral. It can be easily modified to work with any language on the condition that a grammar definition suitable for use by JJTree/JavaCC exists.[6]

CADI implementation: this is a command line tool written in Java that processes two directories of source code files recursively, one containing files from design and the other directory containing files from implementation. By implementing the Visitor Pattern, several methods are invoked while the source files are traversed, and information built in the form of ASTs is received. This method behavior can be modified by altering a system of rules defined in a properties file named "exclusion_rules.properties."

This technique gives the flexibility required for CADI to adapt to quality assurance at different levels of the project. This information provided by methods that implement the Visitor Pattern is used to generate detailed reports on the level of consistence between design and implementation. Reports are executed using a pluggable mechanism which loads at runtime. These reports are executed sequentially and appear in the file "output_config.properties." It provides a very simple, flexible, and powerful system for the generation of all kinds of reports.

At the time of writing this document, only the Java language is supported, but in the next version it is planned to implement a mechanism to handle pluggable syntax definition files, thereby allowing the use of CADI for different programming languages. CADI is fast, it can compare around 24,000 classes per minute using a single processor laptop, thereby allowing not only 100% traceability to be covered but also these checks to be performed as frequently as desired. CADI Java class files are fully documented and there is also a PDF document explaining how it was built (unfortunately both in Spanish). It has been satisfactorily applied in several projects since the end of 2007 and we are currently working in the English version of the tool.

4. The Practical Experience: The Diraya Project

The Diraya project is a complex system currently under development in Andalusia. The practical methodological environment presented in the previous section is used in this project and is described in [9].

Diraya is a system for the management of health information in Andalusia. It is divided into two systems: primary Diraya and specialized Diraya. The former is oriented to manage health information for primary health assistants. The latter offers the functionality to manage health information in hospitals and specialized centers.

---

[6] https://javacc.dev.java.net

The practical environment presented in this chapter is being applied in specialized Diraya. Here, six important companies are working for the Andalusian Health Government[7] to develop this system: Everis, Telvent, Indra, Accenture, Isoft, and Tecnova. The development team is composed of more than 80 people and the use of a suitable methodology and a suitable set of tools must be applied.

The structure of the tools is given in Fig. 26.4. In the requirement, analysis, design, and test phases, NDT-Profile is used. The whole development team uses Enterprise Architect with the special extension for NDT in their daily work.

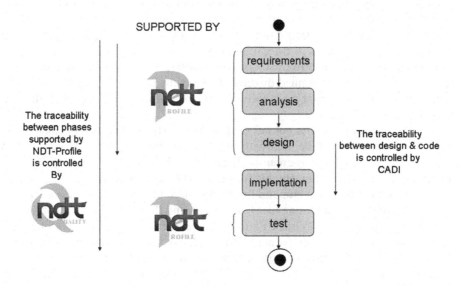

Figure 26.4. Tool solution for Diraya project.

When the design phase is finished, the code is generated in the Java language.

In order to improve and ensure traceability between design results and code, the CADI tool is used.

Furthermore, to assure traceability between requirements and analysis, analysis and design, and requirements and tests are going to be controlled by another new tool called NDT-Quality, which is currently under development and will be presented in the section for conclusions and future work.

This tool environment in Diraya is highly suitable for development support. The collaborative work of several companies, the communication between a highly developed team and the complexity of a system such as specialized Diraya can only be tackled by a mechanical and homogeneous environment such as the one presented.

This environment is being used in other projects in Andalusia and can be observed in detail in www.iwt2.org.

5. Conclusions and Future Works

This chapter presents a practical environment solution to apply model-driven techniques in the enterprise environment. We show how, by using the extension mechanisms of UML and formal metamodels, the two approaches, Métrica and NDT, can be fused in order to attain more suitable results. Furthermore, we provide a tool support solution to help in the application of this methodological environment.

---

[7] http://www.juntadeandalucia.es/servicioandaluzdesalud

As conclusions, the results of the practical applications are very positive. The theoretical fusion of approaches, metamodels, and the profile definition is transparent for the development team which works with only the Enterprise Architect interface. No theoretical lessons about model-driven paradigm have to be learnt by the development team, and the learning time is short since NDT-Profile and CADI offer a very intuitive and suitable interface.

Moreover, the assurance of traceability is a major improvement. In the project, traceability between design and code is 100% guaranteed with the use of CADI. As future work, we are working on the full application of NDT-Quality. This is a new tool developed by the NDT group which analyzes a project developed with NDT-Profile and controls the quality of this project and the traceability between phases. To this end, NDT-Quality controls some rules defined by the QVT transformations of NDT. This tool is fully developed and is starting to be used in specialized Diraya. With this incorporation, the quality assurance is greater. Additionally, the NDT group is working on two further tools. The first, named NDT-Translations, is an implementation of QVT transformations. To date, the development team has had to apply NDT transformations manually, which is not only time consuming but also prone to error. With the use of NDT-Translations the development time will be reduced and the number of manual mistakes will be lower. The second new tool is NDT-Reports. This tool is oriented toward obtaining suitable results from NDT-Profile. Enterprise Architect generates word and html results. However, the adaptation to specific results and format is a little complex and this tool attempts to facilitate this generation. Clearly, we wish to continue this relation with the enterprise environment for our future research. Conclusions obtained from practical applications are essential for the provision of suitable methodological environments.

Acknowledgments

This research has been supported by the project QSimTest (TIN2007-67843-C06_03) and by the RePRIS project of the Ministerio de Educación y Ciencia (TIN2007-30391-E), Spain.

References

1. V. Aho, Ravi Sethi, Jeffrey D. Ullman. "Compilers: Principles, Techniques, and Tools". ISBN: 978-0201100884. Addison Wesley, New York, 1986
2. E. Börger, R. Stärk, "Abstract State Machines: A Method for High-Level System Design and Analysis". ISBN: 978-3540007029. Springer, New York, 2003
3. S. Ceri, P. Fraternali, P. Bongio. "Web Modelling Language (WebML): A Modelling Language for Designing Web Sites". WWW9/Computer Networks 33, 137–157, 2000.
4. C. Cachero. "Una extensión a los métodos OO para el modelado y generación automática de interfaces hipermediales". PhD Thesis. University of Alicante, Alicante, Sapin, 2003.
5. Y. Deshpande, S. Marugesan, A. Ginige, S. Hanse, D. Schawabe, M. Gaedke, B. White. "Web Engineering". Journal of Web Engineering 1(1), 3–17, 2002. Rinton Press.
6. M.J. Escalona, J. Torres, M. Mejías, J.J. Gutierrez, D. Villadiego. The Treatment of Navigation in Web Engineering. Advances in Engineering Software 38(4), 267–282, 2007.
7. M.J. Escalona, J.J. Gutiérrez, J.A. Ortega, I. Ramos. NDT & METRICA V3-An Approach for Public Organizations Based on Model Driven Engineering WEBIST 2008. Proceeding of the 4th International Conference on Web Information Systems, Portugal, Vol. 1, ISBN. 978-989-8111-26-5, 2008.
8. M.J. Escalona, C.L. Parra, F.M. Martín, J. Nieto, A. Llergó, F. Pérez. "A Practical Example From Model-Driven Web Engineering Advance in Engineering Software". Springer Verlag, New York, Vol. 1, ISBN: 978-0-387-30403-8, 2008.
9. M.J. Escalona, G. Aragón. NDT: A Model Driven Approach for Web Requirements. IEEE Transaction on Software Engineering; United States (2008–05), Vol. 34, No. 3, pp. 377–390, ISSN: 0098-5589, 2008.
10. E. Insfrán, O. Pastor, R. Wieringa. "Requirements Engineering-Based Conceptual Modelling". Requirements Engineering Journal 7 (1), 2002.
11. N. Koch. "Software Engineering for Adaptive Hypermedia Applications". Ph. Thesis, FAST Reihe Softwaretechnik 12, Uni-Druck Publishing Company, Munich. Germany, 2001.
12. A. Kraus, N. Koch. "A Metamodel for UWE". Technical Report 0301, Ludwig-Maximilians-Universität München, January 2003.
13. OMG: MDA Guide, http://www.omg.org/docs/omg/03-06-01.pdf. V. 1.0.1, 2003.

14. OMG. Unified Modeling Language: Superstructure, version 2.0. Specification, OMG, 2005. http://www.omg.org/cgi-bin/doc? formal/05-07-04.
15. G. Rossi. "An Object-Oriented Method for Designing Hypermedia Applications". PHD Thesis. University of PUC-Rio. Rio de Janeiro. Brazil, 1996.
16. D.C. Schmidt. "Model-Driven Engineering". IEEE Computer, February 2006.
17. A. Vallecillo, N. Koch, C. Cachero, S. Comai, P. Fraternali, I. Garrigós, J. Gómez, G. Kappel, A. Knapp, M. Matera, S. Meliá, N. Moreno, B. Pröll, T. Reiter, W. Retschitzegger, J.E. Rivera, W. Schwinger, M. Wimmer, G. Zhang. MDWEnet: A Practical Approach to Achieving Interoperatiblity of Model-Driven Web Engineering Methods. 3rd Workshop on Model-Driven Web Engineering. MDWE 07, pp. 246–254, 2007.
18. P. Vilain, D. Schwabe, C. Sieckenius, "A diagrammatic Tool for Representing User Interaction in UML". Lecture Notes in Computer Science. UML'2000. York, England 2002.

27

An Approach to Generating Program Code in Quickly Evolving Environments

Linas Ablonskis

Abstract

In model-driven engineering (MDE) program code generators are used to generate program code from abstract program models, thus bringing the final code closer to program specification and saving time that would be spent in coding. Current approach to program code generation from abstract program models does not work well in quickly evolving environments due to the large amount of work that is required to fully prepare and maintain program code generator. This chapter presents analysis of current approach to program code generation and presents an alternative approach tailored for generating program code in quickly evolving environments by using self-configuring program code generator.

Keywords MDA · MDE · Code generation · Code generator · Reverse engineering · formal concept analysis

1. Introduction

Program code generators are used in model-based software development processes, such as MDA (*model-driven architecture*) or MDE (*model-driven engineering*), to automate the translation of abstract models to corresponding program code [16, 18]. This chapter assumes that program model is written using UML (*Unified Modeling Language*).

We show that standard approach to generating program code is unsuitable for use in quickly evolving environments due to implementation platform and best practices knowledge requirements and prohibitive costs related with configuring and maintaining a program code generator.

An alternative approach to generating program code from abstract program model is presented. The approach relies on relatively static initial code generator configuration that is automatically supplemented with artifacts necessary to generate program code for specific software project. The software project-specific artifacts necessary for code generation are extracted from partial human implementation of abstract program model and applied to generate program code for yet unimplemented parts. This would largely remove the costs related with program code generator configuration and maintenance and would allow to use program code generators in quickly evolving environments.

The method prototype for implementing the automatic code generator configuration in respect to structural program model is described.

This work is supported by Lithuanian State Science and Studies Foundation according to High Technology Development Program Project VeTIS, Reg.No. B-07042

Linas Ablonskis • Department of Information Systems, Kaunas University of Technology, Kaunas, Lithuania.

G.A. Papadopoulos et al. (eds.), *Information Systems Development*, DOI 10.1007/b137171_27,

The following text is organized into three main parts, followed by conclusions and future work. In the first part, a short analysis of standard approach to program code generation from abstract program models is done, together with description of related works that have influenced this chapter. In the second part, the suggested approach to generating program code in quickly evolving environments is presented. The third part describes the draft method for implementing the suggested approach in respect to structural program model.

2. Related Works

Currently there are numerous tools that allow generating program code from abstract program models. Examples of such tools are *OptimalJ*, *Arcstyler*, and *AndroMDA*. All these tools share the same approach to program code generation which we call the *standard approach*.

The standard approach to program code generation follows a predefined pattern and is based on model transformations and template-based program code generators. There is a good taxonomy of template-based code generation methods presented by K. Czarnecki and S. Helsen in [5].

The general idea of software development that involves a standard approach to program code generation can be described by the following figure (Fig. 27.1):

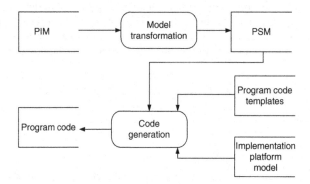

Figure 27.1. Standard approach to program code generation.

An abstract PIM (*platform-independent model*) is enriched with implementation of platform-specific information to yield a PSM (*platform-specific model*). The enrichment is usually done via *marking* [18], for example, by *stereotypes* and *tagged values*. Then program code generation is performed from PSM by using some sort of template-based program code generator. Generated code is then inspected and augmented by developers. In case of errors the program model, code templates, or implementation platform model are adjusted and program code is generated repeatedly [13]. This process iterates until results are satisfactory.

PIM to PSM translations are done either by hand or by applying automatic model transformation tools. Often PSM is considered sufficiently abstract to skip the making of PIM altogether.

Generally template-based program code generators consist of two conceptual parts: a program model walker and parameterized program code templates. The walker traverses program model in predefined fashion feeds to relevant code templates. Code templates use information from model elements to fill the parameterizable parts of code. Another perspective is to view program code generator as a rule engine [5] which executes a set of rules designed to analyze the program model and generate program code.

There are various implementation methods [5, 15, 23] of template-based program code generators each focusing on various user-related aspects such as simplicity of management, extensibility, reusability, and compatibility with some type of metamodel.

The approach to automatic program code generator configuration described in this chapter builds on several areas: software reverse engineering, automatic design pattern detection, and software analysis methods based on *formal concept analysis* [10].

The field of reverse engineering is quite well understood and examples of standard approaches can be found in [9, 19, 22, 29]. This field is closely tied to automatic design pattern detection methods that are used mainly as aids in program understanding.

There are various techniques for detecting design patterns, described in [1–2], [7–8, 12, 14, 20, 24, 26, 33–34], that rely on predefined design pattern database describing design patterns through relations between various types of code entities and additional metrics [8, 12]. Program code is parsed to extract a set of entities and their relations together with a set of metrics and results are compared with information in pattern database.

The exception is the design pattern detection method based on formal concept analysis [33]. It analyzes program code with formal concept analysis techniques by grouping entities into concepts using a predefined set of properties. Concepts are considered to express arbitrary design patterns, which are discovered without a need of predefined pattern database. The ideas in this work served as a basis to method proposal presented in this chapter.

There are other software analysis methods based on formal concept analysis, tailored for discovery of modularities and hierarchies in software code, thus becoming aids in program understanding and legacy system reengineering [6, 17, 25, 27–28, 30–32].

While the widely referenced "no silver bullet" paper [3] has long ago expressed the idea of automatically configurable program code generators that work through expert system techniques; we were unable to find any such systems implemented. Expert systems-related methods are offered for software component matching, an example of which can be [4].

3. Properties and Limitations of Standard Approach to Generating Program Code from Abstract Program Models

In general, program code generation from abstract program models offers numerous benefits over purely hand-written code [13]:

- *savings in coding time, fast prototyping;*
- *reduction in the number of coding errors;*
- *improved correspondence between a program model and the final program code;*
- *increased use of code-related best practices for an application domain and the implementation platform.*

Benefits of the standard approach to program code generation are

- *Faster development of product lines, where program code generators can be applied to generate code for multiple projects in the line without requiring large reconfigurations.*
- *Ability to perform some program changes in an abstract program model and automatically propagate them into the program code by repeated code generation.*

Thus program code generation is an efficient aid in a software development process. However, the availability of program code generator for a specific software project depends on the presence of configuration database for specific implementation platform and technologies used. This obvious requirement is the main limitation of the standard approach as will be shown further in this chapter.

Popular program code generators come with a wide assortment of configurations and modules tailored for generating program codes for most popular implementation platforms and technologies. Sharing of code generation configurations and modules by community is often encouraged and supported by vendors to widen the applicability of code generators furthermore.

However, there are a lot of technologies and programming frameworks that do not have code generator profiles written and new ones emerge constantly. If benefits of code generation are to be utilized by them, someone has to write the necessary profiles for specific code generators. Furthermore, if an application domain evolves quickly, someone has to maintain existing program code generator configurations to keep them up with domain evolution. We define the *quickly evolving environment* as an unstable development environment where new technologies are constantly tried out and application domain knowledge relatively frequently changes.

4. Analysis of Information Required to Configure Program Code Generator

To write a program code generator configuration one must have or write and debug several pieces of information. Some of these pieces are relatively static and can be readily reused in different software projects but some of them may be unavailable for the specific software project because they depend on implementation platform and technologies used (Fig. 27.2).

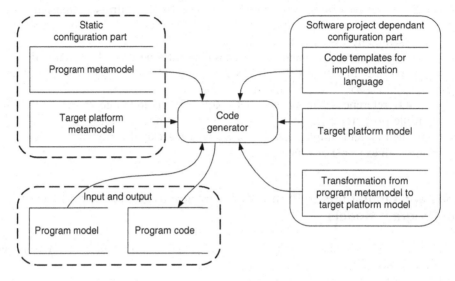

Fig. 27.2. Data flow in program code generation process.

The relatively static aspects of program code generator configuration are metamodels used to model software in question and the implementation platform. Since modeling languages are relatively stable, these two pieces of information can be reused between different software projects.

The relatively dynamic aspects of program code generator configuration are code templates of target platform model and transformation from the program metamodel to the target platform model. They depend on implementation platform, technologies, and programming languages used and must be modified every time when any of those change.

The dynamic artifacts usually contain a lot of information and are costly to make and maintain [11]. Furthermore, some of them cannot be made without expert-level knowledge of program target domain, best code practices, and implementation platform [13]. This knowledge can only be obtained by first creating one or several relevant software products manually [13].

Thus standard approach to program code generation is suitable for use only in well-known, slow changing environments and unsuitable when environment is unstable or not well known, because configuration and maintenance costs of program code generator become prohibitive.

5. Properties of Program Code Exploited by Program Code Generators

It can be observed that most of the real-world program code contains repetitive and unique fragments. The unique fragments depend on the requirements that program fulfils and are usually coded by a human who knows the context involved. When facilities of programming language allow, repetitive fragments can be moved to separate constructs and reused.

Often there are patterns in program code that cannot be efficiently reused by the facilities of programming language only. Consider the typical database persistence code in a class. Such code depends on the attributes of class involved, but otherwise has a clearly defined pattern which is repeated in every persistent class. The reuse of such patterns is achieved with a help of program code generators, which automatically generate the parameterized code expressing the necessary patterns, based on an abstract representation of the entity (class) involved.

However, if program domain evolves quickly or implementation platform is not well known, a standard approach to program code generation requires performing costly program code generator configuration and maintenance and thus is unsuitable to real-world applications. In such a case, the benefits of program code generation are unavailable.

6. An Approach to Generating Program Code in Quickly Evolving Environments

In this section it is assumed that software system is being implemented in an environment which is dynamic or new enough to make standard approach to program code generation infeasible. First an abstract model of such software system is built, using UML [21]-like modeling language, in order to conceive an abstract system which satisfies the requirements of the consumer. It is assumed that the model is correct and consistent. The next step would be implementation of software system in the actual implementation platform, using a specific programming language.

It can be observed that part of the final system is already expressed in abstract model and the implementation of that model is the transformation from abstract expression to platform-specific expression, thus concepts, names, properties, structural and behavioral relationships from program model will be transferred to program code in some form.

A partial implementation of the program model in the program code can be reverse engineered [9, 19, 22, 29] to yield a partial program model. The relationships between the reverse-engineered program model and the program code can be easily traced, thus yielding insights to implementation patterns of original program model. This can be used as the basis for automatic configuration of a program code generator (Fig. 27.3).

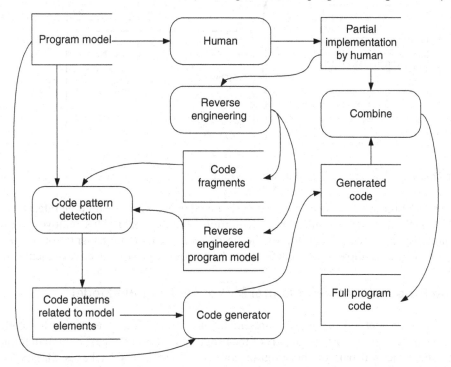

Figure 27.3. Data flow in suggested approach to generating program code in quickly evolving environments.

Such code generator would reverse engineer the partial program model implementation written by humans to extract code fragments related with implementation of model elements. It would analyze code fragments to detect patterns related to properties of model elements being implemented and use those patterns to make general code templates that can be used to automatically generate code for yet unimplemented model elements having the same sets of properties (Fig. 27.3).

In this scenario, the developer would be tasked with providing initial code to analyze and write unique code that requires contextual knowledge beyond that present in program model and not deducible from program code.

Unlike a standard program code generator, an automatically configurable code generator would use a relatively static initial configuration database and extract project-specific data from program model and a partial implementation of that model.

A static part of code generator configuration would consist of a program meta-model, a database of programming language constructs, correspondence rules between program metamodel and programming language constructs, and rules for detection of code patterns. The dynamic part would consist of implementation of program language model, used to reverse and forward engineer program code, and name mangling rule set that would allow detection of correspondence between model elements and their representations in code (Fig. 27.4). It can be seen that even dynamic part, once written, would remain relatively static, because programming languages change slowly and there are relatively few naming conventions.

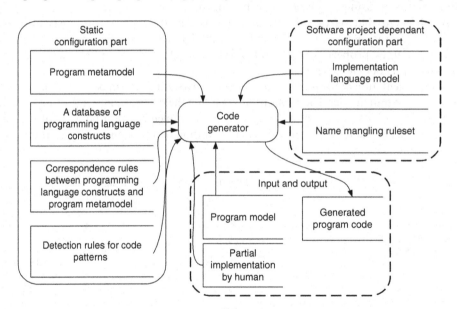

Figure 27.4. Data flow in program generation process when self-configuring program code generator is involved.

Other pieces of information necessary for program code generation would be inferred by observing the program model and partial human implementation of that model. This removes the necessity to manually adapt program code generator to the needs of particular implementation technologies and related best practices, thus allowing its benefits to be had in quickly evolving environments.

7. A Method Proposal for the Structural Part of the Program Model

In this section, a method proposal is presented for achieving automatic program code generator configuration by observing the structural part of the program model and a partial human implementation of that part. The structural part of the program model will consist of packages, classes, components, interfaces, and other declarative elements able to act as containers.

The important property of the structural model is that it usually has more or less straightforward correspondence in the program code. Structural model entities can have 1:1, 1:n, n:1, and n:m relationships with their implementations in the code. In the first two cases (1:1, 1:n), the information from the model is largely not lost in the code. The second two cases are encountered in optimization scenarios and they lose information. However, it is rare to optimize structural constructs manually; usually it is done automatically by code compilers.

It is assumed that we already have a name mangling rule set that allows name transformations between program model and code, and vice versa. A possible example would be a naming convention that uses *Formal English* and a corresponding name mangling rule set that would operate with placeholders and well-known prefixes and suffixes.

An AST (*Abstract Syntax Tree*) can be built from the partial human implementation of structural program model. Then AST can be transformed, so that its nodes represent entities from the programming language construct database – this would yield a programming language-independent AST (Fig. 27.5). Links between model elements and AST nodes can be found by using name mangling and the database of correspondence rules. The nodes that do not depend on the types of super-nodes and model elements would be removed and replaced with special nodes indicating placeholders for human to fill. This would leave only tree fragments that are either self-sufficient or depend only on properties of model elements that they implement.

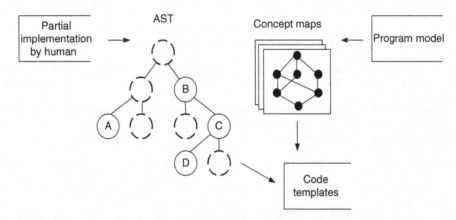

Figure 27.5. Artifacts used in the method.

Techniques of *Formal Concept Analysis* can be employed to make groupings of model elements that depend on the same properties (Fig. 27.5). Such groupings are called *concepts*. Properties relevant for analysis would be such as the presence of the stereotype, tagged values, a type of an attribute, a specific member, and sharing of containment. Concepts can be matched with pruned AST tree and tree fragments that depend on the same set of properties as possessed by concept can be found. Those tree fragments can be parameterized by properties of related concept to serve as code templates for yet unimplemented model elements that belong to the same concept (Fig. 27.5).

Since a possibility still remains to make a concept that actually was never intended by a human and whose members do not share implementation details the method would need to be used with IDE (*Integrated Development Environment*) that would offer the potential code generation candidates in a fashion of auto-completion mechanism, which would react to acceptance or rejection by a human to validate concepts.

8. Conclusions and Future Work

In this chapter it was shown that standard approach to generating program code from abstract models is not well suited to quickly evolving environments because configuring and maintenance costs of a program code generator become a limiting factor in its use.

An approach to generating program code in quickly evolving environments is presented. It would work by employing a relatively static initial program code generator configuration which would be automatically augmented by artifacts necessary to generate program code for specific software project. This would be achieved by observing partial human implementation of abstract software model and detecting code patterns related to groups of model entities. Those code patterns then would be used to generate code for yet unimplemented entities of the model in the same group. A draft method is presented to implement the automatic configuration of program code generator that works with the structural part of the program model.

It is intended to further refine the theory behind this idea for automatic configuration of program code generators by building a working prototype and expanding the method to encompass some types of easy to analyze behavioral models such as sequence and state diagrams.

References

1. Albin-Amiot, H., Cointe, P., Guéhéneuc, Y.G., Jussien, N. (2001) Instantiating and detecting design patterns: Putting bits and pieces together. In *ASE*, pp. 166–173. IEEE Computer Society.
2. Asencio, A., Cardman, S., Harris, D., Laderman, E. (2002) Relating expectations to automatically recovered design patterns. In *Proceedings of the Ninth Working Conference on Reverse Engineering (WCRE'02)*, pp. 87–96. Washington, DC, USA: IEEE Computer Society.
3. Brooks, F.P. (1987) No silver bullet – essence and accidents of software engineering. *IEEE Computer*, April: 10–19
4. Christensen, K., Olesen, T.H., Thomsen, L.L. (2006) Matching semantically described web services using ontologies. *Information Technology and Control*, 35(3A):267–275
5. Czarnecki, K., Helsen, S. (2003) Classification of model transformation approaches. In *Workshop on Generative Techniques in the Context of MD (OOPSLA 2003)*, Anaheim, CA, USA (available at http://www.swen.uwaterloo.ca/~kczarnec/ECE750T7/czarnecki_helsen.pdf)
6. Eisenbarth, T., Koschke, R., Simon D. (2001) Feature-driven program understanding using concept analysis of execution traces. In *9th International Workshop on Program Comprehension*, pp. 300–309. IEEE Computer Society.
7. Fabry, J., Mens, T. (2004) Language independent detection of object-oriented design patterns. *Computer Languages, Systems and Structures*, 30(1–2):21–33
8. Ferenc, R., Beszedes, A.,Fulop, L.,Lele, J. (2005) Design pattern mining enhanced by machine learning. In*Proceedings of the 21st IEEE International Conference on Software Maintenance*, pp. 295–304. Washington, DC, USA: IEEE Computer Society.
9. Gannod, G.C., Cheng, B.H.C. (1999) A framework for classifying and comparing software reverse engineering and design recovery techniques. In *Working Conference on Reverse Engineering*, pp. 77–88.
10. Ganter, B. and Wille, R. (1998) Applied lattice theory: Formal concept analysis. In *General Lattice Theory*, pp. 591–605. Birkhäuser Verlag, Basel.
11. Glass, R.L. (1996) Some thoughts on automatic code generation. *The Data Base for Advances in Information Systems*, 27(2): 16–18
12. Gueheneuc, Y.G., Sahraoui, H., Zaidi, F. (2004) Fingerprinting design patterns. In *Proceedings of the 11th Working Conference on Reverse Engineering*, pp. 172–181. Washington, DC, USA: IEEE Computer Society.
13. Herrington, J. (2003) *Code Generation in Action*. Manning Publications Co.
14. Heuzeroth, D., Holl, T., Högström, G., Löwe, W. (2003) Automatic design pattern detection. In *Proceedings 11th IEEE International Workshop on Program Comprehension IWPC*, pp. 94–104. IEEE Computer Society.
15. Heyse, W., Jonckers, V., Wagelaar, D. (2005) *Generic Code Generation Approaches*, Apprenticeship Report.
16. Kent, S. (2002) Model driven engineering. In *Proceedings of Third International Conference on Integrated Formal Methods (IFM 2002)*, LNCS 2335, pp. 286–298. Springer.
17. Lindig, C., Snelting, G. (1997) Assessing modular structure of legacy code based on mathematical concept analysis. In *Proceedings of the 1997 International Conference on Software Engineering*, pp. 349–359. ACM Press.
18. Miller, J., Mukerji, J. (2003) *MDA Guide Version 1.0.1*, Retrieved June 01, 2007 from: http://www.omg.org/cgi-bin/apps/doc?omg/03-06-01.pdf
19. Niere, J., Wadsack, J., Zundorf, A. (2001) Recovering UML Diagrams from Java Code using Patterns. In *Proceedings of the 2-nd Workshop on Soft Computing Applied to Software Engineering*. Enschede, The Netherlands.
20. Niere, J., Schäfer, W., Wadsack, J.P., Wendehals, L., Welsh, J. (2002) Towards pattern based design recovery. In *Proceedings of the 24th International Conference on Software Engineering*, pp. 338–348. New York, NY, USA: ACM.
21. *OMG Unified Modelling Language (OMG UML) Superstructure* (2008), V2.1.2, Retrieved April 01, 2008 from: http://www.omg.org/spec/UML/2.1.2/Superstructure/PDF/
22. Paradauskas, B., Laurikaitis, A. (2006) Business knowledge extraction from legacy information systems. *Information Technology and Control*, 35(3):214–221

23. Sauer, F. (2002) Metadata driven multi-artifact code generation using frame oriented programming. In *OOPSLA 2002 Workshop "Generative Techniques in the Context of Model Driven Architecture"*, November 5, Seattle, WA.

24. Shi, N., Olsson, R.A. (2006) Reverse engineering of design patterns from java source code. In *Proceedings of the 21st IEEE/ACM International Conference on Automated Software Engineering*, pp. 123–134. Washington, DC, USA: IEEE Computer Society.

25. Siff, M., Reps, T. (1997) Identifying modules via concept analysis. In *Proceedings of the International Conference on Software Maintenance*, pp. 170–179. IEEE Computer Society.

26. Smith, J., Stotts, D. (2002) *Elemental Design Patterns: A Logical Inference System and Theorem Prover Support for Flexible Discovery of Design Patterns*. Department of Computer Science, University of North Carolina, Technical Report TR02-038.

27. Snelting, G. (1998) Concept analysis – a new framework for program understanding. In *SIGPLAN/SIGSOFT Workshop on Program Analysis for Software Tools and Engineering (PASTE)*, Montreal, Canada, pp. 1–10.

28. Snelting, G., Tip, F. (2000) Understanding class hierarchies using concept analysis. In *ACM Transanctions on Programming Languages and Systems*, pp. 540–582.

29. Systa, T. (1999) On the Relationship between static and dynamic models in reverse engineering java software. In *Proceedings of the 6th Working Conference on Reverse Engineering (WCRE99)*, pp. 304–313.

30. Tilley, T., Cole, R., Becker, P., Eklund, P. (2004) A survey of formal concept analysis support for software engineering activities. In *Proceedings of the First International Conference on Formal Concept Analysis ICFCA'03*, LNCS 3626, pp. 250–271. Springer-Verlag.

31. Tonella, P., Ceccato, M. (2004) *Aspect Mining though the Formal Concept Analysis of Execution Traces*, IRST Technical Report.

32. Tonella, P. (2001) Concept analysis for module restructuring. *IEEE Trans on Software Engineering*, 27(4):351–363

33. Tonella, P., Antoniol, G. (1999) Object Oriented Design Pattern Inference. In *Proceedings of the 5th Symposium on Software Development Environments (SDE5)*, pp. 230–238. IEEE Computer Society.

34. Tsantalis, N., Chatzigeorgiou, A., Stephanides, G., Halkidis, S.T. (2006) Design pattern detection using similarity scoring. *IEEE Transanctions on Software Engineering*, 32: 896–909.

28

Devising a New Model-Driven Framework for Developing GUI for Enterprise Applications

Pierre Akiki

Abstract

The main goal of this chapter is to demonstrate the design and development of a GUI framework that is model driven and is not directly linked to one presentation technology or any specific presentation subsystem of a certain programming language. This framework will allow us to create graphical user interfaces that are not only dynamically customizable but also multilingual. In order to demonstrate this new concept we design in this chapter a new framework called Customizable Enterprise Data Administrator (CEDAR). Additionally, we build a prototype of this framework and a technology-dependent engine which would transform the output of our framework into a known presentation technology.

Keywords Enterprise application · Model driven · Graphical user interface (GUI) · Presentation technology

1. Introduction

The model-driven architecture (MDA) [7] provides a technology-independent approach for tackling the effect of technology and business requirements change in software development. As specified in [1], MDA is about using modeling languages as programming languages rather than merely as design languages. Programming with modeling languages can improve the productivity, quality, and longevity outlook. Such approach would be very efficient with enterprise applications due to the major effect of continuous change in technology and business requirements on this type of applications. This chapter will rely on the essence of MDA in order to devise a model-driven framework for building GUI which mainly targets enterprise applications and even smaller line-of-business applications.

Enterprise applications (enterprise resource planning (ERP), customer relationship management (CRM), etc.) usually provide many graphical user interfaces, commonly known as forms or screens, mainly for inputting and viewing data. The large quantity of those GUIs will make the application vulnerable to any change in technology since it was not designed and built in a scalable manner. A model-driven approach will minimize the effect that any technology change could have on enterprise applications. If, for instance, we build the entire GUIs of an ERP system, which could constitute hundreds of forms, using a certain presentation technology without using a model-driven approach, it would be very difficult to shift the product to a different programming language or to another newly released presentation technology within the same language. This is simply because the cost of such move will be very high due to the necessity of having to change every GUI on its own as if it were being newly developed.

Enterprise applications have evolved from small custom-made products into generic off-the-shelf products. This brings up a dilemma concerning some special requirements which each user might request. If

Pierre Akiki • Department of Computer Science, Notre Dame University, Zouk Mosbeh, Lebanon

G.A. Papadopoulos et al. (eds.), *Information Systems Development*, DOI 10.1007/b137171_28,

we consider the GUIs for instance, we could see that different customers might want to visualize their GUIs in different manners due to the different needs and cultures.

The purpose of this chapter is to propose a novel framework that we will call "customizable enterprise data administrator" (CEDAR) that aims at solving the matter of change in the presentation technology by suggesting a model-driven approach rather than a language-specific approach. CEDAR will also aim to solve the different needs in terms of modifying the user interface's layout and human language without having to develop a tailor-made application.

As specified in [7], the MDA unites the Object Management Group's (OMG) well-established modeling standards with every middleware technology – past, present, and future – to integrate what you've built, with what you're building, with what you're going to build. Rather than focusing on yet another "next best thing," MDA raises the bar and designs portability and interoperability into the application at the model level.

Although the MDA has been extensively studied [1, 2, 6], very few studies have investigated and developed tools which could handle the different tiers of enterprise applications. The concept of the MDA discussed in [7] specifies rules for building applications which are based on it. Yet, our study in this chapter is based on the essence of MDA and not on specific implementation rules.

This chapter is divided into five main sections. Section 2 discusses the different commercial presentation technologies and their different usages. Section 3 interprets the dilemma which emerges due to the existence of such diverse presentation technologies on the market and due to their constant change. In Section 4, we discuss the different aspects of our proposed framework CEDAR. Section 5 concludes this chapter and discusses the open possibilities for further work.

2. Presentation Technologies

There are currently many different software development technologies on the market. This means that there are also many different methods for creating a presentation layer, especially since some development technologies might offer several presentation subsystems which might serve for the same or different purposes.

In the case of web-based applications, the dominant presentation technology is based on markup. This could be either the traditional HyperText Markup Language (HTML) or any of its variations such as XHTML. Both .NET's ASP.NET and Java's JSP are technologies for developing web-based applications and provide the capability of developing GUIs using HTML and XHTML. The markup allows developers to build lightweight yet limited GUIs which would be interpreted and displayed by web browsers. Web applications require the usage of more technologies which could enrich them. Such technologies might include Flash, Shockwave, VRML, etc.

In case of desktop applications, each development technology offers its own presentation subsystem. For example, C# and VB.NET offer Windows Forms [5], Java offers Swing [8], and Visual C + + offers its GUI technology as part of the Microsoft Foundations Classes (MFC).

The .NET frameworks 3.0 and 3.5 offered a new presentation subsystem called the Windows Presentation Foundation (WPF) [4]. This subsystem allows C# and VB.NET developers to develop GUIs using a markup language called Extended Application Markup Language (XAML). This new technology would separate the work of developers from that of graphic designers, whereby a graphic designer could design the GUI separately, and then hand it over to the developer who would only have to write the presentation logic behind that GUI. This procedure could also be done the other way around where the developer will create a scrap GUI and write the presentation logic and then hand it over to the graphic designer who would add his/her artistic touch to it. This procedure would allow the designer to use special design tools like Microsoft Expression Blend, for example, while the developer maintains the usage of an integrated development environment (IDE) like Visual Studio. This presentation technology also started bridging the gap between web and desktop applications since it allows developers to use the same syntax in order to create a presentation layer for both desktop applications (WPF applications) and web applications (WPF browser applications known as XBAP). Figures 28.1, 28.2, 28.3, and 28.4 provide a small demonstration on the different commercial presentation technologies which are offered by different development platforms. Figures 28.1 and 28.2 show that Windows Forms and Swing could

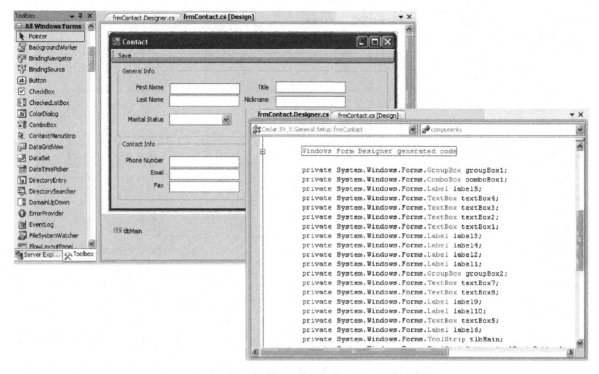

Figure 28.1. Desktop Applications' GUIs using .NET's Windows Forms.

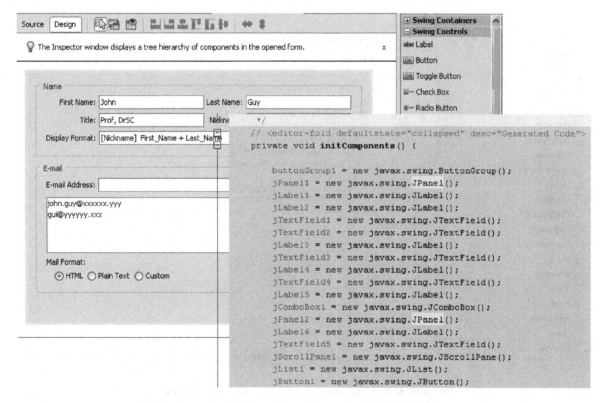

Figure 28.2. Platform-independent GUIs using Java's Swing.

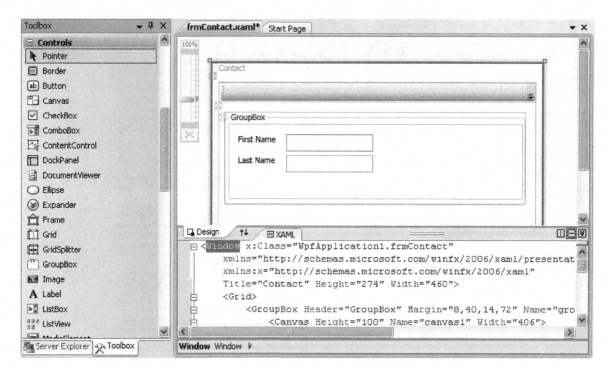

Figure 28.3. Desktop XAML GUIs using .NET's WPF.

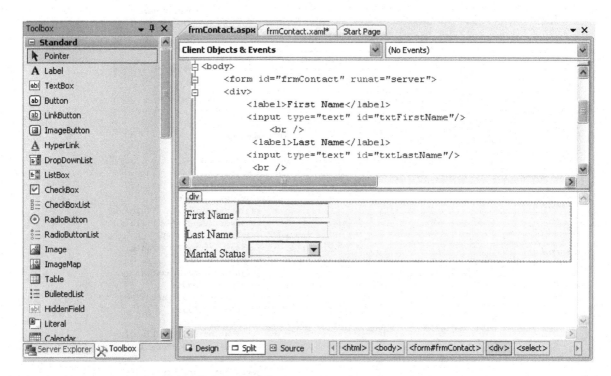

Figure 28.4. Web Applications' GUI using HTML and XHTML.

be created through visual designers that are usually integrated within their supporting IDEs such as Visual Studio.NET and NetBeans. The IDE would, in turn, generate compiled language-specific code (C#, VB.NET, Java, etc.) from the visual design. On the other hand Fig. 28.3 and 28.4 show that other technologies like HTML/XHTML and WPF could also be created using a visual designer which would, in turn, generate certain markup from the visual design. In either case, all the demonstrated presentation technologies are technology specific.

3. Diverse Presentation Technology Dilemma

The basic dilemma is created by the existence and emergence of many development technologies and their constant independent progress. In the case when a software company wants to shift its product from one programming language to another, the GUIs will have to be entirely redone as if they were being written for the first time. This matter remains simple if one can commit to a specific programming language and decide not to shift to a new language unless the used one becomes entirely obsolete. On the other hand, the existence of more than one presentation technology within a single programming language could create a more confusing decision problem. Let us consider .NET for an example. When it was first released .NET offered Windows Forms [5] as the sole presentation technology for creating desktop applications under C# and VB.NET. Currently, Windows Forms is considered by many to be a time-tested and robust solution capable of handling all GUI requirements for enterprise and line-of-business applications. This is partially due to the availability of trained personnel and abundance in third-party components. Upon the release of the .NET framework 3.0, Microsoft released an entirely new presentation subsystem called the Windows Presentation Foundation (WPF). WPF surpassed Windows Forms in several areas and lacked some of the latter's capabilities. Microsoft announced that WPF was not intended as a replacement of Windows Forms and that they will both continue to be supported and will run together side by side for years to come. This is translated with the release of Crossbow, an interoperability technology for building hybrid WPF and Windows Forms applications.

The co-existence of these two presentation technologies within .NET will create confusion among software companies upon which one to choose. This confusion will most certainly exist for newly developed projects since the software company will have to make a choice. It will face some problems if it goes with WPF, due to the lack of the necessary components required for building enterprise applications. This is also accompanied by a lack of expertise among developers, hence the company will have to set up a budget for training its developers quickly. Yet if it goes with Windows Forms it could face the fact that WPF might still replace Windows Forms in the near future. This replacement might not be that expensive for small software tools but it is definitely a problem for enterprise applications with hundreds of forms, especially if those applications were built to be used for years.

Our solution is that this dilemma could not be optimally solved without the usage of a model-driven approach. By using such an approach a software company could choose the technology which best suits it for the coming couple of years and then in case a change is required, the effect on the cost will be minimal.

Another problem is created by the fact that some applications might require the development of the same GUIs using two different technologies. Let us take the example of a desktop enterprise application which requires the development of some of its forms using a web technology. In case no model-driven approach is used, these GUIs will have to be developed each on its own, hence doubling the development and maintenance time.

4. Customizable Enterprise Data Administrator (CEDAR)

In order to apply any model-driven approach a tool must be devised in order to create the models on which the application will be based. CEDAR will be the tool by which we will apply our model-driven approach. We have divided enterprise applications into several tiers starting with the three main tiers discussed in the model view controller (MVC) architecture [3]. Hence CEDAR will have to include several tools in order to handle the different parts of an enterprise application, such as the presentation layer, the business logic layer, the data access layer. In this chapter we will only cover the part related to the presentation layer.

4.1. CEDAR Development Technology

We chose C# as the programming language by which to develop CEDAR due to the different facilities which it offers. The major facility offered in this part of CEDAR is the designer surface component. This component will allow us to develop a visual designer without having to write all the functionality from scratch, and we consider that as a major starting point.

Since CEDAR will require a storage facility for its modeled data, a DBMS has to be chosen. Hence, SQL Server was chosen due its high compatibility with .NET and due to its wide usage with different types of enterprise applications.

4.2. CEDAR Presentation Designer

The major tool provided by CEDAR is the presentation designer which will allow developers to create a technology-independent presentation layer. The main features of CEDAR are the following:

- It is similar in its appearance to the Windows Forms designer provided by Visual Studio.NET. This is considered by many to be an efficient designer.
- Could be considered as a WYSIWYG designer since the generated technology dependent output would be identical to the technology-independent design.
- It is based on the "DesignerSurface" component which is incorporated within the .NET framework. This feature saved us the effort of having to create the designer completely from scratch.

This designer is composed of several components which are the following:

- A designer surface which will allow the user to visually create the GUI and manipulate the controls at will.
- A set of toolboxes containing preset controls from which the developers could easily choose which to add to their user interfaces.
- Different panels including the properties panel that shows the properties of the control, which is currently being edited, and the layouts panel that provides the developer with the ability to choose which layout to edit.
- The "DesignerSurface" component (Fig. 28.5) also incorporates several useful functionalities like "Undo/Redo," "Tab Order," in addition to "Copy and Paste" which could be used in both directions between CEDAR and Visual Studio's Windows Forms designer, since the "DesignerSurface" is basically the Windows Forms designer incorporated in a reusable .NET component. This makes it easy to directly copy existing Windows Forms GUI elements into the CEDAR designer, hence benefiting from its technology-independent capabilities.

4.3. CEDAR Data Storage

Since CEDAR aims to create technology-independent GUIs it should be capable of storing these GUIs in a technology-independent manner. A relational database was chosen to be the storage repository due to the wide usage of relational databases with enterprise applications. CEDAR will basically store all its data in an application database which is separated from the business database. The enterprise

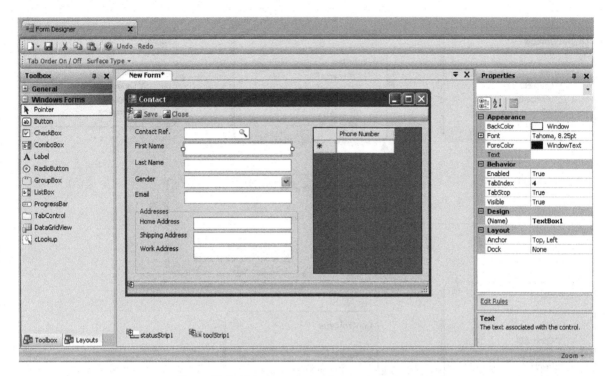

Figure 28.5. Cedar presentation designer (contact screen).

application will have to read its application information from the application database and use it in order to generate its presentation layer. Figure 28.6 shows part of the CEDAR data model, this model is practically a representation of the application database which is used to store all the presentation information.

4.4. CEDAR Application Architecture

Since CEDAR stores its data inside a relational database, CEDAR-based enterprise applications could utilize any application architecture to communicate with the database. Whether the application communicates with its business database using a client–server or a three–tiered architecture it will still be able to communicate with CEDAR application database. As for the CEDAR designer itself it employs a three–tiered architecture in order to communicate with the application database. Figures 28.7 and 28.8 show how CEDAR communicates with its application database and the different options that the enterprise application has in order to communicate with its own business database. On the presentation layer (Figs. 28.7 and 28.8) lies the technology-specific enterprise application which will, in turn, read from the CEDAR application database and use the stored data in order to generate technology-specific GUIs.

4.5. CEDAR Designer Essentials

It is not enough for the CEDAR designer to merely allow developers to create GUIs visually. Due to the ability to control every aspect of CEDAR designer, much more could be done to improve the quality and agility of software development. Some of these aspects could include validation, data binding, etc. The CEDAR designer provides the ability to set up different types of validation without writing any programming language-specific code. Figure 28.9 shows a sample interface which would allow the setting up of rules

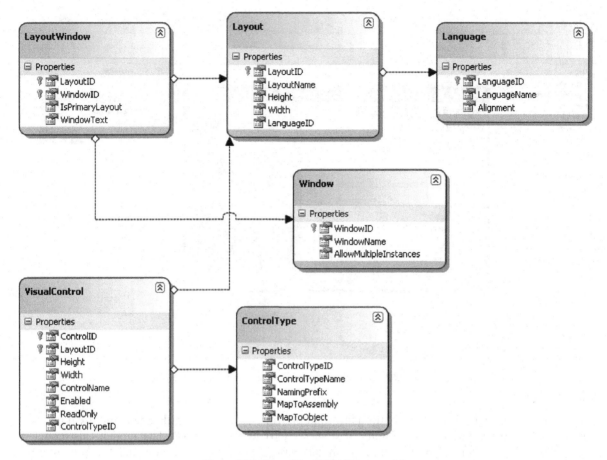

Figure 28.6. Part of the CEDAR data model.

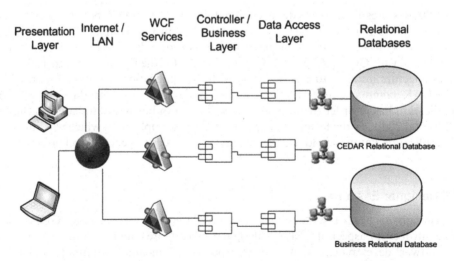

Figure 28.7. CEDAR and enterprise application following the three-tiered architecture.

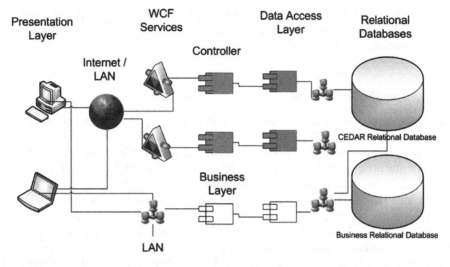

Figure 28.8. Three-tiered architecture CEDAR and client–server enterprise application.

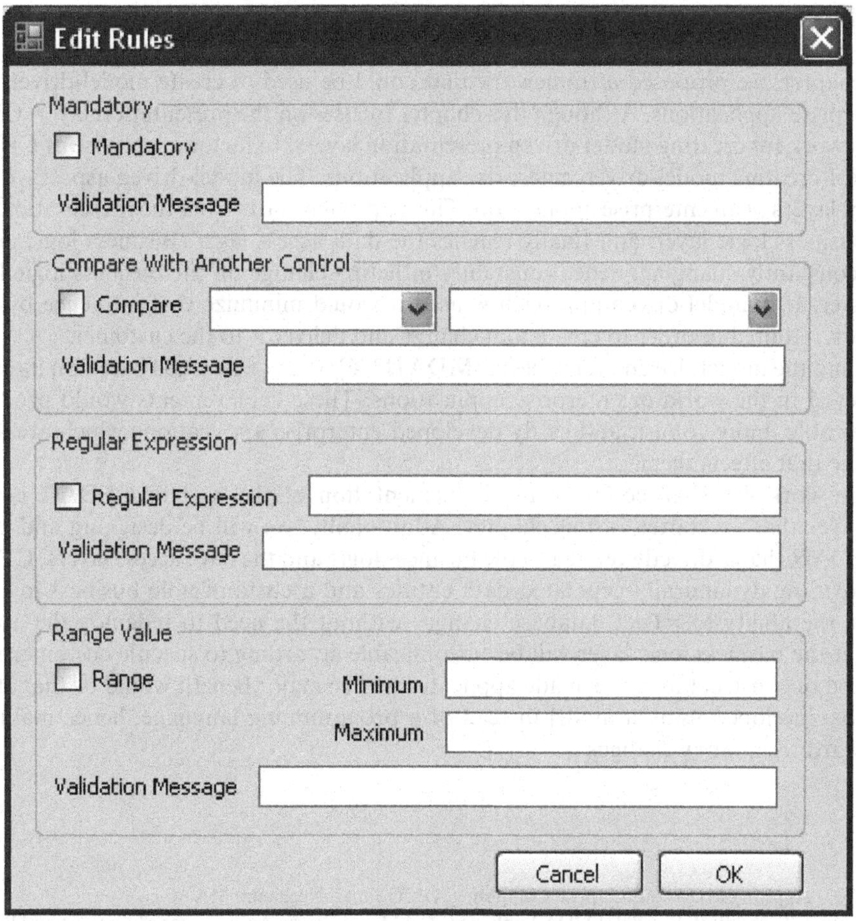

Figure 28.9. CEDAR validation rules.

such as checking mandatory fields, comparing one field with another, comparing fields with regular expressions, and validating field values based on ranges. Additionally, CEDAR would eventually provide the ability to bind the visual controls to a data source.

4.6. Technology-Specific Generation

CEDAR is the tool that will be used for creating all aspects of the presentation layer in a technology-independent manner. But that would merely remain as data inside a database if a technology-specific generator engine is not developed. Let us consider a case where the presentation layer of a certain enterprise application was developed under CEDAR. Next, the choice of presentation technology would be made and a specific engine would be written in order to translate what CEDAR created into that technology. In case the technology changes partially or completely, only the engine will have to be modified or rewritten, hence preserving the presentation layer from constant change. The role of this engine would be to customize any compiled presentation elements if they exist and to create these elements otherwise. This engine will also handle the dynamic generation of all the validation elements and the data-binding components, in addition to setting the data-binding properties.

5. Conclusion and Future Work

In this chapter, we proposed a framework that could be used to create model-driven presentation layers for enterprise applications. Although this chapter focuses on the presentation layer, CEDAR is not merely a framework for creating model-driven presentation layers. In fact, the purpose of CEDAR is to be a framework for creating model-driven enterprise applications. The model-driven aspect would influence all the different layers of an enterprise application. This approach starts from the presentation layer, passes through the business logic layer, and finally reaches the data access layer. Business logic and the data's structure are constantly changing, hence constantly inflicting change on the business logic layer and the data access layer. If a model-driven approach is used it would minimize that influence by reducing the amount of work required in order to create that change and deliver it to the customer.

By applying the model-driven architecture (MDA) [2, 6] or any new ideas based on its essence, much could be achieved in the world or enterprise applications. These achievements would produce scalable, highly customizable, more robust, and easily developed enterprise applications which are less fragile to constant change that affects them.

As future work, we shall complete the implementation of the part of CEDAR concerning the presentation layer that we started in this chapter. Additionally, we will be designing and implementing the part of CEDAR that is directly related to the business logic and the data access layers. CEDAR will be capable of providing dynamically generated data entities and a customizable business logic layer. This would provide the ability to reflect database changes without the need to redeploy the application. In addition to that the business logic layer will be customizable according to specific customer requirements without the need of constructing tailor-made applications. The major benefit would be that all application layers would be developed using a model instead of a programming language, hence making them less vulnerable toward technology changes.

References

1. Frankel, D. (2003) Applying MDA to Enterprise Computing, OMG Press, Needham, MA
2. Kleppe, A., Warmer, J., and Bast, W. (2003) MDA Explained: The Model Driven Architecture™: Practice and Promise, Addison Wesley, New York
3. Ladd, S., and Donald, K. (2006) Expert Spring MVC and Web Flow, Apress, Berkeley, CA

4. MacDonald, M. (2007) Pro WPF – Windows Presentation Foundation in .NET 3.0, Apress, Berkeley, CA
5. MacDonald, M. (2005) Pro .NET 2.0 Windows Forms and Custom Controls in C#, Apress, Berkeley, CA
6. Mellor, S., Scott, K., Uhl, A., and Weise, D. (2004) MDA Distilled: Principles of Model-Driven Architecture, Addison Wesley, New York
7. Object Management Group http://www.omg.org/mda
8. Zukowski, J. (2005) The-Definitive-Guide-to-Java-Swing-Third-Edition, Apress, Berkeley, CA

29

Model-Driven Development of Decision Support Systems: Tackling the Variability Problem

María Eugenia Cabello and Isidro Ramos

Abstract

In this chapter, we present software variability management using conceptual models for diagnostic decision support information systems (DSS) development. We use a software product line (SPL) approach. In the construction of the SPL, two orthogonal variabilities are used to capture domain (i.e., diagnosis) and application domain (i.e., medical diagnosis) particularities. In this context, we describe how variability is managed by using our BOM (baseline-oriented modeling) approach. BOM is a framework that automatically generates applications as PRISMA software architectural models using model transformations and SPL techniques. We use model-driven architecture (MDA) to build domain models (i.e., computational-independent models, CIMs), which are automatically transformed into platform-independent models, PIMs, and then compiled to a executable application (i.e., platform-specific model, PSM). In order to illustrate BOM, we focus on a type of information system, the decision support system, specifically in the diagnostic domain.

Keywords Software product lines · Conceptual models · Variability management · Decision support systems

1. Introduction

The development of families of applications has become increasingly important and with it the need for automatic support. In this context, software engineering must provide tools and methods in order to develop products with varied capabilities and adaptable to different situations. As a response to this, the concept of software product lines (SPL) [1] has been developed with the aim of controlling and minimizing the high costs of the software development process, in order to develop families of products, by means of representing and managing variability.

In this chapter, we describe how variability is managed in our SPL by means of our baseline-oriented modeling (BOM) approach. In order to present BOM we have chosen the decision support systems (DSS) [2] domain as a case study in information systems development, and we selected the diagnosis as the specific domain.

However, DSS are complex and the elements that their software architecture contains can vary significantly. We have found that in DSS, variability management cannot be dealt with by using a single variability model, but rather by using two models in two phases: the first phase using a domain conceptual model (DCM) for capturing the variants that characterize the various base architectures that are derived from a unique domain generic architecture; and the second phase by means of a more classic treatment using an application domain conceptual model (ADCM) and decorating the previous base architectures with different application features, in order to obtain a specific product using product lines and model

María Eugenia Cabello and Isidro Ramos · Polytechnic University of Valencia, Camino de Vera s/n, 46022, Valencia, Spain.

G.A. Papadopoulos et al. (eds.), *Information Systems Development*, DOI 10.1007/b137171_29,
© Springer Science+Business Media, LLC 2009

transformation techniques. In this context, BOM automatically generates DSS in a specific domain using SPL. The products of our SPL are implemented using PRISMA software architectural models [3] having the functionality of the DSS.

Our work integrates the following technological spaces to cope with the complexity of the problem: the generic architecture of the DSS to capture the knowledge of experts; model-driven architecture (MDA) [4] at the abstract modeling level (platform-independent model: PIM); the PRISMA architectural framework as the target software level (platform-specific model: PSM), where aspect-oriented software architectures are used at a design level; software product lines (SPL) as a technique for systematic reuse of products; and feature-oriented programming (FOP) [5] to capture the variability of the application domain.

BOM incorporates techniques and methodologies related to a number of previous works. Batory et al. [6] express the domain features in the Feature Model. In BOM we capture features of the Feature Model in a Decision Tree and then in DCM in order to select the base architectures. Trujillo [5] uses FOP as a technique for inserting the features into XML documents by means of XSLT templates. In BOM we use this technique in the PRISMA architectures (as XML documents). Bachman [7] proposes separation of the variability declaration of the affected artifacts. In BOM, the specification of variability and functionality constitutes separate conceptual models.

The structure of this chapter is as follows: Section 2 presents the variability in the diagnostic domain; Section 3 describes how BOM manages variability; Section 4 presents the model transformations in BOM; and Section 5 presents our conclusions and future work.

2. Variability

In the DSS we have detected a unique generic architecture that captures the functionality of these systems. The generic architecture of DSS has three basic elements [2]: the module that contains the inference process that resolves a problem in a specific domain, the module that contains the knowledge about the domain, and the module that allows communication between user and system.

By capturing the user interaction requirements by means of use case diagrams we have detected the features associated with the DSS structure. This variability is reflected in the construction of the architectural elements and in the final architecture, which is shown in [8]. These features are as follows: the number of use cases: a use case indicates the division of the system based on its functionality, i.e., the various operations of the systems and how the system interacts with the environment (final users); the number of actors: it represents the number of final users of the system; and use cases per actor: a user can access different use cases.

A field study has been realized in a type of DSS (the Expert Systems) in [9]. This chapter explains how in BOM the three basic modules are mapped into the following PRISMA architectural elements:

- The inference motor component – This establishes the system's control and provides the general resolution strategy for decision making. It is independent of system knowledge.
- The knowledge base component – This contains the domain knowledge of the case study using rules of inference (Horn clauses) and facts (information that remains unchanged).
- The user interface component – This establishes the man–machine interaction by allowing communication between users and system.
- The coordinator connector – This contains the choreography of the decision-making process.

We have chosen the diagnostic domain as our domain study. To understand this domain, a field study has been carried out considering five case studies. After finishing the field analysis, we can conclude that a diagnosis consists of an interpretation of the entity states involved (viewed as a set of properties) followed by the identification of the problem by means of these properties.

The features associated with the diagnostic process are as follows:

- Entity views: An entity can be considered to have the same properties (the same view) or to have different properties (different views) during the diagnostic process.
- Property levels: The properties of the entities can have n different abstraction levels. The rules that are used to relate the properties of the entities have n-1 levels, where n is the level of the entity properties.
- Number of hypotheses: The goal of the diagnosis is a single validated hypothesis. There can be one or several candidate diagnostic hypotheses which must be evaluated in order to select the appropriate one.
- Reasoning types: reasoning shows the way in which the rules are applied by the inference motor in order to infer a final diagnosis. The reasoning types can be deductive reasoning (driven by data), inductive reasoning (driven by goals), and differential reasoning (establishing the difference between two or more diagnostic possibilities).

The features that correspond to the application domain are the name and type of entity properties by abstraction level, the rules by abstraction levels (where the entity properties are related through rules), and the level, name, and type of the hypotheses used in the diagnostic process.

3. Variability Management in BOM

Based on the field analysis carried out, we conclude that the variants in DSS are included in two orthogonal types of variability:

- The first variability is given by the specific domain, for example, the iagnosis, (i.e., the features of the domain associated with the behavior of the architectural elements) and the end-user requirements (i.e., features related to the structure of the architectural elements and the system itself).
- The second variability corresponds to the scope of the application domain.

The features of the first variability (which are described in [8]) are represented in the Feature Model for capture of domain variability (see Fig. 29.1a). These features in the Feature Model are represented as

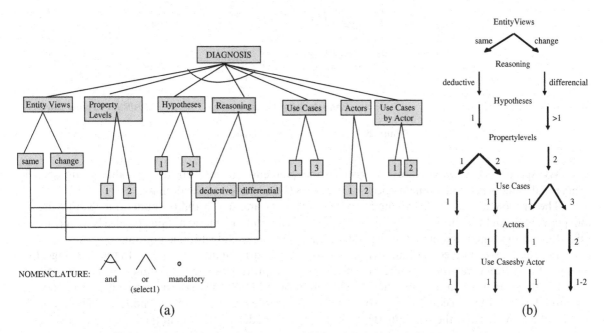

Figure 29.1. The Diagnostic Feature Model (**a**) and the Diagnostic Decision Tree (**b**).

variability points and their variants in a Decision Tree (see Fig. 29.1b). Both the Feature Model and the Decision Tree are computational-independent models (CIMs).

The variability shown in the Feature Model and the Decision Tree is captured in the domain conceptual model (DCM) instances (see Fig. 29.2). The variability of the application domain is represented in the application domain conceptual model (ADCM) instances (see Fig. 29.2). Both DCM and ADCM are platform-independent models (PIMs).

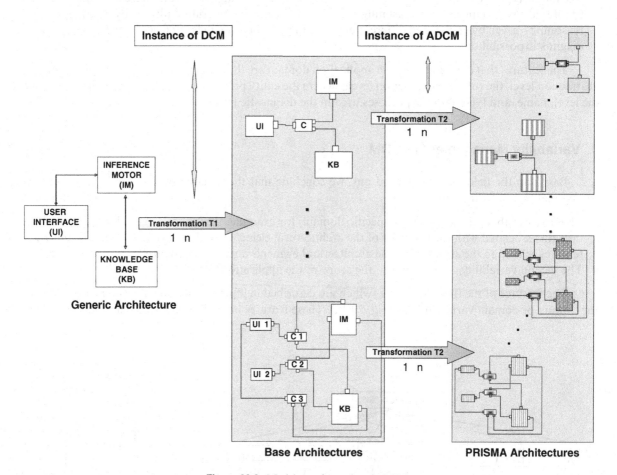

Figure 29.2. Model transformations in BOM.

We specify the variability of the systems independently from their functionality using specific conceptual models defining domain-specific languages (DSL) suited to the domain.

The approach used in BOM models variability by using a variability model and employing an independent model for the functionality of the system (the initial generic architecture). However, in the DSS domain the functional model of the system (i.e., the basic architecture) is not unique.

For this reason it is necessary to divide the variability treatment into two stages. In the first stage, two models of the system are produced: the variability model (capturing domain variability) and the functional model of the system (i.e., a unique generic architecture of the DSS). A first process produces the skeleton functional model. In the second stage, two models are used: the second variability model (variability of the application domain) and the previous skeleton functional model of the system (i.e., the selected skeleton base architecture of the repository of assets or Baseline). A second process is used in order to obtain a PRISMA architecture model, i.e., a final product of the SPL.

Therefore, our approach corresponds to the development of two SPL: the base architecture SPL that shares a generic architecture, i.e., SPL1, and the application SPL in a specific domain that shares a base architecture skeleton, i.e., SPL2.

These SPLs correspond to the two variabilities that are managed in our approach in two stages: the first variability (V1) that includes the domain variability and the user requirements, and the second variability (V2) that includes the application variability.

These variabilities are captured in instances of the two conceptual models, i.e., DCM and ADCMs.

The initial variability is dealt with through variability points embodied in a Decision Tree, which involves selecting a specific base architecture, through an instance of the DCM. The second variability is managed decorating these base architecture skeletons with the features of the application domain, using an instance of the ADCM. This will produce the target PRISMA architecture of the final product (see Fig. 29.2).

3.1. The First Variability in BOM

The initial variability (related to the features of the domain) is represented and managed through two models:

- The first model corresponds to the functional model of the domain, represented by the generic architecture of the DSS (as a PIM) of our SPL (see Fig. 29.2). This architecture is shared by several base architectures skeletons (as PIMs), which represent the SPL1 (see Fig. 29.2).
- The second model is the model of the domain variability, which is represented by the DCM (as a PIM) (see Fig. 29.2). The instances of DCM are used as the variants in the Decision Tree to select the skeleton base architecture that corresponds to the choice made.

The first type of variability involves a family of base architectures, i.e., SPL1. This SPL must be constructed and stored in the Baseline in the domain engineering phase. The Baseline then contains a SPL, formed by all the assets and the know-how necessary to construct the base architectures. Some assets are templates (or skeletons) and others are the configuration information for the base architectures. Thus, when we configure the base architectures, we obtain the first SPL.

3.2. The Second Variability in BOM

The second variability is also represented and managed using two models:

- The first model corresponds to the functional conceptual model of the application domain, which is captured by the skeleton base architecture (as a PIM) of the SPL1 (see Fig. 29.2).
- The second model corresponds to the conceptual model of the variability of the application domain, which is represented by the ADCM (as a PIM) (see Fig. 29.2).

The features used to fill the skeletons in order to obtain the PRISMA types are the features of the application domain (see Fig. 29.2). In this way, the second type of variability involves the SPL of the application in a specific field, i.e., SPL2.

In the application variability management process, the variants of the specific requirements of the application domain should be selected. This selection is made by means of an ADCM instance given by the user. The features are inserted in the base skeletons in order to generate the types of the PRISMA software artifacts. This is shown in Table 29.1.

The PRISMA architectural elements will be used to configure the PRISMA architectural model of the application. This model (as a PIM) is automatically compiled into code (C#) using the PRISMA-MODEL COMPILER [10] and the PRISMA-NET middleware [11]. The generated code contains all aspects of an executable application.

Table 29.1. PRISMA-ADL of the functional aspect of the knowledge base (the different section holes are depicted in bold type).

Functional aspect of the knowledge base of a skeleton	Functional aspect of the knowledge base of a PRISMA type
Functional Aspect FBaseEP using IDomainEP	Functional Aspect FBaseEP using IDomainEP
Attributes	Attributes
Variables	Variables
\<FP.0\>	**laboratories:string, library:string, ...**
Derived	Derived
\<FP.1\>	**infrastructure&services:string,faculty:string,....**
\<FH\>	**developmental_stage:string;**
Derivations	Derivations
\<FR.1\>	**{laboratories = "good" and library = "good"} infrastructure&services: = "good";**
	......
\<FR.2\>	**{infrastructure&services = "good" and faculty="good"}**
	developmental_stage: = "consolidated";
	......
....	
Services	Services
......	......
End_Functional Aspect FBaseEP	End_Functional Aspect FBaseEP

4. Model Transformations in BOM

Figure 29.2 shows the transformations involved in the construction of our SPL architectures. This figure illustrates how the transformation performed at the model level is applied in the transformation processes. The transformations T1 and T2 are executed at the model level (level M1 in OMG-MOF [12]), and they are defined at the metamodel level (level M2 in MOF). In transformation T1, the skeleton model (level M1 in MOF) is obtained from the DSS modular model (level M1 in MOF) and the instances of DCM (level M0 in MOF). In transformation T2, the PRISMA model (level M1 in MOF) is obtained from the skeleton model (level M1 in MOF) generated in T1 and the instance of ADCM (level M0 in MOF). The PRISMA model is the final result (level M1 in MOF).

The generic architecture conforms to the module metamodel, the skeleton base architectures conform to the skeleton metamodel (i.e., the PRISMA metamodel with holes), the PRISMA model conforms to the PRISMA metamodel, and the DCM and ADCM variability models conform to the UML class metamodel.

The transformations can be carried out in two different ways:

(a) With the orthodox method by means of QVT-Relations [13]. In transformation T1, QVT-Relations must take into account the generic architecture DCM and the skeleton base architecture configuration. In transformation T2, QVT-Relations must take into account the base architectures and ADCM giving result as very complex transformation rules. This implies quite a complex and non-scalable transformation as an algorithmic solution calculating variability.

(b) With the BOM approach. In transformation T1, instead of calculating the transformation function using QVT-Relations each time, the function is computed once and the result is stored in the Baseline for each input. In this way, given all the variants, T1 is implemented as a direct access to the table that represents the Baseline. In this way, with Decision Tree techniques we can select the skeleton base architecture of the specific case, given the variants of the variability points (features of the domain) as instances of the DCM. In transformation T2, using FOM techniques, an XSLT decoration process of the skeleton base architectures is implemented employing the application domain features given as instances of the ADCM. The transformation profiles of T1 and T2 are

T1 (GenericArch_model, Instance-V1_model) = BaseArch_model
T2 (BaseArch_model, Instance-V2_model) = PRISMA Arch_model

This solution has the advantage of dealing separately with the functional and the variability models, allowing conversion of a generic architecture into several base architectures, and transforming a skeleton base architecture into a PRISMA architecture. In this approach the transformations are easy, modeling of variability is independent of functionality, and the problem is resolved in a more effective, scalable, friendly way and in addition is expressively richer and clearer.

5. Conclusions and Future Work

We have described how variability is managed in our SPL by means of our BOM framework. BOM automatically generates applications in a specific domain using SPL. However, in order to present our BOM approach, we have selected the DSS as the system domain and the diagnosis as the specific domain.

BOM manages variability at the model level (not at the program level). This approach manages variability in two stages, which correspond to the development of two SPL: the base architecture SPL1 that shares a generic architecture and the application SPL2 in a specific domain, which shares a base architecture skeleton. These SPLs correspond to domain variability and application variability, which are captured by means of BOM by using two compiled conceptual models applications: DCM and ADCM, respectively.

In this context, BOM captures data that characterize the domain variability and the application variability using conceptual models. Using Decision Tree and FOP, these data can be used in the domain engineering and product engineering phases, respectively, in order to obtain a specific application by means of SPL and model transformation techniques. In BOM, the stakeholders (application engineers) introduce the variability data during the execution of the SPL production plan by means of the conceptual model instances.

In BOM thetwo variability kinds are described in two independent conceptual models separated from the functionality models; and the information systems applications are automatically generated in a user friendly way. In doing so, BOM minimizes the high costs of the software development process and reduces the time to market of every new product.

In the future, BOM will be applied in different information system domains (e.g., payroll, accounting) and application domains (e.g., institutions, enterprises). A prototype of the BOM framework (Proto-BOM) [14] has been implemented and will be validated in real case studies. Additionally, we will use benchmarks in order to compare BOM results with other approaches.

Acknowledgments

This work has been funded under the Models, Environments, Transformations, and Applications: META project TIN20006-15175-605-01.

References

1. Clements P., and Northrop L.M., *Software Product Lines: Practices and Patterns,* SEI Series in Software Engineering, Addison Wesley, New York, 2002.
2. Turban, E., and Aronson, J.E., *Decision Support Systems and Intelligent Systems,* Prentice Hall, Upper Saddle River, NJ, 2001, 865 pp. ISBN: 0-13-089465-6.
3. Pérez J., PRISMA: "Aspect-Oriented Software Architectures", *PhD. Thesis of Philosophy in Computer Science,* Polytechnic University of Valencia, Spain, 2006.
4. Model Driven Architecture. http://www.omg.org/mda.
5. Trujillo S., "Feature-Oriented Model Driven Product Lines", *PhD. Thesis*, The University of the Basque Country, San Sebastian, Spain, 2007.

6. Batory D., Benavides D., and Ruiz-Cortés A., "Automated Analyses of Feature Models: Challenges Ahead", ACM on Software Product Lines, 2006.

7. Bachman F., Goedicke M., Leite J., Nord R., Pohl K., Ramesh B., and Vilbig A., "A Meta-Model for Representing Variability in Product Family Development", In *Proceedings in the 5th International Workshop on Product Family Engineering*, pp. 66–80, 2003.

8. Cabello M.E., and Ramos I. "A Generic Solution for the Construction of Diagnostic Expert Systems Based on Product Lines". In Proceedings of HEALTHINF'08, *International Conference of Health Informatics-INSTICC*, Madeira, Portugal. Vol. 2, pp. 237–246, 2008, ISBN 978-989-8111-16-6.

9. Cabello M.E., and Ramos I. "Expert Systems Development Through Software Product Lines Tecgniques". In *Proceedings of ISD08, 17th International Conference onInformation Systems Development, Paphos, Cyprus, Ago.* 2008, (paper accepted).

10. Cabedo R., Pérez J., Carsí J.A., and y Ramos I., "Modelado y Generación de Arquitecturas PRISMA con DSL Tools", en Actas del *IV Workshop DYNAMICA*, Archena, Murcia, España, 2005.

11. Costa C., Pérez J., Ali N., Carsí J.A., and y Ramos I., "PRISMANET: Middleware: Soporte a la Evolución Dinámica de Arquitecturas Software Orientadas a Aspectos", en Actas de las *X Jornadas de Ingeniería del Software y Bases de Datos*, Granada, España, 2005, pp. 27–34.

12. Meta-Object Facility: MOF, http://www.omg.org/mof

13. Query/View/Transformations: OMG Document ad/2005-07-1.

14. Cabello M.E., Gómez M., LLavador M., and Ramos I. "ProtoBOM: A Framework that Semi-Automatically Generates Decision Support Systems Based on Software Product Lines". *Technical Report: DSIC II/02/08*, Polythecnical University of Valencia, Valencia, Spain, p. 68, 2008.

30

Foundations on Generation of Relationships Between Classes Based on Initial Business Knowledge

Oksana Nikiforova and Natalya Pavlova

Abstract

This chapter focuses on the development of the main component of platform independent model (PIM) of Model Driven Architecture, e.g., class diagram defined in Unified Modeling Language (UML), which has necessary details for transformation into platform specific model (PSM). It is important to formulate core principles of development of well-structured class diagram at a conceptual level, using knowledge of the problem domain, which consists of two interrelated models of system aspects – business processes and concept presentation. Definition of relationships of classes is important for PSM generation; therefore, the research on how it could be defined is performed. The hypothesis that it is possible to derive a class structure from initial business information is adduced. Information about the problem domain is presented in the form of two-hemisphere model that describes two interrelated parts of the most important aspects of a system, namely business process and concept models. These models serve as a source model for class diagram receiving. Capacity for the class diagram generation, based on the two-hemisphere model, is represented by a collection of graph transformations and illustrated with examples, where definition of different kinds of relationships (namely aggregation, dependency, generalization) is displayed.

Keywords Business process model · Class diagram · Relations among classes

1. Introduction

The area of software development encompasses many approaches, methods, and techniques. At present, the most frequently used method is Model Driven Architecture (MDA) [1]. MDA [2, 3] is an approach to system specification, which employs three different levels of abstraction. The high-level specification outlining a general purpose of the system (computation independent model or CIM); the specification of the system functionality (platform independent model or PIM); and the specification of the implementation of this functionality on a specific technology platform (platform specific model or PSM) [4]. The above models are detailed in the Object Management Group (OMG), the places of transformations are defined, and the goal of the application of MDA philosophy is indicated. An MDA-based development process can be divided into three domains – a problem domain (CIM), a solution domain (PIM), and a software domain (PSM) [5]. Transformations occur between all models (domains) (see Fig. 30.1). This chapter focuses on transformations inside PIM development between business knowledge and class diagram.

Oksana Nikiforova and Natalya Pavlova • Department of Applied Computer Science, Riga Technical University, Riga, Latvia.

G.A. Papadopoulos et al. (eds.), *Information Systems Development*, DOI 10.1007/b137171_30,
© Springer Science+Business Media, LLC 2009

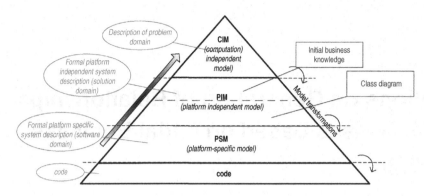

Figure 30.1. Chains of transformations within MDA.

A class diagram is a frequently used visual representation of static aspects of the system in platform independent model [6]. The class diagram is a basic component for PIM representation; however, formal generation of the class diagram from the problem domain is still being researched.

Usually developers start class diagram modeling directly before writing of application code, but still they construct the initial architecture defined in terms of the class diagram in a manual way reading the requirement specification. The problem arranged with two different kinds of models – a user-oriented model and a developer-oriented model – can be solved by generation of the class diagram from the initial knowledge about business [5].

It is very important to receive class diagram in the formal way, because currently it is constructed manually by developers without considering user-oriented models created in the initial project stages. Class diagram also serves as a primary artifact in software development tools based on the idea of MDA.

A lot of organizations are using different tools for business process analysis; therefore, they have complete and consistent models of their organizational structure, employer responsibilities, business processes, and the structure of documentation flows, in other words well-structured initial business knowledge [7]. Therefore, the class diagram received in the formal way from the initial business knowledge serves as a bridge between user-oriented models and developer-oriented models. This class diagram helps to implement software more close to initial description of system processes [5].

If initial business information contains static structure in concept model, then classes and their attributes are predefined. Nothing new is in the definition of classes and attributes without relationships among them. Software development techniques and methodologies propose a lot of methods to indicate classes in problem area or in initial models. For example, entity-relationship diagrams are not new, and they defines how entities should be indicated.

The authors assume that the concatenation of concept model with business process diagram allows to select relationships of classes from initial knowledge. Every concept of concept model defines data structure for one or several data flows on business process diagram in this combination. The idea of common consideration of both models is well known; nevertheless, the usage of combination of business process model and concept model for definition of class responsibilities and relationships among classes in object-oriented approach is not widely published.

The authors of the paper in [5, 8, 9] have proposed how classes and primary associations among them can be defined based on two-hemisphere model [7], which consists of two interrelated models, namely business process model and concept model. The purpose of this chapter is to find a possibility to indicate additional types of relationships among classes (e.g., aggregation, generalization, and dependency) based on combination of business process and concept model.

As the concept model is part of given initial information, definition of classes and its attributes is not a complex task, nevertheless relationship of classes is not obviously defined in initial information. Therefore, it can be investigated to receive possibly more precise static structure of developed system.

During research, business process diagram is presented as a graph with arcs (data flows) and nodes (business processes). The graph presentation gives a possibility to apply graph theory to business process model.

The first section of this chapter describes aggregation relationship of classes, the second section presents the possibilities of dependency definition from combination of business process and data flow, and the third section shows how the generalization is obtained. The last section concludes this chapter, where performed research is discussed.

2. Aggregation

The relationships of classes are defined based on information presented in business process and concept models. The combinations of input and output data flows allow to define how classes corresponding to these data flows are related to each other. During the research of the possibility of indications of class relations a set of combinations of data flows and business processes is investigated, and only combinations which give a possibility to define aggregation, generalization, or dependency are shown in this chapter.

For investigation of obtaining of class diagram elements the business process diagram is split into fragments (or transformation cases), each of which includes one business process and all data flows which are input and output of the business process. These cases are selected so as a lot of combinations would be examined [10].

First discussed relationship is an aggregation. Aggregation is the part-of relationship [11]. Transformation case 1 has one process – "Change room status," which has an input data flow "Room (Found room number)" and an output data flow "Room Status" (see the upper left part of Fig. 30.2), and both data flows have different data types defined with different concepts (upper right side of Fig. 30.2).

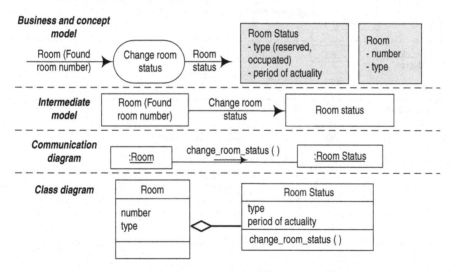

Figure 30.2. The business process, data structure, intermediate, communication, and class diagrams for transformation case 1.

It is assumed that the fragment of business process model is fragment of a graph, where "Change room status" is a node, "Room (Found room number)" and "Room status" are arcs; therefore, graphs transformation could be applied, and arcs could be transformed into nodes, and nodes could be transformed into arcs for receiving of intermediate model [12]. Intermediate model gives a possibility to transit to communication diagram (see Fig. 30.2), for definition of encapsulation of methods for class responsibilities [13].

There are two nodes in intermediate model – "Room (Found room number)" and "Room status" on the example of the described case. The concepts "Room" and "Room status" are defined in the concept model. Making use of the comparison of intermediate nodes with data structures of the concept model, two objects "Room" and "Room status" can be selected; they are shown in Fig. 30.2 as objects in the communication diagram. Interaction between these objects is the process "Change room status" which is transformed in the method "change_room_status ()."

Two classes should be created based on objects in the communication diagram – "Room" and "Room status," and attributes for the classes could be taken from the defined data structure. This kind of business process diagram gives a possibility to define an "aggregation" relation between classes in addition to method definition based on the notational conventions in the UML language [14]. The conclusion that is aggregation is made, since the object room status is adjusted after class room has executed operation from it. And for receiving of room status no external information was used.

One more example of how the aggregation could be defined is presented in transformation case 2; it has three different data flows – two on input and one on output as shown in Fig. 30.3. The data structure consists of three objects: "Client," "Room," and "Reservation Information." The following are the data flows in the process diagram: "Client (Client name)," "Room," and "Reservation information (found room number)."

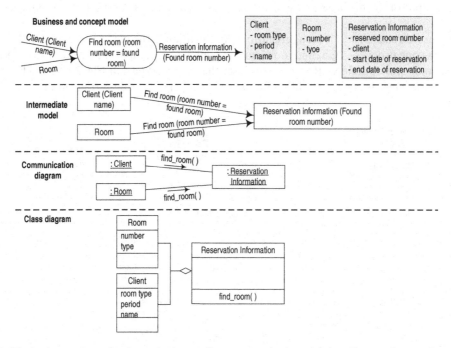

Figure 30.3. The business process, data structure, intermediate, communication, and class diagrams for transformation case 2.

The fragment of business process and concept diagrams gives enough information to the construction of the class diagram fragment [8, 10]. It is important to note that there is an external information missed, except output data flow "Reservation information (found room number)"; therefore, class "Reservation Information" consists of "Client" and "Room."

Construction of intermediate model and the communication diagram is necessary for receiving the class diagram. These models will help to define classes, their operations, and relations between them. Figure 30.3 presents intermediate and communication models. Intermediate model is received similarly as in the previous cases – using issues of graph theory and transformations (see Fig. 30.3).

The attributes of "Reservation Information" are missing in Fig. 30.3, part with communication diagram; therefore, they will be taken from the related classes "Client" and "Room." The operation "find_room" of the class "Reservation Information" is received in the similar way as in the previous cases – from the communication diagram in Fig. 30.3. Thus this transformation case, where two input and one output data flows are presented, allows defining classes and operations, as well as the aggregation among these classes.

One of the complex combinations of initial information (transformation case 3) gives a possibility to define aggregation and has three objects "A," "B," and "C" one process "P" and two data flows where data flows "A'" and "B' " (defined with different objects "A" and "B") are on input, and two data flows "C'" and "C''" (defined with one object 'C') are on output. The sequence of transformations in general case of definition of aggregation relationships is presented in Fig. 30.4.

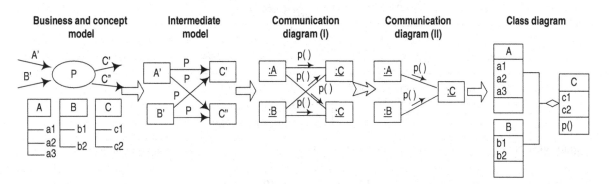

Figure 30.4. Possible transformations for the transformation case 3.

Intermediate model for this transformation case consists of four arcs equal to the data flows in the initial business process – "A," "B'," "C'," and "C''" and four nodes, each of which is "P."

The communication diagram received from intermediate and titled "communication diagram (I)" is shown in Fig. 30.4. There is the same object "C," which has the same operation "p()" on input in the right part of this diagram. Therefore, it can be joined and the next transformation of the communication diagram, "communication diagram (II)", can be received (see Fig. 30.4).

The class diagram for the transformation case 3 is shown in the last place in Fig. 30.4 and includes three classes "A," "B," and "C", where "C" consists of "A" and "B", and "A" and 'B' executes the operation "p()" of the class "C."

3. Dependency

A dependency exists between two elements if changes to the definition of one element (the supplier) may cause changes to the other (the client) [11]. Transformation case 4 presents case with two inputs and one output. There is a variation of one type of data flow on input. And variation of another type of data flow on output. The example chosen for illustration of this case is process of room finding by request from a client. The found room is received as a result of the process "find the required room." Information necessary for this operation is "Room type" and "Period." This information is taken from the object "Reservation Blank" (see the fragment of business process diagram and the according concepts in Fig. 30.5).

According to the proposed graph transformations [8, 12] "Reservation Blank (Room type)," "Reservation Blank (Period)," and "Room (Found room number)" should be transformed to nodes. There is only one process "Find the required room" in Fig. 30.5. It means that nodes "Reservation Blank (Room type)"

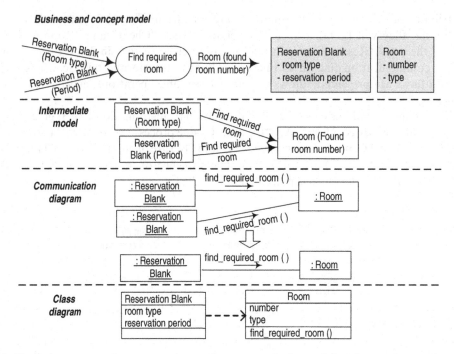

Figure 30.5. The business process, data structure, intermediate, communication, and class diagrams for transformation case 4.

and "Reservation Blank (Period)" should be joined with "Room (Found room number)" using the arc "Find required room" as it is shown in Fig. 30.5. Therefore, intermediate model consists of three nodes and two similar arcs. Figure 30.5 shows duplicated nodes in intermediate model and objects in the first variant of the communication diagram. It is permissible for the intermediate model to have two similar nodes with the same processes on output. This duplication should be got ridden off in the communication diagram. Making use of the concept view, where data structure is defined, the duplicate objects could be "united" in one object "Reservation blank," which sends the message "require_client_data ()" to the object "Room," which is received joining the node of intermediate model "Room (found room number)" and the data structure "Room." Now the communication diagram is received, and it is possible to get classes from it. Based on the communication diagram (see Fig. 30.5) it can be concluded that two classes correspond to the discussed case, one of which executes an operation from another, and change of one class may cause changes to another. Bottom part of Fig. 30.5. presents classes, which are received from initial data of this case, which is shown in upper part of Fig. 30.5. Classes correspond to the objects in the communication diagram, data flows, and data structures in the business process model and concept model (Fig. 30.5).

One more kind of combination of initial information, which gives a possibility to define dependency relationship is presented on upper part of Fig. 30.6 (transformation case 5).

There are two data structures – "Room Status" and "Reservation Information" (right upper part of Fig. 30.6); one process "Give reservation information to client" and three data flows "Room Status" and "Reservation information" twice. Intermediate model is received with graph transformation, the same as discussed above. The same as the previous case, intermediate model has duplicated arcs from the process "Give room information to client" (see Fig. 30.6). Objects of the communication diagram are received using data structure and interactions – using intermediate model. Middle part of Fig. 30.6 shows two similar messages or operations "give_reservation_info ()" that are outputs of different objects "Room Status" and "Reservation Information," and inputs of one object "Reservation Information." Therefore, the operation "give_reservation_info ()" is executed by the object "Room Status." Object "Reservation information" executes operation "give_room_info" from itself. The bottom part of the communication diagram (Fig. 30.6) shows the described situation and the class diagram as the result of transformation case.

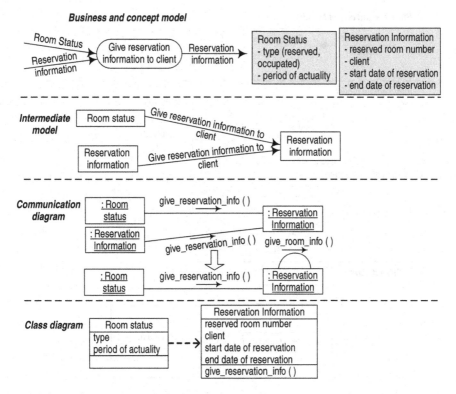

Figure 30.6. The business process, data structure, intermediate, communication, and class diagrams for transformation case 5.

Obtained relationship between "Room Status" and "Reservation Information" is defined as dependency, as class "Room Status" executes operation from "Reservation Information"; and changes of class "Room Status" will cause changes in class "Reservation Information".

4. Generalization

Generalization allows to indicate superclasses and subclasses in class diagram [11]. Transformation case 6 belongs to a series of cases, wherein are multiple outputs. An example chosen for the simplest case is the process "Check room status," where the same object defines data type on input and on output. The input flow for this process is "Room (room number)." Two output flows are here: "Free room" and "Reserved room." One data structure "Room" is defined for the discussed case (see Fig. 30.7).

Applying graph theory [12] the nodes are transformed from arcs of the business process model. The arcs are transformed from the node of the business process diagram. There are three nodes and two arcs in intermediate model. Intermediate model and the received communication diagram are presented in Fig. 30.7. Communication diagram contains three objects – "Room," "Free room," and "Reserved Room" and one operation "check_room_status," which is transformed from the process "Check room status."

Two variants of the communication diagram are in Fig. 30.7. The first variant is received directly from intermediate model "as is." However, as Fig. 30.7 shows, interactions occur among exemplars of one object "Room." The communication diagram allows defining a class diagram and a kind of relations, i.e., "generalization," as bottom part of Fig. 30.7 presents.

Initial model shows that one data flow "Room" is split into two data flows "Free Room" and "Reserved Room." Therefore, class "Room" is related with classes "Free Room" and "Reserved Room" with generalization, where "Room" is superclass, "Free Room" and "Reserved Room" are subclasses.

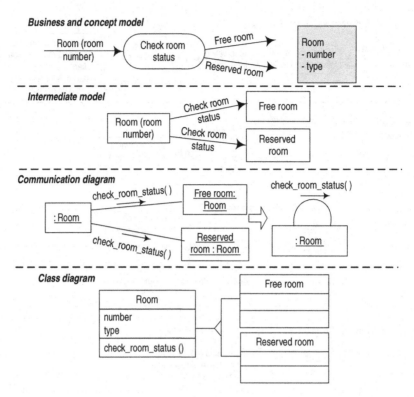

Figure 30.7. The business process, data structure, intermediate, communication, and class diagrams for transformation case 6.

5. Conclusions

After performing all transformations from the initial model of business knowledge, the elements of the UML class diagram are received. The formally received class diagram is the base for further construction of the system architecture. The MDA platform specific model can be obtained by adding platform specific properties to class diagram.

During the investigation of possible combinations of transformations the possibility of definition of class relationships, such as aggregation, dependency, and generalization is discussed in this chapter. To define these relationships during research an example of Hotel room reservation system is examined. All sections of this chapter have illustration of initial information and fragment of target class model.

Business process and concept model is discussed as graphs with arcs and nodes for receiving of class diagram from initial knowledge. Analysis of graphs makes possible to apply graph transformations, where arcs may be transformed into nodes, and nodes may be transformed into arcs. Such analysis gives a possibility to discuss about sharing of responsibilities among classes and defining the relationships between them. Thus making use of the above discussed transformations it is possible to define three kinds of relations: dependency, aggregation, and generalization.

The elements of class diagram are received in the formal way from business process and concept model and include the most part of core elements. It is hopefully that the class diagram elements are received in the formal way, because currently developers construct class diagram manually without considering of user-oriented models created in the initial project stages. A lot of organizations use different tools for business process analysis and therefore they have complete and consistent models of their organizational structure, employer responsibilities, business processes, and the structure of documentation flows. Therefore, the class diagram received in the formal way from the two-hemisphere model serve as a bridge between user-oriented models and developer-oriented models. This class diagram helps to implement software more close to initial description of system processes.

The transformations discussed in this chapter served as a basis for definition of formal algorithm, which gives a possibility to generate structure of class diagram from initial business information. The algorithm allows to develop a tool for the generation of specification of class diagram [15] and is applied for several problem domains defined in the form of two-hemisphere model. These applications make the approbation of defined transformations and have proved the possibility to generate classes, their responsibilities, and three types of relationships in the way described in this chapter.

Acknowledgements

The research reflected in this chapter is supported by the research grant No. R7389 of Latvian Ministry of Education and Science in cooperation with Riga Technical University "Development of tool prototype for generation of software system class structure based on two-hemisphere model." and by the European Social Fund within the National Program "Support for the carrying out doctoral study program's and post-doctoral researches."

References

1. Siegel J. Developing in OMG's Model-Driven Architecture. OMG document omg, 2001. http://www.omg.org/mda/papers.htm
2. Specification of Model Driven Architecture. http://www.omg.org/mda/specs.htm#mdaguide
3. Runde R.K., Stolen K. What is Model Driven Architecture?, Research Report 304, University of Oslo Department of Informatics, 2003. http://heim.ifi.uio.no/~ragnhilk/MDAreport.pdf
4. Mellor S.J., Kendall S., Axel U., et al. MDA Distilled, Principles of Model driven Architecture, Addison-Wesley, New York, 2004.
5. Nikiforova, O., Kirikova M., Pavlova N. Principles of Model Driven Architecture in Knowledge Modeling for the Task of Study Program Evaluation, Databases and Information Systems IV, by IOS Press in the Series "Frontiers in Artificial Intelligence and Applications", Vasilecas, O., Eder, J., Caplinskas, A. (eds.), 2007, pp. 291–304.
6. MDA Guide Version 1.0.1. http://www.omg.org/docs/omg/03-05-01.pdf
7. Nikiforova O., Kirikova M. Two-Hemisphere Model Driven Approach: Engineering Based Software Development, Proceeding of the 16th International Conference Advanced Information Systems Engineering CAiSE'2004, Persson, A., Stirna, J. (eds.), LNCS 3084, Springer-Verlag, Berlin Heidelberg, 2004, pp. 219–233.
8. Pavlova N. Several Outlines of Graph Theory in Framework of MDA, Advances in Information Systems Development, New Methods and Practice for the Networked Society, Vol. 2, Maguar, G., Knapp, G., Wojtkowski, W., Wojtkowski, W.G., Zupancic J. (eds.), Springer Science + Business Media, LLC, New York, 2007, pp. 25–36
9. Pavlova N., Nikiforova O. Formalization of Two-Hemisphere Model Driven Approach in the Framework of MDA, Proceedings of the 9th Conference on Information Systems Implementation and Modelling, Czech Republic, Prerov, 2006, pp. 105–112.
10. Pavlova N. Approach for Development of Platform Independent Model in the Framework of Model Driven Architecture, Ph.D. thesis, Riga Technical University, 2008.
11. Fowler M., Scott K. UML Distilled Applying the Standard Object Modeling Language, Addison-Wesley, New York, 1999.
12. Grundspenkis J. Causal Domain Model Driven Knowledge Acquisition for Expert Diagnosis System Development, Kaunas University of Technology Press, Kaunas, 1997.
13. Larman C. Applying UML And Patterns: An Introduction to Object-Oriented Analysis and Design, Prentice Hall, New Jersey, 2000.
14. OMG Unified Modeling Language Specification. http://www.omg.org/spec/UML/2.1.2/Infrastructure/PDF
15. Nikiforova O., Pavlova N. Development of the Tool for Generation of UML Class Diagram from Two-Hemisphere Model, Proceedings of the Third International Conference on Software Engineering Advances ICSEA 2008, Sliema, Malta, October 26–31, IEEE, Washington, DC, 2008, pp. 105–112.

31

Expert Systems Development Through Software Product Lines Techniques

María Eugenia Cabello and Isidro Ramos

Abstract:

This chapter deals with expert systems (ES) development as the final product of a software product line (SPL). We take into account software variability management in the ES domain. Two kinds of variability emerge: variability in the behavior as well as in the structure of such systems. Experts' knowledge is captured using domain conceptual models in order to manage the variability and functionality of the ES. The ES are constructed using our baseline-oriented modeling (BOM) approach. BOM is a framework that automatically generates software applications as PRISMA architectural models by using SPL techniques. We follow the model-driven architecture (MDA) initiative for building domain models, which are automatically transformed into executable applications.

Keywords Software product lines · Variability · Expert systems · Software architecture · Model transformations

1. Introduction

The development of expert systems (ES) [1] applications has acquired great importance in recent years, and there is therefore a need to properly support them. But these systems are complex because their elements are variant. In order to minimize this problem, we propose to construct the ES using a model-driven architecture (MDA) [2] approach based on software product lines (SPL) [3] techniques. We use SPL techniques in order to control and minimize the time to market and high costs of the software development process. We use MDA approach to automatically generate code.

The representation and management of variability in this case is a key factor. We describe how variability is managed in our SPL by means of our baseline-oriented modeling (BOM) approach. In this context, BOM automatically generates ES in a specific domain by using SPL techniques. The products of our SPL are implemented by PRISMA models [4] capturing the architecture and functionality of the rule-based ES.

To develop BOM, a field study has been done to learn about the structure and functionality of the rule-based ES that carry out tasks in a specific domain. In order to treat in depth a specific field of the ES application, we have selected the diagnosis domain. Some case studies (medical diagnosis, educational diagnosis, video diagnosis, disaster victims diagnosis) have been considered.

The structure of this chapter is as follows: Section 2 presents the different technological spaces that our work integrates and mentions some related works. Section 3 presents our field study in the ES domain. Section 4 describes how BOM manages variability. Section 5 describes ES development by BOM. Section 6 presents our conclusions and proposals for future work.

María Eugenia Cabello and Isidro Ramos • Polytechnic University of Valencia, Camino de Vera s/n, 46022, Valencia, Spain

G.A. Papadopoulos et al. (eds.), *Information Systems Development*, DOI 10.1007/b137171_31,
© Springer Science+Business Media, LLC 2009

2. Foundations

Our work integrates the following technological spaces (TS) in order to cope with the complexity of the problem.

(a) The expert system (ES) TS captures the knowledge of experts and attempts to imitate their reasoning processes when the experts solve problems in a specific domain. Such systems usually have a generic architecture and its components are independent and separate units. Control is independent from the data. The input and output of the information is carried out through the user interface.

(b) Model-driven architecture (MDA) TS is an initiative promoted by the object management group (OMG) for software system development. MDA is based on the separation of the description of the functionality of the system from its implementation on specific software platforms. MDA proposes defining and using models (as first class citizens) at different abstraction levels. From these models we can automatically generate code by means of transformation rules to obtain executable models.

(c) PRISMA framework TS integrates two approaches: component-based software development and aspect-oriented software development. This integration is obtained by defining the architectural elements through their aspects. The PRISMA model consists of three types of architectural elements: components, connectors, and systems.

(d) Software product lines (SPL) TS combines systematic development and reuse of components or assets, i.e., the products are different in some features but they share a generic architecture. In the SPL approach, rather than a single application, the development process produces a family of them. More than creating products, it is a question of storing software assets in a baseline repository and defining a production plan that specifies the process to obtain each one of the individual products.

Our research is related to the following SPL works: (i) Batory et al. [5] express the domain features in a Feature Model (FM). In BOM we capture domain features using FM too. However, we observed that solving the complexity of ES needs two FM, capturing the domain and application domain features, respectively. (ii) Trujillo [6] uses feature-oriented programming as a technique for inserting features into XML documents by means of XSLT templates. In BOM we use this technique but at the model level (i.e., we use feature-oriented modeling), and the features are inserted in the PRISMA architectural models by means of QVT- transformations. (iii) Bachman [7] proposes to separate the artifact's variability declaration of its functionality. In BOM, the specification of the two variabilities and functionality of the ES are captured in separate conceptual models.

3. The Architecture of the Expert Systems

The most important asset (core asset) of our SPL is the generic architecture of the ES product line (also called domain architecture). This is due to the fact that this architecture determines the scope of the SPL and the features of the products that can be developed.

The process of developing an application (member of the product line) begins with a unique generic architecture model that is specific to the domain. The generic architecture model of our SPL is represented in Fig. 31.1 by three fundamental modules: (i) Inference process module, transforming data into useful information for decision making and implementing the inference process. (ii) Knowledge base module, containing the knowledge of the application domain. (iii) User interface module, allowing user interaction with the system.

But as we implement the SPL using PRISMA software architectures models, the generic modules of an ES must be mapped into (skeleton) architectural elements. To be consistent with the PRISMA metamodel, it is necessary to incorporate a new architectural element (the connector) to establish the communication among the components and to define the choreography of the decision process. The choice of this implementation results in a mapping between the two models with a small semantic GAP. As is shown in Fig. 31.1 (using gray arrows), there is a correspondence among the modules and their respective components.

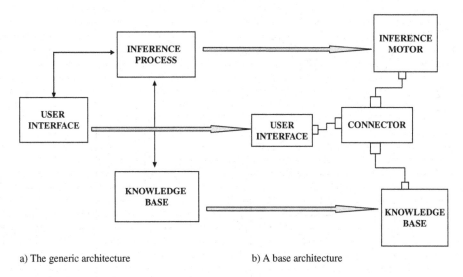

a) The generic architecture   b) A base architecture

Figure 31.1. Mapping between the module generic architecture and a base architecture.

3.1. The Variability in the Architecture of the Expert Systems

We have detected that the base architecture model implementing the generic architecture model is not unique but varies in its behavior, and since we use PRISMA models, in its structure too. In Sections 3.1.1 and 3.1.2 of this chapter, we present the analysis of this variability.

This implies the creation of different base architecture models, every time we start to develop a product line. To obtain the base architecture model from the domain, generic architecture model may require to remove or to add components or relationships between them, re-configure components, and develop specific software elements. This implies the existence of additional features of the base architecture model that are represented in the variability points and whose presence/absence defines the specific product.

3.1.1. Variability in the Expert Systems Structure

In this section, we present the modeling technique that we have developed to configure ES using PRISMA models. This modeling technique shows that an ES as a PRISMA architecture model varies both in the configuration and in the component architectural elements.

Our modeling technique starts with the end user requirements modeled as UML use case diagrams. The number of use cases, the number of actors, and the number of use cases that an actor accesses are the relevant variants.

In the following, we present the step-by-step modeling of an ES using as case study the medical diagnosis.

1) *Specify the functional requirements (at high abstraction level) by using UML use case diagrams.* In our example (see Fig. 31.2a) we have three use cases and two actors, where an actor accesses two use cases and the other one access a single use case.
2) *Create an architectural model for each use case.* In our example (see Fig. 31.2b) we have three use cases, therefore, we build three architectural models.
3) *Build the final architectural model.* The architectural elements of the final model are obtained using the following criteria:

- Connectors: The number of connectors of the final architectural model is equal to the number of use cases.

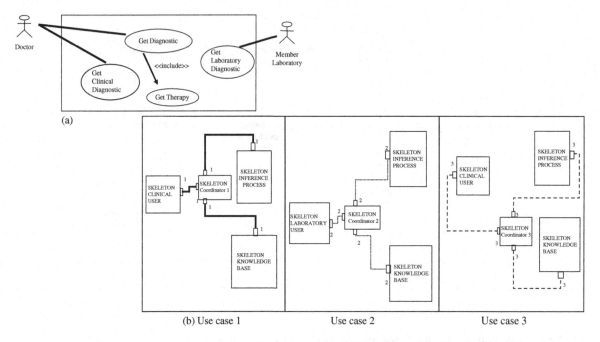

Figure 31.2. Example of a use cases diagram (**a**) and its architectural models, respectively (**b**).

- Components: We have one component per module and to join each component's port we use attachments. The number of ports of a component will be equal to the number of (use cases) connectors where the component is used.

The architectural elements of the final model therefore have the following characteristics: there is one connector connecting all the architectural components for each use case; the number of ports of the inference process component is the same as the number of use cases, the number of ports of the knowledge base is the number of use cases, the number of user interfaces is the number of actors of the use cases, the number of ports of the user interface is the number of use cases that can be accessed by an actor.

In our example, the final architectural model of the ES is presented in Fig. 31.3. It has seven architectural elements with the following characteristics: the inference process component has three ports, the knowledge base component has three ports, the user interface 1 component (i.e., doctor) has two ports, the user interface 2 component (i.e., laboratory member) has one port, the coordinator 1 connector, the coordinator 2 connector, and the coordinator 3 connector.

3.1.2. Variability in the Expert Systems Behavior

The behavior of the architectural elements of an ES varies according to the reasoning strategy used and is part of the inference process component. It contains the process of obtaining a decision or solving a problem. The reasoning strategies simulate the reasoning of experts when performing a task (e.g., diagnosis).We have represented reasoning as processes. In the field analysis of the diagnosis domain, we have detected two types of decision processes: static and dynamic.

In Fig. 31.4a we present a visual metaphor of the static inference process through a graph showing the set of properties (P_i) at level i (gray color), hypothesis (H_i) (black color), as well as deductive reasoning (arrows pointing up) in this process. The inference rules are of the form:

$$p_{j,i} : P_i \leftarrow p_{k,i-1}{}^{*} : P_{i-1} \quad \text{and} \quad h_{j,i} : H_i \leftarrow p_{k,j-1}{}^{*} : P_i$$

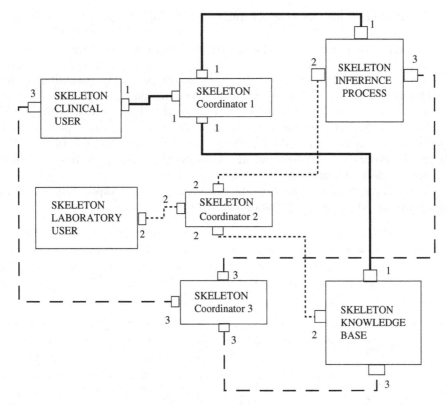

Figure 31.3. Medical diagnosis base architectural model.

where $i = 0 \ldots n$ and $n =$ number of levels, and j,k: nat. For example, in Fig. 31.4a we have (using a natural notation extension for the sake of simplicity): P0, P1 ← P0, P2 ← P1, H ← P2.

In Fig. 31.4b we present a visual metaphor of the dynamic inference process through a graph, showing levels of properties (gray color), several hypotheses (black color), as well as deductive reasoning (arrows pointing up) and inductive reasoning (arrows pointing down) in this process. The inference rules are

$$h_{j,i+1} : H_{i+1} \leftarrow p_{k,i}{}^* : P_i {}^{\wedge} h_{1,i}{}^* : H_i$$

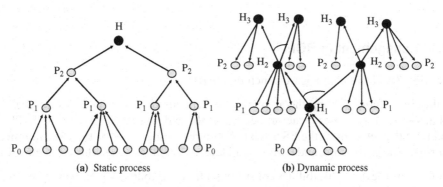

(a) Static process   (b) Dynamic process

Figure 31.4. Inference process diagrams.

where $i = 0, 1, \ldots, n$ and n = number of levels, and j,k,l: nat. For example, in Fig. 31.4b we have

$$H1 \bullet P0, H2 \bullet P1^\wedge H1, \ H3 \bullet P2^\wedge H2 \text{ (extended natural natation).}$$

The behavior of the architectural elements varies according to the reasoning strategy applied. The strategy is closely related to the view of the entity during the diagnosis process, the property levels of this entity, and the number and level of hypotheses involved in this process. In the static process an entity has the same properties (the same view) as during the diagnostic process and only one hypothesis (goal). In the dynamic process an entity has different properties (different views) than during the diagnostic process, and it has several candidate diagnostic hypotheses which must all be evaluated in order to select the valid one.

Figures 31.5a, b show the static and dynamic inference processes respectively, which are modeled using the Business Process Management Notation (BPMN).

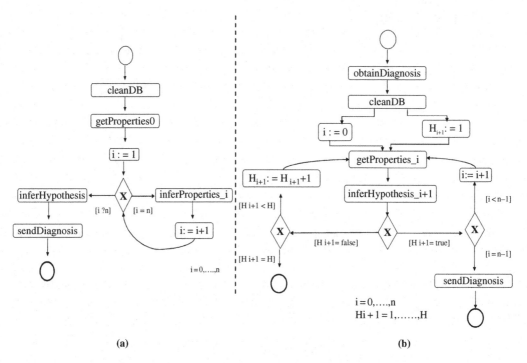

Figure 31.5. Static (**a**) and Dynamic (**b**) inference processes in BPMN.

4. Variability Management in BOM

From Section 3.1 of this chapter, we concluded that

- the variability in structure among the architectural elements of the ES includes number of use cases, number of actors, and uses cases by actor, i.e., this is the end user requirements variability.
- the variability in the behavior of the ES is related with reasoning type, entity views, number of levels of the entity properties to diagnose, and number and level of hypotheses, i.e., this is the domain variability.

The union of the previous variabilities constitutes a first variability: V1. However, we also considered the scope of the application domain to be necessary. Therefore, a second variability emerges: the application domain variability, V2.

These variabilities can be described in terms of features. For this reason and based on the field study carried out, we conclude that the features that define the ES involve two types of orthogonal variability: The first variability (V1) is given by the domain features and the end user requirements, which determine a specific base architecture. The second variability (V2) corresponds to application domain features, which determine the final product of our SPL.

5. Expert Systems Development in BOM

The development in BOM of ES is based on MDA and SPL techniques, the PRISMA model, and the structure and operation of the rule-based ES. This process involves building a baseline (a repository containing all the assets needed to build a product of the SPL) and to model the process of executing the production plan of the SPL.

In Fig. 31.6 we show how an ES is generated by BOM in two steps. In the first step, a skeleton base architecture model is obtained from the modular model (generic architecture of the ES) and a V1 instance (captured by the domain conceptual model: DCM) by means of a first QVT-transformation T1. In the second step, a PRISMA architectural model is obtained from the skeleton base architecture model (which was generated in the previous step) and a V2 instance (captured by the application domain conceptual model: ADCM) by means of a second QVT-transformation T2.

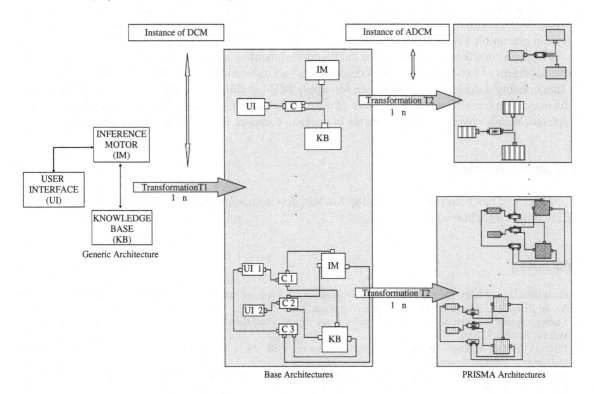

Figure 31.6. Visual metaphor of ES development in BOM.

In BOM, the model transformations T1 and T2 are executed by means of the MOMENT tool [8] using OMG QVT-relational [9] model transformations. At the end, BOM uses the PRISMA–MODEL–COMPILER tool [10] to automatically generate the executable code (in C#.NET) of the generated model. BOM executes the object code over the PRISMA–NET Middleware [11].

In BOM, the user (application engineer) builds an ES (product of SPL), by giving as input the features of the variabilities V1 and V2 using instances of the two conceptual models: DCM and ADCM.

6. Conclusions and Future Work

In this chapter we describe the variabilities of the ES, and how they are managed by means of our BOM framework for automatically generating applications in this specific domain.

In order to cope with the complexity of the ES development, we deal with variability in two stages: in the first stage, variability is reflected in the base architectures of the SPL sharing a generic architecture; in the second stage, variability is reflected in the application features producing the SPL in a specific domain sharing a base architecture. BOM manages the variabilities at the model level (not at the program level). The models are automatically compiled and the generated code is an executable application.

BOM can improve the development of ES in the following ways: By using the characteristics of ES to separate the inference process of the knowledge domain and to incorporate several reasoning strategies in order to solve a problem by applying the most efficient one. By applying SPL techniques to the construction of a design shared by all the members of a program family; in this way cost, time, effort, and complexity are reduced. By developing product line architectures as PRISMA models, and reusing and integrating software components and aspects, in order to facilitate the management of complexity. By applying MDA techniques in order to implement systems on different platforms and to automatically obtain an executable ES.

The main contributions of BOM are the ES development by means of automatically generating code, the management of two variability kinds described in two independent conceptual models separated from the functionality models. In the future, we will apply BOM in different domains, and we will validate its performances in real-life cases by means of our prototype ProtoBOM [12] which we have recently completed. We also plan to use benchmarks in order to compare BOM results with other approaches.

Acknowledgments

This work has been funded under the Models, Environments, Transformations, and Applications: META project TIN20006-15175-605-01.

References

1. Giarratano, J., and Riley, G., *Expert Systems: Principles and Programming.* 4th Edition: (Hardcover), ISBN: 0534384471, 2004.
2. Model Driven Architecture: MDA. http://www.omg.org/mda
3. Clements P., and Northrop L.M., *Software Product Lines: Practices and Patterns,* SEI Series in Software Engineering, Addison Wesley, New York, 2002.
4. Pérez J., *"PRISMA: Aspect-Oriented Software Architectures",* PhD. Thesis of Philosophy in Computer Science, Polytechnic University of Valencia, Spain, 2006.
5. Batory D., Benavides D., and Ruiz-Cortés A., Automated Analyses of Feature Models: Challenges Ahead, ACM on Software Product Lines, 2006.
6. Trujillo S., "Feature-Oriented Model Driven Product Lines", *PhD. Thesis,* The University of the Basque Country, San Sebastian, Spain, 2007.
7. Bachman F., Goedicke M., Leite J., Nord R., Pohl K., Ramesh B., and Vilbig A, "A Meta-Model for Representing Variability in Product Family Development", In *Proceedings in the 5th International Workshop on Product Family Engineering,* pp. 66–80, 2003.
8. MOMENT Project, http://moment.dsic.upv.es/
9. QVT Query/View/Transformations OMG Document ad/2005-07-1.
10. Cabedo R., Pérez J., Carsí J.A., and y Ramos I., "Modelado y Generación de Arquitecturas PRISMA con DSL Tools", *IV Workshop DYNAMICA,* Murcia, España, 2005. (in spanish).

11. Costa C., Pérez J., Ali N., Carsí J.A. y Ramos I., "PRISMANET: Middleware: Soporte a la Evolución Dinámica de Arquitecturas Software Orientadas a Aspectos", *X Jornadas de Ingeniería de Software y Base de datos,* Granada, España, pp. 27–34, 2005, (in spanish).

12. Cabello M.E., Gómez M., LLavador M., and Ramos I. ProtoBOM: A Framework that Semi-Automatically Generates Decision Support Systems Based on Software Product Lines. *Technical Report*: DSIC II/02/08, Polythecnical University of Valencia, Valencia, Spain, pp. 68, 2008.

32

Framework for Using Patterns in Model-Driven Development

Picek Ruben and Strahonja Vjeran

Abstract

This chapter presents a framework for using patterns in promising and emerging paradigm of software industry called model-driven development (MDD). Despite a lot of skepticism and problems, MDD paradigm is being used and improved to accomplish many inherent potential benefits. During the last two decades, patterns are used in SW industry and becoming more and more numerous. So it is natural to ask the question: *How software patterns fits into MDD paradigm?* In this chapter, authors examine the possibilities of using patterns in context of MDD paradigm. Because in the methodological approach of software development it is necessary to use some kind of development process. As the result of this research authors in this chapter presents the framework for using patterns in model-driven development.

Keywords Model-driven development · Software patterns · Framework · Methodology

1. Introduction

Software development is faced with many challenges. Requirements of new and/or existing systems are growing, systems are complex, and it is hard to build them on time and on budget. As an answer to these challenges, a wide spectrum of new paradigms, approaches, and methods have been developed. One of the most promising paradigm is model driven development (MDD). The aim of our work is to examine the possibilities of using patterns in context of that paradigm and define a methodological framework of their use, because during the preliminary research we find out that today's SW methodologies in the context of MDD are insufficient.

2. Model-Driven Development Paradigm and Software Patterns Overview

This section presents a short review of current state in MDD paradigm and in the context of software development; analyze software patterns as reusable artifact.

2.1. Model-Driven Development Paradigm

MDD represents a set of approaches, theories, and methodological frameworks for industrialized software development, based on the systematic use of models as primary artifacts throughout the software development cycle [6]. It targets two roots of software crisis – *complexity* and *ability to change*. The basic

---

Picek Ruben and Strahonja Vjeran • Department of Information System Development, Faculty of Organization and Informatics, University of Zagreb, Varaždin, Croatia.

G.A. Papadopoulos et al. (eds.), *Information Systems Development*, DOI 10.1007/b137171_32,

idea of this paradigm is to move the development efforts from programming to the higher level of abstraction, by using models as primary artifacts and by transforming models into source code or other artifacts. The ultimate objective is the automated development (fully or partly). Models are the key artifacts and the focus shifts from the programming to the modeling.

Traditionally, models are mostly used as sketches that informally convey some aspects of a system or they can be used as blueprints to describe a detailed design that is then manually implemented [15]. In MDD, models are used not just as sketches or blueprints, but as primary artifacts from which efficient implementations are generated, transforming models into programming code or other executable artifacts. According to Selic [11], the essence of model-driven development is about two things. One is abstraction, in terms of how we think about the problem and then how we specify our solutions. Second thing that often gets forgotten is the introduction of more and more automation into the software development by using computer-based tools and integrated environments.

The heart of MDD paradigm makes models, modeling, and model transformation. In order to be suitable for the MDD, models must satisfy additional criteria – they must be machine readable. Machine-readability of models is a prerequisite for being able to generate artifacts. Automated model transformations are the key for realization of the MDD idea.

Benefits and problems which arise in MDD realization are analyzed in author's previous paper [10]. The analysis includes discussion about open questions like *How to transform a model at one level of abstraction into a model or code at a lower level? How to use models? Which notation and modeling language should be used in order to provide automation? Is UML suitable as model programming language?* This is the state of the art. The MDD paradigm brings a lot of open issues on ice and solutions are searched in two directions: methodology and technology. The Object Managements Group (OMG) proposed a approach called model driven architecture (MDA). Industrial leaders are also developing their own solutions, such as the Microsoft's Software Factories (SF) [5].

2.2. Software Patterns

The idea of software patterns has a long history. Maybe the software subroutines in the structural age were the first patterns. In the beginning of the 1990s software patterns became a way of realization of object-oriented main characteristics – reusability.

2.2.1. Definition and Characteristics of Patterns

The term *pattern* evokes a variety of interpretations and definitions, mostly depending on context of use. According to different authors [14, 3, 9] *pattern* is a best practice solution to a recurring problem for a given context. But each solution, algorithm, or best practice is not a pattern. Main characteristic of the pattern is the ability to use it all over again in recurring problems (recurrence). Patterns encapsulate designer's time, skills, and knowledge, and also best practice and domain knowledge. When *recurrence* is a quantitative characteristic which is shown by context and problem definition, *suitability* and *usefulness* are qualitative characteristics where suitability clarifies *how* the pattern will contribute to the problem solution, while usefulness explains *why* pattern will be useful.

Final definition of software pattern used in this chapter is: "software pattern is a recurring structural concept used in context of software development which comprises the problem definition and the solution based on the best practice and can be applied on all levels of abstraction during software development life cycle."

In the context of software development, software pattern is a reusable concept on higher level of abstraction than programming code or individual class. Finally, when used in software development, patterns should improve productivity, reduce development time, minimize complexity, increase quality, improve governance, gain business agility, leverage IT skills, promote open standards, close the gap between business and IT, and improve cost [8]. Two more advantages according to Ackerman and Gonzalez are improved management of developing projects and simplicity of software architecture [1].

Besides, we have included several additional advantages: encapsulation of knowledge and expertise and dissemination of best practice across vertical industries and horizontal problem domains.

2.2.2. Pattern Classification and Standardization

Emerging application of patterns has paid more intention to pattern development and the result is quite a number of new patterns in all segments of software development. Some organizations organize and manage patterns by using their own pattern repositories. Different organizations have developed patterns which are suitable for their way of working and using technology. Direct consequence of that is a large number of different structured patterns and the absence of unified classification.

Relevant references present just a fundamental classification of patterns, where patterns are classified according to *level of abstraction* and degrees *of generality*. According to *level of abstraction* patterns are classified base on architectural patterns, design patterns and language-specific patterns – idioms [14]. According to *degrees of generality,* patterns are classified base on application or domain specific and general design patterns, applicable across application domains [12]. Based on our research we propose an extended classification by: development phases, development aspects and manufacturer (organization) and/or technology platform. The unified classification should enable selection of patterns and their use. To include patterns in MDD scenario, it is necessary to define a standardized way of organization, specification, implementation, and packing.

Toward increasing the return on investment, the term *reusable software asset* is introduced. It includes different artifacts used in development process. Furthermore to ensure their reusability and standardization, reusable asset specification (RAS) was developed for providing a standardized way of *software asset* archiving, searching, organizing, specifying, implementing, packing, and sharing. Futher in this chapter, the authors explore how patterns can be observed as *software asset* and how to implement them by using RAS.

All this indicates a need for a framework for integrating patterns in MDD.

3. Conditions for Using Patterns in MDD

Using patterns in MDD context also sets up some questions: How can advantages that patterns bring to development be identified and used in MDD realization? How to define patterns adequate for using in MDD environment? A closer look at advantages of patterns concerning MDD paradigm suggests that patterns can significantly improve realization of MDD paradigm. Complementary relationship between patterns and MDD can be seen in two forms:

Software patterns provide content for MDD. Expertise captured in patterns represents best practice for the problem solution with opportunity for reuse. That is the main reason why patterns are desirable artifacts for MDD.

Model automation can be easily achieved by using patterns. Traditionally, patterns are written down as documents, often accompanied by UML models and then applied manually. But, if pattern is packed as a reusable asset with encapsulated implementation, it can be automated from conceptual level to programming code.

Results of using patterns in MDD can be visible in reducing time to react, enabling on demand design and development requirements, reducing complexity, and increasing productivity and quality of software [4].

According to all those stated above, we have defined our conditions for using patterns in MDD paradigm, which have to be satisfied for existing patterns, as well as for those that will be developed in future. These conditions are as follows:

- development environment has to support fundamental MDD principles;
- patterns have to be defined in a standard way in the form of reusable software assets that encapsulate both specification and implementation;

- patterns have to be packed and deployed in the pattern repository, equipped with the repository management facility and the import/export to the development environment; and
- development environment must have possibility to use patterns as artifacts for the MDD realization.

On the academic level synergy between patterns and MDD is easily visible. But in real situations and industrial environments a lot of questions are still open. That is the reason why we decided to develop methodological framework for using patterns in MDD paradigm, which has to be a contribution to software development methodology.

4. Framework Development

Despite its merits it is strange how MDD remains insufficient for software development in the sense that it does not provide a concrete and comprehensive process for governing software development activities [2]. We do not suggest that industry should develop a new methodology for MDD, but only emphasize the fact that there is still a lack of formal process for the model-driven development. Therefore, a suitability of modern software development methodologies for MDD development has been evaluated. After that, the framework for using patterns in MDD development was developed. In order that framework becomes methodologically acceptable and applicable, it is necessary that framework's design includes all segments of the pattern life cycle. The pattern life cycle (Fig. 32.1) is developed on the basis of the broader asset life cycle, because one of the condition is that pattern has to be defined as the reusable asset.

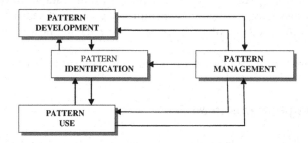

Figure 32.1. Pattern life cycle.

Observing the pattern life cycles, two groups of activities can be identified. First are activities oriented to *development of new patterns* while the second group consist of activities oriented to *MDD development with using patterns*. It is obvious that activities are intertwine, because *developing new patterns* can also be done during MDD development, but it can be separated out of that context and observed independently like classic software development project.

Our standpoint is that it is proper to distinguish these two groups because at development activities the focus is on new patterns. Development includes identification of patterns, their assessment, development, and packing for wider use. On the other hand, *MDD development with using patterns* is focused on new software which has to be realized using concepts of MDD paradigm and patterns. Therefore, it is good to distinguish pattern development from their organizing and using. An ad hoc development and publishing of patterns should also be avoided. Of course, it does not mean a rigid separation of activities, but more like some kind of logical grouping.

The integration framework that we suggest has two dimensions:

Expertise definition in the form of pattern – suitable for the new pattern development within the team of experts.

Model-driven development with patterns – suitable for the new software development projects realized with MDD paradigm.

Figure 32.2 presents both dimensions of the framework. When all segments of pattern life cycle are placed, intertwines of both dimensions are visible. Realization of all segments requires methodological description (who works what, when, and how?) which is presented in the next sections.

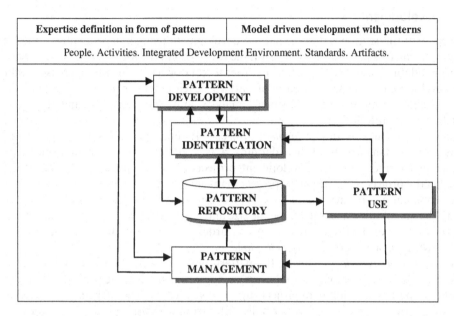

Expertise definition in form of pattern	Model driven development with patterns
People. Activities. Integrated Development Environment. Standards. Artifacts.	

Figure 32.2. Context framework visualization.

4.1. Pattern Identification

The aim of this section is to find existing MDD patterns for perceived and/or new problems, whose solutions can be defined as a pattern. After defining the problem domain or in any other development phase, a question like this can be asked: does any MDD pattern that represents the best practice exists for recognized problems? To find the answer to this question we propose the following activities:

Identifying and locating pattern – For some problems (very small in number) MDD patterns already exist, but for the most of them they have to be developed. To find out if pattern already exists, it is necessary to search in the pattern repository by certain criteria (name, type, etc.). After that, all patterns which satisfy these criteria need to be examined through their specification and implementation to find out their suitability and usability for both the problem and the MDD context. If the pattern does not exist, the problem may become a candidate for the new pattern.

Candidate problem (and solution) for the new pattern – This activity is actually brainstorming – evaluating potential of problems and solutions for new patterns. But all candidates would not be designed as patterns. How to find suitable problem and potential or an existing solution for pattern? We propose a list of questions that may help: What is the importance of this problem? Is the software solution feasible? Is it possible to define the problem and its solution as reusable software asset? Can we reuse the given solution more times? May we expect that this or similar problem will appear in future projects? In cases where candidates would not be realized as pattern, it is possible to encapsulate this knowledge in a form of anti-pattern and store it in the pattern repository. Next time we will have information that this problem or solution has been evaluated in the past. If the candidate is desirable for a pattern, it is necessary to perform initial cost assessment.

Initial cost assessment analysis – It is necessary to determine financial cost of pattern development. Important questions are as follows: What are the costs of development for one use of pattern? Who will pay this development? What is the added value and the cost of reuse? What is the maintenance cost? If this analysis is positive, all documentation is gathered and the result is formal requirements for a new pattern development. New segment of framework – *Pattern development* that can be started.

4.2. Pattern Development

The purpose of this section is that the pattern development team, independently of the MDD phases, creates a new pattern. This pattern should be suitable for MDD in the form of a reusable asset which could be applied in an indefinite number of projects in order to cut down on expenses, increase productivity, and shorten the development time. On the basis of pattern development requirements, e.g., documentation describing a problem, initial cost assessment analysis and additional documentation and models (UML models, etc.) what follows is

The launch of a new pattern development project – It represents the starting point of the pattern development project management. When defining a new pattern development project, a number of activities inherent to other software development projects are determined. They should determine the team involved in the project realization (the project manager, members, tasks, and activities), budget, time schedule, development environment, and development process. The same has to be done at the pattern development. The aim of this stage is to define the size and environment of the pattern development project with a detailed analysis of the project realization, in order to manage it later successfully. The result is a defined project with a *new pattern development plan*.

The development realization – During the pattern development, the key component is the pattern development process. Many companies have their own iterative homemade process which is the result of the best practice of pattern development projects up to now, and which is still being improved by every new pattern. The phases of this process do not normally differ from the classic phases of software development. Therefore we suggest the realization of the new pattern development through following phases:

Analysis – This activity comprises requirements analysis and specification.

Pattern design – This activity includes

(A) *Design solution.* The solution in a clear and unambiguous way defines how the pattern will be developed, i.e., how it will be implemented and at the same time meet all the criteria of MDD paradigm and pattern definition.

   Pattern parameters. It refers to defining their number, type, and possible interrelatedness, as well as possible restrictions of certain parameters. For the purpose of understanding pattern realization, it is also desirable to create some kind of a conceptual UML diagram (class diagram). This stage of the process will iterate a couple of times before it becomes the solution which will be implemented from then on.

(B) *Pattern specification.* It is desirable that the previous activities generate the whole documentation (.doc, .html) constituting the pattern specification. This means that documentation is an artifact which is a product of development.

(C) *Test writing.* The final stage should also comprise the definition of test scripts. Before the organization of a pattern as a reusable asset, it should be tested in order to check the success of its implementation.

After defining the future pattern, architecture follows its *implementation* – that means adding the component of "behavior" which will describe what happens if a value is added to or removed from every pattern parameter. Actually, this is the knowledge which has to be encapsulated in the pattern. It refers to the task which a programmer has to carry out manually every time and which requires to be automated. Based on the specified basic pattern elements, development environment should generate the backbone of the code program which is made up of classes (parameters) with methods for adding and removing parameter's value, as well as description of possible connections between the two parameters.

Testing – the last component of development evaluates the quality of the implementation. Since the basic purpose of every developed pattern is its reusability and automation, a detailed and meticulous approach to testing is necessary. Does the pattern meet our expectations and solve the problem? It means validation. Does the pattern "behave" in a way expected considering the defined specification? It means verification. Test materials written during the pattern design should be checked in order to find out possible errors and mistakes. The result of the previously mentioned activities is feedback which the SW team uses for the improvements in pattern development.

Organizing pattern as a reusable asset – There are some other activities, inherent to MDD, that also a successfully developed and tested pattern should go through. A developed pattern has to be defined as a reusable asset. Therefore the following activities are necessary, *standardization and packing* and *publishing in repository*. In our case, *reusable asset standard (RAS)* is used for the *standardization and packing* of reusable asset (every reusable asset has to contain one manifest file and several artifacts). RAS ensures the existence of the infrastructure for reusability. The point of packing is unification of all artifacts (documentation, model, code) which the reusable asset will make useful for searching, use, etc. Package (reusable asset) is defined by version with *.ras* extension. *Publishing in repository* represents the final step when the produced asset (*.ras*) is placed and becomes ready for wider use.

4.3. Pattern Use

The aim of this section is to define a proper way of using existing patterns for MDD development. It includes

The Import of a pattern from the catalogue and installation in the IDE – This is an initial preparation step for pattern consumption in the context of MDD paradigm. Attention has to be paid to the choice of development environment, IDE, which has to meet the previously defined requirements.

The use during modeling – During this activity models has to be designed in a way suitable for applying certain types of automation. The development of such models implies the use of a standardized modeling language, e.g., UML. The process of use of pattern during the model development includes: *pattern instantiation* and *connecting a pattern instance with model elements*. Pattern instantiation implies the transfer of a pattern into the UML model which is currently being developed (e.g., class diagram). In this way the pattern becomes an UML element. Second step is linking a pattern instance with the model elements (UML concepts) by defining the value of pattern instance parameter.

The use during implementation – The point of MDD is automation by transforming models into other artifacts, primarily the programming code (M2C transformation). In order to do this, IDE should either have already predefined transformation types or the possibility of creating its own transformations. Currently supported transformation types in IBM RSA v6.0.1 are UML–C++, UML–CORBA, UML–EJB, UML–Java and UML–XSD transformation. The implementation process is divided into: *creation and configuration of transformation instances* and *transformation execution with the addition of the manual code programming*. The creation and configuration of transformation instances is conducted by the marking procedure adding details for exact model transformation. Before making this crucial move, it is necessary to create a new transformation instance and later configure it. The configuration of a transformation instance includes determination of basic settings, like configuration name, source, and target (UML model and the code program type), as well as definition of special settings for transformation, related to a certain type of realization. Consistency has to be ensured between the UML elements from the original model and the generated programming code in the target model. Transformation execution with the addition of the manual code programming generates a certain number of files which represent the chosen implementation of the UML model. Currently 100% code program generation from the model is not possible. Therefore follows the final stage of the process and that is the addition of the programming code (programming logic) in generated classes marked as TODO (or some other similar key word). Since transformation can be executed an indefinite number of times, a manually defined code has to be marked by a special tag in order to prevent its erasure during restart.

Defining feedback – It is an important activity since it provides practical experience encompassing information about general impressions of the pattern consumption (its version, its efficiency, simplicity of use, identifying and locating, existing doubts, or worries connected with the use), errors, anomalies to be corrected, and possibilities of pattern reuse or improvement. The information should be gathered through standardized templates for documenting the above-mentioned information. Received information will be crucial for making new decisions in the section *Pattern Management*.

4.4. Pattern Management

The term pattern management can be observed in two senses. In wider sense it represents an environment where different requirements, needs, or tasks are balanced in order to overcome restrictions and risks and to ensure successful development, delivery, and pattern use in the context of MDD. In narrower sense it refers to management activities concerned with patterns (and anti-patterns), i.e., their positioning in the repository, versions, and changes control, etc. In this section, pattern management will be observed in narrower sense through *pattern change management* and *patterns repository management*.

Pattern change management – On the basis of feedback from the consumption segment, a *request for change (RfC)* is formed in order to eliminate anomalies in the course of development, to describe additional possibilities of application of patterns, and to define improvements which have to be made in the new version. RfC represents an artifact by which all the requests during the pattern's life cycle are formally described, followed, and documented. Special attention has to be paid to the content of the RfC document. It should also comprise attributes such as transformation size, alternatives, transformation complexity, time schedule, transformation impact, expenses, and the need for testing after the change.

Patterns repository management – Since the number of patterns in organizations using MDD rapidly grows, the idea is to manage patterns by using some kind of repository. It is obvious that the first step organization and classification of patterns into groups according to some clear criteria, e.g., technology, phases of development, purpose, or some other characteristic. Repository management should provide consistent repository. Some of the possible appearances of inconsistency are redundancy, name conflicts (synonyms, homonyms), inconsistent classification, and generalization/specialization of patterns. Repository management should also provide version/release control of patterns.

5. Conclusions

In this chapter, the authors present short review of current state in model-driven development and software patterns. This chapter points out how patterns fit into the context of MDD paradigm, as well as potential benefits from their use in MDD development. Because, all existing patterns are not suitable for MDD, the authors define conditions that should be fulfilled as a prerequisite for using patterns in MDD development. According to relevant references in authors' research, software methodology which is customized or developed for using patterns in MDD is still missing. The authors in this chapter proposed the pattern life cycle and developed a framework in which they define activities based on the pattern life cycle. The framework is composed from four segments and mainstream activities. Practical realization is based on IBM Rational Software Architect integrated development environment [13]. This framework has been applied and evaluated in a test environment (laboratory) and presents promising results. Future work will be focused on applying it in the industrial environment and integration framework with leading software development methodologies suitable for MDD. The idea is also formally to define a framework using Rational Method Composer.

References

1. Ackerman, L., Gonzalez, C. (2007) *The Value of Pattern Implementations*, DrDobb's Portal, Retrieved March 09, 2008, from: http://www.ddj.com/cpp/199204017
2. Chitforoush, F., Yazdandoost, M., Ramsin, R. (2007) Methodology Support for the Model Driven Architecture, Asia-Pacific Software Engineering Conference. *APSEC 2007* Volume, Issue, Date: 4–7 Dec. 2007, pp. 454–461
3. Elssamadisy, A. (2006) Patterns of Agile Practice Adoption, InfoQ
4. Gardner, T., Yusuf, L. (2006) *Combine Patterns and Modelling to Implement Architecture-Driven Development*, http://www.ibm.com/developerworks/ibm/library/ar-mdd2/
5. Greenfield, J. and Short, K. (2004) *Moving to Software Factories*, http://blogs.msdn.com/askburton/archive/2004/09/20/232065.aspx
6. Greenfield, J., Short, K., Cook, S. and Kent, S. (2004)*Software Factories – Assembling Application with Patterns, Models, Frameworks and Tools*, Wiley Publishing, Indianapolis.
7. Hailpern, B. and Tarr, P. (2006) Model-Driven Development: The Good, the Bad, and the Ugly. *IBM System Yournal*, 45(3), 451–461.
8. IBM developerWorks (2007)*Pattern Solution*, <http://www-128.ibm.com/developerworks/rational/products/patternsolutions/>
9. Larsen, G. (2006) Model-Driven Development: Assets and Reuse. *IBM System Journal* 45(3), http://www.research.ibm.com/journal/sj/453/larsen.html
10. Picek, R. and Strahonja, V. (2007) *Model Driven Development – Future or Failure of Software Development?*, Proceedings of the 18th International Conference on Information and Intelligent Systems, Faculty of Organization and Informatics, Varaždin, pp. 407–413.
11. Pierson, H.(2007) *ARCast #5*, http://channel9. msdn.com/ Showpost.aspx?postid = 132943
12. Rosengard, J.M., Ursu, M. F.(2004) Ontological Representation of Software Patterns
13. Yu, C. (2007) *Model-Driven and Pattern-Based Development Using Rational Software Architect, Part 1: Overview of the Model-Driven Development Paradigm with patterns*, http://www-128.ibm.com/developerworks/rational/library/06/1121_yu/
14. Yu, C. (2007) *Model-Driven and Pattern-Based Development Using Rational Software Architect, Part 2: Model-Driven Development Tooling Support in IBM Rational Software Architect*, 2007, Retrieved April 19, 2008, from: http://www-128.ibm.com/developerworks/rational/library/07/0116_yu/
15. Yusuf, L., Chessel, M. and Gardner, T. (2006) *Implement Model-Driven Development to Increase the Business Value of Your IT System*, Retrieved January 29, 2008 from: http://www-128.ibm.com/developerworks/library/ar-mdd1/

33

Ontology of Domain Analysis Concepts in Software System Design Domain

Robertas Damaševičius

Abstract

The aim of domain analysis is to extract, identify, capture, organize, and make reusable information used in developing new information systems. Many different concepts are used in the area of domain analysis, such as concerns, features, aspects, subjects, intentions, roles. Metamodeling of domain concepts by constructing domain ontologies (ontology engineering), taxonomies, and meta-models of domain concepts supports flexible, concise, and efficient domain knowledge extraction and analysis; provides means for analyzing, representing, and reusing the results of domain analysis; and is an important step toward the development of knowledge-oriented information systems. The aim of this chapter is to analyze the concepts used in domain analysis of software systems and to construct ontology of concepts in software system design domain that describes relationships between analyzed domain concepts and highlights their properties and characteristics.

Keywords Ontology engineering · Domain analysis · Domain metamodeling

1. Introduction

The term *domain* describes a group of related software systems that have similar functionality or share a set of common capabilities or characteristics [17]. *Domain engineering* (DE) affects maintainability, understandability, usability, and reusability of a system or family of similar systems; therefore, DE and especially *domain analysis* (DA) are extremely important for design of domain systems [21]. The aims of DA are to extract, identify, capture, organize, and make reusable information used in developing new information systems [20]. Commonly DA involves (1) definition of the basic domain concepts (boundary, scope, and vocabulary) that can be used to construct domain architecture; (2) description of the domain data (e.g., variables, constants, parameters) that is used to support the functions and state of the domain system or a family of domain systems; (3) identification of relationships and constraints among domain concepts, data, and functions within the domain; and (4) identification, evaluation, and selection of reusable domain artifacts [21].

The analysis of DA methods and concepts, including their relationship, is a case of *metamodeling* [1], *method engineering* [2], and *ontology engineering* [9]. Metamodeling involves construction of a collection of concepts within a certain domain, and development of a meta-model that describes a relationship between analyzed domain concepts highlighting their properties and characteristics. Ontology engineering deals with construction of ontologies that represent domain concepts, entities, abstractions, and relationships between them at a conceptual level of analysis. Ontology construction is especially relevant in the software

Robertas Damaševičius • Software Engineering Department, Kaunas University of Technology, Lithuania.

G.A. Papadopoulos et al. (eds.), *Information Systems Development*, DOI 10.1007/b137171_33,

development domain, because there are a great variety of programming concepts, techniques, methodologies, and paradigms. Ontologies can be used to organize and share this knowledge efficiently in educational [26, 23, 25] and industrial software development [12] contexts as well as in enterprise systems engineering [3]. Specifically, Bunge-Wand-Weber (BWW) ontologies are used to model information systems [11].

The aim of this chapter is to analyze the concepts used in DA methods and to construct the vocabulary, ontology, and taxonomy of DA concepts in software design domain. The ontology is described graphically as well as using OWL (Web Ontology Language), which is a standard language for knowledge representation. The motivation for constructing such ontologies is organization of domain knowledge for educational purposes. The students currently are facing the increasing demands for assimilating large flows of diverse information. Specifically, computer science and programming students are introduced with different software development methodologies and paradigms, whereas no relationship between different concepts of these paradigms is usually provided. This leads to difficulties in knowledge adoption, understanding of software engineering principles and highly subjective views on particular software development methods. The introduction of domain ontologies to students may solve some of these problems.

2. Domain Ontology Engineering: Concepts, Aims, and Definitios

The term 'ontology' is used in computer science as a system of concepts and as a vocabulary (taxonomy) used for building an information system [16] or modeling a domain. Ontologies provide knowledge engineering support for modeling a domain in terms of labeled concepts, attributes, and relationships, usually classified in specialization/generalization hierarchies [18]. In knowledge engineering, the term 'ontology' is used to denote an explicit specification of a *conceptualization* , i.e., a conceptual description of the objects, concepts, other entities, and relationships between them that can exist in a domain. The aims of ontologies are to be used as a common vocabulary for communication and knowledge sharing between designers, for standardization of terminology especially implicit presuppositions/assumptions that make a part of domain knowledge, explication of design rationale, systematization of knowledge about the meaning of domain concepts and domain tasks [16]. The fundamental asset of ontologies is their application independence, i.e., ontology consists of relatively generic knowledge that can be reused by different kinds of applications/tasks within a specific domain [24].

In a context of problem solving, ontologies are divided into two types. (1) *Task ontology* is used for representing system design processes (not considered here). (2) *Domain ontology* is used for representing domain entities and abstractions abstractly and is a concrete representation of a domain conceptualization [9]. A conceptualization is an abstract view of the real world that we wish to represent. The elements constituting a conceptualization of a given domain are used to articulate abstractions of a certain aspect of reality and are called *domain abstractions* .

The construction of ontology (or *ontology engineering*) is an important step in the development of knowledge-based information systems. According to [19], ontology engineering consists of the following steps:

(1) *Domain/requirements analysis*: Analysis of the application domain with respect to a set of predefined requirements.
(2) *Conceptualization*: Domain modeling in terms of ontological primitives, e.g., concepts, relations, axioms. The result is a *conceptual domain model* (meta-model).
(3) *Implementation*: the conceptual model resulted from the previous step is implemented in a (formal or diagrammatic) modeling language such as UML [4].
(4) *Evaluation and usage*: The ontology is evaluated based on designer views and expert opinions. The results of evaluation can be used for ontology refinement at the domain analysis, conceptualization, or implementation level.

Ontology also can be seen as the metamodel specification for an ideal language to represent phenomena in a given domain, i.e., a language which only admits specifications representing possible state of affairs in reality [9]. Development of metamodels or *metamodeling* is the process of knowledge extraction from a given domain using DA methods, i.e., discovery, understanding, and capture the internal structure of a domain and the relationship between its sub-domains and domain entities [6]. The primary stage of metamodeling includes *meta-analysis* (systematic comparison and analysis of DA methods based on selected set of criteria [30] followed by a discovery of domain taxonomy and domain ontology at a higher abstraction level. The *domain taxonomy* outlines the boundaries and the context for metamodeling. The result of metamodeling is a *metamodel*, i.e., a higher level model that describes conceptual relationships between lower level models and their elements, abstractions, and design methods (processes).

3. Domain Concepts in Known DA Approaches

1. *Concern.* A *concern* is a concept of which most software engineers have an intuitive grasp, but no precise definition [7]. Broadly, a concern refers to any particular piece of interest or focus in a program. A concern space encompasses all software in some domain such as a set of software systems or component libraries. It contains a set of software units and a set of all concerns important in this domain. The aim of DA is to identify and segregate design concerns and to provide means for software engineers to use the concerns as the basis for software modularization during development and evolution of domain systems. Separation of concerns refers to the ability to identify, encapsulate, and manipulate parts of software that are relevant to a particular concern. One of the DA methods that deal with separation of concerns is *multi-dimensional separation of concerns* (MDSOC) [18]. MDSOC envisions development of domain programs as composition of separated concerns according to systematic rules. Concerns are understood in terms of a multidimensional design space (*hyperspace*). Each dimension is associated with a set of similar concerns, such as a set of component instances; different values along a dimension are different instances. A *hyperslice* is a set of instances that pertain to a specific concern. A *hypermodule* is a set of hyperslices and integration relationships that dictate how hyperslice units are integrated into a program.
2. *Component.* A software *component* is a unit of a software system, which offers a predefined service and is able to communicate with other components [27]. Components are considered to be a higher level of abstraction than objects and as such they do not share a state and communicate by exchanging messages carrying data. Component-based systems are developed by gluing prefabricated components together. Such components should be usable in multiple systems, context independent, composable with other components, encapsulated (i.e., interface is separated from functionality), and deployed independently.
3. *Aspect.* An *aspect* is a partial representation of some concepts that relate to a concern [5]. Aspects are particularly discussed in a programming paradigm called *aspect-oriented programming* (AOP) [14]. Here, an aspect is a property of the component that affects its performance or semantics in a systematic way and is implemented using the aspect language(s). Aspects describe concerns of a separate set of objects, classes or functions and implement behavior that would normally crosscut the structure and behavior of the core concern of the application. Aspects exist in both design and implementation. A design aspect is a modular unit of the design that crosscuts the structure of other parts of the design. A program or code aspect is a modular unit of a program that crosscuts other modular units of a program.
4. *Class and object. object-oriented aesign* (OOD) paradigm assumes that systems are modeled using a set of classes and relationships between them. A *class* encapsulates the data and the operations applicable to the data. There are three types of relationships between classes: (1) *Inheritance* allows a subclass to incorporate data elements and operations defined in a parent class and to augment it with additional data elements and methods. (2) *Aggregation/Composition* is used when one object (container) physically or conceptually contains another object (component). (3) *Association* represents conceptual relationships between classes and is used for exchange of messages. An instance of a class is an object. An object defines an interface of the services (operations, methods) that it provides and encapsulates data elements

defined in its class. Objects can be viewed at three levels: (1) At the *implementation* level, classes represent blocks of code in a programming language. (2) At the *specification* level, classes specify system interfaces at a high level of abstraction. (3) At the *conceptual* level, classes represent domain concepts such as architectures.

5. *Subject. Subject-oriented programming* (SOP) is a program composition technology that supports building domain systems as compositions of subjects [10]. A *subject* is a collection of classes or class fragments whose hierarchy models a domain in its own subjective way. Each subject encapsulates a single, coherent piece of functionality (e.g., one or more features or components, often cutting across multiple classes). A subject may be a complete application in itself, or it may be an incomplete fragment that must be composed with other subjects to produce a complete application.

6. *Intention. Intention* is used in the context of *Intentional Programming* [22], in which all source code is represented as an abstract syntax tree (AST). Intentions are nodes of an AST that correspond to the semantic constructs of a language. Examples of intentions include if-statements, type declarations, assignment statements. The Intentional Programming system manipulates with the intentions at a higher level of abstraction. The semantics of intentions are described by the tree transformations, which convert the instances into primitive intentions from which native or interpreted code can be generated.

7. *Feature.* The notion of feature is widely used to denote the functional structure and visible properties of a software system. A *feature* is a higher level abstraction of a set of relevant detailed software requirements and is perceivable by users. Features may exist in multiple levels, including business level, user level, and application level. A feature at the business level describes the high-level desire of an organization or a customer for future system. Features at the user level describe services, which a system should provide for user tasks and constraints on the services. In *feature-oriented domain analysis* (FODA) [13], features are user-visible domain characteristics that define both common aspects of the domain as well as differences between related domain systems, and lead to the conceptualization of the set of products that define the domain. Another approach based on the concept of features is *Feature Engineering* [28]. Here, features are a grouping or modularization of particular requirements and their implementation within a specification.

8. *Variation Point and Variant. Variation point model* (VPM) [31] models software variability at the design level in the context of product line development, which provides a systematic approach for software reuse. Variability is modeled using the concepts of Variation Points and Variants. *Variation points* identify locations in a software system (unit, class, component) at which variation occurs. Variation points can exist at all abstraction layers of a software system or product family, such as features, architecture, and component implementations. Variation points in one abstraction layer can *realize* the variability in a higher abstraction level, e.g., an optional architectural component that realizes the choice between two features of a system. Each variation point is associated with zero or more variants. A *variant* is a specific instance of a feature or a set of features. Selection of variants in one or more variation points depends on the application domain (e.g., customer requirements), implementation details, or restrictions on quality attributes.

9. *Role and Collaboration.* Collaboration-based design (CBD) decomposes an OO application into a set of classes and a set of collaborations [29]. Each class encapsulates several *roles*, where each role embodies a separate aspect of the class behavior. The objective is to express an application as a composition of largely independently defined *collaborations*. Viewed in terms of design modularity, CBD acknowledges that a unit of functionality (module) is neither a whole object nor a part of it, but can crosscut several different objects. A cooperating suite of roles is collaboration, which expresses the distinct aspects of an application. Collaboration is a set of objects and a protocol (a set of allowed behaviors) that determines how these objects interact. The part of an object enforcing the protocol that collaboration prescribes is called the object's role in the collaboration. Objects of an application generally participate in multiple collaborations simultaneously and may encode several distinct roles. Essentially, a role isolates the part of an object that is relevant to collaboration from the rest of the object. Different objects can participate in collaboration, as long as they support the required roles. In abstract terms, collaboration is a view of an object-oriented design from the perspective of a single concern, service, or feature.

10. *View and ViewPoint*. ViewPoints are partial requirement specifications, which are described and developed using different representation schemes and development strategies [8]. A distinction can be made between views, perspectives, and viewpoints. A *view* is a representation of a set of system elements and the relationships among them. A view shows a particular perspective of the system (e.g., code units) and may show just part or the entire system. ViewPoints are loosely coupled, locally managed, distributable objects which encapsulate partial knowledge about a system and its domain, specified in a particular, suitable representation scheme, and partial knowledge of the process of development [8]. By explicitly deploying views that encapsulate partial specifications together with the development techniques by which they are produced, the problems of system integration may be addressed.

11. *Design space*. A *design space* is a multidimensional space representing requirements and design choices [15]. Its dimensions identify relevant criteria for characterizing artifacts in a specific domain – components, subsystems, or complete systems. A design space represents taxonomy for variable aspects of systems in a domain. A selection in the design space characterizes a concrete system along this taxonomy.

We summarize our survey of concepts in software design domain by presenting a vocabulary of DA concepts in Table 33.1. The vocabulary is further used to construct domain ontology and taxonomy of concepts in Sections 4 and 5.

Table 33.1. Vocabulary of domain analysis concepts.

Concept	Definition
Concern	Any particular piece of interest or focus in a program
Aspect	A partial representation of some concepts that relate to a concern
Object	An instance of a class
Class	A unit that encapsulates data and the operations applicable to the data
Subject	A collection of classes or class fragments which form a hierarchy
Intention	Nodes of an AST that correspond to the semantic constructs of a language
Feature	A higher level abstraction of a set of relevant detailed software requirements
Variant	A specific instance of a feature or a set of features
Variation Point	Locations in a software system or unit at which variation occurs
Role	A part of an object that is relevant to collaboration from the rest of the object
Collaboration	A set of objects and a protocol that determines how these objects interact
View	A representation of a set of system elements and relationships among them
ViewPoint	Loosely coupled objects which encapsulate partial knowledge about a system, its domain, and the process of its development
Design space	A multidimensional space representing requirements and design choices
Component	A system element offering a predefined service and able to communicate with other components
Dimension	A set of similar concerns within a design space

4. Domain Taxonomy and Ontology

Based on the analysis of various terms and concepts used to express DA concepts in software system design domain, we propose the following domain ontology. Figure 33.1 presents the ontology graphically using a subset of UML, which is more readable and understandable to human learners, whereas Figure 33.2 shows a fragment of a machine-readable ontology described in OWL.

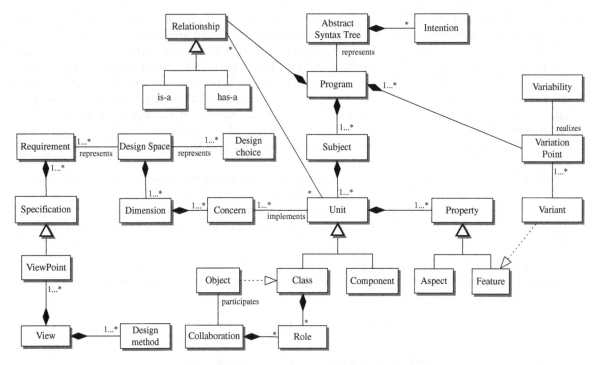

Figure 33.1. Ontology of software design domain concepts.

The design domain represents a universe of design requirements and available design choices. All design techniques, methods, programming languages, abstractions, and tools reside somewhere in the design domain. The designer is ultimately bounded by design problems and solutions residing in this domain. The design domain is multidimensional. A dimension represents a group of related concerns, which characterize certain domain artifacts, such as components, programming methods, languages, data representation. Dimensions are often overlapping. Separation of these dimensions during DA may lead to better comprehensibility of the domain and designed software systems.

Each concern is ultimately implemented in one or several software units such as classes or components (modules, functions, procedures, etc.). The classes are instantiated into objects. Whence the relationship between concerns and objects can be defined as follows: objects are the implementations of concerns (artifacts of DA) mapped into computer memory. Design requirements compose requirement specifications. ViewPoints are partial requirement specifications, of which different views are composed, together with design methods used. Views are similar to concerns, though some implementation details are shown.

Features are important for variability management in software families and product lines. Each feature is an instance of a variant. Variants are dependent on Variant Points, which control variability in specific parts of a software system (unit). Each software unit may have one or several aspects or features. The difference between aspects and features is as follows. An aspect is a property of the component that affects its performance or semantics in a systematic way. Whereas a feature is a distinctive external characteristic of a system that helps characterize it from the user perspective. Aspects are focused on the functionality and/or internal structure, whereas features are more external and user centered.

```
<owl:Class rdf:ID="Component">
  <rdfs:subClassOf rdf:resource="Unit">
</owl:Class>
```

Figure 33.2. A fragment of the software design domain knowledge ontology in OWL.

An object represents the result of OO analysis, when a design problem is decomposed and its functionality is captured in classes. Aspects/features represent an alternative decomposition, when design problem is decomposed not by structure or functionality (designer's view), but rather by external requirements (user's view). Aspects/features may encapsulate concepts that describe high-level desires of a client for a future system. These aspects/features when implemented may be scattered across multiple classes; however, they represent distinctive client's concerns. Whence feature engineering involves identification of commonalities and variability in a domain, rather than real world entities as defined in OOD. Though objects that represent real world entities may be a better representation for the designer, the client is not interested in the implementation details, but rather in different properties and characteristics of what he desires.

A collection of related software units forms a program, though subjects may be introduced as an intermediate layer. A subject may be a complete application in itself, or it may be an incomplete fragment that must be composed with other subjects to produce a complete application. As such, subjects may be seen as possibly incomplete software units described at a higher abstraction layer. The composition of subjects is a program. The relationships between software units may be described in terms of OOD (inheritance, aggregation/composition, association), though other kinds of relationships may be defined and used, too.

A program also may be represented in terms of abstract syntax tree (AST). Nodes of an AST are called intentions, which correspond to the semantic constructs of a language. Thus, intentions represent yet another kind of decomposition of a domain into designer-oriented problem solution artifacts.

Roles are lower level representations of incomplete parts of classes. Roles have some similarity with intentions, which are also lower level parts of programs (though represented not in terms of OOD, but as parts of AST). A composition of roles is collaboration, which represents a set of collaborating objects and describes a part of an OO program. Collaborations are similar to subjects, which are also parts of a programs composed of several related software units.

5. Taxonomy of Domain Analysis Concepts

A taxonomy of analyzed DA concepts is presented in Table 33.2. We classify these concepts according to three criteria: *actor* (*user's view, designer's view*), *design stage* (*domain analysis, implementation*), and *support for variability*.

The user's view represents the design domain concepts as seen by the user (client), who formulates the design requirements. Here we have two similar concepts: Concern and View, which represent the results of DA (Concern) and encapsulate some required design methods or design choices (View).

The designer's view represents design domain concepts as seen by the designer, who performs in-depth DA and implements the required domain systems. During DA, the designer identifies aspects and features of a designed domain systems, which represent the structure, functionality, and properties of

Table 33.2. Taxonomy of DA concepts.

| *Design stage* | *Actor* | | | *Support for variability* |
	User' view	*Designer's view*		
Domain analysis	**Concern**	**Aspect, feature**		
Implementation	**View**	*Higher level*	**Collaboration, Subject**	**Variant, Variation Point**
		Object level	**Class, Object**	
		Lower level	**Role, Intention**	

designed software units and a system as a whole. These aspects (features) are classified according to different categories into, e.g., dominant, overlapping, orthogonal, crosscutting, constant, and variable aspects/features. Based on this classification of domain concepts software units are planned and implemented.

The implementation stage includes development of design artifacts at different levels of abstraction. If we consider Object/Program as the primary unit of software, then at the lower level of abstraction we have Roles/Intentions that are certain incomplete parts of Object/Program representing a single Aspect/Feature.

At the higher level of abstraction, we have Collaboration/Subject, which encapsulates a collection of interacting related objects (programs). These Collaborations/Subjects may be complete applications or syntactically incomplete fragments that must be composed with other Collaborations/Subjects to produce a complete application. Thus Collaborations/Subjects allow customization and integration of domain systems from finer software units and support reuse.

The main difference between implementation-level concepts such as Classes, Subjects, or Intentions, and DA-level concepts such as Concerns, Aspects, and Features is as follows. The implementation-level concepts have predefined semantic properties such as identity, state, or behavior. The DA-level concepts do not have any predefined semantics and can be used to virtually denote anything.

Variability management is addressed at Variation Points, which represent certain locations in a software system or unit. Each Variation Point is associated with one or more variants, which realize specific features of a system. This variability control mechanism allows producing families of related software systems, which share a great deal of commonalty, yet differ by specific features.

6. Conclusions and Further Work

Metamodeling of domain concepts and developing of domain ontologies can lead to benefits in information systems (IS) design by allowing to develop more reusable and scalable quality software. The combination of taxonomies and ontologies of domain concepts allows supporting a flexible, concise, and efficient domain knowledge extraction and analysis, and provides means for analysis, representation, and reuse of the domain analysis results for IS development. Both taxonomy and ontology (metamodel) of domain concepts expressed graphically as well as using OWL serve the same purpose to provide a conceptualization of a domain in order to support domain knowledge extraction, sharing, and reuse.

In further work, the developed ontology is going to be used for in an e-learning system as a domain knowledge representation model. One more direction of future research is the evaluation of the developed ontology from technological and educational perspectives in terms of its structural consistency as a domain knowledge representation mechanism and its subjective understandability by students as a course material supplement.

References

1. Barton, R.R. (1994) Metamodeling: a state of the art review. *Proceedings of the 1994 Winter Simulation Conference* , Lake Buena Vista, FL, USA, 237–244.
2. Brinkkemper, S. (1996) Method engineering: engineering of information systems development methods and tools. *Information & Software Technology* 38(4), 275–280.
3. Caplinskas, A., Lupeikiene, A. and Vasilecas, O. (2003) The role of ontologies in reusing domain and enterprise engineering assets. *Informatica* 14(4), pp. 455–470.
4. Cranefield, S. and Purvis, M. (1999) UML as an ontology modelling language. *Proceedings of the IJCAI-99 Workshop on Intelligent Information Integration* , Vol. 23, July 31, 1999, Stockholm, Sweden.
5. Czarnecki, K., Eisenecker, U. and Steyaert, P. (1997) Beyond objects: generative programming. In *ECOOP'97 Aspect-Oriented Programming Workshop* , Jyväskylä, Finland.
6. Damaševičius, R. (2006) On the application of meta-design techniques in hardware design domain. *International Journal of Computer Science (IJCS)* 1(1), 67–77.
7. Damaševičius, R. and Štuikys, V. (2002) Separation of concerns in multi-language specifications. *Informatica* 13(3), 255–274.

8. Finkelstein, A., Kramer, J., Nuseibeh, B., Finkelstein, L. and Goedicke, M. (1992) Viewpoints: A framework for multiple perspectives in system development. *International Journal of Software Engineering and Knowledge Engineering* 2(1), 31–57.

9. Guizzardi, G. (2007) On ontology, ontologies, conceptualizations, modeling languages, and (meta) models. In Vasilecas, O., Edler, J. and Caplinskas, A., *Frontiers in Artificial Intelligence and Applications, Databases and Information Systems IV*, IOS Press.

10. Harrison, W. and Ossher, H. (1993) Subject-oriented programming – A critique of pure objects. *SIGPLAN Notices* 28(10), 411–428, ACM Press.

11. Herrera, S., Palliotto, D., Tkachuk, G. and Luna, P. (2005) Ontological modelling of information systems from Bunge's contributions. *Proceedings of CAISE'05*, Vol. 2, Philosophical Foundations on Information Systems Engineering, Porto, Portugal.

12. Hruby, P. (2005) Role of domain ontologies in software factories. *International Workshop on Software Factories at OOPSLA 2005*, San Diego, CA, USA.

13. Kang, K., Cohen, S., Hess, J., Novak, W. and Peterson, S. (1990) Feature-Oriented Domain Analysis (FODA) Feasibility Study. Technical Report CMU/SEI-90-TR-021, Software Engineering Institute, Carnegie-Mellon University.

14. Kiczales, G., Lamping, J., Mendhekar, A., Maeda, C., Videira Lopes, C., Loingtier, J.-M. and Irwin, J. (1997) Aspect-Oriented Programming. LNCS 1241, 220–242. Springer-Verlag.

15. Lane, T.G. (1990) Studying Software Architecture through Design Spaces and Rules. Technical Report CMU/SEI-90-TR-18, Carnegie Mellon University.

16. Mizoguchi, R., van Welkenhuysen, J. and Ikeda, M. (1995) Task ontology for reuse of problem-solving knowledge. *Proceedings of the 2nd Internaional Conference on Knowledge Building and Knowledge Sharing (KB & KS'95)*, Twente, The Netherlands, 46–57, IOS Press.

17. Neighbors, J.M. (1984) The draco approach to constructing software from reusable components. *IEEE Transactions of Software Engineering*, SE, 10(5), 564–574.

18. Ossher, H. and Tarr, P. (2000) Multi-dimensional separation of concerns and the hyperspace approach. In Aksit, M. (ed.), *Software Architectures and Component Technology: The State of the Art in Software Development*. Kluwer Academic Publisher, Dordrecht

19. Paslaru-Bontas, E. (2007) *A Contextual Approach to Ontology Reuse: Methodology, Methods and Tools for the Semantic Web*. PhD. Thesis, Freie University Berlin, Germany.

20. Prieto-Diaz, R. (1990) Domain analysis: An introduction. *Software Engineering Notes* 15(2), 47–54.

21. SEI (Software Engineering Institute) (2004) *Domain Engineering and Domain Analysis Roadmap*, http://www.sei.cmu.edu/str/descriptions/deda_body.html

22. Simonyi, C. (1995) The death of computer languages, the birth of intentional programming. *NATO Science Committee Conference*.

23. Sosnovsky, S. and Gavrilova, T. (2006) Development of educational ontology for C-programming. *Information Theories & Applications*, 3, 303–308.

24. Spyns, P., Meersman, R. and Jarrar, M. (2002) Data modelling versus ontology engineering. *SIGMOD Record*, 31(4), 12–17.

25. Štuikys, V., Damaševičius, R., Brauklytė, I. and Limanauskienė, V. (2008) Exploration of learning object ontologies using feature diagrams. *Proceedings of World Conference on Educational Multimedia, Hypermedia & Telecommunications (ED-MEDIA)*, June 30-July 4, 2008, Vienna, Austria, 2144–2154.

26. Su, X., Zhu, G., Liu, X. and Yuan, W. (2005) Presentation of programming domain knowledge with ontology. *Proceedings of the First International Conference on Semantics, Knowledge, and Grid (SKG 2005)*, 27–29 November 2005, Beijing, China, pp. 131.

27. Szyperski, C. (2002) *Component Software: Beyond Object-Oriented Programming*, 2nd ed., Addison-Wesley Professional, Boston.

28. Turner, C.R., Fuggetta, A., Lavazza, L. and Wolf, A.L. (1999) A conceptual basis for feature engineering. *Journal of Systems and Software*, 49(1), 3–15.

29. VanHilst, M. and Notkin, D. (1996) Using role components to implement collaboration-based designs. *Proceedings of OOPSLA'1996*, pp. 359–369. ACM Press.

30. Wartik, S. and Prieto-Diaz, R. (1992) Criteria for comparing reuse-oriented domain analysis approaches. *Journal of Software Engineering and Knowledge Engineering* 2(3), 403–431.

31. Webber, D.L. and Gomaa, H. (2004) Modeling variability in software product lines with the variation point model. *Science of Computer Programming*, 53(3), 305–331.

34

An Anonymity Revocation Technology for Anonymous Communication

Giannakis Antoniou, Lynn Batten and Udaya Parampalli

Abstract

A number of privacy-enhancing technologies (PETs) have been proposed in the last three decades offering unconditional communication anonymity to their users. Unconditional anonymity can, however, be a security threat because it allows users to employ a PET in order to act maliciously while hiding their identity. In the last few years, several technologies which revoke the identity of users who use PETs have been proposed. These are known as anonymity revocation technologies (ARTs). However, the construction of ARTs has been developed in an ad hoc manner without a theoretical basis outlining the goals and underlying principles. In this chapter we present a set of fundamental principles and requirements for construction of an ART, identifying the necessary features. We then propose an abstract scheme for construction of an ART based on these features.

Keywords Privacy · Communication anonymity · PET · Accountability

1. Introduction

There are many technologies which offer privacy services, for example anonymity [15], to their users; these are known as privacy-enhancing technologies (PETs). PETs may offer anonymity at the communication layer (i.e. the source IP Address) or at the data layer (i.e. the name and the home/work address of the user). For the purpose of this chapter, we refer only to those PETs which offer anonymity to the clients (in a client–server communication) at the communication level. Examples of these are Tor [12], anonymizer [6] and crowds [16].

In such a PET scheme a user who wants to act anonymously sends a message to a set of nodes, known as PET entities, which are then responsible for forwarding the message to a destination party such as a server (a responder). PET entities may be located in a country other than that in which the user or destination party reside, and so different legislation about the privacy rights of citizens may apply to these locations. For instance, as described in [17], new legislation in the EU forces the communication providers to store the data exchanged bytheir customers for a specific period of time before destroying it.However, this legislation does not apply to communication providers outside of EU.

A PET protects the right of users who wish to act anonymously, while an anonymity revocation technology (ART) reveals the identity of the users who are suspected of violating some rules and are hiding behind a PET. Therefore, full anonymity is a security threat [13] and the necessity to find a balance between privacy and accountability is great [7]. Although there are ARTs which are applied in an environment

Giannakis Antoniou • The University of Melbourne, Victoria, Australia   **Lynn Batten** • Deakin University, Victoria, Australia   **Udaya Parampalli** • The University of Melbourne, Victoria, Australia

G.A. Papadopoulos et al. (eds.), *Information Systems Development*, DOI 10.1007/b137171_34,
© Springer Science+Business Media, LLC 2009

without a PET, the scope of this chapter focuses on the ARTs which revoke the anonymity of the users who hides their identity by using a PET.

Several papers (e.g. [7, 11] and [9]) identify the problems associated with technologies offering anonymity and agree that there is a need for a system which offers a controllable level of privacy in order to prevent malicious users from abusing PET services. Differing legislative rights make it difficult to determine the most appropriate underlying principles on which such 'controllable' privacy should be based.

Several PETs are currently available over the Internet. Thousand of Internet users around the world can use these technologies for free and in some cases with a very low cost. Examples of available technologies are http://www.anonymizer.com, http://www.idzap.com, http://www.torproject.org and http://www.ano-nymprom.com. Although designing an appropriate ART requires a delicate approach, it is unclear whether any of these PETs have applied an ART in order to discourage users from acting maliciously. Moreover, the necessary theoretical background for ART designers to design such technologies is not available. In this chapter we analyse existing ARTs based on features, we identify as being fundamental to all requirements for such a technology, and we propose an abstract scheme which captures these features.

This chapter is organised as following. In Section 2 we describe the work and the directions in the field of ART, and in Section 3 we propose principles underlying ARTs. In Section 4 we present the conditions required by an ART in order to fulfil the principles introduced in Section 3. In Section 5 we identify a set of parameters which describe an ART, and we propose an abstract scheme for an ART based on the identified parameters. In Section 6 we compare existing ARTs with respect to the principles and requirements of a good ART. In Section 7 we discuss the abstract scheme with respect to the principles introduced in Section 3, and we conclude the chapter in Section 8.

2. Current Work in the Area of Anonymity Revocation Technologies

In [9] the authors mention the important role of trust for an ART, list six requirements of an ART and propose an ART scheme. However, applying that ART scheme over crowds [16] violates one of these requirements because it requires not only the initiator (as the requirement states) but all the PET entities to be aware of the ART. An important requirement, which we will also adopt in the next section, is the necessity to retain the accountability of the actions of the third trusted party who is responsible for revoking the anonymity of a user.

In [18] the authors prove that the majority of communication anonymity schemes can enhance techniques to offer selective traceability. However, in this case, more than one PET entity needs to be aware of the ART.

Existing ARTs can be divided into two categories. In the first category are the ARTs which begin to take action based on the characteristics (e.g. the content and the source/destination address) of the sent message of a user. Examples of ARTs from this category can be found in [14, 3, 1] and [8]. However, most ARTs are included in the second category which takes action based on external or undefined factors; examples of these can be found in [8, 9] and [11]. In [7] the authors study the balance between privacy and accountability and propose that the goal of such a balance is that we should not reveal the identity of honest users but should reveal the identity of dishonest users.

Existing ARTs have been developed without following a concrete set of principles or requirements, as discussed in Section 6. Our aim in the next section is to fill this gap by proposing a set of general principles which should be expected of a good ART.

3. Principles of an Anonymity Revocation Technology

In this section we propose three basic principles expected of a good ART. The two goals proposed in [7] (and described in the previous section) are extended here and chosen as basic principles of a good ART because they both contain clear and reasonable expectations of the participated entities from an ART.

Principle 1

1a. *The identity of a malicious entity must be revealed*and

1b. *Enough information/evidence must be provided to prove its involvement.*

Principle 2   *The identity of an innocent user must be protected.*

In addition to the above, we propose the following as a third principle.

Principle 3   *The desired characteristics of a PET must not be violated by the ART.*

The first principle protects the responders (e.g. servers) from users who want to act maliciously. It has twofold goals. The first goal is to discourage potential malicious users from taking advantage of a PET and acting maliciously against servers. The second goal is to assure servers that those guilty will face the legal consequences. If 1a is not in place, the servers will deny communications coming from PETs; as a result, the communication anonymity of honest users will not be possible. By having in place a PET and an ART which supports the principles 1a and 1b, the servers will be able to communicate securely with users who use PETs, but will be less inclined to communicate with users who do not use PETs.

The second principle protects an honest user from a rogue ART. Although a PET protects the identity of the user from the corresponding server and from all other entities, it should not protect the identity from the administrator of an ART. An ART which does not respect the second principle is unlikely to be accepted by users [5] (an example isthe Clipper chip [10]).

The third principle protects the integrity and the desired [4] characteristics of a PET from an ART. This principle is based on the assumption that a PET cares only about the identity of users who are not malicious. Protecting the identity of users who are malicious lies outside of a PETs' goal. This principle is necessary to ensure that an ART operates as an extension technology of a PET, supporting its goals and not as a contradictory technology. In a client–server communication, both parties should use the system without being discouraged by the system's features.

In the next section we propose six requirements of an ART in order to achieve the three general principles.

4. Requirements of an Anonymity Revocation Technology

In this section we propose six requirements of an ART which guarantee the three major principles. All of these requirements are needed to guarantee all three general principles (as shown in Table 34.1). Thus, in a formal sense, the requirements are complete. For the purposes of this chapter, the administrator of an ART is called investigator. Our requirements of an ART are as follows:

(R1)   *An investigator is responsible, and thus liable, for the decision to begin the anonymity revocation procedure.*

Although the role of an investigator is played by a trusted third party, the less we need to trust somebody, the better. For this reason the investigator must be responsible and liable for its action or lack of action. In

Table 34.1.   The table illustrates which requirements serve specific general principles.

Requirements Principles	R1	R2	R3	R4	R5	R6
Principle 1	•	•	X	X	X	•
Principle 2	•	•	•	X	•	•
Principle 3	•	•	•	•	•	•

case the investigator is not liable, then an investigator could deny revealing the identity of a malicious user (therefore, it protects a malicious user and violates the first general principle) or the investigator could reveal the identity of an honest user which means that it violates the second and the third general principles.

An ART which has the investigator liable for its actions does not prevent but at least discourages the investigator from acting dishonestly.

(R2)   *An investigator decides to reveal the identity of a user based on an agreement which a user has agreed to respect.*

The investigator should not subjectively decide whether to reveal the identity of the user or not based on the criteria of the investigator. A user is considered malicious only in case he/she violates any of the agreements/ rules/ legislations and the user knew about these rules. The user has the right to know what is acceptable and what is unacceptable. This is especially important for cases where the client, the investigator and the server are located in different countries, which follows different legislation rules. Although an action in the country of the client may be considered legal, the same action in the country of the server may be considered as illegal. What is going to happen if the client and server are located in a country where an action of the client is considered legal but that action is considered illegal in the country of the investigator? In order to avoid such surprising results, the client, the server and the investigator should be aware/ acknowledge the same rules (even though the client may not follow them) and the investigator should decide whether the user acted maliciously or not based on these rules. An ART should prevent a user to repudiate that he/she agreed to follow these rules.

(R3)   *An investigator decides to reveal the identity of a user only in case the user violates the agreement.*

In case a user does not violate any agreement, the user is not considered as malicious, and therefore, his/her identity should not be revealed. The ART should employ techniques to offer non-repudiation of the actions of the users. Otherwise, a user may repudiate that he acted like this. Also, if there is no technique offering non-repudiation, a malicious user may be masqueraded, act maliciously by violating some rules and blame innocent users. In case the user did not violate any agreement, the investigator should not be able to reveal the identity of the user.

(R4)   *Before an investigator decides that the identity of a user must be revealed, the level of anonymity of that user should not be reduced.*

An ART need not reveal the identity of the users to multiple entities before determining that these users are honest. This requirement is necessary to prevent an ART violating the functionalities of a PET.

(R5)   *The anonymity revocation of a user should not affect the anonymity of others.*

Without this requirement, the third general principle is violated.

For example, an ART which reveals the identity of one or more clients in order to prove that one client acted maliciously is unacceptable to the users and also violates the second and third general principles.

(R6)   *Only the investigator should be able to detect the identity of the malicious user.*

Otherwise, the reliability of the ART as well as the reliability of the PET is in danger.

All of the above requirements are useless if an entity other than the investigator could reveal the identity of a user.

From a practical perspective, several factors may prevent an ART from achieving its objective and from being applicable in an environment where the client and the server (in client–server architecture) are located in a different country and the PET entities are distributed globally. One implication of this is that an ART should be PET independent, which means that the functionalities, the level of anonymity revocation and the operation of an ART should not be affected by the applied PET.

Another implication is that if an anonymity revocation procedure requires the use of exchanged messages of a user, the ART should store only the required limited volume of information (exchanged messages), for a limited duration. For instance, the legislation in the EU in which a communication provider is required to preserve exchanged messages of its clients for 6 months is impossible from a practical perspective.

In this section we identified a basic set of requirements for achieving the general principles proposed in Section 3. In the next section we will focus on the parameters which characterise any ART and which also affect the fulfilling of some of the identified requirements.

5. Analysis of an Anonymity Revocation Technology

In this section we identify and describe the characteristics based on which we will develop an abstract scheme. Although the characteristics are not exclusive, they give a clear idea about the potentials and weaknesses of an ART. We will not deploy a detailed description of the actual ARTs, but rather focus in an abstract way on their characteristics. Prior to identifying these characteristics, we describe the environment as well as the necessary parameters, which should be involved in an ART.

Alice communicates anonymously with Bob through a PET. Only an attestor A knows Alice and can link her exchanged messages with Alice. An adversary X wants to know the identity of Alice for Re reasons based on information which is held for duration D by entity L. Investigator Inv has a level LoR of responsibility to perform an anonymity revocation investigation based on the request of X. However, X needs to provide proof Pr to Inv that X has the R right to know the identity of Alice. Alice and X have a level LoT of trust in Inv. However, Inv can create problems C for Alice in case Inv is compromised. Inv uses evidence Evi in order to identify Alice. Inv can prove that Alice was the entity who was communicating with Bob by providing strength S of evidence to O entities.

P is the PET to which an ART can be applied. An ideal ART should be applicable to as many PETs as possible. It is important to allow a PET to coexist with an ART.

X is the entity which makes the request to begin the anonymity revocation. For example, the entity X could be a receiver of the message, such as a server, or an intermediate entity such as a PET node. It could also be a government who wants to know with whom a specific client communicated.

Inv is the entity who investigates the requests of the X. More than one entity could play this role. It is a usual practice by some existing ARTs to distribute the responsibilities to multiple entities.

A is any entity that can link an exchanged message with the identity of Alice before the investigation completion.

Re is the reason that X wants to know the identity of Alice. Alice may have sent malicious messages to X or X may suspect that Alice has violated some rules.

R is the right of X to know the identity of Alice. X has the right to know the identity of Alice if X and Alice had an agreement and Alice violated the agreement or if the legislation allows X to identify Alice under some conditions which have been met.

L is the entity at which the necessary information for identified Alice is located.

D is the maximum duration that the entities need to store information to assist the anonymity revocation. In case the duration is too long and too much data are required to be stored, practical problems arise. The smaller the duration is, the more practical the mechanism can be.

LoR is the level of responsibility for the investigator to investigate and identify Alice. An investigator with a low level of responsibility may avoid performing the investigation.

LoT is the level of trust which Alice and X have for the investigator. In case the level of trust is low, Alice or X may avoid using the system. The trust allows Alice and X to believe that the investigator will act honestly based on their agreement.

Pr is a proof that Alice's anonymity must be revealed.

C is the consequence of the dishonest act of the investigator against Alice.

Evi is the strength of information which the investigator relies on in order to identify Alice.

S is the strength of the evidence that the investigator is using to prove, that is, Alice who communicated with Bob.

Table 34.2. The table shows which parameters (except the parameters which represent entities) are useful for achieving the requirements.

Requirements	R1	R2	R3	R4	R5	R6	Practical
Parameters	LoR	R	Re	LoT	LoT	C	P
	LoT	S	Pr	Pr		S	L
	S		Evi	Evi		O	D
			S				

O are the entities who can be convinced by the results of the investigator. It is desired that Alice should not be able to deny her actions. A sub-union of O has an authority on Alice.

The values of some of the parameters affect some of the requirements. These are shown in Table 34.2. We visualise in Fig. 34.1 the interaction of those parameters in an abstract scheme.

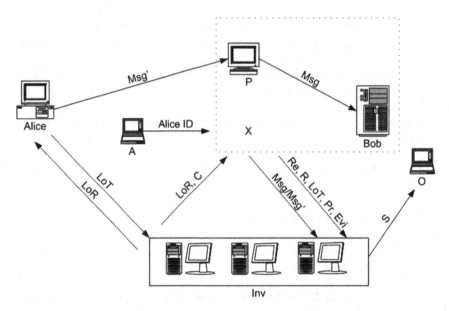

Figure 34.1. An abstract scheme based on parameters of an anonymity revocation technology.

6. Analysis of the Existing ARTs Based on the Requirements

In this section we analyse three ARTs based on the six requirements (Table 34.3) introduced in Section 4. We also describe (Table 34.4) the principles these ARTs follow in regard to the general principles introduced in Section 3. The three selectedpapers found in the literature introducing ARTs are those of Antoniou G. et al. [3] (AntG), Claessens J. et al. [9] (GlaJ) and Kopsell S. et al. [14] (KopS).

In AntG the investigator follows a set of rules in order to decide whether the client acted maliciously or not. These rules have been electronically signed by the client, which confirms the client's agreement to respect these rules. Moreover, exchanged client messages are linked with these rules. The client cannot argue that he/she did not know what is legal and what is not. Further, the exchanged client messages are electronically signed, so the client cannot deny sending the messages. However, a malicious co-operation between

Table 34.3. The table illustrates which requirements are fulfilled for each ART.

ARTs Requirements	AntG	GlaJ	KopS
R1	•	X	X
R2	•	X	X
R3	Partly	Partly	Partly
R4	•	•	•
R5	•	•	•
R6	•	•	•

Table 34.4. The table illustrates which principles are fulfilled for each ART. AntG partly achieves the principles 2 and 3, because it does not completely fulfil the third requirement (R3).

ARTs Principles		AntG	GlaJ	KopS
Principle 1	a)	•	•	•
	b)	•	X	X
Principle 2		Partly	X	X
Principle 3		Partly	X	X

the investigator and the related server can reveal the identity of a client. Moreover, the investigator cannot prove to anyone that an innocent user acted maliciously. After a request from the server, the investigator has no other choice but to check whether the client violated the rules or not. In case the investigator tries to deny revealing the identity of the client, the server has enough information to accuse the investigator.

In GlaJ it is up to the investigator to begin the revocation procedure. The investigator follows its own subjective rules, which the client may not even know their existence. A dishonest investigator can easily reveal the identity of an innocent user.

In KopS, as with GlaJ, the investigator decides whether a message is suspicious (this paper reveals the identity of the users who are just suspicious, not malicious) or not based on the investigator's subjective rules. Therefore, the investigator can reveal the identity of an innocent user.

All three ARTs partly fulfilled (Table 34.3) the third requirement (R3) since no ART can fully prevent a malicious investigator revealing the identity of an innocent user. However, in each ART they employ a mechanism to prevent it from happening.

In AntG, the investigator, who has been selected by the client, needs the malicious co-operation of the related server and it is that server who must first contact the investigator since the investigator is not aware of the server. A similar ART with the AntG is RPINA [1] with an enhanced mechanism [2] to hide the identity of the investigator from the server. That mechanism can also be enhanced in AntG.

In GlaJ, a trustee entity participates in the anonymity revocation procedure; therefore, the client relies on the honesty of that entity.

In KopS, there are two entities (part of the investigation team) who evaluate whether the client is a suspect or not (based on their own criteria), in order to prevent the anonymity revocation of a non-suspect client. However, the client may not trust any of these investigators.

7. Discussion

Anonymity revocation technologies may have difficulty operating in the presence of PETs. The problem is exacerbated when several PET nodes are involved and located in various countries applying differing privacy legislation. For example, PETs such as Crowds and Tor have PET nodes around the world. Therefore, we argue that it is appropriate to apply an ART where the PET nodes are not involved in the anonymity revocation procedure.

It is possible for a user who wants to communicate anonymously to allow intermediate entities to have access to the content of the exchanged message. However, any ART should acknowledge that the messages exchanged between a user and the related responder are confidential and that a PET supports full confidentiality of the forwarded messages.

As previously stated, this work focuses on some key requirements of an ART and analyses them in a standard setting. Examples of some characteristics which were not taken into consideration are the duration of an investigation, the economical aspect and the cost (in respect to the bandwidth and computation) which is required for an ART to function. While these factors may be important when designing an ART, they are not significant to the objectives.

8. Conclusion and Future Work

Anonymity revocation technologies which can collaborate with and complement privacy enhancing technologies are increasingly necessary in an online environment used both for business and social activities. The significant contribution of this chapter is the establishment of a theoretical basis on which to combine both technologies in an appropriate way. We propose three basic principles expected of an ART and its interaction with a PET. We show that these principles can be achieved by the implementation of ARTs with six requirements (Section 4), thus demonstrating that good ARTs are achievable. In Section 6, we consider and compare three recent ARTs from the point of view of the six requirements which form part of our specification.

Our work can help both ART and PET designers to gain a better understanding of the major issues and conflicts between the parties involved. It can also be used to evaluate existing ARTs and PETs in various environments and based on the needs.

In future work, we will design and build an ART adhering to the abstract scheme presented here, which fulfils the proposed requirements and respects the general principles. We also plan to perform an extended analysis of existing and new ARTs based on the characteristics described in Section 5.

References

1. Antoniou, G., Gritzalis, S.: RPINA- Network Forensics Protocol Embedding Privacy Enhancing Technologies. In: Taguchi, A. (ed.): International Symposium on Communications and Information Technologies. IEEE Press, Bangkok, Thailand (2006)
2. Antoniou, G., Jancic, A., Parampalli, U., Sterling, L.: Applying a cryptographic scheme in the RPINA protocol. Digital Forensics and Incident Analysis, 2007. WDFIA 2007. Second International Workshop on (2007) 65–74
3. Antoniou, G., Sterling, L., Gritzalis, S., Udaya, P.: Privacy and Forensics Investigation Process: The ERPINA Protocol. Computer Standard Interfaces 30(2008)229–236
4. Argyrakis, J., Gritzalis, S., Kioulafas, C.: Privacy Enhancing Technologies: A Review. Electronic Government (2003) 282–287
5. Bellin, D.: Who Holds the Keys? The US Government & Cryptography Policy. Computer and Society 24(1994) 6–7
6. Boyan, J.: The Anonymizer: Protecting User Privacy on the Web. Computer-Mediated Communication Magazine 4(1997)
7. Burmester, M., Desmedt, Y., Wright, R.N., Yasinsac, A.: Accountable Privacy. Lecture Notes in Computer Science 3957(2006)83–95
8. Chida, K., Shionoiri, O., Kanai, A.: Secure Anonymous Communications with Practical Anonymity Revocation Scheme. Advances in Information and Computer Security 4752(2007) 352–364
9. Claessens, J., Diaz, C., Goemans, C., Preneel, B., Vandewalle, J., Dumortier, J.: Revocable Anonymous Access to the Internet? Internet Research: Electronic Networking Applications and Policy 13(2003) 242–258
10. Denning, D.E., Smid, M.: Key Escrowing Today. Communications Magazine, IEEE 32(1994) 58–68
11. Diaz, C., Preneel, B.: Accountable Anonymous Communication. Security, Privacy and Trust in Modern Data Management. Springer-Verlag (2006) 15
12. Dingledine, R., Mathewson, N., Syverson, P.: Tor: The second-generation onion router. Proceedings of the 13th Conference on USENIX Security Symposium-Volume 13 Table of Contents (2004) 21–21
13. Farkas, C., Ziegler, G., Meretei, A., Lörincz, A.: Anonymity and accountability in self-organizing electronic communities. Proceedings of the 2002 ACM Workshop on Privacy in the Electronic Society (2002) 81–90

14. Kopsell, S., Wendolsky, R., Federrath, H.: Revocable Anonymity. Proceedings of Emerging Trends in Information and Communication Security: International Conference, ETRICS (2006) 6–9

15. Pfitzmann, A., Hansen, M.: Anonymity, unlinkability, unobservability, pseudonymity and identity management— a consolidated proposal for terminology: 2008: http://dud.inf.tu-dresden.de/literatur/Anon_Terminology_v0.31.pdf: Last Access–8th of May 2008

16. Reiter, M.K., Rubin, A.D.: Crowds: Anonymity for Web Transactions. ACM Transactions on Information and System Security 1(1998)66–92

17. Ticar, K.: A Closer Look at Data Retention. International Journal of Technology Transfer and Commercialisation 6(2007) 87–99

18. von Ahn, L., Bortz, A., Hopper, N.J., O'Neill, K.: Selectively Traceable Anonymity. Designing Privacy Enhancing Technologies, LNCS (pre-proceedings) (2006) 199–213

35

The Fight Against Piracy in Peer-to-Peer Networks: the Sword of Damocles Hanging over ISP's Head?

Evi Werkers and Fanny Coudert

Abstract

During the past few years, copyright holders and holders of related rights have started to legally challenge peer-to-peer networks. Their latest strategy consists of trying to actively involve Internet service providers (ISPs) in this combat, e.g. through the implementation of filters. This development raises legal problems and questions both in terms of the liability of ISPs and the protection of privacy of their clients. This chapter discusses the difficult task of balancing copyright interests and fundamental rights which as the European Court of Justice clearly stated in the *Promusicae* case remains a matter of Member States.

Keywords Copyright enforcement · Liability ISP · Secrecy of communication

1. Introduction

In the 21st century holders of intellectual property rights are confronted with the growing phenomenon of piracy and counterfeiting and have successfully pleaded for more regulatory restrictions/prohibitions and an expansion of copyright protection. As a consequence there has been an extension of the term of protection (70/50 years), an expansion of scope *in materiae* and an expansion of exploitation rights (reproduction, communication of works to the public, distribution). The most eye catching victory, however, has been the implementation of legal protection for digital rights management techniques, the circumvention of which is punishable with high legal penalties. On the other hand, the legislator took into account the interest of users in the information society and expanded the list of exceptions which they can invoke for educational, scientific, private purposes, etc.

The past years copyright holders and holders of neighbouring rights have begun legal actions against developers of peer-to-peer network software such as Napster, Grokster, Kazaa, Bittorent, which led to divergent case law. As a result rightholders have started prosecuting users of these peer-to-peer networks whom they claim have committed copyright infringements. But because of the difficulties in efficiently prosecuting users and the minor impact on the volume of illegal downloads, copyright societies are now trying to convince ISPs to install preventive measures such as the use of filters and to implement specific a posteriori measures such as cutting off Internet access or putting users on black lists.

This chapter will discuss the legal problems and questions both in terms of the liability of ISPs and the protection of privacy of their clients. Before the emergence of the information society the conflict between the enforcement of copyright and the protection of privacy was never so explicit. A black market of illegal copies of works has always existed, but the number of illegal copies and piracy remained relatively small.

Evi Werkers and Fanny Coudert • Interdisciplinary Centre for Law and ICT, K.U.Leuven, Leuven Belgium

G.A. Papadopoulos et al. (eds.), *Information Systems Development*, DOI 10.1007/b137171_35,
© Springer Science+Business Media, LLC 2009

However, thanks to digitization, large numbers of high-quality copies can now be made in a very short time. Also, whereas the exchange of copies between friends of homemade video or cassette recordings from television/radio limited the catalogue of works users could copy, peer-to-peer networks now offer an almost unlimited worldwide catalogue. On the other hand, the technological developments enable us to unmask users making copies.

2. The Role of ISPs as Neutral Intermediaries Endangered?

In a digital context the common rules with regard to liability remain applicable. A person committing a copyright infringement is liable for that act. In other words, the person using peer-to-peer software in an illicit manner by making works available to the public and sharing them with other users can be held liable when such act constitutes a copyright infringement. Copyright societies usually bring legal actions against makers of peer-to-peer software, but given the limited victories, they recently set their minds to suing peer-to-peer users – whom they claim to be infringing copyright whenever making use of this sort of software – to set an example to others. That is when ISPs come into play. Since users are often difficult to identify and/or locate, copyright societies have begun to direct themselves to the technical intermediaries providing the network infrastructure, the access to the infrastructure or the provider hosting their activity.

The E-Commerce Directive of the Internal Market (hereafter referred to as E-Commerce Directive) introduced a conditional exoneration regime (both penal and civil) of liability for certain activities undertaken by ISPs, namely mere conduit, caching and hosting activities [1]. The Directive also determines that Member States cannot impose a general obligation to monitor on ISPs. The reasoning behind this rule was mere practical reasons (ISPs cannot possibly monitor all the content passing on their network) but also out of concern for the freedom of free communication and expression on the Internet. After all, if ISPs were obliged to monitor the content passing or stored on their networks and services to seek for facts or circumstanced indicating illegal activity, this would cause a serious "chilling effect" on Internet communications. It is exactly to avoid this sort of (private) censorship that the European legislator decided to free ISPs of the great pressure of having to monitor, not even in order to enforce copyright protection [2]. On the other hand, the E-Commerce Directive prescribes that Member States may establish obligations for information society service providers to promptly inform the competent public authorities of alleged illegal activities undertaken or information provided by recipients of their service or obligations to communicate to the competent authorities, at their request, information enabling the identification of recipients of their service with whom they have storage agreements. Furthermore, the E-Commerce Directive stipulates that the exoneration for the activities enumerated above shall not affect the possibility for a court or administrative authority, in accordance with Member States' legal systems, to require from the service provider to terminate or prevent an infringement [3]. Finally, the Copyright Directive and the Enforcement Directive stipulate that they do not harm the exoneration provisions of the E-Commerce Directive [4]. It goes without saying that the strained relation between, on the one hand, human rights – namely the right to freedom of expression and the right to privacy – and, on the other hand, the enforcement of copyright causes many divergent legal interpretations and case law among the European Member States. As we will see the "milestone" judgement of the European Court of Justice (hereafter referred to as "ECJ") on this complicated matter in the case *Telefónica v. Promusicae* [5] brought little clarification.

2.1. Developments in European Member States

In France an interprofessional agreement was closed uniting the sector of music, film and ISPs in the battle against piracy and counterfeiting. The agreement installs a gradual approach: the ISP shall (by order of a public authority) send a warning to the client to end his (illicit) activities. In case of recidivism the client risks having his Internet connection suspended or even shut down entirely by the ISP and his name being added to a "black list" database (the latter requiring approval from the CNIL [6]). The "three-strikes-approach", approved by the French Parliament received a significant blow since the Constitutional

Council ruled that cutting of internet access by an administrative authority is not compatible with the French Constitution. Great Britain, Sweden and Ireland seem to be moving in the same direction [7].

The facts of the Belgian case *Sabam v. Scarlet* were quite similar to the *Promusicae v. Telefónica* case, though in this case the copyright society demanded that the usage of filtering or blocking systems be imposed on the ISP Scarlet to put an end to the copyright infringements committed by using peer-to-peer technologies. The President of the Court of First Instance concluded that – given the evidenced infringements and even though the ISP itself could not be held liable – their claim was legitimate and (following the advice of the appointed legal expert) that the ISP filtering system *Audible Magic* had to be installed by Scarlet [8]. But whether or not a copyright exception (e.g. reproductions for educational or scientific goals) is applicable or not is a matter which cannot solely be left into the hands of filtering technologies [9]. Furthermore, ISPs cannot be put on the same level as users committing copyright infringements [10].

2.2. Developments on European Level

A provision was added to the proposal with regard to reviewing the Universal Service Directive which urges providers of electronic communication services and/or networks to inform their clients clearly and at regular intervals regarding their duty to take into account copyright and neighbouring rights as well as the most common infringements and the legal consequences thereof [11]. The value of attractive content has been qualified as the condition sine qua non to ensure both the success of new technologies as well as the preservation of European cultural diversity. A recent study concluded that the income from online content will grow by 400% within the following 5 years. It goes without saying that a coherent legal framework is necessary to support this evolution which is exactly what the European Commission want to provide [14] given that it sees itself as a catalyst to promote win–win situations for all parties concerned with content production and distribution [12]. This has resulted in a communication with regard to creative content online [13]. One of the three goals determined by the communication is to ensure that European content achieves its full potential in contributing to European competitiveness and in fostering the availability and circulation of the great diversity of European content creation and of Europe's cultural and linguistic heritage. Finally, the following four horizontal challenges were analysed:

- *The need to improve the availability of creative content.*
- *How to encourage multi-territorial licenses for creative content.*
- *Ensuring interoperability and transparency of DRM and*
- *The management of online rights and protection against piracy.*

3. The Danger of Private Censorship

If an obligation is to be imposed on ISPs to actively seek for copyright infringements or to use filtering techniques it not only questions their exoneration of liability but also endangers the free circulation of services and the freedom of expression and information. After all, there is still no certainty with regard to the efficiency of filtering techniques. As a consequence legal content and legal uses of copyright protected works can be blocked as well. The judge in the *Sabam v. Scarlet* case specifically recognized this problem but concluded *that such minimal problems do not obstruct the combat against infringements of copyright.* And as the E-Commerce Directive states clearly in recital 9: *this Directive is not intended to affect national fundamental rules and principles relating to freedom of expression.* ISPs have an important role to fulfil in the democratic society now that the Internet has grown into the most important information and communication tool. Everyone, whether professional actor or amateur, can communicate and share content in any form whatsoever with others on a worldwide scale [14].

This led to a proliferation of user-generated content while at the same time enhancing cultural diversity and media pluralism. To a certain extent one might say ISPs have become the new gatekeepers. On the other hand, the emergence of the Internet has also facilitated the reproduction, communication and distribution of content resulting in plagiarism and piracy on a larger scale than the media business was confronted with so far. Many users are not aware of the exact scope of copyright protection/restrictions nor of the penalties attached. Furthermore, as the usage of peer-to-peer technology is not necessarily illegal, they are often used as a legitimate distribution tool [15].

Finally, several institutions expressed dissenting opinions. On 22 January 2008 the initiative report from Guy Bono with regard to the potential of the cultural industry in the context of the Lisbon strategy was adopted by the Commission Culture and Education in the European Parliament. An amendment was submitted to oblige ISPs to implement measures similar to the ones in the Olivennes Agreement [16]. However, in a recent resolution [17], the European Parliament unmistakably rejects the recent developments which we sketched above. The amendment which was finally adopted calls on to Member States to *avoid adopting measures conflicting with civil liberties and human rights and with the principles of proportionality, effectiveness and dissuasiveness, such as the interruption of internet access.* The Council of Europe adopted a Recommendation on 26 March 2008 [18] with a number of guidelines in order to fully protect the exercise of the right to freedom of expression and information of Internet users. When confronted with filters, users must be informed that a filter is active and, where appropriate, be able to identify and control the level of filtering (or even deactivate them). Different tools as such were put forward, among others (a) the need to regularly review and update filters in order to improve their effectiveness, proportionality and legitimacy in relation to the intended purpose, (b) the promotion of raising awareness of the social and ethical responsibilities of the actors designing, using and monitoring filters and last but not least (c) to provide clear and concise information and guidance regarding the manual overriding of an activated filter namely whom to contact when it appears that content has been unreasonably blocked and for what reasons a filter may be overridden for a specific type of content [19].

4. The Protection of the Secrecy of Communications

In the fight against illegal use of peer-to-peer networks, copyrights societies are facing a significant obstacle in the protection of users' right to the secret of correspondence. The measures advocated such as the use of filters all imply the processing of IP addresses which is currently not authorized by the law for these purposes.

User's traffic data, namely, the data processed for the purpose of the conveyance of a communication or for the billing thereof, such as IP addresses, can not be processed when they are no longer needed for those purposes. The interception of communications, understood as "a third party acquiring knowledge of the content and/or data relating to private telecommunications between two or more correspondents, and in particular of traffic data concerning the use of telecommunication services" [20], constitutes a violation of individuals' right to privacy and of the confidentiality of correspondence, as protected by Article 8 of the European Convention on Human Rights (hereafter referred to as "ECHR").

Directive 2002/56/EC [21], the so-called "E-privacy Directive", gives concrete expression to the provisions of the right to the secrecy of correspondence in the field of electronic communications. This Directive does not however affect the ability of Member States to carry out lawful interception of electronic communications, or to take other measures, on the basis of the motives listed in Article 15(1) and in accordance with the Article 8§2 ECHR as interpreted by the ruling of the European Court of Human Rights. It follows that interceptions are unacceptable unless they fulfil three fundamental criteria: the existence of a legitimate legal basis, of a pressing social need and the implementation of measures proportionate to the objective pursued.

These limitations may have a direct impact on the nature of measures adopted to control the exchange of protected works such as filters or of specific sanctions, in particular the disconnection of users from a network.

4.1. Looking for an Appropriate Legal Ground: An Analysis of Article 15(1) of the E-Privacy Directive

The first question resides in defining whether one of the motives listed in Article 15(1) of the E-privacy Directive could ground the monitoring of communication networks for the prevention and detection of infringement of intellectual property rights. The article allows Member States to restrict provisions related to the confidentiality of communications and related traffic data whenever they constitute a necessary, appropriate and proportionate measure within a democratic society for the safeguarding of national security (i.e. state security), defence, public security, and the prevention, investigation, detection and prosecution of criminal offences or of unauthorized use of the electronic communication system, as referred to in Article 13(1) of Directive 95/46/EC, the so-called "Data Protection Directive".

Due to the difficulty to ground such measure on one of the motives of Article 15(1), the ambiguous reference to Article 13 of the Data Protection Directive has been at the core of the ECJ *Promusicae* case [5]. In fact, a broad interpretation that refers to all the motives contained in the latter article would allow Member States to base derogations to the processing of IP addresses on the protection of the rights and freedoms of others and thus on the protection of copyright holders.

General Advocate J. Kokott made a restrictive interpretation considering that only the motives of derogation expressly mentioned by Article 15(1) could be used. To that effect, she takes into account the character of *lex especialis* of the E-Privacy Directive, introducing a specific regulation for the processing of data in the field of electronic communication, with regard to the Data Protection Directive which is meant to apply to all kinds of processing of personal data [22]. She concludes that the legal basis more likely to ground the derogation in this context is public security which narrows considerably the scope of measures that could be adopted.

However, the ECJ does not follow the same reasoning but considers that the reference made to Article 13 of the Data Protection Directive should be understood broadly and that "those provisions of Article 15(1) of Directive 2002/58 must be interpreted as expressing the community legislature's intention not to exclude from their scope the protection of the right to property or situations in which authors seek to obtain that protection in civil proceedings"[5].

This interpretation considerably enlarges the scope of derogations to the confidentiality of communications, and by the same token lowers the level of protection granted to this right to the benefit of other competing legitimate interests. At the same time, the court fails to provide an alternative justification to the reasoning of the General Advocate. However, even if the judgement opens the possibility to ground the processing of IP addresses for measures fighting illegal file sharing on the motives listed in Article 13 of the Data Protection Directive, such measure should be justified on the existence of a pressing social need and be in reasonable proportion to the legitimate aim pursued [22].

4.2. The Existence of a Pressing Social Need

Article 15(1) only allows derogations when the restriction constitutes a necessary measure within a democratic society. The central issue here is whether the damages caused to the cultural industry by the illicit exchange of protected work in peer-to-peer networks constitutes a sufficient threat to copyright holders' interests so as to justify restrictions to the right of secrecy of correspondence.

The question is: Can restrictions such as the ones mentioned above – in the form of filtering content, shutting down private Web-sites collected on black lists or Internet access of private clients – be justified in the name of copyright? Copyright can be qualified as "the rights of others" and thus as an interest of society (legitimate aim) in the context of which the freedom of communication and expression can be restricted. Although it is clear that illegal file-sharing affects copyright, it would be wrong to generalize these problems to all sorts of private file sharing especially when there is no profit or commercial goal involved. In fact, it is quite controversial whether private file sharing threatens the protection of copyright to a sufficient extent to justify the recourse to a restriction on the freedom of expression. To what extent private file sharing causes genuine damage is disputed [22]. Therefore, it would be wrong to place file sharers on the same footing as organized pirates [17].

The different evaluations made by Member States on the impact of such practices will directly influence the response adopted by these states to fight these illegal practices. This has led to the criminalization of serious offences, e.g. in Spain where penal sanctions have been created for the illicit exchange of protected works with an intention to make profit [22], or the adaptation of legislation so as to ease the prosecution in civil and criminal procedures, e.g. in France where the Data Protection Act has been modified to permit copyright societies to collect IP addresses on peer-to-peer networks prior to a judicial process [23]. Other proposed alternatives, based on preventive measures, as currently envisaged in several countries, should, however, first be evaluated in the light of the principle of proportionality.

4.3. The Principle of Proportionality

In the *Promusicae* case [5], the ECJ noted that community law requires that Member States, when transposing the directives, must strike a fair balance between the various fundamental rights protected by the community legal order in conformity with other general principles of Community law, such as the principle of proportionality. The Court merely decided that it cannot be derived from European legislation that Member States are obliged to install a duty to provide personal data in the context of a civil procedure to ensure the effective protection of copyright. It did not, however, provide guidelines on how the balance should be made. In sum, the "hot potato" was passed on to the Member States.

It goes without saying that seeking for the right balance is a heavy task, especially when it concerns the balance between copyright and fundamental rights such as the right to freedom of expression and to the secrecy of correspondence, which has been the subject of heated debates on many occasions in legal literature as well as elaborate case law.

The principle of proportionality requires that the measure taken should be appropriate and necessary to achieve the goal pursued. The measure at stake will have to go through a three-part test: the "suitability" test that defines whether the measure is reasonably likely to achieve its objectives; the "necessity" test that evaluates whether there are other less restrictive means capable to produce the same result; and the proportionality test stricto sensu which consists of a weighing of interests where the consequences on fundamental rights are assessed against the importance of the objective pursued [24]. The more severe the infringement, the more important the legitimate objective in each case will need to be [25].

This principle has been translated into provisions of both the legislation on intellectual property and on data protection. Article 8§1 of Directive 2001/29 and Article 3 of Directive 2004/49 state that measures, sanctions and remedies against infringements to intellectual property rights should not only be effective and dissuasive but also "appropriate", "proportionate", "loyal" and "fair". Moreover, under Directive 2004/48, a court may order the communication of information on the origin and distribution networks of the goods or services which infringe an intellectual property right, only when the request is justified and proportionate (article 8).

In data protection legislation, the principle of proportionality is based not only on the legitimacy of the processing but also on the adequacy and relevance of the means used for the accomplishment of these purposes in a democratic society. In the *Lindqvist* case [26], the ECJ specified that when applying the principle of proportionality, the jurisdiction should take into consideration all circumstances of the case, in particular, the duration of violation of the norms transposing the Data Protection Directive and the significance for data subjects of the protection of the disclosed data. Moreover, the proportionality test should be guided by the more specific safeguards introduced by the applicable legislation.

The Council of Europe [18] explicitly refers to the need to ensure the proportionality of limitations to fundamental rights resulting from the use of filters and stresses the need for Member States to take into account Article 10, Paragraph 2 by (a) introducing regulatory provisions where appropriate and necessary for the prevention of intentional abuse of filters to restrict access to lawful content (b) ensuring the assessment of filters both before and during their implementation to ensure the effects of the filtering are appropriate to the purpose of the restriction and thus necessary in a democratic society in order to avoid unreasonable blocking of content (c) provide for effective and readily accessible means of recourse and remedy including suspension of filters in cases where users and/or authors of content claim content has been blocked unreasonably and (d) avoid the universal blocking of illegal content for users who justifiably demonstrate a legitimate interest to access such content under exceptional circumstances (particularly for research purposes).

It is doubtful whether the preventive measures proposed by copyright societies comply with such principle. Moreover, the implementation of filters goes against the prohibition of all large-scale exploratory or general surveillance of telecommunications and is not compliant with the principle of specificity. To that effect, the Working Party 29, when assessing the conformity of the retention obligation made to ISPs by the Data Retention Directive [27], pointed out the disproportionate nature of a measure which makes surveillance that is authorized in exceptional circumstances – monitoring of communications through the comprehensive storage of all traffic data – the rule, or which covers indiscriminately all natural persons who use electronic communications, irrespective of the fact whether there are intimations that they are infringing the law. It further expressed doubts about the necessity of such measure in a democratic society, *particularly if this leads to the systematic recording of all electronic communications* [28].

By the same token, the cutting off of Internet access as a last resort proposed in the "graduate response" advocated in France has been considered disproportionate by the European Parliament [17].

In addition, to be deemed proportionate, adequate safeguards should surround the interception of communications. In particular, the intervention of an independent supervisory authority monitoring the correct application of the law appears to be crucial for their legality and legitimacy [22]. On the one hand, as pointed out by General Advocate J. Kokott, public authorities are bound by fundamental rights, unlike private individuals, and must respect procedural safeguards [22]. Their participation thus ensures better safeguards for individuals. On the other hand, ISPs cannot replace public authorities in the repression of illicit activities. The participation of public authorities even conditions the constitutional validity of such measures in some countries [29], in particular, when it concerns the identification of IP addresses owners, a competence which is usually reserved for a judge.

5. Conclusion

All recent European as well as national developments point out that the pressure on ISPs is rising and that these "neutral intermediaries" are increasingly obliged to interfere with the content passing through (monitoring) and hence risk loosing their exoneration of liability. Clearly they are implicitly being held responsible for illegal acts conducted by their clients. If we just make an analogy with the offline world it would be like holding the Post Office responsible for the fact that illegal cassettes were delivered by the postman who is unaware of what the letter contains and has to respect the confidentiality of mails as well. In addition ISPs are forced into the position of (private) judge without having the knowledge and tools, or authority to assess the legality of a specific act or content.

We believe that there is no overall solution for the triangular problem between copyright exoneration, privacy and the freedom of expression. However, public authorities should take a central part in the process and act as guide rail of the constitutional safeguards to fundamental rights which remain of vital importance to any democratic system. To that effect, General Advocate J. Kokott considered it more proportionate to limit the communication of traffic data to public authorities. Such communication should be limited to specific situations and subject to strict conditions and procedures which would guarantee the confidentiality of communications. Finally, the interpretation of restrictions to this right should be carefully assessed and should not result in a systematic control of the (il)licit use of electronic communication networks. A control which would lead to monitoring all communications and analysing their content could convert the "glass citizen" into a reality and thus should be avoided.

References

1. Article 12-14 Directive 2000/31/EC of the European Parliament and of the Council of 8 June 2000 on certain legal aspects of information society services, in particular electronic commerce, in the Internal Market ('Directive on electronic commerce'), OJ C 178, 17.07.2000, p. 1
2. Article 15 E-commerce Directive
3. Article 12.3., article 13.2 article 14.3 and article 15.2 E-Commerce Directive
4. Recital 16 Directive 2001/29/EC of the European Parliament and of the Council of 22 May 2001 on the harmonisation of certain aspects of copyright and related rights in the information society (hereafter referred to as Copyright Directive), OJ C 167, 22.06. 2001, p. 10; recital 15 Directive 2004/48 of the European Parliament and of the Council of 29 April 2004 on the enforcement of intellectual property rights (hereafter refered to as Enforcement Directive), OJ L 157, 30.04.2004, p. 45
5. European Court of Justice, *C-275/06, Promusicae vs. Telefónica*, 29 January 2008, OJ C 64, 08.03.2008, p. 9. For a more detailed analysis of the legal implications of this Ruling, see Coudert F., Werkers E., La protection des droits d'auteur face aux réseaux peer-to-peer: la levee du secret des communications est-elle justifiée? Note d'observations sous C.J.C.E. (gr. Ch.) 29 janvier 2008, R.D.T.I. n°30/2008, pp. 76–85.
6. O. Dumons, « Mission Olivennes: signature de l'accord sur fond de grincements de dents », *Le Monde*, 23 novembre 2007; http://www.culture.gouv.fr/culture/actualites/index-olivennes231107.htm. French Constitutional Court, Decision N°2009-580 of 10 June 2009.
7. "Filter or else! Music industry sues Irish ISP", http://www.scl.org/editorial.asp?i + 1786; EDRI-gram: "Sweden wants tougher laws against file sharers", http://www.edri.org/edrigram/number5.14/sweden-file-sharing; D. Carjaval, "Internet providers wary of being cybercrops", *International Herald Tribune*, 13 April 2008; E. Valzey, "An arts flagship going nowhere", *The Times*, 13 February 2008, http://www.timesonline.co.uk/tol/comment/columnists/guest_contributors/article3358697.ece
8. Pres. Court. Brussels 29 June 2007.
9. E. Montero and Y. Cool, « Le peer-to-peer » en sursis?», RDTI, 2005, n 21, pp. 97 and 103.
10. F. Gotzen and M.C. Janssens, *Wegwijs in het intellectueel eigendomsrecht*, Brugge, Vanden Broele, 2007, p. 68.
11. Article 20, paragraph 6 Proposal for a Directive of the European Parliament and of the Council amending Directive 2002/22/EC on universal service and users' rights relating to electronic communications networks, Directive 2002/58/EC concerning the processing of personal data and the protection of privacy in the electronic communications sector and Regulation (EC) No 2006/ 2004 on consumer protection cooperation, COM(2007) 698 definite, http://ec.europa.eu/prelex/detail_dossier_real.cfm?CL = en&DosId = 196419.
12. Speech Viviane Reding, "The European Commission and media industry: the need for a new partnership", Luxembourg, 5 November 2004.
13. Communication from the Commission to the European Parliament, the Council, the European Economic and Social Committee and the Committee of the regions on Creative Content Online in the Single Market, Brussels, Brussels, 3 January 2008, COM(2007)836final.
14. A. Strowel and F. Tulkens, "Les intermédiaires dans la communication, des censeurs malgré eux?" A. Berenboom, E. Derieux et, E. Dommering (eds.), Censuur, Brussels, Larcier, 2003, 107.
15. See for example the European P2P Next project, http://www.p2p-next.org/
16. G. Bono, Report on the cultural industries in Europe – CULT Amendments, Motion for a European Parliament Resolution on cultural industries in the context of the Lisbon Strategy, 22 December 2007.
17. European Parliament Resolution on cultural industries in Europe, 10 April 2008; also see the Stavros Lambridinis Report with a proposal for a European Parliament Recommendation to the Council on strengthening security and fundamental freedoms on the Internet (2008/2160 (INI), A6-0103/2009.
18. Recommendation CM/Rec(2008)6 of the Committee of Ministers to member states on measures to promote the respect for freedom of expresión and information with regard to Internet filtres, adopted by the Committee of Ministers on 26 March 2008 on the 1022nd Meeting of the Ministers'Deputies.
19. A. Strowel and F. Tulkens, *Droit d'auteur et liberté d'expression*, Brussels, De Boeck en Larcier, 2006, 160 p.
20. WP29, Recommendation 2/99 on the respect of privacy in the context of interception of telecommunications, WP18, 3 May 1999.
21. Directive 2002/58/EC of the European Parliament and of the Council of 12 July 2002 concerning the processing of personal data and the protection of privacy in the electronic communications sector, OJ L 201, 31.7.2002, pp. 37–47.
22. Conclusion Adv.-Gen. J. Kokott (2007), *ECJ C-275/06, Promusicae v. Telefónica*
23. Forum des Droits sur l'Internet, Loi Informatique et Libertés, un nouveau cadre juridique pour le traitement des données à caractère personnel, Octobre 2004.
24. T. Tridimas, *The General Principles of EU Law*, 2nd ed., Oxford EC Law Library, p. 139.
25. Liberty, Overlooked: Surveillance and Personal Privacy in Modern Britain, October 2007, available online at: http://www.liberty-human-rights.org.uk/issues/3-privacy/pdfs/liberty-privacy-report.pdf
26. European Court of Justice, Lindqvist, C-101/01, 6 November 2003, OJ C 7, 10.01.2004, p. 3, pt. 89.
27. Directive 2006/24/EC, of the European Parliament and of the Council of 15 March 2006 on the retention of data generated or processed in connection with the provision of publicly available electronic communications services or of public communications networks and amending Directive 2002/58/EC, OJ L 105, 13.04.2006, p. 54

28. Article 29 Data Protection Working Party, Opinion 3/2006 on the Directive 2006/24/EC of the European Parliament and of the Council on the retention of data generated or processed in connection with the provision of publicly available electronic communications services or of public communications networks and amending Directive 2002/58/EC

29. See D. Olivennes, Le développement et la protection des oeuvres culturelles sur les nouveaux réseaux, Rapport au Ministre de la Culture et de la Communication, November 2007; and French Constitutional Court, Decision n°2004-499 of 29 July 2004 with regard to Article 9 of the French Data Protection Act which enable copyright societies to process personal data related to offences, convictions and security measures for purpose of ensuring the defense of their right holders.

36

Information Technology Projects – Leaving the 'Magic' to the 'Wizards'

Peter M. Bednar and Christine Welch

Abstract

In this chapter, we explore the significant challenges relating to investment in IT business. Information technology does not in itself deliver business value. We highlight the complexities that are often ignored in management of IT projects. If the management system in an organization is ineffective, then installing information technologies does not constitute a 'magic wand' that will generate prosperity. It can only generate value if attention is paid to the design of the system for use at the same time that technological systems are developed. The authors explore how IT benefits require attention from management generally and show that investment in IT projects cannot be left to 'IT experts' alone. We point out that undue reliance on rational planning is unsatisfactory, as it ignores contextual dependencies in organizational life. Criteria by which the success/failure of projects is to be judged must go beyond a focus on timescales, budgets, and 'requirement specifications.' We suggest that the criteria need to be expanded to embrace usefulness of resultant systems, as perceived by organizational staff as they attempt to use them in carrying out their work.

Keywords Information Systems development · Contextual dependency · Systems failure · IT projects

1. In Search of the Magic Wand

Despite evidence to the contrary, some people persist in believing that IT provides a solution to all problems. When we look at J.K. Rowling's *Harry Potter* novels, magic can appear to be widely accepted as a panacea for all difficulties. It is every child's dream to possess a magic wand with which any problem can be solved. With a flick of the wand, the bedroom is instantly tidy, the homework is instantly finished, and mummy's precious vase, broken during play, is instantly mended again! It is therefore easy to explain the unprecedented success enjoyed by J.K. Rowling with her novels about *Harry Potter*, the boy wizard, and his adventures at Hogwarts School of Witchcraft and Wizardry. However, a dip into one of these works reveals the deeper mysteries lying behind the magic. In *Harry Potter and the Goblet of Fire* [1], for instance, Harry needs his wand and flying broomstick to fight a dragon in the school tournament. However, he also has to conquer his own feelings of inadequacy, deal with the jealousy of his best friend, and face the embarrassment of asking a girl to dance for the first time. Faced with these challenges, his wand is of any little use to him. Magic just cannot solve the real problems experienced by people in life as it is lived. Many adults might benefit from a reading of these works, since it is not only children who look for a 'magic wand' to save them from troubles and difficulties. In just the same way, in the real world, information technology becomes an object of faith. We notice this phenomenon particularly when

Peter M. Bednar • School of Computing, University of Portsmouth, Portsmouth, UK; Department of Informatics, Lund University, Lund, Sweden   **Christine Welch** • Department of Strategy and Business Systems, University of Portsmouth Business School, Portsmouth, UK.

G.A. Papadopoulos et al. (eds.), *Information Systems Development*, DOI 10.1007/b137171_36,
© Springer Science+Business Media, LLC 2009

organizations set out to exploit the potential of information technologies. Managers often appear to think that IT can be used like a magic spell – just invoke the power of an IT project and suddenly the failing business will thrive, the difficult decisions will resolve themselves and the management practices will meet with success. Such acts of faith possibly seem preferable to the complex processes involved in challenging assumptions and questioning the validity of business 'models'. Our purpose in this chapter is to show that successful management in business requires that complexity must be addressed, and taken-for-granted assumptions must be challenged. In setting out our case, we draw upon a strong, but often ignored tradition of work, exemplified by authors such as Ciborra and Nissen, inter alia. Current agendas in IS strategy continue to focus on a concept of alignment between IS and business objectives – closing a perceived gap. We wish to highlight, in contrast, a need for holistic strategic thinking, in which IS/IT is seen as an integral part of business management and not a separate, serving system to be aligned with it.

In organizational life, people may be confounded by the complexity and uncertainty they experience in 21st century business environments. Benko and McFarlan [2] describe this using a metaphor of an 'information frontier'. In their words:

> "Why a frontier metaphor? Because it aptly captures recent experience: a decades-long period of progressive and lasting change, rich with opportunity and fraught with uncertainty. Frontiers are new terrains in which people roam, settle, and create value. Frontiers fundamentally alter not only what we do, but also how we see the world around us. ... By their nature, frontiers are confusing, volatile and – above all – *unpredictable*. The adoption of new ideas is a social, as well as a business, process. This fact, among others, makes frontiers particularly unsuitable for crystal-ball gazers" [2, p. 6].

We surmise that people yearn for that 'magic wand' to help them reduce complexity to simplicity and uncertainty to predictability. Managers then turn to IT projects in the expectation of finding a solution to life at the frontier. While the rhetoric surrounding control over IT projects emphasizes cognitive dimensions of problem solving; we suggest that the affective domain is relevant to discuss.

Peppard [3] reminds us of a widespread fallacy that ownership of the 'right' IT systems will automatically lead to delivery of value for a business. Unfortunately, in practice, it is only when IT systems are utilized in conjunction with embedded competences of staff throughout the organization that value is created. As Peppard puts it:

> A critical weakness of these approaches is that they assume that the user is the consumer of IT services, failing to acknowledge the value derived from IT is often not only co-created but context dependent [3, p. 338].

Thus, while IS/IT systems are being designed and developed, little attention is being paid to the need to design and develop the business organization at the same time. Nissen [4] points to a difficulty arising through the choice of language developers use when addressing their clientele. If the discourse of development refers constantly to the needs of 'users,' then it is likely that the clientele may not feel ownership of the results. They probably do not regard themselves primarily as users of IT, but as managers, accountants, lawyers, etc. Furthermore, they are not simply 'consumers' of information technologies, but co-creators, since their collaboration is required to create systems which are usable and useful in the first place. The language used leads to a misguided process of development of the system for IS/IT use. Williams and Tanner [5] give an example in the context of Web development:

> By sharing ownership of the project business expectations are more likely to be realized. Disconnection between developers and business can lead to applications being developed out of context [5, p. 20].

It is not uncommon to see business issues discussed using impersonal terms that refer to people as if they were nothing more than intelligent robots. The proposition is that organizations (formed as they are from interactions among people) are manageable by the application of deterministic cybernetic models. Lindblom [6] calls into question the idea that decision making in organizations can be based on rational planning alone. As he points out, the sheer volume of data gathering required to support this would be prohibitive, and that in practice a more intuitive approach is likely. This is supported by Rombach [7], who provides a number of cases to illustrate how organizations attempting management by objectives often flounder. Suggestions that strategy can be formed by a process of rational planning arise naturally if an assumption is made that business activities are founded predominantly in the cognitive domain. However, lust for control can itself be seen as a reflection of the affective domain at work. It can be viewed as a response to uncertainty/complexity (on the 'information frontier') by rising fear for the future. Perhaps an excessive emphasis on cognitive processes reflects a search for a means to regain possession of a comfort zone. Such emotional responses are clearly understandable in a context in which US IT capital spending has reached an estimated 50% of all nominal business capital spending, while an estimated 40% of IT investments in the United States fail to deliver their expected returns [2].

Claudio Ciborra pointed out how situated perspectives in information systems research call for methods of inquiry which capture the inner life of the actor: mind and heart [8]. In this chapter, we look at the mythical search for the 'magic spell' of IT deployment. This chapter pays attention to the relative contributions of cognitive and affective human processes in information systems co-creation and use. It reflects upon the extent to which current agendas in IS strategy appear to be uninformed by previous work, such as research on participatory and socio-technical approaches to design. The authors conclude by drawing out practical implications for information systems development and management.

2. A Cloak of Invisibility

Realizing the benefits promised by creating synergy between IT services and business processes requires change in the business itself and, more particularly, in the interactions between individual groups of people within the business. Furthermore, it is necessary to consider how the business will need to adapt to new ways of working before adoption of any particular technology [9]. This appears to be an obvious requirement. However, in many instances it does not happen. Williams [10] highlights a tendency for IT projects to 'linger on' even after it becomes obvious that they cannot be successful. He suggests this is due to intransigence of managers, since cancellation of a project before completion is seen as a sign of weakness and failure, rather than decisiveness and strength. He draws on research commissioned by the IT Governance Institute. Fifty two percent of the projects sampled were expected to lead to negative returns, while 31% actually destroyed value for the companies concerned. However, only 3% of projects were abandoned before completion. This suggests that managers were continuing to preside over projects that destroyed, rather than created business value. Furthermore, in many cases it was clear that warning signs were available in the form of changes in sponsorship, apathy by proposed users, and lack of engagement from business managers or 'scope creep.' In other words, there was widespread expectation of failure within the organizations concerned, while those specifically charged with governance over the development of IT 'resources' were also those presiding over loss of value. We perceive this to show that managers do not always act as rational beings, drawing upon their cognitive skills to reach decisions informed by all the available evidence (as management literature often suggests). Instead, it is the affective domain that is the key influence on their behavior. Even though reason would suggest abandoning a project, pride, and feelings of commitment lead managers to persist. Why does this occur and how is it allowed to persist? We can draw upon the work of Argyris [11] in seeking for an explanation. Argyris describes a phenomenon of defensive routines which arise in organizational behavior. When faced with the need to address uncomfortable choices or deliver 'bad news,' people often prefer to avoid unpleasantness and confrontation and thus become quite skilled in routines of avoidance (in Argyris' words 'skilled incompetence') which have the effect of ensuring that the status quo is maintained and difficulties are never practically addressed. The phenomenon of defensive routines represents an emotional, rather than a rational response. People may pursue them while scarcely being aware that they are doing so. Even where there is a rhetoric of change, defensive strategies may operate to block progress with projects and plans designed to effect it. Further support for this view comes from Brunsson [12], who points out how organizational discourse (talk) may be at odds with decisions and actions taken. He describes a phenomenon of 'hypocrisy' that is similar to Argyris' idea of defensive routines – decisions are sometimes taken in order to avoid action, rather than to bring it about. However, Brunsson's view is that conflict within organizations is healthy, and that it may be better for problems to remain unsolved, since this leads to more opportunity for reflection and discussion (what Argyris might term opportunities for double-loop learning to occur). In Brunsson's words:

Insoluble problems are a splendid vehicle for the reflection of many ideas and values. They can be endlessly discussed from all sorts of angles and without ever reaching a conclusion. Solutions that can reflect an equal variety of ideas are rare indeed [12, p. 23].

In studies using resource-based theory [13, 14], two factors were found to be crucially important to success in IS/IT strategies. One was commitment of general management toward IS/IT adoption and use and the other was IS/IT capability permeating the organization generally. In those organizations where IT projects were measured as successful, organizational performance was seen to derive from aspects of all business operations including, e.g., sales, marketing, logistics, production, and customer service within which IT was an integral part. IT resources were viewed as a dynamic, constantly changing business variable, requiring organizational competence to manage as *part of overall business management*. Despite all the evidence that IT does not constitute a magic spell to solve all problems, organizations still persist in behaving as if it does. Many chief information officers acknowledge that their task entails not merely installing hardware and software 'resources' into the organization, but interacting with people to support effective deployment of IT in a variety of organizational contexts in order to generate value. They

acknowledge that they are attempting to influence people and decisions as well as encourage involvement and the promotion of actions that do not strictly fall into their realm of authority [3, p. 337].

However, problems arise because chief executives fail to recognize their own responsibility in this area, preferring to leave the process to managers of the 'IT function' (leave the magic to the wizards!). This attitude toward management of IT projects is likely to cascade throughout the organizational hierarchy. This, then, leaves IT managers with no choice but to focus on implementation of IT systems, since they are powerless alone to influence the necessary co-creation of value in context. However, it is only at the level of the business that effective action can be taken to influence organizational values and behavior to enable effective use of available technologies. There is a paradox therefore in that, while elaborate and rigorous plans may be developed for implementation of the technology itself, it is relatively unusual to find similar plans in place for the *realization of benefits* from that technology. Ward and Peppard [15] argue for an iterative process of benefits management. In describing their five-stage iterative model for benefits management, they point out that the starting point assumes an IT-based system that was delivered to specification. However, they emphasize that the benefit management process will impact on the original specification so that modifications to the system will be needed, and that effective change management processes must therefore also be in place. As Ward and Peppard put it:

As the benefits management process proceeds, it may cause revision to the specification, and it is assumed that effective change control processes can deal with this. The other related set of activities are organizational changes of many types that have to be made to deliver the benefits. The benefits management process should be the driving mechanism for these change activities. How to bring them about in detail is addressed in the wealth of change management and organizational development literature [15, p. 441]

This makes clear a need for general management involvement in IT benefits management, in order that these wider areas of competence can be applied effectively. This area cannot safely be consigned to IT 'experts.' It also makes the point that requirements are not static and cannot be captured at the inception of a project to guide its progress to completion. As Ward and Peppard point out, requirements will change with the process of management benefits. We go further than this to suggest that it is insufficient to attempt alignment of IT systems with business processes. Those processes will themselves change as a result of introducing particular technologies. An essential part of benefits management must be to ask in what ways processes are changing, on an ongoing basis. Thus, avoidance of failure cannot simply be about developing systems on time, within budget and fulfilling a specification, because all of these factors are not static, but fluid.

It is not that managers do not understand the need to embed the technology within business processes. However, they have no practical realization of personal responsibility to bring about necessary changes in perspectives and behavior to promote IS capability. Argyris [11, 16] points to a discrepancy that often occurs between espoused theories (i.e., what people think they do) and theories in use (what it appears to other people that they do in practice). This is not to suggest that people are consciously dishonest or stupid. However, emotional responses to experienced situations may be conflicting or may conflict with reasoned assessments of action that is needed. We perceive, here, a difference between development of IT systems and development of *use* of IT in organizational contexts. Evidence for these points can be seen in current popularity of the concept of IT Service Management. This view that IT 'resources' are a separate artifact that can be dealt with by 'experts' outside the main stream of the business leads to inherent difficulties. In Peppard's words:

> This is the conundrum of IT management: how to generate value through IT without having access to authority over necessary knowledge and resources. [3, p. 339].

This is reinforced by, for instance, IBM in their recent White Paper on IT Service Management in which a plea is made for organizations to recognize that IT management cannot be separated from management of the business itself [17]. Consequently, those concerned in IT management must also be concerned in business management [9]. The phenomenon of outsourcing is also symptomatic of a view that IT can be seen as a separate functional artifact. However, instead of asking how the management of IT services can be improved, we argue that the focus should be on managing the production of business value and delivery of this value through IT [3]. Capability to generate value for the business through IT is something that is embedded throughout the organization, i.e., it is a form of knowledge deployed by its entire staff. Management of use of IT is thus *a knowledge management task*, and it is not subsumed within competence to develop IT systems themselves [5].

An example of this can be seen in strategic decisions taken by insurance firm Skandia. The IT departments have been completely restructured, taking the focus away from maintenance of systems. This has led to halving the number of roles for IT specialists through, e.g., outsourcing of routine maintenance, and at the same time significantly increasing the number of business analysts from 15 to 100 [18]. This significant switch in investment toward analysis of business problems, as opposed to IT-specific problems, reflects an enhancement of capability to deal with organizational needs without threatening core competence in IT development. We note that the phenomenon highlighted by Williams, above, where managers persist with IT projects already doomed to failure, is less likely to arise in projects focused on wider business concerns. It is the tendency to consign IT issues to the realm of 'the experts' which lends a 'cloak of invisibility' [19] to projects in the IT field that is unavailable to business managers generally (i.e., IT is regarded as a 'black box' to be taken for granted by all but the experts). The significance of the investment in large numbers of business analysts throughout Skandia may be that it will be impossible for managers to claim lack of awareness of their activities or to retreat from engagement with creation of systems for IT use.

Benko and McFarlan [2] point out that a range of forces 'economic, technological, social, regulatory, and so on' have brought about radical changes in the business environment faced by most firms in Western societies over the past 25 years (p. 7). These changes have led to an increase in complexity of the decisions facing some firms, as managers attempt to seize opportunities provided by a new 'frontier' in which territory is based in multifaceted communications media as well as more traditional business contexts. Evans and Wurster [20] elaborate upon some of the forces for change. In the past, management activities were constrained by their relationship to the physical realities of industrial and commercial processes, e.g., a company's office was likely to be located relatively near to its factory to facilitate 'hands-on' control and to minimize costs. Organizational structures then tended to be constrained by the need to achieve an effective span of control, through division of labor. Collaborative endeavors were hence discouraged. 'Hard-wired' channels for communication, such as fixed periodic reporting and hierarchical relationships, meant that detailed communications could be shared among relatively few, close coworkers, whereas communication to a wider audience was by necessity more terse. Information systems were therefore designed to optimize a necessary trade-off between richness and reach. Organizations of today, within most Western economies, are less constrained by proximity to the physical means of production and modern information and communication technologies make a compromise between richness and reach less necessary. Collaborative working becomes not only possible, but desirable in order to harness creativity, bring about innovation and hence achieve competitive advantage. As boundaries become less fixed, possibilities exist for closer relationships between firms, their suppliers, partners, and customers through systems integration. Managers are effectively obliged to 'deliver for today while adapting for tomorrow's business' [20]. In such periods of discontinuity, it is challenging for managers to develop effective strategies – reflection upon what has worked in the past is insufficient and there is no reliable guide to the future. These authors suggest that companies need to consider a new form of alignment – not IT with business goals, but alignment of a portfolio of projects with company *intentions* to address the 'shifting realities of the larger business context' [20, p. 8]. For Benko and McFarlan [2] company intentions can be perceived through consideration of short-term and long-term objectives in conjunction with a further category, which they term 'traits.' Traits correspond to ideas of business 'capabilities,' e.g., Calderia and Ward's view of IS capability [13] that must permeate the organization as a whole. We can see in the work of these researchers a new emphasis on creating organizations that are flexible and fit to seize on opportunities as they arise by creation of an infrastructure of capabilities.

Thus, management of IT becomes subordinated to management of a portfolio of projects that is future oriented. A number of authors have pointed out that investment in information technology alone will not deliver business value. For example, Teece [21] pointed out that other (complementary) assets are required if a company is to derive benefit from a primary investment in technology. These include a range of organizational, managerial, and social 'assets' such as effective business processes, training programs, decentralized authority, collaborative working environments, intranets and effective telecommunications infrastructures, incentives for innovation, and a management culture that values flexibility. Knowledge held within the organization is also a key factor [22]. It follows, therefore, that a future-oriented portfolio of projects must focus, not simply on the latest hardware and software, but on investment in capability [see, e.g., 23, 24]. Two points follow from this discussion. First, strategy formation becomes a fluid, organic process. Ciborra and Jelassi [25] refer to this in suggesting a key role for improvization (bricolage) in business development. He points out, for instance, that strategic systems such as American Airlines SABRE online booking facility were created through tinkering. What started out as an operational level transaction processing system became, through serendipity, an important revenue generating (strategic) system. An infrastructure for capability, together with organizational activities drawing on that capability, is what forms the organizational information system. As Langefors and Dahlberg [26] points out, since all organizational activity crucially depends upon creating, sharing and using information, the information system and the organization can be viewed as one and the same.

3. Conclusions

In our view, there are a number of important principles to be considered by those who wish to derive advantage from introducing or updating technologies in organizations. The first is a realization that IT alone does not deliver business value or indeed any useful benefit except by lucky accident. In order to derive benefit from use of particular technologies, it is necessary to examine their synergy with other features of organizational life – who are the stakeholders who will use the technology and what is the origin of their desire and enthusiasm for doing so? From what professions are they drawn and what are their opinions about the way in which technologies can support them in carrying out their work. How will their processes for carrying out this work change as a result of changes in technology? Inquiry into these questions involves consideration of multiple levels of contextual dependencies in the experience of real people, and should not be confused with data or process modeling, or drawing up of a 'requirements specification.' Business managers need to plan for realizing those desired benefits which lead to initiation of projects, rather than focusing on the technology in isolation and believing, therefore, that management of IT projects can safely be consigned to 'the experts.' In this way, the 'cloak of invisibility' which has at times been available to IT professionals can be dispensed with in favor of transparency to fellow business professionals with other relevant areas of expertise.

A second aspect to be recognized is the importance of the affective domain in organizational life as it is lived. A person does not leave his psyche at home and travel to work as an automation whose actions are entirely based in reasoned, cognitive processing of data. Just like every other aspect of living, working life is populated by hopes, fears, and dreams. It can be demonstrated that neglect of the affective zone is detrimental to effective action, e.g., as shown by Williams' description [10] of adherence to projects already doomed to failure, which he attributes to emotions of pride, embarrassment, or stubbornness. In the same way, a need to explore desires of stakeholders for potential benefits from IT, and to promote enthusiasm for designed systems, is highlighted by examples such as the NHS IT project. Modern business depends upon collaboration to bring about knowledge creation and sharing. This is argued to be the only sustainable source of competitive advantage. However, people cannot be compelled either to collaborate or to be creative – they can only be empowered and supported to do so. A facilitative approach to management needs to be developed to deal with the needs of life at the 'information frontier' [2]. It can be argued that a facilitative manager needs to be skilled to engage with staff in the affective zone, not just to use cognitive skills for 'decision making'.

Promotion of organizational cultures in which there is tolerance for the ideas, views, and norms of others will be crucial to 21st century management. As boundaries between organizations lose their significance and 'value webs' between firms, their suppliers, customers, and partners are created, success will become dependent on the tolerance for 'entertaining strangers' [27, 28]. A successful organization of the future will need a flexible IT infrastructure so that opportunities can be seized and new 'partnerships' undertaken on a continuous basis. A portfolio of projects will be needed, comprising both technological and non-technological dimensions, and managed as an integral part of the business rather than a separate function [2, 13, 29]. There will also be a need to develop a range of business capabilities permeating the whole organization, including those relating to information systems. In order to bring this about, facilitative management will be needed, emphasizing communications in the form of dialogue between different stakeholders. Only in this way can useful systems be designed and created, and positive relationships based on understanding be sustained. Flexibility in the face of change requires organizations, and the individuals within them, to develop productive learning systems. Through greater attention to the affective dimension of organizational life, and communication within and across its boundaries, it may be possible to encourage learning for success and inhibit learning for failure, overcoming the double bind of defensive routines [11, 16].

All of these points represent significant challenges for organizations. There is no magic wand to remove the complexities and uncertainties from management, whether from technologies or any other source. However, as Brunsson [12] suggests, problems that cannot be resolved may, nevertheless, create dynamic benefits through opportunities to engage in reflection and debate.

References

1. Rowling, J.K. (2000). *Harry Potter and the Goblet of Fire*, Amazon: Bloomsbury Publishing PLC.
2. Benko, C. and McFarlan, W. (2003). *Connecting the Dots*, Boston, MA: Harvard Business School Press.
3. Peppard, J. (2007). The Conundrum of IT Management,' *European Journal of Information Systems*, 16, 336–345.
4. Nissen, H-E. (2002). 'Challenging Traditions of Inquiry in Software Practice,' in Y. Dittrich, C. Floyd and R. Klischewski (editors) *Social Thinking – Software Practice*, Cambridge, MA: MIT Press, pp 69–90.
5. Williams, M. and Tanner, D. (2008). 'Web Development: Get the Process Right,' *Computer Weekly*, March 2nd 2008.
6. Lindblom, C.E. (1959). 'The Science of Muddling Through,' *Public Administration Review*, 19, 79–88.
7. Rombach, B. (1991). *You Cannot Steer with Goals*, Lund: Studentlitteratur.
8. Ciborra, C.U. and Willcocks, L. (2006). 'The Mind or the Heart?' *Journal of Information Technology*, v21i3, 129–139.
9. Chappell, D. (2008). 'The Process of Getting IT to Work for the Business' in IT for Business Process, Sutton: Reed Business Information.
10. Williams, P. (2007). 'Make Sure You Get a Positive Return,' *Computer Weekly*, 13 Nov 2007.
11. Argyris, C. (1990). *Overcoming Organizational Defenses. Facilitating Organizational Learning*, Upper Saddle River, NJ: Prentice Hall.
12. Brunsson, N. (2002). *The Organization of Hypocrisy: Talk, Decisions, Actions in Organizations*, 2nd edition, Norway: Abstrakt/ Liber.

13. Caldeira, M.M. and Ward, J.M. (2003). 'Using Resource Based Theory to Interpret the Successful Adoption and Use of Information Systems and Technology in Manufacturing Small and Medium-Sized Enterprise,' *European Journal of Information Systems*, 12, 127–141.

14. Peppard, J. and Ward, J.M. (2004). 'Beyond Strategic Information Systems,' *Journal of Strategic Information Systems*, 12, 167–194.

15. Ward, J. and Peppard, J. (2002). *Strategic Planning for Information Systems*, 3rd edition, Chichester: Wiley.

16. Argyrols, C. (2004). *Reasons and Rationalisations. The Limits to Organizational Knowledge*. Oxford: Oxford University Press.

17. Salvage, I. and Dhanda, I.S. (2007). *IBM White Paper on IT Service Management*. http://whitepapers.theregister.co.uk/search/?q=IBM viewed 11 Nov 2007.

18. Grant, I. (2007). 'India Deal Clears Skandia's app Maintenance Backlog,' *Computer Weekly*, 6 November 2007, p. 4.

19. Rowling, J.K. (1997). *Harry Potter and the Philosopher's Stone*, Amazon: Bloomsbury Publishing PLC.

20. Evans, P. and Wurster, T.S. (2000). *Blown to Bits*, Boston, MA: Harvard Business School Press.

21. Teece, D. (1998). *Economic Performance and Theory of the Firm: The Selected Papers of David Teece*, London: Edward Elgar Publishing.

22. Davenport, T. and Prusak, L. (1998). *Working Knowledge*, Boston, MA: Harvard Business School Press.

23. Brynjolfsson, E. (2003). 'The IT Productivity Gap,' *Optimize Magazine* 21, July.

24. Marchand, D.A. (2004). 'Extracting the Business Value of IT,' *Capco Institute Journal of Financial Transformation*, 11, 125–131.

25. Ciborra, C.U. and Jelassi, T. (1994). *Strategic Information Systems: A European Perspective*, Chichester: Wiley.

26. Langefors, B. and Dahlberg, B. (1995). *Essays on Infology*, Lund: Studentlitteratur.

27. Hofstede, G. (1991). *Cultures and Organizations*, London: Profile Books.

28. Ciborra, C.U. (2002). *The Labyrinths of Information*, Oxford: Oxford University Press.

29. Bednar, P.M. (2000). 'A Contextual Integration of Individual and Organizational Learning Perspectives as Part of IS Analysis,' *Informing Science – Journal of an Emerging Transdiscipline*, 3(3), 145–156.

37

Analysis of Academic Results for Informatics Course Improvement Using Association Rule Mining

Robertas Damaševičius

Abstract

In this chapter we analyze the application of association rule mining for assessing student academic results and extracting recommendations for the improvement of course content. We propose a framework for mining educational data using association rules, and a novel metric for assessing the strength of an association rule, called "cumulative interestingness". In a case study, we analyze the Informatics course examination results using association rules, rank course topics following their importance for final course marks based on the strength of the association rules, and propose which specific course topic should be improved to achieve higher student learning effectiveness and progress.

Keywords Association rule mining · Education · Academic results · Intelligent data mining

1. Introduction

Data mining is a data analysis methodology that has been successfully employed in many domains such as e-commerce, telecommunication networks, market and risk management, inventory control and bioinformatics, where large volumes of data have to be analyzed [19]. In education and e-learning domains, data mining has been used to analyze by-products (e.g., logs) of the e-learning system sessions and other educational activities to evaluate the quality and efficiency of learning processes and learning management systems (LMS), to assess student learning performance, to build models of students or their interactions with LMS [2, 36]. Data mining is especially important for the educator helping to improve learning content and the quality of studies through learning personalization [22].

Association rule mining is one of the most well-studied data mining methods. Association rules associate one or more attributes of a data set with another attribute, producing an if–then statement concerning attribute values [3, 20]. Originally, mining of association rules between sets of items in large databases was performed in the context of market basket analysis [1]. However, now association rule mining is also applied to educational data from e-learning systems [9].

Educational data mining, in general, and application of association rule mining, in particular, has been a subject of extensive research in recent years [12, 31]. Common data mining tasks include (1) evaluation and classification of educational content [5, 14, 30, 37], e-learning systems [24] and students based on their learning actions [35]; (2) analysis of students' learning behavior for interesting activities and patterns [8, 16, 18, 21, 26, 27, 32, 38, 40, 41, 42]; and (3) personalization of learning processes and environments based on learner characteristics, usage profiles, and a domain ontology [7, 10, 23, 25, 39].

Robertas Damaševičius • Software Engineering Department, Kaunas University of Technology, Kaunas, Lithuania.

G.A. Papadopoulos et al. (eds.), *Information Systems Development*, DOI 10.1007/b137171_37,
© Springer Science+Business Media, LLC 2009

Another direction of research in association rule mining is the evaluation of discovered rules in terms of their "interestingness" or "surprisingness" to the researcher [6, 15, 17].

In this chapter we analyze the application of a particular type of association rule mining for assessing student academic results and extracting recommendations for the improvement of course content. The aim of this chapter is to propose a framework for the application of association rule mining for analysis of Informatics course examination results. The novelty of this paper is a proposed metric for assessing the strength of an association rule, called "cumulative interestingness," which is used to rank course topics according to their importance for final course marks based on discovered association rules.

The structure of the chapter is as follows. We describe the principles of association rule mining in Section 2. We propose a framework of the educational data mining using association rules in Section 3. A case study is presented in Section 4. Finally, in Section 5 we present conclusions and discuss future work.

2. Principles of Association Rule Mining and Rule Metrics

Association rule mining aims to discover interesting relationships (correlations, implications, causalities) between sets of items in the data instance data sets, which relate co-occurring elements and produce if–then statements concerning attribute values [1]. The aim is achieved by reducing a large amount of data to a small and understandable set of statistically supported statements.

Let $I = \{I_1, I_2, \ldots, I_m\}$ is a set of m distinct attributes, T is a data instance that contains a set of items such that $T \subseteq I$, $D = \{T_1, T_2, \ldots, T_n\}$ is a data set of n different data instances. An association rule is an implication in the form of $X \Rightarrow Y$ which means that if X occurs, there is a high probability of having Y as well, here X is the antecedent of the rule (or left hand side – LHS) and Y the consequent of the rule (or right hand side – RHS), $X, Y \subset I$, $X \cap Y = \oslash$.

The aim of the association rules is to reveal *interesting* relations between data, i.e., relations that are empirically true, novel with respect to known relations, understandable but not trivial, and increase our knowledge about an analyzed data set [4]. However, usually a large number of such rules are discovered. To identify novel, relevant, implicit, and understandable rules from the multitude of mined rule, the importance (or interestingness) metrics are used. The importance of each rule can be evaluated using the following metrics:

1. *Confidence*. The confidence of an association rule is the probability $P(Y|X)$ of finding Y for us to accept this rule, i.e., the proportion of data instances with X in the data set that contains the consequent Y also. Values of confidence near value 1 are expected for an important association rule.
2. *Support*. The support of the rule is the probability $P(X \cup Y)$, which is calculated as the proportion of data instances in the data set that contain both the antecedent and the consequent. Sets of items with high support appear frequently together in many data instances.
3. *Coverage*. The coverage of an association rule is the probability $P(X)$, which is calculated as the proportion of instances in the data that have the attribute values or items specified on the antecedent of the rule. Values of coverage near value 1 are expected for an important association rule.
4. *Leverage*. The leverage of an association rule is the probability $P(X \cup Y) - P(X)P(Y)$, which is calculated as the proportion of additional data instances covered by both the antecedent and consequent above those expected if the antecedent and consequent were independent of each other. Leverage values equal or less than 0 indicate a strong independence between antecedent and consequent, and values near 1 indicate an important association rule.
5. *Lift*. The lift of an association rule is the probability $P(Y|X)/P(Y)$, which is calculated as the confidence divided by the proportion of all data instances that are covered by the consequent. This is a measure of the importance of the association that is independent of coverage.
6. *Significance*. The significance of an association rule is the probability that the observed relationship would occur by chance.

This is by no means an exhaustive list of such metrics, for the longer surveys, see [13, 28].

Using just one interestingness metric is not enough to assess the importance of interestingness of a rule. In most cases, it is sufficient to use focus on a combination of support, confidence, and either lift or leverage to quantitatively measure the "quality" of the rule. However, the real value of a rule, an expert selects a combination of metrics applied depending upon the particular domain and his domain knowledge. Since there is no single, formal definition of what an interestingness is, such decision is usually highly subjective [34]. In order to take into account for as much aspects of association rule interestingness, here we propose to use a "cumulative interestingness" metric *CI*, which is calculated as follows:

$$CI = -confidence \cdot support \cdot coverage \cdot leverage \cdot lift \cdot \log(significance) \tag{37.1}$$

The larger value of cumulative interestingness, the more important (interesting) association rule is expected to be.

In the following section, we describe a framework for educational data mining using association rules.

3. Framework for Educational Data Mining Using Association Rules

The general knowledge data mining process has the following next steps: collecting data, preprocessing, applying the actual data mining procedures, and postprocessing of results [11]. However, then applied to the learning domain, the data mining process has to adapted to the specifics of that domain. Here we propose the following framework for mining educational data:

1. *Data collection.* Data is collected from LMS database or log files and may include personal information of the users (user profile), academic results, and the user's interaction data from e-learning systems. Traditional educational data sets are normally small, typically from dozens to several hundred at most, depending on the type of the course (primary, adult, higher, tertiary, academic, and special education).
2. *Problem identification.* The clear aims of data mining should be formulated, what relationships are expected to be discovered in the analyzed data.
3. *Data preprocessing.* The collected data should be preprocessed, to remove superfluous (unnecessary) data or data with missing values, or to fill in missing values of the data, or to perform data cleaning and data discretization (numerical values are transformed to categorical values), to derive new attributes and select attributes (new attributes are created from the existed ones and only a subset of relevant attributes are chosen), to create summary data fields, which represent a sum, average, or other function of other data fields, to transform the data format to format required by the used data mining tools, etc.
4. *Hypothesis formulation.* The hypothesis on the relationships between specific parts of data should be formulated in the form of left hand side rule (antecedent) and right hand side rule (consequent).
5. *Mining parameter selection.* This includes (a) selection of the specific association rule mining algorithm and implementation;(b) configuration of the mining parameters such as selection of mining metrics and their threshold values; and (c) specification of mining restrictions such as the maximum number of discovered rules or what specific attributes can be present in the antecedent or consequent of the discovered rules.
6. *Rule mining.* The application of mining algorithm (tool). In case of lengthy data or complex relationships this step could take for a long time.
7. *Result evaluation and interpretation.* The obtained association rules (often formulated in the natural language as *if–then* rules) are interpreted, evaluated using a selected metric, or a combination thereof and used to make decisions about the changes of learning content and its presentation to improve students' learning effectiveness and the quality of studies, in general.

4. Case Study: Mining Association Rules in "Object-Oriented Programming" Course

Data collection. We have performed association rule mining using academic data from the "object-oriented programming" course [29] lectured for 1st semester bachelor students at Informatics faculty, Kaunas University of Technology (KTU), Lithuania. Summary of a course: to teach students to program simple object programs, to create classes, to teach creating and using dynamic data structures, to provide initial knowledge about data flow analysis, development of program structure, program development, and implementation.

During the semester, the students have 16 theory lectures (32 h) distributed into 12 topics (T1–T12) and 6 labs (L1–L6) (32 h). For examination the students are given three tests (K1–K3) and one theory exam (TE). The summary of course lecture topics and examinations is presented in Table 37.1. The cumulative marking system is used so the final course mark is derived as a weighted sum of L1–L6, K1–K3, and TE. In this research, the academic data from the 2007 Spring semester are used. The course had 357 students enlisted.

Table 37.1. Summary of lecture topics and examinations.

Lecture topics	Labs	Tests	Exam
T0: Introductory lecture	L1: Drawing function graphics	–	–
T1: Classes and objects, UML	L2: Classes. Dynamic array of structures	K1: Array of structures	TE: Theory exam
T2: Menus and dialogs		K2: Dynamic structures	
T3: Pointers		K3: Dynamic lists	
T4: Dynamic lists	L3: Linear dynamic list		
T5: Data flows, files	L4: Processing of data flow		
T6: Class methods, inheritance			
T7: Linear dynamic object list	L5: Dynamic list of objects		
T8: Classes and their properties, copy constructor, operation overriding		–	
T9: Other types of dynamic lists	–		
T10: C++ Builder console mode			
T11: Program debugging and testing			
T12: Design of large programs			
–	L6: Final lab report		

Problem identification. The aim of association rule mining is to discover the relationship between presentation of course topics evaluated based on the interim examination results and final student academic results and to rank the importance of course topics for final course mark in order to improve learning content presentation and student teaching.

Data preprocessing. There are 12 features: 6 labs (L1, L2, L3, L4, L5, L6), 3 tests (K1, K2, K3), 1 theory exam (TE), and final mark (F). Each feature has values from 0 to 10, which represent a 10 grade marking system. A course is considered to be passed by a student if $F \geq 5$. The examination results are summarized in Fig. 37.1.

Hypothesis formulation. The left hand side (LHS) rules may contain eight attributes that indicate student failure during intermediate examinations (L2–L5, K1–K3, TE < 5). L1 was excluded because it was based on the previous semester material, and L6 was excluded, because it is only a summary report of L1–L5. The Right hand side (RHS) attribute indicates student failure to fulfill the entire course ($F < 5$). Our hypothesis is as follows: a student fails the course if he/she fails a specific intermediate examination (L2–L5, K1–K3, TE).

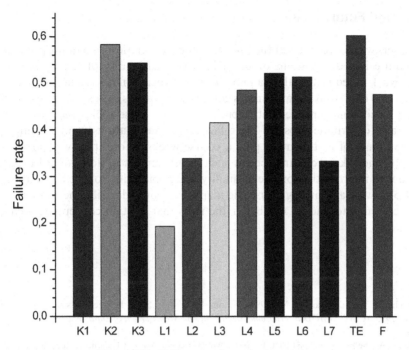

Figure 37.1. Failure rate of examination results.

Mining parameter selection and rule mining. To find association rules, we use Magnum Opus 4.2 [33]. We use confidence, coverage, support, lift, leverage, significance, and newly proposed cumulative interestingness metrics.

Result evaluation and interpretation. The association rules and their assessment using interestingness metrics are presented in Table 37.2. The rules are sorting according to the values of the cumulative interestingness metric (last column). As we can see, the association rule$(L3 < 5) \Rightarrow (F < 5)$ (the student fails the course if he/she fails the *L3: Linear dynamic list* lab) has the largest *CI* value. It also has the largest confidence, lift, leverage, and the smallest significance value, which means that it is highly unlikely that the observed relationship could occur by chance. Based on those results we can claim that a first priority in changing the content and presentation of the course should be assigned to the practical implementation aspects of dynamic lists covered by the lecture *T4: Dynamic lists* (see Table 37.1).

Table 37.2. Mined association rules and their assessment.

| Topic | Association rule | | Interestingness metric | | | | | | |
	LHS	RHS	Confidence	Coverage	Support	Lift	Leverage	Significance	CI
T4	L3 < 5	F < 5	0.872	0.415	0.361	1.83	0.1639	3.16E-039	1.509
T1-T12	Te < 5	F < 5	0.721	0.602	0.434	1.51	0.1474	1.01E-032	1.341
T6-T7	K3 < 5	F < 5	0.753	0.543	0.409	1.58	0.1502	3.92E-032	1.246
T1-T2	K1 < 5	F < 5	0.853	0.401	0.342	1.79	0.1510	1.87E-033	1.035
T7-T8	L5 < 5	F < 5	0.737	0.521	0.384	1.55	0.1357	6.85E-026	0.780
T5-T6	L4 < 5	F < 5	0.751	0.485	0.364	1.58	0.1334	6.18E-025	0.677
T1-T3	L2 < 5	F < 5	0.860	0.339	0.291	1.80	0.1299	9.06E-027	0.517
T3-T5	K2 < 5	F < 5	0.673	0.583	0.392	1.41	0.1147	2.55E-019	0.463

5. Conclusion and Future Work

In this chapter, we have examined the application of association rule mining for identifying course topics, which require improvement, in order to increase learnability of the course content. We also proposed a framework for educational data mining using association rules. The validity of the framework was demonstrated by a case study in Informatics course data analysis. Association rule mining can help the educator in learning content improvement (identification of course topics that cause difficulties to the student learning and contribute most to their failure at examinations) and learning personalization (prediction of the failure of a student to pass a course weeks before it may happen based on interim examination results and take necessary actions such as assignment of additional learning hours, etc. to correct it). In order to improve the comprehensibility and applicability of the association rules, it will be very useful to also provide an ontology (or topic map) that would describe the content of the course and would allow the educator to understand better the rules that contain concepts related to the analyzed domain.

References

1. Agrawal R., Imielinski, T. and Swami, A.N. (1993) Mining Association Rules between Sets of Items in Large Databases. In *Proceedings of the 1993 ACM SIGMOD International Conference on Management of Data*, Washington, D.C., May 26–28, ACM Press, pp. 207–216.
2. Castro, F., Velllido, A., Nebot, A. and Mugica, F. (2007) Applying Data Mining Techniques to e-Learning Problems: A Survey and State of the Art. In Jain, L.C., Tedman, R. and Tedman, D. (Eds.), *Evolution of Teaching and Learning Paradigms in Intelligent Environment*. Springer, pp. 183–221.
3. Ceglar, A. and Roddick, J.F. (2006) Association Mining. *ACM Computing Surveys*, 38(2):1–42.
4. Colton, S., Bundy, A. and Walsh, T. (2000) On the Notion of Interestingness in Automated Mathematical Discovery. *International Journal of Human Computer Studies*, 53(3):351–375.
5. Costabile, M.F., De Angeli, A., Roselli, T., Lanzilotti, R. and Plantamura, P. (2003) Evaluating the Educational Impact of a Tutoring Hypermedia for Children. In *Information Technology in Childhood Education Annual*, Vol. 1, pp. 289–308.
6. Dong, G. and Li, J. (1998) Interestingness of Discovered Association Rules in Terms of Neighborhood-Based Unexpectedness. In Wu, X., Kotagiri, R. and Korb, K. (Eds.), *Proceedings of the Second Pacific-Asia Conference on Knowledge Discovery and Data Mining (PAKDD'98)*, Melbourne, Australia, pp. 72–86.
7. Esposito, F., Licchelli, O. and Semeraro, G. (2004) Discovering Student Models in e-Learning Systems. *Journal of Universal Computer Science*, 10(1):37–47
8. Freyberger, J., Heffernan, N. and Ruiz, C. (2004) Using Association Rules to Guide a Search for Best Fitting Transfer Models of Student Learning. In *Workshop on Analyzing Student-Tutor Interactions Logs to Improve Educational Outcomes at ITS Conference*, pp. 1–10.
9. García, E., Romero, C., Ventura, S. and Calders, T. (2007). Drawbacks and Solutions of Applying Association Rule Mining in Learning Management Systems. In *Proceedings of International Workshop on Applying Data Mining in e-Learning (ADML'07)*, Crete, Greece, pp. 15–25.
10. Ha, S., Bae, S. and Park, S. (2000) Web Mining for Distance Education. In *Proceedings of IEEE International Conference on Management of Innovation and Technology*, Singapore, November 12–15, pp. 715–719.
11. Hamalainen, W., and Vinni, M. (2006) Comparison of Machine Learning Methods for Intelligent Tutoring Systems. In Ikeda, M., Ashley, K. D. and Chan, T.-W. (Eds.), *Proceedings of 8th International Conference in Intelligent Tutoring Systems ITS 2006*, Jhongli, Taiwan, June 26–30, pp. 525–534.
12. Hammouda, K. and Kamel, M. (2006) Data Mining in e-Learning. In: Pierre, S. (Eds.), *e-Learning Networked Environments and Architectures: A Knowledge Processing Perspective*. Springer Book Series: Advanced Information and Knowledge Processing, pp. 1–28.
13. Hilderman, R.J. and Hamilton, H.J. (1999) Heuristic Measures of Interestingness. In Zytkow, J. and Rauch, J. (Eds.), *Proceedings of the Third European Conference on the Principles of Data Mining and Knowledge Discovery (PKDD'99)*, Prague, Czech Republic, pp. 232–241.
14. Hsu, H.H., Chen, C.H. and Tai, W.P. (2003) Towards Error-Free and Personalized Web-Based Courses. In *Proceedings of 7th International Conference on Advanced Information Networking and Applications (AINA'03)*, March 27–29, 2003, Xi'an, China, pp. 99–104.
15. Hussain, F., Liu, H., Suzuki, E. and Lu, H. (2000) Exception Rule Mining with a Relative Interestingness Measure. In *Proceedings of Pacific Asia Conference on Knowledge Discovery in DataBases (PAKDD-2000)*, Kyoto, Japan, April 18–20. LNCS, vol. 1805, pp. 86–97.

16. Hwang, G.J., Hsiao, C.L. and Tseng, C.R. (2003) A Computer-Assisted Approach to Diagnosing Student Learning Problems in Science Courses. *Journal of Information Science and Engineering*, 19:229–248.

17. Jaroszewicz, S. and Simovici, D.A. (2001) A General Measure of Rule Interestingness. In *Proceedings of the 5th European Conference on Principles and Practice of Knowledge Discovery in Databases PKDD 2001*, Freiburg, Germany. LNCS vol. 2168, pp. 253–265.

18. Kay, J., Maisonneuve, N., Yacef, K. and Zaiane, O.R. (2006) Mining Patterns of Events in Students' Teamwork Data. In *Proceedings of Educational Data Mining Workshop at the 8th International Conference on Intelligent Tutoring Systems (ITS 2006)*, Jhongli, Taiwan, pp. 1–8.

19. Klosgen, W. and Zytkow, J. (2002) *Handbook of Data Mining and Knowledge Discovery*. Oxford University Press, New York.

20. Kotsiantis, S. and Kanellopoulos, D. (2006) Association Rules Mining: A Recent Overview. *GESTS International Transactions on Computer Science and Engineering*, 32(1):pp. 71–82.

21. Kumar, A. (2005) Rule-Based Adaptive Problem Generation in Programming Tutors and its Evaluation. In *Proceedings of 12th International Conference on Artificial Intelligence in Education, AI-Ed'2005*, Amsterdam, July 18, pp. 36–44.

22. Loo, K.K. and Cheung, B. (2003) Fuzzy Logic and Data Mining for e-Learning Personalization. In *Proceedings of Conference on Artificial Intelligence and Applications (AIA 2003)*, September 8–10, 2003, Benalmádena, Spain.

23. Lu, J. (2004). Personalized e-Learning Material Recommender System. In *Proceedings of the International Conference on Information Technology for Application*, pp. 374–379.

24. Machado, L.D.S. and Becker, K. (2003) Distance Education: A Web Usage Mining Case Study for the Evaluation of Learning Sites. In *Proceedings of the International Conference on Advanced Learning Technologies (ICALT 2003)*, 9–11 July 2003, Athens, Greece, pp. 360–361.

25. Markellou, P., Mousourouli, I., Spiros, S. and Tsakalidis, A. (2005) Using Semantic Web Mining Technologies for Personalized e-Learning Experiences. In *Proceedings of the International Conference on Web-based Education (WBE 2005)*, February 21–23, Grindelwald, Switzerland, pp. 1–10.

26. Matsui, T. and Okamoto, T. (2003) Knowledge Discovery from Learning History Data and its Effective Use for Learning Process Assessment Under the e-Learning Environment. In C. Crawford et al. (Eds.), *Proceedings of the International Conference on Society for Information Technology and Teacher Education*, pp. 3141–3144, AACE, Chesapeake, VA.

27. Merceron, A. and Yacef, K. (2004) Mining Student Data Captured from a Web-Based Tutoring Tool. *Journal of Interactive Learning Research*, 15(4):319–346.

28. Natarajan, R. and Shekar, B. (2005) Interestingness of Association Rules in Data Mining: Issues Relevant to e-Commerce. *Sadhana – Academy Proceedings in Engineering Sciences*, Vol. 30, Parts 2 and 3, pp. 291–309. Indian Academy of Science.

29. P175B502 (Object oriented programming) module description. Kaunas University of Technology, 2007. Available: http://oras.if.ktu.lt/moduliai/P175B502/

30. Ramli, A.A. (2005) Web Usage Mining Using Apriori Algorithm: UUM Learning Care Portal Case. In *Proceedings of the International Conference on Knowledge Management*, Malaysia, pp. 1–19.

31. Romero, C. and Ventura, S. (2007) Educational Data Mining: A Survey from 1995 to 2005. *Expert Systems with Applications*, 33(1):135–146.

32. Romero, C., Ventura, S. and Bra, P.D. (2004) Knowledge Discovery with Genetic Programming for Providing Feedback to Courseware Author. User Modeling and User-Adapted Interaction: *The Journal of Personalization Research*, 14(5):425–464.

33. RuleQuest (2006) Research Data Mining Tools. Available: http://www.rulequest.com/

34. Sahar, S. (1999) Interestingness via What is Not Interesting. In Chaudhuri, S. and Madigan, D. (Eds.), *Proceedings of 5th International Conference on Knowledge Discovery and Data Mining*, San Diego, CA, USA, pp. 332–336.

35. Shen, R., Han, P., Yang, F., Yang, Q. and Huang, J. (2003) Data Mining and Case-Based Reasoning for Distance Learning. *Journal of Distance Education Technologies*, 1(3):46–58.

36. Tanimoto, S.L. (2007) Improving the Prospects for Educational Data Mining. In *Proceedings of the Workshop on Data Mining for User Modeling, at the 11th International Conference on User Modeling (UM 2007)*, June 25, 2007, Corfu, Greece, pp. 106–110.

37. Tsai, C.J., Tseng, S.S. and Lin, C.Y. (2001) A Two-Phase Fuzzy Mining and Learning Algorithm for Adaptive Learning Environment. In *Proceedings of the International Conference on Computational Science*, San Francisco, CA, USA, May 28–30, 2001. LNCS vol. 2074, pp. 429–438.

38. Wang, F. and Shao, H. (2004) Effective Personalized Recommendation Based on Time-Framed Navigation Clustering and Association Mining. *Expert Systems with Applications*, 27:365–377.

39. Wang, W., Weng, J., Su, J. and Tseng, S. (2004) Learning Portfolio Analysis and Mining in Scorm Compliant Environment. In *Proceedings of 34th Annual ASEE/IEEE Frontiers in Education Conference*, October 23–24, pp. 17–24.

40. Yu, P., Own, C. and Lin, L. (2001) On Learning Behavior Analysis of Web Based Interactive Environment. In *Proceedings of the International Conference on Implementing Curricular Change in Engineering Education (ICCEE)*, Oslo/Bergen, Norway, pp. 1–10.

41. Zaïane, O. (2002) Building a Recommender Agent for e-Learning Systems. In *Proceedings of the International Conference on Computers in Education (ICCE'02)*, December 3–6, 2002, pp. 55–59.

42. Zaïane, O. and Luo, J. (2001) Web Usage Mining for a Better Web-Based Learning Environment. In *Proceedings of the International Conference on advanced technology for education (CATE'01)*, Banff, Alberta, Canada, pp. 60–64.

38

The Automatic Integration of Folksonomies with Taxonomies Using Non-axiomatic Logic

Joe Geldart and Stephen Cummins

Abstract

Cooperative tagging systems such as folksonomies are powerful tools when used to annotate information resources. The inherent power of folksonomies is in their ability to allow casual users to easily contribute ad hoc, yet meaningful, resource metadata without any specialist training. Older folksonomies have begun to degrade due to the lack of internal structure and from the use of many low quality tags. This chapter describes a remedy for some of the problems associated with folksonomies. We introduce a method of automatic integration and inference of the relationships between tags and resources in a folksonomy using non-axiomatic logic. We test this method on the CiteULike corpus of tags by comparing precision and recall between it and standard keyword search. Our results show that non-axiomatic reasoning is a promising technique for integrating tagging systems with more structured knowledge representations.

Keywords Folksonomy · Ontology · Intelligent information systems

1. Introduction

This chapter addresses some limitations inherent in the usage of community-generated tags (or keywords) for electronic resource annotation. Cooperative tagging systems allow their users to annotate resources with short, pithy tags that are relevant to themselves without enforcing a universal vocabulary. This allows users to build up a personal system that facilitates information retrieval as well as allowing searches across all users' tags. The word folksonomy is a portmanteau of the word folk, meaning people, and taxonomy, meaning a system of classification. The word was originally coined by Thomas Vander Wal in August 2004. Folksonomies are a particular type of community tagging system and are essentially comprised of a flat classification system constructed out of the raw tagging data. Each resource is simply classified as being within the classes to which each tag implicitly denotes.

There has been a large increase in the use of folksonomies in recent years; in part this is due to the popularization 'Web 2.0' technologies, of which folksonomies are an example. Folksonomies are often considered as a 'grass-roots' approach to semantic indexing, decentralizing, and democratizing information system organization.

The lack of central control, while an asset in some situations, can lead to problems when the system's users disagree about the tagging of resources. Existing tagging systems treat tags as an all-or-nothing affair with folksonomies based on classical classification. We argue in this chapter that this is partially responsible for the marked deterioration of the quality of large-scale tagging systems.

Joe Geldart and Stephen Cummins • Department of Computer Science, Durham University, Durham, UK.

G.A. Papadopoulos et al. (eds.), *Information Systems Development*, DOI 10.1007/b137171_38,
© Springer Science+Business Media, LLC 2009

Efforts have been made to integrate formal, 'expert' knowledge representations with community-generated folksonomies as part of a solution to the problem of quality. However, current approaches still suffer from the problem of disagreement.

This chapter proposes a solution to the problem of integrating ontological information with folksonomies through the use of a logic with an evidence-based semantics. The main contributions we make are

- An overview of the problem of integration and folksonomy quality (Section 2).
- A proposed solution to this problem using non-axiomatic logic (Section 3).
- Experimental evidence showing the reasoning capabilities of non-axiomatic logic with tagging system data (Sections 4 and 5).

We conclude with a survey of related research and a discussion of future research directions for non-axiomatic tagging systems.

2. The Problem of Integration

Folksonomies are designed to be somewhat resistant to current spamming techniques as they operate as virtual democracies, meaning each tag on a particular resource signifies a single vote [7]. Multiple occurrences of a single tag in a particular resource count as multiple votes and, therefore, increase the recorded value of that particular tag. Usually knowledge representation systems based on folksonomies require a user to have an account in order to contribute to the tagging community. This is an attempt to safeguard against anonymous spammers trying to bias the popularity of particular resources or tags.

However, the older and more popular folksonomy systems have begun to experience problems caused by use of numerous low quality tags during resource annotation. Some of these problems become more apparent when looking at subjects that have commercial relevance where a new form of tag spamming [15, 16] is surfacing.

A problem for traditional tagging systems trying to cope with these issues is that individual tags do not have explicitly defined relationships with each other. That is, there is no explicit classification mechanism between tags within a collaborative tagging system or folksonomy. This leads to further limitations, such as natural language features not being considered in resource searches. For example, the use of plurals, synonyms, and homonyms can change the form of a word and may result in some resources not being retrieved when using standard lexical searches. There is limited amount of literature that addresses the problem of intelligent searching within folksonomies. There are some solutions for the detection and use of natural language features such as homonyms [4]. However, so far only projects that integrate folksonomies with a large natural language ontology such as the WordNet lattice have been able to address them limiting their use to languages where such a lexical resource exists.

The limited ability of computational agents in searching these systems derives from the lack of semantic metadata implicitly defined in folksonomies. This is considered as being one of the main weaknesses of collaborative tagging technologies [9].

One of the most significant issues for the integration of ontological and folksonomic information is that of *disagreement*. Folksonomies are open and tend toward the chaotic with their lack of gatekeepers. This produces a sheer between the pure, formal representation of knowledge in ontologies with necessary and sufficient conditions and the more democratic, evidential approach in tagging systems. While knowledge is presumed to be true and unarguable to the ontologist, the users may disagree over any tag. Bridging this semantic gap is a significant challenge.

In an educational context specifically current folksonomies fail to intelligently represent disagreement between users. In some educational and research disciplines there are various different and often conflicting perspectives on the same subject. These disagreements are often considered valid and indeed valuable to the discipline as a whole. In particular, sociology teaches that learning different theoretical perspectives is fundamental to the field. Even in the physical sciences there are some topics which lack consensus, such as the origins of the universe. The arguments for all theories should be represented in a knowledge management system. A knowledge system that does not cater specifically for the disagreement of its users is surely not a realistic or accurate representation of the knowledge domain. Since folksonomies are simple, flat classification systems they do provide a basic means for representing conflicting tags. However, since the tags have little semantics attached, the folksonomy itself cannot easily identify disagreements to its users; it is left to the users to manually find and identify resources that are tagged with conflicting tags. It is useful for the knowledge management system to identify topics that are contentious or under strong debate to its users, if only to educate the user to the fact that there is a disagreement in that particular topic.

It can be argued that there are very few subjects that have a simple right or wrong (true or false) answer. Allowing concepts to be expressed in different ways and encouraging debates, is considered as being beneficial to one's education. From a knowledge representation perspective there may be cases where disagreement is not desired, but even in these cases we believe that they can be found and handled more efficiently if the knowledge management system is able to automatically detect them and flag them to the user community for discussion. Either way, representing disagreement in large repositories of knowledge, like folksonomies, is an important consideration.

Attempting to integrate the richness of semantic metadata with the ease of use exhibited by folksonomies is not a new concept. There are studies that attempt to do this through using manual and semi-automatic techniques in order to enhance simple tagging-based systems [1, 4, 5]. None of these systems, however, attempt to define a fully automated approach to generating semantic information simply from the tags used in the folksonomy. The focus of these systems is usually on modifying existing folksonomies in order to operate in line with semantic Web or ontology [2] based rules.

By far the most common method of integrating folksonomies with ontological metadata is to require users, at the time of tagging, to also manually position the resource in the ontology [3, 5, 8, 9]. CommonFolks [4] is one such system that is essentially a hybrid of a folksonomy and an ontology; allowing the richer, more structured metadata commonly associated with ontologies to be associated with resources stored in a folksonomy. However, the users must define themselves how the resource relates to other concepts in the WordNet ontology. Techniques exist that speed the whole process up for the users such as making automated ontology suggestions; however, this still requires a human to review them and make corrections, thus requiring manual management and increasing the time overhead. This technique does improve the amount of semantic data recorded but reduces the ease of annotation and still does not specifically cater for disagreements in tags and indeed in relationships between other concepts in the ontology. The resulting decrease in flexibility and speed of adding new resources to the system eliminates many of the advantages of using a folksonomy and will likely adversely affect the likelihood of users participating.

The primary problem with existing hybrid approaches is that there is a change from being a flexible, quick, and easy to use system to being a rigid system, with strict rules and requirements. These systems often require more time and effort from their everyday users in order to be used properly. It is arguably the freedom of expression and ease of tagging resources that makes folksonomies so successful, and any hybrid system should strive to preserve them. The ideal would be to enable a richer metadata for resources to be generated purely from whatever information (tags) the users care to give, thereby making use of what is already being put into the system instead of requiring more work from its users. Providing agents with the ability to perform logical inferences within collaborative tagging systems, given a logic with a semantics appropriate to folksonomies, would bring such systems in line with other more formal mechanisms of resource management, such as ontologies. This chapter takes the position that it is the logic that should be adjusted to match the users' behavior, rather than the users' behavior be changed to match the logic.

3. An Approach to Tagging with Non-axiomatic Logic

As the previous discussion indicated, the main problems with the integration of ontological information with free-form folksonomic information are the flat semantics and potential for conflict of the latter. Previous attempts to integrate ontologies with folksonomies have focused on imposing a clear, universal semantics upon the latter; relegating disagreement to an aberration. As mentioned, this poses unique problems in educational and academic contexts where disagreement must be kept in order to faithfully represent the domain. This chapter, therefore, takes the opposite position; opening ontologies to disagreement using a refined, evidence-based semantics.

A tagging system may be viewed as a collection of asserted pairs, each consisting of a resource and a tag. Each such assertion should have, from a logical perspective, a truth-value which may be used by reasoning mechanisms. Ideally, we want these truth-values to allow a spectrum of belief between true and false and the ability for inference rules to weight assertions by the amount of evidence that backs them. In other words, what we would like is for these truth-values to represent two different things; the degree to which the resource is judged to carry the tag, and the amount of user data which has gone into forming this judgment. A semantics with truth-values defined like this is known as an *evidence-based* semantics. An evidence-based semantics is explicitly partial, making explicit the fact that a user's assignment of truth-values is based upon a limited experience of the world.

In a Boolean truth-functional semantics, such as that used by first-order predicate logic or OWL, truth is taken to be a binary notion. A statement is taken to be either true or false, with no in between state. If a conflict arises between the truth-valuation of the statements of two users, there can be no middle ground and so one or the other of the statements must be thrown away.

Non-axiomatic logic (NAL) is a logic with an evidence-based semantics [12] that operates under an assumption of insufficient knowledge and insufficient resources (AIKIR) [13]; something the authors consider a good fit for the situation of the integration of ontologies and folksonomies. NAL is a term logic, as opposed to a predicate logic, with statements consisting of two terms (a subject and a predicate) linked by one of a small number of statement-forming primitive relations. The most important of these relations is the inheritance relation, which represents a (partial) subclass relationship between the subject and the predicate.

$$S \; - -> \; P \qquad\qquad\qquad (38.1)$$

In (38.1), the term S is the subject while P is the predicate. The arrow represents the inheritance relation. The term S is said to be in the *extension* of P, whereas P is in the *intension* of S. One of the features of NAL is that both extensional and intensional semantics may be represented in a common formalism.

Terms may themselves be built out of smaller parts. NAL defines a number of term-forming operators, generally available in both extensional and intensional forms (which cause different inferences to be made if the term is found in the subject or predicate position of a statement). These operators include intersection, difference, and a product-forming operator that constructs a tuple of other terms. This last operator addresses a common criticism of term logics; their inability to represent arbitrary relations between terms. There are also extensional and intensional image operators that allow statements to be made regarding the components of a product.

NAL also allows statements to be used as terms which, together with independent and dependent variables and implication and equivalence primitive relations, allow higher order knowledge to be encoded; statements about statements. This permits the encoding of arbitrary structural inferences regarding a NAL knowledge base and even the representation of other logics.

The inference rules of NAL are based upon the notion of a syllogism [11]. There are four syllogistic forms: deduction, induction, abduction, and exemplification. The first is familiar to most introductions to logic, but the last three are maybe less so. Induction is the process of generalization from particulars, while its dual, abduction, produces particulars from generals. Exemplification is the dual to deduction and finds more specific terms from general ones. The combination of these four forms of reasoning in one logical formalism provides a powerful tool. From particular tagging patterns, NAL may be used to find relationships among tags by induction and, applying such relationships via abduction. Particular hierarchies of tags can be used through deduction and exemplification. With the compound term constructors of NAL, complex classes (such as the rough equivalents on NAL terms to intersection, union and difference from set theory and many knowledge representation formalisms) may be automatically constructed. With the addition of products and higher order sentences, arbitrary relational knowledge may be represented in the same formalism allowing, for example, the ability to develop refined knowledge based on resource metadata. Such a combination of these forms of reasoning is only possible in a semantics which allows assertions to be revised in a balanced fashion as they are rarely completely accurate.

Due to NAL's AIKIR assumption, a conventional reasoning algorithm would be inappropriate. NAL, therefore, uses a form of anytime reasoner, rather than a proof-theoretic or tableaux one, which is based upon this assumption. The non-axiomatic reasoning system (NARS) is explicitly finite and partial. Rather than attempting to reason over the entire knowledge base simultaneously, it works on tasks (such as input judgments or queries) in a prioritized, probabilistic fashion. The finiteness of the reasoner's memory means that tasks or beliefs with low utility (those which are used very infrequently, or these which have not produced useful results) are forgotten when the system reaches its capacity limits. In this way, not only NARS avoids the issues of knowledge explosion which would otherwise result from having such a powerful and general inference process, but also it should cope well with poor tagging. Only resources and tags which are well linked by inferencing and frequently referred to will persist. The system's judgment of 'well linked' will depend on the contents of its background knowledge, and the system should become more resilient to such poor tagging as it gathers and infers more background knowledge.

The above is, necessarily, only a very brief introduction to the ideas behind NAL and NARS. The interested reader is recommended to read [14] for a thorough introduction to the logic, its reasoning algorithm, and its philosophical inspirations and implications.

4. Experiment

In order to test the efficacy of NAL as a logical basis for tagging systems, we evaluated it against a simple, keyword-based system as a control. The evaluation criteria used are a measurement of the precision and recall of our solution in comparison with existing systems. This allows objective analysis of whether or not the solution presented in this chapter improved the quality of searching in folksonomy-based systems.

The reasoner for the NAL-based tagging system is the open-source OpenNARS reasoner developed originally by Pei Wang and later converted by Joe Geldart into a reusable library. The control was written by Stephen Cummins and uses simple keyword indexing of resources.

The sample data for our experiment comes from CiteULike, a Web-based bibliography manager. CiteULike provides a complete corpus of anonymizsed tagging data extracted from its database in the form of a comma-separated variable file. The file contains a row for each tag attached to each resource identified by article ID. Each row contains a field for the article ID and tag, together with a timestamp and anonymized user identifier. We prepared this data by reducing it to just the article ID and tag, and filtering out stop words, commonly used words which are statistically insignificant on their own for purposes of semantic content analysis. The list of the stop words we used is included in appendix of [6]. We further reduced the size of the corpus to 100 articles, randomly chosen but kept constant throughout the experiments.

The metrics chosen as useful indicators of system performance are precision and recall. Precision is defined as the fraction of the search result that is considered as being relevant for a particular query. Recall is considered as the ability of a particular search system to retrieve all relevant resources in its search results. This metric is typically difficult to measure in large search systems due to the fact that one requires knowledge of all the results retrieved as well as all of the results not retrieved. However, for the purposes of this chapter, we shall only be working with relatively small sets of data in order to demonstrate the concept.

We tested the two systems by comparing their precision and recall under a range of conditions. The precision and recall were calculated by dividing the tagging data in the corpus into two disjoint sets: input and test. The former set was used as input to the tagging systems, providing data about the resources. Queries consisting of random sets of tags were composed using both sets, and the precision and recall calculated. A system with high values for these metrics under this test would be able to predict the human-generated tags with high accuracy.

The experimental conditions consisted of varying the number of reasoning steps taken before querying (essentially, the length of the settling phase used to integrate the data with the reasoner) and the proportional size of the set of input data compared to the set of all data. It was expected that the OpenNARS-based reasoner would show positive correlation of both precision and recall with these conditions.

As NAL has an essentially different notion of membership of a result to a query result set than that of the classical-classification control, a notion of fuzzy cardinality was used for the precision and recall calculations. The two-component truth-value obtained from OpenNARS was reduced to a one-component expectation value, as described in [10]. The sum of these expectation values across the result set was used to define the fuzzy cardinality. For the control, the expectation value for each result was 1, capturing the classical notion of absolute classification. Such a calculation of precision and recall does slightly favor the classical system as each result from the NAL system counts for less (an expectation of 1 being impossible in NAL) and the results should be read with that in mind.

5. Evaluation

The experiment was run over a range of 11 settling lengths (from 0 to 100 in increments of 10 steps, then from 100 to 900 inclusive with increments of 100) and 10 different data proportion sizes. The results were then processed to produce statistics on the recall and precision rates of the two tagging systems.

The statistics are shown in Table 38.1. As can be seen, the NARS-based system shows (as compared to the control) a significantly higher mean recall rate but a significantly lower mean precision rate (across all conditions.) This, we believe, shows both the promise and the problems associated with the use of NARS in a tagging environment.

Table 38.1. Precision and recall statistics

		Control		OpenNARS
Precision	Mean	0.429	Mean	0.017
	Variance	0.245	Variance	0.002
Recall	Mean	0.393	Mean	0.681
	Variance	0.222	Variance	0.198

There were two main contributing factors to the low precision of the NARS-based tagging system. First, the current version of OpenNARS (as of April 2008) was originally designed to be used as a stand-alone Java applet, as opposed to as a reasoner library. This has made the creation of an interface between the experimental harness and the reasoner fraught with difficulties, particularly with the appropriate decoding of statements from the reasoner. The authors decided to err toward overproduction so that they might manually inspect interesting inferences from the system. The authors, having learnt from this experience, are working on a modular rewrite of OpenNARS which will allow for its use in other information systems. Second, the data set we used consisted simply of a list of resource and tag pairs which we encoded as inheritance statements with frequency of 1. A more realistic system would likely include background knowledge (either through explicit inclusion of ontological information or simply by long-term inferencing on a larger set of taggings) which would reduce the judged truth of more spurious inferred taggings. A third possible, and we feel more interesting, reason for the low precision is that OpenNARS is generating entirely novel taggings which have not been expressed by any user of CiteULike. A check of some of the inferences produced has shown a large number of correct (to the authors) taggings which are not found in the corpus. This raises a question of the development of appropriate testing techniques for uncertain, intelligent systems, which the authors leave open for the moment.

The data were also analyzed to find the correlation coefficients of the precision and recall to the experimental conditions. This is shown in Table 38.2. As can be seen, there is a very weak (anti-)correlation between the settling period and both precision and recall, for both reasoners. The very weak anti-correlation between precision and settling time for the NARS-based reasoner could be taken as a first sign of novel generation. This also points to a strategy for detecting novel generation; calculate their (inverse) correlation with the length of the settling period. As may also be seen, recall for NARS is most affected by the data size and to a degree greater than the control. We interpret this as an indication of the inherent growth of inferences as compared to input knowledge.

Table 38.2. Correlation coefficients

Control	Settling	Data size	Precision	Recall
Settling	1.0	6.551	0.0098	0.018
Data size	6.551	1.0	0.270	0.263
Precision	0.0098	0.270	1.0	0.961
Recall	0.018	0.263	0.961	1.0

OpenNARS	Settling	Data size	Precision	Recall
Settling	1.0	6.551	−0.011	0.059
Data size	6.551	1.0	−0.062	0.317
Precision	−0.011	0.270	1.0	0.193

6. Conclusions

This chapter has outlined a method of inferring ontological information from the data already contained in a fully functional folksonomy. Our research indicates that NARS can be used to generate semantic relationships intelligently using nothing more than user-annotated tags as metadata. Therefore, no more information is required from the casual users of the folksonomy in order to use this system. NARS is also able to make inferences based on the information given by users and suggest meaningful tags for resources stored in the system.

The experiment outlined in this chapter has shown that NARS can maintain an active knowledge representation of a folksonomy and make inferences based on its contents. In addition, our results have shown that by using NARS as the backend reasoner for folksonomy searches we yield an improved recall; albeit at the expense of precision. However, we feel that the low precision may be improved, as discussed previously.

With further investigation, the new metadata suggested by the reasoner could be evaluated by a human user in order to determine whether the precision is as low as our experiments would seem to suggest. It is entirely possible that the reasoner has determined that a given resource should be annotated with a tag that a user has yet to devise. Subjective validation of tag quality from a group of users can determine whether or not the tag suggested by the reasoner is valid and of high quality. As already mentioned, the correlation of inferencing and settling time provides another possible test as to whether the changes of behavior of a system such as NARS are due to the processes of inference. As regards the problem of low quality tags degrading the performance of folksonomy searches, NARS is able to 'cleanup' or forget unpopular or less useful tags from the global search space. By having a separate repository used to store individual users' tags for particular 'favorite' resources, the personalization of folksonomy searching could be merged with a better, more intelligent global search mechanism in a fully automated way. This would maintain the personalization element of folksonomy systems and still improve the quality of the metadata shared between users.

The ability for NARS to represent disagreement suggests that the approach outlined in this chapter would be useful to various disciplines where disagreement may be prominent or desirable. Such domains include education, academia, and the open Web, all of which lack a central authority to impose a single classification upon the world.

For the authors, the real potential with the use of NARS lies with its ability to deal with highly structured yet uncertain information such that disagreement and other forms of conflict and agreement can be handled subtly through the use of evidence measures. A more robust, rational Web would allow for more automation and less manual intervention by users. As such, we feel that NAL is a good candidate representation language for the semantics of the Web.

References

1. Al-Khalifa, H. S., and Davis, H. C. (2006). *FolksAnnotation: A Semantic Metadata Tool for Annotating Learning Resources Using Folksonomies and Domain Ontologies.* In Proceedings of The Second International IEEE Conference on Innovations in Information Technology, Dubai, UAE, November 17–21, pp 1–5.
2. Angeletou, S., Sabou, M., Specia, L., and Motta, E. (2007). *Bridging the Gap Between Folksonomies and the Semantic Web: An Experience Report.* In Proceedings of the 4th European Semantic Web Conference (ESWC 2007).
3. Auer, S., and Dietzold, S. (2006). *OntoWiki: A Tool for Social, Semantic Collaboration.* In Cruz, I., Decker, S., Allemang, D., Preist, C., Schwabe, D., Mika, P., Uschold, M. and Aroyo, L. (eds.) Proceedings of the International Semantic Web Conference 2006, Springer Verlag.
4. Bateman, S., Brooks, C., and McCalla, G. (2006). *Collaborative Tagging Approaches for Ontological Metadata in Adaptive ELearning.* Paper presented at the Fourth International Workshop on Applications of Semantic Web Technologies for E-Learning, Dublin, Ireland, 20th June.
5. Bateman, S., Farzan, R., Brusilovsky, P., and McCalla, G. (2006). *OATS: The Open Annotation and Tagging System.* Paper presented at the Third Annual International Scientific Conference of the Learning Object Repository Research Network.
6. Cummins, S., and Geldart, J. (2008). Stop words file. Retrieved 29th April, 2008, from http://www.dur.ac.uk/s.a.cummins/Research/ISD2008/stop_words.txt.
7. Gruber, T. (2007). Ontology of Folksonomy: A Mash-Up of Apples and Oranges. *International Journal on Semantic Web and Information Systems,* 3(1), 1–11.
8. Laniado, D., Eynard, D., and Colombetti, M. (2007). *Using WordNet to turn a Folksonomy into a Hierarchy of Concepts.* Paper presented at the Semantic Web Applications and Perspectives (SWAP).
9. Specia, L., and Motta, E. (2007). *Integrating Folksonomies with the Semantic Web.* Paper presented at the 4th European Semantic Web Conference 2007.
10. Wang, P. (1995). *Non-Axiomatic Reasoning System: Exploring the Essence of Intelligence.* Indiana University.
11. Wang, P. (2000). Unified Inference in Extended Syllogism. *Applied Logic Series,* 117–129.
12. Wang, P. (2005). Experience-Grounded Semantics: A Theory for Intelligent Systems. *Cognitive Systems Research,* 6(4), 282–302.
13. Wang, P. (2006a). The Logic of Intelligence. *Artificial General Intelligence,* 31–62.
14. Wang, P. (2006b). *Rigid Flexibility: The Logic of Intelligence* (Vol. 34), Springer.
15. Weinberger, D. (2005). *Tagging and Why it Matters*: Harvard University - Berkman Center for Internet and Society, Publication No. 2005–07.
16. Xu, Z., Fu, Y., Mao, J., and Su, D. (2006). *Towards the Semantic Web: Collaborative Tag Suggestions.* Paper presented at the 15th International World Wide Web Conference (WWW 2006).

39

Using Rules in an 'Intelligent' Information Retrieval Environment

Gian Piero Zarri

Abstract

The availability of a powerful 'rule system' is an essential requirement for any implemented methodology intended to make use of querying/inferencing techniques according to a knowledge-based approach. In this chapter, we will supply some information about the rule system of NKRL; NKRL (Narrative Knowledge Representation Language) is a powerful information retrieval environment designed to deal with non-fictional 'narratives' of an economic interest. Rules in this context correspond to high-level reasoning paradigms like the search for causal relationships or the use of analogical techniques. Given (i) the conceptual complexity of these paradigms and (ii) the sophistication of the underlying representation language, these rules cannot be implemented in a (weak) 'inference by inheritance' style but must follow a powerful 'inference by resolution' approach.

Keywords Knowledge representation · Knowledge-based systems · Inferences

1. Introduction

The inference techniques represent an essential component of the so-called knowledge-based systems (KBSs). In KBSs – see, e.g. [3, pp.105–170] – these techniques range between two possible basic forms:

- *Rule-based inference techniques making use of* 'inference by resolution'. Within this category, we can distinguish between the 'true' logic programming techniques and the simplest 'production rules' approaches used, e.g. in the expert systems shells of the 1970–1980.
- *Object-based inference techniques making use, basically, of 'inference by inheritance'.* A particular class of inheritance-based procedures, particularly fashionable today, are the 'description logics' [1]. These logics constitute the theoretical basis of the W3C (World Wide Web Committee) languages (or *Semantic Web* languages) like OWL-DL [2].

In its most simple formulation ('chain rule'), the resolution principle can be reduced to an *inference rule* expressed as

$$\text{From } (A \vee B) \text{ and } (\neg A \vee C), \text{ deduce that } (B \vee C). \tag{39.1}$$

The three disjunctions that appear in (39.1) are particularly important types of well-formed formulas (*wff*) of first-order predicate calculus that take the name of '*clauses*'. From (39.1), it is then evident that the resolution process, when applicable, is an *inference process that takes a pair of parent wffs in the form of clauses to produce a new, derived clause* (the 'resolvent'), on condition that one of these clauses contains a

Gian Piero Zarri • Virthualis, Politecnico di Milano, Milano, Italia.

G.A. Papadopoulos et al. (eds.), *Information Systems Development*, DOI 10.1007/b137171_39,
© Springer Science+Business Media, LLC 2009

'*literal*' (atomic formula), ¬A, which is the exact negation of one of the original literals. The resolution principle was originally introduced by J.A. Robinson in an automatic theorem-proving context. When used in this context, it consists then in a form of *proof by contradiction* based on the assumption that, if a theorem follows from its axioms, *the axioms and the negation of the theorem cannot be simultaneously true*. Unification is a key technique in the theorem-proving approaches that make use of the resolution principle.

Logic programming concerns a particular development of the resolution principle approach. It consists of a programming style based on writing programs as *sets of clauses* that have both (i) a *declarative meaning* as descriptive statements about entities and relationships proper to a given domain and (ii) a *procedural meaning* by being executable by an interpreter. The procedural meaning is based mainly on the original resolution principle. As in theorem proving, its central operation is represented then by *unification* involving the use of pattern-matching algorithms. In a logic programming context, clauses are written in general as *implications*. Taking into account that, see (39.1) above, a clause is, in general, *a disjunction of atomic formulas and of negations of atomic formulas*, and making use of logical equivalences like the two de Morgan's laws and the so-called 'contrapositive law' [3, p. 112], a clause can then be written as

$$A_1 A_2, \cdots, A_m \leftarrow B_1, B_2, \ldots, B_n, \quad m, n \leq 0. \tag{39.2}$$

In (39.2), B_1, B_2, ... , B_n are the *joint* conditions of the implication (in this case, the 'comma' connective has the meaning of '*logical and*') and A_1, A_2, ... , A_m are the *alternative* conclusions of this implication (the 'comma' has here the meaning of '*logical or*'). Formula (39.2) is particularly important for at least two reasons:

- *This notation is equivalent to that used for the 'production rules' introduced in symbolic logic by Emil Post.* This notation means that, if a set of different conditions $B_1, B_2, \ldots, B_n$ (the '*antecedent*' of the rule) are all verified, they imply a set of alternative conclusions $A_1, A_2, \ldots, A_m$ (the '*consequent*' of the rule). Production rules constitute the basis of all the *forward-chaining/backward-chaining* rule-based systems (e.g. the expert systems).
- *When* (39.2) *is written as* $A \leftarrow B_1, B_2, \ldots , B_n$ *with* $n \geq 0$, *we obtain the 'Horn clauses' (named after Alfred Horn, who first investigated their properties)*. Horn clauses represent, then, a particular form of implication that contains at most one conclusion. Restriction to Horn clauses is then *conceptually equivalent to disallowing the presence of disjunctions in the 'conclusion' part of the clauses*. Horn clauses are used, e.g. in well-known logic programming languages like PROLOG and DATALOG.

'Inference by inheritance' is a reasoning paradigm *orthogonal with respect to the rule/logic programming paradigm*, popularized in the computer science domain by the object-oriented programming, is normally used in Artificial Intelligence to set up *well-formed hierarchies of concepts (ontologies)*. These are structured as *inheritance hierarchies* making use of the IsA link: when interpreted as (IsA C_2 C_1) – assuming then IsA as a relationship among *concepts* – its semantic reading states that concept C_2 is a *specialization* of the more general concept C_1. In other terms, C_1 subsumes C_2. This assertion can be expressed in logical form as

$$\forall x (C_2(x) \rightarrow C_1(x)). \tag{39.3}$$

Equation (39.3) says that, if any elephant_ (C_2) IsA mammal_ (C_1), and if CLYDE_ is an elephant_, then CLYDE_ is also a mammal_.

In all the *inheritance-based knowledge representation languages* – see, e.g. description logics – 'reasoning' consists then, essentially, in *executing classification operations (by automatically finding the correct position of a concept within an ontology) making use of the* 'subsumption' *principle*, see (39.3). It is possible, in fact, to show that other 'reasoning' operations typical of these languages like 'consistency checking' can be reduced to subsumption. Important theoretical and practical problems derive from the fact that, to be practically useful, concepts in an ontology cannot be simple defined by a conceptual label C_i and the IsA relationships with other concepts as in (39.3), but must also include a 'description' where their 'properties' (roles) are defined. In a modern description logics language as OWL-DL, for example, descriptions are built up making use of 'constructors' like owl:oneOf (some classes may be described by enumeration of the individuals that make up the class), owl:hasValue (a property is required to have a given individual as value), owl:disjointWith (see the classes Man and Woman), owl:unionOf, owl:complementOf, owl:inter-sectionOf. The presence of the descriptions *causes difficulties with respect to the automatic calculation of the subsumption relationships for all the inheritance-based languages.* For example, OWL-DL – like all the other inheritance-based knowledge representation languages – must introduce some *constraints* to give rise to systems that are 'complete' (all the possible deductions are computable) and 'decidable' (all the computations will be executed in finite, linear or polynomial, time, avoiding then any complexity problem of the NP-hard, co-NP-hard and PSPACE-complete, etc., type).

Independently, however, from the above 'tractability' problems, it is evident that the 'inference by inheritance' reasoning paradigm is *weaker* than the 'inference by resolution' one given that, at the difference of this last, *it does not produce actually any new knowledge from the pre-existing one.* This explains why the *native* reasoning mechanisms of the OWL-like languages (Semantic Web languages) are *quite limited* and reduced in practice to offer some form of support for building up 'standard' ontologies like (i) checking the *consistency* of classes/concepts (i.e. determining whether a class can have any instances) and (ii) calculating the *subsumption hierarchy* (i.e. arranging the classes according to their generic/specific relationships). To do this, the W3C scholars have to their disposal several OWL-compatible 'reasoners' like RACER, Pellet or FaCT++.

The interest of being able to make use of 'rules' *in the* 'resolution principle' *style also in an inheritance approach context* has been long since recognized. A pioneer and well-known work in this respect is CARIN [6]. However, building up 'true' rule systems *in a strict W3C languages (OWL, RDF(S)) environment* is a really complex problem. In fact, we can note that, (i), on the one hand, the *lack of the notion of 'variable' in OWL* makes it impossible to rely on this language in its 'native' form to build up 'real' inference engines for rule processing, and (ii) on the other and, *no support for rules and rule processing* has been introduced in the standard descriptions of these languages at the time of their conception. The consequence is that the whole *Semantic Web Rules domain* seems to be in a *very early state of development*, see also [8] in this context. To give only an example, an *operational* inference engine able to make, *directly*, a *full use of SWRL* – SWRL [5] constitutes now a sort of 'standard' in the Semantic Web Rules domain – seems not yet to exist. The 'normal' strategy for executing the SWRL rules is then to make use of 'external' rule engines like Jess or Algernon. This can be done through, e.g. the SWRLJessTab, a plug-in of the Protégé-OWL plug-in and after having separately installed the Jess rule engine.

2. A Rule System for 'Intelligent' Information Retrieval

2.1. Some Information about NKRL

NKRL (Narrative Knowledge Representation Language), see [7, 8, 9] deals with *(multimedia) non-fictional narratives of an economic interest.* These correspond to information embodied into corporate memory documents, news stories, normative and legal texts, medical (or financial, cadastral, administrative) records, many intelligence messages, surveillance videos or visitor logs, actuality photos and video fragments for newspapers and magazines, elearning and cultural heritage material (text, image, video, sound . . .), etc. All these sorts of 'non-fictional narratives' concern, in practice, the *description of spatially and temporally characterized 'events' that relate, at some level of abstraction, the behaviour or the state of some real-life 'actors'* (characters, personages, etc.). These try to attain a specific result, experience particular situations, manipulate some (concrete or abstract) materials, send or receive messages, buy, sell, deliver, etc.

NKRL innovates with respect to the standard ontological paradigm by associating with the usual, 'binary' ontology of concepts (called HClass, Hierarchy of Classes, in NKRL) an 'ontology of events' (a hierarchy of *templates*, HTemp(lates)). HTemp is then a new sort of *hierarchical structure* where the nodes, the templates, *correspond to n-ary structures.* Instead of using, in fact, the traditional *object (class, concept)*

– attribute – value organization, templates are *combinations of quadruples* connecting together the *symbolic name* of the template, a *predicate* (BEHAVE, EXIST, EXPERIENCE, etc.) and the *arguments* of the predicate (a simple HClass concept, or of a structured association of concepts) introduced by named relations, the *roles* (SUBJ(ect), OBJ(ect), SOURCE, etc.). The quadruples have in common the 'name' and 'predicate' components. Denoting then with L_i the symbolic label identifying a template, with P_j the predicate used in the template, with R_k the generic role and with a_k the corresponding argument, the NKRL core data structure for templates has the following general format:

$$(L_i(P_j(R_1a_1)(R_2a_2)\cdots(R_na_n))). \qquad (39.4)$$

Templates correspond formally to *generic classes of elementary events* like 'move a physical object', 'be present in a place', 'produce a service', 'send/receive a message'. When a *particular* event pertaining to one of these general classes must be represented, *the corresponding template is 'instantiated' to produce what, in the NKRL's jargon, is called a 'predicative occurrence'*, see [7]. To represent, e.g. a very simple narrative like: 'British Telecom will offer its customers a pay-as-you-go (payg) Internet service in autumn 1998', we must select firstly the template corresponding to 'supply a service to someone', represented in the upper part of Table 39.1. This is a specialization (see the 'father' code) of the particular MOVE template corresponding to 'transfer of resources to someone'. In a template, the arguments of the predicate (the a_k terms in (39.4)) are represented by *variables with associated constraints* – which are expressed as *concepts or combinations of concepts* ('expansions') using, in both cases, the terms of the HClass standard 'ontology of concepts'.

Table 39.1. Deriving a predicative occurrence from a template.

---

name: Move:TransferOfService
father: Move:TransferToSomeone
position: 4.24
NL description: 'Transfer or Supply a Service to Someone'

MOVE	SUBJ	*var1*: [*var2*]
	OBJ	*var3*
	[SOURCE	*var4*: [*var5*]]
	BENF	*var6*: [*var7*]
	[MODAL	*var8*]
	[TOPIC	*var9*]
	[CONTEXT	*var10*]
	{[modulators]}	

var1, var4, var6 = human_being_or_social_body
var2, var5, var7 = geographical_location
var3 = service_
var8 = process_, sector_specific_activity
var9 = sortal_concept
var10 = situation_

c1) MOVE	SUBJ	BRITISH_TELECOM
	OBJ	payg_internet_service
	BENF	(SPECIF customer_ BRITISH-TELECOM)
	date-1:	after-1-september-1998
	date-2:	

When deriving then a predicative occurrence (an instance of a template) like c1 in Table 39.1, the role fillers must conform to the constraints of the father-template. For example, BRITISH_TELECOM is an *individual* instance of the HClass *concept* company_: this last is a specialization of human_being_or_ social_body. payg_internet_service is a specialization of service_, specific term of social_activity, etc.

About 150 templates are permanently inserted into HTemp: this 'ontology of events' corresponds then to a sort of 'catalogue' of narrative formal structures that are very easy to customize to derive the new templates that could be needed for a particular application. This approach is particularly advantageous for practical applications, and it implies, in particular, that (i) a system-builder does not have to create himself the structural knowledge needed to describe the events proper to a (sufficiently) large class of narrative documents; (ii) it becomes easier to secure the reproduction or the sharing of previous results.

What expounded until now illustrates the NKRL solutions to the problem of representing 'elementary (simple) events'. To deal with those 'connectivity phenomena' that arise when *several elementary events* are connected through causality, goal, indirect speech, etc. links, the basic NKRL knowledge representation tools have been complemented by more complex mechanisms. These make use of *second-order structures* created through the *reification* of the conceptual labels of the predicative occurrences, see, e.g. [7] for some details.

2.2. General Principles about 'Reasoning' in NKRL

Reasoning in NKRL ranges from the *direct questioning* of a knowledge base of narratives represented according to the NKRL format – by means of *search patterns* that unify information in the base thanks to the use of a *Filtering Unification Module (Fum)* – to *high-level inference procedures*. These last make use of the richness of the representation system to automatically establish 'interesting' relationships among the narrative items stored in the base and/or the 'personages' mentioned within them. Given (i) the conceptual complexity of these reasoning techniques and (ii) the sophistication of the underlying representation language, the high-level inference procedures implemented in NKRL – a very detailed paper on this topic is [8] – cannot be limited to the use of 'weak' inference paradigms in the 'inference by inheritance' style. They must use, instead, *powerful 'rules' implemented according to the 'inference by resolution' techniques.*

The NKRL rules are characterized by the following general properties:

- *Using a slight different format from that used in* (39.2), *all the NKRL high-level inference rules can be conceived as implications of the type:*

$$X \text{ iff } Y_1 \text{ and } Y_2 \ldots \text{ and } Y_n. \tag{39.5}$$

- In (39.5), *X* is a *predicative occurrence or a search pattern* and $Y_1 \ldots Y_n$ – the NKRL translation of the *'reasoning steps'* that make up the rule – correspond to *partially instantiated templates*. They include then, see the upper part of Table 39.1 above, *explicit variables* of the form var_i.
- *According to the usual conventions of logic/rule programming (resolution principle), the NKRL InferenceEngine understands then each implication as a procedure.* This reduces *'problems'* of the form *X* to a *succession of 'sub-problems'* of the form Y_1 and $\ldots Y_n$.
- *Each Y_i is interpreted in turn as a procedure call that try to convert – using, in case, backtracking procedures – Y_i into (at least) a successful search pattern p_i.* These last should be able to unify one or several of the occurrences c_j of the NKRL knowledge base.
- *The success of the unification operations of the pattern p_i derived from Y_i means that the 'reasoning step' represented by Y_i has been validated. InferenceEngine continues, then, its work trying to validate the reasoning step corresponding to the sub-problem Y_{i+1}.*
- *In line with the presence of the operator 'and' in (39.5), the implication represented by (39.5) is fully validated iff all the reasoning steps $Y_1, Y_2, \ldots, Y_n$ are validated.*
- All the unification operations p_i/c_j make use only of the unification functions supplied by the filtering unification module (Fum) already mentioned. Apart from being used for the direct questioning operations, Fum constitutes as well, therefore, the 'inner core' of *InferenceEngine*.

NKRL high-level inference procedures concern *mainly* two classes of rules, 'transformations' and 'hypotheses' [8].

2.3. Some Additional Details

Let us consider, e.g. the 'transformations'. These rules try to 'adapt', from a *semantic* point of view, a search pattern p_i that 'failed' (that was unable to find an unification within the knowledge base) to the *real contents* of this base making use of a sort of 'analogical reasoning'. In a transformation context, the 'head' X of formula (39.5) is then represented by a search pattern, p_i. The transformation rules try to *automatically 'transform'* p_i into one or more *different* $p_1, p_2, \ldots, p_n$ that *are not strictly 'equivalent' but only 'semantically close'* to the original one. For example, let us suppose that, in the context of a recent NKRL application about 'Southern Philippine terrorism', see [9], we ask: 'Search for the existence of links between ObL (a well-known 'terrorist') and Abubakar Abdurajak Janjalani, the leader of the Abu Sayyaf' group (a separatist group in Southern Philippines)'. In the absence of a direct answer, the corresponding search pattern can be transformed into: 'Search for the attestation of the transfer of economic/financial items between the two'. This could lead to retrieve: 'During 1998/1999, Abubakar Abdurajak Janjalani has received an undetermined amount of money from ObL through an intermediate agent'.

For clarity's sake, it can be useful to denote the transformation rules as made up of a *left-hand side*, the 'antecedent' – i.e. the formulation, in search pattern format, of the 'query' to be transformed – and one or more *right-hand sides*, the 'consequent(s)' – the NKRL representation(s) of one or more queries (search patterns) to be substituted for the given one. Denoting, then, with A, the antecedent and with Cs, all the possible consequents, a transformation rule can be expressed as

$$A(var_i) \Rightarrow Cs(var_j), \quad var_i \subseteq var_j. \tag{39.6}$$

With respect, then, to formula (39.5) above, X coincides now with A – operationally, a *search pattern* – while the reasoning steps $Y_1, Y_2, \ldots, Y_n$ are used to produce the *search pattern(s) Cs to be used in place of A*. The restriction $var_i \subseteq var_j$ – all the variables declared in the antecedent A *must also appear* in Cs accompanied, in case, by *additional variables* – has been introduced to assure the logical congruence of the rules.

The 'transformation arrow' of (39.6), '$\Rightarrow$', has a *double meaning*:

- *Operationally speaking, the arrow indicates the direction of the transformation.* The original search pattern (which is a specialization of the left-hand side A of the transformation rule) is then *removed* and *replaced* by one or several new search patterns obtained through the updating, using the parameters of the original pattern, of the right-hand side Cs.
- *From a logical/semantic point of view, we assume that between the information retrieved through Cs and the information we wanted to obtain through an instantiation of A there is a sort of implication relationship.* Normally, this relationship denotes solely a possible (a *weak*) implication.

More formal details are given, e.g. in [7]. A representation of the above 'financial transfer' transformation is reproduced in Table 39.2. Note that the left-hand side (antecedent) of this transformation corresponds to a partial instantiation of the template Behave:FavourableConcreteMutual that is routinely used to represent into NKRL format a (positive) mutual behaviour among two or more entities. Many of the transformation rules are characterized by the simple format of Table 39.2 implying only one 'consequent'. This is not true in general: examples of 'multi-consequent transformations' can be found in [8] – and in Table 39.4 below.

With respect now to the *hypothesis rules*, these allow us to build up automatically a sort of 'causal explanation' for a narrative information (a predicative occurrence c_j) retrieved within a NKRL knowledge base using *Fum* and a search pattern in a querying–answering mode. In a hypothesis context, the 'head' X of formula (39.5) is then represented by a predicative occurrence, c_j. Accordingly, the 'reasoning steps' Y_i of (5) – called 'condition schemata' in a hypothesis context – *must all be satisfied* (for each of them, at least one of the corresponding search patterns p_i must find a successful unification with the predicative occurrences of the base) *in order that the set of $c_1, c_2, \ldots, c_n$ predicative occurrences retrieved in this way can be interpreted as a context/causal explanation of the original occurrence c_j*. For example, to mention a 'classic'

Table 39.2.   A simple example of 'transformation' rule.

t1)	BEHAVE	SUBJ	(COORD1 var1 var2)	⇒	RECEIVE	SUBJ	var2
		OBJ	(COORD1 var1 var2)			OBJ	var4
						MODAL	var3
						SOURCE	var1

var1	=	human_being_or_social_body
var2	=	human_being_or_social_body
var3	=	business_agreement, mutual_relationship
var4	=	economic/financial_entity

To verify the existence of a relationship or of a business agreement between two (or more) people, try to see if one of these people has received a 'financial entity' (e.g. money) from the other.

NKRL example, let us suppose we have directly retrieved, in a querying–answering mode, an information like: 'Pharmacopeia, an US biotechnology company, has received 64,000,000 dollars from the German company Schering in connection with an R&D activity' that corresponds then to c_j. We can then be able to automatically construct, using a 'hypothesis' rule, a sort of 'causal explanation' of this event by retrieving in the knowledge base information like (i) 'Pharmacopeia and Schering have signed an agreement concerning the production by Pharmacopeia of a new compound' (c_1) and (ii) 'in the framework of the agreement previously mentioned, Pharmacopeia has actually produced the new compound' (c_2).

2.4. Integrating the Two Inference Modes of NKRL

In Table 39.3, we give the informal description of the reasoning steps ('condition schemata') that, making use of the hypothesis tools, must be validated to prove that a generic 'kidnapping' corresponds, in reality, to a more precise 'kidnapping for ransom' environment. When many reasoning steps must be *simultaneously* validated, as usual in a hypothesis context, a failure is always possible. To overcome this problem – and, at the same time, discover all the possible *implicit information* associated with the original data – the two inferencing modes, transformation and hypotheses, can also be used in an *integrated way*, see again [8]. In practice, we make use of 'transformations' within a 'hypothesis' inferencing environment. This means that, whenever a 'search pattern' is derived from a 'condition schema' of a hypothesis to implement, using *Fum*, one of the steps of the reasoning process, we can use it 'as it is' – i.e. as originally coded when the inference rule has been built up – but also in a *'transformed' form* if the appropriate transformation rules exist within the system.

Making use of transformations, the hypothesis represented in an informal way in Table 39.3 becomes, in practice, *potentially equivalent* to the hypothesis of Table 39.4. For example, the proof that the kidnappers are part of a terrorist group or separatist organization (reasoning step Cond1 of Table 39.3) can be now obtained *indirectly*, transformation T3, by checking whether they are members of a specific subset of this group/organization. Note that transformations T2 and T6 imply only one step of reasoning, whereas all the residual transformations are 'multi-consequent'.

Table 39.3.   Inference steps for the 'kidnapping for ransom' hypothesis.

(Cond1)	The kidnappers are part of a separatist movement or of a terrorist organization.
(Cond2)	This separatist movement or terrorist organization currently practices ransom kidnapping of particular categories of people.
(Cond3)	In particular, executives or assimilated categories are concerned.
(Cond4)	It can be proved that the kidnapped is really a businessperson or assimilated.

Table 39.4. 'Kidnapping' hypothesis in the presence of transformations concerning the intermediary inference steps.

(Cond1) The kidnappers are part of a separatist movement or of a terrorist organization.

    – **(Rule T3, Consequent1)** *Try to verify whether a given separatist movement or terrorist organization is in strict control of a specific sub-group and, in this case,*

    – **(Rule T3, Consequent2)** *Check if the kidnappers are members of this sub-group. We will then assimilate the kidnappers to 'members' of the movement or organization.*

(Cond2) This movement or organization practices ransom kidnapping of given categories of people.

    – **(Rule T2, Consequent)** *The family of the kidnapped has received a ransom request from the separatist movement or terrorist organization.*

    – **(Rule T4, Consequent1)** *The family of the kidnapped has received a ransom request from a group or an individual person, and*

    – **(Rule T4, Consequent2)** *This second group or individual person is part of the separatist movement or terrorist organization.*

    – **(Rule T5, Consequent1)** *Try to verify if a particular sub-group of the separatist movement or terrorist organization exists, and*

    – **(Rule T5, Consequent2)** *Check whether this particular sub-group practices ransom kidnapping of particular categories of people.*

    – ...

(Cond3) In particular, executives or assimilated categories are concerned.

    – **(Rule T0, Consequent1)** *In a 'ransom kidnapping' context, we can check whether the kidnapped person has a strict kinship relationship with a second person, and*

    – **(Rule T0, Consequent2)** *(in the same context) Check if this second person is a businessperson or assimilated.*

(Cond4) It can be proved that the kidnapped person is really an executive or assimilated.

    – **(Rule T6, Consequent)** *In a 'ransom kidnapping' context, 'personalities' like physicians, journalists, artists can be assimilated to businesspersons.*

---

3. Conclusion

In this chapter, we have supplied some information about the rule system of NKRL, a *fully implemented* language/environment designed to deal with the so-called non-fictional narratives of an economic interest. The NKRL software exists in two Java-2 versions, an ORACLE-supported and a file-oriented one. NKRL has been used, among other things, in several EC-funded projects, like NOMOS (ESPRIT P5330); in the legal domain, COBALT (LRE P61-011) in the financial domain; CONCERTO (ESPRIT P29159) in the field of intelligent indexing and retrieval of information stored on Internet and textual databases, EUFORBIA (IAP P26505) in the field of intelligent filtering of information on Internet and PARMENIDES (IST-2001-39023) in the temporal data mining and knowledge management domain.

As already stated, the availability of a powerful 'rule system' is an *essential requirement for any implemented methodology intended to make use of querying/inferencing techniques according to a knowledge-based approach.* NKRL's rules correspond to *high-level reasoning paradigms* like the search for causal relationships or the use of analogical techniques. As we have tried to show in this chapter, given (i) the conceptual complexity of these paradigms and (ii) the sophistication of the underlying representation language, *these rules cannot be implemented in a (weak) 'inference by inheritance' style but must follow a powerful 'inference by resolution' approach.*

The main, future improvements concerning the practical implementation of this rule system concern the introduction of *optimization techniques* with respect to the present, standard *chronological backtracking* that is currently utilized by all the versions of the NKRL's *InferenceEngine*. We plan to make use, in this context, of *efficient pruning strategies* inspired from those – well-known and dependable – developed in a logic programming framework see, e.g. [4]. The aim is here that of reducing considerably the time of processing associated with the *most complex inference procedures*, i.e. those that imply the *integrated exploitation of different types of rules*, see the previous section. For example, in the 'integrated' scenario, the present versions of the NKRL software can take up some minutes to get a result when extended knowledge bases of rules and occurrences are used. Note that a certain 'sluggishness' of the inference procedures when transformations and hypotheses are running together is not a default in itself, given that the possibility of integrating these rules must be conceived *more as a powerful tool for discovering all the possible implicit relationships among the data in the knowledge base than as the support of a standard, real-time question–answering system.*

References

1. Baader, F., Calvanese, D., McGuinness, D., Nardi, D., and Patel-Schneider, P.F., eds. (2002). *The Description Logic Handbook*. Cambridge: University Press.
2. Bechhofer, S., van Harmelen, F., Hendler, J., Horrocks, I., McGuinness, D.L., Patel-Schneider, P.F., and Stein, L.A., eds. (2004). *OWL Web Ontology Language Reference – W3C Recommendation 10 February 2004*.W3C (http://www.w3.org/TR/owl-ref/).
3. Bertino, E., Catania, B., and Zarri, G.P. (2001). *Intelligent Database Systems*. London: Addison-Wesley and ACM Press.
4. Clark, K.L., and Tärnlund, S.-A., eds. (1982). *Logic Programming*. London: Academic Press.
5. Horrocks, I., Patel-Schneider, P.F., Bechhofer, S., and Tsarkov, D. (2005). OWL Rules: A proposal and prototype implementation. *Journal of Web Semantics: Science, Services and Agents on the World Wide Web* 3: 23–40.
6. Levy, A.Y., and Rousset, M.-C. (1998). Combining horn rules and description logics in CARIN. *Artificial Intelligence* **104**: 165–209.
7. Zarri, G.P. (2003). A conceptual model for representing narratives. In: *Innovations in Knowledge Engineering*, Jain, R., Abraham, A., Faucher, C., and van der Zwaag, eds. Adelaide: Advanced Knowledge International.
8. Zarri, G.P. (2005). Integrating the two main inference modes of NKRL, transformations and hypotheses. *Journal on Data Semantics (JoDS)* **4**: 304–340.
9. Zarri, G.P. (2007). An implemented representation and reasoning system for creating and exploiting large knowledge bases of 'Narrative' information. In: *Intelligent Databases, Technologies and Applications*, Ma, Z., ed. Hershey (PA): IGI Global.

40

Genetic Programming Modeling and Complexity Analysis of the Magnetoencephalogram of Epileptic Patients

Efstratios F. Georgopoulos, Adam V. Adamopoulos and Spiridon D. Likothanassis

Abstract

In this work MagnetoEncephaloGram (MEG) recordings of epileptic patients are modeled using a genetic programming approach. This is the first time that genetic programming is used to model MEG signal. Numerous experiments were conducted giving highly successful results. It is demonstrated that genetic programming can produce very simple nonlinear models that fit with great accuracy the observed data of MEG.

Keywords Genetic programming · Magnetoencephalogram (MEG) · Modeling

1. Introduction

Epilepsy is a brain disorder characterized clinically by temporary, but recurrent disturbances of brain function. The observed transient but recurrent unprovoked seizures may or may not be associated with destruction or loss of consciousness and abnormal behavior [1]. More than 1% of the world population is suffering from epilepsy, so, epilepsy is considered as a common neurological disorder. Not all epilepsy syndromes are lifelong – some forms are confined to particular stages of childhood. Epilepsy is usually controlled, but not cured, with medication, although surgery may be considered in difficult cases. One of the most devastating features of epilepsy is its unpredictable nature of epileptic seizures or attacks. Epilepsy manifests itself with a great variety of clinical symptoms, ranging from a momentary lapse of consciousness or destruction and *petit-mal*, to severe tonic-clonic seizures, *grand-mal* and *status epilepticus* [2]. Epilepsy should not be understood as a single disorder, but rather as a group of syndromes with vastly divergent symptoms but all involving episodic abnormal electrical activity in the brain. At the neural level, epileptic activity occurs when the membrane potentials of a population of neurons are synchronized. This abnormal, excessive, and synchronous neuronal activity in the brain, followed by massive neural discharges is associated to a phase transition of the underlying brain dynamics from higher to lower dimensional dynamics [3].

Efstratios F. Georgopoulos • Pattern Recognition Laboratory, Department of Computer Engineering and Informatics; University of Patras Artificial Intelligence Research Center (U.P.A.I.R.C.), University of Patras, Patras, Greece; Technological Educational Institute of Kalamata, Kalamata, Greece. **Adam V. Adamopoulos** • Pattern Recognition Laboratory, Department of Computer Engineering and Informatics; University of Patras Artificial Intelligence Research Center (U.P.A.I.R.C.), University of Patras, Patras, Greece; Medical Physics Laboratory, Department of Medicine, Democritus University of Thrace, Alexandroupolis, Greece. **Spiridon D. Likothanassis** • Pattern Recognition Laboratory, Department of Computer Engineering and Informatics; University of Patras Artificial Intelligence Research Center (U.P.A.I.R.C.), University of Patras, Patras, Greece.

G.A. Papadopoulos et al. (eds.), *Information Systems Development*, DOI 10.1007/b137171_40,
© Springer Science+Business Media, LLC 2009

Brain dynamics can be evaluated by recording the changes of the neuronal electric voltage, either by the electroencephalogram (EEG) or by the magnetoencephalogram (MEG). The EEG recordings represent the time series that matchup to neurological activity as a function of time. On the other hand the MEG is generated due to the time-varying nature of the neuronal electric activity, since time-varying electric currents generate magnetic fields. EEG and MEG are considered to be complementary, each one carrying a part but not the whole of the information related to the underlying neural activity [4]. Thus, it has been suggested that the EEG is mostly related to the inter-neural electric activity, whereas the MEG is mostly related to the intra-neural activity. MEG recordings are obtained using superconductive quantum interference devices (SQUIDs) that are very sensitive magnetometers, capable of detecting and recording biomagnetic fields of the order of femto tesla (FT) ($= 10^{-15}$ T).

To investigate, model, and even more, to predict neural and brain dynamics in epilepsy many efforts have been made in the past. Neural network models have been developed to elucidate the underlying neural and brain modeling of epileptogenesis [5] and propagation of epileptic seizures [6]; dimensionality calculations of the EEG [7] and the MEG [8] of epileptic patients have been performed, considering the emerging brain dynamics with respect to the theory of nonlinear systems and chaos for the analysis of the strange attractors that are observed. Even more, intelligent signal processing methods have been applied, including the use artificial neural networks (ANN) for EEG and MEG signal prediction, as well as the development of nonlinear autoregressive moving average with external inputs (NARMAX) to model these signals [9]. All these methods conclude to a common point, that is, in epileptic brain dynamics, a phase transition does occur, leading from higher to lower dimensional dynamics, emerging self-organization and synchronicity at the neural, as well as at the systemic level.

To our knowledge, none of the previous studies considered the task of modeling epileptic brain dynamics with the use of genetic programming (GP). Introduced by Koza [10, 11], GP faces one of the most important issue in modeling a system, namely to find the right size and shape of the mathematical model of a system. According to the GP approach, obtaining a functional form of a mathematical model can be considered as being equivalent to searching a space of possible computer programs (they can be viewed as mathematical models) for the particular computer program (model) which produces the desired output for given inputs. That is, one is searching for the computer program (model) whose behavior best fits the observed data.

The fittest individual computer programs can be found using the genetic programming evolutionary technique. GP is "a domain-independent problem solving approach in which computer programs are evolved to solve, or approximately solve, problems [12]. Genetic Programming is based on the Darwinian principle of reproduction and survival of the fittest and is in analogy of naturally occurring genetic operations as crossover (sexual recombination) and mutation". In particular, the problem of modeling requires finding a mathematical function, in symbolic form, which fits the given numeric data points representing some observed system. Finding such an empirical model for a system can be used also in forecasting future values of the state variables of the system.

In this chapter we focus on the modeling of MEG recordings of epileptic patients. MEG recordings were obtained from a SQUID unit, model NEUROMAG-122 provided by 4D imaging, which is installed in Medical Physics Laboratory, University Hospital of Alexandroupolis, Greece. MEG recordings were digitized and stored for off-line analysis. The MEG recording can be considered as time series. Therefore the problem of MEG modeling can be considered as a problem of finding a mathematical relationship that associates the value of the MEG at time t (the output) with values of MEG at previous time intervals, $t-1$, $t-2$, and so on.

The problem of MEG modeling is faced using the GP evolutionary method, in order to optimize the nonlinear model fitting to MEG measurements. Specifically, in this chapter we use a variation of traditional genetic programming, namely linear genetic programming. Linear genetic programming (LGP) is a particular subset of genetic programming wherein computer programs in population are represented as a sequence of instructions from imperative programming language or machine language. The graph-based data flow that results from a multiple usage of register contents and the existence of structurally noneffective code (introns) are two main differences to more common tree-based genetic programming (TGP) [13].

Until now there were a lot of efforts to model and predict the MEG of patients and healthy subjects but none of these efforts uses genetic programming. So [14–16] and in [17] an evolutionary neural network with multiple extended Kalman algorithm was used in order to model and forecast the behavior of MEG signals of patients suffering from epilepsy. MEG modeling and prediction, if successful, could provide information on the complexity of the underlying brain dynamics in epilepsy or any other normal or pathological condition of the central nervous system. This information could be of clinical interest [18].

The rest of the chapter is organized as follows. Section 2 is an introduction to genetic programming, while the results are presented in Section 3. Finally, Section 4 discusses the concluding remarks.

2. Genetic Programming

Genetic programming is a domain-independent problem-solving technique in which computer programs are evolved to solve, or approximately solve, problems. Genetic programming is a member of a broad family of techniques called evolutionary algorithms. All these techniques are based on the Darwinian principle of reproduction and survival of the fittest and analogs of biological genetic operations such as crossover and mutation. Genetic programming addresses one of the central goals of computer science, namely automatic programming; which is to create, in an automated way, a computer program that enables a computer to solve a problem [10, 11].

In genetic programming, the evolution operates on a population of computer programs of varying sizes and shapes. Genetic programming starts with an initial population of thousands or millions of randomly generated computer programs composed of the available programmatic ingredients and then applies the principles of biological evolution to create a new (and often improved) population of programs. The generation of this new population is done in a domain-independent way using the Darwinian principle of survival of the fittest, an analog of the naturally occurring genetic operation of crossover (sexual recombination), and occasional mutation [12]. The crossover operation is designed to create syntactically valid offspring programs (given closure among the set of programmatic ingredients). Genetic programming combines the expressive high-level symbolic representations of computer programs with the near-optimal efficiency of learning of Holland's genetic algorithm. A computer program that solves (or approximately solves) a given problem often emerges from this process [12]. Genetic programming generates computer programs to solve problems by executing the following steps, according to [12]:

1. Generate an initial population of random computer programs (these are random compositions of the functions and terminals of the problem).
2. Iteratively perform the following steps until the termination criterion has been satisfied:
   - Execute each program in the population and assign it a fitness value using the fitness measure.
   - Create a new population of computer programs by applying the following genetic operations to computer program(s) chosen from the population with a probability based on their fitness.
   - Darwinian reproduction: reproduce an existing program by copying it into the new population.
   - Crossover: create two new computer programs from two existing programs by genetically recombining randomly chosen parts of two existing programs using the crossover operation (it is described below) applied at a randomly chosen crossover point within each program.
   - Mutation: create one new computer program from one existing program by mutating a randomly chosen part of the program.
3. The program that is identified by the method of result designation is designated as the result for the run (e.g., the best-so-far individual). This result may be a solution (or an approximate solution) to the problem.

Before we apply genetic programming to a problem, we must perform five major preparatory steps [12]:

1. Determine the set of terminals. The terminals can be viewed as the inputs to the as-yet-undiscovered computer program. The set of terminals (or terminal set T, as it is often called), along with the set of functions are the ingredients from which genetic programming constructs a computer program to solve, or approximately solve, the problem.
2. Determine the set of primitive functions. These functions are going to be used to generate the mathematical expression that attempts to fit the given finite sample of data. Each computer program is a composition of functions from the function set F and terminals from the terminal set T. Each of the functions in the function set should be able to accept, as its arguments, any value and data type that may possibly be returned by any function in the function set and any value and data type that may possibly be assumed by any terminal in the terminal set. That is, the function set and terminal set selected should have the closure property so that any possible composition of functions and terminals produces a valid executable computer program (e.g., instead of using the classic division operator we should employ a protected version of division which returns an arbitrary value such as zero when a division by zero is attempted).
3. Determine the fitness measure which drives the evolutionary process. Each individual computer program in the population is executed and then is evaluated, using the fitness measure, to determine how well it performs in the particular problem environment. The nature of the fitness measure varies with the problem: e.g., for many problems, fitness is naturally measured by the discrepancy between the result produced by an individual candidate program and the desired result; the closer this error is to zero, the better the program. For some problems, it may be appropriate to use a multiobjective fitness measure incorporating a combination of factors such as correctness, parsimony (smallness of the evolved program), and efficiency.
4. Determine the parameters for controlling the run. These are the population size, M, and the maximum number of generations to be run, G.
5. Determine the method for designating a result and the criterion for terminating a run. One frequently used method of result designation for a run is to designate the best individual obtained in any generation of the population during the run (i.e., the best-so-far individual) as the result of the run. As a termination criterion is often used, a maximum number of generations that genetic programming is left to run, along with a maximum number of successive generations for which no improvement is considered.

3. Results

In order to apply genetic programming to the particular problem of MEG modeling, we have to specify the above five major preparatory steps [12], as follows:

- Set of terminals: As terminals were used the input variables of the data sets were constructed using the MEG recordings and a number of random constants. Since the MEG recording can be considered as a time series, then the problem of MEG modeling can be considered as a problem of finding a mathematical relationship that associates the value of the MEG at time t (the output) with values of MEG at previous time intervals, $t-1$, $t-2$, and so on. Since it is not known how many previous time intervals are necessary in order to model better MEG, a number of different previous time intervals were used varying from 2 to 7.
- Set of primitive functions: were used as function the classical mathematical functions of addition, subtraction, multiplication, division (a protected version), absolute value, square root, exponential, sine, and cosine as function.
- Fitness measure: As fitness measure the mean square error between the desired output (the observed MEG recordings) and the real output of the model was used.

- Parameters for controlling the run: As population size, M, we used 500 individuals, while the maximum number of generations to be run, G, it was set equal to 300.
- Method for designating a result and criterion for terminating a run: As method of result designation for a run it was used to designate the best individual obtained in any generation of the population during the run (i.e., the best-so-far individual) as the result of the run. While, as a termination criterion it was used the maximum number of 300 generations that genetic programming was left to run.

In all the experiments we used the same parameter values for comparison reasons. The MEG recordings were organized in six data sets according to the number of previous time intervals used (they vary from three to seven). In the sequence, every data set was split in to three other data sets, namely training set consisting of 200 patterns, validation set consisting of 200 patterns, and test set consisting of 1600 patterns. Training set was used; for the training of the individuals (computer programs # models) of the population; the validation set were used to exhibit the generalization performance of the individuals; while the test set was used at the end of the whole evolutionary process in order to appraise the performance of the produced model (the output of genetic programming technique) on unseen data.

In order to evaluate the performance of the produced computer programs three well-known error measures, the normalized root mean squared error (NRMSE), the correlation coefficient (CC), and the mean relative error (MRE) were used.

Table 40.1 depicts the performance of the produced models by the genetic programming technique computer programs (models) on the test set for the six different cases of number of inputs used. Figures 40.1 through 40.6 depict the performance of the generated computer programs (models), at the end of the evolutionary process, on the test set. The produced computer program (model) in the case of six inputs is depicted in Table 40.2.

Table 40.1. Performance of the produced models on the test set.

Number of inputs	NRMSE	CC	MRE	MSE
Two	0.0735	0.9973	0.3603	0.3603
Three	0.0293	0.9996	0.1337	5.9385e–004
Four	0.0288	0.9996	0.1313	5.7302e–004
Five	0.0307	0.9995	0.1410	6.5096e–004
Six	0.0215	0.9998	0.0851	3.1991e–004
Seven	0.0259	0.9997	0.1166	4.6285e–004

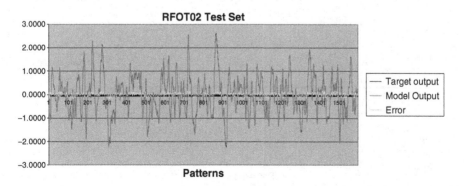

Figure 40.1. Performance on the test set in the case of two inputs.

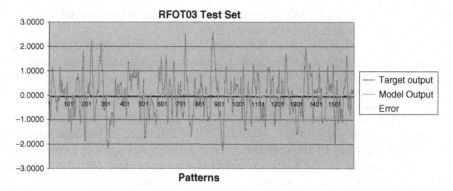

Figure 40.2. Performance on the test set in the case of three inputs.

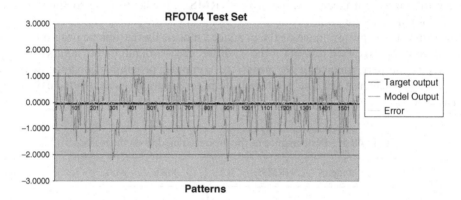

Figure 40.3. Performance on the test set in the case of four inputs.

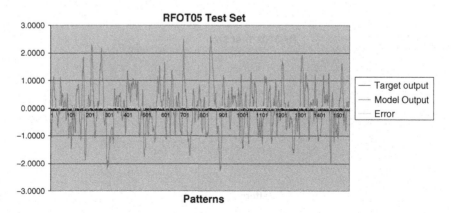

Figure 40.4. Performance on the test set in the case of five inputs.

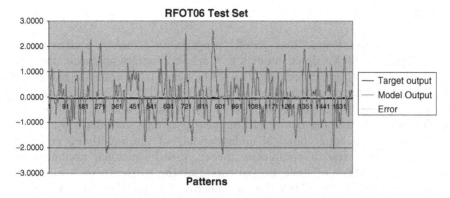

Figure 40.5. Performance on the test set in the case of six inputs.

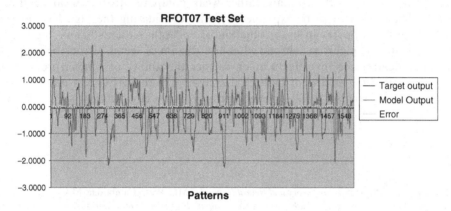

Figure 40.6. Performance on the test set in the case of seven inputs.

Table 40.2. The generated computer program for the case of six inputs.

```
x[t] + = x[t-5];
x[t]- = x[t-7];
x[t]- = x[t-7];
x[t]* = 1.987620830535889f;
x[t] + = x[t-5];
x[t]/ = 0.4281637668609619f;
x[t] + = x[t-2];
x[t]* = 0.03275442123413086f;
x[t] + = x[t-2];
x[t] + = x[t-5];
x[t]/ = 0.9955191612243652f;
x[t]- = x[t-3];
x[t]- = x[t-3];
x[t]/ = 0.1756083965301514f;
x[t]/ = 0.4281637668609619f;
x[t]* = 0.03275442123413086f;
x[t]/ = 0.7790718078613281f;
x[t] + = x[t-2];
x[t]- = x[t-3];
x[t]/ = 0.9177978038787842f;
x[t] + = x[t-2];
```

4. Conclusions

In this work we demonstrated that genetic programming can be used with very promising results to the problem of MEG signal modeling. Genetic programming can produce very simple nonlinear models that fit with great accuracy the MEG signal from epileptic patients. The obtained results are in accordance to the corresponding ones obtained by nonlinear analysis and chaotic methods for the analysis of the epileptic MEG [13, 19]. In those works, signal processing methods based on complexity theory and the theory of nonlinear dynamics and chaos were applied on MEG signals for the purpose of a better physical understanding of the underlying processes in epileptic brain dynamics. From the view of complexity theory, low-dimensional nonlinear dynamics were revealed to undergo the MEG of epileptic patients and the existence of lowdimensional strange attractors in the dynamics of brain function in epilepsy was justified. In addition, in [9], MEG signals of epileptic patients were modeled using NARMAX methods and strong evidence was obtained that the nonlinear coefficients are rather weak compared to the linear coefficients of the obtained models. These results can be explained by only considering the high level of synchronization and rhythmicity that appears in brain function of epileptic patients. Thus, the hypothesis that epileptic behavior is due to highly synchronized neural dynamics seems also to be supported by this work. It is in our intentions to investigate much further the ability of genetic programming evolutionary technique to produce models of biological systems like the MEG and many others. For this reason we have already started to build a genetic programming environment specialized in modeling problems.

References

1. Arbib M. (2003), *The Handbook of Brain Theory and Neural Networks*, MIT Press, Cambridge, MA.
2. Niedermeyer E., and Lopes da Silva F. (2004), *Electroencephalography: Basic Principles, Clinical Applications, and Related Fields*, Lippincott Williams & Wilkins, Philadelphia, PA.
3. Stam C.J. (2005), Nonlinear dynamical analysis of EEG and MEG: Review of an emerging field, *Clinical Neurophysiology*, 116(10): 2266–2301.
4. Dassios G., Fokas A.S., and Hadjiloizi D. (2007), On the complementarity of EEG and MEG, *Inverse Problems*, 23(6): 2541–2549.
5. Anninos P.A., Tsagas N., and Adamopoulos A. (1989), A brain model theory for epilepsy and its treatment: experimental verification using SQUID measurements. In Cotterill, R.M.J. (ed.) *Models of Brain Function*, Cambridge University Press, Cambridge, pp. 405–422.
6. Jouny C.C., Frabaszczuk P.L., and Bergey G.K., Complexity-based analysis of the dynamic of propagation of epileptic seizures, *2nd International IEEE EMBS Conference on Neural Engineering Proceedings*, pp. 155–157.
7. Tsoutsouras V.G., Iliopoulos A.C., and Pavlos G.P. (2006), Non-linear analysis and modelling of EEG in patients with epilepsy, *19th Panhellenic Conference on Nonlinear Science and Complexity*, July 10–22, Thessaloniki, Greece.
8. Adamopoulos A., Pavlos G., Anninos P., Tsitsis D., and Rigas A. (1991), Chaotic analysis of biomagnetic measurements of human brain, *NATO ASI on Chaotic Synamics – Theory and Practice*, July, 11–20, Patras, Greece, 1991.
9. Adamopoulos A.V. (2006), Intelligent adaptive modelling and identification of MEG of epileptic patients, *WSEAS Transactions on Biology and Biomedicine*, 3(2): 69–76.
10. Koza J.R. (1990), A genetic approach to econometric modeling, *Sixth World Congress of the Econometric Society*, Barcelona, Spain, August 27.
11. Koza J.R. (1992),*Genetic Programming: On the Programming of Computers by Means of Natural Selection*, MIT Press, Cambridge, MA.
12. Koza J.R. (1998), Genetic programming. In: Williams, J. G. and Kent, A. (eds.) *Encyclopedia of Computer Science and Technology*, New York, NY: Marcel-Dekker, 39(24): 29–43.
13. Banzhaf W.P., Nordin P., Keller R.E., and Francone F.D. (1998). *Genetic Programming: An Introduction*, Kaufmann, San Mateo, CA.
14. Adamopoulos A., Anninos P., Likothanassis S., and Georgopoulos E. (1998), On the predictability of MEG of epileptic patients using RBF networks evolved with genetic algorithms, *BIOSIGNAL'98*, Brno, Czech Republic, June 23–25.
15. Adamopoulos A., Georgopoulos G., Likothanassis S., and Anninos P. (1999), Forecasting the Magnetoengaphalogram (MEG) of epileptic patient using genetically optimized neural networks, *Genetic and Evolutionary Computation Conference (GECCO'99)*, Orlando, Florida, USA, July 14–17.

16. Adamopoulos A., Georgopoulos E., and Likothanassis S. (2004), Evolutionary neural networks for timeseries prediction, *WSEAS Transactions on Biology and Biomedicine*, 1(1): 137–147.
17. Likothanassis S., Georgopoulos E., and Adamopoulos A. (2000), Structure determination and training of neural networks using evolution programs, *Neural, Parallel and Scientific Computations Journal*, 8(1): 29–48
18. Adamopoulos A., and Anninos P. (1993), Application of chaotic dynamics data analysis methods on the MEG of epileptic and parkinsonian patients, in order to evaluate their improvement using external magnetic fields, *Biophysical Journal* 64(2), *Part 2. Abstracts of 37th Annual Meeting of the Biophysical Society.*
19. Anninos P., Kotini A., Adamopoulos A., and Tsagas N. (2003), Magnetic stimulation can modulate seizures in epileptic patients, *Brain Topography*, 16(1): 57–64.

41

A Three-Layer Approach to Testing of Multi-agent Systems

Tomas Salamon

Abstract

In this chapter, a complex approach to testing of multi-agent systems is presented. Multi-agent testing should be divided into three layers. On the first layer, the individual agents should be tested. A stochastic approach to unit testing and the use of "stages" can be adopted. A stage is a perceptible segment of a virtual world where an agent is placed that is projected for agent unit testing. On the second layer, deadlocks and similar flaws of agent interaction should be fought. Our method of deadlock detection is based on monitoring recurring agent interactions. On the third layer, the behavior of the entire system is evaluated. Bottlenecks and "hot spots" of the system could cause serious performance problems. Stability of multi-agent systems in case of mass collapse of many agents should be tested using stress tests.

Keywords Agent-based simulations · Testing · Methodology

1. Introduction

Multi-agent systems are distributed information systems composed of agents. The agents are independent, autonomous units of code with their own goals that interact, negotiate, collaborate, and communicate with each other in order to reach their objectives. Information is distributed among the particular agents and there is no global control of the whole system. Multi-agent systems are able to solve problems and tasks that are not suitable or performable for "traditional" computing[17]. They can be used in a wide variety of fields, e.g., geographic information systems, cybernetics, robotics, logistics and traffic optimization, and agent-based modeling.

Agent-based modeling is a computational method using multi-agent systems for simulation in social science. Because the properties and behavior of multi-agent systems resemble the characteristics of real social systems, multi-agent systems can be used as an experimental tool in this field [18].

Multi-agent systems are a promising technology. Since the 1990 s they have shifted gradually from theoretical studies to real applications. Although theoretical works about multi-agent systems and their background are relatively abundant, the papers treating practical issues of their design, development, implementation, debugging, testing, deployment, and maintenance are scarcer.

Multi-agent methodologies published so far, such as Prometheus [14], Gaia [21], SODA [13], Tropos [3], seldom deal closely with debugging and testing of multi-agent software. Just a few works published in recent years are concerned with debugging and testing of multi-agent systems, and they are mainly focused on a particular technique or method, not on the testing approach of multi-agent systems as a whole. Jonker and Treur [9] suggest an approach of verification of multi-agent systems based on temporal epistemic logic. However, such a method is suitable only in the phase of system design and does not solve the testing of an

Tomas Salamon · Department of Information Technologies, University of Economics, Prague, Czech Republic

G.A. Papadopoulos et al. (eds.), *Information Systems Development*, DOI 10.1007/b137171_41,

existing system. Others [5, 19] deal with agent-oriented unit testing as a useful technique for testing of multi-agent systems (further elaborated in this chapter) but cover just a part of the problem. Liedekerke and Avouris [10] and Ndumu et al. [12] describe debugging methods of multi-agent systems based on visualizing of their operation that approach could be helpful, but it is not able to cover the entire complexity of the problem. Poutakidis et al. [15] suggest multi-agent system debugging using design artifacts, an approach that is focused on testing agent interaction protocols. Gatti and Staa [8] conducted research focused on the present state of multi-agent debugging and testing, and concluded that there is no single best approach to multi-agent debugging and testing, and that the best solution is a combination of several existing techniques.

Although there are a number of tools and approaches designed for testing various kinds of problems in multi-agent systems, we are still lacking a consistent method for multi-agent testing.

This chapter deals with testing of multi-agents systems generally and with a special interest in testing agent-based models. It is based on our research and the experience with debugging and testing of agent-based models in the JADE multi-agent framework [2] and in our own simple multi-agent framework called *AgEnv*.

This chapter is organized as follows. In the remainder of this chapter, our approach of three layers is introduced. In the following three sections, testing on all three layers is described. Finally, in the last section our conclusions and suggestions for future work are presented.

1.1. Three-Layer Approach

Debugging and testing of traditional applications is founded on testing of the individual parts of the system. Generally, if we can check every single part of the software and their integration, we can theoretically consider the software free of errors. There is indeed a problem that we are not able to check every state and every eventuality of today's complex software, so a perfect testing is not practically feasible. Nonetheless, this problem is outside the scope of this chapter.

In the case of multi-agent systems, the situation is more complicated. Multi-agent systems are composed of the individual agents that are separately testable in the traditional meaning. In addition, however, an integral part of multi-agent systems are the mutual relationships of these agents, their relationships with the agent environment, and incidental emergent properties that appear in the system. Simply said, we cannot deem a multi-agent system just a sum of its parts. The emergent properties of the entire system are even more important than in a "traditional" information system, so a different approach to testing is needed. Possible principles and problems of testing and debugging of multi-agent systems are discussed in this chapter.

Our method is based on testing of a multi-agent system divided into three "layers." In the first layer we conduct unit testing of the individual agents. We test whether functionality of the agents corresponds with their design objectives. Agent unit testing should be indeed an integral part of their development, especially when test-driven development methodology [1] is utilized. In the second layer, the testing of agent interactions is performed. We search there for the errors coming from the agent interactions, because even if the individual agent is working properly, hidden errors could still show up during the interaction of two or more agents. A propensity for deadlocks is a typical problem that is discovered in this phase. The third layer constitutes testing of the entire multi-agent system. Although we may find the individual agents as well as their interactions errorless, the whole system could still fail. On this level, performance problems and bottlenecks of system hubs, and vulnerability to mass collapses of agents could appear.

2. First Layer – Unit Testing

On the first layer we test the individual agents. Coelho et al. [5] offered a method of using *mock agent* based on the concept of mock object by Mackinnon et al. [11] in object-oriented programming. Mock agent is a dummy agent without inner functionality. It possesses a proper interface to communicate with the tested agent. Mock agent can send and receive messages to and from the tested agent and a programmer can evaluate whether the reaction of the tested agent is correct. During testing we can observe the internal states of the test agent using tools like agent inspector, logging, and others if they are present in the agent framework.

The actual process of testing is as follows: the testing environment creates the tested agent, the mock agents (Coelho et al. [5] recommend to create one mock agent for every role of the tested agent), and all other components of the system and starts a *test case* where tests to perform are defined.

Then the mock agent sends messages to the tested agent according to the test plan and receives its responses. The tested agent is monitored by agent monitor (if such tool is present in the system) which logs its activity for the test case. Test case compares records with the plan to find out whether the agent's behavior is correct.

Although it is seldom achievable to test all the possible situations, because the agent's state space is too large, all the relevant types of situations, both desirable and undesirable, should be tested.

2.1. Stochastic Approach

A drawback of this approach is that it is too much inspired by its "object oriented" ancestor. In an object-oriented world, there is no uncertainty about the result of the actual operation (method). Besides various errors and program states covered by exceptions, the behavior of the object is fully predictable. The object has no ability to reject a request to perform a required action. The agent has such ability and it generally can reject or simply ignore an action which is asked for. Although many multi-agent systems are based on simple, reactive agents that do not possess even unsophisticated artificial intelligence, but simply react on the information from the surroundings; agents are often defined as entities with their own intelligence and autonomous decision-making ability [20]. Thus their behavior need not be fully predictable, and we should not test such agents in a traditional, discrete way. A stochastic approach should be adopted instead.

One can have an objection that although the agent's behavior as a black box could outwardly look ambiguous and unpredictable, if we can monitor the agent "inside" and watch its internal states (so-called glass-box testing), there could be no uncertainty.

Nonetheless, agent behavior could be still inherently random in some cases. A good example is agent-based simulation in the social sciences where agents' internal states are often represented by random variables from various probability distributions. Another example of inherent randomness in agents' behavior could be certain methods of deadlock resolution. For example, suppose a traffic management multi-agent simulation, where three car agents come to an intersection of three roads from three directions together, and there is no priority sign. It is a classical example of deadlock, and one of the solutions is that one of the cars simply drives away after a random time period. If agents' decision making was perfectly deterministic, all three cars would either stay there forever or always start driving at once and their smashup would be inevitable.

Due to the reasons mentioned above, we propose using stochastic testing where suitable. The main difference between traditional and stochastic testing is that with "normal" unit testing, the test case is always carried out only once and it is considered successful if all the tests in the test case are passed. In the case of stochastic testing, the test should be repeated many times and its results are recorded. The test is considered successful when the empirical probabilistic distribution of test results fits the expected distribution function. The evaluation of results is done by statistical means (the Kolmogorov–Smirnov test is one of the possibilities). The results of the test cannot be 100% correct by definition, but neither can the results of "traditional" unit testing. We can control the required significance level by adjusting the number of attempts.

A more detailed description of the method of stochastic agent unit testing is as follows:

Step 1: In this step, a testing platform and all its components are created in a test suite and a test case is launched.

Step 2: The test case creates mock agent(s) and the tested agent.

Step 3: Mock agents start to communicate with a tested agent. Resulting states are recorded. Step 3 is repeated multiple times (the number of required repetitions depends on a required level of significance).

A product of such testing is an empirical distribution of results. The test environment performs a goodness-of-fit test to compare whether expected theoretical distribution matches the empirical distribution of test results.

We see two possible drawbacks in this approach. First, it could be sometimes difficult to devise the theoretical distribution function of test results to compare with the empirical one. The second disadvantage is the speed of such testing, which is indeed substantially lower than in the case of the traditional, discrete approach.

2.2. Agent's Perception

The testing approach based solely on mock agents is suitable for multi-agent systems where the only mean of agents' information gathering is their mutual communication. This limitation is a valid assumption for most agent-based simulations in social sciences, where there is no outer environment that the agent should perceive and the only information it could gain is information from the other agents.

In some other types of multi-agent systems such is not a case. For example, the agents in multi-agent systems for traffic management simulation [7] cannot only communicate with other ones, but they gather percepts from their surroundings as well.

Suppose a traffic management simulation where there are various vehicles, roads, buildings, and other entities in the model. There can be two ways of designing such a model. One possibility is that all entities in the simulation would be represented by agents. Another option is that just the entities of our interest (e.g., cars and other vehicles) could be embodied by agents and the rest can be a part of the environment. In the second case, agents gain their information not only by their mutual communication, but they also need to perceive the environment. So, beside their messaging ability, they also need some perception function that must be taken into account in the test environment. In our hypothetical traffic management simulation, the perception function should, for example, allow the simulated car agent to watch the road and nearby buildings.

The test must be conducted in the "production" environment if possible. The production environment in the aforementioned example could be, for example, a virtual landscape crisscrossed by roads. If we have no such environment, it is necessary to build at least a small part of it for testing purposes (let us say, an intersection and its surroundings, in our example) and include it into the test suite.

We call such a piece of environment a *stage* in our research. Stage is an additional part of the test suite. As an example of a stage, we can use a traffic simulation, where agents are the cars and the stage is a part of a "map." It is not meaningful to test traffic simulation just with cars "hung" in space, so we need a stage to put them in. The stage could be quite complex, as in case of the traffic simulation, or somewhat simple, just as a numeric value on an agent's sensor function. The stage has no direct equivalent in object-oriented testing.

A main drawback of using stages is that they are another part of the test suite and so they constitute an extra source of possible failures. Possible ways to mitigate this drawback are to test stages separately before testing agents and to test the agent in more stages.

3. Second Layer – Testing of Agent Interactions

Even if we were able to test the individual agents perfectly, the whole multi-agent system could be still erroneous. A multi-agent system is not just an aggregate of its parts; it possesses emergent properties, too, which begin to appear as soon as two or more agents begin to interoperate. For this reason, failures could show up even in a system with 100% error-free agents. Typical examples of errors of this kind are deadlocks, livelocks, and various other kinds of conflicts.

Deadlock is described as a state of the system when two or more concurrent actions that share a common resource are waiting for the other to finish, but it never occurs. This was first discussed in the case of multitasking in operating systems [6], but it is a pervasive phenomenon in most types of distributed systems including multi-agent systems. Livelock is a similar system state when the actions involved in the livelock hand the activity onto one another, forever, without any progress.

Testing these situations is a challenging task, due to its problematical predictability. In the literature we can find a few works dealing with this specific problem in multi-agent systems. Burkhard [4] discusses the problem of deadlocks from theoretical aspects. Poutakidis et al. [15] suggest a method of testing agent interaction protocols through their transformation into Petri nets. Unfortunately, this does not solve the particular problem of deadlocks and similar situations.

We suggest another method of detecting problems on the second layer. This method is based on the stochastic concept as well, so results cannot be guaranteed.

However, as deadlocks are unpredictable, it is still probably the most feasible and a quite simple solution.

It is based on watching and logging the functions of the existing multi-agent system. We create a table with one line for every type of agent interaction in the system. Every agent is able to make a relationship with at least one another agent. By the interaction we mean a single negotiation scenario. By the negotiation scenario we mean a set of requests and answers in order to solve one type of issue with one other agent (using UML we can depict such a scenario with sequence diagram). Due to the limitations of artificial intelligence, the agents are still not able to perform the negotiations and collaborations with other agents arbitrarily. They always use some scenarios that are "hardcoded" into their program. There is typically a higher number of interactions than agents, but this does not need to be always true.

We log every executed interaction in the running system (see Fig. 41.1), which is defined by a source agent, a destination agent, and a scenario. Every interaction has a score. When the interaction occurs, we examine the table to see whether there is already such an interaction recorded. If so, we increase its score by a so-called s-value; otherwise we add it into the table with the score of s-value (there is an s-value of 2 used in Fig. 41.1). After every simulation round, we decrease the score of every agent by 1. The aforementioned s-value is an integer value determining the sensitivity of the test. We have observed the best results with the s-values between 2 and 4. In Fig. 41.1. we can see an example with communication between A1–B1, A1–A2, and A2–C1. In the case of A1–B1, there was communication in two foregoing rounds as well. In the case of B1–C1 there was communication in the previous round, but there is no communication in the actual round.

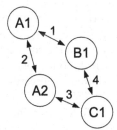

Source	Destination	Scenario	Score
A1	B1	1	4
A1	A2	2	2
A2	C1	3	2
B1	C1	4	1

Figure 41.1. Example of agent communication.

The interactions with the highest (and growing) scores are candidates for deadlocks. We can simply transform this table to a graph where the agents are nodes, the interactions are edges, and every edge is valued by its score. If there are cycles with high and growing scores on their edges in the graph, it is a probable spot of deadlock.

If deadlock candidates are found this way, developers should explore the agents more deeply to reveal the particular cause of the deadlocks and make agents more resistant.

4. Third Layer – Testing of the Whole System

On the third layer, we test problems regarding the entire system. Although we have unveiled all the errors in the individual agents and agent interactions, there could still be problems of the whole system that emerge when the system is populated with a multitude of agents.

4.1. System Bottlenecks

Although multi-agent systems belong to distributed systems, there are often some central points in the system that can turn out into bottlenecks. These points could be messaging services, yellow-pages services (searching for a particular agent according to its characteristics), white-pages services (mapping symbolic names to addresses of particular agents), and others. These services could be working perfectly with the individual agents or even with a certain amount of agents, but as there are more and more agents, the load of these "hot spots" could slow down the entire system.

There could be three main reasons for these problems. First, there could be improper design of such services. If the bottleneck is caused only by this reason, the solution is typically feasible and relatively undemanding. We should optimize the code of this service by common means.

Second, the bottleneck could be caused by improper design of agents. Typically this problem occurs when agents send many more requests to the service than necessary for the purpose of the certain agent-based model or multi-agent system [16]. We have the experience with this problem from research on a particular agent-based simulation. We designed an agent-based model with agents representing people and businesses in a virtual economy. Businesses hired employees. In the first version of the system, during recruitment, business agents tried to send their offers to all people agents in the simulation. In spite of a relatively low number of both businesses (1000) and people (10,000) in the model, the number of messages after the first simulation round was about 10^7, as every business sent a message to every person. The messaging service was flooded with requests and the entire system almost stopped. The problem was indeed in the design of the agents. In fact, there is no need to send so many messages, because sending a message to every single agent in the system constitutes the state of perfect information that is not possible in reality. Individuals cannot communicate perfectly, because they are limited by resources (at least by time constraints), so they have no chance to send more than a certain number of messages in every simulation round. After the implementation of such constraints to our multi-agent system, the number of messages in this particular simulation plummeted to about 5000, a number which was manageable without any impact on system function. However, sometimes the developer needs to distribute information in such massive manner. Then it is better to use another kind of service that is more suitable for mass use (multicast).

Finally, if there is a problem neither in the code of the bottleneck nor in the code of the agents, but the entire system is so huge that bottlenecks are simply unavoidable, then the only solution is to change the architecture of the system, e.g., to turn it into a more advanced distributed architecture and split the load among more hubs. This kind of solution is typically the most difficult.

Testing of the multi-agent system on the third layer should be focused mainly on measuring the performance of the system. The duration of one simulation round, its variance through time, the speed of message delivery, the length of message queues, etc. could be used as measures.

4.2. System Stability during Mass Crashes of Agents

Another issue that should be tested on the third layer is the stability of the system as a whole when a great number of agents crash at once. A multi-agent system is a regular piece of software and it could indeed fail as any other system. If the program is correctly designed, the crash of agents should not have any impact on the system as a whole. Although most multi-agent environments are able to absorb a crash of one or a few agents, when a massive collapse of a great number of agents does occur, the environment need not absorb it. The problem is often in handling a large number of exceptions that are typically highly resource consuming. Multi-agent frameworks have also sometimes a problem with garbage collection and freeing of resources after a mass crash.

Especially if the multi-agent system is designed for a long-running application and its stability is therefore crucial, we recommend using a stress test focused on collapse of a high number of agents as an integral part of testing. The stress test could be performed as follows. We modify regular agents in the system and add the function of an intentional crash caused by throwing some exception. The agents should be able to coordinate their "serial suicide" and to commit it at the same moment (see Fig. 41.2). The easiest way is to trigger such action by a special agent (the grey point in the picture) sending a "suicide command" (dashed arrows in Fig. 41.2) to the other agents. Only some of the agents in the system should be brought down in one moment (let us say one-half – black points in the picture) in order to measure the behavior of the system. Immediately after the "suicide," the same number of agents should be established again in the system.

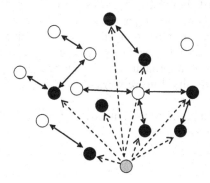

Figure 41.2. "Serial suicide" stress test.

We should measure the number of agents in the system after the test. Their number should be the same as the number of agents before the crash. If their number is lower than expected, it could indicate that some other agents went down unintentionally and that the system could be sensitive to such problems. If their number is greater, it could indicate an error in testing. We should also measure the performance, and other indicators including consumption of memory and other resources, of the system during and after the crash. As well, we should explore the behavior of the agents remaining in the system to see how they are able to reestablish their interactions and how long it takes the system to return to overall stability.

In an ideal case, the system should be robust enough to absorb an agents' collapse of any extent without the impact on global behavior of the system and without loss of its performance.

5. Conclusions and Future Work

In this chapter, the approach to testing of multi-agent systems is presented. Testing of multi-agent systems poses more complex problems than testing of "traditional" computer systems. Emergent properties and behaviors of multi-agent systems are their inseparable traits that add to the system such characteristics that no single one of their parts possess. Hence, the classical approach of dividing the system into atomic units and testing them separately is unsatisfactory with multi-agent systems.

We have developed a three-layer approach to testing multi-agent systems. On the first layer, the individual agents are tested. We adopted the unit testing framework with mock agent, but we propose using a stochastic approach to testing. Because the behavior of agents is not fully deterministic, a deterministic unit testing cannot be successfully applied. Therefore, each test should be repeated several times and for the outcome we need to compare its empirical results with those expected on the basis of the theoretical probability distribution function of the agent.

Those multi-agent systems where agents perform some kind of perception of the environment are not fully testable solely by the use of mock agents. Therefore, we propose a principle of a "stage" that is an environment or a part of an environment for agent testing. However, using stages is problematic due to their complexity and the fact that they can become a source of additional failures. In the future, we plan to elaborate the concept of stages in greater detail.

On the second layer, we are searching for the errors coming from agent interactions that were not possible to find on the first layer. The most common type of such errors is deadlocks and similar phenomena; and the detection that we propose is based on searching for suspiciously repetitious interactions among a small group of agents. Our future work is focused on ways in which the agents could detect and get out of the deadlock automatically.

On the third layer, we should test the errors of the entire system that were not possible to unveil on the lower levels. There can be problems of bottlenecks in the multi-agent system, despite its distributed character, where there are often high-load hubs and central points that can slow down the entire system. Future work should be done on distributed architectures of multi-agent environments.

Furthermore, we recommend stress testing of the system, in order to determine behavior and stability in the case of mass collapse of a great number of agents. Even in such a situation, the multi-agent system should remain stable, without substantial impact on its performance and its global behavior.

The individual methods of our approach were developed during several agent-based simulation projects and used with favorable results. Future work should be done on deeper elaboration of testing methodology and its further evaluation.

This approach is general and it could be used in various types of multi-agent systems, although it was primarily devised for agent-based simulations.

Acknowledgments

This chapter is supported by the European Union in the frame of Unified Program Document 3 under the European Social Fund together with the Czech Republic and the City of Prague.

References

1. Beck, K. (2003) *Test Driven Development: By Example*. Addison-Wesley, Boston.
2. Bellifemine, F., Poggi, A. and Rimassa, G. (2001) Developing multi-agent systems with JADE. In: Castelfranchi, C. and Lespérance, Y. (eds.), *Proceedings of the 7th International Workshop on Intelligent Agents VII. Agent Theories Architectures and Languages*, LNAI, Springer Verlag, London, pp. 89–103.
3. Bresciani, P., Giorgini, P., Giunchiglia, F., Mylopoulos, J. and Perini, A. (2002) Tropos: An agent-oriented software development methodology. *Autonomous Agents and Multi-Agent Systems* 8, pp. 203–236.
4. Burkhard, H. (1993) Liveness and fairness properties in multi-agent systems. In: Bajcsy, R. (ed.), *Proceedings of the 13th International Joint Conference on Artificial Intelligence (IJCAI 93)*, Morgan Kaufmann Publ., pp. 325–330.
5. Coelho, R., Kulesza, U., Staa, A. and Lucena, C. (2006) Unit testing in multi-agent systems using mock agents and aspects. In: *Proceedings of the 2006 International Workshop on Software Engineering for Large-Scale Multi-Agent Systems*, ACM, New York, pp. 83–90.
6. Coffman, E.G., Elphick, M. and Shoshani, A. (1971) System deadlocks. *Computing Surveys* 2, pp. 67–78.
7. Dresner, K. and Stone, P. (2006) Multiagent traffic management: Opportunities for multi-agent learning. In: Tuyls, K. (ed.), *LAMAS 2005*, LNAI, Springer Verlag, Berlin, pp. 129–138.
8. Gatti, M.A.C. and Staa, A.V. (2006) *Testing & debugging multi-agent systems: a state of the art report*. Departamento de Informática, PUC-Rio, Rio de Janeiro.
9. Jonker, C.M. and Treur, J. (1998) Compositional verification of multi-agent systems: A formal analysis of pro-activeness and reactiveness. In: Langmaack, H., Pnueli, A. and De Roever, W.P. (eds.), *Proceedings of the International Workshop on Compositionality, COMPOS'97*, LNCS, Springer Verlag, Berlin, pp. 350–380.
10. Liedekerke, M. and Avouris, N. (1995) Debugging multi-agent systems. *Information and Software Technology* 37(2), pp. 103–112.

11. Mackinnon, T., Freeman, S. and Craig, P. (2000) EndoTesting: Unit testing with mock objects. In: *Extreme Programming and Flexible Processes in Software Engineering – XP2000*, May 2000.

12. Ndumu, D., Nwana, H., Lee, L. and Collins, J. (1999) Visualising and debugging distributed multi-agent systems. In: *Proceedings of the Third Annual Conference on Autonomous Agents*, pp. 326–333.

13. Omicini, A. (2000) SODA: Societies and infrastructures in the analysis and design of agent-based systems. In: *First International Workshop, AOSE 2000 on Agent-Oriented Software Engineering*, Springer-Verlag, New York, pp. 185–193.

14. Padgham, L. and Winikoff, M. (2002) Prometheus: A methodology for developing intelligent agents. In: *Proceedings of the First International Joint Conference on Autonomous Agents and Multiagent Systems: Part 1*, July, pp. 15–19, 2002, Bologna, Italy.

15. Poutakidis, D., Padgham, L. and Winikoff, M. (2002) Debugging multi-agent systems using design artifacts: The case of interaction protocols. In: *Proceedings of the First International Joint Conference on Autonomous Agents and Multi Agent Systems, AAMAS'02*. July 15–19, 2002, Bologna, Italy.

16. Salamon, T. (2008) Dealing with complexity in a multiagent system (in Czech). In: Fi-scher, J. (ed.), *Proceedings of 12th Annual Workshop*, University of Economics, Prague, pp. 60–68.

17. Sycara, K. (1998) Multiagent systems. *AI Magazine* 19(2): Summer, pp. 79–92.

18. Tesfatsion, L. (2002) Agent-based computational economics: Growing economies from the bot-tom up. *ISU Economics Working Paper No. 1*, Iowa State University, Ames, IA.

19. Tiryaki, A.M., Oztuna, S., Dikenelli, O. and Erdur, R.C. (2006) SUNIT: A unit testing framework for test driven development of MASs. In: Padgham, L. and Zambonelli, F. (eds.), *AOSE 2006*, LNCS, Springer Verlag, Berlin, pp. 156–173.

20. Wooldridge, M. (2002) *An introduction to multiagent systems*. John Wiley & Sons, Chichester.

21. Wooldridge, M., Jennings, N. and Kinny, D. (2000) The Gaia methodology for agent-oriented analysis and design. *Journal of Autonomous Agents and Multi-Agent Systems* 3, 285–312.

42

Risk Analysis Based Business Rule Enforcement for Intelligent Decision Support

Olegas Vasilecas, Aidas Smaizys and Ramunas Brazinskas

Abstract

Intelligent information systems are acting by structured rules and do not deal with possible impact on the business environment or future consequences. That is the main reason why automated decisions based on such rules cannot take responsibility and requires involvement or approval of dedicated business people. This limits decision automation possibilities in information systems. However, business rules describe business policy and represent business logics. This can be used in intelligent information systems, together with risk assessment model to simulate real business environment and evaluate possible impact of automated decisions, to support intelligent decision automation. The chapter proposes risk and business rule model integration to provide full intelligent decision automation model used for business rule enforcement and implementation into intelligent software systems of information systems.

Keywords Business rules · Risk analysis · Business rule enforcement · Decision support · Intelligent information systems

1. Introduction

Information system developers force the implementation of simple-structured rules into the software code implementing constraints, ignoring unstructured controversial rules and providing statistical analysis reports at the best. Such way of decision support leads to a large amount of workforce needed to get decisions and even more to implement them. It takes time and leads to mistakes because of human factor. This situation can be explained by avoidance of responsibility of information system developers too, because in traditional way of software engineering, business people creating business rules or influencing rule enforcement cannot see or control decision processing model implemented directly into the software system code. Controversial decisions are especially sensitive and can lead to unwanted results. That is why information system developers avoid them implementing directly into the software code.

In this chapter we discuss the method allowing participation of business people in creation of decision models and using them in the software systems of information systems for automated selection of the best alternate decisions even if they contradict existing business rules. We will discuss what-if analysis using business rules resolution against risk analysis and provide the method for better automated decision implementation into the software systems of information system. For this purpose we use decision model based on statistical risk analysis of historical data and inference engine, together with special technique of setting of enforcement level of business rules and transformation-based implementation, into the information processing rules.

Olegas Vasilecas, Aidas Smaizys and Ramunas Brazinskas • Department of Informatics, Klaipeda University, LT-92294 Klaipeda, Lithuania.

G.A. Papadopoulos et al. (eds.), *Information Systems Development*, DOI 10.1007/b137171_42,

The rest of the chapter is structured as follows. Further sections describe business rule enforcement, risk analysis and introduce risk analysis-based method for business rule enforcement to provide automated selection of the best possible decision from the set of alternatives. Then we provide an implementation example of the model proposed using XForms specification implemented directly into the software system of information system. Finally, the last section concludes the chapter.

2. Related Works

According to business rule manifesto [3] (BRM) "Rules are about business practice and guidance, therefore, rules are motivated by business goals and objectives and are shaped by various influences" and "The cost of rule enforcement must be balanced against business risks, and against business opportunities which might otherwise be lost". Following declarations were not taken into account for long time and only after publication of *Semantics of Business Vocabulary and Business Rules Specification* [9] (SBVR) the definition of enforcement was introduced as "something that represents a position in a graded or ordered scale of values that specifies the severity of action imposed in order to put or keep an operative business rule in force".

The authors in [17] focus on putting the code for rule enforcement inside the database because this approach has the smallest impact on a conventional information system design, but the architecture is planned to have a future enhancement, modules to generate code that will reside outside the database, e.g. in the application interface or in the middle tier.

Many authors claim that business rules should be stated declaratively in some formal language [6, 10, 7]. The authors in [17] proposed use of the standard language for constraint specification – UML Object Constraint Language [14] (OCL) and formally describing business rules over an object-oriented data model. Every business rule, to be enforced by the system and perceived by the user, must be coded somewhere in the system – in the application or in the database – and it is an implicit statement of the rule. Every change in a business rule must be reflected in two different places: in the system and in the documentation. Many times we have to reason about every business rule to discover where to put the code that validates the rule. So, there is a list of events which can fire a rule. When the rule changes, the list of events will change too. We will have many places in the application where the change in the rule must be reflected – a simple mechanical tedious task that is manually done by programmers. This is the usual way we build information systems, but this kind of business rule maintenance waste valuable resources and it is a potential source for errors. When a business rule changes, the new code replaces the old one in the right places and links the rule to its documentation in natural language. Some of the authors provide explanation of how business rule enforcement can be implemented into software systems of information system. However, no one deals with how such rule enforcement should be balanced against business risks as should be according to principles in BRM.

Business motivation model (BMM) [2] provides a range of enforcement levels from "strict" to "guideline". It is important to take into account that this set of enforcement levels is only example and enforcement levels used in a real business system model can be modified depending on the purpose, e.g. discrete enforcement levels assigned according to the risk level of business rule implementation success described in the following sections.

Business systems include institutions or control processes which have power to pursue violation of rules and enforce following the rules, otherwise rules would have no sense. There is a problem of delayed control to be noticed, because controlling process can be involved when unwanted consequences are already unavoidable. For example, if some business rules constraining input of some values are introduced after data model implementation this can lead to consistency problems according to the already entered data stored in database management system (DBMS). However, it can be avoided implementing validation procedure directly in the application instead of DBMS preferring use of externally stored rules.

There are several ways of business rule enforcement implementation into the final software system proposed to implement into relational database constraints [17] or executable code in applications using resolution of separately stored business rules and facts representing entered value instead of validation code [11]. However, database constraints cannot be changed easily and this way of implementation does not suit for our needs of implementation of dynamic rules with rapidly changing enforcement level. In Section 3, we will provide a method for solution of such a problem.

When talking about risk analysis we need to define what the risk is. Under the classical statistical approach, risk is considered to result from a fundamental or inherent randomness in the natural phenomena of the world (aleatory uncertainty). Probabilistic expressions are used to represent this natural variability. Thus, when models are viewed as simplified representations of reality used to estimate system properties, these expressions must be considered as parts of the models. In other words, when logical and physical models are applied under this approach, they include both deterministic and stochastic elements. The deterministic elements capture known coherence in the system, and the stochastic elements represent uncertainty related to quantities viewed to have a random nature [8].

Two main types of risk analysis, quantitative and qualitative, are used. The risk related to an activity is often formulated as the spectrum of consequences C, discrete outcomes which may follow from so-called undesirable events during the activity and the associated probabilities P, i.e. $(C1, P1), (C2, P2), \ldots, (Cn, Pn)$. There are few different approaches to risk analysis based on different methods and principles as traditional approach based on classical statistics, classical approach with uncertainty analysis also referred as the probability of frequency framework approach and a predictive Bayesian approach [8]. The main principle of the analysis used is to describe uncertainty related to quantities occurring in the model and derive the probability of the undesirable consequence in question through the model structure by applying the laws of probability calculus. In qualitative analysis the probability and consequence values are evaluated according to the discrete scale by experts or the quantitative values calculated according to the risk model are discretised, and qualitative risk level value is calculated as follows:

$$R = P' \times C' \tag{42.1}$$

where, R is risk level, P' qualitative P value and C' qualitative C value. There are few typical approaches to the risk assessment: presentation of consequences and risk of selected attributes for the various alternatives, with flexibility in attribute weighting a trade-off and formal Bayesian decision analysis [1]. Modern business intelligence tools, additionally for the same reason, use time series and neural network algorithms [11].

The authors in [5] propose to use expected monetary value (EMV) analysis in decision-making process under risk and uncertainty. The concept of EMV calculates the average outcome for each investment or project to go for when the future includes scenarios which may or may not occur. In the majority of cases, there is no dominant project for all possible scenarios. In reality, higher profits are usually accompanied by higher risks and therefore higher probable losses. At decision-making under risk the probability for each scenario is known. EMV is calculated by multiplying the value of each possible outcome by its probability of occurrence and summing them up together. Other popular methods for evaluating investment decisions are break-even analysis, discounted cash flow calculations, figure of merit calculations, multiple criteria methods and business scenario models [17].

The contribution of a risk analysis to the decision-making process is to clarify or reduce the uncertainty related to activity outcomes by systemising relevant information. The interpretation of analysis models and views on "model uncertainty" does not imply that we can be indifferent about the degree compliance between the model and the real world. The analysis models should be trained using one part of historical data and tuned verifying the model according to another part of historical data set. Analysts doing their work have the responsibility to employ their best engineering judgement to ensure that the differentiation of the models used is adequate for the decision process in question.

3. A Method for Decision Automation Using Risk Analysis Based Business Rule Enforcement

According to [1] if "we have given a set of decision alternatives, A and B. Before a decision can be made, some support is needed, as a basis for the decision. The consequence of choosing one alternative instead of another is needed to be known. Risk analysis provides such decision support. It gives predictions of the performance of the various alternatives with related uncertainty assessments." We agree with such point of view. It is possible for human operator to perform risk-based analysis and select the best possible decision that suites current needs of the business system. However, implementation of such approach in software systems of information systems is not so trivial task. First of all we need to understand decision processing model and have mechanisms for implementation of such dynamic decisions.

The method proposed in this section is an extension of the method provided in [13, 14], where analysing business rule based decision automation we have discovered that sometimes there are situations when business rules and facts loaded into the knowledge base of inference engine cannot lead to the resolution, because there can be conflicting rules loaded and first of all the purification of rule set is needed. In real business it can be represented by the idea of strike, when all the employees start working strictly according to the rules and as the result all the business process is stopped. To avoid such situation in real life human operators of business processes are violating rules which may not lead to big penalty or the risk of being captured is very low. In other words, all the time they are doing risk analysis and based on the results assign different enforcement level to the rules. Such assignment leads to decisions even having contra-dicting rules or no fully suitable decision alternatives provided.

Simulation of real business system behaviour in software systems of information systems can be achieved by using, especially, assigned priorities or enforcement levels. We agree that by using priorities and enforcement levels, we usually try to resolve different problems, e.g. assigning enforcement level to the business, rule we influence possibility of rule violation and in case of such violation determine additional actions to be executed by the system. The priorities on the other hand usually mean some sequence of rule execution. Although according to BRM "A set of statements is declarative only if the set has implicit sequencing" [3]. That is the reason why we avoid setting additional priority attribute for business rules and propose to use enforcement level for rule conflict resolution. The solution of problem can be achieved by simply eliminating contradicting rule with lower enforcement level from the loaded rule set. Acting in this way we will get the result even having contradicting rules in the rule set. This represents a real business system situation, when some rules are better violated to achieve the solution of the problem instead of having no solution at all. To enable this approach we need the setting of enforcement level to be provided on each business rule used for resolution. This is not a trivial task, because of the amount of business rules and dynamic nature of enforcement level for some kind of rules as mentioned before. At the moment we see the only solution of this problem to be the assignment of the enforcement level as some attribute value to the business rule at the moment of formal representation in business rule repository in case of static enforcement level assignment. Automated dynamic enforcement level assignment can be achieved only by providing a special model for each rule. We believe that similar analysis model based on risk assessment as described below can be used for this purpose, but this is left for future research at the moment and is under the scope of this chapter.

Another problem we have discovered is evaluation of alternative decisions which do not contradict any business rule in the current business system situation represented by facts loaded into the knowledge base of inference engine together with business rules and decisions represented as some kind of facts too. Doing resolution we can only evaluate the correctness of decisions proposed to the reasoning subsystem according to the current state of business system. However, we cannot predict the future impact of such decision. That causes the selection of the best suitable decision based on some rational evaluation to be impossible and the intervention of human operator is required. The only one available kind of what-if analysis in this case is the selection of different decision alternatives and its evaluation for correspondence to the business rules in current business situation.

Further in this section, we will show how the proposed method allows selection of the best alternative decision using risk analysis. The main idea of risk analysis involvement together with reasoning for decision automation is represented in Fig. 42.1. The proposed model represents decision processing from decision evaluation to risk assessment and decision selection going vertically down through the layers of the model. All the data carriers and transformation processes are horizontally grouped into four columns by origin according to the method and framework described in [12]. The first horizontal layer is dedicated to represent decision evaluation. At the beginning we have initial business rule set and set of preliminary decision alternatives. First business rules should be checked for completeness and all the conflicting rules should be eliminated. This process is represented as conflict resolution. There are few conflict resolution methods and one of them based on value of enforcement level is presented at the beginning of this section. Decision evaluation process is dedicated to represent logical evaluation when initially predefined preliminary decisions one by one are loaded into the knowledge base of inference engine as some kind of fact for reasoning to check conformance to the current business situation represented by facts and business rules transformed into predicate set. The output of decision evaluation process eliminates preliminary decisions that contradict existing rules and current business state represented by facts. Non contradicting decisions are passed into the next level where future impact of evaluated decisions is analysed according to the risk assessment model. After that each evaluated decision is assigned with its own risk level based on calculated probability and consequence values and passed to the next level for further selection from alternative decisions. Such selection is performed according to the risk level, selection criteria and rules. The implementation of selected decision is performed in two ways. By setting the enforcement level of business rules and changing information or material processing rules using transformations presented in next section. Such dynamically changing information processing rules allows automated changes of decisioning logics of predefined software system processes in information systems.

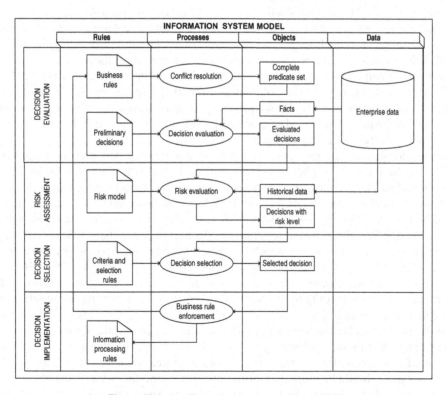

Figure 42.1. Intelligent decision automation model.

The method based on the model proposed in this chapter can be used for decision automation using modern software engineering techniques. However, most of software systems implemented into the business systems today are dedicated only to support decisions of the management staff, there are recurring decision tasks which need automation. Due to large uncertainty and complexity of business systems and frequent changes it is still a very problematic and complicated task.

4. Experimental Validation of the Method Using XForms

In previous section we have described a model for decision automation by business rule enforcement using risk analysis. In this section we will discuss possibility of model implementation into the software systems of the information system using the proposed method. For illustration we will use an example of superstore market.

The problem, which we try to solve implementing decision automation into the ERP software system, can be described as selection of selling price performed by superstore market manager. From first view it is simple task. Manager can simply take prime cost price and add predefined margin in per cent, e.g. 20%. It is a usual business rule not contradicting other business rules together representing business policy like: "sales should be profitable" or "sales price should be more than prime cost price". However, there is another business rule – "It is not allowed to sell expired products". Such rules usually have "strict" enforcement level and cannot be violated because in the contrary case it will directly contradict the main goal of any business system – "get profit doing business" or pursue to penalties. From the first view by increasing margin value we should get more profit. But unfortunately all expired products will reduce the profit more than if they would be sold with lower selling price even less than prime cost price. Such conclusion is not possible to reach using only resolution algorithms operating with decisions based on rule model used for implementation of artificial intelligence. That is the reason why sales are functioning in a complicated way, e.g. in situation with selling goods which are going to be expired. In this case strictly following all the business rules defined before can lead to losses instead of profit because of risk not selling all the goods in time. To increase sales and reduce risk of loss we can decide to lower margin value. However, negative margin values will be allowed only after lowering business rule enforcement level ("sales price should be more than prime cost price"). By this example we demonstrate that enforcement level of business rule can change depending on the real business situation. Moreover violation of this rule (or enforcement level setting to "guideline" or at least to "pre-authorized") can lead to loss of minimisation, better results and bigger total profit allowing achievement of the main business goals. The simplest way for implementation of such a set of business rules can be executable code requiring approval of qualified personnel when margin value used violates rule that "sales price should be more than prime cost price".

However, the decision of what margin value should be to achieve the best sales and biggest profit is more complicated. As we have already explained before, the margin can become any value even with negative meaning discount and selection of the best value based on evaluation of future impact on the business system is needed. Moreover the final decision should be reasonable based on historical results and experience gathered. To simulate such decision behaviour risk analysis model according to the proposed method should be used.

So, we are looking for a decision and selection of sales margin value that will lead to the highest profit or at least to minimise losses of products which are close to expire. We have predefined a set of business rules described before. Then we can predefine some sets of sales margins, e.g. 30%, 20%, 10%, . . . , −10%, −20% as preliminary decisions according to the model in Fig. 42.1. Now the decision evaluation and implementation subsystems according to the model are needed. Some event triggering selection of margin value should collect facts needed for resolution, e.g. profit value. The facts together with business rules should be transformed into a formal form, e.g. predicates and loaded into the knowledge base of inference engine for reasoning. At this stage reasoning engine will select a set of alternative decisions which suit business rules and facts representing current business system state. Negative margin values will contradict business rule "sales price should be more than prime cost price" and the rule conflict resolution should be performed to involve such decisions for further implementation. According to the proposed method of rule conflict resolution it will be allowed by software system only if the enforcement level of business rule "sales price should be more than prime cost price" will be set to different value than "strict" with lower rank and will be eliminated from the rule set in the knowledge base of inference engine. Similar risk model for evaluation of impact of such enforcement level over all the system and selection of most suitable enforcement level according to the business state can be involved too.

As the result from decision evaluation we get a set of alternative decisions about margin value that according to the business policy represented by business rules and according to the current business state represented by facts. All we need to do further is to select one of the best suitable decisions at the next decision implementation level. According to the proposed model we will use risk analysis for this reason. Using predefined analysis model we can get risk value or probability of selling all the goods accordingly for each alternative sale margin values depending on algorithm used and evaluate consequences of every decision. Based on such calculations we have an opportunity to select the best decision available and provide it as a new business rule for sales of evaluated product in the software system of information system.

The question how risk analysis results should be propagated for activation of activities by software system and where the intelligence got should be implemented is open. At present we see several ways, e.g. assignment of different actions to drop down list control in application interface for different set of decisions got and initially preset values corresponding to predefined risk level. This was implemented into the Web-based software system prototype. For automated transformation of business rules and selected decisions, we have represented them in Simple Rule Markup Language (SRML) and transformed into the W3C XForms [14] specification according to the predefined SRML and XForms metamodel-based transformation as displayed in Fig. 42.2.

Such XForms specification was loaded into the Web browser-based user interface to represent information processing rules. According to such rules all the decisions are made automatically by selection of the best decision with balanced or less risk value, but if operator will change the preselected value, software system will act requiring confirmation, sending message to the authorised personal or doing nothing depending on corresponding enforcement level determined by risk level value. This eliminates the need of operator participation in authorisation or selection of margin value, manually row by row in the large set of the pricelist and automates implementation of the best available decision. Such decisions are based on experience discovered analysing historical data, evaluated according to the real business situation represented by facts from real business data and business logics formally represented as business rules instead of just operator experience based manual decisions.

5. Conclusions

Most of software systems implemented into the business systems today are dedicated only to support decisions of the management staff. Although there is a lot of recurring decision tasks which need automation. Due to large uncertainty and complexity of business systems and frequent changes it is still a very problematic and complicated task. In some situations all of the already known preliminary decisions satisfy all the existing rules or all of them can lead to contradictions with business rule set and facts loaded for reasoning disallowing selection of any suitable decision. For solutions of such problems, we have proposed a method based on the risk assessment model to be used for decision automation by the use of risk analysis for selection of the best suitable decision and evaluation of rule violation influence on the entire business system, eliminating business rules with the lowest enforcement level out from knowledge base of inference engine for conflicts resolution.

The method proposed in this chapter was used for experimental implementation of automated decisions in the prototype of Web-based user interface, using automated SRML and XForms metamodel-based transformations for dynamic implementation of business rules into the information processing rules of software system.

The ideas provided in this chapter are at the early stage and requires further research. The practical implementation of the decision automation model proposed in this chapter is complicated, because of missing existing business intelligence tools providing the functionality needed. However, we believe that

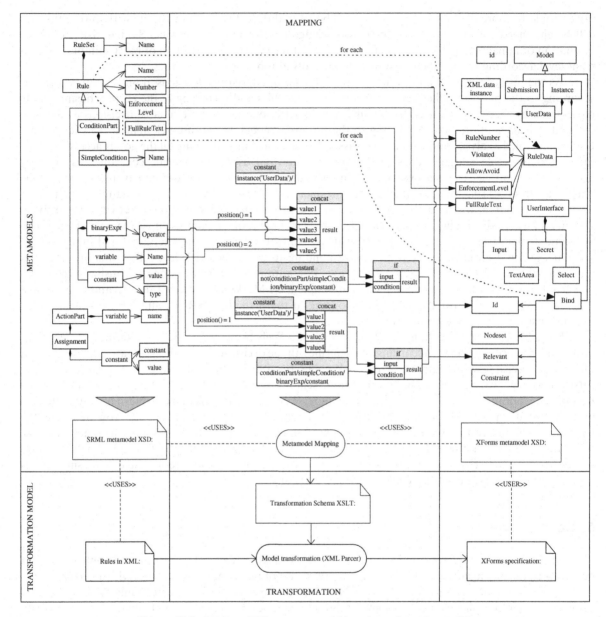

Figure 42.2. SRML and XForms metamodel-based transformation model.

upcoming new releases of business intelligence and data analysis tools and evolving set of inference engines will allow such implementations to be performed at regular basis avoiding complicated risk evaluation scenario model development, tuning and parameterisation. This is the main subject for further research.

Acknowledgements

The work is supported by Lithuanian State Science and Studies Foundation according to High Technology Development Program Project "Business Rules Solutions for Information Systems Development (VeTIS)" Reg. No. B-07042.

References

1. Aven T. and Korte J. On the use of risk and decision analysis to support decision-making, Reliability Engineering and System Safety, 2003, Vol. 79, No. 3, pp. 289–299.
2. Business Rules Group. The business motivation model – business governance in a volatile world [online]. Version 1.2, Ross G. R. (ed.), Business Rules Group, 2005. Available from: http://www.businessrulesgroup.org/bmm.shtml [Accessed 31 January 2008].
3. Business Rules Group. The business rule manifesto – the principles of rule independence [online]. Version 2.0, Ross G. R. (ed.), Business Rules Group, 2003. Available from: http://www.businessrulesgroup.org/brmanifesto/BRManifesto.pdf [Accessed 10 August 2005].
4. Business Rules Group. Defining business rules – what are they really? [online]. Version 1.3, Ross G. R. (ed.), Business Rules Group, 2000. Available from: http http://www.businessrulesgroup.org/first_paper/br01c0.htm [Accessed 31 January 2008].
5. Chapman R. J. Simple Tools and Techniques for Enterprise Risk Management, John Wiley & Sons, NY, 2006.
6. Date C. J. What Not How: The Business Rules Approach to Application Development, Addison-Wesley Longman Publishing Co., Inc., Boston, MA, 2000.
7. Halle B. Business Rules Applied: Building Better Systems Using the Business Rules Approach, John Wiley & Sons, Inc., NY, 2001.
8. Nilsen T. and Aven T. Models and model uncertainty in the context of risk analysis, Reliability Engineering and System Safety, 2003, No. 3, Issue 79, pp. 309–317.
9. Object Management Group. Semantics of Business Vocabulary and Business Rules Specification [online], Object Management Group, 2006. http://www.omg.org/docs/dtc/06-03-02.pdf [Accessed 31 January 2008].
10. Ross R. The business rule book: Classifying, defining and modelling rules, Business Rule Solutions, 1997.
11. Tang Z., Maclennan J. and Kim P. P. Building data mining solutions with ole db for dm and xml for analysis, SIGMOD Rec, 2005, Vol. 34, No. 2, pp. 80–85.
12. Vasilecas O. and Smaizys A. The framework for business rule based software modeling: An approach for data analysis models integration. Frontiers in Artificial Intelligence and Applications, Databases and Information Systems IV, V 155, IOS Press, Amsterdam, 2007, ISSN 0922-6389, pp. 175–188.
13. Vasilecas O. and Smaizys A. Business rule based data analysis for decision support and automation. In B. Rachev, A. Smirkarov (eds.), Proc. of the International Conference on Computer Systems and Technologies "CompSysTech'06", Varna, Bulgaria, 15–16 June, 2006, pp. II.9-1–II.9-6.
14. Vasilecas O. and Smaizys A. The framework for adaptable data analysis system design. In G. Magyar et al. (eds.), Proc. of the 15th International Conference on Information Systems Development 2006, Advances in Information Systems Development: New Methods and Practice for the Networked Society, V 1, Springer, 2007, ISBN-13 978-0-387-70760-0, pp. 101–109.
15. Warmer J. B. and Kleppe A. G. The Object Constraint Language. Addison-Wesley, Boston, MA, 1999.
16. Web A. Risk analysis for business decisions Part1. Engineering Management Journal, 1994, Vol. 4, pp. 177–182.
17. Zimbrao G., Miranda R., Souza J. M., Estolano M. H. and Neto F. P., Enforcement of business rules in relational databases using constraints. In: Proceedings of XVIII Simposio Brasileiro de Bancos de Dados/SBBD 2003, UFAM, 2003, pp. 129–141.

43

Sound Processing Features for Speaker-Dependent and Phrase-Independent Emotion Recognition in Berlin Database

Christos Nikolaos Anagnostopoulos and Eftichia Vovoli

Abstract

An emotion recognition framework based on sound processing could improve services in human–computer interaction. Various quantitative speech features obtained from sound processing of acting speech were tested, as to whether they are sufficient or not to discriminate between seven emotions. Multilayered perceptrons were trained to classify gender and emotions on the basis of a 24-input vector, which provide information about the prosody of the speaker over the entire sentence using statistics of sound features. Several experiments were performed and the results were presented analytically. Emotion recognition was successful when speakers and utterances were "known" to the classifier. However, severe misclassifications occurred during the utterance-independent framework. At least, the proposed feature vector achieved promising results for utterance-independent recognition of high- and low-arousal emotions.

Keywords Emotion recognition · Sound/speech processing · Neural networks

1. Introduction

Human–computer interaction (HCI) is a developing field of science aimed at providing natural ways for humans to interact with computers. Feedback from the user has traditionally been through the keyboard, mouse, or specialized interfaces, such as data gloves and touch screens. Recently, the information provided by cameras and microphones enable the computer to "see" and "hear" the user through advanced image and sound processing techniques in systems similar to the one presented in Fig. 43.1. Therefore, one of these skills that computer potentially can develop, is the ability to understand the emotional state of the person. The most expressive way humans display emotions is through facial expressions. However, it is proven that speech also caries meaningful information concerning the emotional state of the speaker. In the field of human–computer interaction (HCI), emotion recognition from the computer is still a challenging issue, especially when the recognition is based solely on voice, which is the basic mean of human communication. In human–computer interaction systems, emotion recognition could provide users with improved services by being adaptive to their emotions. Therefore, emotion detection from speech could have many potential applications in order to make the computer more adaptive to the user's needs.

Most of the approaches that have been tested in the literature assess their performance in a speaker-dependent or a speaker-independent framework. Usually speaker-dependent tests achieve high level of

Christos Nikolaos Anagnostopoulos and Eftichia Vovoli • Cultural Technology and Communication Department, University of the Aegean, Aegean, Greece.

G.A. Papadopoulos et al. (eds.), *Information Systems Development*, DOI 10.1007/b137171_43,

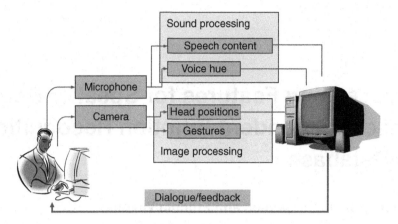

Figure 43.1. Increased human–computer interaction through an emotion recognition system.

accuracy since the speaker is "known" to the classifier. In this way, the phrases in the testing set are also "known" to the classification scheme, imposing a positive bias to the results. The novelty in this research is that emotion recognition is tested in an utterance-independent framework. This framework indicates that the classification performance will be tested in phrases that are "unknown" to the emotion classifier.

2. Basic Emotions

According to a dimensional view of emotions, large amounts of variation in emotions can be located in a two-dimensional space, with coordinates of valence and arousal [1]. The valence dimension refers to the hedonic quality of an affective experience and ranges from unpleasant to pleasant. The arousal dimension refers to the perception of arousal associated with the experience and ranges from very calm to very excited at the other.

A common way to measure the emotions of others is via their emotional expressions. These include facial expression, vocal expression, and bodily posture. For the emotional expressions, MPEG-4 set

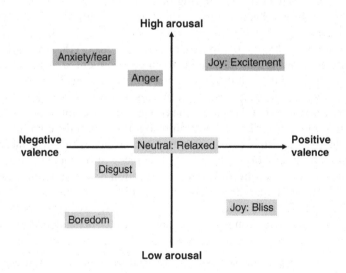

Figure 43.2. Emotions of Berlin database according to valence and arousal.

includes joy, anger, disgust, fear, sadness, surprise. In Berlin database (EMO-DB) [2], surprise utterances were not recorded. Instead, two more emotions are supported, namely boredom and neutral.

The above set of seven emotion classes can also be well separated into two hyperclasses as shown in Fig. 43.2: high arousal containing anger, happiness, anxiety/fear and low arousal containing neutral, boredom, disgust, and sadness. The classification of disgust into low arousal can be challenged, but according to the literature, disgust belongs to low-arousal emotions [3].

In Berlin emotional database, 10 German sentences have been acted in the above 7 emotions by 10 professional actors, 5 of them female. The database contains 535 phrases representing all the possible emotional instances. In our experiments, always whole utterances were analyzed. Table 43.1 depicts the speaker and utterance codes, while Table 43.2 contains the context of the 10 utterances that have been recorded by the actors. Berlin Emotional Database was selected since it is the most complete and rich database which is freely available to the scientific community.

Table 43.1. Speaker codes, utterance codes, and emotions in Berlin database.

Speaker code (gender)	Utterance code	Emotion code (emotion)
03 (male)	a01 (utterance 1)	W (anger)
08 (female)	a02 (utterance 2)	L (boredom)
09 (female)	a04 (utterance 3)	E (disgust)
10 (male)	a05 (utterance 4)	A (anxiety/fear)
11 (male)	a07 (utterance 5)	F (happiness)
12 (male)	b01 (utterance 6)	T (sadness)
13 (female)	b02 (utterance 7)	N (neutral)
14 (female)	b09 (utterance 8)	
15 (male)	b09 (utterance 9)	
16 (female)	b10 (utterance 10)	

Table 43.2. Utterance code and context in Berlin database.

Utterance code	Context of utterance
a01	Der Lappen liegt auf dem Eisschrank.
a02	Das will sie am Mittwoch abgeben.
a04	Heute abend könnte ich es ihm sagen.
a05	Das schwarze Stück Papier befindet sich da oben neben dem Holzstück.
a07	In sieben Stunden wird es soweit sein.
b01	Was sind denn das für Tüten, die da unter dem Tisch stehen?
b02	Sie haben es gerade hochgetragen und jetzt gehen sie wieder runter.
b03	An den Wochenenden bin ich jetzt immer nach Hause gefahren und habe Agnes besucht.
b09	Ich will das eben wegbringen und dann mit Karl was trinken gehen.
b10	Die wird auf dem Platz sein, wo wir sie immer hinlegen.

3. Sound/Speech Features

Many diverse acoustic features have been tested and assessed in the literature considering their performance. The fundamental frequency (F0), often referred to as the pitch, is one of the most important features for determining emotion in speech [4–7]. Bäzinger et al. argued that statistics related to pitch conveys considerable information about emotional status [8]. However, pitch was also shown to be most gender-dependent feature [9]. If the recognition system ignores this issue a misclassification of utterances might be the consequence. It should be noted that most of the features that will be described below are gender dependent to varying degrees.

Beside pitch, other commonly employed features are related to energy, speaking rate, formants as well as spectral features such as mel-frequency cepstral coefficients (MFCCs). Wang and Guan [10] and Thurid and Elisabeth [11] used prosodic, mel-frequency cepstral coefficient (MFCC) and formant frequency features to represent the characteristics of the emotional speech, while the facial expressions were represented by Gabor wavelet features. According to Kostoulas et al. [12], an individual's emotional state is strongly related to pitch and energy, while pitch and energy of a speech signal expressing happiness or anger is, usually, higher than those associated with sadness. Mel-frequency cepstral coefficients have been widely used for speech spectral representation in numerous applications, including speech, speaker, gender, and emotion recognition [4]. They are also increasingly finding uses in music information retrieval applications such as genre classification and audio similarity measures [13].

Energy, often referred to as the volume or intensity of the speech, is also known to contain valuable information. Energy provides information that can be used to differentiate sets of emotions, but this measurement alone is not sufficient to differentiate basic emotions. In [14] it is referred that fear, joy, and anger have increased energy level, whereas sadness has low energy level. Therefore, it can be assumed that energy is a distinguishing characteristic for the classification of emotions with high arousal (e.g., joy, anger) or low arousal (e.g., neutral, sadness).

3.1. Sound Feature Selection

In order to select the most important prosodic features and optimize the classification performance, a subset evaluator was used. Subset evaluators take a subset of features and return a number which measure a quality of the subset and guides the further search. For the selection of the method, the WEKA data mining tool was used [15]. WEKA is a data mining workbench that allows comparison between many different machine learning algorithms. Moreover, WEKA offers many feature selection and feature ranking methods, where each method is a combination of feature search and evaluator of currently selected features. Several combinations have been tested as shown in Table 43.3 in order to assess the feature selection combination that gives the optimum performance for our problem. The shaded cells in Table 43.3 show the feature evaluator and search method that presented the best performance in the data set (CfsSubSetEval and BestFirst).

Table 43.3. Feature evaluators and search methods that were studied. Shaded cells correspond to the selected combination for feature selection in this chapter.

Feature evaluator (offered in WEKA)	Feature search method (offered in WEKA)
CfsSubSetEval	GeneticSearch
ChiSquaredAttributeEval	BestFirst
GainRatioAttributeEval	Ranker
InfoGainAttributeEval	RaceSearch

Based on the acoustic features described above and the literature relating to automatic emotion detection from speech, 76 features are calculated based on four prosodic groups which are represented as contours: the pitch, the 12 MFCCs, the energy, and the first 5 formant frequencies (F1–F5). From these 19 contours, we calculated the mean and the standard deviation of the original contour and the mean and standard deviation of the contour gradient. The 76 measurements are shown in Table 43.4.

All 76 measurements contribute to decision making, but the influence of specific measurements is much bigger than others. In Table 43.4, shaded cells indicate the features selected by the feature evaluator and the search method as the most important for the classification problem. On the basis of this selection,

Table 43.4. The 76 sound features. Shaded cells indicate the selected features by the feature selection method as the most important.

Prosodic group	Prosodic Feature	Mean	Std	Mean of derivative	Std of derivative
1	Pitch	1	2	3	4
	MFCC1	5	6	7	8
	MFCC2	9	10	11	12
	MFCC3	13	14	15	16
	MFCC4	17	18	19	20
	MFCC5	21	22	23	24
2	MFCC6	25	26	27	28
	MFCC7	29	30	31	32
	MFCC8	33	34	35	36
	MFCC9	37	38	39	40
	MFCC10	41	42	43	44
	MFCC11	45	46	47	48
	MFCC12	49	50	51	52
3	Energy	53	54	55	56
	F1	57	58	59	60
	F2	61	62	63	64
4	F3	65	66	67	68
	F4	69	70	71	72
	F5	73	74	75	76

we estimated that the classification should be based on statistical measurements of pitch, energy, and the first 4 MFCCs. This selection is in accordance with similar approaches [11]. In addition, since measurements in only six rows are selected (as can be seen in Table 43.4), we chose to include all the measurements in each selected row in the feature set. Therefore, the final 24-feature vector [F1, F2, ..., F24] is shown in Table 43.5.

Table 43.5. The final 24-feature vector.

Feature	Mean	Std	Mean of derivative	Std of derivative
Pitch	F1	F2	F3	F4
Energy	F5	F6	F7	F8
MFCC1	F9	F10	F11	F12
MFCC2	F13	F14	F15	F16
MFCC3	F17	F18	F19	F20
MFCC4	F21	F22	F23	F24

3.2. Calculation of Sound Features

Pitch was extracted from the speech waveform using a modified version of the algorithm for pitch tracking proposed in [16], which is offered in the VOICEBOX toolbox [17]. Using a frame length of 100 ms, the pitch for each frame was calculated and placed in a vector to correspond to that frame. If the speech is unvoiced the corresponding marker in the pitch vector was set to zero.

For energy, the choice of the window in short-time speech processing determines the nature of the measurement representation. A long window w would result in very little changes of the measurement in time, whereas the measurement with a short window would not be sufficiently smooth. The energy frame size should be long enough to smooth the contour appropriately, but short enough to retain the fast energy changes which are common in speech signals and it is suggested that a frame size of 10–20 ms would be adequate. Two representative windows are widely used, Rectangular and Hamming. The latter has almost twice the bandwidth of the former, for the same length. Furthermore, the attenuation for the Hamming window outside the passband is much greater. Short-time energy is a simple short-time speech measurement. It is defined as

$$E_n = \sum [x(m) \cdot w(n - m)]^2,$$

where m is the overlapping length of the original signal x and Hamming windowed signal w with length n. For the length of the window a practical choice is 160–320 samples (sample for each 10–20 ms) for sampling frequency 16 kHz. For our experiments the Hamming window was used, taking samples every 20 ms.

In addition, for each 5 ms frame of speech, the first four standard MFCC parameters were calculated by taking the absolute value of the STFT, warping it to a mel-frequency scale, taking the DCT of the log-mel spectrum and returning the first four components. The Matlab Code which performs the above calculation was provided in [18].

4. Classification

Classification was performed using WEKA (Waikato Environment for Knowledge Analysis). Beside feature selection, WEKA has also functionality for data preprocessing, classification, and visualization. In this research, the classifier was always a multilayer perceptron (MLP) whose size depends on the size of the input vector and the number of possible classes. For all the tests, MPLs with one hidden layer are used, while the number of the hidden neurons h = 15 was calculated using the well known formula:

$$h = \frac{i + o}{2},$$

where i and o correspond to the number of inputs and outputs, respectively. Input was always a 24 vector containing the values of [F1, F2, ... , F24], while the number of classes are 7 as the number of emotional states in Berlin database. Error backpropagation was used as a training algorithm. Moreover, all neurons follow the sigmoid activation function, while all attributes have been normalized for improved performance of the network.

4.1. Utterance-Dependent Emotion Recognition

In this section, the classification performance in Berlin database for emotion recognition when the phrases (utterances) and the speaker are known to the classifier is discussed. A MLP classifier with topology 24-15-7 was trained using 66% of all samples as training set and the remaining 34% as test set, with sigmoid neurons in middle and output layer, n = 0.3, m = 0.2, and epochs = 1500. Table 43.6 portrays the experimental results. The percentage in every row totals 100%, while the cells in the diagonal positions indicate successful recognition.

From these results, it can be clearly observed that high arousal emotions present extremely high performance (i.e., 100% for anger and happiness). In addition, 2 over 28 anxiety patterns were classified as disgust, which is acceptable.

On the other hand, low-arousal emotion recognition tends to be less accurate, especially for disgust, where the discrimination ability was approximately 77%, with the remaining percentage classified as anxiety/fear. Interestingly, the two hyperclasses of emotions (high and low arousal) did not overlap significantly. Merging the results in shaded cells of Table 43.6, the performance reaches 97.8% for high arousal and 95.7% for low arousal emotions.

Table 43.6. Confusion matrix, emotion recognition, and utterance dependent.

	High-arousal emotions			Low-arousal emotions			
	Anger	Happiness	Anxiety/fear	Boredom	Disgust	Sadness	Neutral
Anger	43 (100%)	–	–	–	–	–	–
Happiness	–	18 (100%)	–	–	–	–	–
Anxiety /fear	–	–	26 (92.9%)	–	2 (7.1%)	–	–
Boredom	–	1 (2.9%)	–	30 (85.7%)	–	2 (5.7%)	2 (5.7%)
Disgust	–	–	3 (23.1%)	–	10 (76.9%)	–	–
Sadness	–	–	–	1 (4.8%)	–	20 (95.2%)	–
Neutral	–	–	–	2 (8.3%)	–	–	22 (91.7%)

4.2. Utterance-Independent Emotion Recognition

For this experiment, the test case consists again of 100 utterances with identification code "a01" and "b01." After the training procedure with the 435 phrases of the training set (all the phrases except "a01" and "b01"), the testing data was presented to the MLP with topology 24-15-7 with sigmoid neurons in middle and output layer, n = 0.3, m = 0.2, and epochs = 1500. The results are presented in Table 43.7.

Table 43.7. Confusion matrix, emotion recognition, and utterance independent.

	High-arousal emotions			Low-arousal emotions			
	Anger	Happiness	Anxiety/fear	Boredom	Disgust	Sadness	Neutral
Anger	23 (100%)						
Happiness		12 (75%)			1 (6.3%)	3 (18.8%)	
Anxiety /fear		7 (53.8%)	2 (15.4%)			4 (30.8%)	
Boredom				2 (15.4%)	3 (23.1%)	5 (38.5%)	3 (23.1%)
Disgust		5 (38.5%)			2 (15.4%)	6 (46.2%)	
Sadness				9 (69.2%)		4 (30.8%)	
Neutral					4 (44.4%)	3 (33.3%)	2 (22.2%)

Judging from the main diagonal of the confusion matrix of Table 43.7, the MLP performance is very low in all classes except from the emotions of anger (100%) and happiness (75%). Overall, we are witnessing 47% correct assignment within the seven emotions, meaning that the 24-feature vector is not sufficient to distinguish the seven emotions accurately. On the other hand, observing the results in the two hyperclasses (low and high arousal), the recognition rate reach 84.6% for high arousal and 87.8% for low arousal emotions which seems quite promising. Nevertheless, it seems that the proposed vector is not sufficient enough to describe the intraclass variations of the two hyperclasses and, therefore, this feature vector should be enriched with more sound descriptors.

5. Conclusion and Future Work

The literature in speech emotion recognition is not very rich and researchers are still debating what features influence the recognition of emotion in speech. There is also considerable uncertainty as to the best algorithm for classifying emotion and which emotions to class together.

Although it is impossible to accurately compare recognition accuracies from this study with others due to different data sets used, the feature set implemented in this work seems to be promising for further research. The proposed feature set contains 24 high-level features, which provide information about the prosody of the speaker over the entire sentence. In the related literature, the input to the classifier usually contains more kinds of features and in many cases more features. In Table 43.8, important issues such as number of features, number of classes, and overall performance of similar researches are briefly presented. It should be emphasized again that there is a lack of uniformity in the way that methods are evaluated and, therefore, it is inappropriate to explicitly declare which methods demonstrate actually the highest performance.

Table 43.8. Related literature.

Reference	No. of features used	No. of emotions/classes	Overall performance
[3]	Up to 26	8	80.0% (speaker dependent)
[5]	Up to 34	6	72.2%
[11]	30	7 (Berlin database)	81.1% (speaker independent)
[12]	20	8	85.4% (speaker dependent)
[19]	20	7 (MPEG-4 + neutral)	71.6% (speaker independent)
[20]	3	4	75.7%
[21]	16	4	74.3%
This paper	24	7 (Berlin database)	92.9% (utterance dependent) 47% (utterance independent)

Moreover, as feature analysis shows significant speaker dependence, we will focus to improve speaker and utterance independence. A first experiment was conducted in this chapter, presenting unknown utterances to the classifier. Ultimately, samples of various speech databases could be assessed from the classifier in order to tackle also the problem of multilingual context. The latter was interestingly addressed in [3].

The researchers usually deal with elicited and acted emotions in a lab setting from few actors. However, in the real problem, different individuals reveal their emotions in a diverse degree and manner. There are also many differences between acted and spontaneous speech. Speaker-independent detection of negative emotional states from acted and real-world speech was investigated in [22]. The experiments demonstrated some important differences on recognizing acted vs. non-acted speech, which cause significant drop of performance, for the real-world data.

Concluding this work, we should emphasize the difficulty of the speech emotion recognition problem. In this interdisciplinary field of research, aspects of psychology and physiology are not always considered and literature still offers ideas rather than solutions.

References

1. P. J. Lang, "The Emotion Probe: Studies of Motivation and Attention", American Psychologist 50(5), 1995, pp. 372–385.
2. V. Hozjan and Z. Kacic, "Context-independent multilingual emotion recognition from speech signals", International Journal of Speech Technology 6, 2003, pp. 311–320.
3. F. Burkhardt, A. Paeschke, M. Rolfes, W. Sendlmeier, and B. Weiss. "A database of german emotional speech". In Proceedings Interspeech, Lisbon, Portugal, 2005.
4. S. Kim, P. Georgiou, S. Lee, and S. Narayanan. "Real-time emotion detection system using speech: Multi-modal fusion of different timescale features", Proceedings of IEEE Multimedia Signal Processing Workshop, Chania, Greece, 2007.
5. D. Morrison, R. Wang, and L. C. De Silva. "Ensemble methods for spoken emotion recognition in call-centres", Speech Communication 49, 2007, pp. 98–112.

6. J. Ang, R. Dhillon, A. Krupski, E. Shriberg, and A. Stolcke. "Prosody-based automatic detection of annoyance and frustration in human–computer dialog". Proceedings of the International Conference on Spoken Language Processing (ICSLP 2002), Denver, Colorado.

7. V. Petrushin, 2000. Emotion recognition in speech signal: experimental study, development, and application. In: Proceedings of the Sixth International Conference on Spoken Language Processing (ICSLP 2000), Beijing, China.

8. T. Bänziger and K. R.Scherer, 2005, "The role of intonation in emotional expression", Speech Communication 46, pp. 252–267.

9. W. H. Abdulla and N. K. Kasabov, 2001, "Improving speech recognition performance through gender separation", In Proceedings of ANNES, Dunedin, New Zealand, pp. 218–222.

10. Y. Wang and L. Guan, "Recognizing human emotion from audiovisual information," Proceedings ICASP 2005, pp. 1125-1128.

11. T. Vogt and E. Andre, 2006, "Improving Automatic Emotion Recognition from Speech via Gender Differentiation" In Proc. of Language Resources and Evaluation Conference, 2006, pp. 1123–1126.

12. T. P. Kostoulas and N. Fakotakis, 2006, "A Speaker Dependent Emotion Recognition Framework", CSNDSP Fifth International Symposium, Patras, July 19–21, pp. 305–309.

13. M. Fingerhut, 2004, "Music Information Retrieval, or how to search for (and maybe find) music and do away with incipits", IAML-IASA Congress, Oslo (Norway), August 8–13.

14. K. R. Scherer, 2003, "Vocal communication of emotion: a review of research paradigms. Speech Communication 40, pp. 227–256.

15. Waikato Environment for Knowledge Analysis (WEKA), [Computer program]. Retrieved January 24, 2006, from http://www.cs.waikato.ac.nz/ml/weka/

16. D.Talkin, "A Robust Algorithm for Pitch Tracking (RAPT)", Speech Coding & Synthesis, 1995.

17. http://www.ee.ic.ac.uk/hp/staff/dmb/voicebox/voicebox.html

18. http://www.ee.columbia.edu/~dpwe/resources/matlab/rastamat/

19. B. Schuller, S. Reiter, R. Müller, M. Al-Hames, M. Lang, and G. Rigoll, 2005, "Speaker independent speech emotion recognition by ensemble classification", Proc. of IEEE International Conference on Multimedia and Expo, pp. 864–867.

20. E. H. Kim, K. H. Hyun, and Y. K. Kwak, 2005, "Robust emotion recognition feature, frequency range of meaningful signal", Proc. of 2005 IEEE International Workshop on Robots and Human Interactive Communication, pp. 667–671.

21. F. Yu, E. Chang, Y.-Q. Xu, and H.-Y. Shum, Emotion Detection from Speech to Enrich Multimedia Content, H.-Y. Shum, M. Liao, and S.-F. Chang (Eds.): PCM 2001, Lecture Notes in Computer Science, vol. 2195, 2001, pp. 550–557.

22. T. Kostoulas, T. Ganchev, and N. Fakotakis, "Study on speaker-independent emotion recognition from speech on real-world data", Cost2102 Workshop, Lecture Notes in Computer Science, 2007, (in press).

44

An Approach for Implementation of Project Management Information Systems

Solvita Bērziša and Jānis Grabis

Abstract

Project management is governed by project management methodologies, standards, and other regulatory requirements. This chapter proposes an approach for implementing and configuring project management information systems according to requirements defined by these methodologies. The approach uses a project management specification framework to describe project management methodologies in a standardized manner. This specification is used to automatically configure the project management information system by applying appropriate transformation mechanisms. Development of the standardized framework is based on analysis of typical project management concepts and process and existing XML-based representations of project management. A demonstration example of project management information system's configuration is provided.

Keywords Project management information systems · Systems configuration · XML

1. Introduction

Project management (PM) is a complex process involving planning, decision-making, execution, and control activities. In order to ensure quality of PM processes, it is guided by various methodologies and standards. These methodologies usually define PM processes, organizational structure of project, project deliverable, templates, and other items. Project management body of knowledge (PMBOK) [9] describes generic PM processes along with data and document flows and techniques used for PM. The PRINCE methodology developed by the UK Computer and Telecommunications Agency (CCTA) is other generic PM used as the UK Government standard for PM [8]. Besides generic methodologies, there are domain-specific PM methodologies such RUP and MSF in the software development area. These domain-specific methodologies cover PM issues as well as product development issues. Specific PM methodologies and guidelines are also developed by individual organizations and funding agencies, which often present their own set of PM requirements.

Regardless of PM methodology used, successful PM requires an appropriate project management information system (PMIS). PMBOK defines PMIS as "an information system consisting of the tools and techniques used to gather, integrate, and disseminate the outputs of PM processes." It provides a framework to help guide the progress of project, because accurate, timely, and relevant information is essential to the decision-making process of a project and inadequate information puts a project at risk. Large automated and integrated PMIS are usually developed on the basis of commercial-off-the-shelf (COTS) PM software. Ideally PMIS would adhere to all requirements of PM methodology used for a particular project.

Solvita Bērziša and Jānis Grabis · Faculty of Computer Science and Information Technology, Riga Technical University, Kalku 1, Riga, LV-1658, Latvia.

G.A. Papadopoulos et al. (eds.), *Information Systems Development*, DOI 10.1007/b137171_44,

However, organizations have multiple projects often governed by different methodologies and regulatory requirements and implementation, and modification of PMIS becomes a complex task plagued by similar problems as implementation of COTS systems. Although some project methodologies have associated set of software tools for PM (e.g., RUP), that is not always the case and integration of these tools into the overall PMIS is complicated.

An objective of this chapter is to develop an approach for implementation and configuration of PMIS according to requirements of specific PM methodologies. If organization initiates a new project, which requires use of specific PM methodology, this approach would enable for quick configuration of PMIS to support new requirements. In order to achieve this objective, a standardized framework for specification of PM methodologies is proposed. This framework is built on the basis of generic PM methodologies. If a PM methodology is specified in this standardized manner, its definition can be loaded into PMIS using appropriate transformation tools. This chapter describes the general approach to implementation and configuration of PMIS, presents an initial version of the standardized framework for specification of PM methodologies, and describes a simple configuration example.

The contribution of this research is simplification of configuration of PMIS and extension of existing PM specification languages to incorporate both static and dynamic aspects of PM. Additionally, it demonstrates use of informally specified industry standards in configuration of enterprise systems.

The rest of the chapter is organized as follows. Section 2 discusses the state of art in implementation of PMIS. Section 3 describes the implementation and configuration approach. Specification of PM methodologies is discussed in Section 4. The configuration sample is provided in Section 5 and Section 6 concludes.

2. State of Art

Despite importance of PMIS in PM, these systems have gained relatively little attention in scientific literature and many developments are largely industry based. At the same time from the perspective of information systems development, PMIS are just one type of information systems and the same principles apply to their development and implementation. This state-of-art review initially discusses selected PM methodologies to identify main specific requirements for configuration of PMIS. Afterward, it reviews some of existing PMIS and their implementation issues.

2.1. Project Management Methodologies

As already mentioned, PM is governed by PM methodologies. Thus, PMIS should support usage of specific PM methodologies and these methodologies pose requirements to implementation of PMIS. Some of the best-known generic PM methodologies are PMBOK and PRINCE and domain-specific methodologies in software development are RUP and MSF.

PMBOK [9] describes general guidelines for PM. It presents PM as closed loop of planning, executing, and controlling. Nine PM areas (e.g., scope, quality, cost, risk management) are defined. Each area is described by presenting the management process and defining activities of the process by their inputs, tools and techniques used, and outputs. Inputs and outputs are some sort of information items produced and used during PM. RUP [6] is one of the most complete software development methodologies developed by Rational Software (now part of IBM). It describes organization and execution of software development project. The methodology defines project roles. Each role performs a number of activities using specific tools and produces certain artifacts. Roles, activities, and artifacts are described in a standardized manner. For instance, each role is defined by description, required skills and activities, and artifacts it is responsible for. Thus, the methodology has well-defined structure, which can be used to configure PMIS. It also defines general PM and software development workflows. The structure of MSF [14] is also very similar to RUP. This methodology defines roles, typical work items and work products, and PM and product development workstreams. MSF is tightly coupled with the developers' tools family of Microsoft software. PM activities are supported by Microsoft Team Foundation Server and Microsoft Project Server.

There are two technical solutions for specification of PM. PMXML Consortium developed a Project Management Extensible Markup Language (PMXML) [3], which is used to define typical PM data and aimed at supporting data exchange among different PM tools. The Microsoft Project XML schema is other similar development. Both definitions describe projects using three main entities – task, resource, and assignment. These solutions have too narrow scope for representation of PM methodologies and contain tool specific data (in the case of Microsoft Project). They can be used as a starting point for development of the methodology specification.

Another development to define the PM domain is PM ontologies. Abels et al. [1] propose the PM ontology PROTON, which is put forward as a reference ontology to support collaboration among multiple enterprises working on common projects. A similar ontology has been proposed also by Ruiz and Dolado [11].

2.2. Project Management Information System

Von Schoultz et al. [15] describe an integrated project management information system, which contains plan building tools, simulation tools, planning tools, reporting tools, and communication and progress control tool. The authors provide a short description of PMIS usage throughout the project life cycle. Raymond and Bergeron [10] survey several project managers to determine contribution of PMIS to efficiency of PM. Their survey confirms positive impact of PMIS on PM efficiency. Several investigations have focused on improving planning and decision making capabilities of PMIS. Jaafari and Manivong [5] discuss the need to improve capabilities of existing PMIS. One of their conclusions is that PMIS need to enhance representation of project-specific information. Stewart et al. [13] discuss implementation of PMIS from the strategic perspective with emphasis on managerial decision making on system's implementation rather than technical issues of implementation.

To our knowledge, there are no papers addressing configuration of PMIS according to requirements of specific PM methodologies.

2.3. Implementation of COTS Systems

Implementation of PMIS shares many commonalities with implementation of other types of COTS systems [7]. Enterprise resource planning (ERP) systems are one of the most widely studied types of COTS systems. In order to reduce complexity of their implementation [2], best practice configuration scenarios can be used. However, PM modules of existing ERP systems essentially implement their vendors' PM methodologies and modification of these modules is complex and time consuming. From the perspective of implementation of COTS systems, to some extent the proposed approach can be perceived as definition and usage of best practice scenarios. Model-driven approaches also have been proposed for implementation of ERP systems [12, 4]. These approaches currently constitute a rapidly expanding research area. The proposed PMIS implementation approach also can be perceived as a model-driven approach. From this perspective, the paper also contributes to investigation of model-driven implementation of COTS and enterprise applications.

3. Approach

PMIS ideally would comply with all requirements of the PM methodology and provide means for facilitating PM processes. However, COTS PM systems provide just an overall framework for PM, which does not necessarily be the best fit for the particular project and PM methodology used. Therefore, PMIS should be appropriately adjusted. The general approach for configuring and implementing PMIS proposed in the papers is to specify the PM methodology in a standardized manner and then to apply software tool-specific transformations to load this standardized representation into the software tool. The PM specification can be used to structurally modify the PM system or to populate PMIS with master data. For instance, a PM methodology specifies data fields describing project tasks as well as some mandatory project activities. In this case, both necessary data fields can be created and the predefined activities can be loaded.

The PMIS configuration and implementation process is shown in Fig. 44.1. It starts with definition of the PM methodology. The PM methodology can be defined as an XML document (for instance, MSF already is defined using XML) or using some kind of visual tool (for instance, UML diagramming tools) capable of producing XML outputs. The PM definition is transformed using XSL to produce the PM methodology's specification in a standardized form. This transformation is performed with regards to the standard PM methodology's specification (SPMS) XML schema discussed in the following section. SPMS is loaded into the PM software by applying software tool specific transformations. It is assumed that software vendors would be responsible for developing these transformations. During the transformation process, the methodology-specific content also could be loaded into the PM system. That includes predefined data values, document templates, and process guides. These are retrieved from the methodology's template database.

The configuration and implementation process is further elaborated in Section 5 using an example.

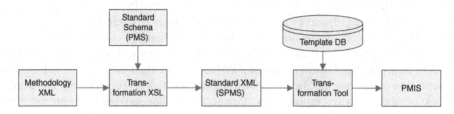

Figure 44.1. The PMIS configuration and implementation process.

4. Project Management Methodology Specification

The key part of the implementation process is specification of the PM methodology. The specification must cover both static and dynamic characteristics of PM. Static characteristics are represented similarly as in PMXML, while dynamic characteristics are structured according to process groups defined in PMBOK.

In order to identify entities to be included in the specification of PM methodologies, existing methodologies and standards are analyzed. Table 44.1 lists key entities relevant to PM and indicates whether these have been considered in the selected methodologies and standards (of course, the complete list of all PM entities is substantially longer).

The table shows four major types of entities: (1) simple entities (e.g., roles and activities); (2) composite entities (e.g., change management); (3) methods entities (e.g., earned value analysis); and (4) operational and transactional entities (e.g., calendar and baseline). The simple entities can be directly represented in the PM specification. The composite entities consist of multiple simple entities. The operational and transactional entities generally are not used for PMIS configuration and implementation purposes. However, some of them are represented indirectly through attributes of other entities.

The table shows only entities while methodologies also define attributes of these entities. Identification of common attributes is complex although, for specification building purposes, a generic attribute type can be used.

This table is used to produce an XML schema defining the standardized framework for specifying PM methodologies. This schema is referred to as PMS (project management schema). At current stage of this investigation, only main principles of designing PMS are laid out and further development and

Table 44.1. Entities considered in selected PM methodologies.

Entities	PMBOK	RUP	MSF	PRINCE	PMXML
Roles	−	+	+	+	−
Activities	+	+	+	+	+
Assignments	+	+	+	+	+
Artifacts/documents/deliverables	+	+	+	+	−
Resources	+	+	+	+	+
Reports	+	+	+	+	−
Measurements/checkpoints	+	+	+	+	−
Procurement management	+	−	−	−	−
Change management	+	+	+	+	−
Issue management	+	+	+	+	−
Quality management	+	+	+	+	−
Communications management	+	−	+	+	−
Risk management	+	+	+	+	−
Work order/project network diagram/schedule	+	+	+	+	+
Milestones	+	+	+	+	+
Cost management /budgeting	+	−	+	+	+
Corrective activities/lesson learned	+	+	−	+	−
Project charter/vision	+	+	+	+	+
Constraints/assumptions/exceptions	+	+	+	+	−
WBS	+	+	+	+	+
Earned value analysis	+	−	−	+	+
Calendar	+	−	−	−	+
Baseline	+	+	+	+	+

refinement is subject of further research to be conducted in relation with other ongoing PM domain formalization efforts (e.g., ontology development).

Figure 44.2 shows main top-level elements of the PMS describing static characteristics of PM. These elements are *roles*, *activities*, *assignments*, *artifacts*, *measurements*, *risks*, and *tools*. The *artifacts* element is used to refer any information item used or produced during the project. It has an attribute *artifact Type* to identify the type of artifact. Artifacts include documents, models, deliverables, components, PM guidelines, and others. It is possible that further refinement of this element is needed. The *risks* element already is separated from the *artifacts* element due to increasing importance of risk management in PM. The *measurements* element describes various performance measurements used in various PM disciplines. The *assignments* element describes not only roles to activities assignments but also other relationships among the elements of PMS.

The *views* element is used to describe views of the PM methodology. The view is perceived as a set of related PM entities.

The *processes* element describes dynamic PM processes such as change management or status reporting processes. This element has the attribute *workflowReference* referencing to a document defining the process workflow. Workflows by themselves are defined using the workflow description XML-based standard XPDL [16]. Necessary mapping between elements of the PM specification elements and elements of the workflow definition in XPDL are established using the *bindings* element. PM constraints, assumptions, and business rules currently are not explicitly represented in PMS though these are important during implementation of PMIS. Some of them can be represented within workflows while a special constructs are needed for others.

The *knowledgeArea* element defines well-established PM knowledge areas describing knowledge, skills, and processes needed for successful PM. This element is structured according to guidelines provided by PMBOK.

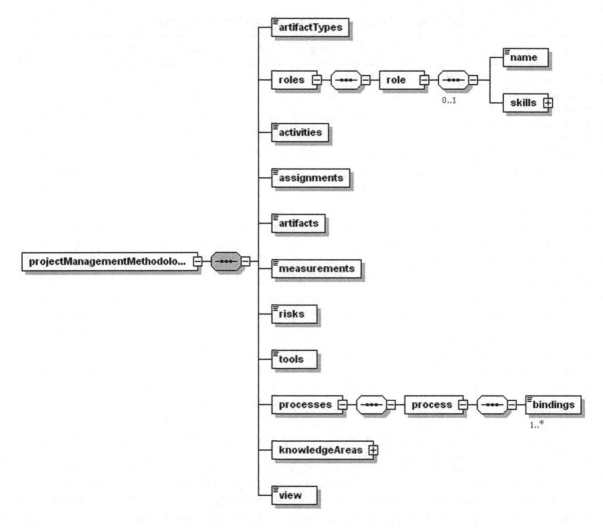

Figure 44.2. Main elements of the PMS.

The *knowledgeAreas* element (Fig. 44.3) includes child elements defining a generic knowledge area and all nine knowledge areas from PMBOK (for illustration purposes, the figure shows only two knowledge area child elements). PMBOK based knowledge area elements are used because these can be used as starting points for defining a custom PM methodology. The knowledge area element has the *alias* attribute, which is used for custom labeling. Each knowledge area is defined by artifacts, roles, processes, and methods as well as other entities to be specified. The *methods* element is used to resemble methods used in the particular PM area. For instance, it is used to indicate usage of WBS or earned value analysis, which were identified as important PM entities in Table 44.1. The simplest implementation of this element in PMIS would be references to guidelines about using these methods. However, if the selected PM software supports a particular method, means for utilizing this functionality are provided.

The generic knowledge area element is provided to enable specification of custom knowledge areas, especially, domain-specific knowledge areas.

The proposed standardized PM methodology specification is used to describe particular PM methodologies. During specification of a particular methodology, the standard specification can be augmented to include missing information and truncated to exclude irrelevant information. The specification also included references to the project methodology templates database, which stores methodology specific content.

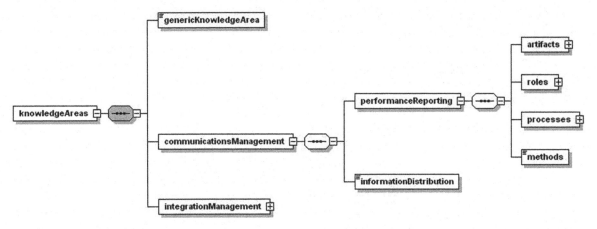

Figure 44.3. The knowledge areas element of PMS.

5. Sample Application

In order to demonstrate application of the proposed approach, a simple sample is elaborated. It shows configuring PMIS by loading team roles as defined by the RUP methodology. It is assumed that an organization uses RUP in their software development projects and wants using Microsoft Project for building and managing the project team. In order to do that, team roles and their skills should be defined into the Microsoft Project based PMIS.

The first step is definition of the methodology. Roles defined in the RUP are described using a diagramming tool supporting UML. Figure 44.4 shows the roles represented as actors in the UML diagram. Each actor has specific attributes including name, description, and required skills.

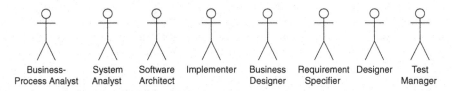

Figure 44.4. Definition of PM methodology using a diagramming tool.

The next step is transformation of the definition into SPMS. The definition of PM methodology is saved as an XML document according to schema supported by the diagramming tools (in this case, the XMI format is used). Appropriate XSL transformation is defined and applied to produce the specification of PM in the standardized format according to the PMS schema. The resulting XML documents or SPMS of the part of RUP methodology is shown in Fig. 44.5.

The last step is loading the SPMS document into PMIS, in this case Microsoft Project Server. The loading is performed using software specific transformation scripts. In the example, the list of roles is created in Microsoft Project Server. This list is populated with the roles from the RUP methodology (bottom left panel of Fig. 44.6). The roles are also added to the resource center as generic resources in order to enable personal selection according to their skills (upper panel of Fig. 44.6). The hyperlink field is used to associate the roles list and the resource center. Skills defined for the roles are added as custom enterprise

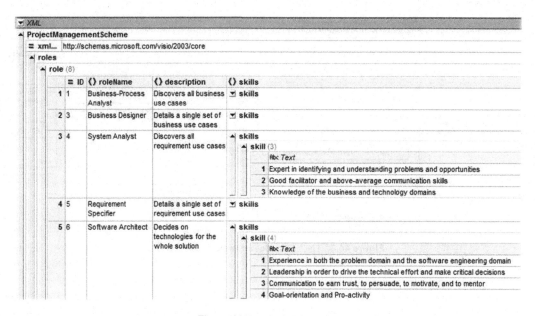

Figure 44.5. SPMS document.

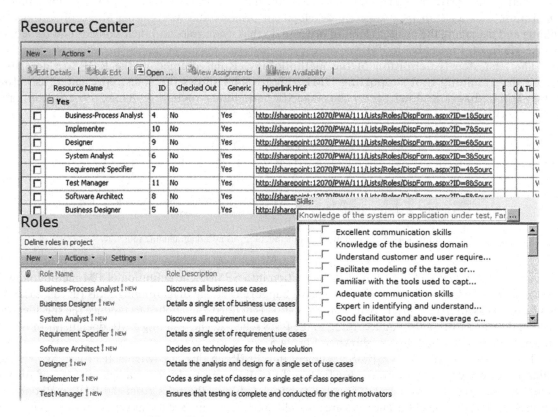

Figure 44.6. PMIS configured to support the RUP roles.

fields (Fig. 44.6, bottom right panel). This way PMIS contains both role-specific information not included in the resource center and team building functionality of MS Project Server can be used.

6. Conclusion

This chapter described the approach for configuration and implementation of PMIS. This approach is aimed at improving fit between functionality of out-of-box PM systems and PM methodologies and reducing efforts needed to start using PMIS according to new PM requirements.

The key part of the approach is PMS, which provides the standardized framework for specifying PM methodologies. Development of PMS is in early stages and only some basic principles have been presented in this chapter. This representation will be further refined and steps to approbate it will be taken. This effort is to be conducted in relation with other attempts to standardized representation of PM, for instance, developing PM ontology. Thus, the main steps of future research are elaboration and approbation of PMS as well as validation of the approach.

Acknowledgments

This work has been partly supported by the European Social Fund within the National Program "Support for the carrying out doctoral study programs and post-doctoral researches" project "Support for the development of doctoral studies at Riga Technical University" (2004/0002/VPD1/ESF/PIAA/04/NP/3.2.3.1/0001/0002/0007).

References

1. Abels S, Ahlemann F, Hahn A, Hausmann K, Strickmann J (2006) PROMONT – A Project Management Ontology as a Reference for Virtual Project Organizations. On the Move to Meaningful Internet Systems 2006, OTM 2006 Workshops, 813–823.
2. Botta-Genoulaz V, Millet PA, Grabot B (2005) A survey on the recent research literature on ERP systems. Computers in Industry, 56: 510–522.
3. Cover Pages (2005) Project Management XML Schema (PMXML), http://xml.coverpages.org/projectManageSchema.html.
4. Dugerdil PH, Gaillard G (2006) Model-driven ERP implementation. 8th International Conference on Enterprise Information Systems (ICEIS'2006). Workshop on Model-Driven Enterprise Information Systems (MDEIS), Paphos, Cyprus, May 23–27, 2006.
5. Jaafari A, Manivong K (1998) Towards a smart project management information system. International Journal of Project Management, 16: 249–265.
6. Kroll P, Kruchten P (2005) The Rational Unified Process Made Easy: A Practitioner's Guide to the RUP. New York: Addison-Wesley.
7. Meyers BC, Oberndorf P (2001) Managing Software Acquisition: Open Systems and COTS Products. New York: Addison Wesley Professional.
8. Office of Government Commerce (2005) Managing Successful Projects with PRINCE2, The Stationery Office.
9. Project Management Institute (2003) Guide to the Project Management Body of Knowledge (PMBOK), Project Management Institute, Newton Square.
10. Raymond L, Bergeron F (2008) Project management information systems: An empirical study of their impact on project managers and project success. International Journal of Project Management, 26: 213–220.
11. Ruíz FJ, Dolado J (2007) A domain ontology for project management, Software Quality Management XV: Software Quality in the Knowledge Society, E. Berki, J. Nummenmaa, I. Sunley, M. Ross, G. Staples (eds.), 15: 317–326.
12. Rosemann M, Van der Aalst WMP (2007) A configurable reference modelling language. Information Systems, 32: 1–23.
13. Stewart RA, Mohamed S, Daet R (2002) Strategic implementation of IT/IS projects in construction: a case study. Automation in Construction, 11: 681–694.
14. Turner MSV (2006) Microsoft Solutions Framework Essentials: Building Successful Technology Solutions. Redmond: Microsoft Press.
15. Von Schoultz F, Malzahn U, Schulz R (1996) An Integrated Project Management Information System, Turku Centre of Computer Science, Technical Reports, No. XX.
16. WFMC (2005) Workflow Management Coalition Workflow Standard: Process Definition Interface XML Process Definition Language, http://www.wfmc.org/standards/docs.htm.

45

From Standard Application Packages to Enterprise Systems – A Matter of Opportunities

Anders G. Nilsson

Abstract

The purpose of this chapter is to make clearer the meaning behind the concepts of "standard application package" and "enterprise system." There is today a confusion in our IS field about the connection between the two concepts and how they have appeared historically? The main idea is to contrast them against each other and in this sense to study which opportunities organizations and companies can achieve with these two different IT environments. This transparency will give business and IT people a better understanding for managing investments in information systems more professionally. The research approach is characterized as "consumable research" (Robey, and Markus, *Information Resources Management Journal*, 11(1): 7–15, 1998) based on theoretical knowledge integrated with business practice from the IS field. Our background is through working with practical methods for customer involvement (purchasing, implementation, maintenance) as well as performing vendor studies of the software application industry.

Keywords Enterprise systems · IT environments · Standard application packages

1. Historical Review

Computer-based information systems or IT systems emerged in the end of the 1950s to render the administrative routines more effective in companies. The first IT systems were in-house solutions and tailor-made for various business activities in organizations. These systems were based on bespoke software ordered from internal computer departments or external data consultants.

In the beginning of the 1970s the idea of reusing existing software applications between different companies developed [9]. This possibility to purchase or buy software on the market was an alternative to make or produce software individually. The concept of "standard application packages" was introduced in the IT industry. The original standard application packages were generalizations of former successful in-house solutions further developed by professional IT consultants in the field. Standard packages for financial and accounting applications as well as for logistics and material planning control (MPC) applications were launched on the market [12, 14]. As a pioneering package solution from the early stage we can mention Mapics from the vendor IBM.

An interesting trend since the middle of 1990s is that we gradually introduced a new concept in the IT industry labeled "enterprise systems" or "ERP systems" [5, 7]. A new approach emerged for having more holistic and integrated systems solutions as opposed to the existing standard application packages that were more focused on delimited business areas within a company. The main idea was to increase the quality of interfaces and interactions between applications from several former standard packages on the market. As a pioneering ERP system we can mention the R2/R3 systems from the vendor SAP.

Anders G. Nilsson • Department of Information Systems, Karlstad University, Karlstad, Sweden.

G.A. Papadopoulos et al. (eds.), *Information Systems Development*, DOI 10.1007/b137171_45,

2. Standard Application Packages

Standard application packages have for a long time been used as advanced tools to increase the business capacity in companies and organizations. They consist of standardized software that has been developed by a vendor to meet the business requirements of several users (customers). A significant potential in the packages is the fact that well-tried experience and skills are built into the system from previous installations. There are scale economy benefits in standard application packages, inasmuch as a large number of companies are using the same system. The idea behind the packages is that several organizations should use a common application package instead of having to "re-invent the wheel." Thus time, costs, and efforts may be divided among many customer companies [8].

A standard application package is more or less finished software that can be plugged in directly into the business operations of a company, as opposed to systems developed in house, which need to be built up from scratch. Normally certain adaptations are required in the package, as well as in the customer business, to obtain a working IT solution. As a rule vendors have prepared their packages with a great number of pre-adjustable parameters ("adjusting knobs") to facilitate the customer's own adaptations. A standard application package could be regarded as a packed system solution – another common expression is, therefore, packaged software. It is an existing information system that has been used before in another organization.

Standard application packages are thus manifested as program packages that can be run in different technical environments such as mainframes, minicomputers, and PCs. Normally this involves a main path of choice for companies, as most packages are associated with particular platforms. A standard application package can be acquired in different ways, for example, by purchase, leasing, loan, gift, or exchange of software between companies. The most frequently used approach is that vendors sell software licenses, which from a legal point of view is a form of leasing. There are a number of different types of arrangements for the packages, such as

- *External standard application packages*
  Sold by established national and foreign vendors in the open market
- *Internal standard application packages*
  Provided by an IT department for business units within a company group
- *Procured standard application packages*
  Between companies with or without third link broking organizations

3. Enterprise Systems

A current trend since the 1990s is that a growing number of packages are classified as "enterprise systems" [10]. By enterprise systems we, here, refer to large integrated standard application packages that fully cover the provision of information required in a company. Enterprise systems are made up of extensive administrative solutions for management accounting, human resource management, production, logistics, and sales control. An important criterion is that the included parts are closely integrated with each other through a central database [4]. From that standpoint, we can conclude that enterprise systems are all-embracing IT supports for the whole business in companies and organizations [2, 6].

An advantage of enterprise systems is that the vendor guarantees that different functions in the package are connected, with thoroughly tested interfaces. A disadvantage is that the different parts in the vendor's enterprise system are often of varying quality. For this reason it may be wise to combine an enterprise system with one or more niche packages. Because of their extensiveness, enterprise systems are also called mega-packages [3] or enterprise resource planning (ERP) systems [15].

Nowadays many organizations are facing a complex existence, with mixed system environments (platforms) and multiple IT solutions for the same applications in the business. It is not unusual in large companies to find perhaps five different MPC packages running parallel – often operating on different platforms – as a result of previous organizational mergers. It is, therefore, tempting to start afresh, replacing existing IT solutions by a new, "fresh" enterprise system. Most of the enterprise systems or ERP systems on the market have traditionally been designed with a focus on manufacturing companies, but during the last years the supply of various enterprise systems for service-oriented business organizations has gradually increased [11].

4. Opportunities

For gaining a deeper understanding of the practical use of standard application packages and enterprise systems in organizations, it is essential to highlight the opportunities or potentials behind the two IT environments. This will be done from five different dimensions that have emerged from our working with practical methods for customer involvement [8, 10] and from performing vendor studies of the software application industry [1]. Each dimension comprises two different opportunities; one opportunity for standard application package (left part) and one opportunity for enterprise system (right part) are as follows:

- *Quality dimension*
  function quality vs. integration quality
- *Way of working dimension*
  customer-driven work vs. vendor-driven work
- *View dimension*
  component view vs. portfolio view
- *Changeability dimension*
  expandability vs. adaptability
- *Concept dimension*
  promoting system concept vs. controlling system concept

In such a case for emphasizing the opportunities with standard application packages and enterprise systems, we can contrast the two concepts against each other as a basis for analyzing the connection between them.

4.1. Function Quality vs. Integration Quality

The quality of an IT system is of vital importance for achieving a successful information provision in companies and organizations. A system, in general, consists of a number of parts and certain relationships between these parts. Usually the parts of an IT system are labeled functions or applications. The relationships between the parts are normally labeled integrations or interfaces. In consideration of this insight, it is essential to assess both the function quality and the integration quality of an IT system.

For minor IT systems in a company the *function quality* is the center of attraction. A strength with delimited IT systems is that the vendor can guarantee peak competence for built-in applications. As examples of such niches for IT systems, we can emphasize applications regarding human resource management, general ledgers, and sales control. An additional benefit with minor IT systems is the accessibility of different special variants for including applications; for instance an unusual variant of index invoicing within management accounting. It has been evident that vendors of minor IT systems often have difficulties to achieve satisfactory quality of necessary interfaces to surrounding systems solutions in the organization. The great opportunity with a *standard application package* is the high degree of function quality that normally is achieved for this IT investment in the company.

For larger IT systems in organizations the *integration quality* is the center of attraction. A benefit with large-scale IT systems is that the vendor can guarantee that different functions or applications are connected with well-tested interfaces. A disadvantage is, however, that the vendor often has a varying quality for different parts of its IT system. The more comprehensive IT systems contain two fundamental parts in the form of administrative support for management accounting (incl. sales control) and material flow control (incl. service management) in a company. Vendors tend to place a quality accent on one of these fundamental parts. They have started by perfecting an "excellent" part and subsequently tried to extend the IT system with the other part at an adequate level. The great opportunity with an *enterprise system* is the high degree of integration quality that normally is achieved for this IT investment in the company.

4.2. Customer-Driven Work vs. Vendor-Driven Work

Working with an IT system can be regarded from two aspects: vendor and customer, respectively. The vendor is marketing and selling the system in the IT industry. A customer is acquiring and using the IT system within the business. In this respect, we will discuss the opportunities of a customer-driven work as opposed to a vendor-driven work with IT systems.

A *customer-driven work* implies that a systematic way of working or methodological support is guiding the customer to purchase, implement, operate, and maintain the IT system in order to make the business operations as efficient as possible. The customer should have a support for questioning if the different vendors can offer a usable IT solution. Moreover, a systematic way of working should guide when a dialogue is needed between the customer and the vendor as well as how a customer can prepare the vendor contacts in a suitable way. A situation with a *standard application package* is more appropriate and gives a good opportunity to assist a customer-driven work. The reason behind this is that the vendor seems to be more respectful in a standard application package case and by that way is trying to attain a successful implementation at the customer. An exception is, however, the so-called "off-the-shelf" systems where the vendor is selling prefabricated IT systems directly from the counter.

A *vendor-driven work* implies that a systematic way of working or methodological support is guiding the vendor to emphasize its IT system and to achieve successful implementations at the customers. This systematic way of working should also guide the vendor to assess the customer's qualifications for gaining benefits of the IT system within its business. Moreover, a systematic way of working should guide how an IT system can be rolled out and disseminated in a proper way to different business units and to different countries within a customer company's group. A situation with an *enterprise system* is more appropriate and gives a good opportunity to assist a vendor-driven work. The reason behind this is that the vendor seems to have a more rigid attitude and by that way want the implementation to go on as quickly and smoothly as possible. A customer who purchases a certain set of delimited standard application packages could be freer to choose various vendors than a customer who is considering purchasing of an enterprise system from one and the same vendor.

4.3. Component View vs. Portfolio View

Today, more and more vendors start developing IT systems in line with principles for component-based approaches with or without possibilities for open source solutions. A component view should be contrasted against a portfolio view that is needed when the IT systems are put into use and later on maintained. A component view has primarily a development focus and a portfolio view primarily a maintenance focus.

A *component view* during systems development facilitates the selection phase as well as the adaptation phase that will take place when a customer purchases re-usable IT systems. The systems analysis work will be concentrated on lots of comparisons between the business demands and the systems properties for selected vendor candidates. A careful vendor assessment is also an important stage in order to acquire the right type of IT system from the market. Working with a component-based approach promotes to a large extent an offensive systems development process for designing a business support with powerful effects in the organization. There seems to be evident that for minor *standard application packages* have it so far been easier to adopt a component view thinking – which gives these packages distinctive opportunities in this respect. A delimited systems size could give a more perceivable situation in order to put together IT solutions with the help of standardized components. Even if enterprise systems have become more component based during recent years so are still these characterized by a "monolith" view thinking in larger modules.

A *portfolio view* during systems maintenance facilitates the work with handling of new releases of the IT systems from vendors. The vendors have a conscious strategy of bringing out new systems releases on the market after a period of approximately 12–18 months. There is a special problem complex that maintenance normally contains a large portfolio of systems and applications from in-house as well as reusable software. This will put great demands on efficient systems coordination. Usually, the professional competence of the systems functionality and structure is kept by the vendor, in other words outside the user (customer) organization. Systems maintenance comprises measures for retaining and reinforcing the usefulness and value of the IT system for the supporting business to a reasonable cost. These measures consists of surveys, corrections, improvements, adaptations, and phasing outs. There seems to be evident that for larger *enterprise systems* have it so far been easier to adopt a portfolio view thinking – which gives these systems distinctive opportunities in this respect. An all-encompassing business support with help of a holistic IT solution simplifies the management of the company's systems portfolio where all applications are assembled under one and the same surface.

4.4. Expandability vs. Adaptability

In the case of reusing and purchasing an existing IT system, it is important to do necessary comparison. We need access to a requirements specification of the demands from the business side together with a systems description from the vendor side illustrating contents and structure of the IT system. From this point of departure, we can create a comparitive description which among other things can highlight the necessary expansions and adaptations that are needed for the IT system. Considering this we approach the issue to what degree expandability and adaptability are built-in for the IT system.

The issue on *expandability* concerns various additions that can be included in the acquired IT system from the vendor. By this we mean implementing new software applications or program modules to meet the business requirements of several users or customers. These parts do not exist in the earlier version of the IT system but is essential in order to make the business operations more effective for the customer. These expansions can be regarded as a renewal of the IT system for the vendor. Rather, often the vendor is charging for such expansions of the IT system even if they are launched as innovations in the next release of the IT system. For *standard application packages* there are opportunities to create a powerful expandability of the IT system for various customer groups which will render an extra favor. This has to do with the easiness to add new functionality in minor systems.

The issue on *adaptability* concerns various distinctive changes and modifications that can be performed in the acquired IT system both by the vendor and the customer. These concern adaptations of inputs, outputs, and program modules which will be negotiated with the vendor. The goal is that the changes and modifications would meet the specified requirements for the business information and the business processes. These adaptations can be characterized as exact adjustments or tunings as opposed to the expansions mentioned above that are more comprehensive in character. A vendor can choose not to charge for smaller adaptations of the IT system but instead let it be a part of the normal service and support to the customer. For *enterprise systems* there are opportunities to create a powerful adaptability of the IT system for various customer groups through a high degree of configurability with the help of a parameter setting which will render an extra favor. Moreover, it could be easier to make changes in existing program modules and software applications for more comprehensive IT systems that contain well-integrated solutions.

4.5. Promoting System Concept vs. Controlling System Concept

There seems to be evident that standard application packages and enterprise systems are based on different philosophies or system concepts. By this we mean how an IT system should behave in relation to the working practice of business operations. On a crude level we can distinguish between a promoting system concept and a controlling system concept. There are opportunities for both of these philosophies.

A *promoting system concept* implies that the vendor is open to various setups or business scenarios. The IT system "follows" the business method of work. This philosophy allows greater customer adaptation of the system instead of purely business adaptations. These IT solutions are general with no specific suggestions for layout from the vendor's side. In concrete terms we, here, are open for different sets of parameters. Some vendors create best practice models or application templates to facilitate the customer's work in adapting business operations and IT systems to each other. When using a promoting system concept, the customer should work from the hypothesis of how the company should work and adapt the IT system to this. This freedom can be a big advantage in some instances where there is a clearly developed corporate strategy. In other cases, however, it can be a limitation if the customer is unsure how business can be improved and expects the vendor to make concrete suggestions on the work methods. A potential strength with *standard application packages* is that they are designed around a principle to be more of a promoting system concept for customer or user organizations.

A *controlling system concept* means that the customer accepts the business concept that the vendor has built into the package. The IT system "guides" the business method of work. This philosophy is dependent upon the customer's acceptance of the vendor's "built-in" concept of business. This does not necessarily exclude a degree of flexibility within the concept. Starting from an overview of the customer company's business, the vendor supplies a large set of parameters which are included in the IT system when it is installed and which can be altered during the maintenance phase. A controlling system concept can be beneficial to customers with limited ability to develop their own businesses. They are, however, a disadvantage for companies with a good understanding of their business or where the business concept of the IT system is at odds with the company's methods of work. The potential strength with *enterprise systems* is that they are designed around a principle to be more of a controlling system for customer or user organizations.

5. The Connection

We have above described five dimensions that illustrate different opportunities with standard application packages and enterprise systems, respectively. In such a way we have a basis for analyzing what unites and separates the two concepts. We can regard *the connection* between standard application packages and enterprise systems from a Venn diagram perspective with joint and disparate parts (see Fig. 45.1). The leading idea behind both of these IT environments is the overall principle of reusing software applications within and between customer (user) organizations. The difference between the two concepts could be of somewhat varying character which will be evident from the discussion below.

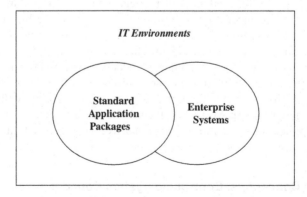

Figure 45.1. The connection between standard application packages and enterprise systems.

A *standard application package* could be of varying range or "granularity" all the way from a simple computer program (software component) to a holistic program complex (software monolith). From this point of departure an enterprise system is a subset of a standard application package, in other words belongs to an extreme variant of extensive and all-embracing systems solutions with strongly integrated applications. But there exists a vast supply of standard application packages that could not be characterized as genuine enterprise systems. By this we mean software for delimited applications such as for invoicing, payroll processing, project management, and sales control. Furthermore, there exist some areas for standardization that are not business oriented in character. In this context we can mention standard packages for data technical processing in companies such as operating systems, programming aids, database tools, and communication platforms.

An *enterprise system* could be of varying character. They could be universal or general for all types of business in companies and organizations or they have an industry-specific design for handling business logics within medical care sector, hotel business, electronic industry, transport services, and car manufacturing. Enterprise systems could be oriented toward financial and accounting management or material and logistics control as well as directed to both these areas. They could also have a focus on manufacturing or service management. For all these nuances the enterprise systems have a character of being standard application packages. Conceptually an enterprise system could consist of a set of minor standard packages labeled program modules or software applications.

Do we have situations where enterprise systems do not at all include some elements of a standard application solution? On this matter there have been a real confusion regarding the use of the concept "enterprise system"! General managers or CEO's normally associate the term "enterprise system" to comprehensive IT systems that serve the overall information provision in their companies. Therefore, it is unimportant from a management perspective if the IT system is constructed as a standard package, tailor-made system, component-based solution, or a mixture of these approaches. There is also an intermediary form labeled "best of breed" solutions that represent a combined architecture with portions of two or more enterprise systems on the market. Such a combined IT solution constitutes an enterprise system on a "macro" level.

An important conclusion from our review of the connection between standard application packages and enterprise systems is that we conceptually need them as two specifically distinct concepts. The two concepts are not exchangeable! Instead these concepts can occur in various fruitful combinations for practical IT use in private companies as well as in public organizations. As an example, we can mention that one or more standard application packages could be sharp niche systems to a more comprehensive enterprise system. This means that the desired IT system will come from several vendors on the market which implies a demand for coordination and integration of the systems solution [1].

References

1. Andersson, R. and Nilsson, A. G. (1996) The standard application package market: An industry in transition. In Lundeberg. M. and Sundgren, B. (eds), *Advancing Your Business: People and Information Systems in Concert*, Stockholm School of Economics and Lund, Sweden: Studentlitteratur. (available at: http://www.hhs.se/EFI/IM/Publications/ayb.htm).
2. Askenäs, L. (2004) *The Roles of IT: Studies on Organising When Implementing and Using Enterprise Systems*, Dissertation, Department of Economic Information Systems, Linköping University, Sweden.
3. Davenport, T. H. (1996) *Holistic Management of Mega-Package Change: The Case of SAP*, Working Paper CB1309, Center for Business Innovation, Ernst & Young, Boston, MA.
4. Davenport, T. H. (1998) Putting the enterprise into the enterprise system, *Harvard Business Review*, July–August, 76(4): 121–131.
5. Davenport, T. H. (2000) *Mission Critical: Realizing the Promise of Enterprise Systems*, Boston, MA: Harvard Business School Press.
6. Ekman, P. (2006) *Enterprise Systems & Business Relationships: The Utilization of IT in the Business with Customers and Suppliers*, Dissertation, School of Business, Mälardalen University, Sweden.
7. Hedman, J. (2003) *On Enterprise Systems Artifacts: Changes in Information Systems Development and Evaluation*, Dissertation, Department of Informatics, Lund University, Sweden.
8. Nilsson, A. G. (1990) Information systems development in an application package environment. In Wrycza, S. (ed), *Proceedings of the Second International Conference on Information Systems Developers Workbench*, September, 25–28, 1990, University of Gdansk, Poland, pp. 444–466.

9. Nilsson, A. G. (1996) Evolution of methodologies for information systems work: A historical perspective. In Wrycza, S. and Zupancic, J. (eds), *Proceedings of the Fifth International Conference on Information Systems Development – ISD'96*, September, 24–26, University of Gdansk, Poland, pp. 91–119.

10. Nilsson, A. G. (2001) Using standard application packages in organisations: Critical success factors. In Nilsson, A. G. and Pettersson, J. S. (eds), *On Methods for Systems Development in Professional Organisations: The Karlstad University Approach to Information Systems and its Role in Society*, pp. 208–230, Lund, Sweden: Studentlitteratur.

11. Nilsson, A. G. (2007) Enterprise information systems – eight significant conditions. In Knapp, G., Magyar, G., Wojtkowski, W., Wojtkowski, W. G. and Zupancic, J. (eds), *Information Systems Development: New Methods and Practices for the Networked Society*, Proceedings of the Fifteenth International Conference on Information Systems Development – ISD'2006, August, 31–September, 2, 2006, Budapest, Hungary, pp. 811–821. New York: Springer.

12. Rapp, B. (1989) *A Reference MPC System: A Language Tool for Vendors and Buyers of Computerized MPC Systems*, Research Report, Department of Production Economics, Linköping University, Sweden.

13. Robey, D. and Markus, M. L. (1998) Beyond rigor and relevance: Producing consumable research about information systems, *Information Resources Management Journal*, 11(1): 7–15.

14. Samuelson, L. A. (1990) *Models of Accounting Information Systems: The Swedish Case*. Lund, Sweden: Studentlitteratur.

15. Sumner, M. (2005) *Enterprise Resource Planning*. Upper Saddle River, NJ: Pearson Prentice Hall.

46

The Total Picture – A Framework for Control of IT Investments

Mats-Åke Hugoson, Björn Johansson and Ulf Seigerroth

Abstract

Evaluation of IT investments is a difficult and complicated issue. This chapter presents a framework for control of IT investments with the aim of providing decision-makers with a clear picture of individual IT investments as well as an aggregated level where all IT investments are combined into a total picture. The framework has been developed using an action–research approach.In a number of workshops intermediate results have been presented, and reactions from practitioners have influenced the development. Participants in the project come from different EU countries all directly concerned with IT investments. The framework, that is being tested by authorities in different EU countries, is considered by participants to have the potential to improve the decision-making processes. The framework can also potentially be used in academic teaching in IT economics. The framework is based on a lifetime perspective in which established investment models can be applied. A main dimension is to consider interrelations between different IT investments through aggregation into a total picture, in order to control total spending on IT in organisations.

Keywords Benefits from IT investments · Delayed investments · Evaluating framework · Lifetime perspective · Management of IT investments · Total picture

1. Introduction

Evaluating IT investments has a high priority in organisations at the same time such evaluations are considered difficult to carry out [5, 4]. It can be stated that IT investments have received [13] and still receive great attention [5, 4]. This attention can be compared to the discussion on IT productivity and the productivity paradox [2, 3], and at least two questions could be asked: (1) What is a successful IT investment? and (2) How can decisions on IT investments be improved in order to achieve success?

To give an exact answer to the first question is not easy, for several reasons. First, judgement of success depends on expectations. Second, IT investments need to be evaluated regarding both tangible and intangible benefits [5, 14]. And, third, since IT is more or less necessary for most organisations today and to a great extent intertwined in most organisations' business processes [12], it becomes hard to evaluate. This could be compared to the statement by Brynjolfsson [3] that organisations lack supporting tools for being able to follow up IT investment decisions. The lack of support when it comes to evaluation of IT investments is also stated by Ross and Beath [11] when they claim that there is a need for support on two issues in IT investments: How to distribute funds across investment types? and How to establish

Mats-Åke Hugoson • Department of Informatics, Jönköping International Business School, Jönköping, Sweden. **Björn Johansson** • Copenhagen Business School, Center for Applied Information and Communication Technology, Frederiksberg, Denmark. **Ulf Seigerroth** • Department of Informatics, Jönköping International Business School, Jönköping, Sweden.

G.A. Papadopoulos et al. (eds.), *Information Systems Development*, DOI 10.1007/b137171_46,
© Springer Science+Business Media, LLC 2009

priorities within investment types? This is the focus of the framework that we suggest. The aim is to support executives in their decision-making by keeping track of the effect of total investments in the organisation.

Despite the fact that Renkema [9] identified as many as 65 distinct methods aiming at assisting an organisation and its decision-makers in evaluating IT investments, we argue that there is still a need for improved support for management of IT investments. Nagpal et al. [8] state that there is a gap of knowledge about IT productivity in terms of return on investment (ROI). They stipulate that four questions need to be answered: (1) How can IT investments be conceptualised?; (2) What is or should be included in costs?; (3) What level of analysis should be chosen?; and (4) At what time horizon should ROI be estimated?

Based on the discussion above, an idea of how to control IT investments is suggested from the assumption that a lifetime perspective and an aggregation into a total picture is useful when controlling IT investments. In order to validate this, we have developed and tested a framework with the following characteristics: (1) the framework applies a lifetime perspective, (2) the framework is independent of specific accounting principles and calculation practice, (3) the framework makes a distinction between investment and costs during development and operations, and the concept of delayed investments is introduced, and (4) the framework aggregates all instances of all types of IT investments into a total picture for evaluation of total IT spending. All these aspects are relevant to the second of our two basic questions: How can decisions on IT investments be improved? In order for the framework, with its two levels (project and total picture), to be useful in different situations and in different EU countries, the aggregations in the framework must rise above existing methods, calculations, and principles specific for different countries. The data sources that feed the framework can be based on local application of established financial methods like cost–benefit analysis, net present value (NPV), annuity methods, and payback. It is the quality of the application of these methods and principles that will set the quality that can be achieved with the proposed framework. The framework also adopts thoughts from non-financial approaches as described by Renkema and Berghout [10], and then mainly from the portfolio approach.

This chapter is structured in the following way. The next section describes the research method and the project setting. After that we describe the framework; first, the individual project level for different types of separate IT investments and second, the total picture where all IT investments are aggregated. In the next section, the framework is analysed and discussed. The final section summarises the discussion, gives some conclusions and presents future research directions that can be drawn from the framework, its development and initial usage.

2. Research Method and Project Setting

The choice of method is action research since this method is suited to study technology in a human context [1], which is the focus of this project. Our aim of the knowledge endeavour has been to develop knowledge that is useful to both research and practice, in this case exploring the potential in applying a lifetime perspective and a total picture as a means of controlling IT investments. We rely on the same arguments as Lindgren et al. [6] express (based on [7]), "Merely studying a real-world problem without assisting to resolve or ameliorate it is perceived as unhelpful. In other words, action researchers see it as their responsibility to assist practitioners by not only developing but also applying knowledge" (p. 441), in this case, the presented framework. Formulated in terms of action research, the framework is presented as an explicit contribution to local practice and the application has been a way to explore the working hypothesis that a lifetime perspective and a total picture are suitable approaches for controlling IT investments.

The starting point for this research project was a project that should help agricultural public agencies in the EU to "get a grip on their IT investments". In 2005 the Panta Rhei association for EU's agricultural agencies gave the assignment to the Swedish Board of Agriculture (SBA) to be the coordinator of a project called "IT costs". At this point SBA involved Jönköping International Business School in the project. The development and application of the proposed framework has implied a close cooperation between researchers and practitioners. It has been a fruitful approach to bring knowledge and experiences from practice face to face with academic knowledge and experiences in the development of the framework. There have been many challenging meetings and discussions about practical implications of existing theories as well as theories on practical applications. During the development of the framework we have had 15 joint working meetings with SBA. Between these working meetings both parties have been working individually with the development of different parts of the framework. Four other EU countries have also been involved during the development phase in five working meetings. These countries have mainly functioned as a test bench for the growing framework. These countries have mainly evaluated the applicability of the framework. The framework has been applied in different cases (already conducted IT investment projects) in these countries. This gave valuable information about the applicability and showed that local principles and methods for accounting and calculation could be applied within the framework. During the development phase a consultant supported us with implementing the framework into an IT tool for testing different cases in different countries. The IT tool was used and tested during the working meetings and the case applications with the four other EU countries. The usage of the tool also contributed to the information about the applicability of the framework.

3. Proposed Framework

The basic idea of the framework is to aggregate all IT-related investments, lifetime costs for maintenance, lifetime costs for IT operations and lifetime benefits (both monetary benefits and non-monetary benefits) into a structure which will be repeatedly updated, revised and used to support assessment and decisions concerning IT investments. The framework adapts to the ideas presented by Ward et al. [15] about creating a rigorous and systematic exploration of benefits expected from investments.

3.1. The Project Level in the Framework

The first step is to deal with different types of IT investments, which are categorised into five different types, as shown in Table 46.1. General objectives have been specified for each type of IT investment, and it is indicated where the expected impact of the investment most probably will occur. The basic reason for doing this is to provide a clear distinction between *Business process*, *IT process*, *General practice* and *Usage by external clients* as means of making decisions about IT investments. On the individual project level the framework will deal with IT investments within these five categories. The normal case is that an organisation has several IT investments within each category.

Information systems call for investments both in the IT process and in the business process, which should be specified separately. Some benefits in the business process are monetary. Other benefits, some of which can be quantified and measured, are attached as a text document to the framework. Cost for IT

Table 46.1. Different types of IT investments.

Investment type	General objectives
Information systems	To increase efficiency in a specific business process
(Business application)	To improve interaction with end users
Common infrastructural information systems	To support users throughout the organisation, general practice (for instance, an e-mail system)
IT infrastructure hardware and software	To make operation and interaction between information systems possible
	To improve efficiency in IT operations (for instance, through investments in hardware)
Pre-development/ procurement of packaged software	Reuse of components or (possibly) standardised information (sub)systems
Strategic IS/IT planning	To create suitable architectures
	To coordinate application projects and projects for infrastructural development

operations is estimated as *additional* or *changed cost*, caused by the new, changed or replaced system. Maintenance costs, both estimated and real, can be specified for each system.

Infrastructural information systems refer to general IT support, oriented to general practice, and not a specific business process. The objective is to support users in the entire organisation. This type of investment can be handled in the same way as investments in information systems, but there are some differences. First, it is often difficult to estimate, and to evaluate, benefits which are distributed over several/all business processes. On the other hand, such investments may have a strong impact, as many users are affected. Second, projects of this type are often initiated for technical reasons, in order to make the IT process more efficient. It is, however, crucial that investments in the business process for implementation and the effect on the whole organisation (changes for end users) are not neglected.

Investments in IT infrastructure are often necessary to facilitate operations of applications. Other infrastructural projects, for instance new general hardware, can have the purpose of improving efficiency in IT operations. In both cases, other benefits may also be estimated, such as capacity, availability, and security that mainly refer to the IT process. Infrastructural investment can also affect end users in the business process. This is generally difficult to specify in monetary terms, but estimated impact, for instance on improved service level for users, should as far as possible be described (textual documents) and entered into the framework.

Investments in pre-developed components and software packages are based on the expectation that systems development will be more efficient, for instance through reusable components. The aim is to cut lead time and decrease investments in the system development process. There are no direct monetary benefits until reuse really takes place in other projects. Some other benefits, such as expected shorter lead time, can be pointed out and specified in textual documents.

Efforts related to strategic IS/IT planning and coordination of the IS/IT infrastructure must also be regarded as IT-related investments since they go beyond the strategic goals for a single investment. There is a need to set the total scene (the city plan) for the IS/IT structure. The expected outcome is an appropriate IS/IT infrastructure that can ensure expected benefits in both the business process and the IT process. As with predevelopment, the benefits will not appear in this specific project, but later on in relation to other projects.

3.1.1. Different Types of Benefits

For these types of IT investments, we need to address different types of benefits. The benefits in the framework are divided into two categories: monetary benefits and non-monetary benefits. Monetary benefits can be both internal monetary benefits received within the own organisation and external monetary benefits that external users receive. The non-monetary benefits can be divided into quantifiable/measurable and not quantifiable/ measurable. These benefits can occur in the business process, in the IT process, generally throughout the organisation or for users outside the organisation.

3.1.2. Principles of the Framework

An overview of the framework, illustrating the principles of the framework, is shown in Fig. 46.1. The framework is divided into two basic phases, a *development* phase and a *system-in-use* phase. The development phase is divided into three steps: analysis, IT development and implementation, without a specific time scale. For systems in use there is a timescale in years, which is the normally used timescale in accounting and calculations. Investments in the IT process and in the business process occur during the development phase, but we cannot account for any benefits until the system is in use. Below the time axis in the figure various investments and costs are specified, and above the axis benefits in the business process are shown.

The figure describes how managers should deal with investments in the IT process and costs for IT operations. It is also indicated how investments and benefits in the business process as well as costs for maintenance and delayed investments should be treated. There is also a possibility to register other benefits (the white area), thereby indicating that these should be considered when making decisions about IT investments. Delayed investments are planned investments that remain after the system has "gone live".

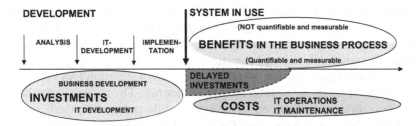

Figure 46.1. The principles of the framework.

Usually delayed investments are dealt with and included in maintenance even though they have nothing to do with maintenance. The framework makes a point of separating remaining investments that are necessary to achieve anticipated benefits from what really is maintenance.

The main principle in the framework is to work with estimations and follow-up reports during the life cycle. There is a need to estimate planned investments, benefits and costs of various kinds. As time passes, these estimations are replaced with reported values, i.e. the actual outcome, which may call for revision of remaining estimations for the rest of the life cycle.

On the project level, the underlying practice and methods used for accounting and calculation to feed the framework are of less interest. What is important is that the quality of these activities will have a direct effect on the quality that we will get out of the framework.

3.2. The Total Picture Level in the Framework

In the section above, the framework deals with benefits, investments and costs in terms of instances of different types of IT investments. In this section the framework will be extended in order to (1) give an overview of total IT investments and costs related to their values for the total activities in the organisation, and (2) give the person in charge a clear picture of the organisation's total IT investments and how these may be influenced.

The primary task is to analyse the total impact on the business process from the total IT spending. In order to do this, benefits, investments and costs from all different types of projects are combined into a total picture. When the framework is used over a period of time, the total picture will show the outcome related to earlier plans and estimates. Different types of investments have different consequences, but the investments are usually related to each other in various ways. Benefits from one investment can perhaps only be achieved if some other investments are made. The framework argues that investments should always be handled separately from costs for IT operations. The main reason is that investments should always be related to possible benefits, in the business process and in the IT process. It can be a good decision to increase investments in order to either increase benefits or reduce costs. On the other hand, costs for IT operations should always be as low as possible (cost cutting).

Another issue to consider is how to treat investments in a lifetime perspective when all investments are aggregated into a total picture. In this chapter, we have adopted a cash flow approach since most public authorities apply an allotment funding principle. An alternative could be to distribute investment over the period of use, which may be more suitable for loan-financed investments. The framework can easily be adjusted for this alternative.

3.2.1. The Total Picture – from a Cash Flow Perspective

Total expected impact from IT investments. When all IT-related investments and their impact are captured in a life cycle perspective at project level, it is possible to aggregate these to form a total picture. In Fig. 46.2 monetary benefits are summarised and shown along the time axis. Also non-monetary benefits are specified when they occur in order to provide the total picture. Resources to be used to reach these benefits are shown below the time axis. Only remaining investments (in the business process and in the IT process) are shown (as a cash flow approach is used). Gradually paid investments will disappear (the striped project in Fig. 46.2), but an effect is still to be expected. Total estimated effect on costs for IT operations and maintenance can be summed distributed over time.

The total picture related to the current situation. The current situation (AS IS) must be the starting point, which cannot be derived from the total picture framework. The main purpose is to show *changes*. Changes in the business processes will of course have many different sources; the figure shows only what changes can be achieved from IT investments. Total spending in the IT process can, however, be more precisely predicted as shown at the bottom of Fig. 46.2. The actual total cost for IT operations and maintenance (captured from general accounting) plus investments in the IT process plus (or possibly minus) changes in costs for operations will give the estimated TO BE situation.

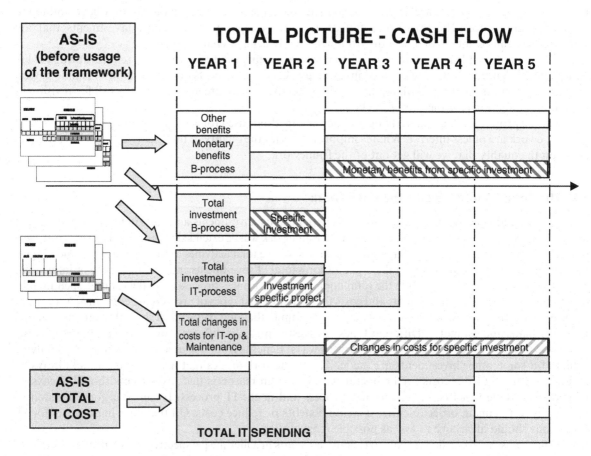

Figure 46.2. The total picture in a cash flow perspective.

4. Discussion: Applying a Lifetime Perspective and a Total Picture to Control IT Investments

The framework and its usage are to a great extent dependent on the data that are entered into the framework. It can be stated that the quality of making decisions on different investments and the possibility to follow up the results of investments depend on a reliable process for the analysis of different types of investments, benefits and costs for operations. It is necessary to have clear and understandable principles for identifying benefits as well as costs and the relation between them. The framework supports this, but the framework by itself is not enough. The underlying calculation practice such as a cost/benefit analysis must be considered as an essential aspect of IT investments in order to serve as a basis for the total picture. The underlying calculation practice needs to be taken seriously, since the quality of these analyses sets the quality that can be achieved in the total picture.

The framework indicates which investment gives most value for invested money. It is, therefore, important to make the business value (including non-monetary benefits) visible for all parties involved when making decisions. To succeed with this, it is important to have a simple and reliable collection of data and an efficient basis for follow-up, but also clear the responsibilities for actions in order to achieve the estimated impact both in the business process and in the IT process. The basic idea in the framework is to continuously serve decision-makers with information on the actual and estimated future situation as long as the IT investment is in use. The analysis shows that the framework can be a tool for benefit management during the whole life cycle.

Another aspect is how to handle benefits that cannot directly be expressed in monetary terms, often referred to as "soft benefits". In most investment models the approach is to attribute a monetary value to all benefits. The calculation then reveals if the investment is profitable or not. It is evident that this monetary evaluation of soft benefits sometimes makes the total calculation unreliable. The presented framework puts an emphasis on the collection of "all" benefits and also makes soft benefits available to the decision-maker through textual documents. This opens up for the use of more qualitative-oriented alternatives in investment decisions. The value of this feature in the framework has not yet been fully tested, but it anyhow eliminates false monetary benefits that can never be followed up.

Whatever alternative is used for investment decisions, the framework maintains a clear distinction between investments and costs for operations and maintenance. The main reason for this is that total investment should always be related to potential impacts (of different kinds) considering changes in costs for operations and maintenance. An increase in investment may be favourable if benefits are still evaluated as higher. Costs for IT operations and maintenance (for specified functionality) should instead be kept as low as possible, which means a cost-cutting perspective.

The overall intention of the developed framework is to support decision-makers with a tool for evaluating the estimated and achieved impact from IT investments both during the development phase and when systems are in use. It is shown that the framework has some special features to improve decisions on IT investments: the framework (1) applies a lifetime perspective on IT investments, costs and benefits; (2) makes a clear distinction between investments and costs, in the business process and in the IT process; (3) introduces the concept and usage of delayed investments from a lifetime perspective; (4) supports handling of non-monetary benefits; (5) supports different practices for evaluation, calculations and decisions regarding IT investments; and (6) compiles and sums up all types of IT investments into a total picture for evaluation of the total spending on IT in organisations. This means that the developed total picture framework aims at being a general framework for evaluating IT investments from a lifetime perspective, independent from whatever accounting principles and calculation practice the organisation uses or wants to use. It supports financial control by managing planned and reported investments as well as delayed investments related to estimated and achieved benefits of various kinds, including non-monetary benefits, especially when they are possible to measure.

5. Conclusions and Future Research

It is difficult to evaluate IT investments, and in the introduction three different reasons for this were presented [4, 5, 12]. It is argued that the framework presented deals with these reasons. The framework supports managers' expectations about IT investments since it gives an overview of expectations in a lifetime perspective, both at project level and at an aggregated level. It also supports management of tangible and intangible benefits, and it emphasises the fact that IT is heavily intertwined in the business processes of organisations. The framework also deals with the questions put forward by Nagpal et al. [8] and, especially, the question of time horizon by suggesting the lifetime perspective. But, despite the fact that the framework has many strengths, there are some weaknesses that could act as a basis for future research. A major difficulty when evaluating IT investments is the quality of data. The framework does not support decision-makers in their collection of correct data, and this could definitely be a future development of the framework. Another weakness of the framework, regarding the total picture and area of development, is that it has to be used for sometime before the framework shows "correct" data. Today the framework needs to be initiated at usage start-up with an AS IS situation, i.e. the legacy needs to be handled. The handling of the AS IS situation will then need to be done every year until the pre-framework legacy has diminished and been phased out of the lifetime framework. The framework also states that it is independent of calculation method and, therefore supports different practices. This statement has to be empirically tested in more depth. Future research also calls for further development of the IT tool so that it, to a greater extent, can implement the framework with its principles.

However, from the development and use of the framework (it has so far been used/tested on cases in five different EU countries), some conclusions can be drawn. First, the framework emphasises the total net impact or influence that investments have on the business processes. It can be stated that benefits from projects intended to support the business process are often specified as cost savings in the business process. Even if these benefits do not give full return on the investment, the project should/must be started to meet requirements in the business process. A help for the decision-makers is, then, that also non-monetary impact is as far as possible identified and followed up in the framework. Second, the framework offers the possibility to relate different types of IT investments to each other in the total picture which can prevent gains in the business process from a profitable project from being wiped out by necessary investments in an infrastructural project leading to increased costs in the IT process.

The final conclusion is that a lifetime perspective and the total picture has a clear potential to provide different decision-makers with a clear image of all different types of IT investments and total management of IT investments.The total picture goes beyond the individual IT investment view when investments are compiled so that an effect of total IT investments in organisations can be derived.

References

1. Baskerville, R. L. and Wood-Harper, A. T. (1996) A Critical Perspective on Action Research as a Method for Information Systems Research. *Journal of Information Technology 11*(3):235–246.
2. Brynjolfsson, E. (1992) The Productivity Paradox of Information Technology: Review and Assessment. *Working paper. MIT Sloan School of management.* http://ccs.mit.edu/papers/CCSWP130/CCSWP130.html May 18, 2005./Also published in *Communications of the ACM*, December, 1993/
3. Brynjolfsson, E. (2003) The IT Productivity Gap. *Optimize 21*:26–43. http://www.optimizemag.com April 19, 2005.
4. Gammelgård, M. (2007) Business Value Assessment of iIT Investments: An Evaluation Method Applied to the Electrical Power Industry. *Industrial Information and Control Systems*, KTH, Royal Institute of Technology, Stockholm.
5. Lech, P. (2007) Proposal of a Compact IT Value Assessment Method. *Electronic Journal of Information Systems Evaluation 10*(1):73–82.
6. Lindgren, R., Henfridsson, O. and Schultze, U. (2004) Design Principles for Competence Management Systems: A Synthesis of Action Research Study. *MIS Quarterly 28*(3):435–472.
7. Mathiassen, L. (2002) Collaborative Practice Research. *Information Technology & People 15*(4):321–345.
8. Nagpal, P., Lyytinen, K. and Helper, S. (2006) I.T. Investment and Complements in Value Creation: A Meta-Analytic Replication. *Proceedings of the 14th European Conference on Information Systems. Gothenburg, Sweden*, June 12–14, 2006.
9. Renkema, T. J. W. (2000) *The IT Value Quest: How to Capture the Business Value of IT-based Infrastructure.*Chichester: Wiley.
10. Renkema, T. J. W. and Berghout, E. W. (1997) Methodologies for Information Systems Investment Evaluation at the Proposal Stage: A Comparative Review.*Information and Software Technology 39*(1):1–13.
11. Ross, J. W. and Beath, C. M. (2002) Beyond the Business Case: New Approaches to IT Investment. *MIT Sloan Management Review 43*(2):51–59.

12. Smith, H. and Fingar, P. (2003) IT Doesn't Matter – Business Processes Do: A Critical Analysis of Nicholas Carr's I.T. Article in the *Harvard Business Review*. Tampa, Fla: Meghan-Kiffer.
13. Svavarsson, D., Björnsson, H., Ekström, M. and Bergendahl, G. (2002) Evaluating IT Investments in the AEC Industry. *Proceedings of the Ninth European Conference on Information Technology Evaluation*. Université Paris-Dauphine, France, July 15–16 2002, pp 415–424.
14. Ward, J. and Peppard, J. (2003) *Strategic Planning for Information Systems*. Third Edition, New York, NY: John Wiley & Sons, Inc.
15. Ward, J., Daniel, E. and Peppard, J. (2008) Building Better Business Cases for IT Investments. *MIS Quarterly Executive* 7(1):1–15.

47

Design Patterns Application in the ERP Systems Improvements

Bojan Jovičić and Siniša Vlajić

Abstract

Design patterns application have long been present in software engineering. The same is true for ERP systems in business software. Is it possible that ERP systems do not have a good maintenance score? We have found out that there is room for maintenance improvement and that it is possible to improve ERP systems using design patterns. We have conducted comparative analysis of ease of maintenance of the ERP systems. The results show that the average score for our questions is 64%, with most answers for ERP systems like SAP, Oracle EBS, Dynamics AX. We found that 59% of ERP system developer users are not familiar with design patterns. Based on this research, we have chosen Dynamics AX as the ERP system for examination of design patterns improvement possibilities. We used software metrics to measure improvement possibility. We found that we could increase the Conditional Complexity score 17-fold by introducing design patterns.

Keywords Design patterns · ERP systems · Comparative analysis · Software metrics

1. Introduction

ERP (**E**nterprise **R**esource **P**lanning) systems are such information systems which are oriented toward information support of most of common business processes, such as purchase, sales, warehouse management, finances, and their planning.

Today there is a huge number of ERP systems. Some of ERP systems with most market share are [1, 2]: mySAP ERP (SAP), Oracle E-Business Suite (Oracle), Dynamics (Microsoft), Accpac ERP and Pro ERP (Sage), and SSA ERP (Infor).

In software engineering, a design pattern is a general reusable solution to a commonly occurring problem in software design. A design pattern is not a finished design that can be transformed directly into code. It is a description or template for how to create **solution** for given **problem** in given **context**. Object-oriented design patterns typically show relationships and interactions between classes or objects, without specifying the final application classes or objects that are involved. This chapter will try to shed some light on design patterns usage in ERP systems and possibilities of improving ERP systems using design patterns. First a comparative analysis of ease of maintenance was performed. Based on this research, Dynamics AX was chosen as the ERP system for examination of design patterns improvement possibilities, because it was one of the ERP systems that scored best at comparative analysis and it has most of its code open, so design patterns application and improvement possibilities could be investigated.

Bojan Jovičić · Delta Sport, Belgrade, Serbia. **Siniša Vlajić** · Faculty of Organizational Sciences, University of Belgrade, Belgrade, Serbia.

G.A. Papadopoulos et al. (eds.), *Information Systems Development*, DOI 10.1007/b137171_47,
© Springer Science+Business Media, LLC 2009

2. Review of Business Functionalities Analysis

Existing comparative analysis of ERP systems focused on comparison of business functionalities and divisions based upon price category. Some examples of research like this are as follow:

- One of the first analysis is given in [3]. It was done in 1999 and compares SAP, Oracle, PeopleSoft, and Baan.
- The research which compares bigger number of ERP systems based on basic, out of the box, and all functionalities with focus on production and distribution areas is given in [4].
- One of the most complex researches is given in [5]. This research compares a big number of ERP systems and lasts for 3 years. Besides the results for the year 2007 (available at [5]), results are also available for the year 2006 [6] and the year 2005 [7].
- The research which compares Microsoft Dynamics and SAP based on user productivity is given in [8].

Although not a research, a central place where you can track all changes and acquisitions of ERP systems and their vendors is ERP graveyard [9].

3. Analysis of Ease of Maintenance and Design Patterns Usage

This is one of the pioneer attempts in researching some of the characteristics of ease of maintenance and design patterns usage in ERP systems. The research was conducted in two phases.

- In first phase, answers were collected by direct contact. Answers were gathered from 28 examinees in this manner. Some of these examinees had experience in several ERP systems, making the total number of completed questionnaires 42. Total experience of these 28 examinees in working with ERP systems is 102 years, making an average of 3.64 years.
- In second phase, answers were collected using anonymous "online" questionnaire, which is available at [10]. Answers were gathered from 96 sessions in this manner. Total experience in working with ERP systems gathered from these 96 sessions is 568 years, making an average of 5.87 years.

In the questionnaire, each examinee was required to provide answers for each of ERP systems he/she is proficient with.

Questionnaire had 11 mandatory questions:

1. Number of years of experience in ERP system
2. Ease of creating/modifying reports
3. Ease of creating/modifying forms
4. Ease of modifying business processes
5. Database model (Direct / Metamodel)
6. Ease of integration with other applications
7. Level of support for XML
8. Level of support for Web services
9. Ease of Web development
10. Level of support for automated testing
11. Check question if examinee is familiar with design patterns

For questions 2–4 and 6–10 answers were provided by choosing a score from 1 to 5, where 1 means no support, or hardest way of achieving, and 5 means best support, or easiest way of achieving.

Besides these questions, examinee was to provide six additional answers, if he answered check question about design patterns familiarity positively. These six answers were given in response to following two questions:

1. Can you identify some of design patterns in this ERP system (up to three answers)?
2. Which design patterns can improve development in this ERP system (up to three answers)?

3.1. Analysis of Combined Results

In this part, results of analysis of combined research for both phases will be presented. For all questions, T test was performed and it was determined that there are no statistically important differences between anonymous and direct parts of research.

In our research ERP systems with highest number of answers were Dynamics AX, SAP, Dynamics NAV, Oracle EBS, and Dynamics GP.

In Table 47.1 answers are presented for asked questions. For each question, number of answers for each option is show, with question averages.

Table 47.1. Answers by options with question averages.

		No support (worst)	2	3	4	Best support (easiest)	No answers	Average score
Ease of creating/ modifying reports	Answers	10.00	21.00	42.00	39.00	26.00		3.36
	Percent	7.25	15.22	30.43	28.26	18.84		
Ease of creating/ modifying forms	Answers	4.00	17.00	40.00	27.00	50.00		3.74
	Percent	2.90	12.32	28.99	19.57	36.23		
Ease of modifying business processes	Answers	4.00	19.00	51.00	42.00	22.00		3.43
	Percent	2.90	13.77	36.96	30.43	15.94		
Ease of integration with other applications	Answers	7.00	20.00	51.00	37.00	23.00		3.36
	Percent	5.07	14.49	36.96	26.81	16.67		
Level of support for XML	Answers	15.00	29.00	42.00	29.00	22.00	1.00	3.10
	Percent	10.87	21.01	30.43	21.01	15.94	0.72	
Level of support for Web services	Answers	18.00	28.00	38.00	35.00	18.00	1.00	3.05
	Percent	13.04	20.29	27.54	25.36	13.04	0.72	
Ease of Web development	Answers	22.00	24.00	48.00	28.00	14.00	2.00	2.91
	Percent	15.94	17.39	34.78	20.29	10.14	1.45	
Level of support for automated testing	Answers	26.00	25.00	52.00	18.00	12.00	5.00	2.74
	Percent	18.84	18.12	37.68	13.04	8.70	3.62	

As in results from separate phases, here we can also see that the level of support for automated testing is weakest. Besides that, Web development is weakly supported, and Web services too. The best supported activity is creating and/or modifying forms and modification of business processes.

In Fig. 47.1 graphical representation of average scores for five ERP systems with most answers is shown.

From Fig. 47.1 we can see that examinees have given answers that indicate that creating/modifying reports is easiest in Dynamics NAV and hardest in Oracle EBS. Forms are easiest to create/modify in Dynamics AX and hardest in Oracle EBS.

Business processes are easiest to modify in Dynamics AX and hardest in Dynamics GP. Integration with other applications is easiest to achieve in Dynamics AX and hardest in Dynamics GP.

XML is best supported in Dynamics AX and worst in Dynamics GP. Web services are best supported in SAP ERP system and worst in Dynamics NAV. Web development is easiest in Oracle EBS and hardest in Dynamics NAV.

Automated testing in best supported in SAP ERP system and worst in Dynamics GP.

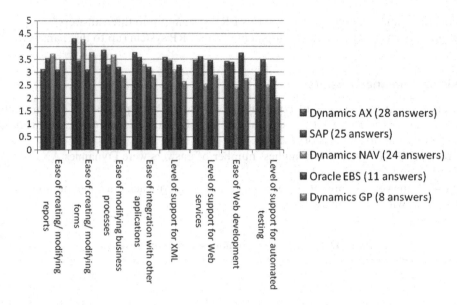

Figure 47.1. Analysis of answers for five ERP systems with most answers.

3.1.1. Design Patterns Familiarity

Many of the examinees have stated that they are not familiar with design patterns, way up to 58.7%. Examinees who stated that they are familiar with design patterns could list three patterns that they recognize as being used in ERP system for which they are providing answers, and three patterns for which they think that their introduction could improve ERP system for which they are providing answers. Most of the answers for these questions do not represent design patterns at all.

4. Analysis of Existing Patterns in Dynamics AX

In this part we will show results of identification of some of the design patterns from GoF, *Gang of Four: Gamma, Helm, Johnson, Vlissides*, book [11] in Dynamics AX ERP system.

For each pattern we will show the original description from [11] with analysis of implementation and structure in Dynamics AX.

4.1. Strategy

4.1.1. Intent

Define a family of algorithms, encapsulate each one, and make them interchangeable. Strategy lets the algorithm vary independently from clients that use it [11].

4.1.2. Application in Dynamics AX

Application of this design pattern is very common in Dynamics AX. One of the examples is class *AddressZipCodeImport* and classes that inherit it. Class *AddressZipCodeImport* represents both *Context* and *Strategy* from original structure in [11].

Class *AddressZipCodeImport* has abstract method *readFile* which is implemented by all classes that inherit it. This is the manner as with method *AlgorithmInterface* from original structure in [11]. In method *Construct*, this class instantiates object from one of the classes that inherits it, based on parameters. Afterward the method *Run* calls the method *readFile* in order to activate concrete implementation of strategy.

One of the classes that represent concrete strategy in this example is class *AddressZipCodeImport_NL*. This class inherits the class *AddressZipCodeImport* and implements the strategy method *readFile*.

4.2. Iterator

4.2.1. Intent

To provide a way to access the elements of an aggregate object sequentially without exposing its underlying representation [11].

4.2.2. Application in Dynamics AX

Some of the basic collection classes which are available inside X + + (Dynamics AX programming language) are *set*, *map* (hash table), and *list*. These classes are part of kernel and it is not possible to see their implementation (as it is with classes which are not part of kernel, which in total make more than 1.2 million lines of code available to developers). Classes *set* and *list* have their iterator classes: *SetIterator* and *ListIterator*. These classes are also part of kernel and it is not possible to access their implementation. For classes which are part of kernel we can see documented part of their interface in help system.

But, it is possible to use reflection classes to examine if these classes are part of hierarchy which can be considered as implementation of iterator design pattern. For this need a "job" (Dynamics AX name for small X + + piece of code) was implemented which can be downloaded from [10].

In last part of this script, we examine which classes implement given class, and we have found error in internal implementation, because the reflection method *implementedBy* always returns a list of classes which implement given class as if give class implements itself. We have written about this on [10]. This script contains a workaround, so this error is avoided.

When this script is run upon classes *ListIterator* and *SetIterator*, we see that neither of the given two classes is abstract, that neither is interface, that both are parts of kernel, and both inherit base class *Object*. Besides that the class *InventDimOnHandIterator* inherits class *SetIterator*.

Based on the above results, we can conclude that hierarchy of shown classes cannot be considered iterator design pattern, since there is no connection between given classes.

But, both of this collection classes have methods that return objects of class *Enumerator*. *Enumerator* class in Dynamics AX is by functionalities and interface very similar to definition of iterator design pattern (it contains such methods as: *current( )*, *moveNext( )*, *reset( )*).

As in iterator case, enumerators are also part of kernel, so we must use reflection in order to confirm if this is a part of bigger hierarchy. Because these classes are part of kernel, we are also restricted of possibility to create class diagram by using reverse engineering (one of good functionalities of Dynamics AX).

For examining class hierarchy between classes *Enumerator*, *MapEnumerator*, *SetEnumeratora*, and *ListEnumerator*, it is enough to perform analysis upon *Enumerator* interface, using the script we have created, because it also shows which classes implement given interface.

In MorphX IDE (Integrated Development Environment) of Dynamics AX, interfaces are created in same part where classes are created, i.e. in classes part. Even in help system, interfaces are shown as classes.

Results of script execution show that *Enumerator* is not abstract, that it is interface, that it is part of kernel, and that it inherits base class *Object*. *Enumerator* is implemented by exact three classes which are considered as part of hierarchy. This hierarchy looks like iterator design pattern class hierarchy.

What remains is to check if there is class hierarchy for collection classes themselves. Since these classes are also part of kernel, we will use reflection script once again. Results show that collection classes do not have common base interface.

Based on previous research, we can conclude that shown classes do not have exact iterator design pattern, but that very little modification is needed to make this happen and to certainly improve class hierarchy in both collection classes and iterator classes (*SetIterator*, *ListIterator*). Hierarchy of enumerator classes is implemented with good object-oriented principles in mind. We have provided some guidelines for these modifications in Dynamics AX ERP system kernel:

- Create common interface for classes *SetIterator* and *ListIterator*. We will call this interface *IIterator*.
- Change classes *SetIterator* and *ListIterator*, so that they implement (in X + + for interface implementation keyword *implements* is used) *IIterator* interface.
- Create class *MapIterator* which will implement given interface for class *Map* and support iteration upon its key collection.
- Create one or two common interfaces for classes *Map*, *Set*, and *List*. It is possible to create one interface to support both iterator and enumerator classes or to create two separate interfaces.
- Change classes *Map*, *Set*, and *List* so that they implement given interfaces.

4.3. Template Method

4.3.1. Intent

Define the skeleton of an algorithm in an operation, deferring some steps to subclasses. Template method lets subclasses redefine certain steps of an algorithm without changing the algorithm's structure [11].

4.3.2. Application in Dynamics AX

This design pattern is widely used in Dynamics AX ERP system. Classes such as *RunBase*, *RunBaseBatch*, and *RunBaseReport* represent abstract classes, and implementation of new functionalities and reports is often reduced to inheriting these classes, and implementing methods that form template method (hook methods).

Template method inside *RunBaseReport* (base class for working with reports) operates in the following manner:

1. First method *Init* is triggered upon activation of report.
2. Afterward the method *Run* is called.
3. Method *Prompt* is activated in order to allow interaction with user.
4. Afterward the method *Fetch* is called.
5. Finally the method *Print* is called.

5. Improvement Possibilities for Dynamics AX Using Design Patterns

We have already provided some guidelines for improvement in part where we examined iterator design pattern.

In this part, we will try to improve quality of this ERP system by introducing design patterns. In order to perform exact comparison, we will use software metrics.

5.1. Software Metrics

Dynamics AX ERP system does not have built-in support for software metrics, so we will use cyclomatic complexity software metric from [12].

Cyclomatic complexity is often used metric from group of static software metrics. This metric can be considered as a good measure of quality and reliability of software. It measures the number of linearly independent path through code, and as results return the number which can be compared with complexity of other programs [13].

A huge number of programs have been analyzed using this metric, and some base ranges have been established which can measure risk and stability of program. Low cyclomatic complexity adds to easier understanding of code and indicates easier modification with lesser risk than more complex program [13].

5.2. Example in Dynamics AX

For concrete example, we will take classes *CustPaymFormatCtrl* i *VendPaymFormatCtrl* and their method *availableFormats*. Cust is common prefix for parts of Dynamics AX ERP system that deal with customers, and Vend for parts that deal with vendors. Both of these two classes inherit abstract class *CustVendPaymFormatCtrl*.

Abstract class *CustVendPaymFormatCtrl* uses **strategy** pattern so that in run time it can create proper object of one of the classes *CustPaymFormatCtrl* or *VendPaymFormatCtrl*, based on parameters, and call its abstract method *allAvailableFormats* which is implemented by both classes and called by method *availableFormats*.

Implementation of both versions of method *availableFormats* in X++ is very long (79 and 100 lines of code, respectively). Number of lines of code is also one of software metrics.

Conditional complexity of method *availableFormats* of class *CustPaymFormatCtrl* is **22**. Conditional complexity of method *availableFormats* of class *VendPaymFormatCtrl* is **17**. Both values are outside recommended range.

In rest of this chapter, we will show how using refactoring techniques it is possible to introduce design patterns, then we will measure new software metrics of these methods and present comparison results.

For refactoring patterns, we will use guidelines presented in [14] and [15].

Some of the facts that are to be taken into consideration while refactoring are

- Both implementations have certain number of very similar parts which create container collection objects based on contents of a given list.
- Implementation of *CustPaymFormatCtrl* version uses objects of classes *CustOutPaym*, *CustInPaym*, *CustOutPaymRemittance*, and *CustPaymReconcilationImport*.
- Implementation of *VendPaymFormatCtrl* version uses objects of classes *VendOutPaym* and *VendPaymReconcilationImport*.
- Both implementations uses certain objects of classes which are very similar: container collections, *SysOperationProgress* (for showing status of executing long running operation), *DictClass* (for reflection), and *ListEnumerator*.

Since there are certain parts of code which are repeated and which look like template method, we will try to introduce template method pattern, using guidelines for creating template method design pattern from [14] and [15] taking into consideration the analysis of class hierarchy in Dynamics AX ERP system.

First we will perform analysis of classes whose objects represent difference in implementation of these two methods. In order to grasp the best manner of introducing template method, we must examine wider hierarchy which includes base classes and interfaces if there are any. As it is shown in Fig. 47.2, base of this hierarchy is interface *CustVendBankPaymFormat*.

Since all template parts of existing implementation often use method *interfaceName*, as base we will create interface *IPaymInterfaceName* which will contain only this method.

We will change interface *CustVendBankPaymFormat* so that it extends our new interface *IPaymInterfaceName*.

Next step is creating abstract class which will be the base of template method. The main problem is that we need to separate the base of template method, whose behavior will change. Sample of this class (*CustVendPaymAvailableFormat*) implementation in X++ is given below:

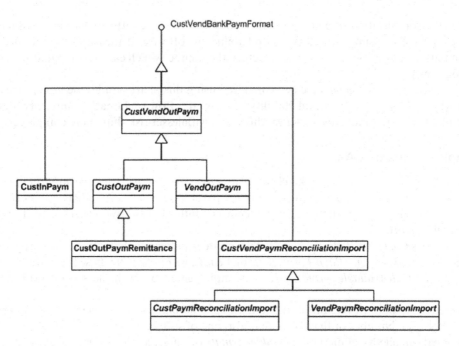

Figure 47.2. Class hierarchy for classes used in AvailableFormats method implementation.

```
final container AvailableFormats(List targetList, SysOperationProgress progress)
{
    ListEnumerator                listEnumerator;
    DictClass                     dictClass;
    container                     conPaymentIds;
    container                     conPaymentNames;
    IPaymInterfaceName            payment;
    ;

    listEnumerator = targetList.getEnumerator();
    while (listEnumerator.moveNext())
    {
        progress.incCount();
        dictClass = new DictClass(listEnumerator.current());

        if (this.CheckPayment(dictClass, payment) && payment.interfaceName() &&
CustVendPaymFormatCtrl::checkConfigurationKey(payment))
        {
            conPaymentIds += this.GetClassId(dictClass);
            conPaymentNames += payment.interfaceName();
            progress.setText(payment.interfaceName());
        }
    }

    return [conPaymentIds, conPaymentNames];
}
```

During this class implementation it has been decided that method *GetClassId* has default implementation. Template method (*availableFormats*) has been declared as final.

New version of method *availableFormats* in class *VendPaymFormatCtrl* now has 30 lines of code, compared to initial 100, making it more then three-fold improvement. The new value of cyclomatic complexity software metric is 1, which represents 17-fold improvement in comparison with original value. Same method in class *CustPaymFormatCtrl* now has 35 lines of code, making it two-fold improvement in comparison with 79 original lines of code. The new value of cyclomatic complexity software metric is now 1, which represents 22-fold improvement in comparison with original value.

6. Conclusions

Based on performed analysis, we can provide answer to the first question which represents the essence of this chapter:

Do existing ERP systems provide mechanisms for developing specific processes and in which measure?

The answer to this question is that existing ERP systems provide solid mechanism for easy and fast development of specific processes and their introduction into business system. But, when we take into consideration the needs in some actual trends in business systems (Web development, support for Web services, support for XML, integration) and needs in actual trends in software development (need for automated testing support), we can say that **existing mechanism are mostly not so solid**. ERP systems should improve their support for actual trends in development, in fast implementation of new functionalities and easy maintenance.

Second question that we have answered is:

Can Dynamics AX ERP system be improved by introducing design patterns?

We have found out that it can, and that improvement can in some parts of system be 17-fold. The question is raised why developers who use Dynamics AX ERP system do not use design patterns, or why developers who create Dynamics AX ERP system do not use design patterns? One possible answer is that for successful work in ERP systems, business processes familiarity is important, and that it is possible that many of these developers do not come from formal software development education. Because of high importance of business process understanding and grasping the manner in which they are implemented in given ERP system, it is totally possible that some concepts of software engineering are slipping through their radar as secondary effects.

References

1. Reilly, Kevin (2005) *AMR Research Releases Report Showing Overall European Market for ERP Vendors to Grow 7% Annually Through 2009*. AMR Research. Retrieved December 16, 2006 from http://www.amrresearch.com/Content/View.asp?pmillid = 18386
2. Bailor, Coreen (2006) *For CRM, ERP, and SCM, SAP Leads the Way*. destinationCRM.com. Retrieved December 15, 2006 from http://tinyurl.com/2ndaon
3. Peasley, Sean (1999) *Introduction to ERP: Overview of ERP Systems*. Internal Audit: Resources for Internal Auditors. Retrieved 15 May, 2007 from http://tinyurl.com/5tzeyf
4. Chewning, Charles (2006) *The Accounting Library: Research Which Business Management Application is Best for You*. Microsoft. Retrieved 22 January, 2007 from http://tinyurl.com/6cu7ah
5. 180 Systems (2007) *2007 Accounting and ERP Survey*. CAMagazine. Retrieved 01 September, 2007 from http://tinyurl.com/58zelg
6. 180 Systems (2006) *Accounting/ERP Comparison*. 180 Systems. Retrieved 16 August 16, 2007 from http://www.180systems.com/ERP-Comparison2006.xls
7. 180 Systems (2005) *Accounting/ERP Comparison*. 180 Systems. Retrieved 22 July 22, 2007 from http://www.180systems.com/ERP-Comparison2005.xls
8. Iansiti, Marco (2007) *ERP End-User Business Productivity: A Field Study of SAP & Microsoft*. Microsoft. Retrieved 15 May, 2007 from http://tinyurl.com/6o68y5
9. Lilly, Ned (2005) *The ERP Graveyard Scorecard*. The ERP Graveyard Blog. Retrieved 04 September, 2007 from http://www.erpgraveyard.com/tombs.html
10. Jovičić, Bojan (2007) http://www.bojanjovicic.com/. Bojan Jovičić – Blog about Software Lifecycle, Design Patterns, Electronic Business and ERP systems.
11. Gamma, Erich, et al. (1999) *Design Patterns: Elements of Reusable Object-Oriented Software*. Addison-Wesley, Boston, MA.
12. Sørensen, Anders Tind (2006) *Measuring Complexity in X + + Code*. IMM Publications. Retrieved 19 January, 2007 from http://tinyurl.com/5tb4an
13. VanDoren, Edmond (2000) *Cyclomatic Complexity*. Carnegie Mellon, Software Engineering Institute. Retrieved 22 August, 2006 from http://tinyurl.com/ydjs7x
14. Kerievsky, Joshua (2004) *Refactoring to Patterns*. Addison-Wesley, Boston, MA.
15. Fowler, Martin (1999) *Refactoring: Improving the Design of Existing Code*. Addison-Wesley, Boston, MA.

48

Determinants of Open Source Software Adoption – An Application of TOE Framework

Tomasz Przechlewski and Krystyna Strzała

Abstract

Open source software (OSS) is currently one of the most debated phenomena in both academia and the software industry. Several OSS systems have achieved significant market success but they are rather server-side applications, such as the Apache Web server, MySQL database server, or other components of IT infrastructure. On the other hand, penetration of OSS systems on the market of desktop applications is rather limited and it is virtually dominated by products of one software vendor, i.e., Microsoft. In this chapter, the benefits and barriers of OSS implementation in Poland are investigated. Based on the well-known technology–organization–environment model of IT technology adoption of a simple model was developed and evaluated empirically, based on the data from the survey of 178 enterprises and public institutions. Statistical analysis using partial least squares (PLS) was performed. Of the four factors considered to determine adoption decisions (benefits, costs, environment, and organization), it was found that only perceived benefits and environment are significant.

Keywords Open source software · Software adoption · Statistical survey

1. Introduction

Open source software (OSS) refers to any IT system whose source code is freely accessible [1, 2]. There is a huge interest in OSS movement recently both from business and academia, cf. [3–5]. However, the main research interest in OSS so far has been to explain the incentives of individuals, so organizations get engaged in OSS projects [6–9]. Other contributions approach OSS phenomenon from a diversity of angles; among these are social organization of OSS projects [10, 8], economics of OSS and OSS business models [11], or OSS software development methods [12]. The literature focusing on the implementation issues, motivation, and benefits of organizational users is relatively scarce [13–15].

In this study a simple conceptual model of OSS adoption based on the technology–organization–environment (TOE) theoretical framework is verified using data from the survey of Polish public institutions and enterprises.

The rest of the chapter is organized as follows. A brief overview of OSS is presented in the subsequent section. Conceptual models of users' acceptance of IT, including technology–organization–environment model is discussed next. Then research method and survey design is described, followed by results of the data analysis. Discussion of the findings concludes the chapter.

Tomasz Przechlewski · Katedra Informatyki Ekonomicznej, Uniwersytet Gdański, Sopot 81-864, ul, Piaskowa 9, Poland **Krystyna Strzała** · Katedra Ekonometrii, Uniwersytet Gdański, Sopot 81-824, ul Armii Krajowej 119/121, Poland

G.A. Papadopoulos et al. (eds.), *Information Systems Development*, DOI 10.1007/b137171_48,

2. Research on IT Adoption and Implementation

A great variety of IT systems are used in business and public institutions nowadays and thus IS innovations can be of various types – some are technical in nature and concerns organization's IT department only while others may affect whole of the organization. From mere technical point of view, IT systems can be divided onto two broad categories: server systems, which are part of the infrastructure and are usually transparent for ordinary users and desktop applications. Swanson [16] divided IT systems into the following three groups: Type I innovations are confined to the technical tasks; Type II are concerned with business administration; and Type III innovations are embedded in the core of the business. Based on strategic importance of IT systems to organization, Kwan and West [17] classified IT systems into the following categories: *strategic, mission critical, support,* and *laboratory*. They argue that evaluation criteria used during procurement process, such as risk, system features, and costs depend heavily on the relative importance of the system for the organization. In particular, they claim minimizing risk not costs and maximizing features are of primarily concern for strategic systems.

A popular model explaining IT adoption at the organizational level, developed by Tornatzky and Fleischer [18], identifies three aspects that influence the process by which technological innovations are implemented: technological context, organizational context, and environmental context. Technological context describes technologies relevant to the organization. Organizational context concerns firm size and scope, centralization, formalization, managerial issues, slack resources available, and the skills of organization's staff. Prior studies indicate larger organizations on the average have more slack resources and are more likely to achieve economies of scale and thus are more innovative [19, 20]. On the other side, the association between adoption and formalization reported in most innovation studies is negative. Environment factors concern organizations surroundings, such as type of industry, legal settings, environmental uncertainty, external pressure. Both external pressure and uncertainty is consistently recognized as innovation facilitators.

The TOE framework was employed in a number of empirical studies[1] to explain adoption in various organizational contexts (SMEs, large organizations) of different technologies, such as Open Systems [22, 23], Internet technologies [20], EDI/IOS systems [24–27], or e-CRM implementation/ adoption [28].[2]

Particularly relevant to OSS adoption are studies concerned with Open Systems, or EDI to IOS migration. For example, perceived barriers and satisfaction with existing systems appeared to be significant to adoption of open systems while perceived benefits were not [22]. The difference between the beliefs concerning the benefits of open systems of adopters and non-adopters was insignificant. Explaining this phenomenon Chau and Tam [22, 23] claim that the most prominent obstacle of OSS migration is the lack of skilled personnel. They argued that adoption of complex technologies is (primary) a process of reducing knowledge barriers. This claim is supported by several other studies [31, 32].

Dedrick and West [29] developed a TOE-based model explaining adoption of OSS-server platforms and tested it empirically with series of semi-structured interviews. Technological factors include *relative advantage* perceived primarily in terms of *lower costs* and *improved reliability, compatibility* and *complexity*; organizational context consists of *IT innovativeness, IT centrality, slack*; and environmental factors contains *external support and availability of skilled IT personnel* and *legitimacy*. It is claimed that *cost savings* are most important driver of OSS adoption while such benefits as possibility to modify source code[3] appeared to be negligible.

---

[1] For the overview of various IT adoption surveys using TOE framework see [21].

[2] It should be noted, however, that TOE framework still does not represent well-developed model [29, 30]. A vast span of variables was included and inconsistency of variable selection may be observed (For example, costs belong to "technology context" in [22, 29] or to "organizational context" in [27].)

[3] The benefit often raised by OSS advocates and developers.

3. Conceptual Model of Open Source Adoption

Most successful OSS application belongs to IT infrastructure and desktop applications, thus they can be classified as Type I or Type II innovation according to Swanson taxonomy [16]. Desktop usage is dominated by proprietary applications, and OSS programs are introduced usually as replacements for them, such as OpenOffice for MS Office or Mozilla Firefox in place of MSIE browser. As concerns most valuable systems (Type III or strategic/mission critical), it is obvious there are no ready to download OSS applications that could provide strategic advantage to the organization; however, such systems based on OS components can be developed or bought from external integrator/developer. Most OSS implementations can be regarded as an organizational innovation that requires both technical and administrative innovation.

Although open source software presents an interesting example of IT adoption by organizations, there are quite a few quantitative studies describing this phenomenon [29, 14]. Based on the TOE framework discussed above, we propose a conceptual model for OSS adoption, as illustrated in Fig. 48.1. Drawing upon empirical evidences combined with prior research on IT adoption [17, 14, 22], we believe that TOE framework is appropriate for explaining adoption of OSS systems. Variable selection to maximum extent possible is based on previous studies on adoption of similar technologies [22].

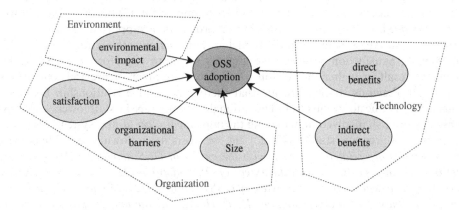

Figure 48.1. Proposed model of OSS adoption based on TOE framework.

In our model OSS adoption is determined by the following variables: *perceived benefits*, *perceived barriers*, *organizational*, and *environmental factors*. Perceived benefits refer both to more tangible *direct* or *acquisition benefits* as well as *indirect benefits*. The former includes OSS benefits, frequently mentioned by OSS advocates, namely *low acquisition cost*, *source code availability*, and *more software/hardware choices*. OSS can be acquired without costs as license fees are eliminated. Next, availability of source code allows – at least potentially – for better customization, thus allowing for more software/hardware choices. The anticipated advantages that OSS systems can provide to organization are *cost savings* and *better software quality*. Several reports indicate OSS adoption can result in significant cost savings [33]. The administrative/legal overhead of software ownership is significantly reduced (i.e., no need for troublesome software audit). Upgrading/maintenance costs are lower too. Excessive upgrade expenditures often force users to upgrade only a part of their IT infrastructure.[4] Hardware costs may be reduced too as Linux is often used on inexpensive Intel computers (Wintel platform) replacing Unix systems running on expensive hardware.

---

[4] In result the organization exploits several versions of the systems. Obviously, such heterogeneous IT infrastructure is more expensive to maintain. Alternatively, one could pay for unnecessary upgrades. Frequently hardware replacement is needed for new software to work properly which enlarge upgrade expenditures even further.

Except *cost savings* many OSS systems are attributed with superior quality (superior reliability, functionality, and security). Raymond [34] argues obscurity of the source code and typical vendor's policy toward releasing (infrequently) patches/upgrades hinders both reliability and security of the software. Bugs are reported to vendors but cannot be fixed properly (as source code is not accessible), so frequently some quick-and-dirty way arounds are devised to cope the problems. Such practices degrade the quality of the source code, in result may cause reliability and security problems. In the case of OSS patches and security, upgrades are fixed much quicker. With the public accessibility to the source code there is little room for *back doors*.

Following Attewell [35] many authors emphasize the role of know-how and organizational learning in the adoption process and divide perceived barriers of IT adoption into the following dimensions: *overall financial migration costs, knowledge of the IT personnel*, and *compatibility problems* [22]. Costs and technical knowledge[5] have been reported as important factors that significantly hinder IT implementation in a number of studies [30, 22, 23]. We posited the above mentioned three cost dimensions (financial costs, compatibility, and knowledge) in our model.

Environment context embraces external services and external support, and peer adoption. It is reported in many previous studies that these factors are positively related to IS adoption [37, 13, 24]. Both dimensions are related to the economic concept of network effect. Even there is frequently no direct network effect, one can list several positive indirect ones. The larger is the net of users of particular (OSS) system, the greater are incentives: (1) for the developers to improve it, (2) for organizations to adapt it as hiring skilled workforce is cheaper, and (3) for external providers of support services.

Two additional variables included in the model are *satisfaction with existing systems* and *IT human resources availability*. Satisfaction provides the impetus to improve performance [38] so low level of satisfaction should result in higher motivation to change. A number of previous studies confirm this assumption [23, 22]. Previous studies indicate that there is a positive relationship between *IT human resources availability* and the adoption of IT. The rationale is that larger IT staff lowers knowledge barriers and could absorb more risk involved in managing the implementation of new systems [20].

Consistently with previous studies [23, 22, 26], we posit the following set of hypotheses: *Higher perceived direct benefits are related positively with the extent of OSS adoption (H1a), Higher perceived indirect benefits are related positively with the extent of OSS adoption (H1b), Higher perceived organizational barriers are related negatively with the extent of OSS adoption (H2), IT human resources availability is related positively with the extent of OSS adoption (H3a), Higher satisfaction with proprietary systems results in lower extent of OSS adoption (H3b), and Environmental impact is positively related with the extent of OSS adoption (H4).*

A statistical survey was performed to verify the research hypotheses.

4. Research Method, Survey Design, and the Sample Description

The targets of the survey were twofold: provide accurate figures concerning OSS use in Poland in general, and provide data to verify our TOE-based model of OSS adoption. The *target population* consisted of *all the enterprises which manage non-trivial IT systems*. This definition excluded enterprises which outsourced IT systems or those who used only very simple applications (i.e., PC for word-processing or Web browsing). Practically speaking, the sampling unit was an enterprise which had some sort of IT department and hired IT professional(s). Eligible respondents were IT managers best qualified to speak about organization's IT infrastructure. As vast majority of small firms (with employment less than 50) had no IT staff they were excluded from the target population.

The sample frame for the study was taken from the BJS register which contains all establishments operating in Poland and is maintained and used by Polish Central Statistical Office (GUS). Using BJS a random sample was taken from the population, stratified for NACE groups and firm size. The robust

---

[5] Following Iacovou et al. these factors are defined as technological readiness in a number of studies [36].

procedure used enable for estimation of OSS usage in Poland. The pre-test and pilot survey was conducted in September 2005 and the main study was conducted in October 2005.

In two-step approach the establishments were approached by phone with the question whether they manage ITC on their own, and if so, whether they are using or planning to use OSS within a year. In total, 994 respondents were asked. As expected, many establishments do not have IT department – thus do not manage their IT systems on their own, rely on service outsourcing, or use only very simple applications, like Office ones (391 establishments or 39.3%). Usage ratios were computed based on answers of 553 enterprises declaring to manage ITC systems on their own. In total, 336 respondents (60.8% of establishments managing ITC systems) declared that they use OSS systems, while 217 (39.2%) use only commercial software. Further 50 respondents refuse to take part in the survey (approximately 5%). The details of the survey – one of a few of such an extent and statistical soundness – can be found in [39]. Overall, the sample represented a wide range of establishments, increasing the generalizability of the results.

The second part of the survey was designed as a self-administered, Web-based one. Of those 336 respondents declaring to use OSS systems, 216 completed the questionnaire (64.3%).

The study revealed a number of interesting features. Number of IT stuff is surprisingly low with 80% of the enterprises have three or less persons employed in ITC department (the mode within mid-sized and large establishments is 1.0 and 2.0, respectively). The survey shows not only that OSS usage is high (60.8% establishments declares to use OSS) but also the usage of OSS in the public sector is higher than the average (77.0%).[6] Finally OSS usage ratios by application type are the highest for server applications (45% of those using OSS claims that). Again the figures are consistent with other surveys [14].

Subsequent analysis and the estimation of the model are based on the sample of 178 OSS users. Table 48.1 presents selected descriptive statistics of the final sample.

Table 48.1. Sample description (employment, number of IT Staff, number of computers used).

Statistic	Employment	No. of IT Staff	No. of Computers
Mean	365.29	5.16	162.40
Standard deviation	584.37	17.89	428.69
Mode	162.50	2.00	50.00

Measurement items for the model presented in Section 3 were developed from prior studies on OSS, Open Source, EDI/IOS migration/adoption, as well as expert opinions and from OSS-oriented magazines, advocates of this software, and practitioners. Perceived benefits were measured using five items and the respondents were asked to give their level of agreement or disagreement with the following potential benefits of adopting OSS: *available source code; higher number of applications; no license fee* (direct benefits); and *cost savings regarding maintenance, support, and administration, higher performance, stability and security, better quality to TCO ratio* (indirect benefits).

Perceived organizational barriers were operationalized with the following three items: *high migration costs, compatibility problems within organization's IT infrastructure, personnel are only familiar with commercial applications*, and *satisfaction with proprietary systems is high*. Finally, environmental factors include the following four items: *availability of external support, integration in another acquired product, recommendation of integrator/IT provider*, and *adoption of OSS systems in peer organizations*. All but two construct (satisfaction, IT staff) are operationalized by multiple items.

---

[6] These figures are consistent with the results of the FLOSS survey which shows that public-sector organizations in Germany, Sweden, and the United Kingdom have above-average use and planned use rates compared to commercial firms (37% versus 31%, cf. [14]).

A five-point Likert scale was used in most items. Server systems (operating systems, database management systems, Web-based systems) and desktop applications were evaluated separately by informants. To estimate the *extent* to which OSS is used in the organization-dependent variable in the model is a multi-item construct measuring perceived overall importance of OSS as well as OSS adoption in a few key application areas, such as servers, database management systems, Web-based systems, and desktop applications (respondents were asked to select between *using/planning to use OSS in important applications, using/planning to use OSS in auxiliary applications,* and *not using and do not plan to use OSS*).

5. Estimation of the TOE Model

Partial least squares path modeling (PLS), as implemented in SMARTPLS [40], was used to empirically evaluate the model of OSS acceptance. PLS is a structural equation modeling technique that allows for formative as well as reflective indicators, small sample sizes and does not imply assumptions of multivariate normal distribution [41]. In this study *all* measurement relationships between indicators and constructs are specified as *formative.*[7] Formative indicators are not expected to be unidimensional and correlated with each other. Therefore, "traditional" measures of validity and reliability are not applied to them. Formative constructs are evaluated in terms of significance of weights only [24, 42].

Moreover, PLS is more appropriate when the research model is in an early stage of development and has not been tested extensively [24]. The review of the literature presented in Section 2 clearly indicates that TOE-based models are still not well-established theory. Hence, PLS seems the appropriate estimation method for our model.

The relevant statistics for the multi-item constructs of the measurement model are presented in Table 48.2. Separate models for server systems and desktop applications were estimated. Most measurement items have significant loadings.

The structural model in PLS is assessed by examining the path coefficients and its significance with *t*-statistics. Standard R^2 coefficient is used as an indicator of the overall goodness-of-fit measure of the model. The path coefficients and *t*-values for server applications are shown in Fig. 48.2a.

As concern's server systems coefficient values associated with *direct benefits, indirect benefits, environmental impact,* and the *availability of IT staff* were significant (thus *H1a, H1b, H4,* and *H3a* hypotheses are supported) while impact of *organizational barriers* and *satisfaction with proprietary systems* were not (*H2* and *H3b*). Model shows acceptable fit to data with $R^2 = 33.1\%$.

In case of desktop applications all coefficients were insignificant except *environmental impact* and *indirect benefits* so only *H1b* and *H4* are supported. Fit to data is lower than in the previous model with $R^2 = 28.8\%$ (cf. Fig. 48.2b).

It should be noted that (1) *organizational barriers* were consistently insignificant in both estimated models and (2) *environmental impact* and *indirect benefits* were shown to be the most significant factors as indicated by their path coefficients magnitude. The results obtained are exactly opposite to those reported in [22] where the perceived barriers (of open systems adoption) were significant while perceived benefits were not. The authors explain this phenomenon by lack of knowledge concerning new technologies such as Unix or TCP/IP. It seems that nowadays both proprietary and OSS software are based on many common open standards, so migration between them often do not require radically new knowledge or skills. On the other hand, in case of most popular OSS desktop applications there is a application-level interface standard (Gnome/KDE is similar to MS Windows desktop, Firefox to MS Internet Explorer, and OpenOffice to MS Office). Both proprietary and OSS systems employ the same protocols, formats and interfaces which facilitate migration.

The other significant factor consistently shown both for server and desktop applications was environmental impact, namely external support and peer adoption. Respondent's positive attitude

---

[7] There is a tendency to use reflective constructs in majority of MIS research. For example, perceived benefits/barriers were defined as reflective in [36, 27, 30], although it is in our opinion disputable to classify such multifaceted construct in that way.

Table 48.2. Summary of the measurement models of server and desktop applications.

Construct/measure	Servers		Desktop	
	Loading	t	Loading	t
Adoption extent:				
OSS importance to organization	0.8823	11.2198	0.7839	5.8083
OSS server or desktop usage	0.7370	7.3087	0.7688	6.0324
Indirect benefits:				
Higher performance, stability	0.8231	11.6999	0.6103	4.1677
Better quality to TCO ratio	0.8952	7.6990	0.8031	6.7566
Cost savings regarding maintenance	0.7014	5.3467	0.8649	6.8828
Organizational barriers:				
Personnel familiar with commercial...	0.5766	2.6927	0.3671	1.2563*
High migration costs	0.8571	5.0982	0.8943	4.1267
Compatibility problems	0.6361	2.6913	0.6353	2.2296
Environment impact:				
Peer adoption	0.7566	5.5844	0.8869	9.7348
Integration in another product	0.0813	0.3708*	0.0645	0.3122*
Availability of external support	0.6918	5.1039	0.4763	2.9750
Acquisition (direct) benefits:				
Higher number of applications	0.6469	4.7551	0.8743	5.5867
No license fee	0.0671	0.4325*	0.3839	1.6254*
Source code available	0.9318	10.0504	0.6654	3.3260

* Insignificant at α = 0.1 level

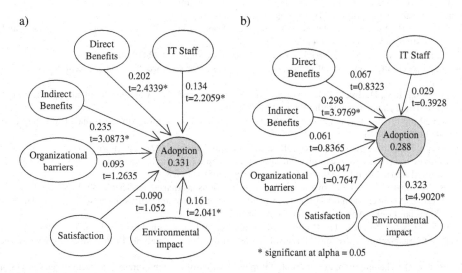

Figure 48.2. Coefficients of the structural model for server systems (**a**) and desktop applications (**b**).

manifested by relative importance of perceived advantages and external support, together with insignificance of perceived organizational barriers is an important hint both for IT developers and integrators as well as IT managers.

6. Summary

In this chapter, a conceptual model of open source software adoption was developed based on technology–organization–environment. The model was subsequently empirically verified using data coming from statistical survey performed in Polish public institutions and enterprises.

Separate models were estimated for server and desktop applications. For both models significant relation was shown between perceived indirect benefits and organizational factors (external support, peer adoption pressure) and the extent of OSS adoption. The impact of organizational barriers was insignificant for both categories of software. Our study raises important implications for managers and practitioners. The relative unimportance of perceived barriers seems encouraging for open source implementation perspectives within governmental institutions.

As the study is subject to number of limitations, including small sample size, the findings should be interpreted with caution when generalizing the results.

References

1. Weber, S.: The Success of Open Source. Harvard University Press, Cambridge, MA (2004).
2. Raymond, E.S.: The Cathedral and the Bazaar. O'Reilly Media, Inc. (2001) http://www.catb.org/~esr/writings/cathedral-bazaar/.
3. AlMarzouq, M.: Open source: Concepts, benefits, and challenges. Communications of AIS 16 (2005) 1–49.
4. Nelson, M.L., Sen, R., Subramaniam, C.: Understanding open source software: A research classification framework. Communications of AIS 2006 (2006) 2–37.
5. Niederman, F., Davis, A., Greiner, M.E., Wynn, D., York, P.T.: Research agenda for studying open source II: View through the lens of referent discipline theories. Communications of AIS 18 (2006) 2–45.
6. Holck, J., Larsen, M.H., Pedersen, M.K.: Identifying business barriers and enables for the adoption of open source software. Technical report, Copenhagen Business School (2004)
7. Shah, R., Goldstein, S.M.: Use of structural equation modelling in operations management research: Looking back and forward. Journal of Operations Management 24 (2006) 148–169.
8. Crowston, K., Li, Q., Wei, K., Eseryel, U.Y., Howison, J.: Self-organization of teams for free/libre open source software development. Information and Software Technology 49 (2007) 564–575.
9. Wu, C.G., Gerlach, J.H., Young, C.E.: An empirical analysis of open source software developers' motivations and continuance intentions. Information and Management 44 (2007) 253–262.
10. Fielding, R.T.: Shared leadership in the apache project. Communcation ACM 42 (1999) 42–43.
11. Mustonen, M.: Copyleft–the economics of Linux and other open source software. Information Economics and Policy 15 (2003) 99–121.
12. Mockus, A., Fielding, R.T., Herbsleb, J.D.: Two case studies of open source software development: Apache and Mozilla. ACM Transaction of Software Engineering Methodology 11 (2002) 309–346.
13. Goode, S.: Something for nothing: management rejection of open source software in Australia's top firms. Information and Management 42 (2005) 669–681.
14. Berlecon Research: Free/libre and open source software: Survey and study (2002) http://www.infonomics.nl/FLOSS.
15. Waring, T., Maddocks, P.: Open source implementation in the UK public sector: Evidence from the field and implications for the future. International Journal of Information Management 25 (2005) 411–428.
16. Swanson, E.B.: Information systems innovation among organizations. Management Science 40 (1994) 1069–1092.
17. Kwan, S.K., West, J.: A conceptual model for enterprise adoption of open source software. In Bolin, S., ed.: The Standards Edge: Open Season. Sheridan Books, Ann Arbor, MI (2005) 274–301.
18. Tornatzky, L.G., Fleischer, M., eds.: The Processes of Technological Innovation. Lexington Books, Lexington, KY (1990)
19. Lee, G., Xia, W.: Organizational size and IT innovation adoption: A meta-analysis. Information and Management 43 (2006) 975–985.
20. Grover, V., Goslar, D.: The initiation, adoption, and implementation of telecommunications technologies in US organizations. Journal of Management Information Systems 10 (1993) 141–163.
21. Zhu, K., Kraemer, K.L., Xu, S.: Electronic business adoption by Europen firms: A cross country assessment of the facilitators and inhibitors. European Journal of Information Systems 12 (2003) 251–268.
22. Chau, P.Y.K., Tam, K.Y.: Factors affecting the adoption of open systems: An exploratory study. MIS Quarterly 21 (1997) 1–24.
23. Chau, P.Y., Tam, K.Y.: Organizational adoption of open systems: A 'technology-push, need-pull' perspective. Information and Management 37 (2000) 229–239.
24. Zhu, K., Kraemer, K.L., Gurbaxani, V., Xin Xu, S.: Migration to open-standard interorganizational systems: Network effects, switching costs, and path dependency. MIS Quarterly 30 (2006) 515–539.

25. Zhu, K., Kraemer, K.L., Xu, S.: The process of e-business assimilation in organizations: A technology diffusion perspective. Management Science (2006).

26. Chwelos, P., Benbasat, I., Dexter, A.: Research report: Empirical test of an EDI adoption model. Information Systems Research **12** (2001) 304–321.

27. Kuan, K.K.Y., Chau, P.Y.K.: A perception-based model for EDI adoption in small businesses using a technology-organization-environment framework. Information and Management **38** (2001) 507–521.

28. Chang, T.M., Liao, L.L., Hsiao, W.F.: An empirical study on the e-CRM performance influence model for service sectors in taiwan. In: EEE '05: Proceedings of the 2005 IEEE International Conference on e-Technology, e-Commerce and e-Service (EEE'05) on e-Technology, e-Commerce and e-Service, Washington, DC, USA, IEEE Computer Society (2005) 240–245.

29. Dedrick, J., West, J.: An exploratory study into open source platform adoption. In: Proceedings of the 37th Annual Hawaii International Conference on System Sciences. (2004)

30. Hong, W., Zhu, K.: Migrating to internet-based e-commerce: Factors affecting e-commerce adoption and migration at the firm level. Information and Management **43** (2006) 204–221.

31. Teo, H.H., Wang, X., Wei, K.K., Sia, C.L., Lee, M.K.O.: Organizational learning capacity and attitude toward complex technological innovations: An empirical study. Journal of the American Society for Information Science & Technology **57** (2006) 264–279.

32. Fichman, R.G., Kemerer, C.F.: The assimilation of software process innovations: An organizational learning perspective. Management Science **43** (1997) 1345–1363.

33. Shankland, S., Kane, M., Lemos, R.: How Linux saved amazon millions (2001) http://news.com.com/2100-1001-275155.html.

34. Raymond, E.S.: The Art of UNIX Programming. Pearson Education (2003) http://www.catb.org/~esr/writings/taoup/.

35. Attewell, P.: Technology diffusion and organizational learning: The case of business computing. Organization Science **3** (1992) 1–19.

36. Iacovou, C., Benbasat, I., Dexter, A.: Electronic data interchange and small organizations: Adoption and impact of technology. MIS Quarterly **19** (1995) 465–485.

37. Larsen, M.H., Holck, J., Pedersen, M.K.: The challenges of open source software in IT adoption: Enterprise architectures versus total cost of ownership. In: IRIS'27, Falkenberg, Sweden (2004)

38. Rogers, E.M.: Diffusion of Innovations. 5th edn. Free Press, NY (2003)

39. Strzala, K., Przechlewski, T.: Analiza wykorzystania oprogramowania otwartego w polskich przedsiebiorstwach i instytucjach publicznych. Wyzsza Szkoa Zarzadzania w Kwidzynie, Kwidzyn (2005) http://wsz.kwidzyn.edu.pl/.

40. Ringle, C.M., Wende, S., Will, A.: Smartpls, 2.0 (beta) (2005) http://www.smartpls.de.

41. Chin, W.W., Marcolin, B.L., Newsted, P.R.: A partial least squares latent variable modeling approach for measuring interaction effects: Results from a Monte Carlo simulation study and an electronic-mail emotion/adoption study. Information Systems Research **14** (2003) 189–217.

42. Chin, W.W.: Issues and opinion on structural equation modeling. MIS Quarterly 22 (1998) vi–xv.

49

Hybridization of Architectural Styles for Integrated Enterprise Information Systems

Lina Bagusyte and Audrone Lupeikiene

Abstract

Current enterprise systems engineering theory does not provide adequate support for the development of information systems on demand. To say more precisely, it is forming. This chapter proposes the main architectural decisions that underlie the design of integrated enterprise information systems. This chapter argues for the extending service-oriented architecture – for merging it with component-based paradigm at the design stage and using connectors of different architectural styles. The suitability of general-purpose language SysML for the modeling of integrated enterprise information systems architectures is described and arguments pros are presented.

Keywords Information system architecture · Information system component · Component-based paradigm · Service-oriented architecture

1. Introduction

Integrated enterprise information systems (IEIS) encompass human-oriented, process-oriented, and technology-oriented elements. They must be able to quickly respond to changes in business processes and emerging technologies, thus development of such systems becomes complex. Therefore, simple and flexible IEIS modification, complexity management should be ensured. In other words, theory should support the development of information systems on demand.

During the last years component-based and service-oriented development has been widely used for building flexible enterprise-scale systems. Service-oriented architecture (SOA) structures IT assets as a series of reusable services that perform business function. However, SOA is still software architectural style and is not always suitable for systems, which include hardware, software, personnel, and facilities.

Applying service way of thinking to enterprise information system means that problems are shifted from information system development to service system, which aligns business processes with information system development. So, SOA should be specialized to use it in particular enterprise engineering methodology and systems integration projects.

Assembling systems from existing components has already proved its importance. Component-based engineering is mature enough and helps to solve practical problems of software systems development. However, component-oriented theory does not provide adequate support for information systems development. To say more, the theory is forming.

Architectural styles tend to focus on solving one type of design problem. Due to complex nature of IEIS, it is necessary to combine different architectural styles in order to develop such systems.

Lina Bagusyte and Audrone Lupeikiene · Software Engineering Department, Institute of Mathematics and Informatics, Vilnius, Lithuania

G.A. Papadopoulos et al. (eds.), *Information Systems Development*, DOI 10.1007/b137171_49,
© Springer Science+Business Media, LLC 2009

This chapter discusses architectural decisions for enterprise information systems, which are integral part of any enterprise system. It argues that in a service-oriented enterprise system, information system (IS) should be arranged as a set of interacting components to enable easy modifiable IEIS. This chapter presents the proposal to combine service-oriented architecture style with component-based paradigm and connectors from different architectural styles. It provides arguments for considering components and services as architecture level concepts. The suitability of general-purpose language SysML for IEIS architecture modeling is described and arguments pros are presented.

The rest of the chapter is organized as follows. Section 2 clarifies our position at the start point – explains our conceptual framework. Section 3 discusses service-oriented architecture and provides arguments for its extension to use in enterprise systems engineering. Section 4 describes hybrid integrated enterprise information systems architecture. Finally, in Section 5 we present concluding remarks.

2. Component-Based Integrated Enterprise Information System

A variety of approaches and multiplicity of different terminology sets are in use by the developers of enterprise systems. First of all, we will present a short explanation to clarify our terminology and consequently – our conceptual framework.

Any enterprise is organization of resources, which carries out activities in accordance with its purpose. An enterprise system (in other words, activity) is a three-layered system consisting of business systems, information systems, and supporting software systems [1]. Any enterprise information system is a constituent part of business system and any software system is an essential part of a particular information system. Information system is a set of information processing processes performed by functional entities in order to provide information services required to support business processes. We thought of software system as consisting of software programs (the executable parts of a software system), files, databases, etc., designed to perform a well-defined set of tasks or to control processes and equipments. A set of hardware is necessary to execute a software system. Enterprise information system is integrated if and only if the lower level systems are aware of higher level systems and the lower level systems are constrained by rules governing processes in higher level systems.

The first design decision in the development of an enterprise system is the choice of its architectural style. The development of the whole enterprise system from the scratch is rather exceptional case. Moreover, a permanently changing environment requires endless changes in business processes and even complete reengineering of the whole enterprise system; and it is a quite natural state of affairs. Hence, componentization and service-orientation are essential principles that enable to realize information system on demand, i.e., to develop easily customized and dynamically modifiable system.

There exist various definitions of a component [2–5] showing that the term denotes different entities – subsystems, packages of software, binary code, etc. Assembling systems from existing components has already proved its importance in industry. Today components are popular in hardware and software engineering. However, a component should not be constrained in physical centricity [6], for example, in one chip or package. It is advantageous to encapsulate processes, supporting infrastructure within a component. Therefore, different kinds of components are distinguished – hardware–software, application infrastructure, communication infrastructure, and even social–technology components [6–8].

Component-based approach structures enterprise information system to a set of reusable elements that provide functionality meaningful to business system. IEIS component first of all is a component, i. e., an autonomous unit that has defined interface (or interfaces) and can be plugged into a system. Second, as an IEIS component, it encapsulates hardware, software, communication medium, processes, and organizational elements (Fig. 49.1).

Operation encapsulates processes or series of actions that certain functional resource performs, and is thought of as functional aspect of IEIS component (Fig. 49.1). This constituent focuses on the activities performed by the information system, produces the required effects, and changes the state of informational resources. IEIS components interact through their interfaces. Two types of interfaces can be

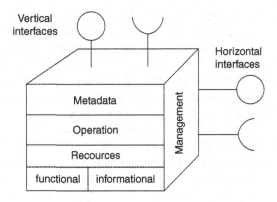

Figure 49.1. Constituents of IEIS component.

distinguished – horizontal and vertical. The horizontal interfaces are necessary to ensure relationships with the other components of the same level. The vertical interfaces are necessary to define interactions between the components of different levels and types, for example, between the computer platform and software components or between the IEIS and business components.

3. Service-Oriented Architecture: Characteristics and Open Questions

Service-oriented architecture emerged as a software architectural style for linking heterogeneous resources on demand. Nowadays there are attempts to extend and apply service-oriented thinking to the whole enterprise system. According to [9] SOA has to be raised up to business domain level, i.e., business-aligned software services should be organized into an enterprise-scale SOA. Although SOA gained recognition of software developers and was widely used during recent years, there still are ambiguities and problems to solve.

First of all, the term "service" and therefore integration architecture approach based on the concept of a service are interpreted differently. Further we will present clarifications for two most commonly used meanings of this concept: a service as linking of resources and a service as function.

Some entity (system, component, person, etc.) creates capabilities to solve or support a solution of others problems, i.e., to meet their needs [10]. The purpose of using the capability is to realize one or more real-world effects. Services are perceived as the means, which bring needs and capabilities together. It should be emphasized that in this interpretation the capabilities are not part of service – they exist independently and are arranged on demand. Figure 49.2 illustrates how the needs of business system are linked to the capabilities of IEIS components. So, service is perceived as linking means of heterogeneous

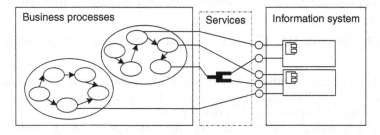

Figure 49.2. Service as linking means.

resources and can be analyzed as a system having different implementations (e.g., one person, group of persons, technological solutions, such as enterprise service bus, broker, messaging mechanisms).

Significant contribution in the development of SOA reference architecture, also called SOA solution stack, was made by IBM [11]. Service-oriented architecture is based on the idea that business function is provided as a series of services, which are assembled together to create solutions that serve a particular business need. The applied meaning of service differs from the previous one. A service is defined as a discrete function that is offered to an external consumer. The consumer may be a Web page, another business function, or a collection of functions that together form a process.

SOA solution stack resembles client–server architecture and the differences are not obvious. In other words, IBM's SOA reference architecture can be perceived as a derivative from the client–server architecture. The service consumer (e.g., business process) makes service request to the service provider through the complementary integration layer (usually realized by enterprise service bus) and gets service as the response. Service encompasses the service delivery mechanism with the service providers, i.e., capabilities. So, in this interpretation service is the functionality that a system offers for its environment.

Second, SOA is still software architectural style. SOA reference architecture provides a solution to support business needs with existing software components [11]. Software components encapsulate operational resources (monolithic applications, legacy systems, databases, enterprise resource planning (ERP) and customer relationship management (CRM) packages) and provide the realization of services. This implies that composite software systems are being organized to provide the overall business process functionality using the descriptions of services.

We perceive business system as a set of interrelated business processes that are performed by an enterprise (a set of functional entities) to achieve certain goals while delivering products and/or services to its customers. Three kinds of business processes are separated:

- management processes, that govern operation of the system,
- operational or core processes, that create real business value for customers,
- supporting processes, including information processing.

Integrated enterprise information system is composed of interrelated information processing processes and supports the whole enterprise system. However, currently main attention in SOA is focused on linking business processes with software, i.e., development of enterprise application systems.

Third, SOA is to be considered as generalized reference architecture. Therefore, service-orientation can be used as the key principle to design enterprise-scale systems, which encompass human-oriented, process-oriented, and technology-oriented elements. But for specific class of systems this general approach should be specialized and applied with the other types of architectures.

To summarize, our position can be explained as follows. SOA is an enterprise-scale architecture which emphasizes linking of business processes and IT services on demand. SOA has many desirable pros:

- provides high flexibility – reconfiguration of the business processes and applications that support them,
- allows business and information system convergence through set of services,
- enables to integrate existing software systems, including monolithic custom applications, legacy systems, packaged applications, to solve problem of islands of information within enterprises, where data is replicated over multiple systems.

However, SOA solution stack [11, 12] focuses on the specific types of problems and leaves open questions:

- Service-oriented architecture stands for the service way of thinking, i.e., linking of resources on demand. It means that problems are shifted from information system development to service system, which aligns business processes with information system development.
- Service-oriented architectures can be typical for software systems (to say more precise, for linking business processes with supporting software); and this pure architectural style is not always suitable for systems, which include hardware, software, personnel, and facilities.

- SOA is generalized reference architecture and should be adapted, refined, or specialized to use it, in particular enterprise engineering methodology and systems integration. In other words, it defines the most general approach recommended for the use in enterprise engineering and integration projects.

4. Hybrid Architecture for Integrated Enterprise Information Systems

Pure architectural styles focus on solving one type of design problem, so it is necessary to combine different architectural styles in order to build complex systems. This implies the development of hybrid architectures and their modeling languages.

4.1. Components and Services as Architecture Level Concepts

IS development is a process that comprises multiple stages, including analysis (which contains modeling), design, implementation, and deployment. The concept "component" is utilized in all these stages; for that reason components merge different aspects: a component as architectural abstraction and a component as implementation [13, 14].

Components in their most abstract form are interchangeable units of functionality, which are accessed through the interfaces. Viewed as architectural abstraction, they conform to an architectural component model that impose what constituents a component should have, as well as how they should be exposed. Viewed as implementation, components are the physical pieces of a system. They can be deployed in environments and assembled into larger packages.

The same is true for the concept "service". This term is used to denote at least two different meanings: a service as architectural abstraction and a service as implementation. Services in their abstract form are entities capable to perform tasks and provide a coherent functionality from the point of view of provider and requester entities [10, 15]. Viewed as architectural abstraction, services express design rules that prescribe their constituents and impose the interaction models. Viewed as implementation, services are concrete functional entities that bring together the needs of consumers with the capabilities of providers. Depending on the implementation technology, this role is played by software and/or hardware and/or employee.

We strongly separate two distinct perspectives mentioned above. It is obvious that components and services are to be considered as architectural abstractions in the design stage of an enterprise system. It should be noted that architectural components and architectural services are not contradictory; they complement each other. In service-oriented paradigm emphasis is placed on the development of loosely coupled systems. So, building an enterprise system, and hence an information system, involves the transfer of data, the coordination of transactions, and the composition of services to support business processes. Component-based paradigm strongly espouses the "building block" position – emphasis is placed on the reusable artifacts and the management of complexity. So, building a system becomes the selection or development and the assembling of encapsulated elements. Components add value when they are assembled to form the required units of functionality and the whole information system.

Complementary use of component-based and service-oriented paradigms is presented in [16, 17]. However, Service Component Architecture (SCA) extends and supplements prior approaches to implementing services. It has proposed the programming model and the framework for implementing SOA. In other words, components and services are "employed" at different architectural layers, i.e., components are implementation decision of service-oriented architecture – they implement services that can be invoked.

4.2. Main Architectural Decisions to Build IEIS

Our architectural design to develop an enterprise system, and hence an integrated information system, can be characterized as follows:

- SOA style is global for the enterprise system,
- components and services are "employed" as architectural abstractions in the design stage of IEIS development,
- IEIS architecture is hybridized; i.e., pure styles are amalgamated (namely, connectors from SOA, pipes and filters, data centered, and call and return architecture styles).

To paraphrase M. Jackson [18], activity in information systems development is an activity of building machines to solve problems. It is emphasized the distinction between the world, in which problems are located, and the effects one would like a system, located in the same world, to achieve. We use this conception as analogue to motivate service-oriented enterprise system architecture in which services are the means by which the needs of consumers are brought together with the capabilities of providers. Analogical problem solving suggests that

- business system is the world where the problems (in other words, needs) are located,
- information system is the machine which is to be designed,
- service system connects the problem world and the machine – business and information systems; on the other hand, service stands for the requirement (i.e., the effects to achieve) – the behavior to be established and maintained in the problem world.

Service-oriented architecture is a derivative from the layered client–server architectural style. To be more precise, the primary building blocks of service-oriented architecture are service description manager, service provider, service consumer, and service producer. It should be noted that service description manager is generalized term to denote broker or repository or registry and is optional constituent. The services communicate with each other by passing messages/requests from one service to another or by coordinating an activity. All messages/requests are sent to the same service endpoint, which decides how to process them.

In a service-oriented enterprise system, the information system should be arranged as a set of interacting components to enable an easily modifiable IEIS. Because of heterogeneous nature of IEIS components, it should be permitted a single component to use a mixture of architectural connectors – to represent invocation of component services and flow of different kinds of resources (Fig. 49.3). The arguments are as follows:

- IEIS component includes hardware components, so items such as signals or energy may flow between the components.
- IEIS can be based on different technologies, including people, manual processing, and paper documents.

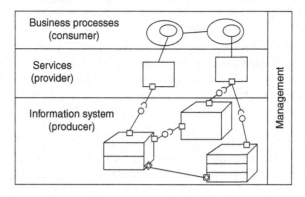

Figure 49.3. Different architectural styles of the SOA layers.

Component's provided interface defines the capability of the component exposed to outside and required interface defines the needs of component. Links (see Fig. 49.3; the information system's layer) are used to achieve communications and cooperation, local or distributed, between components in general via infrastructures, which can be componentized as communication link components or network connection components.

To summarize, our proposal is heterogeneous enterprise system architecture: SOA for the whole enterprise system and heterogeneity at same layer, where individual components are connected using a mixture of architectural connectors.

4.3. Using SysML for IEIS Architectural Modeling

The choice of a suitable language to model architectural decisions has an effect on the result that is produced. The evaluation and selection of the most appropriate language is not trivial problem. We use two main requirements in the first step of this selection:

- ontological completeness and expressive adequacy,
- correlation with the unified enterprise system development environment.

Language for the modeling needs of architectural level decisions should be able to represent all phenomena of interest and enable user to formulate statements about the architecture under consideration in adequate terms.

Unified development environment (i.e. tools, languages, repositories, techniques, and technologies used to support system development) is necessary to build the whole enterprise system – systems of all three layers [1]. Besides, componentization is meaningful at all three layers of an enterprise system. So, selected language to model IEIS components should be consistent with the other modeling languages and other elements of the unified enterprise system engineering environment.

Unified Modeling Language UML [19] enables user to specify, visualize, and document models of software systems, including requirements and design solutions. This language is also widely used for modeling business processes and data structures. However, UML provides an insufficient basis for modeling IEIS components and their interaction. First, comparing to objects IEIS components consist of the heterogeneous constituents. Second, IEIS components can demonstrate proactive behavior. Third, IEIS components need to exchange messages as well as different types of resources.

We argue for SysML as a language to model the proposed IEIS architectural decisions. The main distinguishing characteristics are (a) SysML provides constructs for the modeling of units and systems, which include hardware, software, information, processes, personnel, and facilities and (b) SysML extends UML 2.1 and provides additional constructs for the asynchronous and broadcast interactions, for representing different resources that flow between the constituents [20]. Moreover, SysML reuses and extends UML 2.1 (uses UML 2.1 extension mechanisms). Therefore, inclusion of SysML into the unified development environment, where UML is preferable for software-intensive systems, does not cause additional problems.

SysML supports the development activities (analysis, design, verification, etc.) of a broad range of complex systems. This language provides construct *block* – unified modular element – to model structure of a system or its constituent. Blocks may include both structural and behavioral (including proactive behavior) features. They provide the ability to represent a system hierarchy. *Port* is special construct to specify the allowable types of interactions between blocks. It should be noted that SysML lets the system designers to model connectors of different architectural styles. Standard (i.e., typical for UML) ports are interaction points through which block provides and requires set of "services," and flow ports – interaction points through which data or material entity can enter or leave the block. The "services" are specified by a set of interfaces (interface may specify the operations or signals).

Thus, components can be adequately represented as blocks (Fig. 49.4). Standard ports are typically used in the context of synchronous request/response communications; flow ports are used for broadcast or send and forget interactions. Figure 49.4 represents the data flow – broadcasting data to mobile component of Help Desk, the material flow form emergency service, and "traditional" message passing.

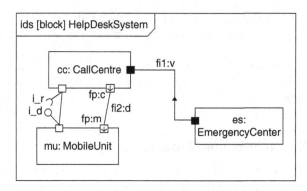

Figure 49.4. Example of modeling connectors from different architectural styles.

5. Concluding Remarks

Changes in enterprise systems are natural state of affairs. Consequently, we need suitable development methodologies that could be used to design and redesign the whole enterprise system including its integrated information system. In order to develop easy modifiable IEIS, proper architectural decisions should be made.

Architecture of such IEIS is inevitably heterogeneous. Services and components can be used as complementary architectural constructs. Hybrid architecture of the IEIS can be realized as follows: SOA for the whole enterprise system and heterogeneity at the same architectural layer – using a mixture of the architectural connectors of different styles to provide all necessary mechanisms for interaction of IEIS components. SysML stands for suitable language to model IEIS heterogeneous architecture.

References

1. Caplinskas, A., Lupeikiene, A., and Vasilecas, O. (2002) Shared conceptualisation of business systems, information systems and supporting software. In H.-M. Haav and A. Kalja (eds.), *Databases and Information Systems II*, Kluwer Academic Publishers, Dordrecht, pp. 109–320.
2. Cheesman, J. and Daniels, J. (2001) *UML Components: a Simple Process for Specifying Component-Based Software*. Addison_Wesley, Boston, MA.
3. D'Souza, D. F. and Wills, A. C. (1999) *Objects, Components, and Frameworks. The Catalysis Approach*. Addison-Wesley, Boston, MA.
4. Herzum, P. and Sims, O. (2000) *Business Component Factory: a Comprehensive Overview of Business Component Development for the Enterprise*. John Wiley & Sons, New York.
5. Wang, A. and Qian, K. (2005) *Component-Oriented Programming*. Wiley-Interscience, New York.
6. Messerschmitt, D. G. (2007) Rethinking components: from hardware and software to systems. *Proceedings of the IEEE*, 95(7): 1473–1496.
7. Cherbakov, L., Galambos, G., Harishankar, R., Kalyana, S., and Rackham, G. (2005) Impact of service orientation at the business level. *IBM Systems Journal*, 44(4): 653–668.
8. Lupeikiene, A. (2007) Integrated enterprise information systems: Thinking in component concepts. In O. Vasilecas, J. Eder, and A. Caplinskas (eds.), *Databases and Information Systems IV*, Selected Papers from the Seventh International Baltic Conference DB&IS'2006, IOS Press, Amsterdam, pp. 203–215.
9. Zimmermann, O., Schlimm, N., Waller, G., and Pestel, M. (2005) Analysis and Design Techniques for Service-Oriented Development and Integration. In *INFORMATIK 2005 - Informatik LIVE! Band 2, Beiträge der 35. Jahrestagung der Gesellschaft für Informatik*, pp. 606–611, 2005.
10. OASIS (2006) *Reference Model for Service Oriented Architecture*. Architecture 1.0, Committee Specification 1, 2 August 2006, OASIS.
11. Arsanjani A., Zhang, L.-J., Ellis, M., Allam, A., and Channabasavaiah, K. (2007). Design an SOA solution using a reference architecture.*IBM Developer Works*, March 2007 (available at http://www.ibm.com/developerworks/library/ar-archtemp/#).
12. Papazoglou, M. P. and van den Heuvel, W.-J. (2007) Service oriented architectures: approaches, technologies and research issues. *The VLDB Journal*, 16(3): 389–415.

13. Wang, G. and MacLean, A. (1999) Software components in contexts and service negotiations. In *Proceedings of the 1999 International Workshop on Component-Based Software Engineering*, Software Engineering Institute, Carnegie-Mellon University, Pittsburgh, PA, pp. 83–88.

14. Bachmann, F., Bass, L., Buhman, Ch., Commella-Dorda, S., Long, F., Robert, J., Seacord, R., and Wallnau, K. (2000) *Volume II: Technical Concepts of Component-Based Software Engineering*. Technical Report CMU/SEI-2000-TR-008 ESC-TR-2000-007, Software Engineering Institute.

15. Booth, D., Haas, H., McCabe, F., Newcomer, E., Champion, M., Ferris, Ch., and Orchard, D. (2004) *Web Services Architecture*. W3C Working Group Note, 11 February 2004, W3C (available at http://www.w3.org/TR/ws-arch/).

16. Barcia, R. and Brent, J. (2005) Building SOA solutions with the service component architecture: Part 1, *IBM WebSphere Developer Technical Journal*, October 2005 (available at http://www.ibm.com/developerworks/websphere/techjournal/0510_brent/0510_brent.html).

17. Swithinbank, P., Bandaru, S., Crooks, G., Ferrier, A., Krishnaswamy, R., He, J., Mann, V., and Viale, M. (2007) *Connecting Applications to WebSphere Enterprise Service Bus*. IBM.

18. Jackson, M. (1995) Problem architectures. Position paper for the *ICSE-17 Workshop on Architectures for Software Systems*.

19. UML (2007) *Unified Modeling Language: Superstructure*. Version 2.1.1, Object Management Group.

20. SysML (2007) *OMG Systems Modeling Language OMG SysML*. Version 1.0, Object Management Group.

50

Proposing a Formalised Model for *Mindful* Information Systems Offshoring

Gabriel J. Costello, Chris Coughlan, Brian Donnellan and Andreas Gadatsch

Abstract

The central thesis of this chapter is that mathematical economics can provide a novel approach to the examination of offshoring business decisions and provide an impetus for future research in the area. A growing body of research indicates that projected cost savings from IT offshoring projects are not being met. Furthermore, evidence suggests that decision-making processes have been more emotional than rational, and that many offshoring arrangements have been rushed into without adequate analysis of the true costs involved. Building on the concept of *mindfulness* and *mindlessness* introduced to the IS literature by Swanson and Ramiller, a cost equation is developed using "deductive reasoning rather than inductive study" in the tradition of mathematical economics. The model endeavours to capture a wide range of both the quantitative and qualitative parameters. Although the economic model is illustrated against the background of a European scenario, the theoretical framework is generic and applicable to organisations in any global location.

Keywords Offshoring · Outsourcing · Mathematical economics · Mindfulness

1. Introduction

The central thesis of this chapter is that mathematical economics can provide a novel approach to the examination of offshoring business decisions and provide an impetus for future research in the area. The description of IT outsourcing performance as "worrying" by Kern & Willcocks together with the conclusion that most organisations are getting less cost benefits than expected surely calls for some theoretical reflection. Furthermore, cost was one of the six areas identified in their research, where companies had experienced severe or difficult problems [1] . This chapter argues that more precision is required in IS offshoring decision-making given the growing importance of services in the knowledge economy and the resulting value chain re-alignment from selling product to providing integrated customer solutions [2]. Building on the concept of "mindfulness" and "mindlessness" introduced to the IS literature by Swanson and Ramiller [3], a cost model is developed using "deductive reasoning rather than inductive study" in the tradition of mathematical economics. To address the issues of relevance, the theoretical economic model is presented in the context of German companies looking, like the two-headed Janus, to the East and the West. These companies are increasingly being driven to offshore IS in order to remain competitive. The focus of the German lens is Ireland, an important location within the European Union for information

Gabriel J. Costello • Galway-Mayo Institute of Technology, Galway, Ireland; Centre for Innovation and Structural Change, National University of Ireland, Galway, Ireland. Chris Coughlan • Hewlett-Packard Galway Limited, Ireland. Brian Donnellan • National University of Ireland, Galway, Ireland. Andreas Gadatsch • Bonn-Rhein Sieg University of Applied Sciences, Sankt Augustin, Germany.

G.A. Papadopoulos et al. (eds.), *Information Systems Development*, DOI 10.1007/b137171_50,
© Springer Science+Business Media, LLC 2009

systems offshoring in software applications, financial services and areas such as call centres and shared services [4]. However, although the economic model is illustrated using a European scenario, the methodology is generic and applicable to organisations in any global location. This chapter proceeds as follows: at the outset an overview is given of Ireland as an offshore location in a period of economic transition and following this the business reasons which are driving German companies to offshore IS are presented. A literature review and some theoretical perspectives are then discussed. Subsequently, a formalised economic model is introduced using the approach of mathematical economics that builds on the concept of mindful and mindless decision-making. This is followed by a consideration of the variables in the model. Next, the implications of the proposed model are discussed and finally, suggestions for future research are proposed.

2. Background and Motivation

First, this chapter will set the scene by providing an overview of Ireland as an offshore location in a time of economic transition and of Germany where a growing number of agencies are being faced with the decision to offshore. The general objective of this opening section is to claim that our economic model follows Chiang's [5] proposition that the development of theory is by its very nature "an abstraction from the real-world". Consequently, we initially present the "real world" scenario that provided the impetus for our work and from which the later theoretical framework was abstracted.

2.1. Offshoring: The Case of Ireland and Germany

In the closing decades of the 20th century Ireland leapfrogged from a traditional agrarian economy to a deliberately created information economy [6]. The initial impetus was fuelled by foreign direct investment (FDI) from North American multinational corporations (MNCs) setting up offshore manufacturing facilities to avail of low-tax incentives, a young educated workforce and proximity to their growing number of European customers. However, this successful model is increasingly being threatened by the low-cost economies of Eastern Europe, India and China assertively competing for offshoring and outsourcing business. Irish enterprises rapidly need to build new sources of competitive advantage to sustain employment and standards of living. Ireland is now entering a new era which, according to Michael Porter, requires a transition to an innovation economy [7].

In Germany many companies in the industrial and service sectors – ranging from large corporations to SME (small to medium sized enterprises) – are evaluating how to reduce IT costs by permanently purchasing their IT services from countries such as India, China or Eastern Europe, which presently have relatively low labour costs. When looking at the cost of labour only, the German IT manager sees an immediate large reduction due to the very high personnel costs at home. However, the evidence suggests that many projects cannot achieve these initial over-optimistic financial projections because outsourcing decisions are "much more complicated than expected, have to be reversed, and in some cases lead to failure" [8].

2.2. Literature Context

There have been a number of comprehensive reviews of the literature relating to IT outsourcing and offshoring. For example, Dibbern et al. [9] have provided thorough reviews of publications in this area. Their analysis demonstrate that the literature draws from contributions across a wide range of academic fields that encompass traditional economics (production costs), transaction cost economics, institutional theory, theories on social influences, resource dependence theory, psychological contracts, theories on property rights, agency theory, governance inseparability, organisational learning, the resource-based view of the firm and path dependence. Willcocks et al. (2006) identify three distinct phases of publications on outsourcing. In the period from 1991 to 1994 the publications on IT outsourcing were focused on the identification of characteristics regarding firms that outsource. The current era appears to be characterized by a multitude of theories, case work and assertions with little evidence of the emergence of a coherent, comprehensive framework. In light of the rather eclectic landscape of IS offshoring research outlined above, we will argue in the next section that there is a gap for some rigorous theoretical reflection on the subject of IS offshoring.

3. Research Framing

In this section, we first discuss some theoretical considerations that emerged from the literature review and the academic–practitioner interactions that provided the impetus for our work. Subsequently, we introduce the approach of mathematical economics and argue that it can provide a novel lens to enable the development of theory in the area of IS offshoring. In particular, we suggest that the concept of *mindfulness*, recently proposed to the IS community by Swanson and Ramiller [3], provides a theoretical conceptualisation for the deductive development of our offshoring model.

3.1. Theoretical Considerations

Many publications have argued that current outsourcing decisions are based on minimalist considerations by purchasing departments [10], insufficient assessment of risk factors [11] and the need to develop multi-dimensional perspectives in an international business context [12]. Models have been developed that simulated offshoring relationships at the country level [13], while Wehrmann and Gull [14] proposed a decision support model for offshore software development projects using the COCOMO (COnstructive COst MOdel) estimation technique that cosidered cost, effort, and schedule for their emprical study. However, this chapter takes a deductive approach and argues that the concepts of *mindfulness* and *mindlessness,* proposed by Swanson and Ramiller [3] for decisions on IT innovation can be profitably applied to decisions on offshoring.

3.2. Research Approach

According to Chiang [15] *mathematical economics* is the application of mathematics to economic analysis through "deductive reasoning rather than inductive study" and as a result principally deals with "theoretical rather than empirical material". More recently, he emphasises that mathematical economics is an approach to economic analysis and is not a distinct branch of the discipline such as the study of international trade [5]. Also he points out that the main difference of this approach vis-à-vis *literary economics* is that "assumptions and conclusions are stated in mathematical symbols rather than words, and in equations rather than sentences". Furthermore, Chiang argues that a good theoretical framework– "preferably in a mathematical formulation"– is required prior to undertaking any empirical statistical or econometric studies. Mathematical economic equations are characterized by two types of variables [16]:

- Exogenous variables that are beyond the control of the agents in the model. These variables are also referred to as parameters.
- Endogenous variables that are subject to or determined, directly or indirectly, by agents' choices.

Another important concept in the field is the term "elasticity" where the elasticity of variable y with respect to another variable x is "defined as the percentage change in y for a percentage change in x". These concepts will be utilized in the next section, where the formalized economic model will be presented.

4. Towards a Mindful Offshoring Model

To assist practitioners to guard against "bandwagon" phenomena, a *mindless* model is first presented. This situation typically results when offshoring strategies have been decided at a senior level in an organisation, with little business analysis, and then presented to purchasing department as a fait accompli. Many such corporate directives are committed to work force reduction over short periods of time with an underlying assumption that such actions will lead to cost reductions. The term *equation* is used interchangeably with the term *model* in this section of this chapter.

4.1. Mindless Offshoring Equation

First, a relationship between parameters that express a simplistic cost model for offshoring is developed which is termed a *mindless* offshoring equation:

$$T_{OC} = \sum_{j=1}^{p} Q_j(L_j - R_j) + \sum_{j=1}^{p} Cs_j, \tag{50.1}$$

where

T_{OC} = total annual cost savings realized by outsourcing to an offshore location;
Qj = annual quantity of product or service of type j;
Lj = local cost (incumbent location) of product or service j;
Rj = offshore (remote) cost of product or service j;
p = total number of products (or services) under consideration for offshoring;
Cs = savings in shipping cost to deliver the product: the slowest boat or the telecoms/network with the poorest QoS (Quality of Service) level;
and
$Lj - Rj$ = the unit cost differential for product (or service) j between locations.

4.2. Mindful Offshoring Equation

Second, based on the literature referred to above, a relationship is proposed that, we argue, expresses a more realistic cost model for offshoring. This new equation incorporates some of the many costs and business critical factors that are often conveniently ignored when an emotive or mindless decision-making process is pursued.

$$T'_{OC} = \sum_{j=1}^{p} Q_j L_j + \sum_{j=1}^{p} C's_j - \Omega_{AB}\left(\sum_{j=1}^{p} Q_j R_j + \sum_{k=1}^{m} C_k\right), \tag{50.2}$$

where

T'_{OC} = total annual cost savings realized by outsourcing to an offshore location (*mindful* case);
Ω_{AB} = the offshoring coefficient (parametric constant) between local location A and remote location B;
$C's$ = Differs from Cs in Equation (50.1) in that a nominal cost (rather than lowest) is used that includes consideration of extra "expediting" costs;
C_k = additional *endogenous* variable costs within the firm's locus of control;
and
$Lj - \Omega_{AB}Rj$ = the adjusted unit cost differential for product (or service) j between local location A and remote location B.

Now that we have deductively developed an offshoring model (equation) based on *mindful* and *mindless* concepts using the approach of mathematical economics, we will proceed to discuss possible attributes of the parameters and variables. It is proposed that these suggestions can provide the basis for empirical testing and further refinement of the model.

5. Analysis and Suggestions

In this section, we will first discuss possible *endogenous* variable costs that need to be considered by the firm but that were not included in the mindless Equation (50.1). Then we will attempt to analyze the offshoring coefficient Ω in terms of potential constituent parameters. Finally, we will evaluate the coefficient intuitively and in terms of the concept of elasticity used in the mathematical economic approach.

5.1. Possible Endogenous Variables

C_k in Equation (50.2) represents additional endogenous variable costs that are in the control of the firm but which are not considered in the formulation of *mindless* offshoring models. Here, we suggest a number of such costs that could be included in the *mindful* model that originated from the authors' experience as academics and practitioners in the area.

C_1 = vendor assessment costs
C_2 = increased auditing costs
C_3 = increased local overhead costs per unit due to the transfer resulting in a loss of cost efficiency in the local site
C_4 = increased travel, training, co-ordination and project management costs
C_5 = increased warranty costs due to supplier's inexperience
C_6 = increased cost due to time to market delays
C_7 = increased communication cost due to online meetings, telephone calls and e-mail communication (including preparing, reading and executing tasks from e-mails, meetings)
C_8 = Management Attention Units (MAU), i.e. the co-ordination overhead costs associated with management having to intervene to ensure that projects are meeting performance and schedule targets
C_9 = increased quality costs

5.2. Offshoring Coefficient

In Equation (50.2), we introduced the concepts of an offshoring coefficient or parametric constant, Ω_{AB}, between local location A and remote location B. The purpose of this coefficient is to capture the qualitative attributes that, we argue, need to be taken into account in order to make a *mindful* offshoring decision. Here, we propose that Ω_{AB} consists of a number of *exogenous* variables that are outside the firm's locus of control. Now we will suggest a possible way of capturing these parameters and linking them to the overall offshoring coefficient. Therefore, let

$$\Omega_{AB} = \prod_{i=1}^{n} \mu_i, \tag{50.3}$$

where μ_1 to μ_n represent the exogenous variables that are outside the control of the firm.

Note: These parameters can be applied to the economic equation such that setting a parameter to 1 indicates a neutral effect. The factors could be estimated in relation to the local location (from where product or service is currently supplied) and the proposed remote location. This will also allow a comparison of a number of scenarios in the cost model.

Now we will suggest possible attributes of these parameters.

μ_1 = projected labour costs inflation factor for offshore location due to influx of business annualised over a typical 5-or 10-year investment

μ_2 = political stability/instability factor

μ_3 = globalization/location attractiveness/unattractiveness of offshore location where unattractiveness will be expressed as >1

μ_4 = time zone inefficiency factor

μ_5 = risk factor due to theft or piracy, or of losing intellectual property to a supplier becoming a competitor, since both data security and IP protection are growing concerns for companies [17].

μ_6 = currency fluctuation risks

μ_7 = cultural compatibility factor F_1: the cultural compatibility of the offshore company with the parent company.

μ_8 = cultural compatibility factor F_2: the cultural compatibility of the offshore company with the customers of the parent company. This can be very significant in situations where the offshore location will provide IT services such as direct customer support.

μ_9 = Staff churn rate (taking account of the transient nature of staffing level in offshore locations)

μ_{10} = Turnaround time or speed of execution of projects

μ_{11} = Quality of software product or service

5.3. Elasticity Analysis of the Equation Parameters

The purpose of this section is to propose a method to test the sensitivity of the qualitative factors μ_1 to μ_n when the estimates are included in an offshoring business decision using the mathematical economic concept of *elasticity*. We also have a secondary objective to provide some intuitive *feel* when the concepts are transposed into the empirical domain.

Let the domain of the overall offshoring factor (the product of the individual factors μ_1 to μ_n) Ω_{AB} be set as follows:

$$Domain = \{\Omega | 0.90^n \leq \Omega \leq 1.10^n\}. \tag{50.4}$$

Here limits are allocated to the domain from 0.90 to 1.10.

Let $n = 11$ as in Section 5.2, resulting in the minimum and maximum cumulative impact of the factors to be calculated as follows:

$$Domain = \{\Omega | \ 0.90^{11} \leq \Omega \leq 1.10^{11}\} \quad = > 0.31 \leq \Omega \geq 2.85. \tag{50.5}$$

Note that in this case $n = 11$ which assumes that all factors have been estimated. However, in practice, companies can choose to include only the number of these factors that suit their business situation or to set a factor at the neutral level of 1 until further approximations become available internally or externally. Also the formula allows the number of factors to be increased or decreased according to the business requirements. The upper and lower limits above indicate that the maximum effect of applying all the factors ($n = 11$) is to increase or decrease the offshore costing approximately by a factor of 3. This analysis of Equation (50.4) results in a first cut approximation that we argue can be used to assist simulation of the elasticity of dependant and independent variables. In this example, the offshoring coefficient Ω varies with respect to the μ parameters from 31 to 285 %. Thus Equation (50.4) can test the sensitivity impact on Equation (50.2) by increasing or decreasing the number of factors (n) and their values. Furthermore, in the analysis above, the resulting decrease of the accumulated costs by a maximum of one-third raises the intriguing possibility that this equation could be used by companies in the present low-cost zone to *reverse-shore* IT products or services to higher cost locations (such as Germany, Ireland, the United States) because the overall factor analysis indicates that this is the best business decision. Also, similar IT products and services could increasingly originate in the traditional offshore locations and be transferred to the established higher cost locations as outsourcing companies seek to move up the value chain based on the analysis proposed here.

This section has attempted to fill the present gap in the financial business case analysis of offshoring decisions by providing a *mindful* equation that can be built into decision spreadsheets to ensure that managers capture and use realistic figures. Again, as in the previous section, the approach is to provide a tool to assist practitioners make the correct decision rather than providing another *mindless* solution, where the equation is expected to make the decision by itself.

6. Discussion

In the previous two sections, we have introduced the concept of a *mindful* offshoring model and then suggested some attributes of the parameter that could provide further theoretical reflection and empirical investigation. We now discuss some implications and limitations of our work.

6.1. Assignment of Values to the Parameters

The *mindful* equation contains a large number of parameters some which are typical quantitative financial measurement and some which are of a qualitative kind. We argue that the former can be determined using existing cost management mechanisms and then modeled using a financial spreadsheet to support the company level offshoring business decision. For example, the vendor assessment cost for an IT offshoring project is quoted in the literature as being of the order of $500,000 [11].

An important question at this stage is how to obtain figures for the factors μ_1 to μ_n proposed in the equation, and which are in the qualitative category. A number of suggestions to address this include the company itself could initially provide its own estimates using a cross-functional focus group drawn from expertise within its organisation; it could also utilize existing reputable indices currently available such as the AT Kearney globalisation [18] and location attractiveness indices [17].

6.2. Implications for Theory and Practice

This chapter argues that the approach of mathematical economics provides a novel methodology to contribute to the evaluation of IT investment outsourcing and offshoring decisions. Furthermore, we propose that the offshoring equation developed using the approach has the advantage of generalisation and can be iterated and refined by repeated use and updating of the parameters. Hence it has the potential of contributing to the area of offshoring theory. It is also suggested that the logic and reasoning under-pinning the equation will open up possibilities for future work in this area. Furthermore, we argue that the incorporation of qualitative parameters in the equation is supported by recent evidence on the importance of taking into account factors such as customer relationships when making offshoring decisions.

In the area of practice, Chief Information Officers of many US and European companies are under increasing pressure to reduce their IT costs. However, outsourcing decisions often seem to be made based on emotion or bandwagon phenomena rather than grounded in factual evidence and based on sound business decision logic. A major obstacle has been the lack of a universally applicable "tool-set" to support companies faced with making outsourcing decisions. Our chapter has attempted to address this salient problem.

6.3. Limitations and Suggestions for Future Work

This conceptual chapter is proposed as a novel theoretical reflection on IS offshoring using the approach of mathematical economics. However, there are a number of limitations such as the critique that the contents of the model seem just a "mathematical" listing of practitioner decision-making factors that is already amply covered in the literature. Our defence here is that the main contribution of this chapter is to introduce the precision inherent in the approach of mathematical economics to offshoring research. The attributes of the model were proposed as a starting point in order to facilitate further development both in the areas of complexity and of mathematical operations. Many of the exogenous variables are extremely qualitative, for example μ_2, and would be difficult to measure or estimate. However, as this is a conceptual and theoretical chapter we chose to include as many parameters as possible and leave further refinements of this chapter open to a wide range of empirical investigation and debate.

Suggestions for future work include investigating other major offshoring locations, such as India or China, to understand whether different endogenous or exogenous parameters apply; or if the equation needs to be localised. In general, the model needs to be moved from the theoretical to the empirical domain to test the underlying propositions and assumptions.

7. Conclusions

This chapter has argued that the ever-increasing demands on IT managers to outsource services to a global marketplace requires economic models to support the decision-making process and further develop theory in the field. Consequently, we proposed that the precise approach of mathematical economics can provide a novel method to examine offshoring business decisions and provide an impetus for future research in the area. This study is the result of an international collaboration, between Germany, where large corporations and increasingly SME are moving a significant portion of IT business to remote locations, and Ireland which is still an important international offshore location. This chapter proposed to contribute something novel to the debate by introducing the approach of mathematical economics using deductive reasoning in contrast to the prevalent inductive empirical studies that dominate the field. We provided an example of how the methodology could be used to develop a theoretical cost model that replaces the present minimalist business case analysis with a comprehensive equation that captures the wide range of quantitative expenditures and qualitative parameters that must be included in offshoring decision-making. Finally, the authors suggested that the propositions advanced in this study can promote further work to develop the concepts, both theoretically and practically.

Acknowledgements

The authors would like to thank the following people for their helpful suggestions during the development of this chapter: Deirdre Quin, Lecturer in Mathematics and Clare Lundon Lecturer in Mathematics, Galway-Mayo Institute of Technology; Prof. Dr. Reiner Clement, Professorship of Economics and Innovations, Bonn-Rhein Sieg University of Applied Sciences; John Cullinan, Department of Economics, National University of Ireland, Galway.

References

1. Kern, T. and L.P. Willcocks, *The relationship advantage: information technologies, sourcing, and management.* 2001, Oxford: Oxford University.
2. Grimes, S., Ireland's emerging information economy: Recent trends and future prospects. *Regional Studies,* 2003, **37**(1): pp. 3–14.
3. Swanson, E.B. and N.C. Ramiller, innovating mindfully with information technology. *MIS Quarterly,* 2004, **28**(4): pp. 553–583
4. Barry, F. and D. van Welsum. *Services FDI and offshoring into Ireland: Panel session on ICT-enabled offshoring: Country experience and business perspectives.* 2005, OECD Committee for Information, Computer and Communications Policy, Paris 9–10 June 2005.
5. Chiang, A.C., *Fundamental methods of mathematical economics (4th Edition).* Third ed. 2005, Auckland: McGraw-Hill.
6. Trauth, E.M., *The culture of an information economy: Influences and impacts in the Republic of Ireland.* 2000, Norwell, MA: Kluwer Academic Publishers.
7. Porter, M., Irish competitiveness: Entering a new economic era, In *IMI top management briefing, Dublin, Ireland, 9 October 2003 (available on-line through* www.isc.hbs.edu*)* 2003.
8. Ciborra, C., A critical review of the literature on the management of the corporate information infrastructure, In *From control to drift: The dynamics of corporate information infrastructures,* C.U. Ciborra, Editor. 2000, Oxford: Oxford University Press. pp.15–40.
9. Dibbern, J., et al., Information Systems Outsourcing: A Survey and Analysis of the Literature. *The Data Base for Adavances in Information Systems* 2004. **35**(4): pp. 6–102.

10. Womack, J.P. and D.T. Jones, *Lean thinking: banish waste and create wealth in your corporation.* 2003, London: Free Press.
11. Tafti, M.H.A., Risk factors associated with offshore IT outsourcing. *Industrial Management & Data Systems,* 2005. **105**(5): pp. 549–560.
12. Niederman, F., International business and MIS approaches to multinational organizational research: The case of knowledge transfer and IT workforce outsourcing. *Journal of International Management,* 2005. **11**: pp. 187–200.
13. Dutta, A. and R. Roy, Offshore outsourcing: A dynamic causal model of counteracting forces. *Journal of Management Information Systems,* 2005. **22**(2): pp. 15–35.
14. Wehrmann, A. and D. Gull, Ein COCOMO-basierter Ansatz zur Entscheidungsunterstützung beim Offshoring von Softwareentwicklungsprojekten (A COCOMO-based Approach to Decision Support in Offshoring Software Development Projects). *WIRTSCHAFTSINFORMATIK,* 2006. **48**: pp. 407–417.
15. Chiang, A.C., *Fundamental methods of mathematical economics (3rd Edition).* 1984, Auckland: McGraw-Hill.
16. Baldani, J., J. Bradfield, and R.W. Turner, *Mathematical economics.* 1996, Fort Worth: Dryden Press.
17. ATK Offshore Index, *ATKEARNEY Offshore Location Attractiveness Index: Making Offshore Decisions (available on line at* www.atkearney.com*).* 2004.
18. ATK Globalisation Index, *ATKEARNEY Globalisation Index (available on line at* www.atkearney.com*).* 2004.

51

Negotiating a Systems Development Method

Fredrik Karlsson and Karin Hedström

Abstract

Systems development methods (or methods) are often applied in tailored version to fit the actual situation. Method tailoring is in most the existing literature viewed as either (a) a highly rational process with the method engineer as the driver where the project members are passive information providers or (b) an unstructured process where the systems developer makes individual choices, a selection process without any driver. The purpose of this chapter is to illustrate that important design decisions during method tailoring are made by project members through negotiation. The study has been carried out using the perspective of actor-network theory. Our narratives depict method tailoring as more complex than (a) and (b) show the driver role rotates between the project members, and design decisions are based on influences from several project members. However, these design decisions are not consensus decisions.

Keywords Method tailoring · Method engineering · Actor-network theory

1. Introduction

Systems development methods (or methods for short) are rarely applied as described in method textbooks. In most situations they are tailored to fit the actual needs of development projects [5]. During systems development projects, method parts are added, omitted, exchanged or modified when necessary. The need to tailor methods is acknowledged by the two schools of information systems development methods [1]: method engineering and method-in-action.

The school of method(ology) engineering [4, 14] represents a rigorous approach for creating and tailoring methods. Within this school, it is possible to make a distinction between static and dynamic method adaptation [2]. Static method adaptation is carried out during a project's initial stage resulting in an initial route map. A wide range of approaches (e.g. [7, 22, 10]) can be found. Dynamic tailoring, or what Rossi et al. [23] term evolutionary method engineering, means changing the method during the development process. Hence, the method requirements are not viewed as known at the start and these approaches rely on shorter feedback loops. However, the method tailoring still seems to be driven by the method engineer.

The second school, method-in-action [6], focuses on the relationship between method-in-concept and methods actually used [8]. Several studies discuss that methods are not used, at least not as they are described in the textbooks (e.g. [9, 27]). Fitzgerald et al. [6] provide a more elaborated view. They have shown that method use is U-shaped in relation to experience. When inexperienced developers become more experienced they tend to discard methods. But as developers become even more experienced they start using methods again. This use differs from their initial use, however. Experienced developers use selections of methods based on their needs, experience and viewpoints. Consequently, we find that the concept of the

Fredrik Karlsson and Karin Hedström • MELAB, Swedish Business School, Örebro University, SE-701 82, Örebro, Sweden.

G.A. Papadopoulos et al. (eds.), *Information Systems Development*, DOI 10.1007/b137171_51,

reflective practitioner [24] is embodied in method-in-action research. Method tailoring is, therefore, an integrated activity in the systems developer's use of methods.

Consequently, method tailoring is viewed as either (a) a highly rational process with the method engineer as the driver, where the project members are passive information providers or (b) as an unstructured process where the systems developer makes individual choices, a selection process without any driver. Both these perspectives describe method tailoring as a non-collaborative activity, without social influences. Riemenschneider and Hardgrave [21], however, show that acceptance of methods is dependent of 'the opinions of developers' coworkers and supervisors towards using the methodology.' This means that method tailoring is a highly social activity, where cooperation between coworkers constitute an important aspect of the method tailoring process.

Designing methods is an act of making social and technological design choices. We believe that method tailoring, due to the cooperative of method use [11], is best viewed as a negotiating activity, where different interests and values are presented and discussed. The emergent method is a result of negotiation, where different actors hold and promote various and sometimes conflicting values influencing the design. These values are exposed to negotiations during the systems development process, where some values become accepted and part of the method-in-use, while others are excluded [17].

The purpose of this chapter is to illustrate that important design decisions during method tailoring are made through negotiation. It is based on a case study of an information systems development project in a public organization. We provide a rich description of the interplay that takes place during an information systems development project analyzing the impact on the emergent method. For this purpose we apply actor-network theory (ANT) [15, 26], which has been used before in the information systems field (e.g. [18, 20].

This chapter is structured as follows. In the second section, we outline our interpretation of ANT as our research approach and theoretical background. Section 3 contains four narratives and analysis from the case concerning different method tailoring activities. Finally, this chapter ends with reflections on method tailoring as negotiation and a short conclusion.

2. Research Design

2.1. Theoretical Underpinnings

Considering the purpose of this chapter, which puts the focus on different actors' sense-making, this study is classified as interpretative [25, 12]. The case unfolds the negotiation process of method tailoring from the perspectives of different actors. This is important as different actors hold and negotiate different values, influencing the emergent method. By following the translation process through the actions of the actors taking part in the method tailoring process, we disclose how negotiation has formed the emergent method. The analytical units are important design decisions influencing the emergent method.

The analytical units as well as the analysis were based on the perspective of ANT (e.g. [15]), but also influenced by the early writings of Mumford [19] and Kling [13]. Mumford [14] illustrated how different actors' values influenced the development and use of IT systems. This made us view the tailoring of methods as an intrinsically social activity influenced by peoples' interests and values. ANT has given us, not only theoretical but also methodological support. The consequence being that we have focused on analyzing the translation process by following the actors. We have focused on actors and their actions by studying the method tailoring process as a process of negotiation, where actors try to 'transcribe' or include their values and interests in the emergent method by means of interventions.

ANT is a social theory that focuses how actors' relations evolve and changes the coherence in networks [15]. Using this theory as a frame of reference makes it possible to study how existing relations in actor-networks change and new relations as well as networks arise. These relations are of significant importance to understand when analyzing how a method evolves during a project based on the involvement of different actors. These changes are captured through the narrative approach of ANT, where different actors are allowed to express their view. In other words, ANT is an appropriate frame of reference for investigating the role of negotiation in method tailoring.

Our interpretation of this framework is inspired by Walsham [25] (see Table 51.1). This framework does have a specific characteristic; it does not contain any a priori distinction between human and non-human actors. Both concepts are viewed as active makers of actor-networks and are specializations of the actant concept. Furthermore, networks are changed through translation. A translation is establishment of a new relation between actors. Latour [16] describes it as coexisting in a network to achieve a common goal, for example, when a system analyst and a tester agree to document an information system's external behaviour using use cases. Often translation requires enrollment where an actor seeks to influence how another actor should act. An example of enrollment during method tailoring is when a tester tries to influence a system analyst to write pre-conditions in the use cases – because they are important information when writing test cases. Enrollment and translation can result in inscriptions, where interests are inscribed into written material or technical systems. If we continue our example above, a tester and a system analyst can decide to create a use case template containing a pre-condition paragraph. This template then becomes an inscription of the method.

Table 51.1.   Key Concepts in the ANT framework.

Concept	Interpretation of the concept
Actor or actant	Both human and non-human actors such as systems analysts, information systems and methods.
Actor-network	A heterogeneous collection of aligned interest, including people and methods.
Translation	The creation of an alliance concerning a specific issue between humans and non humans, for example, an agreement to use test cases during testing.
Enrollment	When an actor seeks to influence another actor to act in a particular manner. For example, when a tester provide arguments for the use of use cases because they are excellent starting points for test case writing.
Delegate	An actor who represents the viewpoints of others. For example, if an implementer argues for the use of use cases on the behalf of the tester.
Inscription	A frozen organizational discourse. For example, the decision and use of use cases to capture requirements.

2.2. Case Description and Data Collection

The empirical base is an information systems development project undertaken in a public organization. The case is selected as an illustration of the negotiating character of method tailoring. We have chosen to demonstrate the negotiations that occur during the process of method tailoring by the use of design decisions that have had impact on the emergent method.

A content management system (CMS) was implemented and an existing Web site was migrated to this platform. The CMS purchased was a framework that needed tailoring in order to fit the organizational needs. It meant creating complementing functionality, integration with existing information systems and designing page layouts (Web page templates). The first author participated as one of 13 regular team members in this project, playing the role as implementer. The project lasted 3 years and the first author spent 1, 200 man hours during the project's first 18 months. Consequently, the first author participated in the tailoring process as a normal team member, which can give rise to a certain bias. However, the research has been carried out as a retrospective study based on existing data. Furthermore, the high degree of involvement was a trade-off in order to get access to the project.

This research is based on several data sources: intermediate project artefacts, e-mails, project notes, the CMS, and the new Web site. Intermediate project artefacts show what has actually been documented with the method-in-use and what kind of templates were used. Furthermore, these artefacts are time-stamped making it possible to analyse how they have evolved over time. That is to say, they show the result of method tailoring and how they have affected the method's product model. The e-mails and the project notes are used to capture tailoring decisions and arguments behind these decisions. Hence, these documents contain traces of the project members' different viewpoints about the emergent method. Finally, the CMS and the new Web site contain the results of the project work.

3. The Negotiating Process of Method Tailoring

The CMS project was carried out as, mainly, an in-house project at the public organization. As described above, the regular project team consisted of 13 people who are the basis for the analysis below. One of the project members was a hired consultant. The project was carried out at three different locations, two locations inside the public organization and one location at the consulting firm. The actors are categorized according to the main roles that have been identified in the project: project manager, systems administrator, implementer, requirements engineer and content manager. No explicit method had been chosen as the starting point for the tailoring activities.

The size of this project and the details needed to unfold the negotiation process of the emergent method is to some extent incompatible; it is impossible to provide a description of the complete method tailoring process. Accordingly, we are forced to make a selection of examples based on four negotiation situations where design decisions have had a major impact on the emergent method. This selection covers the project start, requirements, testing and deployment. Hence, we have made an illustration that covers different stages of the development process.

3.1. Negotiation 1 – Basic Principles

This example is from one of the initial project meetings. No development work has been carried out, yet. The CMS has been bought and is still waiting to be installed on the development server. Hence, the emergent method is still in its bud.

The project manager addressed the need for a starting point at a project meeting. He proposed a basic philosophy anchored in the agile community (e.g. [3]). This proposal is viewed as an enrollment including all project members. Furthermore, this is an enrollment of parts of agile methods. During this project meeting the philosophy was summarized in three bullet points (which do not necessarily correspond to the common understanding among scholars): (1) the use of short timeboxes (iterative development) (2) face-to-face communication and (3) interaction with the end users (who the content managers represented).

The proposal was well received by the project team and is part of the negotiation results found in Table 51.2. However, one concern was raised by the implementers. They concluded that they would sometimes be working at two or three different locations, making face-to-face communication difficult. Still they agreed, that this principle should be guiding when possible. Furthermore, they made the suggestion to define the timebox as a week. This suggestion was in line with the project manager's viewpoint and the remaining project members did not object. In addition, the project manager suggested 1 hour project meetings each Friday. These meetings had two purposes (1) to discuss current status of the project and (2) to decide the work package for the forthcoming timebox. During most of the project the 1 week length of the timeboxes was a good choice. However, during some stages of the project the implementers had problems implementing larger user stories within 1 week (for example, the debate forum discussed below).

Table 51.2.   Negotiation 1 – Summary.

Actors	The project manager, the implementers, the content managers, the systems administrators and the requirements engineer
Negotiation results	Three basic method principles and their initial implementation

3.2. Negotiation 2 – Storyboards

Much of the requirement work during this project concerned the Web page templates in the CMS, because these templates determined what type of Web pages that could be built and their possible layouts. For example, the purpose of a Web page template could act as the starting point for building personal Web pages. Simple sketches were used to capture such layout requirements and the different options that had to be available. This work was carried out by the requirements engineer together with the content managers.

However, when it came to more advanced Web page templates, containing interaction possibilities, sketches did not provide enough information. For example, one Web page template concerned a debate forum. The Web page template had to contain functionality to create subject threads, make contributions to the discussion and so forth. The emergent method's inadequacy was acknowledged by both the requirements engineer and the implementers, for example, in an e-mail conversation: 'what are the options in this listbox', 'how are these [Web] pages linked to each other', 'how shall we display the thread overview' and 'I know we did not include it [the classification of contributions] in the sketch.'

In a later e-mail the requirements engineer concludes 'that several options exist' and she suggests the use of either use cases or storyboards to capture the more advanced requirements. The suggestions she makes are anchored in her knowledge about methods. Hence, she enrolls other methods as a support in this discussion. Through the proposal she tried to enroll both the content managers and the implementers in use of one of these techniques. Two of the implementers preferred storyboards to use cases. This was expressed in an e-mail reply 'use cases tend to become cluttered ... difficult to show how [web] pages are related.' Consequently, the two implementers seem to be concerned, based on their knowledge about other methods, with the amount and the type of details that are captured if they chose to use, use cases. Furthermore, the implementers needed to know how Web pages were related to each other in order to determine possible navigation paths and when to provide a specified functionality.

In an additional e-mail to the implementers and the content managers, the requirements engineer referred to a discussion with some of the content managers (it is unclear with whom). She stated that the content managers preferred storyboards as well, 'since they are easier [to read]'. We can conclude that there exists a mutual agreement between the requirements engineer, the content managers and the implementers about which option to choose. Therefore, the requirements engineer concludes in the above-mentioned e-mail that she would use storyboards to document more advanced requirements. This decision changed the emergent method and is viewed as a negotiation result in Table 51.3.

Table 51.3. Negotiation 2 – Summary.

Actors	The requirements engineer, the implementers and the content manager
Negotiation results	The use of storyboards to capture more advanced requirements

The project managers and the systems administrators had, so far as the e-mail conversation can reveal, not been aware of method tailoring activity. The use of storyboards was presented on a project meeting later on. Neither the project managers nor the systems administrators had any objections.

3.3. Negotiation 3 – Bug Report Template

The point of departure for this example of negotiation is a situation where there was a need to begin testing some parts of the implemented CMS. The purpose of these tests was to see if implemented Web page templates meet the layout as well as the functional requirements. The implementers concluded that the emergent method lacked support for test reports. The content managers, who are responsible for migrating the Web content and testing the Web page templates, had just begun building Web pages. They gave oral reports to the implementers about the flaws they found. In some cases they documented them on post-it notes. In addition, the project manager, the systems administrators and the requirements engineer did not expressed any concerns with this way of working.

One of the implementers addressed this issue with the content managers via e-mail. In an e-mail, the implementer tried to enroll the content manager as he presented the need for one shared artefact for documented bugs, because 'I believe we can not keep trace of all the bugs we have found.' The content managers' answers to this e-mail can be divided as follows: (1) two persons did acknowledge the problem, (2) one person did not acknowledge this as a problem and (3) two persons did not answer. In an e-mail reply to the content managers the implementer proposed 'a simple Excel sheet ... on a shared domain'. The implementer received three positive replies on this invitation. In one reply we find '... we have to discuss the layout [of this document]'. The person who did not acknowledge the need for a formal test report document did not answer the implementer's e-mail.

The implementers discussed the need for a formal test report document with the project manager, arguing that they were not able to manage the change requests with the current way of working. Hence, they enrolled the project manager in the method tailoring process. At this meeting the implementers presented a document template, which was later e-mailed to the content managers. The e-mail conversation shows that the project manager acted as delegate for the implementers: 'I believe this [the document layout] looks good.' However, he did not state that the team members had to use the template.

The document template was further discussed during a Friday meeting. All project members participated in this meeting except the systems administrators. In the first document layout, which had been sent out via e-mail, we find four columns: serial number as identification, bug description, who has found the bug and status. One of the content managers brought forward the argument that it would be good to see 'who is or have been working with the bug'. Hence, he suggested an additional column for this purpose. In addition, he suggested three classes for the status column: unsolved, in progress and solved. Two of the implementers explicitly agreed that this was a good improvement.

One of the implementers made an additional suggestion – to include a column containing the name of the Web browser that had been used when the problem occurred. He argued this was important information, because Web browsers are implemented differently. A second implementer objected arguing that this information could be provided in the bug description. The first implementer provided a counter-argument 'it is not obvious [that we need such information]'. The second implementer aligned with this argument. One of the content managers thought it was a good idea to include an extra column.

A decision was taken by the project manager to report identified bugs in this document template, and that the template had to include the two improvements described above. This decision was explicitly supported at the meeting by the implementers as well as two of the content managers. Consequently, an inscription in the emergent method was done, see Table 51.4.

Table 51.4. Negotiation 3 – Summary.

Actors	The implementers, the content manager and the project manager
Negotiation results	Bug report template

Project documentation, however, shows that two of the content managers disagreed with the decision and the inscription. In most cases, they continued to report bugs via post-it notes, e-mail and orally. This snap shot shows that the emergent method was not shared by all project members when it came to method-in-action, despite that all project members had possibilities to influence the method design.

Finally, the e-mail analysis unfold that the implementers tried to enroll the requirements engineer in this part of the method tailoring process. She was carbon copied several of the initial e-mails.

3.4. Negotiation 4 – Standardization of Web Page Template Documentation

The content managers in the project team represented a larger group of content managers. One of the aims with the CMS was to simplify Web publication, allowing all employees of the organization to edit Web pages within their area of responsibility. However, to enable such a deployment in the organization there was a need for user manuals. They had to include advice on when a Web page template was appropriate to use and what layout options that existed for each template.

The content managers were responsible for producing the user manuals beside the task to migrate the old Web site to the new platform. However, in order to write these manuals they needed input from the implementers about the meaning of input boxes, options and the dimension that each option had. This information was not evident from using the Web page templates. Consequently, the content managers' task was made difficult because of lacking documentation routines.

The content managers called the project manager's attention to this issue. At this stage he acted as a delegate and via an e-mail he called the implementers to a meeting 'concerning the documentation of the Web page templates.' The implementers agreed with him that they had a backlog, but they argued that much of the documentation was available in the source code. However, the source code was unavailable to the content managers. In addition, the implementers concluded that they had no structured way of documenting the needed information. Hence, this meeting unfolded that neither the implementers nor the content managers were satisfied with the emergent method.

One of the implementers created a document template in order to standardize the structure of the Web page template documentation. He e-mailed this template as a suggestion to the content managers and the project manager, which is considered as an enrollment. The suggestion only received positive replies. When the implementers started using the documentation template they made an inscription to the emergent method, which is found as the negotiation results in Table 51.5. The requirements engineer and the systems administrators were still aligning with the emergent method, since this issue did not concern them.

Table 51.5. Negotiation 4 – Summary.

Actors	The content managers, the project manager and the implementers
Negotiation results	Document template to standardize the structure of the Web page template documentation

4. Reflections on Method Tailoring as Negotiation

All four snap shots of the method tailoring process show that the emergent method is modified based on the needs of project members and the insufficiencies they have identified. Often such problems occur in the intersection between different actor categories, for example, between the implementers and the content managers in third example. The driver of the method tailoring process shifts depending on the problem areas. For example, in the first example the project manager was the driver, while the implementers drove the tailoring process in the second and third example. Consequently, these examples show a problem with the method engineering view with the method engineer as the driver, and where project members are passive information providers.

In addition, the examples show two types of enrollments during method tailoring: direct and indirect. Direct enrollment occurs when project members address other project members that are concerned with the problem. One example is when the implementers addressed the requirements engineer about more elaborated requirement specifications. Indirect enrollment, on the other hand, occurs when project members try to involve actors that are not directly concerned with the problem. For example, the implementers addressed the project manager with their concern about the bug report template. Hence, project members try to influence each other using own arguments as well as the arguments of others.

Negotiation, however, is no guarantee that the emergent method will become method-in-action. The third example, concerning the bug report template, shows that the decided method was not used by all project members. First, as shown in the example it is not always that negotiation results in consensus. Second, even though the analysis has not explicitly focused this issue, one can suspect that project members are not always involved in the negotiation process under the same conditions. Both these concerns can affect the will to use the method.

5. Conclusion

Most of the existing literature view method tailoring as either (a) a highly rational process with the method engineer as the driver where the project members are passive information providers or (b) an unstructured process where the systems developer makes individual choices, a selection process without any driver. The purpose of this chapter is to illustrate that important design decisions during method tailoring are made through negotiation. Our narratives depict method tailoring as more complex than (a) and (b) show; results that are relevant both for the method engineering and the method-in-action communities.

Method engineering, being the more normative of the two schools, is often concerned with method tailoring approaches and tools. Our study shows that method engineering tools should enable all project members to be drivers of the method tailoring process – to let them address their needs for design decisions. In addition, the negotiations in our study have been about intersections between actor categories. Hence, method engineering tools should support identification of such intersections, to help identify the need for design decisions and negotiation.

To the method-in-action school we contribute with a deeper understanding of the method-in-action concept itself. Our results show that project members try to influence design decisions direct and indirect; direct through their own involvement and indirect through the use of delegates. Furthermore, we found that method tailoring is not a consensus process and is no guarantee that the emergent method, the design decisions, will be followed by all project members.

References

1. Ågerfalk, P. J. and Fitzgerald, B. (2006). Exploring the concept of method rationale: A conceptual tool for method tailoring. In Siau, K. (ed.) *Advanced Topics in Database Research*. pp. 63–78, Hershey, PA: Idea Group.
2. Aydin, M. N., Harmsen, F., Van Slooten, K. and Stegwee, R. A. (2005). On the adaptation of an agile information systems development method. *Journal of Database Management*, 16(4): 24–40.
3. Beck, K. (2000). *Extreme Programming Explained: Embrace Change*, Reading, MA: Addison-Wesley.
4. Brinkkemper, S. (1996). Method engineering: Engineering of information systems development methods and tools. *Information and Software Technology*, 38(4): 275–280.
5. Fitzgerald, B., Russo, N. L. and O'kane, T. (2003). Software development method tailoring at Motorola. *Communications of the ACM*, 46(4): 65–70.
6. Fitzgerald, B., Russo, N. L. and Stolterman, E. (2002). *Information Systems Development – Methods in Action*, Berkshire, UK: McGraw-Hill.
7. Harmsen, A. F. (1997). *Situational Method Engineering*, Utrecht, The Netherlands: University of Twente.
8. Iivari, J. and Maansaari, J. (1998). The usage of systems development methods: Are we stuck to old practice? *Information and Software Technology*, 40: 501–510.
9. Introna, L. D. and Whitley, E. A. (1997). Against method-*ism*: Exploring the limits of method. *Information Technology & People*, 10(1): 31–45.
10. Karlsson, F. and Ågerfalk, P. J. (2004). Method configuration: Adapting to situational characteristics while creating reusable assets. *Information and Software Technology*, 46(9): 619–633.
11. Karlsson, F. and Wistrand, K. (2006). Combining method engineering with activity theory: theoretical grounding of the method component concept. *European Journal of Information Systems*, 15(1): 82–90.
12. Klein, H. K. and Myers, M. D. (1999). A set of principles for conducting and evaluating interpretive field studies in information system. *MIS Quarterly*, 23(1): 67–94.
13. Kling, R. (1987). Computerization as an ongoing social and political process. In Bjerknes, G., Ehn, P. and Kyng, M. (eds.) *Computers and Democracy. A Scandinavian Challenge*. Aldershot: Avery.

14. Kumar, K. and Wellke, R. J. (1992). Methodology engineering: A proposal for situation specific methodology construction. In Cotterman, W. W. and Senn, J. A. (eds.) *Challenges and Strategies for Research in Systems Development*. pp. 257–269, Washington, DC: John Wiley & Sons.

15. Latour, B. (1991). Technology is society made durable. In Law, J. (ed.) *A Sociology of Monsters: Essays on Power, Technology and Domination*. pp. 103–131, London: Routledge & Kegan Paul.

16. Latour, B. (2007). *Reassembling the Social: An Introduction to Actor-Network-Theory*, Oxford: Oxford University Press.

17. Mcmaster, T., Vidgen, R. and Wastell, D. (1998). Information system development and 'due process': The case of the Van Sant map. In Buch, N. J., Damsgaard, J., Eriksen, L. B., Iversen, J. H. and Nielsen, P. A. (eds.) *Information Systems Research in Collaboration with Industry. Proceedings of the 21st Information Systems Research seminar in Scandinavia (IRIS)*. Aalborg, Danmark: Department of Computer Science, Aalborg University.

18. Monteiro, E. and Hanseth, O. (1996). Social shaping of information infrastructure. In Orlikowski, W., Walsham, G., Jones, M. and Degross, J. (eds.) *Information Technology and Changes in Organisational Work*. pp. 327–343, London: Chapman & Hall.

19. Mumford (1981)

20. Quattrone, P. and Hopper, T. (2006). What is IT? *Information and Organization*, 16(3): 212–250.

21. Riemenschneider, C. K., Hardgrave, B. C. and Davis, F. D. (2002). Explaining software developer acceptance of methodologies: A comparison of five theoretical models. *IEEE Transactions on Software Engineering*, 28(12): 1135–1145.

22. Rolland, C. and Prakash, N. (1996). A proposal for context-specific method engineering. In Brinkkemper, S., Lyytinen, K. and Welke, R. (eds.) *IFIP TC8, WG8.1/8.2 Working Conference on Method Engineering on Method Engineering: Principles of Method Construction and Tool Support*. Chapman & Hall, Atlanta, Georgia, United States, pp. 191–208.

23. Rossi, M., Ramesh, B., Lyytinen, K. and Tolvanen, J.-P. (2004). Managing evolutionary method engineering by method rationale. *Journal of Association of Information Systems*, 5(9): 356–391.

24. Schön, D. A. (1983). *The Reflective Practitioner: How Professionals Think in Action*, New York: Basic Books.

25. Walsham, G. (1995). Interpretive case studies in IS research: Nature and method. *European Journal of Information Systems*, 4: 74–81.

26. Walsham, G. (1997). Actor-network theory and IS research: Current status and future prospects. In Lee, A. S., Liebenau, J. and Degross, J. I. (eds.) *The IFIP TC8 WG 8.2 International Conference on Information Systems and Qualitative Research*. Chapman & Hall, New York, pp. 466–480.

27. Wynekoop, J. L. and Russo, N. L. (1995). Systems development methodologies: Unanswered questions. *Journal of Information Technology*, 10(2): 65–73.

52

A Hybrid Peer-to-Peer Solution for Context Distribution in Mobile and Ubiquitous Environments

Xiaoming Hu, Yun Ding, Nearchos Paspallis, Pyrros Bratskas,
George A. Papadopoulos, Yves Vanrompay, Manuele Kirsch Pinheiro
and Yolande Berbers

Abstract

With the proliferation of mobile devices such as PDAs and smart-phones, users get accustomed to using them in their daily life. This raises the expectations for user-customized and environment-aware services. However, mobile context-aware systems inherently feature characteristics of distribution and heterogeneity which pose great challenges to their developers. In this chapter, we focus on context distribution in mobile and ubiquitous computing environments. After describing the requirements in such environments, we propose a hybrid peer-to-peer based context distribution approach, which is built on top of the JXTA framework, a standard for peer-to-peer systems. We categorize context-aware system entities into three types of peers according to their device capabilities and their roles in context distribution. The peers are able to dynamically discover each other along with their offered services, form groups, and communicate with each other. The proposed approach is evaluated against the derived requirements and illustrated through a motivating scenario.

Keywords Context awareness · Context distribution · P2P systems · JXTA

1. Introduction

The proliferation of embedded sensors and mobile devices increases the importance of context-aware services. Consider, for example, a train station where the context conditions are monitored from distributed sensors, travelers are guided according to their current location and trip plan, entertainment programs are proposed to groups of travelers according to their common interest and location, etc. Along with a wealth of context information becoming available, a key challenge which is faced by developers is to enable wider dissemination of such context information across distributed sensors, application components, and context-processing components that manage the flow of context information between the sensors and the applications. Apparently, in mobile and ubiquitous environments, allowing individual context-aware devices to communicate with each other can provide increased levels of synergy in terms of power conservation and reusability (rather than replication) of hardware

Xiaoming Hu • European Media Laboratory GmbH, Schloss-Wolfsbrunnenweg 33, 69118 Heidelberg Germany
Yun Ding • European Media Laboratory GmbH, Schloss-Wolfsbrunnenweg 33, 69118 Heidelberg Germany
Nearchos Paspallis • Department of Computer Science, University of Cyprus, CY-1678, Nicosia, Cyprus
Pyrros Bratskas • Department of Computer Science, University of Cyprus, CY-1678, Nicosia, Cyprus
George A. Papadopoulos • Department of Computer Science, University of Cyprus, CY-1678, Nicosia, Cyprus
Yves Vanrompay • University of Leuven, Celestijnenlaan, 200A B-3001 Leuven, Belgium
Manuele Kirsch Pinheiro • University of Leuven, Celestijnenlaan, 200A B-3001 Leuven, Belgium
Yolande Berbers • University of Leuven, Celestijnenlaan, 200A B-3001 Leuven, Belgium

G.A. Papadopoulos et al. (eds.), *Information Systems Development*, DOI 10.1007/b137171_52,
© Springer Science+Business Media, LLC 2009

equipment (such as context sensors). In this respect we, here, endeavor to study and propose a hybrid peer-to-peer (P2P) [1] infrastructure solution to the problem of context distribution within mobile and ubiquitous computing environments.

Unlike the pure P2P paradigm, which employs the flooding technique in completely decentralized manner to decide how to route query messages by letting nodes broadcast query messages to all of their neighbors, in our hybrid model, some *super-peers* with rich computing resources are selected to maintain meta-information, such as the identity of other peers on which certain context is stored. The same peers are also responsible for processing raw sensor data to generate high-level context information, which can then be retrieved by surrounding resource-limited peers to enable their own context-aware applications.

We performed an early analysis of the basic requirements for a context distribution system by interviewing several pilot application developers and by examining the state of the art. We have identified the following requirements:

- *Heterogeneity*: Inherently, mobile and ubiquitous computing environments imply the involvement of multiple heterogeneous devices (e.g., context sensors, mobile devices, and service nodes), a plethora of available networking configurations, and protocols (such as Bluetooth, Wi-Fi), as well as different context-modeling technologies.
- *Scalability*: Mobile and ubiquitous environments can involve large numbers of participating devices, which implies the need for a decentralized approach enabling scalability. This can be partly achieved by using approaches which enable *localized scalability* [2] for context dissemination.
- *Security*: Security provisions are needed to guarantee the *privacy* of sensitive context information. Such information includes user-related data like their mood, location, activity, and preferences.
- *Robustness*: Due to the mobile nature of targeted environments, context providers and consumers spontaneously appear and disappear. Unreliability of the wireless network connections (e.g., drop of bandwidth and network partition) is generally the rule, rather than the exception. Thus, the system must be able to detect these changes dynamically and cope with them.
- *Light weight*: The context system must be light weight to be capable of being deployed in embedded devices of various sizes and capabilities.
- *Ease of use*: A main objective of any context distribution system is to reduce the complexity which is inherent in the development of context-aware applications. For this purpose, the context system must be easy to use.

The rest of this chapter is organized as follows. We describe our hybrid peer-to-peer infrastructure for context distribution in Section 2. Then we compare our approach with related work in Section 3, and evaluate it against the aforementioned requirements in Section 4. Finally, we summarize our results and provide pointers to our plans for future work in Section 5.

2. A Hybrid Peer-to-Peer Based Context Distribution System

In mobile and ubiquitous environments, context data may be transferred and disseminated among several system entities. Such data can be generated by context sensors, refined and reasoned by context processors, and consumed by context clients. This can be achieved in a highly distributed system using peer-to-peer (P2P) computing. According to their resources (e.g., computing power and memory use) and roles, we classify system entities into three categories (see Fig. 52.1a):

Sensor peers are the sources of context data. They generate low-level raw context data. These distributed sensors can be physical sensors such as thermometers installed in a room or software sensors monitoring the system performance.

Disseminator peers are resource-rich devices which act as context processors, distributors, and consumers. Playing an important role in the proposed context distribution system, each disseminator peer has four main responsibilities:

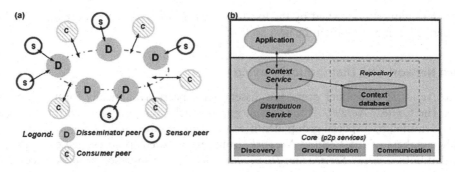

Figure 52.1. (a) Three types of peers in the context distribution system (b) A hybrid peer-to-peer infrastructure for context distribution.

- First, it can search for available sensors to acquire the raw context data.
- Second, it can extract, reason about and transform low-level context data to higher level abstractions in order to meet the different application needs.
- Furthermore, it can record context data for retrieval of history context data.
- Finally, it delivers and distributes context information to other peers.

Consumer peers are only context consumers. Usually, they have limited resources. Thus, they can neither afford to aggregate low-level context data nor reason about it.

2.1. A Hybrid Peer-to-Peer Infrastructure for Context Distribution

Figure 52.1(b) illustrates the proposed P2P-based infrastructure for context distribution. This framework is hosted by every disseminator peer, while a consumer peer can omit the repository due to its resource constraints. Adapters or software drivers are necessary to integrate the sensor peers. The infrastructure services are described as follows:

The *Core* provides the essential services required in P2P systems, which can be divided into three categories:

- *Discovery* includes peer discovery and service discovery. It allows a peer to be discovered by other peers, and to search for other peers and services. A peer can actively poll for other peers or services using certain criteria. Moreover, a peer can be notified of the arrival or departure of peers and services. Each peer is associated with a self-description, which is published to announce its presence and the context information it can offer.
- *Group formation* enables peers to create, join, and leave peer groups dynamically. Peers of a group will be notified of new or lost group members. A transient peer group can be built to let the peers collaboratively compose and provide a group service. A group self-description is also published for each group.
- *Peer communication* provides communication primitives for a peer to send messages to other peers or propagate messages within a peer group.

The *Context Service* is designed as a single interface for context providers to insert context information and for context clients (e.g., a context-aware application) to acquire context information. Context clients can either actively pull context data, or alternatively they can subscribe for context update events which are then pushed to them. Context clients are not concerned about the location of their required context information as this is encapsulated inside the *Context Service* and thus it is transparent for them. The task of the *Repository* is to maintain context information.

The *Distribution Service* is an internal service, which enables federated context services. Context requests which cannot be satisfied by the local *Context Service* are forwarded to connected remote *Context Services* via the *Distribution Service*. As already mentioned, it remains transparent for context clients whether a context request is satisfied by the local *Context Service* or by a remote one. The Distribution Service is described in more detail in the next section.

2.2. Context Network and Distribution Service

Context Network. Consumer peers and disseminator peers dynamically form groups to exchange context data. The *Context Network* is the default group which each peer joins during its bootstrap. This root group is identified by a special group identifier and provides the *Context Service* and the *Distribution Service.* Only members of the *Context Network* group are allowed to access these services. It is worth mentioning that both *Context Service* and *Distribution Service* are so-called group services, meaning that they are provided collectively by the members of the group. In our case, the disseminator peers dynamically form a federation. If one of them fails, other disseminator peers can still continue providing services to the consumer peers.

Whenever entering into the network, a disseminator peer publishes its self-description (see Fig. 52.2). Each peer has a unique peer ID and by default joins the *urn:music:ContextNetwork* group. This default group ID is used to limit the scope of discovery, meaning that only peers having the specified group ID can be discovered. Each disseminator peer also declares the context elements it requires in order to be discoverable by the corresponding sensor peers. Additionally, it searches for existing disseminator peers. Disseminator peers are *super-peers* in the system and stay relatively stable in the network. Each peer maintains a disseminator view which is a list of known disseminator peers in the group. This is achieved by using the *Discovery Service* provided by the *Core.* Since each disseminator peer can disappear and new ones can appear at any time, we use the following algorithm to converge local views of peers. Each disseminator peer periodically computes a list of randomly selected disseminator peers from their local view and sends the list to a random list of their known disseminator peers. Additionally, each disseminator peer periodically pings a list of randomly selected disseminator peers and purges the non-responding ones from their local view. In this way, the local views are kept loosely consistent among the peers. The algorithm described above is similar to the algorithm used by rendezvous peers of JXTA [3]. In contrast to rendezvous peers, the local view of each disseminator peer includes not only peer information but also the context elements which these peers can provide. In this way, the disseminator peer is easy to locate another proper disseminator peer to forward a context request which cannot be satisfied locally.

```
<jxta:PA xmlns:jxta="http://jxta.org">
   <PID>
      urn:jxta:uuid-59616261646162614A787461503250334F29B8E8818E46A7B7F7F98AFE71C68503
   </PID>
   <GID>urn:music:ContextNetwork</GID>
   <Type>music:DessiminatorPeer</Type>
   <Name>dp1</Name>
   <Desc>
     <RequestContext>
       <MetaContextElement>
          <ContextElement UpdateMode="trigger" Type="temperature">
             <Threshold Relatvie="false">32</Threshold>
          </ContextElement>
          <ContextElement UpdateMode="trigger" Type="humidity">
             <Threshold Relatvie="true">3%</Threshold>
          </ContextElement>
          <ContextElement UpdateMode="trigger" Type="CO2Concentration">
             <Threshold Relatvie="true">4%</Threshold>
          </ContextElement>
       </MetaContextElement>
       <MetaContextElement>
          <ContextElement UpdateMode="poll" Type="freeURBAMs"></ContextElement>
       </MetaContextElement>
     </RequestContext>
   </Desc>
</jxta:PA>
```

Figure 52.2. Self-description of a disseminator peer.

Whenever a consumer peer first appears in the network, it joins the *Context Network*. In fact, it connects to one or multiple disseminator peers in this group through the infrastructure. As a result, a virtual group is created on top of the existing P2P infrastructure (see Fig. 52.3a).

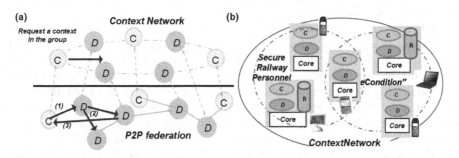

Figure 52.3. (a) Distribution Service maintains a physical network to a virtual Context Network (b) Hierarchically organized Context Groups.

Context Service. Instances of the *Context Services* are connected via the federation of their associated peers. As illustrated in Fig. 52.3a, when a consumer peer searches for a certain context, it uses its *Distribution Service* to propagate a *request* message within the group. Actually, the message is merely sent to its known disseminator peers by utilizing the peer *Communication Service* provided by the *Core* (step 1). Upon receiving the request for context information, the *Context Service* of a disseminator peer checks the local context repository. If the required information is not available, the *Context Service* utilizes the *Distribution Service* to find the information from remotely connected *Context Services* (step 2). Obviously, the *Distribution Service* relies on the P2P interaction among the peers. The receiving remote disseminator peer passes the incoming request to its local *Context Service* for processing and possibly sends a positive answer directly back to the requesting consumer peer (step 3).

Distribution Service. According to the requirements of the application and the characteristics of context information, the Distribution Service of each peer provides two mechanisms to distribute the context. By *polling*, any context change event will be propagated to remote peers within the group (e.g., any available URBAM[1] public display nearby). And *triggers* are used to enable asynchronous feedback on specific events (e.g., CO_2 concentration arising above a certain threshold in the waiting hall). The way context dissemination should be handled is also reflected by the *UpdateMode* context property in the peer description (see Fig. 52.2).

2.3. Scope of Context Distribution

The default group *Context Network* can be divided into subgroups to restrict information sharing. Each subgroup *Context Group* consists of a dynamic set of peers that have common interests for certain context data and have agreed upon a set of policies (e.g., group authentication). For example, assume a disseminator peer *A* which produces *environmental condition* data by combining measurements of the ventilated temperature from a thermometer, the humidity from a hygrometer and the CO_2 concentration from an infrared gas analyzer. Furthermore, assume that peer *A* would like to share this information with other peers. So peer *A* searches for a subgroup with the name "envCondition" and tries to join it. If this group does not exist, peer *A* creates an *urn:music:ContextNetwork:envCondition* group and publishes its group advertisement. Then, another peer *B* can discover this "envCondition" group and become its

---

[1] URBAM terminals are special Internet-connected devices which are made available in some RATP metro stations to offer information services to the passengers.

member, thus enabling the acquisition of shared preprocessed information. Obviously, each peer may belong to several subgroups simultaneously.

Whenever joining the network, a consumer peer registers a list of context data (more precisely, a list of types of context data) of interest to the *Context Service*. During run time, its interest may change. The *Distribution Service* maps the interests of consumer peers to dedicated subgroups and joins them on behalf of the associated consumer peers.

Groups and subgroups can be hierarchically organized (Fig. 52.3b). A subgroup inherits all the group services of its parent. As a group member, a disseminator peer can propagate messages either to request context information or to notify a context update within the group. *Context Groups* serve to subdivide the context network into regions, providing a scoping mechanism for restricting the propagation of search requests and update events. Thus, context clients will not be bothered to handle irrelevant context information. Context information required by context clients might change from time to time. They join or leave the corresponding *Context Group* according to the information they need to receive.

Moreover, taking into account the protection of private or sensitive context information, a specific policy can be enforced within a Context Group to control access rights. Peers, which would like to join a Context Group, should be approved by a group authentication service. For example, a "Railway Personnel" subgroup provides work forces in the station. Only peers which can provide a registered identifier are permitted to join the group and obtain the right to use these resources.

3. Comparison with Related Work

A plethora of related work studies both centralized and distributed context systems. According to Baldauf et al. [4], centralized approaches with one or more centralized components remain the most common in the literature. Centralized context-aware systems use a local service which provides applications with contextual information. Such a local service is usually part of a middleware which acquires raw contextual data from sensors and provides interpreted context to applications via a predefined interface. Furthermore, the middleware is assigned to monitor particular context changes and dispatch relevant events to interested applications as needed. Two well-known examples are the Context Toolkit [5] and CoBrA [6]. In contrast to centralized approaches, distributed context-aware systems allow the generation and management of context information at several locations, thus avoiding potential bottlenecks and unnecessary hardware duplication. Despite the fact that decentralized architectures increase the communication cost, they are more resilient to errors as they do not require a central server to maintain the context information.

The context management system of the PACE [7] middleware consists of a distributed set of context repositories. Context-aware components are not statically linked to a single repository, but they can discover repositories dynamically. However, scalability or tolerance for node failures is not provided.

Paganelli et al. [8] propose a multi-domain approach for context management, in which local domains handle geographically bounded context entities, and application domains manage context entities within organizational or application defined boundaries. However, this approach remains centralized, since context management inside each domain is performed by a server and coordination between different domains is based on a set of Web services allowing the exchange of context information among servers.

A different approach partly based on message multicasts is described by Abdelaziz et al. [3]. In this approach clients broadcast their location queries to all the members of a group, while interested parties anonymously listen to the queries. When they match a query and their privacy policy allows it, they reply to the query. The main disadvantage of this approach lies in the increased computation and communication cost of broadcasting context information. This is also the case for the approach proposed by Ye et al. [9]. The authors adopt a P2P approach for context sharing, in which context information remains locally stored on the peers and only an access reference, represented by a *Context Database Agent* (CDA), is registered on remote peers. The discovery of new peers is performed by broadcasting messages and context queries to remote peers are sent through unicast messages. The broadcasting of registering messages and the flat structure may raise scalability and security issues in ubiquitous environments, since every peer potentially registers its available context information on every known peer.

Reichert et al. [10] propose a distributed architecture with context sources, context processors, and context sinks. Context coordination and management are carried out in a distributed and self-organized way by means of P2P overlay networks. A context association is a directed link between a context source and a context sink. A centralized Context Coordinator is used as a registry for context source locations and resolver of context queries. Distributed context querying is possible, but the Context Coordinator stays the central node from which the query starts.

Paspallis et al. [11] describe the architecture of the distributed context management system used in the MADAM middleware. Providers and subscribers of context can reside on different network-connected nodes. Localized scalability is enabled by assigning higher importance to local context and by limiting the number of hops (i.e., transitions) to which specific context types can be communicated. Information in the local repositories is shared between nodes. The approach is based on the periodic broadcast of heartbeat messages which are used for both the formation of loosely coupled membership groups and for disseminating context information of selected types. The main drawback of this approach, however, is that it limits the participating nodes to the full MADAM nodes only, which limits the possibility for synergies. In contrast to this approach, this chapter proposes an approach which enables devices of varying sizes and capabilities (i.e., laptops, smart-phones, and embedded sensors) to accommodate the required software and act as either context providers, context consumers, or both.

Considering traditional P2P works on content dissemination, Delmastro et al. [12] argue that the P2P paradigm is particularly suitable for creating ad hoc networks to share content. They designed a cross-layer optimized protocol (XScribe) to enable P2P multicast services for sharing content among groups of users interested in the same topics. Group membership is managed and a light weight structure-less approach based on a *Distributed Hash Table* to deliver data to group members is used. This work focuses on the protocol and does not propose architectures for context dissemination.

Bisignano et al. [13] have designed a middleware layer over JXTA, named *Expeerience*. This middleware provides high-level support for MANET (Mobile ad hoc network) developers exploiting P2P technology and the mobile agent programming paradigm over mobile ad hoc networks. This approach fulfills requirements for code mobility, discovery of services, and intermittent connectivity.

Bonificacio et al. [14] propose a peer-to-peer architecture for distributed knowledge management on top of JXTA in which so-called K-peers provide services needed to organize local knowledge from an individual's or group's perspective. Protocols of meaning negotiation are introduced to achieve semantic coordination between peers. The system allows each individual or community of peers to build their own knowledge space within a network of autonomous K-peers, to make knowledge available to other K-peers, and to search for relevant knowledge.

The majority of the works in [12–15] do not explicitly focus on context dissemination or context-aware systems. Consequently, they often ignore intrinsic characteristics of context systems such as the highly dynamic environments, uncertainty, and error proneness which affect context distribution.

4. Evaluation

A prototype of the proposed system is currently under development. The Core functionality has already been implemented (http://www.igd.fhg.de/igd-a1/dynamite-project/software/tools/ubinet.zip). It is based on JXTA, which is a standard for P2P systems. JXTA defines a set of open protocols that allow any devices connected to the network to communicate and collaborate in a peer-to-peer manner [16]. To illustrate the motivation for this work, we present a scenario where context distribution is needed. This example validates the requirements mentioned in Section 1 and explains how the proposed approach satisfies these requirements.

The example is partly based on a pilot application developed by the MUSIC [17] consortium. It refers to an application designed for passengers of the Paris Metro. The application is an intelligent guide which senses the location of the user along with her or his agenda and automatically displays relevant information. For example, consider a user who is heading to a football game. Since there is sufficient time for a drink before the game, the application shows a map of the area with bars serving beers and snacks. Furthermore, because the user's smart-phone is equipped with a small display, the smart-phone detects a nearby URBAM terminal and delegates its visual output to it.

To enable this kind of scenario, it is assumed that a number of context information is needed. For instance, a RFID sensor is needed to provide location information (GPS normally does not work in roofed areas such as metro stations or tunnels). Furthermore, a specialized software sensor is needed to access and analyze the user's agenda. For example, such a sensor can be designed to access the user's syndicated calendar feed (as it is available from services like Google's Calendar), and infer the user state. In this example, the system combines the location information (e.g., Metro station adjacent to the football stadium of the upcoming game) and the user's agenda entry (e.g., "attending the PSG football game at 7 p.m.") and, combined with the current time, it infers that Bob is going to the game and that he has 1 hour free before that. Additional context information needed is the availability of devices and network connectivity in the Metro station. In terms of devices, for example, the smart-phone detects a nearby URBAM terminal which is free and notifies the user about it. The user walks to the URBAM terminal and accepts the smart-phone's suggestion to delegate the user interface (UI) to its touch-screen display. At that point, the UI is delegated to the URBAM terminal and the user analyzes his options for a quick drink and snack before the game.

The proposed hybrid P2P-based approach is requirements-driven, and as such, we briefly discuss how these requirements identified in Section 1 have been satisfied by the proposed mechanisms within the scope of this example.

- *Heterogeneity*: Because of the multiple types of devices involved in this scenario (smart-phone, URBAM terminal, and Metro RFID sensor), it is important to enable a common method for interoperability among these devices. Our proposal is based on the JXTA framework, which provides different implementations suitable for varying device types like embedded sensors, smart-phones and PDAs, laptops, desktops. As such, different and varying implementations of the proposed mechanism can be installed on the RFID sensor, the URBAM terminal and the smart-phone, each one fitting the appropriate category. The former acts as a *sensor peer*, the URBAM terminal as a *disseminator peer*, and the latter as a *consumer peer*. In this chapter we are primarily concerned with the *communication aspects* of heterogeneity, but in practice more aspects need to be tackled. Most notably, interoperability at the *model level* is needed to guarantee that the devices have a common understanding of the exchanged data. In this perspective, the MUSIC project follows an ontology-based approach [18].

- *Scalability*: Because of the large number of users expected in such scenarios (i.e., passengers with smart-phone trying to detect available RFID sensors or URBAM terminals), it is important that the proposed solution is scalable, allowing dozens or even hundreds of users exchanging context information. Our approach tries to limit the increased communication cost by using a hybrid P2P infrastructure solution. Resource-rich devices running as "super-peers" (disseminator peers) contribute by organizing and limiting the propagation of context information. The feature of group formation prevents the replication of already available context data sensors. In addition, it defines the boundaries for the dissemination of specific context data. This ability, together with the ability of context clients to join and leave groups according to their context needs, protects from delivering redundant information to uninterested peers.

- *Security*: Context information such as *location* and *available URBAM terminals* can safely be published, because there are no privacy concerns in sharing this information. On the other hand, the user's agenda is private information and thus access to that data should be limited to authorized entities only. To mitigate security concerns, the proposed context distribution system provides the notion of protected groups which provide access to authorized users only. In this example, a Calendar application running on the desktop of the user can form a subgroup containing information about the user's agenda. Access to that group is restricted, and only users with authorized access can join it.

- *Robustness*: Taking advantage of the discovery service provided by JXTA, our proposed system satisfies the requirement for *robustness*, arising from the instability of network connections which is common in mobile networks. This service allows for the discovery of both dynamically appearing and disappearing peers as well as of peer groups. In the proposed scenario, new smart-phones (consumer peers) can connect and disconnect as needed and dynamically discover URBAM terminals.
- *Light weight:* The implementation on top of JXME [19], which offers a light weight JXTA implementation targeting mobile devices, allows the proposed solution to be deployed on resource-constrained devices. In this scenario, the distinction between consumer and disseminator peers offers the possibility of selecting the implementation that best fits the capabilities of the devices.
- *Ease of use*: The proposed solution provides a single interface (the *Context Service* interface) that enables prospective context clients and context providers to access (i.e., insert and query) context information both synchronously and asynchronously, in an easy and intuitive manner.

5. Conclusions

This chapter introduces a hybrid peer-to-peer based context distribution system. We have argued that this approach offers significant improvements over related solutions. The approach builds on top of a thoroughly studied standard JXTA framework. This framework provides many facilities for discovering, communicating, and safeguarding information. We have shown that our approach meets the identified requirements as examined with a motivating scenario. Concerning future plans, the implementation of this approach is already in progress, and plans have been made for validating and testing it in the context of a set of field trials.

Acknowledgements

This chapter was financially supported by the European Union (MUSIC-IST project, 6th Framework Programme, contract number 35166). The authors from the European Media Laboratory GmbH are supported by the Klaus Tschira Foundation.

References

1. D. Milojicic, V. Kalogeraki, R. M. Lukose, K. Nagaraja, J. Pruyne, B. Richard, S. Rollins, and Z. Xu, Peer-to-peer computing. Technical report HPL-2002-57 20020315, Technical Publications Department, HP Labs Research Library, Mar. 2002. http://www.hpl.hp.com/techreports/2002/HPL-2002-57.html.
2. M. Satyanarayanan, Pervasive computing: Vision and challenges, IEEE Personal Communications, pp. 10–17 (2001).
3. M. Abdelaziz, E. Pouyoul, B. Traversat, Project JXTA, A Loosely-Consistent DHT Rendezvous Walker (Available at: http://research.sun.com/spotlight/misc/jxta-dht.pdf).
4. M. Baldauf, S. Dustdar, F. Rosenberg, A survey on context-aware systems. International Journal of Ad Hoc and Ubiquitous Computing, Vol. 2, No. 4, pp. 263–277 (2007).
5. A. Dey, D. Salber, G. Abowd, A conceptual framework and a toolkit for supporting the rapid prototyping of context-aware applications, Human Computer Interaction, Vol. 16, No. 2–4, pp. 97–166 (2001).
6. H. Chen, An Intelligent Broker Architecture for Pervasive Context-Aware Systems, PhD Thesis, University of Maryland, Baltimore County. (2004).
7. K. Henricksen, J. Indulska, T. McFadden, S. Balasubramaniam, Middleware for distributed context-aware systems, International Symposium on Distributed Objects and Applications (DOA) (2005).
8. F. Paganelli, G. Bianchi, D. Giuli, A context model for context-aware system design towards the ambient intelligence vision: Experiences in the eTourism domain. In Stephanidis, C. and Pieper, M. (eds.), Universal Access in Ambient Intelligence Environments, 9th ERCIM Workshop on User Interfaces for All (ERCIM UI4ALL), Lecture Notes in Computer Science, Vol. 4397, Spring-Verlag, pp. 173–191 (2006).
9. Ye, Jian, Li, Jintao, Zhu, Zhenmin, Gu, Xiaoguang, Shi, Hongzhou, PCSM: A context sharing model in peer-to-peer ubiquitous computing environment. International Conference on Convergence Information Technology, 21–23 Nov. 2007, pp. 1868–1873 (2007). 20. D. Milojicic, V. Kalogeraki, R. M. Lukose, K. Nagaraja, J. Pruyne, B. Richard, S. Rollins, and Z. Xu. Peer-to-peer

computing. technical report HPL-2002-57 20020315, Technical Publications Department, HP Labs Research Library, Mar. 2002. http://www.hpl.hp.com/techreports/2002/HPL-2002-57.html.

10. C. Reichert, M. Kleis, R. Giaffreda, Towards distributed context management in ambient networks, 14th IST Mobile & Wireless Communications Summit. Proceedings (2005).

11. N. Paspallis, A. Chimaris, G. A. Papadopoulos, Experiences from developing a distributed context management system for enabling adaptivity, J. Indulska and K. Raymond (Eds.) DAIS 2007, LNCS 4531, pp. 225–238 (2007).

12. F. Delmastro, A. Passarella, M. Conti, P2P Multicast for pervasive ad hoc networks, Pervasive and Mobile Computing, Vol. 4, No. 1, pp. 62–91 (2008).

13. M. Bisignano, A. Calvagna, G. Di Modica, O. Tomarchio, Design and development of a JXTA middleware for mobile ad hoc networks, 3rd International Conference on Peer-to-Peer Computing (P2P 2003), Linkopings, Sweden, September1–3 (2003).

14. M. Bonifacio, P. Bouquet, G. Mameli, M. Nori, Peer-mediated distributed knowledge management, Technical Report DIT 03-032 Department of ICT, University of Trento (2003)

15. F. Delmastro, A. Passarella, M. Conti, P2P Multicast for pervasive ad hoc networks, Pervasive and Mobile Computing, Vol. 4, No. 1, pp. 62–91 (2008).

16. JXTA, https://jxta.dev.java.net.

17. The MUSIC project, http://www.ist-music.eu/

18. M. Wagner, R. Reichle, M. Ullah Khan, K. Geihs, J. Lorenzo, M. Valla, C. Fra, N. Paspallis, G.A. Papadopoulos, a comprehensive context modeling framework for pervasive computing systems, 8th IFIP International Conference on Distributed Applications and Interoperable Systems (DAIS), 4–6 June, 2008, Oslo, Norway, Springer Verlag, to appear.

19. https://jxta-jxme.dev.java.net/.

53

Rules Transformation Using Formal Concept Approach

Darius Jurkevicius and Olegas Vasilecas

Abstract

One important part of modern information systems is rules. Rules that define or constrain some aspects of activities in an application domain are usually written using natural language in declarative form. However, for applying rules in information systems we need to use formal rules. In this chapter we propose a method that allows the transformation of declarative rules represented in natural language into formal rules. For transformation we used formal context. In that formal context are described all concepts required for transformation of rules. The suggested method allows simplifying the input and transformation of rules.

Keywords Formal concept analysis · Formal concept · Formal context · Rules transformation

1. Introduction

Designing information systems and seeking to implement projects successfully are important to establish cooperation and understanding between businessmen and designer of information systems. A user describes the system requirements and constraints using the rules or the business rules. By Gottesdiener [5], a business rule is "a statement that defines or constrains some aspect of the business. It is intended to assert business structure or to control or influence the behaviour of the business".

According to the principles of rules independence [1] of the Business Rules Manifesto released by the Business Rules Group, rules must be declarative: rules must be expressed declaratively in natural-language sentences for the business audience; if something cannot be expressed, then it is not a rule; a set of statements is declarative only if the set has no implicit sequencing; any statements of rules that require constructs other than terms and facts imply assumptions about a system implementation; a rule is distinct from any enforcement defined for it. A rule and its enforcement are separate concerns; rules should be defined independently of responsibility for the *who*, *where*, *when*, or *how* of their enforcement; exceptions to rules are expressed by other rules.

When a user describes business rules, then those rules can be ambiguous and without definition. We can remove indefinites and ambiguity, if each business rule is resolved into elementary or atomic rules. Atomic business rule is declaratively written, using natural language, easily understudied by businessmen, and it is not ambiguous. Information system designers write atomic rules using formal language. During this stage of rules transformation, cross-purposes can occur because businessmen have their own language, and system creators have their own. Mistakes occurring during the stage of the rules transformation process can be removed if a user himself writes the declarative rule by the template proposed in natural language.

Darius Jurkevicius and Olegas Vasilecas • Department of Information Systems, Faculty of Fundamental Sciences, Vilnius Gediminas Technical University, Lithuania.

G.A. Papadopoulos et al. (eds.), *Information Systems Development*, DOI 10.1007/b137171_53,
© Springer Science+Business Media, LLC 2009

2. Related Works

For example, the Semantics of Business Vocabulary and Business Rules specification [8] of OMG consortium is proposed, and we can find the information how to describe business rules using Semantics of Business Vocabulary and Business Rules structured English natural language. The example above includes three key words or phrases, two designations for noun concepts and one for a fact type (from a form of expression), as illustrated below (Fig. 53.1).

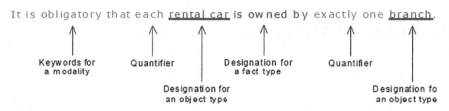

Figure 53.1. Rule represented in Semantics of Business Vocabulary and Business Rules structured English.

Below are examples of two statements of a single rule:

1. A rental must have at most three additional drivers.
2. It is obligatory that each rental has at most three additional drivers.

Using the font styles of SBVR Structured English, these rule statements are:

1. A **rental** must *have* at most three **additional drivers**.
2. It is obligatory that each **rental** *has* at most three **additional drivers**.

It shows that using expression of sentence we can write different business rules using templates. We can automatically transform the declarative rule into the formal rule using templates.

3. Understanding of Formal Concept Analysis

One of the ways to transform available data in hierarchic aspect is formal concept analysis. Dau [2] noticed that scientists in making plots could not lean on them as on arguments. To separate formally the mathematical structure from its scheme presentment, the work environment was created in which diagrams could be used to make formal substantiations. Now we define some terms used in this article:

Concept can be defined as

- an abstract or general idea inferred or derived from specific instances [13];
- a concept is an abstract idea or a mental symbol, typically associated with a corresponding representation in language or symbology, that denotes all of the objects in a given category or class of entities, interactions, phenomena, or relationships between them [11];
- has an intention (deep definition), extension (set of objects or exemplars) [6];
- the definition of a type of objects or events. A concept has an intensional definition (a generalization that states membership criteria), and an extension (the set of its instances) [7];

Formal Concept Analysis (FCA) [10] method is

- a mathematization of the philosophical understanding of concept;
- a human-centred method to structure and analyze data;
- a method to visualize data and its inherent structures, implications and dependencies.

FCA is based on the philosophical understanding that a concept can be described by its extension, that is, all the objects that belong to the concept and its intension which are all the attributes that the objects have in common [9];

Formal context – the mathematical structure which is used to formally describe these tables of crosses (or briefly a context) [12].

FCA is a method used in data analysis, knowledge imaging and information control. Rudalf Wille suggested FCA in 1981 [10], and it is successfully developed nowadays. For 10 years FCA was researched by small groups of scientists and Rudalf Wille's students in Germany. FCA was not known worldwide because the biggest part of publications was presented at mathematicians' conferences. After getting the sponsorship, some projects were implemented in this area. Most of them were knowledge research projects used in work. This system was known only in Germany. During the last 10 years, FCA became the research object of international scientists' community. FCA was used in linguistics, psychology, also in projecting the software, in the areas of artificial intelligence and information search.

Some of the structures of FCA appear to be fundamental to information representation and were independently discovered by different researchers. For example, Godin et al.'s [4] use of concept lattices (which they call "Galois lattices") in information retrieval.

Now, we introduce the formal concept analysis definition [3].

For example, G is the set of objects that we are able to identify in some domain (e.g. if, when, than). Let M be the set of attributes. We identify the index I as a binary relationship between two sets G and M, i.e. $I \subseteq G \times M$. A triple (G, M, I) is called a formal context. For $A \subseteq G$, we define:

$$A' := \{m \in M | (g, m) \in I \text{ for all } g \in A\} \tag{1}$$

and dually, for $B \subseteq M$

$$B' := \{g \in G | (g, m) \in I \text{ for all } m \in B\} \tag{2}$$

A formal concept of a formal context (G, M, I) is defined as a pair (A, B) with $A \subseteq G$, $B \subseteq M$, $A \subseteq B$ and $B \subseteq A$. Sets A and B are called extend and intend of the formal concept. The set of all formal concepts of a context (G, M, I) is called the concept lattice of context (G, M, I).

4. Process of Rule Transformation

Now we will describe our proposed method to transform declarative rules into formal rules (Figs. 53.2 and 53.3).

Making the rule input in the declarative form, it is suggested to make the input using the template or this rule can be written using semi-structured natural language.

Using the template input proposed by the system the initial component of the rule (ex. If) is suggested (Fig. 53.3). Then other terms that are kept in the formal context are suggested. It is a step-by-step constructed rule. The mistake can be avoided using the first method, when the templates are suggested, and the rule can be immediately transformed into the formal form. This method is designed mainly for the businessmen. Hereunder we show that different rules have generic form. Rules can be defined by declarative IF-THEN form with the priority, start date, finish date, for example:

First rule:

If customer is from Vilnius, then 1 DVD will be proposed for free;

Second rule:

If customer's age is > 65, then 1 ticket will be proposed for free.

At the first sight these rules don't have much common. After analysing the rules it was recognized what condition and action of the rule can be made from some components.

If customer characteristic comparison value, then value commodity will be proposed for free.

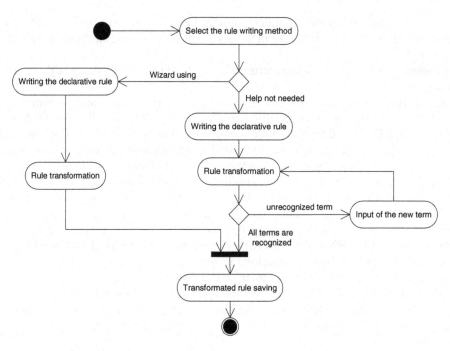

Figure 53.2. Transformation process of the declarative rule.

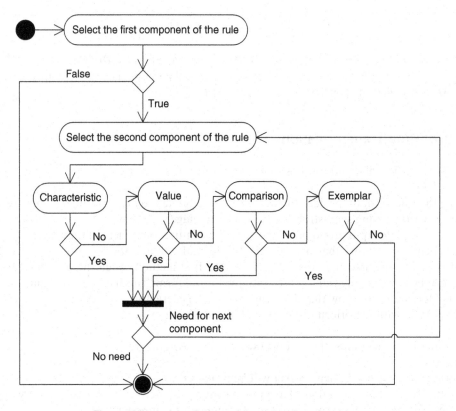

Figure 53.3. Activity diagram of the declarative rule writing.

If we write this rule in the more common way, it would be

If exemplar characteristic comparison value, then action value characteristic exemplar.

If we write this rule in the most common way, it would be:

If condition, then action.

There are not so many ways to formulate the condition and action.

The second method is designed to input new terms to write the new kind of rules in the system.

For understanding in Fig. 53.4 we show an example of how some statements in natural language of a single rule transform in one rule in formal language.

Exapmle of 1 condition

Form of representation		Exemplar	Characteristic	Comparison	Value
Natural language	if	customer's	age	is more than	65 metu
	when	customer	is older	then	65 metai
	if	customer	yave year	more then	65 m.
Formal language	If	customer!= ''	and age	>	'65'

Exapmle of 2 condition

Form of representation		Exemplar	Characteristic	Comparison	Value
Natural language	if	customer	bay	more than	200 lt
	when	customer	baying	more than	200 lt
Formal language	If	customer!= ''	and sum_of_bay	>	'200'

Figure 53.4. Examples of some statements of a single rule.

Written declarative rule is transformed, and if there are variances or unknown words, then we propose to input this word into the formal context. When word is saved, the rule transformation is made one more time (Fig. 53.2).

When programmer working with application program (in edit mode), his first steps are creating objects (terms of specific domain, e.g. business). He gets terms from declarative rules and input in attributes fragment of SQL code (e.g. can be another language: RuleML, OCL). They have relationship represented by binary relation. And additionally they have relationship with another attributes that describe terms (objects) characteristics, e.g. verb, noun, characteristic, comparison, value or another. Information about exemplars can be retrieved from databases or can be kept separately as metadata. Using terms saved in formal context, we can transform declarative rule into formal represented rule. Using formal concept analysis, we can represent the formal concepts in concepts hierarchical tree.

Now we shall demonstrate how one component of the rule can be transformed using formal concepts (Fig. 53.5). Fig. 53.5 shows the use of attribute's type (ex. SQL_). That type of attribute needs separate SQL sentence from natural language text (ex. SQL_If and Text_If). And we can use those types of attributes for different tasks: show the SQL code, show the RuleML code, for search task, etc.

The creating form of rules of application program proposes for user to sequent design the rule in the sentence form. The form gets terms and conditions from the formal context. The then declarative rule is transformed into formal rule, it must be saved.

Our proposed general function architecture of system is shown in Fig. 53.6. Functions of components are

- declarative rules management component: compose of declarative rules with or without system help; transformation of declarative rules; saved transformed declarative rules;
- objects management component: manage objects of formal context;

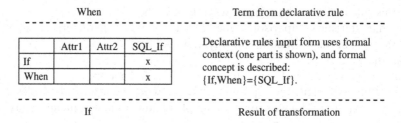

When				Term from declarative rule

	Attr1	Attr2	SQL_If
If			x
When			x

Declarative rules input form uses formal context (one part is shown), and formal concept is described: {If,When}={SQL_If}.

If   Result of transformation

Figure 53.5. Example of rule transformation.

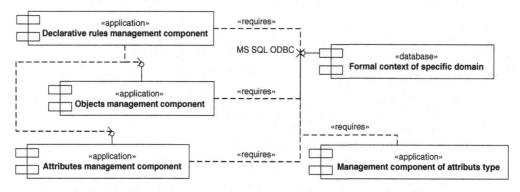

Figure 53.6. Function architecture diagram of rules transformation system.

- attributes management component: manage attributes of formal context;
- management component of attributes type: manage type of attributes;

5. Storage of Formal Concepts in Formal Context and Experiment Overview

We propose collecting the set of rules (in formal representation) in the formal context splitting it into two parts: condition and action, where conditions are objects and attributes are actions. From our point of view formal concepts that are collected in the formal context can be represented in three levels (Fig. 53.7). In the first level are collected the set of rules, in the second level are collected the set of simple transformed rules and in the third level are collected the compound rules. This solution avoids duplication of rules.

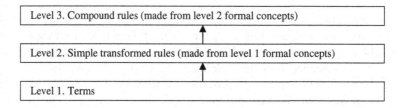

Figure 53.7. Formal concepts represented in formal context in 3 levels.

A tool (prototype) has been created to manage the formal context and rule composition and transformation. This tool, a Web application, is called Formal Context Manager (FCM) (Fig. 53.8).

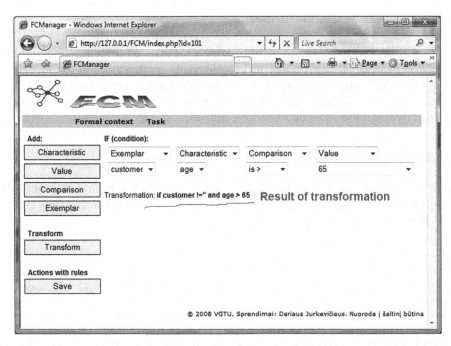

Figure 53.8. Rule' composing and his transformation.

FCM allows collecting formal concepts in relational database (MS SQL, MySQL 5.0) and to create a conceptual system on top of it. The whole program is database-aware and tries to support the user by supplying relevant information from the database at each step.

FCM has a complete feature set to enable you to create your own conceptual systems.

Some features of FCM are

- Editing of contexts
- Can use different databases (MS SQL, MySQL)
- Supporting of editing and using type of attributes

6. Discussions

In this section, we want to debate typical questions that may show up during discussions about the subject of this chapter.

- What are the business cases of the approach? A "business case" for our approach is to reduce the work of programmers inputting business rules into the system. The user can himself insert declarative rules into the system using natural language.
- Why use the type of attributes? The type of attributes is needed for conceptual splitting. That approach allows
  - Keep set of context from different domain in one formal context;
  - Separate formal concept for representation of concept. For example, we have formal concept {If,When} = {SQL_If}. The problem is how to extract and represent the part of the formal concept (for example, If).

7. Conclusions

Using our proposed method, the user (businessman) is allowed to compose action rules without requiring specific knowledge. It is proposed to keep formally written rules in the formal context. The conclusion was made that using type of attributes to describe formal concepts can facilitate the usage of formal concepts in practice. Keeping the formal concept in formal context allows the representation of concepts in hierarchical form to show dependences, equivalences, repeated structures, exceptions, etc.

Acknowledgements

The work is supported by Lithuanian State Science and Studies Foundation according to High Technology Development Program Project "Business Rules Solutions for Information Systems Development (VeTIS)" Reg. No. B-07042.

References

1. Business Rules Group (2002). Business Rules Manifesto. [Overviewed on 2007-11-16]. http://www.businessrulesgroup.org/brmanifesto.htm.
2. Dau F. (2004). Types and tokens for logic with diagrams. In K. E. Wolff, H. Pfeiffer, and H. Delugach (Eds.), *Conceptual Structures at Work: 12th International Conference on Conceptual Structures*. Springer, Berlin, pp. 62–93.
3. Ganter B., Wille R. (1999). *Formal Concept Analysis: Mathematical Foundations*. Springer, Berlin-Heidelberg.
4. Godin R., Gecsei J., Pichet C. (1989). Design of browsing interface for information retrieval. In N. J. Belkin and C. J. van Rijsbergen (Eds.), *Proc. SIGIR '89*, pp. 32–39.
5. Gottesdiener, E. (1997). Business rules. Show power, promise. *Application Development Trends*, Vol. 4, No. 3. [Overviewed on 2007-12-20]. http://www.ebgconsulting.com/Pubs/Artcles/BusinessRulesShow-PowerPromise Gottesdiener.pdf.
6. Martin J., Odell J. (1994). *Object-Oriented Methods: A Foundation*. Prentice-Hall, Upper Saddle River, NJ, p. 52.
7. Mayers A., Maulsby D. (2004) Glossary. [Overviewed on 2007-12-11].http://acypher.com/wwid/BackMatter/Glossary.html.
8. OMG consortium (2006). *Semantics of Business Vocabulary and Business Rules Specification*. [Overviewed on 2007-12-14]. http://www.omg.org/docs/dtc/06-03-02.pdf.
9. Tilley T. (2003). *Formal Concept Analysis Application to Requirements Engineering and Design*. [overviewed on 2007-11-15]. http://www.int.gu.edu.au/~inttille/publications/ tilley04formal.pdf.
10. Wille R. (1982). Restructuring Lattice Theory: an approach based on hierarchies of concept. *Ordered sets/editor I. Rival.— Reidel, Dordrecht-Boston*, pp. 445–470.
11. Wikipedia (2008). *Concept, Wikipedia. The Free Encyclopedia*. [Overviewed on 2008-02-22]. http://en.wikipedia.org/wiki/Concept.
12. Wolf K. (1993). A first course in formal concept analysis. In: Faulbaum, F. (Ed.), *SoftStat'93 Advances in Statistical Software 4*, pp. 429–438.
13. WORDNET (2008). *A Lexical Database for the English Language*. [Overviewed on 2008-01-08]. http://wordnet.princeton.edu/perl/webwn?s = concept.

54

Agreements in Virtual Organizations

Malgorzata Pankowska

Abstract

This chapter is an attempt to explain the important impact that contract theory delivers with respect to the concept of virtual organization. The author believes that not enough research has been conducted in order to transfer theoretical foundations for networking to the phenomena of virtual organizations and open autonomic computing environment to ensure the controllability and management of them. The main research problem of this chapter is to explain the significance of agreements for virtual organizations governance. The first part of this chapter comprises explanations of differences among virtual machines and virtual organizations for further descriptions of the significance of the first ones to the development of the second. Next, the virtual organization development tendencies are presented and problems of IT governance in highly distributed organizational environment are discussed. The last part of this chapter covers analysis of contracts and agreements management for governance in open computing environments.

Keywords Virtual organization · Virtualization · Agreements · SLAs · Governance

1. Virtualization

Modern computer systems are now sufficiently powerful to present users with the illusion that one physical machine consists of multiple virtual machines, each one running separate and possibly different instance of an operating system. Today, virtualization can apply to a range of system layers, including hardware, operating system and high-level language virtual machines. Virtual machine concept was in existence since 1960 when it was first developed by IBM to provide concurrent, interactive access to a mainframe computer [6]. The fundamental idea behind virtualization is to introduce an additional layer of indirection in accessing resources so that a lower level resource can be transparently mapped to multiple higher level resources or vice versa. Each level has its own virtualization control layer which is responsible for management and enforcement of mapping between level n and level $n + 1$ of virtualized resources. So virtualization decision may be performed during the system configuration phase or even in the run time. The lowest layer of the hierarchy represents physical resources. The virtualization of resources is a powerful tool for creating advanced data network services. A major advantage to the virtualization of network functionality through abstraction techniques is increased flexibility in service creation, provisioning and differentiation.

The main purpose of the infrastructure-level virtualization is to provide an abstracted view of a collection of discrete computer, data, application, network and storage resources for the purpose of hiding complexity and improving flexibility and productivity. An important beginning to the virtualization process is to recognize that series of components could be better managed if they are abstracted. As these abstractions are crafted in an appropriate and ultimately productive manner, the predominant interactions remain with the individual components. In this way, virtualization also provides both an

Malgorzata Pankowska · University of Economics, Katowice, Poland.

G.A. Papadopoulos et al. (eds.), *Information Systems Development*, DOI 10.1007/b137171_54,
© Springer Science+Business Media, LLC 2009

opportunity and the means to abstract away complexity. It offers customers the opportunity to build more efficient IT infrastructures. Virtualization is seen as a step on the road to utility computing. With virtualization, the logical functions of the server, storage and network elements are separated from their physical functions (e.g. processor, memory, controllers, disks and switches). In other words, all servers, storage and network devices can be aggregated into independent pools of resources. Elements from these pools can then be allocated, provisioned and managed, manually or automatically, to meet the changing needs and priorities of one's business [24].

2. Virtual Organizations and Their Development

A virtual organization is a set of individuals and institutions, with some common purposes or interests, that need to share their resources to pursue their objectives. According to Burn and Ash [4] a virtual organization is recognized as a dynamic form of interorganizational systems and hence one where traditional hierarchical forms of management and control may not apply. Franke [16] suggests that the organizational concept of virtual organizations encompasses three organizational elements. The first element is a relatively stable Web platform from which dynamic virtual corporations are derived. Second, virtual corporations are interorganizational adhocracies that consist temporarily of independent companies in order to serve a particular purpose, such as joint R&D, product development and production. The third element of the organizational construct is the management organization that initiates and maintains the Web platform and facilitates the operation of dynamic virtual corporations. Byrne [5] defines the virtual organization as a temporary network of independent companies which are fluid and flexible groups of collaborators that quickly unites to exploit a specific opportunity. Lewis and Weigert [21] state that the pillars of virtual organizations comprise (1) standardizing interactions, (2) standardizing metadata, (3) treating knowledge separately from the individual and (4) abstracting information from operations. According to Dirksen and Smit [13], Prusak [28] and Kisielnicki [18] the real value of the virtual organization is in the spontaneous gathering of people with shared interests and aims emerging during the development process. Virtual organization is made up of a plurality of socio-technical resources, which always maintain their independence and their former legal status. Virtual organization creates social environment where virtualization of IT infrastructure resources would be realized.

Virtual organizations now find a new way for further development in grid environment. Grid technology provides means for harnessing the computational and storage power of widely distributed collections of computers. Computing grids are usually very large-scale services that enable the sharing of heterogeneous resources (hardware and software) over an open network such as the Internet. A grid organized in virtual organizations, collection of computational and storage resources, application software, as well as individuals (end users) that usually have a common research area. Access to grid resources is provided to virtual organization members through the grid middleware, which exposes high-level programming and communication functionalities to application programmers and end-users, enforcing some level of resource virtualization. Virtual organization membership and service brokerage are regulated by access and usage policies agreed among the infrastructure operators, the resource providers and the resource consumers.

Grid computing has emerged as an attempt to provide users with the illusion of an infinitely powerful, easy-to-use computer, which can solve very complex problems. This very appealing illusion is to be provided (1) by relying on the aggregated power of standard (thus inexpensive), geographically distributed resources owned by multiple organizations and (2) by hiding as much as possible the complexity of the distributed infrastructure to users. Grid computing is the technology that enables resource virtualization, on-demand provisioning and service (or resource) sharing between organizations. Using the utility computing model, grid computing aims at providing ubiquitous digital market of services. Frameworks providing these virtualized services must adhere to the set of standards ensuring interoperability, which is well described, open and non-proprietary and commonly accepted in the community. Grid computing is the logical step on the IT market to the ubiquitous connectivity, virtualization, service outsourcing, product commoditization and globalization [26]. Examples of grid computing virtual organizations are widely described in literature [3].

Both resources of the virtual organization and its users can be widely distributed, spanning multiple organizations (and crossing multiple administrative domains) and connecting users from even larger set of organizations and countries. In order to ensure its operation, each virtual organization utilizes several grid services that allow to perform user management or provide access to the resources. These services are often configured and administrated by the virtual organization itself, but a virtual organization can also arrange to share the services with another virtual organization [10].

In essence, grid computing is aiming to help standardize the way for distributed computing. A standards-based open architecture promotes extensibility, interoperability and portability because it has general agreement within the community. To help with this standardization process, the grid community has the successful and popular Global Grid Forum (GGF). A key parameter in grid systems is the Quality of Service (QoS). When a grid job has QoS requirements, it is often necessary to negotiate a service-level agreement beforehand to enforce this certain level of service. Broadly speaking, there are three types of grid:

1. Computational grids
2. Data grids
3. Service grids

A computational grid is a distributed set of resources that are dedicated to aggregate computational capacity. A data grid is a collection of distributed resources that are specifically set up for processing and transferring large amounts of data. Here, the European DataGrid project, http://www.eu-datagrid.org, is a good example, focusing on the development of middleware services to enable distributed analysis of physics data from CERN. A service grid is a collection of distributed resources that provides a service that cannot be achieved through one single computer. An important benefit of the grid is its capability for supporting not only individual applications and services but also complete large-scale distributed environments for collaborative communities, thereby enabling scalable virtual organizations [20, 32].

Virtual organization is an open and temporal integration of autonomic units. The openness, temporality, adhocratism and heterogeneity of resources are the reasons why the organizations act in On Demand Operating Environment (ODOE) [15]. It defines a set of integration and infrastructure management capabilities that enterprises can utilize, in a modular and incremental fashion, to become an in-demand business. These are each unique services that work together to perform a variety of on-demand business function. ODOE must be responsive to dynamic and unpredictable changes, variable to adapt to processes and cost structures to reduce risk, focused on core competencies and differentiated capabilities, resilient to manage changes and external threats, flexible, self-managing, scalable, economical, resilient, based on open standards. ODOE may be the construction of the future, nethertheless, autonomic computing is focused on the most pressing problem facing the IT industry today: the increased complexity of the IT infrastructure that typically accompanies the increased business value delivered through computing advancements. The problem is contributing to an increasing inability of business to absorb new technology and solutions.

Decentralized autonomic computing is achieved when a system is constructed as a group of locally interacting autonomous entities (i.e. virtual organizations) that cooperate in order to adaptively maintain the desired system-wide behaviour without any external or central control. Such a system is also called a self-organizing emergent system. Self-organization is achieved when the behaviour is constructed and maintained adaptively without external control. In virtual organizations as ad hoc networks, decentralized control is the only possible way to manage the system behaviour because all necessary information to make appropriate decisions is inherently distributed and decentralized.

3. Virtual Organizations' Management Problems

One of the prominent problems in large-scale distributed computing is the management of virtual organization, i.e. uniform views over pools of distributed computing and storage resources that are controlled by multiple, often autonomous organizations. The ability to address the large-scale computational problems that require ad hoc configurations of resources depends largely on the rapid and effective creation of virtual organizations. For the owners of virtual organization resources it is essential to

- generate incentives for the constant provision of computing services to meet the needs of resource consumers;
- enabling them to quest offers of resources of other providers when their own capacities are insufficient;
- allowing them to maximize their resources utilization by offering a competitive service access price in order to attract consumers, and as a consequence;
- reducing their Total Costs of Ownership (TCO).

It is essential for the setup and administration of a computing infrastructure that the participants share the costs resulting from the use of hardware, software, maintenance and administration in a fair way. To realize this basic idea of autonomic computing it is necessary to establish a comprehensive billing solution for the mutual provision and usage of computing resources [34].

On the other hand, in a competitive and transparent market, the users (resource consumers) have the option of choosing the providers that best meet their requirements or to choose between rental and self-procurement of computing resources. The billing mechanism must support various payment mechanisms, such as payment after job submission, pay as you go and prepayment. It must ensure necessary support from job submission up to payment between user, resource broker, resource provider, and clearing institutions, various mechanisms of pricing for the resource providers such as prices based on different metrics, flat price models, ability to handle various currencies, existence of clearing institutions (bank service, account management), installation of a procedure for the settlement of disputes and conflicts, independency of the utilized middleware. To assure secure access to any computer resources one must provide an adequate level of authentication, authorization, job isolation and possibility of auditing users' needs. This should be realized with as little administrative effort as possible, through providing the administrators and virtual organizations managers with enough control on their resources and users. The Public Key Infrastructure-based approach is suitable for use in well-structured and trusted environments like scientific communities, but it has demonstrated to be unable to effectively or efficiently support secure interactions when deployed in an open and dynamic environment like the Internet, both for technical and organizational reasons [1]. For confidentiality and integrity services in autonomic computing environment a mechanism similar to SSL is used for guaranteeing integrity and confidentiality of exchanged messages. Early being transmitted over an insecure communication channel, TCP packages are encrypted by using cryptography based on session keys which are generated anew for each session and exchanged between communicating parties using asymmetric cryptography. In autonomic computing environment the quality of service measuring and monitoring as a business cooperation requirement needs techniques, which measure and certify actual application level performance of service flows spreading on a network in consequence of a service request [25]. To obtain precise measurements, it is then needed to record the actual behaviour of IP packets corresponding to service flows in the network.

Virtual organization constitutional norms describe the terms of cooperation that parties adhere to. Their first approach considers that each partner states workloads and prices for its contribution and that a general business process outline is specified. This umbrella agreement represents a set of norms parties commit to and which set up the ground for the virtual organization operation phase. Specific contracts indicating actions to be performed make up the third normative layer. Operational contracts are proposed and signed within the context of virtual organization contractual agreements, and their creation and execution are subject to enforcement and monitoring procedure [8].

Virtual organization management covers evaluation issues. An approach for evaluating companies comprises three types of evaluation: (a) evaluation of enterprise components (products, processes and capabilities), (b) identification of core competencies and (c) evaluation of infrastructure elements [33]. Another approach suggests resource considerations as it is in project management. However, the noticeable difference to virtual organizations is that in this case the methods tend to operate not at the company level but at the employee level or project level and do not adequately support an evaluation of virtual organization efficacy.

4. Virtual Organization's Evaluation by Contracts and Agreements

Information technology governance is a framework that supports the effective and efficient management of information resources (e.g. people, funding and information) to facilitate the achievement of corporate objectives. The focus is on the measurement and management of IT performance to ensure that the risks and costs associated with IT are appropriately controlled [30]. The governance framework encompasses the IT governance domains representing the management-related responsibilities:

- IT strategic alignment
- IT value delivery
- Risk management
- IT resource management
- Performance measurement

Without establishing and monitoring performance measures, it is unlikely that the previous phases (IT strategic alignment, IT value delivery, risk management and IT resource management) will achieve their desired outcomes. The performance measurement domain closes the loop and provides feedback to the alignment domain by providing evidence that the IT governance initiative is on track and creating the opportunity to take timely corrective measures. Virtual organizations, although they are temporal, exist on a long-term basis. Therefore, participating companies find agreements, for example, on the goals, on the internal rules of transferring goods and services or on the cooperative marketing. On the basis of the agreements, virtual organization can act as temporal operational teams configured uniquely for each type of order. A cost accounting system for a virtual organization needs to consider specific requirements. They may be described as follows:

- Distributed, shared performance: Virtual organizations do not possess any own resources. For any market order, the most competent companies have to be selected from the pool of partners to perform a suborder with their own resources.
- Flexible process-oriented configuration: In contrary to traditional organizations, tasks are not necessarily assigned to a partner but are allocated for every type of order. In consequence, the process to be performed to fulfil an order is the main planning and control object.
- Autonomy of the partners: In decentralized organizations, the organizations' units (e.g. profit centres) act autonomically to a certain extent.

All members have to agree upon rules on how to allocate rules and tasks in the value net and consequently on how to share profit and losses, also for tax purposes in compliance with applicable rules and regulations [9]. As a general principle, partners can regulate their relationships by agreement, but agreements cannot possibly cover each and every present and future task and interaction of virtual organizations. They may be renewed or rewritten but not continuously – otherwise the stability of rules would be lost. For what is not specifically provided for in the agreements, codes and law in force can be applied. In the absence of a clear solution, each partner might be potentially subject to the law of every other virtual organization member which contributes to the same product or service and also to the law of every country in which products and services are provided. In virtual organization the contribution of the individual partners to the final product or service may be impossible to distinguish, also because cross-company groups may work on the same project. Every partner contributes to the final goal by concentrating on specific competencies. The framework agreement is the strongest tool in the hands of the partners of a virtual organization. The principle of contractual freedom allows them to regulate their interactions in the ways they deem best, thus leaving the least possible situations to chance. What virtual organization partners can do is to reduce the margin of uncertainty as much as possible by signing carefully drawn framework agreements in which both applicable law and competent court are commonly decided upon. They do not necessarily have to choose the national law of one of the partners but can freely opt for another legislation, provided that it best suits the activities and interactions of the virtual organization. Virtual organizations as network organizations exemplify the decomposability of organizations and the conditions established by the information growth dynamics and the technological infrastructure sustaining such a dynamics. By subcontracting and outsourcing the overwhelming variety of production tasks, organizations of this type concentrate on their core competencies and higher quality product deliveries.

A contract is a legally enforceable agreement in which two or more parties commit to certain obligations in return for certain rights. Contracts guarantee rights (protection) and impose obligations (demanding the requirements' fulfilment) concerning exchanged values, i.e. information, knowledge, service, money, digital product (music, information, expert's report) and material product [27, 2].

The essential characteristics for a modern form of contract are following:

- A specific duty for all parties to deal fairly with each other, and with their subcontractors, specialists and suppliers, in an atmosphere of multilateral cooperation.
- Involvement of a general presumption to achieve "win–win" solutions to problems which may arise during the course of the project.
- A wholly interrelated package of documents which clearly defines the roles and duties of all involved and which is suitable for all types of projects and for any procurement route.
- Separation of the roles of contract administrator, project and lead manager and adjudicator.
- A choice of allocation of risks, to be decided as appropriate to each project but then allocated to the party best able to manage, estimate and carry the risk.
- Taking all reasonable steps to avoid changes in preplanned works information, but where variations do occur, they should be proceeded in advance, with provision for independent adjudication if agreement cannot be reached.
- Express provision for assessing interim payments by methods other than monthly valuation, i.e. milestones, activity schedules or payment schedules. Such arrangements must also be reflected in the related subcontract documentation. The eventual aim should be to phase out the traditional system of monthly measurement or re-measurement, but meanwhile provision should still be made for it.
- Clearly setting out the period within which interim payments must be made to all participants in the process, failing which they will have an automatic right to compensation, involving payment of interest at a sufficiently heavy rate to deter slow payment.
- While taking all possible steps to avoid conflict on site, providing for speedy dispute resolution if any conflict arises, by a predetermined impartial adjudicator [14, 23].

A contract is an agreement between two or more competent parties in which an offer is made and accepted and each party benefits. A contract defines the duties, rights and obligations of the parties, remedy clauses as well as other clauses that are important to characterize the goal of the contract. An agreement is an arrangement between parties regarding a method of action. The goal of this arrangement is to regulate the cooperation actions among partners and it is always associated to a contract [7]. Partners of virtual organizations funded by UE 7th Framework Programme can be presented with several models for consortium agreements. The models are all based on FP7 predecessors. Interest groups of industries, academia and research organizations have developed several models, e.g. IPCA by ICT and Telecom industries, DESCA by academia and research organizations, EU-Car by the automotive industries, IMG by the aerospace industries [11]. Significant issues included in IPCA model cover as follows: rights for affiliates, joint ownership rights, open access structure for Foreground, clauses for using open source software. In a maturing IT governance environment, service level agreements (SLAs) and their supporting service level management (SLM) process need to play an important role. The functions of SLAs are

1. to define what levels of service are acceptable by users and attainable by the service provider;
2. to define the mutually acceptable and agreed upon set of indicators of the quality of service.

A special language for service level agreements for Web services, the Web Service Level Agreement (WSLA) language, just for edition of SLAs, has been elaborated by IBM [12]. The SLM process includes defining an SLA framework, establishing SLAs including level of service and their corresponding metrics, monitoring and reporting on the achieved services and problems encountered, reviewing SLAs and establishing improvement programs. The major governance challenges are that the service levels are to be expressed in business terms and the right SLM/SLA process has to be put in place. The roles most commonly given to SLAs can generally be grouped into six areas:

1. Defining roles and accountability. In virtual organizations a service provider in one SLA can be the customer in another SLA and vice versa. Service level agreements will be used to re-establish the chain of accountability.
2. Managing the customer's expectations regarding a product's delivery on three performance levels (from the top): engineered level, delivered level, guaranteed level.
3. Control implementation and execution, although customers tend to use SLAs to ensure preferential treatment for their particular service requirements relative to all the others in the service provider's network.
4. Providing verification on the customer side. This is especially important to companies that opt for higher levels of QoS.
5. Enabling communications for both service providers and customers to address their needs, expectations, performance relative to those expectations and progress on action items [19, 29, 31].

The goal of SLM is to maintain and improve IT service quality through a constant cycle of agreeing, monitoring, reporting and reviewing IT service achievements [22, 17]. The SLM process is responsible for ensuring the service-level agreements and any underpinning operational level agreements (OLAs) or contracts are met and for ensuring that any adverse impact on service quality is kept to a minimum. The process involves assessing the impact of changes upon service quality and SLAs, both when changes are proposed and after they have been implemented. Some of the most important targets set in the SLAs will relate to service availability and thus require incident resolution within agreed periods.

5. Conclusions

Virtual organizations are open, highly distributed, decentralized, heterarchical, temporal, adhocratic and knowledge-based network organizations acting as collaborative environments for science and technology development. Originally, they were developed in the Internet, however, now they are based on grids and individual access is permitted only to identified and authorized users. Their demands are specified in contracts and agreements. Management of highly decentralized and distributed organizations cannot be based on hierarchy of orders and reports; the best way for management is the general acceptance of rules and regulations by all potential virtual organizations' partners and contractors. Usually contracts are developed for strategic alliances, but for particular services SLAs can be widely applied as a tool for control and management.

References

1. Arcieri, F., Firavanti, F., Nardelli, E. and Talamo, M. (2004) A Specification for Security Services on Computational Grids. In *Grid Services Engineering and Management, First International Conference, GSEM 2004* Erfurt, Germany, Springer, Berlin, pp. 119–135.
2. Bravard, J.L. and Morgan, R. (2006) *Smarter Outsourcing*, Prentice Hall, Dorchester, MA.

3. Bubak M., Turala M. and Wiatr M. (2008) *Cracow'07 Grid Workshop Proceedings*, Cracow, Academic Computer Centre Cyfronet AGH, Cracow.

4. Burn, J.M. and Ash, C. (2002) Knowledge Management Strategies for Virtual Organizations. In Kisielnicki J. (ed.), *Modern Organizations in Virtual Communities*, IRM Press, Hershey, PA, pp. 1–18.

5. Byrne, J.A.(1993) The Virtual Corporation, *Business Week*, February 8, pp. 98–102.

6. Cala, J. and Zielinski, K. (2007) Influence of Virtualization on Process of Grid Application Deployment – CCM Case Study. In Bubak M., Turala M., Wiatr M. (eds.), *Cracow'06 Grid Workshop Proceedings*, Cracow, Academic Computer Centre Cyfronet AGH, Cracow, pp. 367–375.

7. Camarinha-Matos, L.M., Silveri, I., Afsarmanesh, H. and Oliveira, A.I. (2005) Towards a Framework for Creation of Dynamic Virtual Organizations, In Camarinha-Matos L.M., Afsarmanesh H. and Ortiz A.(eds.), *Collaborative Networks and Their Breeding Environments*, Berlin, Springer, pp. 69–80.

8. Cardoso, H.L., Malucelli, A., Rocha, A.P. and Oliveira, E. (2005) Institutional Services for Dynamic Virtual Organizations, In Camarinha-Matos L.M., Afsarmanesh H., Ortiz A. (eds.), *Collaborative Networks and Their Breeding Environments*, Berlin, Springer, pp. 521–528.

9. Cevenini, C. (2002) What Regulation for Virtual Organizations? In Franke U. (ed.), *Managing Virtual Web Organizations in the 21st Century Issues and Challenges*, IGP, Hershey, PA, pp. 318–339.

10. Chudoba, J., Fiala, L., Kmunicek, J., Kosina, J., Kouril, D., Lokajicek, M., Matyska, L., Ruda, M.and Swec J. (2006) VOCE – A Grid Environment for Central Europe. In Bubak M., Turala M., Wiatr, M. (eds.), *Cracow'05 Grid Workshop Proceedings*, Academic Computer Centre Cyfronet AGH, Cracow, pp. 322–328.

11. *Consortium Agreements for Participation under FP7* (2007) IPR-Helpdesk, CIP Programme of the European Commission, Retrieved October 29, 2007, http://www.ipr-helpdesk.org

12. Dan, A., Davis, D., Kearney, R., Keller, A., King, R., Kuebler, D., Ludwig, H., Polan, M., Spreitzer, M. and Youssef, A (2004) Web Services on Demand: WSLA-driven Automated Management, *IBM Systems Journal*, Volume 43, Number 1, Retrieved July 11, 2008 http://www.research.ibm.com/journal/431/dan.html.

13. Dirksen, V. and Smit B. (2002) Exploring the Common Ground of Virtual Communities: Working Towards a "Workable Definition". In Kisielnicki J. (ed.), *Modern Organizations in Virtual Communities*, IRM Press, Hershey, PA, pp. 67–76.

14. Eggleston, B. (1996) *The New Engineering Contract*, Blackwell Science, London.

15. Fellenstein, C. (2005) *On Demand Computing, Technologies and Strategies*, Prentice Hall, Upper Saddle River, NJ.

16. Franke, U.J. (2002) The Competence-based View on the Management of Virtual Web Organizations, In Kisielnicki J. (ed.), *Modern Organizations in Virtual Communities*, IRM Press, Hershey, PA, pp. 19–48.

17. Gatial, E., Balogh, Z., Seleng, M. and Hluchy, L. (2008) Knowledge-Based Negotiation of Service Level Agreement. In Bubak M., Turala M., Wiatr M. (eds.), *Cracow'07 Grid Workshop Proceedings*, Academic Computer Centre Cyfronet AGH, Cracow, pp. 134–139.

18. Kisielnicki, J. (2002) Virtual Organization as a Chance for Enterprise Development. In Kisielnicki J. (ed.), *Modern Organizations in Virtual Communities*, IRM Press, Hershey, PA, pp. 100–115.

19. Lee, J.J. and Ben-Natan, R. (2002) *Integrating Service Level Agreements, Optimizing your OSS for SLA Delivery*, Wiley Publishing Inc, Indianapolis, Indiana.

20. Levermore, D.M. and Hsu, Ch.(2006) *Enterprise collaboration, On-Demand Information Exchange for Extended Enterprises*, New York, Springer Science + Business Media, NY, 2006.

21. Lewis, J. and Weigert, A.(1985) Trust as a Social Reality, *Social Forces*, 4(63), pp. 967–985.

22. Maestranzi, P., Aay, R. and Seery, R.(2002) A Business-Focused Service Level Management Framework. In van Bon J. (ed.), *The Guide to IT Service Management*, Addison-Wesley, London, pp. 778–798.

23. Marcolin, B.L. (2006) Spiraling Effects of IS Outsourcing Contract Interpretations. In Hirschheim R., Heinzl A., Dibbern J. (eds.), *Information Systems Outsourcing*, Springer, Heidelberg, Berlin, pp. 223–256.

24. Minoli, D. (2005) *A Networking Approach to Grid Computing*, John Wiley & Sons, Hoboken, NJ.

25. Pastore, S. (2004) Using Web Service Architecture of a Grid Infrastructure: An Early Implementation of Web Services Actors, Programming a Grid Application to Access Astronomical Databases, In *Grid Services Engineering and Management, First International Conference, GSEM 2004 Erfurt*, Springer, Berlin, pp. 1–15.

26. Plaszczak, P. and Wellner, R.(2006) *Grid Computing, The Savvy Manager's Guide*, Elsevier, Amsterdam.

27. Power, M.J., Desouza, K.C. and Bonifazi, C.(2006) *The Outsourcing Handbook, How to implement a Successful Outsourcing Process*, Kogan Page, London.

28. Prusak, L. (1997) *Knowledge in Organizations*, Butterworth-Heinemann, Boston, MA.

29. Ruijs, L. and Schotanus, A. (2002) Managing the Delivery of Business Information. In van Bon J. (ed.), *The Guide to IT Service Management*, Addison-Wesley, London, pp. 165–177.

30. Saaksjarvi, M. (2006) Success of IS Outsourcing as a Predicator of IS Effectiveness: Does IT Governance Matter? In Hirschheim R., Heinzl A., Dibbern J. (eds.), *Information Systems Outsourcing*, Heidelberg, Berlin, Springer, pp. 283–302.

31. Scholz, A. and Turowski, K. (2002) Enforcing Performance Guarantees Based on Performance Service Levels. In van Bon J. (ed.), *The Guide to IT Service Management*, Addison-Wesley, London, pp. 302–311.

32. Travostino, F., Mambretti, J. and Karmous-Edwards, G.(2006) *Grid Networks Enabling Grids with Advanced Communication Technology*, Chichester, John Wiley &Sons, Ltd, New york.

33. Tsakopoulos, S., Bokma, A. and Plekhanova, V. (2003) Partner Evaluation and Selection in Virtual Enterprises Using a Profile Theory Based Approach. In Camarinha-Matos L.M., Afsarmanesh H. (eds.), *Processes and Foundations for Virtual Organizations*, Kluwer Academic Publishers, Boston, pp. 73–84.
34. Voight von, G., Ruckemann, C-P. and Muller, W. (2006) Development of a Billing Framework for D-Grid. In Bubak M., Turala M., Wiatr M. (eds.), *Cracow'05 Grid Workshop Proceedings*, Academic Computer Centre Cyfronet AGH, Cracow, pp. 467–474.

55

Applying Utility Functions to Adaptation Planning for Home Automation Applications

Pyrros Bratskas, Nearchos Paspallis, Konstantinos Kakousis and George A. Papadopoulos

Abstract

A pervasive computing environment typically comprises multiple embedded devices that may interact together and with mobile users. These users are part of the environment, and they experience it through a variety of devices embedded in the environment. This perception involves technologies which may be heterogeneous, pervasive, and dynamic. Due to the highly dynamic properties of such environments, the software systems running on them have to face problems such as user mobility, service failures, or resource and goal changes which may happen in an unpredictable manner. To cope with these problems, such systems must be autonomous and self-managed. In this chapter we deal with a special kind of a ubiquitous environment, a smart home environment, and introduce a user-preference-based model for adaptation planning. The model, which dynamically forms a set of configuration plans for resources, reasons automatically and autonomously, based on utility functions, on which plan is likely to best achieve the user's goals with respect to resource availability and user needs.

Keywords Pervasive computing · Ubiquitous environment · Utility function · User preferences · Smart home

1. Introduction

Ubiquitous computing environments are characterized by frequent and unpredictable changes. To retain their usability, usefulness, and reliability in such environments, systems must adapt to the changing context conditions. Consequently, there is a growing demand for software systems to be deployed in such environments. In this case, many constraints and requirements must be taken into consideration in order to provide a fair utility to the users. Furthermore, mobile computing environments include a huge spectrum of computation and communication devices that seamlessly aim to augment peoples' thoughts and activities with information, processing, and analysis. Devices such as Personal Digital Assistants (PDAs) and smart-phones have gained a lot of popularity and are increasingly being networked. On the other hand, people use different software development and deployment platforms to design and create applications for such devices. These applications must be context-aware to meet the requirements of the highly dynamic and distributed environment. These types of context-aware systems adapt not only to changes in the environment but also to the user requirements and needs.

But even though the device capabilities become more and more powerful, the design of context-aware applications is constrained not only by physical limitations but also by the need to support a plethora of features such as distribution, scalability, fault tolerance. Indeed, mobile devices will continue to be battery

Pyrros Bratskas, Nearchos Paspallis, Konstantinos Kakousis and George A. Papadopoulos • Department of Computer Science, University of Cyprus, Nicosia, Cyprus.

G.A. Papadopoulos et al. (eds.), *Information Systems Development*, DOI 10.1007/b137171_55,

dependent and operate in an environment where more and more devices will be present and will need to communicate or share resources for the foreseeable future.

A special kind of a ubiquitous environment is a smart home environment where a large number of devices are used for a wide set of purposes. Examples include lighting control modules, heating control panels, light sensors, temperature sensors, gas/water leak detectors, motion detectors, video surveillance, healthcare systems, and advanced remote controls. As in ubiquitous environments, a smart home environment faces challenges like adaptability and context-aware reconfiguration, mobility (user mobility, device mobility and information mobility ([14, 21]) However, unlike them the smart home environment is very much user oriented and thus sensible to user preferences and needs.

In this chapter we describe a self-adaptive distributed approach that automates the configuration and reconfiguration in a ubiquitous computing environment. This approach provides home users with the ability to set up an advanced home environment taking into account user preferences and needs. We focus on a home automation application and we present a model of adaptation in such an environment. In this respect, utility functions are used to choose from a set of dynamically constructed configuration plans. The primary aim is to choose the one that best meets the user preferences and needs while respecting the limitations imposed by the resources availability.

The main contributions of this work include that it makes explicit representations of user preferences and needs with respect to quality dimensions offered by the devices, so that the system can automatically determine what service qualities are required for any given configuration. The system is dynamic and performs reactive adaptation: the application defines which aspects of context are of interest to the application itself, identify dynamically which context changes are relevant, and choose the best configuration to execute. Some of these configurations could be predefined and some others could be created on demand during execution. Furthermore, the system enables the decoupling of user preferences from the lower level mechanisms that carry out those preferences, which in result provides a clean separation of concerns (from an engineering perspective) between what is needed and how it is carried out.

This chapter is organized as follows: Section 2 describes a motivation scenario that illustrates our idea. Then, in Section 3 we discuss about the architecture of the system, how the user's preferences are considered in our chapter, and how we use utility functions to map them into numerical values. Section 4 presents a case study scenario and Section 5 describes the related work and outlines the research challenges of the preference and task-driven computing, but also the use of utility function in some existing middleware systems in the area of ubiquitous computing. Finally, we provide conclusion and outlook for future work in Section 6.

2. Motivating Scenario

In order to better illustrate the motivation for this work, this section describes an application scenario to demonstrate the problem aspects. We have chosen a home automation system which is composed of devices and services operated by users. This includes the air-conditioning system, a multimedia home entertainment sys-tem, a digital lighting system, additional electrical devices. This environment also includes user-carried devices like smart-phones, PDAs, laptops. It is assumed that these devices discover and communicate with each other, using technologies such as Jini [19] and UPnP [18].

When a user returns back to his home, he would like an automatic adjustment of the heating, cooling, and lighting levels in the living room, or the control of the home entertainment system. In this case, the devices can sense the presence of a user, his or her identity, and thus set appropriate values to the different features of the room based on a set of factors (e.g., the day of the week or the time of the day). The values of the different features may also vary given the preferences of the individual user.

In the scenario, we consider four home devices: the stereo, the TV, the air-conditioning, and the digital lighting system. Related to these systems, we also consider the following characteristics: the volume of the stereo system, the room temperature, the TV brightness, and the room luminosity. These devices offer information to the users about their characteristics and functionalities so that the users can configure them. This can be done using any technology such as an electronic house key, a mobile phone, or a PDA.

When the user enters the room, he can activate a command to tune the lights and the temperature in the room, and the volume of the multimedia entertainment system. Several decisions have to be made though. For example, if there is enough natural light, the digital light system can be switched off. Due to this decision, the TV contrast and the room temperature have to be tuned properly during summer or winter months. The TV volume has to be tuned considering the state of the stereo, for example, if the stereo is switched on the TV volume should be muted. On the other hand, if privacy is needed, the user can shut the drapes which influences all other device settings, i.e., the lighting systems must be adjusted again, etc. The scenario is described by the user's point of view and we must map all these operations into system's services. As these environments are user oriented, the user preferences are of high importance, the services must satisfy them taking into ac-count the context constraints and the QoS required by the user.

Our approach suggests the use of a user-preference management application that adapts the home automation environment to the user. To apply adaptation, we need a model which takes into account the user preferences during reasoning and decision making. For instance, there could be a situation with the user leaving home. The system will detect if the user is leaving and pass the control from its remote control or PDA to the home control system. When leaving, all lights should turn off automatically (which saves the user from having to go in each room and switch off the lights manually), and the video surveillance system will be enabled. In the case of detecting movements in the home, the home control sys-tem has two choices depending on the available bandwidth: it will send a video stream to the user's PDA via Internet if there is enough bandwidth, otherwise it will store the video stream to the home control computer.

The adaptation model we introduce in this chapter attempts to make the best choice among all possible ones, by applying a utility function and taking into account the preferences of the user and resource availability. In this model, the user specifies his preferences and then the system maps them onto the services offered in the ubiquitous environment.

3. System overview

The main idea of our approach is to enable users to make requests for tasks to be achieved, which must implicitly take into consideration the user preferences. These preferences guide the selection of a plan capable of executing the task.

When a user enters a room, he selects his preferences based on a set of options. This set can be predefined depending on a common set of user tasks. The selection of preferences also depends on a set of constraints, which can be divided in to logical and context constraints. For example, a logical constraint is that the TV and the stereo cannot be switched on and tuned to different inputs at the same time (i.e., another media is played by the TV and another by the stereo system). A context constraint is related to the resources, i.e., if there is not enough bandwidth, some Internet-based TV channels might not be available.

In this section, we first discuss device and service discovery protocols, as they are basic requirements for enabling synergies. Then, we discuss about the configuration plans and how the user preferences are taken into account by the system. We also present how the utility functions are constructed, and how the system operates based on the selection of the best plan using the utility function.

3.1. Device and Service Discovery

In a home automation environment with devices that provide services without requiring any user attention, service discovery is essential to achieving such sophistication. It enables devices and services to discover, configure, and communicate with each other. Device interaction protocols like UPnP, Bonjour [5], SLP [10], Bluetooth SDP [4], and Jini allow the dynamic discovery of devices in a home environment network without any need for user interaction. These technologies al-low interested clients to dynamically discover available services in a network and also they supply the needed mechanisms for browsing through services, as well as for detecting and using the desired service. Dynamic and automatic service discovery is particularly challenging in ad hoc communication networks, where no fixed infrastructure exists. Such networks are characterized by devices which connect to each other, spontaneously offer and acquire services and then disconnect [3].

3.2. Configuration Plans

Our system uses configuration plans which are applied to achieve the user goals. A configuration plan is a plan which defines how the components are connected to each other in order to provide the functionality required by the application. Thus, a plan can be formally thought of as being like a protocol which defines the communication of the user with the environment.

The resources in the environment are subject to dynamic changes concerning their values and/or properties. Also, new devices can be added and others can be deactivated, the luminosity in the environment may increase or decrease, batteries discharge, etc. Taking that into account, the choice of configuration plans can make the adaptation process easier. In order to perform adaptations, we decouple the preference specification from the middleware specification which provides a separation of concerns. In this way, the "adaptation logic" is one level higher than the middleware. That means that the users do not deal with the values and names of resources, but its viewpoint over the system are the configuration plans. Some of these plans can be predefined based on a set of user preferences. On the other hand, other plans can be redefined if changes occur in the system, as well as new configuration plans that can be added.

We make the following assumptions:

- Plans vs utility: For any particular adaptation, there may be multiple configuration plans that can achieve it. The choice of a particular plan is based on the utility it offers to the system.
- Plans vs resources: Each plan requires a set of resources with values defined by user preferences in order to provide a certain QoS to the user.
- Utility vs user goals: The utility offered by a plan may not satisfy the user at a certain moment. For example, the user in a room may want to prefer natural light to the privacy by opening the drapes. It is up to the user to decide his preference priorities and guide the plan execution accordingly.
- User needs vs offered utility: Each device defines its domain of the offered value. The utility of a plan will be evaluated with respect to user needs for a certain utility and to the utility offered by the configuration plan. The difference between them will be weighed in order to prefer one plan to another.
- Plans vs distributed, dynamic planning: Plans are not predefined but rather they are dynamically generated at run time by discovering and coordinating with the set of available, distributed devices. To achieve this, we assume a component-based approach, where applications are formed as component compositions and where components might become available or unavailable dynamically [9].

Based on these assumptions the system operates as follows: the user-attached de-vice performs device discovery as the user enters the home. Then a set of variation points is defined based on context and logical constraints. The decision on which variation point is the best one is driven by the user preferences. As a result, the system performs adaptation after the selection of a new variation point. This operation is depicted in Fig. 55.1.

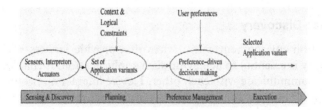

Figure 55.1. The system lifecycle.

3.3. User Preferences

The problem of modeling preferences has been widely researched in other fields. For instance, Agrawal and Wimmers in [1] present a preference model that allows users to supply preferences and be combined, using preference functions, for decision making. Hafenrichter and Kie&#ßling in [11] represent preferences as strict partial orders for the efficient integration of preference querying. Both approaches are used in the field of database research.

In our case, we use a simplified version of the preference model introduced by Henricksen et al. in [12]. This preference model employs a scoring mechanism, which is loosely based on the scheme proposed by Agrawal and Wimmers. Each preference is assigned with a score which is a numerical value in the range of [0, 1] where larger score indicates higher preference. Four special scores represent prohibition, indifference, obligation, and error conditions.

Applying this preference model to our scenario yields the following preferences:

p_1 = when Privacy (public) and Light (natural, 30)
$w_1 = 0.7$
p_2 = when Privacy (public) and Light (natural, 10)
$w_2 = 0.2$
p_3 =when Privacy (public) and Light (artificial)
$w_3 = 0.7$

The value W_i is used by the utility function in order to compute the utility of a configuration. In fact, W_i is a weight that reflects how much the user cares about the user preference W_i

3.4. Utility Functions

To perform adaptation, the selected plan must meet the user's preferences in order to receive a good utility and also to minimize the use of shared resources. To achieve this, we use utility functions to map the user preferences for QoS to a function that defines how a selected plan satisfies the user preferences. The aim of the utility functions is to express the quality of the adaptation for the user. Its input includes the user preferences taking into account the current context and the available resources, while its output is the degree to which a variation point satisfies the user goals. Utility functions are in general n-dimensional functions taking as arguments values from an n-dimensional utility space [2]. In our work, we adopt a simple approach, which defines the overall utility as a weighted sum of the set of utility functions.

Let $P = \{cp_1, \ldots, cP_n\}$ be the set of configuration plans and let q_i for $i = 1 \ldots n$ be the corresponding utility of the adaptation when the plan p_i is selected. Then $Q = \{q_1, \ldots, q_n\} q_i$ is the set of utility dimensions related to these plans. This utility depends on the availability of resources and on the logical and context constraints. To express this with a mathematical formula, let R be the set of resources and C the set of constraints. We assign to each resource a weight w which expresses its availability as well as its value. As user preferences express user constraints and needs, they can be thought of as predicates that must be maximized.

Thus, the utility function F related to the QoS q_i is expressed as

$$F(q_i) = f_{user\_need}(x_1, \ldots, x_m) \text{ where } x_i \in R \cup C \quad \forall i \in 1 \ldots m.$$

Then, the utility function associated to a configuration plan cp_i is expressed as the normalized, weighted sum of the dimensional utilities as follows:

$$U(cp_i) = \frac{\sum_{i=1}^{n} w_i F(q_i)}{\sum_{i=1}^{n} w_i} \quad \forall cp_i \in P.$$

The utility function $U : P \rightarrow [0, 1]$ is a function that maps and transforms a set of configuration plans into a numerical values and the weight w_i reflects how much the user values the particular user preference p_i. This process also takes into account the availability of resources and context constraints.

For any particular adaptation, there may be multiple configuration plans that can achieve it. The choice of a plan variant is based on the utility it offers to the system. Each configuration plans requires a set of resources with values defined by user preferences in order to provide a certain QoS to the user. On the other hand, its utility may not satisfy the user at a certain moment. It is up to the user to decide his preference priorities and guide the plan selection accordingly.

4. Evaluation

Existing solutions for self-adaptation consider all configurations of applications and choose the ones that best fit the user's preferences and needs. In a highly dynamic environment where the number of such configurations is quite numerous, the task of managing them can be time consuming.

In this section, we show that our approach offers some benefits as opposed to other approaches. For example, in the comparison with the MADAM approach [7], the main advantage is that the plans can include adaptation at the server side (assuming a client–server model), whereas in MADAM adaptations were limited to local only. This is important because it enables adaptations in ubiquitous computing environments, which otherwise (i.e., in MADAM) is very difficult.

4.1. Case Study Example

Let us revisit the application scenario of Section 2. Given the smart home environment, we consider three context types: *temperature* which corresponds to the room temperature, *luminosity* which corresponds to the room light, and privacy which express the user's need for privacy. Let W_t, W_l, and W_p be the weights indicating how the user may specify the relative importance of the quality dimensions for the context types, temperature, luminosity, and privacy, respectively. Table 55.1 illustrates the importance that the user gives to any of these dimensions for three different configurations and Table 55.2 the dimensional utility function for the user, defined as a set of coefficient values where each coefficient specifies the utility value for a quality layer of a QoS dimension.

Table 55.1. Dimensional weights.

Configuration	W_t	W_l	W_p
1st	0.7	0.3	.0.5
2nd	0.3	0.8	0.5
3rd	0.2	0.2	0

Table 55.2. Dimensional utility functions.

Configuration	$F(t)$	$F(l)$	$F(p)$
1st	0.8	0.6	0.5
2nd	0.7	0.5	0.4
3rd	0.6	0.4	0.3

The temperature and luminosity properties take their values in the ranges [10, 40] and [0, 40], respectively, while the privacy property is a binary variable taking the values *true* or *false* according to the user's preference for privacy. If we consider that the user goal is to illuminate the room, then the first service variant will be whether the light is natural or artificial. This is closely related with privacy since opening the drapes will have an impact not only on the privacy property but also on the temperature property because the sunny light will impact it as well.

As can be seen from Table 55.1, the first configuration perceives the temperature dimension as the most important ($w_t p_l$) while the second configuration gives more importance to the luminosity dimension. We assume that privacy is needed for these two configurations which is not the case for the third one. The utility for each configuration is shown in Table 55.3.

Table 55.3. Utility for each configuration.

Configuration	1st	2nd	3rd
Utility	0.66	0.5	0.5

5. Related Work

The notion of task-driven computing was first introduced by Wang and Garlan in [20]. The approach is based on two basic concepts, tasks and sessions, and that it is possible to let users interact with their computing environments in terms of high-level tasks and free them from low-level configuration activities.

Implementing this notion, the Aura infrastructure [16] performs automatic con-figuration and reconfiguration in ubiquitous computing environments according to the users' tasks. For that, the infra-structure needs to know what the user needs from the environment in order to carry out his tasks. It also needs mechanisms to optimally match the user's needs to the capabilities and resources in the environment. Aura infrastructure addresses two principles of autonomic computing as they were introduced in [13]: self-optimization and self-healing from the point of view of user's task in a ubiquitous environment.

In [17], the authors describe an approach to self-configuring in computing environments. Their adaptation architecture allows explicit representation of user's tasks, preferences, and service qualities.

Henricksen et al. present an approach involving the use of preference information as a basis for making flexible adaptation decisions in [12]. Their work focuses on generic preference and programming models that can be used for arbitrary context-aware applications and can facilitate preference sharing among applications. They introduce a preference model and a programming model to support a common form of context-dependent choice problem. The authors consider preferences as a link between the context and appropriate application behaviors placing them in a layer of separation between the application and its context model allowing them to evolve independently of one another.

In MADAM, utility functions were used to enable self-adaptive behavior in mobile applications. Basic composition plans were provided by the developer and were dynamically used to from the set of possible configurations (variants). Then, the MADAM middleware was used to evaluate them at run time, based on the con-textual and resource conditions, and automatically select the most suitable option. Naturally, the MADAM approach is very similar to this approach, as our approach builds on it and attempts to extend it. The main limitation that we attempt to over-come is that of limited support for ubiquitous computing. While MADAM enabled the adaptation of locally hosted applications, it fails to support adaptation of remotely hosted services (i.e., an application running on a different host). This limits the domain of possible applications to locally deployed software only, with apparent limitations concern-ing ubiquitous computing.

MUSIC middleware builds on the legacy of MADAM and attempts to extend its scope to ubiquitous computing environments. As described in [15], the MUSIC planning framework is an extension of the MADAM planning framework, which supports the adaptation of component-based architectures. The extension proposed supports self-adaptation of ubiquitous applications to changes in the service provider landscape. The planning middleware evaluates discovered remote services as alternative configurations for the functionalities required by an application. In the case of services, the planning framework deals directly with SLA protocols supported by the service providers to negotiate the appropriate QoS for the user, while our approach deals with utility functions and uses an explicit representation of user preferences allowing users to supply their own preferences and providing flexibility and spontaneity, in response to changes in user needs and operating conditions. As MUSIC is still work in progress, there has been no real-world evaluation of it, yet.

6. Conclusions

In this chapter we address the self-adaptation in a home automation environment. The adaptation is performed through the use of configuration plans which are selected using a utility function mechanism. The choice of a plan, which best meets the user requirements and needs, is made by taking into account the user preferences which are represented explicitly during the calculation of the utility. This makes the system dynamic and offers transparency to the users.

A future direction of this work will be the study of issues like diagnosis and recovery by introducing a mechanism supporting fault tolerance. On the other hand, as a good starting point over the adaptation for a home automation application, another future direction of this work could be the context and service discovery routing in such a system. Home automation applications represent a special segment of networked wireless devices with its unique set of requirements related to the set of home networking applications and the perceived operation of the system.

Acknowledgments

The authors of this chapter would like to thank their partners in the IST-MUSIC project and acknowledge the partial financial support given to this research by the European Union (6th Framework Programme, IST 035166).

References

1. Agrawal, R., Wimmers, E. L. 2000. A framework for expressing and combining preferences. *ACM SIGMOD Conference on Management of Data*, Dallas, TX, 2000. ACM Press, New York.
2. Alia, M., Eide, V. S. W., Paspallis, N., Eliassen, F., Hallsteinsen, S., Papadopoulos, G.A. 2007. A utility-based adaptivity model for mobile applications. *21st International Conference on Advanced Information Networking and Applications Workshops (AINAW'07)*, Niagara Falls, Ontario, Canada, May 21–23, 2007, IEEE Computer Society Press, pp. 556–563
3. Bettstetter, C., Renner, C. 2000. *A Comparison of Service Discovery Protocols and Implementa-tion of the Service Location Protocol.* EUNICE 2000, Sixth EUNICE Open European Sum-mer School, Twente, Netherlands, September 2000.
4. Bluetooth Special Interest Group, Bluetooth Core Specification – Version 2.1. 2007
5. Bonjour Protocol Specification. http://developer.apple.com/networking/bonjour/specs.html
6. Edwards, W. K. 2006. Discovery systems in ubiquitous computing. *IEEE Pervasive Computing* 5, 2, 70–77, April 2006.
7. European IST-FP6 project MADAM (Mobility And aDaptation enabling Middleware) http://www.ist-madam.org
8. European IST-FP6 project MUSIC (Self-adapting applications for Mobile Users In ubiquitous Computing environments) http://www.ist-music.eu
9. Floch, J., Hallsteinsen, S., Stav, E., Eliassen, F., Lund, K., Gjorven, E. 2006. Using architecture models for runtime adaptability. *IEEE Software* 23, 2, 62–70, March 2006.
10. Guttman, E., Perkins, C., Veizades, J., and Day, M. 1999. Service Location Protocol, Version 2. RFC. RFC Editor.

11. Hafenrichter, B., Kießling, W. 2005. Optimization of relational preference queries. 16th Austral-asian Database Conference – Volume 39 (Newcastle, Australia). H. E. Williams and G. Dobbie, Eds. *ACM International Conference Proceeding Series*, vol. 103. Australian Computer Society, Darlinghurst, Australia, 175–184.

12. Henricksen, K., Indulska, J., Rakotonirainy, A. 2006. Using context and preferences to implement self-adapting pervasive computing applications. *Journal of Software Practice and Experience, Special Issue on Experiences with Auto-Adaptive and Reconfigurable Systems*, 36(11–12), 1307–1330. Wiley, New York, 2006

13. Kephart, J., Chess, D. M. 2003. The vision of autonomic computing. *IEEE Computer Magazine* 36, 1, 41–50, January 2003.

14. Labrinidis, A.., Stefanidis, A. 2005. Panel on mobility in sensor networks. *6th International Conference on Mobile Data Management (MDM'05)*, pp. 333–334. Ayia Napa, Cyprus, May 2005.

15. Rouvoy, R., Eliassen, F., Floch, J., Hallsteinsen, S., Stav, E. 2008. Composing components and services using a planning-based adaptation middleware. *7th International Symposium on Software Composition (SC'08)*. pp. 52–67 of LNCS 4954 (Springer). Budapest, Hungary. March 29–30, 2008.

16. Sousa, J. P. and Garlan, D. 2002. Aura: An architectural framework for user mobility in ubiquitous computing environments. *IFIP 17th World Computer Congress – Tc2 Stream/3rd IEEE/IFIP Conference on Software Architecture: System Design, Development and Maintenance* (August 25–30, 2002). J. Bosch, W. M. Gentleman, C. Hofmeister, and J. Kuusela, Eds. IFIP Conference Proceedings, vol. 224. Kluwer B.V., Deventer, The Netherlands, 29–43.

17. Sousa, J. P., Poladian, V., Garlan, D., Schmerl, B., Shaw, M. 2006. Task-based adaptation for ubiquitous computing. IEEE Transactions on Systems, Man, and Cybernetics, Part C: *Applications and Reviews, Special Issue on Engineering Autonomic Systems* 36(3), May 2006.

18. UPnP Forum 2007. Universal Plug and Play. http://www.upnp.org

19. Waldo, J. 2000 The Jini specifications. *2nd Addison-Wesley Longman Publishing Co.*, Inc, Boston, MA.

20. Wang, Z., Garlan, D. Task-driven computing. Technical Report CMU-CS-00-154 School of Computer Science Carnegie Mellon University http://reports-archive.adm.cs.cmu.edu/anon/2000/CMU-CS-00-154.pdf

21. Zachariadis, S., Mascolo, C., Emmerich, W. 2002. Exploiting logical mobility in mobile computing middleware. *22nd International Conference on Distributed Computing Systems – Workshops (ICDCS 2002 Workshops)*. July 2002, Vienna, Austria.

56

Current Trends in Testing XMLMSs

Irena Mlynkova

Abstract

   Since XML technologies have become a standard for data representation, a huge amount of XMLMSs have emerged as well. Consequently, it is necessary to be able to experimentally test and compare their versatility, behaviour and efficiency. In this chapter we provide an overview of existing approaches to testing XMLMSs and we discuss respective consequences and recommendations.

Keywords XML benchmarking · XML test suites · XML data generators

1. Introduction

Since XML [10] has become a de facto standard for data representation and manipulation, there exists a huge amount of so-called XML processing tools, or more comprehensive *XML Management Systems* (XMLMSs) dealing with efficient management of XML data. They usually involve methods for storing, validating and querying of XML documents, nevertheless, there may also exist XMLMSs which support more complex operations with XML data, such as transforming, updating, exchanging, compressing. Consequently, being users, we need to know which of the existing XMLMSs is the most sufficient for our particular application. On the other hand, being vendors who develop a new XMLMS, we need to test correctness and performance of our system and, especially, to compare its main advantages with competing SW. And being analysts, we are especially interested in comparison of various aspects of existing systems from different points of view.

   A natural solution is to find results of an appropriate analysis. But, although there currently exists a number of such analytical papers, the speed of development of new XMLMSs is high and, hence, their results soon become obsolete. On the other hand, if we manage to find reasonably up-to-date analytical results, the testing scenarios usually do not fit well to all our use cases. Hence, in most situations we still need to prepare our own testing sets of data and operations that reasonably represent our situation.

   The aim of this chapter is to provide an overview of possibilities how to acquire or prepare XML testing scenarios and what are the limitations of the current approaches. We focus on existing conformance test suites, repositories of real-world XML data, XML benchmarking projects and data generators and we describe and discuss their main characteristics and especially issues related to their versatility. Finally, we provide an overview of the key findings and related recommendations. We will not compare particular XMLMSs, but systems and methods using which they can be tested and compared. We will show that the solutions for basic XML technologies are common, but in case of advanced or new ones the situation is much worse.

Irena Mlynkova • Department of Software Engineering, Charles University in Prague, Czech Republic.

G.A. Papadopoulos et al. (eds.), *Information Systems Development*, DOI 10.1007/b137171_56,

The text is structured as follows: The second section classifies and describes the existing approaches. Section 3 provides a summary of the findings and recommendations. And, finally, Section 4 provides conclusions.

2. Overview of Existing Approaches

Currently, there exists a number of approaches to experimental testing of XMLMSs and they can be classified variously. In general, a *benchmark* or a *test suite* is a set of *testing scenarios* or *test cases*, i.e. data and related operations which enable to compare versatility, efficiency or behaviour of *systems under test* (SUT). In our case the set of data involves XML documents, possibly with their XML schemes, whereas the set of operations can involve any kind of XML-related data operations.

From the point of view of the type of data we can distinguish benchmarks which involve real-world data and benchmarks involving synthetic data. Though the former type seems to have more reasonable application, the problem is that according to analyses [35] real-world XML documents are quite simple and do not cover most of the constructs allowed by W3C specifications. For instance, there are methods whose space complexity is closely related to depth of XML documents [22] or methods that require training a neural network on particular data [42]. And acquiring such specific real-world XML data can be difficult. A different type of classification distinguishes approaches involving a fixed set of testing data sets and approaches which enable to create them dynamically on the basis of user-specified parameters.

On the basis of the purpose of an XML benchmark, we can further distinguish benchmarks which deal with various types of data operations, such as parsing, validating, querying, updating or transforming. And in particular areas, we can establish also more finer classification on the basis of exploited languages and constructs, such as DTD [10] vs. XML Schema [43, 6] benchmarks, XQuery [7] vs. XPath benchmarks, XPath 1.0 [17] vs. XPath 2.0 [5] benchmarks.

2.1. XML Data Sets

Currently, one of the most typical approaches to XML benchmarking is exploitation of fixed sets of real-world XML data that represent a particular field of XML processing. Apart from rather interesting than useful examples of XML documents, such as the Bible in XML [24], Shakespeare's plays [9], classic novels in XML [46], the most common types of testing data sets are usually XML exports of various databases, such as *IMDb* [28] database of movies and actors, *FreeDB* [26] database of musical CDs, *DBLP* [18] database of scientific papers, *Medical Subject Headings* [34] database of medical terms, or repositories of real-world XML data coming from various resources, such as project *INEX* [29], *Open Directory Project* [37]. There also exist examples of rather special XML data, such as human genes [27], protein sequences [45], astronomical NASA data [47], linguistic trees in XML [44], having very uncommon structure and, hence, requiring special processing. Some of these collections were not originally in XML format, but they were converted and stored in XML repositories.

As mentioned before, the real-world XML data have two disadvantages. They are usually very simple and most of them are provided without respective operations. Hence, though they represent a realistic resource of information, they enable to test only a limited set of aspects or situations.

2.2. XML Data Generators

A natural solution to the previous problem is to generate the testing data sets synthetically. Currently, we can find several implementations of XML data generators which generate XML data on the basis of user-provided setting of parameters.

The methods can be classified on the basis of the input parameters. The most general classification differentiates so-called *schema-unaware* and *template-based* generators. The schema-unaware generators, such as *NiagDataGen* [1], support general structural parameters (e.g. number of levels of the required XML trees, numbers of subelements at each level) and exploit various strategies, such as Zip's law, Markov chains, statistical distributions, to generate as realistic structure as possible randomly, but within the parameters. On the other hand, the template-based generators, such as *ToXgene* [4], *VeXGene* [30], *MemBeR* [2], get as input a kind of annotated XML schema and generate XML documents valid against it. The structure of the resulting data is specified using the schema more precisely (although the full generality of DTD or XML schema languages is not usually supported), whereas the annotations provide even more specific information, such as probability distributions of occurrences of elements/attributes or lengths of string literals.

Apart from specification of structure of the required data, the generators also often deal with problems such as where to get the textual data or element/attribute names to achieve as natural result as possible. For some applications, such as XML full-text operations or XML compressing, may be the content of textual data important, but for techniques related to parsing, validating or querying the aspects are of marginal importance.

In general, the biggest advantage of the data generators is that they usually support a huge number of parameters a user can specify and, hence, provide quite a precise result. But, on the other hand, this is also a big disadvantage, because the user must know all these parameters of the required data. And this is of course realistic only in case of XML experts. Similarly to the case of real-world XML data, the synthetic XML data are not accompanied with respective operations as well. In fact, there seems to be no generator of XPath queries over the given data having specified features.

2.3. Parsing and Validating XML Data

The basic operations with XML data are parsing and validating, i.e., checking their correctness. It involves conformance to W3C recommendations and, eventually, existing XML schemes. Naturally, the testing scenarios consist of correct and incorrect data and the aim is to test whether the SUT recognizes them correctly.

2.3.1. XML Conformance Test Suites

The W3C consortium provides so-called *XML Conformance Test Suites* [33], i.e. a set of metrics to determine how well a particular implementation conforms to *XML 1.0 (Second Edition)*, *XML 1.0 (Third Edition)*, *XML 1.1 (First Edition)* and *Namespaces in XML 1.1*. It consists of a set of 2000 XML documents which can be divided into two basic types – *binary* and *output tests*. Binary tests contain a set of valid XML documents, invalid XML documents, non-well-formed XML documents, well-formed errors tied to external entities and XML documents with optional errors. Depending on the category, the tested parser must either accept or reject the document correctly (therefore, the tests are called binary). On the other hand, the output tests enable to test whether the respective applications report information as required by the recommendations.

2.3.2. XML Parsers

On the other hand, the key users' interest in XML parsing and validating is efficiency and space overhead. Currently, we can distinguish so-called *event-driven* and *object-model* parsers. The former ones read the document and while reading they return the respective fragments of data, whereas the latter ones read the document and build its complete model in memory. The former ones can be further divided into *push-parsers* and *pull-parsers*. In case of push-parsers the reading cannot be influenced, whereas pull-parsers read the next data only if they are "asked" to. And, later, there have also occurred their various combinations. Naturally, each of the approaches has its (dis)advantages and limitations that need to be experimentally tested.

Currently, there exist analyses [e.g., 23, 38] comparing either same or distinct types of XML parsers. But, they all involve only a selected subset of real world or synthetic XML data. Although the authors usually make the testing sets as well as *test harnesses*[1] available, there seems to be no true benchmarking project which would enable to analyse all aspects and especially bottlenecks of XML parsing.

2.4. Querying XML Data

Since the key operation with XML data is undoubtedly querying, the biggest set of conformance test suites and XML benchmarks focuses on it. The W3C provides the *XML Query Test Suite (XQTS 1.0.2)* [40] which contains over 15000 test cases, i.e. queries and expected results, which enable to test whether the W3C XML Query Language is fully supported. There also exists a set of W3C *XML Query Use Cases* [15], i.e. examples illustrating important applications for an XML query language. Though they are not considered as test cases, they are often used as minimal requirements for an XML benchmark.

In general, there exists a large set of true XML query benchmarking projects. Their aim is to analyse versatility and performance of XML querying tools, i.e. the amount of query constructs they support and how efficiently they are processed. The seven best known representatives are *XMark* [12], *XOO7* [11], *XMach-1* [8], *MBench* [41], *XBench* [48], *XPathMark* [25] and *TPoX* [36]. The overview of their key features according to which they can be classified is depicted in Table 56.1.

The first characteristic of a benchmark is its type. We differentiate so-called *application-level* and *micro* benchmarks. Since an application-level benchmark is created to compare and contrast various applications, a micro benchmark should be used to evaluate performance of a single system in various situations. Consequently, the operations respectively differ. In the former case the queries are highly different trying to cover the key situations, whereas in the latter case they can contain subsets of highly similar queries which differentiate, e.g. in selectivity. Note that the only representative of micro benchmarks is MBench project.

Another set of benchmark characteristics describe the general purpose of the benchmark, i.e. the number of users it is intended for, the number of applications it simulates and the number of documents within its data set. As we can see, most of the benchmarks are single-user, single-application and involve only a single-document. This observation meets the general criteria that a benchmark should be simple. Nevertheless, while the single-document data set is not of a great problem, the single-application feature can be highly restrictive. The only exception, XBench, involves four classes of XML applications with different requirements – text-centric/single-document (TC/SD), text-centric/multiple documents (TC/MD), data-centric/single-document (DC/SD) and data-centric/multiple documents (DC/MD). Nevertheless, there are XML use cases that cannot be simulated only using various data sets. XMach-1 and TPoX projects are multi-user and enable to test other XML management aspects, such as indexing, schema validation, concurrency control, transaction processing, network characteristics, communication costs. They both consist of four parts – an XML database, application server(s), loaders and browser clients. The SUT is represented via the application server which interacts with the XML database. The loaders load and delete various XML data into/from the database via the application servers. And browser clients are assumed to query and retrieve the stored XML data. In addition, since most of the features of the systems can be controlled via parameters, they can be even set to query-only, single-user, single-document.

Another important aspect of XML benchmarking projects are characteristics of the data sets. As we can see, all the representatives involve a data generator that enables to influence parameters of the synthetic data and various default data sets. But, on the other hand, in most cases the only parameter that can be specified is the size of the data. Most of the benchmarks involve own simple data generator, some of them (i.e. XBench and TPoX) exploit a more complex data generator (in the two cases ToXgene), but pre-set a subset of its parameters. Also note that all the projects involve also one or more DTDs or XSDs[2] of the data.

---

[1] A software that tests a set of programs by running them under varying conditions and monitor their behavior and outputs.
[2] XML Schema definitions

Table 56.1. Main characteristics of XML query benchmarks.

	XMark	XOO7	XMach-1	MBench	XBench	XPathMark	TPoX
Type of benchmark	Application-level	Application-level	Application-level	Micro	Application-level	Application-level	Application-level
Number of users	Single	Single	Multiple	Single	Single	Single	Multiple
Number of applications	1	1	1	1	4	1	1 but complex
Documents in data set	Single	Single	Multiple	Single	Single/ multiple	Single	Multiple
Data generator	✓	✓	✓	✓	✓	✓	✓
Key parameters	Size	Depth, fan-out, size of textual data	Number of documents /elements /words in a sentence, probability of phrases /links	Size	Size	Size	Size + number of users
Default data set	Single 100 MB document	3 documents (small, medium, large) with pre-defined parameters	4 data sets of 10000/ 100000/1000000/ 10000000 documents	Single-document with 728000 nodes	Small (10 MB)/ normal (100 MB)/large (1 GB)/huge (10 GB) document	1 XMark document and 1 sample document from a book	XS (3.6 millions of documents, 10 users), S, M, L, XL, XXL (360 billions of documents, 1 million users)
Schema of documents	DTD of an Internet auction database	DTD derived from OO7 [13] relational schema	DTD of an document having chapters, paragraphs and sections	DTD/XSD of the recursive element	DTD/XSD	DTD	XSD
Number of schemes	1	1	Multiple	9	1	2	1 consisting of multiple
Number of queries	20	23	8	49	19, 17, 14, 16	47 + 12	7
Query language	XQuery	XQuery	XQuery	SQL, XPath	XQuery	XPath	XQuery
Number of updates	0	0	3	7	0	0	10

The last important set of characteristics describes the operation set of the projects. All the projects involve a set of queries, some of them (i.e. XMach-1, MBench and TPoX) also a set of update operations. As we have mentioned before, the two multi-user benchmarks also support additional, less XML-like operations with the data. Nevertheless, the most popular operations are XQuery queries or in some cases (i.e. MBench and XBench) the queries are specified abstractly and, hence, can be expressed in any language, though their XQuery expression is usually provided as well. The queries try to cover various aspects of the language, such as ordering, casting, wildcard expressions, aggregations, references, constructors, joins, user-defined functions.

2.4.1. Analysis of Benchmarking Projects

Paper [3] analyses the first five benchmarking projects and deals with their purpose, versatility, current usability, etc. The authors have found out that only 1/3 of papers on XQuery processing use a kind of benchmark which is probably caused by the fact that 38% of benchmark queries are incorrect or outdated. In addition, 29% of the queries are XPath 1.0 queries, 61% are XPath 2.0 queries and only 10% cannot be expressed in XPath. An important finding is that the most popular benchmarking project seems to be the simple XMark. It indicates that users do not want to bother with complicated setting of parameters.

2.4.2. Benchmark Repository

From the overview of the benchmarks and their various features it is obvious, that a single fixed set of queries cannot allow testing of various aspects of applications. Hence, the main aim of the *MemBeR repository* [2] of micro-benchmarks is to allow users to add new data sets and/or queries for specific performance assessment tasks. The repository has a predefined structure involving XML documents and their parameters, XML queries and their parameters, experiments and their parameters (i.e. related documents and/or queries), micro-benchmarks (i.e. sets of experiments) and micro benchmark result sets. A new micro benchmark or a new result set must be specified as an XML document conforming to a predefined DTD which describes all the related characteristics.

Currently the repository contains three categories of benchmarks – XPath, query stability and XQuery. The benchmarks can be further classified into performance, consumption, correctness and completeness benchmarks on the basis of the resulting metric, type of scalability (data/query), usage of schema, query processing scenarios (e.g. persistent database, streaming), query language and tested language feature.

2.5. Transforming, Updating and Other Operations with XML Data

Since the key aspects of XML processing are undoubtedly parsing, validating and querying, most of the existing benchmarking projects focus mainly on them. But, there are also other popular and useful XML technologies, such as XSL transformations [16], XML compression methods and, hence, there also occur benchmarks determined for other purposes. Surprisingly, the number of such special-purpose projects is low or the only existing representatives are quite old and, hence, obsolete. An example of the situation is benchmarking of XSL transformations. The only known benchmarking project is XSLTMark [31] which is not maintained anymore and supports only constructs of version 1.0 from 1999. Similarly, there exist several analytical papers which compare a subset of XSLT processors [e.g. 32, 14], nevertheless, most of them are based on the obsolete XSLTMark data set or distinct sets of real-world data.

From one point of view the situation may be caused by the fact that most of other technologies, such as XSLT, XPointer [19], XLink [20], are based on one of the basic ones, mostly XPath queries. Thus, an argument against special benchmarking projects may be that projects for benchmarking XML queries are sufficient enough. But, on the other hand, the exploitation of, e.g. XPath in XSL can be quite different from typical exploitation in data retrieval. And, in addition, there are other important aspects of XSL transformations than the path queries which influence their correctness and efficiency. Furthermore, if we consider even more special operations on XML data, such as XML compressing, the respective benchmark may deal with features which are for other types of XML processing marginal. However, the amount of these special-purpose benchmarks is still low – we can hardly find at least a single representative for each of the areas.

On the other hand, there are XML technologies that have become popular only recently and, consequently, their benchmarking projects are relatively rare. A representative of this situation is XML updating. As we can see in Table 56.1, some of the existing query benchmarks involve few update operations, but a true XML update benchmarking project has been proposed only recently [39]. And a similar situation can be found in case of technologies related to semantic Web [21].

3. Summary

We can sum up the state of the art of existing XML benchmarking projects into the following findings and recommendations:

- The most typical source of testing XML data are repositories with fixed, real-world XML data. But though the data are realistic, they are usually too simple to cover all possible XML constructs and, mostly, they are not accompanied with respective operations.
- A solution to this problem can bring various generators of synthetic XML data. They enable to specify the precise structure of the target data and exploit various approaches to simulate real-world situations. Nevertheless, the problem is that such systems require a user well skilled in XML technologies and, especially, data characteristics. And, naturally, these data are not accompanied with respective operations as well.
- Since parsing and validating are two most important basic operations with XML data, the W3C has defined appropriate conformance test suites which enable to test their correct behaviour. Hence, this area of testing sets is well covered.
- On the other hand, the key users' interest of XML parsing is efficiency and space overhead. Although there exist several papers and projects dealing with this topic that provide results of respective analyses, there seems to be no true test suite that would cover the key influencing aspects and bottlenecks.
- The second key operation on XML data is undoubtedly querying. The W3C provides the XML Query Test Suite and XML Query Use Cases which enable to test the full support of the language and provide a set of typical application of XML querying. Furthermore, there exist several well-known and verified benchmarking projects with different purposes, features, advantages and disadvantages.
- Although all the query benchmarking projects involve a kind of data generator, the most popular ones seem to be those which are of simple usage (e.g. XMark), i.e. having only few parameters to specify. On the other hand, these benchmarks usually provide only very simple data, of one special type and complexity.
- In general, the area of query benchmarks is relatively wide and the projects usually try to cover the key query operations. But if we consider other XML technologies which involve path queries, such as XSLT, XPointer, XLink, the typical usage can strongly differ. Hence, these technologies require special treatment and special benchmark projects. Surprisingly, in these areas the amount of respective benchmarks is surprisingly low. Mostly there exists no appropriate benchmark project.

The general observation of our analysis is that the basic XML data operations, i.e. parsing, validating and querying, are well covered with respective test suites and benchmarking projects. The situation in case of other technologies is much worse. Nevertheless, in these cases we can always exploit either real-world XML data or, if they do not cover our test cases, synthetically generated data sets.

On the other hand, this situation opens a wide research area of both proposing special-purpose benchmarking projects and test suites, as well as performing respective analyses of existing implementations.

4. Conclusion

The main goal of this chapter was to describe and discuss the current state of the art and open issues of ways how to test XMLMSs. We have dealt especially with the problem of gathering or preparing the testing data sets and operations. We have focussed mainly on conformance test suites, repositories of real-world XML data, XML benchmarking projects and data generators. We have provided an overview and classification of the existing approaches and their features and summed up the key findings and recommendations. In general, this chapter should serve as a good starting point for users, developers and analysts who are interested in testing a selected subset of XMLMS implementations.

Acknowledgments

This work was supported by the National Programme of Research (Information Society Project 1ET100300419).

References

1. Aboulnaga, A., Naughton, J.F. and Zhang, C. (2001): Generating Synthetic Complex-structured XML Data. In WebDB'01: Proc. of the 4th Int. Workshop on the Web and Databases. Santa Barbara, California: Informal proceedings.
2. Afanasiev, L., Manolescu, I. and Michiels, P. (2005): MemBeR: A Micro-Benchmark Repository for XQuery. In XSym'05: Proc. of 3rd Int. XML Database Symp., LNCS: Springer-Verlag.
3. Afanasiev, L. and Marx, M. (2006): An Analysis of the Current XQuery Benchmarks. In ExpDB'06: Proc. of the 1st Int. Workshop on Performance and Evaluation of Data Management Systems, pp. 9–20, Chicago, Illinois, USA: ACM.
4. Barbosa, D., Mendelzon, A. O., Keenleyside, J. and Lyons, K. A. (2002): ToXgene: A Template-Based Data Generator for XML. In SIGMOD'02: Proc. of the 2002 ACM SIGMOD Int. Conf. on Management of Data, p. 616, Madison, Wisconsin, USA: ACM.
5. Berglund, A., Boag, S., Chamberlin, D., Fernandez, M. F., Kay, M., Robie, J. and Simeon, J. (2007): XML Path Language (XPath) 2.0. W3C. http://www.w3.org/TR/xpath20/.
6. Biron, P. V. and Malhotra, A. (2004): XML Schema Part 2: Datatypes (Second Edition). W3C. www.w3.org/TR/xmlschema-2/.
7. Boag, S., Chamberlin, D., Fernandez, M. F., Florescu, D., Robie, J. and Simeon, J. (2007): XQuery 1.0: An XML Query Language. W3C. http://www.w3.org/TR/xquery/.
8. Bohme, T. and Rahm, E. (2001): XMach-1: A Benchmark for XML Data Management. In BTW'01: Datenbanksysteme in Buro, Technik und Wissenschaft, 9. GI-Fachtagung, pp. 264–273, London, UK: Springer-Verlag.
9. Bosak, J. (2007): Jon Bosak's XML Examples. http://www.ibiblio.org/bosak/.
10. Bray, T., Paoli, J., Sperberg-McQueen, C. M., Maler, E. and Yergeau, F. (2006): Extensible Markup Language (XML) 1.0 (Fourth Edition). W3C. http://www.w3.org/TR/REC-xml/.
11. Bressan, S., Lee, M.-L., Li, Y. G., Lacroix, Z. and Nambiar, U. (2003): The XOO7 Benchmark. In Proc. of the VLDB 2002 Workshop EEXTT and CAiSE 2002 Workshop DTWeb on Efficiency and Effectiveness of XML Tools and Techniques and Data Integration over the Web-Revised Papers, pp. 146–147, London, UK: Springer-Verlag.
12. Busse, R., Carey, M., Florescu, D., Kersten, M., Manolescu, I., Schmidt, A. and Waas, F. (2003): XMark – An XML Benchmark Project. Centrum voor Wiskunde en Informatica (CWI), Amsterdam. http://www.xml-benchmark.org/.
13. Carey, M. J., DeWitt, D. J. and Naughton, J. F. (1993): The OO7 Benchmark. SIGMOD Record (ACM Special Interest Group on Management of Data), 22(2), pp. 12–21.
14. Caucho (2005): XSLT Benchmark. Caucho Technology, Inc. http://unsemaul.sportsseoul.com/resin-doc/features/xslt-benchmark.xtp.
15. Chamberlin, D., Fankhauser, P., Florescu, D., Marchiori, M. and Robie, J. (2007): XML Query Use Cases. W3C. http://www.w3.org/TR/xquery-use-cases/.
16. Clark, J. (1999): XSL Transformations (XSLT) Version 1.0. W3C. http://www.w3.org/TR/xslt.
17. Clark, J. and DeRose, S. (1999): XML Path Language (XPath) Version 1.0. W3C. http://www.w3.org/TR/xpath/.
18. DBLP (2008): Digital Bibliography & Library Project. http://dblp.uni-trier.de/.
19. DeRose, S., Daniel, R., Grosso, P., Maler, E., Marsh, J. and Walsh, N. (2002): XML Pointer Language (XPointer). W3C. http://www.w3.org/TR/xptr/.
20. DeRose, S., Maler, E. and Orchard, D. (2001): XML Linking Language (XLink) Version 1.0. W3C. http://www.w3.org/TR/xlink/.
21. Dokulil, J., Yaghob, J. and Katreniakova, J. (2008): Everything You Ever Wanted to Learn from the Semantic Web, but Were Unable to Ask. In ADVCOMP'08: Proc. of the 2nd Int. Conf. on Advanced Engineering Computing and Applications in Sciences, Valencia, Spain: IEEE.

22. Dvorakova, J. and Zavoral, F. (2008): Xord: An Implementation Framework for Efficient XSLT Processing. In IDC'08: Proc. of the 2nd Int. Symposium on Intelligent Distributed Computing, Catania, Italy: Springer-Verlag.

23. Farwick, M. and Hafner, M. (2007): XML Parser Benchmarks: Part 1 & 2. XML.com. http://www.xml.com/pub/a/2007/05/09/xml-parser-benchmarks-part-1.html. http://www.xml.com/pub/a/2007/05/16/xml-parser-benchmarks-part-2.html.

24. Fields, M. (1996): Mark Fields's Ebooks. http://www.assortedthoughts.com/downloads.php.

25. Franceschet, M. (2005): XPathMark – An XPath Benchmark for XMark Generated Data. In XSym'05: Proc. of 3rd Int. XML Database Symposium, LNCS: Springer-Verlag.

26. FreeDB (2008): http://www.freedb.org/.

27. H-InvDB (2007): Annotated Human Genes Database. http://www.jbirc.aist.go.jp/hinv/.

28. IMDb (2008): The Internet Movie Database. http://www.imdb.com/.

29. INEX (2007): INitiative for the Evaluation of XML Retrieval. http://inex.is.informatik.uni-duisburg.de/.

30. Jeong, H. J. and Lee, S.H. (2006): A Versatile XML Data Generator. International Journal of Software Effectiveness and Efficiency, 1(1), pp. 21–24.

31. Kuznetsov, E. and Dolph, C. (2000): XSLT Processor Benchmarks. XML.com. http://www.xml.com/pub/a/2001/03/28/xsltmark/index.html.

32. Kuznetsov, E. and Dolph, C. (2001): XSLT Benchmark Results. XML.com. http://www.xml.com/pub/a/2001/03/28/xsltmark/results.html.

33. Martinez, S. I., Grosso, P. and Walsh, N. (2008): Extensible Markup Language (XML) Conformance Test Suites. W3C. http://www.w3.org/XML/Test/.

34. MeSH (2008): Medical Subject Headings. http://www.nlm.nih.gov/mesh/meshhome.html.

35. Mlynkova, I., Toman, K. and Pokorny, J. (2006): Statistical Analysis of Real XML Data Collections. In COMAD'06: Proc. of the 13th Int. Conf. on Management of Data, pp. 20–31, New Delhi, India: Tata McGraw-Hill Publishing Company Ltd.

36. Nicola, M., Kogan, I. and Schiefer, B. (2007): An XML Transaction Processing Benchmark. In SIGMOD'07: Proc. of the 2007 ACM SIGMOD Int. Conf. on Management of Data, pp. 937–948, New York, NY, USA: ACM.

37. Open Directory Project (2004): http://rdf.dmoz.org/.

38. Oren, Y. (2002): SAX Parser Benchmarks. SourceForge.net. http://piccolo.sourceforge.net/bench.html.

39. Phan, B. V. and Pardede, E. (2008): Towards the Development of XML Benchmark for XML Updates. In ITNG'08: Proc. of the 5th Int. Conf. on Information Technology: New Generations, pp. 500–505, Las Vegas, Nevada, USA: IEEE.

40. Rorke, M., Muthiah, K., Chennoju, R., Lu, Y., Behm, A., Montanez, C., Sharma, G. and Englich, F. (2007): XML Query Test Suite. W3C. http://www.w3.org/XML/Query/test-suite/.

41. Runapongsa, K., Patel, J. M., Jagadish, H. V., Chen, Y. and Al-Khalifa, S. (2006): The Michigan Benchmark: Towards XML Query Performance Diagnostics (Extended Version) http://www.eecs.umich.edu/db/mbench/mbench.pdf.

42. Stanclova, J. (2006): The Associative Recall of Spatial Correlated Patterns. In CIARP'06: Proc. of 11th Iberoamerican Congress on Pattern Recognition, pp. 539–548, Cancun, Mexico: Springer-Verlag.

43. Thompson, H. S., Beech, D., Maloney, M. and Mendelsohn, N. (2004): XML Schema Part 1: Structures (Second Edition). W3C. www.w3.org/TR/xmlschema-1/.

44. Treebank (1999): The Penn Treebank Project. http://www.cis.upenn.edu/~treebank/.

45. UniProt (2008): Universal Protein Resource. http://www.ebi.uniprot.org/index.shtml.

46. Wendover, A. (2001): Arthur's Classic Novels. http://arthursclassicnovels.com/.

47. XDR (2002): XML Data Repository. www.cs.washington.edu/research/xmldatasets/www/repository.html.

48. Yao, B. B., Ozsu, M. T. and Keenleyside, J. (2003): XBench – A Family of Benchmarks for XML DBMSs. In Proc. of the VLDB 2002 Workshop EEXTT and CAiSE 2002 Workshop DTWeb on Efficiency and Effectiveness of XML Tools and Techniques and Data Integration over the Web-Revised Papers, pp. 162–164, London, UK: Springer-Verlag.

57

Service-Oriented Software Development Value Chain and Process

Yuan Rao, Shumin Lu and ZhiXiong Yang

Abstract

SOA provides a new method to optimiz software development process with value chain. A formalized definition and a meta-model about value chain were introduced for analysing the difference between traditional software development process and service-oriented reusable software process. Furthermore, some metrics in software development value chain was proposed and compared in value matrix. The results show that the service-oriented reusable development process has more value improvement than traditional software process, which collaborate all the resources and roles in software process together under an open environment.

Keywords Service-oriented architecture · Software development process · Value chain · Value matrix

1. Introduction

Software reuse is always an important issue to research for improving the productivity of software development in software engineering field. Freeman [1] considered that the software reuse was the technology of assembling the existent software artifacts to build a new software system. From this viewpoint, software reuse promoted COTS-based [2] software application development and changed the development process and methodology from traditional requirement, analysis, design, coding and testing process to selection, customization, adaptation, extension and assembly process [3] for reusing software artifacts. Caldieri [4] introduced a factory pattern for software development, which is an integration environment for rapid development and configuration of specific application, to satisfy the requirements of global software development process. Furthermore, the change about software development pattern with reusing software artifacts in SOA environment, which is based on a series of XML-based protocols (e.g., SOAP, WSDL, BEPL, UDDI) and traditional Internet standard protocols, will make great effect upon the quality about software products and development efficiency, which also affects the core competency of both the users and the software vendors. Therefore, in order to realize the objectives of software reuse, which includes how to improve the competency and quality level, to decrease the cost and to optimize the software development process, the whole value chain of the service-oriented software development resources should be integrated and be divided into different logical levels for analysis. The meta-model of value chain was proposed to compare the traditional software development with service-oriented software development process.

Yuan Rao · College of Software Engineer, Xi'an Jiaotong University, China.   **Shumin Lu** · The Key Lab of Electronic-Commerce, Xi'an Jiaotong University, China.   **ZhiXiong Yang** · Zhongguancun Haidian High-Technique Park Postdoc Workstation-UFIDA Substation, Beijing, 100085, China.

G.A. Papadopoulos et al. (eds.), *Information Systems Development*, DOI 10.1007/b137171_57,
© Springer Science+Business Media, LLC 2009

2. Service-Oriented Reusable Software Development Process

The traditional software development process is a close process, which emphasizes the integration of inner development resources and process specification of software vendor. Therefore, this process always considers a primary activity in the value chain of software product. Service-oriented software development process is an open process, which not only extends the traditional software process but also stresses more on the outer software resources for reusing. So, a value chain of software development is formed, which includes four kinds of different roles, such as the user, the developer, the customer, and the software/service component vendor (SCV), and integrates some business phases into the development process, such as SCVs' relationship management, requirement management, production definition and design, production assembly, supply chain management, and so on. The whole process of service-oriented software development is illustrated in Fig. 57.1.

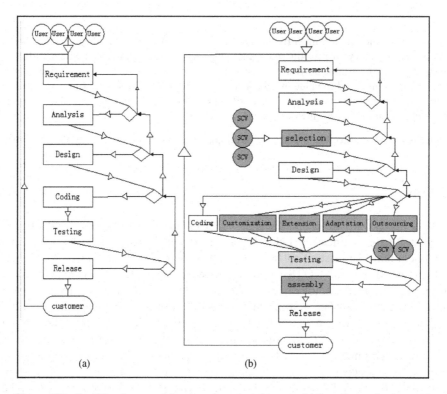

Figure 57.1. Traditional process (**a**) and service-oriented process (**b**) for software development.

After requirements collection from many users, the system analyst must define the boundary and function of software system, then they must select the list of suitable functional components and services from SCVs or those existed software products of themselves for reuse. Brownsword [5] suggested that the COTS-based software development process was a continuous trade-off among several factors: the requirements for the component-based software (CBS), the COTS products offered by the marketplace, and the architecture of the CBS. Therefore, it is important for the system designer to evaluate these reusing software artifacts and design component-based (i.e., assembly-based) software architecture. This architecture will define which parts must be coded by programmers for developing a reusable component, connector or others, which parts will adopt the reusable component from the SCV or COTS, which parts will be customized, adapted, extended, and outsourcing, and how to assemble all these parts together. Based on these definitions, the system is divided into different aspects for programmer to realize in parallel and asynchronous method. Because these reusable software artifacts have been tested as a unit, the testing work of the assembly system focuses on the system integration test and function test. In addition, the programming process can be divided into five kinds of tasks in service-oriented software development process, such as coding, customization, adaptation, extension, and outsourcing. The optimized objective of the whole development process can be clearly defined as follows: the most rapid response time for user's requirements with minimization of the coding work and maximization of reusing the reusable software artifacts.

3. Value Chain Model of Service-Oriented Software Process

3.1. Meta-Model of Value Chain

Definition 1: Value Chain is a business system and analysis tool, which describes the production and knowledge activities, the relationship between these activities, the metrics of value-added activity under certain conditions, and rules within or around an organization. Based on those fundamental elements, we can analyze the competitive strength of the organization. Therefore, the definition of value chain is formalized as follows:

```
<Value Chain>:: ==<VC_Entity> <rule> {"," <rule>}
<VC_Entity> ::==Entity_name <Activity> <Relationship> <Metric> <Role>
<Activity>:: ==<Production Activity>|<knowledge Activity>
<Production Activity>::== inbound logistics| product| outbound logistics| market &
sale| service
<Knowledge Activity>::==gathering| organizing| selecting| synthesizing| distributing
<Relationship> ::== between activities| between roles| between activity and role
<Metric>::==<objective>{<index>{<value>}}
<Role>::==< Value chain role>|< Activity role>
<Value chain role >::== value chain owner| value chain supporter
<Activity role>::==activity planner| activity executor| activity valuator
```

Today, there are two strategies, i.e., low-cost strategy and differentiation strategy to help enterprises to keep their competitive strength and maximize the shareholder value under the global severe competition pressure. Value chain model can provide an opportunity and tool to put these strategies into practice. From the above-mentioned formalized definition, we can clearly understand the core elements of value chain. At the same time, we can analyze and measure which part is a weakness or virtue point to add more value for production and service of enterprise in the whole chain. In general, product value-added activity always mixes with knowledge creation activities. In addition, value matrix is a good tool to evaluate value-added activity in IT industry [5]. The metrics in value matrix mainly depend on the objective selection for optimization. A meta-model of value chain, described by UML, was illustrated in Fig. 57.2.

3.2. Value Chain-Based Software Development Process

Definition 2: Software Development Process (SDP) is a method or a process to convert the users' requirements into software product, which also includes four key activities: an explicit development specification, programming, validation, and software evolvement under this specification.

Definition 3: Software Development Value Chain (SDVC) is a value-added process based on the SDP, which is an instance of meta-model of value chain used in software development process.

From these definitions, SDP is a product-oriented development process and emphasize to establish the process standard and management specification for software development. However, SDVC not only need

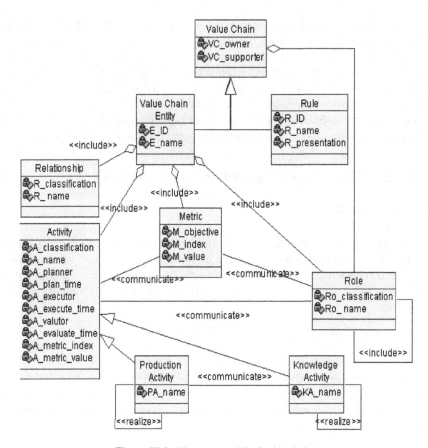

Figure 57.2. The meta-model of value chain.

the specification to manage the software process but also need to refine the whole process and add more values into the different development activities. SDVC involves process entity and development rule. Meanwhile, the process entity also is composed of four kinds of elements as follows: software development activity, role, relationship, and software process metric. Furthermore, these two kinds of activities are always closely mixed together and knowledge activities can add more values into software development process, which is very different from traditional manufacture process or supply chain process. The role in software development process includes users, user requirement analyst, product manager, system analyst, system designer, tester, coordinator and customers. Owing to the participation, competition, and collaboration among the different roles in SDVC, the software development pattern is changed. Furthermore, openness is one of the essential difference between the SDVC and the traditional SDP. The metrics is an important element for improvement of the software process. In general, the optimized objective of software process is to improve software product's competitive strength by lower cost, shorter development life cycle, and better quality.

3.3. The Establishment of SDVC Based on Different Processes

Based on the above mentioned definitions and the theory of virtual value chain, we build the value chain model for traditional SDP and service-oriented SDP, respectively. The different SDVCs based on the different processes are illustrated in Fig. 57.3, where the denotation about "$\sqrt{}$" means that the development activity exists knowledge-based value improvement or else we can use null. Therefore, in order to describe the value-added from SDP to SDVC, a value matrix is denoted as follows:

$$V = \begin{bmatrix} V_{11} & V_{12} & \cdots & V_{1\,m} \\ V_{21} & V_{22} & \cdots & V_{2\,m} \\ V_{31} & V_{32} & \cdots & V_{3\,m} \\ \cdots & & & \\ V_{51} & V_{52} & \cdots & V_{5\,m} \end{bmatrix}$$

where $\{1 \le i \le 5,\ 1 \le j \le m\}$ means the added value when the No. i knowledge activity was mixed into the No. j development activity in different indexes of SDP. As a non-negative integer, "m" means the number of development activities. The added value of each node can be evaluated by cost, quality, customer response time, the ratio of new product, the productivity of reusable software, and others. All these indexes were defined as follows:

Definition 4: Customer Response Time T_{ack} means the interval time from the proposed user requirements to the completed software product, where $T_{ack} = T_{dew} + T_{imp}$; $T_{dev} = T_{ana} + T_{deg} + T_{cod} + T_{test}$. Under the perfect condition with non-defect, i.e., when the maintain time about software application is zero, $T_{main} \approx 0$, then, the life cycle about software is $T_{LC} = T_{ack} + T_{main} \approx T_{ack}$.

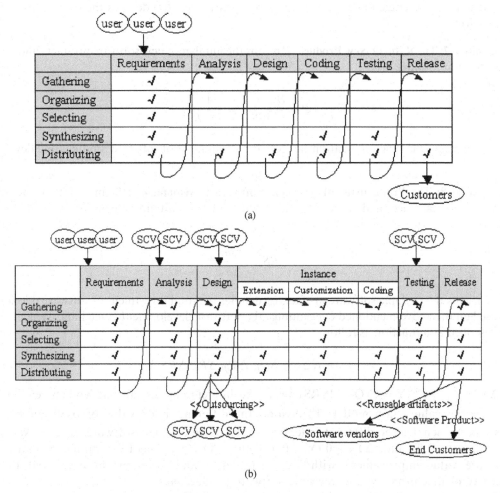

Figure 57.3. Value chain-based software development process model.

Definition 5: Software Development Cost C means the quantity of software development resource engrossed in unit time, i.e.,

$$C = \int_0^{T_{LC}} R(t)dt = \sum_{k=1}^n \int_0^{T_{LC}} r_k(t)dt$$

where, $R = \{r_k | 1 \le k \le n\}$ denotes the software development resource; T_{LC} means the life cycle of software development and maintenance. Therefore, the more resources used in unit time or longer than T_{LC}, the more cost spent on software development.

Definition 6: Software Qualify Q means the detected probability of software defects or failures in certain time under the suitable requirement overlay and correctness of requirement. Let us suppose that the probability distribution of software defect obeys the exponential distribution [6], then

$$Q(t) = \frac{1}{t_0} e^{-\frac{t}{t_0}} \{t \ge 0\}$$

where t_0 denotes the average time of software defect occurrence, $Q(t)$ denotes the probability density of software defect.

Definition 7: The Ratio of New Product P means the number of new software products under the unit time and the unit resource.

$$P = \frac{\partial^2 n(t,r)}{\partial t \partial t} = \frac{1}{T_{LC} R}$$

where, n (t, r) means the function relationship between the number of software products and development time.

Definition 8: The Productivity of Reusable Software Development RS_e means that the reusable software artifacts are acquired under the unit time and the unit investment in every development process, i.e.,

$$RS_e = \frac{rsa}{i_{all}}$$

where rsa means the reusable software artifact, i_{all} denotes the total investment of software development.

Based on the above-mentioned conceptions, the software development value improvement, i.e., V_{ij}, can be described as a function as follows:

$$V_{ij} = f(\Delta C_{ij}, \Delta Q_{ij}, \Delta T_{ij}, \Delta P_{ij}, \Delta RS_{ij})$$

where $\Delta Y_{ij} = Y_{ij} - Y_{ij}^0$ ($Y = C, Q, T, P, RS$) means the different indexes value-added between SDVC and SDP under the value chain model. Y_{ij}^0 denotes the different index value of traditional software process and Y_{ij} denotes the different index value of service-oriented software process. Whereas, if $\Delta Y_{ij} \le 0$ ($Y = C, Q, T$) and, $\Delta Y_{ij} \ge 0$ ($Y = P, RS$) then $\Delta Y_{ij} \ge 0$. This function means that it would create more value improvement with less cost, defect and development cycle and the more productivity of new products and reusable software productivity.

Therefore, the total value-added between the two kinds of software development processes can be expressed as follows:

$$V = \sum_i \sum_j V_{ij} = \sum_j \left(\sum_i f(\Delta C_{ij}, \Delta Q_{ij}, \Delta T_{ij}, \Delta P_{ij}, \Delta RS_{ij}) \right)$$

4. Value Chain Analysis of Software Development Process

Based on the above-mentioned conception and definition, the cost of software development depends on the software resources and development life cycle, where the software resources include development of human resources $R_h = \{r_{hk} | 1 \le k \le z\}$, the development of tool resources $R_t = \{r_{tk} | 1 \le k \le m\}$, reusable software resources $R_r = \{r_{rk} | 1 \le k \le l\}$, and $n = z + m + l$. Because the reusable software resources R_r comprises some reusable resources developed by software vendors themselves $R_r^d = \{r_{rk}^d | 1 \le k \le a\}$ and the COTS or some reusable software artifacts provided by the third parties $R_r^c = \{r_{rk}^c | 1 \le k \le b\}, l = a + b$. Therefore, the total cost of the whole software development process can be described as follows:

$$C = \int_0^{T_{LC}} R(t)dt = \int_0^{T_{LC}} (R_h(t) + R_t(t) + R_r(t))dt$$

$$= \sum_{k=1}^{z} \int_0^{T_{LC}} r_{hk}(t)dt + \sum_{k=1}^{m} \int_0^{T_{LC}} r_{tk}(t)dt + \sum_{k=1}^{a} \int_0^{T_{LC}} r_{rk}(t)dt + \sum_{k=1}^{b} \int_0^{T_{LC}} r_{rk}^c(t)dt$$

where the cost of developer C_h means the sum of work time in SDP. Therefore,

$$C_h = \sum_{k=1}^{z} \int_0^{T_{LC}} r_{hk}(t)dt = \sum_{k=1}^{z} \int^{T_{dev} + T_{imp} + T_{main}} r_{hk}(t)dt$$

$$= \sum_{k=1}^{z} \int_0^{T_{ana} + T_{deg} + T_{cod} + T_{test} + T_{imp} T_{main}} r_{hk}(t)dt$$

$$= \sum_{k=1}^{f} \int_0^{T_{ana}} r_{hk}(t)dt + \sum_{k=1}^{g} \int_0^{T_{deg}} r_{hk}(t)dt + \sum_{k=1}^{s} \int_0^{T_{cod}} r_{hk}(t)dt + \sum_{k=1}^{p} \int_0^{T_{ama}} r_{hk}(t)dt$$

$$+ \sum_{k=1}^{q} \int_0^{T_{deg}} r_{hk}(t)dt + \sum_{k=1}^{z-f-g-s-p-q} \int_0^{T_{cod}} r_{hk}(t)dt$$

$$= C_{hana} + C_{hdeg} + C_{hcod} + C_{htest} + C_{himp} + C_{hmain}$$

where $z - f - g - s - p - q \ge 0$. At the time of $z = f - g - s - p - q$, the human maintenance cost maybe zero, i.e., $C_{hmain} = 0$, which means that we need not provide the programmer resources for maintaining software product because of the perfect product quality and other factors.

For the same reason, the cost of equipment and tool can also be denoted as the consumed time by the equipment and tools in the development process. as follows:

$$C_t = \sum_{k=1}^{m} \int_0^{T_{LC}} r_{tk}(t)dt = C_{tana} + C_{t\,deg} + C_{tcod} + C_{ttest} + C_{timp} + C_{tmain}$$

The cost of reusable software resource can be composed of the cost for developing the reusable software and the trade cost for purchasing the COTS or other reusable components. Let us suppose the component provider is the undertaker for system maintenance. Furthermore, owing to adopting the whole system analysis and design in the process of developing the reusable software resources, the cost of analysis and design can be omitted for the corresponding activities in development. Then

$$C_r = C_r^d + C_r^c = \sum_{k=1}^{a} \int_0^{T_{LC}} r_{rk}^d(t)dt + \sum_{k=1}^{b} \int_0^{T_{LC}} r_{rk}^c(t)dt = C_{rcod}^d + C_{rtest}^d + C_{rimp}^d + C_{rmain}^d + C_{trade}^d$$

Therefore, let us suppose that the total quantity of resource as well as the number of components and modules all are invariable in every development process. C_1, C_2, and C_n denote the cost for the first development, second development, and the nth development process, respectively. If latter development process may effectively reuse the resources developed in the preceding time, then

$$C_1 = C_{1h} + C_{1t} + C_{1r}$$
$$= C_{1hana} + C_{1hdeg} + C_{1hcod} + C_{1htest} + C_{1himp} + C_{1hmain} + C_{1tana} + C_{1tdeg} + C_{1tcod}$$
$$+ C_{1ttest} + C_{1timp} + C_{1tmain} + C_{1rcod}^d + C_{1rtest}^d + C_{1rimp}^d + C_{1rmain}^d + C_{1trade}^c$$

$$C_2 = C_{2h} + C_{2t} + C_{2r} - C_{1r}$$
$$= C_{2h\,ana} + C_{2h\,deg} + C_{2hcod} + C_{2htest} + C_{2himp} + C_{2hmain} + C_{2tana} + C_{2t\,deg} + C_{2tcod}$$
$$+ C_{2ttest} + C_{2timp} + C_{2tmain} + C_{2rod}^d + C_{2rtest}^d + C_{2rimp}^d + C_{2rmain}^d + C_{2trade}^c$$
$$- C_{1rcod}^d - C_{1rtest}^d - C_{1rimp}^d - C_{1rmain}^d - C_{1trade}^d$$

and, $C_n = C_{nh} + C_{nt} + C_{nr} - \sum_{j=1}^{n-1} C_{jr}$

This function can be easily proved by the method of mathematics induction (omitted here). Suppose the situation is invariable for putting the human resources and the equipment resources into every development process. Then

$$C_n = C_{(n-1)h} + C_{(n-1)t} + C_{(n-1)r} - \sum_{j=1}^{n-1} C_{jr} \quad \text{and} \quad C_n - C_1 = -\sum_{j=1}^{n-1} C_{jr}$$

The cost of traditional software development process is similar to the cost of the first development process. Because there is not enough accumulation of the software property, the cost of the traditional process is always high in each time of development. But compared with the traditional software development process, the cost of nth times the service-oriented development process may approximately reduce to $\sum_{j=1}^{n-1} C_{jr}$.

Based on the definition about development cost, we can conclude that the service-oriented software development process can develop the whole project with the quicker development speed and the smaller customer response time than traditional method under the same cost and the resources condition. Moreover, the enterprise not only can use the reusable software property to avoid the waste of duplicating development but also can straight sale those reusable components to users or can develop the new product with those resources saved by using the reusable components. Thus the new productivity rate P will be enhanced and the development income also will be increased too.

Although the above analysis is under one kind of perfect condition, namely, all resources, especially for reusable software resources, obtained or developed in the previous time could be used in the next development process. But, there is another index to evaluate the practical process, i.e., the reuse ratio of software resource λ, which means that the probability of every software artifact can be reused in the new process. Therefore, in the above-mentioned results we also need to multiply λ, i.e., $\sum \lambda_j C_{jr}$. To enhance the value of λ, one has to shorten the product development and maintenance cycle, decrease the development cost, reduce the number of software defects, and promote the new productivity ratio P and the development efficiency. Therefore,

$$V = \sum_i \sum_j V_{ij} = \sum_j \left(\sum_i f(\Delta C_{ij}, \Delta Q_{ij}, \Delta T_{ij}, \Delta P_{ij}, \Delta RS_{ij}) \right) > 0$$

is right, which means that more values increment in the service-oriented software process than that in traditional process.

5. Related Work

Indeed, there are some important research results in the software development process. For example, CMU/SEI proposed CMM and CMMI for improving the software process. IBM delivered a uniform process methodology (rational uniform process, RUP) for guiding the whole process of software development with UML tools, 6 Sigma-based software development [7], and agile software development process [8], etc. mainly focused on the process specification, visualized software architecture management, software quality and time-sensitive development, respectively. Whereas, this kind of closely loop development pattern, without the participation of users and other partners, limited the software productivity. PACE theory and PACE-based IPD [9] practice also promoted the software development process to the market, which incorporates the market management with the reengineering of products and business processes for optimizing the resources and activities in software development process. But, all these works not only did not research on the detailed metrics of service-oriented software reuse and on the quantitative analysis of software development, but also did not provide the bottleneck problems, optimized strategies, and factors for value improvement.

In 1985, Porter was first the introduce to the concept of value chain in his book *Competitive Advantage*. Many researchers [10, 11] used this theory to analyze the value-added factors in certain industry or certain application domain of supply chain. The objective of value chain is to coordinate the different parts in value chain for the best performance and to enhance the value improvement of the whole chain. Rayport [12] proposed the concept of virtual value chain, which mixed the information and knowledge into the product activities with new value improvement. The realization process of virtual value chain can be divided into three phases, namely visualization, mirror, and new customer relationship. Then, all these value-added activities can be analyzed and optimized by value matrix. Whereas, these research works emphasize on the level of enterprises management strategy with qualitative analysis. How to use the value chain to research certain software development process with accurate method is an important issue. McGrath [13] delivered a new thought to next generation about software development process with the conception of development chain management (DCM), which means that the software development process is similar to the supply chain. Therefore, this chapter incorporates the value chain with software development process for providing a new approach to evaluate the value-added activity in development process.

6. Conclusion

As a new management theoretical method, value management was widely used in supply chain management, enterprise information integration, and enterprise process optimization, etc. This chapter proposed a formalized definition and a meta-model about value chain to analyze the different software development processes. Furthermore, some metrics in service-oriented software development value chain were proposed and compared in value matrix. The results show that the service-based development process has more value improvement than traditional software development process, which collaborates all the resources and roles in software process together under an open environment.

Acknowledgments

Foundation Item: This work was co-granted by National High-Tech Research Development Plan of China (No. 863-2006AA04A118) and Zhongguancun Postdoc Research Fund.

References

1. J. Freeman, K. Brune, P. McMillan, et al., Software Technology Review [R], CMU/SEI, June 1997.
2. L. BrownSword, T. Oberndorf and C. A. Sledge, Developing New Processes for COTS-Based Systems [R], IEEE Software, 2000, Vol. 17, pp. 48–55.
3. J. Greenfield, Software Factories: Assembling Applications with Patterns, Models, Frameworks, and Tools [EB/OL], http://msdn.microsoft.com/library/default.asp? url = /library/en-us/dnbda/html/softfact3.asp, November 2004.
4. G. Caldiera and V. R. Basili, Identifying and Qualifying Reusable Software Components [J], IEEE Computer, 1991, Vol. 24, No. 2, pp. 61–70.
5. L. Brownsword, T. Oberndorf and C. A. Sledge, Developing New Processes for COTS-Based Systems [J], IEEE Software, 2000, Vol. 17, pp. 48–55.
6. J. O. Wilder, Assessment of Execution Behavior Using the Static Measure of Defect Density, http://spacecoretech. org/core tech2002/Papers/SystemsReliability/pdfs/EVD-%20SW %20R%20Modelrev1%20paper.pdf.
7. G. Gack, Six Sigma Software Development Case Study [EB/OL], http://software.isixsigma.com/library/content/c030528a.asp.
8. S. BeiJun, C. Cheng and J. DeHua, Research on Agile Software Process, Journal of Computer Research and Development (in Chinese) [J], 2002, Vol. 39 (11): 1456–1463.
9. Integrated Product Development Technical Handbook (V1.0), UFIDA Software Corporation (in Chinese), 2005, 11.
10. J. F. Shapiro, V. M. Singhal and S. N. Wagner, Optimizing the Value Chain [R]. INTERFACES23: March–April 1993, pp. 102–177.
11. C. Xiaoying and X. Guoliang, Summarization on the Research of Value Chain [J], Foreign Economies & Management (in Chinese), 2000, Vol. 22(1): 25–30.
12. J. F. Rayport and J. J. Sviokla, Exploiting the Virtual Value Chain [J], Harvard Business Review, Nov–Dec. 1995, pp. 75–85.
13. M. McGrath, Next Generation Product Development: How to Increase Productivity, Cut Costs, and Reduce Cycle Times [M], McGraw-Hill, 1 edition, April 23, 2004.

58

A Content Markup Language for Data Services

Noviello C., Acampa P. and Mango Furnari M.

Abstract

Network content delivery and documents sharing is possible using a variety of technologies, such as distributed databases, service-oriented applications, and so forth. The development of such systems is a complex job, because document life cycle involves a strong cooperation between domain experts and software developers. Furthermore, the emerging software methodologies, such as the service-oriented architecture and knowledge organization (e.g., semantic web) did not really solve the problems faced in a real distributed and cooperating settlement. In this chapter the authors' efforts to design and deploy a distribute and cooperating content management system are described. The main features of the system are a user configurable document type definition and a management middleware layer. It allows CMS developers to orchestrate the composition of specialized software components around the structure of a document. In this chapter are also reported some of the experiences gained on deploying the developed framework in a cultural heritage dissemination settlement.

Keywords Distributed Content Management Systems · Information grid · Distributed systems

1. Introduction

Thanks to diffusion of low-cost high-speed Internet connections, institutions and organizations face increasing demands to cooperate in sharing common knowledge. While the Internet side is undergoing the Web 2.0 revolution, the machine side is likewise experiencing a major transformation from an application based to a *service-oriented architecture* (*SOA*). The SOA approach does away with monolithic applications, in fact in the case an application is structured as a set of services orchestrated by business processes then a new application may be built by recomposing the enterprise's services. Data services are thus an important class of services that warrant explicit consideration in designing, building, and maintaining SOA applications, but application data models are missing in SOA architecture. A typical data service will provide a set of operations that encapsulate different ways to access business objects in order to simplify data access for service' consumers. Because data will always be central to applications, it is likely that it will enrich the SOA model by letting application developers more easily and quickly understand the enterprise's sea of services, facilitating service discovery and reuse. Consequently, systems that make easier building and managing data services will become an increasingly significant piece of enterprise information integration puzzle. Moreover, data-service modeling will become a design discipline in need of sound new methodologies and supporting tools.

There are applications, e.g., hypermedia applications, that critically depend on the domain informational contents and on the explicit representation of the structure of these contents. The maintenance of these applications typically involves the addition of new contents and the modification of the existing ones, as well as the customization of other relevant features. In [10] these kind of applications are called *content*

Noviello C., Acampa P. and Mango Furnari M. • Istituto di Cibernetica "E. Caianiello", Consiglio Nazionale delle Ricerche, Italy.

G.A. Papadopoulos et al. (eds.), *Information Systems Development*, DOI 10.1007/b137171_58,
© Springer Science+Business Media, LLC 2009

intensive. Since domain experts are the owners and/or the authors of the contents and they have a deep knowledge of the structure of these contents and of the other aspects of the application domain then the content maintenance process supposes their active involvement. In turn, developers have good skills in computer science, but they are not necessarily proficient in the application domain.

Contents production and maintenance for content - intensive applications are costly tasks. The development process of this kind of applications usually proceeds through several iterations, where experts provide the contents and developers delivery new versions of the application, which are in turn evaluated by the experts, notifying developers of their modifications and/or improvements [3, 4].

Contents delivery and documents sharing across enterprise or institutions boundaries are today possible using a variety of technologies. However, technologies for sharing content are only one aspect of contents management in cooperative and distributed settlements. In fact, contents not only need to be created, managed, revised, and finally published, but they may also need to be organized and aggregated in more complex structures, e.g., collections. Modern *content management system* (*CMS*) has a complete environment to support users in content production and publishing for the web. However, most CMSs have poor support for cross systems interoperability and to promote cooperation over the network, in fact they mainly focus the attention on the users' interaction and documents usage.

Prerequisite to share documents, in machine understandable way, is the adoption of de facto standards for content and metadata representations. Standards play many important roles and provide a body of "portable knowledge" that IT application developers can use and hopefully reuse across multiple projects and products. Aside of the use of standards, document representations must provide both user-and machine-oriented representations and must play an active role in data sharing process.

The current semantic-oriented exploitation attempts are mainly oriented to cope with the conceptualization of a single knowledge source, they use document semantic models as monolithic entities providing little support to specify, store, and access them in a modular manner.

In this chapter we describe one possible way to map document conceptual models onto an object-oriented programming (*OOP*) model and how to exploit the OOP methodological and technological features to simplify the documents sharing process. We address the problem of making distributed document collection repositories mutually interoperable. The design methodologies here described are based on the hypothesis that it is yet necessary to develop an adequate treatment for distributed and heterogeneous document model interpretation to promote knowledge sharing on the semantic web. Appropriate infrastructures for representing and managing distributed document model interpreters will also be described. To pursue these goals we introduced the notion of *knowledge stakeholders community* that exchange modularized *document model interpretation* together documents using a *document middleware*. Experimental implementation and tools were developed to check the adequacy of the proposed methodologies; their deployment for the cultural heritage promotion arena is also described.

The rest of this chapter is organized as follows: in Section 2 the architecture and the implementation of the proposed distributed contents management system is described. In Section 3 the document type definition language designed to cope with document description and document models are described. In Section 4 the implemented test bed is described and the proposed architecture advantages are summarized.

2. Octapy3 a Distributed and Cooperative Content Management System

In order to design the Octapy3 distributed and cooperative *content management system* (*CMS*) we adopted the document-oriented development approach. This approach promotes the use of documents to describe the contents, the structure of the managed knowledge, and the customizable CMS features. These different facets are described by means of a set of documents and different description languages used to represent them. Document description languages make possible to automatically process these documents in order to rebuild the applications when they change. Documents are not restricted to text but they include application contents and other customizable features of the application.

The main Octapy3's functionalities are oriented to support both an easy and fast process to define new document types, and the management and deployment of documents aggregation through the network. Contents are implemented in this way for playing the roles of data and active software components. They expose a well-defined API, on doing so we allow implementing different kinds of end-user and machine-oriented document representations. The way of defining document types has been one of the most intriguing aspect coped with the design of software platform. In fact, we need to describe document and its components in such a way that they could be easily processed to produce software modules that manage them as digital objects. We solved this problem defining a document descriptive command-oriented language to represent the logical structure of a document, see Section 3, and defines the document structure, the associated persistency, its user presentation, and so on. Summarizing, to create a knowledge community we need software systems and middleware having a number of key features including

- *Support to semantic web technologies*: it should push semantic web technologies into CMS, allowing interoperability with other systems. It should use document models suitable for semantic-oriented interoperability.
- *Extensible metadata management*: the document models should contain metadata to be used to express any type of digital collections membership, parent–child or taxonomic relationships. Moreover, document repositories should be conformant with metadata exchange protocols, such as the *open archive initiative protocol for metadata harvesting* (OAI-MPH).
- *Multiple document representations*: for each managed document type multiple representations should be available, representations that must be adequate for both user and machine processing. Using the XML and RDF widespread standard, documents could be exchanged across different document repositories even if they did not directly manage the data model of the transferred documents.
- *Powerful component model*: it should have a flexible software component model in order to make easy the development of content-oriented extensions. Extensions that should be generic and not tightly coupled with document models.

Octapy3 has been designed to bring functionalities for content-based interoperability to create knowledge communities of distributed content providers that share common knowledge. In Octapy3, contents play a central role since they are active parts of interoperability among different systems, information sharing is achieved by exchanging documents, and each document may have multiple representations and interpretations.

From architecture point of view we adopted the Zope3/Plone *zope component architecture* (ZCA), see [11] and [12] *ZCA* is a Python framework that supports component-based design and programming [6]. For managing complexity the *ZCA* central idea is the use of components rather than multiple-inheritance, where components are reusable objects with introspectable interfaces. A component provides an interface implemented in a class or any other callable object. It does not matter how the component is implemented, the important part is that it complies with its interface contracts. Using *ZCA*, we can spread the complexity of systems over multiple cooperating components. However, *ZCA* is not about the components themselves, rather it is about creating, registering, and retrieving components. The component architecture provides both ways to look up various kinds of components based on *interfaces*, *names* and two basic kinds of components, *adapter* and *utility*.

We developed the *document content component (DCC)* to automatically generate software components starting from document type description written using the OCML language, see Section 3 below. In Octapy3 documents are represented as digital objects, that in turn are implemented as classes. More specifically, all objects that provide the *IOctapyContent* interface (described later) are documents living locally in a document repository node, while the class *RemoteContent is* used to manage, on a given repository node, documents that are located in other nodes of a knowledge community.

The software generation process is carried out by YODA[1] module that generates both the code and interfaces describing the document structure [7]. This interface is an enumeration *content type description* field associated attributes to each and the class that implements this interface. Summarizing, Octapy3 have been organized around three main application levels:

---

[1] The acronym means *Yoda is octapy document assembler*.

- *Documents definition layer*: it contains software modules that add functionalities that simplify the definition of new document types. To pursue this goal the document description language *Octapy Configuration Markup Language (OCML)* was defined and used to specify both the application and the associated presentation logic.
- *Content components layer*: one of the main goals of Octapy3 is to abstract from the content structure introducing a clear separation among application layers. Octapy3 generates specific software components (*document content components*), which represent the managed documents. These components expose the interfaces used, for example, to manage documents structure and the relationships among documents.
- *Distributed and cooperative layer*: Octapy3 is designed with the aim to build communities of cooperating knowledge node providers. Special attention has been paid to support standards for interoperability, such as RDF/RDFS [5] for semantic interoperability, Dublin core metadata set and open archive initiative protocol (OAI-PMH) for metadata exchanges.

A *DCC*, see Fig. 58.1, has at least two interfaces: one describing the *content type definition* and the *IOctapyContent, which is the* generic interface common to all *DCC* components. *IOctapyInterface* exposes the method getContentInteface () to capture the effective interface describing the document content type, i.e., it allows to search for a specific data interface. Handling and managing generic content type extensions is also allowed in Octapy3, in this case an adapter to the fixed interface *IOctapyContent* could be used to add the required functionalities. For example, a presentation interfaces may be built using the *browser pages* Octapy3 component that adapts and accesses the content through the *IOctapyContent* and getContentInterface () method. Furthermore, it is also possible to write an extension module for a given data schemata adapting only the generated content component interfaces.

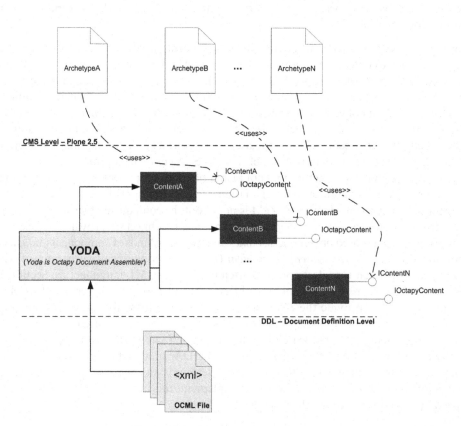

Figure 58.1. The Octapy component model.

Different machine "understandable" document rapresentations are available in Octapy 3 to make effective the cooperation and to share document across documents stakeholders' boundaries. Some of them are oriented to the semantic web and are based on RDF/RDFS languages and their derivatives; others are oriented to facilitate the interoperability using standard protocol for metadata sharing, like the OAI-PMH protocol, see OAI-PMH. Starting from the information provided by the document serialization the *OctapyProxy* base class manages the content interface creation of a remote document. *RemoteContent* (the corresponding Plone conten type) is a subclass of the class *OctapyProxy*, and it is used by users to handle contents coming from other document repositories.

As documents, in Octapy3 every document of type *container* implements the *IOctapyContainer* interface. Containers can be also exported to other document repository and/or aggregated using the corresponding *RemoteContainer* class.

3. OCML Specification

To make possible to extend the content type definition during the CMS configuration phase a document type definition language was defined. This language is called *Octapy content markup language (OCML)* [1] and it allow: to define new document types; to choose documents storage methods for each document type or parts of it; to assign some sort of semantics to the document components associating a document interpretation models so that the system can correctly process them; and to assign user presentation logic for each content type.

OCML is a command-oriented language whose commands are represented as a set of XML tags, called *directives*, and grouped into three main XML namespaces: `data`, `storage`, and `view`. In order to assign an operational semantic to directives, an OCML tag interpreter may be associated to each one. A valid OCML file must contain at least one content definition, to which is assigned a symbolic name (attribute `name`) and a unique identifier (`id` attribute). It is possible to define structured documents, namely compound documents, using the `data:document` attribute `subDocs`.

The content management directives (`data:document`, `data:section`, and `data:field`) tell to the system which type, structure, constraints, and functionalities the content must have and how they are grouped inside the `data` namespace. `data:document` directive is used to define new types of documents. The directive `data:section` represents a section of a document, which may contain any number of fields (`data:field`). The attribute `name` assigns a symbolic name to a section. The directive `data:field` denotes a field of a section and it has a number of attributes to specify the allowable values.

A document may be composed of any number of subdocuments. This functionality allows documents to be organized in a hierarchical way with arbitrary nesting. Another interesting feature is the ability to add subdocuments, both local and remote, whose types are computed dynamically at run time. This is done with the subdocument type "object reference," whose special OCML tag is `#REF`. This is not a trivial functionality, since modern CMSs introduce a sort of content "type system" like CMF types in Plone. This lead to user inability to structure documents as they want, and this is a strong restriction for a document system that aims to be distributed. This functionality is also used in handling remote documents via RemoteContent and RemoteContainer content types. Octapy does not require that the type of a remote document must be known a priori, introducing a kind of document "lazy evaluation." This is achieved adding new important functionalities to the Zope/Plone type system.

Suppose, for example, that we want to describe archeological goods, then a new document type *archeology* may be defined using OCML, and the software components necessary to manage it will be automatically be produced processing YODA the document specification. A fragment of the OCML document for the new *archeology* document type is shown in Fig. 58.2.

In general, the application data layer does not assign a meaning to the collection of fields, since they are considered only containers for "values" and used to store fixed data. In other words, this kind of information is interpreted as a pair of a *name* and an uninterpreted *value*. Nevertheless, in order to be semantic oriented we must assign an interpreted value to a metadata name, i.e., it is necessary to make explicit both the domain from which the values are chosen and the valuation function (interpreter) used to assign a value.

```
<octapy
xmlns:view="http://namespaces.remuna.org/octapy-view"
        xmlns:data="http://namespaces.remuna.org/octapy-data"
        xmlns:storage="http://namespaces.remuna.org/octapy-storage">
    <data:document name="Oggetto Archeologico" id="OggettoArcheologico"
        subDocs="((localizzazione, *), (condizionegiuridica, 1))>
      <data:section name="generale">
        <data:field name="id" type="Int" languageIndependent="True"
                default="1000" mode="r" />
        <data:field name="titolo" type="String" searchable="True"
                languageIndependent="false" required="True"
                default="Titolo"/>
        <data:field name="descrizione" type="Text" searchable="true"
                languageIndependent="false" required="false"
                metadata="{'uiuse':'description'" />
        <data:field name="immagine" type="Image" searchable="false"
                languageIndependent="true" required="true"/>
      </data:section>
    </data:document>
  </octapy>
```

Figure 58.2. The OCML document for an *Archeology* document type.

In such a semantic-oriented scenario it is possible to define, for example, a document whose content is of type *ArtisticObject* and the fields `oss` and `title` not only are simply container for lines of text but also have meanings that depend on its use context. For example, we may interpret the field *oss* as the "description" of an *Artistic Object*, in one context, and as "caption" for a picture in another one, with a different formatting and typesetting rules. This means that a document, or part of it, may have a special interpretation that must be correctly handled by the Octapy3 run-time software. In OCML the attribute `metadata` of the directive `field` has been introduced to specify which interpretation model has to be associated to a field. For example, the value `<data:field name="oss "type="Text" metadata="{'uiuse':'description'}"/>` instructs the run-time presentation layer, to interpret the field `oss` as the *Artistic Object* field `description`, and therefore it must be accordingly processed.

The interpretation model is implemented annotating the *DCC* model attributes and methods with tags. The corresponding content interfaces, generated by YODA, are annotated with the information provided by the `metadata` attributes, and the extension modules can access this information using the `getTaggedValue` () method. It is important to underline that then interpretation models are not only used to implement the presentation logic, but also may be used whenever it is necessary to associate a special meaning to a field in other component, some sort of *metadata cross-walk* mechanism. For example, the Octapy3 Dublin core subsystem uses `metadata` attribute to map fields defined by the stakeholders metadata set to the DC [2] metadata set, as shown by the following example:

```
...
    <data:field name="descrizione_breve"
            type="Text'' metadata="{' dc' :' title' "/>
    <data:field name="autore_scheda"
            type="Text'' metadata="{' dc' :' author' "/>
...
```

The directive `data:vocabulary:` defins the vocabulary as collections of reserved words to be used as fields' domain. This directive is specified by the parameter (`id`), a unique identifier for the specified vocabulary; the `name` that will appear into the user interface, and the parameter `description` that provides a brief vocabulary description. Suppose, for example, we want to create a new vocabulary, called *Material and Technology*, the corresponding OCML fragment is shown in Fig. 58.3.

```
...
<data:vocabulary
   id="RA.MTC"
   name="Material and Technology"
   description="Il vocabolario di Materia e Tecnica per un oggetto RA"
   type="Simple">
</data:vocabulary>
...
</octapy>
```

Figure 58.3. Fragment of an OCML definition for the vocabulary *Material and Technology*.

The directives belonging to the `storage` namespace instruct Octapy3 run time about persistence mechanisms to be used for a document or for an individual document field. The directive `storage:apply` defines the type of storage to be applied to a content or a portion of it; this directive may have an arbitrary number of optional parameters specified through the attribute `storage:param`. This last directive specifies any parameter for storage. The lexical form `document{.Field}` is used to indicate the name of the field to which is applied the storage mechanism.

In Fig. 58.4 is shown the OCML fragment for a document of type `ArcheologicalGood` whose associated storage is of type Relational DataBase (i.e., `Postgres`) for all the fields except the `image` that has the File System (`FS`) storage mechanism type.

```
<storage:apply
     for=''ArcheologicalGood''
     type=''Postgres''>
     <param name=''dbname''>marcheo</param>
     <param name=''user''>remuna</param>
</storage:apply>
<storage:apply
     for=''ArcheologicalGood.image''
     type=''FS''>
     <param name=''path''>/usr/octapy/marcheo-locale</param>
</storage:apply>
```

Figure 58.4. OCML fragment that specifies the document persistence.

Using OCML it is also possible to specify the GUI to be associated to a user defined document type. To achieve this functionality a set of directives have been defined and grouped into the application namespace `view`. The directive `view:configure` allows to configure the widget associated to a document and/or a field. This directive may take an arbitrary number of optional parameters specified by `view:param`. The code shown in Fig. 58.5 is an example of a GUI configuration where the directive `view:widget` associates a `StringWidget` to a new document type and the `TextAreaWidget` to one or more fields of a document. The `fordata` attribute associates a widget to a document type while the `forattribute` associates a widget to a field of a document type. The attributes `label` and `description` (to be used only in conjunction with attribute `for`) allow to specify how labels of a particular field should be shown, while the attribute `i18n` allows to set the language translation mechanism. The directive may take an arbitrary number of optional parameters specified with the directive `view:configure`.

```
<view:widget
    fordata="Text"
    type="StringWidget"
    <view:configure>
        view:param name="maxlength">255</view:param>
    </view:configure>
</view:widget>
<view:widget
    for="OggettoArcheologico.descrizione"
    type="TextAreaWidget"
    label_msgid="label_descrizione"
    i18n="octapymus"
    <view:configure>
        <view:param name="cols">50</view:param>
        <view:param name="rows">30</view:param>
    </view:configure>
</view:widget>
```

Figure 58.5. OCML fragment for GUI description.

4. The Museo Virtuale Test Bed

In this section we shortly describe the cultural heritage environment where the developed framework has been tested and deployed. The aim of any ordinary museum visitor is something quite different from trying to find certain objects. In physical exhibitions, the cognitive museum experience is often based on the thematic combination of exhibits and their contextual information. To foster the museums cooperation, software tools were developed to aggregate, both locally and remotely, knowledge about cultural heritage goods. Using these tools the knowledge stakeholders could organize virtual exhibitions according to some physical or logical criteria either in the case where the information is directly managed or shared with other stakeholders. The information provider[2] could also organize a set of related documents, as document collections, according to some relationships.

To assure the necessary museum manager operational autonomy, without reducing the cooperation opportunities, we deployed a cooperation schema as intermediate coordination organization that is in charge to register, syndicate, and guarantee the document contents quality.

From technical point of view the main goal pursued with this test bed was to concretely verify the possibility to create knowledge cooperating communities, where each participating museums could exchange its own managed knowledge so as to improve their institutional cooperation. Currently more than 100 Octapy3 nodes, spread over the geographic region of Campania, are organized in knowledge clouds; [9] each cloud covers the territories around the main cities of Campania, i.e., Naples, Benevento, Salerno, Caserta, and Avellino. The cultural heritage knowledge offering is organized according to thematic topics, such as the *First civilizations in Campania*, the *Roman civilization periods*, the *Gran Tour period*.

From the museum manager's perspective each information system allows him to make available the managed artifacts' information through the Octapy3 node, where no assumption about fixed attributes names' schemata is taken, so the application builder can create new attributes as needed by just modifying the associated document interpretation model without changing the internal CMS schemata. The deployed *cultural heritage circuit* is included in the Italian cultural heritage portal because the Octapy3 framework allows exchanging contents through the OAI-PMH protocol.

---

[2] In this chapter we assumed that *museum manager* means one who is responsible, inside the museum organization, of the cultural heritage goods information production and organization.

5. Conclusions

One of the most interesting technological aspect investigated and described in this chapter was how to design document repository systems that allow the content stakeholder managers to organize heterogeneous document repositories spread over many autonomous organizations.

Our work successfully showed that Octapy3 could be used as document repository back end for distributed CMSs, where a central role is played by the cooperation middleware on deploying such kind of systems. We also verified that tools to define the Octapy content markup languages could significantly improve the domain experts and software developers' interaction. In fact these tools drastically reduce the costs required to adapt the documents to the domain expert needs along the document life cycle.

Furthermore, as semantic web begins to take fule shape, this type of distributed CMS implementation will enable agents to understand what is actually being presented in distributed CMS, since all content within the system is modeled in machine-understandable RDF/OWL documents.

References

1. Acampa P. and Noviello C. (2007) *Specifica OCML*, Technical Sheet Octapy CMS.
2. DC (1995) *The Dublin Core Metadata Initiative*, http://www.purl.org/dc/
3. Fraternali P.(1999) Tools and approaches for developing data intensive web applications: A survey, *ACM Computing Surveys* 3 227–263.
4. Juristo N. and Pazos J. (1993) Towards a joint life cycle for software and knowledge engineering, *IFIP Transactions* A-27, pp. 119–138.
5. Lassila O. and R. Swick (1998) Resource Description Framework (RDF) Model and Syntax, *World Wide Consortium Working Draft*.
6. von Mayrhauser A. and A. M. Vans (1995) Program understanding: models and experiments, *Advances in Computers* 40, pp. 1–38.
7. Noviello C. (2007) Il Component-Model di Octapy 3, Technical Sheet Octapy CMS.
8. OAI-PMH (2008), *Open Archives Initiative*, http://www.openarchives.org
9. CIR-Campania (2008), http://www.campaniabeniculturali.it
10. Sierra J., Fernàndez-Manjòon B., Fernàndez-Manalyor A., Navarro A. (2005) *Document-oriented development of Content-Intensive Applications*, International Journal of Software Engineering and Knowledge Engineering 15(6), pp. 975–994.
11. von Weitershausen P. (2007) *Web Component Development with Zope 3* – 2nd Edition, Springer, Berlin, Heidelberg.
12. ZCA (2007) http://wiki.zope.org/zope3/ComponentArchitecture

59

Organizational Learning Literature Visited – Fresh Lenses to Study Practices in ISD Organizations?

Pasi Juvonen and Päivi Ovaska

Abstract

This chapter presents results of a study, in which the literature related to organizational learning (OL) and learning organization (LO) also in disciplines outside information systems (IS) was studied. The results of the literature review were classified based on the proposed framework. Based on the framework, organizations tend to learn from direct experience, from the experience of others, or by developing conceptual frameworks or paradigms for interpreting that experience. This chapter also represents some expressions from empirical data related to the subjects. The results suggest that studies made in other disciplines might provide the IS community some fresh lenses and insights to study OL and LO. The results also suggest that there exists a difference between canonical practices and non-canonical practices in the ISD organizations studied. Implications of these differences and the need for more empirical research related to the OL and LO are also discussed in this chapter.

Keywords Organizational learning · Learning organization · Information systems development · Grounded theory

1. Introduction

During the recent decade rapid ICT development in Eastern Europe and Far East has affected the business models and the value chains in the ICT industry worldwide. As a part of the change, learning and innovativeness have become crucial factors in the organizations survival. Furthermore, management of the change has become one of the major challenges for the organizations [27]. In the same time it has been reported by several authors that organizations have failed to learn from their previous experiences (i.e., [16, 25]).

Organizational learning (OL) studies have its origins in management studies. Parallel with OL the concept of learning organization (LO) has been developed being strongly emphasized by consultants. During the past decade OL and LO have become more popular subjects for study also in IS discipline. The subjects for the OL-related studies have varied from knowledge creation and management to intelligence information retrieval systems and groupware. These approaches that usually try to build an organizational memory by information systems are usually referred to as "ICT approach" [7] or "technical approach" [15]. The approach has its advocates but the results gained have in many cases been controversial or in certain organizational settings even detrimental. It is in place to argue that these approaches are still lacking real success stories and some fresh lenses might be useful in future. Furthermore, studies using so-called social approach have shown us some fruitful results (i.e., [17, 14, 12]).

The evaluation of the research made in other disciplines such as organization science and management science has showed that there are numerous different lenses used to study organizational learning

Pasi Juvonen and Päivi Ovaska · South Karelia University of Applied Sciences, Finland.

G.A. Papadopoulos et al. (eds.), *Information Systems Development*, DOI 10.1007/b137171_59,

from social viewpoint also. Furthermore, when preparing a manuscript for an article the literature study is usually restricted only to the literature related to researchers' own discipline. Although learning rate has been proven to be dependent, i.e., on time, industry, and product [13] viewpoints from other disciplines might be useful also to IS discipline to recognize. Therefore, the motivation for this study was to familiarize ourselves to some fresh viewpoints to OL and LO concepts that have been studied in other disciplines than IS. The empirical data collected were also analyzed in the light of these viewpoints. Implications of the literature study and the observations made from the empirical data collected in ISD organizations are also discussed.

This chapter is organized as follows. Next section gives the results of the literature study related to organizational learning. In Section 3 the research process and empirical data are introduced. Furthermore, we present the observations on the empirical data. In Section 5, the results of the study are discussed along with its limitations. Finally, summary and future work is presented.

2. Organizational Learning Literature

The objectives of the literature study were to also look around to the studies that have been made related to OL within other disciplines and provide some results from studies emphasizing social view to the IS community.

The literature study was made between August 2007 and January 2008. Articles related to OL and LO were searched from six journals (MISQ, Organizational Learning, Management Learning, Organization science, European Journal of Information Systems, and Information Technology & People). In addition some conference article databases (i.e., ACM) were used. The first round of the information retrieval process provided us about 180 interesting articles. After selecting a proper blend of articles, theoretical sampling [30, 11] was used to make another round of information retrieval. The criteria used in the selection process were that the article should present either interesting results from social viewpoint or present constructive criticism of past OL or LO research. The objective of this second round was to find out where well-known and referenced articles of this area were and what kind of criticism has been presented against the mainstream of the research area.

2.1. Concepts and Terminology

OL has been defined in many different ways. In general, learning and knowledge are seen interrelated to each other. In several studies learning is seen as a process and knowledge is seen as a product of this process (learning).

OL has concentrated to address the observation and analysis of individual and collective learning inside organizations [15]. Learning organization (LO) is seen as counterpart for OL [17]. LO is also seen as an organization that is continually expanding its capacity to create future; Senge [28] sees learning either as adaptive (learning to cope) or as generative (learning to create). Furthermore, learning has been seen either as a single-loop or as a double-loop learning [3]. Terms incremental and radical have also been widely used to describe different learning types.

Another essential definition in OL/LO field is relation between learning and knowledge. It has been well defined by Vera and Crossnan [32]: "*Learning and knowledge are intertwined in an iterative, mutually reinforcing process. While learning (the process) produces new knowledge (the content), knowledge impacts future learning.*" Traditionally, formal training is seen to produce learning and new knowledge. In practice, this is not always the case; training is rather a possibility to learning [31].

2.2. Literature in IS Discipline

The OL and the LO have also been studied in the IS discipline. This chapter will shortly represent some previous studies made related to the subjects. Lyytinen and Robey [23] have pointed out that ISD organizations have failed to learn because of barriers of learning and limits of organizational intelligence. They argue that in the course of time organizations even tend to accept failure and learn to fail. Furthermore, Lyytinen and Rose [24] have made an empirical study of ISD agility as OL.

They found out that agility to move from exploring new technologies to exploit new technologies is valued in organizational context as a part of three other factors: innovativeness of the content, quality, and cost.

Social defences in information systems development have been studied by Wastell [33]. Wastell has found out that there exists several social defence modes of group behavior that hinder or even paralyze the learning processes that are crucial for successful ISD project. When employees are stressed of problematic situations they tend to operate defensively which creates a negative feedback loop. In a normal learning situation a problematic situation poses a problem-oriented action that fosters learning [33]. The practices of how to break through the defences and release the learning process are discussed in his study.

OL opportunities during advanced ISD have been studied by Stein and Vandenbosch [29]. They argue that systems development and implementation are an opportunity for OL, especially double-loop learning, because during the development and implementation the underlying values and norms are often questioned at that stage. Stein and Vandenbosch [29] have identified five critical success factors that affect the learning. These factors were orientation of developers (technical or managerial), development focus (process vs. product), development paradigm (learning vs. engineering), view of expertise (expert in context vs. expert in isolation), and developer–expert interaction (double-loop vs. single-loop learning behaviors).

2.3. Literature in Other Disciplines

Lave and Wenger [21] have presented a concept "Community of practice" (CoP) that has also been referred as "Community of practioners." Lave and Wenger have situated learning in the trajectories of participation in which it takes on meaning. They see that these trajectories must themselves be situated in the social world. The concept of CoPs has been expanded by Brown and Duguid [6]. In their study an organization is seen as a community of communities, where OL and CoPs are tied together to present unified view of working, learning, and innovation [6]. This approach is called a socio-cultural perspective and its sees human contact and social setting as drivers for OL. Orr's studies of service technicians are also referred to show how training of technicians and what they do in practice (non-canonical practices) are far from the ways that organizations describe their (canonical) practices in, i.e., manuals [26].

Unsystematic and unintentional learning seems to be very common [19]. However, there are still quite few studies that have been focused on this. Lave and Wenger [21] have studied several different CoPs. They have argued that conventional teaching or training within CoPs has almost no significance. The context of learning and informal community as part of it has been found essential in learning by doing [21, 6, 26, 20].

2.4. Classification of Organizational Learning Literature

A good review of OL literature and its theoretical roots has been conducted by Levitt and March [22]. They have presented that the ways how organizations learning can be classified into three categories that are (1) *from direct experience*, (2) *from the experience of others and* (3) *develop conceptual frameworks or paradigms for interpreting that experience*. A short summary of literature that was evaluated during the literature study is presented in Table 59.1.

3. Research Process and Revisited Empirical Data

A total of 36 in-depth interviews lasting from 1 to 3 hours were made in six Finnish ISD organizations during the previous research project we were participating. The interviews concentrated on processes, methods, and practices in ISD organizations. During this study the data from the past research project were revisited and a new viewpoint to the data was taken for analysis.

Table 59.1. A summary of the literature found from other disciplines.

Type of learning [22]	Author(s)	Scope of the study	Key suggestions(s) interpreted
1,2	Orr [26]	Service technicians in training and in work	Actual practices are far from canonical practices
1,2	Senge [28]	Concept of LO–LO is seen as an ultimate target for an organization	Five disciplines: (1) Personal mastery (2) Mental models (3) Shared vision (4) Team learning (5) Systems thinking
1,2,3	Lave and Wenger [21]	Learning within several different communities of practioners (CoPs)	All knowledge is socially constructed, learning is socially situated
1,2,3	Argyris [2–4]	Single-and double-loop learning	Organizational defences in individual level and lack of openness play a major role in inhibiting OL
1,2,3	Argyris and Schön [5]	Two ways to handle conflicts in organizations	Differences exist between espoused theory and theory-in-practice
1,2	Brown and Duguid [6]	Differences between canonical and non-canonical practices	An organization is a community of communities where practice, learning, and innovativeness cannot be separated
1,2	Newell et al. [25]	Knowledge sharing between ICT projects	"Re-inventing the wheel" in ISD projects is common
1	Edmondson [16]	Group level learning	Types of groups: (1) No reflection of practices (2) Reflection of practices but no changes (3) Reflection and change of practices
1	Adler and Cole [1]	A tale of two auto plants	In car industry "democratic taylorism" seems to be superior method to gain efficiency and foster learning
1,2,3	Hardagon and Bechky [18]	Interactions that benefit creativeness among communities	Four basic interactions: (1) Help seeking, (2) Help giving, (3) Reflective reframing, and (4) Reinforcing

The data were analyzed with grounded theory method [30]. When using grounded theory method researchers need theoretical sensitivity [10]. When interesting phenomenon is met a theoretical sampling is used to gather more data of it to be able to understand what is going on. Hence, to be able to better understand the phenomena found during the analysis it was decided to carry out five expert interviews in Midlands, Ireland, in Irish ISD organizations. During the interviews in Ireland a new seed category, *usefulness of the created knowledge during ISD project*, was emphasized. The objective of this new category was to first enquire the interviewees what kind of practices they use in their organization (canonical practices) and after that, ask them to evaluate those practices. The interviewees were eager to evaluate their canonical practices and in the same time also to express strengths of their hands-on (non-canonical) practices. Differences in these practices and reasons for the differences were also discussed during the interviews made in the Irish ISD organizations.

Based on the methodological instructions related to grounded theory method, the data collection should be continued until the data are saturated [30]. In other words when the same phenomena start to repeat themselves in the extra interviews made, there is no reason to continue data collection for that category. In this case the category *usefulness of created knowledge during ISD project* was saturated after five extra interviews. For the analysis of the empirical data the research question was formulated as follows:

What kind of evidence of organizational learning theories can be seen in information systems development projects?

The analysis of the empirical data included open coding, axial coding, and selective coding phases [30]. First the interviews were transcribed to ACSII text and stored to Atlas.ti program. After that a three-phase analysis was started. In the open-coding phase all the interesting phenomena related to seed category were marked (as a code). The open-coding phase produced almost 1600 codes. The analysis continued with the axial coding where these codes were regrouped and relations (is cause of, is associated with) between them were searched. The analysis ended with the selective coding. During the selective coding the most interesting phenomena were selected and an interpretation of "what is going on" was written.

4. Observations on Empirical Data

Re-inventing the wheel has been found to be common in all kinds of organizations all over the world despite their location and across the industries. When a new project is starting, there is a tendency to reinvent the wheel rather than learn from the experiences of previous projects [25]. Furthermore, companies tend to store product information rather than problem-solving experiences to their databases. This has been one of the reasons why individuals do not feel the stored knowledge useful for themselves. These previous findings are also supported by our empirical data. In Table 59.2 there are some examples of expressions from the interviews.

These expressions presented in Table 59.2 support the results gained in previous studies. It seems that employees tend to use practices they find useful and ignore those that they find useless as has been stated in behavioral theory of the firm [9]. These expressions also might implicate that there probably exists a difference between canonical practice that has been written to organizations manuals or certificates and actual practices used among different communities of practice inside an organization. Formal documentation is in some cases avoided by using unofficial ways to store useful information.

Another viewpoint that was taken during the analysis of the empirical data was the existence of communities of practice and team learning among organizations studied. We were interested if it was possible to recognize CoPs or team-level work practices based on the empirical data. Furthermore, we were interested if we could be able to find out how individuals in CoPs felt the managerial interventions directed on them. This viewpoint also includes team working and innovativeness. Before individuals commit themselves to teamwork, appropriate conditions have to exist [28]. Innovativeness is seen to be developed within CoPs [6, 18]. The expressions from the interviews presented in Table 59.3 show how interviewees saw the situation in their organization.

An interpretation that emerges from citations 6 and 7 is that in "crisis" situations managers in case company Y seem to increase surveillance and bureaucracy. These kinds of actions are not seen to foster problem-solving skills and capacity among employees; instead it is likely to raise defensiveness in individual level and increase barriers of learning [2–4].

An interpretation of citation 8 is that a project manager of company X probably tried to build a project group of suitable employees from different locations inside the company. A proper set of suitable

Table 59.2. Citations from the interviews related to usefulness of documentation.

#	Citation	Role and Company
1	"...The problem is that after ten weeks you don't remember what was agreed. Documentation does not much help the situation because the documents are not usually read..."	CRM manager, company X
2	"...We have also predefined documents but we are not using them very much..."	Project manager, company X
3	"...When we are in hurry the documentation is not updated and it becomes useless..."	Project manager, company Y
4	"...Sometimes I think the processes could have been streamlined better in XXXXXX. Seemed to be an awful lot of unnecessary documentation..."	Analyst, company Z
5	"...It's strange because when you had something like... it's like you don't really want to let management know about it because you think if this becomes a formal process; it becomes something else that has to be reviewed and will this be better that way, I don't know..."	Analyst, company W

employees from different positions around the company would make it possible to have fruitful brain-storming sessions in the beginning of a new project and also to use reflective reframing to cope with

Table 59.3. Citations from the interviews related to CoPs.

#	Citation	Role and Company
6	"Q: Do you see any areas where you could do better? A: Nothing special… but at least management should bear in mind that we are all human beings. Some of us communicate more than others. Too much surveillance and control cannot be good. We have already continuous rush, continuous lack of resources. Mainly stick instead of carrot is used for motivate employees. Employees will in longer burn out…"	Project manager, company Y
7	"….Our organization chart changes about once per year. These changes cause uncertainty and it decelerates our working…"	Project manager, company Y
8	" …I tried to get people from XXXXX and YYYYY into my small project but I couldn't do that because project managers said that they don't have time and they are very jealous of their work and so on…"	Project manager, company X
9	"… Employee has to be able to work with those methods and processes that we have, or she will not work for us any longer. We approve that one is slower than another but work has to be done according to our processes and quality requirements…"	Vice president, company W
10	"… You don't in many cases have time to make documentation or design tests…"	Analyst, company W

upcoming challenges during the project. When employees from different positions would form a project organization they could be able to reflect their previous experiences in a new situation [18]. Furthermore, if organizations policy would allow one to utilize appropriate employees from different CoPs it would inevitably foster learning by increasing information sharing across CoPs.

Citations 9 and 10 raise a question if management in company W sees ISD as "a software factory" or is it seen as a practice of creative human beings. It seems that the manager interviewed sees a company as a software factory where analysts strictly follows the processes, methods, and quality standards given from the management (canonical practices). Respectively, an analyst of company W from his own viewpoint sees that the most important issue is to "handle the job in hand" whether the quality requirements are met or not. As it was argued before, if documentation that is done during ISD project is seldom accessed after project is done, the differences between described practices and actual practices in company W might never be exposed.

5. Discussion

The empirical data gave us some evidence that hands-on practices in ISD organizations are far from official practices of how organizations describe their way of operating. Employees in ISD organizations tend to abandon practices and rules they find useless and replace them with ones they find useful. In some cases this is done in a way that the organizations management does not even know about it.

If organizations structure is continuously changing and CoPs are broken or employees are pressed to follow strict canonical processes it will break the soil for motivation, commitment, and innovativeness to develop. Most of the ISD organizations worldwide are nowadays seeking for short-term business profits and searching more productivity by developing their canonical methods, processes, and practices. We suggest that more concern should be paid on long-term objectives such as well-being of the personnel.

The OL and LO and numerous concepts that relate to them in several disciplines will probably remain fuzzy for most of the IS researchers until more empirical research is made to gain more insights to the area. As several studies have already pointed out, nature of learning in organizations varies across industries and time, so when, i.e., organizational structure or technology used in ISD projects changes in the same time new challenges of OL emerge.

There are naturally several limitations in this study. First, we were able to conduct only a minor intersection of the OL and LO literature. There would be numerous additional interesting results available, i.e., in knowledge management and IS discipline to explore. Though the literature review was limited, this is usually the case in most of the studies made so we do not see this as a major limitation.

Another limitation of the study obviously is the nature of empirical data we used to make our observations. The data were originally collected to study information systems development methods, processes, and practices used in Finnish ISD organizations. However, when our interest started to wheel toward OL and LO we were able to use theoretical sampling and adjust interview questions before interviews in Irish ISD organizations. When a retrospective examination to the original data collected in Finland was made, we felt that totally fresh lenses were provided to us for the analysis and we supposed that there were not much bias in the interviews. Anyway, we believe that the data would have been much richer if the original focus in the all interviews were been in OL and LO.

As a third limitation of this study we have to admit that part of the literature study was made before analyzing the data. This was because at first OL and LO were studied as separate subjects but in a later phase we became interested to combine lenses provided by OL and LO literature to the past research concerning methods, processes, and practices. If the grounded theory method would be strictly followed there should not have been any previous literature study of the subject that was studied. This instruction is unquestionably given to avoid any bias in interviews and data analysis. This third limitation was mitigated by utilizing investigator triangulation [10] during the analysis of the data.

As has been pointed out in several previous studies made outside IS disciple, learning depends on context where it takes place [21]. These studies also suggest that learning is usually far from canonical procedures, i.e., how the manuals and training programs [6] describe working procedures. In addition, learning varies at least across industries, products, and time [13]. Therefore, there is doubtless need for more empirical research related to OL and LO in the IS discipline.

6. Summary and Future Work

In this chapter, we have tried to provide the IS community some fresh lenses to OL and LO research. The creation, managing, communicating, and retrieving new knowledge are in any case focal part of any project. Therefore, we analyzed the OL and LO literature in different disciplines. We also used OL lenses to the empirical data gathered from six Finnish ISD organizations.

Our study suggests that within the IS discipline OL and LO subjects might have some unexplored areas. The study also argues that there is some theoretical diversity related to the subjects, also discussed in [8]. The study also suggests that other disciplines have provided us ample interesting results that have helped several organizations to learn and solve new challenges in their ISD projects.

The empirical data analyzed suggest that differences between canonical and non-canonical practices in ISD organizations might be useful to explore in more detailed level. The useless processes, methods, and practices may even be detrimental to organization in the longer run because when employees find canonical methods, processes, or practices useless they tend not to follow them. In addition, organizations will probably miss opportunities to learn when useful hands-on practices are not discussed or even recognized by the managers of an organization.

There are inevitably several similarities in practices of ISD organizations in Western European organizations; even differences in organizational culture and culture-related issues have shaped the organization in the course of the time. However, there are not so much studies related to differences in practices in ISD organizations operating worldwide where OL and culture have been used as lenses in the same time. A deep culture-related analysis between, i.e., Finnish and Irish ISD organizations might provide us some fresh insights to understand phenomena related to OL and LO in organizations that operate in different cultural districts. Though its limitations, the study gave the authors a good entry point to OL and LO studies and will serve as a baseline for further empirical studies related to the subjects.

References

1. Adler, P. and Cole, R. (1993). Designed for learning: A tale of two auto plants. *Sloan management review*, Spring 1993, Vol. 34, No.3., pp. 85–94.
2. Argyris, C. (1990). *Overcoming Organizational Defences – Facilitating Organizational Learning.* Prentice-Hall, Englewood Cliffs, NJ.
3. Argyris, C. (1992). *On Organizational Learning.* Blackwell Publishers Ltd, Malden, MA.
4. Argyris, C. (1993). *Knowledge for Action – A Guide to Overcoming barriers to Organizational Change.* Jossey Bass, San Francisco, CA.
5. Argyris, C. and Schön, D. (1996). *Organizational Learning II – Theory, Method and Practice.* Addison-Wesley, Reading, MA.
6. Brown, J. and Duguid, P. (1991). Organizational learning and communities of practice; toward a unified view of working, learning and innovation. *Organization Science*, February 1991, Vol. 2, No. 1., pp. 40–57.
7. Chen, J., Lee, T., Zhang, R. and Zhang Y. (2003) System requirements for organizational learning. *Communications of the ACM*, December 2003, Vol. 46, No. 12., pp. 73–78.
8. Chiva, R. and Alegre, J. (2005). Organizational learning and organizational knowledge: towards the integration of two approaches. *Management Learning*, March 2005, Vol. 36, No. 1., pp. 49–68.
9. Cyert, R. M. and March J. G. (1963) *Behavioral Theory of the Firm.* Prentice Hall, Englewood Cliffs, NJ.
10. Denzin, N. (1978). *The Research Act: A Theoretical Introduction to Sociological Methods.* McGraw-Hill, New York.
11. Denzin, N.K. and Lincoln, Y.S. (eds.) (2003). *Collecting and Interpreting Qualitative Materials.* Sage Publications, Thousand Oaks, CA.
12. Dierkes, M., Antal, A., Child, J. and Nonaka, I. (eds.) (2001). *Handbook of Organizational Learning and Knowledge.* Oxford University Press, Oxford.
13. Dutton, J. M. and Thomas, A. (1984). Treating progress functions as managerial opportunity. *Academic Management Review*, Vol. 9, pp. 235–247.
14. Easterby-Smith, M., Antonacopoulou, E., Simm, D. and Lyles, M. (2004). Constructing contributions to Organizational Learning. *Management Learning*, Dec 2004, Vol. 35, No. 4., pp. 317–380.
15. Easterby-Smith, M. and Araujo, L. (1999) Organizational learning: Current debates and opportunities In: Easterby-Smith, M., Burgoyne, J. and Araujo, L. (eds.) *Organizational Learning and the Learning Organization.* Sage Publications, Thousand Oaks, CA.
16. Edmondson (2002). The local and variegated nature of learning in organizations: A Group-level Perspective. *Organization Science*, March/April 2002, Vol. 13, No. 2., pp. 128–146.
17. Elkjaer, B. (1999). In Search of Social Learning Theory. In: Easterby-Smith, M., Burgoyne, J. and Araujo, L. (eds) *Organizational Learning and the Learning Organization.* Sage Publications, Thousand Oaks, CA.
18. Hargadon, A. and Bechky, B. (2006). When collections of creatives become creative collectives: a field study of problem solving at work. *Organizational Science*, July/August 2006, Vol. 17, No. 4., pp. 484–500.
19. Huber, G. P. Organizational learning: the Contributing processes and the literatures. *Organization Science*, February 1991, Vol. 2., No. 1., pp. 88–115.
20. Kolb, D. (1984). *Experimental Learning. Experience as The Source of Learning and Development.* Prentice Hall, Englewood Cliffs, NJ.
21. Lave, J. and Wenger, E. (1991) *Situated Learning: Legitimate Peripheral Participation.* Cambridge University Press, Cambridge.
22. Levitt, B. and March, J. (1988) Organizational learning. *Annual Review of Sociology,* Vol. 14, pp. 319–340.
23. Lyytinen K. and Robey, D. (1999). Learning failure in information systems development. *Information Systems Journal*, April 1999, Vol. 9, No. 2., pp. 85–101.
24. Lyytinen, K and Rose, G. M (2006). Information system development agility as organizational learning.*European Journal of Information Systems*, April 2006, Vol. 15, No 2., pp. 183–199.
25. Newell, S., Bresnen, M., Edelman, L. Scarbrough, H. and Swan, J. (2006). Sharing knowledge across projects: Limits to ICT-led project review practices. *Management Learning*, June 2006, Vol 37, No 2., pp. 167–185.
26. Orr, J. (1987). *Narratives at Work: Story Telling as Cooperative Diagnostic Activity.* Field Service Manager, pp. 47–60.
27. Schein, E. (1993). How can organizations learn faster? The challenge of entering the Green Room. *Sloan Management Review*, Winter 1993, Vol. 34, No.2.
28. Senge, P. (1990). *The Fifth Discipline – The Art & Practice of the Learning Organization.* Sage, New York.
29. Stein, E, and Vandenbosch, B (1996). Organizational learning during advanced system development: Opportunities and obstacles. *Journal on Management Information Systems*, Vol. 13, No. 2., pp. 115–136.
30. Strauss, A. L. and J. Corbin (1990). *Basics of Qualitative Research: Grounded Theory Procedures and Applications.* Sage Publications, Newbury Park, CA.
31. Tosey, P. (2005). The hunting of the learning organisation: A paradoxical journey. *Management Learning*, September 2005, Vol. 36, No 3., pp. 335–352.

32. Vera, D. and Crossnan, N. (2003). Organizational learning and knowledge management: Toward an integrative framework. In M. A. Lyles and M. Easterby-Smith (eds) *The Blackwell Handbook of Organizational Learning and Knowledge Management*, pp. 122–142., Blackwell Publishing, Oxford.

33. Wastell, D. (1999). Learning dysfunctions in information systems development: overcoming the social defenses with transitional objects. *Management Information Systems Quarterly*, Vol. 23, No. 4., pp. 581–600.

Contract Negotiations Supported Through Risk Analysis

Sérgio A. Rodrigues, Marco A. Vaz and Jano M. Souza

Abstract

Many clients often view software as a commodity; then, it is critical that IT sellers know how to create value into their offering to differentiate their service from all the others. Clients sometimes refuse to contract software development due to lack of technical understanding or simply because they are afraid of IT contractual commitments. The IT negotiators who recognize the importance of this issue and the reason why it is a problem will be able to work to reach the commercial terms they want. Therefore, this chapter aims to stimulate IT professionals to improve their negotiation skills and presents a computational tool to support managers to get the best out of software negotiations through the identification of contract risks.

Keywords Negotiation · Risk assessment · Decision support systems · Software contract negotiation

1. Introduction

Many negotiations of software development's contract seem successful from the seller's point of view; however, these contracts often show failures which appear only in the development process [1].

This fact occurs because many negotiators have been neglecting inherent software development risks and they have focused only on the sale's progression.

The lack of prior risk reviews may lead a promising business to fail early. It is common to find failures of IT professionals who think that they have created such an innovative solution that they have avoided the criticism and sharing of ideas.

This behavior often results in disappointments once many IT professionals do not consider that software sale is much different than software development.

A good IT negotiator must be skilled and experienced in software contract negotiations; indeed, it is necessary that a huge knowledge of the context and the product that is being negotiated, besides the risks, is involved.

However, in most IT contracts, the negotiator only tries to sell the software while the development risks are often transferred to the technical staff.

Negotiating requires ability for measuring risks which, when neglected, can unexpectedly lead to project failure. Negotiating software development can be seen as an instance of the act of negotiating something once it has parties, interests, alternatives, criteria for selection, relationships, and time to close an agreement.

Sérgio A. Rodrigues and Marco A. Vaz • COPPE/UFRJ - Computer Science Department, Graduate School of Engineering, Federal University of Rio de Janeiro, Brazil.

G.A. Papadopoulos et al. (eds.), *Information Systems Development*, DOI 10.1007/b137171_60,

To be efficient in these negotiations, it is suggestive to seek preponderant information about the parties, technical characteristics, and quality parameters besides the services expected, aiming at adding value to each new negotiation held.

In the course of software negotiating contracts, the points of conflict ordinarily focus on scope definition, cost, and quality parameters.

In this type of trading, the risks involved should be considered to form acceptable values to avoid future conflicts. Thus, the preparation of these negotiations tends to be more productive with the prior review of risks.

Accordingly, this chapter will present the approaches used for knowledge acquisition and software's contract risks identification as well as some criteria used to classify them.

The work will also present a tool whose objective is to support IT professionals in the negotiation preparation step. A case study is presented in order to examine the tool usability and to show advantages of using risk management in the software contract negotiation's context.

2. Risk Management

Failure situations found in software development projects are often linked to one or more unidentified risks in the early stages of negotiation, which could have been avoided if they had been identified and assessed correctly [2].

In [3], the author states the risk of focusing on closing contract negotiations. The author also claims that the negotiator must recognize that contract closing is only the beginning of the process of value creation. The real challenge is not to ensure small victories before the signing, but the projection of an agreement that works in practice.

The perception of risks in some negotiations is more significant, but risk is an element found in all negotiations, no matter their nature [4]. In addition, all risks have costs involved and can take huge or small impact on some project's elements such as timeline, scope, quality, resources, and relationships [5].

According to [6], even though a survey of methodologies tackles different types of risks management, there is no established standard. Because of this, many risk management methods have been used in the market such as Project Management Institute (PMI), Failure Mode and Effect Analysis (FMEA), Hazard and Operability Analysis (HAZOP), and Financial Risk Management. On the other hand, all of them show qualitative and quantitative risk analysis, which permit to identify, evaluate, prioritize, and measure the project negotiation risks.

In the set of procedures for risk managing, described in PMBOK [5], this work uses the processes to quantify the risks through the cost estimate (monetary value), the threats and opportunities and values involved in the actions to mitigate the risk. As shown in Fig. 60.1, after risk assessment and response, the negotiator will be prepared to go to negotiation table.

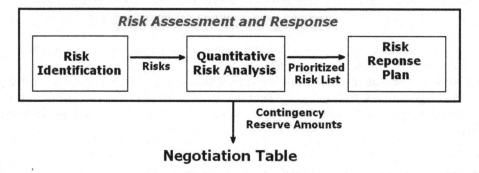

Figure 60.1. Risk assessment and response.

Risk assessment is a process that evaluates risks through qualitative and quantitative analysis. According to PMBOK [5], the expected value is the importance obtained by the multiplication of impact and probability of risk occurrence and can be used to estimate the risk importance (i.e., risk = probability × impact).

The risk analysis process, associated to different points of view, is one of the motivations to create methods to evaluate risk relevance. This type of method can use financial values to appraise risk significance. The idea is to build an instrument, based on quantitative analysis, which considers the probability of risk event occurrences in IT contract negotiations, taking into account elements such as contract, scope, requisites, and quality.

As a quantification metrics, the negotiator will indicate the probability and impact of each risk stored and, based on this information, it is possible to calculate the cost of threats and the value of opportunities through the Expected Monetary Value Formula (Probability × Impact).

$$EVM = PR * Ic$$

EVM - Expected Monetary Value
Pr - the probability that the risk will occur
Ic - Ic for the cost impact

The Total Risk Value (TRV) is the sum of the Expected Values of all threat and opportunities risks. Threats are negative and opportunities are positive values.

$$TRV = \sum_{n=1}^{N} EVM_n$$

EVM - Expected Monetary Value
TRV$_1$ - Total Risk Value

The Expected-Value calculation must be added to the initial contract cost to be computed on the total project Expected Monetary Value before risk management.

Once the Total Risk Value for Threats (TRVT) and Total Risk Value for Opportunities (TRVO) have been calculated, the Base Value Expected (BVE + TRVT – TRVO) can be achieved as well as the Best and Worst negotiation case.

The Worst Case considers a situation in which all threats happen and no opportunities appear. On the other hand, the Best Case takes into account only the opportunities and not the threats. The risk quantification, calculated through the expected value, identifies these negotiation limits: the worst and the best case.

The interval between the values assessed as best and worst can be called ZOPA – Zone Of Possible Agreement. As showed in Fig. 60.2, ZOPA involves the range that satisfies both negotiation counterparties [7–9]. In this work, ZOPA is considered the range where the agreement may happen between the minimum acceptable and the maximum desired.

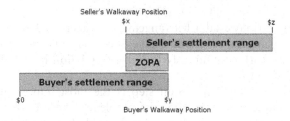

Figure 60.2. Zone of possible agreement.

The negotiation process involves seeking an alternative within a set of actions to risk response. These actions are designed to provide alternatives to negotiators to establish alternative paths of action when the negotiable agreement is far [8].

These alternatives can be compared to the BATNA concept (Best Alternative To a Negotiated Agreement) which is used to assist negotiators to keep the focus on the objective and to present different ways of achieving the planned interests [7, 9].

A systematic process to manage risks provides enough information to IT professionals and has been considered a key factor to determine the project success degree. In this context, the negotiation process appears to be the main aspect to any organization entrepreneur. Besides, the negotiation can be more productive if the negotiator knows that there are risks involved and realizes that risks can be not only threats but also opportunities.

3. The Negotiation Process

Both in organizations and daily life, situations involving negotiations permeate the relationship between individuals. It is common to experience circumstances in which, spontaneously, people create new relationships that often results in opportunities to make coexistent relations or business agreements.

In spite of premeditated or unexpected events, a good negotiator has a natural capacity to find opportunities. The ability to anchor agreements is commonly acquired over time; as a result, experienced negotiators have, theoretically, more chances to be successful [10]. This often occurs because the experienced negotiator is fast at discovering the main points of conflict, as well as the interests of each party.

In general, negotiation is an activity that requires training, practice, coaching, strategy, preparation, and allows the execution of agreements that are mutually acceptable for counterparts, even though different conflicts may occur and external help may be needed [7].

According to [11], a conflict can be defined as a concurrent situation in which counterparts are aware of future incompatibilities related to potential positions. In this case, a conflict occurs when one party takes an incompatible position in relation to the other counterpart's desires. In IT context, the main points of conflicts are scope, time, cost and quality, and the challenging resource management [5].

It is important to emphasize that the negotiations can be divided into steps. As said in [11], in a negotiation process four stages can be identified: preparation, value creation, value division, and execution.

Preparation is the phase where negotiators should point out their positions clearly and try to comprehend the counterparts' relationship [7]. Besides, in the preparation step, the negotiation should define the ZOPA (Zone Of Possible Agreement), or simply zone of potential agreements, which involves the counterparts' satisfaction range [9]. The ZOPA must also consider cultural aspects [12] and elaboration of mutual gain suggestions [13].

In the Value Creation step, it is important to explore counterpart's interests and to create alternatives that extend mutual gains [14]. At this stage, it is imperative to avoid criticism and encourage the use of neutrality to facilitate the relationships and to enable the creation without prior commitments.

The Value Division is a step to propose contingent agreements and to project future agreements [11]. At this stage, the neutrality must be used to suggest possible ways of distribution and discuss standards and criteria for distributing the generated value [14, 15].

Finally, the Execution step may establish arrangements to keep track or check adopted decisions and facilitate the commitments maintenance. At this stage, incentives and organizational controls must be aligned, and it is essential to work continuously to improve relationships and use neutrality to resolve disagreements as well [11, 16].

Among these four phases, the Preparation step is the most important once it gathers enough information to facilitate the agreement, to define the problem to be solved, and to position clearly the counterparties' interests. Great negotiators have already said that this step is the key to success in negotiations [17–20] because it prevents the consolidation of counterparts' inflexible positions and focuses on the main interests of the involved parties [21, 22] and power [23].

Therefore, IT contract negotiation preparation is a moment to identify positions, strengths, and weaknesses, and cannot be a stage to try to impose or to persuade. The negotiators should know how to describe their interests in an ethical way and, when possible, they may rescue characteristics of similar negotiations.

Then, it is important to highlight that there are similarities in the best practices used by the major negotiators [24], so that it is possible to imagine a group of negotiation reports and interfaces, based on best practices, which support even inexperienced negotiators.

These aspects denote a necessity in organizing the IT contract negotiations on systematic steps and provide reports to create a negotiation diagnostic. This approach can support not only experienced negotiators, through the negotiation knowledge management, but also inexpert professionals. During negotiations, the turnover of negotiators is common and the lack of information is the attenuation factor to maintain the negotiation productivity.

In this work, it is also proposed a series of steps whose goal is to guide the IT contract negotiation process, using risk management and negotiation knowledge management, especially in the preparation phase.

Naturally, the negotiation process is very dynamic and, as stated in [25], there is no mathematical formula to find the best negotiation practice since its attributes do not obey mathematical functions that can be transcribed into regular curves. The negotiation attributes derived from unequal and irregular sets and only the best practices can be considered to guide the negotiator and increase the chances of an agreement [26].

In the negotiation context, the scope of this chapter aims to show a viable alternative to structure IT contract negotiations, considering the IT professional as the negotiator.

4. IT Contract Negotiation

The competitive globalization environment has led negotiations to conflict situations, in which counterparties are competing in a zero-sum game [7]. The competition between suppliers can help to reduce cost due to negotiators tendency to make concessions that may change the product value. On the other hand, the negotiators are often neglecting the risks of such actions.

From the client's point of view, the developing software outsourcing is motivated by the possibility of transferring the technological risk. However, these factors often cause a breach of the budget, problems with deadlines, and features that do not satisfy the customer needs.

Inexperience in the negotiation context can also be a problem. Frequently, the sale of software is done by professionals who are not from the IT area, which raises difficulties to anticipate risks in the project's execution phase.

On the other hand, it is also interesting to note that the aspiration for new careers conducts IT professionals to migrate to sale areas. This alternative requires capacity to broaden their knowledge in other subjects, such as trading, risk analysis, and negotiation performance.

In this context, Bosworth [27] introduces the sale engineering concept as a training to transform an IT technician into an IT seller. Thus, the sale engineer will be the professional with IT background and expertise in software contract negotiations.

In this type of contracts, it is crucial that customer and supplier are in consensus about the software requirements. While the seller or the technologist is concerned with speaking tactically about terms of applications or tools, the customer wants to talk in strategic terms – the benefits, risks, and returns [28].

As pereira [29] said, when a technical IT professional is the leader of the software contract negotiation, he becomes a natural candidate to have credibility and, as a result, is a candidate more accessible to discover the client's interests.

It is important to emphasize that the word seller is still mystified as a person who only wants the clients' money. This fact creates a necessity for IT professionals to assume this role through expertise in trading, risk management, and software sale engineering [27, 10, 29].

Therefore, this work also shows a computational tool which supports IT professionals in the negotiation's preparation through functionalities, such as negotiation knowledge management, risk identification, and risk quantification.

This tool was experimented in some IT contracts and will be explained in the next section. The negotiations' context and results will also be illustrated.

5. Case Study and Results

The objective of this section is to evaluate the tool proposed through a real negotiation case. The negotiation was supported by RisNeg software and this section will clarify this tool and illustrate how the prototype functionalities influenced in the agreement.

The negotiation analyzed in this chapter was carried out during software development contract. The negotiation was considered complex once it involved groups with different interests and negotiation behaviors, several issues, and unexpected results. In the description, the real names will be changed to guarantee the confidentiality of the involved entities: MarSer and BraxPetrol.

5.1. Negotiation Context

This negotiation aimed at renewing an IT contract, in which MarSer was the supplier and BraxPetrol the client.

MarSer is an Information Technology institution which researches and develops software. MarSer has around 120 professionals (managers, developers, and researchers), including this chapter's authors. The client of this negotiation was BraxPetrol institution, a company which deals with petroleum exploration, production, and commercialization in whole world, especially in Brazil.

In general, contract renovations used to be easier than new deals but, in this case, some elements were influenced to difficult the agreement. The main aspects were the political environment once the principal sponsor was changed and the constant trials to decrease costs and increase software requisites.

At that time, MarSer negotiators decided to use the RisNeg software to manage risks and to store negotiations data. The objective was to identify threats and opportunities and set up the negotiation preparation step.

5.2. Using RisNeg in the Negotiation

The preparation phase indicated that the BraxPetrol negotiators were not in consensus. One group was defending the renewing and the other opposing the contract continuity.

Therefore, some trade risks were previously identified by MarSer negotiators and RisNeg was applied to manage them, as illustrated in Fig. 60.3.

RisNeg is a computational prototype to manage negotiation's risks. After storing basic negotiation data (client, goals, stakeholders), the negotiator can manage threats and opportunities risks, as showed in Fig. 60.3. Afterward, based on the survey on potential risks, the software suggests some measurement parameters to evaluate the threats and opportunities as well as the reaction priority for each risk.

In BraxPetrol's negotiation, the main threat stored in RisNeg was the possibility of the client deciding to purchase another proprietary software. The effect would be the loss of the capital and time invested on the negotiation.

On the other hand, a good identified opportunity was the use of MarSer's great knowledge on the client's business to keep the contract and to negotiate staff financing in the period without contract.

These examples allow the negotiator to visualize the quantified impacts. The negotiator will then be able to prepare the negotiation strategy. Besides, RisNeg allows recalculations through the "Variation Analysis" field which guarantees high flexibility for the measured data.

Fig. 60.4 illustrates a summarized analysis considering the Expected Values of threats and opportunities. Based on this graph, MarSer's negotiators could study the real chances of agreement, the threat and opportunity effects, and the worst and best negotiation cases. This diagram helped BraxPetrol's negotiators choose the best alternative to the contract closing.

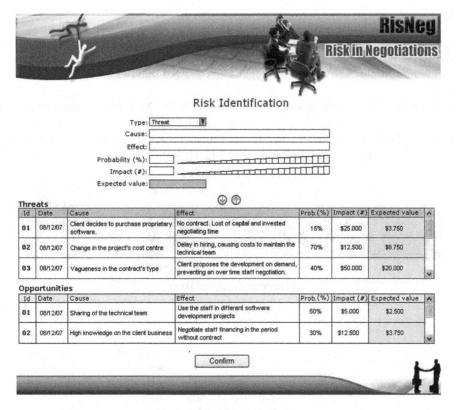

Figure 60.3. Risk identification.

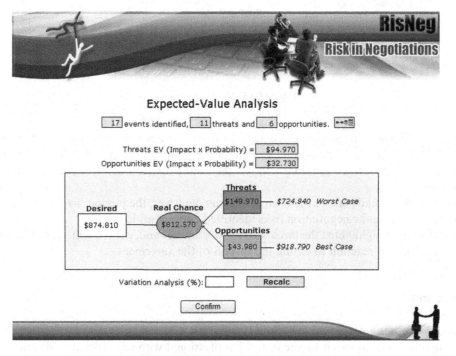

Figure 60.4. Expected-value analysis.

5.3. Results

During the negotiation, the client's perception on the intangible variables was positive, especially about the MarSer's services quality. Although the change of the sponsor had affected the negotiation beginning, the method employed by MarSer's negotiators showed that the contract continuity would bring mutual benefits.

Moreover, the BraxPetrol's business understanding allowed MarSer to maintain positions, such as requirements and development time; then, the zone of conflict focused on the proposal price.

Consequently, the use of RisNeg favored the agreement once the negotiators had the visualization of possible threats and opportunities at hand, as seen in Fig. 60.4 and 60.5.

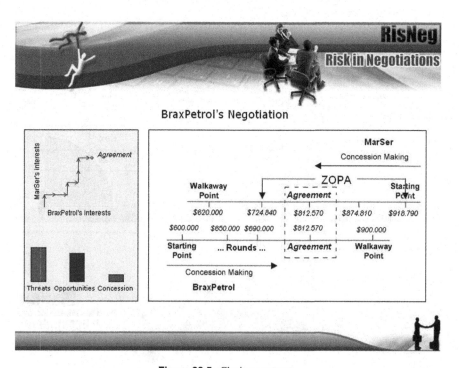

Figure 60.5. Closing contract.

As a result, MarSer's negotiators managed to close the agreement within the Zone Of Possible Agreement (ZOPA). The final resolution, as well as the variables arranged for each round could be increased gradually in RisNeg. Figure 60.5 shows the final provision of the agreement considering the planned parameters.

Some rounds were made before the contract closing; however, the predominant factor of success was the convenience of having the negotiation risks identified and quantified.

The use of RisNeg highlighted the threats and opportunities and, consequently, MarSer's negotiators could take their shares of reaction to ensure the success of the agreement.

6. Conclusions

Overall, IT projects are exposed to various types of risks. In software contract negotiations, the seller can have competitive advantages if he/she is an IT professional with negotiation skills due to the understanding of the context and client interests.

This work aims at presenting the software contract negotiation through the prism of risk management. This approach attempts to develop a strategy to facilitate risk identification and quantification, inferring risk probabilities and impacts.

Even though it seems to be difficult for many professionals to quantify the attributes of IT negotiations, risk quantification is an important metric to identify what the priority in the deal is.

The case study showed that it is possible and suggestive to use risk management methods in IT contract negotiation. In this chapter, a computational tool was applied to map the threats and opportunities in the negotiation preparation step and to show the chances of an agreement.

Therefore, the obtained results attempted to demonstrate the use of RisNeg as IT negotiation risk and knowledge management, aiding the identification of preponderant elements and leading to successful negotiation. The systematic use of this software makes the IT negotiations more objective because of the welldefined risk criteria. Then, the negotiation is faced as more productive and the negotiators do not feel they are wasting their time due to lack of compliance.

As a future work, the proposed system would easily accept the allocation of values from simulation tools such as Monte Carlo. A further alternative would be the use of data mining to rescue similarities in old stored negotiations.

Another example of the advance is to supplement RisNeg with negotiation workflows and data warehousing to observe the negotiation and risk background.

References

1. Boehm, B., 1996. Anchoring the software process, *IEEE Software*, Vol. 13, Issue 4, 73–82.
2. Boehm, B.; Ross, R., 1989. Theory-W software project management: Principles and examples. In: *IEEE Transactions on Software Engineering*, Vol. 15, No. 7.
3. Ertel, D., 2004. *Getting Past Yes: Negotiating as if Implementation Mattered.* Harvard Business Review, Boston MA.
4. Bartlett, J., 2004. *Project Risk Analysis and Management Guide*, Second Edition ed., Apm Publishing Limited, London.
5. PMBOK, 2004. *Project Management Body of Knowledge*, 2004 Edition. Project Management Institute, http://www.pmi.org.
6. Hillson, D., 2007. *Managing Project Risks.* World PM Magazine. Rio de Janeiro, Feb. 2007.
7. Fisher, R.; Ury, W., 1991. *Getting To Yes*: Negotiating an Agreement Without Giving In. Century Business, Boston.
8. Raiffa, H., 1982. *The Art and Science of Negotiation.* Harvard University Press, Cambridge, Massachusetts.
9. Harvard Business Essentials, 2003. *Negotiation*, The Harvard Business Essentials Series (Paperback), Harvard Business School Publishing Corporation, Boston.
10. Chapman, M. R., 1999. *The Product Marketing Handbook for Software.* Aegis Resources, Glastonbury, Connecticut.
11. Duzert, Y. org., 2007. *Manual de negociações complexas.* Editora FGV, Rio de Janeiro.
12. Faure, G. O.; Rubin, J. Z., 1993. *Culture and Negotiation.* Sage Publications, Newbury Park.
13. Susskind, L.; Cruikshank, J. L., 2006. *Breaking Robert's Rules.* Oxford University Press, Oxford.
14. Bazerman, M. H., 2002. *Judgment in Managerial Decision Making.* 5 ed. New York: Wiley.
15. Rawls, J., 1971. *A Theory of Justice.* Harvard University Press, Cambridge.
16. Susskind, L.; Cruikshank, J., 1987. *Breaking the Impasse: Consensual Approaches to Resolving Public Disputes.* Basic Book, New York.
17. Adams, C. R.; Hicks, R. D., 2001. *Preparation for Trial.* The Harrison Company, New York, 300 p.
18. Tardy, T., 2004. *The Brahimi Report: Four Years On.* Proceedings of a Workshop held at the GCSP, June 2004, 18p.
19. Kennedy, G., 2004. *Essential Negotiation*, The Economist Newspaper Ltd. 240 p.
20. Baker, J., 2006. *Ask the Negotiator.* The Negotiation Magazine, March 2006. Available in <http://www.negotiatormagazine.com/article315_1.html>, 03/23/2008.
21. Rothman, J., 1992. Conflict management policy analysis. In: Rothman J (ed) *From Confrontation to Cooperation.* Sage, Newbury Park.
22. Zartman, I. W.; Rubin, J. Z., 1999. *Power and Negotiation.* University of Michigan, Ann Arbor.
23. Boulding, K. E., 1989. *Three Faces of Power.* Sage Publications, Newbury Park, CA.
24. Lewicki, R.; Saunders, D.; Minton, J., 1999. *Negotiation*, 3rd ed., McGraw-Hill, Boston, 202 p.
25. Leontief, W. W., 1958. Factor Proportions and the Structure of American Trade: Further Theoretical and Empirical Analysis. *The Review of Economics and Statistics*, Vol. 40, No. 1, Part 2. Problems in International Economics. pp. 119–122.
26. Raiffa, H., 1985. Post-Settlement Settlements. *Negotiation Journal*, Vol. 1, Issue 1, pp. 9–12.
27. Bosworth, M. T., 1995. *Solution Selling.* Mc-Graw-Hill, New York.
28. Page, R., 2002. *Hope Is Not a Strategy.* Nautilus Press, Atlanta.
29. Pereira, A., 2004. *Selling Software.* São Paulo, Novatec Editora.

61

Instantiating Software Processes: An Industry Approach

Peter Killisperger, Georg Peters, Markus Stumptner and Thomas Stückl

Abstract

Software processes are used for organizing work in software development projects. In order to use them for a number of projects they are described in a generic way. Since software development is highly individual, they have to be particularized (i.e., instantiated) in turn for becoming applicable in projects. A number of instantiation approaches have been proposed in recent years, but none has become a de facto standard in industry. Therefore instantiation in many software developing organizations is still manual and lacks standardization, making the procedure time consuming and expensive. This chapter describes a standardized and semi-automated instantiation approach developed at Siemens. The approach supports instantiation by ensuring that the resulting process is syntactically correct and consistent.

Keywords Software development processes · Semi-automation · Tailoring · Standardization

1. Introduction

Most organizations use processes for developing software. According to ISO 15504 [10] a software process is "the process or a set of processes used by an organization or project to plan, manage, execute, monitor, control, and improve its software related activities." Organizations choose an existing approach as their standard (e.g., the Rational Unified Process [12]), adapt one, or define their own process according to their individual needs.

In order to apply processes to a spectrum of projects they are described in a generic way as reference processes. However, software projects are highly individual. To be able to use a process in a project it has to be instantiated. Instantiation is the representation of an abstraction by a concrete instance [14]. In other words, the generic description of the software process is specialized and adapted to the needs of a particular project. Recent studies show that instantiation of software processes is still a wide open field for research [16].

Within Siemens, software developing business units define reference processes which are applied in any software project within that business unit. They are intended to be a guideline and basis from which the actual process is derived. This instantiation is done manually and only partly standardized which is time

---

Peter Killisperger • Competence Center Information Systems, University of Applied Sciences–München, Germany; Advanced Computing Research Centre, University of South Austrlia, Adelaide, Australia.   **Georg Peters** • Department of Computer Science and Mathematics, University of Applied Sciences-München, München, Germany.   **Markus Stumptner** • Advanced Computing Research Centre, University of South Australia, Adelaide, Australia.   **Thomas Stückl** • Siemens Corporate Technology, Software and System Processes, Munich, Germany.

G.A. Papadopoulos et al. (eds.), *Information Systems Development*, DOI 10.1007/b137171_61,

consuming and thus expensive. Siemens Corporate Technology, the University of South Australia, and the University of Applied Sciences–München are collaborating to improve current practice.

A standardized and semi-automated approach has been developed supporting project managers when instantiating software processes. By executing basic instantiation operations, a process is adapted step by step to project specific needs. It is guaranteed that the resulting process is syntactically correct and consistent. The process can then be applied more effectively as described in Killisperger et al. [11].

The contribution of this chapter is to introduce to Siemens' Software Processes, their current instantiation, and the developed approach. The fundamentals of the approach are described in detail, basic instantiation operations forming the elementary building blocks of the approach are defined, and its application is demonstrated in a use case.

This chapter is structured as follows: Section 2 gives an overview of related work. Section 3 introduces to Siemens' processes, describes their current instantiation, and clarifies the need for a standardized and semi-automated instantiation approach. The fundamentals of the developed approach are detailed in Section 4. Its implementation is described, a use case of its application is given, and the approach is evaluated. This chapter ends with a conclusion in Section 5.

2. Related Work

Instantiation of processes to project specific needs has been subject to intensive research in recent years. However, in early software process approaches it was thought that a perfect process can be developed which fits all software developing organizations and all types of projects [5]. It was soon recognized that no such process exists [15, 3]. Due to the dynamics of software development, every project has individual needs. Therefore, the description of the general software process (i.e., the reference process) has to be adapted to be applicable.

Early approaches to overcome this problem have been developed, for example, by Boehm and Belz [5] and Alexander and Davis [2]. The former used the Spiral Model to develop project-specific software processes. The latter described 20 criteria upon which the best suited process model for a project can be selected.

Many different adaptation approaches have been proposed since then and the need for adaptation of processes is recognized in industry which is shown by publications about tailoring approaches in practice, e.g., Bowers et al. [6], Fitzgerald et al. [8].

Although a lot of effort has been put into improving the adaption of software processes to project-specific needs, only few approaches offer a completely standardized and semi-automated method and none has become accepted in industry as the standard so far.

An important reason is the variety of processes used in practice. Instantiation approaches depend heavily on the meta model underlying the processes. For instance, Yoon et al. [19] developed an approach for adapting processes in the form of Activity–Artifact–Graphs. Activities have a name, type, input and output artifacts and are consequently connected by artifacts. Since the process is composed of activities and artifacts, only the operations "addition" and "deletion" of activities and artifacts are supported, as well as "split" and "merge" of activities. Another example is the V-Model [4], a process model developed for the German public sector. It offers a toolbox of process modules and execution strategies. Process modules comprise related activities and define work products, activities, and roles. The execution strategy defines the chronological and organizational flow. The approach for developing a project-specific software process is to select required process modules and an execution strategy. Due to these dependencies on the meta models, none of the existing approaches offers a fully standardized and semi-automated method for instantiating Siemens' processes.

Because of the close relationship between Siemens' processes, business processes, and workflows, also adaptation approaches for the latter two are of interest. However, the approaches for processes and workflows of higher complexity are often restricted to only a subset of adaptation operations. For instance, Rosemann and Aalst [17] developed configurable EPCs (C-EPCs) enabling the customization of reference processes. Also, concepts and tools supporting users in using C-EPCs have been developed [7, 13]. However, the approach only allows activities of the process to be switched on/off, the replacement of gateways, and the definition of dependencies of adaptation decisions. A comprehensive and flexible adaption of processes as required for Siemens' software development is not supported.

3. The Siemens Software Processes

Processes at Siemens cover the whole life cycle of a software product. They are similar to workflows but their focus is to be read and understood by humans and not to be automated by IT. The process definition language XPDL [18] is used for their definition. Because of the high number of elements associated with activities and the size of Siemens' processes it is advantageous to use two types of diagrams for visualization. We use UML activity diagram like models but extended them for our needs by distinguishing between models describing the temporal order of activities and models specifying participants and artifacts associated with activities. We call the diagram for the former Control-Flow-Model and the visualization for the latter Activity-Allocation-Model.

In the Control-Flow-Model the elements start events, activities, milestones, gateways (i.e., splits and joins) and end events can occur. They are connected by transitions which form the control flow. A process has only one start event and at least one end event. Between start event and end events all remaining objects can occur by meeting the defined constraints. Splits and joins of the type AND, OR, and XOR can be used to start and end parallel and alternative paths. Milestones have similar characteristics to activities. However, because of the importance of milestones for project management, milestones are defined as their own type.

The Activity-Allocation-Model specifies participants and artifacts associated with activities. Participants can be either human or an application. Human participants are of the type *person*, *role*, *organizational unit*, or *group*. Applications can only be of the type *system*. The association of a participant with an activity has an additional attribute expressing the relationship (e.g., "is responsible for" or "executes") and is subject to constraints (e.g., there can only be one participant with the relationship "responsible for"). Artifacts are associated with files implementing them and can be input and output of activities. The direction of the arc connecting the artifact and the activity indicates whether it is input or output. If an artifact is updated, it is both input and output.

Figure 61.1 shows a simplified example of a part of a Siemens process. The Control-Flow-Model describes the development of components. The marked sub process has to be executed for every component of the system to be developed while it is monitored by the activity "Plan, Monitor & Control Development of Components." An Activity-Allocation-Model is only detailed for "Develop Test Specification" but exists for all activities.

In these reference processes the development of a system is only described generically. Since the development of a system is subject to individual requirements the process has to be instantiated. Instantiation of Siemens' processes comprises in a narrow sense (1) tailoring, (2) resource allocation, and (3) instantiation of process artifacts.

1. *Tailoring.* Tailoring is "the act of adjusting the definitions and/or of particularizing the terms of a general process description to derive a new process applicable to an alternative (and probably less general) environment" [9]. That means, tailoring is not restricted to cutting away unneeded parts but also includes the addition and change of parts of the process.
2. *Resource Allocation.* The assignment of resources to activities to carry them out is called resource allocation [1]. In most cases human participants are allocated, because only few activities can be completely executed by applications in software development.
3. *Instantiation of Artifacts.* The general artifacts have to be individualized for a project at hand and associated with files implementing the artifacts.

Figure 61.2 shows the example process of Fig. 61.1 instantiated for the development of a system "xyz." Since the system requires two components to be developed, the marked sub process of Fig. 61.1 is

Section of Control-Flow-Model

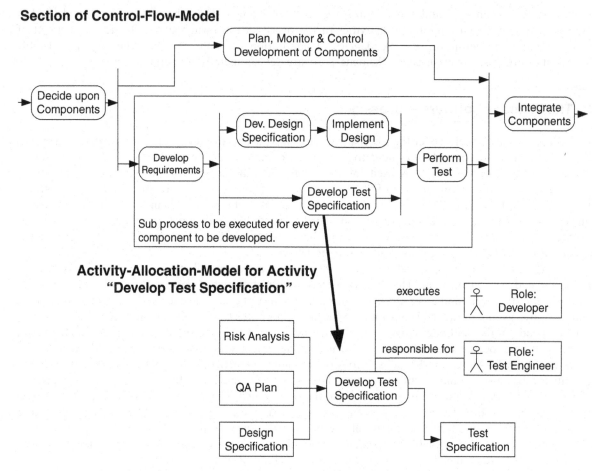

Figure 61.1. Example of a reference process.

duplicated and instantiated. In addition, project management decided to adapt the sub process for the development of component B by adding an additional activity "Check Safety Relevance of Component." Beside the Control-Flow-Model the Activity-Allocation-Models are instantiated, too. Figure 61.2 contains only Activity-Allocation-Models for the activities "Develop Test Specification" of the sub processes but they exist for every activity.

Until now, this instantiation is manual and only partly standardized at Siemens. However, using a fully standardized and semi-automated approach for instantiating software processes has strong advantages:

- Semi-automated adaptation ensures maintenance of consistency of complex processes. In addition, it is less time consuming and less expensive than manual instantiation.
- Due to the existence of a standardized instantiated software process model, project participants can be better supported in applying processes. It helps to reduce the various perceptions and applications of the process and implies more effective and efficient software projects.
- Decisions made in the instantiation of the reference process can be automatically documented and therefore are reproducible.
- Standardization of the instantiation approach enables easier and better improvement of the reference process.

In order to improve practice, Siemens' current approach of instantiating and applying software processes has been analyzed and an improved method developed.

Section of Control-Flow-Model

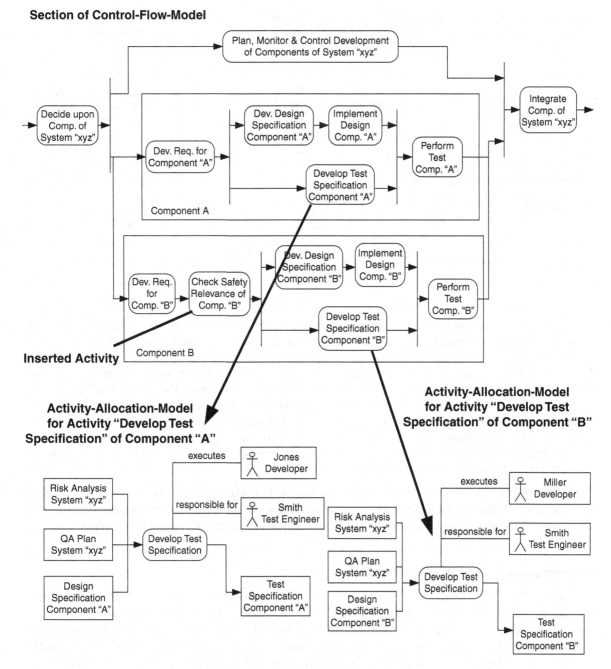

Figure 61.2. Example of an instantiated process.

4. Standardized and Semi-automated Instantiation of Processes

The developed approach supports project members by offering an instantiation procedure which guarantees a resulting process that is syntactically correct and consistent. It consists of three layers as illustrated in Fig. 61.3. The objects forming the three layers are the building blocks for implementing a system for semi-automated instantiation of software processes.

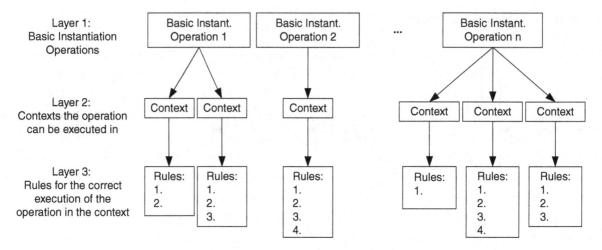

Figure 61.3. Three-layer instantiation approach.

1. *Basic Instantiation Operations.* They are the elementary building blocks of the approach. Examples are the deletion of an activity in the process or the association of an artifact with an activity. They are encapsulated operations on a process. By executing them, a process is step by step adapted to project-specific needs.
2. *Contexts.* Each operation can be executed in one ore more contexts. Restrictions on the execution depend on the context. For instance, the execution of the operation "Inserting an Activity" depends on the preceding and successive elements in the control flow. Thus every possible combination of preceding and successive element is considered as a context when inserting an activity.
3. *Rules.* Rules are defined, restricting the execution of an operation in a specific context and thus guaranteeing that the resulting process is syntactically correct and consistent. However, they do not check for semantic correctness.

The approach is not restricted to Siemens processes. However, since the basic instantiation operations, the contexts and the rules depend on the meta model of the software process, the objects of the three layers have to be adapted to be applicable to processes with a different underlying meta model.

4.1. Implementation of the Approach

On the basis of an analysis of the given reference processes and their current and desired application in projects, basic instantiation operations have been identified. The operations are as elementary as possible in order to reduce complexity and avoid dependencies with other operations. Because of this simplicity, it might be necessary to execute more than one basic operation to accomplish a complex adaptation step. Operations can be executed several times and in any order. They are grouped in the categories (A) control flow, (B) information flow, and (C) resources.

A. Control Flow

1. *Inserting an Activity.* An additional activity specified by the user is inserted in the control flow. The user provides the required information, i.e., selects the control flow where the activity is to be inserted and provides the necessary information for creating a new activity.
2. *Deleting an Activity.* An activity selected by the user is deleted in the process.
3. *Inserting an Alternative/Parallel Path.* An additional parallel or alternative path is inserted into the process. The user has to select a control flow from where the new path diverges, a control flow where

the path rejoins the process again (in case it rejoins the process), and the type of split and join to insert for the diversion.

4. *Duplicating a Sub Process*. The user marks a number of elements connected by control flows to be duplicated. The operation "Duplicating a Sub Process" creates copies of the elements including control flows, resource connections and information flows. The connection, to elements of the main process is established.

5. *Inserting a Milestone*. A new milestone is inserted in the process. The user provides the information necessary for the creation and selects the control flow where the milestone is to be inserted.

6. *Deleting a Milestone*. A milestone selected by the user is deleted in the process.

B. Information Flow

7. *Creating an Information Flow*. An existing artifact is associated with an activity as input and/or output. The user has to specify the required information.

8. *Deleting an Information Flow*. An association of an artifact with an activity as input or output selected by the user is deleted.

9. *Adding an Artifact to the Process*. A new process artifact is added to the process. The user has to provide all information required.

10. *Removing an Artifact from the Process*. An artifact selected by the user is deleted in the process (the process artifact itself and all associations with activities).

11. *Instantiating an Artifact with a File*. A template or an existing implementation of a process artifact is associated with a process artifact. The user has to specify process artifact and file.

C. Resources

12. *Creating a Resource Connection*. A participant is associated with an activity. The user has to select both elements.

13. *Deleting a Resource Connection*. The association of a participant with an activity selected by the user is deleted.

14. *Adding a Participant to the Process*. An additional participant (abstract or real person) is added to the process. The user has to specify all necessary information.

15. *Removing a Participant from the Process*. A participant selected by the user is deleted in the process.

Contexts have been identified in which the basic instantiation operations can be executed in and rules for the correct execution of the operations in the contexts have been defined. However, not all contexts require specific rules, i.e., for a number of contexts the same rules can be used. This led to the definition of standard rules for each operation which guarantees a syntactically correct and consistent resulting process for the majority of contexts an operation can be executed in.

Because of space limitations we cannot describe all contexts with their corresponding rules in this chapter. Instead, the notion of contexts and rules is described by means of a use case.

4.2. Use Case "Inserting a Milestone"

Below a use case is given for executing the basic instantiation operation "Inserting a Milestone" on the process of Fig. 61.1. The following scenario is the basis for the use case:

Project management decides to insert an additional milestone "M1"at the end of the development of a component.

For inserting a milestone the basic instantiation operation "Inserting a Milestone" has to be run. The user Selects the control flow connecting the activity "Perform Test" with the following AND join. The following context is identified:

Instantiation Operation:	Inserting a Milestone
Context:	Preceding element: Activity
	Successive element: AND Join

This context is associated with the standard rule as defined in Section 4.1. The input parameters are the control flow (cf) connecting the activity with the following AND join and the information (info) required for the creation of the milestone.

```
InsertMilestone (ControlFlow cf, MilestoneInfo info)
    m = new Milestone (info)
    new ControlFlow (cf.source, m)
    new ControlFlow (m, cf.target)
    delete (cf)
```

Figure 61.4 shows the control flow model of the resulting process after adapting the example process of Fig. 61.1 as described in the use case.

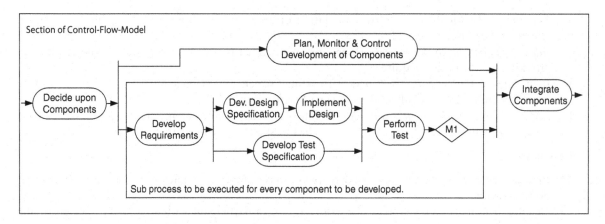

Figure 61.4. Resulting process of use case.

A new milestone "M1" is created and connected by control flows with the activity "Perform Test" and the following AND join. The originally selected control flow is deleted in order to maintain a syntactically correct process.

4.3. Evaluation of the Approach

The basic instantiation operations were evaluated by a selected group of process experts by asking them for their opinion about the usefulness and completeness.

The validation showed that experts view the instantiation operations from different perspectives. Some argued for the inclusion of more complex operations, e.g., for the assignment of a real-world participant to an abstract participant of an activity. Such operations are not included in the current list since our intention was to define operations as elementary as possible. In some cases more than one operation has to be executed in order to achieve a complex instantiation step. For example, the assignment of a real-world participant to an abstract participant of an activity can be accomplished by executing the operations "Associating a (real world) Participant with an Activity" and "Deleting an Association of an (abstract) Participant with an Activity".

Conversely, some experts also viewed particular operations as outside the scope of instantiation. For instance, adding an additional abstract participant to the process could be seen as improvement of the reference process but not as particularizing a process to project needs. However, the operations required for instantiation depend on the process and the organization applying it. Organizations can choose which basic instantiation operations they want to use or can define additional operations if necessary. For our current purpose, a comprehensive catalog is therefore important, and future work will include identifying the usefulness of particular operations depending on the domain.

The complexity of Siemens' processes results in a high number of contexts. Therefore the identified contexts have to be verified regarding their completeness. The complexity of processes also results in a high number and in complex rules for the execution of an instantiation operation in a particular context. Verification of rules comprises completeness and correctness. In order to exclude any incompleteness and insufficiency, a tool-supported approach is necessary which is being developed at the moment.

5. Conclusion

Siemens' software processes have been introduced, their current instantiation described, and the necessity of a standardized and semi-automated instantiation approach identified. An approach using elementary building blocks called basic instantiation operations has been developed. The execution of the operations is restricted by the context the operation is nested in. Rules regulating the execution of an operation in a particular context guarantee that the resulting process is syntactically correct and consistent. The application of the approach was demonstrated by a use case. The approach has already been evaluated, but verification will continue by implementation of an instantiation system.

References

1. Aalst, W. and Hee, K. (2004), Workflow Management – Models, Methods, and Systems, The MIT Press, Cambridge, MA.
2. Alexander, L. and Davis, A. (1991), Criteria for Selecting Software Process Models, in 'Proceedings of the Fifteenth Annual International Computer Software and Applications Conference', pp. 521–528.
3. Basili, V. and Rombach, H. (1991), 'Support for Comprehensive Reuse', *Software Engineering Journal* **6**(5), 303–316.
4. BMI (2004), 'The new V-Modell XT – Development Standard for IT Systems of the Federal Republic of Germany', URL: http://www.v-modell-xt.de (accessed 25.03.2008).
5. Boehm, B. and Belz, F. (1990), Experiences with the Spiral Model as a Process Model Generator, in 'Proceedings of the 5th International Software Process Workshop "Experience with Software Process Models"', pp. 43–45.
6. Bowers, J.; May, J.; Melander, E. and Baarman, M. (2002), Tailoring XP for Large System Mission Critical Software Development, in D. Wells and L. Williams, ed., 'Extreme Programming and Agile Methods – XP/Agile Universe 2002, Second XP Universe Conference Chicago', pp. 100–111.
7. Dreiling, A.; Rosemann, M.; Aalst, W.; Sadiq, W. and Khan, S. (2005), Model-Driven Process Configuration of Enterprise Systems, in 'Wirtschaftsinformatik', pp. 687–706.
8. Fitzgerald, B.; Russo, N. and O'Kane, T. (2000), An Empirical Study of System Development Method Tailoring in Practice, in 'Proceedings of the Eighth European Conference on Information Systems'; pp. 187–194.
9. Ginsberg, M. and Quinn, L. (1995), 'Process Tailoring and the Software Capability Maturity Model', Technical report, Software Engineering Institute (SEI).
10. ISO/IEC (1998), 'ISO/IEC 15504-9 Technology Software Process Assessment – Part 9: Vocabulary'.
11. Killisperger, P.; Peters, G.; Stumptner, M. and Stückl, T. (2008), Challenges in Software Design in Large Corporations – A Case Study at Siemens AG, in 'Proceedings of the Tenth International Conference on Enterprise Information Systems, Vol. ISAS – 2', pp. 123–128.
12. Kruchten, P. (1999), The Rational Unified Process, Addison-Wesley, Boston, MA.
13. Mendling, J.; Recker, J.; Rosemann, M. and Aalst, W. (2005), Towards the Interchange of Configurable EPCs, in 'EMISA', pp. 8–21.
14. Merriam-Webster's Collegiate Dictionary (2005), Encyclopedia Britannica.
15. Osterweil, L. J. (1987), Software Processes Are Software Too, in 'ICSE', pp. 2–13.
16. Pedreira, O.; Piattini, M.; Luaces, M. and Brisaboa, N. (2007), 'A Systematic Review of Software Process Tailoring', *ACM SIGSOFT Software Engineering Notes* **32**(3), 1–6.
17. Rosemann, M. and Aalst, W. (2007), 'A Configurable Reference Modelling Language', *Information Systems* **32**(1), 1–23.
18. Workflow Management Coalition (2005), 'Workflow Standard – Process Definition Interface – XML Process Definition Language', URL: http://www.wfmc.org/standards/documents/TC-1025_xpdl_2_2005-10-03.pdf (accessed: 03.07.2008).
19. Yoon, I.; Min, S. and Bae, D. (2001), Tailoring and Verifying Software Process., in 'APSEC', pp. 202–209.

62

A Language for Modelling Trust in Information Systems

Kamaljit Kaur Bimrah, Haralambos Mouratidis and David Preston

Abstract

It has been argued in recent research that trust is an important issue for modern information systems and that it should be considered from the early stages of the development process. Nevertheless, little effort has been put into understanding how trust can be modelled and reasoned when developing information systems. Equally little effort has been put into developing modelling languages to support trust modelling. Our motivation comes from this situation and we aim to develop a trust-aware modelling framework that will enable information system developers to consider trust and its related concepts collectively during the development of information systems. In this chapter we re-enforce the argument about the need to consider trust during information systems development and we describe a modelling language that supports trust modelling. We employ a case study from a trust critical domain to demonstrate the application of our language.

Keywords Trust Information systems development · modelling language

1. Introduction

Trust is a catalyst for human cooperation. It allows people to interact spontaneously and helps the economy to operate smoothly [1]. If there is no trust in relations then this could have severe adverse effects. Discussing the Internet and its mechanism for enforcing a security policy, [2] states that if the security mechanisms for enforcing authentication, authorisation, privacy, integrity and non-repudiation policy do not appear to be sufficiently strong to the users, then users may hesitate to use the Internet for conducting business. An important reason for people to be hesitant regarding information systems is because they do not appear or the user does not perceive the system to be safe.

But what exactly is trust? According to the literature, "...Trust is a term with many meanings" [2] that is difficult to define, convey, measure or specify. In some cases, trust is frequently defined and described in terms of confidence, expectation, belief and faith [3]. For example, if a ladder looks wobbly, one is unlikely to trust it to hold ones weight [2]. It is defined in [4, 5] that trust is the belief that an entity has about another entity, from past experiences, knowledge about the entity's nature and/or recommendations from trusted entities. It is stated in [6] that to trust someone is to be confident that in a situation where you are vulnerable, one will be disposed to act benignly towards you. Similarly, [7] states that trust is the firm belief in the competence of an entity to act dependably, securely, and reliably within a specified context. Although these definitions use different terms and define trust differently they all agree that trust is related to a number of other concepts and it should not be considered in isolation.

Kamaljit Kaur Bimrah, Haralambos Mouratidis and David Preston • Innovative Informatics, School of Computing and Technology, University of East London, London, UK.

G.A. Papadopoulos et al. (eds.), *Information Systems Development*, DOI 10.1007/b137171_62,

As information systems are widely employed in every area of human life and are increasingly used by organisations and individuals, trusting such information systems is therefore becoming a central issue for the effective usage of such systems and the appropriate dissemination of the large amounts of sensitive information stored in them. Developing trustworthy information systems is important not only for the right operation of these systems but also for their social acceptance and the advancement of information networking. As argued by [8] *Trust is becoming an increasingly important issue in the design of many kinds of information systems.* Recent research by [9, 3] goes even further to state that trust should be considered from the early stages of the information systems development process. It is highlighted in [9] that *design and trust intersect in two ways.* He argues that information system users will have a positive experience only if the systems are designed so the users trust them. This role is to be fulfilled by good design [9]. Some form of "ownership" should also be allowed in such systems, which allows the user to customise them and adapt according to his/her needs; this in turn actually *facilitates trust.* The second way that [9] mentions that design and trust are intersected is by having "technology acting as a mediator of trust between people, organisations or products". In essence, Sutcliffe means that the uncertainty that is present in relationships should be reduced by technology, this in return will make information more accessible; enhancing trust.

However, [10, 11] conclude that in information systems development, trust is either not considered by the software system developers or if it is considered, it is usually considered as a sole concept isolated from the rest of the development process. A main reason for this situation is the lack of conceptual modelling support to model and reason about trust and its related concepts when modelling information systems. This situation provides the foremost motivation for our research. In particular, our aim is to develop a modelling framework to assist information systems developers to consider trust during the development of information systems. In this chapter we introduce a modelling language for modelling trust during information systems development.

The subsequent section discusses the related work and the resultant limitations of them. In Section 3 we introduce the proposed modelling language; the modelling language concepts; the modelling language notation and then closing the section with a description of the links and associations. The penultimate section introduces the case study we are to use in the validation of the modelling language. Section 5 concludes this chapter and indicates directions for future work.

2. Related Work

Although the literature provides a large number of works related to modelling languages, little effort has been reported on modelling languages that consider trust. Reference [12] defines a modelling framework to model trust relationships using the Tropos methodology [13]. The framework supports (limited) identification of trust relationships and provides some concepts that allow developers to (partially) model such relationships. Similarly, in [14], trust relationships are identified with no supplementary enlightenment on *how* they exist. The TrustCoM project [15] has developed a framework that supports trust, security and contract issues related to dynamic virtual organisations. We appreciate the fact that these works emphasise the need to acknowledge and model trust relationships and provide an initial step towards this direction but we believe it is an important limitation that they lack conceptual support and appropriate reasoning mechanisms to allow developers to understand explicitly how trust relationships are formed and what are the core dynamics and features that form the foundation and might affect such trust relationships. In particular, a number of questions can be raised such as *why does a trust relationship exist? What might affect the trust relationship? Is there a consequence to this trust relationship? Does this trust relationship impose any constraints on the functional requirements of the system?* We believe that an information systems modelling language for trust should allow developers to understand in detail the trust relationships and provide answers to these questions.

A number of works are related to security and risk aware modelling languages. UMLsec [16] is an extension of UML, which allows developers to express security-relevant information alongside a system specification. Similarly, SecureUML [17] provides a language for specifying access control policies for actions on protected resources. Secure Tropos [18] is a security-aware methodology that enables developers to model and reason about security issues from the early stages of the development process. CORAS is a European project which is developing a tool-supported framework for precise, unambiguous and efficient risk assessment of security critical systems [19]. All of these works are important and provide a number of advantages. However, they do not support modelling and/or reasoning of trust. We consider our work to be complimentary to these approaches.

3. A Modelling Language for Trust

Our modelling language is based on previous work on the development of an ontology for trust [20], which was based on an ontological analysis that took into account a number of existing ontologies [21–27]. Our modelling language includes a number of concepts and associated links and it is supported by a metamodel that provides an explicit description of the constructs and the rules of the language. To better explain the language-supported concepts and their relationship we employ a running example from the banking domain. In particular, we are using a scenario where a *Customer* wants to invest a large number of cash into a *Bank* with the maximum possible return. The next few sections describe our language.

3.1. Modelling Language Concepts

As stated above the modelling language is supported by a metamodel that defines the abstract syntax of the language. The metamodel is based on the standard four level architecture as defined by the OMG [28] where the *Meta-Metamodel* level specifies the language structural elements, the *Metamodel* level provides constructs for modelling an instance of the meta-metamodel structural elements, the *Domain* level defines instances of the metamodel models for specific application domains, and the *Instance* level contains instances of the domain model elements. In particular, the metamodel (shown graphically in Fig. 62.1) supports the following concepts:

Actor: We adopt the concept of an actor from existing approaches in requirements engineering such as the i* framework [8]. According to the definition of the concept within the i* framework, *an actor represents an entity that has intentionality and strategic goals* [8]. For the purpose of our work we extend this definition as follows: *An actor represents an entity, within a system or an organisational setting, which has intentionality and strategic goals and also is able to perform an action and raise a request.* Considering the running example, a number of actors can be identified, such as the Customer and the Bank Employee.

Goal: The concept of a goal is also adopted from the i* framework [8] and it is used to represent an actor's strategic interests. Referring to our running example a goal of the Customer actor is to *get maximum return from the investment*.

Request: A Request is defined as *the act of an actor asking another actor for something to be done or given*. It is the state of an appeal posed at any one time by an Actor and it is usually associated with a goal of an actor. A Request is raised by an Actor, and it might trigger an Action. Referring to our running example, the Customer actor might raise a request with the Bank Employee actor for a specific investment return on their money. Most likely such request will trigger an action from the Bank Employee actor.

Action: An Action defines a specific activity carried out by an Actor as a response to a request from another actor. An Action is a duty that an Actor performs. Referring to our running example, the Bank Employee might authorise the specific investment asked from the Customer actor; might deny it, or might trigger a further action with another actor, such as the Bank Manager.

Resource: A resource represents, as in the i* framework [8], a physical or an informational entity. A resource might be required by an actor in order to perform an action. In the running example, a resource could be the signature of the Bank Manager to a potential action raised by the Bank Employee actor.

Security Constraint: We define the concept of security constraint as in the Secure Tropos methodology [13]. In particular, in our language a security constraint might restrict an action or a request by imposing security-related constraints. In our running example, the Bank Employee actor might not be able

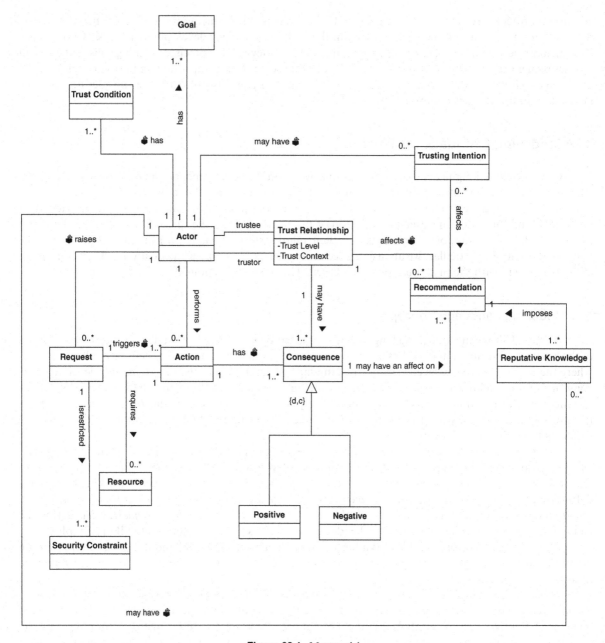

Figure 62.1. Metamodel.

to carry out the specific action corresponding to the Customer actor request because they might not have the necessary security clearance.

Trust Relationship: A trust relationship indicates that an actor trusts another actor. As indicated in [29] the essential components of a trust relationship are the trustor, the trustee, a specific context with associated level of trust and the conditions under which this relationship becomes active. In our metamodel, trust level and context are represented as attributes of the trust relationship. In the context of our running example, there might be a trust relationship between the Customer and the Bank Employee within the context of investing money. Coming to trust levels, there are two levels of trust, one is Forced Trust and the other is Independent Trust. Forced Trust is when one Actor is forced to trust another Actor because they are in a position of duty. For example, the Customer is forced to trust the Employee. Independent Trust is an Actor trusting another Actor of ones own accord. For example, an Employee may not trust another Employee. Forced Trust is represented by Trust Level 1; however, Independent Trust scales from 0.1 upwards depending on the degree of trust involved.

Trusting Intention: Trusting Intention is the intent on the Actor's behalf on how far he/she actually trusts another Actor to carry out the Request/Action beneficially to them; in a way that is not detrimental to them. Trust Intention affects the Recommendation. For example, reverting back to our bank scenario, how can the Customer trust the Bank? The Bank can be trusting as they are in a position of duty; so the Customer assumes trust (Initial Trust). Initial trust can be present without experience, not knowing the reputation of the Bank, just simply trusting based on Banks position. Likewise for Bank being able to trust Customer.

Reputative Knowledge: Reputative Knowledge is the knowledge that one has about the object they are going to trust. In regard to our bank scenario, the Customer may have an experience (good or bad) of liaising with the Bank; the Bank may have an experience (good or bad) of liaising with the Customer. Looking at the experience of the Bank from the Customers point of view; the Customer may need to check with other Customers, Bank reviews, other Banks, in regard to the reputation of the Bank the Customer is thinking to invest with. If the reputation of the Bank is not acceptable to the Customer, then this may affect the trust relationship before it is even established or the Customer may give the Bank the benefit of the doubt and decide about trusting the Bank, the Customer may ask others for to get an "idea", but ultimately the decision is the Customer's, whether to trust or not.

Recommendation: Recommendation is representation in favour of a person or thing [30]. Recommendation is affected by Trust and is also the result of a Consequence of an Action that has been carried out by an Actor. The Customer may recommend a third person to trust the Bank based on the Customers Reputative Knowledge of the Bank. The Recommendation may be enforced by the Reputative Knowledge.

Consequence: Consequence is the effect of Trust. Consequence is the result of an Action which has been carried out by the Actor. If the Customer has a good experience with the Bank then it will be a Positive Consequence however, if the Customer has a bad experience with the Bank then it will be a Negative Consequence. Prior to commencing onto the finer details of the modelling language, we would like to stress that we presently deliberate on a small part of the metamodel rather than the whole metamodel due to lack of space; this small part being the trust relationship.

3.2. Links/Associations

As can be observed in the metamodel in the preceding section, there are numerous links connecting each of the concepts. Due to lack of space, we focus on three links related to the actor concept. In particular, an Actor is involved in a trust relationship either as a trustee or as a trustor and he/she can raise a request and/or perform an action as shown in Fig. 62.2.

In particular, we can identify the following links:

Raises. One actor may raise zero or many requests as shown in the metamodel part in Fig. 62. 2: Link 1 (Please see Fig. 62.3 for the corresponding actor raises request link analysis diagram).

Triggers. One request triggers one or more actions as shown in the metamodel part in Fig. 62. 2: Link 2. We say at least one action must be carried out in order for the request to be satisfied (Please see Fig. 62. 4 for the corresponding Request triggers action|Link analysis diagram).

Performs. One actor performs zero or more actions as shown in the metamodel part in Fig. 62.2: Link 3. (Please see Fig. 62.5 for the corresponding actor performs action link analysis diagram).

3.3. Modelling Language Graphical Notation

To enable developers to use the language, we have defined a number of graphical notations to depict the concepts and links of the language, as can be viewed in Fig. 62.6. As discussed earlier in this chapter we only focus on the links related to the Actor concept as shown in Fig. 62.2.

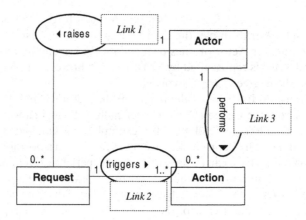

Figure 62.2. Actor Links.

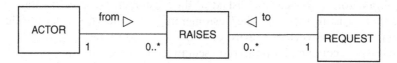

Figure 62.3. Actor raises request link analysis.

Figure 62.4. Request triggers action link analysis.

Figure 62.5. Actor Performs Action Link Analysis.

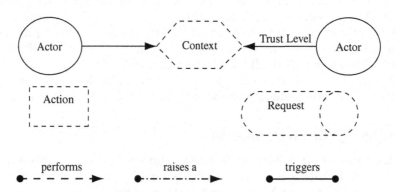

Figure 62.6. Trust modeling language notation.

Considering the running example, a trust relationship is formed between a customer and a Bank employee within the context of opening an account. Graphically, this trust relationship can be depicted using the proposed language as shown in Fig. 62.7. In particular, following the metamodel a trust relationship exists between two actors, for a given context and for specific trust levels. In the presented example, the customer trusts the employee more than what the employee trusts the customer.

Figure 62.7. Trust relationship between employee and customer.

As mentioned above, it is important to understand how a trust relationship is satisfied and analyse that information. In the proposed language, this analysis takes place by understanding the requests raised due to a trust relationships and the relevant actions that are triggered to satisfy such requests.

Going back to the running example, and for the account opening trust relationship the customer might raise a number of request relevant to that trust relationship. Such requests might trigger many actions, which the employee performs in order to satisfy the customer requests. Graphically, this is shown in Fig. 62.8.

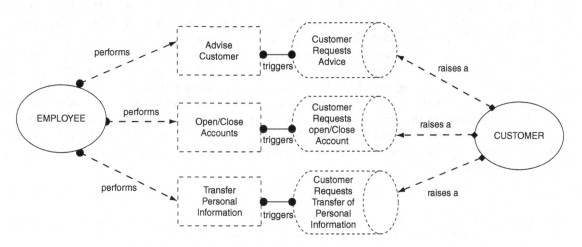

Figure 62.8. Actor raises many requests – triggering many actions from one actor.

After further analysis, we have assumed that the customer has a request, which has one Action, fulfilled by one employee; however, this is not necessarily the case, as we highlighted in Fig. 62.8, however, there is no written rule that only one employee has to complete all of the raised actions, two employees may complete them. Also, once a request has been raised, it may trigger many actions. Many actions may need to be completed, by one or more actors in order for the initial request to be satisfied. For example, in Fig. 62.9, the Customer raises a request of opening an account. This triggers three separate actions. Action A (Open Account) and Action C (Confirm Account Details) are to be carried out by the Cashier; however, Action B (Get Authorisation of Account) needs to be carried out by the Customer Manager.

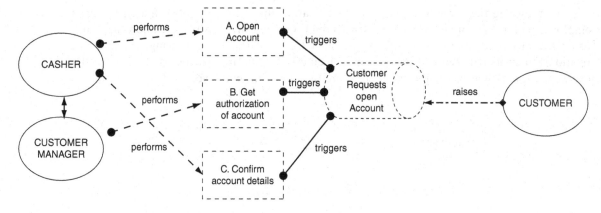

Figure 62.9. Actor raises one request – triggering many actions rrom multiple actors.

4. Case Study

Here we shall introduce a case study and venture to capture the factors affecting the scenario and demonstrate how the language and the framework can be used to model trust relationships in that case study. The case study is from a paper by Giorgini et al. [12] used to demonstrate the applicability of the secure Tropos methodology for modelling trust. A case study from the health domain was employed to illustrate Giorgini et al., [12] approach. Their case study includes five actors: a Patient, the Department of Health, the Health Research Agency, the General Practitioner (GP) and the Nurse. In our analysis we are using the latter two.

Using Secure Tropos Giorgini et al. have tried to model the various trust considerations that exist in such network of actors. In particular, they state in the paper *The General Practitioner not only depends on the Nurse to Provide Primary Care, but he/she trusts the Nurse to achieve this goal.*[12]. However, one of the important limitations of their approach is the lack of modeling all the components of a trust relationship as discussed in previous sections. Using our language we are able to improve on this limitation by making explicit the components of the trust relationship. In particular, let us consider the above relationship between the General Practitioner and the Nurse. The trust relationship between these two actors is shown in Fig. 62.10. Since both the actors are in a position of duty, a forced trust is assumed and therefore a trust level of 1 for both actors.

Figure 62.10. Trust relationship between GP and Nurse.

It is also important to understand how the trust relationship is operationalised within the network of actors in an information system. In doing so, we use the language to model the requests raised by the actors, due to the trust relationship, and the relevant actions. A partial analysis of this is shown in Fig. 62.11 where the General Practitioner (GP) raises a request to provide primary care.

Such request triggers an action, which the nurse actor performs. Using the language in a similar way, we are able to model all the trust relationships between the network of actors and analyse alternative ways of operationalising them.

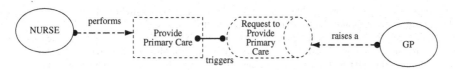

Figure 62.11. As per our trust modeling language.

5. Conclusions and Future Work

In this chapter we have argued for the need to model trust during information systems development. Our argument is consistent with a number of arguments presented in the literature. We have reviewed a number of related works and we have identified a number of important limitations. To overcome these limitations we have concentrated our efforts in developing a modelling language that enables the modelling of trust and its related concepts in one framework. In this chapter we have presented such modelling language and we have illustrated with the aid of a case study from the health sector how our modelling language can assist information systems developers to analyse a number of trust issues related to the environment of a potential information system. However, our work is not complete. We are yet to validate the language on a large case study and develop appropriate methods to form a complete trust-aware framework.

Acknowledgements

First, we would like to show gratitude to EPSRC for their funding with regard to this project and second we would like to express thanks to the staff at St Patrick's College (London) for their support in our research.

References

1. Jøsang, A., Patton, M.A. (2004)."Technologies for Trust in Electronic Commerce." Electronic Commerce Research Journal 4(1&2): 9–21.
2. Michael, J.B., Hestad, D.R., Pedersen, C.M., Gaines L.T (2002). "Incorporating the Human Element of Trust into Information Systems." IAnewsletter 5: 4–8.
3. Chopra, K., Wallace, W.A. (2003). Trust in Electronic Environments. Proceedings of the 36th Hawaii Conference on System Sciences (HICSS'03), Hawaii.
4. Almenarez, F., Marın, A., Campo, C., Garcıa, C. (2004). PTM: A Pervasive Trust Management Model for Dynamic Open Environments. First Workshop on Pervasive Security, Privacy and Trust, PSPT'04 in conjunction with Mobiquitous, Boston, USA.
5. Robinson, S. L. (1996). "Trust and Breach of the Psychological Contract." Administrative Science Quarterly 41: 574–579.
6. Alford, J. (2004). Building Trust in Partnerships Between Community Organization and Government. Changing the Way Government Works Seminar, Melbourne.
7. Maarof, M. A., Krishna, K (2002). A Hybrid Trust Management Model For MAS Based. Information Security Group, Faculty of Computer Science and Information System University of Technology Malaysia, 81310 Skudai, Johor.
8. Yu, E., Liu, L (2001). Modelling Trust for System Design Using the i* Strategic Actors Framework. Proceedings of the workshop on Deception, Fraud, and Trust in Agent Societies held during the Autonomous Agents Conference: Trust in Cyber-societies, Integrating the Human and Artificial Perspectives.
9. Sutcliffe, A. (2006). Trust: From Cognition to Conceptual Models and Design. 18th International Conference, SE 2006, June 5–9, 2006 Proceedings, Springer-Verlag Berlin Heidelberg, Luxembourg.
10. Kethers, S. E. A. (2005). Modelling Trust Relationships in a Healthcare Network: Experiences with the TCD Framework. In Proceedings of the Thirteenth European Conference on Information Systems, Regensburg, Germany.
11. Li, X., Valacich, J. S., Hess, T. J. (2004). Predicting User Trust in Information Systems: A Comparison of Competing Trust Models. The Proceedings of the 37th Hawaii International Conference on Systems Sciences, Hawaii.

12. Giorgini, P., Mouratidis, H., Zannone, Z. (2006). Modelling Security and Trust with Secure Tropos. In Integrating Security and Software Engineering: Advances and Future Vision, Idea Group: 160–189.
13. Mouratidis, H., Giorgini, P. (2004). Enhancing secure Tropos to effectively deal with security requirements in the development of multiagent systems. 1st International Workshop on Safety and Security in Multiagent Systems, NY, USA.
14. Grandison, T., Sloman, M (2001). SULTAN – A Language for Trust Specification and Analysis. In: Eighth Workshop of the HP OpenView University Association, Berlin.
15. Wilson, M., Arenas, A., Schubert, L., Ed. (2007). TrustCoM Framework V4. AL1 – TrustCoM Framework.
16. Jürjens, J. (2004). "Developing Security-Critical Applications with UMLsec. A Short Walk-Through." The European Journal for the Informatics Professional 5(2).
17. Basin, D., Clavel, M., Doser, J., Egea, M. (2007). A Metamodel-Based Approach for Analyzing Security-Design Models. MODELS 2007, Nashville, TN.
18. Mouratidis, H., Giorgini, P., Manson, G. (2005). When Security Meets Software Engineering: A Case of Modelling Secure Information Systems, in Information System. Elsevier 30(8): 609–629.
19. Dimitrakos, T., Ritchie, B., Raptis, D., Stølen, K. (2002). Model Based Security Risk Analysis for Web Applications: The CORAS Approach. EuroWeb 2002 Conference, Oxford, UK.
20. Bimrah, K., Mouratidis, H., Preston, D. (2007). Trust Ontology for Information Systems Development. 16th International Conference on Information Systems Development Ireland, Galway.
21. Viljanen, L. (2005). Towards an Ontology of Trust. Lecture Notes in Computer Science, Springer Berlin/Heidelberg, Copenhagen, Denmark.
22. Kim, A., Luo, J., Kang, M. (2005). Security Ontology for Annotating Resources. Lecture Notes in Computer Science, Springer-Verlag Berlin/Heidelberg, Agai Napa, Cyprus.
23. Cuske, C., Korthaus, A., Seedorf, S., Tomczyk, P. (2005). Towards Formal Ontologies for Technology Risk Measurement in the Banking Industry. Proceedings of the 1st Workshop Formal Ontologies Meet Industry, Verona, Italy.
24. Simmonds, A., Sandilands, P., Ekert, L.V. (2004). An Ontology for Network Security Attacks. Lecture Notes in Computer Science, Springer Berlin/Heidelberg, Kathmandu, Nepal.
25. Casare, S., Sichman, J. (2005). Towards a Functional Ontology of Reputation. International Conference on Autonomous Agents Archive Proceedings of the Fourth International Joint Conference on Autonomous Agents and Multiagent Systems, The Netherlands.
26. Martimiano, A. F. M., Moreira, E. S. (2005). An OWL-based Security Incident Ontology. In: Proceedings of the Eighth International Protege Conference 43–44 Poster.
27. Mouratidis, H., Giorgini, P., Mansoon, G (2003). An Ontology for Modelling Security: The Tropos Approach. Proceedings of the 7th International Conference on Knowledge-Based Intelligent Information & Engineering Systems, Oxford, England.
28. Siegel, J. (2001). "Developing in OMG's Model-Driven Architecture." Developing in the MDA.
29. Grandison, T., Sloman, M (2000). "A Survey of Trust in Internet Applications." IEEE Communications Surveys and Tutorials 3(4).
30. Random House (2006). Random House Unabridged Dictionary, Random House, Inc., New York.

63

Modeling the Contribution of Enterprise Architecture Practice to the Achievement of Business Goals

Marlies van Steenbergen and Sjaak Brinkkemper

Abstract

Enterprise architecture is a young, but well-accepted discipline in information management. Establishing the effectiveness of an enterprise architecture practice, however, appears difficult. In this chapter we introduce an architecture effectiveness model (AEM) to express how enterprise architecture practices are meant to contribute to the business goals of an organization. We developed an AEM for three different organizations. These three instances show that the concept of the AEM is applicable in a variety of organizations. It also shows that the objectives of enterprise architecture are not to be restricted to financial goals. The AEM can be used by organizations to set coherent priorities for their architectural practices and to define KPIs for measuring the effectiveness of these practices.

Keywords Enterprise architecture · Organizational effectiveness · Cause effect · Key performance indicator · Design research · Architecture effectiveness model

1. Effectiveness of Enterprise Architecture

Enterprise architecture, the practice of developing and applying a consistent set of rules and models that guide the design and implementation of processes, organizational structures, information flows, and technical infrastructure within an organization [22], is a relatively young, but well-accepted discipline [4, 14]. The discipline is in a stage of development as is evidenced by the many practitioners conferences dedicated to the practice of enterprise architecture, the rapid emergence of books on the topic, and the emergence of standardization efforts [10, 18].

Establishing the effectiveness of enterprise architecture, however, appears difficult [10, 16]. The effect of architecture on the business goals is indirect and the difficulty in linking the two may be compared to the difficulty of linking learning and growth efforts to strategic objectives [8]. The wide-ranging nature of enterprise architecture makes it difficult to quantify the impact of architecture [10], though the need for clearly expressing the contribution of architecture to the organization's goals is increasingly felt. Enterprise architecture teams are under constant pressure to demonstrate their value to the organization [23]. The topic of architectural effectiveness also starts to appear on professional conferences [5, 19]. Some statistical evidence of effectiveness is appearing [1]. However, statistical evidence alone does not help an organization to clearly define the contribution of architecture to their business goals. In addition, much effectiveness research concentrates on financial benefits [1, 15]. We will argue that this is too limited a view.

In this chapter we present an architecture effectiveness model (AEM) that can be used to model the contribution of the architectural practice to the organization's business goals. The AEM is based on the

Marlies van Steenbergen • Architecture and Business Solutions, Sogeti Netherlands B.V., The Netherlands. **Sjaak Brinkkemper** • Institute of Information and Computer Sciences, University of Utrecht, Utrecht, The Netherlands.

G.A. Papadopoulos et al. (eds.), *Information Systems Development*, DOI 10.1007/b137171_63,
© Springer Science+Business Media, LLC 2009

concept of cause-and-effect. As such we work in the tradition of the balanced scorecard [7, 9, 11, 16] and especially the strategy map [8]. Other applications of the cause–effect model in the field of enterprise architecture are [3] and [12]. Though the cause–effect model can occasionally be encountered in the architecture profession to express the objectives of the architectural practice in a specific organization, extensive research into its use as an instrument to express intended and actual effectiveness of architecture has as yet not been done. Our research is akin to research on the maturity of enterprise architecture [3, 14, 17]. However, we focus on the contribution of architecture to business goals, rather than on how well the architecture processes are performed.

The approach we took in developing the AEM is that of design-science research [6, 21]. We tested the concept of the AEM in three cases. We found that the AEM is applicable as an instrument in all three cases, but that the exact instantiations of the AEM in the three cases varies. It appears that the three cases differ in their objectives of practicing enterprise architecture and that these objectives are not limited to financial gains. In terms of the three domains of business performance of [20], architecture contributes to business performance, or even organizational effectiveness, not only to financial performance.

In Section 2 the structure and aim of the AEM is discussed. Its application in three cases is described in Section 3. Section 4 compares the three applications. In Section 5, we discuss conclusions and suggestions for further research.

2. The Architecture Effectiveness Model

The goal of our research is to develop an instrument for making explicit the intended and actual contribution of the architectural practice to the organizational goals. As we are dealing with a new solution to a hitherto unsolved problem: the explication of the effectiveness of an enterprise architecture practice, this may be considered a case of design-science research [6]. From our goal we defined requirements, assumptions, and specifications for the instrument as recommended by [21]. Examples of the requirements we formulated are (1) *the formulation of the intended contribution of the architectural practice to the business goals must be tuned to the organization.* If the contribution of architecture is stated in general terms only, it is very difficult to make the connection to what is actually happening in the organization. (2) *the line of reasoning from architecture to business goals must be transparent.* The instrument must be crystal clear as architecture is often considered rather abstract. From the formulated requirements we reasoned that a cause–effect network seemed a suitable design, as such a network allows us to build an explicit link between architectural practice efforts and business goals by means of a number of intermediate steps. The choice for this kind of solution was strengthened by its similar kind of use in the strategy map of [8]. The AEM that resulted relates architectural efforts to business goals by building a cause–effect-based network. Figure 63.1 shows the general structure of an AEM.

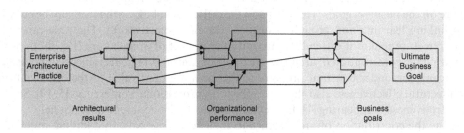

Figure 63.1. The general structure of an architecture effectiveness model.

The basic concepts of an AEM are the effect, represented by a rectangle, and the cause–effect relation, represented by an arrow between two rectangles. An effect in this context is defined as an intended result. A cause–effect relation represents the purposeful contribution of one effect to another effect.

The AEM is intended to reflect the objectives of architecture for an organization in the next couple of years. It shows what the architecture practice strives for. This implies that it represents a choice: there is not one right model, only a model that is agreed upon within the organization. The instantiation of an AEM differs between organizations. As Fig. 63.1 shows, an AEM contains on the left the enterprise architecture practice, the whole of activities, responsibilities, and actors involved in the development, and application of enterprise architecture within the organization. On the right it contains the ultimate business goal: the primary goal of the organization. The steps in between link the two.

An AEM can be modeled as an acyclic directed graph. It consists of nodes and directed edges. The nodes represent effects that are desirable for the organization. Examples are 'having overview' or 'better project control', or 'reduced costs'. The edges represent the unidirectional relation 'contributes to'. The word 'contributes' is used instead of 'causes' to reflect the fact that the contributing effect need not be the sole factor influencing the resulting effect. Experience with enterprise architecture in many organizations suggests that the effects (the nodes) can be divided into three types. The architectural results are positioned at the left hand of the graph. These are the effects that are fully determined by the architectural practice. The business goal effects are positioned at the right hand of the graph. These are the business results defined by senior management. The enterprise architecture practice is one of the factors contributing to these goals. In between we find effects in the area of the operations of the organization: the internal processes. We call these effects the organizational performance effects. This division into three types of effects echoes the categories of learning and growth, internal process, and customer perspective of the balanced scorecard strategy map [8].

$$AEM = (N, E) \text{ with } N = (AR \cup OP \cup BG) \text{ the set of nodes,}$$

where AR = architectural result effects; OP = organizational performance effects; BG = business goal effects and E the set of edges on N (i.e., E is a subset of $N \times N$) satisfying

$$OP \times AR \cap E = \phi \text{ and } BG \times OP \cap E = \phi \text{ and } BG \times AR \cap E = \phi.$$

An AEM has only one source (node with indegree 0), the enterprise architecture practice node, and usually also only one sink (node with outdegree 0), the ultimate business goal, though more than one sink is possible if an organization has multiple purposes. Note that the model does not preclude AR effects to be related directly to BG effects. In an AEM the following key effects may be distinguished.

- *Key step.* A key step is defined as an effect that has both an indegree and an outdegree of a specified minimum s. In other words, it has at least s contributing effects and it contributes itself to at least s other effects. So $n \in N$ is a key step iff indegree(n) $\geq s$ AND outdegree(n) $\geq s$. The exact value of s is to be determined yet. On the basis of the three cases we have studied so far, we have set s to 3, for the time being. This seems a reasonable value with respect to the total number of nodes and edges in each of the three cases.
- *Key motivator.* A key motivator is defined as an effect with the largest indegree (i.e., the largest number of contributing effects). So $n \in N$ is a key motivator iff indegree(n) = max (indegree(m)), $m \in N$. It is an effect that is the aim of many other effects. Note that there may be more than one key motivator.
- *Key enabler.* A key enabler is defined as an effect with the largest outdegree (i.e., the largest number of effects it contributes to). So $n \in N$ is a key enabler iff outdegree(n) = max (outdegree(m)), $m \in N$. It is an effect that contributes to many other effects. There also may be more than one key enabler.

The model as such presents the intended contribution of architecture to the business goals by way of a number of intermediate results. By attaching key performance indicators (KPIs) to the effects, the actual contribution over time can be measured. Regarding the effects as goals, an approach like the Goal Question Method [2] can be adopted to formulate KPIs.

3. Three Applications of the AEM Concept

The AEM concept has been applied in three organizations: a large municipality, a university of professional education, and an international financial institution. The three organizations have in common that they had all been engaged in organization-wide enterprise architecture initiatives for 2 to 3 years. The building of the AEM was done by the architects of the organization, assisted by either business strategy documents or opinion leaders. The researcher only fulfilled a moderator role, asking questions, and recording results. In each occasion the AEM went through at least two versions. The final version was accepted by the person in charge of the enterprise architecture practice. It was generally felt, however, that the AEM should always remain open to extension from new insights or needs.

The three organizations are of different type, one of them being a commercial profit organization, one an educational institution with a not-for-profit goal, but with some goals of growth and a limited sense of competition, and one a municipality strongly ruled by government regulations. This variation was intentionally sought, as our objective was to test the use of the AEM in different circumstances.

3.1. Case 1: A Municipality

The first application of the AEM is in a municipality of more than 200,000 citizens. The municipality has about 2200 employees, about 100 of which work in IT. Architecture is the responsibility of the Policies, Standards and Programs team which is positioned within the IT department and consists of seven employees, three of which have the role of enterprise architect.

A preliminary AEM was established in a workshop with eight participants. The lead architect selected the participants from the various architecture stakeholder groups: architects, program managers, controllers, information managers, IS management. Brown paper techniques were used to build the AEM. At the far left of the brown paper a card was put with the text 'enterprise architecture practice'. At the far right a card was put with the text 'coalition charter', as the realization of the coalition charter was the primary goal of the municipality organization. The purpose of the exercise was explained as filling the gap between the two, or in other words, determining what the architectural practice should contribute to realizing the coalition charter. Participants were first asked to write down on cards the results they thought architecture should deliver or contribute to. These were used as a base to build the model together. Starting at the right, the moderating researcher asked if anyone had written down a result that would contribute to realizing the coalition charter. One participant volunteered a card with the text 'customer service' which was added to the brown paper to the left of the 'coalition charter' card. This called forth other cards from other participants. Each card was discussed and after consensus was reached it was added in the right place on the wall. When the flow of cards stagnated attention was turned to the left side of the wall. This time the question was to indicate the results of practicing enterprise architecture. This brought forth a new flow of cards, with architectural results like 'standards', 'common framework', and 'overview'. When the participants felt they had no more cards to add, the group turned to closing the gap between left and right. This constituted the final stage of building the AEM. After the workshop, the AEM was distributed among the participants for review. A few simplifications were suggested, which were finalized in a second workshop. These simplifications dealt with combining a number of cards into one. For instance, the combination of 'data consistency', 'data integrity', 'data reliability', and 'data security' into the one result 'trusted information'. In Fig. 63.2 the final AEM is shown. The shadings reflect the three types of effects, grey-(dotted line) for architectural results, dark grey-(solid line) for organizational performance effects, and light grey-(striped line) for business goals.

Effects like 'employee satisfaction', 'personal development', 'organizational development', and 'identity' show a focus on employees and organization. The key nodes are all in the categories of architectural results ('common framework') and organizational performance ('project performance' and 'trusted information'). This case was the only one with two end nodes: 'coalition charter' and 'municipality as government outlet', reflecting the dual character of the municipality in having its own coalition goals as well as being a representative of government.

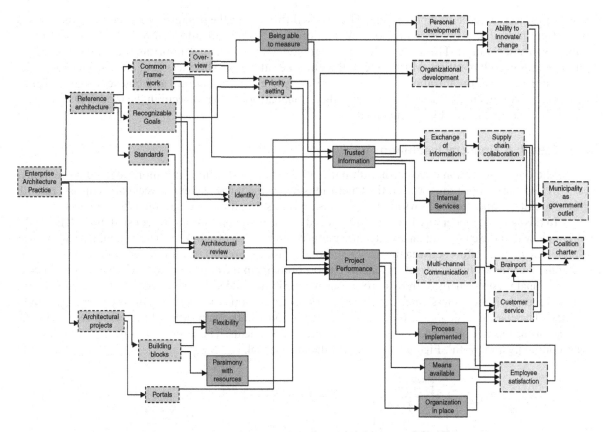

Figure 63.2. The AEM of a municipality.

After it was completed, the AEM was used to define paths from the start node to the end node, in order to set priorities in architecture activities. An example is the path 'enterprise architecture practice', contributes to 'architectural review' contributes to 'project performance' contributes to 'process implemented', 'means available', and 'organization in place' contribute to 'employee satisfaction' contributes to 'customer service' contributes to 'coalition charter'. It was decided to define KPIs on this path for the effects 'project performance', 'process implemented', 'means available', 'organization in place', and 'employee satisfaction'.

3.2. Case 2: A University of Professional Education

The second application of the AEM concerns a university of professional education with more than 16,000 students and about 1500 employees. The university has an IT department of about 50 employees. Architecture is taken care of by the one information architect. The preliminary model was established in a joint effort between the information architect and one of the researchers. The researcher mainly asked questions for elaboration to sharpen the reasoning of the information architect, whereas the information architect built the actual model. In this case too, the building process started at the right, then turned to the left, and finally closed the gap. The ultimate business goal for this organization was 'playing its role in society'. Building the preliminary model took 6 hours. The resultant model was validated by the director of one of the divisions, the centre of innovation and knowledge distribution, a key stakeholder of enterprise architecture. The architect was also present in this discussion. We explained the purpose and structure of the model. Then we concentrated on the business goals and asked the director if he recognized the goals and if he had any additions. Apart from fine-tuning some of the goals, the director made two main additions concerning accreditation and partnering. This worked through in the organizational performance effects by putting more focus on 'exchange of information' and 'quality of information'. Architectural result effects were not changed. The focus in the emergent model was much on supporting the primary processes and facilitating collaboration. Most nodes fall within the category of business goal effects. The key nodes are all in the areas of organizational performance ('exchange of information') and business goals ('aligned process', 'more students'). As with the municipality, financial goals do not occur in the model. Due to space limitations the actual AEM is not included.

3.3. Case 3: A Financial Institution

The third application concerns a multinational financial institution with more than 60,000 employees. Architecture is positioned within the Operations department (14,000 employees) and consists of both global architects and architects within the various divisions. In all there are about 175 architects.

In this case, the model was discussed and revised by various people in varying constellations. The model was made within the context of an architecture maturity improvement program. The preliminary model was established in a joint effort between the person responsible for the architecture improvement program and the researcher and then refined over seven versions, incorporating input from discussions with various architects, until the final version emerged. In this process each contributor added his own concerns to the model. One person focused on the professionalizing effect of architecture, another introduced effects concerning simplification. These additions concerned architectural result nodes and organizational performance nodes. The source for the business goal nodes was existing strategic documents. The ultimate business goal in this case was 'continuity and profit'. Figure 63.3 contains the final model.

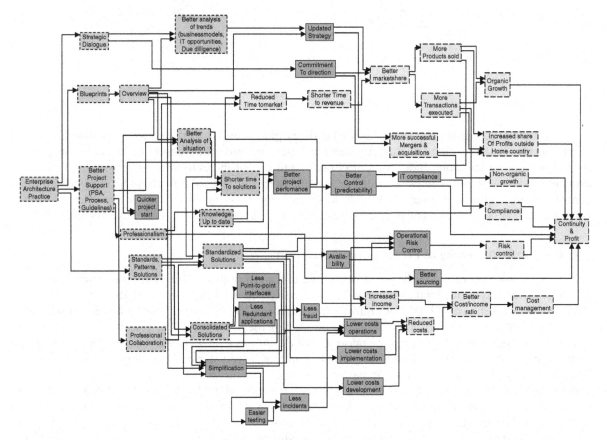

Figure 63.3. The AEM of a financial institution.

The focus in the financial AEM is on organizational processes and control. The key nodes are in the architectural results area ('standardized solutions', 'overview') and organizational performance area ('simplification'). Professionalism and control are two areas that are unique to this case.

4. Discussion

The AEM instrument could be applied to all three cases. In all cases the distinction between architectural results, organizational performance effects, and the business goal effects could be established. And though the actual definition of the nodes in these three categories differed, we can identify a common core: nodes like 'overview', 'standards', 'flexibility', 'exchange of information', and 'project performance' are shared among two or all three of the models. Though the model does not preclude a direct relation between architectural results and business goal effects, the three cases show no such direct link. In the cases, all architectural results are linked to business goals via organizational performance effects. It is a matter for further research to investigate whether this is the case in general.

The differences between the three instantiations reflect the characteristics of the organizations. In terms of the value dimensions of [13], the municipality exhibits a more internal focus than the university which is more externally focused. On the structure dimension the financial institution exhibits a greater tendency to control than the municipality. Though the number of three is too small to draw any definite conclusions, the cases do indicate that the intended contribution of the enterprise architecture practice to the business goals is partly organization specific and can not be expressed fully in general terms. In only one case financial results play an important role.

Table 63.1 shows some figures for the three cases. The numbers between brackets show the number of incoming (key motivator) or outgoing (key enabler) edges.

Table 63.1. Statistics of findings of cases.

Characteristic	Municipality	Education	Financial
Number of effects	32	48	48
Distribution over EA/OP/BG	12 / 9 / 11	17 / 11 / 20	14 / 18 / 16
Number of relations	52	78	83
Key steps	Project performance	Aligned process	Simplification Standardized solutions
Key motivator	Project performance (5)	More students (5)	Standardized solutions (4)
Key enabler	Common framework (4) Trusted information (4)	Exchange of information (6)	Overview (6)

A number of additional observations can be made. The three cases do not differ greatly in AEM size and the distribution of nodes over the three categories is quite evenly. The cases do differ in key node type: architectural results ('standardized solutions' and 'overview') and organizational performance ('simplification') for the financial institution, organizational performance ('project performance' and 'trusted information') and architectural results ('common framework') for the municipality and business goals ('aligned process' and 'more students'), and organizational performance ('exchange of information') for the university. The number of three cases is too small to draw any definite conclusions from these observations, so we will leave that to further research.

Much of the benefit of the AEM lies in the process of building the model. The three cases showed that building the cause–effect chain from the enterprise architecture practice to the primary business goals stimulates the architecture stakeholders to reflect on the real value of architecture for their organization. As the cases also show, the development of an AEM can be done in various settings, varying from a sequence of bilateral exercises to a workshop with up to ten participants. As the AEM is a normative model, essential in the process is the final acceptance of the model by the person responsible for the architectural practice.

An AEM can not only be used to show the intended contribution of the enterprise architecture practice to the business goals. It can be taken one step further in defining key performance indicators to measure this contribution over time. From the model we can select effects we wish to measure. Criteria for selecting these effects are the importance of the effect in the organization, the extent of influence of architecture on the effect, and the feasibility of measuring KPIs for the effect. A good practice is to select two or more effects that are directly linked, at least one that is largely determined by the architecture practice and at least one that lies in the organizational performance or business goal area. In this way progress in an architectural result is linked to progress in an organizational result. In any AEM, many paths can be chosen from the start node to the end node. Each path represents a line of reasoning connecting the architecture practice to the business goals. By choosing KPIs on one path, a coherent priority setting is achieved.

5. Evaluation and Conclusions

We evaluated the design of the AEM against the seven guidelines formulated by [6]. Table 63.2 summarizes the results of this evaluation.

Table 63.2. Applying the guidelines of Hevner et al. [6] to the AEM.

Guideline 1: design as an artifact	Our research delivered a construct, a model, and a method as described in Sections 2 and 3
Guideline 2: problem relevance	The AEM definitely seems to fulfill a need, as expressed in Section 1 of this chapter
Guideline 3: design evaluation	The AEM is applied in three types of cases (external validity). Construct validity is striven for by using multiple participants in building the model. Reliability is achieved by describing the process by which the different AEMs were built. Internal validity is not applicable as the case studies were exploratory in nature [24]
Guideline 4: research contributions	The contribution is mainly to the design foundation in that it presents a novel way of making explicit the contribution of enterprise architecture to the business goals
Guideline 5: research rigor	The approach is in the tradition of the balanced scorecard
Guideline 6: design as a search process	Requirements were defined excluding certain approaches as described in Section 2
Guideline 7: communication of research	This chapter to the research community

There are some limitations to our research so far. The AEM has been applied to a municipality, a professional university, and a financial institution. From these applications some interesting similarities and differences can be derived. However, the number of three cases is very limited. We intend to extend the number of AEMs in the future which will make it possible to analyze a larger sample. Also the three applications differed somewhat in the actual manner the AEM was built. Though in all cases the approach of starting at the right, moving to the left, and then closing the gap was followed, this was done in a workshop setting in one case, in a face-to-face meeting with an information architect in the second case, and in a number of consecutive sessions with varying participants in the third case. These differences sprang from practical reasons mainly. As an anonymous reviewer pointed out to us, it might be interesting to investigate whether a standard implementation model could be developed.

It must be borne in mind that architecture is not the only factor contributing to the organizational performance and business goals. In practice this means that actual KPIs have to be closely investigated to explain their actual values. But this is good practice for any KPI measurements.

In this chapter we presented an instrument for modeling the contribution of the enterprise architecture practice to the organizational goals, the AEM. We tested the AEM in three very different organizations. The AEM appeared applicable to all three organizations, resulting in instantiations that clearly reflect the characteristics of the organization and provide a transparent connection between the enterprise architecture practice and the ultimate business goal. The AEM presents a novel way of making explicit the contribution of enterprise architecture to the business goals and as such enables further research into the effectiveness of enterprise architecture. It fills a gap that up till now existed between the architecture practice and the area of achieving business goals.

The three cases show that not every organization is focused on financial goals. Our conclusion is that the focus of much research on financial results is therefore excluding whole categories of use of enterprise architecture in organizations. In our view a purely financial approach to architecture effectiveness is too restrictive.

The AEM shows similarities with the balanced scorecard (BSC) strategy map in that it links organizational efforts to organizational objectives by a cause–effect relation. The BSC perspectives of customer and internal process are recognizable in the business goal effects and organizational performance effects, respectively. The architectural result effects are comparable to the learning and growth perspective. In organizations that have implemented the BSC, the AEM can be linked to the strategy map. If no BSC is implemented, the AEM might be a first step in doing so. As architects are usually very knowledgeable about the organization, they are likely candidates to initiate such an initiative.

The AEM adds to the existing research on architecture maturity [3, 14, 17] by focusing on the contribution of architecture to the business goals (effectiveness), rather than on how well the architecture processes are performed (maturity). It would be interesting to relate maturity and effectiveness. The hypothesis being that a greater maturity should lead to a greater effectiveness. We intend to perform a longitudinal study to investigate precisely this relation.

Acknowledgment

The authors wish to thank Rik Bos, Wiel Bruls, and Ralph Foorthuis for their stimulating discussions during the execution of this research.

References

1. Bahadur, K., Desmet, D. and Bommel, E. van (2005) *Smart IT Spending: Insights from European Banks*, McKinsey on IT, No.6, pp. 23–27.
2. Basili, V.R., Caldiera, G. and Rombach, H.D. (1994) *The Goal Question Metric Approach.* Encyclopedia of Software Engineering, Wiley, New York.
3. Berg, M. van den and Steenbergen, M. van (2006) *Building an Enterprise Architecture Practice.* Springer, Dordrecht.
4. Bucher, T., Fischer, R., Kurpjuweit, S. and Winter, R. (2006) Enterprise architecture analysis and application – An exploratory study. In *EDOC Workshop TEAR 2006.* Hong Kong.
5. EACE (2007) *Enterprise Architecture Conference Europe*, London. www.irmuk.co/ eac2007.
6. Hevner, A.R., March, S.T., Park, J. and Ram, S (2004) Design research in information systems research, *MIS Quarterly*, Vol. 28, No. 1, pp. 75–105.
7. Kaplan, R.S. and Norton, D.P. (1992) The balanced scorecard: measures that drive performance, *Harvard Business Review,* Vol. 70, No. 1, pp. 71–79.
8. Kaplan, R.S. and Norton, D.P. (2000) Having trouble with your strategy? Then map it, *Harvard Business Review*, September–October 2000, pp. 1–11.

9. Kaplan, R.S. and Norton, D.P. (2006) *Alignment: Using the Balanced Scorecard to Create Corporate Synergies*. Harvard Business School Publishing Corporation, Boston, MA.
10. Lankhorst, M.M. et al. (2005) *Enterprise Architecture at Work*. Springer, Heidelberg
11. Martinsons, M., Davison, R. and Tse, D. (1999) The balanced scorecard: a foundation for the strategic management of information systems, *Support Systems*, Vol. 25, pp. 71–88.
12. Op 't Land, M. and Proper, H.A. (2007) Impact of principles on enterprise engineering. In *Proceedings of the 15th European Conference on Information Systems*, pp.1965–1976.
13. Quinn, R.E. and Rohrbaugh, J. (1983) A spatial model of effectiveness criteria: towards a competing values approach to organizational analysis, *Management Science*, Vol. 29, No. 3, pp. 363–377.
14. Raadt, B. van der, Slot, R. and Vliet, H. van (2007) Experience report: assessing a global financial services company on its enterprise architecture effectiveness using NAOMI. In *Proceedings of the 40th Annual Hawaii International Conference on System Sciences (HICSS'07)*, Big Island, Hawaii.
15. Schekkerman, J. (2005) *The Economic Benefits of Enterprise Architecture*. Trafford Publishing, UK.
16. Schelp, J. and Stutz, M. (2007) A balanced scorecard approach to measure the value of enterprise architecture, *Journal of Enterprise Architecture*, Vol. 3, No. 4, pp. 8–14.
17. Steenbergen, M. van, Brinkkemper, S. and Berg, M. van den (2007) An instrument for the development of the enterprise architecture practice. In *Proceedings of the 9th International Conference on Enterprise Information Systems*, pp. 14–22.
18. The Open Group (2007) *The Open Group Architecture Framework (TOGAF) Version 8.1.1*, Enterprise Edition.
19. TOGAF (2007) *14th Enterprise Architecture Practitioners Conference*. www.opengroup.org/ paris2007.
20. Venkatraman, N. and Ramanujam, V. (1986) Measurement of business performance in strategy research: a comparison of approaches, *The Academy of Management Review*, Vol. 11, No. 4, 801–814.
21. Verschuren, P. and Hartog, R. (2005) Evaluation in design-oriented research, *Quality & Quantity*, 39, pp. 733–762.
22. Wagter, R., Berg, M. van den, Luijpers, L. and Steenbergen, M. van (2005) *Dynamic Enterprise Architecture: How to Make It Work*. Wiley, Hoboken.
23. Weiss, D. (2006) *Enterprise Architecture Measurement Program, Part 1: Scoping*. ID Nr G00142314.
24. Yin, R.K. (2003) *Case Study Research, design and methods*, third edition. SAGE Publications, London.

64

Organizational Culture and ISD Practices: Comparative Literature Review

Päivi Ovaska and Pasi Juvonen

Abstract

This chapter reports results from a study that aims to analyze and compare the literature related to custom IS, packaged, and open source software organizational cultures, and their systems development practices. The comparative analysis is performed using a framework for organizational culture as lenses to the literature. Our study suggests that the beliefs and values of these three communities of practice differ remarkably and make their organizational culture and systems development practices different. The most important differences were found in business milieu, ISD team efforts, ISD approaches, and products and quality. Based on the study we can question the widely held wisdom of methods, techniques, and tools in systems development and managing its efforts. Our study has several implications for research and practice, which are discussed in this chapter.

Keywords Information systems development · Organizational culture · Communities of practice

1. Introduction

Relatively new stream of literature is emerging that examines the organizational work cultures and IS [1]. The studies have revealed a multitude of ways organizational culture affects organizational change efforts, e.g., [2, 3]. Some studies have suggested problems in the IS implementation due to a mismatch between unique organizational culture and implementation effort [4, 5].

As regards ISD in organizational context, a literature examining and comparing custom IS and packaged software development is enormous. Lately, the newest research subject has been open source software (OSS) development and OSS community of practice. Our objective of this chapter is to analyze and compare the literature related to these three different communities of practice, namely custom IS, packaged, and open source. Based on the results of the analysis, practitioners and researchers are in a better position to understand various approaches to ISD and the organizational culture behind them. For these purposes, an analytic organizational culture framework is used to guide our analysis and comparisons.

This chapter is organized as follows. Next section gives an overview of related research. In Section 3, three communities of practice based on literature are given. Furthermore, we present the results of the comparative analysis. Fifth section discusses the findings and their theoretical and practical implications. Finally, summary of the study is presented.

Päivi Ovaska and Pasi Juvonen · Saimaa University of Applied Sciences, Lappeenranta, Finland.

G.A. Papadopoulos et al. (eds.), *Information Systems Development*, DOI 10.1007/b137171_64,
© Springer Science+Business Media, LLC 2009

2. Community of Practice and Organizational Culture

A community of practice (CoP) is a group of people who share similar goals, interests, beliefs, and value systems in a common domain of recurring activity or work [6, 7]. Because they grow out of human sociability and efforts to meet job requirements (especially those not anticipated and supported by the formal organization and formal training for work), a CoP is typically not an authorized group nor a role identified on an organization chart. People in CoPs might perform the same job (technical representatives) or collaborate on a shared task (software developers) or cooperate on a product (engineers, marketers, and manufacturing specialists). There are typically many communities of practice within a single company, and most people belong to more than one of them.

Much like social cultures have beliefs and values manifested in norms that form behavioral expectations, organizations have cultures that form and give its members guidelines for the way of developing information systems, called an organizational culture perspective [8]. Organizational culture helps individuals and groups deal with uncertainties and ambiguities while offering some degree of order in social life. The substances of such cultures are formed from ideologies, the implicit sets of taken-for-granted beliefs, values, and norms. Members express the substance of their cultures through the use of cultural forms in organizations, acceptable ways of expressing and affirming their beliefs, values, and norms. Organizational cultures, like other cultures, evolve as groups of people struggle together to make sense of and cope with their worlds [8]. It is through the interaction between ideologies and cultural forms that cultures maintain their existence. Most organizational culture researchers view work culture as a kind of consensus-making system [8]. However, some researchers view organizational culture as an emergent process [8].

In this study, the organizational culture is viewed as a phenomenon manifested in an organization's work practices, norms, beliefs, values, and artifacts defined below [8].

- *Beliefs – Express cause and effect relations (i.e., behaviors lead to outcomes)*
- *Values – Express preferences for certain behaviors or for certain outcomes*
- *Norms – Express which behaviors are expected by others and are culturally acceptable ways to attain outcomes.*

We analyze the connections between content themes and cultural manifestations in the custom IS, packaged IS, and OSS communities of practice by using the Martin's framework [8]. According to this framework, the substance of a culture is its ideology – shared, interrelated sets of emotionally beliefs, values, and norms that bind people together and help them to make sense of their world [9].

There exist many other approaches to organizational culture, which differs greatly in relation to how this complex concept culture is defined [8, 9].

3. Overview of Three Communities of Practice

Custom information systems (IS) are those made by either an organization's internal IS staff or by direct subcontract to a software firm (such as Andersen Consulting or Computer Associates). Custom IS are made-to-order systems and are typically built for specific users. This definition of custom IS also includes most government work [10]. The degree of customization varies within this kind of IS. Some IS are totally constructed from scratch while others, like ERP (enterprise resource planning) systems, are more software products that are tailored to customer needs [11]. Custom information systems development is typically done by internal to the organization information technology departments or consulting/ service firms (e.g., EDS, IBM, ISSC, or Anderson Consulting) who build custom systems on a contract basis [10].

Packaged software (also known as shrink-wrapped, COTS, and commercial software) means all software sold as a tradable product (purchased from a vendor, distributor, or store) for all computer platforms including mainframes, workstations, and microcomputers, e.g., [12]. Typically, packaged software is licensed for use, not sold.

Most packaged software firms function in an environment of intense time-to-market pressure. Packaged software firms are under constant pressure to innovate and beat out the competition in delivering their products to market. When a firm releases some critical functionality in the latest release, all other firms developing for this marketplace are compelled to modify their development to include this functionality in the next release, even if it is relatively late in their development cycle.

Open source software (OSS) sometimes referred also as FOSS (Free/Open Source Software) is usually seen as an antonym to commercial software. Commercial software is generally sold for a fee, with restrictions on use, and in binary format only. In contrast, OSS is software released under a license conforming to the open source definition (OSD) given by open source initiative. The key conditions of OSD are that the source code must be available to user and the software must be redistributable [13].

In the OSS development the main focus has always been in the technology and the people developing it. The OSS community wants to develop technologically superior tools with high quality.

4. Comparative Analysis

In this section, custom IS, packaged, and open source software organizational cultures are compared using framework described below. In the analysis, the most important differences of their organizational culture were found from four categories: business milieu, team efforts, software development approaches, and products and quality. In the following, the results of this comparison are summarized in each of these categories.

4.1. Analytic Framework for Comparisons

In order to compare the literature related to custom IS, packaged, and open source software organizational cultures, we used Martin's framework with beliefs, values, norms, and artifacts (Table 64.1).

4.2. Business Milieu

Relative to packaged software, cost pressures (not time-to-market pressures) dominate the custom IS development industry. In OSS community, the belief of code quality dominates their work. These differences influence remarkably to the ISD management practices. While custom IS development the project management and planning becomes very important, in packaged software development the release management and planning forms the most important practice in managing ISD practices. In relation to these, OSS development teams rely on change management systems to organize and track their development work. By effective change management, OSS teams try to achieve the highest possible code quality of the product. Release management means that the software evolves through a planned set of releases and the efficient release planning insure the soft-ware product coming to the market in a right moment and scope.

Third difference between these communities of practice is their relationships with their customer. Custom IS company's objective is usually to stay "on the skin" of its customer. The customer relationship is tight and the customer has lot of power in the relationship. Packaged and OSS communities of practices tend to have the distant relationships with their customers. This separation means that intermediaries – such as consultants or implementation firms – mediate the information from customers. This relationship also influences on how they measure their success in systems development: custom IS communities of practice seek customer satisfaction, packaged software firms seek "killer application" or "mind share" positions in the markets, and OSS communities seek software and information freedom.

Yet another difference between custom IS, packaged, and OSS CoPs is their organizational structure. Custom IS companies are mostly big hierarchical formal organizations, which share the roots from former IS departments and they are closely aligned with the business culture of their former owner. Package software firms are individualistically oriented with legend of hackers and "code cowboys" personifying and mythologizing the industry. OSS communities are more loosely coupled virtual teams that are kept

Table 64.1.   Beliefs, values, norms, and artifacts in the framework.

Cultural concepts	Custom IS	Packaged software	Open Source software
Beliefs	Customer satisfaction, user satisfaction [14, 15]	Profit and revenues, market-share [16]	Software and information freedom [13], [17]
	Importance of costs [18]	Importance of time to market [19]	Importance of code quality [17].
	Hierarchical formal organization, project culture [20]	Individualism, "made-in-my-garage," long-lasting teams [12, 21]	Loosely coupled communities kept together by strong common values [22]
	Customer is close, user is near [14]	Customer is far, user is far [10, 16]	Customer is far, user is inside [13]
Values	Business domain knowledge [14, 15]	Software development talent [23]	Software development talent [24]
	Solving a tough problem, doing things right [14]	Financial rewards [23]	Career advancement, improving programming skills [24]
Practices	Process view of development, separate design, and coding [25]	Product view of development, iterative development [26]	Product view of development, iterative development [27]
	Project planning and management [28]	Release planning and management [15]	Change management [29]
	Big distributed projects [10]	Small, co-located long-lasting teams [30, 31]	Big distributed virtual teams, forking is forbidden [24, 32]
	Implementation included [33, 34]	Implementation left to third party consultants [10, 16]	Implementation not included [17]
	Meeting requirements and budget [14, 34]	Meeting new market opportunities [15]	Meeting high-quality requirements [32, 33, 35]
Artifacts	Trusted partner, IS that meets customer requirements [14]	Innovative, "killer" application [15]	IRQ achieves, mailing lists, downloadable source code [22]

together by strong common beliefs and values such as software and information freedom, sharing, helping, and cooperation. When the success of the packaged and OSS CoPs is tied, in a large part, to the software development talent, the most valuable skill of custom IS developers is the domain or business expertise.

4.3. Team Efforts

At the level of software development team, differences between custom IS, packaged, and open source software development domains are manifested in the structure and conduct of the software developers.

Both custom IS and OSS teams tend to be big and distributed over several sites, whereas packaged software development teams are smaller and typically co-located. Packaged and open source development teams tend to have stable teams where members remain committed to the product over several versions or releases. In open source development there is a norm against forking a project meaning that splitting the project into two or more projects developed separately is forbidden. Custom IS development teams are more like ad hoc work groups, in where their members do not work full time belonging to the several projects in the same.

Packaged software teams have possibility of financial rewards, which seems to be reason for hard work in these firms. This financial incentive seems rare for those developing custom IS. Custom IS developers are more motivated by non-financial rewards such as solving a tough problems of their customer or doing things in a right way. Either OSS teams are motivated by financial rewards, but their motivation comes from career advancement, increased peer reputation, and improving programming skills. Firms looking for a particular skill in the labor market can easily find qualified programmers by examining code contributions in the OSS community. Participants also improve their programming skills through the active peer review that is prevalent in OSS projects.

There exists also another difference between the teams of these CoPs, namely the difference between social dynamics of the team. Package and OSS teams reflect contention, not consensus as is the situation in custom IS teams. Contention orientation along with the product orientation leads in packaged and OSS teams that the software development is driven by one person or a small core team. In custom IS teams the development does not lay in the head of one person, but the development revolves around building a shared, consensus-oriented view of needs and functions. This consensus-based approach also relies on formal "sign-offs" and documentation to assist those involved in the development effort to maintain a shared view.

4.4. Software Development Approaches

Several factors underscore the differences between custom IS, packaged software, and open source software development approaches.

Custom IS developers tend to have a process view of development unlike packaged software and OSS developers which have product view of development. Process focus means the belief in the importance of process, not the final system and therefore in most cases custom IS organization process tends to be more central and mature. A product focus means that the dominant goal of the software development effort is to ship a product and all the other activities are secondary. The product focus is also reflected in the belief that hacking (the attention to coding as a defining art) is good: whatever it takes to get the product out is more important than how it is done. On the contrary, in custom IS communities of practice the coding is seen more routine work which can be outsourced easily. The hacking culture also is supported by accepted wisdom that all products are driven by a person and the process that evolves is based around particular people whereas the routine work culture appreciate the work of project people working together and having specified roles (like project manager, designer, coder, tester) within this project. The best hackers are seen as visionaries in the packaged software and OSS communities of practice and it is their vision that drives the development of the product.

It is also typical in personalized and product-focus culture that design and development are intertwined. The resulting process is highly iterative, flexible, and constantly evolving. In process-oriented environment the process is quite often more waterfall style with separate design and development. The reason for this kind of process is the contract-based development of custom IS firms but also the reason that customers are used to this kind of process. Custom IS development process also includes implementation – the introduction, rollout, and host-organization acceptance of the system. Implementation stands separate from the work of the both packaged and open source software developers.

Yet another area where this comparison of practices challenges norms is the role of users. In custom IS they are seen as critical to successful implementation whereas users are not integral to contemporary packaged software development efforts. In OSS development the situation is more complex. Users are seen very valuable in OSS development if they own ISD competencies. They can act, i.e., as beta-testers, bug fixers, or even co-developers. In the cases where a user is not willing to participate to the work of community, the situation is the same as in the packaged development community.

4.5. Products and Quality

Underlying beliefs in these different communities of practices highlight the quality in totally different ways. In custom IS development concentration is clearly in the customer relationship and process quality. The developed IS does not have to be superior but it has to be good enough to satisfy the customer. In packaged software community the quality can be expressed as by innovation quality, meaning the aim to build a killer application that would dominate the market. OSS community concentrates on the technological quality of the product, namely producing as good code as possible downloadable for anyone who wants to use it or participate to its further development.

5. Discussion

In this section, the results of the comparative analysis are discussed. The purpose is to identify the principal implications for research and practice. Table 64.2 summarized these implications.

Table 64.2. Summary of results and implications of the study.

Category	Description of the results	Implications
Business milieu	Different success factors for business (cost, time to market, code quality)	New and different business models for IS organizations
	Different organizational structure (big, small, virtual)	Diversity of organizing systems development efforts
	Different kind of relationship with customer (near, far)	Customers and users awareness of these differences
Team efforts	Differences in social dynamics of the team (consensus, content)	More research in different kinds of social dynamics of ISD teams
	Differences in developers motivators (non-financial rewards, financial rewards, reputation)	Considered in recruiting software developers
Software development approaches	Different view for development (process, product)	Diversity of ISD processes, questioning the wisdom of ISD methods, techniques, and tools
	Differences in relationships with user (near, far, inside)	More research about different types of user roles in ISD
	Differences of systems development management (project, release, change)	Diversity of managing systems development efforts
Products and quality	Different quality criteria for final product (technical, innovation, business domain)	Diversity of needed skills for developers

In making the comparison between custom IS, packaged, and OSS communities of practice, the evidence is compelling enough to suggest questioning cherished beliefs regarding at least four elements of contemporary ISD wisdoms: the importance and form of ISD processes, method, techniques, and tools, the one-sided view of users role in development, the social dynamics of ISD teams, and the importance of project management in managing ISD efforts.

The results of the comparison suggest also the implications for education of software developers due to the importance of different kind of skills in these three domains. Factors such as the individualistic culture, the product and innovation orientation, and centrality of programming skills in packaged and OSS domains are very different than skills needed in custom IS domain, such as business understanding, teamwork skills, and client interactions.

What emerges from this comparative study is a picture of three different ISD approaches. Based on this argument, the study has several implications for ISD business. There exists different kind of business models for IS organizations and even new business models arises for packaged domain in implementing software and for OSS domain implementing and supporting the software.

Besides differences in business models of these organizations, also their organization cultures with beliefs and values vary a lot. Customers and users should be aware of the differences. For example, if a customer wants rapid reaction for changes in software requirements from their software vendor, it is very hard to get those changes rapidly from package software and OSS organizations, but a lot more easier from custom IS firms because of their closer relationship with customer.

6. Conclusions

In this chapter, we have illustrated how different systems development organizational cultures differ from each other. We analyzed and compared the literature related to custom IS, packaged, and open source software development and used organizational culture framework as a lens to the data.

Our study suggests that the beliefs and values of these three communities of practice differ from each other remarkably and make their development practices different. The most important differences were found in business milieu, ISD team efforts, ISD approaches, and products and quality.

The results of the study have many implications for research and practice. The results of the study questions the widely held wisdoms of systems development and the management of its activities, such as the importance and form of ISD processes, method, techniques, and tools, the one-sided view of users role in development, the social dynamics of ISD teams and the importance of project management in managing ISD. The results provide practitioners and researchers a better position to understand various approaches to ISD and the organizational culture behind them.

References

1. Avison, D.E. and Myers, M.D. (1995). Information systems and anthropology: an anthropological perspective on IT and organizational culture. *Information Technology & People*, 8(3), 43–56.
2. Harrington, S. and Rubbel, C.P. (1999). Practical and value compatibility: their roles in the adoption, diffusion, and success of telecommuting. *Proceedings of the 20th International Conference on Information Systems*, pp. 103–112, December 12–15, Charlotte, North Carolina, United States.
3. Dellana, S.A. and Hauser, R.D. (1999). Towards defining the quality culture. *Engineering Management Journal* 11(2), 11–15.
4. Pliskin N., Romm T., Lee A.S. and Weber Y. (1993). Presumed versus actual organizational culture: managerial implications for implementation of information systems. *The Computer Journal* 36(2), 143–152.
5. Krumbholz, M. and Maiden, N. (2001). The implementation of enterprise resource planning packages in different organizational and national cultures. *Information Systems* 26(3), 185–204.
6. Brown, J.S. and Duguid, P. (1991). Organizational learning and communities-of-practice: Toward a unified view of working, learning and innovation. *Organization Science* 2(1), 40–57.
7. Wenger E. (1998). *Communities of Practice: Learning, Meaning and Identity*, Cambridge, Massachusetts: Cambridge University Press.
8. Martin J. (2002). *Organizational Culture: Mapping the Terrain*, Thousands Oaks: Sage Publications.
9. Smirchich L. (1983). Concepts of Culture and Organizational Analysis. *Administrative Science Quarterly*, 28, 339–358.
10. Carmel, E. and Sawyer, S. (1998). Packaged software development teams: What makes them different? *Information Technology and People*, 11(1), 7–19.
11. Carmel E. and Bird B. (1997). Small is beautiful: a study of packaged software development teams. *The Information Society* 13(1), 125–142.
12. Carmel, E. (1997). American hegemony in packaged software trade and the culture of software. *The Information Society*, 13(1), 125–142.
13. Feller, J. and Fitxgerald, B. (2000). A Framework Analysis of the Open Source Software Development Paradigm. *Proceedings of the twenty first international conference on Information systems*, Brisbane, Queensland, Australia, pp 58–69.
14. Ovaska,P (2008): A Case Study of Systems Development in Custom IS Organizational Culture. In Barry, C., Lang, M., Wojtkowski, W., Wojtkowski, G., Wrycza, S., and Zupancic, J. (eds) *The Inter-Networked World: ISD Theory, Practice, and Education*. Springer-Verlag: New York.
15. Sawyer, S. (2000). Packaged software: implications of the differences from custom approaches to software development. *European Journal of Information Systems*, 9, 47–58.
16. Keil, M and Carmel, E (1995). Customer-developer links in software development. *Communications of the ACM*, 8(5), 33–44.
17. Stewart, K. and Gosain, S. (2006). The impact of ideology on effectiveness in open source software development teams. *MIS Quarterly*, 30(2), 291–314.
18. Boehm, B. (1987). Improving software productivity. *IEEE Computer*, 20(8), 43–58.
19. Carmel, E. (1995). Cycle-time in packaged software firms. *Journal of Product Innovation Management*, 12(2), 110–123.

20. Walz, D.B., Elam, J.J. and Curtis, B. (1993). Inside a software design team: Knowledge acquisition, sharing, and integration. *Communications of the ACM*, 36 (10), 63–77.
21. Constantine, L. (1995). *Constantine on Peopleware*, Englewood Cliffs, NJ: Yourdon Press.
22. Augustin, L., Bressler, D. and Smith, G. (2002). Accelerating software development through collaboration. *ICSE'02*, May 19–25, Orlando, FL.
23. Zachary, G. (1994). *Showstopper: The Breakneck Race to Create Windows-nt and the Next Generation at Microsoft*. New York: The Free Press.
24. Sawyer, S. (2004). Software development teams. *Communications of the ACM*, 47(12), pp. 95–99.
25. Humphrey, W. (1989). *Managing the Software Process*. Reading, MA: Addison-Wesley.
26. Heckman, R. (1998). Planning to solve the 'skills problem' in the virtual information management organization. *International Journal of Information Management*, 18(1), 3–16.
27. Ye, Y. and Kishida, K. (2003). Towards an understanding of the motivation of open source software developers. *Proceedings of the 25th International Conference on Software Engineering*, Portland, Oregon, May 3–10, pp. 419–429.
28. Larson, E. and Gobeli, D. (1988). Organizing for product development projects. *Journal of Product Innovation Management*, 5, 180–190.
29. Gosain, S. (2003). Looking through a window on open source culture: Lessons for community infrastructure design. *Systémes d'Information et Management*, 8(1), pp. 11–42.
30. Cusumano, M. and Selby, R. (1995). *Microsoft Secrets: How the World's Most Powerful Software Company Creates Technology, Shapes Markets, and Manages People*. New York: Free Press/Simon & Schuster.
31. Cusumano, M. and Smith, S. (1997). Beyond the waterfall: Software development at microsoft. In *Competing in the Age of Digital Convergence* (Yoffie D., Ed.), 371–411. Boston, MA: Harvard Business School Press.
32. Ljungberg, J. (2000). Open source movements as a model for organizing. *European Journal of Information Systems* (9:4), 208–216.
33. Markus, M.L. and Robey, D. (1988). Information technology and organizational change: Causal structure in theory and research. *Management Science*, 34 (5), 583–598.
34. Kling, R. and Iacono, S. (1984). Computing as an occasion for social control. *Journal of Social Issues* 40 (3), 77–96.
35. Elliott, M. and Scacchi, W. (2003). *Free Software Development: Cooperation and conflict in A Virtual Organizational Culture*. Open Source Software Development, IDEA Publishing, Hershey, PA, 2004.

65

Metadata to Support Data Warehouse Evolution

Darja Solodovnikova

Abstract

The focus of this chapter is metadata necessary to support data warehouse evolution. We present the data warehouse framework that is able to track evolution process and adapt data warehouse schemata and data extraction, transformation, and loading (ETL) processes. We discuss the significant part of the framework, the metadata repository that stores information about the data warehouse, logical and physical schemata and their versions. We propose the physical implementation of multiversion data warehouse in a relational DBMS. For each modification of a data warehouse schema, we outline the changes that need to be made to the repository metadata and in the database.

Keywords Data warehouse · Schema evolution · Changes · Metadata · Repository

1. Introduction

Data warehouses often evolve due to changes in data sources and business requirements. These changes influence existing schemata and data extraction, transformation, and loading (ETL) processes of the data warehouse. This is why these changes need to be handled properly. Often the existing schema and ETL processes can be adapted to changes automatically or with minimal manual work.

Simple adaptation of the data warehouse schema can cause a loss of history. Therefore, it is necessary to keep versions of data warehouse schemata. According to [7], 'schema version is a schema that reflects the business requirements during a given time interval, called its validity, that starts upon schema creation and extends until the next version is created.' In this chapter metadata of the multiversion data warehouse are discussed. The metadata include physical and logical information about data warehouse schema versions. The impact of changes of data warehouse schema on metadata is also discussed.

The rest of this chapter is organized as follows. In Section 2 the related work is presented. In Section 3 the proposed data warehouse framework is outlined. The main contribution of this chapter is presented in Sections 4 and 5, where the metadata model for a multiversion data warehouse is described and changes of the data warehouse schema that are supported by the proposed framework and their results are discussed. We conclude with directions for future work in Section 6.

2. Related Work

In the literature there are various solutions for the data warehouse evolution problems, which are the data warehouse adaptation after the changes in source data and schemata as well as business requirements.

Changes in dimensions of a data warehouse are discussed in [8]. Dimension structural and instance update operators are formally specified and their effect is studied over materialized views over dimension levels.

Darja Solodovnikova • University of Latvia, Raina bulv. 19, Riga, Latvia.

G.A. Papadopoulos et al. (eds.), *Information Systems Development*, DOI 10.1007/b137171_65,
© Springer Science+Business Media, LLC 2009

In [1, 9] the primitive evolution operations that occur over the data warehouse schema are defined. In [9] the semantics of the changes for star-and snowflake schemata are given for each operation.

The above-mentioned papers do not address the problems of the data warehouse adaptation after changes in data sources. Several approaches have been proposed for solving these problems [10, 11, 18]. These approaches are based on mappings that specify how one schema is obtained from the other schema. This specification is used to adapt one schema after changes in the other schema.

In several papers [3, 14] a data warehouse is defined as a set of materialized views over data sources. These papers study the problems of how to rewrite a view definition and adapt view extent after changes in source data and schemata.

In all these approaches schema versioning is not supported. Several authors [6, 8, 19] propose versioning approach. The main idea in [7] is to store augmented schemata together with schema versions to support cross-version querying. When a new version is created, for all previous versions, augmented schemata are created and populated with data. Though the physical storage and metadata of schema versions are mentioned, the details are not explored. In [15] the definition of a multidimensional schema that supports schema versioning is given. This definition is very similar to the one given in [2], the difference is that the first one supports versioning. In [4, 5] a method to support data and structure versions of dimensions is proposed. The method allows tracking history and comparing data, using temporal modes of presentation that is data mapping into the particular structure version. In [6] the metadata model that supports schema versioning for data warehouses is introduced. Metadata management solutions in a multiversion data warehouse are also proposed in [19], where one of the discussed issues is metadata support for detection of changes in sources and propagation of them to the designated data warehouse version. Issues related to queries over a multiversion data warehouse are considered in [12]. These papers do not address the problem of physical storage of multiversion data warehouse.

The above-mentioned papers consider only one kind of evolution problems, for example, changes in a schema raised by evolving business requirements, adaptation of a data warehouse after changes in data sources or data warehouse versioning, and querying multiversion data warehouse. In our approach we propose the framework that is able to solve all these kinds of evolution problems.

3. Data Warehouse Evolution Framework

To handle data warehouse evolution problems, we propose the data warehouse framework depicted in Fig. 65.1. In this section the general issues of the framework are discussed. The detailed description of the framework is given in [16].

The framework is composed of the development environment and user environment. In the development environment the data warehouse metadata repository and other metadata management components are located and ETL processes and change processing is conducted. In the user environment reports on one or several data warehouse versions are defined and executed by users.

The metadata of the data warehouse schema versions and database structure are stored in the mapping repository. Also the repository includes metadata, which define the logics of ETL processes, and metadata used for data warehouse adaptation. The description of these metadata and the adaptation process is found in [17]. The schema metadata are presented in Sections 4.1 and 4.2.

4. Data Warehouse Metadata

Common Warehouse Metamodel (CWM) [13] was used as a basis of the proposed metamodel of multidimensional data warehouse. CWM is a metadata standard produced by Object Management Group to simplify metadata interchange between data warehousing applications. CWM consists of packages, which describe different aspects of a data warehouse.

Using the following metamodel, it is possible to model a data warehouse schema at physical and logical level. In the physical metamodel an implementation of a data warehouse in RDBMS is specified, but

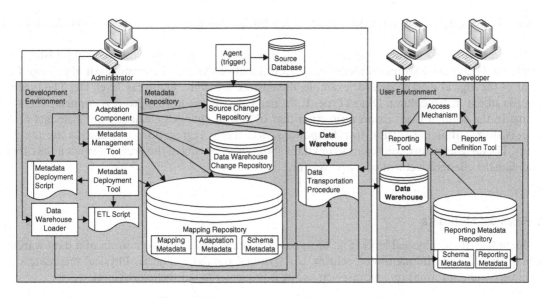

Figure 65.1. Data warehouse evolution framework.

the logical metadata describe schema versions of a data warehouse. The physical level metadata are based on the relational package of CWM. The logical level metadata are based on the OLAP package. These two levels are connected by objects defined in the Transformation package of CWM. Due to space limitations, the description of elements of the physical and logical metadata that are taken from CWM is not given.

4.1. Logical Metadata

Metadata at the logical level describe the multidimensional data warehouse schema. The logical metamodel is depicted in Fig. 65.2.

To reflect multiple versions of a data warehouse schema, two objects were introduced: *schema version* and *version transformation*, which are not included in CWM. If, as a result of any change in a data warehouse schema, a new schema version is created, a new record is inserted in the table schema version. Each schema version has a validity period defined by the columns ValidFrom and ValidTo. The column

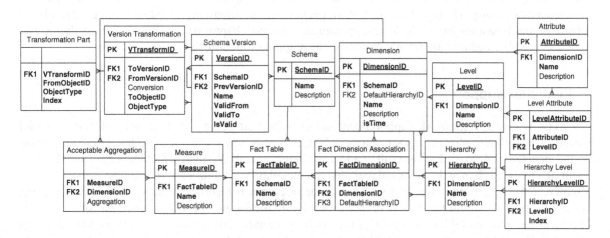

Figure 65.2. Logical metamodel.

IsValid indicates whether a version is currently valid. Each version, except for the first one, has a link to a previous version.

Elements of a version are connected to the table schema version by the table version transformation. The column ToObjectID stores an identifier of an element of the current version. An object can be any element of the logical metamodel, for example, dimension, attribute, hierarchy level, etc. The type of an element is stored in the column ObjectType. If an element remains unchanged it is connected to several versions. In the column Conversion a function that obtains a changed element from elements of other version is stored. Building version transformations, acceptable aggregations of elements are taken into account. The table transformation part stores data about the elements of the previous version that are used to calculate the changed element of a new version.

4.2. Physical Metadata

Metadata at the physical level (Fig. 65.3) describe relational database schema of a data warehouse and mapping of a multidimensional schema to relational database objects. Physical metadata do not include versioning information, because versioning is implemented at the logical level.

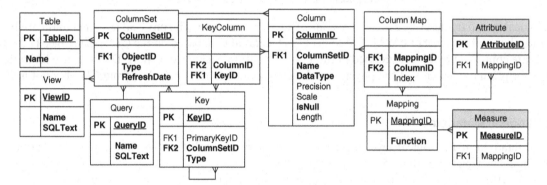

Figure 65.3. Physical metamodel.

CWM metadata were extended by the additional type of column set, a result of SQL *query*. The column RefreshDate was introduced to store the date of the last update of the table or base tables of a view or a query. *Mappings* (FeatureMap in CWM package transformation) specify formulas that obtain attributes and measures from one or several columns. In this chapter it is assumed that attributes and measures are obtained directly from columns by the mapping function "copy."

5. Evolution Support

The evolution framework supports physical changes that operate with tables and columns, and logical changes that modify mainly schema metadata. In this section a result of each change and its' impact on the metadata is described. As a result of a logical change, mainly the logical metadata are adapted. As a result of a physical change, both logical and physical metadata are modified. When a new schema version V_N is created from the previous version V_P, the time of change is recorded in the column ValidTo of the version V_P and the column ValidFrom of the version V_N. In the following sections the corresponding tables of dimensions and fact tables are the tables that include columns that are transformed by a mapping into attributes of dimensions and measures of fact tables in the physical metadata.

5.1. Physical Changes

New Dimension Attribute. When a new attribute A is added to the dimension D, in the database a new column K is added to the corresponding table T. In the physical metadata a new column K is created in the column set T. In the logical metadata a new schema version V_N is constructed from the previous version V_P.

A new attribute A is attached to the dimension D. A mapping with a function "copy" is created to connect the column K at the physical level with the attribute A at the logical level. If A can be calculated from other attributes of the dimension D, then the version transformation is constructed for A from version V_P to version V_N.

Deletion of Dimension Attribute. When an attribute A is deleted from the dimension D, in the database the corresponding column K of the table T is not removed but is no longer updated by ETL processes. The physical metadata remain unchanged. In the logical metadata a new schema version V_N is constructed from the same objects from the previous version V_P except for the attribute A. If the attribute A can be calculated from the remaining attributes of the dimension D, then the version transformation is constructed for A from version V_N to version V_P.

An attribute can be deleted only if it is not connected to any level. If a connection persists, at first an attribute must be disconnected from all levels. It is not allowed to delete an attribute that corresponds to a primary key column.

Change of Datatype of Attribute. When datatype of the attribute A of the dimension D is changed, a new column K with a new datatype is added to the corresponding table T. The column K is updated instead of the changed column. In the physical metadata a new column K is created in the column set T. In the logical metadata a new schema version V_N is constructed from the previous version V_P, but the datatype of A is changed to a new value. A mapping with a function "copy" is created to connect the column K at the physical level with the attribute A at the logical level. Version transformation, which transforms the attribute A in the version V_P to the attribute A in the version V_P by conversion function is created. This means that semantically the attributes in both versions are identical.

Renaming Dimension Attribute. When an attribute A of the dimension D is renamed, in the database and in the physical metadata a corresponding column K is renamed. In the logical metadata a new schema version V_N is constructed from the previous version V_P, but the attribute A is created with a new name. A mapping with a function "copy" is created to connect the column K at the physical level with the attribute A at the logical level. Version transformation with an empty function, which connects the attribute A in the version V_P to the attribute A in the version V_P is created. This means that semantically the attributes in both versions are identical.

New Dimension. When a new dimension D is added, in the database a new corresponding table T with a primary key is created. In the physical metadata the table T and the corresponding column set is created, metadata about columns and keys of the table T are recorded. In the logical metadata a new schema version V_N is constructed from the previous version V_P. A new dimension D with attributes that correspond to columns of the table T is added. Mappings with a function "copy" are created to connect columns of the table T at the physical level with attributes of the dimension D at the logical level. Version transformation is not constructed. Reports that use the dimension D can run only from the time it was created.

Deletion of Dimension. When a dimension D is deleted, in the database the corresponding table T is not removed but is no longer updated by ETL processes. The physical metadata remain unchanged. In the logical metadata a new schema version V_N is constructed from the same objects from the previous version V_P except for the dimension D, attributes, hierarchies and levels of it.

A dimension can be deleted only if it is not connected to any fact table. If a connection persists, at first a dimension must be disconnected from all fact tables.

Renaming Dimension. When a dimension D is renamed, in the database and in the physical metadata a corresponding table T is renamed. In the logical metadata a new schema version V_N is constructed from the previous version V_P, but the dimension D is created with a new name. A mapping with a function "copy" is created to connect columns of T at the physical level with attributes of D at the logical level. Version transformation with an empty function which connects the dimension D in the version V_P to the dimension D in the version V_P is created. This means that semantically the dimensions in both versions are identical.

New Measure. When a new measure M is added to the fact table F, in the database a new column K is added to the corresponding table T. In the physical metadata a new column K is created in the column set T. In the logical metadata a new schema version V_N is constructed from the previous version V_P. A new measure M is attached to the fact table F. A mapping with a function "copy" is created to connect the column K at the physical level with the measure M at the logical level. If the measure M can be calculated from other measures of the fact table F, then the version transformation is constructed for M from version V_P to version V_N.

Deletion of Measure. When a measure M is deleted from the fact table F, in the database the corresponding column K of the table T is not removed but is no longer updated by ETL processes. The physical metadata remain unchanged. In the logical metadata a new schema version V_N is constructed from the same objects from the previous version V_P except for the measure M. If the measure M can be calculated from the remaining measures of the fact table F, then the Version transformation is constructed for M from version V_N to version V_P.

Change of Datatype of Measure. When datatype of the measure M of the fact table F is changed, a new column K with a new datatype is added to the corresponding table T. The column K is updated instead of the changed column. In the physical metadata a new column K is created in the column set T. In the logical metadata a new schema version V_N is constructed from the previous version V_P, but the datatype of M is changed to a new value. A mapping with a function "copy" is created to connect the column K at the physical level with the measure M at the logical level. Version transformation which transforms the measure M in the version V_P to the measure M in the version V_P by conversion function is created. This means that semantically the measures in both versions are identical.

Renaming Measure. When a measure M of the fact table F is renamed, in the database and in the physical metadata a corresponding column K is renamed. In the logical metadata a new schema version V_N is constructed from the previous version V_P, but the measure M is created with a new name. A mapping with a function "copy" is created to connect the column K at the physical level with the measure M at the logical level. Version transformation with an empty function, which connects M in the version V_P to the measure M in the version V_P is created. This means that semantically the measures in both versions are identical.

New Fact Table. When a new fact table F is added, in the database a new corresponding table T is created. In the physical metadata the table T and the corresponding column set with the type "table" is created, metadata about columns of the table T are recorded. In the logical metadata a new schema version V_N is constructed from the previous version V_P. A new fact table F with measures that correspond to columns of the table T is added. Mappings with a function "copy" are created to connect columns of the table T at the physical level with measures of the fact table F at the logical level. Version transformation is not constructed. Reports that use the fact table F can run only from the time it was created.

Deletion of Fact Table. When a fact table F is deleted, in the database the corresponding table T is not removed but is no longer updated by ETL processes. The physical metadata remain unchanged. In the logical metadata a new schema version V_N is constructed from the same objects from the previous version V_P except for the fact table F, its measures and connections with dimensions.

Renaming Fact Table. When a fact table F is renamed, in the database and in the physical metadata a corresponding table T is renamed. In the logical metadata a new schema version V_N is constructed from the previous version V_P, but the fact table F is created with a new name. A mapping with a function "copy" is created to connect columns of the table T at the physical level with measures of the fact table F at the logical level. Version transformation with an empty function which connects the fact table F in the version V_P to the fact table F in the version V_P is created. This means that semantically the fact tables in both versions are identical.

5.2. Logical Changes

Connection of Dimension to Fact Table. To connect a dimension D to a fact table F, in the database and the physical metadata a foreign key column K (or columns) is added to the corresponding table T_F, which will be connected to the primary key column (or columns) of the table T_D that corresponds to the dimension D. In the database in the table T_D a new fictive record (for example, with data "all together") is created with an identifier I. If there are data in the table T_F the new column K is filled with I. In the database and the physical metadata a foreign key is created to connect the column K to the primary key of the table T_D or column set T_D. Depending on requirements, in the database and in the physical metadata the column K can be included in the primary key of the table T_F and column set T_F or a new primary key can be created if there is no primary key in the table T_F.

In the logical metadata a new schema version V_N is constructed from the previous version V_P. A fact dimension association is created between the fact table F and dimension D. Version transformations are created for measures of the fact table F if it is possible. One transformation with the function that transforms (divides) measure data to correspond to the version V_N is recorded. Another transformation with the function that transforms (aggregates) measure data in respect of the dimension D to correspond to the version V_P is recorded. If conversion is not possible, reports that span both versions can be run only until or after the change of a schema using only one of the versions V_P or V_N.

Disconnection of Dimension from Fact Table. To disconnect a dimension D from a fact table F, in the database in the table T_D that corresponds to the dimension D a new fictive record (for example, with data "all together") is created with an identifier I. During ETL processes the identified I is stored in the table T_F that corresponds to the fact table F in the foreign key column that was connected to the table T_D. The physical metadata remain unchanged. In the logical metadata a new schema version V_N is constructed from the same objects from the previous version V_P, except for the fact dimension association between the fact table F and the dimension D. Version transformations are created for measures of the fact table F if it is possible. One transformation with the function that transforms (aggregates) measure data in respect of the dimension D to correspond to the version V_N is recorded. Another transformation with the function that transforms (divides) measure data to correspond to the version V_P is recorded. If conversion is not possible, reports that span both versions can be run only until or after the change of a schema using only one of the versions V_P or V_N.

New Dimension Hierarchy. When a new hierarchy H is added to the dimension D, in the logical metadata a new schema version V_N is constructed from the previous version V_P. A new hierarchy H is attached to the dimension D. Version transformation is not constructed. Reports that use the hierarchy H can run only from the time it was created.

Deletion of Dimension Hierarchy. When a hierarchy H is deleted from the dimension D, in the logical metadata a new schema version V_N is constructed from the same objects from the previous version V_P except for the hierarchy H. Version transformation is not constructed. Reports that use the hierarchy H can run only until the time it was deleted.

New Hierarchy Level. When a new level L is added to the hierarchy H, in the logical metadata a new schema version V_N is constructed from the previous version V_P. A new level L is attached to the dimension D, which contains the hierarchy H. The level L is connected to the hierarchy H and the corresponding index of the level L is recorded. If there are any other levels in the hierarchy H that have the index, which is the same or bigger than the index of the level L, their index is increased by 1. Version transformation with an empty conversion is constructed for all changed levels, except for the level L. Version transformation is not constructed for the level L. Reports that use the level L can run only from the time it was created.

Deletion of Level from Hierarchy. When a level L is deleted from the hierarchy H, in the logical metadata a new schema version V_N is constructed from the same objects from the previous version V_P except for the connection between the hierarchy H and the level L. If there are any other levels in the hierarchy H that have the index which is the bigger than the index of the level L, their index is decreased by 1. Version transformation is not constructed. Reports that use the connection between the hierarchy H and the level L can run only until the time it was removed.

Deletion of Level from Dimension. To delete a level L from a dimension D, at first it must be deleted from all hierarchies where it is used. Then in the logical metadata a new schema version V_N is constructed from the same objects from the previous version V_P except for the level L. Version transformation is not constructed. Reports that use the level L can run only until the time it was deleted.

Connection of Level to Hierarchy. To connect a level L to a hierarchy H, in the logical metadata a new schema version V_N is constructed from the previous version V_P and the level L is connected to the hierarchy H and the corresponding index of the level L is recorded. If there are any other levels in the hierarchy H that have the index which is the same or bigger than the index of the level L, their index is increased by 1. Version transformation with an empty conversion is constructed for all changed levels, except for the level L. Version transformation is not constructed for the connection between the hierarchy H and the level L. Reports that use the connection between the hierarchy H and the level L can run only from the time it was created.

Connection of Attribute to Level. To connect an attribute A to a level L, in the logical metadata a new schema version V_N is constructed from the previous version V_P and the attribute A is connected to the level L. Version transformation is not constructed for the connection between the attribute A and the level L. Reports that use this connection can run only from the time it was created.

Disconnection of Attribute from Level. To disconnect an attribute A from a level L, in the logical metadata a new schema version V_N is constructed from the same objects from the previous version V_P, except for the connection between the attribute A and the level L. Version transformation is not constructed for the connection between the attribute A and the level L. Reports that use the connection between the level L and the attribute A can run only until the time it was removed.

6. Conclusions and Future Work

The main contribution of this chapter is a data warehouse repository that describes data warehouse schema at the logical and physical level. The model is based on the CWM standard, which was supplemented with metadata to describe data warehouse schema versions. The proposed metamodel is used in the framework that supports data warehouse evolution caused by changes of business requirements and data.

The physical implementation of the multiversion data warehouse in relational DBMS is proposed. It allows to store all schema versions in one physical schema. Changes that can happen with multidimensional data warehouse and create new schema versions are discussed. Necessary modifications in the proposed metamodel and in the database are given. It would be desirable to evaluate the completeness of the supported changes.

The future research could be connected with querying multiple data warehouse schema versions. The open issues are the construction of SQL queries based on the proposed metadata, processing of results of these queries, and presentation of reports. It is planned to develop a reporting system to allow to execute reports on one or several data warehouse versions using metadata from the presented data warehouse metamodel.

Acknowledgments

This work was supported by the European Social Fund (ESF).

References

1. Blaschka, M.: FIESTA: A Framework for Schema Evolution in Multidimensional Databases. PhD thesis, Technische Universitat Munchen, Germany (2000)
2. Blaschka, M., Sapia, C., Hofling, G.: On Schema Evolution in Multidimensional Databases. In: DaWaK 1999. LNCS, Vol. 1676, pp. 153–164. Springer, Heidelberg (1999)
3. Bellahsene, Z.: Schema Evolution in Data Warehouses. Knowl. Inf. Syst. 4, 283–304 (2002)
4. Body, M., Miquel, M., Bedard, Y., Tchounikine, A.: A Multidimensional and Multiversion Structure for OLAP Applications. In: ACM 5th International Workshop on Data Warehousing and OLAP, pp. 1–6. ACM, McLean, VA (2002)
5. Body, M., Miquel, M., Bedard, Y., Tchounikine, A.: Handling Evolutions in Multidimensional Structures. In: 19th International Conference on Data Engineering, pp. 581–594. IEEE Computer Society, Los Alamitos, CA (2003)

6. Eder, J., Koncilia, C., Morzy, T.: The COMET Metamodel for Temporal Data Warehouses. In: CAiSE 2002. LNCS, Vol. 2348, pp. 83–99. Springer, Heidelberg (2002)
7. Golfarelli, M., Lechtenbörger, J., Rizzi, S., Vossen, G.: Schema Versioning in Data Warehouses: Enabling Cross-Version Querying Via Schema Augmentation. Data Knowl. Eng. 59(2), 435–459 (2006)
8. Hurtado, C. A., Mendelzon, A. O., Vaisman, A. A.: Maintaining Data Cubes Under Dimension Updates. In: 15th International Conference on Data Engineering, pp. 346–357. IEEE Computer Society, Sydney (1999)
9. Kaas, C. E., Pedersen, T. B., Rasmussen, B. D.: Schema Evolution for Stars and Snowflakes. In: 6th International Conference on ICEIS, pp. 425–433. Porto, Portugal (2004)
10. Marotta, A.: Data Warehouse Design and Maintenance through Schema Transformations. Master thesis, Universidad de la República Uruguay (2000).
11. McBrien, P., Poulovassilis, A.: Data Integration by Bi-directional Schema Transformation Rules. In: 19th International Conference on Data Engineering, pp. 227–238. IEEE Computer Society, Bangalore (2003)
12. Morzy, T., Wrembel, R.: On Querying Versions of Multiversion Data Warehouse. In: ACM 7th International Workshop on Data Warehousing and OLAP, pp. 92–101. ACM, Washington, DC (2004)
13. Object Management Group. Common Warehouse Metamodel Specification, v1.1 http://www.omg.org/cgi-bin/doc?formal/03-03-02
14. Rundensteiner, E. A., Koeller, A., Zhang, X.:Maintaining Data Warehouses over Changing Information Sources. Commun. ACM. 43(6), 57–62 (2000)
15. Shahzad, M. K., Nasir, J. A., Pasha, M. A.:CEV-DW: Creation and Evolution of Versions in Data Warehouse. Asian J Information Technol. 4(10), 910–917 (2005)
16. Solodovnikova, D.: Data Warehouse Evolution Framework. In: Spring Young Researcher's Colloquium on Database and Information Systems, Moscow, Russia (2007)
17. Solodovnikova, D., Niedrite, L.: Data Warehouse Adaptation after the Changes in Source Schemata. In: 7th International Balt. Conference DB & IS, pp. 52–63, Vilnius, Lithuania (2006)
18. Velegrakis, Y., Miller, R.J., Popa, L.: Mapping Adaptation under Evolving Schemas. In: 29th International Conference VLDB, pp. 584–595. Morgan Kaufmann, Berlin, Germany (2003)
19. Wrembel, R., Bebel, B.: Metadata Management in a Multiversion Data Warehouse. In: OTM Conferences (2) LNCS, Vol. 3761, 1347–1364. Springer, Heidelberg (2005)

66

The Morning After: What Happens When Outsourcing Relationships End?

Hamish T. Barney, Graham C. Low and Aybüke Aurum

Abstract

Many firms are reevaluating their initial outsourcing decisions for various reasons, including whether the goals set for the outsourcing effort were achieved, changes in the business environment, internal changes, and/or mergers. An increasing number of outsourcing deals are being terminated and backsourced or re-outsourced. According to a recent international industry survey 49% of companies engaged in outsourcing have terminated outsourcing contracts prematurely. Research has not reflected this trend with few studies concentrating on what firms do after they terminate or fail to extend an outsourcing contract. It is argued that there is a need to study this important and increasingly frequent decision. The main contribution of this chapter is to present an outsourcing decision model and demonstrate its applicability with respect to a recent sourcing decision.

Keywords Information technology outsourcing · Information technology backsourcing · Information systems sourcing decisions

1. Introduction

Outsourcing has been, and continues to be, big business. There, however, has been a recent move to backsource, or bring back in-house, information systems functions. Firms discover that their outsourcing decisions were wrong or that the circumstances have changed in such a way as to make a previously sound outsourcing deal untenable [28, 37].

According to a recent industry survey on information systems outsourcing [10], 49% of companies who engage in outsourcing have terminated outsourceing contracts prematurely, i.e., before the end of the contract period. Furthermore, in 43% of those cases where contracts are abnormally terminated, the decision is made to backsource the previously outsourced function. Similarly, Lacity and Wilcocks [23] found that a third of the 79 firms surveyed had cancelled their outsourcing contracts.

For instance in May of 2002, to great fanfare, JP Morgan Chase (JPMC; a large North American bank) and IBM signed a $5 billion (USD) 7-year outsourcing deal in what was, up till then, one of the largest information systems outsourcing deals ever agreed [31]. About 20 months into the outsourcing contract with IBM, JPMC merged with Bank One [5]. Bank One had a previous unhappy outsourcing experience with IBM but had subsequently become one of the most efficient banks in terms of their delivery of information systems services [34]. Shortly after this merger and after less than 2 years, JPMC decided to end the outsourcing deal and backsource, or bring back in-house, their information systems functions. It is speculated in the media that in the process JPMC had to pay large, unspecified, contractual penalties to

Hamish T. Barney, Graham C. Low and Aybüke Aurum • School of Information Systems Technology and Management, The University of New South Wales, Sydney, Australia.

G.A. Papadopoulos et al. (eds.), *Information Systems Development*, DOI 10.1007/b137171_66,

IBM. The backsourcing process also apparently had a very negative effect on employee morale, in what has been described as a 'whiplash effect' [30].

How should information systems function be managed after an outsourcing contract has been prematurely terminated or not extended in such cases as the one described above? Should it be backsourced (i.e., returned in-house) or should it be re-outsourced? Whether backsourced or outsourced, how should the information systems function be governed (as a partnership, a profit centre or something else) so that the problems of the old, now defunct outsourcing relationship do not reoccur? There is very little academic information systems research that explicitly deals with these post-outsourcing questions. The question remains why is the decision about how a particular information systems function should be sourced after an outsourcing contract has been terminated different from other information systems sourcing decisions?

One difference is that the firm has gained some experience about what works within the context of outsourcing and how outsourcing (or backsourcing) can be better organized. It seems likely that firms with more outsourcing experience make better decisions about outsourcing and, assuming theories about the causes of outsourcing are correct, these decisions will be better predicted by the theory. Mayer and Agyres [27], for example, detail how an outsourcing relationship evolved over time as the two firms learnt more about how to collaborate. Similarly, Fleming and Low [9] describe a case where a contract was renegotiated to be more beneficial to both parties.

On the other hand, an acrimonious end to the old outsourcing relationship could bias the firm against the further outsourcing of information systems functions despite its potential advantages. There is a well-known psychological bias called the availability heuristic [6, 35, 36] whereby a salient example of a particular phenomenon becomes the rule of thumb for future decisions about that phenomenon. Conversely, negative experiences, with the internal information systems department could, for example, bias decision makers against backsourcing in a similar way.

Having outsourced the particular information systems function, the firm may no longer have the capability to fulfill the function internally in the short to medium term at reasonable cost. The internal capabilities that the firm maintained during the outsourcing deal or the firm's ability to increase its internal capabilities to perform the previously outsourced function may play a role in determining its ability to backsource. This short-to medium-term cost may influence the decision to backsource or to find a new outsourcing vendor despite a different form of governance being more appropriate in the long-run [37].

Organizational reshuffles are costly and often harm employee morale. Overby [30], for instance, refers to the whiplash effect of changing sourcing strategies in the case of the case of JP Morgan Chase and IBM, where after only a short while after outsourcing their information systems function to IBM, JP Morgan Chase decided to backsource the function. The costs of switching sourcing strategies make getting this decision right crucial

Despite the apparent frequency of abnormal contract termination and the high levels of backsourcing there is only a small body of research on this important topic (e.g. [28, 37]). If the statistics, quoted above, are even close to being accurate it seems apparent that what happens after an outsourcing contract is terminated prematurely or not renewed is of significant interest for both industry and academy.

This research at develops and validates an outsourcing decision model. The results of this research will also be of interest not only directly to firms who are terminating an outsourcing contract but also to firms considering outsourcing. It is hoped that this research will help them to consider ways of structuring their outsourcing agreements in light of potential contingencies that may occur should they decide to terminate their outsourcing contract.

Similarly the results of this research may be of interest to outsourcers. It may help them to identify outsourcing deals that are at high risk of being backsourced in the future. The results may also aid in the identification of customers that are at risk of ending their outsourcing contract to either backsource or find an alternative vendor.

The related literature on backsourcing, outsourcing, and vertical integration will be reviewed. Based on the literature a preliminary model of the factors that appear to be relevant to the decision about what to do after terminating an outsourcing contract will be discussed. Finally, a validation of the model will be presented based on a recent sourcing decision.

2. Reported Findings on Sourcing Decisions

There is relatively little research on what firms should do once they have decided to end or prematurely terminate an outsourcing relationship. First, definitions of the important terms will be discussed. Second, related research on backsourcing and outsourcing will be reviewed.

Since a number of terms in this topic are new or have been subject to differing definitions, it seems worthwhile to review the definitions of these terms.

Outsourcing. The first reported case of information systems outsourcing is generally accepted to Eastman Kodak [1]. The definition of outsourcing adopted here is as follows:

> ...the commissioning of a third-party (or a number of third-parties) to manage a client organzation's IT assets, people and/or (or part thereof) activities for required results [pp. 92, 9].

This definition makes it clear that authority for managing the service is taken over by the outsourcer. This definition has two notable aspects that the information systems function is managed by the third-party and that the ownership of assets and the identity of the employer are not specified.

Backsourcing. The term backsourcing is relatively recent but is gaining widespread acceptance [28]. Authors have also referred to backsourcing as 'insourcing' using the term ambiguously to mean both back- and insourcing. Alternatively, some authors have used the term 're-insourcing.' Backsourcing can be defined as "pulling back in-house [previously outsourced] activities as outsourcing contracts expire or are terminated" [12, 20]. This means that the management of the particular information systems function that was previously outsourced has been returned in-house.

Insourcing. Insourcing has been defined as, "the practice of evaluating the outsourcing option, but confirming the continued use of internal IT resources to achieve the same objectives of outsourcing" [13]. This definition is given to clarify the meaning of insourcing within this chapter, given the ambiguous way the term has sometimes been used in the past.

2.1. Related Research

The research conducted by Whitten and Leidner [37] is the closest to the current research. They analyzed the perceptions of information technology executives in a recent decision about outsourcing contracts. A combination of transaction cost economics [39] and social exchange theory [15] was used as the theoretical underpinning of their research.

They sent surveys to 650 executives and received 160 responses. They broke the respondents into three groups: those who continued with the current outsourcing relationship, those who backsourced, and those that switched to a different outsourcer. Their results showed a significant difference between the three groups summarized in Table 66.1.

Table 66.1. Comparison of continuers, backsourcers, and switchers [37].

Decision	Product quality	Relationship quality	Service quality	Switching costs
Continuers	High	High	High	High
Backsourcers	Low	Low	Low	Low
Switchers	High	Low	High	Low

Whitten and Leidner's [37] research differs from the current research in several ways. They look at the qualities of previous outsourcing arrangement as a predictor of the next outsourcing arrangement. The current research broadens the focus to incorporate the characteristics of the tasks involved in the information systems function itself. Their research suggests that product and service quality are useful predictors of whether the firm will decide to backsource or to outsource the information systems function after the end of the previous outsourcing relationship. Switching costs seem to play a smaller role in this decision according to their data but a measure more focused on the cost of backsourcing may yield different results.

McLaughlin and Peppard [28] reviewed publicly available records on high-profile backsourcing deals and their causes. In their analysis they encountered six main reasons given for backsourcing decisions: problems arose during the contract and/or specific objectives were not achieved, information technology had come to be seen as strategic, changes in the business environment or business change and evolution, changes in the available technologies and changes in the management. This research gives some interesting preliminary clues about the difference between an initial decision to outsource and the subsequent decision about what to do after a contract with an outsourcer has been terminated.

Hirschheim and Lacity [13] describe a qualitative analysis of 14 different firms' insourcing and backsourcing deals. In this chapter they refer to both backsourcing and insourcing (as defined above) as 'insourcing.' For their study they interviewed a total of 41 participants in 14 firms. Twelve of the firms studied had insourced while two had backsourced their information systems functions. In both cases of backsourcing, the cost savings expected of the previous outsourcing deal did not eventuate. As a result, the firms both backsourced their information systems function and apparently achieved cost reductions over the previous outsourcing relationship. It is, however, noted that neither firm formally reviewed the comparative performance of the two arrangements.

This previous research forms the basis of a model of the decision about the appropriate way to source information systems functions after an outsourcing contract has ended.

3. Proposed Model

Figure 66.1 shows the proposed model of how individual sourcing options are evaluated after an outsourcing contract has been terminated. It is expected that each sourcing option, whether it be backsourcing or re-outsourcing would be evaluated on these dimensions and then the most appropriate sourcing option chosen. The individual constructs in the proposed model are discussed below.

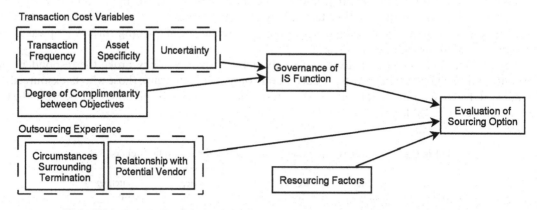

Figure 66.1. Proposed model of sourcing decision after the end of an outsourcing relationship.

Governance of IS Function: One potential factor in the evaluation of a sourcing option is the most appropriate form of governance to adopt in the relationship between the firm and the information systems function (whether internal or external). Most outsourcing research has used a simple binary or linear measures to delineate between sourcing options, from provided in-house to outsourced (e.g., [2, 33]). Some researchers have called for a more nuanced view of outsourcing relationships [19]. Some research points toward one important dimension of the outsourcing relationship being a hard versus a soft contracting approach [9, 19]. Hard contracting is distinguished by a strict adherence to agreed upon contractual obligations and service level agreements. While soft contracting is based more on mutual accommodation between the two parties and has been mainly observed in more mature relationships [9, 19].

Research originating from several different disciplines [3, 14, 26, 40] identifies the three key dimensions on which the governance of a relationship can be measured: authority (who determines how the work is to be done), ownership (who owns the key assets), and incentives (whether compensation based on output). Prototypical market exchange is distinguished by weak authority, the agent owning the key assets and compensation being directly based on output, while employee empowerment, a hybrid form of organization, is distinguished by weak authority, principal owning the key assets and weak productivity incentives. This characterization of governance seems to be a potentially useful way of formally describing the governance of outsourcing and backsourcing relationships. These alternative characterizations of governance will be evaluated in light of interviews and case studies.

Transaction Cost Variables: Transaction cost framework is a potential determinant of the most appropriate form of governance to be used in the relationship with the information systems function. It would be difficult to ignore this framework given the widespread use of the transaction cost economics framework and its success in both information systems outsourcing research [29, 33] and vertical integration research [24]. Poppo and Zenger [33], for instance, directly compared transaction costs, knowledge-based/resource-based, property rights, agency, production cost, institutional agency, and hybrid theories about the information systems functions outsourcing. Transaction cost economics was the theory with the most explanatory power in the survey they conducted. The transaction cost variables of transaction frequency, asset specificity, and uncertainty, suggested by Williamson [38, 39], will be incorporated into the model.

It is worthwhile noting that the transaction cost variable of asset specificity subsumes various concepts including the number of providers who are able to offer the same service; whether the required assets and resources are standardized or highly customized; and whether any specialized organizational structures that need to be developed in order to work productively with the outsourcer [38, 39].

Degree of Complimentarity between Objectives: Another potential determinant of the appropriate form of governance for the information systems function is the degree to which the organizational objectives to be performed by the sourcing option are compliments. Makadok and Coff [26] argue that the appropriate form of governance (using the three dimensional characterization discussed above) will be influenced by the degree to which the objectives (or tasks in their terminology) to be achieved are complimentary. They present a theoretical model of the circumstances under which different forms of governance will be appropriate based on the degree to which the different objectives are complimentary (extending the work of [14]). They divide the required objectives into four conceptual categories: current production, asset maintenance, lever-less objectives (e.g., cooperation), and private activities. This work is unique in that most theoretical models of organization have only shown that the only viable forms of governance sit on a continuum between market and hierarchy [14, 40]. Their research points to potential explanation for alternative forms of organization outside this narrow continuum. Franchises and piece-rate are two forms of governance that do not fit in this market-hierarchy continuum [14, 40]. This model appears to have potential for explaining the choice of the form of information systems governance after an outsourcing relationship has ended.

Outsourcing Experience: It is also anticipated that a firm's prior experience with outsourcing may influence its evaluation of a particular sourcing option in several ways. For instance if there is an existing relationship with the particular sourcing option provider then this may impact on the perceived desirability of this option [9, 25]. It seems plausible that a firm would be more likely to transfer the recently terminated outsourcing contract to a vendor with whom the firm already has a good relationship. Research that examines relationship quality and its determinants includes Lee and Kim [25] who examine the outsourcing relationship using a behavioral attitudinal model which incorporates both a behavioral and a psychological dimension [17, 18]; Kim and Chung [21] who examine relational exchange characteristics and task characteristics, Kern and Wilcocks [19] who examine an outsourcing relationship using the IMP Group's interaction model [11]; and Fleming and Low [9] who extended the model proposed by Lee and Kim [25] and examined the outsourcing relationship from the perspective of both the outsourcer and the client. The preceding research points to a number of factors that are important determinants of an outsourcing relationship, these include trust, cultural similarity, organizational linkage [9].

Whitten and Leidner's research [37] also indicates that experience with the previous outsourcing provider may influence the decision to backsource or to find a new outsourcer after an outsourcing relationship ends (either prematurely or by failing to renew the contract). They showed that product quality and service quality are the dimensions on which backsourcers systematically differ from people who switched outsourcers.

As discussed above, learning effects may mean that firms learn to make better sourcing decisions just as some researchers have shown that firms learn to contract with one another [27]. Alternatively memorable experiences with other outsourcers (or the internal information systems department) may lead to judgments biased by the so-called availability heuristic [35, 36].

Resourcing Factors: There may be an ideal way of organizing the new sourcing effort but achieving this in the short to medium term may prove too expensive or conflict with short-term objectives or constraints. As such resourcing factors may play a role in the evaluation of a particular sourcing option. Despite Whitten and Leidner [37] finding that resources had little influence on backsourcing versus re-outsourcing it is possible that a more finely tailored measure may find a larger effect.

4. Model Applied to Case Study

In order to demonstrate the applicability of the model developed above, it will be applied to the case briefly introduced in the introduction. JP Morgan Chase (JPMC) originally signed a 5 billion US dollar 7-year outsourcing contract with IBM in May 2002, in what was, up till then, one of the largest outsourcing deals. In August 2004, after less than 2 years and a recent merger with Bank One, JPMC decided to backsource their entire information systems function [5]. Although the results of this analysis cannot be conclusive or authoritative, given that media reports (albeit from a variety of sources) have been used to ascertain the details of what transpired. Nevertheless it is felt that this analysis demonstrates the worth of this program of research and the proposed model.

Transaction Cost Variables: The merger with Bank One had an impact on the transaction cost factors. With the increased size of the bank, frequency of information systems transactions would have increased. The increased size and complexity of the merged firms' information systems is likely to have increased the relationship-specific investment required on the part of IBM. Assuming uncertainty specificity remained relatively unchanged, this increase in transaction frequency and asset specificity increases the desirability of backsourcing the information systems function [38].

Degree of Complimentarity between Objectives: From the reports in the media it is apparent that IBM did not invest in capital and many projects were delayed or cancelled [31]. It appears that IBM did not have sufficient incentive to invest in asset maintenance and as such the structure of the outsourcing arrangement chosen appears to have been inappropriate and that backsource may be a better way to achieve JPMCs goals [26].

Governance of IS Function: Transaction cost measures suggest that backsourcing the information systems function had become more desirable since the merger with Bank One, while the objective complimentarity measures suggest that the operation of the outsourcing agreement revealed that the organization of the outsourcing effort was inappropriate. The mismatch between the optimal form of governance and the current situation is confirmed by IBM's ability to hold up JPMC by refusing to make infrastructure investments unless they were paid for by JPMC [31].

Outsourcing Experience: The experience of both JPMC and Bank One may have played a role in the decision to backsource. Bank One had a negative experience when they outsourced their information systems function to IBM [31]. Bank One's information systems function appeared to perform much better after it was backsourced than when it was outsourced to IBM [34]. JPMC appeared to be unhappy with

IBM's performance as an outsourcer [31] which may have caused decision makers to be biased against trying further outsourcing.

　　Resourcing Factors: With the acquisition of Bank One there was an increase in information systems resources within JPMC. This would reduce the short-term cost of backsourcing. JPMC also used backsourcing as a way of getting rid of the deadwood and to cut salaries as they rehired the staff who had been transferred to IBM [31]. Against these putative benefits the organizational restructure had a negative impact on staff morale [30]. Adverse effects on staff morale probably would have occurred regardless of whether the information systems function was backsourced or outsourced again. This consideration should therefore play a minor role in differentiating between sourcing options.

　　In the case of JPMC, the model does appear to have explanatory power and seems to be a good way of organizing the main factors that led to the decision to backsource the entire information systems function. Given this confirmation of the value of the proposed model, it seems appropriate to continue research on this question, using this model as a starting point.

5. Conclusion and Future Work

　　It has been argued that the decision about what to do after an outsourcing contract has been prematurely terminated or has not been extended is an important question that has not been adequately answered by the existing body of research. This chapter presented a model aimed at explaining the information systems sourcing decision-making process. This model draws from literature on outsourcing, backsourcing, psychology, and governance. The explanatory power of this model was briefly demonstrated by applying it to a case study drawn from the literature. A program of research based around this model is currently in progress.

　　Deciding what to do after an outsourcing contract has ended is also a relatively recent phenomena, previously, almost all outsourcing projects were "green-fields" projects. It is only recently that a significant number of firms have started to reevaluate their sourcing strategies. Given these circumstances, the limited research on the specific question, the use of new constructs, and the relative recency of the phenomena, case studies seem to be the most appropriate research technique to apply [7, 41].

　　Over the coming months a series of interviews will be conducted with information systems professionals employed by both outsourcers and client firms. These interviews will inform a series of case studies focusing on firms who have recently ended outsourcing agreements. Based on the data gathered, the proposed model may be modified. Organization-specific factors may be added to the model depending on the results of the case studies. For instance some research indicates that internal politics may play a role in influencing decisions in certain contexts [4, 16, 22, 32].

　　Although outsourcing has been thoroughly studied, little research has focused on sourcing decisions that are made after an outsourcing contract has been ended. The measure of organizational type has also not previously been used in outsourcing research and a case study affords the opportunity to test the value of this construct. The key contribution of this chapter is the development of a model that will enable firms to better understand the decision process following the premature termination of or failure to extend an outsourcing contract.

References

1. Applegate, L.M., Montealegre, R.: Eastman Kodak Company: Managing Information Systems Through Strategic Alliances. Harvard Business School Case (1991) 9–192
2. Aubert, B.A., Rivard, S., Patry, M.: A Transaction Cost Model of IT Outsourcing. Information and Management 41 (2004) 921–932
3. Brandach, J.L., Eccles, R.G.: Price, Authority and Trust: From Ideal Types to Plural Forms. Annual Review of Sociology 15 (1989) 97–118
4. Buchowicz, B.S.: A Process Model of Make-vs.-Buy Decision-Making. The Case of Manufacturing Software. Engineering Management, IEEE Transactions on 38 (1991) 24–32

5. Chase, J.P.M.: Annual Report 2005. (2005)
6. Combs, B., Slovic, P.: Newspaper Coverage of Causes of Death. Journalism Quarterly 56 (1979) 837–843
7. Darke, P., Shanks, G., Broadbent, M.: Successfully Completing Case Study Research: Combining Rigour, Relevance and Pragmatism. Information Systems Journal 8 (1998) 273–289
8. Fitzgerald, G., Willcocks, L.P.: Contracts and Partnerships in the Outsourcing of IT. Proceedings of the 15th International Conference on Information Systems, Vancouver, Canada (1994) 91–98
9. Fleming, R., Low, G.C.: Information Systems Outsourcing Relationship Model. Australasian Journal of Information Systems 14 (2007) 95–112
10. Global IT Outsourcing Study. Diamond Management Technology Consultants (2006)
11. Hakansson, H.: International Marketing and Purchasing of Industrial Goods: An Interaction Approach. John Wiley, New York (1982)
12. Hirschheim, R.: Backsourcing: An Emerging Trend? Outsourcing Journal (1998)
13. Hirschheim, R., Lacity, M.C.: The Myths and Realities of Information Technology Insourcing. Communications of the ACM 43 (2000) 99–107
14. Holmstrom, B.R., Milgrom, P.R.: The Firm as an Incentive System. The American Economic Review 84 (1994) 972–991
15. Homans, G.C.: Social Behavior as Exchange. American Journal of Sociology 63 (1958) 597–606
16. Hung, P., Low, G.C.: Factors Affecting the Buy vs. Build Decision in Large Australian organizations. Journal of Information Technology (2008)
17. Kappelman, L., Mclean, E.: The Respective Roles of User Participation and User Involvement in Information System Implementation Success. 12th International Conference on Information Systems. (1991)
18. Kappelman, L.A., Mclean, E.R.: Promoting Information System Success: The Respective Roles of User Participation and User Involvement. Journal of Information Technology Management 3 (1992) 1–12.
19. Kern, T., Willcocks, L.: Exploring Relationships in Information Technology Outsourcing: The Interaction Approach. European Journal of Information Systems 11 (2002) 3–19
20. Kern, T., Willcocks, L.P.: The Relationship Advantage: Information Technologies, Sourcing and Management. Oxford University Press, Oxford (2001)
21. Kim, S., Chung, Y.S.: Critical Success Factors for IS Outsourcing Implementation Form an Interorganisational Relationship Perspective. Journal of Computer Information Systems 43 (2003) 81–90
22. Kurokawa, S.: Make-or-Buy Decisions in R&D: Small Technology Based Firms in the United States and Japan., IEEE Transactions on Engineering Management 44 (1997) 124–134
23. Lacity, M.C., Willcocks, L.P.: Global Information Technology Outsourcing: In Search of Business Advantage. Wiley, Chitchester (2001)
24. Lafontaine, F., Slade, M.: Vertical Integration and Firm Boundaries: The Evidence. Journal of Economic Literature 45 (2007) 629–685
25. Lee, J.N., Kim, Y.G.: Understanding Outsourcing Partnership: A Comparison of Three Theoretical Perspectives. IEEE Transactions on Engineering Management 52 (2005) 43–58
26. Makadok, R., Coff, R.: Both Market and Hierarchy: An Incentive-Systems Theory of Hybrid Governance Forms. Proceedings of the Academy of Management Annual Meeting, Best Papers, Philadelphia, PA (2007)
27. Mayer, K.J., Argyres, N.S.: Learning to Contract: Evidence from the Personal Computer Industry. Organization Science 15 (2004) 394–410
28. McLaughlin, D., Peppard, J.: IT Backsourcing: From 'Make or Buy' to 'Bringing IT Back In-House'. In: Ljungberg, J., Andersson, M. (eds.): Proceedings of the Fourteenth European Conference on Information Systems, Goteborg (2006) 1735–1746
29. Miranda, S.M., Kim, Y.-M.: Professional Versus Political Contexts: Institutional Mitigation and the Transaction Cost Heuristic in Information Systems Outsourcing. MIS Quarterly 30 (2006) 725–753
30. Overby, S.: Backsourcing Pain. CIO Magazine (2005)
31. Overby, S.: Outsourcing-and Backsourcing-at JPMorgan Chase. CIO Magazine (2005)
32. Peled, A.: Outsourcing and Political Power: Bureaucrats, Consultants, Vendors and Public Information Technology. Public Personnel Management 30 (2001) 209–225
33. Poppo, L., Zenger, T.R.: Testing Alternative Theories of the Firm: Transaction Cost, Knowledge-Based, and Measurement Explanations for Make-or-Buy Decisions in Information Services. Strategic Management Journal 19 (1998) 853–877
34. Strassman, P.: Why JP Morgan Chase Really Dropped IBM. Baseline (2005)
35. Tversky, A., Kahneman, D.: Availability: A Heuristic for Judging Frequency and Probability. Cognitive Psychology 5 (1973) 207–232
36. Tversky, A., Kahneman, D.: Judgment Under Uncertainty: Heuristics and Biases. Science 185 (1974) 1124–1130
37. Whitten, D., Leidner, D.: Bringing IT Back: An Analysis of the Decision to Backsource or Switch Vendors. Decision Sciences 37 (2006) 605–621
38. Williamson, O.E.: Transaction-Cost Economics: The Governance of Contractual Relations. Journal of Law & Economics 22 (1979) 233–261
39. Williamson, O.E.: The Economic Institutions of Capitalism. Free Press, New York (1985)
40. Williamson, O.E.: Strategizing Economizing and Economic Organization. Strategic Management Journal 12 (1991) 75–94
41. Yin, R.K.: Case Study Research: Design and Methods. Sage Publication, Thousand Oaks, CA (1994)

67

Method Engineering: A Formal Description

Ali Sunyaev, Matthias Hansen and Helmut Krcmar

Abstract

The development of information systems (IS) requires methods that recommend how to act during the development process. In some cases existing methods cannot cope with the requirements of the project situation at hand. Therefore, new methods must be developed. Method engineering (ME) attends to this application field. In this chapter, we provide a detailed overview of IS method engineering approaches in order to describe the concept of method engineering. Based on a literature review we derive a formal description of methods that can be used to describe them in a basic way and transfer them to other fields of application. With the formal description of methods this chapter facilitates the process of understanding method engineering both for method user and its engineer.

Keywords Method engineering · Formal description · Information systems · Method development · Method

1. Introduction

The development of IS often demands a methodical approach in order to know which steps have to be taken in which order at which time in the development process (e.g. [1, 4]). While in many cases the method and its included steps as a whole are the objects of research, this chapter in detail examines the fundamental parts and elements of methods as well as their interplay among each other. The research subject is set in the discipline method engineering. In this context the development of a formal description, which overviews the structure of methods and its corresponding building blocks, shall be emphasised. The formalisation of methods on the one hand helps explain existing methods and method parts and on the other hand facilitates the transfer of methods to other application fields. Furthermore the formal described methods become more transparent, traceable and understandable for both method users and its engineers.

This chapter is organised as follows: Since this research is based on a comprehensive literature review of relevant journals and articles, Section 2 overviews the research approach used. Section 3 describes the concept of method engineering and the existing building blocks and elements that can be used to build a method. Section 4 deals with the formalisation of the concept of methods. The application of the formalisation on the basis of an example will be the subject of Section 5. The last section concludes this chapter and provides an outlook.

Ali Sunyaev, Matthias Hansen and Helmut Krcmar • Department of Informatics, Technische Universität München, München, Germany.

G.A. Papadopoulos et al. (eds.), *Information Systems Development*, DOI 10.1007/b137171_67,
© Springer Science+Business Media, LLC 2009

2. Research Approach

In order to describe the concept of method engineering we examined description of IS method engineering approaches currently receiving attention in the literature. The literature review was based on the approach by Webster and Watson [23]. After the identification of relevant journals the examination of appropriate articles was performed. Therefore, a search by keywords was carried out to identify relevant articles. By examining the title and abstract of each article, a total of 41 articles have been found to be relevant. A further in-depth review resulted in an assortment of 24 articles that were relevant and of importance for the research (Table 67.1).

Table 67.1. Analysed articles.

Journal	Keywords	Abstract	In-depth review
Accounting, Management & Information Technologies	40	1	0
ACM Computing Surveys	3	1	1
Communications of the ACM	7	5	0
Computers & Security	41	1	1
European Journal of Information Systems	87	4	0
Information Management & Consulting	1	1	0
Information and Software Technology	39	6	1
Information Systems	31	6	2
Information Systems Journal	37	7	0
Information Systems Management	12	1	0
Information Systems Research	5	1	0
Information Technology & People	15	4	0
International Journal of Software Engineering and Knowledge Engineering	10	1	0
Knowledge-Based Systems	10	1	1
MIS Quarterly	14	1	0
Total journals	**352**	**41**	**6**
Dissertations/Master's Theses/Working paper	5	5	3
Conferences/Workshops	19	19	8
Total	**376**	**65**	**17**

3. Description of the Method Elements

Methods are the cornerstone of goal-oriented and tactical action in many application fields and different kinds of projects. The use of methods is very important for the development of IS, because they support the developers of IS by providing systematic development approaches [1]. However, the simple existence of development methods is not always a guarantee for successful acting. The environment in which companies are located is changing over time and forces the companies to conform their development work to the increasing complexity of IS. In this context, the need for comprehensive methods that cover a wide range of situations within the development process is emphasised [16].

However, the application of comprehensive IS development methods to specific situations as well as the application of detailed methods to a broad project context is problematic. Rather, methods have to be adapted to the situation at hand. This process is part of the discipline method engineering. Brinkkemper [5] defines method engineering as follows: "Method engineering is the engineering discipline to design, construct and adapt methods, techniques and tools for the development of information systems."

In the majority of cases a method consists of several parts, which divide the development process in manageable and ordered steps. This division of methods into parts supports the clarity and eases the responsibility assignment. The following section will show and explain the basic concepts and elements regarding methods.

3.1. Method Chains and Alliances

In some cases it can be necessary to connect methods and method parts, respectively. This can be done with method chains and method alliances [16].

Nilsson defines method chains as "integration of methods between different levels of development work[1]". This approach to combining methods is a kind of vertical integration. For example, there can be a higher level dealing with conceptual modelling and a lower level dealing with object modelling. The latter can in turn be used for database scheme definition. Method alliances are a method integration within the same abstraction level and thus can be called horizontal integration. Method alliances cover several aspects of problem domains or perspectives at a specific level.

Cronholm and Ågerfalk [8] state that in their opinion Nilsson means method fragments (see next section) when he speaks of methods. We subscribe to this view.

3.2. Method Fragments

Since a fragment is a detached, broken off or an incomplete part of something [18], Harmsen, Brinkkemper and Oei [10] call the building blocks of methods method fragments. These can be classified according to the dimensions perspective and granularity layer[2] [6].

The dimension perspective considers the product and process view on method fragments. Product fragments are goal oriented and are deliverables, milestone documents, models, diagrams, etc. Process fragments are process oriented and are stages, tasks and activities to be carried out [20].

The granularity layer is very important for the description of the type and structure of a method fragment. A fragment can reside on one of the layers *method, stage, model, diagram* or *concept* [6]. The *method* layer addresses the complete method for developing the IS. For instance, the information engineering method [15] resides on this granularity layer. The *stage* layer addresses a segment of the life cycle of the IS. An example of a method fragment residing on the stage layer is a Technical Design Report. The *model* layer addresses a perspective of the IS. Such a perspective is an aspect system of an abstraction level. Examples of method fragments are the Data Model and the User Interface Model [17]. The *diagram* layer addresses the representation of a view of a Model layer method fragment. For instance, the Object Diagram and the Class Hierarchy [17] both address the data perspective, but in another representation. For instance, the Statechart [9] resides on this granularity layer, as well as the modelling procedure to produce it. The *concept* layer addresses the concepts and associations of the method fragments on the diagram layer, as well as the manipulations defined on them. Concepts are subsystems of diagram layer method fragments. Examples are Entity and Entity is involved in Relationship [7]. Ter Hofstede and Verhoef [22] add that the sensible arrangement of method fragments on the respective granularity layer is very important in order to avoid negative consequences in the form of monetary or organisational costs.

Concluding the concept of method fragments the relations of method fragments will be explained. Relations clarify the interrelation of method fragments and divide the development of methods in logic steps. Relations between fragments of the same layer and relations between fragments of different layers exist [10].

The relevant relation between fragments of the same layer is the predecessor relation. It says that one step can be done not until the previous step is done. This relation is only defined for process fragments, but can be derived for product fragments. The important relation between fragments of different layers is the input/output relation. It says that on the one hand process fragments require product fragments and on the other hand process fragments produce product fragments.

---

[1]Nilsson makes a difference between strategic, process-oriented and system-oriented development, see [16].

[2]The third dimension *abstraction level* is not the subject of consideration.

3.3. Method Chunks

Ralyté and Rolland [19] choose an approach that builds up on the concept of method fragments. The existing process and product fragments get combined to a method chunk, which guarantees the close coupling between the process part and its correspondent product part. This is supposed to emphasise the consistency and independence of method chunks [2]. Thus a single method consists of several loosely coupled and already existing method chunks.

3.4. Method Components

Röstlinger and Goldkuhl [21] [3] consider methods as exchangeable and reusable components. Karlsson and Wistrand [14] amend that method components are the smallest meaningful part of methods and consist of a process, notation and concept.

A process describes rules and recommendations for the IS development and informs the method (component) user what actions to perform and in what order. Notation means semantic, syntactic and symbolic rules for documentation. Concepts are categories included in the process and the notation [8]. They support the description of the problem domain and the method itself [13].

4. Formal Description of the Concept of Method

At this point, the concept of method will be described in a formal way for a better understanding. This will facilitate a concise and logical explanation of the construction of methods and its consisting method elements. In addition the formalisation will ease the transfer of the concept of method to other areas and the application there.

The method concepts considered in the formalisation are method chains and alliances, method fragments, method chunks and method components and will be aggregated under the collective term "method fragments". Since the involved elements in the mentioned concepts largely vary only by name[4] and not by content, the aggregation avoids recurrences when formulating the formal description.

Annotation

METHOD: Method itself	TASKS: Set of tasks
S_{MF}: Set of method fragments	ACTIVITIES: Set of activities
P: Set of process fragments	STAGES: Set of stages
R: Set of product fragments	DOCUMENTS: Set of documents
REL: Set of relations between method fragments	MODELS: Set of models
MBL: Set of method blocks	DIAGRAMS: Set of diagrams

Additionally, we define the function returning the level of a particular method fragment as

$$level : S_{MF} \geq \{n|n \in N\} \tag{67.1}$$

Since a method fragment is either a process fragment or a product fragment, for

$$S_{MF} \; applies : S_{MF} = P \cup R \tag{67.2}$$

A process fragment $p \in P$ is process oriented and provides guidelines. For p applies

---

[3]Cited in [8].

[4]Process and product fragments in [10, 19], process and notation in [21].

$$P = \{p | p \in TASKS \oplus p \in ACTIVITIES \oplus p \in STAGES\} \tag{67.3}$$

A product fragment $r \in R$ is goal oriented and provides the results of process fragments. For r applies

$$R = \{r | r \in DOCUMENTS \oplus r \in MODELS \oplus r \in DIAGRAMS\} \tag{67.4}$$

For the set of relations REL between method fragments the following applies:

$$REL = \{produces, requires, precedes, I_{vert}, I_{hor}\} \tag{67.5}$$

Relations between method fragments are meaningful and necessary for the method construction. The following relations exist:

Input/Output relations: either for the case that a process fragment requires a product fragment (rule (67.6)) or for the case that any process fragment produces a product fragment (rule (67.7)).

$$requires = \{(p \in P, r \in R) | r \text{ is required by } p\}^5 \tag{67.6}$$

$$produces = \{(p \in P, r \in R) | r \text{ is produced by } p\} \tag{67.7}$$

Predecessor relations for consistency checking [10]: if a process fragment requires an existing product fragment, the product fragment has to be produced by a preceding process fragment.

$$precedes = \{(p_1, p_2 \in P) \, | \, \exists r \in R : produces(p_1, r) \wedge requires(p_2, r)\} \tag{67.8}$$

While relations show the relationships between method fragments, the following concepts are used to link method fragments to logical units. These concepts are the integration between method fragments and the development of method blocks.

The integration of method fragments leads to the development of method chains and method alliances. The vertical integration produces method chains by linking method fragments of different levels of granularity. Connecting method fragments with same granularity is called horizontal integration. The following two rules show these concepts in a formal way.

$$connects = \{(mf_1, mf_2 \in MF) | ((mf_1 \text{ and } mf_2 \text{ are connected}))\} \tag{67.9}$$

$$I_{vert} = \{(mf_1, mf_2 \in connects) \, | \, ((level(mf_1) = level(mf_2) + 1) \, V(level(mf_1) = level(mf_2) - I))\} \tag{67.10}$$

$$I_{hor} = \{(mf_1, mf_2 \in connects) \, | \, level(mf_1) = level(mf_2)\} \tag{67.11}$$

The distinction whether it is a vertical (67.10) or horizontal (67.11) integration can be made with the help of the granularity level of the involved method fragments. Rule (67.10) states that the number of the granularity level of the method fragment must be one number higher or lower than the number of the granularity level of the preceding method fragment.

The development of method blocks is one more way to link method fragments to logical units. In this case it is the connection of a process fragment with its respective product fragment. The following applies:

$$MBL = \{(p \in P, r \in R) \, | \, r \text{ is produced by } p\} = produces \tag{67.12}$$

---

[5] To be read: for a process fragment p element of P there exists (at least) one product fragment r element of R, for that applies: p requires r.

In this context the following rule states the fact that a process fragment and its respective product fragment are always on a higher granularity layer than the method block that is constructed of them:

$$\forall mbl \in MBL, \forall p \in P, \ \forall r \in R | (p,r) = mbl \Rightarrow level(mbl) = level(p) - 1 \wedge level(mbl) = level(r) - 1 \quad (67.13)$$

After the explanation of the method elements now the formal description of the global method concept will follow.

$$METHOD := \{mf_1, mf_2, mf_3, \ldots, mf_n, rel_{1,2}, rel_{2,3}, rel_{3,4}, \ldots, rel_{m-1,m}\}$$
$$\text{with } mf_n \in S_{MF}, rel_{m,n} \in REL$$

The rule states that a method consists of several method fragments, which are connected among each other by relations.

5. Application of the Formal Description

To show the application of the formal description an appropriate method will be drawn on. Risk analysis methods [11] like CRAMM[6] or ISRAM[7] do suit for this. The application of the formal description will be performed on the basis of ISRAM because of its broad range of application and its ease of use. ISRAM is a quantitative, paper- and survey-based risk analysis method that allows effective participation of managers and staff into the process. Structured in seven steps, ISRAM provides a guideline for risk assessment that considers the probability of occurrence as well as the consequences of occurrence of security breaches. In this chapter, only the sub-process for the probability of occurrence of security breaches is taken into account (see Fig. 1). In the following due to the lack of space only the first three steps of ISRAM will be described to show the application of the formalisation. The remaining four steps of ISRAM are developed in the same way as shown below.

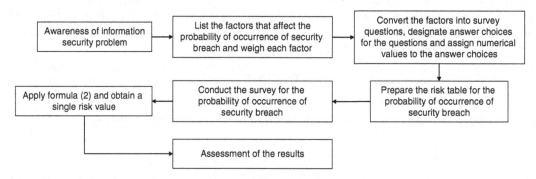

Figure 67.1. Basic flow diagram of ISRAM – Sub-process for the probability of occurrence of security breach (according to [12][8]).

(1) Awareness of the problem

Process fragment (PCF) "Realize information security problem(s)"
Within this phase people realise information security problems and decide to perform a risk analysis.

---

[6]CCTA's (Central Computer and Telecommunications Agency of the UK Government) Risk Analysis and Management Methodology, see Baskerville [3].
[7]Information security risk analysis method, see Karabacak and Sogukpinar [12]
[8]For details to the mentioned formula (67.2), see Karabacak and Sogukpinar [12].

Knowing that a process fragment always produces a product fragment because of the output relation, according to rule (67.7) $produces = \{(p \in P, r \in R) \mid r\ is produced\ by\ p\}$ the following applies:

> produces(PCF "Realize information security problem(s)", PDF "Information security awareness")

Product fragment (PDF) "Information security awareness"
Since a product fragment is the result of a preceding process fragment, the "Information security awareness" fragment deals with the situation of the awareness of potential security breaches.

For consistency reasons the process and product fragments get connected to logical units, called method blocks. These blocks can be chosen and reused in any other project where their application makes sense. Applying rule $(67.12)MBL = \{(p \in P, r \in R) | r\ is\ produced\ by\ p\} = produces$:

> MBL "Information security awareness" = (PCF "Realize information security problem(s)", PDF "Information security awareness")

A method step (MS) consists of several method blocks: $MS \in 2^{MB}$. Hence for the method step (MS) "Awareness of information security problem" of the ISRAM we can state:

> MBL "Information security awareness" $\in$ MS "Awareness of information security problem"

(2) Listing and weighing the factors

PCF "Categorise factors"
Within this fragment separate analyses are made for two risk parameters to determine the factors, which affect these parameters. After determining and listing all the factors, different weight values are assigned to the factors [12].

> produces(PCF "Categorise factors", PDF "Weighted security breach factors")

PDF "Weighted security breach factors"
As a result the corresponding product fragment shows all the factors that should be included in the survey developed in the next step.

Both the process and the product fragment together form the MBL "Security breach factors" which in turn provides the MS "List the factors that affect the probability of occurrence of security breach and weigh each factor".

> MBL "Security breach factors" = (PCF "Categorise factors", PDF "Weighted security breach factors")

> MBL "Security breach factors" $\in$ MS "List the factors that affect the probability of occurrence of security breach and weigh each factor"

(3) Converting factors into questions, designating answer choices and assigning numerical values to answer choices

Before the PCF "Develop survey" can be executed, existing relations must be considered. In this case there is an input relation between the PDF "Weighted security breach factors" from the last step and the PCF "Develop survey" in this step. According to rule (67.6) the input relation can be expressed like *requires* = {(*p* ∈ *P*, *r* ∈ *R*)|*r isrequired by p*}. Since the process fragment and its corresponding product fragment is encapsulated in the MBL "Security breach factors", we need first to decompose the method block into its corresponding method fragments. The following applies:

> MBL "Security breach factors" = (PCF "Categorise factors", PDF "Weighted security breach factors")

> requires(PCF "Develop survey", PDF "Weighted security breach factors")

To ensure the consistency of the method fragments the predecessor relation between the involved process fragments has to be checked. Applying rule (67.8) *precedes* = {(*p*₁, *p*₂ ∈ *P*)|∃*r* ∈ *R* : *produces*(*p*₁, *r*) ∧ *requires*(*p*₂, *r*)} :

> requires(PCF "Develop survey", PDF "Weighted security breach factors") produces(PCF "Categorise factors", PDF "Weighted security breach factors") → precedes(PCF "Categorise factors", PCF "Develop survey")

PCF "Develop survey"

The factors analysed in step 2 are converted into appropriate survey questions and answer choices are designated. Subsequent answer choices are converted into numerical values according to a given schema [12].

> produces(PCF "Develop survey", PDF "Survey with questions and corresponding numerical values")

PDF "Survey with questions and corresponding numerical values"

The finished process fragment provides the complete survey with questions and numerical values. The corresponding MBL is called "Survey development" and facilitates the development of the MS "Convert the factors into survey questions, designate answer choices for the questions and assign numerical values to the answer choices".

> MBL "Survey development" = (PCF "Develop survey", PDF "Survey with questions and corresponding numerical values")

> MBL "Survey development" ∈ MS "Convert the factors into survey questions, designate answer choices for the questions and assign numerical values to the answer choices"

The graphical overview of the three described method steps is shown in Fig. 67.2.

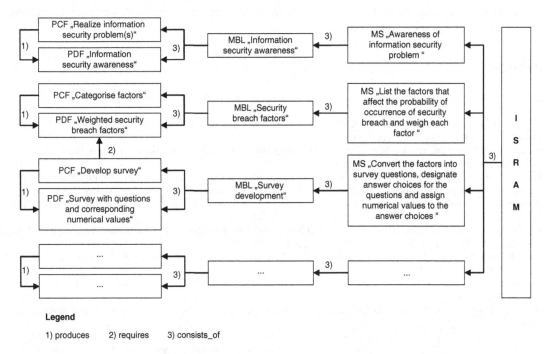

Legend

1) produces   2) requires   3) consists_of

Figure 67.2. Structure of the first three steps of ISRAM.

To finish the description of the formal application the rule for the global method concept $METHOD := \{mf_1, mf_2, mf_3, \ldots, mf_n, rel_{1,2}, ref_{2,3}, ref_{3,4}, \ldots, rel_{m-1,m}\}$ is applied. For the set of process fragments P and the set of product fragments R the following applies:

$P = \{P_1, P_2, P_3\}$ with $P_1 = \{$ "Realize information security problem(s)"$\}$, $P_2 = \{$ "Categorise factors"$\}$, $P_3 = \{$ "Develop survey"$\}R = \{R_1, R_2, R_3\}$ with $R_1 = \{$ "Information security awareness"$\}$, $R_2 = \{$ "Weighted security breach factors"$\}$, $R_3 = \{$ "Survey with questions and corresponding numerical values"$\}$

With the sets of process and product fragments given, the following does apply for the global method concept METHOD of the first three steps of ISRAM:

$METHOD_{ISRAM} = \{P_1, R_1, P_2, R_2, P_3, R_3, produces = \{(P1, R1), (p2, R2), (P3, R3)\}, requires = \{(P3, R2)\}\}$.

6. Summary and Outlook

This chapter introduced a formal description of method engineering. Using a structured research approach we first examined the existing literature on IS method engineering approaches. Based on the literature review we discussed the construction and description of the concept of method engineering. We then presented a detailed approach for formalising the concept of method engineering, unveiling the method fragments and its relations that underlie formalisation design. As a next step we provided an illustration of an example for formal description of methods in order to show its possible application in research and practice.

The introduced formalisation of the concept of method engineering can be used to describe each part or element of almost any IS method. Therefore, it can be applied to get information about the structure and the underlying assembling technique. This knowledge can help to develop new methods and to reconstruct existing methods in order to adapt them to the project situation at hand. Furthermore due to the formal description of methods and in comparison to descriptive texts as used today, method engineering becomes more traceable. This modular approach allows a transparent and understandable design of the processes and method development itself. In particular, formal description of methods enables the automated (computer-assisted) method engineering.

References

1. Avison, D.E., Fitzgerald, G. (1995) Information Systems Development: Methodologies, Techniques and Tools. McGraw-Hill, New York.
2. Ayed, M.B., Ralyté, J. and Rolland, C. (2004) Constructing the Lyee Method with a Method Engineering Approach. In: Knowledge-Based Systems, Vol. 17, pp. 239–248.
3. Baskerville, R. (1993) Information Systems Security Design Methods: Implications for Information Systems Development. In: ACM Computing Surveys, Vol. 25, No. 4, pp. 375–414.
4. Braun, C., Wortmann, F., Hafner, M. and Winter, R. (2005) Method Construction – A Core Approach to Organizational Engineering. In: ACM Symposium on Applied Computing SAC'05, March 13–17, Santa Fe, New Mexico, USA.
5. Brinkkemper, S. (1996) Method Engineering: Engineering of Information Systems Development Methods and Tools. In: Information and Software Technology, Vol. 38, No. 4, pp. 275–280.
6. Brinkkemper, S., Saeki, M. and Harmsen, F. (1999) Meta-Modelling Based Assembly Techniques For Situational Method Engineering. In: Information Systems, Vol. 24, No. 3, pp. 209–228.
7. Chen, P. Pin-Shan (1976) The Entity-Relationship Model – Toward a Unified View of Data. In: ACM Transactions on Database Systems, Vol. 1, No. 1, pp. 9–36.
8. Cronholm, S. and Ågerfalk, P.J. (1999) On the Concept of Method in Information Systems Development. In: http://citeseer.ist.psu.edu/283885.html.
9. Harel, D. (1987) Statecharts: A Visual Formalism for Complex Systems. In: Science of Computer Programming, Vol. 8, pp. 231–274.
10. Harmsen, F., Brinkkemper, S. and Oei, H. (1994) Situational Method Engineering for Information System Project Approaches. In: A.A. Verrijn-Stuart, T.W. Olle (Eds.), *Methods and Associated Tools for the Information Systems Life Cycle*. Elsevier Science B. V., Amsterdam 1994, pp. 169–194.
11. Huber, M., Sunyaev, A. and Krcmar, H. (2008): Security Analysis of the Health Care Telematics Infrastructure in Germany. In: ICEIS 2008 – Proceedings of the Tenth International Conference on Enterprise Information Systems, Barcelona, Spain, Vol. ISAS-2, pp. 144–153.
12. Karabacak, B. and Sogukpinar, I. (2005) ISRAM: information security risk analysis method. In: Computers & Security Vol. 24, pp. 147–159.
13. Karlsson, F., Ågerfalk, P.J. and Hjalmarsson, A. (2001) Method Configuration with Development Tracks and Generic Project Types. In: 6th CaiSE/IFIP8.1 International Workshop on Evaluation of Modeling Methods in System Analysis and Design (EMMSAD'01), Interlaken, Switzerland, 4–5 June 2001.
14. Karlsson, F. and Wistrand, K. (2004) MC Sandbox – Tool Support for Method Configuration. In: http://www.nuigalway.ie/acc/documents/fredrik_karlsson_NUIG-seminar-21052004.pdf.
15. Martin, J. (1990) Information Engineering, Book II – Planning and Analysis. Prentice Hall, Englewood Cliffs 1990.
16. Nilsson, A.G. (1999) The Business Developer's Toolbox: Chains and Alliances between Established Methods. In: A.G. Nilsson, C. Tolis and C. Nellborn (Eds.), *Perspectives on Business Modelling, Understanding and Changing Organisations*. Springer-Verlag, Berlin, Heidelberg 1999, pp. 217–241.
17. Object Management Group OMG (2008) The Object Management Group. In: http://www.omg.org/.
18. Oxford Online Dictionary (2008) Fragment. In: http://www.askoxford.com/concise_oed/fragment?view = uk.
19. Ralyté, J. and Rolland, C. (2001) An Approach for Method Reengineering. In: H.S. Kunii, S. Jajodia, A. Solvberg (Eds.), *Conceptual Modeling. Proceedings of the 20th International Conference on Conceptual Modeling, Yokohama, Japan, November 27–30, 2001*. Springer-Verlag, Berlin, Heidelberg 2001, pp. 471–484.
20. Rolland, C. (1997) A Primer for Method Engineering. In: http://citeseer.ist.psu.edu/rolland97primer.html.
21. Röstlinger, A. and Goldkuhl, G. (1994) In Swedish: Generisk flexibilitet – På väg mot en komponentbaserad metodsyn. Presenterat på VITS Höstseminarium 1994. Institutionen för datavetenskap, Linköpings universitet.
22. Ter Hofstede, A.H.M., Verhoef, T.F. (1997) On the Feasibility of Situational Method Engineering. In: Information Systems, Vol. 22, No. 6/7, pp. 401–422.
23. Webster, J. and Wason, R.T. (2002) Analyzing the Past to Prepare for the Future: Writing a Literature Review. In: MIS Quarterly, Vol. 26, No. 2, pp. xiii–xxiii.

68

A Methodological Framework for Enterprise Information System Requirements Derivation

Albertas Caplinskas and Lina Paškevičiūtė

Abstract

Current information systems (IS) are enterprise-wide systems supporting strategic goals of the enterprise and meeting its operational business needs. They are supported by information and communication technologies (ICT) and other software that should be fully integrated. To develop software responding to real business needs, we need requirements engineering (RE) methodology that ensures the alignment of requirements for all levels of enterprise system. The main contribution of this chapter is a requirement-oriented methodological framework allowing to transform business requirements level by level into software ones. The structure of the proposed framework reflects the structure of Zachman's framework. However, it has other intentions and is purposed to support not the design but the RE issues.

Keywords Enterprise engineering · Strategic alignment · Requirements engineering · Requirements elicitation

1. Introduction

In this chapter, IS is understood as "a set of information processing processes performed by enterprise functional entities in order to provide a number of information services required to support business processes." [1]. The IS may consist of both manual and automated process. Unfortunately, different computer-based ISs operating in one enterprise still often are developed as stand-alone systems and are weakly integrated. However, such style of working is already outdated. The new generation of IS, enterprise information systems, is thought as an integral part of enterprise system (ES) that is designed to support strategic goals of an enterprise, with the goal to integrate business processes, computer-supported and manual information processing procedures, and ICT components in order to improve business efficiency. ES should maintain alignment of business, information processing (IP), and ICT activities. However, most of authors discuss business and ICT alignment only. For example, Jerry Luftman writes that "Business-IT alignment refers to applying Information Technology (IT) in an appropriate and timely way, in harmony with business strategies, goals and needs" [2]. As a rule, IP level is not considered as a separate system level. Often (e.g., in [3]) manual IP procedures are considered as a part of business processes, software supported procedures as a part of ICT. We argue that it is purposeful to consider IP as a separate level of enterprise system comprising manual as well as software supported IP procedures. Only in this way it is possible to eliminate the gap between business processes and supporting IP procedures on the one hand and the gap between IP procedures and application software on the other hand. Besides, all IP activities should be designed and optimized together.

Albertas Caplinskas and Lina Paškevičiūtė • Software Engineering Department, Institute of Mathematics and Informatics, Vilnius, Lithuania.

G.A. Papadopoulos et al. (eds.), *Information Systems Development*, DOI 10.1007/b137171_68,
© Springer Science+Business Media, LLC 2009

The main purpose of this chapter is to discuss a methodological framework for definition of enterprise information systems requirements allowing in a systematic way to derive requirements of all levels, including IS and software levels, from business level requirements. The chapter does not pretend to propose a new RE process nor a new RE methodology. Consequently, it does not consider requirements traceability, process scalability, and many other issues that should be considered describing RE process or methodology. These issues are out of the scope of this chapter.

The remaining part of this chapter is organized as follows. Section 2 describes the related works and states the problem. Section 3 discusses the proposed methodological framework in details. Finally, Section 4 concludes this chapter.

2. Related Works

The main methodological approach to gather business and IT together is enterprise architecture. Unfortunately, the term is ill-defined, used in different senses. For example, IS engineers define it in terms of information architecture, data architecture, technical architecture, etc., and business people in terms of mission, strategy, business models, business processes, etc. However, in any case the goal is to fit together business, IP and ICT components in order to constitute a seamless system. A framework may present a model for architectural descriptions as well as a process to produce such descriptions [4]. Some frameworks focus on the descriptions, others on the process, and finally there are frameworks that encompass both architectural descriptions and the way to produce them.

A number of frameworks have been proposed [4–6], from which one of the most popular is the Zachman's framework [5]. However, any, including Zachman's framework does not describe how to produce detail functional or non-functional requirements [7] and does not mandate or recommend any RE process. This process should be defined at the lower than an architectural level. On the other hand, some attempts to adapt the Zachman's framework for the needs of RE have been done by David Hay [8]. He considers the Zachman's framework as a tool for requirement analysis, which allows translating enterprise business owner's view into architect's view. Hay emphasizes the importance of strategic planning and even insists that it should be considered as the first step in building any system [8]. On the other hand, Hay is influenced by Oracle CDM methodology [9]. He supposes that at each level provided by Zachman's framework first of all the data requirements should be specified and data model should be developed. So, requirements are not derived from motivation but, vice versa, the motivation only explains reasons of already defined requirements. Hay also blurs the information processing level between business and software levels. We argue that such approach is not fully correct. To perform requirements flowdown from business to software level not violating business and IT alignment, the information processing level (usually it is called IS level) should be considered as a separate one. By the way, Zachman considers this level (he calls it "System level") as separate one, too.

A significant attempt to develop a requirements definition approach helping to derive software requirements from business ones has been done by Karl Wiegers [10]. He does not refer to any enterprise architecture and even does not pretend to propose "an elaborate methodology that purports to solve all of your requirements problems" [10], nevertheless his scheme to organize requirements of different levels is related to Zachman's framework because requirements are grouped into layers using criteria of views. Wiegers considers three requirements levels: business requirements, user requirements, and software requirements. Information processing requirements do not belong to any of these groups and are considered as "system requirements", which are treated as external information source to be used defining software level requirements. It seems, that Wiegers follows here the IEEE Std 1223-1998 [11] approach. His book is valuable source for any requirements engineer, but it does not describe in details how one can perform requirements flowdown from business to software level correctly. He mentions both business and software visions, but explains how to explore further the software vision only. How business vision and other deliverables of the strategic planning should be used, it is not explained. There is also some obscurity in how software requirements can be derived from user requirements.

3. The Proposed Methodological Framework

The aim of the proposed framework is to define exhaustive organizational scheme that organizes requirements of different levels, including technology independent information processing requirements, in a way, which allow to flowdown requirements from business to software level preserving their business-orientation and as a rule enabling to derive lower level requirements from higher level ones in a systematic way. The main structure of this framework (Fig. 68.1) – its views and aspects – is suggested by Zachman's framework. However, the meaning of cells is changed completely. The set of requirements produced using this approach forms a hierarchical structure defining required properties of enterprise-wide information system as it is seen by business consultants, users, IS engineers, and software requirements engineers. It is important to mention that deliverables of the strategic planning serve as the *Why* aspect of business level requirements describing rather business needs and goals that should be supported by enterprise-wide IS than business system itself.

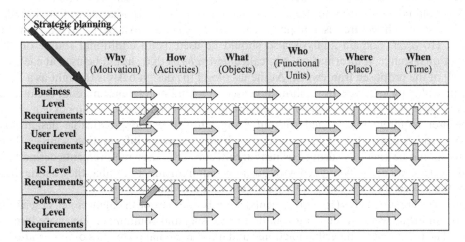

Figure 68.1. Methodological framework for requirements derivation.

The proposed framework defines the order in which the requirements are derived (Fig. 68.1) and provides additional sources of information that should be used deriving requirements. In Fig. 68.1 these sources are shown as shaded zones. They will be discussed later in this chapter.

The derivation of requirements starts from the upper left cell that contains deliverables of strategic planning process. The derivation of all other requirements is performed row by row from top to down and on each of rows going through all aspects from left to right. Each step (activity used to produce results described in the corresponding cell) makes use of the results of the already performed steps described in the neighboring cells straight above and to the left of the current one and additional sources of information provided by the framework. Such spiral-like process ensures that all needed information for all requirement types would be eventually gathered and at the same time, the requirements allocated to all the cells would be aligned to each other. The methods provided by quality function deployment [12], goal-oriented requirements analysis [13, 14], and other requirements flowdown approaches can be used successfully for requirements derivation. However, because of the limited space of this chapter we are not able to explain these issues in more details here.

Most of the traditional RE approaches do not consider IS (more exactly information processing) level as a separate level. It is supposed that the user requirements should be formulated in terms of services required to support business needs, later the scope and the depth of the project should be defined, and that after this it is already possible to start to specify software requirements. We argue that such approach would almost certainly lead to misalignment because the requirements of IS reflecting the point of view of

IS engineer in terms of the IS architecture implementing required services should be defined before. Despite the fact that modern approaches (including TOGAF [4]) provide phases dealing with the IS architecture, they treat this architecture in IT oriented way and, in contrary to our framework, cannot ensure that misalignment will be prevented.

Let us discuss briefly the framework presented in Fig. 68.1. The rows of the table describe different views. In order to avoid the gap between business requirements and software requirements the process of requirement definition should be started on business level and the requirements describing the view of business engineer on the enterprise system should be specified. It means that first of all the business architecture requirements aligned with business mission, vision, aims, and goals should be defined. Only after then business-oriented requirements of lower levels can be derived.

The next level requirements (user requirements) describe the view of domain professionals' and other direct and indirect users of services provided by the enterprise information system, including business clients, suppliers, and governmental institutions. They reflect operational needs of users and are formulated in terms of information processing, communication, and other services required to satisfy those needs. They should take into account user requests and wishes, too. Because operational needs primarily depend on business architecture, user requirements can be for the most part derived from higher level requirements. However, domain analysis also should be used as an additional source of information. Another additional source of information is so called *design basis* that should be used at each level (except business level) of the proposed framework. At the user level the design basis is thought as a list of services that can be provided by a today's IS. It should be used as a kind of reference manual because most of the users and even the part of IT professionals are unfamiliar with the modern technologies (e.g., RFID) and as a result the user requirements defined without using innovative and practicable design basis can be outdated. All requirements that at least partly are based on other information sources than business requirements should be validated using business architecture. So, user requirements define IS as a set of interrelated services and are fully aligned with business requirements. Inter alia, they define the scope and the depth of the project and it is done in terms of services provided by IS, too.

The third level requirements (IS requirements) describe the view of IS engineer i.e., describe IS in terms of organizational memory and a set of information processing and communication procedures defined on this memory. The requirements describe functional and non-functional properties of information processing system, and its subsystem level architecture including manual subsystems, too. Inter alia, the architecture requirements should define what application systems supporting IS should be developed and what high level requirements they should meet. It is possible because the depth of the project is already defined on the user level. So, indeed, the IS level consists of two sublevels. The first sublevel describes requirements of information processing system itself; the second one describes high-level requirements of its subsystems. Requirements of IS are derived from user requirements. As additional information sources are used as description of current information system, information processing rules in force (e.g., accounting rules) and design basis that at the IS level is thought as a list of capabilities of modern IS. User requirements are used to validate requirements that are at least partly based on additional information sources.

Last level requirements (software requirements) describe the view of software engineers. They are defined for each application system supporting information processing level procedures. Requirements mainly are derived from IS level requirements. As additional information sources are used stakeholders' opinions about priorities of non-functional properties of IS and design base that on this level is thought as an implementation platform.

Let us discuss now briefly the columns of the proposed framework. They represent aspects (types of requirements) each of which is shared by all the views represented in the framework. The aspects are ordered in such a way that going from left to right and defining requirements related to a particular aspect all required information of this level under consideration would be already known. On the other hand, requirements flow down from one level to another through the columns.

The first column states the goals. It answers the question "*Why* the system should be built?". Then the question "*How* to achieve the goals stated in the first column?" or more exactly "What services should be provided by the system?' should be answered. The next question is "*What* are requirements of the objects used to implement required services?" and, after answering this question, the question "*Who* will use the services supported by the system and what rights they will have?" is raised. Answering this question at the IS and software requirements levels the interface and security requirements are defined. The next one question is "*Where* (at what workplaces) the services will be delivered?". Answering this question at the IS and software requirements levels the software and hardware requirements for each workplace are defined as well as the requirements of spatial distribution of the workplaces including the deployment of computerized ones over the computer network. The answer also defines how well the resources should be utilized delivering each of the services. The last question is "When should the service be delivered" supposing that the answer will specify how quickly the system should deliver each service provided by it.

Let us discuss now each aspect more in details.

The definition and derivation of business level requirements is presented in Fig. 68.2. The "**Why**" aspect describes the results of strategic planning phase. More exactly, it describes at business level the vision of the enterprise system under development and the economic, policy, ethical, and legal constraints that constraint implementation of this vision. The "**How**" aspect describes functional requirements in terms of business transactions that can be seen as goals that should be achieved in order to implement the vision. It is done in the form of a goal tree. Additionally the constraints defining the reliability and safety for each transaction are stated. Mainly they are derived from the vision implementation constraints. The "**What**" aspect describes requirements of business objects required to implement business transactions. Object requirements are formulated in terms of business ontology and describe the business rules which constraint properties, states, and usage of the objects. The rules partly are derived from the business vision and partly inherited from old business system.

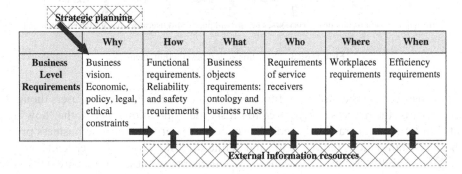

Figure 68.2. Definition of business level requirements.

The "**Who**" aspect describes requirements of service receivers. On the one hand, services are required by functional units (positions, departments, processes, equipment, etc.) that process the business objects and execute business transactions. On the other hand, the services are required by external users of the system, including business clients, business partners, and governmental institutions that initiates business transactions. All "who" requirements are formulated in terms of competency and rights. The rights are derived from policy constraints constraining the vision implementation and for every "who" define what business objects he can access and what he can do with them. The requirements also describe what business transactions by which functional units must be supported. Describing the "**Where**" aspect the workplace requirements are derived from the requirements of service receivers. The "where" requirements define what workplace is required for each "who," for execution of which business transactions it will be used, where it should be placed, and through which kind of enterprise communication networks (internal networks, restricted external access networks, public networks) it may access enterprise system resources. The "**When**" aspect describes efficiency requirements defining maximal allowed processing time for each business transaction. They are derived from vision constraints, functional requirements, and workplaces requirements.

The definition and derivation of user level requirements is presented in Fig. 68.3. The **"Why"** aspect describes the results of the business level "why" requirements flowdown. First, the vision is restated in terms of business processes and business tasks. It is verified according to business level functional requirements. Priorities to business transactions are assigned. From the restated vision each business process requirements are derived. They are formulated in terms of transactions (business goals). The vision implementation constraints stated at the business level are transformed into appropriate constraints constraining the implementation of business processes and transactions. All "why" requirements are contrasted with information gathered from users.

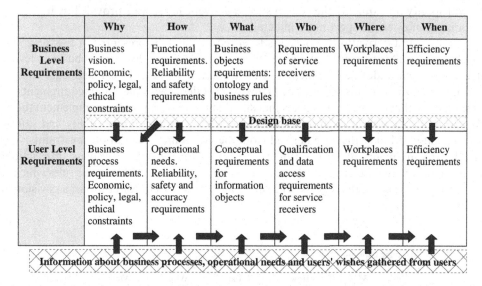

Figure 68.3. Definition of user level requirements.

The **"How"** aspect describes user level functional requirements. Because the users thought the system in services and because the services are required to satisfy their operational needs, the "how" requirements are formulated in terms of operational needs that mainly are derived from the business process requirements and business transactions requirements and define what IS services are needed to support business transactions. The reliability, safety, and accuracy requirements of these services are derived from corresponding higher level requirements. Finally, the scope of the project is defined, i.e., the extent to what each IS service should be computerized taking into account user requests and wishes as well as financial and other project constraints. The **"What"** aspect describes conceptual requirements of information objects modeling corresponding business objects. They are produced contrasting business level "what" requirements with user level "how" requirements. For all information objects (records, events descriptions, contents, pictures, maps, video, etc.) stored in the organizational memory these requirements describe what data or other information should be used to model corresponding business objects, modeling accuracy, integrity constrains, delivery mode as well as where and how each of information objects would be created and how they would be put into the organizational memory. The requirements also define what contents should be accessible in the IS and what information architecture every accessible content should have. The **"Who"** aspect elaborates, refines, and concretizes "who" requirements stated at the business level. At the user level they are considered as high-level interface, usability, and security requirements defining what abilities and skills IS services receivers, including other information processing systems and equipment, should be expected to have, what information objects are permitted to access for each of them and what they can do with accessed objects. Besides the requirements define how frequent (in a regular way, occasionally, etc.) each service receiver is using each from delivered services what is crucial for the further refinement of usability requirements. The **"Where"** aspect refines workplaces requirements with regard of "how" and "what" requirements defined at the user level. They define what business tasks in which workplaces should be performed, what information processing services are required for this aim, and what communication modes (data transferring, data exchange, etc.) among the workplaces should be provided. They also define where each kind of information objects should be stored because it is purposeful to treat information storages as a special kind of workplaces. So in this way services are allocated in workplaces provided for official positions, terminals to serve business clients (e.g., ATM system), and access to system points provided for other users (business partners, other systems, etc.). The "**When**" aspect refines the efficiency requirements stated at the business level with regard to user level "what" and "where" requirements defining maximal allowed processing time for each business task.

The definition and derivation of information system level requirements is presented in Fig. 68.4. The "**Why**" aspect at the IS level states the vision of IS as a product, i.e., describes information processing and communication capabilities that are required to implement user-oriented services. The economic, policy, ethical, and legal constraints constraining the implementation of this vision also are described. The vision is derived from the user-oriented vision taking into account the information processing rules in force as an additional information source. The "**How**" aspect describes first of all the functional requirements of IS. The vision is decomposed into tree of capabilities taking into account operational needs of users. The tree is constrained by productivity, accessibility, and quality requirements. Further, the capability tree is decomposed down into information processing tasks. In this step the architectural requirements for IS should be defined and the system should be decomposed into subsystems. The information processing tasks are allocated to the subsystems and the reliability, safety, and accuracy requirements flowdown to subsystem level is performed. The "**What**" aspect details information objects requirements, including security requirements, taking into account the IS capability tree. These requirements state what information storages should be created in the IS, how they should be organized, how their security should be ensured, and what accuracy and integrity constraints should meet the information objects stored in each of the storages. The "**Who**" aspect defines usability and interface requirements of IS. They describe external interfaces of each IS subsystem and of what kind these interfaces should be that they were convenient to use for particular service receiver. The "**Where**" aspect defines what kind of equipment, hardware, and system software should be installed in each workplace and what ergonomic requirements should meet each of the workplaces. Besides requirements describing in what communication networks each of the workplaces should be included also are defined. The "**When**" aspect describes efficiency requirements for each information processing task taking into account the "where" requirements.

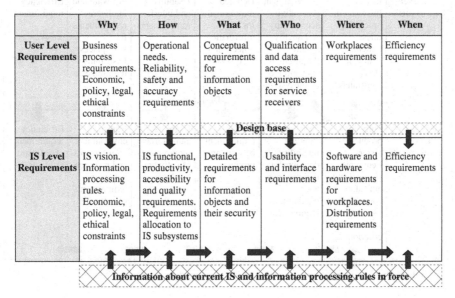

	Why	How	What	Who	Where	When
User Level Requirements	Business process requirements. Economic, policy, legal, ethical constraints	Operational needs. Reliability, safety and accuracy requirements	Conceptual requirements for information objects	Qualification and data access requirements for service receivers	Workplaces requirements	Efficiency requirements
			Design base			
IS Level Requirements	IS vision. Information processing rules. Economic, policy, legal, ethical constraints	IS functional, productivity, accessibility and quality requirements. Requirements allocation to IS subsystems	Detailed requirements for information objects and their security	Usability and interface requirements	Software and hardware requirements for workplaces. Distribution requirements	Efficiency requirements
			Information about current IS and information processing rules in force			

Figure 68.4. Definition of IS level requirements.

The definition and derivation of software level requirements is presented in Fig. 68.5. Software requirements should be defined for each application system supporting IS and for each other software components of IS. The **"Why"** aspect describes the visions of the software product. First, the IS vision elements are allocated to software products and flowdown to software level. Decisions on what IS system vision elements each software product will support are made according to "how" requirements formulated at IS level, especially according to the tree of capabilities and to the allocation of these requirements to subsystems. The economic, policy, ethical, and legal constraints constraining the implementation of IS also are allocated to software products and constraints flowdown is made (i.e., corresponding constraints are derived for each software product from the allocated IS constraints). In addition, quality evaluation criterions (priorities) for non-functional properties of each software product are defined taking into account the gathered and generalized stakeholders' opinions. The **"How"** aspect describes functional, safety, reliability, deployment, maintenance, and operation requirements of each software product. The requirements are produced allocating IS requirements and performing flowdown of allocated requirements. The allocation should be done taking into account the allocation of "why" requirements. The **"What"** aspect describes data requirements for each software product. First, IS level "what" requirements are allocated to the software products and flowdown of allocated requirements is performed. The flowdown is performed taking into account the functional requirements of corresponding product and constraints constraining the implementation of its vision. The **"Who"** aspect defines usability and interface requirements for each software product. This is done in an analogical way: higher level requirements are allocated and their flowdown is performed taking into account the "how" and "what" requirements of the corresponding software product. The **"Where"** aspect describes run-time environment requirements (system software, hardware, network environment, etc.) and resource behavior requirements, the **"When"** aspect describes efficiency requirements. The "where" and "when" requirements are produced in an analogical way, too. The requirements also are produced in an analogical way. The "where" requirements flowdown is performed taking into account IS level "why" requirements, especially economical constraints as well as the "how" and "what" requirements of the corresponding software product, and the "when" requirements flowdown – taking into account to the run-time environment requirements.

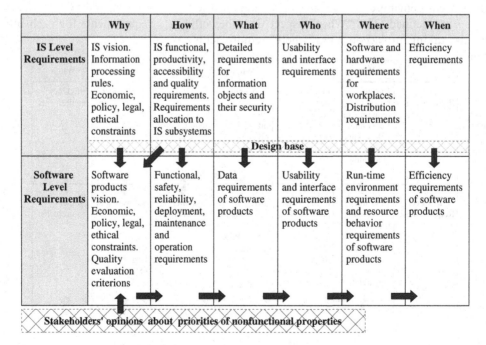

	Why	How	What	Who	Where	When
IS Level Requirements	IS vision. Information processing rules. Economic, policy, legal, ethical constraints	IS functional, productivity, accessibility and quality requirements. Requirements allocation to IS subsystems	Detailed requirements for information objects and their security	Usability and interface requirements	Software and hardware requirements for workplaces. Distribution requirements	Efficiency requirements
Software Level Requirements	Software products vision. Economic, policy, legal, ethical constraints. Quality evaluation criterions	Functional, safety, reliability, deployment, maintenance and operation requirements	Data requirements of software products	Usability and interface requirements of software products	Run-time environment requirements and resource behavior requirements of software products	Efficiency requirements of software products

Design base

Stakeholders' opinions about priorities of nonfunctional properties

Figure 68.5. Definition of software level requirements.

4. Conclusions

This chapter discusses a requirement-oriented methodological framework that is purposed to be used as a part of enterprise engineering process and supports software requirements derivation from business level ones. This framework facilitates producing software requirements, which are aligned with strategic goals of the enterprise and its operational business needs. It also bridges the gap between the strategic planning and the requirements engineering. The main structure of the proposed framework reflects the structure of Zachman's framework. However, it is used in a completely different way. One of the distinguishing features of this framework is strong separation of IS requirements from business as well as from software level requirements. It seems that after the work of Tom DeMarco [15] this question was nearly ignored. Only few of the current RE methodologies consider information processing requirements as separate ones. However, including part of requirements of this level into business level requirements and another part into software level requirements we violate the concerns of separation principle and as a result requirements misalignment problems arise. The proposed framework solves this problem. It has been tested in several enterprise engineering projects and proved out to be as acceptable one. However, at the moment the gathered statistical evidence is insufficient to do the final conclusions.

References

1. Caplinskas, A.; Lupeikiene, A.; Vasilecas, O. (2002) Unified enterprise engineering environment: ontological point of view. In *Proceedings of the Baltic Conference, BalticDB\&IS 2002*, Institute of Cybernetics at Tallin Technical University, pp. 30–50.
2. Luftman, J. (2000) Assessing business-IT alignment maturity. *Communications of the AIS*, 4(14), pp. 1–50.
3. Henderson, J. C.; Venkatraman, N. (1993) Strategic alignment: leveraging information technology for transforming organizations. *IBM Systems Journal*, 32(1), pp. 4–16.
4. The Open Group (2003) *The Open Group Architecture Framework TOGAF*. Version 8.1, Enterprise Edition.
5. Sowa, J. F.; Zachman, J. A. (1992). Extending and formalizing the framework for information systems architecture. *IBM Systems Journal*, 31(3), pp. 590–616.
6. Capgemini (2007) *Enterprise, Business and IT Architecture and the Integrated Architecture*,Capgemini. Consulting, Technology, Outsourcing, Brochure. Available from <http://www.capgemini.com/services/soa/ent_architecture/enterprise_arch/> [accessed 29 April 2008].
7. Sousa, P; Pereira, C. M.; Marques, J. A. (2005) Enterprise architecture alignment heuristics. *The Architecture Journal* (Microsoft Architect Journal), Journal 4. Available from <http://msdn2.microsoft.com/en-us/library/aa480042.aspx> [accessed 29 April 2008].
8. Hay, D. C. (2002) *Requirements Analysis, From Business Views to Architecture*, Prentice Hall PTR, Upper Saddle River, NJ.
9. Oracle Corporation (2000) *CDM Quick Tour*, Release 2.0.0.
10. Wiegers, K. E. (2003) *Software Requirements*. 2nd edition, Microsoft Press, Redmond, WA.
11. IEEE (1998) *Std 1233-1998: IEEE Guide for Developing System Requirements Specifications*. Software Engineering Standards Committee of the IEEE Computer Society, USA.
12. Karlsson, J. (1997) Managing software requirements using quality function deployment. *Software Quality Journal*, 6, pp. 311–325.
13. Chung, L.; Nixon, B. A.; Yu, E.; Mylopoulos, J. (2000) *Non-Functional Requirements in Software Engineering*, Kluwer Academic Publishers, Boston.
14. Lamsweerde, A. v. (2001) Goal-oriented requirements engineering: a guided tour. *Proceedings of the 5th IEEE International Symposium on Requirements Engineering (RE'01)*, Toronto, Canada, pp. 249–261.
15. Demarco, T. (1979) *Structured Analysis and System Specification*, Prentice Hall PTR, Upper Saddle River, NJ.

69

Measuring Communication Heterogeneity Between Multiple Web-Based Agents

Maricela Bravo and Martha Coronel

Abstract

Communication between multiple agents is essential to achieve cooperation, negotiation, and take decisions for mutual benefit. Nowadays there is a growing interest in automating communication processes between different agents in dynamic web-based environments. However, when agents are deployed and integrated in open and dynamic environments, detailed syntax and semantics of their particular language implementations differ, causing the problem of communication heterogeneity. Therefore, it is necessary to measure heterogeneity among all participating agents and the number of required translations when heterogeneous agents are involved in communications. In this chapter we present a set of measures with the objective to evaluate the minimal computational requirements before implementing a translation approach. Our measures are based on set theory, which has proved to be a good representation formalism in other areas. We showed how to use the set of measures for two highly heterogeneous set of agents.

Keywords Multi-agent systems · Heterogeneity · Ontologies

1. Introduction

Communication between multiple agents is essential to achieve cooperation, negotiation, and take decisions for mutual benefit. Nowadays there is a growing interest in automating communication processes between different agents in dynamic Web-based environments. Traditionally autonomous agents have been implemented independently of each other in local environments, where agents exchange messages following a protocol based on standard language specifications. However, when agents are deployed and integrated in open and dynamic environments, detailed syntax and semantics of their particular language implementations differ, causing the problem of *communication heterogeneity*.

There are two traditional solutions to support communication interoperability: one is the use of a common communication protocol and the second is a translation approach with the use of a shared ontology. The use of a common communication protocol consists of defining syntax and formal semantics of primitives for all participating agents, the main drawback of this approach is the lack of flexibility, and the required time and effort for coding each agent every time that it is going to be deployed on a different agent community, with different communication rules; therefore this solution is not suitable for dynamic environments.

The second approach consists of automatic translation of exchanged messages by means of a shared ontology populated with all the communication primitives. However, there are certain computational considerations when selecting this approach, because it requires the use of a shared ontology and a translator. To help the developer to decide which approach better suits its requirements, it is necessary to measure heterogeneity among all participating agents and the number of required translations when

Maricela Bravo and Martha Coronel · Informatique Department, Morelos State Polytechnic University, Morelos, México.

G.A. Papadopoulos et al. (eds.), *Information Systems Development*, DOI 10.1007/b137171_69,
© Springer Science+Business Media, LLC 2009

many heterogeneous agents are involved in translation. In this chapter we present a set of measures that will provide such information.

The rest of the chapter is organized as follows. In Section 2 we present related work with the subject of this research. In Section 3 we describe a set of measures to evaluate the main requirements of a translation approach. In Section 4 we apply the measures to a case study, in order to clarify the measures usage. In Section 5 we conclude and give future direction of this work.

2. Related Works

Many authors agree on the importance of communication interoperability and the correct interpretation of exchanged messages in multi-agent systems. Malucelli and Oliveira [1] stated that a critical factor for the efficiency of communication processes and the success of potential settlements is an agreement between parties about how the issues of a communication are represented and what this representation means to each of the parties. In [2] authors explain that interoperability is about effective use of system services. They argue that the most important precondition to achieve interoperability is to ensure that the message sender and receiver share the same understanding of the data in the message and the same expectation of the effect of the message. Rueda [3] argues that the success of an agent application depends on the communication language, allowing agents to interact and share knowledge. In [6] authors state that communication deals with how to represent agent's requirements and constraints on a product and service and how to convey intentions by passing messages between parties.

There has been a common interest among multiple researchers, in providing communication interoperability between agents using an ontology to support translation. Gruber [4] presented Ontolingua, a system for describing ontologies in a compatible form with multiple representation languages. He used Ontolingua to translate definitions written in KIF (Knowledge Interchange Format) into different representation languages. Willmott et al. [5] presented an abstract ontology representation (AOR) to capture models of communication to deal with the interoperability problem between multiple agents. Hübner [6] described Saci (Simple Agent Communication Infrastructure) a tool for programming communication between multiple agents using KQML messages. Fourlan et al. [7] designed a CORBA interface to Saci to support communication interoperability between Saci- and CORBA-based agents. In [8] the author proposed a translation approach to facilitate agent communication, where agents use partially shared ontologies for muli-agent communication. In [9], authors propose a common ontology for defining semantics for agent communication languages, based on public mental attitudes. In [10], we presented a shared ontology to support communication in electronic systems, invoking a translator only when necessary.

In the above related works we can see a common trend in using ontologies to support communication interoperability. But we need to evaluate heterogeneity among a set of agents, in order to decide if a translation solution approach will need high computational requirements.

3. Measuring Heterogeneity

Communication among multiple agents in Web-based environments is executed through the exchange of messages following a protocol. A protocol is a sequence of exchanged messages conforming to a set of shared rules. For this work we are considering that a message has the following elements:

    *<Sender, Receiver, **Primitive**, Parameters, Other data>*
Where

- **Sender** *identifies the agent that is issuing the message,*
- **Receiver** *is the target agent, which will receive and analyze the incoming message,*
- **Primitive** *is a basic communication act, which has syntax, semantics, and pragmatics.*
- **Parameters** *are the rest of input data, these parameters depend on the primitive.*
- **Other data** *is left for additional information.*

To measure heterogeneity between multiple agents we considered the set of communication primitives of each agent and designed a set of measures, which will be described next.

a) *Universal set of communication primitives*

Given a set of heterogeneous agents

$$A = \{a_1, a_2, a_3, \ldots, a_n\},$$

The universal set of communication primitives is represented by

$$CP = \{CPa_1, CPa_2, \ldots, CPa_n\}, \tag{69.1}$$

where $CPa_n = \{p_1, p_2, p_3, \ldots, p_i\}$ is the set of communication primitives of agent n.

b) *Number of communication links*

Considering a set of n agents, the possible number of peer-to-peer communication links among them is n^2. However, as we are evaluating heterogeneity, we need to extract the number of communication links where agents are equal, which is n. We also considered that a communication link between agents (a, b) has the same heterogeneity as a communication link of agents (b, a), thus we reduced the number of different communication links dividing by 2.

The number of different communication links between n agents is given by

$$CL = (n^2 - n)/2 \tag{69.2}$$

c) *Set of different communication links*

Considering a set of agents, the set of different communication links is given by

$$DCL = \{(a_1, a_2), (a_1, a_3), \ldots (a_i, a_j)\}, \tag{69.3}$$

d) *Number of communication primitives*

The total number of communication primitives is obtained from the union operation of all sets of communication primitives.

$$CPT = |CPa_1 \cup CPa_2 \cup \cdots \cup CPa_n| \tag{69.4}$$

e) *Number of different communication primitives*

The total number of different communication primitives results from extracting the intersection of common communication primitives from CPT.

$$DCPT = |CPa_1 \cup CPa_2 \cup \cdots \cup CPa_n| - |CPa_1 \cap CPa_2 \cap \cdots \cap CPa_n| \tag{69.5}$$

f) *Level of heterogeneity*

The level of heterogeneity results from dividing $DCPT$ by CPT, which is the ratio that will serve as an indicator for evaluating heterogeneity.

$$\textbf{\textit{Level of heterogeneity}} = DCPT/CPT \tag{69.6}$$

g) *Number of required translations*

Considering that for each pair (x_i, y_i) of communication links the necessary translations among them is the number of communication primitives that are unknown for each agent. This is, the number of translations that agent x_i needs to be translated is the set of communication primitives from agent y_i, minus the set of communication primitives that are common for both. For this formula we considered the sum of required translations of each agent independently, because translation is required independently of the translations of other agents.

$$\sum \forall(x_i, y_i) \in DCL = |x_i \cup y_i| - |x_i \cap y_i| \tag{69.7}$$

4. Case Studies

In this section, we present two case studies to apply the set of measures and evaluate the resulting values. We selected the set of communication primitives from the agents presented in [11]. We utilized three agents for the first case, and eight agents for the second, this decision was taken to discriminate if the number of agents has a considerable impact on the heterogeneity among them.

4.1. Case One. Measuring Communication Heterogeneity with Three Agents

Given a set $A = \{a_1, a_2, a_3\}$, of three autonomous agents developed independently of each other and deployed on the Web, and their respective set of communication primitives.

$CPa_1 = \{Initial\_Offer, RFQ, Accept, Reject, Offer, Counter\_Offer\}$
$CPa_2 = \{CFP, Propose, Accept, Terminate, Reject, Acknowledge, Modify, Withdraw\}$
$CPa_3 = \{Requests\_Add, Authorize\_Add, Require, Demand, Accept, Reject, Unable, Require-for, Insist\_for, Demand\_for\}$

We first calculate the number of different communication links between them using Formula 2.

$$n = 3$$
$$CL = (3^2 - 3)/2 = 3$$

The resulting set of different communication links is

$$DCL = \{(a_1, a_2), (a_1, a_3), (a_2, a_3)\}$$

Using Formula 4, we calculate the total number of communication primitives.

$$CPa_1 \cup CPa_2 \cup CPa_3 = \quad \{Initial\_Offer, RFQ, Accept, Reject, Offer,$$
$$Counter\_Offer, CFP, Propose, Terminate,$$
$$Acknowledge, Modify, Withdraw,$$
$$Requests\_Add, Authorize\_Add, Require, Demand,$$
$$Unable, Require-for, Insist\_for,$$
$$Demand\_for\}$$
$$CPT = |CPa_1 \cup CPa_2 \cup CPa_3|$$
$$CPT = 20$$

Using Formula 5 we calculate the total number of different communication primitives..

$$|CPa_1 \cup CPa_2 \cup CPa_3| = 20$$
$$|CPa_1 \cup CPa_2 \cup CPa_3| = 2$$
$$\textbf{\textit{DCPT}} = 18$$

We apply Formula 6 to calculate the level of heterogeneity for this set of heterogeneous agents.

$$\textbf{\textit{Level of heterogeneity}} = 18/20 = 0.9$$

The level of heterogeneity results too high for these agents; then we should analyze if a translation approach will have higher computational requirements to support communication interoperability. To select a translation approach we need to measure the number of individuals in the shared ontology. For our case study the number of individuals is equal to the total number of communication primitives, which is **CPa$_1$** $\cup$ **CPa$_2$** $\cup$ **CPa$_3$** = 20, we should also consider the size of definitions and semantic relations among them.

In the first case, we represent the three sets of communication primitives, and we can clearly see that the two common primitives for all agents are *accept* and reject primitives. To calculate the number of required translations, we considered the set of different communication links $DCL = \{ (a_1, a_2), (a_1, a_3), (a_2, a_3) \}$, and the worst case where each agent needs the translation of all communication primitives from the other agents in a peer-to-peer communication.

Using Formula 7, the number of required translations for agents a_1, a_2, a_3 is given by:

$$\sum \forall(x_i, y_i) \in \textbf{\textit{DCL}} = |CPx_i \cup CPy_i| - |CPx_i \cap CPy_i|$$

$$|CPa_i \cup CPa_i| - |CPa_i \cap CPa_i| = 12 - 2 = 10$$
$$|CPa_i \cup CPa_i| - |CPa_i \cap CPa_i| = 14 - 2 = 12$$
$$|CPa_i \cup CPa_i| - |CPa_i \cap CPa_i| = 16 - 2 = 14$$

$$\sum \forall(x_i, y_i) \in DCL = \textbf{36}$$

The minimal number of required translations in the worst case, for this scenario is 36, with a 0.9 level of heterogeneity. For minimal we mean that the translator translates only once for a communication session, considering that each participating agent has the ability to temporarily learn a communication primitive that has been translated. The worst case represents the communication session into which all the different communication primitives will be issued, then causing the translator to execute the maximal number of translations for this scenario.

We consider this scenario as a high heterogeneity case. However, the implementation of the translation approach will not be too costly, because the number of required instances in the ontology is 20, and the number of required translations is 36.

4.2. Case Two. Measuring Communication Heterogeneity with Eight Agents

Given a set $B = \{ a_1, a_2, a_3 \}$, of eight autonomous agents developed independently of each other and deployed on the Web, and their respective set of communication primitives.

CPa$_1$ = {*Initial_Offer, RFQ, **Accept, Reject**, Offer, Counter_Offer*}
CPa$_2$ = {*CFP, Propose, **Accept**, Terminate, **Reject**, Acknowledge, Modity, Withdraw*}
CPa$_3$ = {*Requests_Add, Authorize_Add, Require, Demand, **Accept, Reject**, Unable, Require-for, Insist_ for, Demand_for*}
CPa$_4$ = {*accept-offer, what-is-price, what-is-item, add-sell-agent, add-buy-agent, add-potential-customers, add-potentil-sellers, agent-terminated, deal-made*}

CPa_5 = {*Call for proposal, Propose Proposal, Reject proposal, Withdraw proposal, Accept proposal, Accept proposal, Modify proposal, Acknowledge message, Terminate negotiation*}

CPa_6 = {*request-quotation, give-quotation, order, delivered, paid*}

CPa_7 = {*Accept Proposal, Agree, Cancel, Call for Proposal, Confirm, Disconfirm, Failure, Inform, Inform If, Inform Ref, Not Understood, Propagate, Propose, Proxy, Query If, Query Ref, Refuse, Reject Proposal, **Request**, Request When, Request Whenever, Subscribe*}

CPa_8 = {*Propose, Arrange, **Request**, Inform, Query, Command, Inspect, Answer, Refine, Modify, Change, Bid, Send, Reply, Refuse, Explain, Confirm,*}

We first calculate the number of different communication links between them using Formula 2.

$$n = 8$$
$$CL = (8^2 - 8)/2 = 28$$

The resulting set of different communication links is given by:

$$DCL = \{(a_1, a_2), (a_1, a_3), (a_1, a_4), (a_1, a_5), (a_1, a_6), (a_1, a_7), (a_1, a_8),$$
$$(a_2, a_3), (a_2, a_4), (a_2, a_5), (a_2, a_6), (a_2, a_7), (a_2, a_8),$$
$$(a_3, a_4), (a_3, a_5), (a_3, a_6), (a_3, a_7), (a_3, a_8),$$
$$(a_4, a_5), (a_4, a_6), (a_4, a_7), (a_4, a_8),$$
$$(a_5, a_6), (a_5, a_7), (a_5, a_8),$$
$$(a_6, a_7), (a_6, a_8),$$
$$(a_7, a_8)\}$$

Using Formula 4, we calculate the total number of communication primitives.

$$CPa_1 \cup CPa_2 \cup CPa_3 \cup CPa_4 \cup CPa_5 \cup CPa_6 \cup CPa_7 \cup CPa_8 =$$

{*Initial_Offer, RFQ, Accept, Reject, Offer, Counter_Offer, CFP, Propose, Terminate, Acknowledge, Modify, Withdraw, Requests_Add, Authorize_Add, Require, Demand, Unable, Require-for, Insist_for, Demand_for, accept-offer, what-is-price, what-is-item, add-sell-agent, add-buy-agent, add-potential-customers, add-potential-sellers, agent-terminated, del-made, Call for proposal, Reject proposal, Withdraw proposal, Accept proposal, Modify proposal, Acknowledge message, Terminate negotiation, request-quotation, give-quotation, order, delivered, paid, Accept Proposal, Agree, Cancel, Call for Proposal, Confirm, Disconfirm, Failure, Inform, Inform If, Inform Ref, Not Understood, Propose, Proxy, Query If, Query Ref, Refuse, Reject Proposal, Request, Request When, Request Whenever, Subscribe, propose, Arrange, Query, Command, Inspect, Answer, Refine, Modify, Change, Bid, Sent, Reply, Explain, Confirm, Promise, Commit, Grant, Agree*}

$$CPT = |CPa_1 \cup CPa_2 \cup CPa_3 \cup CPa_4 \cup CPa_5 \cup CPa_6 \cup CPa_7 \cup CPa_8|$$
$$CPT = 82$$

Using Formula 5 we calculate the total number of different communication primitives.

$$|CPa_1 \cup CPa_2 \cup CPa_3 \cup CPa_4 \cup CPa_5 \cup CPa_6 \cup CPa_7 \cup CPa_8 \cup| = 82$$
$$|CPa_1 \cap CPa_2 \cap CPa_3 \cap CPa_4 \cap CPa_5 \cap CPa_6 \cap CPa_7 \cap CPa_8| = 0$$
$$DCPT = 82$$

We apply Formula 6 to calculate the level of heterogeneity for this set of heterogeneous agents.

$$\textit{Level of heterogeneity} = 82/82 = 1$$

Although there are some agents which share some communication primitives among them, for example the subset of agents $\{ a_1, a_2, a_4, a_8 \}$ have in common the primitives $\{$ Accept, Reject $\}$; the level of heterogeneity among the eight agents resulted in the maximal possible heterogeneity. Therefore we need to calculate the number of translations required in peer-to-peer communications for all the different communication links to evaluate the computational requirements for this set of heterogeneous agents. The sum of all required translations is equal to 599.

Another important aspect that must be considered for a translation approach is the number of required individuals in the ontology. For this case the number of terms that must be defined in the ontology is equal to the total number of communication primitives.

$$|CPa_1 \cup CPa_2 \cup CPa_3 \cup CPa_4 \cup CPa_5 \cup CPa_6 \cup CPa_7 \cup CPa_8| = 82$$

5. Evaluation of Results

Figure 69.1 shows that more than the 70% of the 28 different communications links of the second case are totally heterogeneous, which represents a very difficult interoperability problem. To analyze if a translation approach would be a better solution we need to evaluate the number of required translations.

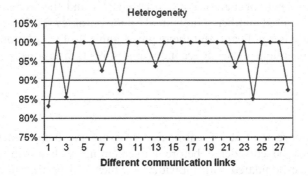

Figure 69.1. Level of heterogeneity of the second case.

Figure 69.2 shows the number of primitives and the number of different communication primitives for each different communication link.

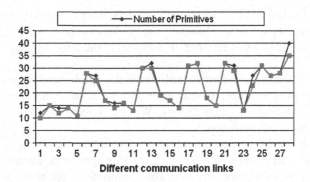

Figure 69.2. Number of different communication primitives of the second case.

Figure 69.3 shows the number of required translations of each different communication link.

Comparing the three graphics we can see that there is a relation between the numbers of different communication primitives of Fig. 69.2 with the number of required translations of Fig. 69.3. However, there is not a direct relation between the level of heterogeneity and the number of required translations, as we would have supposed.

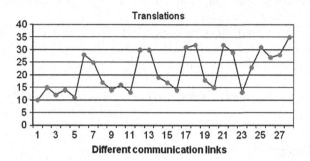

Figure 69.3. Number of required translations of the second case.

Both cases are highly heterogeneous, the first case is 0.9 and the second is 1, which represents a minimal difference. The required number of individuals in the ontology for the first case is 20, while for the second is 82, this difference is significant. But the required number of translations has a bigger difference, the first case needs 36 translations while the second requires 599 translations.

6. Conclusions

Many authors propose the use of ontologies to overcome heterogeneity. However, there are certain aspects that must be considered before implementing such a solution. An ontology-based solution will require to be populated with individuals, which will be the support of a translator. We need to measure the number of individuals in that ontology solution and the number of required translations.

In this chapter we have presented a set of measures with the objective to evaluate the computational requirements before implementing an interoperability solution for a given set of heterogeneous agents. Our measures are based on set theory, which has proven to be a good representation formalism in other areas.

We showed how to use the set of measures with two sets of highly heterogeneous agents. The first case represents a high heterogeneity scenario. However, the implementation of a translation approach for this case will not be too costly, due to a low number of instances in the ontology and a low number of required translations.

For the second case, we can appreciate that although the number of individuals is low, the number of required translations is high. Therefore, we may infer that an increase in the number of participants will cause lower performance during communications. We evaluated the results and obtained significant information for the developer of a solution.

To continue with this work we are extending our measures, considering a pragmatic approach to evaluate the differences and their impact in selecting a solution approach. There is also the need to evaluate communication scenarios in web-based environments populated with more agents, and modeling the dynamics of such environments, where agents enter and leave communications any time.

References

1. Malucelli, A., and E. Oliveira, Towards to Similarity Identification to Help in the Agents' Negotiation, Proceedings of 17th Brazilian Symposium on Artificial Intelligence, São Luis, Maranhão, Brazil, 2004.
2. Pokraev, S., M. Reichert, M. Steen, and R. Wieringa, Semantic and Pragmatic Interoperability: A Model for Understanding, Proceedings of the Open Interoperability Workshop on Enterprise Modelling and Ontologies for Interoperability, Porto, Portugal, 2005.
3. Rueda, S., A. García, and G. Simari, Argument-Based Negotiation Among BDI Agents, Computer Science & Technology, 2(7), 2002.
4. Gruber, T. R., A Translation Approach to Portable Ontology Specifications. Knowledge Acquisition, 5(2):199–220, 1993.
5. Willmott, S., I. Constantinescu, and M. Calisti, Multilingual Agents: Ontologies, Languages and Abstractions, Proceedings of the Workshop on Ontologies in Agent Systems, Fifth International Conference on Autonomous Agents, Montreal, Canada, 2001.
6. Hübner, J. F., Um Modelo de Reorganização de Sistemas Multiagentes. Ph.D. Dissertation, Universidade de São Paulo, Escola Politécnica, 2003.
7. Furlan de Souza, M. A., J. F. Hübner, J. S. Sichman, and M. A. Varella Ferreira, Interoperability in Multi-Agent Systems: Lessons Learned
8. Heiner, S., Exploiting Partially Shared Ontologies for Multi-Agent Communication, In Proceedings of the 6th International Workshop on Cooperative Information Agents VI, 2002.
9. Boella, G., R. Damiano, J. Hulstijn, and L. van der Torre, A Common Ontology of Agent Communication Languages, Applied Ontology, (2): 217–265, 2007.
10. Sosa, V. J., M. Bravo, J. Pérez, and A. Díaz, An Ontological Approach for Translating Messages in E-Negotiation Systems, In Proceedings of the 7th International Conference on Electronic Commerce and Web Technologies EC-Web, Krakow, Poland, 2006.
11. Bravo, M., J. Pérez, J. Velázquez, V. Sosa, A. Montes, and M. López, Design of a Shared Ontology Used for Translating Negotiation Primitives. International Journal of Web and Grid Services, Vol. 2, No. 3, pp. 237–259, 2006.

70

Requirements Modeling with Agent Programming

Aniruddha Dasgupta, Aneesh Krishna and Aditya K. Ghose

Abstract

Agent-oriented conceptual modeling notations are highly effective in representing requirements from an intentional stance and answering questions such as what goals exist, how key actors depend on each other, and what alternatives must be considered. In this chapter, we review an approach to executing i* models by translating these into set of interacting agents implemented in the CASO language and suggest how we can perform reasoning with requirements modeled (both functional and non-functional) using i* models. In this chapter we particularly incorporate deliberation into the agent design. This allows us to benefit from the complementary representational capabilities of the two frameworks.

Keywords Early-phase requirements engineering · BDI · i* · Agentspeak, Constraints · Softgoal

1. Introduction

The early phase of requirements engineering [12] is usually done informally, possibly with the help of informal diagrammatic notations. i* [15] is one such notation. It supports the modeling of stakeholders, their goals, the intentional dependencies that exist in the organization, as well as the reasoning each actor goes through while attempting to achieve its goals. As problems grow in size and complexity, the need for formal analysis during the early requirements engineering (RE) phase may increase. Hence it is often desirable to include mechanisms which allow simulations of different scenarios which would be useful in analyzing its properties and could serve as a decision support tool. However, formal support for the early-phase RE has been relatively sparse. Formal Tropos [5] adds model checking support for i*s Strategic Dependency diagrams, while another approach [17] uses the ConGolog [7] action programming language to animate and verify i* models. Here the i* framework is used to model the environment of the system-to-be, analyze the dependencies among the actors in the environment, explore alternative system configurations, and the rationale behind agent processes and design choices, while ConGolog is used to formally specify and analyze agent behavior described informally in i*. Lapouchnian et al. in [11] presents an agent-oriented requirements engineering approach that combines informal i* models with formal specifications written in the CASL language [10]. A methodology for the combined use of i* and CASL is proposed and applied to a meeting scheduling process specification. Co-evolution of i* models with 3APL is described in [9] where agent programs are concurrently maintained and updated. In another notable system called SNet [6], extended i* diagrams are automatically translated into executable ConGolog programs in inter-organizational networks in business process management. One major drawback of most of the existing approaches is that the agents themselves are limited in the kinds of choices they

Aniruddha Dasgupta, Aneesh Krishna and Aditya K. Ghose • Decision System Laboratory, School of Computer Science and Software Engineering, University of Wollongong, Wollongong, NSW, Australia.

G.A. Papadopoulos et al. (eds.), *Information Systems Development*, DOI 10.1007/b137171_70,
© Springer Science+Business Media, LLC 2009

are able to make during a simulation. During a particular simulation run, the agents simply commit reactively to the choices required by the design of the agent network and do not themselves engage in deliberation about what the most appropriate course of action might be. It is to be noted that SNet [6] also uses softgoals to model alternates in ConGolog; however, our approach uses the technique of BDI [14] agent programming with CASO [2], which incorporates constraints into a reactive BDI agent programming language that may lead to better expressive capabilities as well as more efficient computation. This work presents an agent-oriented requirements engineering approach that combines informal i* models with formal specifications written in the CASO language which is an agent programming language with logic-based formalism. This extends and builds upon our earlier work on co-evolution of i* model and CASO agent programs [3] and [4]. Unlike most of the other approaches we particularly focus on modeling non-functional requirements also known as softgoals. We use CASO to incorporate preferences or soft constraints to map to the softgoals in i* model which are used as selection criteria. A methodology for the combined use of i* and CASO is proposed and applied to a meeting scheduling process specification. Since fully developed CASO agent programs are executable, CASO system specification can be validated by simulation. The goal of our approach is to devise a method for the analysis and validation of requirements models represented in i* with CASO.

The remainder of this chapter is organized as follows. Section 2 gives some background i* and CASO. Section 3 shows how CASO is used to incorporate user preferences and Section 4 discusses how softgoals in i* can be extended to include some measurable metrics. Section 5 describes how i* and CASO can be combined by a set of mapping rules and discusses the co-evolution of these two models. Section 6 uses a meeting scheduler system to discuss the methodology and shows by examples, how one can benefit from combining the two frameworks. Finally, concluding remarks are presented in the last section.

2. Background

We briefly provide an overview of the i* and CASO in this section. Considerable detail has been omitted in this section due to space limitations but examples and full versions of the text can be found in [15] and [2].

2.1. The i* Framework

The i* framework [15] for agent-oriented conceptual modeling was designed primarily for early-phase requirements engineering. An i* model consists of two main modeling components: the Strategic Dependency (SD) Model and the Strategic Rationale (SR) Model. The SD diagram consists of a set of nodes and links. Each node represents an actor, and each link between the two actors indicates that one actor depends on the other for something in order that the former may attain some goal. The depending actor is known as depender, while the actor depended on is known as the dependee. The SD diagram represents the goals, task, resource, and softgoal dependencies between actors. There are four types of dependencies in i* – goal dependency, task dependency, resource dependency, and softgoal dependency. The notion of softgoals (quality goals) is related to the notion of non-functional requirements [1]. Softgoals are the goals that do not have a clear-cut satisfaction condition. Each contribution link toward a softgoal is characterized by a label that specifies the contribution type and strength. The positive contribution types for softgoals are HELP (positive but not by itself sufficient to meet the higher goal), MAKE (positive & sufficient), SOME + (partial positive contribution), and ? (unknown). The dual negative types are HURT, BREAK, and SOM, respectively.

2.2. CASO

CASO (Constraint AgentSpeak with Objectives) [2] is a programming language based on the popular BDI (belief-desire-intention) language AgentSpeak [13]. It incorporates constraints and objectives into the symbolic approach of BDI model. CASO is based on a logical formalism and is very expressive. It can be well adapted to the early-design stages of system development, when detailed alternative process designs have to be specified and need to be compared. CASO incorporates constraint solving and optimization (CSOP) techniques where the optimization is based on the objective function (softgoal). An agent program in CASO consists of a set of beliefs B, a set of constraints C, an objective function O, a set of events E, a set of intention I, a plan library P, a constraint store CS, an objective store OS, and three selection functions S_E, S_P and, S_I to select an event, a plan, and an intention, respectively, to process and n_p and n_i are parameters which denote the number of steps to look-ahead for plan and intention selection respectively. Transition of agent program to process events depends on the event triggers. An event trigger, t, can be addition ($+$) or removal ($-$) of an achievement goal ($\pm!gi$) or a belief($\pm$ bi). The CASO interpreter manages set of events, a constraint store, an objective store, and a set of intentions with three selection functions. The usefulness of using preferences comes when a CASO agent has to perform an option selection operation in choosing a particular plan to pursue.

3. Modeling Softgoals as Preferences in i*

In order to decide among different courses of action, it is important to rank them according to some measure of utility. This decision involves the categorization of the softgoals according to the importance to the system. We extend the approach put forward in [8] for goal analysis in which simple preference scores are given to softgoals based on the contributions. A value of 1 is added for each positive contribution to a preference, 0 to each unmarked preference, and -1 for each negative contribution to a preference. Note that these numbers are arbitrary and depends on the modeler who may wish to give any other weights depending on the domain requirements. It is to be noted that although softgoal decomposition is possible, we are only concerned about the lowest level of softgoal decompositions here. Using this notion we observe that in Fig. 70.1 which describes the Meeting Initiator (MI) agent, using the task *UseMeetingScheduler* is going to have a positive contribution (value of 1) toward the softgoal *MinimizeEffortSubsequent* and the task *ScheduleManually* is going to have a negative contribution (value of -1) toward the same softgoal.

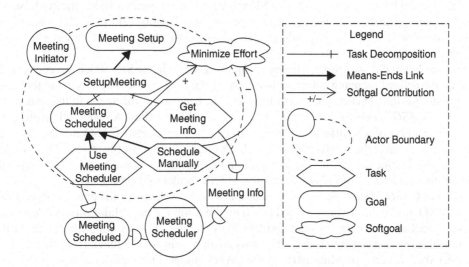

Figure 70.1. SR diagram for meeting initiator agent.

If there are many softgoals in the system say p1, p2 p3 and tasks T1, T2, T3, and T4 then i* could be extended to incorporate a preference value associated with each softgoal. We annotate each softgoal with a weight (say between 0 and 1) such that p1 = 0.5, p2 = 0.7, and p3 = 0.7. Let us further assume that the tasks have contribution toward each softgoal as given in Table 70.1.

Table 70.1. Task-softgoal contribution.

Task	p1	p2	p3
T1	3	0	−1
T2	2	1	1
T3	−1	2	0
T4	1	1	1

Now if we further assume that each of the tasks T1, T2, T3, and T4 are alternate ways of achieving the same goal, then using simple weighted sum for calculating the task contribution values (ConVal) toward all the softgoals, we get the following values for each task:

$$ConVal(T1) = 3*0.5 + 0*0.7 + (−1)*0.7 = 0.8$$
$$ConVal(T2) = 2*0.5 + 1*0.7 + 1*0.7 = 2.4$$
$$ConVal(T3) = −1*0.5 + 2*0.7 + 0*0.7 = 0.9$$
$$ConVal(T4) = 1*0.5 + 1*0.7 + 1*0.7 = 1.9$$

4. A Methodology for Combined Use of the i* and CASO Frameworks

Our methodology for the combined use of i* and CASO frameworks includes six steps described below.

1. *Building the strategic Dependency Model (SD) for the System.* The analyst develops a SD model that specifies the agents, roles, positions, and the intentional dependency.
2. *Building the Strategic Rationale Model (SR) for the System.* The analyst further analyzes the requirements of the system based on the developed SD model, focusing on identifying the goals, softgoals, and tasks to be accomplished inside agents. It also specifies the decompositions of the tasks/goals, and the contributions to softgoals. The dependency relationships will be specified between nodes inside the related agents.
3. *Developing the Initial CASO Model.* The analyst maps elements in the SR model into entities in the CASO model using the defined mapping rules and builds the initial CASO model by specifying the actions, tasks, softgoals, plans, the initial beliefs and constraints, and the behavior of the agents in the system.
4. *Validating the CASO Model by Simulation.* The analyst evaluates the CASO model through simulation. Given a specification of an initial state for the system, the developed CASO model will be simulated using the interpreter and the results are used to check the correctness of the model. Then, we identify the shortcomings and refine the CASO model based on the results of the evaluation. This step will help the analyst find those mistakes and revise the annotated SR model in the next step.
5. *Refining i* and CASO Models Based on Validations Results.* Whenever the analyst observes that the i* model or CASO models has to be modified based on the results of the validation step, he will refine both the CASO model and the corresponding part of the i* model. Also by communicating with the client about the current i* and CASO models, the analyst can obtain the feedback from the client and revise the i* model and the corresponding parts of the CASO model. This brings out new specification of the system of interest. Another case is when the analyst needs to add new features into the designed system after he finds some missing requirements have to be modeled, such as loops, exogenous actions, etc. He must modify the i* model and the corresponding part of the CASO model to ensure consistency between these two models.
6. *Producing the Requirements Analysis Document.* The models and specifications are collected in a document with appropriate explanations and discussion. The results of simulation and verification are also described.

5. Case Study: Meeting Scheduling Process

In this section, our methodology for the combined use of i* and CASO frameworks will be applied. This case study concerns a process that is used to support the scheduling of meetings. The idea for the example comes from [16] which gives the details of the meeting scheduling process. The interested reader may refer to the original work to get an overview of how i* has been used to model the meeting scheduling process.

5.1. Building i* Models for Meeting Scheduler

Figure 70.1 (in Section 3) shows the strategic rational (SR) model of the actor Meeting Initiator. We will use this actor to describe our combined methodology of using i* and CASO. A Strategic Dependency (SD) model of this meeting scheduling process is shown in Fig. 70.2. which was originally presented in [16].

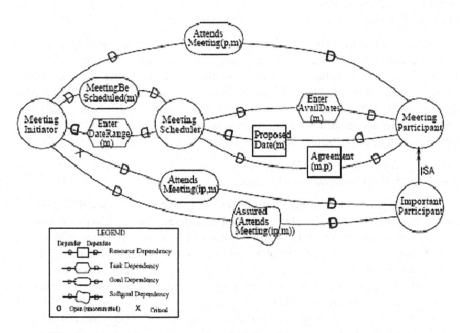

Figure 70.2. SD diagram for meeting scheduling with computer-based scheduler.

5.2. Developing the Initial CASO Model

A first step in developing the CASO model is to define a mapping from i* to CASO. For sake of continuity, we provide the results from the earlier work [3] where this mapping was initially defined. A multi-agent system (MAS) is defined as a pair {Agents, ESA} where Agents = a_1 ..., a_n, each a_i is a CASO agent and ESA is a specially designated environment simulator agent implemented in CASO. ESA holds the knowledge about the actions that might be performed by actors in SD model and the possible environment transformation after the executions of those actions. The environment agent can verify fulfillment properties such as creation conditions, invariant conditions, and fulfillment conditions of those actions associated with each agent. While ESA is a CASO agent, it must be provided with necessary beliefs as well as the plans. The context of the plans determines the constraints that must hold and actions in the body are how to react to the situation.

The agents in the MAS are Meeting Scheduler, Meeting Participant, and Meeting Initiator. We map the edges and nodes for each agent from the SR diagrams for each actor which defines the goal, task, and resource dependencies into CASO plans. It is to be noted here that besides the four agents, the ESA is also supplied by the analyst of the system (not shown here) which monitors all of the actions/tasks performed by each agent, all of the messages exchanged and all of the beliefs communicated by individual agents for consistency and constraint violations. In CASO we use decision-theoretic planning which investigates alternatives with the aim of finding the best solution in terms of some measure of utility. For this purpose a softgoal is given a numeric value, which can then be incorporated into the utility computation. The mapping of softgoals in i* to the soft constraints extended CASO model as described earlier is quite straightforward. The option selection function S_O determines the particular plan to follow in case there are alternatives by calculating the task contribution toward each softgoal.

Let N_G, N_T, and N_R are goal, task, and resource node, respectively, in SR and SD diagrams. Given two goal predicate symbols, goal, task, a belief predicate symbol resource and a term t: !goal(t) is a valid goal iff t N_G; !task(t) is also a valid goal iff t N_T; resource(t) is a valid belief atom iff t N_R. Given four action predicate symbols, *RequestAchieve*, *RequestPerform*, *RequestResourse*, *Supply* and a term t:

RequestAchieve(t) is a valid action iff t N_G;
RequestPerform(t) is a valid action iff t N_T ;
RequestResource(t) is a valid action iff t N_R;
Supply(t) is a valid action iff t N_R.

We now briefly describe the hybrid modeling approach from the mapping rules mentioned earlier. This hybrid modeling is composed of i* model and CASO agents, that is, when we have an i* model constructed for a given system, then we can also get the CASO agents of this system using the proposed mapping rules. Our problem representation is an executable specification because it is an operational CASO programming which could therefore check the initial i* model by executing CASO agents. In this hybrid model, these two basic models, i* and CASO agents, might co-evolve. At each stage, the i* model and CASO agents are consistent. Using translation steps, they can be translated into each other. This co-evolution process will involve two aspects:

(1) *reflect the changes of i* model on CASO agents and*
(2) *reflect the changes of CASO agents on i* model.*

There are 16 categories of possible changes that may occur to i* model. These are the addition and deletion of the following eight elements: Dependencies, Tasks, Goals, Resources, Softgoals, Means-end links, task-decomposition links, and Actors. As for our work to reflect the changes of i* model to CASO program, we only put emphasis on nodes, goals, tasks, softgoals, dependencies. The changes of those nodes will also bring the changes to the links. These changes have been described in detail in [3] and are not described here for lack of space. The result of applying these rules generates the three CASO agents as mentioned above. We show the Meeting Initiator (MI) CASO agent in Fig. 70.3. Note that some of the plans that do not have any body do not exist in the actual

Beliefs
ConVal(ScheduleMeeting,=,-1).
ConVal(SchedulerScheduleMeeting,=,1).
Plans
(p1) +task((OrganizeMeeting):True ← !task(MeetingBeScheduled),
RequestAchieve(AttendMeeting).
(p2) +task(MeetingBeScheduled):True ← !task(ScheduleMeeting).
(p3) +task(MeetingBeScheduled):True ← !task(SchedulerScheduleMeeting).
(p4) +task(ScheduleMeeting):ConVal(ScheduleMeeting , >=, 0) ←.
(p5) +task(SchedulerScheduleMeeting):ConVal(SchedulerScheduleMeeting. >=, 0)
←
RequestAchieve(MeetingBeScheduled), RequestPerform(EnterDateRange).

Figure 70.3. CASO Meeting Initiator Agent.

programs. However, we show them in this figure to avoid the confusion and improve the clarity of the paper. There are five plans – p1, p2, p3, p4, and p5 as shown in the figure. There are two beliefs in the belief base of the agent which quantifies the contribution of two tasks toward the softgoals as described in Section 5. *ConVal(ScheduleMeeting, = ,−1)* signifies that the task *ScheduleMeeting* has a contribution of −1 toward all existing softgoals (here only one softgoal "minimize effort" exits without any weight associated with it). Similarly, *ConVal(SchedulerScheduleMeeting, = ,1)* implies that the task *SchedulerScheduleMeeting* has a contribution of +1. Now, plans p4 and p5 which describe the alternates that MI can choose from has constraints as the context of the plans. In plan p4, the context *ConVal(ScheduleMeeting,•, 0)* means that this plan will be pursued if and only if the task contribution of *ScheduleMeeting* is • 0. In our example, the belief base has the contribution as −1 and hence this plan will not be selected. Thus plan p5, whose context clearly satisfies the constraint, will be selected as the alternate. It is to be noted here that it is purely up to the modeler to decide the context constraint of the plans when dealing with softgoals. Thus any plan context of the form *ConVal(T, cond, val)* could be used by the modeler where *T* refers to the task, *cond* could be any of $>$, $=$, •, $<$, •, and *val* refers to a number. Thus CASO captures the softgoal contribution of each task into its plans as shown here.

5.3. Validating and Refining the CASO Model by Simulation

The modeler can evaluate the CASO model through simulation. First, we specify an instance of the system and then we run a simulation. By checking and comparing the results of simulation on different system instances or initial states, we can see whether the system behaves as expected. Unforeseen occurrences may cause revisions in the model. In our example, the modeler first creates an instance of ESA, Meeting Initiator (MI) and Meeting Scheduler (MS), and several instances of Meeting Participant (MP) agents depending on the number of participants for the meeting. We summarize below the result of our simulation run under different conditions.

Scenario 1: In this scenario we give values of scheduling dates which are conflicting such that the meeting scheduler fails to find an agreeable date. The above trace shows that after obtaining available dates from participants, the MS finds out that the merged date list, which is merged from the lists of available dates of the participants and the proposed meeting dates offered by the initiator, is empty. So he cannot schedule the meeting and notifies the initiator of his failure. This shows that the specification produces the expected behavior in this case. We also make changes to the plan such that MI now decides to do schedule meeting manually. Since no automated MS is needed we compare the information exchanged among the agents in the automated case with the manual case. By comparing the two efforts, one can arrive at an optimal number, n, of meeting participants which signifies that manual scheduling may be better in case the number of participants is • n.

Scenario 2: Here we give values of scheduling dates which are not conflicting such that the meeting scheduler is able to find an agreeable date. We let MS agent a date given the initial dates as obtained from the MP agents. However, while MS is trying to find a date, we deliberately change one of the available dates (beliefs) for one of the MPs (say MP1). Meanwhile MI may find the particular date as suitable and sends it back to all the MPs for acceptance. MP1 rejects this date as it conflicts with its belief and send this information as a new event to the MI agent. MI now sends this information to all other MPs and starts to find another agreeable slot. This simulation shows that MI may still be trying to find an agreeable slot with the initial available date set even though an available date has changed in MP1. One way to remodel the system would be to send the new condition immediately to the MI as a new event so that MI is able to do a belief revision and abandon its current intention and start working with the new set of available dates. This kind of scenario is not captured in i* but is captured quite well using CASO.

Scenario 3: Here we try out scheduling multiple meetings with the same set of participants which result in one of the meetings being scheduled and the other fail. The CASO model is certainly helpful for modeling repetitive processes, complex tasks, goals, and even dependencies. Also in the initial SR model, the possibility of failing to achieve a goal is not clearly shown, but in the CASO model, this is handled. Moreover the CASO model gives hints about how to achieve the softgoals using quantitative modeling. However, the softgoal *LowEffort* is not mentioned anywhere in the CASO program but only the total contribution of the tasks toward all the softgoals are shown here. Thus the two models really complement each other well.

5.4. Refining i* and CASO Models Based on Validation Results

The first five steps described in Section 4 will need to be repeated if errors are found or if aspects of the i* model and CASO model do not satisfy the clients needs. Based on the CASO model and simulation experiments, if the i* model lacks some part of the desired requirements, modifications to the i* model will be performed. Similarly if the CASO model needs to specify additional details or aspects of the i* model, modifications to the CASO model will be made. Once a satisfactory model of the required system has been developed, a requirements specification document is produced. In our example, in scenario 2 of the previous section, we see that if one of the MPs has one of the date changed, the MS has to compute a new schedule again. The modeler may choose to put a constraint into the MPs such that they cannot change the available dates, once they have sent it to the MS. This refinement process could be applied to both i* and CASO and again the simulation can be run to see if this refinement is reflected into the models.

6. Conclusion

In this chapter, we review an approach to executing i* models by translating these into set of interacting agents implemented in the CASO language and suggest how we can perform reasoning with the requirements modeled (both functional and non-functional) using i* models. In this chapter we particularly incorporate deliberation into the agent design. The methodology allows the requirements engineer to exploit the complementary features of the two frameworks to develop better models of the application of interest and produce requirements specifications that fulfill the client's goals. A CASO model can be used both as a requirements analysis tool and as a formal high-level specification for a MAS that satisfies the requirements because it is possible to produce a high-level, formal model of the MAS right from the i* diagrams. Our work particularly focuses on modeling alternatives using softgoals which is different from most other approaches where softgoals and softgoal dependencies are abstracted out from SR diagrams before annotations are introduced and softgoal nodes are dropped from the i* diagrams along with the accompanying contribution links. We can analyze the system behavior and especially reason with the alternates, using real-life examples which is otherwise not possible by only looking at the i* model and CASO agents separately. Using the CASO interpreter, one can run this high-level model of the system on some sample environment/agent parameters and determine if the behavior of the program corresponds to the expected behavior of the system-to-be. If discrepancies are found, they can be analyzed and appropriate changes can be made to the original SR diagram. Due to the tight mapping between SR diagrams and the CASO models, it is easy to find parts of the SR diagram that are related to specific parts of the CASO program and vice versa. Using this technique one can specify requirements, define architecture, model behavior as well as perform simulation. Our future work is to build an automated tool which can help toward achieving this exercise.

References

1. L. Chung, B. A. Nixon, E. Yu, and J. Mylopoulos. Non-Functional Requirements in Software Engineering. Kluwer Academic Publishers, Boston, 2000.
2. A. Dasgupta, and A. K. Ghose. CASO: A framework for dealing with objectives in a constraint-based extension to Agentspeak(L). In Proceedings of the 2006 Australasian Computer Science Conference, 2006, pp. 121–126.

3. A. Dasgupta, A. Krishna, and A. K. Ghose. Co-evolution of agent-oriented conceptual models and CASO agent programs. In IEEE/WIC/ACM International Conference on Intelligent Agent Technology, Hong Kong, China (IAT'06), 2006, pp. 686–689.

4. A. Dasgupta, A. Krishna, and A. K. Ghose. Agent based executable conceptual models using i* and CASO. In Proceedings of ER Workshops, NZ, 2007. pp. 276–285.

5. A. Fuxman, R. Kazhamiakin, M. Pistore, and M. Roveri. Formal Tropos: language and semantics. 2003.

6. G. Gans, M. Jarke, G. Lakemeyer, and D. Schmitz. Deliberation in a metadatabased modeling and simulation environment for inter-organizational networks. Information Systems, 30(7), pp. 587–607, 2005, Elsevier Science Ltd.

7. G. D. Giacomo, Y. Lesperance, and H. J. Levesque. Congolog, a concurrent programming language based on the situation calculus. Artificial Intelligence, 121, pp. 109–169, 2000.

8. B. Hui, S. Liaskos, and J. Mylopoulos. Requirements analysis for customizable software goals-skills-preferences framework. In International Requirements Engineering Conference, RE (2003). IEEE, 2003, pp. 117–126.

9. A. Krishna, Y. Guan, and A. K. Ghose. Co-evolution of i* models and 3apl agents. In Sixth International Conference on Quality Software (QSIC'06), 2006, pp. 117–124.

10. A. Lapouchnian. Modeling mental states in requirements engineering an agent-oriented framework based on i* and CASL. MSc Thesis, York Univeristy, Canada, 2004.

11. A. Lapouchnian, and Y. Lesperance. Modeling mental states in the analysis of multiagent systems requirements. In Proceedings of the Fifth International Joint Conference on Autonomous Agents and Multiagent Systems(AAMAS 2006). ACM, New York, USA, pp. 241–243.

12. B. Nuseibeh, and S. Easterbrook. Requirements engineering: a roadmap. In Proceedings of 22nd International Conference on Software Engineering-Future of SE Track, June 4–11, 2000, Limerick, Ireland, pp. 35–46.

13. A. Rao. Agentspeak(L): BDI agents speak out in a logical computable language. In Agents Breaking Away: Proceedings of the 7th European WS on Modelling Autonomous Agents in a Multi-Agent World. Springer, Berlin, 1996.

14. A.S. Rao and M. Georgeff. BDI agents: from theory to practice, In Proceedings of First International Conference on Multi-Agent Systems (ICMAS-95), San Francisco, 1995, pp. 312–319.

15. E. Yu. Modelling strategic relationships for process reengineering, PhD Thesis. University of Toronto, Canada, 1995.

16. E. Yu. Towards Modelling and Reasoning Support for Early-Phase Requirements Engineering. In Proceedings of the 3rd IEEE International Symposium on Requirements Engineering (RE'97), Washington D.C., USA, January 6–8, pp. 226–235, 1997.

17. X. Wang and Y. Lesperance. Agent-oriented requirements engineering using ConGolog and i*. In Proceedings of the 3rd International Bi-Conference Workshop AOIS-2001, 59–78, iCue Publishing, Berlin, 2001.

71

BPMN, Toolsets, and Methodology: A Case Study of Business Process Management in Higher Education

Balbir S. Barn and Samia Oussena

Abstract

This chapter describes ongoing action research which is exploring the use of BPMN and a specific toolset – Intalio Designer to capture the "as is" essential process model of part of an overarching large business process within higher education. The chapter contends that understanding the efficacy of the BPMN notation and the notational elements to use is not enough. Instead, the effectiveness of a notation is determined by the notation, the toolset that is being used, and methodological consideration. The chapter presents some of the challenges that are faced in attempting to develop computation independent models in BPMN using toolsets such as Intalio Designer^{TM}.

Keywords BPMN · Process modelling · Process management · Methodology

1. Introduction

Business process modeling is experiencing a resurgence of activity and its importance to the successful deployment of IT systems is now being again widely recognized. This is the so-called 'third wave' of business process activity coined by Smith and Fingar [21] which follows on from previous business process modeling initiatives. The first wave of business process thinking originates back to seminal papers published by Davenport and Short [6] and Hammer [10] where process innovation was achieved by re-engineering organizations by focusing on a complete re-design of processes in order to achieve dramatic performances [23]. While there was some success, high failure rates of 50–70% [10] meant that this clean slate approach was subsequently questioned. The second wave of business process activity sometimes called X-engineering focused on processes that cut across functions rather than the machine metaphor leading to functional silos traditionally adopted by organizations. This second wave was aimed at continuous, incremental change rather than the radical approaches adopted in the first wave.

The third wave of business process modeling initiatives [21] is a return to business process modeling where organizations will rapidly adapt a business process to address a new need, measure the performance of the new business process, and then make further changes to the business process to optimize the performance of the process – business process management (BPM). Thus BPM is not just about the past; it is also about the future. In order to make this happen, important technologies need to be in place. These technologies will enable processes to be designed, implemented, executed, and evaluated (from a performance perspective) and then changed in real time on business management servers. A key aspect is thus the notion of a model that is the process definition (and thereby its documentation) and its execution specification. BPM technical infrastructure includes standards for notations for business process modeling,

Balbir S. Barn • Middlesex University, London, UK.   **Samia Oussena** • Thames Valley University, London, UK.

G.A. Papadopoulos et al. (eds.), *Information Systems Development*, DOI 10.1007/b137171_71,
© Springer Science+Business Media, LLC 2009

standards for translation of models into executable languages, and the building of systems from multiple process definitions. The last 2 years have seen the Object Management Group – authors of the Unified Modeling Language (UML) – publish the Business Process Modeling Notation BPMN 1.0 standard [4] which includes mappings to the execution language BPEL4WS [1] itself, a unification of multiple approaches to process execution. Alongside this notion of an executable business process model (from analysis to design) is the emergence of service-oriented architecture [7, 15] leading to a move toward a stronger focus on new systems development and application integration led by business process modeling [9]. Correspondingly then, there has been the emergence of new forms of toolset – BPM tools that are model based and allow a process to be taken from analysis through to execution in a single environment. These toolsets are being billed as key disruptive technologies for organizations to use in managing change.

Recently, higher education (HE) in the United Kingdom has seen a significant level of interest in process mapping. This has been reflected in the range of activities that have been scheduled in order to better understand the domains with HE. For example, there are projects funded by the Joint Information Systems Committee (JISC) in the United Kingdom that are mapping timetabling requirements, course validation (see later), customer relationship management systems, and many more. The need to develop process maps of key functional areas within HE has placed a need for a greater understanding of the potential role of BPMN as a standard that can help document such processes in HE.

2. Motivation for This Chapter

Business Process Modeling Notation (BPMN) has been the recipient of considerable recent research, particularly in the efficacy of the notation (see Section 3), but what has not received as much attention is the usage of the notation in conjunction with implementations of BPMN and the use of methods and techniques. Specifically, there is relatively little evaluation of the effectiveness of BPMN from analysis through to implementation using a BPM toolset to meet the needs of the third wave of business process management.

This chapter thus sets out to provide experimental data of the use of BPMN to implement a business process using an open source BPM toolset. Section 3 provides a review of relevant recent literature around BPMN. Section 4 describes the methodology adopted for this research and provides details of the case study on which this chapter is based. Given that the nature of the research approach is partially action research, the challenges and issues raised by an earlier stage of this research are introduced. Section 4 presents an evaluation of the results of our use of BPMN and finally Section 5 concludes the chapter with key recommendations, lessons learnt, and an outline of future research.

3. Background and Related Work

The focus of this chapter is the efficacy of Business Process Modeling Notation to support the needs of process-driven model-based approaches to systems implementation. The review of relevant literature is constrained by that viewpoint.

The history of business process modeling presents a cornucopia of modeling approaches, notations, and tools. A survey by Knutilla et al. [13] provides an example of the notations that existed when process modeling was a central tenet of business analysis activity. Historically process modeling notations have included IDEF0, petri-nets, Merise, and UML activity diagrams. But it is only recently (ratified by the OMG in 2006) that the Business Process Modeling Notation (BPMN) [4, 3] has emerged as probably the most important standard for describing business processes. A recent inspection of the OMG web site indicates that there are 44 implementations of BPMN [3], with six further planned, suggesting that the IT industry is aligning with the new standard.

While BPMN would appear to have its origins driven by the need to have a visual representation that could be used alongside executable descriptions of business processes – BPEL [1] – the goals of the BPMN designers are quite emphatically aimed at the business environment as well as at technology implementation. Thus the notation and the specification provide a distinction between a core set of notations and an extended set. The core set of notations provides a lightweight introduction to BPMN for capturing and describing analysis models (essentially flow charts of activity) and is expected to be used by business analysts and the like. The extended notation provides more complex capability which approximates to programming language constructs and is aimed at mapping to an execution layer (targeted to be the BPEL4WS specification). For description of the notation, the reader is directed to the full BPMN specification [4].

Currently there are 44 implementations of BPMN and as the BPMN specification does not mandate how diagrams should be stored electronically, the tools implementing BPMN have chosen to store diagrams in different proprietary standards or they have chosen to translate the diagrams into a BPEL model. This has the potential to have a negative impact on the widespread use of BPMN and goes against some of the key divers for initiating the BPMN standardization process. The OMG is now addressing this issue with the development of a Business Process Definition Meta model that will allow the translation of BPMN diagrams into an XML model interchange format defined by the OMG.

Given the size of the BPMN specification, research has largely focused on the notation and its efficacy. In particular the expressiveness of BPMN was subject to an examination by Recker et al. [19] using the so-called BWW representational model developed by Wand and Weber [24] based on an ontology originally defined by Bunge [5]. The notation set was reviewed from perspectives of construct deficits (lack of notation support for modeling requirement), construct excesses (notations which may not be needed), and construct overloads (notation for which there are multiple meanings). While the research indicated that not all theoretical problems were seen as critical, some issues identified by the research were a lack of business rules, a lack of a structuring capability, and ambiguity around the definitions of Lane and Pool constructs. Further research by Muehlen and Recker [26] explored the subset of notations actually used based on empirical study of BPMN models derived from the Internet. While this research provides an interesting study of constructs that must be used in conjunction there are several shortcomings, for example, the semantics of the models are not part of the analysis – the notational elements are simply counted; the core elements identified also appear to be nothing more than simple flowcharting – the original purpose of BPMN seems to have been discarded.

Studies of uses of BPMN for specific problems have been limited, but one example is the study by Muehlen and Ho [25] which explored the use of BPMN to the re-design of service management process in a truck dealership. Some of the observations noted in this study, for example, the deliberate misuse of constructs to help in explanation of models, are also noted by the research described in this chapter.

Evaluations of BPMN from a tools' perspective in the academic literature have also been limited. A significant source of toolset evaluation has been the commercial sector – Bruce Silver, in conjunction with the BPMinstitute.org, has published a series of reports on a number of leading commercial vendors of BPMN toolsets. Each report provides a detailed description of the toolset but there is lack of consistency in approaches between reports on the toolsets so it is difficult to make effective comparisons based on this secondary research. Tool evaluation is important, as noted by Recker et al.,

'The moderating effect of tool support on the perceived criticality of identified representational deficiency aligns with previous studies (Davies et al., 2004; Green and Rosemann, 2000)'.

Thus, it is likely that perceived representations of notation deficit, excess, and overload can all be modified depending upon the toolset being used. This comment manifested itself in our use of the Intalio Designer Toolset (http://www.intalio.com). For example, while BPMN provides an exhaustive set of variants of event type, Intalio has chosen to limit the number of event types and so reduce the notation excess issues reported by Recker et al.

In summary then, BPMN provides a more abstract representation (and ostensibly more usable) of process models while still supporting an implementation requirements. The notation currently is large, with redundancy, overloading, and has gaps notably in the area of business rules support and data representation. These issues present challenges in its application and more experimental evaluation data are required. The impact of the selection of the toolset has further implications on these restrictions and it is these limitations that this chapter addresses in the following sections.

4. Approach Taken

The work described in this chapter refers to and follows from earlier work on process modeling, service-oriented architecture, and associated methodologies. Thus the research approach follows a conjunction of a number of research methods.

First, the work draws upon principles of action research in that we are attempting to integrate theory and practice by a process of experimentation, reflection, and iteration [14]. In this chapter we describe an implementation of a process using BPMN, whereas in an earlier iteration we implemented the same process using UML activity diagrams and BPEL. In both cases, our ongoing experiences were documented as a series of reflective blogs designed to provide us with an ongoing source of qualitative discussion.

The second research method adopted is that of case study research as there are several examples in IS research where there is evidence that case study-based methodologies are well suited for exploring business processes in an organizational setting. Examples include those described in Huang et al. [12] and Sedora et al. [20]. Case studies provide an opportunity to take an interpretivist stance on how the systems and structures in place are based on the meanings of concepts and how people use those concepts. A case study also allows in-depth exploration of issues.

Finally, it was important to provide experimental data that was derived from the implementation of the case study business process using a BPMN toolset. We chose to implement our case study process using the Intalio Designer Community Edition. This version provides full expressive model-based capability to produce BPMN diagrams which can be executed, provided enough model-based information is entered. The toolset includes a server for executing workflows of a specified process. A full description of the toolset is outside the scope of this chapter.

The action research element meant that we already had a diagrammatic description of the case study process drawn as a UML activity model. Further, as the process had already been implemented, the execution of the process was handled using BPEL and a series of WSDL services. This meant that our implementation approach was one of translating the existing process into BPMN description and then an implementation of the BPMN process within the Intalio toolset.

It is important to note that we were not attempting to make any "improvements" to the BPMN process model, that is, we were trying to describe the process from UML activity diagram to BPMN diagram "as is."

Consistent with our first iteration, we continued our efforts to adhere to model-driven architectural principles. Thus we saw the original UML model as our platform-independent model and our translation into BPMN (Intalio) as our platform-specific model.

5. Case Study

This section provides a short description of the context of the case study for which the business process modeling and subsequent application design was performed.

The e-Framework (http://www.e-framework.org) is an initiative by the UK's Joint Information Services Committee (JISC) and Australia's Department of Education, Science, and Training (DEST) to build a common approach to service-oriented architectures for education and research across a number of domain areas including course validation.

The course validation process is one of the most important business processes within Higher Education Institutions (HEIs) and between HEIs and other institutions. New courses and the continuation of existing courses are the direct outputs of this process. Activities within the validation process are knowledge centric and collaborative. Each instance of the process is a case and will focus typically on different subject domains and therefore require different knowledge bases and experts to support the process. The end result of the process is a course specification that addresses areas such as rationale, appropriateness, justification, marketing analysis, resources required, economic viability of the courses, and detailed descriptions of the courses in terms of outcomes, aims and objectives.

In this research, the purpose of the COVARM project was to define and implement the course validation business process using SOA. Systems analysis was undertaken at four institutions using a case study approach. Visual models were constructed and evaluated and an approach to synthesizing the models from each institution into a single canonical model was developed and then applied. This approach includes rules for identifying variances between processes and is described in more detail elsewhere [2]. These models were used as input to the software design and implementation stages to develop a set of software services that allowed us to automate a part of the business process.

As the overall business process was large it was necessary to decompose the process into a series of sub-processes. We used a rationale based on business events [17]. Two of the sub-processes formed the basis of the experimental data for conversion into BPMN. One such sub-process is shown in Fig. 71.2. Key points here are compactness of the diagram and the ability to capture data structural information.

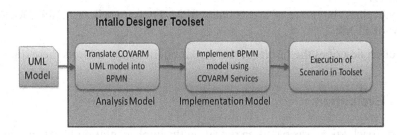

Figure 71.1. Process.

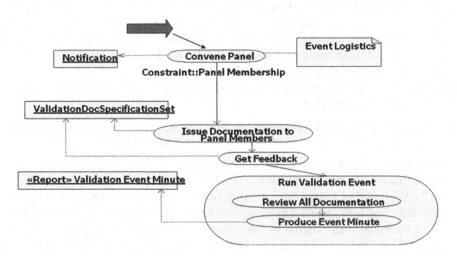

Figure 71.2. UML activity diagram for the "run validation event" sub-process.

5.1. Experimentation with UML Activity Diagrams and BPEL

Before we describe the results of this iteration aimed at implementing a BPMN process, we provide a short reflection on our earlier experiment. A more detailed description of this experiment is available at [17]. Having identified a number of sub-processes, two of the sub-processes were selected for implementation. Scenarios were used to elaborate the descriptions of the processes and to help identify WSDL services that would implement the activities in the processes. BPEL was used to provide a choreography of the implemented services that conformed to the process specification documented in UML activity diagrams. From this earlier experiment the following summary of issues emerged:

- BPEL Toolsets and their linkages with WSDL presented problems with complex data types in message flows thus it was necessary to breakdown complex structures into simple data types.
- The WSDL code generation and re-compilation with BPEL meant that there were overheads in maintaining code consistency.
- There were multiple model transforms because of our use of a number of toolsets (Rational XDE, Rational Software Architect, JBuilder, BPEL process manager). We had elected to use specific tools for specific purposes based on best in class principles. However, this meant that multiple transforms created significant overheads and opportunity for error.

Thus the purpose of experiment forming the focus of the research in this chapter was to address some of these issues which have been expressed as two research questions listed below:

Q1: How can the BPMN elements be used to in documenting common administrative processes in Higher Education?

Q2: What impact does the usage of a particular BPM Toolset such as Intalio Designer have on the effectiveness of BPMN?

The next section describes the results of the work undertaken to address these questions.

6. Results and Evaluation

While the approach taken was based on repeating the implementation of existing specified processes in BPMN there were also key model-driven principles [8, http://www.omg.org/mda/] that we wanted to apply to our implementation work – namely the various model viewpoints of computation independence, platform independence, and platform specific models.

We wanted to describe a computation independent model which captured the essential description of the process without concern of any implementation issues specific to technological platform. Our original UML model served that purpose so we expected our BPMN model to also serve that purpose. Instead we observed the issues discussed further below.

Both Muehlen et al. and Recker et al. have identified semantic issues with the use of Pools and Swim Lanes. Recker in particular, notes that

'BPMN construct Lane maps to the BWW construct *thing, class, system*. . .a question whether a Lane in BPMN model represents a specific organizational entity. . .or set of entities such as a group of activities'.

In our modeling we needed to represent concepts such as a Panel – a structure comprising of several individuals each with a specific role. A validation panel would have internal reviewers, external examiners, members of the Registry, and a Chair person. A panel, however, does not sit neatly with the definition of an organizational entity. Similarly, while University is clearly an organizational entity, roles within the university have to be modeled as external to the university because a role is a Pool within BPMN. This created the need to show a linkage between roles that the notation did not support directly. This was done by using additional semantics on the naming of Pool names. An example is shown below:

- University:Registry
- University:Computing Dept

Here the use of <<Parent-role>>:<<sub-role>> is used to model the requirement that while Registry and Computing Dept are part of the organization unit – University – they need to exchange data. A more natural usage of the BPMN specification would have been to use the notion of Pools and Swimlanes. However, using Swimlanes would not have allowed the exchange of data.

A BPMN rule is that Flow Objects (Activities, Events, and Gateways) can only be connected to each other in the same Pool using a Sequence Flow. Further a Sequence Flow cannot go across a Pool boundary. A Message Flow on the other hand can only connect Flow Objects that reside in different Pools. The naming convention and the use of multiple Pools allows us to model the situation where different roles within the same organizational unit need to exchange data.

Where a Task in one Pool needs to connect to a Task in a separate Pool (for example when the documentation set is not complete and the course team needs to update the documents) then it is necessary insert an additional coordinating Task. These Tasks add to the verbosity of the "essential" process and are thus an overhead in the computation independent model of the process in BPMN (see Fig. 71.3). The draw the essential model in BPMN we also need to capture sequence constraints across two Pools (not possible using the standard semantics). Thus it was necessary to use Link events and further naming conventions (Fig. 71.4).

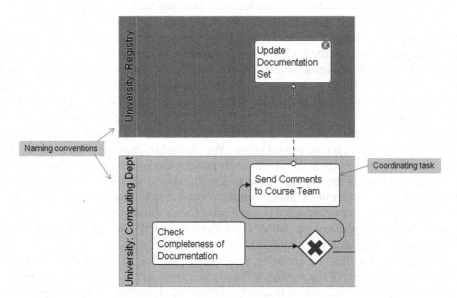

Figure 71.3. Linking pools together and the need for coordinating tasks.

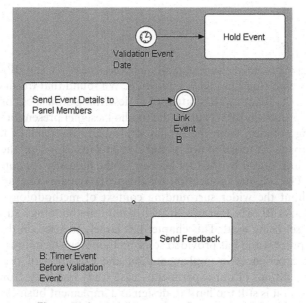

Figure 71.4. Modeling sequence flows across pools.

The use of a BPM toolset such as Intalio raises interesting issues about the nature of the documented process. For example, our goal was to capture the "essential" characteristics of the as is process – further, as this process was not implemented in any form, this process was to be documented as a *specification* business process. However, the toolset supports and implements those features of BPMN, which will support potential implementation in the future. So it is actually hard to document an essential business process in the toolset without the implementation features polluting the process model.

Activities that are jointly performed by more than one role have always been difficult to model in flowchart-based process modeling approaches. In previous research we have used stereotypes on flows between two activities (owned by two different roles) to model joint activities. Ould [16] in his work on the Role Activity Diagram (RAD) approach to process modeling repeats the same activity with a link between the two activities to indicate joint activity. More recently, Muehlen and Ho [25] places an activity over two Pools. This particular approach is not scalable and is only suitable for BPMN tools that are essentially only flowcharting tools, e.g., Visio templates. Our approach has been to document multiple roles in the same Pool to imply that all the names roles in the Pool jointly participate in carrying out activities. This approach also has shortcomings in that it introduces additional Pools that add yet more verbage to the essential model.

Sub-processes present further challenges to using BPMN effectively. The BPMN specification describes three types of sub-processes: embedded/re-usable/referencing. These seem to mimic the containment and assembly semantics for composition in Class or Use Case diagrams in UML. Embedded sub-processes are essentially a diagram structuring mechanism as the scope of the sub-process is the same as the containing process. Such a sub-process cannot cross a Pool boundary making them even less useful (except from a diagram handling perspective). A re-usable sub-process has its own independent existence it has its own scope/data and exhibits all the characteristics of a main process. Ideally it should be defined on a new diagram. We found that we were only using embedded processes in the same pool – i.e., for diagrammatic convenience only. Sometimes we were forced to use a sub-process simply to include a loop constraint as the Intalio Designer does not implement the BPMN specification exactly. We observe that sub-processes in Intalio are difficult to manage and use within our timescales.

We have been conscious that we are using a community edition of the Intalio Designer toolset. We also note that during the lifetime of the project, we have seen the toolset progress through multiple versions. As these versions have progressed, missing features have become available. None the less, the toolset while providing generally competent diagramming capability has several shortcomings which only really manifest themselves when moving from essential to execution models.

7. Conclusion

In this chapter we have provided a summary of our experiences in using BPMN for a complex process from reasonably complex case study in higher education. We found that during our action research, the translation of a UML activity diagram (first attempt at describing a business process) to a computation-independent model of the process in BPMN using the Intalio Designer presents a number of key challenges. These range from missing notation from the Intalio implementation (lack of timer events), the need to introduce additional "verbage" in terms of notational elements for capturing the required essential model to additional complexity introduced by the tool because of the necessity for considering implementation/execution requirements. The original motivation for this work remains relevant. The use of BPMN, its efficacy of notation without the wider surrounding context of methodology, and toolset moderation requires further research. As BPMN matures, it will require methodology support which is specific to the notation and the toolset being used. This chapter has largely focused on the capture of computation independent models of a process and has provided some methodology techniques for their capture. Future papers will describe our experiences in implementation and execution of processes within the Intalio toolset. Even given the limitations of our experiment – case study numbers, from a 3rd wave perspective, our experiences indicate that it is still too hard to design and implement business processes within a single model-driven environment.

Acknowledgements

This work has been supported by funding from JISC – Joint Information Systems Committee http://www.jisc.ac.uk. For further details of the COVARM and COVa projects see: http://covarm.tvu.ac.uk/covarm and http://samsa.tvu.ac.uk/cova

References

1. Andrews, T., Curbera, F., Dholakia, H., Goland, Y., Klein, J., Leymann, F., Liu, K., Roller, D., Smith, D., Thatte, S., Trickovic, I., and Weerawarana, S. (2003). Business Process Execution Language for Web Services. Version 1.1. BEA Systems, International Business Machines Corporation, Microsoft Corporation, SAP AG and Siebel Systems, available at: http://xml.coverpages.org/BPELv11-May052003Final.pdf
2. Barn, B.S., Dexter, H., Oussena, S., and Petch, J. (2006). An Approach to Creating Reference Models for SOA from Multiple Processes. In: IADIS Conference on Applied Computing, Spain.
3. BPM. (2005). http://www.omg.org/news/releases/pr2005/06-29-05.htm
4. BPMI.org. (2006). OMG: Business Process Modeling Notation Specification. Final Adopted Specification. Object Management Group, available at: http://www.bpmn.org
5. Bunge, M. (1997) Treatise on Basic Philosophy, Volume 3: Ontology I: The Furniture of the World, Boston: Reidel.
6. Davenport, T. and Short, J. (1990). The New Industrial Engineering: Information Technology and Business Process Redesign. Sloan Management Review, 31(4), 11–27.
7. Erl, T. (2005). Service Oriented Architecture – Concepts, Technology and Design, Englewood Cliffs, NJ: Prentice-Hall.
8. Frankel, D. (2004). Model Driven Architecture, Needham, MA: OMG Press
9. Frankel, D. (2005). Business Process Trends. BPTrends http://www.bptrends.com/publicationfiles/07%2D05%20COL%20BP%20Platform%20%2D%20Frankel%2Epdf
10. Hammer, M. (1990). Reengineering Work: Don't Automate, Obliterate. Harvard Business Review, 68(4), 104–112.
11. Hammer, M. and Champy, J. (1993). Reengineering the Corporation, A Manifesto for Business Revolution, London: Nicholas Brealey.
12. Huang, J.C., Newell, S., Poulson, B., and Galliers, R.D. (2005). Deriving Value from a Commodity Process: A Case Study of the Strategic Planning and Management of a Call Center. In: Proceedings of the Thirteenth European Conference on Information Systems (Bartmann, D., Rajola, F., Kallinikos, J.,Avison, D., Winter, R., Ein-Dor, P., Becker, J., Bodendorf, F., and Weinhardt, C., eds.), Regensburg, Germany.
13. Knutilla, A., Schlenoff, C., Ray, S., Ployak, S.T., Tate, A., Cheah, S.C., and Anderson, R.C. (1998). Process Specification Language: An Analysis of Existing Representations, National Institute of Standards and Technology (NIST), Gaithersburg (MD), NISTIT 6160
14. Lau, F. (1997). A Review on the Use of Action Research in Information Systems Studies. In: Information Systems and Qualitative Research (Lee, A.S., Liebenau, J., and DeGRoss, J.I., eds.), Berlin: Springer.
15. Ort, E. (2005). Service-Oriented Architecture and Web Services: Concepts, Technologies, and Tools. http://java.sun.com/deve loper/technicalArticles/WebServices/soa2/
16. Ould, M. (1997). Designing a Re-engineering-proof Process Architecture. Business Process Management Journal, 3(3).
17. Oussena, S. and Barn, B. (2007). Applying Component Concepts to Service Oriented Design: A Case Study. Conference: Presented at 2nd International Conference on Software and Data Technologies (ICSOFT 2007) 22–25 July 2007 Barcelona, Spain.
18. QAA: http://www.qaa.ac.uk/
19. Recker, J., Indulska, M., Rosemann, M., and Green, P. (2006). How Good is BPMN Really? Insights from Theory and Practice. In: Proceedings of the 14th European Conference on Information Systems. Association for Information Systems (Ljungberg, J. and Andersson, M., eds.), Goeteborg, Sweden, 1582–1593.
20. Sedera W., Rosemann M., and Doebeli, G. (2003). A process modelling success model: insights from a case study. In: Proceedings of the Eleventh European Conference on Information Systems (Ciborra, C.U., Mercurio, R., de Marco, M., Martinez, M., and Carignani, A., eds.), Naples, Italy.
21. Smith, H. and Fingar, P. (2003). Business Process Management: The Third Wave, Tampa, FL: Meghan-Kiffer Press.
22. UCAS: http://www.ucas.ac.uk/
23. Vidgen, R. and Wang, X. (2006). From Business Process Management to Business Process Ecosystem. Journal of Information Technology, 21, 262–271.
24. Wand, Y. and Weber, R. (1995). On the Deep Structure of Information Systems. Information Systems Journal, 5(3), 203–223.
25. Zur Muehlen, M., and Ho, D.T. (2008). Service Process Innovation: A Case Study of BPMN in Practice. In: Proceedings of the 41st Hawaii International Conference on System Sciences.
26. Zur Muehlen, M. and Recker, J. C. (2008). How Much Language is Enough? Theoretical and Practical Use of the Business Process Modeling Notation. In: Proceedings 20th International Conference on Advanced Information Systems Engineering, Montpellier, France.

72

Incorporating Spatial Data into Enterprise Applications

Pierre Akiki and Hoda Maalouf

Abstract

The main goal of this chapter is to discuss the usage of spatial data within enterprise as well as smaller line-of-business applications. In particular, this chapter proposes new methodologies for storing and manipulating vague spatial data and provides methods for visualizing both crisp and vague spatial data. It also provides a comparison between different types of spatial data, mainly 2D crisp and vague spatial data, and their respective fields of application. Additionally, it compares existing commercial relational database management systems, which are the most widely used with enterprise applications, and discusses their deficiencies in terms of spatial data support. A new spatial extension package called Spatial Extensions (SPEX) is provided in this chapter and is tested on a software prototype.

Keywords Spatial data · Enterprise applications · Line-of-business applications · Vague spatial data · Relational DBMS · Crisp spatial data

1. Introduction

The term spatial data signifies all geometric objects of different dimensions and the relations that could bind these objects together. Spatial data is, in general, divided into two parts: crisp spatial data and vague spatial data. Crisp spatial data has determinate coordinates and boundaries (districts, lakes, rivers, roads, cities, buildings, etc.), whereas vague spatial data has indeterminate ones (oceans, vegetation, English speaking population, etc.).

Enterprise applications and smaller line-of-business applications, which are categorized as information systems, mostly rely on traditional data which could be represented by text and numbers. Yet these systems could also benefit from spatial data support in order to represent some non-traditional aspects. Most enterprise applications rely on relational database management systems in order to store and manipulate their relational data. That is why it would be very useful if these database management systems get promoted from merely relational to post-relational, hence support non-traditional data like spatial data.

Both crisp and vague spatial data were analysed in this chapter, and their usage and major aspects were highlighted. We also studied existing support for spatial data in commercial DBMS and pointed out the existing lack of functionality in these systems. We deduced that providing a common storage repository and generic visualization components for all the applications that deal with spatial data saves development companies time and money which is otherwise consumed by developing custom solutions, and provides standards for everyone to follow.

Pierre Akiki and Hoda Maalouf • Department of Computer Science, Notre Dame University, Zouk Mosbeh, Lebanon.

G.A. Papadopoulos et al. (eds.), *Information Systems Development*, DOI 10.1007/b137171_72,

Major contributions in this domain can be found in [1, 2] where M. Schneider and R. Gutting studied crisp spatial data and laid the foundations for the implementation of spatial data in commercial DBMS. Although most commercial DBMS are currently natively supporting crisp spatial data, yet much work still need to be done regarding vague spatial data and 3D spatial data in general.

This chapter is divided into seven main sections. Section 2 briefly states the importance of spatial data for enterprise applications. In Section 3 we discuss spatial data support in enterprise applications. Section 4 sums up the role of the Open Geospatial Consortium (OGC) and the importance of following standards. In Section 5 we discuss different techniques for visualizing spatial data in enterprise applications. In Section 6 we elaborate on Spatial Extensions (SPEX) which is our own spatial extension package. Finally, we conclude this chapter in Section 7 and discuss the required future advancements.

2. Spatial Data Usage in Enterprise Applications

Most enterprise applications generally rely on RDBMS in order to store their relational data which is mostly composed of text and numbers. Hence one would think that text-and number-based storage would suffice for the basic functionalities required by such applications. Yet incorporating spatial data into such applications would give them new perspectives. This incorporation currently exists, however, many organizations have separated the storage of the business-related data, and the spatial data, resulting in inefficiency in several matters [3]. These inefficiencies appear mainly in the replication of data and their complicated replication schemes and most importantly the inability to perform certain types of business tasks. Due to these problems and the fact that most enterprise applications rely on RDBMS, rather than other types (object oriented, multimedia, etc.), many DBMS providers have extended their products' functionality by adding spatial data support. We will discuss this support in the following section.

3. Spatial Data Support in Commercial Relational Database Management Systems

While some DBMS do not natively provide spatial data manipulation capabilities, others do provide such functionality but merely handle basic crisp spatial data and cannot handle vague or complex crisp spatial data [1].

For instance the SQL Server 2005 SDK provides an example of how to use some of its basic functionalities in order to store spatial data. Yet, this does not provide a generic solution but merely a specific solution using a custom-made methodology, which needs to be re-implemented according to each case [4, 5]. For this reason native spatial data support has been added to SQL Server 2008.

Oracle started supporting spatial data through its spatial extension called "Oracle Spatial". Yet this support is merely restricted to 2D crisp spatial data, whereas vague spatial data and 3D spatial data are still not supported.

The spatial data types that are provided by PostgreSQL's PostGIS [6] extension are based on the OGC standards [7, 8]. PostgreSQL also provides the ability to extend the spatial operators it offers [9].

DB2 provides several spatial capabilities through its Spatial Extender. Some of these capabilities include standard-based geometry model using object-relational technology, standards-based geometry functionality, spatial indexing, etc. [10]

Finally, MySQL5 provides means for storing and manipulating 2D crisp spatial data based on the OGC standards but it neglects 3D and vague spatial data [11].

As the Table 72.1 demonstrates many commercial DBMS do support crisp spatial data, yet none of them provides native support (built in support developed by the company that owns the product) for vague spatial data. And, although some might support 3D spatial data in the sense that one can store locations on the earth's surface, similar to the GEOGRAPHY type provided by SQL Server 2008, however, none of these DBMS provides support for 3D objects.

Before RDBMSs started natively supporting spatial data, software applications used to rely on spatial data management products in order to store and manage their spatial data. Another solution was

Table 72.1. Spatial data support in commercial RDBMS [12].

	SQL Server	Oracle	MySQL	PostgreSQL	DB2
Natively supports spatial data	YES	YES	YES	YES	YES
Supports spatial indexing	YES	YES	YES	YES	YES
	R-Tree	Z-Ordering	R-Tree	R-Tree	Grid
Supports vague spatial data	NO	NO	NO	NO	NO
Natively supports 3D spatial objects	NO	NO	NO	NO	NO
Based on OGC standards	YES	YES	YES	YES	YES

to adopt an existing spatial extension package or to develop new one. A spatial extension package would extend the basic functionalities of an RDBMS in order to make it spatially enabled by supporting spatial data types and by providing the necessary spatial operations which are used to manipulate these types, in addition to the necessary spatial indexing mechanisms.

4. The Open Geospatial Consortium (OGC)

The Open Geospatial Consortium (OGC) is an international organization that is leading the development of standards for geospatial and location-based services [7]. The OGC provides common standards for developing any spatial extension package. Such standards include the implementation of a common set of methods which are required for the manipulation of spatial data, the usage of a common class hierarchy, etc. For instance, the following methods are used to test spatial relations between regions: Equal, Disjoint, Intersect, Touch, Within, Contain, Overlap, etc. And, additional methods are used to perform spatial analysis of geometries: Distance, Buffer, Intersection, Union, Difference, etc. [8]. Figure 72.1 shows a representation of the geometry class hierarchy which is proposed by the OGC.

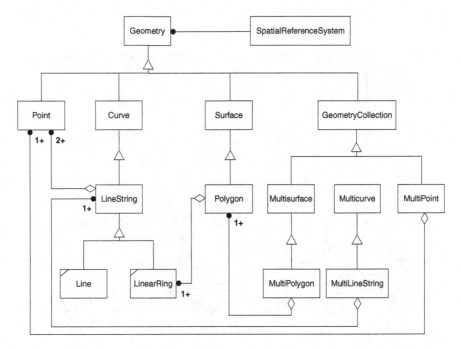

Figure 72.1. Geometry class hierarchy [7, 8].

5. Spatial Data Visualization in Enterprise Applications

Visualizing spatial data is as important as storing it in the database. Enterprise applications could rely on existing technologies in order to visualize their spatial data or they can rely on custom built visualizing controls. Existing techniques include passing spatial coordinates to existing web-based services such as Virtual Earth which could yield a map including the specified coordinates as shown in Fig. 72.2, or the usage of embedded visual components (Fig. 72.3).

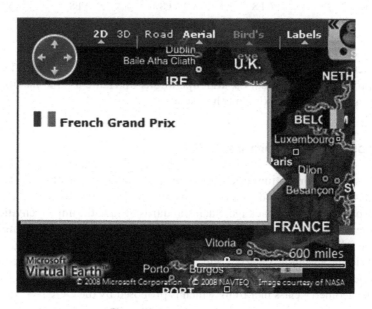

Figure 72.2. Virtual Earth result.

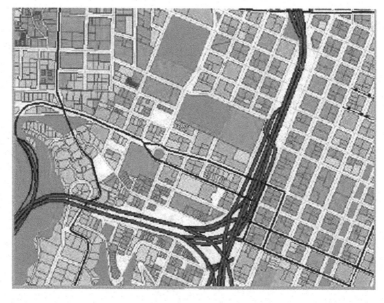

Figure 72.3. Embedded visual component

The development of new visual components might serve as solutions for specific requirements. In order to develop such components we need to rely on a robust fully featured presentation technology. Dot NET's Windows Presentation Foundation (WPF) could be considered as a good candidate for such types of components. This is because WPF allows its users to represent and manipulate vector-based shapes in addition to its capability to represent 2D and 3D geometric shapes. The development of such custom component could allow enterprise applications to host statistical maps, which are based on spatial data stored within the enterprise's relational database. Such maps could include brand sales by region, region sales per salesman, number of employees in each region, etc. Additionally, enterprises could visualize items of interest such as delivery routes, customers' addresses, etc.

6. Spatial Extensions (SPEX)

Most RDBMSs have started recently the support of 2D crisp spatial data. For example SQL Server 2005 did not natively support spatial data but this support started with SQL Server 2008. Since crisp spatial data is now being widely supported we decided to focus on vague spatial data. In this work, we have developed a spatial extension package that we called SPEX that will be used on RDBMS and could support both crisp and vague spatial data. Details on SPEX are given next.

6.1. SPEX Development Technology

The programming language chosen for the development of our proposed package SPEX is C# and the database management system is SQL Server 2008. C# was chosen due to the wide range of features which it provides. These features include the usage of the Windows Presentation Foundation (WPF) presentation subsystem in addition to the creation of CLR stored procedures, user-defined functions and user-defined types under SQL Server 2008. WPF provides SPEX with the capability of creating the necessary advanced visualization components. SQL Server 2008 in an RDBMS which currently supports crisp spatial data, making it a good candidate for a spatial extension package that would support vague spatial data as well.

6.2. SPEX Visual Components

The visual components provided by any spatial package should include the capabilities of visualizing both 2D and 3D crisp and vague spatial data. The following figures demonstrate the startup prototype component proposed by SPEX in order to use WPF to visualize spatial data which is stored inside an SQL Server database. Figure 72.4 for instance shows several crisp points and polygons that represent different Lebanese cities and districts, respectively. Figure 72.5 shows several vague regions representing different degrees of oil spills along the coast, in addition to two crisp polygons marking the coastline and the sea.

The visual components also provide the ability to manipulate the different visual spatial elements as shown in Fig. 72.6.

It is also necessary to be able to manipulate non-spatial elements. Such elements might include text and other visual elements which could be displayed on the same canvas as the spatial elements. In order to do so SPEX utilizes a visual designer called CEDAR which we designed and developed to use with enterprise application forms. This designer would allow us to manipulate both spatial and non-spatial elements and then save them side by side in a relational database. The usage of this designer is illustrated in Fig. 72.7.

Such designer could be shipped with enterprise applications to do its native job of manipulating enterprise application GUIs in addition to any non-spatial elements which exist on a spatial surface.

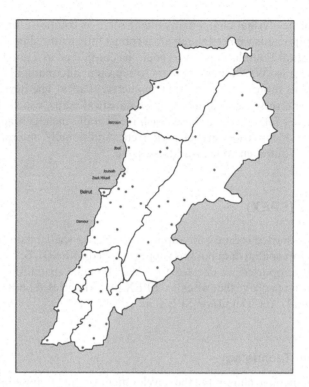

Figure 72.4. SPEX WPF canvas visualizing crisp spatial data on Lebanon's map.

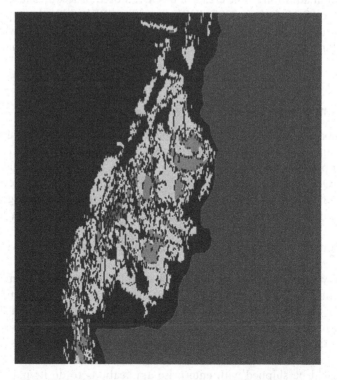

Figure 72.5. SPEX WPF canvas visualizing vague spatial data on Lebanon's map.

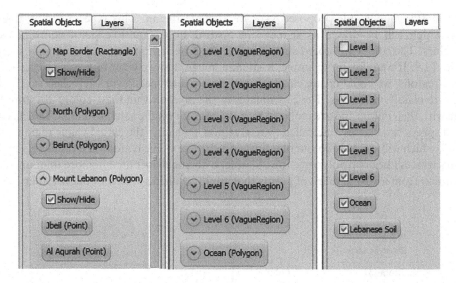

Figure 72.6. Listing of the different spatial elements on the SPEX visual canvas.

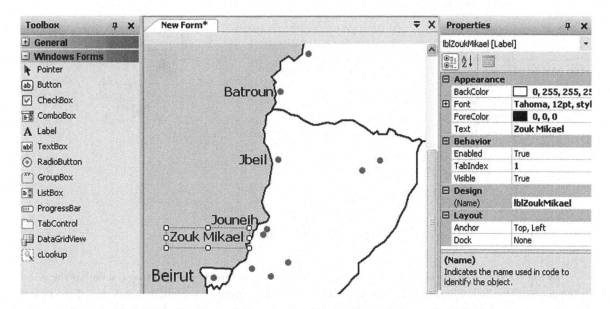

Figure 72.7. Visual designer for non-spatial objects represented alongside spatial objects.

6.3. SPEX Vague Spatial Data Support

Vague spatial data is usually modeled as raster data. This is what we followed in our proposition for storing such types of data alongside the native crisp spatial data support in SQL Server 2008.

Figure 72.8(a) models our proposed view of a vague region. This type of region does not store coordinates, which will be drawn as shapes but instead stores multiple point coordinates and their significant colors. The colors are stored since they are the criteria that are used to classify such regions as shown in Fig. 72.9. If we take, for example, a satellite image that we want to use as a basis for specifying several vague regions, we could create classification classes and specify for each class several colors that could be used to classify that class. The coordinates of the pixels within these colors are stored in a vague region along with their colors and are replaced by a single color on the satellite image. The class diagram in Fig. 72.8(a) displays two classes: one called "vague region", which is the actual vague region and the other called "color", which will store the colour of a single pixel in the vague region. The vague region differs from regular crisp surfaces like crisp polygons, for example, by being distributed in more than one place and by being constituted from a vast amount of points that could be dislocated from one another.

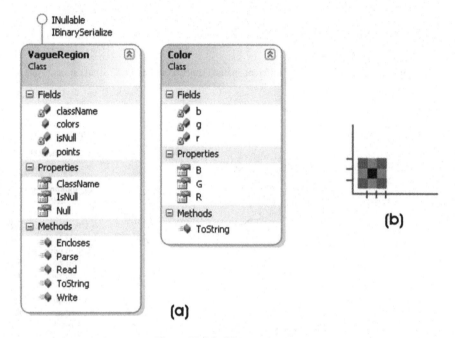

Figure 72.8.(a, b) Vague region.

In Fig. 72.8(b), a vague region is represented by different colours. If we want to test whether the point at the center actually belongs to this region, we have to test it in order to see whether it is one of the points that are stored in the region user-defined Type (UDT). After that, we must check the surrounding points to decide whether they belong to this region as well. If so we could say that our vague region encloses the point at the center.

The proposed method for storing vague spatial data as raster data is based on the fact that vague spatial regions are very interconnecting and cannot be exactly determined. Although this method works very well with small sizes of data, its drawback becomes evident when this data gets bigger. This led us to the suggestion of a new method that uses image segmentation in order to represent each vague spatial region as a crisp polygon collection. So the combination of both raster and vector representation would make a near ideal manner for storing vague spatial data that could sometimes be very interconnecting. Hence, raster would be better in case the data is very interconnecting otherwise vector representation would be better since it requires less storage space and shorter time to load.

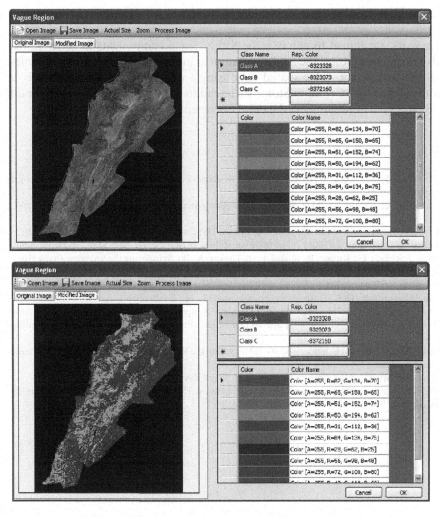

Figure 72.9. Classifying satellite images based on colours.

7. Conclusion

Even though much advancement has been made recently in the area of spatial data support in relational database management systems, yet much work still needs to be done. If we look at the entire picture of the DBMS market, we could see Relational DBMSs, object-oriented DBMSs, object relational DBMSs and Multimedia DBMSs, in addition to extensions to existing DBMSs created by the software companies that own these DBMSs or third-party companies. But what the market really lacks is a single-layered DBMS, which could support relational, object-oriented, spatial and multimedia data. Such "Common Store" could provide a major leap especially for enterprise applications which could open up towards new aspects. DBMSs should aim more towards providing native support for vague spatial data in addition to simple and complex 3D spatial objects. In this chapter we designed and implemented visualization techniques for both crisp and vague spatial data. We also suggested, designed and implemented data storage techniques for vague spatial data in relational databases. We discussed in general how enterprise applications could benefit from spatial data especially if it is stored side by side with the business data inside a relational database. We conclude by saying that whenever relational database management systems grow in terms of supporting non-traditional data, new windows will be open in the world of enterprise applications.

As future work, we intend to enhance the SPEX visual components in order to make them more generic. We also intend to continue the implementation of the SPEX vague spatial data types, especially the part concerning the storage of vague spatial data using a vector representation. Finally in order to aim more towards the idea of the "Common Store" we intend to work on other extensions for different types of non-structured data such as multimedia data and documents.

References

1. Schneider, M. (1997) Spatial Data Types for Database Systems. Finite Resolution Geometry for Geographic Information Systems, Springer-Verlag, Berlin.
2. Hartmut Gutting, R., and Schneider, M. (1995) Realm-Based Spatial Data Types: The ROSE Algebra, VLDB Journal, 4(2), 243–286.
3. Betlehem, A.W. (2005) Enterprise Wide Integration of Spatial Data into Core Business Practices, Proceedings of SSC.
4. Szalay, A., Fekete, G., and Gray, J. (2005) HTM Interface Release 4, SQL Server 2005 SDK – Spatial Sample.
5. Szalay, A., Gray, J., Fekete, G., Kunszt, P., Kukol, P., & Thakar, A. (2005) Indexing the Sphere with the Hierarchical Triangular Mesh, SQL Server 2005 SDK – Spatial Sample
6. PostGIS http://postgis.refractions.net/
7. Open Geospatial Consortium (OGC). http://www.opengeospatial.org
8. Elmasri, R., and Navathe, S. (2007) Fundamentals of Database Systems Fifth Edition, Addison Wesley, Reading, MA.
9. Rigaux, P., Scholl, M., and Voisard, A. (2002) Spatial Databases with Applications to GIS, Morgan Kaufman Publishers, San Fransisco, CA.
10. Adler, D. (2001) IBM DB2 Spatial Extender – Spatial Data within the RDBMS, Proceedings of the 27th International Conference on Very Large Data Bases.
11. MySQL Community, MySQL 5.0 Reference Manual, 2006. http://dev.mysql.com/doc/refman
12. Akiki, P. (2007) The Design and Implementation of Two Dimensional Spatial Data Types and Their Integration into a Relational Database Management System, M.S. Thesis NDU.

73

The Development of Mobile Services – The Impact of Actor Groups in the Standardization Process

Endre Grøtnes and Steinar Kristoffersen

Abstract

This chapter presents the impact of actor groups in the development of new mobile services. We have taken a micro view and collected actual data from a standardization process to contrast the general macro perspective in use. We develop four metrics: strength, openness, depth and efficiency to measure the impact of groups. Our findings indicate that contrary to popular belief the manufacturers and operators still dominate the development process. They score highest on all aspects while the application vendors score low on almost all aspects. We also find that governments and content providers are almost absent from the standards development process for new mobile services.

Keywords Actor groups · Mobile services · Standardization · Development process

1. Introduction

The telecommunication sector is one of the largest service sectors with an annual revenue of over 1 trillion USD [11] in the OECD area. During the last decade and especially since the downfall in 2000, the sector has undergone a transformation. This is most profound in the development of new mobile services and infrastructures. The 3G infrastructure has been developed in many markets, connecting the mobile infrastructure to the fixed Internet, and new enhanced handsets give the opportunity for a whole range of new Internet-related services. New and possible disruptive technologies, like VoIP, Wi-Fi and WiMax are also altering the existing landscape. Into this environment comes large actors from the IT, media and broadcasting industries as well as new actors from emerging new markets like China and South Korea. The operators, regulators and telecom vendors are striving to find their place and role in this transformed environment. What used to be a market with national monopolies, and standards that were developed by operators and regulators through the International Telecommunication Union (ITU), have now become a many-sided market where each country has many operators, the operators and vendors operate globally, and standards are developed by a multitude of standards organizations, alliances and consortia.

The changes are affecting the development of new mobile services and the constellation between the actors. One pivotal factor in this changing landscape is standards. Standards are essential for the reconfiguring of the actor constellations and the development of new mobile services [6, 9, 10, 18, 19, 20].

This chapter addresses the research question: *How do different actors influence the development of new mobile services within standardization organizations?* To address this question we have compiled a number of metrics from the involvement and contribution of actor groups within the Open Mobile Alliance, the largest standardization consortium in the mobile sector. Our findings show that the operators and

Endre Grøtnes · Department of Informatics, University of Oslo, Oslo, Norway. **Steinar Kristoffersen** · Faculty of Computer Science, Østfold University College, Halden, Norway.

G.A. Papadopoulos et al. (eds.), *Information Systems Development*, DOI 10.1007/b137171_73,
© Springer Science+Business Media, LLC 2009

manufactures have a larger impact than their numbers should indicate and that some groups like govern-ments and content providers are absent from the process. A macro perspective on the actors involvement in the development of new mobile services suggests that new actors have a large impact on the development of new mobile services [14, 15]. Our findings contradict this belief and we conclude that the "old" alliance of operators and manufacturers still dominate the process.

The rest of the chapter is structured as follows. In Section 2 a framework on group involvement in mobile service development is presented. We then present our research methods, framework and findings in the following Sections. The chapter ends with a discussion of the findings and finally draws some conclusions.

2. A Framework for Showing Standardization Involvement

Lately a theoretical perspective (framework) has been used to analyse the dynamics and changes in the mobile industry [7, 15, 20]. The framework has a macro perspective and uses some terminology like actor and actor-network from Actor-Network Theory [8], to track the different actors and the changes in the actor constellations. The framework divides the mobile industries institutional environment into the following parts (see also Fig. 73.1).

- *The Innovation system* is the interlinked network of sites, competencies, ideas and resources that over time is able to develop new services and technologies. Exploitation of the new services and technologies in a wider system is according to the framework dependent of the creation of standards.
- *The marketplace* is a set of actors that produce services or technologies by exploiting the technological potential defined within standards and technical innovations.
- *The regulatory regime* is any type of authority that can influence, direct, limit or prohibit any activity in the innovation system, the marketplace or the regulatory regime itself.

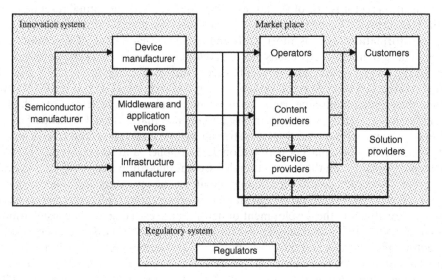

Figure 73.1. The mobile industries institutional environment with the main participants (adapted from Tilson and Lyytinen [15]).

These domains form the institutional environment in which mobile services are created, and the domains are situated around and interlinked with the standards creation regime. The standards are not merely a technical component but act as an important mechanism for coordination among the actors [7]. Yoo et al. [20] calls this network an innovation and diffusion system for mobile infrastructures.

It is possible to place the different actors in mobile services standardization into this framework. Tilson and Lyytinen [15] do this in their study of the US mobile industry, see Fig. 73.1. In the innovation system you have different types of manufacturers. This can be infrastructure, device (handset) and/or semiconductor manufacturers. The manufacturers are the traditional actors in the innovation system. With the introduction of 3G and new mobile services actors like system integrators, application providers, and middleware vendors have entered the innovation system. Thus, while the marketplace used to consist of operators and their customers new mobile services have introduced new actors like service and content providers into the marketplace. The convergence of telecommunication, data and broadcast has also triggered a convergence of the regulatory authorities in some places [3].

The above picture shows the industry participants within the institutional environments in the mobile industry. As the picture shows the constellations between the actors are many and they are interlinked. Some companies are expanding and take on more than one role. This is a macro view and gives one perspective of the involvement of the actors. With our metrics we will add a more nuanced and alternative perspective on the actors actual involvement in the standardization process since it will be based on actual contribution not mere presence.

3. Our Framework and Research Methods

The data for this chapter are from the Open Mobile Alliance (OMA) and are gathered during the period October 2006 until December 2007. The data are based on participant observation in OMA, interviews with participants and to a large extent analysis of the documents found in the OMA portal. The OMA meetings and the OMA document portal are only available for OMA members. The access to OMA and the portal was secured when a large international operator let us participate as a part of their delegation. This was cleared with the OMA staff. Participation in OMA was necessary in order to determine which standards to look at and how to find the relevant data in the OMA documents.

Finding out what factors we should develop metrics for was done by examining previous research [1, 12, 17] and talking with the OMA participants. We decided on four factors/aspects that we developed metrics for. There are of course more factors that can be measured, but for the purpose of this chapter we focussed on the following four:

- *Strength*. The number of essential IPR each company/actor group holds. This metric indicates the technical strength of a company. The more essential IPR a group has the more it can influence the technical content of a standard.
- *Openness*. The number of new work items supported by each company/actor group. This metric indicates the cooperation efforts of a company. In OMA four companies must support a proposal for a new work item, while in ITU five companies must support a proposal for a new work item. This metrics indicate how well a company cooperates with other companies in creating new work items. The more proposals it supports the more cooperative and open is that company.
- *Depth*. The number of positions each company/actor groups holds. This metric indicates the ability to steer the standardization process of a company. Holding a position as a chair, vice chair or editor of a working groups give influence in the actual shaping of a standard. A company with more positions can influence the standard setting process in more ways. The have a greater depth and reach in the way they can alter and shape the standards.
- *Efficiency*. The number of contributions each company/actor group gets approved and included in the requirement specifications. This indicates how good a company is at getting their requirements and solutions into a standard. The more contributions a company get accepted the more the end result ends up the way they want.

The first three metrics are calculated for the organization as a whole, while the number of contributions is calculated for each work item/standard individually.

Even if the data were collected for individual companies we grouped the data into groups of companies. OMA has the following categories of companies: Operators, Telecom vendors, IT vendors and others (meaning content providers, financial institutions, etc.). We took this as a starting point, but since the distinction between telecom vendors and IT vendors can be a little blurred we decided to categorize them according to if they provided handset/infrastructure or applications. This distinction is also in accordance with von Hippel [16] categorization of sources of innovation: lead users, manufactures, suppliers and others. In this setting the operators can be thought of as lead users, the chip, handset and infrastructure providers as manufacturers, the application vendors as suppliers and the rest as others. We ended up with the following categories of companies:

- *Operators.* This is companies that provide mobile subscriptions and mobile services to the end users.
- *Manufacturers.* Handset, infrastructure or equipment vendors. This is vendors that provide mobile handsets (devices) to the market, vendors that provide parts to mobile devices or vendors that provide the technical infrastructure for mobile networks.
- *Application vendors.* This is vendors that provide IT solutions to the operators and handset vendors.
- *Others.* This is companies that provide content to mobile services, financial institutions providing financial solutions for mobile services, test laboratories, other standard organizations and governmental agencies.

The framework used for the analysis of the influence of actor groups in the development of mobile services is presented in Table 73.1.

Table 73.1. The metrics framework for measuring the impact of user groups in the mobile domain.

Factors/group	Operators	Manufacturers	Application vendors	Others
Strength				
Openness (towards new work)				
Influence/depth				
Efficiency				

Every step of proposing, creating or altering a standard in OMA is done formally through a document, and the document is placed in the OMA portal. The portal is a repository of all OMA documents and includes over 66,000 documents. Associated with the documents are also the companies that are supporting the proposal.

To find out which companies were supporting proposals for new work items in OMA we looked at the final proposal document that was sent to the OMA technical plenary and registered the companies that supported the proposal. We went through the 40 last new work item proposal. This is approximately for the last 2.5 years. To find which companies got their contributions approved we did the same for two sets of final requirements proposals, the Mobile Email and Push to talk Over Cellular standards.

The number of work group leaders and the number of IPR each company had was found by a simple count of all the IPR declarations and by going through the name of the leaders of all the work groups. The actual numbers in the metrics could have come about because the number of companies in each actor group was unbalanced and tilted towards some actor group. To counter for this we also present what would be an expected number based on the distribution of companies among the actor groups. The expected number for each actor group is the same for all metrics and based on the size of each actor group.

Below we present the distribution (both in numbers and in percentage) of the voting members of OMA per July 2007. The percentage will be used to measure the expected result of the metrics and will be constant for all metrics (Table 73.2).

Table 73.2. The distribution of voting companies in OMA for different actor groups.

	Operator	Manufacturer	Application vendor	Other	Total
Numbers	35	46	31	6	118
Percentage	30	39	26	5	100

4. Findings – Presentation of the Data

First we present the data for the strength, openness and depth metrics. Then we present data for the efficiency metrics through two examples.

4.1. Technological Strength – The Number of Essential IPR

In OMA 25 companies have declared that they have essential IPR. Ten companies are manufacturers (40%), 11 companies are application vendors (44%), 2 companies are operators (8%) and 2 companies can be regarded as content providers (others) (8%). This shows an almost even distribution between the number of application vendors and manufacturers that have declared essential IPR.

If we count the numbers of essential IPR the different types of companies hold, the numbers show another story. The manufacturers hold 182 essential IPR (79%), the application providers hold 43 essential IPR (18%), the operators hold 5 essential IPR (2%) and others hold 3 essential IPR (1%). The manufacturers are the dominant actor when it comes to the number of declared IPR.

There are great differences in the expected distribution and the actual distribution when it comes to IPR. Each manufacturer holds more IPR compared to all other groups. The manufacturers have the highest strength, the operators have the lowest strength while the application vendors and others have a low strength (Table 73.3).

Table 73.3. The strength metric.

	Operators	Manufacturers	Application vendors	Others
Distribution of companies that have declared essential IPR	8%	40%	44%	8%
Expected distribution	30%	39%	26%	5%
Actual distribution of declared IPR per actor group	2%	79%	18%	1%
Impact	Lowest	Highest	Low	Low

4.2. The Depth Metric – Number of Chairs and Editors

Thiry-seven different companies have a position as a chair, co-chair or editor (chair for short) of a working group. Fourteen (38%) of the companies are manufacturers, 14 (38%) are application vendors, 8 (22%) are operators and 1 company (2%) is defined as others.

If we count the numbers of chairs held be each actor group the numbers again show some differences. Fifty-eight percent of the positions are held by manufacturers, 18% are held by application vendors and 23% are held by operators and 1% is held by others.

The distribution between manufacturers and application vendors are even when it comes to the number of companies that holds chairs, but each manufacturer holds more chairs. The manufacturers' numbers of chair rises, the application vendors' numbers drop while the operators have the same number of chairs compared with their distribution. The others group is hardly present. The manufacturers have the highest depth, the operators a medium depth, the application vendors a low depth while the others group have the lowest depth (Table 73.4).

Table 73.4. The depth metrics.

	Operators	Manufacturers	Application vendors	Others
Distribution of companies that hold a chair	22%	38%	38%	2%
Expected distribution	30%	39%	26%	5%
Actual distribution of chair per actor group	23%	58%	18%	1%
Impact	Medium	Highest	Low	Lowest

4.3. The Openness Metric – Number of Proposals Supported

Ninety-five different companies have supported one or more of the 40 latest work item proposals in OMA. There can be an unlimited number of companies supporting a work item, but there has to be a minimum of four. Twenty-one operators have supported one or more proposals (22%), 30 manufacturers have supported one or more proposals (32%), 41 application vendors have supported one or more proposals (43%) and 3 other companies have supported a proposal (3%).

When we look at the number of proposal that has been supported by the different types of companies the numbers are a little different. Thirty-eight percent of the companies backing a proposal have been manufacturers, 28% have been application vendors, 32% have been operators and 2% have been others.

The actual numbers are close to the expected numbers. Each operator supports more work items than the application vendors and a little more than the manufacturers while the others group again has little impact. The operators have the highest impact, the manufactures and application vendors a medium impact while the others group have the lowest impact (Table 73.5).

Table 73.5. The openness metrics.

	Operators	Manufacturers	Application vendors	Others
Distribution of companies supporting a new work item	22%	32%	43%	3%
Expected distribution	30%	39%	26%	5%
Actual distribution of new work items supported per actor group	32%	38%	28%	2%
Impact	Highest	Medium	Medium	Lowest

4.4. The Efficiency Metric – Two Cases

Two cases will be presented here to show how efficient the different groups are at getting their contributions into the specifications; Mobile Email and Push to talk Over Cellular. There are both small and large companies in every group. The operators have companies like Vodaphone, Sprint and NTT DoCoMo, the application vendors companies like IBM and Microsoft, while the manufacturers have companies like Nokia and Intel. Size alone cannot explain any difference in influence in the contributions. First we provide the distribution among the actor groups for the participating companies, and then we present the number of accepted contribution from each group.

4.4.1. Mobile E-mail

Looking at the number of participants gives us these numbers: Operators 21%, manufacturers 42%, application vendors 32% and standard organizations 5%. Summarizing the contributions per type of company shows that 23% of the approved contributions are from operators, 49% are from manufacturers, 23% are from application vendors and 5% are input from other standardization organizations.

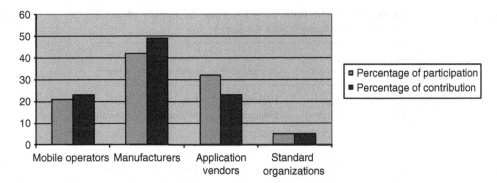

Figure 73.2. The participation and contribution in the mobile email standard development.

The effectiveness of a group is an indication of the difference in the number of companies participating and the number of contributions each group get accepted. Here we can see that the manufacturers are the most efficient group, the application vendors have the lowest efficiency while the operators and standard organizations (others) have a medium efficiency (Fig. 73.2).

4.4.2. Push to Talk Over Cellular (POC)

The POC standard is a typical new service specification. It requires new functionality in the handset and new offerings from the operators. Looking at just the number of participants the distribution is manufacturers 50%, operators 37% and application vendors 13%. In this working group both the chairman and the co-chair are manufacturers. Summarizing the contributions per type of company show that 19% of the approved contributions are by operators, 79% are by manufacturers and 2% are by application vendors. Here we again can observe that the manufacturers are the most efficient group of actors, while the operators have a low efficiency and the application vendors the lowest. This data give another perspective on the contribution by the application vendors. With a contribution of 2% the actual influence of the application vendors is almost negligible (Fig. 73.3).

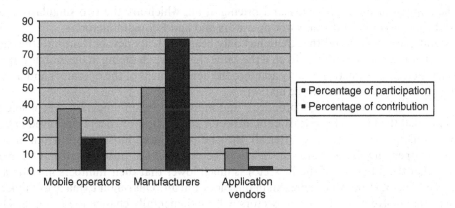

Figure 73.3. The participation and contribution in the POC standard development.

4.5. Summary of Our Metrics

Our findings show that the manufacturers have the highest impact in the development of new mobile services while the application vendors score low on almost every aspect. The others group have the lowest impact, almost zero (Table 73.6).

Table 73.6. The framework showing the impact of actor groups in developing mobile services.

Factors/ group	Operators	Manufacturers	Application vendors	Others
Strength	Lowest	Highest	Low	Low
Openness (towards new work)	Highest	Medium	Medium	Lowest
Influence/ depth	Medium	Highest	Low	Lowest
Efficiency	Medium	Highest	Low	Lowest

5. General Observation and Discussion

A first observation is that the group others, including governments and content providers are almost absent from the standard setting process. This is in contrast to what macro perspectives (e.g., [15]) suggest. Why this is the case should be researched further but is outside the scope of this chapter.

From the previous we can see that manufacturers are more efficient and have higher strength and depth than other types of companies. Overall the hardware manufacturers/vendors seem to be most efficient. Since these companies have to produce physical goods they have a longer production setup than the application vendors and they also have a higher initial production cost. According to our interviewees the manufactures have the most to gain by getting their standards into the specifications, since this can shorten their production line setup and give them a shorter time to market. The following statement from one participant illustrates this. "The vendors and the operators have different reasons to participate. The operators want to influence the requirements, and know what products they can expect from the vendors. The vendors want to reduce time to market and get their functionality (and IPR) into the specifications."

Reading the standards documents carefully, we find corroborating evidence. The standards do not enter into the domain of interoperability and pricing at all, which are the two singularly most pressing concerns for the parties outside the network operators and handset manufacturers.

Whally and Curwen [19] find that there has only been one truly new entrant into the European 3G market. This is in line with our findings. Even if the value chains are changing in the mobile industry [10, 13] and include new actors, these actors mainly adapt to the development of the operators and manufacturers. For them this is just a new channel to the market.

In view of the convergence of IT, broadcast and mobile telecommunication, one would perhaps be inclined to think that the IT and broadcast/content sector should be more deeply involved in the specifications of new mobile services. They are, after all, the ones who stand most to gain from interoperability standards and an open interface towards the means of getting paid for mobile content. Our metrics on the contrary show that the influence of the IT sector is much lower that their numbers indicate and that the broadcast/content sector is almost not present in this picture at all. This ought to make us think twice on the statement that the involvement of the new sectors will fundamentally change the business. Our research indicates that the manufacturers and the operators still control the business models and key features of new services trough the specification process.

IPR is essential in the development of mobile infrastructures [2]. Controlling this gives influence in the development process. The strength of the manufacturers is an indication of their control of the process. After all four companies hold more than 2/3 of the essential IPR for the 3G infrastructure [5].

Gaynor and Bradener [4] have contributed towards a quantitative theory for standards, which complement nicely the framework that we have suggested in this chapter. It is different in as much as it is concerned with the standards themselves, rather than, like ours, the process of standardization. Comparing our metrics with the framework of Tilson and Lyytinen [15] shows that some general trends can be found using their framework, but to get the more detailed picture one must use a metrics framework, like the perspective that we have presented in this chapter.

6. Conclusion

Our findings indicate that the view in existing research that new actors have a large impact on the development of new mobile services is not entirely true. The manufacturers and the operators still dominate the process. Governmental presence is absent in the consortia setting as well as the influence of content providers. The manufacturers are the group with greatest strength and also the most efficient group in terms of getting their requirements into specifications while the operators are the most open group in terms of collaboration with others. The application vendors main influence is through the creation of new work items within the standardization process.

The metric presented here provides a complementary view compared with existing macro perspectives on the mobile service industry and can be a good starting point for further discussions on the impact of actor groups in the development of mobile services.

References

1. Axelrod, R., W. Mitchell, et al. (1995). "Coalition formation in standard-setting alliances." Management Science 41(9): 1493–1508.
2. Bekkers, R., B. Verspagen, et al. (2002). "Intellectual property rights and standardization: the case of GSM." Telecommunications Policy 26(3–4): 171–188.
3. García-Murillo, M. (2005). "Regulatory response to convergence: experiences from four countries." INFO 7(1): 20–40.
4. Gaynor, M. and S. Bradner (2001). The real options approach to standardization. Proceedings of the 34th Annual Hawaii International Conference on System Sciences.
5. Goodman, D. J. and R. A. Myers (2005). 3G cellular standards and patents. 2005 International Conference on Wireless Networks, Communications and Mobile Computing, IEEE.
6. Iversen, E. J. and R. Tee (2006). "Standards dynamics and industrial organization in the mobile telecom sector." INFO 8(4): 33–48.
7. King, J. L. and K. Lyytinen (2002). "Around the cradle of the wireless revolution: the emergence and revolution of cellular telephony." Telecommunications Policy 26: 97–100.
8. Latour, B. (2005). Reassembling the Social. An Introduction to Actor-Network-Theory. Oxford University Press, Oxford.
9. Lyytinen, K. and V. V. Fomin (2002). "Achieving high momentum in the evolution of wireless infrastructures: the battle over the 1G solutions." Telecommunications Policy 26: 149–170.
10. Maitland, C. F., J. M. Bauer, et al. (2002). "The European market for mobile data: evolving value chains and industry structure." Telecommunication Policy 26: 485–504.
11. OECD (2007). OECD Communication Outlook 2007, OECD, Paris.
12. Shapiro, C. and H. R. Varian (1999). "The art of standards wars." California Management Review 41(2): 8–32.
13. Steinbock, D. (2003). "Globalization of wireless value system: from geographic to strategic advantages." Telecommunications Policy 27(3–4): 207–235.
14. Steinbock, D. (2005). The Mobile Revolution: The Making of Mobile Services Worldwide. Kogan Page, London and Philadelphia.
15. Tilson, D. and K. Lyytinen (2006). "The 3G transition: changes in the US wireless industry." Telecommunications Policy 30: 569–586.
16. von Hippel, E. (1988). The Sources of Innovation, Oxford University Press, New York.
17. Weiss, M. B. H. and M. Sirbu (1990). "Technological choice in voluntary standards committees: an empirical analysis." Economic of Innovation and New Technology 1: 111–133.
18. Werle, R. (2001). "Institutional aspects of standardization – jurisdictional conflicts and the choice of standardization organizations." Journal of European Public Policy 8(3): 392–410.
19. Whally, J. and P. Curwen (2006). "Third generation new entrants in the European mobile telecommunication industry." Telecommunication Policy 30: 622–632.
20. Yoo, Y., K. Lyytinen, et al. (2005). "The role of standards in innovation and diffusion of broadband mobile services: The case of South Korea." Journal of Strategic Information Systems 14: 323–353.

74

Reducing Health Cost: Health Informatics and Knowledge Management as a Business and Communication Tool

Regina Gyampoh-Vidogah, Robert Moreton and David Sallah

Abstract

Health informatics has the potential to improve the quality and provision of care while reducing the cost of health care delivery. However, health informatics is often falsely regarded as synonymous with information management (IM). This chapter (i) provides a clear definition and characteristic benefits of health informatics and information management in the context of health care delivery, (ii) identifies and explains the difference between health informatics (HI) and managing knowledge (KM) in relation to informatics business strategy and (iii) elaborates the role of information communication technology (ICT) KM environment. This Chapter further examines how KM can be used to improve health service informatics costs, and identifies the factors that could affect its implementation and explains some of the reasons driving the development of electronic health record systems. This will assist in avoiding higher costs and errors, while promoting the continued industrialisation of KM delivery across health care communities.

Keywords Knowledge management · Information processing · Innovation · Information systems · Information technology · Health informatics · Electronic patient record · ICT

1. Introduction

Health care computing or medical informatics is one of the fastest growing areas of information and communication technology (ICT) application [1]. Health informatics (HI) is a multifaceted discipline concerned with electronic patient records, performance indicators, paramedical support, emergency service, computer-aided diagnosis, clinical governance, research support and hospital management which aims to promote good practice without conflict with the fundamental medical ethical principles of beneficence and respet for patients' autonomy [1].

The Electronic Patient Record (EPR) in particular is indicative of the advances in medical informatics and allows providers, patients and payers to interact more efficiently and in life-enhancing ways [2]. EPR offers new methods of storing, manipulating and communicating medical information of all kinds, including text, images, sound, video and tactile senses, which are more powerful and flexible than current paper-based systems [2].

Regina Gyampoh-Vidogah • Care Services Improvement Partnership, Department of Health, London, UK. Robert Moreton • University of Wolverhampton, Wolverhampton, UK. David Sallah • University of Wolverhampton, Wolverhampton, UK.

G.A. Papadopoulos et al. (eds.), *Information Systems Development*, DOI 10.1007/b137171_74,
© Springer Science+Business Media, LLC 2009

Despite the potential of health informatics epitomised by EPR, many clinicians are ambivalent about the benefits of EPR [3]. A review suggests that, people are suspicious of technology because it makes medicine cold and impersonal. In the opinion of Humber et al., [4] this is due to the fact that little attention is given to the potential benefit of clinical research to using EPR. It was further suggested that electronic records could facilitate new interfaces between care and research environments, leading to great improvements in the scope and efficiency of research. These benefits range from systematic generation hypotheses for research to undertake entire studies based only on electronic records [4].

While no single entity or sector originated the idea of harnessing EPR technology to address health care issues, purchasers (e.g., health management organisations), physicians, other practitioners, health care delivery systems, patients (users), developers and academics all bring unique perspectives to, and have sometimes divergent opinions about, maximising health informatics (HI) potential in behaviour change and disease management. There had been an increasing call to explore research methodologies for health evaluation research. In this context the issue is to investigate how HI technologies based on EPR will be able to reach traditionally unserved populations [4].

This chapter contributes to the development of HI by settling out reasons driving the development of electronic health record systems and further examines how knowledge management (KM) can be used to cut and reduce health service informatics costs, and identifies the factors that could affect its implementation. KM within the health informatics context is the strategic use of technology and knowledge to manage process, maintain and protect key assets of the health service by measuring the impact and outcome that knowledge has on the health service knowledge community in terms of access to information and appropriate services [5]. This will assist in avoiding higher costs and errors, while promoting the continued industrialisation of KM delivery across health care communities based on EPRs.

1.1. Research Approach

The perceptions and practices of knowledge management were examined through literature review. The literature review was chosen to match the objectives and description of theory building [6].

1.2. Knowledge Management in the Medical Health Informatics Service of Business

In the absence of KM when an organisation expands, it is difficult to hire and train employees to meet the expectations of stakeholders and customers for performance. In such cases, knowledge management serves as a system that identifies, captures, organises and disseminates critical knowledge to help enterprises to deal with economic fluctuations [7, 8].

According to research [9] any organisation that can find an efficient way to mine, share and manage an intellectual capital improves employee productivity, increase stakeholder and customer satisfaction and retention, distinguishes the organisation among competitors. This suggests that the efficient utilisation of the intellectual capital via KM initiative is imperative for any successful support organisation. Accordingly the support required for KM is composed of elements namely interaction management; resource management; performance management [10, 11].

2. Health Informatics and Evidence-Based Medicine

Figure 74.1 is an attempt to illustrate the process by which patient data are transformed into HI evidence. Three stages are identified. First, the data are created. It is worth clarifying the claim that is being made here. Data are not just waiting to be gathered, collected or recorded. Data are created. Recording information is not a simple matter of writing down observed facts. The observations emerge from the conversation between the clinician and the patient and thus a product of that conversation and take their

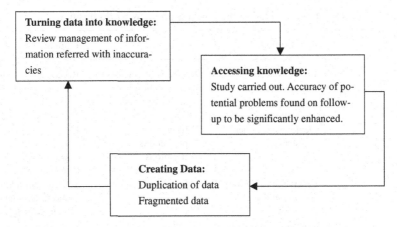

Figure 74.1. Stages in a virtuous circle of health knowledge management.

meaning from it. Similarly when information and/or data are transmitted from one location to another, the simplest statements will be reinterpreted in the light of new information, new possibilities and changing priorities [12].

The process of care comes to a conclusion if treatment is successful, when the patient stops being a patient and returns to being an active healthy individual. However, this is not necessarily the end of the story for the data. Details recorded in the management of this information are coded and classified to compile statistics about the management of patients' information with disease at different locations and used to answer a range of questions. This is because clinical audit, clinical information and knowledge management all depend on data [13].

The second stage in the process is the transformation of clinical data into various forms of medical knowledge. In the third stage, the loop is closed and the knowledge obtained from the data is used to inform the management of future patients. Again, the ideal of evidence-based medicine is that the essence of the aggregated data about past patients provides the empirical basis for decisions about current and future patients.

3. The Role of Health Informatics in Knowledge Management Environment

The role of HI as the memory within the learning organisation has been specified [14]. However, HI can be used for knowledge acquisition support research and competitive intelligence system [15] while the role that IS implementation within the health service can play to ensure proper information and/or knowledge management has been identified [16]. This means that the programs are designed to identify and correct errors, jobs get done and the action staying aligned with the organisation policies. Research suggests that, some of the problems affecting implementation of HI are due to traditional form of doing business and the rules and regulations governing such traditional business [17].

Today's business world does not reward playing by pre-defined rules but rewards understanding and keeps pace with changes [18]. Table 74.1 represents the difference between the traditional business and the new world of business according to selected domains. Related to the strategic notion of knowledge and informatics, there are some *paradigm shifts* that characterised the transformation from the old world of business to the new [19]. These relate to business strategy, business models, knowledge processes, management, use of technology, regulation and design. As such the KM process needs to shift from deployment of best practices to efficiency in predictable situations which is critical for the health service.

Table 74.1. Traditional business and new world business.

Paradigm	Shift from	Shift to	Emphasis	References
Business strategy	Faster cycle of knowledge	Realise value. Access to information base; authority to act	Rapid detection and correction of discrepancies	[20, 21]
Business models	Static models	Dynamic models	Measure outcomes	[22]
Knowledge processes	Deployment of best practices	Efficiency and predictable situations	Ingenious suggestions and effective knowledge management	[23]
Management	Change of role from command and control	Sense and respond	Strategy formulation and technology management	[17]
Use of technology	Transaction processing, integrated logistics and work flows	Systems support, networks communication building	Competencies, people network on the job learning	[24]
Regulation	Limited control	Organisational vision; few rules freedom of information	Responses to dynamic changes of the business environment	[25]
Design	Self designing	Participate and define problems and generate solutions	Rethink and promote knowledge creation	[26]

Adapted from [19].

4. Cutting Health Service Costs

Potential problems have been identified [18] that can result in expensive EPR systems. These are lack of funding, costly dependence proprietary technology companies, monopoly, learning curves, traditional and technological-mediated models working in parallel, KM implementation costs, design or other operational flaws, insufficient training and indirect legal costs.

The net effect of these issues is that there are considerable uncertainty regarding the costs associated with HI implementation that mediated health initiatives and their allocation [27]. Costs rise as both traditional and technological models work in parallel [28]. Most immediately, the health care service will have to adjust to costs associated with *evolving technologies* and short system lives. An example is the recent controversy in the United States over the rejection of governments' initiative to expand funding for the Office for National Health Information Technology coordination of the Department of Health and Human Services. This is likely to jeopardise public sector projects that should have been funded out of that office [29]. This is different in UK because the UK government has put in place funding for health service IT. However, because service providers and IT vendors do not allow the right expertise and developers to do the job in-house, the increased cost deters the progress that could have been made in implementation.

Equally, there are practical, economic, political and professional barriers that impede the acceptance of HI implementation. Individual physicians or small practice groups have particular concerns about the costs and learning curves associated with informatics [30]. Additionally, there are questions about whether to convert records retrospectively or whether it should be prospective. Predictably, the medical community is concerned about costly dependence on proprietary technology companies, who potentially could monopolise the hardware and software required. One possible solution would be for the mechanism of implementation of HI in KM environment to be a public service built to public standards and/or under patient control [18].

5. Information Technology and Information System Use

Information technology and information systems promise to address the above problems. This requires construction of a suitable tool and/or framework to establish a standard way of measuring results that will allow high quality of what is needed to sustain and improve that high quality [31, 32] and to assess an organisation's compliance with KM initiative [1] based on six point domains for assessing KM, namely strategy, using technology, knowledge management culture, management, processes and on-going maintenance and protection.

5.1. Strategy

This refers to the definition of business and customer value propositions and focuses on whether the organisation is committed to a KM improvement programme, its funding and how it is managed to ensure business benefit [33].

5.2. Using Technology

This refers to the level of IT sophistication available. This should have the minimum weight since it is only a tool that cannot work without a deployment strategy. This focuses on whether the IT infrastructure is sufficient and used effectively enough to support knowledge management to avoid design or other operational flaws [25].

5.3. Knowledge Management Culture

This refers to the degree of IT utilisation in everyday work, with emphasis on the learning techniques and knowledge transferring mechanisms [34]. This also indicates whether the behaviours within an organisation enable exploitations of knowledge inherent in the company in an effective manner such that the organisation can identify the best experts for different areas of key knowledge and has a training strategy set in place that will allow expertise to codify tacit knowledge into explicit knowledge [34].

5.4. Management

Refers to the role of management, communication and different interpretation of data. This indicates whether staff understands the concept of knowledge management and whether management is committed to its use. This will assist in minimising KM implementation costs and properly rewarding those that support its efforts towards knowledge management by using incentives [35].

5.5. Processes

Refers to the availability of systematic processes for gathering, organising, exploiting and protecting key knowledge assets, from external and internal sources. This will help avoid monopoly and costly dependence on proprietary technology companies and focuses on whether specific roles have been identified and assigned, in such a way that all senior managers and professionals are trained in knowledge management techniques [36].

5.6. Ongoing Maintenance and Protection

Refers to how well the organisation protects and maintains its information and knowledge assets. This focuses on whether there is a strictly maintained knowledge inventory, with a knowledge tree, and clear ownership of knowledge entities, that is readily accessible across the organisation [34]. This also focuses on whether the organisation measures the impact of KM particularly the management of intellectual assets. This will avoid indirect legal costs.

6. Recommendation

The health care services need to set out to provide good services to patients in terms of access to information and appropriate services. KM deals with the value of work in terms of explicit knowledge creation, defining, participating, deployment and value realisation of data. Out of this value of work implicit knowledge of expertise, judgement, innovation and creativity can be delivered by HI using KM. This means, users and carers, stakeholders and partners will be able to access appropriate services deployed and communicate effectively. This will enable the health service reduce cost, build skills and produce quality and speed up work (Fig. 74.2).

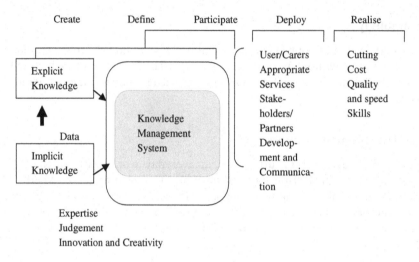

Figure 74.2. Good services model: *could knowledge management provide an organization with a competitive advantage?* Adapted from [37].

7. Summary and Further Research

The new world witnessed the materialisation of interest in health informatics and its adoption by information technology vendors and solution providers. This fact triggered the need for developing better and more accurate understanding of knowledge management as enabler of information strategy for the new world.

This chapter (i) provides a clear definition and characteristic benefits of knowledge management in the context of health care delivery, (ii) identifies and explains the difference between HI managing knowledge in relation to business strategy and (iii) elaborates the role of information technology and information systems in transferring knowledge and further examined factors affecting implementation in the health care service.

Further research is, however, underway on exploring potential problems and finding solutions by using an empirical study. This is being explored using combination of quantitative, action and qualitative research. The aim is to address in detail the reasons driving the development of electronic health records systems; how knowledge management can be used to cut and reduce health service informatics costs in detail; and how HI will conquer technical problems they pose and avoid the security and privacy costs. The researchers are exploring research methodologies for e-health evaluation that could be adopted to reach traditionally undeserved health populations that will avoid higher costs and errors, while promoting the continued industrialisation of health care delivery and subordinating patient autonomy and professional ideals to expressionless systems.

In conclusion, this chapter has focused on three factors that the researchers believed highly affect health care. The only sustainable source of competitive advantage is the rate at which organisations learn. KM content and its relation to business and customer value are considered as an ultimate competitive edge. It is therefore proposed that an evaluation tool is needed to assess and evaluate the performance towards an effective KM to scan the environment for improvement opportunities.

References

1. Bergamaschi, W., Rapone, L., and Sorda, E. (2006) New national healthcare information system. *Clinical Chemistry and Laboratory Medicine*, 44 (6).
2. Hippisley-Cox, J., Pringle, M., Cater, R., Wynn, A., Hammersley, V., Coupland, C., Hapgood, H., Horsfield, P., Teasdale, S., and Johnson, C. (2003) The electronic patient record in primary care regression or progression? A cross sectional study. *British Medical Journal*, 326: 1439–1443.
3. Taylor, P. (2006) *From Patient Data to Medical Knowledge: The Principles and Practice of Health Informatics*. London: Blackwell BMJ Books.
4. Humber, M., Butterworth, H., Fox, J., and Thomson, R. (2001) Medical decision support via the internet. *Medinfo*, 10 (1): 464–468.
5. Moteleb, A. A., and Woodman, M. (2007) Notions of knowledge management systems: a gap analysis. *The Electronic Journal of Knowledge Management,5* (1): 55– 62.
6. Myers, M. D. (1997) Qualitative research in information systems. *MIS Quarterly MISQ Discovery*, archival version 21 (2): 241–242.
7. Tsai, J., and Bond, G. (2008). A comparison of electronic records to paper records in mental health centers. *International Journal of Quality Health Care*, 20 (2): 136–143.
8. Tobin, T. (2003) Ten principles for knowledge management success. (Available at http://www.serviceware.com/whitepapers/main.asp
9. Özkan, S. (2006) Process based information systems success model: assessment of the information technology function in three healthcare organizations. *European and Mediterranean Conference on Information Systems* (EMCIS) 2006, July 6–7 2006, Costa Blanca, Alicante, Spain.
10. Zack, M. (1999) Developing a knowledge strategy. *California Management Review*, 41(3): 125–145.
11. Tarabanis, K., and Peristeras, V. (2003). Knowledge management requirement models for pan-European public administration service delivery. In Wimmer, M.A. (Ed.): KMGov, pp. 37–47.
12. Gunter, T.D., and Terry, N.P. (2005) The emergence of national electronic health record architectures in the United States and Australia: models, costs, and questions. *Journal of Medical Internet Research*, 7 (1): 14.
13. Malhotra, Y. (2004) *Why Knowledge Management Systems Fail? Enablers and Constraints of Knowledge Management in Human Enterprises*. American Society for Information Science and Technology, Silver Spring, MD, Monograph Series, pp. 87–112
14. Huber, G. (1991) Organizational learning: the contributing processes and the literatures. *Organization Science*, 2: 88–125.
15. Malhotra, Y. (2000) Knowledge management for e-business performance. *Information Strategy: The Executives Journal*, 16 (4): 5–16.
16. Gyampoh-Vidogah, R., Moreton, R., and Sallah, D. (2007). Improving information management in the health service: the role of information systems development. *European and Mediterranean Conference on Information Systems (EMCIS)* June 24–26, 2007, Valencia, Spain.
17. Malhotra, Y., and Galletta, D. (2003) Role of commitment and innovation in knowledge management system implementation: theory, conceptualization, and measurement of antecedents of success. *Proceeding of the 36th Hawaii International Conference on System Science,* IEEE.
18. Mandl, K.D., Szolovits, P., and Kohane, I.S. (2001) Public standards and patients' control: how to keep electronic medical records accessible but private. *British Medical Journal*, Feb 3; 322(7281): 283–287.
19. Malhotra, Y. (2002) *Why Knowledge Management Systems Fail? Enablers and Constraints of Knowledge Management in Human Enterprises. Handbook on Knowledge*. Springer-Verlag. Heidelberg, Germany.
20. Bolinger, A., and Smith, R. (2001) Managing organizational knowledge as strategic asset. *Journal of Knowledge Management*. 5 (1): 8-18, MCB University Press.
21. Mintzberg, H. (1987) Crafting strategy. *Harvard Business Review*. July-August, 6–75.
22. Martensson, M. (2000) A critical review of knowledge management as a management tool. *Journal of Knowledge Management*, 4 (3): 204–216.
23. McDermott, R. (1999) Why information technology inspired but cannot deliver knowledge management. *California Management Review*, 41 (4): 103–117.

24. Argyris, C. (1977) Double loop learning in organizations. *Harvard Business Review*, September–October.
25. Hodgson, L., Farrell, C.M., and Connolly, M. (2007) Improving UK public services: a review of the evidence. *Public Administration*, 85 (2): 355–382.
26. Grayson, C., and O'Dell, C. (1999). Knowledge transfer: discover your value proposition. *Strategy & Leadership*, March–April, 10–15.
27. Hawryluk, M.P. (2004) Electronic health records. Bills set the foundation for action in the next Congress. *American Medical News*. 2004 June 14. (Available at http://www.ama-assn.org/amednews/2004/06/14/gvsc0614.htm)
28. Lohr S. (2004) Health care technology is a promise unfinanced. *New York Times*, 5.
29. Health Connect (2004) Australian Government: Department of Health and Ageing (Available at http://www.healthconnect.gov.au/)
30. Richmond, R. (2004) Small business: doctors see healthy returns in digital records. *Wall Street Journal*, B1.
31. Department of Health (2007) Our NHS Our future. *NHS Next Stage Review*. Interim Report. (Available at http://www.ournhs. nhs.uk/fromty pepad/283411_Our NHS _summary_ v2acc.pdf)
32. Harrison, W., Marshall, T., Singh, D., and Tennant, R. (2006) *The Effectiveness of Healthcare Systems in the UK – Scoping Study*, Department of Public Health and Epidemiology and HSMC University of Birmingham, Birmingham.
33. Carroll, J., Rowlands, B., Standing, C., Frampton, K., and Smith, R. (2006) *European and Mediterranean Conference on Information Systems (EMCIS)*2006, July 6–7 2006, Costa Blanca, Alicante, Spain.
34. Powell, J., and Buchan, I. (2005) Electronic health records should support clinical research. *Journal of Medical Internet Research*, 7 (1).
35. Ritterband, L.M., Andersson, G., Christensen, H.M., Carlbring, P., and Cuijpers, P. (2006) Directions for the International Society for Research on Internet Interventions (ISRII). *Journal of Med Internet*, 8 (3): 23.
36. Mack, R., Ravin, Y., and Byrd, R.J. (2001) Knowledge portals and the emerging digital knowledge workplace. *IBM Systems Journal*, 40 (4): 925–955.
37. Taher, A., and Ismail El-Kayaly, D. (2005) Could knowledge management provide an organization with a competitive advantage? *European and Mediterranean Conference on Information Systems*, June 7– 8, Egypt, Cairo.

75

The Information Architecture of E-Commerce: An Experimental Study on User Performance and Preference

Wan Abdul Rahim Wan Mohd Isa, Nor Laila Md Noor and Shafie Mehad

Abstract

Too often, designers of e-commerce web sites use models, concepts, guidelines, and designs that focus on the artifacts while ignoring the context in which the artifacts will be used. Furthermore, the link between culture and usability in web site IA phenomenon is still considered as uncharted area, as it lacks much theoretical consideration. In an effort toward addressing the aforementioned issues, our study provides a theoretical and empirical link between cultural and usability through the application of 'Venustas' (Delight) drawn from the architectural field and Hofstede's cultural dimensions. We use Islamic culture as the case study and report on the experiment to investigate the effect of the IA designs based on the cultural dimensions on e-commerce web sites. The result provides partial empirical support to the theorized link between culture and usability based on the usability measurement on user performance and preference. In addition, practical web site IA cultural design prescriptions are also provided.

Keywords Web site information architecture · Culture · Usability · Business-to-consumer (B2C) · E-commerce

1. Introduction

With the increasingly fierce and competitive environment of the international market, clearly the companies that produce culture-specific designed products could benefit the most [23]. This is because culture and its impact on usability are considered an important factor that directly influences international users [18]. The sooner designers begin to assimilate the cultural diversity of users into product development, the faster products become more appropriate for a global market [22]. However, despite the ongoing development on the culture-oriented design, the localization process for culture-centered design will continue to be a challenge for researchers and practitioners [22]. This is due to the difficulties to design one interface or product that will work throughout the world and taking into account the diversity of cultural background [9].

Web site IA is the organization and structure of information [3, 24, 27] and is considered an important process of interaction design [2]. Therefore, it is our intention in this study to provide primary focus on web site IA as it is primarily treated as a new field [3], with much research on multidisciplinary areas to be conducted. In addition, although the IA literature contains numerous arguments on the influence of cultural dimensions in the context of using web sites, the link between culture and web site usability is far from clear. Therefore, our research would also come to response of perceived lack of common understanding or shared reference on cultural usability. This is because

Wan Abdul Rahim Wan Mohd Isa, Nor Laila Md Noor and Shafie Mehad · Department of System Science, Universiti Teknologi MARA, Malaysia

G.A. Papadopoulos et al. (eds.), *Information Systems Development*, DOI 10.1007/b137171_75,

the growing number of design frameworks and models from multi-disciplinary areas does not justify having any single approach [15].

In an effort to address these issues, we proposed a conceptual model of cultural dimension and web site usability. We then conducted an experiment to observe links between our prescribed cultural dimension of web sites and their usability by using the Islamic culture as our cultural case study. We used two sub-cultural groupings of Muslim subjects to represent Islamic culture. A controlled experiment was conducted to determine the usability of the business-to-consumer (B2C) e-commerce prototype web site incorporated with IA cultural design against a control web site. The usability measures are based on user performance for time-on-task completion and their preference captured from a survey questionnaire. The experiment is conducted to provide empirical support to the theorized link between culture and usability and practical design indications. The next section presents research framework and method. We then provide results to the derived research questions and hypotheses followed by conclusion.

2. Research Framework

2.1. Conceptual Model

Based on this understanding, we delineate the understanding by suggesting a conceptual model of the interaction design process between culture and usability, by bringing forward the theoretical understanding of *venustas* into the interaction design process, as shown in Fig. 75.1. The descriptions for this conceptual model are as follows:

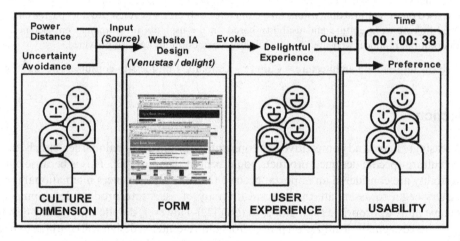

Figure 75.1. Conceptual model between culture and usability.

- *Input: Culture Applies (Source) to 'Form' (Venustas)*
  Architects think of buildings in terms of structure, function, and form [5]. Similarly, we can view web sites as such. The construct 'Form' in Fig. 75.1, represents the IT artifact under investigation, i.e., the cultural-centered web site IA. The 'form' adopted consists of web site content, navigation, and context. In general, the dimension of content refers to the properties, dimension, and principle of the information content. The dimension of navigation relates to the elements and system path of information hypertext space and the dimension of context refers to the appropriateness of the underlying surface it provided. Therefore, by applying the theoretical understanding of *venustas* in this study, the designed object is experienced through usage and perception [16] as *venustas* is primarily treated as the experiential value in building [21].

- *Evoke: Form (Web site IA) Ignite Delightful User Experience*

  In general, the Cultural Cognition Theory (CCT) provides the linkage among culture, cognition, and web site design, under the assumption that the information processing is affected by the cultural context via culturally designed web sites [6, 7]. Therefore, the sense of delight may be evoked through the usage of web site IA design that represents its cultural values. As noted by Garrett, user experience is an important element that forms the customer's impression of the company's offerings, differentiates the company from its competitors, and determines whether your customer will ever come back [11]. Therefore, the impression may be created by the representational delights provided for the user's experience through the reflection of the cultural dimensions of Power Distance (PD) and Uncertainty Avoidance (UA) in web site IA design.

  According to Hofstede and Hofstede, PD dimension relates to the state of which weaker member of the society accepts inequality in power distribution in which, Low-Power Distance (LPD) suggests equality; High-Power Distance (HPD) suggests inequality in power distribution. Accordingly, UA refers to the state of which a society feels vulnerable of taking risks in unknown situation where Low Uncertainty Avoidance (LUA) takes risks, whereas High Uncertainty Avoidance (HUA) is uncomfortable with uncertainty and usually avoids taking risks [13]. The example of the attached IA design prescriptions to cultural dimensions is as shown in Table 75.1.

Table 75.1. Summary of IA design prescriptions [25].

Cultural dimensions	IA design traits	Cultural dimensions	IA design traits
HPD	Content – Tall hierarchy in mental models [19]	LPD	Content – Shallow hierarchy in mental models [19]
	Content – Highly structured access to information [19]		Content – Low structured access to information [19]
	Context – Significant and frequent emphasis on the social and its symbols [19]		Context – Infrequent use of social and its symbols [19]
HUA	Content – Chunk info by topic/module [20]	LUA	Content – Chunk information by task [20]
	Content – Beauty value: unity, balance, symmetry, harmony [17]		Content – No present elements of beauty
	Navigation – Navigation schemes to prevent users from getting lost [19]		Navigation – Less control of navigation [19]

- *Output: Delightful User Experience Increase Usability*

  The sense of delight experienced by the user may influence the usability level of web site IA. This may be determined through the assessment of the user performance and preference for using culture-centered web site. Here, we refer performance based on the time required to perform the task and the preference selection based on the web site IA design. The representational delight experienced by the user may ease the tasks and lead toward increasing the usability level of web site IA.

2.2. Research Questions

The primary research goal for our study is to gain a better understanding of the culture-centered web site influences on the usability of the web site IA from the measurement of performance and preference. Here, the culture-centered web site is referred as web site that is accentuated with the design of cultural dimensions of the target user. In the pursuit of this main goal, we propose two main research questions (RQ):

RQ1: Do web sites that have been designed for a particular target culture produce better usability results when tested by members of that particular target culture?

RQ2: Do users prefer the web site targeted for their own culture?

3. Research Method

The research method consists of a controlled one-to-one experimental session. The experiment was conducted to investigate the usability of IA for two business-to-consumer (B2C) e-commerce prototype web sites that reflect the incorporation of IA cultural design prescriptions against a control web site. Our study involved using the Islamic culture as the case study with 44 Middle East and 44 Malaysian students as the Muslim subjects. A post-study survey questionnaire to assess user preference followed subsequently after the experimental session.

3.1. Subjects

Our approach of using the sub-cultural groupings is not a new phenomenon in cross-cultural studies. The notion to study from the subculture groupings perspective had slowly emerged in cross-cultural studies, such as using Chinese sub-cultural groupings [8, 14]. As the study uses Muslims as a case study, we engaged Middle East and Malaysian subculture groupings to represent the Islamic culture, under the assumption that both groups were predominantly associated to the Islamic culture. Forty-four Middle East and 44 Malaysian students from the Information Technology and Engineering postgraduate faculties from local universities were used as our subjects. Using students as the subject was useful for concept identification, construct analysis, and the homogenous nature of the student sample allowed for more exact theoretical predictions [4]. The sample size used in our study was also in accordance with Hofstede's recommendation of at least 20–50 samples for each country or even region [12]. The subjects were selected using convenient sampling through bulletin announcements, e-mail and short text messaging invitations. The data gathering process lasted for about 1 month from December 2007 until January 2008.

3.2. Experimental Web sites

Two Business-to-consumer (B2C) e-commerce prototype web sites that reflect the incorporation of IA cultural design prescriptions were used in the experimental session. Two versions of B2C web sites that sell Islamic books were constructed using a free e-commerce tool called 'Zen-Cart,' available at the URL http://www.zen-cart.com/. Several available open source coding and designs were also used in the development of the web site design to maintain the color consistency. For example, 'Cascading Style Sheet' (CSS) template design and a user tracking behavior module were installed as an additional function inside the 'Zen-Cart' tool. Additional tools such as the EasyPHP were used to install the local apache web server and 'PHP,' 'PHPMyAdmin,' and MySQL database were used to develop the web site together with Macromedia Dreamweaver Version 8 and Adobe Illustrator CS. The functionality included in both web sites was the e-commerce elements such as product view, shopping cart, and a transaction tool to purchase using credit card payment. However, for this study, the analysis was concentrated only on the product view. The dimensions of 'Power Distance' and 'Uncertainty Avoidance' were incorporated into the IA of both the treatment web site and the control web site with the opposing values as shown in Figs. 75.2 and Fig 75.3, respectively.

As we use Islamic culture as the case study, the treatment web site (Iqra Book Store Web site 1) is based on the theorized cultural dimensions that may provide contextual cues for representing Islamic culture dimensions as suggested by Wan Abdul Rahim et al. [26]. Here, Islamic culture dimensions are High Power Distance (HPD) and High Uncertainty Avoidance (HUA) [26]. In contrary, Iqra Book Store Web site 2 will incorporate the opposite dimensions as the control web site. We used the IA design prescriptions as earlier shown in Table 75.1 in the treatment and control experimental e-commerce web sites.

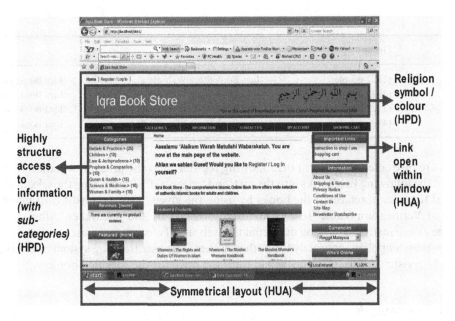

Figure 75.2. Iqra book store web site 1.

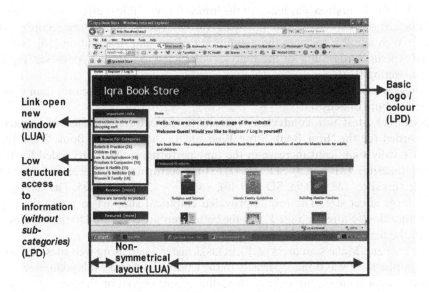

Figure 75.3. Iqra book store web site 2.

3.3. Experimental Design and Procedure

In our experiment we used the within-subjects design approach. Specifically, we used a 2×2 Latin square experimental design or also known as crossover design as shown in Table 75.2 [1]. This design was used to minimize the order effects where, the first treatment may influence the response to the second treatment through warm-up, practice, learning, interference, adaptation, assimilation, contrast, fatigue, and so on [1]. In general, group 1 and group 3 were required to perform tasks on the 'Iqra Book Store Web site 1' first, followed by the 'Iqra Book Store Web site 2.' Group 2 and group 4 were required to perform tasks on the 'Iqra Book Store Web site 2' first, followed by the 'Iqra Book Store Web site 1.'

Table 75.2. 2×2 Latin square experimental design.

Subject	Group	Web sites	
Middle East	(1) 22 people	'Iqra Book Store Web site 1'	'Iqra Book Store Web site 2'
	(2) 22 people	'Iqra Book Store Web site 2'	'Iqra Book Store Web site 1'
Malaysia	(3) 22 people	'Iqra Book Store Web site 1'	'Iqra Book Store Web site 2'
	(4) 22 people	'Iqra Book Store Web site 2'	'Iqra Book Store Web site 1'

Subjects are instructed to perform the following register, find the price information of the specified two books, add the following two books into the cart, and 'check out' after making the selection. Then, they were instructed to make purchase of the books by using the given 'dummy' credit card number, expired date, and 'Card Verification Value' (CVV) number, provided by the researcher. After completing the transaction, they were instructed to 'log out' from the web site. To capture the user performance data, the user tracking system is applied separately for both web sites. The user tracking system tracks the time after user successfully registered into the web site and finds the price for the specified books.

4. Research Framework

4.1. Experimental Result

Initially, data transformation was made to the 'timesite1' variable (performance time recorded while using the 'Iqra Book Store Web site 1') and 'timesite2' variable (performance time recorded while using the 'Iqra Book Store Web site 2'), to meet the assumption of normal distribution [10]. Subsequently, the following are the experimental results for the analyses conducted to test the hypotheses (H_1, H_2, H_3) as the counterpart of answering RQ1.

H_1: Web sites for a particular target culture produce better time performance than web sites with the opposite culture dimension.

A paired-samples t-test was conducted to evaluate the cultural dimensions impact on the time performance recorded for the 'Iqra Book Store Web site 1' and the 'Iqra Book Store Web site e.g.2.' There was a statistically significant increase in the time performance score recorded for the 'Iqra Book Store Web site 1'; 'timesite1' ($M = 0.20$, SD $= 0.47$) to time performance score recorded for the 'Iqra Book Store Web site 2'; 'timesite2' ($M = 0.95$, SD $= 0.46$), $t(87) = -13.79$, p<.0005. The Eta squared statistics (0.69) showed a large effect size. The results provided empirical support to prove the hypothesis as it showed that the 'Iqra Book Store Web site 1' was the better web site compared to the 'Iqra Book Store Web site 2' in terms of the time recorded to perform tasks.

H_2: Middle East and Malaysian users perform tasks faster when using web sites of their own cultures

A paired-samples t-test was done separately to the Middle East and Malaysian users. First, a paired-samples t-test was conducted to evaluate the cultural dimensions impact on the time performance recorded for the 'Iqra Book Store Web site 1' and the 'Iqra Book Store Web site 2' for the Middle East group users. There was a statistically significant increase in the time performance score recorded for the 'Iqra Book Store Web site 1'; 'timesite1' ($M = 0.45$, SD $= 0.41$) to the time performance score recorded for the 'Iqra Book Store Web site 2'; 'timesite2' ($M = 1.21$, SD $= 0.37$), $t(43) = -9.92$, p<0.0005. The Eta squared statistics (0.70) showed a large effect size.

Second, a paired-samples t-test was conducted to evaluate the cultural dimensions impact on the time performance recorded for the 'Iqra Book Store Web site 1' and the 'Iqra Book Store Web site 2' for the Malaysian group users. There was a statistically significant increase in the time performance score recorded for the 'Iqra Book Store Web site 1'; 'timesite1' ($M = -0.06$, SD $= 0.38$) to the time performance score recorded for the 'Iqra Book Store Web site 2'; 'timesite2' ($M = 0.68$, SD $= 0.39$), $t(43) = -9.474$, p<0.0005. The Eta squared statistics (0.68) showed a large effect size. The results provided an empirical support for H_2. Both results showed that the Middle East and Malaysian group performance (in terms of time performing task) were much better for the 'Iqra Book Store Web site 1' compared to the 'Iqra Book Store Web site 2.' This assumption was based on the time performance score which recorded an increase for the 'Iqra Book Store Web site 2' for the Middle East ($M = 1.21$, SD $= 0.37$), $t(43) = -9.92$, p<0.0005 and also for Malaysian users ($M = 0.68$, SD $= 0.39$), $t(43) = -9.474$, p<0.0005.

H_3: Middle East and Malaysian users' performance differ in doing tasks when using web sites of their own cultures

A one-way between-groups multivariate analysis of variance (one-way MANOVA) was performed to investigate the Middle East and Malaysian users, performing tasks in two different web sites. Two dependent variables were used: 'timesite1' and 'timesite2.' The independent variable was 'region group' (by Middle East or Malaysian). Preliminary testing was conducted for normality, linearity, univariate and multivariate outliers, homogeneity of variance–covariance matrices and multicollinearity, with no serious violations. There was a statistically significant difference between the Middle East and the Malaysian users on the combined dependent variables: $F(2, 85) = 34.16$, p $= 0.014$; Wilks' Lambda $= 0.554$; partial Eta squared $= 0.45$. When the results for the dependent variables were considered separately, both the dependent variables reached the statistical significance using a Bonferroni adjusted alpha level of 0.025. The first dependent variable was 'timesite1': $F(1,86) = 36.46$, p $= 0.000$, partial Eta squared $= 0.30$. The result supported H_3 that the task time performance would show that the Middle East and the Malaysian users' time performance differed when using the web sites targeted for their own culture ('Iqra Book Store Web site 1'). Although there was significant support from previous hypothesis that the Muslim users performed better in culture-centred web sites, however, the performance time between the Middle East and Malaysian users was different. This was suggested based on the findings of the inspection of the mean scores which showed that the Middle East users reported higher levels of time performance for the 'Iqra Book Store Web site 1' (M $= 0.45$, SD $= 0.41$) than the Malaysian users (M $= -0.06$, SD $= 0.38$).

4.2. Post-Study Result

The following are the post-study result for the set of hypotheses (H_4, H_5) used to answer RQ2. Generally, the hypotheses were used to determine whether the users would prefer the web site targeted for their own culture.

H_4: Middle East and Malaysian users are more satisfied with the design of the web site of their own cultures.

The 'Kruska Wallis' test was conducted to compare the difference in the satisfaction level of the Middle East and Malaysian users on their culture-centered web sites. Only three constructs: 'structure/ organization of information for the 'Iqra Book Store Web site 1' (p $= 0.018$), 'Ease of finding information site 1' (p $= 0.014$), and 'Ease of finding information site 2' (0.003) met the significance level set at less than 0.05. Further analysis was conducted on these constructs by using an inspection of mean ranks. An inspection of the mean ranks for the Middle East and Malaysian groups suggested that the Middle East had the highest preference for 'Structure/organization of information site 1' (50.50) compared to the Malaysians (38.60). Furthermore, the inspection of the mean ranks also suggested that the Middle East group had the highest preference for 'Ease of finding information site 1' (50.61) compared to the Malaysians (38.39). However, there were also mixed results on the findings as the inspection of the mean ranks also suggested that the Middle East users also showed the highest preference (52.16) compared to the Malaysian users (36.84) for 'Ease of finding information site 2.' Therefore, the evident results in this analysis provided a partial support that Muslims were more satisfied with the design elements of web site incorporated into their culture ('Iqra Book Store Web site 1') in terms of the structure or organization information.

H_5: Middle East and Malaysian users are more satisfied with the web site of their own cultures.

The Median test was conducted to test the hypothesis if the user prefers web sites from their cultural background. The results show that all the constructs were not statistically significant as they did not meet the threshold of less than 0.05. Therefore, there was no evidence support that could be provided for H_5.

5. Conclusions

This research sought to explore whether IA design imposed with specific cultural dimensions for B2C e-commerce may affect the usability level. To achieve the objective, this study was specifically designed to use Islamic culture as the context of the study. Two B2C e-commerce prototype web sites that reflect the incorporation of IA cultural design prescriptions against a control web site were used in the experimental session. Based on our literature and the result of the present study, we provide theoretical and empirical support that showed e-commerce web sites designed with targeted cultural background of the user has a positive influence toward the time-on-task performance. In addition, we manage to provide partial empirical support from the preference measurement used in the usability assessment of the web site IA design.

Furthermore, our research came to response to the perceived lack of common understanding or shared reference on cultural usability within the scope area of web site IA. We had managed to provide the conceptual model of the interaction design process between cultural and usability and showed that this conceptual model may have been leverage to design the guidelines for the B2C e-commerce from the cultural perspectives, for the benefit of the designers and practitioners. Thus, our work may provide the platform for researchers and practitioners to decide which IA designs and cultural dimensions that might be relevant to their context of study toward increasing the usability level. Researcher might find exploring the dimensionality of cultural dimensions highlighted in our work to be a continuing line of fruitful inquiry.

We believe that the main value of this study is in its contribution to the building body of knowledge in the web site IA domain. We also hope that our work will continue to encourage researchers to move beyond usability assessment by focusing more on the cultural perspective. It is our intention that our study will provide a bridge between research and practice due to the multi-disciplinary approaches ranging from conceptual model, empirical support, and design prescriptions, as illustrated in our study. These approaches are necessary and useful and together they will guide us to a better understanding of the intersection between IA and cultural usability.

References

1. Anderson, N. H. (2001) *Empirical Direction in Design and Analysis*, Lawrence Erlbaum Associates, Mahwah, NJ.
2. Barfield, L. (2004) *Design for New Media: Interaction Design for Multimedia and the Web*, Pearson Addison Wesley, New York.
3. Dijck, P. V. (2003) *Information Architecture for Designers: Structuring Websites for Business Success*, RotoVision, Hove.
4. Douglas, A. C., Mills, J. E., and Kavanaugh, R. (2007) Exploring the Use of Emotional Features at Romantic Destination Websites. In M. Sigala, L. Mich and J. Murphy (Eds.), *International Conference in Ljubljana, Slovenia, 2007*, Springer Vienna.
5. Ehn, P., Meggerle, T., Steen, O., and Svedemar, M. (1997) What kind of car is this sales support system? On styles, artifacts and quality-in-use. In M. Kyng and L. Mathiassen (Eds.), *Computers and Designs in Context*, pp. 111–144. The MIT Press, Cambridge, MA.
6. Faiola, A. (2006) Toward an HCI theory of cultural cognition. In C. Ghaoui (Ed.), *Encyclopedia of Human-Computer Interaction*, pp. 70–77. Idea Group: Hershet, PA.
7. Faiola, A., and Matei, S. A. (2006) Cultural cognitive style and web design: beyond a behavioral inquiry into computer-mediated communication, *Journal of Computer-Mediated Communication*, 11(1): 375–394.
8. Fan, Y. (2000) A classification of Chinese culture. Cross cultural management, *An International Journal*, 7(2): 3–10.
9. Fernandes, T. (1995) *Global Interface Design: A Guide to Designing International User Interfaces*, Academic Press, Inc., San Diego, CA
10. Field, A. (2005) *Discovering Statistics Using SPSS*, SAGE Publication Ltd, London.
11. Garrett, J. J. (2003) *The Elements of User Experience*, Aiga New Riders Publishing, New York.
12. Hofstede, G. (2001) *Culture's Consequences: Comparing Values, Behaviors, Institutions and Organizations Across Nations*, Sage Publications, Thousand Oaks, CA.
13. Hofstede, G., and Hofstede, G. J. (2005) *Cultures and Organization*, McGraw-Hill, New York.
14. Huo, Y. P., and Randall, D. (1991). Exploring subcultural differences in Hofstede's value survey: the case of the Chinese. *Asia Pacific Journal of Management*, 8(2): 159–173.
15. Knight, J., and Jefsioutine, M. (2006) Design frameworks. In C. Ghaoui (Ed.), *Encyclopedia of Human Computer Interaction*, pp. 150–153. Idea Group Reference, Hershey, PA.
16. Lash, S., and Lury, C. (2007) *Global Culture Industry: The Mediation of Things*, Polity, Cambridge, MA.

17. Lawrence, D., and Tavakol, S. (2006) *Balanced Website Design: Optimising Aesthetics, Usability and Purpose,* Springer, London.

18. Lodge, C. (2007) The impact of culture on usability: designing usable products for the international user. In N. Aykin (Ed.), *Usability and Internationalization, Part 1, HCII 2007,* pp. 365–368. Springer-Verlag, Berlin, Heidelberg.

19. Marcus, A. (2003). Global and intercultural user-interface design. In J. A. Jacko and A. Sears (Eds.), *The Human-Computer Interaction Handbook,* Lawrence Erlbaum, Mahwah, NJ.

20. Mccool, M. (2006) Information architecture: intercultural human factors. *Technical Communication,* 53.

21. Ozkan, S. (2001) *Development of Thinking and Theory in Architecture,* Retrieved January 22, 2007 from: http://www.csbe.org/e_publications/theory_in_architecture/essay10.htm

22. Rose, K. (2006). Cultural diversity and aspects of human machine systems in mainland China. In C. Ghaoui (Ed.), *Encyclopedia of Human Computer Interaction,* pp. 136–142. Idea Group Reference, Hershey, PA.

23. Rose, K., and Zuhlke, D. (2005) Localization of user-interface-design for mainland China: empirical study results and their description in a localization model and language issues. In X. Ren and G. Dai (Eds.), *Evolution of the Human-Computer Interaction,* Nova Publishers, Hauppauge.

24. Rosenfeld, L., and Morville, P. (1998) *Information Architecture for the World Wide Web,* O' Reilly, Sebastopol, CA.

25. Wan Abdul Rahim, W. M. I., Nor Laila, M. N., and Shafie, M. (2007) Incorporating the cultural dimensions into the theoretical framework of website information architecture. In N. Aykin (Ed.), *Usability and Internationalization, Part 1, HCII 2007, LNCS 4559,* pp. 212–221. Springer-Verlag, Berlin, Heidelberg.

26. Wan Abdul Rahim, W. M. I., Nor Laila, M. N., and Shafie, M. (2008) Inducting the dimensions of islamic culture: a theoretical building approach and website IA design application. In W. Khong, C. Y. Wong and B. V. Niman (Eds.), *21st International Symposium Human Factors in Telecommunication: User Experience of ICTs,* pp. 89–96. Prentice–Hall, Englewood Cliffs, NJ.

27. Wodtke, C. (2003) *Information Architecture: Blueprints for the Web,* New Riders Publishing, New York.

76

Computer Literacy of Population 50+ – A Case from Slovenia

Barbara Vogrinec

Abstract

The contribution refers to two projects of computer/ICT literacy of older adults in Slovenia that are also linked one to another. The first is the Slovenian national project "Computer literacy of population" – that was actually the first project of this kind in Slovenia, and that brought a new, innovative, i.e. the so-called brain learning-based curriculum. The second project is the European international project "Specific experiences in collaborative work using ICT – Photographic Internet gallery project" – that brought a curriculum developed on the basis of the one of the first project.

Keywords Computer literacy · Population 50 + · Brain learning

1. Introduction

In the period 2001–2004, CPZ-International, Centre for Knowledge Promotion, in collaboration with the Institute Jozef Stefan, carried out the project "Computer literacy of population" (the CLP project). This was the Slovenian national targeted research program project, funded by the Ministry of Education, Science and Sport and the Ministry of Information Society. A series of projects of computer (or ICT) literacy of population, that already exists in Slovenia, thus became enrichened by one project. But the CLP project is also the project that is worth to be set out. This is first of all because of two reasons. The first reason is that this project was actually the first of this kind in Slovenia, pertaining older adults – adults, older than 50 years – and mass of population. And the second reason is that it brought a new, innovative programme or curriculum for training of older adults for (and with) the use of ICT, i.e. the so-called brain learning-based curriculum – which then also became the basis for the development of another curriculum of the same kind, curriculum developed within another project.

2. The CLP Project and the PIG Project

2.1. The CLP Project

The goal of the CLP project was then the development of the curriculum (programme, approach ...) for mass basic computer literacy of adults 50 + and still or not anymore working. The target group was then the population characterized by the following:

– It represents an increasing part of today's so-called ICT (European, or rapidly ageing European) society.
– Mostly it is not well acquainted with or does not well master ICT.

Barbara Vogrinec • CPZ-International, Centre for Knowledge Promotion, Ljubljana, Slovenia.

G.A. Papadopoulos et al. (eds.), *Information Systems Development*, DOI 10.1007/b137171_76,
© Springer Science+Business Media, LLC 2009

- It also have negative attitude to ICT (including the conviction/prejudice that they are too old for learning).
- As a part of today's ICT (European, rapidly ageing European) society, this is the population for which the mastery of ICT is necessary – as far as it is necessary for its working performance and for keeping jobs (or for bigger employment possibilities), in case of those still working, or for raising the quality of life and enabling active ageing, in case of those not anymore working (i.e. in case of the retired people).

Further, the goal was the pilot version of the programme and educational materials.

The programme that was developed within the project is conceived in a way to effectively train older adults to acquire the basic competences of the use of ICT, and also to influence on the abolition of their fear of ICT, and on the development of positive attitude to ICT, and, consequently, to influence that these people become (more) active, creative, useful, and satisfied, also healthy, members of today's ICT (European) society. What is very important here is the proper training approach. Within the CLP project, an approach that considers the following three important issues was developed:

- psychological principles of older adult education
- senSorical-motorical and cognitive characteristics of older adults, and
- health and social condition

Or the CLP project brought a new, innovative, i.e. a brain learning-based curriculum.

This curriculum was then checked in three experimental workshops. Prior to each of them, two things were carried out:

- An interview with each of the participants to test, first of all, the individual's interests and his/her previous knowledge (which includes not only the individual's acquaintance with ICT, but also his/her interest for learning and the acquaintance with novelties), and
- A capability test to test the individual's sensorical-motorical and cognitive capabilities.

In this way the programme was able to be prepared or developed in cooperation with participants, or in accordance with their interests, capabilities.

Previous knowledge and the mentioned capabilities are actually the core criteria. The individual, for example, knows what he or she has to do, but is hindered by the fact that is dealing for the first time with the issue, or by sensorical-motorical and cognitive problems that he or she has because of his or her age (he or she does not see or hear well, for example, or does not remember how to do something). (As it was also able to be observed on the workshops, these two criteria are also very connected. For example' those without bigger problems with working with a mouse and a keyboard were in most cases active users of mobiles, etc., while the others were reserved towards these issues.)

On the workshops the learning environment defined first of all by the more personal attitude of trainers – including lecturer (mentor) and assistants (co-mentors) – to the trainees was set up. This means the following. Their role was, as it is used to say, being the "guide by the side" rather than being the "sage on the stage" [5]. Thus the trainers were not simply transferring new knowledge, new information, answers to the questions, problem solutions, to the trainees, but were helping them to get new knowledge, new information, answers, solutions by themselves – on the basis of their previous knowledge, information, answers, and solutions. This was taking place first of all in the form of the dialogue between the trainers and the trainees, in which, however, the questioner is the trainer rather than the trainee. It was then a matter of the dialogue similar to the dialogue that was taking place between philosopher Socrates and his students. Or, it was a matter of the dialogue where praising of trainees is also very important. The role of the trainers was then actually threefold: to be the mentor, the trainer and the facilitator. It was then a matter of the learning process defined first of all by the following: it is an active process; it evolves on a spiral – the trainee is continually building, creating on the basis of his/her previous knowledge, information; it is a process where the trainee is becoming more and more autonomous [3, 2].

Besides, the explanation was tried to be as simple and clear as possible, and oriented towards concrete problem solutions. As it was also able to be observed, the interest of the participants declined immediately, when the explanation became more complex. Also the material was tried to be good, organized and clear, with important information emphasized.

Of course, the success and progress of each (individual) trainee also depends on independent work out of the workshop. So, the participants were also stimulated to this kind of work – either at home or in libraries and cybercafés (in case of those not having computer at home).

Yet, a word concerning the proper extent of course hours. For the group of beginners, the 36 pedagogical hours course was taken. Some shorter time was taken for the advanced students in order that they acquaint themselves with the same issues, and the same time was taken for these students in order that they acquaint themselves also with other issues. And concerning the distribution of hours: taking into account two issues – first, that very intensive course may be too tiring for the participants, and, second, that the course that is time-extended enables the participants to master the issues properly (for example, it enables them the proper number of task repetitions) – three pedagogical hours per day, three times a week, for 4 weeks, was taken as the optimal distributon.

2.2. The PIG Project

Two years after the CLP project, in the period 2006–2007, CPZ-International, this time within the partnership of Ajuntament de Manresa from Spain, VUC Nordjylland from Denmark, and E-ÜLIKOOL/ Estonian e-university, carried out another project of computer literacy of (also) older adults – the project "Specific experiences in collaborative work using ICT – Photographic Internet gallery project" (the PIG project). This was the European International Lifelong Learning Programme (LLP) project or Grundtvig project.

The main goals of the project were to build transnational European network to share experiences in the use of ICT in adult education/training and to carry out workshops/courses on the collaborative work using ICT in each of the project partner countries.

In Slovenia these courses were carried out according to the curriculum developed on the basis of the CLP project curriculum. This curriculum – the PIG project curriculum – could be summarized as follows.

It is dedicated to the following target groups: adults 50+; unemployed.

The main programme goals are the following. On the first level: to acquire the basis of computer use. On the second level: to acquire the basis of moodle technology use. And on the third level: to realise the photographic Internet gallery project.

And the programme contents – that are chosen on the basis of the previous knowledge of students, etc. – are the following.

On the first level:

– computer and other equipment (like printer, modem, scanner)
– connecting computer to the world net
– using programmes for electronic mail
– exploring Internet
– editing texts with text editor

On the second level:

– access to information about e-courses, time table and pedagogical staff (e-mentors), access to e-contents and other tools of particular course
– communication with e-mentors and other e-students (adding comments and notes to the whole e-content, participating in forums, chats and so on – like audio and audio/video conferences)
– receiving exercises, homeworks, sending them to e-mentor, reviewing work results and so on.

And on the third level:

– realization of the photographic Internet gallery project, with the first proposal for the realization as follows. Concerning content – chosen also on the basis of the cooperation, between e-mentor and e-students: exploring the capital of Slovenia, Ljubljana, and concerning other tools: forum, chat and audio or audio/video conferences.

However, there are three more things about the courses carried out in Slovenia that have to be mentioned. The first is that the first of (the three of) the courses was a lab course. The second thing is that during the courses the competences for e-learning and e-mentors were tried to be developed. And the third thing, the courses – the second and the third – were taking place also online. In this way, the courses were taking place in different regions in Slovenia. This was also one of the ways of dissemination of the information concerning the project – that was taking place also in the following (two) ways. Pamphlets describing the courses were provided and disseminated to different relevant institutions (including employment services, lifelong learning institutions) in different regions in Slovenia. And the project was presented at the Regional Development Centre in Zagorje – where an interest for the introduction of the courses for unemployed persons was expressed.

3. Conclusions

To conclude this contribution – which refers to two projects of computer/ICT literacy of older adults in Slovenia that are also linked one to another – the (Slovenian national) CLP project and the (European international) PIG project – let us set out the Slovenian PIG project partner's future plans. These plans could be summarized as follows:

– to continue with courses on collaborative work using ICT
– to develop several e-learning courses on the basis of the (PIG and also CLP) project experiences and
– to develop the competences for e-learning and e-mentors.

References

1. Gabrscek, S., Ursic, M., Piscuric, J., Golob, P., Soklic, A. (2004) *Computer literacy of population. Final project report.* Slovenia, CPZ-International, Centre for Knowledge Promotion, Ljubljana.
2. Litou, N. (2008) *The development of teaching-learning materials in an e-learning environment.* In Roceanu, I. (ur.), *The 4th International Scientific Conference "eLearning and Software for Education"*, 17–18 April, Bucharest, Romania, pp. 321–327.
3. Moisil, I., Pah, I. (2008) *Challenges and opportunities in e-learning.* In Roceanu, I. (ur.), *The 4th International Scientific Conference "eLearning and Software for Education"*, 17–18 April, Bucharest, Romania, pp. 95–103.
4. Ursic, M., Vogrinec, B., Caf, H. (2007) *Specific experiences in collaborative work using ICT – Photographic internet gallery project. Final project report.* Slovenia, CPZ-International, Centre for Knowledge Promotion, Ljubljana.
5. Wolfson, G. (2007) *Preface.* In *Proceedings of the International Conference on Information Communication Technologies*, 12–14 July, Heraklion, Crete, Greece.

77

A Taxonomy of E-Health Standards to Assist System Developers

Emma Chávez, Padmanabhan Krishnan and Gavin Finnie

Abstract

Building e-health systems requires a good understanding of the range and characteristics of many relevant standards. These standards play an important role in the promotion of coordination amongst the key players in the technical and administrative areas of the e-health arena. Many entities including government, information technology professional bodies and medical organizations have developed a large number of e-health standards initiatives. Because of this broad range of initiatives, we propose a classification of standards to simplify the process to find out relevant information. The main objective is to facilitate the retrieval of e-health standards information by limiting the searching of classes or categories based on the applicability that the standards have in particular domains. Thus, we offer a framework to classify documents "standards" by assigning them to a predetermined set of categories and domains.

Keywords E-health · Standards · Taxonomy · E-health software · Accreditation

1. Introduction

Although the benefits of information technology in health care have been considered obvious for several decades, the successful implementation of e-health and national health care initiatives has been fraught with difficulty. IT health care programs have consistently failed to deliver, been over budget and/or late. In the UK, the NHS IT project [12] was intended to keep electronic records of 30 million patients. By 2006, it was £6bn over budget and 2 years behind schedule with the collapse of the software developer iSoft. Furthermore, according to the IHE survey [16] the cost of integration represents 20% of hospital IT budget. The main cause of this is the lack of "adequate health care IT standards".

Standards set specifications, formats, terminologies and others to enable information exchange. There are standards which have been developed for the same purpose offering two or more solutions. Nevertheless, none of them may be universally acceptable. On the other hand, multiple standards are also important as this leads to competition and helps to promote the quality of the e-health system environment [3]. Thus, it is not easy to select the best or most relevant standard.

During the last few years the focus on standardization has been mainly to achieve interoperability. For instance approximately 50% of the 88 standards considered provided guidance in the semantic area, such as information exchange and messaging. The general goal is to establish a set of parameters which can make the digital transmission/exchange and storage of health care information interoperable. To achieve

Emma Chávez • School of Information Technology, Bond University, Australia.; Departamento de Ing. Informática, Universidad Católica de la Ssma. Concepción, Chile. **Padmanabhan Krishnan and Gavin Finnie** • School of Information Technology, Bond University, Australia.

G.A. Papadopoulos et al. (eds.), *Information Systems Development*, DOI 10.1007/b137171_77,
© Springer Science+Business Media, LLC 2009

this interoperability standards are focussed in different areas such as message exchange, terminology and vocabulary, EHR object model (content and structure) and security [4, 9].

Nevertheless, standards are helping to assure only a part of the interoperability process. Therefore, it is necessary to identify essential requirements of quality and safety issues in other e-health-related areas such as clinical information system development. E-health applications are the basis in which patient information is stored, exchanged, processed and managed. The poor quality of e-health solutions can lead to inappropriate treatments, service delays, exposures of privacy and confidentiality and others which finally damage the patient outcomes [6]. Questions like What are the standards used to assure the quality of the process in e-health software developments? and What is the standard that states key functionalities for some specific e-health products? are not answered easily because of the great amount of information and standards developed and the diverse and large number of players involved in the e-health standardization arena.

Thus, accreditation, certification and standards compliance of e-health applications are some of the recommended solutions to ensuring quality. Consequently, the main aim of this chapter is to develop a taxonomy of e-health standards which can provide guidance to identify standards information in the specific IT domain of software engineering. The taxonomy has been designed to enable a wide variety of users (e.g. IT developers, e-health vendors and IT acquirers) to identify relevant standards.

In Section 2, a brief background and evolution of e-health standardization is showed. Section 3 introduces the framework based on five software engineering domains. In Section 4, we present a classification of various e-health standards as an example of how the taxonomy can be used. We also describe the use of a software prototype which has been developed to maintain and make usable the taxonomy proposed. We finally conclude this chapter in Section 5 with the research conclusions and the future research possibilities.

2. Background and Evolution of E-Health Standardization

2.1. Principal Standards and Stakeholders

There are at least six principal organizations which have developed e-health international standards including ASTM-E31, ANSI-HL7, CEN-TC 251, ISO-TC 215, NEMA-DICOM, and IEEE with the family of 1073.X standards. ASTM, the American Society for Testing and Materials based in the United States, is mainly used by commercial laboratory vendors. Its committee E31 is focused in developing e-health standards. ANSI, the American National Standards Institute operating in the United States, is developing HL7 which is a family of standards for the exchange, integration, sharing and retrieval of electronic health information. CEN, the European Committee for Standardization, has formed the Technical Committee CEN/TC 251 Health Informatics, which has created a series of European pre-standards and standards covering the electronic exchange of medical data principally focussed on Electronic Health Records. ISO, the International Organization for Standardization, develops e-health standards through the technical committee ISO TC215, which involves a number of other organizations such as CEN and HL7. The American College of Radiology (ACR) and the National Electrical Manufacturers Association (NEMA) have published DICOM, a standard that addressed the methods for data transfer in digital medical images in the United States. Finally IEEE, the Institute of Electrical and Electronics Engineers, is establishing a series of standards related with medical device communications. Table 77.1 summarizes some of the relevant standards proposed by different stakeholders.

Due to an extensive number of players in the e-health standardization area, the focus has been to work co-operatively to develop new standards and to obtain a general agreement and global consensus with the participants of the e-health community from many countries around the world. Thus, the establishment of the e-health Standardization Coordination Group (eHSCG) was proposed by the Workshop on Standardization in e-health (Geneva, 23–25 May 2003) with representatives of different standards bodies and the World Health Organization (WHO). Now stakeholders such as the WHO, ITU, ISO/TC

Table 77.1. Stakeholders vs. standards.

	Messaging	EHR obj. Model	Terminology	Security and others
ASTM	ASTM E1238, ASTM 1394	ASTM E1384	ICD9, SNOMED	ASTM E1762
HL7	HL7 V2	HL7 CDA	SNOMED CT	–
CEN	ENV13606-4, ENV 13607	ENV 13606-5, MEDICOM	ENV 12017	ENV 12251
NEMA	–	DICOM	–	–
ISO	ISO/TR 18307	–	–	ISO/TR 27809
IEEE	IEEE 1073.2.1.2	–	–	–

215, CEN/TC 251, IEEE/1073, DICOM, HL7 and OASIS "are working to promote stronger coordination amongst the key players in the e-health Standardization area" [9].

2.2. E-Health Standardization Problems

The main problems with standards are overlapping issues, the lack of a base of common terminology, several versions and the marketplace [4, 15, 18, 21]. Overlapping issues refer to different definitions and terminology properties in the reference models. Several versions make upgrades difficult and some of the versions of the same standard are incompatible. The lack of agreement in the use of standards causes different countries to implement different standards exacerbating the interoperability problems. All of these problems will be illustrated in more detail in the following paragraphs through the use of examples.

As the Medical Technology Policy Committee Interoperability Working Group states [11], standards should specify format (content and structure of the medical information) and access services (i.e. communication protocol). Nevertheless, EHR standards differ widely in scope and content [4, 15]; the only standards that specify both are DICOM SR and ENV 13606-5. Furthermore, there are differences in the core structures required for interoperability of health records or specific messages between HL7 data types and those developed by other organizations such as ISO and CEN [18].

Terminology differences between these standards can be seen in the reference model: in ENV 13606-5, the constraint rules are called "archetypes" while equivalent concepts in HL7 CDA are called "templates". Hence it is difficult to assess interoperability even though they can be made compatible [17].

The problem with several versions is highlighted by HL7. The basic HL7 standard, which is one of the most used standards for linking e-health data, is maintained by the American National Standards Institute (ANSI). Nevertheless, HL7 has a large number of affiliates and contributors in different countries. This standard has moved through several versions and is difficult to upgrade because new functionalities added by newer versions cannot be supported by an older version [13]. Moreover, HL7 has optional parts in its implementation, which generate "new specifications" for each HL7 implementation. Different interpretation and understanding of the key concepts in standards because of multiple versions of HL7 make the information exchange difficult.

The fourth problem identified is that even though a general agreement is necessary, not all the EHR standards are planned for an international market. Content EHR standards such as Medical Markup Language (MML), DICOM and HL7 could be used in many countries; however, MML has been developed particularly for the Japanese Market [15] whilst Australia has decided to use HL7.

To solve some of these problems standards organizations are moving towards a co-operative effort recognizing the work of others and providing the possibility to combine standards to cover different functions and make them more usable and accessible. For example, SNOMED International and HL7 have signed an agreement formalizing a joint venture in which SNOMED enables the harmonization between SNOMED Clinical Terms (SNOMED CT) and the HL7 Reference Information Model (RIM).

Similarly, ISO and CEN are signatories to the Vienna Agreement which allows technical cooperation between ISO and the European Committee for Standardization. As a result, e-health aspects such as patient safety have been covered by ISO/TS 23258:2006 Classification of Safety Risks from Health Informatics Products. This standard is now in the process of being published as an ISO Technical Specification and is a modified version of a near-equivalent European document (CEN/TS 15260:2006) [11].

Thus, there are a large number of standards which are incompatible in a number of ways. So, we have developed a system which can guide the various participants to pick the most relevant standards.

2.3. Software Development Standards in E-Health

Although e-health promises accessibility, effectiveness and efficiency of health care delivery, Dumay [8] argues that there is no structured framework of essential requirements of quality and safety issues. Consequently, the lack of consensus on standards [19], which can help the system as a whole, and particularly the necessity of a structured framework or set of activities with regulated software development can result in products with poor design and implementation being used and the most dangerous problem is the potential to harm patients [5]. It is essential that requirements with respect to quality and safety are complied with.

Even though some initiatives have been undertaken since the United States department of human and health services promoted the discussion about the future regulation of stand-alone clinical software systems in 1996 [10], there is no clear evidence about the formal use of either software safety standards or software development process standards in e-health.

Developers of e-health solutions are a heterogeneous group. They consist of software development companies, system integrators and in-house developers. In the commercial sector, the need to be ahead of the competition and financial pressures to be cost-effective may result in released products that have not been completely tested [14, 20]. According to Cooper and Pauley [7], clinical decision support systems currently have not being tested and reviewed in-depth; consequently, the most rigorous of assurance processes should be employed.

Thus, the most appropriate model of governance over the safety and quality of the development processes and product is far from clear [1] and "may involve elements of industry self-regulation, legislation and best practice guidance, to be safe certification might have to include the skills of those using the software, and the organisational processes in which the software is embedded" [5].

2.4. E-Health Standards' Main Categories

Some current efforts have been applied to structure the large number of e-health standards. These are the taxonomy of the National Health Information Network (NHIN) [18] and the e-health standards classification defined by Blobel [2]. Both will be briefly explained in the following paragraphs.

- The taxonomy of the NHIN: The IEEE-USA's Medical Technology Policy Committee Interoperability Working group [11] developed taxonomy of core standards. The two main categories are "medical terminology standards" such as the SNOMED-CT and LOINC terminology databases and "electronic health records standards", which digitally store information about laboratory test, observations, drugs, therapies and others, such as DICOM, Clinical Document Architecture (CDA) and ENV 13606.
- Blobel's e-health standards classification: The Blobel's classification [2] not only includes e-health standards but also includes technical IT formats and standards to cover different functions to achieve interoperability such as architecture standards (e.g. HL7 versions 2.x/3 and CORBA), modelling standards (e.g. UML and the CEN 15300 report "Framework for formal modelling of healthcare security policies") and communication standards (e.g. CEN 13608: "Security for health care communication").

It is also important to show the definition of interoperability provided by IEEE 1073, point of care of medical device communications [18], which specifically characterized two different types of interoperability and the aspects that they need to cover which are *Functional interoperability,* which is defined as "the capability to reliably exchange information without error", and *Semantic interoperability,* which is defined as "the ability to interpret, and therefore, to make effective use of the information exchanged".

3. The Taxonomy

Because of the need to assure the quality of e-health products and services, we focussed the classification mainly in the activities involved to carry out the development of software products and services. Thus, the classification discussed below has its basis under the e-health application (software and products) developments domain to assure quality of health care delivery.

As there is no terminology agreement between standards the process of classification is manual. Domains are characterized by definitions given by others and the categories of each domain will be based on comparing definitions, standard descriptions and scope and studies also conducted by others.

Domains consist of more than one category and represent processes, a set of activities or a collection of things. Each category by definition belongs to a specific domain. As a consequence, a standard will belong to one or more domains because it has determined features that apply to certain categories.

3.1. Taxonomy Domains

Software development process standards: According to ISO 12207, the software processes in general (e.g. waterfall, OOD) contains a set of activities such as requirement, design, operation, implementation, feasibility and planning testing. All of these activities have a set of tasks to develop new software or to maintain existing software. The categories for this domain are as follows:

- Software requirements: Description of the tasks that facilitate determining the needs (environmental and purpose including data formats) of the product under development. What are the necessities that the system or entity needs to cover.
- Software design: This activity describes the system architecture as an abstract representation addressing the depiction of interfaces between the software system and the other software products, as well as the hardware and operative system needed. Thus, e-health standards in this category should specify content such as interfaces, data structures and the representation of system functions.
- Software implementation: Generally represents the software coding but also the documentation of it. In this, an e-health standard represents the design reduced to code and shows the ways in which the software requirements will be implemented.
- Software testing: This activity has a number of tasks that identify whether the e-health product satisfies its defined requirements.

Quality assurance standards: Quality assurance involves a number of activities necessary to provide evidence of quality. In the case of e-health, both the supplier and the customer need to be satisfied with the quality and consistency of the services provided. Therefore, the requirements to establish desirable levels of quality must be defined in advance. To assure quality is necessary to provide confidentiality and integrity of the e-health services, which according to ISO 12207 are safety- and security-related issues. Thus, the categories for this domain are the following:

- Patient Safety: e-health standards can apply to this category if they provide guidelines to establish desirable levels of system security for patient safety.
- Data Security: e-health standards can apply to this category if they provide guidelines to establish desirable levels for authentication and data integrity of electronic health records and general issues for system security such as secure storage and transmission.

Interoperability standards: According to IEEE 1074, interoperability is defined as the ability of two or more systems or components to exchange information and to use the information that has been exchanged. Its definition splits into two categories which are:

- Semantic interoperability: It is the ability to interpret, and, therefore, to make effective use of the information. E-health standards in this category should share data types; such as types of data exchanged, messaging formats and programming languages, terminologies; such as common vocabularies for the interchange of information and coding; mechanisms to encode software functions, medical diagnoses and procedures.
- Functionality interoperability: It is the capability to reliably exchange information without error. E-health standards in this category should share architectures, such as design of the system; methods, such as process and procedures that the system performs; and frameworks, which represent a set of goals and strategies to ensure interoperability.

Other general domains:

- Communication standards: Communication can be defined as the transmission of data and information exchange between computers and/or devices. Thus, e-health standards in this category should provide specifications to control the exchange of information, the data representation, the signals and the authentication and error detection required to send and receive information between technology devices. This category includes network and protocol standards which facilitate the interoperability and support data transmission.
- Privacy standards: According to Clark (2003), privacy is "the interest that individuals have in sustaining a "personal space", free from interference by other people and organisations". Thus, e-health standards apply in this category if they provide guidelines and mechanisms to maintain, store and transmit private data (generally electronic health records) related to individuals and individual behaviour.
- Modelling standards: According to IEEE610.3-1 standard glossary of modelling and simulation terminology, modelling refers to the design and representation of decisions. This includes the actions and activities of existing or prospective organization or system. Thus, e-health standards apply in this category if they provide conceptual and contextual descriptions of systems and organizational processes. Additionally, standards in this category should represent e-health real-world interactions between services or processes and the entities involved (users) in these.

4. E-Health Standards Classification

Only a few standards were selected to illustrate the key aspects of the taxonomy. These are shown in Table 77.2. More information about these standards is provided in the taxonomy tool.

After the classification, a prototype application was developed to make the classification of standards proposed accessible. By providing a search engine tool, using simple or advanced search, e-health consumers, IT developers and vendors will be able to find a list of standards for each domain or category defined. Furthermore, this system was designed to allow the management of e-health document standards information and is intended to give information about the standards' use rather than the implementation of them. If additional information is required for a standard with a simple click on its name, information such as organization developer, contact and compliance tools are provided. A snapshot from the tool is given in Fig. 77.1.

5. Conclusions

The consistent implementation of health informatics standards is critical to achieving an information technology-enabled health sector. Furthermore, the integration practices of software quality assurance, safety analysis and formal activities for the development of e-health systems and products will greatly enhance the safety, reliability and quality of the e-health applications.

Table 77.2. Standard's classification.

Domain	Category	Standard	Explanation
Software process	Requirements	ANSI/AAMI SW68 Medical device software	It can be used to specify the life cycle processes including the requirements for software development, software maintenance and others for medical device software
	Design implementation	None e-health-specific WADO Web Access to DICOM	This defines a web-based service that can be used to retrieve DICOM objects (images, waveforms and reports) via HTTP or HTTPS from a web server
	Testing	CEN/TC 251 N 96018(prCEN/TS) Testing Physiological measurement software	This pre-standard describes a framework for specifying a set of test data, its documentation and use to be submitted to a medical software application
Quality assurance	Patient safety	ISO/TS 23258:2006 Classification of safety risks from health informatics products	This provides a framework for classifying safety risks associated with the use of health software based on patient's potential risk
	Security	ASTM-E31.20 Data and System Security for Health Information ISO 27799 Security management in health using ISO/IEC 17799	This offers guidelines to develop security services and mechanism standards for health care information and systems This provides general guidelines for identifying a range of security controls needed for health information systems
	Gnarl assurance	None e-health-specific	
Interoperability	semantic	DICOM (Shared Data)	This shares data such as the data structures dictionary and the messaging formats to transfer, to query, to retrieve, to store and to print digital images and associate documents
		SNOMED - CT (clinical terminology)	This is a clinical terminology database which contains approximately 325000 concepts, 800000 terms in English, 350000 in Spanish, 150000 in German and 1,200,000 relationships
		ISO/TR 18307:2001 (shared framework)	This is a framework that describes a set of key characteristics for developing messaging and communication systems in health care. It is a guide for software developers, vendors, and health care providers and set criteria for standards developers and implementers
	Functionality	IEEE P11073-00103	This describes the landscape of transport independent applications and information profiles for personal telehealth devices
Other	Communication	prENV 1064:2000	This pre-standard specifying the data format and means for electrocardiogram digital transmission among digital electrocardiographs, computer electrocardiogram, management systems and other computer systems that store electrocardiographs
	Privacy	ISO/TS 22600-1:2006	This provides guidelines to define methods for managing authorization and access control of sharing health information among unaffiliated providers of health care, health care organizations and others.
	Modelling	None e-health specific	

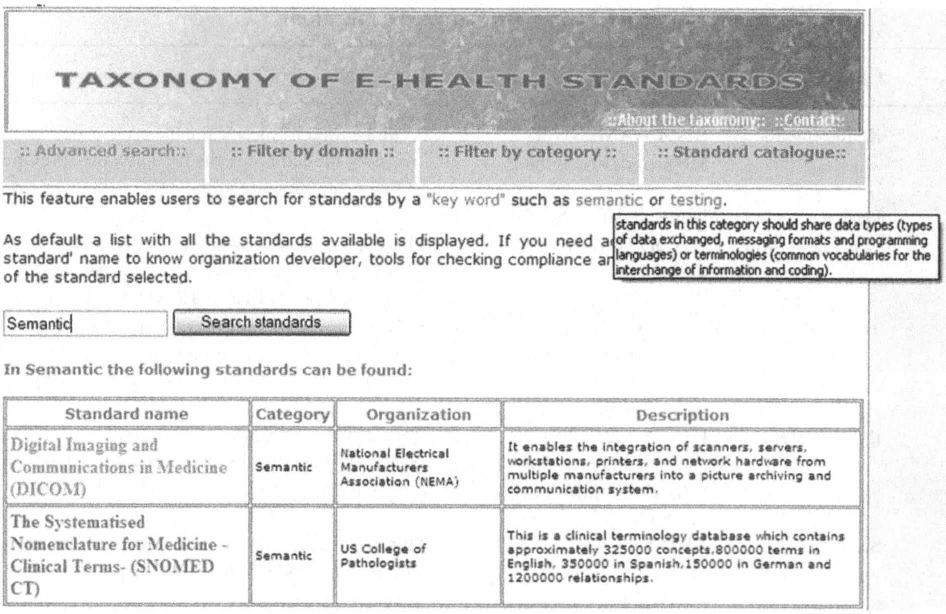

Figure 77.1. Taxonomy of e-health standard tool.

Thus, the validation of standards implementation requires measurement of the product or software applications' conformance relative to a set of points set out in the standard. In this manner, how to identify the relevant standards is one of the main contributions of the taxonomy proposed. The taxonomy provides guidance to those in the health sector who are responsible for improving care delivery through information technology by identifying the applicability of health informatics standards in different domains of the software engineering arena. It is likely that the understanding in the domains defined by the taxonomy will minimize risk and development costs because suppliers, developers and purchases may identify the areas to obtain standards' conformance. Thus, the standards applicability of main features and information necessary to start with an implementation were identified. However, the evaluation and effectiveness of the standards are issues for future work. The prototype tool also provides general guidelines, tools for checking compliance, accredited standards and the application areas in which a standard can be used.

Achieving interoperability through standards implementation is a consideration for every aspect of an implementation. Therefore, more than 50% of the standardization activities studied comprised functionality. Consequently, it can be possible to find more standards which are formally accredited in this category which apply to systems implementation rather than activities such as project design, testing or management. Although there are areas in which specific e-health standards were not identified, there are general information technology standards that can be applied. Therefore, the harmonization between general IT standards and specific e-health standards to complete the taxonomy are activities for future research.

References

1. AMA Position Statement. (2006). *Safety and quality of e-health systems.* Retrieved January 13, 2007 from: http://www.ama.com.au/web.nsf/doc/WEEN-6VD2PW
2. Blobel, B. (2007). *RIDE project workshop.* Retrieved June 12, 2007 from: http://www.imu.iccs.gr/events/semhealth/presentations/06-RIDE-BerndtBlobel.pdf
3. Chheda, N. (2007). *Standardization and certification: The truth just sounds different.* Retrieved January 29, 2008 from: http://www.nainil.com/research/whitepapers/Standardization_and_Certification.pdf

4. Cohen, S. and Shabo, A. (2001). *Electronic health record (EHR) standards survey*. Retrieved June 29, 2007 from: http://www.haifa.ibm.com/projects/software/imr/papers/EHRSurvey.pdf

5. Coiera, E., Westbrook, J. I. and Wyatt, J. C. (2006). The safety and quality of decision support systems. *IMIA Yearbook of Medical Informatics*, 20(5): 20–25.

6. Coiera, J. I. and Westbrook, E. W. (2006). Should clinical software be regulated? *Medical Journal of Australia*, 184(12): 600–601.

7. Cooper, J. G. and Pauley, K. A. (2006). Healthcare software assurance. In: *Annual Symposium of the American Medical Informatics Association*, pp. 166–170.

8. Dumay, A. C. M. (2007). Improving ehealth quality and safety. *Proceedings of Med-e-Tel*, pp. 151–159.

9. Eichelberg, M., Aden, T., Riesmeier, J., Dogag, A. and Laceli. G. B. (2005). A survey and analysis of electronic healthcare record standards. *ACM Computing Surveys,* 37(4): 273–315.

10. Food, Drug Administration Center for Devices, and Radiological Health. (1996). *Announcements and minutes of meetings on future regulation of stand-alone clinical software systems*. Retrieved January 13, 2007 from: http://www.fda.gov/cdrh/

11. IEEE-USA's Medical Technology Policy Committee Interoperability Working Group. (2006). *Interoperability for the NHIN*. IEEE-USA Books.

12. IHE. (2005): *Development priorities survey*. Retrieved April 29, 2007 from: http://www.ihe.net/pcd/survey_2006.cfm

13. Health Level Seven Inc. *What is HL7?* http://www.hl7.org/about/.

14. Miller, R. A. and Gardne, R. M. (1997). Recommendations for responsible monitoring and regulation of clinical software systems. In: *Journal of the American Medical Informatics Association*, 4(6):442–457.

15. *National E-Health Transition Authority: Standards for e-health interoperability*. (2007). Retrieved November 25, 2007 from: http://www.nehta.gov.au/index.php?option = com_docman&task = doc_download&gid = 252&Itemid = 139

16. *Report by the Comptroller and Auditor General*, HC 1173. (2006). Retrieved January 29, 2008 from: http://www.nao.org.uk/publications/nao_reports/05-06/05061173.pdf

17. *RIDE D.5.3.1 – Proposals to Standardization Bodies*. (2007) Retrieved December 12, 2007 from http://www.srdc.metu.edu.tr/webpage/projects/ride/deliverables/RIDE-D5_3_1_Proposals_to_standardization_Bodies_version_II.doc

18. Rowlands, D. (2007). *Standards Australia, report on ISO TC215*. Retrieved June 12, 2007 from: http://www.e-health.standards.org.au/downloads/TC215%20Montreal%20Report.pdf

19. Tan, J. (2005). *E-health Care Information Systems*. Jossey-Bass, New York.

20. Thomas, R. (2001). *The ehealth landscape: A terrain map of emerging inf. and com. technologies in health and health care*. Princeton, NJ: The Robert Wood Johnson Foundation.

21. World Health Organization. (2005). *Basic operational framework on ehealth for health care delivery*. Retrieved April 29, 2007 from: http://www.who.int/eht/eHealthHCD/en/print.html

78

Mobile Location-Based Services for Trusted Information in Disaster Management

Lemonia Ragia, Michel Deriaz and Jean-Marc Seigneur

Abstract

The goal of the present chapter is to provide location-based services for disaster management. The application involves services related to the safety of the people due to an unexpected event. The current prototype is implemented for a specific issue of disaster management which is road traffic control. The users can ask requests on cell phones or via Internet to the system and get an answer in a display or in textual form. The data are in a central database and every user can input data via virtual tags. The system is based on spatial messages which can be sent from any user to any other in a certain distance. In this way all the users and not a separate source provide the necessary information for a dangerous situation. To avoid any contamination problems we use trust security to check the input to the system and a trust engine model to provide information with a considerable reliability.

Keywords Disaster management · Location-based services · Trust management

1. Introduction

The wireless technology becomes important in our daily life because it provides a lot of services. The World Wide Web gives the opportunity to people to connect mobile phones or portable devisces to Internet. Universal Mobile Telecommunication System (UMTS) with the new smart phones enable more services. The number of people that use the Web and the wireless technology is increasing rapidly.

User location was difficult to find out but with the usage of global positioning system (GPS) new possibilities are open. The integrated technology of GPS devices gives the location of the people quickly and with accuracy. That means that we can have location-based services (LBS) which connect, in principle, the geographic location with user requests.

There are several approaches that show personalized LBS services for different applications: in the area of tourism [1, 14, 16] or navigation [10]. There are also some approaches for LBS which discuss the connection to databases [6, 7].

Disaster management is an important topic for local authorities, governments and disaster managers because they try to manage efficiently all the information provided mainly from people on the field to provide directions to the public. LBS for disaster management is extremely useful for the citizens since they can have great benefits having the right information in the appropriate time. In the scientific area of disaster management there are appro7aches which simulate a pre-disaster phase [9] or demonstrate an open source software especially for natural hazards [4]. Application for LBS for disaster management can be

Lemonia Ragia, Michel Deriaz and Jean-Marc Seigneur • Advanced Systems Group, Centre Universitaire d'Informatique, University of Geneva, Geneva, Switzerland.

G.A. Papadopoulos et al. (eds.), *Information Systems Development*, DOI 10.1007/b137171_78,
© Springer Science+Business Media, LLC 2009

found on the area of health care [13]. There are different aspects for services for disaster management. We can classify them in the following categories:

- Services for Natural hazards. This service provides information about the natural physical phenomena which can happen at any time. Earthquake, flood, cyclones, fire, etc. belong to this category. These information use *historical data* and try to make prediction for local authorities or other responsible offices to share the information and advise people how to avoid such a situation and protect themselves.
- Safety-related services. In this category the information is related to the safety of the people in unexpected events. Man-made disasters such as car accidents or a plane crash are included. It provides information for a dangerous situation and it uses *real-time data*. These *real time data* are related to this event and can be provided by any user.

In our approach we deal with the safety-related services. An important issue in disaster management is for instance the traffic control. This service gives information about a safe and free travel and helps the users to avoid any kind of unexpected difficult occasion. It does not include the normal traffic jams during rush hours but it is related to unexpected events happening in special conditions. It takes into account a big area of infrastructure and it is updated by the users living through the event.

The mobile LBS application in our system is based on spatial messages. A spatial message is a message which refers to a specific geographic location. It allows a mobile user to publish a geo-referenced note so that any other user close and affected can get the message. Let us consider a community of car drivers. For example, an accident can happen or there is a fire next to the road. The car drivers would like to communicate about such event-related dangers in specific places.

Spatial messaging has been already used. We could site for instance E-Graffiti [2]. E-Graffiti is a spatial messaging application that allows a user to read and post geo-localized notes. These notes can be either public or private, meaning that only the set of people defined by the author are able to read the note. E-Graffiti has been designed to study the social impact on spatial messaging.

Another interesting example is GeoNotes [12]. GeoNotes has more functionalities than E-Graffiti. While posting a note, the user can choose how he is going to sign it (for privacy reasons the user can write any text he wants as a signature), decide whether people are allowed to comment on it and decide whether anyone can remove this message. For the readers, the graphical interface of the application provides some interesting functionalities like showing all the neighbouring messages or sort them according to different criteria. Inspired by the E-Graffiti evaluation, GeoNotes discarded the remote authoring of tags as well as the possibility to "direct" notes to certain users.

In our system the mobile location based-services include the connection to a central database and in principle every user can send data to the central database using virtual tags. The virtual tags include any spatial messages which are related to a geo-referenced context related to disaster information. An important issue in our system is the use of a trust engine that gives information with considerable reliability to the users. We develop a framework that provides, among other things, a set of generic trust engines and a tool box providing geo-related tools. This framework, called LBSDisMan (location-based services for disaster management), should provide APIs (application programming interfaces) in order to ease future development of applications using virtual tags. The results can be presented in a cell phone or any other Internet appliance.

In the next section we present the system architecture and give some details for the server and the client part. Sections 3 and 4 focus on security and trust in the system. Section 5 gives an example of a real application and Section 6 discusses results and further work to improve the system.

2. System Architecture

In order to share the spatial data among the users, we use a centralized architecture. The data are organized in small units that we call virtual tags. Each tag contains geo-related information, that means its position, and a content that is written in HTML.

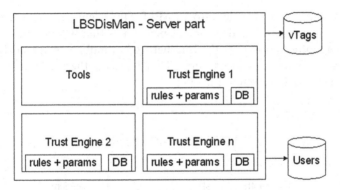

Figure 78.1. LBSDisMan server part of the framework.

The server part of our framework is represented in Fig. 78.1. The application designer starts by choosing the trust engine according to the kind of tag he is dealing with, then customizes it with code (if needed) and parameters and finally defines how the tags have to be stored (memory, flat files, database). For the storage, template classes should be provided in order to ease the development but still lets the possibility for the developer to implement his own specifications.

The trust engines are generic and easily extensible. Each trust engine proposes a set of parameters in order to adapt its behaviour according to a given application, and all the trust computations are made in a standard and formalized way. This means that an application designer is able to adapt a trust engine by adding, modifying or removing the rules used to compute a trust value. Roughly speaking, the designer of a new application will have to code "how much a specific behaviour in a specific context costs in terms of trust value". He will therefore only have to code behaviours directly related to its application, leaving the framework doing all the job of maintaining and managing the trust information. This should guarantee that our trust engines can be adapted to any situation and therefore really be generic.

The Tools box is used by the trust engines and can also be accessed by the application. It contains mostly geographical-related tools, like methods allowing conversions or methods handling tags of different formats.

All accesses to the database (vTags contains the virtual tags and Users contains the ID of the users) are done via the trust engines. It can be of any storage solution, including no permanent storage (information is kept in memory), flat files or a SQL standard database. Throughout this document, we will use the term "database" or its abbreviation "DB" to mention any storage system, and use the term "SQL database" or "SQL DB" if we talk about a "traditional" relational database using the SQL language to interact with.

Each trust engine provides a box allowing it personalization through rules and parameters, as well as a DB box responsible to store the tags in a permanent way. The latter should provide classes that can be adapted for the main storage architectures but also provide a generic solution that can be extended by a developer willing to implement its own storage architecture.

The trust engine should be accessed via three main primitives:

- *setTag*. This primitive simply creates a new tag. No trust mechanism is used.
- *getTags*. Returns a list of tags. The requester specifies which filter he wants to apply to the result. For instance, a user can ask to get all the tags in a certain radius, with updated trust values for the author and the reviewers, and let the application decide what to do. But he can also ask to get only the tags that are above a certain trust level and ignore the others. Or he can apply a personal filter and not use the trust mechanism at all, like asking all the tags that are authored or reviewed by a user.
- *reviewTag*. Reviewing a tag means to rate it, optionally to add a comment, and then update the trust tables of the reviewer, the author and the former reviewers. The way the trust tables are updated is defined through the rules and the parameters. The framework splits all the behaviours so that the application developer can simply write the rules according to the needs of its application.

The LBSDisMan framework provides also an API for the client part. This API provides geo-related tools, tools to manage virtual tags and also some general tools that will be needed by spatial messaging applications like sending information over the Internet from a mobile device storing information on the local device, or accessing to an external or internal GPS (or another positioning device). A graphical representation of the client part is given in Fig. 78.2.

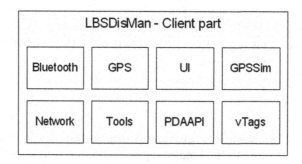

Figure 78.2. LBSDisMan client part of the framework.

3. System Security

In a secured spatial messaging system, a user can be sure that the message he is reading is really written by the mentioned author, that nobody has modified the content of the original message and that all other available messages at this place are available. More precisely, a secured spatial messaging system has to respect the "traditional" security services that are the following [3]:

- Confidentiality: Protection of the information against divulgations.
- Integrity: Protection of the information against modifications.
- Availability: Information is always available.
- Entity authentication: The author can be identified.
- Data origin authentication: Information can be linked to its author.
- Non-repudiation: The author cannot repudiate a message.
- Non-duplication: Protection against copying the information.
- Anonymity: The real-life identity of the users must be preserved.

Our aim is to focus on specific security services, the ones that are required for spatial messaging (in addition to the "traditional" ones). These are centered on the *pseudonym concept* [8]. What we would like is a system in which an author can be identified, but at the same time we would like to prevent any link with his real-life identity. A new user is therefore able to get a pseudonym in an anonymous way, but only one. If the person can obtain an unlimited number of pseudonyms, then the system can be victim of a Sybil attack [5]. The user must also be able to change its pseudonym. Again, this must be done in an anonymous manner and it must be impossible to link a former pseudonym with the new one.

A secured spatial massaging system must therefore respect, in addition to the "traditional" security services, the following "specific" ones:

- A user has only one pseudonym at a time.
- A user must be able to change its pseudonym.
- It is impossible to link a pseudonym to a real-life identity.
- It is impossible to link two pseudonyms of the same real-life identity (an old one with a new one).

Each pseudonym is unique, it is impossible that two different real-life identities share the same pseudonym. This is even true over time; if a user changes its pseudonym, the old one is locked and can never be used again. If in our application, we have a small community of users, we could choose to base the security of the database, its access and the users information via the use of a Public Key Infrastructure (PKI).

4. Trust in the System

The previous section discussed the security aspects of spatial messaging. A reader can be sure that a given message is really posted by its signer and that the content has not been modified since. But even if the reader can be sure about the author's identity, it is useless if they do not know each other. This section discusses how to add trust information on spatial messages so that the reader can evaluate the reliability of a message.

Trust is a very complex concept. Even if it is part of everyday life, different people give also different definitions of what trust is. This observation is even strongly accentuated when we try to explain how to build a trust relation between machines or between humans and machines. One reason is that most models are only designed and specialized for peer-to-peer file sharing systems. For example, these models do not take time into account. In spatial messaging time is very important. For example a message indicating a high risk of avalanches posted yesterday has to be taken more seriously than the same message posted 6 months ago.

Spatial messaging needs a specific trust model that takes time into account, as discussed previously, and that is sufficiently flexible to be adapted to different situations. For example, in a mountain guide example, we suppose that the community of users is quite small and that a Web-Of-Trust trust model [14] will be sufficient. If user A trusts user B at 0.8 (out of 1), and user B trusts user C at 0.5, then user C rating (in user A's eyes) will only count for $0.8 \times 0.5 = 0.4$. This does not mean that user A's trust in user C is only 0.4. It is only the number by which user C's rating will be multiplied.

However, this model does not work for large communities. In this case we need to know the global reputation of the author. We could of course provide two different models depending on the size of the community. There is also a third trust model, the one that informs about the reliability of the message itself, without taking care of the author's reputation. Even a very reputable author can make a mistake and publish wrong information. Or, even more likely, a message signed by a reputable editor can contain outdated information.

We use a trust model which is actually the model that will combine the former ones. Its role is to answer the "How to trust the different trust models" question. The three previous models will give us three different trust values, and the fourth model's role is to determine, according to the current situation, how much weight to give to each value. In this way we obtain a trust engine that is generic and can be easily applied to any situation.

5. Implemented Prototype

We have developed a system for mobile location-based services for disaster management according to the architecture outlined in the previous section. We applied it in a specific topic of disaster management which is road traffic control. We used a central database including traffic data and additional data related to unexpected events and disaster phenomena. For the geometry we follow the standards of Open Geospatial Consortium [11] using their geometrical attributes.

The system incorporates spatial queries including requests regarding the content, the geographical position, the address and the time. The content describes all the information about this specific theme, e.g. "give all the fires in a distance of 50 km of the place with coordinates X and Y". The geographical position is based on the longitude and latitude of a location which can be taken by a navigation system or GPS, e.g. a spatial query can be "car stops at a position with X and Y coordinates, is there any problem in the highway". An address refers to a street (name, number or code), to postal code, to a name of a city, e.g. "give all information about traffic jam in the highway number 5 in Switzerland" and the date can be a day, a month, week, year, part of day, hour, minute, e.g. "show all the accidents positions during April 2006". Or when car driver is on a forest road can ask "is any fire in a specific part of a road". The content will also be chosen by the service and there will be a lot of possibilities to make different kind of queries.

The system allows the user to enter data via virtual tags using a location. Then spatial messages can be sent to other users. In this case a user can ask for a user profile. The trust engine provides a trust value which is between [0,1]. Zero means totally unreliable, 0.5 neutral and 1 highest reliability. We developed an application running on mobile phones that helps the user to find the closest exit from the centre of a city (Fig. 78.3). Something unexpected happened and the traffic stops for some time. A Bluetooth GPS connected to the mobile phone gives the current position of the user, and the GPRS protocol is used by the mobile in order to connect to the server that hosts the data. The user receives spatial messages in his cell phone "there are flames in a building" with high trust value.

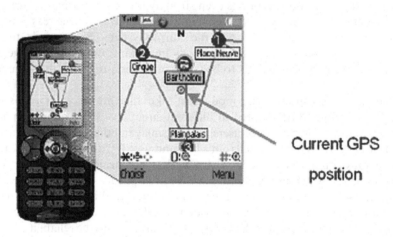

Figure 78.3. Visualization of the information.

In this example the user using a GPS system provides his/her coordinates to the system and asks the query "which are the next exits from this specific location in the centre of Geneva". The green point with a circle shows the position of the user. Then the system shows the exit 1, 2, 3 with blue colour (Fig. 78.3). Due to the security part of the system and after analysing the data the system gives only one solution to the user which is the number 3 in this case and highlighted in green on the mobile phone display. The visualization of the results can be displayed in a mobile electronic device like a cell phone (Fig. 78.3).

The implementation of our system includes spatial queries in SOAP protocol and in XML language and answers can be shown via XML or SOAP. The system uses suitable methods for selecting, storing and detecting user profiles according to their location.

6. Conclusions

We present a system for mobile location-based services for disaster management and its application for traffic control. The system uses spatial messages to share geo-referenced information to the users. It incorporates a central database and every user is allowed to feed data in the database. The users can use the services to ask queries at a given spatial location and receive the messages real time in a smart phone or other Internet device. Our system integrates trust engines and its security is also taken into account. In this way we improve the quality and reliability of the services. We implemented a disaster management scenario using real examples and we used the cell phone display to show the results of the spatial messages.

Currently we work on the implementation of the designed services to improve the results. We would like to use a bigger scenario with more real data. We envision a system applied in other applications of disaster management. From the database perspective we will work more in database integration and try to use the system with real data provided by other sources. In addition, we investigate the model of the trust engine as a general framework for open applications.

Acknowledgments

This work is sponsored by the European Union, which funds the FP7-ICT-2007-2-224024 PERIMETER project.

References

1. Antikainen, H., Rusanen, J., Vartiainen, S., Myllyaho, M., Karvonen, J., Oivo, M., Similä, J. and Laine, K., 2006: Location-based Services as a Tool for Developing Tourism in Marginal Regions. Nordia Geographical Publications, 35: 2, pp. 39–50.
2. Burrell, J., Gay, G. K., 2002: E-graffiti: evaluating real-world use of a context-aware system. In Interacting with Computers, 14: 4, pp. 301–312.
3. Charton, E., 2005: Hacker's Guide, Edition DeLuxe. Campus Press, Boulder, CO.
4. Currion P., Silva de, C., and Walle Van De, B., 2007: Open source software for disaster management. Communications of the ACM, 50: 3, pp. 61–65.
5. Douceur J. R., 2002: The Sybil attack. In Proceedings of the IPTPS02 Workshop, Cambridge, MA, USA, March.
6. Gruber, B., Winter, S., 2002: Location based services using a database federation. In: Ruiz, M., Gould, M., and Ramon, J. (Eds.), 5th AGILE Conference. Universitat de les Illes Balears, Palma, Spain, pp. 243–252.
7. Jensen, C. J., Christiensen, A. F., Pedersen, T. B., Pfoser, D., Saltenis, S. and Tryfona, N., 2001: Location based services – A database perspective. In: Bjorke, J. T. and Tveite, H. (Eds), Proceedings of 8th Scandinavian Research Conference on Geographical Information Science, pp. 59–68.
8. Lubinski, A., 1998: Security issues in mobile databases access. In Proceedings IFIP WG 11.3 12th International Conference on Database Security
9. Meisner A., Luckenbach T., Risse T., Kirste T., and Kirchner H., 2002: Design challenges for an integrated disaster management communication and information system. In the IEEE DIREN 02, The First IEEE Workshop on Disaster Recovery Networks.
10. Müller J., 2006. Location based services indoor navigation. Presentation, ifgi.uni-muenster.de/~muellerj/lbs06/vortraege/8-IndoorNavigation.ppt
11. Open Geospatial Consortium, http://www.opengeospatial.org/
12. Persson, P., Espinoza, F., Fagerberg, P., Sandin, A., and Cöster, R., 2000: GeoNotes: a location-based information system for public spaces. In: Höök, K., Benyon, D., and Munro, A. J. (Eds.), Readings in Social Navigation of Information Space, Springer, London.
13. Rahman A. A. and Zlatanova S., 2006: Pre-hospital location based services (LBS) for emergency management. In: Fendel, E., and Rumor, M. (Eds.), Proceedings of UDMS'06 Aalborg, pp. 11.49–11.57
14. Zimmerman P., 1994: PGP User's Guide, The MIT Press, Cambridge, MA.
15. Zipf A., Malaka R., 2001: Developing location based services for tourism the service providers. In: Sheldon, P., Wöber, K., Fesenmaier, D. (Eds.), Information and Communication Technologies in Tourism, Proceedings of ENTER 2001, 8th International Conference. Montreal, Springer Computer Science, Wien, New York, pp. 83–92.
16. Zipf A., 2002: User adaptive maps for location based services (LBS) for tourism. In Proceedings Conference for Information and Communication Technologies in Travel & Tourism (ENTER). Springer-Verlag, Berlin.

79

Resolution of Complexity in ISD Projects

Jill Owen and Henry Linger

Abstract

ISD projects are characterised by complexity because they are situated in an unstructured environment where requirements are dynamic and the technical solution is potentially unknown. In this context existing tools, routines and methodologies may not be sufficient to resolve the complexity that emerges during the project life span. The resolution of complex issues requires access to a broad range of experience and knowledge and the ability to apply that knowledge to the specific requirements of the project. Knowledge processes, such as experimentation, sense making and learning, amongst others, represent an innovative and flexible means to address the intrinsic complexity of ISD projects. In this chapter we argue that knowledge processes must be explicitly incorporated into project management in order to resolve emergent issues and integrate knowledge created by those practices into project management tools, techniques and methodologies. The chapter presents a study of the rollout of an enterprise project management software project in an Australian government department to illustrate the role of knowledge processes to resolve complex issues and how these processes became incorporated into the emergent methodology used to manage the project.

Keywords ISD projects · Complexity in ISD projects · Knowledge processes

1. Introduction

Businesses are continually responding to a competitive environment by utilising innovative techniques to deliver business strategies and goals [1]. Implementation of innovation requires an iterative or experimental approach [2]. As organisations respond to competition and innovation, information systems development (ISD) projects play a key role in this process [6]. These projects are complex endeavours.

Complexity is intrinsic to the development process of ISD projects as often requirements and technical solutions evolve throughout the project. This complexity gives rise to high failure rates in ISD projects. One aspect of the high failure rates is that existing approaches to the management of ISD projects are insufficient to deal with the intrinsic complexity of these projects.

Knowledge processes (KP) represent one approach to address complexity. Such processes incorporate learning and knowledge into the management of project, supplementing the tools and techniques derived from scientific management and the methods of soft systems. In this chapter we contend that KP techniques are key to the resolution of intrinsic complex issues in ISD projects [11]. This approach contributes to the development of a theoretical explanation of issues resolution in project management [3]. The chapter is structured as follows: a background on complexity in ISD projects is discussed and a theoretical framework introduced. This is followed by a case study of a project to roll out an enterprise project management software tool in a large Australian Government Department. This case study is then analysed through the lens of the theoretical framework.

Jill Owen • School of Business, Australian Defence Force Academy, University of New South Wales, Canberra, Australia.   **Henry Linger** • Faculty of Information Technology, Monash University, Melbourne, Australia.

G.A. Papadopoulos et al. (eds.), *Information Systems Development*, DOI 10.1007/b137171_79,
© Springer Science+Business Media, LLC 2009

2. Complexity in ISD Projects

Complexity is inherent in the development of ISD projects [9] as these projects are characterised by a very large number of elements, a variety of stakeholders [17], a diversity of technological issues and organisational factors [21], the dynamic or emergent nature of requirements or specifications and the technology to deliver the project [19]. A number of problems of ISD emanate from this complexity.

ISD projects can be characterised in terms of people, technology, processes and the situated nature of the project: its context. Complexity in the technology domain is manifested in terms of its novelty, application and integration with other systems. From the people perspective complexity emerges from the size of the project, the diversity of the project team, the skill sets of the team and the number of stakeholders and users. ISD projects follow a development cycle that is usually prescribed and integrates with an organisation, other business processes and organisational structures. Projects differ in terms of their scope, requirements, size, the volume of new information and the complexity of that information [9, 17, 21].

The complexity of the process domain is tied to how these factors influence the prescribed process in terms of how it is adapted to the specific conduct of the project. While complexity is intrinsic to each domain, it is compounded by the interactions between the domains and with the social and organisational contexts that influence the project. The complexity intrinsic to ISD projects is manifested in the domains and the patterns of interactions as represented in Fig. 79.1.

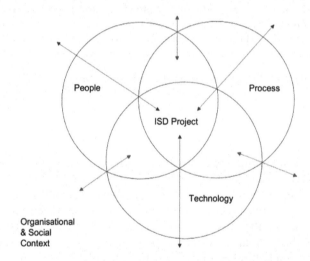

Figure 79.1. The complex nature of ISD projects.

3. A Theoretical Framework for ISD Complexity

Complexity can be characterised by a number of important characteristics such as self-organisation, non-linearity and emergence [15]. A complex system requires a meta-level understanding that includes an account of its inherent dynamics and the ability to incorporate unanticipated and unforeseen features. Snowden's Cynefin model, shown in Fig. 79.2 [15], provides a framework as a knowledge space conceptualised as three sectors of order, unorder and disorder. The model implies that complex phenomena co-exist in the order and unorder sectors but are not viable in the disorder sector. Within the order sector are the domains of the known and the knowable, while complexity and chaos domains exist in the unorder sector. Each domain has a different mode of community behaviour and each implies a different form of management and leadership style as well as requiring different tools, practices and conceptual understanding of the phenomena [7].

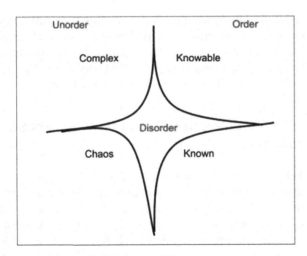

Figure 79.2. The Cynefin framework (adapted from Snowden [15]).

The usual normative approaches to project management are grounded in the known domain. Work in this domain is characterised by standard operating procedures and techniques based on rational processes. Project management has a BoK for the management of projects [12] that is underpinned by assumptions from hard systems, scientific management and systems thinking [10, 20]. It includes various tools and techniques that do not allow for situations such as unstable requirements and complex interactions of the project to be effectively addressed [10, 20]. However, project management also operates in the knowable domain as it needs to respond to unforeseen and unanticipated aspects of the project. In these situations, systems thinking needs to be applied and an analytical approach to problem solving that implicitly draws on experience but is usually expressed within the confines of the adopted methodology.

What is evident is that projects also exist in the unorder sector and this is particularly evident in ISD projects. The challenge is to deal with issues in this sector so that they can be transposed into the order sector and so addressed in a normative manner. Knowledge processes (KP) are the main tools used in this sector as these processes are able to make sense of emergent behaviour, explicitly drawing on experience and learning. It is the way that we think about moving between domains [7]. What is also evident is that such activities are usually not articulated but are only evident when expressed in the order sector.

4. Research Approach

ISD projects often involve outsourcers or third-party providers to implement, integrate or develop ISD. The case presented in this chapter is a study of the nature of complex issues in an ISD project involving outsourcing the implementation of a software tool at an Australian Government Department. The project provides an ideal venue in which to study complexity. In outsourced projects, complexity is compounded by the fact that there are two parties (actors) involved in the implementation process – the commissioning authority and the outsource provider.

The study used a number of different sources to view the phenomena in different ways [16] that enabled us to crosscheck our findings [13]. The study was conducted by observations, background discussions, document analysis (including publicly available documents), analysis of internal and external business processes and in-depth interviews. A framework was developed for recording and analysing the relevant project documentation and business processes. In addition an interview guide was developed for conducting in-depth interviews, and key themes were covered in the background discussion.

Observations and background discussions allowed the framework and an in-depth interview guide to be constructed and for further interviews to occur as necessary. Nine in-depth interviews were conducted with the outsource provider employees at all levels, including the senior management team representatives and the two consultants from the case study project team. This provided a background as to how the provider conducted projects using the government department as a concrete example. Interviews with the department staff responsible for the project were done informally due to imposed restrictions. Detailed analysis of business processes and documentation were conducted for the provider and the government department, restricted to publicly available documentation for the latter.

5. Case Study – Rollout of an Enterprise Project Management Software in a Government Department

The study discussed below provides an illustration of how ISD projects are characterised by complexity, because they are situated in an unstructured environment where requirements are dynamic. While existing tools and techniques are not sufficient to resolve intrinsic issues, knowledge processes provide an innovative way to resolve them. The study was completed in a large Australian Federal Government Department (Department XYZ), comprising a number of divisions, that outsourced the rollout of an enterprise project management software tool to Primavera Australia (Primavera), the outsource provider. Our approach to the study identified that three actors were involved – the government department, the service provider and the project. From this perspective, the study comprises a network of heterogeneous actors who are both humans and nonhumans [8]. We elected to look at the project as an actor because we are interested in the interaction between the other actors with the technical details and social aspects that constitute the project.

5.1. Department XYZ

Department XYZ is charged with the delivery of social services support to the community and other government departments via branches located throughout Australia. Department XYZ continually readjusts its services based on government legislation and budgetary initiatives introduced by the government. The divisions that provide internal support are IT, corporate services, finance and human resources. These divisions support the strategic themes for Department XYZ of strengthening customer focus, building a networked organisation and building capability for government. Implementation of budget initiatives means that projects need to be implemented in a timeframe dictated by legislation. In addition to budget initiatives, Department XYZ also implements internal initiatives to deliver strategic initiatives. These projects usually involve a number of stakeholders (other government agencies) and use emerging technologies. Projects are used to deliver these services and strategic initiatives.

A large number of the department's projects have a significant IT component to support service delivery throughout Australia and to enable the concept of a networked organisation. All divisions are involved in projects as the types of projects range from IT replacement initiatives to delivery of budget and legislative initiatives, people and planning capability, customer service and service delivery.

To meet these demands, Department XYZ has introduced a project management methodology based on PMI's [12] project management body of knowledge (PMBOK) but adapted to reflect Department XYZ's projects and operational requirements and to incorporate a parallel life cycle for IT components of projects. The methodology is scalable depending on the size of the project and prescribes the documentation that should be produced. These documents are then to be kept in a central repository.

To improve management of its large IT spend the department recognised the need to formalise the way it ran increasingly expensive, complex and mission-critical IT projects. A corporate project office (CPO) was created to support all projects and to manage the project management practice, to coordinate the management of projects and to centralise project management activities.

The CPO has responsibility for resource allocation, including staffing, to projects. To manage competing demands for resources between different projects the CPO relied on approximation from project managers that was more of a gut feel. The result was inappropriate planning that regularly caused resource conflicts. This is compounded as projects are plagued by frequent scope changes and milestone slippage.

The CPO recognised the need to adopt an enterprise level, top-down approach to managing resources. Department XYZ decided to outsource the application and delivery of an enterprise project management tool and undertook a closed tender process to select an enterprise project management tool. Primavera Australia (Primavera) was contracted to deliver this software.

5.2. The Third Party – Primavera Australia

Primavera is a major provider of enterprise project management software. It is a privately owned, locally run organisation, with a professional service culture and informal but developing business processes. The background of the principles is predominantly engineering, providing them with a background that facilitates a rational decision-making process. Primavera employs approximately 20 consultants (implementation and technical) throughout Australia and employs contract staff as required via their professional networks.

Primavera's strategy is to be the leading software integrator of enterprise project management software in Australia and Asia Pacific. It has integrated enterprise project management software into some large organisations, both government departments and publicly listed companies in Australia and New Zealand.

The management structure of Primavera is a matrix structure reflecting the regional and functional business structures. A board of management consisting of executive and nonexecutive members governs the strategic direction and finances of the organisation. Primavera utilises a methodology that focuses on software implementation and systems integration. The project management methodology is based on PMI's [12] project management body of knowledge (PMBOK).

5.3. The Project

Department XYZ was in a crisis that their existing tool for configuration of project management software and time sheeting was unsustainable and could not handle the volumes of projects. The official reason for the rollout of the Primavera Enterprise Project Management Software (PEPMS) was to better manage and allocate resources, but the prime driver was the fact that the existing tool was no longer suitable.

The initial scope of the project was to implement PEPMS within the IT division. The scope of the project was the implementation of the software, managing change, providing training and communication about the project and use of PEPMS. The scope and project requirements were broadened to include both the internal and customer facing divisions due to the range of projects they had and to support good strategic project management. In addition there was a requirement to allow financial and resource data to be imported from PEPMS to Department XYZ's ERP system. Requirements changed between a number of divisions in terms of configuration requirements or they required additional functionality that was outside the initial requirements and scope of the project.

The initial duration of the project was 8 months but was extended by another 9 months to cover the extended scope. As requirements changed and rollout occurred from IT to other business units the budget was increased. Each time the software was rolled out to another division additional budget had to be obtained from Department XYZ's investment committee.

The structure of the project was as an interaction between Primavera and the internal project team from Department XYZ. The initial project team consisted of three staff from Department XYZ and one implementation consultant from Primavera (the consultant). As requirements broadened two technical consultants from Primavera were allocated to develop the integration between PEPMS and the ERP. As requirements emerged in the business divisions additional Primavera consultants were deployed for short-term assignments to meet the timeline. The project reported to a project steering group comprising senior managers in Department XYZ and the Primavera consultant reported to the Primavera management team. Initially the project was implemented using Primavera's methodology. As requirements changed neither the Department's methodology nor Primavera's methodology was followed. Instead an informal methodology emerged that drew on both methodologies and the experience of Primavera consultants and departmental staff.

Divisions within Department XYZ resisted the rollout as users did not understand why they had to use a new system because they assumed that the existing project management systems were sufficient and allowed them to effectively and efficiently manage projects. To overcome this resistance, the consultant developed a communication strategy that identified how and why PEPMS was being implemented. Training was provided to all the users. Champions in each division were identified to assist with the rollout and improve the usage of the tool. These champions were not part of the project team but were identified as key stakeholders who could influence the usage of PEPMS. The Primavera technical consultants working on the integration with ERP did not understand the nature of the differing customer requirements in different divisions, nor did they communicate with the customer to try and understand the customer requirements. To bridge this gap, the consultant established weekly meetings with Department XYZ's project team and relevant stakeholders to understand and resolve the issues. These meetings were then broadened to include other issues that emerged.

6. Discussion

Within both Primavera and the department complex issues were explicitly addressed and their resolution integrated into project management routines, tools and methodologies.

One feature of this study was that technology, in itself, was not an issue that presented any problems. It did not contribute to the complexity of the project but it is also evident that the technology was used, in a political sense, to resist organisational change. The impact of standardisation of procedures and reporting, as well as the centralisation of control over projects, was facilitated by the implementation of the new application. Thus the contention within the department was not around user needs, usability and functionality, the typical issues of complexity intrinsic to technology, but on the organisational and social impact of the technology. This highlights the layered understanding of complexity that is inherent in technology and its interaction with the people and process domains.

The standard methodology employed by both Primavera and the Department was based on the normative PMBOK model and could not deal with the complexity of the project. As issues emerged the consultant and the department project team utilised an emergent methodology that was adjusted to the situation. As Kautz et al. [4] point out, such emergent methodologies are in fact normal practice in project management. This tailored methodology enabled both actors to effectively address project complexity in the implementation process.

Such tailored methodologies are based on techniques that emerge to deal with the complexity of the project, are made explicit by the project team and incorporated into an emergent methodology. These techniques utilised Schön's [14] concept of reflection in action, in that they are constructed from an understanding of how the methodology should be applied in the current situation. This understanding is based on learning, sensemaking, exploitation of organisational memory and personal experience [14]. These flexible approaches overcome the limitations of standard methodologies but remain informal in that they are not explicitly identified in the contractual arrangements and are not documented and included in the organisational routines and methodologies.

The project became even more complex as more divisions were included in the project and the inevitable increase in the number of stakeholders with differing agendas and requirements. Complexity was manifested in resistance to the project and a lack of stakeholder buy-in within the divisions throughout the project's life span. The project team addressed this issue by deescalating it out of the project and appointing a champion in each division. The intention was for the champion to try to influence the use of PEPMS within the division and to help the team understand the division's requirement. A network that included the project team and the divisional champions was formed to function as a community of practice (CoP) [18]. The champions' knowledge of each divisions was used to create a shared understanding within the network and this understanding was propagated by the champions back to their divisions to facilitate the acceptance and use of PEPMS. The CoP provided the expert opinion that was relied on by the Divisions to ensure their acceptance and use of PEPMS.

The main feature of the organisational context was the discrepancy between the stated aim and implied agenda of Department XYZ that contributed to the changing requirements throughout the project. This discrepancy became evident to all parties as a gap in the scope making the project unbounded [7]. From the department's perspective, the resolution of this discrepancy was to renegotiate the contract terms. Primavera only became aware of the discrepancy after the contract was awarded. One consequence of the discrepancy was that Primavera lacked an understanding of what was needed, the areas that required it and when it was required. To resolve the different perspectives between the contracted project and what the department expected, the issue was deescalated to a meta-level – the project steering group and Primavera's management team where the issue was reviewed and resolved within the framed situation of the meta-level, that is the negotiation of a revised scope of the project, the cost, resource requirements and the revised schedule [5].

The integration of PEPMS with other technology was not in itself complex rather it became complex with the interaction of the integration consultant with stakeholders and users from Department XYZ. Primavera recognised that their understanding of the requirements was based on assumptions about what the customer wanted. This recognition led Primavera's lead consultant to deescalate the issue to resolve the requirements. Complexity in the project was further exacerbated because the integration consultant developed what he thought Department XYZ required, rather than what they required. In an effort to resolve the confusion and reduce the complexity, the Primavera's lead consultant organised an initial meeting to make sense of the requirements and agree on a set of requirements. This led to the establishment of a weekly meeting between department representatives and Primavera. These meetings were not concerned with the practicalities of the conduct of the project per se but with the meta-level understanding of the project through reflective practice and sense making [14] in order to construct a shared understanding of the issues. These meetings were quickly expanded to deal with all emergent issues with the meeting assuming explicit responsibility to develop a comprehensive understanding of the issues, assign an owner to each issue and to ensure that the issues were resolved. These meetings became part of tools and techniques used in the emergent methodology.

6.1. Addressing Complexity

The Cynefin framework is a useful lens to look at how complex issues in ISD projects are resolved as it helps determine the context in which they are operating and the type of KP or action that is required to resolve the issue. It recognises that different KPs are required to resolve issues depending on the domain in which they are situated. Complex issues cannot be resolved utilising standard rational tools and techniques; rather, the KPs of experimentation, sensemaking and learning are used to resolve the issue. The complexity that emerged during the project was due to the contextual nature of the project: changing requirements, resistance to change and stakeholder agendas. Project management tools allow such issues to be dealt with when they have limited impact on the overall project and are within the discretionary power of the project manager. However, the complexity of a project often means that the tools, techniques and knowledge available to the actors are insufficient to resolve the issue. Such issues exist in the unorder sector requiring different conceptualisation and tool set. In our study, the meta-level understanding needed to address these issues meant that the project was deescalated to actors who were authorised to address them at an appropriate level. The actors could draw on broader knowledge and experience and were able to exercise power in order to resolve the issue. The resolution was articulated as additional tools and techniques involved in the management of this project, thus transposing the issues into the order sector. This is summarised in Table 79.1.

The KP recognised the emergence of issues in the complex domain allowing for reflection and discussion to occur in meetings generating innovative ideas to deal with the issue and moving it back to the ordered domains [7]. The deescalation of issues provided the cognitive, conceptual, power and authority space in which senior actors were able to re-define the project by negotiating a shared

Table 79.1. Resolution of issues during the implementation of PEPMS.

Nature of complex issue	Manifestation in study	Resolution in study
Process	Methodology	Emergent methodology used
Interaction between people and project context	Change in project scope – scope broadened to include business divisions	Meeting between Primavera and Department XYZ management
Interaction between people and project context	Changing requirements	Meeting between Primavera and Department XYZ management
		Weekly meetings between department and Primavera
Interaction between people and project context	Organisational resistance to a new tool being introduced	Communication plan
		User training
		Champion appointed
Interaction between people and project context	Change management	Communication – user training
		– Champion appointed
People	Difference between what Primavera thought they were delivering and what department wanted	Deescalation to a higher forum

understanding and the practicalities that characterise the real project. This in turn provided the context for the Primavera consultant and Department representatives to construct techniques and tools that effectively addressed the issues as they were manifested in the conduct of the project. Both these activities involved KPs in their ability to exploit knowledge and even to construct new knowledge. These KPs were expressed in a manner that was relevant to the project and was able to be incorporated into the methodology and practices by which the project was conducted.

7. Conclusion

The objective of our research was to study the nature of complexity in ISD projects and to understand how complexity can be resolved in practice. Our study showed that complex issues are not resolved within the traditional project management model that is dependent on existing tools, techniques and methodologies. The resolution of complexity in our study relied on the ability of actors to engage in knowledge processes outside the traditional project management model. Significantly, the outcomes of these processes are expressed in terms of tools and techniques that can be re-integrated into the project management model.

Our approach suggests that project management needs to be conceptualised more broadly in order to incorporate complex, and even chaotic, phenomena and extend the assumptions that underpin project management practices to include emergence, self-organisation and adaptation. The implications of this shift in thinking are that knowledge processes need to play an overt and visible role and the project management model needs to incorporate knowledge-based practices. In ISD, such a shift in thinking is consistent with the historical evolution of the development of methods, tools and techniques to address the intrinsic issue of complexity in ISD.

References

1. Drucker, P. (2006). Classic Drucker: Wisdom from Peter Drucker from the Pages of Harvard Business Review, Harvard Business School Press, Boston, MA.
2. Eisenhardt, K. and Tabrizi, B. (1995) Accelerating adaptive processes: product innovation in the global computer industry. *Administrative Science Quarterly* 40 (1), 84–110.
3. Gregor, S. (2006). The nature of theory in information systems. *MIS Quarterly* 30 (3), 611–642.
4. Kautz, K., Hansen, B. and Jacobsen, D. (2004). The utilization of information systems development methodologies in practice. *JITCA* 6 (4), 1–19.

5. Keil, M. and Robey, D. (1999) Turning around troubled software projects: an exploratory study of the deescalation of commitment to failing courses of action. *Journal of Management Information Systems* 15 (4), 63–87.

6. Keil, M., Tiwana, A. and Bush, A. (2002) reconciling user and project manager perceptions of IT project risk: a Delphi study, *Information Systems Journal*, 12(1), 103–119.

7. Kurtz, C. F. and Snowden, D. J. (2003). The new dynamics of strategy: sensemaking in a complex and complicated world. *IBM Systems Journal* 42 (3), 462–483.

8. Latour B. (1999). On recalling ANT. In: Law J, Hassard J, editors. Actor Network Theory and After, Blackwell, Oxford, pp. 15–25.

9. Mathiassen, L. and Stage, J. (1992). The principles of limited reduction. *Information Technology and People*. 6 (2), 171–185.

10. Morris, P. (2002). Science, objective knowledge, and the theory of project management. ICE James Forrest Lecture. http://www.bartlett.uc/.ac.uk/research/management/ICE.paper.pdf on 22/12/2007.

11. Owen, J. and Linger, H (2006). The Nature of a Program Through a Knowledge Management Lens, IRNOP Project Research Conference Xi'an, China, October 2006, 411–418.

12. Project Management Institute. (2004). A Guide to the Project Management Body of Knowledge. Project Management Institute, Seattle, VA.

13. Sabherwal, R., Hirschheim, R., and Goles, T. (2001). The dynamics of alignment: a punctuated equilibrium model. *Organization Science* 12 (2), 179–197.

14. Schön, D. A. (1991) The Reflective Practitioner: How Professionals Think in Action. Arena Ashgate Publishing Ltd, Aldershot.

15. Snowden, D (2002), Complex acts of knowing: paradox and descriptive self-awareness. *Journal of Knowledge Management* 6 (2), 100–111.

16. Stake, R. E. (2000). Case studies. In N. K. Denzin and Y. S. Lincoln (Eds.), Handbook of Qualitative Research (2nd ed.), (pp. 435–454), Sage Publications, Thousand Oaks, CA.

17. Vigden, R. (1997). Stakeholders, soft systems and technology: separation and mediation in the analysis of information systems requirements. *Information Systems Journal* 7, 21–46.

18. Wenger, E. (1996). Communities of practice: the social fabric of a learning organization. *The Healthcare Forum Journal* 39 (4), 20–26.

19. Williams, T. (2002). Modelling Complex Projects. John Wiley & Sons, Chichester.

20. Winter, M. and Checkland, P. (2003). Soft systems: a fresh perspective for project management, *ICE Civil Engineering* 156 (Nov), 187–192.

21. Xia, W. and Lee, G. (2005) Complexity of information systems development projects: conceptualization and measurement development, *Journal of Management Information Systems* 22 (1), 48–83.

80

Business Architecture Development at Public Administration – Insights from Government EA Method Engineering Project in Finland

Katariina Valtonen and Mauri Leppänen

Abstract

Governments worldwide are concerned for efficient production of services to customers. To improve quality of services and to make service production more efficient, information and communication technology (ICT) is largely exploited in public administration (PA). Succeeding in this exploitation calls for large-scale planning which embraces issues from strategic to technological level. In this planning the notion of enterprise architecture (EA) is commonly applied. One of the sub-architectures of EA is business architecture (BA). BA planning is challenging in PA due to a large number of stakeholders, a wide set of customers, and solid and hierarchical structures of organizations. To support EA planning in Finland, a project to engineer a government EA (GEA) method was launched. In this chapter, we analyze the discussions and outputs of the project workshops and reflect emerged issues on current e-government literature. We bring forth insights into and suggestions for government BA and its development.

Keywords E-government, Enterprise architecture, Business architecture, Enterprise architecture method engineering

1. Introduction

The diffusion of e-commerce technologies in the private sector has made public administrations (PA) foster e-government initiatives and programs [4]. E-government refers to the deployment of information and communication technologies (ICT) to promote more efficient and effective provision of high-quality government services [4, 24]. This yields a wider array of services for customers, as well as better and more secure communication between customers and government agencies. E-government is expected to bring administration closer to citizen's everyday life [19] and make government more accountable and transparent to customers [10, 24].

Implementation of e-government is challenging in many ways. Much of government work is carried out by multiple government agencies working as vertically rigid "silos" [24, 29]. This results in poor coordination, poor performance, and poor quality of services. For mature e-government development, there is a need for a sophisticated and centrally managed strategy function [20] based on a comprehensive view of processes, information, systems, and technology in PA. This kind of view is provided by the notion of enterprise architecture (EA). *Enterprise architecture* is seen as a collection of artifacts that define and describe the structure and processes of an enterprise, the information being stored, processed, and communicated, the systems used for these activities, and the technologies and the infrastructure that the

Katariina Valtonen and Mauri Leppänen • University of Jyväskylä, Computer Science and Information Systems, Jyväskylä, Finland.

G.A. Papadopoulos et al. (eds.), *Information Systems Development*, DOI 10.1007/b137171_80,
© Springer Science+Business Media, LLC 2009

systems are implemented with [13]. Here, an enterprise is regarded as a public organization, a private company, or a virtual organization in the form of a network of organizational actors aiming at a common goal.

Enterprise architecture planning and development is particularly difficult in PA, due to a large number of government agencies, a wide and heterogeneous set of customers, as well as a formal, hierarchical structure of authority with a detailed, rationalized division of labor. *EA planning* means the definition of the overall target state of an enterprise, including a transition plan as a road map of transition projects for achieving the target state [23]. *EA development* refers to an execution process of one of the transition projects for new EA arrangements, either as new organization structures, processes, information assets, e-Business solutions, information systems, technology platforms, etc. *Business architecture (BA) development* focuses on designing and implementing business change in services, organization structures, business processes, etc.

Various frameworks, models, and methods have been suggested for EA planning and development (see reviews in [23, 27, 35]), some of which have been largely applied at PA as well. Due to differences in laws, organizational structures, degree of privatization, culture, etc., no framework or method as such is applicable in all the countries or even among various branches of administration. The EA methods have to be customized.

In Finland, interoperability development program (IDP) was launched to implement a part of a government policy decision on the development of IT management [14]. One of the most important goals of the IDP was to engineer a method for government EA (GEA) planning and development, called GEA method in the chapter. The project group consisted of representatives from Finnish state administration, municipalities, and consultants. The GEA method is composed of a large conceptual framework, a general-level process model, and normative instructions for how to apply the framework. Due to the strict time limit provided for the method engineering, the outcome can be seen as a first version of the GEA method. The intention by the Finnish state government has been to develop the GEA method further, for instance by applying it in pilot projects.

Our purpose is to search for deeper insight into BA in PA and suggest improvements into methodical guidelines of BA development at PA. We do this by analyzing the recorded and transcribed discussions of the workshops of the GEA method engineering group and by comparing the emerged BA development issues with the literature. In this way we pursue to bring forth new ideas to be included in any EA method. Our analysis covers a small part of themes considered in the workshops. We focus on BA visions, customer activation at BA design, and BA implementation models.

The remainder of the chapter is structured into four sections. In Section 2 we outline the GEA method engineering project and the GEA method. Section 3 describes the research method used. In Section 4 we analyze selected issues raised at the project workshops and compare them with conceptions in the literature. In Section 5 we present implications from the analysis and suggest improvements into methodical guidelines of BA planning. The chapter ends with a summary and conclusions.

2. CASE: The GEA Method Engineering Project

In autumn 2006, interoperability development program (IDP) was launched at the Ministry of Finance in Finland to implement a part of the government policy decision on the development of IT management [14]. The IDP involved five sub-projects: (1) to analyze the state of the art of the information systems architecture of the state administration, (2) to engineer a government EA (GEA) method and describe a high-level target architecture, (3) to develop a GEA governance model and a GEA maturity model, (4) to model the logical integration architecture of the target state, and (5) to analyze obstacles and potentials for reusing the current state repositories and databases.

In this study, we focus on the project pursuing the GEA method engineering (addressed in [8] too). The project group consisted of administratives and IT management of Finnish PA (i.e., the Ministry of Finance, the Council of State, Population Register Center, National Board of Taxes, Finnish Road Administration and the Ministry of Justice, the University of Helsinki, Turku town as a representative of municipalities) and the liable consultancy (TietoEnator Oyj), all bringing their expertise on different fields to the project. The work in the project comprised five tasks: (1) the selection of a suitable EA method or EA methods, (2) the adaptation of the EA methods for Finnish PA, (3) writing a user manual for the resulting GEA method, (4) applying the GEA method to a small-scale case and thus producing an exemplar document of the method use, and (5) planning and describing a high-level target architecture. The project group worked in 15 workshops from late autumn 2006 until April 2007 led by the consultancy. The GEA method was produced exploiting existing EA methods (e.g., [7, 17]) and published in June 2007. The method is composed of a conceptual framework (the GEA grid), a process model with stepwise and normative instructions for proceeding, and an array of description models [15].

The GEA grid is structured by three description levels and four architectural viewpoints (Table 80.1). The description levels are PA, domains (e.g., a branch of administration), and sub-domains (e.g., a government agency). For the description of the target state EA, the domain level was thought to be, for example, a common goal of a network of organizations (called "cluster" at the GEA method document [15] and at the project workshop). Sub-domains in that case were, respectively, denoted as sub-areas of the development goal of the cluster.

Table 80.1. Overview of the generic GEA grid in Finland.

GEA grid in Finland	B A	I A	S A	T A
PA level				
Domain level				
Sub-domain level				

The EA viewpoints correspond to four common sub-architectures: business architecture (BA), information architecture (IA), systems architecture (SA), and technology architecture (TA) (cf. [7, 17]). The sub-architectures include descriptions of, for example, stakeholders, customers, organizations, services, and processes to describe BA, whereas strategic data warehouses, information assets, and vocabularies describe IA. In SA, IS portfolios, IS life cycles, and systems services are typical descriptions, whereas technology policies, standards, and reference models are typical of TA descriptions [15].

The GEA method is aimed to be applied situationally [15]. This implies, for instance, that a suitable approach to the situation at hand is selected. If the process-driven approach is selected, the first steps are taken to develop BA and IA focusing on services, processes, and information related to them. In the systemdriven approach the EA development may start with describing current information systems and how they might be harmonized or integrated.

The GEA process model [15] is composed of three phases. In the first phase, the scope of the EA work is defined, descriptions of the current state EA are collected, needs for the change are explored, the vision of the target state is outlined, and the development project is established. The second phase is to produce primary designs of selected viewpoints and levels concerning the target state EA. Stakeholders are thus identified, suitable description models are selected, issues affecting the EA at hand are analyzed, the target state EA is modeled, the target state plans are reconsidered, and the defect analysis is carried out. The last phase is to make a transition plan of the implementation projects, assess andprioritize them, and distribute the outcomes to the stakeholders [15].

3. Research Method

This study was conducted as a case study [36] to reveal the intricate phenomenon of BA development at PA, and by reflecting the case on e-government literature, to suggest improvements into methodical guidelines of BA development.

Data gathering and validation. The primary data were collected by the first author who was acting as a participatory observer at 13 workshops of the GEA method engineering project. The researcher acted partly as an outside observer and partly as an involved researcher commenting on issues (cf. [1], orig. [32]). Discussions were written down as field notes in the first four workshops and tape recorded in nine consequent workshops. The recorded discussions (in average ca. 3 h) were transcribed (altogether ca. 500 pages) and coded during data analysis. As secondary data, the project documentation, minutes of meetings, and results of the workshops were extensively exploited in data synthesis and analysis. In addition to these, all materials of the overall interoperability program and its subprojects were available in a shared workspace of the Ministry of Finance. The researcher could not attend two of the workshops, and some of the tapes suffered from minor technical problems. Although the work at the consultancy was not followed, the outcomes were reported in the workshops and shared also at the shared workspace. The primary data were in most cases checked by the group members in the beginning of the workshop that followed the one where the data were collected. All the delivered data were shared for the group members also in a shared workspace, and corrections were welcomed also by e-mail. This arrangement enabled the validation of the data regardless of time and place.

Data analysis. The primary data were subjected to in-depth textual analysis. Secondary data allowed cross-checking with the aim of a stronger substantiation of analysis and conclusions [1]. The primary data were organized as a thick text repository and analyzed interpretatively by semi-open coding to uncover the salient issues of the workshops. Therefore, a process of quoting, coding, and categorizing was carried out in an iterative and converging fashion, forming the final themes by confirming or absorbing the previous ones. By a theme we mean a bunch of categories and their attached quotations which have been formed iteratively and converged based on the whole database. Representative quotations were selected by the authors through reflection with the literature and writing of results. The results were validated by stakeholder reviews and comparing them with the results of a parallel qualitative study at Finnish PA with independent data set [9].

4. Results

In this section we bring forth e-government issues related to BA planning based on e-government literature, the interpretative analysis of project discussions, and the document analysis of the GEA method. Three themes arise: (a) e-government business models, (b) customer-driven development, and (c) business process modeling.

4.1. E-Government Business Models

A large variety of e-business models have been suggested for private sector (e.g., [25, 34], cf. a review in [6]). In recent years, e-business models have excited interest in PA as well [11, 12]. E-business models reflect the core business of an organization and describe the organization from the perspective of its main mission and the products and services that it provides to its customers [11], orig. [33]. Applying an e-government business model helps to define service strategies; to identify, categorize, and structure the services; and to view the service production as a more organized set of processes (cf. [11]). It may lead to changes in functions, roles, responsibilities, organization structures, and infrastructures [31] also in PA. Janssen, Kuk et al. [11] discuss the e-business model taxonomy of Weill et al. [34] applying it for e-government. In the following, we shortly describe some of these e-government business models.

Based on the *full service provider* model, a full range of services is provided to an Internet user in one service domain (e.g., health domain), directly or via allies. The *value net integrator model* supports establishing the coordination of processes across a value net by gathering, synthesizing, and distributing information. Applying the *content provider* model means that information, digital products, and services are provided via intermediaries. The content comes from one single organization and can be customized. Weill et al. [34] also suggest the *direct to consumer model*, which provides "goods or services directly to the customer, often bypassing a traditional channel [11]." For a Finnish customer, this kind of service already exists, for example, a tax deduction card can be ordered online bypassing officers as a matter of course. In the *virtual community model,* an online community of people with a common interest enables interaction to enhance service provision. This has to be considered, since Internet users are getting more accustomed to advanced services (e.g., eBay [26]; future service production [2]).

In the project, e-government business models were not explicitly mentioned, although several examples of online services were highlighted to illustrate the possibilities of e-government. For instance, supporting the various phases of building process online was outlined resembling the value net integrator model. This e-service would collect information such as blueprints of the design firm and support license case processing of builders and officials. A consultant: "It is known, that with the help of an electrical desktop, you can nicely try to guide or even force making of more thorough [licence] applications. .... Thus, you get more prepared text, thus the officials of the supervision of the building might concentrate more on assessment . . . and not using their time on information collection and chasing it after."

The GEA method does not refer to any specific e-government business model. The vision of the target state BA is created using a scenario technique of the GEA method. Thereafter, to put it simply, the GEA method guides BA development: (a) to take legislation, visions, trends, and strategies as a starting point; (b) to identify customers and their needs; and (c) to outline services for customer profiles. Guidelines for e-government business models should be an integral part of any GEA method. The scenario technique, for example, might present different choices for e-government business models. This might provide managers with an analytical tool set for thinking through potential e-government business models and the consequences for realization. Weill et al. [34] suggest this kind of approach as a tool for enterprise managers. E-government business models can also be seen to have clear impacts on how business processes should be structured, interrelated, and designed.

4.2. Customer-Driven Development

The importance of customers' role in the development of e-services and processes is commonly recognized [31]. The literature on e-government brings forth this issue too (e.g., mapping customers' needs-to-services [21] and involvement of potential users in the co-production of new content and services [11]). Application of the customer-driven approach manifests itself, for example, as the provision of pro-active services. Web sites could be personalized, for example, to alert before the expiration of one's driving license [11]. At the workshop discussions a PA customer was referred to as an individual, whether citizen or non-citizen, a private sector organization, a non-profit organization, or another government agency inside PA. The government agency acts either at a local, state, or European Union level [22]. An agency was recognized in a role of a customer and service provider. Similarly, the roles of other actors may alter from service customer to service provider in different occasions in PA.

The customer-driven approach was seen quite essential to BA development in the project workshops. The recognized dimensions of customer-driven issues were transparency, automation of the non-value adding actions, pro-activity of services, and the mapping of provider and customer processes. Transparency of services was seen beneficial, since it enables a customer to follow up steps of her/his service request proceeding in a network of actors: "If it's a lengthy process, like applying an exceptional permit for a summer cottage, which may take even a year . . . I would have liked to see, if the case is at a standstill there at the municipality." Automation of service processes was seen as a means to eliminate non-value-added operations. A citizen could be, for example, automatically subsidized by housing allowance, or at least informed about this possibility, if her/his income meets the stated income limits. The subsidy could be even channeled directly to her/his lessor: "They know it very well who owns the rental apartment, and the money can go straight to there." Several cases related to pro-active services were also discussed. For example, a security guard might routinely make an offer to help a victim in reporting of an offence. Special attention was given to the notion of life cycle. E-services might be based on the life cycles of the publicly maintained information. For instance, based on the life cycle of a building (and building information, respectively), several services were identified, including counseling construction planning, location registration, license services, accepting building process supervisors, and customer involvement in local area development planning. A life cycle view may thus help to recognize essential life events [30] to be implemented as e-services.

The customer-driven approach is clearly visible in the GEA method [15]. The method guides principally to take customers and their needs as a starting point in the identification of customer profiles and service portfolios. Services are then to be described and among other things categorized into different service types (like core online service and information service). Services are also to be characterized, for example, in terms of iterativeness measuring the number of interactions between customers and officials needed to conclude one case [15].

4.3. Business Process Modeling

PA is commonly afflicted by separate silos, having negative influence on the performance of processes and their coordination [24, 29]. Many services require actions from more than one agency. To cope with that, agencies have to be interoperable, not only at the technological level but at the semantic and organizational levels too [21]. Co-operative service production requires cross-agency processes, i.e., inter-organizational processes (IOPs) [10]. The IOPs (or cluster processes, as the group also put it) were largely discussed in the workshops. An IOP was defined to mean a process which crosses the boundaries of branches of administration or service provider organizations. A service provider could also be a private or non-profit organization. "Silo" problems were recognized to be quite recurrent, as noticed: "At present, the processes break immediately when the boundary of an organization is encountered. . . . the responsibility is passed to a customer who is expected to act respectively [i.e. to trigger a process with another agency]."

There are many challenges related to the implementation of the IOPs. First, it is difficult to define a strategy for an IOP, as stated in the group: "Even if a [IO] process was identified, it has no formal strategy." The group concluded that when developing an IOP co-operatively, you have to take into account and adapt the different BA requirements originating from several strategies of participating organizations. A PA representative: "But how do you cope with that in future, if you have a priority of one organization, and still all the others are supposed to act accordingly?" The consultant: "Then you have performed the requirements engineering and management wrong. You have to specify all the stakeholders and users, whether it is a bunch of three organisations or actors. . . .."

Second, special principles are needed to implement an IOP. Punia et al. [24] list three ways to structure workflows of IOPs. In *sub-process integration* organizations link their sub-processes together, creating a new process that spans all the organizations. Alternatively, a new *public process* is developed for the organizations, or bought from a third party, for linking their internal sub-processes. Sub-process execution could also be implemented *through bidding*. Organizations that want to use a service providing a sub-process make bids for the latter, and organizations that want to sell respond to the bids. For us, it seems that implementation of a public process would result in extra administrative work in a long run, whereas integration of sub-processes, although more demanding for developers, would enhance and smooth current processes as a positive by-product.

The group elaborated another notion in addition to IOP, called a shared process, to promote organizational interoperability. A shared process means a chain of operations which are executed in the similar way in several agencies. Examples of typical shared processes are case processing, licensing (i.e., certification, cf. [20]), and financial administration. The group saw it important to harmonize practices through a process which could be shared, supported, and possibly automated by a centralized system. For instance, "The process related to a building license is actually a generic licensing process containing parts that could be reused." Of course, implementation of a shared process into an agency may necessitate its re-localization, possibly re-configuration. One should, however, be aware of risks resulting from going too far in centralization, as experienced in the NHS project in England where local socio-technical needs were not allowed in local implementation of some health processes, even though it would have been possible technically [5].

The GEA method guides categorizing business processes into two types, core processes and support processes. A core process refers to the way of how an organization aims at fulfilling its purpose of existence. A support process creates good conditions for core processes. In addition, management processes are mentioned but neither defined nor discussed. Each process is to be identified, represented in a process chart, and described in a process diagram with sub-processes, customer and service provider roles, services and information system(s). The GEA method presents the IOPs and shared processes but gives no instructions to identify, organize, and implement them. We suggest that any EA method should advice how to select a suitable implementation strategy for an IOP or a shared process. A choice is situational and must be dependent, for example, on the goals and the applied e-government business models.

Furthermore, we suggest that any EA method should address how to identify and model not only "coal-face processes" but also management and strategy processes [18]. In the group: "Through [EA] descriptions [e.g., process maps] we are aiming at understanding. . . . to make better decisions. . . . Details, however annoying, have to be brought forth somehow, since they have to be EXECUTED somewhere." Describing the management and strategy processes was seen as a tricky task: "There are some issues, for instance planning, monitoring, concern reporting, and official statistics, . . . such things where this kind of [administrative] hierarchy – a state administration, a branch of administration and an agency – creates us services which transfer information and understanding from a hierarchical level to another. And where have we described them? It is as they would not exist at all." Although this demand was recognized in the project, it is neither mentioned in the GEA method nor operationalized into instructions for the identification and modeling of management and strategic processes. We suggest that a normative technique [18] would be exploited for this purpose.

Including the coal-face, management, and strategy processes in BA descriptions would increase understanding, for example, of the organization structure and implementation strategy of an IOP, a shared process, and/or an e-government business model. In IOP planning an implementation strategy should be chosen in a deliberate manner in order to involve and commit the concerned parties with sufficient resources. Developing shared processes implies the centralization of IS support with a few alternative options. One can aim to, for instance, harmonizing the way of action among all parties to deploy the same IS for all or, alternatively, harmonizing the process only to a chosen level and support it by a configurable system where taking into account the local socio-technical needs is possible (cf. [5]).

5. Implications

Based on the workshop discussions, the analysis of the GEA method, and literature on e-government, we conclude with the following suggestions for BA development.

Elaboration of a shared vision among the involved organizations. A number of studies (e.g., [28]) show that technology-driven e-government implementation fails because of stakeholder resistance at the time when changes in processes and organizational structures should be made. We suggest the use of e-government business models as a means to direct discussions toward strategic issues in order to establish a shared vision at the organizational level among the concerned government agencies and business enterprises or other service providers. E-government business models may guide the concretization of the selected vision into new arrangements of organizational structures and processes. In addition to those referred to in Section 3 [34], the literature provides other e-government business models (e.g., life-event portals and one-stop shops, cf. [3, 16]) that might be considered in a situational manner.

Customer-driven requirements engineering. In order to provide customer-oriented e-services, requirements engineering should be carried out in a customer-driven way. We suggest that the notions of life cycle process and life-event workflow are used to find a proper match between the customers' and the provider's views in the following way: (1) Model the service provider's view (i.e., life cycle process) and the customers' view (i.e., life-event workflow) and try to find out which part of the life cycles and information maintained by PA could support e-services for customers. (2) Look for "blind spots" in the customer process that could be smoothed. Typically these are situations where the customer is obligated to patronize with several officials or agencies in order to get one single case to be handled. (3) Ask the customers how they could be served pro-actively by relevant information, products, or services. (4) Ask the customers to which information they would like to have an access through electronic self-service channels, such as Internet, mobile phone, or digital television.

Identification and description of processes. One of the conclusions from the GEA method engineering project was lack of understanding of business processes, especially management and strategy processes. We suggest that the identification and modeling of the management and strategy processes are to be supported by a systematical approach developed by Ould [18].

Planning inter-organizational processes (IOPs). To support the planning of IOPs when service production necessitates co-operation among several agencies, or private organizations, we suggest that inter-organizational processes are carefully planned based on a specific strategy and a conscious development approach. As mentioned above, there are many alternative strategies (e.g., integrating sub-process, public processes, and e-marketplaces by [24]).

Designing IS support for shared processes. One of the issues discussed in the GEA method engineering project group concerned shared processes and how these are recognized and re-designed in local agencies and municipalities in practice. IS support for shared processes may mean (1) the use of the same IS to enforce the agencies to act in the same way in their service provision, (2) the use of the same IS to support different instances of a shared process differentiated by customers' needs, and (3) the use of different IS implementations based on socio-technical factors and adapted situationally from one common IS (cf. [5]).

6. Conclusion

Enterprise architecture planning is a big challenge in PA due to a large number of stakeholders, a wide set of customers with heterogeneous needs, and solid and hierarchical structures of organizations. To support EA planning in Finland, a project to engineer a government EA (GEA) method was launched in 2006. A part of the discussions in the workshops of the project addressed the PA business architecture (BA). In this study we have analyzed the project discussions and the GEA method documents and reflected the emerged issues on current e-government literature. The aim was to find new insights and suggestions for BA and its planning at PA. The suggestions are related to elaboration of a shared vision among the service providers through the use of e-government business models, customer-driven requirements engineering, identification and description of relevant processes, and designing implementation strategies and IS support for different types of public processes.

BA planning contains many other important issues we had to exclude in the chapter. For instance, questions about managing the inter-organizational processes and relating legislation and architecture management and planning are vital. In our future research we aim to enlarge our analysis to cover these issues, as well as to reveal the themes of overall EA planning and method adaptation for PA. The lack of a proper theoretical framework for possible e-government business models seems evident. Also a more careful consideration of consequences of applying of an e-government business model is an interesting issue for future research (e.g., the use of different modeling approaches, depth of customer involvement, and process implementation strategies) in order to devise a systematic way for enhancing BA at PA.

Acknowledgments

The authors thank the workshop members of the GEA method engineering project for inspiring work. The research was funded by the ValtIT Research Project, Finnish Enterprise Architecture Research (FEAR) Project, and COMAS Graduate School.

References

1. Berger H. and Beynon-Davies P. (2004) Issues impacting on the project management of a RAD development approach of a large, complex government IT project. Pacific Asia Conference on Information Systems.
2. Bjoern-Andersen, N. (2007) The never ending story of IT impact on the organization – the case of ambient organizations. In: *Proceedings of 30th Information Systems Research Seminar in Scandinavia* (IRIS30), Tampere, Finland, www.cs.uta.fi/reports/dsarja/D-2007-9.pdf
3. Chatzidimitriou, M. and Koumpis, A. (2007) Matters of conceptualization and security in the building of one-stop-shop e-government solutions in Europe: experiences from the European OneStopGov project. ICISIE 2007 Conference, London, UK, July 2–4.
4. Cordella, A. (2007) E-government: towards the e-bureaucratic form? *Journal of Information Technology 22*, 265–274.
5. Eason, K. (2007) Local sociotechnical system development in the NHS national programme for information technology. *Journal of Information Technology 22*, 257–264.
6. Hedman, J. and Kalling, T. (2003) The business model concept: theoretical underpinnings and empirical illustrations. *European Journal on Information Systems 12(1)*, 41–48.
7. Hirvonen, A. and Pulkkinen, M. (2004) A practical approach to EA planning and development: the EA management grid. In: W. Abramowicz (Ed.), *Proceedings of 7th International Conference on Business Information Systems*. Poznan, Poland, pp. 284–302.
8. Hirvonen, A., Pulkkinen, M. and Valtonen, K. (2007) Selection criteria for enterprise architecture methods. ECIME Conference 2007, Montpellier, France.
9. Isomäki, H., Liimatainen, K. and Valtonen, K. (2008) *Challenges and Collaboration Opportunities of Enterprise Architecture Work*. Ministry of Finance, Public Management Reforms 10/2008 (In Finnish. Abstract in English) http://www.vm.fi/vm/en/04_publications_and_documents/01_publications/04_public_management/20080227Challe/name.jsp
10. Janssen, M. and Cresswell, A. (2005) Enterprise architecture integration in e-government. *Proceedings of the 38th Hawaii International Conference on System Sciences*.
11. Janssen, M., Kuk, G. and Wagenaar, R.W. (2005) A survey of e-government business models in the Netherlands. ICEC'05 August 15–17, 2005, Xi'an, China, pp. 496–504.
12. Lee, K.J. and Hong, J-H. (2002) Development of an e-government service model: a business model approach. *International Review of Public Administration 7(2)*, 109–118.
13. Leppänen, M., Valtonen, K. and Pulkkinen, M. (2007) Towards a contingency framework for engineering an enterprise architecture planning method. *Proceedings of 30th Information Systems Research Seminar in Scandinavia* (IRIS30), Tampere, Finland. http://www.cs.uta.fi/reports/dsarja/D-2007-9.pdf
14. Ministry of Finance (2006) *Government Policy Decision on the Development of IT Management in State Administration*. Public Management Department Publications 3c/2006, Finland, www.vm.fi/publications
15. Ministry of Finance (2007) Finnish Government Enterprise Architecture Method. Käyttöohje, User manual, version 1.0, 28th June 2007 (in Finnish), http://www.hare.vn.fi/upload/Asiakirjat/12260/104939_Loppuraportti_Liite_02_Arkkitehtuurimenetelmä.pdf
16. Momotko, M., Izdebski, W., Tambouris, E., Tarabanis, K. and Vintar, M. (2007) An architecture of active life event portals: generic workflow approach. In: M.A. Wimmer, H.J. Scholl and A. Grönlund (Eds.), *Electronic Government*. Springer-Verlag, Heidelberg, Berlin, pp. 104–115.
17. OpenGroup (2003) *The Open Group Architecture Framework* (TOGAF) Version 8.1 "Enterprise Edition". [online, referred on 4.12.2006] http://www.opengroup.org/togaf
18. Ould, M. (2005) *Business Process Management – A Rigorous Approach*. British Computer Society. Meghan-Kiffer Press, Tampa, Florida, USA.
19. Peristeras, V. and Tarabanis, K. (2000) Towards an enterprise architecture for public administration using a top-down approach. *European Journal of Information Systems 9*, 252–260.
20. Peristeras, V. and Tarabanis, K. (2004) Governance enterprise architecture (GEA): domain models for e-governance. In: M. Janssen, H.G. Sol, and R.W. Wagenaar (Eds.), *Proceedings of Sixth International Conference on Electronic Commerce* (ICEC'2004), pp. 471–479.
21. Peristeras, V., Tarabanis, K. and Loutas, N. (2007) Cross-border public services: analysis and modeling. *Proceedings of the 40th Annual Hawaii International Conference on System Sciences*, Jan. 2007.
22. Peters, R.M., Janssen, M. and van Engers, T.M. (2004) Measuring e-government impact: existing practices and shortcomings. In: M. Janssen, H.G. Sol, and R.W. Wagenaar (Eds.), *Proceedings of the 6th International Conference on Electronic Commerce* (ICEC'04), pp. 480–489.

23. Pulkkinen, M. and Hirvonen, A. (2005) EA planning, development and management process for agile enterprise development. *Proceedings of the 38th Hawaii International Conference on System Sciences*, IEEE Computer Society, Washington, DC.

24. Punia, D.K. and Saxena, K.B.C (2004) Managing inter-organizational workflows in egovernment services. ICEC'04. In: M. Janssen, H.G. Sol, and R.W. Wagenaar (Eds.), *Proceedings of Sixth International Conference on Electronic Commerce*, pp. 500–505.

25. Rappa, M. (2002) *Business Models on the Web*. http://digitalenterprise.org/models/models.html

26. Resnick, P., Zeckhauser, R., Swanson, J. and Lockwood, K. (2006) The value of reputation on eBay: a controlled experiment. *Experimental Economics 9(2)*, 79–101.

27. Schekkerman, J. (2003) *How to Survive in the Jungle of Enterprise Architecture Frameworks – Creating or Choosing an Enterprise Architecture Framework*. Trafford, Victoria, Canada.

28. Scott, M., Golden, W. and Hughes, M. (2004) Implementation strategies for e-government: a stakeholder analysis approach. In: T. Leino, T. Saarinen, and S. Klein (Eds.), *Proceedings of the Twelfth European Conference on Information Systems* (ECIS'2004). Turku, Finland. pp. 1719–1731.

29. Tarabanis, K., Peristeras, V. and Fragidis, G. (2001) Building an enterprise architecture for public administration: a high-level data model for strategic planning. *Proceedings of the 9th European Conference on Information Systems* (ECIS'2001) "Global Co-Operation in the New Millennium". Bled, Slovenia.

30. Trochidis, I., Tambouris, E. and Tarabanis, K. (2007) An ontology for modeling life-events. *Proceedings of IEEE International Conference on Services Computing* (SCC' 2007*)*, July 9–13, Salt Lake City, Utah, USA.

31. Vitale, M., Ross, J. and Weill, P. (2002) From place to space: migrating to profitable electronic commerce business models. *Series/Report no: Center for Information Systems Research; 324*, MIT Sloan School of Management Working Paper; pp. 4358-01. http://hdl.handle.net/1721.1/711

32. Walsham, G. (1997) *Interpreting Information Systems in Organisations*. Wiley, New York.

33. Wand, Y., Woo, C. and Hui, S. (1999) Developing business models to support information system evolution. *Proceedings of the Ninth Workshop on Information Technologies and Systems* (WITS'99), December 11–12, Charlotte, North Carolina.

34. Weill, P. and Vitale, M. (2001) *Place to Space: Migrating to EBusiness Models*; Harvard Business Press, Watertown, MA.

35. Whitman, L., Ramachandran, K. and Ketkar, V. (2001) A taxonomy of a living model of the enterprise. *Proceedings of the 33rd Conference on Winter Simulation* (Arlington, Virginia, December 09–12, 2001). Winter Simulation Conference. IEEE Computer Society, Washington DC, pp. 848–855.

36. Yin, R.K. (2003) *Case Study Research: Design and Methods*. Sage Publications, Beverly Hill, CA.

81

A Standardization Framework for Electronic Government Service Portals

Demetrios Sarantis, Christos Tsiakaliaris, Fenareti Lampathaki
and Yannis Charalabidis

Abstract

Although most eGovernment interoperability frameworks (eGIFs) cover adequately the technical aspects of developing and supporting the provision of electronic services to citizens and businesses, they do not exclusively address several important areas regarding the organization, presentation, accessibility and security of the content and the electronic services offered through government portals. This chapter extends the scope of existing eGIFs presenting the overall architecture and the basic concepts of the Greek standardization framework for electronic government service portals which, for the first time in Europe, is part of a country's eGovernment framework. The proposed standardization framework includes standards, guidelines and recommendations regarding the design, development and operation of government portals that support the provision of administrative information and services to citizens and businesses. By applying the guidelines of the framework, the design, development and operation of portals in central, regional and municipal government can be systematically addressed resulting in an applicable, sustainable and ever-expanding framework.

Keywords eGovernment · eGIF · Interoperability · Electronic Service Portals

1. Introduction

As yet, there is no generally accepted definition of a portal and the definition and characteristics of a government portal are even less well specified; no existing definition fits the unique requirements of a government portal. Government service portals are not the same as public portals that have a strong commercial aspect and they provide structured access to web sites across the whole of the World Wide Web. They are not vertical portals that attempt to provide comprehensive access to information on a defined topic or function to a defined audience, even though there are vertical specialist portals in the government sector. Although they may focus exclusively on government information and services, government has much broader scope than does the normal range of a specialist portal. They have a challenging and unique mission, focused on public access, for an unknown group of users who vary greatly in terms of the information and services they seek, as well as their education, background and access to technology. Within this context government portals must try to channel users and inquiries through hundreds of thousands, and in some cases millions, of web pages, with maximum efficiency and with user satisfaction.

Demetrios Sarantis • Decision Support Systems Laboratory, National Technical University of Athens, Athens, Greece. **Christos Tsiakaliaris** • Planet, 64 L.Riencourt Str., Apollon Tower, 115 23 Athens, Greece. **Fenareti Lampathaki** • Decision Support Systems Laboratory, National Technical University of Athens, Athens, Greece. **Yannis Charalabidis** • Decision Support Systems Laboratory, National Technical University of Athens, Athens, Greece.

G.A. Papadopoulos et al. (eds.), *Information Systems Development*, DOI 10.1007/b137171_81,
© Springer Science+Business Media, LLC 2009

A new definition of information portal seems to best capture their purpose, but what is needed most of all is an understanding of the very specific requirements and standards of electronic government service portals and the unique range of roles they play [1].

Most governments see the use of a gateway or portal web site as a means of providing a one-stop-shop entry point to government information and services as a significant advancement in the maturity of eGovernment [2]. Many countries include the development of such a portal in their eGovernment objectives [3] and base one measure of eGovernment success on the effectiveness of their portal. However, the concept of a portal has not yet been standardized, and government portals around the world address the task of creating a central gateway to government information and services in a variety of ways.

A standardization framework for electronic government service portals allows for the definition of conventions and agreements and provision of the essential guidelines and directives in the eGovernment domain. In July 2005, the Greek government presented an integrated "Digital Strategy" [4] policy for the period 2006–2013. The new digital strategy places ICT high in the country's agenda and treats new technologies as a strategic priority for Greece, adhering to the principles of the EC "i2010" Information Society action plan [5]. The aim is to perform a "Digital Leap to Productivity and Quality of Life." Two of the six main directions of the above policy are to offer a large number of digital services to businesses and to develop e-services for the citizen. To reach this goal, the Greek government has embarked on development and implementation of a central governmental portal (Hermes) – a portal that will be constructed based on the guidelines of the Greek standardization framework for electronic government service portals.

In the second section of this chapter we present the need behind the development of standardization frameworks for electronic government service portals. In the third section we examine some of the most remarkable government frameworks worldwide that provide guidelines and define standardization characteristics of electronic government service portals. After presenting the structure and the basic concepts of the recently developed Greek standardization framework (in Section 4), in Section 5 we examine and evaluate the compliance of two government portals with the framework. finally we present our conclusions and some thoughts about the necessity, usability and applicability of a standardization framework for electronic government service portals.

2. The Driving Force

In the past decade, the Greek government and especially several important public agencies (e.g. Ministry of Economy/General Secretariat for Information Systems [6], the Greek Social Security Organization [7], government administrations at central, regional or local level) initiated many efforts towards the development of government portals in order to offer electronic services to citizens and businesses. However, even if these efforts were in most cases successful, the portals that were developed did not follow a common set of specifications. On the contrary, each public agency did its own design, set its own functional and technical specifications and most of all put its own needs before the needs of its customers, i.e. citizens and businesses.

These rather dispersed, uncoordinated and heterogeneous efforts for the development of Greek government service portals resulted in several problems and discrepancies for both public agencies and citizens and businesses. More specifically, different solutions were adopted for issues such as content organization and presentation, navigation, search functions, accessibility, domain name registration, user authentication or personal data protection. On top of these issues, probably the most significant area that raises difficulties for citizens and businesses is the identification of, registration to, authentication to and use of eGgovernment services offered via government portals. In many cases, eGovernment services are not either well designed or not suitably promoted by public agencies that provide them, resulting in a very low level of usage.

The Greek standardization framework for electronic government service portals aims at providing effective and efficient solutions to the above problems/issues defining strategic directions, standards and specifications for the design, development and support of the operation of government portals that offer electronic services to citizens and businesses.

3. State of the Art

Nowadays, building a standardization framework for electronic government service portals must oppose the tendency to "reinvent the wheel" and requires examination and extended review of related research and standardization efforts undertaken in other countries focusing on work achieved in the EU, the UK, the USA and Australia. Each standardization endeavour brings a remarkably different approach to the task of designing and implementing electronic government service portals defining its own guidelines, best practices, characteristics and having its own strengths and weaknesses.

At European level, the European interoperability framework – EIF [8], published by the interoperable delivery of European eGovernment services to public administrations, businesses and citizens programme (IDABC), provides some general directions. The eEurope Action Plan 2005 [10] and the Decisions of the European Parliament, the Council and the Commission have adopted and promote a set of general principles which should be respected for any eGovernment services set up at a pan-European level. Accordingly, we can distinguish the following principles of EIF that are relative to a standardization framework for electronic government service portals: accessibility, multilingualism, security, privacy (personal data protection), use of open standards and use of multilateral solutions.

EIF represents the highest ranking module of a comprehensive methodological tool kit for implementing pan-European eGovernment services. National standardization frameworks develop further the emerging requirements for electronic government service portals. At country level, United Kingdom appears as a pioneer in implementing a standardization framework. Recently a new, revised version of the UK-eGIF framework [11] has been issued, covering the following sections: buying and selling advertising space and sponsorship, web site evaluation usage and analysis, minimum technical standards for government web sites, making PDF files usable and accessible, how to use cookies on government web sites, building in universal accessibility, legal issues, registering .gov.uk domain names and guidance on securing web sites.

The US framework is based on Web Design & Usability Guidelines [12] (209 guidelines), which were developed by the U.S. Department of Health and Human Services (HHS), in partnership with the U.S. General Services Administration. The content of the framework is based on the results of research that have been completed in the individual sectors that are related with the design and implementation of web sites.

On the other hand, Australia has chosen to focus on the compliance of governmental web sites with the National Privacy Act. Therefore, the Australian government guidelines [13] aim to assist Federal and Australian Capital Territory (ACT) government agencies to adopt best privacy practice and comply with the privacy act in respect to their web sites. These guidelines are organized in the following categories: openness, collection of personal information via web sites, security and publication.

The Australian government guidelines do not regulate state or territory agencies, except for the Australian Capital Territory (ACT). Western Australia, an Australian state, follows a simplified approach for the description of its web guidelines, defining 13 principles [14] that government agencies should follow when developing their web sites.

The New Zealand government has compiled a set of web standards and recommendations [15], which apply to any web site that is intended for the public and financed by the public through the crown or through public agencies. The standards are a combination of those devised specifically for NZ government web sites and accessibility standards derived from the W3C web accessibility initiative (WAI). So, the New Zealand framework includes standards for images, colour, site markup, special purpose documents, writing content, site content, page layout, navigation, style sheets, etc.

Having considered analytically the provided guidelines of the above frameworks we could classify them in the following five categories:

- *General Principles*, describing topics related to principle of equality and isonomy (equality of laws, or of people before the law), principle of completeness and credibility, principle of trustfulness and principle of proper use of public resources.
- *Portal Administration and Optimization*, describing topics related to organizational, management issues of the government portal, user support, evaluation and statistics.
- *Content Organization and Presentation*, describing topics covering the information presented on the portal, web design choices, design layout and usability-related issues.
- *eGovernment Services Support and Interoperability*, which covers the electronic services provision from the government portal, interoperability issues and compliance with interoperability standards.
- *Security Requirements and Legal Issues*, which covers the secure operation, secure data administration and data exchange via the government portal as well as authentication issues, privacy statement definition, guidelines about the compliance with national, European and international laws related to electronic communications.

In Table 81.1 we present a comparison among the above-mentioned frameworks. Each SF characteristic receives a full coverage a partial coverage or a no coverage mark. During the analysis phase of each SF, evaluators determine the overall coverage indicator for each characteristic. If the majority of evaluators do not agree on the level of coverage, partial coverage is assigned as the consensus value. In order to assess each characteristic's coverage degree, the individual components comprising it are examined.

Table 81.1. Framework coverage.

Country/ framework	General principles	Portal administration and optimization	Content organization and presentation	eGovernment services support and interoperability	Security requirements and legal issues
EU-EIF	PC			PC	PC
UK	EC	PC	EC	PC	EC
USA	EC	PC	EC		PC
Australia	PC		EC		PC
Western Australia	PC		EC		EC
New Zealand	PC				PC

EC/PC: extended/partial coverage, blank: no coverage

As shown by the analysis, most of the frameworks deal with the "General Principles", the "Security Requirements and Legal Issues" and the "Content Organization and Presentation" issues. On the other hand, there are substantial differences on the magnitude that each SF addresses areas like "Portal Administration and Optimization" and "eGovernment Services Support and Interoperability". In contrast with the results of the above analysis, the Greek standardization framework for electronic government service portals (SF or SFEGSP) covers all the above areas providing specific and detailed guidelines.

4. The Greek Standardization Framework

The Greek SF is part of the Greek eGovernment framework [16], which aims at meeting the demands of the Greek Digital Strategy [4], contributes to the Lisbon economic and societal objectives and harmonizes with the pan-European policies and directions of i2010 [5]. The eGovernment framework also complies with the recommendations for national interoperability frameworks issued by the European interoperability framework [8]. Finally, the eGovernment framework takes into account the results of standardization efforts performed by international organizations and initiatives such as W3C, OASIS, IETF.

The SF consists of five areas; one area is generic describing the basic principles to be followed by public agencies when designing, developing or operating eGovernment portals while the other four areas include directions and standards as regards specific issues. These rest four areas cover portal administration and optimization, content organization and presentation, eGovernment services support and interoperability and security requirements and legal issues (Fig. 81.1).

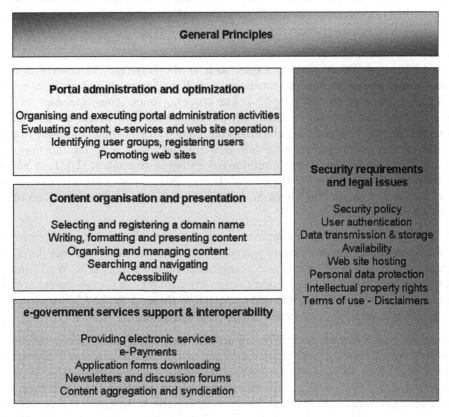

Figure 81.1. The Greek standardization framework for electronic government service portals.

According to SF, all government portals should adhere to the following general principles: principle of equality and isonomy, principle of completeness and credibility, principle of trustfulness and principle of proper use of public resources. The compliance of a portal with the general principles assures – at least at a basic level – that the portal is accessible to several user groups including people with disabilities [17] through the use of different well-accepted technology platforms and tools, its content is correct and up to date and electronic services are offered in a secure and trustworthy manner to citizens and businesses.

The "portal administration and optimization" part of the SF tries to regulate all issues related to the roles and the procedures that the public agency owner of the portal should establish in order to assure that the portal is functioning properly. So, this part describes the roles and the procedures for content management, eGovernment services support and content, e-services and web site evaluation. The procedures and measures used for the registration of users to eGovernment services as well as their authentication to them are also described in this section. Last but not least, this section includes guidelines for the promotion of eGovernment service portals pertaining to their registration to search engines and web directories, as well as other advertising or dissemination activities according to the magnitude of the user group(s) they target.

The second major group of SF's guidelines refers to the organization and the presentation aspects of the content hosted in governmental portals [18]. First of all, it is very important that the content of governmental portals meets the needs of its users [19]. To this direction, the SF includes guidelines about the actual content of the portals, i.e. what information should exist on a governmental portal and how it should be organized. Two facets for the content organization are introduced:

- a government category list (GCL), developed based on the services public administrations offer to citizens and business;
- an organization based on life events and business episodes, which allows citizens and businesses locate information and services without needing to remember which public administration is responsible for them.

As far as the organization and storage of the content in the IT systems of public agencies, tree structures should be used. Other relevant issues, such as the language the content is written in, the procedures that assure its correctness and timeliness as well as the search and navigation functionalities supported, are also discussed in this part [20]. The colours, fonts, icons, graphics and other effects employed by public agencies in order to make their portals attractive form another significant section of a standardization framework. These conjectural aspects along with guidelines about the size and length of web pages form the first impression a web user gets from accessing a portal and may influence him positively or negatively on his decision to continue navigating in its content [21]. Last but certainly not least, the selection of a domain name and the accessibility of a governmental portal are two topics that a SF should in any case try to regulate. The Greek SF includes guidelines for both of them, according to which all government service portals should

- register a name that is easy to find and remember and automatically relate to the agency that owns the portal. Domain names such as www.agencyname.gov.gr should be the first choice for public agencies.
- be compliant with World Wide Web's web accessibility initiative [22] (W3C/WAI) and web content accessibility guidelines [23] (WCAG) version 1.0. Government service portals should at least satisfy the requirements of the "A" level of WCAG and try to satisfy those of the "AA" level in order to be truly accessible by different technological means and several user groups.

A fundamental part of the SF is the eGovernment services support and interoperability section. This section provides guidelines about the way of presenting and granting access to services via government service portals and how the portals should communicate and exchange data with back office systems [24]. Since interoperability and authentication [9] are the two concepts hidden behind the words here, the SF simply describes the basic requirements and cross-references to other parts of the Greek eGovernment framework.

5. Application of the Standardization Framework

To test the maturity and applicability of the Greek standardization framework, two case studies are presented. A case study approach was used as it would allow insight into the practices and experiences of actual web portal implementations in public sector and provide an opportunity to extend the research into a longitudinal study as application of the SF in governmental portals continues to be promoted by central government and becomes an established method used in the transformation of government. The research investigation principally utilized the analysis of the web portals by SF experts although this was supplemented by interviews of the web portal administrators to generate data. In each case study, the compliance of a specific government service portal with the SF is examined.

5.1. The Case of Civil Personnel Selection Portal

The Supreme Council for Civil Personnel Selection (ASEP) in Greece works as an independent public body and is not subject to government control. ASEP's mission is to monitor and supervise the selection of permanent personnel for the public sector. ASEP's web site [25] hosts information with respect to the procedures for employment in the public sector, announcements of vacancies and publishes the results of written examinations and announcements. Apart from information about vacancies, the web site also offers a set of electronic services for citizens (candidates for employment in the public sector) and public agencies: calculation of credits for the participation in a written examination, publication of work positions, electronic completion and submission of applications for the participation in examinations, vacancies selection, etc. Examining ASEP's web site, the following conclusions and comments (Table 81.2) can be derived as regards its compliance with the SF's guidelines.

Table 81.2. ASEP compliance with Greek SF's guidelines.

SF's standards categories	Assessment/comments
General principles	Full compliance
Portal administration and optimization	
Organizing and executing portal administration activities	Partial compliance. ASEP has not established the required roles and procedures for the organization and administration of the portal
Evaluating content, e-services and web site operation	No compliance. No such features have been implemented
Identifying user groups, registering users	Full compliance
Promoting web sites	No compliance. Promotion or dissemination activities have not been exercised
Content organization and presentation	
Selecting and registering a domain name	No compliance. ASEP has not registered a name in the domain .gov.gr. Moreover, the domain name should be a translation rather than a transliteration of the agency's official name
Writing, formatting and presenting content	Partial compliance. There is no content in a language other than Greek
Organizing and managing content	Partial compliance. Metadata are not kept for content and services
Searching and navigating	Compliance
Accessibility	Compliance. The portal is compliant with W3C's WCAG guidelines (A-level)
eGovernment services support and interoperability	
Providing electronic services	Partial compliance
ePayments	Not applicable
Application forms downloading	Full compliance
Newsletters and discussion forums	No compliance
Content aggregation and syndication	No compliance
Security requirements and legal issues	
Security policy	Partial compliance. A security policy has been defined but it is not published on the portal
User authentication	Full compliance
Data transmission and storage	Partial compliance. HTTPS is not used
Availability	It is not clarified whether the portal fulfils the relevant requirements of the SF
Web site hosting	Not applicable
Personal data protection	Partial compliance. It exists but is not published
Intellectual property rights	Not applicable
Terms of use – disclaimers	Not applicable

5.2. The Case of Fireservice Portal

The Fireservice is a public agency supervised by the Ministry of Internal Affairs. Through its portal [26], it presents basic information about fire hazards and how to protect against them, describes some fundamental security measures citizens and businesses can take against fires, etc. The portal also allows businesses to fill in and submit electronic applications for several public certificates issued by the Fireservice. Table 81.3 shows the compliance with SF.

Table 81.3. Fireservice compliance with Greek SF's guidelines.

SF's standards categories	Assessment/comments
General principles	Full compliance
Portal administration and optimization	
Organizing and executing portal administration activities	Partial compliance. The established roles and procedures for the organization and administration of the portal do not meet the requirements of the SF
Evaluating content, e-services and web site operation	No compliance. No such features have been implemented
Identifying user groups, registering users	Full compliance
Promoting web sites	No compliance. Promotion or dissemination activities have not been exercised
Content organization and presentation	
Selecting and registering a domain name	Partial compliance. Fireservice has not registered a name in the domain .gov.gr
Writing, formatting and presenting content	Partial compliance. There is no content in a language other than Greek
Organizing and managing content	Partial compliance. Metadata are not kept for content and services
Searching and navigating	Compliance
Accessibility	Compliance. The portal is compliant with W3C's WCAG guidelines (A-level)
eGovernment services support and interoperability	
Providing electronic services	Partial compliance
ePayments	Not applicable
Application forms downloading	Partial compliance
Newsletters and discussion forums	Not applicable
Content aggregation and syndication	No compliance
Security requirements and legal issues	
Security policy	It is not clarified whether the portal fulfils the relevant requirements of the SF
User authentication	Partial compliance. Username/password combinations are used as user credential whereas digital certificates should be used for some electronic services
Data transmission and storage	Compliance
Availability	It is not clarified whether the portal fulfils the relevant requirements of the SF
Web site hosting	Not applicable
Personal data protection	It is not clarified whether the portal fulfils the relevant requirements of the SF
Intellectual property rights	Not applicable
Terms of use – disclaimers	Not applicable

Overall, both these portals are considered to be the results of positive efforts to move administrative services online.

6. Conclusions

Concluding we should underline that the development of an effective standardization framework for electronic government service portals depends on extensive research into user needs and the ability and political willingness to portray a citizen's or a business perspective of government on a government portal, rather than purely a government's perspective [27]. This is a challenge for governments and for the design of government portals and is possibly only ever partially achievable, due to the nature of government. However, the more a standardization framework makes the architecture of a government service portal transparently clear, the more easily users will be able to find the information and electronic services they seek. If government portals cannot reflect the mental models that users bring to the site, they can at least make clear the mental model lying behind the site, in the architecture, design, policies and even data and metadata used, so that users can make their own translation into the world of government. Simple techniques of web portal architecture, navigation and design, the use of site maps, good labelling and mouse-over explanations of headings and links can reveal the mental model to users, but these basics of good web practice are not always observed.

The development of standardization frameworks for electronic government service portals seems to be still in its infancy, and those working in the field predict a new generation of government portals with enhanced capabilities. Framework developments are dependent on technologies that are already available and are starting to be used in some of the most advanced commercial, educational and enterprise-based portals; they are being tentatively applied to government portals. However, on top of all reasons, it is the political willingness that will drive the effort of developing a standardization framework for electronic government service portals. Governments that have realized the anarchy in the electronic facet of public administration have the opportunity to correct the situation, or at least try to improve it, by issuing a standardization framework that defines a common set of principles and guidelines to be considered by all public agencies when they design and develop their portals. This is exactly the case for the Greek SF as well. The SF is ready and known to market and it remains for the Greek government to define how and when it will be set as the basis for the development of government service portals. At the end, the compliance of all government service portals with the standardization framework will result in achieving homogeneity in eGovernment and providing effective eGovernment services to citizens and businesses, which are easily located and used and accessible to a wide range of user groups.

References

1. Hernon, P., Cullen, R., Relyea, H., Comparative perspectives on eGovernment, 2006.
2. Wimmer, M. A., European Development towards Online One-stop Government: The "eGOV" Project, Proceedings of the ICEC2001 Conference, Vienna, 2001.
3. Varavithya, W., Esichaikul, V., The Development of Electronic Government: A Case Study of Thailand, Electronic Government, Springer, Berlin/Heidelberg, 2004
4. Digital Strategy 2006-2013, http://www.infosoc.gr/infosoc/en-UK/sthnellada/committee/default1/top.htm
5. EU: i2010 eGovernment Action Plan, Commission of the European Communities (CEC), i2010 e-Government Action Plan: Accelerating e-Government in Europe for the Benefit of All, COM (2006) 173 final, Retrieved February 15, 2007 from http://europa.eu.int/eur-lex/lex/LexUriServ/site/en/com/2006/com2006_0173en01.pdf
6. General Secretariat for Information Systems is operating the Taxisnet portal (www.taxisnet.gr), which is the national portal for all tax related services.
7. IKA is operating the IKAnet portal (www.ikanet.gr), where employers can declare the social security contributions for their employees as well as fulfil several other social security related obligations.
8. IDABC, European Interoperability Framework for pan-European eGovernment Services, Version 1.0, Retrieved February 5, 2007 from http://europa.eu.int/idabc/en/document/3761
9. Lambrinoudakis, C., Gritzalis, S., Dridi, F., Pernul, G., Security requirements for e-government services: a methodological approach for developing a common PKI-based security policy, 2003, Computer Communications, 26(16):1873–1883.
10. eEurope 2005:An information society for all, http://ec.europa.eu/information_society/eeurope/2005/all_about/action_plan/index_en.htm
11. Guidelines for UK Government Websites, http://www.cabinetoffice.gov.uk/government_it/web_guidelines.aspx
12. Web Design & Usability Guidelines, http://www.usability.gov/pdfs/guidelines.html
13. Guidelines for Federal and ACT Government Websites, http://www.privacy.gov.au/internet/web/index.html
14. Premiers Circular 2002/14:Website Standards, http://www.dpc.wa.gov.au/psmd/pubs/legis/premcirculars/2002_14UPAug061.pdf
15. New Zealand Web Guidelines, http://www.e.govt.nz/archive/standards/web-guidelines/listing_archives
16. Greek e-Government Framework, http://www.e-gif.gov.gr/
17. Huang, C.J., Usability of e-government web-sites for people with disabilities, Proceedings of the 36th Hawaii International Conference on System Sciences (HICSS'03)

18. Wimmer, M.A., Holler, U., Applying a holistic approach to develop user-friendly, customer oriented eGovernment oriented portal interfaces, 7th ERCIM International Workshop on User Interfaces for All, Paris, 2002.

19. Gant, J.P., Gant, D.B., Web portal functionality and State government e-service, Proceedings of the 35th Hawaii International Conference on System Sciences – 2002.

20. Eschenfelder, K.R., Behind the web site: an inside look at the production of web-based textual government information, Government Information Quarterly, Vol. 21, No. 3, 2004, pp. 337–358.

21. The MIT usability guidelines, http://web.mit.edu/is/usability/usability-guidelines.html

22. World Wide Web's Web Accessibility Initiative, http://www.w3.org/wai

23. Web Content Accessibility Guidelines, http://www.w3.org/TR/WCAG10/

24. Hammer, M., Reengineering work: don't automate, obliterate, Harvard Business Review, Vol. 68, No. 4, 1990, pp. 140–112.

25. Supreme Council for Civil Personnel Selection (ASEP), http://www.asep.gr

26. Fireservice, http://www.fireservice.gr

27. Younis, T., Customers' expectations of public sector services: does quality have its limits? Total Quality Management, Vol. 8, No. 4, 1997, pp. 115–129.

82

Elaborating the WARE Method for eParticipation Requirements

Øystein Sæbø, Tero Päivärinta, Jan Helge Austbø and Svein Sundfør Scheie

Abstract

eParticipation systems are often directly targeted at citizens. However, as a group of potential users, citizens form a heterogeneous and unpredictable group, which makes requirements elicitation a challenging issue. Based on recently developed ideas for wide audience requirement engineering (WARE), this chapter discusses and elaborates a method for eliciting citizen requirements for eParticipation. The method elaboration was conducted in connection with a project in southern Norway, where young people's requirements for becoming active e-participants in society were mapped. Based on these experiences, we discuss the use and usefulness of the WARE method and suggest ideas on how to further develop the WARE method for eParticipation purposes.

Keywords Ware method · eParticipation

1. Introduction

eParticipation involves the extension and transformation of democratic communication and decision-making processes mediated by information and communication technologies in society [11]. eParticipation projects have, in a majority of cases, had only modest impact on public participation [4]. One reason for this is the lack of understanding the demand side requirements of eParticipation, that is, the public's incentives and needs to participate [1].

As a potential means to tackle this issue, we discuss and elaborate the wide audience requirement engineering (WARE) method [13]. The WARE method is designed to address information system development (ISD) projects where stakeholders may not be able to express their needs specifically, the target group may be scattered outside a single ISD environment and end users may be difficult to reach [15]. This chapter focuses on the use and usefulness of the WARE method in an eParticipation project. The project explored young people's interests in eParticipation in local matters. We wanted to find out (whether and) how the WARE method could be used to elicit requirements for eParticipation from young people. Based on our experiences we suggest potential improvements to the WARE method.

The chapter is organised as follows. After a short introduction to the eParticipation area we briefly sketch the WARE method literature. Then we present results on how WARE was utilised when analysing requirements held by the youth in southern Norway on eParticipation. We suggest potential improvements to the method, and we summarise by suggesting further research on WARE itself and on utilisation of the WARE method for eParticipation purposes.

Øystein Sæbø, Tero Päivärinta and Jan Helge Austbø • ***Department of Information Systems, University of Agder, Kristiansand, Norway. **Svein Sundfør Scheie** • The Norwegian Post and Telecommunications Authority, Norway.

G.A. Papadopoulos et al. (eds.), *Information Systems Development*, DOI 10.1007/b137171_82,
© Springer Science+Business Media, LLC 2009

2. eParticipation

By definition, eParticipation aims at reversing the trends of declining political engagement, disconnections between citizens and their elected representatives and a consequent decline in the legitimacy of political institutions. The democratic idea depends fundamentally on effective communication among citizens, politicians, officers and other stakeholders [3, 16]. Information and communication technologies (ICT) and, particularly, Internet technologies are often considered to represent a potential solution to these problems—offering new possibilities and opportunities for political participation [4]. A variety of technologies have been used to help with these initiatives—including discussion forums, blogs, wikis, chat rooms, geographical information systems, decision support systems, voting systems and web and pod casts, in addition to the standard web sites and e-mail services routinely provided.

Except in a handful of success stories, eParticipation projects have rarely had any large influence on public participation [10]. Reluctant key stakeholders [7] and a lack of knowledge on how ICT could be designed to support various democratic systems and ideas [9] are some reasons for the limited success. eParticipation projects are often characterised by unclear and poorly formulated objectives [11] by a large variety of stakeholders, including citizens, politicians and government officials, possessing a wide variety of requirements and interests [1] and by lack of knowledge on how ICT relates to varying democratic ideals and objectives [10].

Little research has focused on young people's perspective on online participation for democratic purposes [6]. But what are such interests of the youth concerning online participation? How could we elicit their interests concerning eParticipation purposes? These questions were investigated in a qualitative case study, whose objective was to investigate young people's needs and expectations towards eParticipation projects. Based on these characteristics, the WARE method was chosen to study young people's interests and requirements in eParticipation.

3. Wide Audience Requirement Engineering (WARE)

The WARE method is designed to address major challenges in requirement elicitation for ISD projects aimed at heterogeneous end users and has the following characteristics [14]:

- (potential) users have little knowledge on how to describe functionality for the suggested product and technology;
- end users may not be available or controllable (as assumed by many traditional ISD methodologies);
- end users' and the developers' cognitive ideas may vary substantially, complicating the opportunity to develop aggregated models of the suggested system;
- it appears difficult to develop requirement specifications based on traditional techniques.

Tuunanen [13] suggests an eight-step WARE model to address these shortcomings. The model is illustrated in Fig. 82.1 and further explained based on Tuunanen's work.

In phase 1, the pre-study phase, the objective is to define the scope of the study and provide stimuli for the actual requirement gathering [13]. The stimuli list influences phase 2, where the project is defined more in detail and participants are selected to identify a broad range of ideas to continue working with. To accumulate a satisfactory range of various ideas (around 80–90%), about 30 persons should be investigated [2]. A laddering technique [5] is utilised for phase 3, the requirement-gathering phase. Based on the stimuli list from phase 1, each participant is asked to describe a quality which she finds important. The input is organised as a chain of arguments and is further aggregated in phase 4, the model aggregation phase, where the main objective is to identify themes, organise chains of arguments accordingly and develop semantic maps, which graphically introduce findings and relationships.

Semantic maps are further adapted in phase 5 to introduce findings to the audience. Chains of arguments could be presented in a way that allows participants to look at general themes as well as detailed data and to see how these themes arise from the interviews. A seminar (phase 6) could be used to present

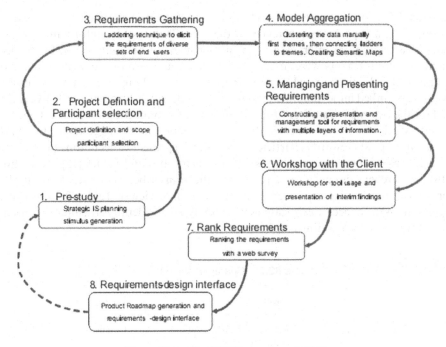

Figure 82.1. The WARE process model [13].

these semantic maps to decision makers and developers. Thus far, ideas are not prioritised, which is the main objective of phase 7. Tuunanen [13] suggests conducting a survey among potential users to prioritise and validate findings. Finally, in the requirement design interface phase, requirement analysis could be presented based on the WARE method and data-gathering activities.

4. Implementing the WARE Method in an eParticipation Project

In this section, we illustrate our implementation of the WARE method, lessons learned from using the techniques and ideas on how to improve it, as well as reflection on the use and usefulness of WARE techniques for eParticipation purposes.

In the pre-study phase (phase 1) focus group interviews were conducted to gather data to create the stimuli list. Focus group interviews may identify unforeseen circumstances and a wide variety of ideas [8]. To obtain well-informed data, students attending an eDemocracy course at Master's level were interviewed, and data were analysed according to the focus group kit developed by Morgan and Krueger [8]. Based on transcriptions of these interviews, a stimuli list was developed (Table 82.1).

Table 82.1. Stimuli list.

Ongoing activities
One-stop integration
Well-developed user interface
Design
Marketing
Personal benefits (for participants)
Opportunity to influence
Adapted information

In the project definition and participant selection phase (phase 2), participants were selected based on access to informants and expected competence on the area. Twenty-three informants, secondary school students aged 17–18 years, were interviewed. To further increase the outcome of the project definition phase, four additional informants were interviewed. These four were resource personnel from the local municipality and the local university, who were experienced in working on eParticipation projects.

The informants ranked important themes based on the stimuli list from phase 1. Every informant was asked in detail on the two most important topics and asked to comment on important characteristics for these two themes. Attributes, consequences and values were identified as suggested by the WARE method. Attributes represent requests towards eParticipation, values represent expectations on what to achieve by participating and consequences represent links between attributes and values [13]. To identify chains of arguments, two researchers discussed and processed the transcribed data, resulting in 897 individual statements organised into 89 chains of arguments (from 27 interviews). Table 82.2 illustrates how these chains of arguments were coded. Each statement is analysed to identify attributes, consequences, and values and coded towards open-coding categories [12].

Table 82.2.   Coding of statements.

	Statement	Coding
Attribute	"…reward good articles about specific topics"	Competition
Consequence	You should be rewarded for being active	Reward activities
Value	"Youngsters become engaged if activities are rewarded"	Reward activities

Aggregation of data is necessary to utilise such large amount of data, which is the main objective in phase 4. The WARE method does not explicitly suggest any structured way to aggregate data. Here informed grounded theory techniques were used [12]. In an iterative process where two researchers conducted open coding of 89 chains of arguments individually and in comparison with each other, 11 themes were identified. By using axial coding techniques, these 11 themes resulted in 6 overall themes, illustrated in Table 82.3.

Table 82.3.   Six main themes based on axial coding.

Themes identified from axial coding
Ongoing activity
Engagement
Attract attention
Fortify the message
Communicate
Adaptation of information towards young people

The chains of arguments were distributed to the overall themes. Two researchers conducted the analysis individually and compared the results afterwards, resulting in an initial agreement of 71.9%. The 25 chains of arguments reflecting the disagreement between the researchers were discussed and full agreement was achieved. Finally in the data aggregation phase, first drafts of semantic maps were developed to be able to communicate findings and illustrate relations between themes and chains of arguments (see Section 5).

The drafted semantic maps include relationships among attributes, consequences and values for each of the six themes (presented in Table 82.2). An online presentation tool was developed (http://ware.austboe.com/, in Norwegian only) in phase 5 to help decision makers and developers grasp an overview of young people's expectations and requirements towards eParticipation services.

A seminar was conducted in phase 6 of the project. The development group from a regional project, which aims at increasing youth participation in politics, was invited and presented with the preliminary results based on the semantic maps and the presentation tools. The group's input influenced the final results of the study. A short survey among the participants at the seminar showed that they found the results useful, but found the amount of information overwhelming.

A group of secondary school students (different from those included in phase 3) was asked to rank the requirements in phase 7. Based on their input we could rank the five most important elements (Table 82.4). The WARE method includes no formal test to validate the ranking. In order to check the statistical validity of the relative ranking in our case, Kendall's W was calculated. The test unveiled only weak (or non-existent) similarities among the participants' rankings, thus weakening the strength of argument. This implies that the requirements and reasoning for them vary greatly among the participants.

Table 82.4. Top-ranked themes from the rank requirement phase.

Relevance for the target group
User friendly design
Categorisation to ease navigation
Designed to claim attention
Bring in some kind of competition to market the
    eParticipation service

Finally the end objective for the WARE method is to come up with requirement design interface. These results are illustrated by introducing the process of developing semantic maps for one of these six major themes, which is presented in the next section.

5. Developing Requirement Design Interface to Support "Ongoing Activities"

The chain of arguments and statements as analysed to identify patterns and relationships. Figure 82.2 introduces one sub-category of "ongoing activities" including quotations to illustrate the coding process.

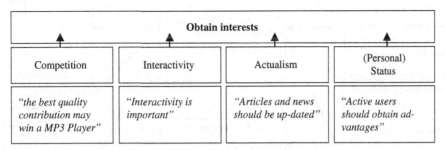

Figure 82.2. Examples of aggregated statements.

Based on the coding process of the chains of arguments, semantic maps for the six major themes were developed. Quotations and chains of arguments were allocated to these categories, as illustrated in Fig. 82.3. Here, the first two numbers identify a participant, the next two identify a chain of argument and the last two identify a statement. Thus 010402 refers to the first respondent's fourth chain of argument, statement two.

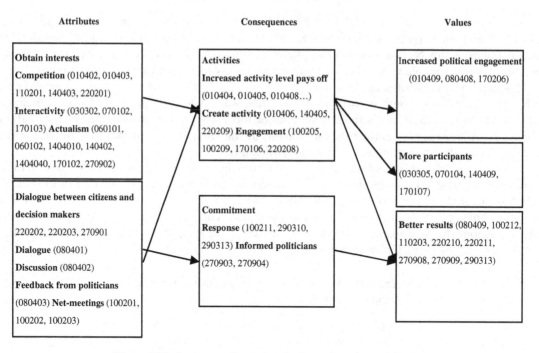

Figure 82.3. Statements allocated to the theme, "ongoing activities".

Findings indicate that it is important to establish some interests based on dialogues between young people and those involved in making decisions. Politicians should be present since the driving force for continued participation is to achieve some results from previous contributions. The eParticipation project could introduce some benefits for active participants, e.g. by introducing various status levels. Figure 82.4 introduces the summarised semantic map for the topic.

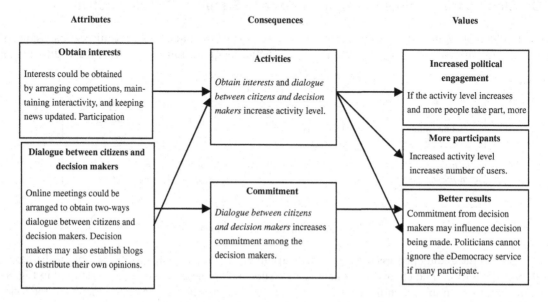

Figure 82.4. Semantic map for "ongoing activities".

6. Discussion

The WARE method was introduced in the eParticipation research project since the characteristics of the project coincide with the characteristics of the methodology. The youth area of eParticipation research still lacks integration and structure [1], where a number of case studies are presented without any well-organised data-gathering techniques. The WARE method suggests stepwise data-gathering approach, which may address some of these shortcomings. Due to our experiences we argue that the WARE method has proved to be a promising candidate for further research projects similar to the eParticipation project introduced here.

Primarily the WARE method offers structure to the research projects and the data-gathering techniques. The stepwise approach systematises the analytical process, focusing on relations between various elements. Moreover, the WARE technique also introduces the semantic maps, simplifying the presentation to decision makers and major interest groups at the end, and increases the opportunity to discuss findings with participants dynamically throughout the project since these semantic maps present a large amount of data in a structure which is (hopefully) well suited for communicative purposes.

The WARE method focuses on relationships among attributes, consequences and values. Thus, for ISD purposes, the WARE method could help identify connections among characteristics of the system (attribute), the purpose (the value) of including these characteristics and how to achieve these purposes (the consequences). Some of the findings in our case study relating to the eParticipation area are already discussed in existing research literature (which is not introduced here due to our focus on the WARE methodology, not on eParticipation). But the WARE methodology and the semantic maps identify relationships between these elements, which are not present in existing literature.

The structure and relationships identified by introducing the WARE method appear clear and convincing. Thus it is timely to question the strengths of these relationships as they arise from a qualitative study. Both the starting argument (the stimuli list) and the end product (the semantic maps) are based on qualitative and interpretative approaches. These semantic maps should be seen as one interpretation of the data, not *the only* way to structure the data.

6.1. Suggested Improvements to the WARE Method

The WARE method in the contemporary research literature is still in its infancy. Hence, a few adaptations may appear useful for its adoption and further application. Based on our experiences we suggest some improvements on how to utilise the WARE methodology in projects similar to our eParticipation project.

First, the WARE method does not suggest any formal techniques to develop the stimuli list in phase 1. The stimuli list is highly important since participants are asked to comment and prioritise topics based on this list. Explorative data-gathering approaches could be utilised. Focus group interviews could explore a wide variety of ideas [8] and have proved to be a promising approach in our research project.

Second, the WARE method lacks clear indications on how to analyse raw data into aggregated data models. We argue that formal data analysis approaches are needed. Here we introduced a grounded theoretical approach. Although we admit that a full-scale grounded theoretical analysis is neither conducted nor possible (since the study is arguably well informed by theories and approaches), the coding techniques from grounded theory were useful.

Third, more effort should be made on continuous presentation of findings to both participants and decision makers. The online presentation tool (http://www.austboe.com/webware/modell.htm, in Norwegian only) made it possible for interested parties to look at the aggregated models (illustrated in Fig. 82.4) and, at the same time, look at details like chains of arguments and individual statements. The simplified presentation of findings presented as semantic maps is, from our point of view, an important strength of the WARE method since these maps allow for continuous discussion and feedback on findings from various stakeholders.

Fourth, our experiences suggest re-ordering phases 6 and 7. Participants at the seminar (phase 6) found the results interesting but overwhelming. The rank requirements in the following phase (phase 7) might help organise a large amount of data, based on importance.

Finally, as mentioned above, calculating Kendall's W did not support the ranking in phase 7. These tests are usually introduced in more quantitative studies. Despite this, we argue that the test is relevant for our purposes since a major contribution from utilising the WARE method is supposed to be ranking of identified elements based on importance. In our study we could not rank importance based on any evident input. To be able to rank importance, more work is needed to develop (or utilise) better ranking techniques.

7. Conclusion

This chapter introduces and elaborates the WARE method for eliciting citizen requirements in eParticipation projects. The conducted study on identifying young people's interests in eParticipation projects explored the method and gained insights on its strengths and weaknesses. Based on our experiences we argue that the WARE method is a promising candidate for analysing eParticipation projects, since such projects (focusing on the public's needs) are characterised by heterogeneous users, unclear ideas on what to achieve and non-controllable end users. The WARE method introduces a structured approach to identifying requirements, unveiling relationships that are not currently present in the eParticipation literature.

More effort is needed to further develop the WARE method for eParticipation purposes. More formal data-gathering techniques should be introduced in several phases to further validate the method. Better presentation techniques could improve the communication strength of the method, by presenting semantic maps for interested parties throughout the process.

The WARE method is still in its infancy and should be developed further for increased practical usefulness. More studies are needed to improve the WARE method and our knowledge on how the WARE method could be used for eParticipation purposes.

References

1. Flak, L., Sein, M., and Sæbø, Ø. (2007). Towards a cumulative tradition in e-government research: going beyond the Gs and Cs. In Electronic Government (pp. 13–22).
2. Griffin, A., and Hauser, J. R. (1993). The voice of the customer. Marketing Science, 12(1), 1–27.
3. Habermas, J. (1996). Between facts and norms: contributions to a discourse theory of law and democracy. Cambridge, MA: MIT Press.
4. Hoff, J., Lofgren, K., and Torpe, L. (2003). The state we are in: E-democracy in Denmark. Information Polity: The International Journal of Government & Democracy in the Information Age, 8(1/2), 49–66, IOS Press.
5. Kelly, G. A. (1991). The psychology of personal constructs. London: Routledge.
6. Macintosh, A., Robson, E., Smith, E., and Whyte, A. (2003). Electronic democracy and young people. Social Science Computer Review, 21(1), 43–54.
7. Mahrer, H., and Krimmer, R. (2005). Towards the enhancement of e-democracy: identifying the notion of the 'middleman paradox'. Information Systems Journal, 15(1), 27–42.
8. Morgan, D. L., and Krueger, R. A. (1998). The focus group kit. Thousand Oaks, CA: Sage.
9. Päivärinta, T., and Sæbø, Ø. (2006). Models of e-democracy. Communication of Association of Information Systems, 17, 818–840.
10. Päivärinta, T., and Sæbø, Ø. (Forthcoming). The genre system lens on eDemocracy. Scandinavian Journal of Information Systems.
11. Sæbø, Ø., Rose, J., and Flak, L. S. (2008). The shape of eParticipation: Characterizing an emerging research area. Government Information Quarterly 25, 400–428.
12. Strauss, A. L., and Corbin, J. M. (1990). Basics of qualitative research: grounded theory procedures and techniques. Newbury Park, CA: Sage.
13. Tuunanen, T. (2005). Requirements elicitation for wide audience end-users. Helsinki.
14. Tuunanen, T., Peffers, K., and Gengler, C. E. (2004). Wide audience requirements engineering (WARE): a practical method and case study.
15. Tuunanen, T., and Rossi, M. (2004). Engineering a method for wide audience requirements elicitation and integrating it to software development. Paper presented at the System Sciences, 2004. Proceedings of the 37th Annual Hawaii International Conference on.
16. Van Dijk, J. (2000). Models of democracy and concepts of communication. In K. L. Hacker and J. Van Dijk (Eds.), Digital democracy, issues of theory and practice. London: Sage Publications.

83

Web Tools for Geospatial Data Management

Petr Horak, Karel Charvat and Martin Vlk

Abstract

The systems that are able to work with data from remote sources are becoming more and more important. Management and the usage of data stored on remote sources (external servers) without the necessity of data replication give us the chance to try to solve some of the problems that requirements for fast and easy data usage present. This solution is based on the principles of remote data retrieval through data management systems. The main objective of the chapter is to present unique web solution for spatial data management in the form of integration using different kinds of spatial web services together with internal data sources (files, databases). A very important point is also the collaboration of this tool with other web tools in the same portal solution. Map Project Manager and the Uniform Resource Management system are the programmes able to provide geodata integration and SW tools collaboration within a web environment.

Keywords Web service · Spatial data · OGC · Catalogue · Metadata · Map Project Manager

1. Introduction

Present society is "data dependent" on all counts – data accessibility is necessary in business, for internal data usage within official government bodies, public free time activities as well as basic conditions for good government–public communication. The expanse of data sources also demands far better information management facilities and publication systems are increasing more and more. Technical solutions covering these general requirements are important mainly for institutions dealing with data processing and data publication or for institutes which provide information on other subjects. New systems should have the possibility of faster access to updated information, better search options, publication and sorting facilities for data and the possibility of using other systems or subsystems.

Thanks to the progress in the development of web services, users (people, institutions) now have the possibility to not only work with their own geographical data saved on their computers but also use the data stored on external servers. Users are now able to include much more information in their ongoing work and the data are continually kept up to date (that means that the data in the user's application will be as up to date as the data on the source server).

The systems that are able to work with data from remote sources are becoming more and more important. Users can combine their own data with the newest available data on the Internet, thereby they have an up-to-date information base for decision support processes, analyses and evaluation. Currently, external geospatial data sources management systems, which work on the web service basis, are mostly implemented into desktop applications.

Petr Horak • Wirelessinfo, Cholinska 1048/19, 784 01 Litovel, Czech Republic.   **Karel Charvat** • Czech Centre for Science and Society, Radlicka 28, Praha, Czech Republic.   **Martin Vlk** • Help forest, Slovanska 21, Sumperk, Czech Republic.

G.A. Papadopoulos et al. (eds.), *Information Systems Development*, DOI 10.1007/b137171_83,
© Springer Science+Business Media, LLC 2009

2. Objectives

The problem of how to solve the management of the external remote sources on the web is one of the main goals of the technological research being carried out by the Czech Living Lab association. The main idea of the work has been to find solutions based mainly on web server technology. The solution should cover the requirements for functionality which have not been implemented on the server side or implementation (and usage) of which is too expensive for smaller users.

This objective has been split up into three main groups:

- how to gather together data from different sources (files, databases, web services) that are stored on different external or internal servers
- how to make results easily available to users
- how to create a link between web tools used for geospatial data operation

One of the solutions to the above-mentioned problem is the Map Project Manager (MapMan) web tool and its integration into the Uniform Resources Management portal.

3. Methodology

New technology tools have been developed by the work of several international projects, where experts from the Czech Living Lab have participated – NATURNET-REDIME, AMI4FOR and C@R. The general objective of NATURNET-REDIME project (NNR) is the improvement of knowledge and the provision of education concerning all aspects of sustainable development. The project has been developed and has demonstrated prototype technology and educational programmes towards implementing the European Union's strategy for sustainable development (SSD). The components of the project will focus on building an interoperable Internet architecture, through which users can access and visualize much of the data on sustainable development that currently exist in a scattered, non-integrated form throughout the world. The AMI4FOR project has been focused on integration of a spatial data infrastructure as part of a forestry and agriculture knowledge system on the basis of standards and recommendations of OGC (Open Geospatial Consortium).

The next aim of the AMI4FOR has been the usage of new methods for data mining, modelling and analysis for improving forestry and agriculture management. Collaboration@Rural (C@R) is an integrated project, funded by the IST Priority of the European Commission's 6th Framework. The main goals of the C@R project regarding technology development are to provide a collaborative platform for rural communities, defined in cooperation with other collaborative working environment communities; demonstrate the use of the same platform integrating various tools for various rural user communities; promote the user-centric open collaborative architecture (OCA) in the industrial, new business opportunity and emerging rural sectors, demonstrating its affordability and usability.

A proposed system for the integration of different sources is being developed on the basis of open web services, mainly on web services agreeing to Open Geospatial Consortium standards. OGC (a non-profit, international, voluntary consensus standards organization) is leading the development of standards for geospatial and location-based services. This organization enables other organizations that adhere to the same standards, accessibility to data sources. The communication between web tools inside of the portal is provided by XML or sometimes directly through TCP/IP protocol.

An openly available Internet site guarantees that no installation on a user's desktop is needed. The main installation is placed on servers separately for each project and access to the application is supported by an independent authorization service.

The design of the spatial data management system has been created on the basis of requirements to make data easily available, which is not stored on the user's own servers, but which is available through web map service or web feature service.

These remote data can be combined together with data saved on an internal server (in database or files) into new map compositions. Publication of the composition is provided using standard web visualization clients (Java, DHTML, GoogleMap and Google Earth) or as a new web service. The combination of different types of data sources on the web and follow-up publication of new web services are the most important recent innovations in this field.

Strong emphasis is placed on metadata functionality. Each new map project contains its metadata label, which is registered in independent metadata systems. The Czech Living Lab uses the Micka metadata system, which meets ISO 191XX standards regarding INSPIRE directives.

Communication between several independent tools is provided either directly (one to one communication) or through integration into a Uniform Resource Management (URM) portal solution, which is described below.

4. Technology Description

A system for the management of geospatial data, MapMan has been created to cover requirements for the integration of data which are available through geospatial web services (WMS, WFS) and internal user's data stored in different data formats (databases, shp or dgn files). The data sources are used for the creation of new map compositions using web technology. These new map compositions can be published in different map visualization programmes or can be offered on the web as a new web map service. Some of the most important developments in information management facilities and publication systems are the utilization of a web environment and the follow-up publication of new web services.

Map Project Manager works together with UMN MapServer to create an environment for building spatially enabled Internet applications. The MapServer project is hosted by the TerraSIP project, a NASA-sponsored project between the UMN and consortium of parties with land management interests. Map Project Manager uses the common function ability of MapServer and creates a user interface for the easier creation of multi-source maps.

The core component of the spatial data management system is the Project Editor (Fig. 83.1), which brings together connectors of data sources with the publishing functionality of the system and provides an interface for users. Project Editor is linked to Layers and Symbols Storage (where it is saved in the Layer and Symbol libraries) and also to the external metadata catalogue. Data sources can be connected in

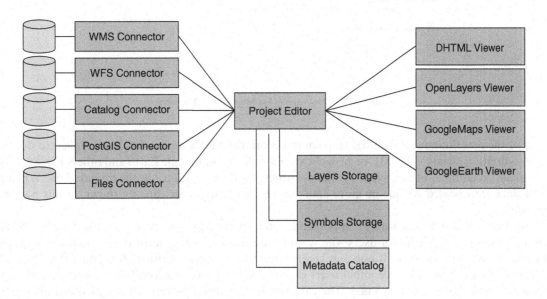

Figure 83.1. Map Project Manager components.

different ways depending on the type of available data. Internal data sources can be stored on databases or files. Database data are available through database connectors; currently a PostGIS database connector is implemented, but also other databases can be joined for relevant tasks. From data files, SHP files are supported.

Data files have to be stored in pre-defined server folders which are available for MapMan. External data (data stored on remote servers) can be connected through standard web services (web map services, web feature services). Catalogue connector links metadata catalogues, enables data searching possibilities and makes it available without the knowledge of fixed data source addresses. The final map composition is displayed using a map visualization client (e.g. DHTML client, GoogleMap, Google Earth or Open Layers). This new composition also contains metadata labels and can be published as a web map service.

5. Developments and Results

5.1. Generation of Map Compositions

Map Project Manager is able to work with different coordination systems. If a user wants to create a new map composition, he first of all needs to define a coordination system and specify an area of interest. Next, the user must define the data sources available through web map services (WMS), web features services (WFS), metadata catalogue or data stored on an internal data server Fig. 83.2. The data would be in raster or vector form. (In vector the colour and symbol of objects can be altered.) If the user does not know the addresses of an external data source, he can use the search function of the metadata catalogue.

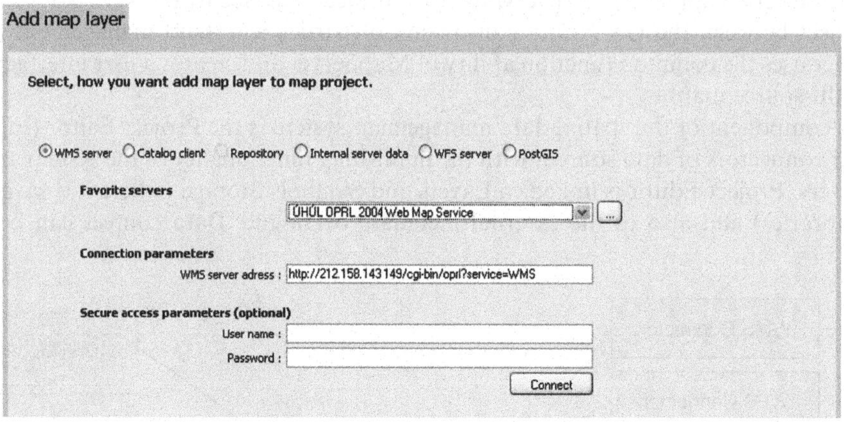

Figure 83.2. Data sources for Map Project Manager.

For the presentation of the final map composition, the MapMan can be closely linked to different map visualization clients–DHTML or Java clients, Google Maps, Google Earth and others Fig. 83.3. One of the main advantages of this system is the possibility to have actual up to the minute data. When the source data are updated on one or more data sources, all changes are directly shown in this new map composition.

As mentioned above, new map compositions can be published as a new web map service WMS. This functionality is really helpful for users who want to use this composition for background or referential data in their own applications. If one user creates new thematic compositions from different layers and publishes it as a new web service, other users do not need to look for several different data sets on the Internet or work together for each task. They are able to take this pre-prepared composition and use it in their own work.

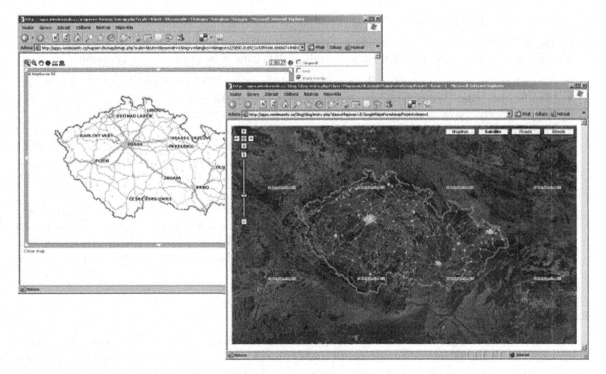

Figure 83.3. Map visualization clients.

5.2. Example of composition

The idea and technological possibilities of Map Project Manager should be clearer in the following example (Fig. 83.4):

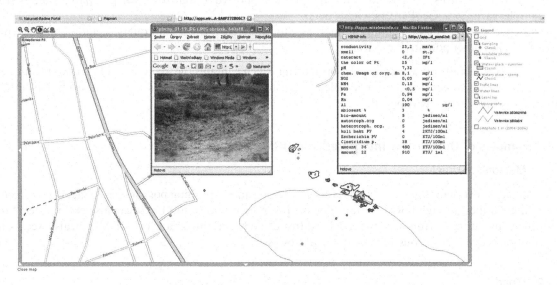

Figure 83.4. Example of a new map composition.

This map project shows a small locality near the city of Hradec Kralove, where students from the grammar school provided biotope research of protected plant and animal species.

The map composition consists of data stored on different servers:

1. Public WMS layers (these reference layers come from different external servers that created a background for a new map composition). These kinds of data cannot be updated by a common user.

   - "Ortophoto" is stored on the Czech environmental agency's CENIA (not displayed in the figure).
   - "Traffic lines" and "Water lines" are stored on the server of the HSRS company.
   - "Hypsography" layer is stored on the Forest Management Institute Vector data files.
   - "Watery place" layers show what the water level in lakes is during different seasons (spring, summer). The data files are stored on internal servers in a pre-defined directory. These kinds of data can be updated by users who have the authorization to edit the data on the internal MapMan server.

2. Vector data through WFS

   - "Sampling" and "Available photo" layers are stored in the server of the Help forest company. These layers are available through web feature service (WFS). These layers' contents point to descriptions of samplings and descriptions of the locality with reference photos. The data can be edited remotely, e.g. from PDA – in this case, the map composition which has been created in MapMan still shows the current data.

5.3. Integration with Other Web Tools

Map Project Manager can be used as a single tool, but it is integrated into URM portal solutions in many cases. Uniform Resource Management (URM) provides a simply understood, well–designed and user-friendly framework within which communities can easily share information and knowledge. In order to effectively share information and knowledge, there has to be a standardized system, which will enable a uniform description of information.

The basic components of URM can be divided into the followings areas:

- Metadata scheme, which defines a universal structure, which can be used for the giving of information.
- Thesaurus – represents a database or list of semantically orthogonal topical search keys.
- Geospatial thesaurus – The Geospatial thesaurus supported search tools for geospatial objects (for example, gazetteers, GeoParcers, Geocoders).
- Catalogue service – defines common interfaces to discover, browse, and query metadata about data, services and other potential resources.

URM is generally presented in web portal form, which contains the main search functions mentioned above and several supporting tools available for registered users. These tools support direct publishing of information through a URM portal.

5.4. Examples of Other Tools Integrated into URM Portals

5.4.1. Metadata Extractor

Metadata extractor is a tool that gives access, editing and publishing possibilities to metadata directly from different files through URM portals (documents, presentation, etc.) Users can also extract metadata (and then edit) directly from existing URL addresses and store metadata on URM portals. Access to information is available through direct URL addresses.

5.4.2. Moodle

A course management system (CMS), Moodle is an Open Source software package which helps educators to create effective online learning courses and web sites. The software is used all over the world by universities, schools, companies and independent teachers.

5.4.3. Video Lecture

The objective of video lecture modules is to support online lectures given by tutors using video streaming. The technology was developed by a NATURNET-REDIME project using VLC library and currently is published under Open Source license. It supports online training.

6. Business Benefits

Common problems of spatial data infrastructure have come to light also during the technology development. The following were found to be important problems that need to be solved during preparation of new map composition:

- Identification of the geospatial data available through web services
- Lack of data available through web services (only WMS available, much less WFS, WCS)
- Lack of data sets description
- Problems with data in different projections
- Non-performance of standards for geospatial web service
- Problems with object customizing (colour, symbol)
- Lack of harmonization between data sets at different geographical scales
- Duplication of data sets from different sources

Most of the problems mentioned above could be solved by uncompromising application of uniform standards and principles – in the case of geospatial data for example, INSPIRE directive.

7. Conclusions

Source exploitation through web services will become more important in the future. The possibility of utilizing existing web services to help establish new web services represents a chance for meaningful and efficient data source usage.

Map Project Manager is a web tool for the management of geospatial data where data can be stored in different external or internal servers in different data formats. Data from external servers are made available through standard web service (WMS and WFS) and can be easily found thanks to a connected catalogue system. New map compositions created in Map Project Manager can be displayed using several map visualization clients (Open Layers, GoogleMap, DHTML) using standard internet browsers or can be offered to other users as a new web map service (WMS).

The collaboration functionality between these geospatial web tools is provided by a special web portal system, which is called Uniform Resource Management (URM). URM enables open searching facilities for information, a uniform description of information and the integration of various web tools into one system.

The developed technologies have been tested on simple use cases which demonstrated the possibility of the creation of new services for the end user – in this case, the creation of new map compositions compiled from external and internal data and their publication through web service. Also communication with some other web collaborative tools (metadata and catalogue system, Moodle, Videolecture) and their integration into web portal solution have been successful. Future development and potential market implementation are planned after detailed tests from users and the processing of their comments regarding technological functionality and user-friendly interface. These activities are currently being carried out in the framework of current projects Collaboration@Rural and also EarthLookCZ – one of the pilot projects developed in the ERA-STAR regions framework focused on verification of spatial data infrastructure quality for GMES support in the Czech Republic.

References

1. New Education and Decision Support Model for Active Behaviour in Sustainable Development Based on Innovative Web Services and Qualitative Reasoning, D3.4.4, Release 4 of NaturNet-Redime portal – final release 30/10/2007,Praha.
2. AMI4FOR project, D3.1DESIGN OF FORESTRY KNOWLEDGE ANDPRECISION FARMING MANAGEMENT SYSTEM
3. Karel Charvat at all Uniform Resource Management, at Naturnet Redime Newsletter vol 6, December 2007, ISSN 1801–6480
4. Collaboration@Rural, ONTOLOGIES FOR RURAL ENVIRONMENTS, Madrid 2007
5. http://www.naturnet.org, http://portal.naturnet.org
6. http://www.ami4for.org
7. http://mapserver.gis.umn.edu/

84

Exploring the Role of Method Rationale in the Context of Teaching Information Systems Development Methods

Kai Wistrand, Fredrik Karlsson and Pär J. Ågerfalk

Abstract:

Research has shown that traditional education in systems development has its limitations. This chapter draws on recent research on a component-based view of systems development methods. The aim is to explore the impact of applying a method rationale perspective during method teaching with regards to student's abilities to reason about the suitability of a particular method to various development settings. A qualitative research approach was adopted, which used two different approaches to teaching a particular method to two groups of students. The students' ability to reason about the method in modelling seminars and follow-up interviews was analysed. The results indicate that explicating method rationale in teaching methods may have a positive impact on students' ability to reason about methods and method tailoring.

Keywords Method rationale · Method component · Method teaching · Systems development

1. Introduction

Successful enactment of an information systems development method (or method for short) requires good working knowledge of that particular method and how it relates to other methods [5]. Research has shown that traditional education and formal training in systems development have its limitations [10, 12] and that true systems development competence will be achieved only through long-term engagement with systems development in practice [5]. According to Stolterman and Russo [21], the appreciation of a method is related to how well the rationality of that method matches the rationality of the developer. They refer to this as a state of *rationality resonance*, where the public rationality, inherent in the method, is in harmony with the individual method user's private rationality. That is, when the underlying philosophy of the method is truly embraced by the method user so that method prescriptions make intuitive sense.

As suggested by Fitzgerald [5], rationality resonance is more likely to occur after having used one or several methods for a long time—just as any knowledge, methods in use are part of an ongoing institutionalization process whereby the knowledge is continuously integrated into our world and eventually becomes part of who we are as social beings (cf. [3]). The rationality inherent in methods and their use— a.k.a. *method rationale*—thus appears to be central to how method users learn to appreciate methods. One reason that extensive practical method experience is supposedly required in order for rationality resonance

---

Kai Wistrand and Fredrik Karlsson · MELAB, Swedish Business School, Örebro University, SE-701 82, Örebro, Sweden. Pär J. Ågerfalk · Department of Information Science, Uppsala University, Uppsala, Sweden; Lero – The Irish Software Engineering Research Centre, Limerick, Ireland.

G.A. Papadopoulos et al. (eds.), *Information Systems Development*, DOI 10.1007/b137171_84,
© Springer Science+Business Media, LLC 2009

to occur might be that method rationale is seldom explicitly dealt with in method textbooks and thus not in traditional education and formal training.

The question, then, is if a better foundation for understanding methods *can be* laid already during the initial learning phase (as opposed to the lifelong *in situ* learning by doing) by explicating method rationale and, by doing so, training future developers in thinking about methods at a more abstract "philosophical" level. Teaching this type of method knowledge would then prepare students (the future systems developers) for their use of methods and facilitate their lifelong learning process—giving them a deeper understanding of the practice of systems development and a solid foundation for becoming competent method users. While previous research on method rationale [2, 18] points in this direction, no empirical work on the role of method rationale in teaching and learning has been reported in the literature. Therefore, the aim of this chapter is to explore the impact of explicating method rationale in method teaching on students' ability to understand the suitability of a particular method to a specific development setting and thus helping them to reach rationality resonance.

This chapter proceeds as follows. The next section introduces our theoretical framework in terms of method rationale and a component-based view of methods. The following section describes the adopted research approach. Thereafter we describe the teaching and the students' interpretations of the method thought. This presentation is divided into three sections: lectures, modelling seminars and interviews. Each section opens with an elaboration on the research approach used in that specific part of the study. Finally, the chapter ends with a concluding discussion.

2. Theoretical Framework

This section introduces the theoretical framework used, which is based on the concept of method rationale and a component-based view of methods.

2.1. Method rationale

The concept of method rationale has received increasing attention in recent years, specifically in relation to information systems development [14, 21] and method engineering [8, 17, 18]. The concept as used in this chapter is anchored in Weber's [22] notion of practical rationality, which emphasizes that, when engaging in social interaction, people choose means in relation to ends, ends in relation to values and act in accordance with certain ethical principles [2]. Method rationale thus captures central aspects of what has been termed a method's "philosophy" [6], "way of thinking" [4] and "the method creator's design rationale" [15].

As mentioned above, Stolterman and Russo [21] distinguish between public and private rationality. Public rationality concerns the objective (or inter-subjective) understanding of methods and the results they produce. This aspect of method rationale thus relates to the method in concept [11]—to the way the method is described and communicated in, for example, method textbooks. Private rationality, on the other hand, relates to the method in action [6, 11] to the way methods are enacted in actual development practice.

An obvious function of method education is to influence method learners' private rationality—to affect the fundamental thinking of the method user by raising awareness as to why method users should apply specific parts of a method in particular settings. Method users have to find the method meaningful in their development practice—to find what [20] terms *rationality resonance*. He exemplifies rationality resonance with a detailed recipe for baking a cake and the advantages of expressing the rationality of each step. The baker then has the possibility to tailor the baking to the particular situation. The same thoughts can be applied to the use of methods and should affect how methods are taught. Much like a recipe, a large method is complex and contains a wide range of prescribed actions possible to perform, to perform modified or not to perform at all, depending on the situation. To continue the example, when baking a cake it is crucial to take into consideration that certain ingredients may have to be omitted and be replaced with something else should some of your guests have food allergies, for example.

2.2. Method Components

The method component concept is a construct used to demarcate parts of a method into manageable units to be selected and combined by method users. The selection and combination is based on the components' expressed method rationale: *A method component is a self-contained part of a systems development method expressing the transformation of one or several artefacts into a defined target artefact, and the rationale for such a transformation.*

The method component construct consists of an internal view and an external view. Below we will provide a brief introduction to these both views and how method rationale is operationalized in the construct. For a more thorough elaboration, see Karlsson and Wistrand [9].

2.2.1. The Internal View

The content of a method component is an aggregate of method elements: *A method element is a part of a systems development method that manifests a method component's target state or facilitates the transformation from one defined state to another.*

Method elements are specialized (sub-classed) to reflect the complex content of a method: prescribed action, concept, notation, artefact, and actor role. Prescribed actions and sequence restrictions together constitute a pattern for systems development in specific situations—for example, how to draw a business use case model. In carrying out prescribed actions, method users' attention is directed towards specific phenomena in the problem domain through the use of method-specific concepts. In the case of a business use case model, concepts include business actor and specializations. The actor concept directs the method users' attention to the actors in the business and to the business context. The specialization concept tells method users that it is possible to model inheritance between business use cases. The set of concepts helps method users to describe the problem domain and record the results in artefacts using a specific notation that gives the concepts a concrete representation—for example, a business actor is drawn as a stick figure. Thus, the artefact is a deliverable from the transformation process. Finally, actor roles describe the roles played by actors, such as analyst, developer, etc.

The rationale part of the method component is represented by a set of interrelated goals and values. Each method element is included in the method component for reasons. These are made explicit by associating method elements to goals. For example, the business actor concept in a business use case model has been included in the method in order to capture who is interacting with the business.

Furthermore, the goals are anchored in values of the method's creator. They reflect what the method's creator regarded as important during method development. Together these goals and values reflect the underlying philosophy of the method and the method creator's design rationale. Through this method rationale it is possible to address the goals that are essential in order to fulfil the overall goal of a specific project. The goals and values inside the method component exist in supporting hierarchies (goal achievements and value anchoring). Prescribed actions and artefacts are viewed as means to achieve these goals and adhere to values, just as in Weber's [22] notion of practical rationality. Thus, method rationale can help developers not to lose sight of the ultimate result and also help them to find alternative ways forward. For further elaboration on this view of method rationale and its relation to other views, see Ågerfalk and Fitzgerald [2].

2.2.2. The External View

The method component concept also facilitates the hiding of unnecessary details when working with the method. Hence, it provides encapsulation that draws on how the component concept is traditionally used in software engineering [19]. From the external view of a component its details are not of interest during all parts of a development project or during all parts of a teaching situation. For example, it has been shown that the method rationale and the artefacts are more important during method configuration (tailoring) than concepts and notation [7]. In other words, a user of a method component is primarily interested in the results offered by the component and the input required to achieve those results. This reduction of complexity is achieved through the method component interface: *A reference to a selection of method elements and rationale that is relevant for the task at hand.*

The external view of method components also addresses how method components are interconnected to structure a complete method. Each selected method component contributes to a chain of goal achievements adding to the overall goal of the project at hand. The use of method rationale in the external view also provides a possibility to emphasize the goal achievements (and possibly goal contradictions) between method components.

3. Research Approach

Given that little research has been conducted in the area of method rationale and method teaching, an exploratory qualitative approach was deemed appropriate, as suggested by Miles and Huberman [13]. Thus, we seek to develop a rich understanding that can be used in subsequent research as a basis for formulating more specific research questions and research models. The concept of the method component, including its focus on method rationale, was used as a descriptive framework that guided data collection and analysis [16]. The exploratory approach undertaken focused on actions taken and students' behaviour and verbal accounts during lectures, modelling seminars and follow-up interviews, e.g., error rates, number of teacher interventions and the degree of activity during seminars. To facilitate analysis, the interviews were taped and transcribed and the modelling seminars were video recorded. More details about the lectures, modelling seminars and interviews are provided below.

The systems development method used was VIBA/SIMM [1]. A thorough description of VIBA/SIMM is not necessary to communicate the rationale of our study. VIBA/SIMM was chosen for this research because (a) the systems development method was already part of a regular university course, (b) the course included practical assignments, (c) VIBA/SIMM is explicitly grounded in an articulated theoretical framework—actability theory [1] and (d) it is well suited to be structured as a collection of method components.

Only 28 students took part in the study which can be regarded as a limitation in our study. This study should be regarded an exploration of the potential of the method component concept and method rationale in the area of method teaching. For this task the number is sufficient. Furthermore, the theoretical framework can be applied to any systems development method and the proposed approach to teaching can be applied in any method course which enables repeatable studies in order to improve the possibilities for generalization.

4. Lectures

The students were randomly assigned to two groups, henceforth referred to as G1 and G2. The G1 lectures focused on reflection and the method's underlying rationale using the method component concept. The G2 lectures focused on the method's normative dimension and the students were only taught the process of the method through the suggested step-by-step workflow. These lectures ignored any reflection and reasons for why the method was constructed the way it was. Both groups were given equal number of lectures and time devoted to hands-on training. The students were aware that they were participating in a research project and that the lectures differed. Furthermore, they were asked to refrain from discussions across the group boundaries concerning the lectures and experiences during the course.

4.1. G1 Lectures

The G1 students received a total of three, 3-hour, lectures on VIBA/SIMM. The method was presented as a collection of connected method components fulfilling individual as well as process-related goals. For every method component, the inherent rationale was explicitly discussed and presented. References were made to actability theory to explain what goals the individual method components were supposed to fulfil. The students also received documents showing how the components were related to each other in terms of input and output. This map showed how the components together could contribute to overall project goals.

The G1 students were also given method component documents with the following structure: the first four rows addressed the method component's name, the overall goal of the method component, the recommended input artefacts and references to the components using the method component as input. The rest of the document was devoted to any notes the students deemed important for their own understanding of the method component in question. These notes could, for example, be what the notation looked like or general thoughts about the method component. The students were encouraged to use the note area in any way they liked as long as they used it in a way that would help them to grasp the method component more easily. A fitting analogy would be to view the method component documents as templates for method component knowledge. Working with the method component documents was easily grasped by the group and they asked many different kinds of questions, seeking feedback on what they had made notes of. Overall, there was a feeling of creativity as the students internalized the method by establishing the method component perspective through their own personalized notes.

4.2. G2 Lectures

The lectures received by the G2 students focused on VIBA/SIMM as a step-by-step process. An analogy is viewing the method as a cookbook, telling a novice chef how to prepare a certain meal. This normative view focused on telling the students how to perform the actions in order to drive a project further. They were not introduced to any of the goals behind the intermediate artefacts or how these artefacts help to realize goals elsewhere in the development process. No references were given to actability theory. The three G2 lectures were an hour shorter than the G1 lectures due to the lack of explanations of the underlying perspective. This is natural, because it takes less time telling someone what to do than explaining why.

The method was presented in a very straightforward manner and the students were very focused during these lectures. However, this form of presentation resulted in fewer questions from the students as compared to the G1 lectures. Our interpretation is that the G2 students regarded the method to be less problematic and easier to comprehend.

5. Modelling Seminars

Two weeks into the course, G1 and G2 had to demonstrate their VIBA/SIMM skills on a fictitious analysis and design task. The purpose was not to produce a complete solution, but to show that they could use selected parts of VIBA/SIMM and that they had understood how these work. Both groups were given a text describing a business as a starting point and the teacher acted as a business stakeholder answering any business-related questions. Each seminar lasted 4 hours, and during these seminars the students were told to move on when they had shown their skills in a part of the method that they had deemed necessary to use. In addition, G1 and G2 were divided into smaller groups consisting of four individuals each who took turns leading the modelling. The rest of the students acted as analysts and designers providing input and support to the modelling leaders.

Data were collected using video cameras and a logbook. Two video cameras were used during the seminars. One camera was directed towards the white board where the students carried out the actual modelling and created intermediate results. The second camera was facing the remaining part of the classroom capturing the discussions. In addition, the second teacher took notes during both seminars.

5.1. G1 Modelling Seminar

On several occasions during the G1 seminar, the modelling leaders expressed statements such as "Perhaps we should go back and review what we have done earlier?" and "This is something we can pick up again later." Throughout the seminar discussions arose about central concepts in the case and how the various method components could be used to deliver the required results. These discussions were not confined to the modelling leaders but involved the whole classroom. Notation issues seldom appeared to be problematic. The knowledge about how the results were to be documented according to VIBA/SIMM resulted in very few errors and other G1 members often corrected errors made. Consequently, the types of statements exemplified above and the discussions showed an iterative work pattern. Hence, the students displayed a fair understanding of how the various components in VIBA/SIMM could be used in relation to each other.

At times the teacher had to intervene when errors were missed or when a state of confusion arose. In total the teacher intervened 22 times during the 4-hour seminar. The general atmosphere was positive and the students appeared to have good confidence in their task. A lot of laughter and jokes during the seminar vindicated this. Very often the groups wanted to anchor decisions by asking questions like "Do we agree?" or "Does anyone have any objections?" These types of questions tell us that they felt a natural ambition to reflect upon what had been done and what needed to be done—to create an inter-subjective understanding of the task, the method and the situation.

The use of study materials (method textbook, personal notes and method component documents) during the seminar was very limited. They were mostly used in situations when the students wanted to verify that they actually took the actions recommended by VIBA/SIMM.

5.2. G2 Modelling Seminar

The G2 group perceived the modelling task to be more cumbersome. At times, the whole group was sitting silently, simply watching each other and hoping that someone could figure out what to do. At other times, the videotapes show large parts of the G2 group frantically flipping pages in the method textbook. They were looking for answers to what they should do or how to document a result they had agreed upon. The following student voices reflect a feeling of confusion: "OK... does anyone have a suggestion?" "Is this really how you draw?" "I need some help here!".

In situations where the work stopped completely it became necessary for the teacher to intervene— just as during the G1 seminar. The teacher intervened at 49 occasions during this 4-hour session. The general atmosphere of the seminar was uncomfortable. At frequent occasions the only active students were the drivers of the modelling activities. Moreover, often only one or two students in the driver group were in charge.

The iterative ideas that the method suggested were often forgotten or misunderstood. The students had difficulties in grasping how and where they should use their previously conceived results later on in the process. As a result some of the tasks were performed twice.

6. Interviews

Two days after the modelling seminars the students were interviewed. The time-stamped logbook made it possible to retrieve and analyse video segments before the interviews. These video clips were shown to the groups during the interviews while questions were asked about their individual actions, or non-actions, capturing their understanding of VIBA/SIMM and their internalization of the underlying method rationale. The questions concerned the underpinning principles of the method, how elicited results could be used later on in the process, which parts of the method fulfilled certain goals, aspects that the method user could not find any methodological support for in the method and the students' experiences during the seminar.

6.1. G1 Interviews

From the interview sessions with the G1 students we find long rather insightful answers concerning the method rationale of VIBA/SIMM. Furthermore, the answers they provided were rarely completely off the wall. Almost all of the students participated in answering the questions and very few sat quietly for any longer periods of time. Most of the answers came quickly and most of the time they seemed confident in their answers. When the questions that addressed issues not covered by VIBA/SIMM came up there was confusion, as they initially did not know how to answer. However, all the respondents from G1 eventually realized that the method rationale asked for could not be provided by VIBA/SIMM.

When the G1 students were shown video clips from the seminar and were asked about what they were thinking at the time, most of them gave insightful and elaborate answers. This is illustrated by the following answer given to a question concerning why the students chose to have a particular discussion about the current state of an activity diagram: "Well, you perceive things differently and all of us have certainly read and understood differently. Then it is important to figure out a solution together. This is a model that is supposed to reflect reality and the actions that are important in reality. All of our interpretations of the case had to be considered so that we could get a coherent picture." This type of answer tells us that there indeed was an ambition to arrive at consensus and that they deemed it important that everyone's voice should be heard.

6.2. G2 Interviews

The interviews with the G2 students gave a different picture. The students sat quietly to a larger extent than during the G1 sessions and they seemed more uncertain when providing answers. Very often they sought confirmation from each other, which indicates uncertainty. Similar to the modelling seminar, the G2 students appeared less comfortable than the G1 students. Several of the students were reluctant to give an answer and preferred to sit quietly, hoping for someone else to step forward. Their answers varied from well grounded to answers that revealed major flaws in their understanding of the method. However, the answers from the G2 students were in general inferior to the G1 counterparts. When asked questions concerning issues not addressed by VIBA/SIMM, only one respondent group came to the correct conclusion. The other groups were ignorant of the fact that the problem addressed could not be solved using the method and took their chances guessing instead.

The G2 students were also shown video clips to recall modelling events from the seminar. At times the students could not explain why they took certain actions during the seminar. During the interviews some respondent groups considered certain method components they used as "Waste of time". This indicates that they did not find that particular method component meaningful or useful in that particular situation—rationality resonance never appeared to emerge.

7. Concluding Discussion

The purpose of this chapter was to explore the impact of explicating method ration-ale in method teaching on students' ability to reason about the suitability of a particular method to a specific development setting. The concept of method rationale was operationalized through the method component construct during teaching.

To explore the potential of achieving rationality resonance we split the class in to two groups: G1 and G2. The G1 students received teaching using the method component concept, while the G2 students received a more traditional presentation of VIBA/SIMM, the method in question. When summing up the lectures, the modelling seminars and the interviews, we can conclude that the G2 students had a shallower understanding of VIBA/SIMM than the G1 students; G1 students made fewer errors, required fewer teacher interventions and showed a higher degree of activity overall.

Altogether we find support for the idea that explicating method rationale in teaching information methods may have a positive impact on students' ability to reason about methods. An emphasis on method rationale may better prepare the students for their professional life as they reach a deeper understanding of how methods convey knowledge and how they can combine that knowledge with their own rationality. This would make systems developers more capable in the complex business of systems development. A component perspective and the use of method component documents can be added to the curriculum to help the students to develop a deeper understanding of methods and appreciate their underlying rationality.

Although the empirical validation reported in this chapter is limited to VIBA/SIMM, there is nothing to suggest that the method component concept would not also work in other contexts. In fact, the possibility to map the construct onto any existing method was one of the design goals of method component from the outset. However, it should be acknowledged that the results are based on a small study. The conclusions may be biased by the quality of the teacher as well as the students. These limitations certainly call for more comprehensive future research.

References

1. Ågerfalk, P. J. (2003). *Information Systems Actability – Understanding Information Technology as a Tool for Business Action and Communication,* Linköping: Linköping University.
2. Ågerfalk, P. J. and Fitzgerald, B. (2006). Exploring the concept of method rationale: a conceptual tool for method tailoring. In Siau, K. (ed.) *Advanced Topics in Database Research.* pp. 63–78, Hershey: PA: Idea Group.
3. Berger, P. L. and Luckmann, T. (1967). *The social construction of reality: a treatise in the sociology of knowledge,* New York: Anchor Books.
4. Brinkkemper, S. (1996). Method engineering: engineering of information systems development methods and tools, *Information and Software Technology,* 38(4): 275–280.
5. Fitzgerald, B. (1997). The use of systems development methodologies in practice: a field study, *The Information Systems Journal,* 7(3): 201–212.
6. Fitzgerald, B., Russo, N. L. and Stolterman, E. (2002). *Information Systems Development – Methods in Action,* Berkshire, UK: McGraw-Hill.
7. Karlsson, F. (2005). *Method Configuration – Method and Computerized Tool Support,* Linköping: Linköping University.
8. Karlsson, F. and Ågerfalk, P. J. (2004). Method configuration: adapting to situational characteristics while creating reusable assets, *Information and Software Technology,* 46(9): 619–633.
9. Karlsson, F. and Wistrand, K. (2006). Combining method engineering with activity theory: theoretical grounding of the method component concept, *European Journal of Information Systems,* 15(1): 82–90.
10. Lee, J. and Truex, D. P. (2000). Exploring the impact of formal training in ISD methods on the cognitive structure of novice information systems developers, *Information Systems Journal,* 10(4): 347–367.
11. Lundell, B. and Lings, B. (2004). Method in action and method in tool: a stakeholder perspective, *Journal of Information Technology,* 19(3): 215–223.
12. Mathiassen, L. and Purao, S. (2002). Educating reflective systems developers, *Information Systems Journal,* 12(2): 81–102.
13. Miles, M. and Huberman, M. (1994). *Qualitative Data analysis: An Expanded Sourcebook,* Thousand Oaks, CA: Sage.
14. Nilsson, A. G. (1999). The business developer's toolbox: chains and alliances between established methods. In Nilsson, A. G., Tolis, C. and Nellborn, C. (eds.) *Perspectives on Business Modelling: Understanding and Changing Organisations.* pp. 217–241, Heidelberg: Springer Verlag.
15. Oinas-Kukkonen, H. (1996). Method rationale in method engineering and use. In, Brinkkemper, S., Lyytinen, K. and Welke, R. J. (eds.) *Proceedings of the IFIP TC8, WG8.1/8.2 Working Conference on Method Engineering on Method Engineering.* pp. 87–93, Atlanta, USA: Chapman & Hall.
16. Patton, M. Q. (1990). *Qualitative Evaluation and Research Methods,* Newbury Park, CA: Sage.
17. Rolland, C. and Prakash, N. (1996). A proposal for context-specific method engineering. In Brinkkemper, S., Lyytinen, K. and Welke, R. (eds.) *Proceedings of the IFIP TC8, WG8.1/8.2 Working Conference on Method Engineering on Method Engineering.* pp. 191–208, Atlanta, United States: Chapman & Hall.
18. Rossi, M., Ramesh, B., Lyytinen, K. and Tolvanen, J.-P. (2004). Managing Evolutionary Method Engineering by Method Rationale, *Journal of Association of Information Systems,* 5(9): 356–391.

19. Stevens, P. and Pooley, R. (2006). *Using UML – Software Engineering with Objects and Components,* Essex, England: Addison Wesley.

20. Stolterman, E. (1991). *Designarbetets dolda rationalitet: en studie av metodik och praktik inom systemutveckling,* Umeå, Sweden: Umeå University.

21. Stolterman, E. and Russo, N. L. (1997). The paradox of information systems methods – public and private rationality. *British Computer Society 5th Annual Conference on Methodologies*, Lancaster, England.

22. Weber, M. (1978). *Economy and Society,* Berkeley, CA: University of California Press.

85

Four Levels of Moral Conflict in ISD

Tero Vartiainen

Abstract

This study introduces a literature-based classification of moral conflicts in information systems development (ISD). The classification describes what moral conflicts an IS professional confronts in ISD as a whole and includes intentional, functional, managerial, and societal levels. The internal structure of moral conflicts is exemplified by means of a philosophical and a business ethics theory. The limitations of the study are considered and practical implications for the teaching of computer ethics are discussed.

Keywords ISD · Moral conflicts · Ethics teaching

1. Introduction

Information systems (IS) are used to capture data and transform them into information and knowledge in order to support processes in organizations and to control production and traffic systems, for instance. Computerized information systems consist of software and the hardware upon which the software functions. Because of the logical malleability and universal nature of the computer as a tool [24], it has been integrated into our societal systems to such an extent that if it were to be factored out societies would be fatally impaired [11, 39]. While decisions made by IS professionals may be restricted to particular projects or organizations, on the collective level of information systems development (ISD) they affect the whole of society. Indeed, professional ethics have been incorporated into curricula in computing disciplines [12], frameworks for ethics teaching in computing have been proposed [e.g., 23, 33], textbooks on ethics education have been published [e.g., 15, 28], and techniques for teaching computer ethics have been presented [e.g., 2, 4, 8, 13, 22, 31]. What is missing in these frameworks and techniques is that they do not take a holistic approach to the moral conflicts a computer professional confronts in her or his (working) life. For this purpose we should offer students at least the following kinds of framework: (1) descriptive theories of what moral conflicts they will confront when they enter working life in computing; (2) descriptive theories of human moral behavior for understanding the process of conflict resolution; and (3) normative theories that enhance the process of moral conflict resolution. All these frameworks would be large and complicated, and therefore, perhaps paradoxically, we need simplified solutions covering all the significant perspectives to support the practice of ethics teaching. This study presents a simplified classification of moral conflicts in ISD. The descriptive classification consists of four levels – intentional, functional, managerial, and societal – and is derived from the literature on computer science, information systems, and management. Descriptions of moral conflicts by Finnish IT professionals (coded Examples 1...4) exemplify the levels. Two theories, one from philosophy and one from business ethics, shed light on the internal structure, the source of moral requirements, on each level.

Tero Vartiainen • Pori Unit, Turku School of Economics, Turku, Finland

G.A. Papadopoulos et al. (eds.), *Information Systems Development*, DOI 10.1007/b137171_85,

The chapter is organized as follows. The concept of ISD is introduced in the next section, and the classification is described in Section 3. Section 4 introduces the philosophical theory and three normative business ethics theories. Section 5 discusses the results.

2. Information Systems Development

An information system (IS) is a work system supporting other work systems by processing data (capturing, storing, etc.). In a work system a business process is performed by human participants and/or machines to produce products or services for customers [1, p. 6]. Information systems development (ISD) is defined as follows (Fig. 85.1) [14, p. 15]: "[ISD is] a change process taken with respect to object systems in a set of environments by a development group to achieve or maintain some objectives."

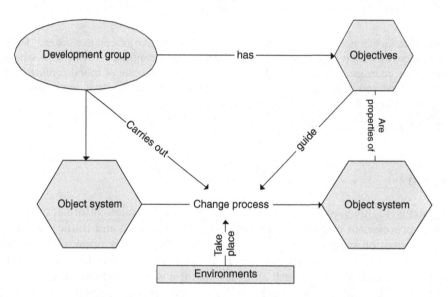

Figure 85.1. Information systems development [14, p. 16].

ISD is an intentional change process aimed at changing an object system toward desirable ends. An object system identifies a target of change. There may be more than one object system a development group can identify, and a change in one may cause a change in others. The change process is carried out by a formally organized group, and there are social processes affecting it (e.g., roles, authority questions). ISD is surrounded by a variety of environments, webs of conditions and factors, such as labor, the economy, and normative and technological environments. Objectives relate to general value orientations and represent desirable ends. They may be explicitly agreed upon through open negotiation, and they may be clear or conflictual, for example. The description of ISD forms a complicated web of social and technological phenomena, and there are dependencies between the components. In addition, ISD may be in-house or external: IS may be developed from scratch through programming a solution, an existing system may be purchased off the shelf, a system may be used but is managed outside the organization (hosted solution), or the off-the-shelf or hosted system may be tailored according to the needs of the organization [6, p. 343].

3. Four Levels of Moral Conflict in ISD

Table 85.1 summarizes the four levels of moral conflict confronted in information systems development (ISD). The levels are generic in the sense that they do not take into account whether the IS is built in-house or for an external client. The intentional level concerns the moral assessment of the purpose of the IS

Table 85.1. Four levels of moral conflict in ISD.

Level	Description
Intentional	Moral acceptableness of the IS and of the surrounding work system.
Functional	Morally significant decisions concerning the quality of the IS and of the utilizing system, and the consequences of those decisions.
Managerial	Morally significant decisions concerning production- and people-related issues.
Societal	Reactions to moral claims promulgated by actors from outside the organization.

and of the surrounding system using it. On the functional level the decisions involving quality factors are taken into account as they affect the stakeholders when the IS is in use. The managerial level concerns production and work place issues, together with questions on introducing good working methods into the process. The focus on the societal level is on laws, regulations, and ideologies put forward by outside actors (e.g., governments and associations).

3.1. Intentional Level

The moral acceptableness of the IS and of the surrounding work system [1] utilizing it may concern an ISD professional involved in its development. What the IS and the surrounding larger system (or the object system as Hirschheim et al. [14] put it) are intended to accomplish should therefore be morally evaluated. In addition, for a professional the business line of the employer or client may cause moral conflicts if the values conflict with his or her values. Compare the values upheld by the military industry to those of health care or forestry, for example. Additionally, any tool such as an IS or the utilizing system may be used for the particular purpose for which it was created, or for other purposes (compare using a hammer for cutting wood or for killing people). This kind of deliberation is diametrically opposed to the concept of affective neutrality put forward by Parson [referenced in 17]: a professional should not allow his or her assessments of the client's purposes to affect the services she or he as a professional offer. This concept is untenable in that if it were to be accepted professionals would become guns-for-hire for anyone. In the following extract a Finnish computer professional recognizes the needs of the health-care center and she or he also indirectly recognizes the conflict between the interests of the software firm and its social responsibility:

Example 1. "A health-care center and a big delivery company offer a software-production contract the same time. We know that the health-care center has a desperate need for a new solution, and we also know that the delivery company wants to maximize its profits. We chose the delivery company because it's a bigger client and therefore we got a bigger deal."

3.2. Functional Level

The functional level describes morally relevant decisions involving the quality factors of IS (e.g., security vs. usability of the software) and which are made during the change process [14]. The decisions are moral in nature as they affect the stakeholders when the object system is in function (cf. penubra in [7]). The stakeholders are affected to a greater extent if the work systems or even the organizational structures are redesigned to achieve the necessary changes [25]. Next, as an exemplification of functional-level moral conflicts a theory of software quality factors is presented, together with a claim that decisions related to them are moral ones.

Quality factors. Software quality factors are divided into internal and external qualities, and the internal qualities affect the external qualities: accuracy and consistency affect reliability, for example [10] (Fig. 85.2). As the external qualities may have harmful effects on the parties in the surrounding system the decisions concerning internal qualities have moral significance. The two aspects of Fenton's [10] division are considered next.

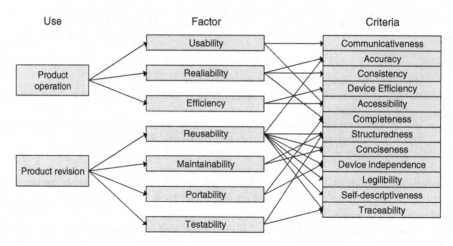

Figure 85. 2. Factors and criteria [10].

The aspect of product operation [10, p. 17] concerns the operation of the software and its effects on stakeholders. Fenton's approach to product operation – the recognition of high-level quality factors such as usability, reliability, and efficiency – could be interpreted as values or the desired end states [30] of software. Every information system is ideally intended to be usable, reliable, and so on, but in practice ISD projects involve making decisions concerning these values. Decisions related to lower-level criteria made in professional practice affect high-level quality factors. For example, completeness, accuracy, and consistency affect reliability. These decisions have moral significance as they may affect stakeholders negatively. For example, poorly implemented IS in business may cause financial loss, and poorly implemented user interfaces may be detrimental to the quality of working life.

The aspect of product revision [10, p. 17] concerns maintaining the software or transferring it to different environments. Whereas factors of product operation concern users, factors of product revision affect the work of ISD professionals, and also indirectly the users. Here, lower-level decisions, for example, the structuredness of the code, affect the reusability and maintainability of the software (Fig. 85.2).

In the next extract the computer professional considers software and hardware compatibility a major ethical problem in the field. This could be interpreted to imply that compatibility of software is considered a quality characteristic, which may be prioritized for financial reasons (aim to benefit with closed systems):

Example 2. "One very significant ethical problem is perhaps the fact that genuine compatibility in software and hardware is not sought in the field. In my own circles I try to produce as consistent solutions as possible – if it doesn't contribute anything, well, perhaps controllability and understandability at least are developed."

3.3. Managerial Level

This level covers all morally significant decisions made when managing a work community such as a software house or a development group in ISD. Indeed, the development of an ethical corporate culture [34, p. 592] is a major challenge in business. It is noteworthy that the moral conflicts at this level do not only concern managers, they concern all members of any work community. The following definition of management shows its complexity [27, p. 6]: "Management is the process of achieving organizational objectives, within a changing environment, by balancing efficiency, effectiveness and equity, obtaining the most from limited resources, and working with and through other people."

The above definition can be simplified to incorporate the two concerns presented by Blake and Mouton in their classical managerial grid: concern for production (management) and concern for people (leadership). Moral conflicts perceived by students on a project course held in collaboration with industry were studied [37]. The students were expected to implement real-life IT projects for industry clients. The moral conflicts they reported were classified as task, human, and context related. The distinction between task and human conflicts resembles the division into concern for production and concern for people. Although these concerns are highly interwoven in practice, the moral problems are next introduced in the order of production and people.

Production. ISD is typically managed in projects. IS managers are faced with huge pressures to deliver quality software on time and within budget [16], and due to these difficulties project success and failure have been studied in the context of IS and project management [e.g., 20, 32]. Westerveld [40] reviewed the literature on project management and constructed a "Project Excellence Model." The results area of the model cover the project outcomes (budget, schedule, quality) and the level of appreciation of the client (e.g., customer benefit), the project personnel (e.g., the team is happy), the users (e.g., their needs are satisfied), the contracting partners (e.g., the project is profitable for contractors), and the stakeholders (e.g., their needs are satisfied). This model shows project management to be a complex phenomenon involving interplay among different actors (e.g., development team members, project managers, the client organization). It is clear from Westerveld's model and the following extract that there are major moral challenges involved in IT projects. In the extract the IT professional confronts a loyalty-related moral conflict between the benefit of the provider and that of the client organization (his or her employer):

Example 3. "It is hard to relate the benefit of the client organization and that of one's own organization in a large project in which there are major pressures on the timetables and the budget. -> To what extent does loyalty to the paying client take precedence over loyalty to the firm, which pays (a good) salary?"

Decisions about the introduction of work methods and approaches may be interpreted as moral ones. Using a participatory approach in ISD is recognized as a moral choice [25]. Similarly, the adoption of good practices such as walkthroughs and inspections in the ISD project process is a moral decision that has a significant effect on the quality of the IS.

People. Managing and leading a working community such as a software house or an ISD project team is a moral challenge (see managerial dilemmas in [21]; peopleware in [9]). How managers and foremen apply principles of distributive justice, how rewards and resources are distributed, and how procedural justice and fairness are used in the distribution [19] are moral concerns in all work communities. Workplace health and safety issues (see the analysis of bullying in [18]) and balancing the demands of work life with other significant life elements (e.g., family, hobbies) could be interpreted as moral conflicts by anyone involved in working life. The following example suggests that the human issues are a moral challenge in the whole IT field in Finland:

Example 4. "Usually we work in terms of technology and the constant (even large) changes do not give people in IT or in the user sector time to 'manage' their own work and 'lead a human life'. You are not able to have a normal gestation process any more. The constant change process is transformed to a constant panic – knock-out competition – no one dares to opt out from 'the technological development'."

3.4. Societal Level

Reacting to moral claims promulgated by actors outside of the organization (or from ISD environments in the terms of [14]) in which ISD is developed is of concern at this level. The environment of any organization is complex. The organizational environment consists of the operating environment, a wider environment, and the international environment [27, p. 65]. The operating environment relates to parties with which organizations have clear and direct interactions: regulators, suppliers, investors, competitors, customers, and distributors. The two-way interactions with these parties include the exchange of products, money, information and influence. The wider environment relates to factors that indirectly affect organizations, such as the economic, political and legal, technological, and social environments. The international environment is a dimension of both the operating and the wider environments: competitors may exist in other countries and political pressure may be international. Complying with IS-related regulations, laws (e.g., privacy laws), standards, ethical codes [3], and the ideologies [e.g., 36] promoted or enforced by societal actors such as governments and associations are examples of moral claims from outside the organization. IS professionals working for transnational enterprises [22] should understand the global markets and international law and the characteristics of the different cultures, for example.

4. Theories Describing the Internal Structure of Moral Conflicts

To better understand the moral conflicts in ISD in business context we need theories describing the internal structure of moral conflicts in general and the sources of moral requirements that collide in conflict situations. Two exemplary theories are presented next.

4.1. A Philosophical Theory

Thomas Nagel [26] perceived moral conflicts as conflicts between types of values and conflicts within those values. Values come from many different viewpoints on life, and we can view the world from many perspectives – individual, relational, ideal, for example. Each of these viewpoints and perspectives makes different kinds of claims on us. Nagel suggests that the conflicts between different types of values are more difficult to resolve than those within the same type. He identified five fundamental types of value that give rise to basic conflicts:

- There are obligations to other people or institutions, depending on the subject's relation to others, e.g., obligations to patients, to one's family, the university.
- There are general rights to do certain things or not to be treated in certain ways, e.g., freedom from assault and coercion.
- One's actions have effects on others' welfare: one could benefit or harm other people. Utility is consideration about these effects.
- Perfectionist ends or values refer to the intrinsic value of certain achievements or creations apart from their value to individuals. For example, there is intrinsic value in a scientific discovery and an artistic creation.
- The last category is that of commitment to one's own projects or undertakings: It is partly a matter of justifying earlier investment of time and energy. These projects make autonomous claims on us.

Nagel divides the above-mentioned values into two types: agent centered and outcome centered. Obligations, general rights, and commitment to one's own projects or undertakings are of the former type. Utility and perfectionist ends or values are outcome centered. In Nagel's view, the major distinction between these sources of conflict (agent centered vs. outcome centered) is too profound to allow unification. These types of values are formally and fundamentally so different from each other that resolution of conflicts among them is not possible. These and within-value conflicts may be genuine moral dilemmas.

4.2. Three Normative Theories of Business Ethics

Three major normative theories of business ethics, the stockholder theory, the stakeholder theory, and the social contract theory [5, 35], are considered next. The first of these holds that managers have an obligation to maximize profits because in that way stockholders get the greatest value from their investments. The basic idea is that the firms that provide the goods and services that are the most valuable to society are rewarded, and in the long run the stockholders of these firms get the profits. According to the stakeholder theory, a corporation has to take into account all those who are affected by its actions: employees, consumers, suppliers, the surrounding community, and society at large. Social responsibility toward these parties is considered as much a concern as its responsibilities toward its investors or owners. There is a fundamental distinction between the normative stakeholder theory and the stockholder theory. This distinction is summarized as follows [35, p. 14]: "Stakeholder theory demands that interests of stakeholders other than stockholders be considered along with those of the stockholders even if it reduces firm profitability." The third major theory, the social contract theory, obliges managers to consider not only the interests of consumers and workers, but also the canons of justice. The implication is that there exists a hypothetical contract between society and certain individuals who form an enterprise. This contract would include expectations and obligations between these parties: the individuals forming the enterprise would ask society for legal recognition as a single agent (e.g., authorized to sign contracts) and for the right to use resources to hire employees. Society, in turn, requires firms to promote social welfare, which means looking after consumers' and workers' interests by maximizing advantages and minimizing disadvantages. Managers of firms should also take into account the societal consequences of their actions: they should avoid pollution and should not misuse political power, for example.

4.3. An Exemplary Application of the Theories

The professional in Example 2 most probably perceives the conduct of software and hardware providers as harmful to the larger whole (all actors in the IT field) and aims to fight against the trend in her or his personal actions. This deliberation and action are in accordance with stakeholder theory. As Nagel would see it, the professional may confront a conflicting situation if her or his employer, a software house for example, demanded that its employees develop closed systems. This being the case, the professional would confront a conflict between an agent-centered claim, an obligation toward the employer, and an outcome-centered claim, in other words what the professional perceives is best for the larger whole.

5. Discussion

This study described a classification of moral conflicts confronted in ISD, which incorporates intentional, functional, managerial, and societal levels. The goal of ethics education in our field should not be restricted to technology-laden problem solving in computing (e.g., privacy and IPR), and we should direct students' deliberation to the complex whole of being an IS professional and a human being in a society. This classification is a step toward this goal. Reference theories – like the two exemplary theories described in this study – offer analytical tools that allow a better understanding of the emergence of moral conflicts and their internal structure. Carefully selected and in combination with the classification, they help students to acquire a fine-grained understanding of the moral conflicts that may arise during their future working lives. The classification resembles, to some extent, the categorization put forward in [38]. They interviewed experienced project managers of morally successful IT projects and found three categories in their responses: initiation (choosing the client, making a project proposal), execution (meeting the objectives, ensuring the well-being of the team), and context (laws and regulations, effects on the stakeholders). The similarities in the two systems are as follows: initiation resembles the intentional level, execution the managerial level, and the context the societal level. The functional level was not determined in the above-mentioned study. One reason for this difference lies in the fact that it concentrated on project management, whereas the present study takes into account the product and its qualities. In other respects, it could be said that the results of the two studies support each other.

Evaluation. The results of this study have some limitations. The classification does not comprehensively describe the moral problem in computer ethics and is restricted to ISD. It is also tentative in that it has not been tested empirically. It is intended to sensitize the individuals concerned to moral conflicts and does not account for resolving them. More reference theories would be needed to support this process: a moral psychology theory describing human moral behavior (starting from sensitizing to moral conflicts to implementing what one perceives is the right solution) [29] and classical theories of ethics (e.g., utilitarianism, Kant, virtue ethics) are potential candidates. The stories of Finnish computer professionals were collected along with a questionnaire ($n = 500$) at the end of the 1990 s. Fifteen subjects responded to the additional question and they described moral conflicts both in their professional practice and in the end use of information systems. Although the response rate was minimal, the single descriptions have exemplary value. The Finnish language version of the framework has been presented to students during three computer ethics courses and for an unofficial review to the ethics workgroup of The Finnish Information Processing Association. It made sense to both of these parties. The members of the workgroup gave some critical comments and suggested adding to the contents of the levels.

References

1. Alter, S. 2002. *Information Systems, Foundation of E-Business*. Fourth edition. Upper Saddle River: Prentice Hall.
2. Applin, A.G. 2006. A learner-centered approach to teaching ethics in computing. *SIGCSE'06*, March 1–5, Houston, Texas, USA, pp. 530–534.
3. Berleur, J., Brunnstein, K. 1996. *Ethics of Computing, Codes, Spaces for Discussion and Law*. London: Chapman & Hall.
4. Botting, R.J. 2005. Teaching and learning ethics in computer science: walking the walk. *SIGCSE'05*, February 23–27, St. Louis, Missouri, USA, pp. 342–346.
5. Branco, M.C., Rodrigues, L.L. 2007. Positioning stakeholder theory within the debate on corporate social responsibility. *EJBO Electronic Journal of Business Ethics and Organization Studies*, Vol. 12, No. 1, pp. 5–15.
6. Chaffey, D., Wood, S. 2005. *Business Information Management. Improving Performance Using Information Systems*. Harlow, England: Prentice Hall.
7. Collins, W.R., Miller, K.W., Spielman, B.J., Wherry, P. 1994. How good is good enough? *Communications of ACM*, Vol. 37, No. 1, January, pp. 81–91.
8. Dark, M.J., Winstead, J. 2005. Using educational theory and moral psychology to inform the teaching of ethics in computing. *Information Security Curriculum Development (InfoSecCD) Conference '05*, September 23–24, Kennesaw, GA, USA, pp. 27–31.
9. DeMarco, T., Lister, T. 1987. *Peopleware: Productive Projects and Teams*. New York: Dorset House Publishing Co.
10. Fenton, N.E. 1991, *Software Metrics a Rigorous Approach*. London: Chapman & Hall.
11. Gibbs, W. 1994. Software's chronic crisis. *Scientific American*, Vol. 271, No. 9, pp. 72–81.
12. Gorgone, J.T., Davis, G.B., Valacich, J.S., Topi, H., Feinstein, D.L. Longenecker, H.E. Jr. 2002. IS 2002: model curriculum and guidelines for undergraduate degree programs in information systems. *Communications of the Association for Information Systems*, Vol. 11, No. 1, pp. 1–53.
13. Grodzinsky, F., Gehringer, E., King, L.S., Tavani, H. 2004. Panel: responding to the challenges of teaching computer ethics. *SIGCSE'04*, March 3–7, Norfold, Virginia, USA, pp. 280–281.
14. Hirschheim, R., Klein, H.K., Lyytinen, K. 1995. *Information Systems Development and Data Modelling, Conceptual and Philosophical Foundations*. Cambridge: Cambridge University Press.
15. Johnson, D.G. 2001. *Computer Ethics*. Upper Saddle River, NJ: Prentice Hall.
16. Jurison, J. 1999. Software Project Management: the Manager's View. *Communications of Association for Information Systems*, Vol 2, Article 17.
17. Ladd, J. 1991. Collective and individual moral responsibility in engineering: some questions. In Johnson, D. (ed.) *Ethical Issues in Engineering*. Upper Saddle River, NJ: Prentice Hall.
18. Lee, D. 2000. An analysis of workplace bullying in the UK. *Personnel Review*, Vol. 29, No. 5, pp. 593–612.
19. Leventhal, G. 1980. What should be done with equity theory? New approaches to the study of fairness is social relationships. In Gergen, M., Greenberg, M., & Wills, R. (eds.) *Social Exchange: Advances in Theory and Research*. New York; Plenium Press.
20. Lyytinen, K., Hirschheim, R. 1987. Information systems failures – a survey and classification of the empirical literature. *Oxford Surveys in Information Technology*, Vol. 4, pp. 257–309.
21. Manning, F.V. 1981. *Managerial Dilemmas and Executive Growth*. Reston, VA: Reston Publishing.
22. Marchant, A. 2004. Teaching ethics in the context of IT and globalization. *SIGITE'04*, October 28–30, Salt Lake City, Utah, USA, pp. 227–230.
23. Martin, C.D., Huff, C., Gotterbarn, D., Miller, K. 1996. Implementing a tenth strand in the CS curriculum. *Communications of the ACM*, December, Vol. 39, No. 12, pp. 75–84.
24. Moor, J.H. 19 What is computer ethics? *Metaphilosophy*, Vol. 16, No. 4, pp. 266–275.
25. Mumford, E. 2003. *Redesigning Human Systems*. Hershey, PA: IRM Press.
26. Nagel, T. 1987. The fragmentation of value. In Gowans, C.W. (ed.) *Moral Dilemmas*. New York: Oxford University Press, pp. 174–187.
27. Naylor, J. 1999 *Management*. Harlow, England: Prentice Hall.
28. Quinn, M.J. 2006. *Ethics for the Information Age*. Boston, MA: Addison Wesley.
29. Rest, J. 1984. The major components of morality. In Kurtines, W.M., Gewirtz, J.L. (Eds.) *Morality, Moral Behavior, and Moral Development*. New York: A Wiley-Interscience Publication, pp. 24–38.
30. Rokeach, M. 1973. *The Nature of Human Values*. New York: The Free Press.
31. Schwarz, S.J. 2005. Teaching ethics and computer forensics: the Markkula center for applied ethics approach. *Information Security Curriculum Development (InfoSecCD) Conference '05*, September 23–24, Kennesaw, GA, USA, pp. 66–71.
32. Shenhar, A.J., Levy, O. 1997. Mapping the dimensions of project success. *Project Management Journal*, Vol. 28, No. 2, pp. 5–13.
33. Siponen, M.T., Vartiainen, T. 2002. Teaching end-user ethics: issues and a solution based on universalizability. *Communications of the Association for Information Systems*, Vol. 8, pp. 422–443.

34. Small, M.W. 2006. Management development: developing ethical corporate culture in three organisations. *Journal of Management Development*, Vol. 25, No. 6, pp. 588–600.

35. Smith, H.J. 2002. Ethics and information systems: resolving the quandaries. *The DATA BASE for Advances in Information Systems* Vol. 33, No. 3, pp. 8–22.

36. Stallman, R. 1995. Why software should be free. In Johnson, D.G., Nissenbaum, H. (eds.) *Computers, Ethics & Social Values*. Englewood Cliffs, NJ: Prentice Hall.

37. Vartiainen, T. 2006. Moral conflicts perceived by students of a project course. In Berglund, A., Wiggberg, M. (eds.) *Proceedings of 6th Baltic Sea Conference on Computing Education Research, Koli Calling 2006*. Uppsala University, Uppsala, Sweden, ISSN 1404-3203.

38. Vartiainen, T., Pirhonen, M. 2007. Morally successful IT project. Proceedings of 16th International Conference on Information Systems Development (ISD2007) Galway, Ireland, August 29–31, 2007. In Barry, C., Lang, M., Wojtkowski, W., Wojtkowski, G., Wrycza, S., Zupancic, J. (eds.) *The Inter-Networked World: ISD Theory, Practice, and Education*. New York: Springer-Verlag.

39. Weizenbaum, J. 1976. *Computer Power and Human Reason: From Judgment to Calculation*. San Francisco: W. H. Freeman.

40. Westerveld, E. 2003. The Project Excellence Model: linking success criteria and critical success factors. *International Journal of Project Management*, Vol. 21, pp. 411–418.

86

Specification of Learning Content Using Feature Diagrams

Robertas Damaševičius

Abstract

The main idea of a learning object (LO) is to break educational content down into small chunks that can be reused in various learning environments. When reused, such small chunks of educational content are combined in various ways leading to a great variability of the learning content. We propose using feature diagrams (FDs) for the specification of learning content at different layers of abstraction starting from the organization of teaching material in a lecture down to the specification and demonstration of particular software/hardware components. FDs can be used by (1) designers, teachers, and learners for graphical representation of domain knowledge in LOs; (2) programmers to specify and express variability–commonality relationships of LOs at a higher abstraction level to allow the development and implementation of generative LOs; and (3) researchers as a vehicle for analysis and better understanding of the e-Learning domain itself.

Keywords Learning object · Feature diagram · Feature modeling · e-Learning

1. Introduction

Currently, an instructional technology, called "learning objects" (LOs) [24], is leading as a technology of choice for e-Learning support due to its potential generativity, adaptability, and scalability [37]. LOs are computer-based teaching components that are influenced by the object-oriented (OO) paradigm in computer science [16]. LOs are generally understood to be digital entities deliverable over the Internet where they can be accessed and used simultaneously by many learners. Furthermore, LOs can be reused multiple times in different contexts, used independently, or grouped into larger collections of content, including traditional course structures.

However, the development of LOs remains a vague issue, because still there is no clearly defined and widely adopted LO specification and development methodology as, e.g., in software engineering, where classes and objects are modeled using UML [12], a standardized graphical specification and modeling language. There have been several efforts to adopt UML in e-Learning domain, e.g., for modeling the interaction between LOs and a specific learning management system (LMS) [14] or to describe the content and process within "units of learning" in order to support reuse and interoperability [21]. However, these efforts have not been fully successful, because of inherent UML's orientation toward a very specific technological paradigm with specialized concepts such as "concurrency" or "polymorphism" [13].

The main idea of LO is to break educational content down into small chunks that can be reused in various learning environments [38]. When reused, such small chunks of educational content are combined in various ways leading to a great variability of the learning content. Such variability cannot be modeled

Robertas Damaševičius • Software Engineering Department, Kaunas University of Technology, Kaunas, Lithuania.

G.A. Papadopoulos et al. (eds.), *Information Systems Development*, DOI 10.1007/b137171_86,

using UML, which has no adequate means for expressing different variants of configurations of a system. Given the likelihood of the broad deployment of LO-based technology and the dangers of employing it in an instructionally unprincipled manner, there is a clear need for a solid methodological and technological background of a graphical modeling notation and associated methodology for modeling variability of learning content in general and LOs in particular.

The outline of the chapter is as follows. We discuss motivation for graphical knowledge modeling in the educational domain and review known graphical modeling languages in Section 2. Feature modeling and feature diagrams (FDs) are described in Section 3. The motivation for using FDs in the LO domain is given in Section 4. The capabilities and limitations of using FDs in the LO domain are discussed in Section 5. A case study is presented in Section 6. Finally, conclusions are presented in Section 7.

2. Use of Graphical Modeling Languages in Educational Domain

Graphical knowledge modeling is a way of representing knowledge structures in a domain by linking domain concepts, procedures, and entities in a way that describes the domain content and its processes. Paquette et. al [30] summarize the benefits of graphical knowledge representation: it illustrates relationships among components of a complex phenomenon, makes evident the complexity of actor interactions, facilitates the communication of the reality studied, ensures the completeness of the studied phenomena, and helps searching for a general idea because it minimizes the use of text.

In the educational technology, graphical modeling languages can be used for representing domain knowledge, learning outcomes, LO aggregation, learning paths (sequences) or learning activities, learning scenarios, architecture of LMS, and semantics of learning content.

Known graphical notations for course design knowledge modeling include *goal trees* [23] to represent learning goals and sub-goals on many levels such as course or lecture; *topic maps* [34] to represent information using topics (representing any concept, from people, countries, and organizations to software modules, individual files, and events), associations (which represent the relationships between them), and occurrences (which represent relationships between topics and information resources relevant to them); UML for modeling the interaction between LOs and a specific LMS [14], or to describe the content and process within "units of learning" in order to support reuse and interoperability [21]; Petri Nets [31] to describe the structure and mutual dependence of a set of learning objects and to model course plans and learning paths; business process modeling notation [19] for defining graphical representations of educational processes (learning flows) modeled with the IMS learning design specification; MOT graphical language [30] for modeling knowledge objects; and ontological modeling notation [3] for developing an ontology for a course subject.

In such context, we propose using feature diagrams (FDs) for modeling learning content. Originally, FDs were introduced in the FODA methodology in 1990 [17]. Since then, they have undergone several extensions [11, 18] intended to improve their expressiveness for specific domains of application. Feature diagrams first were applied in the context of industrial manufacturing product lines (PLs), e.g., for modeling car assembly lines. Later, the idea was extended to software PLs. A software PL is a set of software systems that share a common, managed set of features satisfying the specific needs and that are developed from a common set of core assets in a prescribed way [6]. The concept, if applied systematically, allows for dramatic increase of software design quality and productivity, provides a capability for mass customization, and leads to the "industrial" software design [25].

Based on the success of feature modeling and the PL approach in industrial manufacturing and software engineering domains and intention to introduce product families to the System-on-Chip (SoC) design [1], we propose using FDs in the e-Learning domain for specification, representation, and structuring of learning content. We hope that feature modeling of learning content would ease maintenance of learning content, reduce its redundancy and duplication, allow for easy customization when applying for different teaching aims, student groups, and e-Learning environments, and provide a global framework for coordinating the re-engineering and reuse of LOs. Furthermore, FDs are also important for constructing domain ontologies by providing views on ontologies [8, 36] in order to acquire a common understanding of the learning domain. Ontology is a conceptual specification that describes knowledge about a domain [15]. The construction of such ontologies allows providing a shared and common understanding of a specific domain and facilitates knowledge sharing and reuse.

Related works in the e-Learning domain concern the application of a software PL approach for the creation of new courseware [28], analysis of cross-cutting concerns of LOs to improve conceptual design, modularity and maintenance of e-Learning material contained in LOs [27], and feature modeling for adaptation of learning units [10]. The novelty of this chapter is the systematic application of FDs for the specification of learning content at different layers of abstraction starting from the organization of teaching material in a lecture down to the specification and demonstration of particular software/hardware components in the context of the microelectronics course.

3. Features, Feature Modeling, and Feature Diagram

There are several definitions of a feature. Informally, features are key distinctive characteristics of a system. Feature-oriented domain analysis (FODA) defines a feature as a prominent and distinctive user-visible characteristic of a system [17]. Ontology definition metamodel (ODM) defines a feature as a distinguishable characteristic of a concept (e.g., artifact, area of knowledge) that is relevant to some stakeholders (e.g., analysts, designers, and developers) [26]. When comparing to other conceptual abstractions (such as function, object, or aspect), features are externally visible characteristics of a system, whereas functions, objects, and aspects have been mainly used to specify the internal details of a system. Therefore, feature modeling focuses on identifying and specifying the externally visible characteristics of products in terms of commonality and variability [22], rather than describing all details of a system.

The result of feature modeling is a feature model. Features are identified and classified in terms of capabilities, domain technologies, implementation techniques, and operating environments. Capabilities are user-visible characteristics that can be identified as distinct services, operations, and non-functional characteristics. Domain technologies represent the way of implementing services or operations. Implementation techniques are generic functions or techniques that are used to implement services, operations, and domain functions. Operating environments represent environments in which applications are used. Features are primarily used in order to discriminate between product instances (configuration choices). Common features among different products are modeled as mandatory features, while different features among them may be optional or alternative. Optional features represent selectable features for products of a given domain and alternative features indicate that no more than one feature can be selected for a product.

A FD is a graphical AND/OR hierarchy of product features that captures structural or conceptual relationships among features. A FD consists of a set of nodes, a set of directed edges and, a set of edge decorations. The nodes and edges form a tree. The edge decorations are drawn as arcs connecting subsets or all of the edges originating from the same node. Effectively edge decorations define a partitioning of the sub-nodes of a node (divide sub-nodes into a number of disjoint subsets). The root of a FD represents a domain concept (learning topic). Features can be mandatory (and-features), optional, and alternative (case-features or or-features) (see Table 86.1). And-features are denoted with a filled circle. Or-features are denoted with an empty circle. Extension points are features that have at least one optional sub-feature, an edge ending in an empty circle, or at least one set of (sub-)features. Extension points with optional features are denoted as edges ending in an empty circle. Extension points with or-features use a filled decorated edge arc. The edges ending in a filled circle denote the mandatory features.

Three types of relations are represented in a FD. The *composed-of* relation is used if there is a whole-part relation between a feature and its sub-features. In cases where features are generalization of sub-features, they are organized using the *generalization/specialization* relation. The *implemented-by* relation is used when a feature is necessary to implement another feature. Moreover, features have dependencies: the

Table 86.1. Feature attributes for feature model representation.

Feature type	Definition and examples	Graphical notation
Mandatory	Feature is included if its parent feature is included. **if A then B**; **if A then B and C**	
Optional	Feature may be included if its parent feature is included. **if A then** B or *no feature* **if A then** C **or** D **or** *no feature*	
Alternative (case-selection)	Exactly one feature has to be included if its parent feature is included. **if A then** *case of* (B, C) **if A then** *case of* (B, C, D)	
Alternative (or-selection)	At least one feature has to be included if its parent feature is included. **if A then** *any of* (B, C) **if A then** *any of* (B, C, D)	

selection of one feature may rule out (mutual exclusion constraint) or assume (require, include constraints) the inclusion of another feature.

The derivation of a product consists of traversing the feature tree in an orderly manner and selecting the optional features. The result is a product description containing all the features in the product (a feature configuration). In the PL terminology, a product is fully specified when all of its variation points are bound, i.e., the product specification is complete when all its features have been selected.

FDs provide a concise and explicit representation of variability. They guide the choices to be made for determining the features of specific products and facilitate the reuse of software components implementing these features. We apply FDs as a tool for representing learning content and connecting between learning aims, teaching materials, and software/hardware components. FDs also satisfy a minimal set of requirements (concepts, relations, axioms, and instances) for the construction of ontology as defined by [7]. Therefore, FDs also can be used to describe lightweight ontologies in the educational domain.

4. Motivation of Using Feature Diagrams for LO Domain

There are at least three reasons why FDs are beneficial for the LO domain:

1) *Methodological.* In the LO development domain, there is the need for specification of requirements and provided services at a higher abstraction level. Because FD is a graphical language, which is domain and application independent and independent of the implementation technology of LOs, the language can

be seen as a tool for specification and modeling of LOs. In contrast to the UML notation, the syntax and semantics of FDs are simpler and thus can be easily learnt by different stakeholders (course designers, course experts, teachers and learners, etc.). In the e-Learning domain FDs can be used to promote reusability and interoperability in analysis, sharing, and distributing of knowledge related to LOs. Also, FDs can contribute to the formation of the formal theory of LOs.

2) *Ontology-based knowledge representation.* LO is a breakdown of a teaching content into small chunks that can be reused in various learning environments [37]. When reused, such knowledge units of the content are combined in various ways leading to a composition of complex relationships that can be seen as *domain ontology*. In the e-Learning domain as well as in various other domains (e.g., computer science, information science, artificial intelligence), an ontology is usually understood as a data model that represents a set of concepts within a domain and the relationships between those concepts. For example, OMG [26] defines ontology as "common terms and concepts (meaning) used to describe and represent an area of knowledge." Specifically, an ontology-based model is a form of knowledge representation about the world or some part of it. It is used to reason about the objects within that domain. As a feature can be treated as a chunk of knowledge to be learnt using LOs, FDs contribute to explicit structuring of learning content (chunks of knowledge) at the different level of abstraction. FDs allow expressing the representation of relationships between basic knowledge chunks (features) explicitly, thus they are related to the representation of knowledge and may contribute to better understandability and perception. Knowledge of LO are usually represented using some knowledge-based approach, such as ontology trees of LOs [5]. Domain ontologies, where domain knowledge is represented as *ontology trees*, have some syntactic and conceptual resemblance with *feature hierarchies* represented using FDs. However, FDs have weaker capabilities to express various relationships in representing knowledge [8]. Therefore, FDs currently can be used for representation of *lightweight* ontologies only.

3) *Variability management.* LOs are complex entities entailing many different aspects with a great deal of variants. FDs allow expressing and grasping the common and variable features of LOs explicitly. Variability is especially important for representation and development of the generative LOs [4, 9]. FDs also can be used for modeling LO product lines [29].

5. Capabilities and Limitations of Feature Diagrams in Learning Object Domain

First, we evaluate the capabilities of FDs as a modeling language for the LO domain, then we outline limitations of using FDs in LOs domain, and describe how these limitations can be reduced or overcome. We evaluate FDs as a tool for specification, representation, and structuring of learning content in the e-Learning domain based on a set of general requirements formulated by Koper and Es [20]:

1. *Formalization.* FDs can be seen as a tool for formalization of LOs, though the syntax and semantics of FDs have not become standard, yet. There are efforts to describe generic semantics of FDs formally [33].
2. *Pedagogical flexibility.* FDs allow modeling LOs based on different pedagogical theories.
3. *Explicit expression of meaning.* FDs allow explicitly specifying commonalties and variabilities of LOs.
4. *Completeness.* FDs are a complete specification system that can be used to describe all types of LOs, the relationships between different LOs, and the pedagogical activities related to LOs development and usage.
5. *Reproducibility.* The LO specification described using FDs can be used to reproduce learning content.
6. *Personalization.* FDs allow describing personalization aspects with LO as a part of variability management.
7. *Media neutrality.* FDs are independent of LO-publishing formats such as web or e-books.
8. *Interoperability and sustainability.* FDs as a description method are independent upon the implementation technology of LOs.
9. *Compatibility.* FDs do not contradict of using the existing LO standards such as LOM or SCORM.

10. *Reusability*. FDs promote the reusability of LOs.
11. *Life cycle*. FDs can be used throughout the entire lifecycle of LOs.

The limitations and restrictions of FDs are as follows:

1. *Non-standard notation*. Although FD has been known since the 1990s, its syntax and semantics are still being extended [2, 33]. FDs are evolving toward domain ontologies [8].
2. *Immaturity*. There is a lack of maturity and experience of using FDs (except the PL development in software engineering), and the e-Learning community is not yet familiar with FDs at a large scale.
3. *Lack of expressiveness*. FDs may lack of expressiveness, e.g., to describe domain ontology more comprehensibly or to describe heavyweight domain ontologies. In this case, FDs can be combined with more powerful methods for knowledge representation [32].

6. Case Study: A Learning Object for Teaching Shift Registers

As a case study we have selected a LO that is used in the MSc-level "Reuse Technologies" course at Kaunas University of Technology (KTU). The topic of the course is reuse technologies in microelectronics and hardware design domain.

As a teaching object we have selected shift registers. A shift register is a group of flip-flops set up in a linear fashion which have their inputs and outputs connected together in such a way that the data are shifted down the line when the circuit is activated. Shift registers can have a combination of serial and parallel inputs and outputs, including serial-in/parallel-out (SI/PO) and parallel-in, serial-out (PI/SO) types. There are also types that have both serial and parallel inputs and types with serial and parallel outputs. There are also bi-directional shift registers which allow to vary the direction of the shift register. The serial input and outputs of a register can also be connected together to create a circular shift register. One could also create multi-dimensional shift registers, which can perform more complex computation. Thus, there is a great variability of types and parameters in a domain of shift registers. We use FDs to represent such variability (see Fig. 86.1).

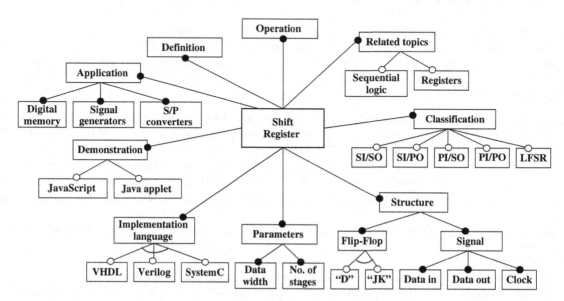

Figure 86.1. Feature diagram of the shift register topic.

The students are introduced with a definition of a shift register, its operation principles, structure, classification, and parameters. The implementation of shift registers using a hardware description language (VHDL, Verilog or SystemC) is presented. The behavior of shift registers is demonstrated using JavaScript or Java applet. Finally, applications of shift registers are explained.

The FD of the shift register topic also has been used to develop parameterized generative components, which specify a family of similar shift registers. A specific shift register description can be generated on demand by specifying metaparameter values. An example of such generative component is presented in Fig. 86.2.

```
$
"Enter data width"                                        {8,16,32}    width:=8;
"Enter input type (0 - parallel, 1 - serial)"            {0,1}        itype:=1;
"Enter output type (0 - parallel, 1 - serial)"           {0,1}        otype:=0;
"Select shifting direction (1 - left, 2 - right)"        {1,2}        dir:=2;
[itype/=1] and [otype/=1]
"Select shifting type (1 - logical, 2 - arithmetical, 3 - cyclical)"
                                                          {1,2,3}      type:=3;
$
entity SHIFT_REGISTER is
  port(CLK    : in std_logic;
       SI     : in std_logic@if[itype=0,{_vector(0 to @sub[width-1])}];
       SO     : out std_logic@if[otype=0,{_vector(0 to @sub[width-1])}]);
end SHIFT_REGISTER;
architecture model of SHIFT_REGISTER is
       L      : in std_logic_vector(0 to @sub[width-1]) := "@rep[width,{0}]";
       LOUT   : in std_logic_vector(0 to @sub[width-1]) := "@rep[width,{0}]";
  begin
@if[otype=0,{
@if[itype=0,{
@- parallel input, parallel output shift register
@case[type,{  @- logical
@case[dir,{
       L <= SI(1 to @sub[width-1]) & '0';        },{
       L <= '0' & SI(0 to @sub[width-2]);        }]
},{            @- arithmetical
@case[dir,{
       L <= SI(1 to @sub[width-1]) & '1';        },{
       L <= '1' & SI(0 to @sub[width-2]);        }]
},{            @- cyclical
@case[dir,{
       L <= SI(1 to @sub[width-1]) & SI(0);           },{
       L <= SI(@sub[width-1]) & SI(0 to @sub[width-2]);     }] }]
},{  @- other types of shift registers ...      }] }]
       SO <= LOUT;
       R1: REGISTER port map (D => L, CLK => CLK, Q => LOUT);
end model;
```

Figure 86.2. Generative shift register specification (a fragment).

Here, the common parts of the shift register description are implemented in VHDL and the variable parts are implemented in a metalanguage Open PROMOL (metalanguage functions are shown in bold) [35]. The interface of the generative component specifies its metaparameters (in italic) and their value space. The metalanguage functions describe specific modifications of the domain implementation language (VHDL, in this case) code in the component's variation points. These variation points represent locations in source code, where variability reveals itself. The modifications implemented at variation points depend upon the specified values of the metaparameters. Such separation of features (which are specified as metaparameters), variation points (which capture variability and are specified using a metalanguage), and common code (which represents commonalty across a specific learning topic and is specified using a domain language) based on the FD models allows to better explain commonality–variability relationships across a specific learning topic.

Specific shift register instances representing different types and variants of a shift register can be generated by the metalanguage processor automatically. Such generative components based on the FDs of learning topics allow to capture and distribute domain knowledge to students in a more efficient and systematic way.

7. Conclusions

Feature diagrams can be used by (1) *designers, teachers, and learners,* as a means for graphical representation of knowledge contained in learning objects by providing domain ontologies using feature concepts, their types, values, and relationships; (2) *programmers,* to specify and express variability–communality relationships of learning objects at a higher abstraction level in order to develop and implement generative learning objects systematically; (3) *researchers and other domain actors,* as a vehicle for analysis and better understanding of the learning object domain itself, because feature diagrams enable to express granularity, compositionality, and context explicitly to support reusability of learning materials.

Since learning objects are entities that contain a variety of attributes with complex relationships (e.g., between various parts of a learning object and between learning object and metadata) and have to be considered from different contexts (e.g., design, retrieval, learning) and perspectives (e.g., designer's, teacher's, learner's), learning objects can be represented and modeled using feature diagrams. In a feature diagram, the root represents a learning topic (concept), intermediate nodes represent compound features, and leaves represent atomic features. Branches describe various kinds of relationships between features. There are mandatory, optional, and alternative features. Using feature diagrams, we can identify and model lightweight ontologies related to learning objects.

Feature diagrams also have some limitations (e.g., not standardized yet, not enough maturity). The application of feature diagrams for the learning object domain requires some extension of the feature diagram notation (e.g., the introduction of contextualization and more rich relationships to express various types of ontologies may be useful). Further research is needed in order to exploit benefits and overcome limitations of feature diagrams in the e-Learning domain.

References

1. Bailey, B., Martin, G. and Anderson, T. (Eds.) (2005) *Taxonomies for the Development and Verification of Digital Systems.* London: Springer.
2. Batory, D.S. (2005) Feature models, grammars, and propositional formulas. In Obbink, J.H. and Pohl, K. (Eds.), *Proc. of 9th Int. Conf. on Software Product Lines,* SPLC 2005, Rennes, France, September 26–29, 2005, pp. 7–20.
3. Boyce, S. and Pahl, C. (2007) Developing domain ontologies for course content. *Educational Technology & Society* 10 (3), pp. 275–288.
4. Boyle, T., Leeder, D. and Chase, H. (2004) To boldly GLO – towards the next generation of learning objects, *World Conference on eLearning in Corporate, Government, Healthcare and Higher Education,* Washington USA.
5. Brace, J. and Nejdl, W. (2004) Ontologies and metadata for elearning. In Staab, S. and Studer, R. (Eds.), *Towards an Ontological Support for eLearning Courses.* LNCS vol. 3292, pp. 555–574. London: Springer-Verlag.
6. Clements, P. and Northrop, L. (2002) *Software Product Lines: Practices and Patterns.* Boston, MA: Addison-Wesley.
7. Corcho, O. (2006) Ontological engineering: principles, methods, tools and languages. In Calero, C., Ruiz, F. and Piattini, M. (Eds.), *Ontologies for Software Engineering and Software Technology,* p. 5. London: Springer.
8. Czarnecki, K., Kim, C.H.P. and Kalleberg, K.T. (2006) Feature models are views on ontologies. In *Proc. of 10th Int. Software Product Line Conference, SPLC'06,* Baltimore, USA, pp. 41–51.
9. Damaševičius, R. and Štuikys, V. (2008) On the technological aspects of generative learning object development. In Mittermeir, R. T., and Syslo, M.M. (Eds.), *Proc. of 3rd Int. Conf. on Informatics in Secondary Schools Evolution and Perspectives ISSEP 2008,* 1–4 July, 2008, Torun, Poland. LNCS vol. 5090, pp. 337–348. London: Springer-Verlag.
10. Dodero, J.M., Zarraonandia, T., Fernández, C. and Díez, D. (2007) Generative adaptation and reuse of competence development programmes. *Journal of Interactive Media in Education* (Special Issue on Adaptation and IMS Learning Design), Vol. 4, pp. 1–3.
11. Eisenecker, U.W. and Czarnecki, K. (2000) *Generative Programming: Methods, Tools, and Applications.* Boston, MA: Addison-Wesley.
12. Fowler, M. (2003) *UML Distilled: A Brief Guide to the Standard Object Modeling Language,* 3rd ed., Boston, MA: Addison-Wesley.
13. Friesen, N. (2004) Three objections to learning objects and e-learning standards. In McGreal, R. (Ed.), *Online Education Using Learning Objects.* London: Routledge, pp. 59–70.
14. Gao, J., Marchetti, E. & Polini, A. (2005) Applying advanced UML based testing methodology to e-learning. In *Proc. of the IADIS Int. Conf. on Applied Computing,* Algarve, Portugal, February 22–25, 2005, pp. 74–79.

15. Guizzardi, G. (2007) On ontology, ontologies, conceptualizations, modeling languages, and (meta)models. In Vasilecas, O., Eder, J. and Caplinskas, A. (Eds.), *Frontiers in Artificial Intelligence and Applications, Databases and Information Systems IV*, pp. 18–39. Amsterdam: IOS Press.

16. Holzinger, A., Smolle, J. and Reibnegger, G. (2005) Learning objects (LO): an object oriented approach to manage e-learning content. In: Lazakidou, A. (Ed.) *Encyclopedia of Informatics in Healthcare & Biomedicine*. Hershey (PA): Idea Group Reference, pp. 89–98.

17. Kang, K., Cohen, S., Hess, J., Novak, W. and Peterson, S. (1990) Feature-Oriented Domain Analysis (FODA) Feasibility Study. Technical Report CMU/SEI-90-TR-21, Software Engineering Institute, Carnegie Mellon University, November 1990.

18. Kang, K.C., Lee, J. and Donohoe, P. (2002) Feature-oriented product line engineering. *IEEE Software*, 19(4), pp. 58–65.

19. Karampiperis, P. and Sampson, D. (2007) Towards a common graphical language for learning flows: transforming BPEL to IMS learning design level a representations. In *Proc. of the 7th IEEE Int. Conf. on Advanced Learning Technologies (ICALT 2007)*, Niigata, Japan.

20. Koper, R. and van Es, R. (2004) Modelling units of learning from a pedagogical perspective. In McGreal, R. (ed.), *Online Education Using Learning Objects*. New York: Routledge.

21. Laforcade, P. (2005) Towards a UML-based educational modeling language. In *Proc. of 5th Int. Conf. on Advanced Learning Technologies, ICALT 2005*, 5-8 July 2005, pp. 855–859.

22. Lee, S.-B., Kim, J.-W., Song, C.-Y. and Baik, D.-K. (2007) An approach to analyzing commonality and variability of features using ontology in a software product line engineering. In *Proc. of 5th ACIS Int. Conf. on Software Engineering Research, Management & Applications, SERA 2007*, 20–22 Aug. 2007, pp. 727–734.

23. Lin, F.O. (2004). Knowledge modelling for designing learning objects. In McGreal, R. (Ed.). *Online Education Using Learning Objects*. London: Routledge, pp. 314–330.

24. LTSC (Learning Technology Standards Committee) (2002) *IEEE Standard for Learning Object Metadata*. IEEE Standard 1484. 12.1. IEEE, New York.

25. MacGregor, J. (2002) Requirements engineering in industrial product lines. In *Proc. of Int. Workshop on Requirements Engineering for Product Lines, REPL*, Essen, Germany, pp. 5–11.

26. OMG (Object Management Group) (2003) *Ontology Definition Metamodel*. Available at: www.omg.org/docs/ontology/03-03-01. rtf

27. Pankratius, V. (2005) Aspect-oriented learning objects. In *Proc. of the 4th IASTED Int. Conf. on Web-based Education (WBE2005)*, February 21–23, Grindelwald, Switzerland.

28. Pankratius, V. (2007) *Product Lines for Digital Information Products*. Karlsruhe: Karlsruhe University Press.

29. Pankratius, V. and Stucky, W. (2006) A strategy for content reusability with product lines derived from experience. In Inverardi, P. and Jazayeri, M. (Eds.), *Online Education, Software Engineering Education in the Modern Age: Challenges and Possibilities*. LNCS 4309, pp. 128–146. London: Springer Verlag

30. Paquette, G., Léonard, M., Lundgren-Cayrol, K., Mihaila, S. and Gareau, D. (2006) Learning design based on graphical knowledge-modelling. *Educational Technology & Society*, 9 (1), pp. 97–112.

31. Risse, T. and Vatterrott, H.-R. (2004). The learning objects structure Petri net. In Auer, M. and Auer, U. (Eds.), *Interactive Computer Aided Learning – The Future of Learning ICL 2004*, Villach, September 29–October 1, 2004. Kassel: Kassel University Press.

32. Robak, S., and Pieczynski, A. (2003) Employing fuzzy logic in feature diagrams to model variability in software product-lines. In *Proc. of the 10th IEEE Int. Conf. and Workshop on the Engineering of Computer-Based Systems (ECBS'03)*, pp. 305–311.

33. Schobbens, P.-Y., Heymans, P., Trigaux, J.-Ch. and Bontemps, Y. (2007) Generic semantics of feature diagrams. *Computer Networks: The International Journal of Computer and Telecommunications Networking* 51(2), pp. 456–479.

34. Scott, B. and Johnson, Z. (2005) Using topic maps as part of learning design – some history and a case study. In *Proc. of 3rd Int. Conf. on Multimedia and Communication Technologies in Education*, Caceres, Spain, June 7-10.

35. Štuikys, V., Damaševičius, R. and Ziberkas, G. (2002) Open PROMOL: an experimental language for target program modification. In Mignotte, A., Villar, E. and Horobin, L. (Eds.), *System on Chip Design Languages – Extended Papers: Best of FDL'01 and HDLCON'01*, pp. 235–246. Boston, MA: Kluwer Academic Publishers.

36. Štuikys, V., Damaševičius, R., Brauklytė, I. and Limanauskienė, V. (2008) Exploration of learning object ontologies using feature diagrams. In *Proc. of World Conference on Educational Multimedia, Hypermedia & Telecommunications (ED-MEDIA 08)*, June 30–July 4, 2008, Vienna, Austria, pp. 2144–2154.

37. Wiley, D.A. (2000) *Learning Object Design and Sequencing Theory*. PhD Thesis, Department of Instructional Psychology and Technology, Brigham Young University, Provo.

38. Wiley, D.A. (2002) Connecting learning objects to instructional design theory: A definition, a metaphor, and a taxonomy. In Wiley, D.A. (Ed.), *The Instructional Use of Learning Objects*. Bloomington, IN: Association for Educational Communications and Technology.

87

Understanding Service-Oriented Architectures in the Classroom: From Web Services to Grid Services

D. Petcu and V. Iordan

Abstract

The main challenges in today's teaching of service-oriented architectures at graduate and undergraduate levels are discussed and several approaches are analyzed. Teaching web and grid services is treated as special cases. Based on a positive experience in teaching service-oriented architecture using grid services, we advocate the usage of grid services in classroom for graduate students.

Keywords High education · Service-oriented architecture · Web and grid services

1. Introduction

Service-oriented architecture (SOA) is a recent evolution in distributed middleware. There are many definitions of SOA in the literature. A good representative for the aim of this chapter is the following: SOA is an IT strategy that organizes the discrete functions contained in enterprise applications into interoperable, standards-based services that can be combined and reused quickly to meet business needs. The SOA paradigm is currently increasing its role in the industry. Investigation in SOA is growing in importance and the subject is of high relevance to software engineering education. The pedagogical challenges are mainly in the arena of those who teach programming, management information systems, or organizational design.

The SOA's services are building blocks that relate to activities in organizations and to the functions supported by software systems. Therefore, the ability to think in terms of services is a challenge to both programmers and educators. From the perspective of software engineers, this challenge may be the equivalent of the transition from structured procedural programming to the object-oriented paradigm. Moreover, according to [11], it forces a closer association between programming and organization theory.

Student projects in software engineering courses must often integrate disparate components across a heterogeneous networked infrastructure using concepts such as SOA. While SOA promises to successfully accomplish this task, mastering the design, development, and deployment of SOA-based systems places a considerable pedagogical burden on teachers and students [8].

We discuss in this chapter a series of challenges that were identified in the process of creating lectures and labs for students that effectively develop skills necessary for confronting SOA in professional practice.

The chapter is organized as follows. Section 2 presents the challenges in building a curriculum for SOA teaching and the approaches that were reported in the literature. Section 3 treats the special case of

D. Petcu • Institute e-Austria Timisoara, Timisoara, Romania, Computer Science Department, West University of Timisoara, Timisoara, Romania.   **V. Iordan** • Computer Science Department, West University of Tiomisoara, Timisoara, Romania.

G.A. Papadopoulos et al. (eds.), *Information Systems Development*, DOI 10.1007/b137171_87,
© Springer Science+Business Media, LLC 2009

teaching web services. Section 4 describes our experience in teaching SOA through grid services. Finally, Section 5 points to the most important conclusions of the chapter.

2. SOA Education

The following section discusses the main issues encountered in SOA teaching.

2.1. Importance of SOA Education

The advantages of SOA were underlined in several books and papers in the last decade. For example, the authors of [16] discussed in detail the advantages of using SOA pointing to the following aspects:

- appropriate services can be used as required;
- new services (including third-party services) are relatively easy to integrate; and
- less danger of technology "lock in" due to the easiness of integrating services.

Another important aspect is the one underlined by [15]: the costs of developing SOA applications are less than that of traditional application development. SOA applications are usually not write from scratch. Or, if it is writing it from scratch, some components can be used by other peoples. This opens the door for smaller companies to get involved in the market. Moreover, SOA allows them to afford more development projects with reduced costs of managing outsourcing. Another fact is that many companies are heavily investing in converting legacy systems into valuable corporate assets in the guise of business services.

In this context, the education must be aligned with the overall SOA initiatives and the current industry trend toward SOA. The education is the central pillar for the enterprise shift toward SOA, as stated in [7]. Currently SOA education is strongly promoted by vendors of specific SOA tools such as IBM. The personalities participating at the discussions on SOA education in colleges and universities presented in [10] agreed that it needs to be flexible and adaptable and new methodologies and strategies for instruction may be necessary.

2.2. Requirements of SOA Education

SOA is not only in widespread use by the industry, but is also a current area of interest for research. A currently open area of investigation is how to properly introduce SOA in a curriculum for computer science, information technology, or software engineering. Common is the fact that the students must develop a series of abilities and skills related to SOA for effective professional practice.

The SOA concept subscribes to the idea of modular design of software applications, having several familiar benefits [11]:

- divide and conquer approach to complexity;
- facilitates coordination of team members;
- Project easier to document and comprehend;
- Opportunities for code reuse; and
- Application easier to maintain.

SOA refers to distributed systems in which some of the modules of software are services. It involves the concept of service that is not necessarily intuitive to the programmers. The design goal of a SOA is not only to design the software code but also to integrate the design of processes into the design of the software code. Therefore, SOA blurs the distinction between analysis and design [11] that complicates more the placement of the SOA education in a specific curriculum.

As future professionals the students must develop skills in three areas to be able to implement SOA solutions in the real world [7]:

– Ability to explain business conditions that require SOA and what restrictions they impose.
– Ability to use the underlying infrastructure that supports SOA environments and choose and justify the selection of one standard, technology or implementation over another.
– Ability to integrate real world applications in an SOA environment understanding the complexity involved.

Taking into consideration the above remarks, we consider that a SOA introduction has as perquisites at least object-oriented programming skills, software engineering knowledge, and business understanding.

2.3. Initiatives for SOA Education

SOA education was already included and tested as part of several software architecture courses in an undergraduate technical program. The challenges mentioned in [7] in following this way are related to restrictions of undergraduate programs, intricacy of current technologies, implementations and standards for SOA, complexity to create business scenarios in SOA, and high exigency of skills required from instructors for proper SOA teaching.

SOA education at earlier time in professional formation, at the level of high schools, was proposed and analyzed by [15].

Promoting SOA to non-technical students is reported in [11]. The article describes the experiences introducing web services, SOA, and workflow modeling to a class of graduate students in a public administration program. The position paper [7] discusses what a learning environment should provide for students and instructors to develop skills that will enable SOA practice in the business world.

The fourth International Symposium on Software Engineering Course [8] explored in 2007 how educators and industry can work together to develop a more rewarding educational experience for all stakeholders involved.

To fit SOA education into a crowded curriculum can be a challenge. The IEEE/ACM Computing Curricula 2005 does not specify explicitly the SOA topics as relevant, but "net centric principles and design" and "net centric use and configuration" as well as "distributed systems" or "computer architecture and organization" can encompass several parts of a SOA-specific course. For example, in a course on distributed systems the SOA can be presented as a kind of concept that enables the integration of resources from third-party organizations. A course indicated in the Curricula from 2005 that must deal with web-based systems is "system administration." On the other hand, "systems development through integration" is marked as a necessary skill of a graduate.

2.4. Comments on the Current Content of SOA Education

According to the survey [5], the area of most interest for education is SOA design, much more relevant than technologies such as component models or vendor specific tools. The same survey also reveals that topic areas of most relevance were organization, policies and governance, SOA design, and standards.

The key steps in a SOA design are the following:

– design both the processes and the software that automates the processes;
– define roles, rules, and activities;
– identify paths between activities; and
– identify sub-processes to address complexity.

An activity can be implemented as a service and can exist remotely. A service may be used to tap into part of the functionality of a legacy system lying locally or remotely.

The students must understand what SOA provides for them. A good starting point is to underline the current high complexity IT infrastructure and the key challenges in handle it, like:

1. Scale in number of resources, users, objectives, goals, management and provisioning options handled by sophisticated algorithms.

2. Heterogeneity expressed in variations in resources, resource types, interfaces, management systems.
3. Distribution and federation expressed in geographically dispersed resources and management systems, multiple players from the organization and outside, and multiple administrative domains and policies.

Simple interfaces through which all resources can be provisioned and managed uniformly are needed to hide (according [9]):

– Different levels of abstraction (business processes, applications, servers, network).
– Different types of resources (operating systems, application servers, web servers, databases, custom logic, switches, routers, firewalls, load balancers, disk arrays).
– Different management interface standards (configuration files, scripting).
– Constant change (interfaces change for improved functionality and design, resources change for replacing the old ones).

The students should be able to identify situations where integration might be achieved using an SOA approach independently of technology. This requires that students must follow real-world scenarios [7]. These scenarios should be simple enough from a business perspective since the students need to spend more time in the integration exercise than in understanding the business processes.

A useful exercise according to the authors of [7] would focus on the identification of business processes and their relationship with concrete process support applications. In this type of exercise students would have to identify which applications are candidate for SOA integration, what services would be necessary from each application, and how would these services be orchestrated. Another type of exercise proposed in [7] can have as goal the identification of potential risks of SOA migration.

Student team projects are the cornerstone of many software engineering courses, including SOA education, since the students learn the importance of topics such as project management and issues of scale that separate software engineering from program development. The focus of such projects is not on learning about a particular technology, but on using it as a means to an end. However, this cannot be achieved without a sufficient understanding of the underlying technologies. Therefore, the teacher must carefully balance the effort needed to learn about SOA with the effort to learn about other aspects of software engineering required to finalize the project. This may be particularly difficult to achieve considering the complexity of SOA. Related to this subject, the paper [2] presents a project-based course: the project is an online shopping mall that links retailers and customers over the Internet; services should be built for collective negotiation with suppliers, advertising agencies, search engines, payments-handling services, and credit agencies. A similar web-based e-commerce project is proposed by [7]; to simulate real conditions, students are divided so that some groups developed the product providers, while others develop the package couriers, and the online intermediary is developed by teacher assistants; each group is in charge of creating the SOA environment independently of which implementations are used.

In what concerns the integration exercises, a learning environment is needed where students can easily use SOA infrastructure. The topics of SOA infrastructure must be covered, at least service call and discovery, as well as orchestration with process execution languages. In this context it is needed to provide tools and frameworks based on standards used in SOA. They should also provide visual and easy-to-use monitoring so students can actually witness the execution of an SOA scenario [7]. The author of [11] advocated the teaching of workflow design using computer-based modeling tools, as appropriate response to the pedagogical challenges of SOA being at the intersection between application design and organization design.

In the real world, the legacy applications are the best candidate for SOA integration. Integration scenarios of legacy applications in a classroom are very difficult because most of the real-legacy applications are functionally complex. The time dedicated by students to one course is not sufficient to learn how to use a legacy technology. An interesting proposal is presented in [7]: to use pseudo-legacy applications having a closed implementation and providing only interfaces for their access. Students can work then for extending the pseudo-legacy applications without modifications to the original source code. The extensions must focus on aspects such as data transformation, concurrency of service calls, or availability of the application. One exercise can focus on extensions to transform the platform-specific calls to services exposed by the application and transform service responses to specific calls to the application.

Unfortunately, the tools for SOA industry are currently too complex to be used in labs, and there is a clear need for specific tools with simplified functions for teaching. The paper [3] mentions an initiative to build portals for SOA teaching. Providing environments where students go beyond learning some concepts and specific technologies to truly apprehend the complexity involved in SOA is still an important challenge for SOA education [7].

3. Web Service Education

The following subsections are pointing toward the current approaches for education in web services.

3.1. Importance of Web Services for SOA Education

Web services have become recently important enough that all software professionals should know something about them. Moreover, a prediction mentioned in [4] states that web services will become the dominant distributed computing architecture in the next 10 years. This tendency will create a demand for computing professionals with expertise in this field. In this context, universities will begin teaching web services in their distributed programming course, or as a separate course [4].

Understanding the path that has lead to web services and the relation of web services with existing technology are key elements to master web services and how they might evolve is [1].

The term service-oriented architecture was coined by a Gartner analyst in 1994 and is not exclusive to the brand of web service that is dominant today. Several technologies can serve as a basis for SOA such as CORBA, but these have failed to become universally adopted. According to [1], web services are the result of the natural evolution of middleware and enterprise application integration platforms as they try to leverage the WWW, the Internet, and the globalization of society as a whole, particularly in its economic aspects.

Web services standards, built on Internet protocols, facilitate the creation of distributed applications and are currently used to implement SOAs. The notion of service in the conventional middleware is translated into the notion of web service based on the access channel to that service [11]; the service in fact can be a pre-existing middleware service, e.g., stored procedures in databases made available as web services. From a technical perspective, a web service is a software piece accessed using particular technologies including SOAP, WSDL, and UDDI. Important is the fact that in the middleware and enterprise application integration world only few details need to be changed so that they match the needs of exchanges through the Internet rather than a LAN [1] using

- XML as the data representation format;
- SOAP as a protocol wrapper to allow conventional communication protocols of middleware platforms to cross the Internet and firewalls (turns invocations into document exchanges);
- WSDL as the XML version of IDLs from CORBA; and
- UDDI as the WWW version of basic name and directory services.

The major advantages of web services are that they are platform independent and can be accessed using freely available resources rather than by using more specialized or proprietary resources. The disadvantage is that these distributed applications tend to run relatively slowly, in part because of a dependence upon XML.

3.2. Initiatives for Web Service Education

Common approaches for web service education require teaching the standards and several APIs.

Currently, two platforms dominate the market for developing web services: Java Enterprise Edition (J2EE) and Microsoft's .NET. The authors of [4] compared the two platforms using parameters such as features present in each platform, tools and resources offered by the two, and compatibility with the classical curriculum in software engineering or computer science. According to [4], the arguments in favor of J2EE are platform independence, multiple vendor support, the popularity of Java in universities, and a larger number of tools and resources from which to choose. Points favoring .NET include support for multiple languages and integrated support for web services.

The simplest web service to be developed in the classroom is presented in [4]: it is similar to the ubiquitous "Hello World" program used to teach any new programming language and takes a name of a person as a parameter and returns the greeting "Hello," appended with the person's name. The exercise illustrates the process of building and deploying a web service. The same process would be used to build and deploy complex web services.

Several special tools can be also used in the teaching process. The authors of [7] mention the use of Tongo as a platform that integrates, summarizes, and simplifies technologies and architectures related to web services. The object-oriented Water language proposed by [6] is designed for rapidly prototyping XML-based web services and it provides a very concise encoding of web services functionality, making it ideal for teaching, as students can learn very fast to write web services.

The course associated with the book [1] goes beyond the technologies aiming to develop a critical understanding of web service technology and its possibilities today. The goal is for participants to be able to look at current and future developments with enough background to be able to judge how much of a contribution they have and what their true potential is.

3.3. Comments on the Current Content of Web Service Education

Unfortunately, the simple Hello World example that was mentioned in the previous section is not sufficient to understand how technologies are used in the real world.

A big problem related to web service education (identified also in [7]) is that the technologies to support it are too complex and implementation oriented. Moreover, the reference manuals can be very long and students have problems filtering all the information and separating concepts from implementation-specific details. A student faced with the challenge of using web services has to spend so much time with implementation details that would not be able to grasp how they can be used effectively in an enterprise.

Other issues that can hinder the success of web service education are, according to [7], the following:

- difficulty to understand how technology accomplishes its roles such as platform independence without having access to concrete implementation details;
- what is the right technology that students must use if the industry lacks widespread standards;
- standards are becoming increasingly more complex;
- instructors rarely have time to use real-world scenarios (due to many applications to be involved, the need of comprehension of the business, and the time restrictions for a course); and
- the instructor needs to have a whole set of skills: knowledge and abilities in SOA practice in the real world; should have faced the problems of integration of new and legacy applications; should be an expert in the technologies, but should not be partial to any of them; should constantly study new technologies and standards; should be able to spot trends in the industry; and should bring best practices to the classroom.

4. Grid Services in the Context of SOA Education

The current popular version of web services based on SOAP, UDDI, and WSDL is a very poor and limiting view on what true web services should be. Alternative proposals such as ebXML, xCBL, or RosettaNet provide a much deeper insight on what is needed for electronic commerce through web services [1]. Moreover, general web services do not hold state and tend to be slow because of overhead required by use of SOAP and XML. The first drawback is removed by using the grid services and statefull web services for resource management.

The grid technologies, originally, a set of protocols and conventions for sharing cycles for compute-intense scientific applications is becoming now oriented to sustain a service-oriented connecting architecture for collaborative applications requiring access to global resources.

The current grid service architecture is defined on top of the web service standards and includes common characteristic with SOA. Grid services extend basic web services by introducing explicit service creation and lifetime management, by defining a two-layer naming scheme that enables support for distributed system transparencies, and by requiring a mandatory set of functions and data elements that support discovery [12]. It is possible, using standard web services, to manage and name statefull services using ad hoc methods, like extra characters placed in URLs or extra arguments to functions; however, this is not done in a uniform and consistent manner; grid services are bringing uniformity and consistency in this topic.

Grid education was the subject of our recent papers [13,14]. In this chapter we discuss the issue related to the grid service training in the course sustained in the last 3 years to PhD students.

The grid computing course provides both a practically oriented introduction to current technologies, focusing on grid technologies and standards, including web and grid services, and a theoretical overview of the underlying issues that arise in supporting grid-based e-infrastructures.

Understanding the fundamental principles of distributed systems (such as would be obtained from a senior undergraduate course in computer networks and security and a first-year graduate course on distributed systems) is the main prerequisite for this course. Students should be also competent in Java programming, need to have experience with parallel and distributed algorithms, need to be accommodated with Unix operating systems, and should be done some work on databases to the level of detail covered in an undergraduate computing science curricula.

The course content is focusing on understanding the grid architectures, standards, tools as well as the specific topics related to resource management, security, and data management. Mandatory lab assignments include developing a web service and a grid service.

An individual semester project consists in the requirement to port a legacy code into SOA by exposing it as a grid service. The application fields have varied over the 3 years, depending on the subject of the grid-related research projects that were executed in the corresponding academic year. The legacy codes involved were computer algebra systems, codes implementing a metaheuristic algorithm, image processing tools, and computational fluid dynamic simulation codes.

The common characteristics of these legacy codes involved in the wrapping exercise was the fact that despite their usual interaction with the human client through a nice graphical user interface, they are also able to be called through a command line. A grid service has been designed and implemented to accept the running parameters from the service's client and to translate them into command line parameters or input files for the legacy code. Moreover, the benefits of using grid services instead of web services by creating different instances of the grid services for different users and interacting in several successive sessions with these statefull services (keeping the history of interactions) is proved, e.g., by the wrappers of computer algebra systems.

One difficult task during the lectures is to draw some borderlines between the grid and web services and the other exciting fields like utility computing, virtualization, cloud computing, autonomous computing, global computing, pervasive computing, ubiquitous computing, mobile computing, peer-to-peer computing, volunteer computing, service-oriented knowledge utility, and so on. For each of them practical examples are needed to be provided which is a highly time-consuming task, but the effect is a better understanding of what grid and web services can provide for their users.

Accustomed to use integrated development environments to build and to launch their projects, the students found as unpleasant the classical batch processing and the classical tools for remote access to their department accounts. To overcome this situation, the usage of the eclipse tools for designing web services and the usage of a special workflow editor for grid services were promoted. Moreover, the grid services were registered by the students in the local Tomcat container in which services are made visible through a service portal. This special portal allows to inspect the operations that a service exposes in its standard web service description and to launch automated generated clients for selected operations that has been very useful in understanding the interactions with web and grid services.

5. Conclusions

We pointed several issues that hinder the development of SOA skills of the next generation of professionals in information technologies, computer science, and software engineering. While the current SOA technologies are dominated by web services, we advocate the usage of grid services as more proper for teaching SOA technologies, especially in what concerns the resource management and virtualization, despite the missing tools specially designed for teaching grid services.

Acknowledgments

This study was partially supported by the Romanian research projects funded by the Ministry of Education and Research: project no. CEEX-I 47/2005 in the case of the first author and project no. PN II 91-047/2007 in the case of the second author.

References

1. Alonso G., Casati F., Kuno H. and Machiraju V. (2004) *Web Services Concepts, Architectures and Applications.* Springer Verlag, Berlin.
2. Alrifai R. (2008) A project approach for teaching software architecture and web services in a software engineering course. *Journal of Computing Sciences in Colleges* 23 (4), pp. 237–240
3. Gilbert L., Sitthisak O., Sim Y.W., Wang C. and Wills G. (2006) From collaborative virtual research environment to teaching and learning. In: *TENcompetence Workshop: Learning Networks for Lifelong Competence Development*, March 2006, Sofia, Bulgaria, http://eprints.ecs.soton.ac.uk/12088/. Accessed April 2008
4. Kachru S. and Gehringer E.F. (2004) A comparison of J2EE and .NET as platforms for teaching web services. *Frontiers in Education*, Vol. 3, FIE 2004: S3B, pp. 12–17
5. Kemsley S. (2006) SOA education. *ebizQ* 4/2006. http://www.ebizq.net/blogs/column2/ar chives/2006/04/soa_education.php. Accessed April 2008
6. Kendall M.D. and Gehringer E.F. (2006) Teaching web services with water. *Frontiers in Education*, 36th Annual Conference, pp.7–12
7. Lopez N., Casallas R. and Villalobos J. (2007) Challenges in creating environments for SOA learning, *Procs. SDSOA'07*, pp. 9–15
8. Lyons K. (2007), Workshops of CASCON 2007, *Proceedings of the 2007 Conference of the Center for Advanced Studies on Collaborative research*, ACM, New York, pp. 356–365
9. Machiraju V. (2003) Grid services: web services for resource management, *Proceedings of 4th VLDB Workshop on Technologies for e-services* (TES 2003).
10. Miron D. (2006) SOA education in colleges and universities, *ASU Workshop on Service-Oriented Architecture and Applications.* May 2006, Tempe, Arizona. http://asusrl.eas.asu.edu/srlab/activities/SOAworkshop/. Accessed April 2008
11. Neubauer J. (2007) Introducing SOA and workflow modeling to non-technical students, *Journal of Computing Sciences in Colleges* 22 (4), pp. 101–107
12. Petcu D. (2006) Between web and grid-based mathematical services. *Procs. ICCGI*, August 2006. IEEE Computer Society Press, pp. 41–47
13. Petcu D. (2008) Teaching grid technologies to PhD students, Part 1: using best practices to build the course, *IEEE Distributed Systems Online* 9 (3), 2008, art. no. 0803–o3002.
14. Petcu D. (2008) Teaching grid technologies to PhD students, Part 2: course structure and experiences, *IEEE Distributed Systems Online* 9 (4), 2008, art. no. 0804–o4001
15. Thompson A. (2006) SOA education in high schools. *ASU Workshop on Service-Oriented Architecture Education, Research, and Applications.* May 2006, Tempe, Arizona, http://asusrl.eas.asu.edu/srlab/activities/SOAworkshop/. Accessed April 2008
16. Wilson S., Blinco K. and Rehak D. (2004) *Service-oriented Frameworks: Modelling the Infrastructure for the Next Generation of E-learning Systems.* JISC position paper, http://www.jisc.ac.uk/uploaded_documents/AltilabServiceOrientedFrameworks.pdf. Accessed April 2008

88

Refactoring of Learning Objects for Mobile Learning

Robertas Damaševičius

Abstract

We analyze the problem of refactoring of learning object (LO) for m-Learning. We apply methods adopted from software engineering domain for redesigning the structure and user interface of a LO and aim both at increasing usability and accessibility of the learning material. We evaluate usability of a LO from the user interface point of view, following the user interface development principles that are common both for human–computer interaction (HCI) and e-Learning domains. We propose the LO refactoring framework based on user interface usability principles. In a case study, we demonstrate the refactoring of an array-sorting LO for a mobile device.

Keywords Learning object · m-Learning, Refactoring

1. Introduction

e-Learning is learning that uses computer networks as the delivery mechanism [22]. However, the Internet technologies are only a prerequisite for e-Learning. e-Learning considers content, technologies, and services for delivering learner-centered, interactive, and facilitated learning environment to anyone, in anyplace, at anytime by utilizing the attributes and resources of various digital technologies along with other forms of learning materials tailored for open, flexible, and distributed learning environments [14].

Currently, "learning objects" (LOs) are leading as an instructional technology of choice for e-Learning support due to its potential generativity, adaptability, and scalability [29]. LOs are digital teaching components that were introduced following the object-oriented (OO) paradigm in software engineering. LOs can be delivered over the Internet where they can be accessed and used by many learners simultaneously. Furthermore, LOs can be reused multiple times in different contexts, used independently, or grouped into larger collections of content, including traditional course structures. From the technological point of view, a LO consists of (1) teaching material and (2) technologies that are used to provide a view of a LO to the user, i.e., a user interface (UI).

The design and development of LOs for e-Learning and, especially, m-Learning solutions are time consuming, cumbersome, and usually based on concrete models, scenarios, and recommendations, but not on general framework or methodology. Despite the great potential advantages, the methodologies for developing LOs for m-Learning environments are still underdeveloped. The analysis of m-Learning is still in its infancy, and most attention is paid to benefits, possible uses, used technologies, and case studies.

LO adaptability is a critical requirement to accommodate a large variety of learners that will be accessing LOs through web-based learning management systems (LMS). The adaptive features of LOs include a LO language, inclusion of optional material, size or information content granularity of LO states, ordering of examples, general rules, selection of visual metaphors and icons, adjustments in colors, fonts,

---

Robertas Damaševičius • Software Engineering Department, Kaunas University of Technology, Kaunas, Lithuania.

G.A. Papadopoulos et al. (eds.), *Information Systems Development*, DOI 10.1007/b137171_88,
© Springer Science+Business Media, LLC 2009

and size, etc. [27]. Therefore, adaptation of LOs is not a trivial task and requires a solid methodological background.

In this chapter, we adopt a concept of *refactoring*, known from software engineering, to the e-Learning domain. Refactoring is a disciplined technique for restructuring an existing body of code, altering its internal structure without changing its external behavior [10]. As such, refactoring is a part of re-engineering process [17].

Recent work in LO refactoring and reengineering includes the development of reengineering frameworks for e-Learning systems [5], reengineering of e-Learning systems [3], reengineering learning materials for electronic platforms [21], refactoring of learning software with mobile extensions [18], refactoring of e-Learning resources based on a competence model and instructional roles [31], pedagogical reengineering of distance learning courses using new technologies [6], restructuring of courseware to allow reuse of learning material for different pedagogical scenarios and adaptation of courseware for delivery in a computer network [24], reengineering of learning scenarios [26], redesign of courses using reusable lesson modules or objects to achieve cost reduction [12], reengineering legacy processes such as lectures, tutorials, group activity, discussion groups for use with online learning [9], and case studies in reengineering of LOs for e-Learning and m-Learning [28]. Reengineering of LOs is still an underdeveloped topic and LO reengineering processes are to be improved [23]. Our prior work concerned the definition of common HCI and e-Learning principles for designing usable user interface (UI) for LOs [7] and analysis of the problem of LO reengineering [8] based on common usable UI design principles.

The aim of this chapter is to demonstrate how the concept and methodology of refactoring adopted from software engineering can be used in adapting learning materials for m-Learning. Section 2 discusses technological and educational issues related to m-Learning. Section 3 analyzes a concept of refactoring in software engineering, describes basic techniques of learning content refactoring, and proposes a framework for LO refactoring. Section 4 demonstrates an application of the framework for refactoring a LO for a mobile device. Section 5 discusses open research issues in LO refactoring. Section 6 presents conclusions.

2. Technological and Educational Issues in m-Learning

2.1. Technological Constraints of Mobiles

A mobile device (such as PDA, mobile phone, smart phone) is a small (pocket-sized) computing device comprised of a small visual display screen for user output and a miniature keyboard or touch screen for user input. The technological challenges for designing UIs for mobile devices are as follows [13]:

1) *Limited input facilities:* PDA users can input text and control functions with a stylus and a miniaturized on-screen, separate, or add-on keyboard. Handwriting recognition software can be used to type text, but it is often quite inaccurate and works slowly. Mobile phones typically use a 12-button keypad.
2) *Small screen size, low resolution, and number of colors:* Small screens with short lines slow down the speed of reading. The display resolution of a PDA screen is poor: typically 240×320 or 320×320, and for mobile phones the resolution is even smaller. Current mobile devices with color displays support either 4,096 (12-bit) or 65,536 (16-bit) colors while PCs can display over 16 million (32-bit) colors.
3) *Slower CPU and smaller memory:* The processing power is behind that of a desktop computer and thus limits the ability of running multimedia applications on mobile devices. CPU may have $600+$ MHz speed, but this characteristic can be very misleading, because mobile devices run an "emulation layer," which makes application code 5–20X slower than the same code running in the native processor mode. The amount of data that can be stored in a mobile device is limited: typically, there is 64 MB RAM on a handheld, while 32 MB of it is dedicated to the file system.
4) *Lack of persistent storage:* PDAs and mobile devices can lose data if the battery power is allowed to run low for long periods. Lack of persistent storage such as hard disks is a major drawback for these devices. There is a trend to solve this problem in mobile devices by including a solid-state flash memory. Expanded memory can be provided via secure digital/SDIO/MMC memory card slots.

5) *Battery life:* The development in the performance of batteries continues to lag that of the other elements of the hardware such as processor speed and storage sizes. Most devices use rechargeable lithium polymer cells which have limitations in life cycle and levels of power provided. The restrictions in battery power limit processing and communication facilities of mobile devices [1]. Thus power consumption is a major issue with handhelds.

6) *Data connectivity:* While connectivity bandwidth in most cases is not an issue, the cost of it limits the widespread use of this technology.

Mentioned restrictions are cited very often, but mobile devices are evolving very quickly, and they become less relevant to the problem.

2.2. Educational Issues in Using Mobile Devices

m-Learning can be defined as user-centered learning supported through the usage of mobile devices. These devices are used to deliver a wide range of educational content to users without dealing with time and location restrictions associated with traditional learning methods such as attendance of classrooms, time scheduling of lectures, or connection to a specific network associated with many e-Learning activities [15]. The main advantage of m-Learning is the ability to perform training and assessment tasks using any device connected to any network. Another advantage is a learning style that is novel, attractive, interactive, and engagement supportive amongst the students [20].

The main challenge for a teacher in m-education is to provide pedagogical support to mobile students independent of time and location [25]. Since the educational content is readily available to the learner on the mobile device or can be accessed using a wireless Internet connection, the role of an educator shifts toward online collaboration and interaction with students aiming to support active learning activities (such as surfing the web for information) rather than passive assimilation of learning content.

The student's role is to actively seek for information that includes educational materials provided by an educator as well as materials available on Internet. m-Learning enhances the learning experience by supporting more frequent student–educator and student–student interactions. It enables students to participate more actively in discussions and provides the educator with better feedback on his/her topic. The studying becomes more frequent, but takes shorter periods of time. m-Learning encourages both independent and collaborative learning experiences, helps remove some formality from the learning process, helps to raise self-esteem and self confidence of a learner, engages reluctant learners, provides a material tailored to the needs of an individual learner, and raises concentration on the learning subject [2]; however, there are memorability problems related to assimilation of rapid flows of information.

The main aims of adapting learning content when migrating from traditional learning and e-Learning environments to m-Learning should be (1) to provide adaptation of learning content to the technological capabilities and constraints of the mobile devices and (2) to utilize the pedagogical advantages and mitigate disadvantages of a learning style associated with m-Learning. These aims could be implemented by refactoring the existing LOs for mobile devices, which is discussed in the following section.

3. Refactoring of Learning Objects

3.1. Concept of Refactoring in Software Engineering

In software engineering, refactoring of a program means the modification of its code in order to improve its readability, understandability, internal consistency, and clarity without changing its external behavior. Note that external behavior is understood here in terms of functionality and services delivered by a program to external users or systems, but not in terms of user interfaces, which are a representation of user interaction with a system. Refactoring can be regarded as the object-oriented equivalent of restructuring, which is defined as "the transformation from one representation form to another at the same relative abstraction level, while preserving the subject system's external behavior (functionality and semantics)" [4].

The principal goals of refactoring include increasing understandability, flexibility, and dependability, while at the same time preserving the functional behavior of the artifact [30]. Refactoring is not concerned with fixing errors or adding new functionality. Rather it is aimed at improving the understandability of the code or changing its internal structure in order to make it more maintainable. An example of a trivial refactoring is to change a variable name into something more meaningful.

Refactoring is an important activity in the software development process. Software developers often alternate between adding new functionality and refactoring source code to improve its internal consistency and clarity. As software is enhanced, modified, and adapted to new requirements during its life cycle, the code becomes more complex and drifts away from its original design, thereby lowering the quality of the software. In the context of software evolution, refactoring is used to improve the quality of the software (e.g., extensibility, modularity, reusability, complexity, maintainability, efficiency) [17].

Refactoring is also used in the context of reengineering, which is the analysis and alteration of a software system in order to implement it in the new form. In this context, refactoring is needed to convert legacy or deteriorated code into a more structured form or to migrate code to a different programming language [4]. Although refactoring is often understood as the modification of source code only, it also can be applied to any type of software artifact such as UML models or software requirements [17].

3.2. Learning Content Refactoring Techniques

When applied to learning content, refactoring may mean content cleaning (the removal of redundant and superfluous content), reformatting (improvement of content formatting using, e.g., colors, capitalization, or font style), adding of summaries at the end of separate parts of the content, adding an overview for the learners, who may not want to have in-depth explanation of the topic, insertion of headings, subheadings, or paragraph titles to attract attention and increase understandability of content, re-arrangement of content, breaking of content into smaller more manageable parts, referencing (linking to specific parts of the existing content as well as to the external material), and layering of content using bullets or tables. Note that learning content is understood here as static open source learning materials, which are described using a markup language and are available for editing.

The main characteristics of learning content refactoring are as follows:

1) Refactoring deals with the internal structure of learning content. Thus, the techniques of refactoring are applied to teaching artifacts such as learning assets.
2) Refactoring explicitly preserves the meaning of learning content and observable behavior of a LO.
3) Refactoring aims at improving learning content according to an informally expressed goal, e.g., improvement of readability, clarity, and maintainability.
4) Refactoring steps are fine grained and can be described in a catalog using a description template similar to that used by design patterns [11].

3.3. Framework of LO Refactoring

Considering the learning content refactoring techniques introduced in Section 3.2, we propose a framework for learning object refactoring (see Fig. 88.1):

(1) *Identification:* Identify the location for refactoring in the learning object.
(2) *Determination:* Determine which refactorings (selected from a catalogue of known refactorings; for an initial list of such refactorings; see Table 88.1) should be applied for the refactoring location. Determination should be based on the objectives (what we aim to achieve?) and expectations (what result we expect?).
(3) *Meaning preservation:* Ensure that refactoring does not change the meaning of learning material. In the absence of more formal guarantees, a comprehensive testing procedure should be set up to ensure that each refactoring is behavior preserving.
(4) *Application:* Apply the selected refactorings to the LO.

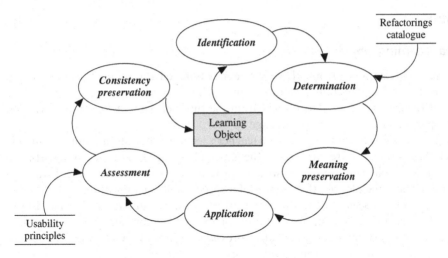

Figure 88.1. A framework of LO refactoring.

Table 88.1. Learning content refactoring techniques.

Refactoring technique	Description	Advantage
Cleaning	Removal of redundant and superfluous content	Increases clarity
Reformatting	Improvement of content formatting	Improves readability
Summarizing	Adding of summaries at the end of separate parts of the content	Improves understandability
Overviewing	Adding an overview/preview	Improves content assimilation
Breaking	Breaking of content into smaller, more manageable parts	Attracts attention, improves understandability
Headlining	Insertion of headings, subheadings, or paragraph titles	Attracts attention
Referencing	Linking to specific parts of the existing content as well as to the external material	Improves understandability
Layering	Representation of content in layers: vertically (using bullets) or horizontally (using tables)	Improves understandability

(5) *Assessment:* Assess the effect of the refactoring on the quality of the refactored LO using a LO evaluation model based on usability principles.

(6) *Consistency preservation:* Maintain consistency between refactored elements and other parts of the LO.

An important part of the refactoring process is identification of locations, where refactoring is needed, and assessment of the effects of the performed refactorings. We claim that such identification and assessment should be made based on the LO usability principles. The usability problem is especially important when new technologies (in our case, mobile technologies) and new ways to use these technologies are considered. When evaluating technical usability, the basic assumption is that it should be easy to learn to use the main functions of the system, which should be efficient and convenient in use.

Different artifacts and instruments are employed to solve the problems concerning the achievement of higher usability such as recommendations, guidelines, standards, and principles [16, 19]. Here we use the common principles for usable user interface design formulated for HCI/e-Learning domains [7].

4. Case Study

4.1. Original Learning Object

In our case study, adopted from [7], we consider LOs aimed at teaching the array-sorting algorithms. Such LOs can be used in different programming teaching courses to demonstrate the principles and effectiveness of the array-sorting algorithms within the Internet-based e-Learning environment independently from a particular programming language.

The original LO was assembled from the teacher's lecture materials and implemented in HTML and Javascript. HTML is used for presentation of the natural language description of a sorting algorithm and presentation of its implementation in a specific programming language, while Javascript is used for demonstration of the principles or effectiveness of a specific sorting algorithm.

The original LO as seen via the Internet browser is shown in Fig. 88.2a. The LO introduces the student with the description and implementation of the bubble sort algorithm and demonstrates it in action. The array for sorting is generated after pressing the button "Generate." The sorting process is demonstrated after pressing the button "Bubble sort."

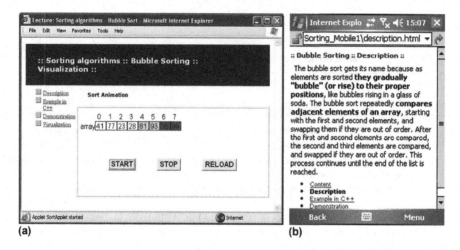

(a)   (b)

Figure 88.2. LO: **a)** original LO, **b)** LO after refactoring for m-Learning (a fragment).

4.2. Refactoring of a LO to a Mobile Device

Our aim is to perform the refactoring of the available LO to a mobile device (Pocket PC, Qtek S200, 195 MHz, RAM 64 MB, LCD 240×320, 65536 col.). When the LO was ported to the mobile device due to the limitations of the mobile device, the interface of the LO had many shortcomings such as low visibility, therefore, though the UI was designed following the common HCI/e-Learning domain principles [7], it required further adaptation and modification.

During adaptation we considered the following constraints of the mobile devices: limited input facilities, small screen size, low resolution and number of colors, and slower CPU and small memory. We apply the refactoring techniques and the learning object refactoring framework described in Section 2. The refactorings applied to the LO are described in Table 88.2. The refactored LO as seen via the display of Pocket PC is shown in Fig. 88.2b.

All refactorings of the LO were made considering small screen size only. This is impacted by the nature of our example LO, because it is aimed for presentation of learning information rather than for interactive activities. Limited input capabilities in this case were not as important, because this LO required no large amount of input data.

Table 88.2. Refactorings of the learning object.

Modification	Refactoring technique
Tables were eliminated and content was represented in one column. The main purpose is to eliminate horizontal scrolling. Now elements are layered vertically instead of horizontally	Layering
Site structure was renewed. Title page with content was made as a separated element, which shows an overall structure of the LO	Headlining
Scrolling from title page was eliminated. Direct access is realized as follows: each function (part) is accessed by one link (with one click)	Referencing
The overall amount of material on one page was reduced. Unnecessary elements used for better appearance were eliminated	Cleaning
Font size was reduced. Students remain able to modify the size of the LO elements using browser capabilities	Reformatting
Color scheme was modified, in order to meet requirements to better use in poor visibility environments	Reformatting
Some text labels (titles of pages) were shortened	Cleaning
Key phrases were accentuated in bold, in order to gain better readability	Reformatting
The smaller version of the link list is included in every page. It also concerns that users usually scroll only down but not up	Overviewing

5. Open Research Issues in LO Refactoring

LO refactoring is still a novel research direction in e-Learning. Therefore, there are many open research problems that are required to be solved:

1) Formal description of refactorings in e-Learning domain: what formal language/notation should be used?
2) Definition of relationships between refactorings: how to manage dependencies between LO refactorings? Detection of dependencies is important for ensuring that all dependent refactorings are applied where they are needed.
3) Formal definition of the concept of "behavior" in the e-Learning domain. The definition of refactoring is based on the concept of the external behavior, which states that "for the same input, we should obtain exactly the same output." The external behavior is not the same as the user interface, because the user interface only provides a representation form (textual, graphical, audio/video, etc.) for an interaction between a user and a system. It is not always clear what are the inputs and outputs of a LO. This implies that we need a more precise definition of LO behavior that may or may not be preserved by refactoring, depending on specific concerns of an educator or a learner.
4) Development of an ontology of LO refactorings. There are many primitive refactorings as well as a number of composite refactorings. We need to define a hierarchy of such refactorings and a sequence of their application based on their effect on the quality of a LO.
5) Development of a comprehensive LO testing methodology, which provides for management of LO behavior consistency during refactoring. Since we cannot test a LO after every refactoring, we need to define levels of LO change after which a testing of a LO should be performed.
6) Definition of the quantitative LO quality metrics to allow evaluating the effect of the application of refactorings on the LO quality. Such quality metrics can be based on the quality attributes used for evaluating software quality (such as ease of use, robustness, adaptability, reusability, compatibility, performance, portability, and understandability) as well as on the learning-oriented quality attributes of a LO.
7) Evaluation of the educational value of the performed LO refactorings. It is hard to prove that the use of any technology-based facility really improves the quality of learning. Due to complicated nature of the education domain there and its social implications (learning is a social process) usually various forms of questionnaires are used to assess student satisfaction and learning effectiveness.

6. Conclusion and Future Work

In this chapter, we have analyzed the problem of refactoring of learning objects (LOs). We have identified the following learning content refactoring techniques (refactorings): cleaning, reformatting, summarizing, overviewing, breaking, headlining, referencing, and layering. The refactorings can be applied to LOs independently or collectively following the proposed learning object refactoring framework, which includes six major steps: identification, determination, meaning preservation, application, assessment, and consistency preservation. The framework is based on the usability principles, formulated in the HCI and e-Learning domains. The proposed LO refactoring framework allows to increase adaptability and usability of LOs for m-Learning.

Future work will focus on the open research problems in LO refactoring: formal description of refactorings, definition of relationships between refactorings, development of ontology of LO refactorings, and definition of quantitative metrics for evaluation of LO refactorings.

References

1. Anderson, P. (2005) Mobile and PDA Technologies: Looking around the corner. *JISC Technology and Standards Watch*. JISC.
2. Attewell, J. (2005) From Research and Development to Mobile Learning: Tools for Education and Training Providers and their Learners. In *Proc. of 4th World Conf. on mLearning (mLearn 2005)*, Cape Town, South Africa.
3. Barre, V., Chaquet, C. and El-Kechaï, H. (2005) Re-engineering of collaborative e-Learning systems: evaluation of system, collaboration and acquired knowledge qualities. In *Proc. of the 12th Artificial Intelligence in Education AIED, Workshop "Usage Analysis in Learning Systems"*, 18–20 July 2005, Amsterdam, The Netherlands, pp. 9–16. IOS Press, Amsterdam.
4. Chikofsky, E.J. and Cross, J.H. (1990) Reverse Engineering and Design Recovery: A Taxonomy. *IEEE Software* 7 (1), pp. 13–17.
5. Choquet, C. and Corbière, A. (2006) Reengineering Framework for Systems in Education. *Educational Technology and Society* 9 (4), pp. 228–241.
6. Cruz, D.M., de Moraes, M. and Barcia, R.M. (1998) Tele-Learning and Distance Learning Re-Engineering Process. In *Int. Conf. on Engineering Education (ICEE 98)*, Rio de Janeiro, Brazil, August 17–20, 1998.
7. Damaševičius, R. & Tankelevičienė, L. (2008a) Merging HCI and e-Learning Domain Oriented Design Principles for Developing User Interfaces for Mobile Devices. In *Proc. of Int. Conf. on Innovations in Learning for Future e-Learning*, March 27–29, 2008, Istanbul, Turkey, pp. 155–166.
8. Damaševičius, R. and Tankelevičienė, L. (2008b) Learning Object Re-engineering Based on Principles for Usable User Interface Design. In *Proc. of 10th Int. Conf. on Enterprise Information Systems (ICEIS 2008)*, Vol. HCI, June 12–16, 2008, Barcelona, Spain, pp. 124–129.
9. Ferguson, J.D., McGettrick, A.D., Wilson, J. and Weir, G.R.S. (2002) Reengineering for Quality On-Line. In *Proc. of Computers and Advanced Technology in Education (CATE 2002)*, May 20–22, 2002, Cancun, Mexico.
10. Fowler, M. (1999) *Refactoring: Improving the Design of Existing Code*. Addison Wesley, Reading, MA.
11. Gamma, E., Helm, R., Johnson, R. and Vlissides, J.M. (1994) *Design Patterns: Elements of Reusable Object-Oriented Software*. Addison-Wesley Professional, Reading, MA.
12. Im, J.H. (2008) Educational Reengineering For E-Education. In *Proc. of College Teaching and Learning (TLC) Conference and International Applied Business Research (IABR) Conference*, March 17–20, 2008, San Juan, Puerto Rico, USA.
13. Kadirire, J. (2006) Learning with Mobile Devices – A Microportal Design Experience. *Recent Research Developments in Learning Technologies* 2, pp. 792–797.
14. Khan, B.H. (2005) *Managing e-Learning: Design, Delivery, Implementation and Evaluation*. Information Science Publishing, Hershey, PA.
15. Marcos, L., Hilera, J.R., Gutiérrez, J.A., Pagés, C. and Martínez, J.J. (2006) Implementing Learning Objects Repositories for Mobile Devices. In *Proc. of First Int. Conf. on Ubiquitous Computing (ICUC)*, June 7–9, 2006, Alcalá de Henares, Spain, pp. 31–38.
16. Mariage, C., Vanderdonckt, J. and Pribeanu, C. (2004) State of the Art of Web Usability Guidelines. In Proctor, R. and Vu, K. (eds.), *The Handbook of Human Factors in Web Design*. Lawrence Erlbaum Associates, Mahwah, NJ.
17. Mens, T. (2004) A Survey of Software Refactoring. *IEEE Transactions on Software Engineering* 30 (2), pp. 126–139.
18. Mohan, P. (2007) Using m-Learning Technologies to support tertiary-level education in the Caribbean. In *Proc. of CADE/ACED Int. Conf.*, Winnipeg, Canada, May 12–16, 2007.
19. Nokelainen, P. (2004) Conceptual Definition of the Technical and Pedagogical Usability Criteria for Digital Learning Material. In *Proc. of World Conf. on Educational Multimedia, Hypermedia and Telecommunications (EDMEDIA 2004)*, pp. 4249–4254.
20. Nyíri, K. (2002) Towards a Philosophy of M-Learning. In *Proc. of IEEE Int. Workshop on Wireless and Mobile Technologies in Education WMTE'02*, Växjö, Sweden, pp. 121–124.

21. Pankratius, V. & Vossen, G. (2005) Reengineering of educational material: a systematic approach. *International Journal of Knowledge and Learning (IJKL)* 1 (3), pp. 229–248.

22. Piskurich, G.M. (2003) *The AMA Handbook of e-Learning: Effective Design, Implementation, and Technology Solutions.* AMACOM, New York.

23. Polsani, R.P. (2003) Use and Abuse of Reusable Learning Objects. *Journal of Digital Information* 3 (4), pp. 164.

24. Ponta, D. and Da Bormida, G. (1996) Re-engineering a computer-based learning course in digital electronics for flexibility, re-use and network delivery. In *Proc. of Frontiers in Education Conference (FIE'96),* November 6–9, 2006, Vol. 3, pp. 1203–1207.

25. Quinn, C. (2000) *M-Learning. Mobile, Wireless, In-Your-Pocket Learning.* Linezine.

26. Randriamalaka, N., Iksal, S. and Choquet, C. (2007) Indicators' Elicitation Process for Re-Engineering of Learning Scenario: Tracks Approach Based on Usage Tracking Language. In *Proc. of the 7th IEEE Int. Conf. on Advanced Learning Technologies, ICALT 2007,* July 18–20, 2007, Niigata, Japan, 492–496.

27. Rodriguez, O., Chen, S. and Shang, Y. (2003). Open Learning Objects: The Case for Inner Metadata. *The Journal of Computing in Small Colleges,* 18 (4), pp. 56–64.

28. Scalera, M., Convertini, V.N., Marengo, A., Marengo, V. and Serra A. (2007) Re-Engineering of a Flash Based Application for Mobile Learning. In *Proc. of the 2007 Computer Science and IT Education Conference,* November 16–18, 2007, Mauritius, pp. 635–647.

29. Wiley, D.A. (2000) *Learning Object Design and Sequencing Theory.* PhD Thesis, Brigham Young University.

30. Wohlfarth, S. and Riebisch, M. (2006) Evaluating Alternatives for Architecture-Oriented Refactoring. In *Proc. of 13th Int. Conf. and Workshop on the Engineering of Computer Based Systems (ECBS06),* Potsdam, Germany, March 2006, pp. 73–79.

31. Zouaq, A., Nkambou, R. and Frasson, C. (2007) Using a Competence Model to Aggregate Learning Knowledge Objects. In *Proc. of 7th IEEE Conf. on Advanced Learning Technologies (ICALT 2007),* July 18–20, 2007, Niigata, Japan, pp. 836–840.

89

Early Orientation Toward Future Profession: A Case Study of Introduction into Information Systems Development for the First-Year Students

Alla Anohina, Janis Grundspenkis and Evita Nikitenko

Abstract

The chapter describes an experience of the Institute of Applied Computer Systems of Riga Technical University in the implementation of a business game related to the information system development project within the course "Introduction to study area" for the first-year bachelor-level students. The conception of the business game and its implementation scenario, as well as results of processing of students' questionnaires evaluating organization of the game, and changes in students' knowledge about the information system development are discussed.

Keywords Information system development · Project · Business game · Introduction to study area

1. Introduction

At the end of the 20th century many countries, including Latvia, entered the so-called information era and started to develop knowledge societies which require well-educated and high-skilled workforce especially in engineering. At the same time due to permanently low birth rate the number of graduates from secondary schools starts to decrease. Moreover, one can notice serious changes in priorities of those who are entering universities. There are more and more young people all over the world who prefer to study languages, philosophy, sociology, psychology, or law, instead of engineering and natural science disciplines demanded by industry. In this situation all interested parties (governments, industry, universities, etc.) must dedicate much more efforts to motivate schools' graduates to choose curricula which refer to engineering and natural studies. In [1] it is pointed out that despite an economic downturn information technology positions represent the fastest growing job segment and, as a result, the number of qualified graduates produced by computing curricula may be insufficient to meet increasing industry demands.

Several years ago at Riga Technical University (RTU), inter alia on the Faculty of Computer Science and Information Technology (FCSIT), a new compulsory study course "Introduction to study area" was introduced for freshmen with the purpose to acquaint them with specific features of studies in the university and to show perspectives of the chosen profession in the labor market. According to [2] one of the keys to successfully recruit undergraduates into information systems programs is the introductory information systems course for which an instructor(s) and a content should be carefully chosen. However, the main problem of FCSIT all these years was related exactly to the selection of the course content and methods of

Alla Anohina, Janis Grundspenkis and Evita Nikitenko • Department of Systems Theory and Design, Riga Technical University, Riga, Latvia.

G.A. Papadopoulos et al. (eds.), *Information Systems Development*, DOI 10.1007/b137171_89,

teaching. Different approaches were used which, unfortunately, did not give results for reaching the intentional goals of the course.

During the year 2007 a new initiative was carried out by the Institute of Applied Computer Systems (IACS) which is an integral part of FCSIT. The initiative is based on the belief that it is possible to motivate students to pursue the chosen degree and to master the speciality by showing as early as possible the most significant roles in real information system development projects and stressing on wide opportunities for further students' professional activities. In this case students can focus on their interested job position already at the early stage of the study process and, thus, purposefully direct their learning towards, the mastering of such skills and knowledge which are necessary for the chosen job. Moreover, they receive understanding of the organization of the pedagogical process within the university, namely, why specific courses are included in the curriculum, how different activities contribute to their knowledge and skills, etc. One of the rational ways how to put this idea into practice is to organize a business game in which the information system development project is implemented. It gives students an opportunity to acquire necessary knowledge at the theoretical level, as well as to master needed skills at the practical level.

The chapter describes an experience of IACS in the implementation of the business game related to the information system development project within the course "Introduction to study area" for the first-year bachelor-level students. Section 2 gives the general information about the mentioned course. Section 3 shares the institute's experience in teaching of the course. The conception of the business game is presented in Section 4. Section 5 describes the scenario of the business game implemented in the year 2007. Results of processing of students' questionnaires are discussed in Section 6. The last section presents conclusions.

2. Context

One of the important purposes of the extension of curricula at RTU by the compulsory study course "Introduction to study area" was an effort to decrease the percentage of dropouts for the first-year students which is around 25% in average. Such a quite high percentage of dropouts can be explained by some specific challenges for schools' graduates. Students are coming from different secondary schools located in different parts of the country. Frequently they were the best in their class and habituated to an individual attitude and a regular knowledge assessment. At the university they unexpectedly meet a rather different style of teaching and learning. Due to the large number of first-year students it is impossible to practice an individual approach to each student. Young people do not know each other and frequently feel lonely, but in case of difficulties they feel even helpless. Another important factor is that even those who chose their curriculum knowingly have haziest notion of their future profession. Thus, the mentioned challenges very often decrease students' motivation to continue the study process. So, offering the course "Introduction to study area" administration of RTU strongly believed that the course will facilitate early adaptation of students to university requirements, will add confidence to study and, as a consequence, will rise their motivation to pursue the chosen degree.

The mentioned course is taught in the autumn semester in the first year of the bachelor studies at all faculties. FCSIT consists of three institutes offering different curricula (Fig. 89.1): a study program "Computer Systems" belongs to IACS, a curriculum "Information Technology" is implemented by the Institute of Information Technology, and a study program "Automation and Computer Engineering" is offered by the Institute of Computer-Aided Control, Automation and Computer Engineering. Generally, the purpose of the course "Introduction to study area" is to acquaint students with the faculty's structure, to give general knowledge about the implementation and basic requirements of the study process, to present information about pedagogical and scientific activities within the faculty, and to show perspectives of the chosen profession in the labor market. Eight lectures compose the course. The first three lectures are delivered to all students (in average 350 per year) of FCSIT. During the first two lectures students are introduced into the history and structure of the faculty, informed about the library, and pedagogical and scientific activities. The third lecture is devoted to the implementation and requirements of the study process, as well as activities of student self-government. In some cases the lecture is attended by representatives from industry who give information about their companies and student possibilities to work there. After the third lecture all students are divided in sub-groups according to the chosen institute. Each institute is free to implement its own strategy for the remaining five lectures in the course.

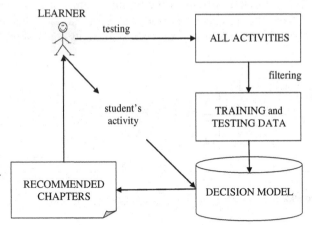

Figure 89.1. The structure of the Faculty of Computer Science and Information Technology.

3. Previous Experience

The curriculum "Computer Systems" [3] offered by IACS has the $3 + 2 + 3$ scheme, i.e., 3 year bachelor, 2 year master, and 3 year doctoral studies. Its objective is to provide academic education in computer science and to prepare highly qualified professionals in the fields of systems analysis, software engineering, design of databases, and information systems with fundamental knowledge based on engineering science, which includes mathematics, physics, chemistry, electrical engineering, and electronics [4]. IACS has tried the following approaches in the implementation of the course "Introduction to study area":

- The general information about the institute (the history of foundation, the director and staff, the location, the offered curriculum, and departments) was given to students at the first lecture. After that, representatives of separate departments presented research directions, teachers, and courses of their department.
- All lectures were devoted only to IACS without presenting separate departments. During these lectures the following information was given to students: the history of the institute, the offered curriculum, teachers, available computer classes and laboratories, the software development process and possible job positions in this area, offered courses and their correspondence to the stages of the software development process, directions of scientific research within the institute, and the process of the development of the bachelor thesis.

However, in both described cases the following problems were revealed: students are not motivated to master this course, students do not keep the discipline, and it is very difficult for teachers to read lectures and to keep students' attention. The main reasons were twofold. Firstly, very often the lectures were nothing more than the advertising of the departments and/or the institute. Secondly, the lectures were conducted speaking about things (magistracy, doctoral studies, scientific activities, software life cycle, etc.) which are not understandable for the first-year students.

The mentioned problems led to the development of a new conception for the study course "Introduction to study area" by the course-organizing group which includes three young researchers, seven Ph.D. students, one master student in the field of computer science, and one master student in the field of pedagogy in order to ensure correspondence of the developed conception to pedagogical principles. The business game related to the implementation of the information system development project underlies the conception which is described in the next section.

4. Conception

Taking into account that the first-year students do not have knowledge about the information system development process the most simple and widely known information system life cycle model, namely the waterfall model (Fig. 89.2), is chosen as a basis of the business game. Such stages as implementation and maintenance are excluded from the practical, but not the theoretical part of the course, because of time limits. The following roles are chosen: a project leader, a system analyst, a designer, a tester, and a technical writer.

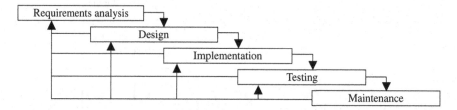

Figure 89.2. The waterfall model of the information system development process.

All students are divided into groups of 10–12 students. Each group forms a team of project developers. The supervisor is appointed to each team from the course-organizing group. Responsibilities of the supervisor are the following:

- to participate in all five lectures;
- to study all documents which will be used during the lecture before the beginning of each lecture in order to be able to answer students' questions and to give necessary explanations;
- to distribute handouts to team's participants and to introduce them to tasks of the lecture when a new stage of the development process starts;
- to encourage students' activity, to answer questions, to give explanations, to provide help during the execution of tasks, to solve problems and conflicts, to keep discipline, to direct activities of students to the achievement of the goal;
- to sign the agreement with the students' team; the agreement is introduced in order to make the project more realistic; and
- to play the role of the client by answering students' questions during the stage of the requirements analysis.

A project leader is chosen from students of a team. The project leader of the team is responsible for the following:

- to convince that all participants of the team have studied the agreement, to give a project's title, and to sign the agreement with the supervisor; and
- to organize and supervise activities of the team, to distribute tasks (if necessary), to keep discipline, and to follow the involvement of each participant into the project development.

Each team receives its own description of a system for development. After that the agreement between the project leader and the supervisor, which concurrently plays the role of the client, is signed.

The stage of requirements analysis is carried out on the basis of students' questions. Members of a particular team receive a template of the interview protocol (Fig. 89.3). On the basis of the mentioned protocol and previously given description of the system students must prepare questions in order to conduct an interview with the client. Each team's member asks the prepared questions and fixes all answers (given both on his/her questions and on other participants' questions) in the template of the interview protocol. Further, on the basis of the interview protocols, each team must prepare a requirements specification, using a special template (Fig. 89.4). Thus all students play the role of the system analyst.

Interview protocol

Name of the system _____

Time _____

Interviewer_____

Client _____

1. Purpose of the system

2. External environment of the system

3. System's users

4. Functional requirements

No	Name	Description	Input	Output	User
1					
2					
3					
...					

5. Non-functional requirements

Figure 89.3. The template for the interview protocol.

Requirements specification

1. INTRODUCTION

1.1. Name of the system

1.2. Purpose of the system

1.3. Users of the system

2. GENERAL DESCRIPTION

3. SPECIFIC REQUIREMENTS

3.1. Functional requirements
- Name of the function
- Goal
- Input
- Processing
- Output

3.2. Non-functional requirements

Figure 89.4. The template for the requirements specification.

When the requirements specification is finished, the team continues with the design stage. In this stage the students' task is to draw interface windows of the system on the basis of the previously defined requirements and to show transitions between windows, as well as to describe possible erroneous situations. Thus all students play the role of the designer.

In the testing stage each team verifies the drawn windows against the described requirements. Verification results must be fixed in a template of the testing protocol (Fig. 89.5). Thus students play the role of the tester.

Testing protocol

Requirement	Conformity assessment	Comments
...		

Figure 89.5. The template for the testing protocol.

Preparing of the project documents allows students to play the role of the technical writer.

Each stage is accompanied by reading of handouts about the stage, its documents, and roles, and by the demonstration of video interviews with 2–3 representatives of the corresponding role.

The following resources were developed for the implementation of the strategy: handouts, working documents, video interviews, and an advertising video clip of IACS. The purpose of the handouts is to give students basic theoretical information about the development stages of an information system project. They include the following descriptions:

- the development stages: an information system development process, a requirements analysis, a design stage, an implementation stage, and a testing stage;
- documents for the development stages: a project agreement, a requirements specification, a design document, and a testing document;
- roles within the project: a project leader, a technical writer, a system analyst, a designer, a programmer, and a tester.

The working documents include

- description of systems for the development: a library management system, a computer class visitors management system, a cinema ticket reservation system, a retail department management system, a wholesale department management system, and a warehouse management system;
- tasks for each lecture; and
- document templates: the project agreement, the interview protocol, the requirements specification, and the testing protocol.

Two or three short videos of interviews with former graduates of IACS who work on a job position considered in the current stage were prepared for each stage of the project. The interviews contained the information on how the person got the job, what are his/her responsibilities, what knowledge and skills are important for the job, and what is contribution of the education acquired in IACS into the job performance.

The goal of the advertising clip of IACS is to give information about the institute and its departments, showing the main research directions and aspects of the pedagogical process.

5. Implementation of the Conception

The previously described conception was realized during five lectures within the course "Introduction to study area" in the year 2007. Totally 12 teams participated in the offered business game. The general scenario is given in Table 89.1.

Some conditions were defined in relation to the game: all students of a particular team must contribute to all activities of the project and the spirit of the competition must be maintained among

Table 89.1. The scenario of the business game.

Activities	Necessary resources	Outcomes
First lecture		
Informing students about the organization of lectures	Short presentation	
Formation of teams		
Reading of handouts	Handouts about the information system development process and the role of the project leader	
Demonstration of interviews with project leaders	Video recorded interviews	
Selection of the project leader of each team		
Delivery of the description of the system and its reading by students	Descriptions of the systems	
Reading of handouts	Handouts about the project agreement	
Signing of the agreement between the project leader and the supervisor	Template of the agreement	Project agreement
Second lecture		
Reading of handouts	Handouts about the stage of requirements analysis, the roles of the system analyst and the technical writer, the requirements specification, and the content of the lecture	
Demonstration of interviews with system analysts and technical writers	Video recorded interviews	
Interviewing of clients	Template of the interview protocol	Interview protocols
Development of the requirements specification	Template of the requirements specification	Requirements specification
Third lecture		
Reading of handouts	Handouts about the design stage, the role of the designer, the design document, the implementation stage, the role of the programmer, and the content of the lecture	
Demonstration of interviews with designers and programmers	Video recorded interviews	
Drawing of windows	Paper, pencils	System's windows
Fourth lecture		
Reading of handouts	Handouts about the testing stage, the role of the tester, the testing documentation, and the content of the lecture	
Demonstration of interviews with testers	Video-recorded interviews	
Testing	Template of the testing protocol	Testing protocol
Discussion of the results between two teams who have the description of the same system		
Fifth lecture		
Comments of the supervisors		
Demonstration of the video clip of the institute	Video clip of the institute	
Questioning of students	Questionnaires	Questionnaires
Awarding of the best teams	Awards	

teams in order their activities would be directed toward an achievement of the best possible result. The first condition was achieved by the double control both from the leader of the team and from the supervisor. In order to maintain the spirit of the competition three additional activities were included in the scenario:

- Discussion of results between two teams which have the description of the same system. As was mentioned in Section 4 six different system descriptions were developed. So there were two teams for each system. At the end of the fourth lecture both teams compared their results by inspecting the developed documents and by discussing the overall process of the development. In this way students made their own conclusions about missing things and drawbacks of the development process of their team.

- Awarding of the best three teams at the last lecture. The best three teams were chosen by the course-organizing group taking into account two things: evaluation of each team by the team's supervisor and evaluation of results of each team by other members of the course-organizing group. The team's supervisor evaluated his/her team by using the scale from 1 (worse) to 3 (best) and by considering the following criteria: the activity level of the project leader, the organizational level of the interview, the degree of detailed elaboration of interview protocols, the requirements specification and system's windows, and the completeness of the testing protocols. After the evaluation given by supervisors teams with maximum points were selected and their results, namely, interview protocols, the requirements specification, system's windows and the testing protocol were examining by each of other supervisors using their own subjective criteria. The voting process allowed the selection of the three best teams.

- Comments of supervisors. Each supervisor characterized his/her team at the beginning of the fifth lecture by pointing out the most essential drawbacks of the development process.

6. Evaluation Results

At the end of the last lecture a questionnaire was offered to students. Its purpose was to evaluate organization of lectures, supervisors' work, and changes in students' knowledge about the information system development process. The questionnaire had 16 questions. Totally 87 questionnaires were processed. Let us consider some of students' answers.

Fig. 89.6 shows that half the students had only fragmentary knowledge about the information system development process before the lectures, but one-third did not have any knowledge about the mentioned process.

Students were asked to evaluate activities offered in the business game by taking into account two aspects: whether an activity was interesting and whether it was useful. For this purpose they used a 5-point scale, where 5 is the highest value and 1 is the lowest value. Figure 89.7 demonstrates the obtained results. We can conclude that the most interesting activities were drawing of system's windows and interviewing of the client, but the most useful ones were development of the requirements specification, interviewing of the client, and signing of the agreement.

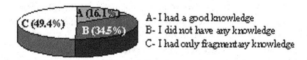

A- I had a good knowledge
B- I did not have any knowledge
C- I had only fragmentary knowledge

Figure 89.6. Distribution of students' answers on the question "What was your level of knowledge about the information system development process before the lectures".

Figure 89.8 displays how well students understood the essence of each stage of the information system development process. Each stage is evaluated using the same 5-point scale. It is possible to conclude that in general the preliminary work done by the course-organizing group and materials and supervisors' explanations during lectures allowed for the greatest part of students to understand the design and testing stages. Exception is the requirements analysis stages which one-third of students evaluated as hardly understandable. This should be taken into account for the next study year.

Students' evaluation of the experience obtained during the lectures is shown in Fig. 89.9. These results are especially pleasing for the course-organizing group showing that the main goal of the course is achieved. Students get valuable experience which as we hope more strongly will motivate them to continue their studies.

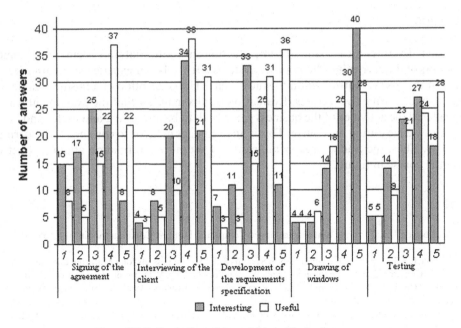

Figure 89.7. Evaluation of the activities of the business game.

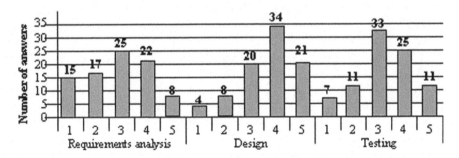

Figure 89.8. Evaluation of the comprehensibility of stages.

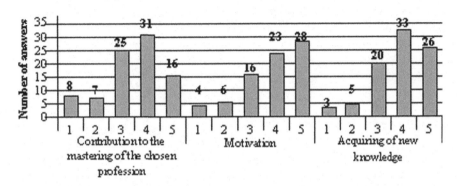

Figure 89.9. Students' evaluation of the experience obtained during the lectures.

7. Conclusions

The chapter describes a case study of introduction into information systems development for the first-year students of the curriculum "Computer Systems." It is a 1-year experience got after reorganization of the content of the course "Introduction to study area." The conception of a business game was worked out and implemented during five lectures. Evaluation results manifest that the experiment was successful. Students considered the activities of the business game both to be interesting and useful and answered that they got new knowledge during the course. This is an argument in favor to continue the experiment for the next year as well. Thus, the course-organizing team will get more information about student wishes and may improve the course in future.

References

1. Akbulut, A.Y., Looney, C.L. Inspiring Students to Pursue Computing Degrees. Communications of the ACM, Vol. 50, No. 10, 2007, pp. 67–71.
2. George, J.F, Valacich, J.S., Valor, J. Does Information Systems Still Matter? Lessons for a Maturing Discipline. Proceeding of the 25th International Conference on Information Systems, Washington, DC, USA, December 12–15, 2004, pp. 1039–1048.
3. Study Programme "Computer Systems" (in Latvian). Riga Technical University. Available online at: https://info.rtu.lv/rtupub/prg?ukNoteikId = 1268.
4. Study Programme "Computer Systems (academic studies)": self-evaluation report (in Latvian). Riga Technical University. Available online at: http://www.cs.rtu.lv/ldi/files/pasnovert jumi/Pasnz06a.pdf.

90

Embedding Knowledge Management into Business Logic of E-learning Platform for Obtaining Adaptivity

Dumitru Dan Burdescu, Marian Cristian Mihaescu and Bogdan Logofatu

Abstract

Obtaining adaptivity is one of the main concerns in current e-Learning development. This chapter proposes a methodology for obtaining adaptivity by embedding knowledge management into the business logic of the e-Learning platform. Naïve Bayes classifier is used as machine learning algorithm for obtaining the resources that need to be further accessed by learners. The analysis is accomplished on a discipline that is well structured according to a concept map.

Keywords Knowledge management · e-Learning · Concept maps

1. Introduction

Personalized content delivery as a goal for improving learner's proficiency represents one of the most important goals of e-Learning systems. We consider that learner's activities represent very important data and may be successfully used in estimating preferences and learning styles. The overall analysis process will finally give advice regarding the resources that need to be accessed and studied.

Every e-Learning platform has implemented a mechanism for assessing the quantity of accumulated knowledge for a certain discipline. A problem that frequently arises is that the system in place may not be fair regarding the ordering of learners according to accumulated knowledge. Usually, there are situations when the distributions of grades are not normal, such that many learners are clustered although there are differences regarding their accumulated knowledge.

The evaluation environment is represented by the setup put in place within an e-Learning platform for assessment of learners. The setup consists of course materials and test quizzes that are set up by course managers. Learner's activities are obtained by specific methods embedded in our e-Learning platform, called Tesys [1]. The main goal of the application is to give students the possibility to download course materials, take tests or sustain final examinations, and communicate with all involved parties. To accomplish this, four different roles were defined for the platform: sysadmin, secretary, professor, and student.

Concept maps are a result of Novak and Gowin's [2] research in human learning and knowledge construction. Novak [3] proposed that the primary elements of knowledge are concepts, and relationships between concepts are propositions. Novak [4] defined concepts as "perceived regularities in events or objects, or records of events or objects, designated by a label." Propositions consist of two or more concept labels connected by a linking relationship that forms a semantic unit. Concept maps are a graphical two-dimensional display of concepts (usually represented within boxes or circles), connected by directed arcs

Dumitru Dan Burdescu and Marian Cristian Mihaescu · Department of Software Engineering, University of Craiova, Craiova, Romania. **Bogdan Logofatu** · CREDIS Department, University of Bucharest, Bucharest, Romania.

G.A. Papadopoulos et al. (eds.), *Information Systems Development*, DOI 10.1007/b137171_90,

encoding brief relationships (linking phrases) between pairs of concepts forming propositions. The simplest concept map consists of two nodes connected by an arc representing a simple sentence such as "flower is red", but they can also become quite intricate.

Naïve Bayes is one of the most effective and efficient classification algorithms. In classification learning problems, a learner attempts to construct a classifier from a given set of training examples with class labels. Assume that $A_1, A_2, \ldots, A_n$ are n attributes. An instance E is represented by a vector $(a_1; a_2; \ldots; a_n)$, where a_i is the value of A_i. Let C represent the class variable, which takes two values: P (the positive class) or N (the negative class). We use c to represent the value that C takes. A Naïve Bayesian classifier, or simply Naïve Bayes, is defined as

$$C_{NB}(E) = \text{argmax } p(c) \prod_{i=1}^{n} p(a_i \mid c)$$

Because the values of $p(a_i|c)$ can be estimated from the training examples, Naïve Bayes is easy to construct. It is also, however, surprisingly effective [5].

Naïve Bayes is based on the conditional independence assumption that all attributes are independent given the value of the class variable. It is obvious that the conditional independence assumption is rarely true in reality. Indeed, Naïve Bayes is found to work poorly for regression problems [6] and produces poor probability estimates [7].

The concept that needs the attention of learner is returned by the classifier according to the learner's performed activity. The activity is represented by the number of answers to questions regarding that concept, the average result of answered questions, and the final result at the discipline. Each filtered concept is classified as "displayed" or "not displayed." The values of each feature will be defined.

The second outcome of the chapter is represented by an analysis procedure that has as input data representing the performed activities by learners. As learning algorithm Naïve Bayes classifier was employed [8]. The classifier will predict the concepts that the learner needs to access and study for improving his proficiency regarding the studied subject.

2. Methods and Materials

The next paragraphs present the Tesys e-Learning platform and some things about concept maps. The process of data filtering is also presented and the way recommendations are obtained.

2.1. Tesys e-Learning Platform

The main goal of the platform is to give students the possibility to download course materials, take tests or sustain final examinations, and communicate with all involved parties. To accomplish this, four different roles were defined for the platform: sysadmin, secretary, professor, and student.

The main task of sysadmin users is to manage secretaries. A sysadmin user may add or delete secretaries, or change their password. He may also view the actions performed by all other users of the platform. All actions performed by users are logged. In this way the sysadmin may check the activity that takes place on the application. The logging facility has some benefits. An audit may be performed for the application with the logs as witness. Security breaches may also be discovered.

Secretary users manage sections, professors, disciplines, and students. On any of these a secretary may perform actions like add, delete, or update.

These actions will finally set up the application such that professors and students may use it. As conclusion, the secretary manages a list of sections, a list of professors, and a list of students. Each discipline is assigned to a section and has as attributes a name, a short name, the year of study and semester when it is studied, and the list of professors that teach the discipline which may be a maximum of three. A student may be enrolled to one or more sections.

Tesys application offers students the possibility to download course materials, take tests and exams, and communicate with other involved parties like professors and secretaries.

Students may download only course materials for the disciplines that belong to sections where they are enrolled. They can take tests and exams with constraints that were set up by the secretary through the year structure facility.

Students have access to personal data and can modify it as needed. A feedback form is also available. It is composed of questions that check aspects regarding the usability, efficiency, and productivity of the application with respect to the student's needs.

2.2. Concept Maps

Concept mapping may be used as a tool for understanding, collaborating, validating, and integrating curriculum content that is designed to develop specific competencies. Concept mapping, a tool originally developed to facilitate student learning by organizing key and supporting concepts into visual frameworks, can also facilitate communication among faculty and administrators about curricular structures, complex cognitive frameworks, and competency-based learning outcomes. To validate the relationships among the competencies articulated by specialized accrediting agencies, certification boards, and professional associations, faculty may find the concept mapping tool beneficial in illustrating relationships among, approaches to, and compliance with competencies [9].

According to this approach, the responsibility for failure at school was to be attributed exclusively to the innate (and, therefore, unalterable) intellectual capacities of the pupil. The learning/ teaching process was, then, looked upon in a simplistic, linear way: the teacher transmits (and is the repository of) knowledge, while the learner is required to comply with the teacher and store the ideas being imparted [10].

Usage of concept maps may be very useful for students when starting to learn about a subject. The concept map may bring valuable general overlook of the subject for the whole period of study. It may be advisable at the very first meeting of students with the subject to include a concept map of the subject.

2.3. Data Filtering

The decision model helps to determine whether a given concept is appropriate to be displayed to the learner as a recommendation for study. The obtained Bayes classifier and its behavior are quite similar to a content-based recommender system. A recommender system tries to present to the user the information items he/she is interested in. To do this the user's profile is compared to some reference characteristics. These characteristics may be from the information item (the content-based approach) or the user's social environment (the collaborative filtering approach). Our approach is close to the latter approach.

The information about the concept and the user's activity are presented to the classifier as input, having as output a probability that represents the appropriateness of the concept for this student (or how interesting the item is for this user). Building the initial model needs the authors to specify that match the learner's activity with the concept and overall result in order to determine how necessary is more study to the concept in discussion.

The training and testing data that are used for building the model are represented by instances. Each instance represents the activity of a learner regarding a concept. The structure of an instance is

instance(conceptId, noOfTests, avgTests, finalResult, recomend)

The *conceptId* feature represents the concept for which the other features are valid. This is a numeric field. The *noOfTests* feature represents the number of tests that were submitted by the learner regarding the *conceptId* concept. The *avgTests* feature represents the average grade of tests that were submitted by the learner from the *conceptId* concept. The *finalResult* feature represents the grade obtained by the learner at the discipline to which *conceptId* belongs. The *recommend* feature represents the recommendation made by course manager. The result set of available concepts will be partitioned into these two classes. For Naïve Bayes algorithm these are the values of the target function.

2.4. Obtaining Recommendations

Obtaining recommendations is the last step of the analysis process. Once the model has been obtained and its quality has been acknowledged the effective process of obtaining recommendations may run.

The acknowledgement of the quality of model is done by specifying thresholds regarding the percentage of correctly classified instances. These values are set up in a configuration file of the analysis module. In our setup, the model system stared making recommendations after the percentage of correctly classified instances raised above 80%.

Obtaining recommendations for students is accomplished by finding the concepts that obtain "yes" as estimation of target function. The current status of the student is evaluated at the moment he logs in the LMS. Then, the model selects the concepts that have as estimated target value "yes" and displays those concepts.

Each time the learner accesses the LMS the current performed activity is matched against the current model and the corresponding concepts that end up as *recommended* are displayed.

After each week of running, the new data are considered for being included in training and testing data. These new data are added and new data and a challenger model are obtained. If the challenger model has better accuracy regarding the percentage of correct classified instance, it will replace the old model.

Sometimes it happens that during the usage of the system, the student could change his/her type of interaction with LMS. The problem of changes of the users' preferences is known as concept drift and has been discussed in several works about the use of machine learning for user modeling [11, 12]. Concept drift can occur either because the acquired learning information needs to be adjusted or because the student simply changes his/her habits. In these scenarios, adaptive decision models, capable of better fitting the current student's preferences, are desirable.

If a concept drift is observed, the model is adapted accordingly. The improvement of the approach is proposed in [13], where the learning style once acquired was no more refined and the decision model was modeled using an adaptive Naïve Bayes classifier. In this approach a dynamic Bayesian network was used for modeling learning styles and a 2-DBC (dependence Bayesian classifier) [14] to initialize the decision model.

3. Analysis Process and Experiments

The analysis process for building the model is presented in Fig. 90.1.

First, the cold-start problem is solved. This means the data are collected such that the decision model is created. All performed activities are filtered such that training and testing data are obtained. Because we use Weka the data are extracted and translated into a standard format called ARFF, for attribute relation

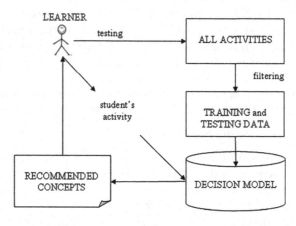

Figure 90.1. The selection of recommended concepts.

file format [15, 16]. This involves taking the physical log files and database relations and processing them through a series of steps to generate an ARFF data set.

The values of attributes are computed for each instance through a custom-developed off-line Java application. The outcome of running the application is in the form of a file called *activity.arff* that will later be used as source file for Weka workbench [17].

The *activity.arff* file has a standard format which is composed of two sections. In the first one the name of the relation and the attributes are defined. For each attribute the set of nominal values it may have is defined. In the next lines the first section of the file is presented.

```
@relation activity
@attribute conceptId {1, 2, 3, 4}
@attribute noOfTests {1, 2, 3, 4, 5}
@attribute avgTests {1, 2, 3, 4, 5}
@attribute finalResult {1, 2, 3, 4, 5}
@attribute recommend {yes,no}
```

In this section of the file all attributes are defined. An important decision that is needed is to establish the granularity for each attribute which is represented by the number of nominal values it may take. As can be seen from the above presented lines we consider five possible values for *noOfTests* feature. In the same the set of possible values are defined for each of the features.

The second section of the *activity.arff* file is represented by the data itself. Here there are all the instances that will enter the classification process. In the next lines few instances are presented which may be found in this section.

```
@data
1, 1, 2, 3, no
1, 2, 3, 2, no
2, 3, 4, 3, yes
```

Each row represents an instance. For example, the first row represents an instance (a learner) which took many tests at concept 1, obtained high grades for tests regarding this concept, and obtained an average result at final examination. For this student the decision is not to show concept 1 in the set of recommended concepts. In the same way all other instances can be interpreted. At this point we may say we have obtained useful data that may be used for experimentation with machine learning schemes.

The Naïve Bayes algorithm was run in Weka. The original data set was divided into a training of 90% of instances and a test set of 10% of instances. The model was constructed using four attributes: *conceptId*, *noOfTests, avgTests, and finalResult*, and *recommend* as the value of the target function.

More detailed results regarding the obtained model are presented below.
```
=== Run information ===
Scheme:      weka.classifiers.bayes.NaiveBayes
Relation:    activity
Instances:   850
Attributes:  5
             conceptId, noOfTests, avgTests, finalResult, recommend
Test mode:   evaluate on training data
=== Classifier model (full training set) ===
Naive Bayes Classifier
Class yes: Prior probability = 0.45
conceptId: Counts = 85 122 152 135 (Total= 530)
noOfTests: Counts= 100 118 134 95 60(Total= 512)
avgTests:  Counts= 110 105 130 124 93(Total= 565)
finalResult:Counts= 90 122 132 130 86 (Total = 560)
```

Class no: Prior probability = 0.55
conceptId:Counts=75 159 106 80 110 (Total = 520)
noOfTests: Counts=70 161 101 105 108(Total= 545)
avgTests:Counts = 72 152 110 99 114 (Total = 547)
finalResult:Counts=72 122 120 109 124(Total= 547)
=== Evaluation on training set ===
=== Summary ===
Correctly Classified Instances   690   81.1764 %
Incorrectly Classified Instances   160   18.8235 %
Kappa statistic   0.6271
Mean absolute error   0.3153
Root mean squared error   0.1951
Relative absolute error   41.4597 %
Root relative squared error   75.8637 %
Total Number of Instances   850
=== Confusion Matrix ===
 a b <– classified as
 150   110 | a = yes
 50 540 | b = no

The performance of the model was evaluated by using ten fold cross-validation technique. The results are presented as percentage of correctly classified instances (81.17%) and incorrectly classified instances (18.82%) and confusion matrix.

4. Conclusions and Future Works

In this chapter we have presented an analysis process that creates an user model aimed at discovering the student's needs regarding the concepts that need more study. This model was used in an e-Learning system for filtering the concepts of a discipline the learner needs to study. To discover the user's needs we use the information about learner's performed activities. The advantages of using these information are that this allows refining the initial beliefs acquired by the system by observing the student's performed actions over time thus computing up-to-date learning activity for each student. On the other hand, we use Naïve Bayes as the decision model for determining whether a concept is appropriate to be recommended for a specific learner. We described the experiments carried out to obtain an initial model thus solving the cold-start problem.

For each learner we initialize the decision model from data obtained from previous learner's performed activities.

Each individual decision model is then adapted from the observations of the student's performed activities. Moreover, the model is also able to adapt itself to changes in the student's performed activities.

At the e-Learning platform setup 375 students were registered. After 6 months of running the platform there were over 40,000 recorded actions that represent the raw data. Filtering this data had as output an arff file with 850 instances.

References

1. Burdescu, D. D., Mihăescu, M. C., Tesys: e-Learning Application Built on a Web Platform, In Proceedings of International Joint Conference on e-Business and Telecommunications, INSTICC Press, Setubal, Portugal, 2006, pp. 315–318.
2. Novak, J. D., Gowin, D. B. "Learning How to Learn", New York: Cambridge University Press, 1984.
3. Novak, J. D. "A Theory of Education", Ithaca, NY: Cornell University Press, 1977.
4. Novak, J. D., "Learning, Creating, and Using Knowledge: Concept Maps as Facilitative Tools in Schools and Corporations". Mahwah, NJ: Lawrence Erlbaum Associates, 1998.

5. Kononenko, I., Comparison of Inductive and Naive Bayesian Learning Approaches to Automatic Knowledge Acquisition, "Current Trends in Knowledge Acquisition". Amsterdam: IOS Press, 1990.

6. Frank, E., Trigg, L., Holmes, G., Witten, I. H.,Naive Bayes for Regression, Machine Learning 41(1), 2000, pp. 5–15.

7. Bennett, P. N., Assessing the calibration of Naive Bayes' posterior estimates, Technical Report No. CMU-CS00-155, 2000.

8. Mitchell, T., "Machine Learning". New York: McGraw-Hill, 1997.

9. McDaniel, E. Roth, B., Millar, M. (2005) Concept Mapping as a Tool for Curriculum Design, Issues in Informing Science and Information Technology Education Joint Conference, 505–513, Flagstaff, AZ, June 16–19, 2005.

10. Vecchia, L., Pedroni, M., Concept Maps as a Learning Assessment Tool, Issues in Informing Science and Information Technology, 4, 2007.

11. Koychev, I., Schwab, I., Adaptation to Drifting User's Interests. Proceedings of ECML2000 Workshop: Machine Learning in New Information Age, Spain, 2000.

12. Webb, G., Pazzani, M., Billsus, D., Machine Learning for User Modeling. User Modeling and User-Adapted Interaction, 11, 2001, 19–29.

13. Castillo, G., Gama, J., Breda, A.. An Adaptive Predictive Model for Student Modeling. In "Advances in Web-based Education, Personalized Learning Environments", eds: Magoulas, G.D. and Chen, S.Y.; Chapter IV. Chicago: Information Science Publishing, Idea Group Inc., 2005.

14. Sahami, M., Learning Limited Dependence Bayesian Classifiers. Proceedings of the Second International Conference on Knowledge Discovery and Data Mining, KDD-96 AAAI Press, 1996, 335–338.

15. Garner, S.R., Cunningham, S.J., Holmes, G., Nevill-Manning, C.G., Witten I.H., Applying a Machine Learning Workbench: Experience with Agricultural Databases, Proceedings of the Machine Learning in Practice Workshop, Machine Learning Conference, Tahoe City, CA, USA, pp. 14–21, 1995.

16. Holmes, G., Donkin, A., Witten, I.H., Weka: a machine learning workbench. Proceedings of the 1994 Second Australian and New Zealand Conference on Intelligent Information Systems, Brisbane, Australia, pp. 357–361, 1994.

17. www.cs.waikato.ac.nz/ml/weka

91

Problem-Based Learning in a Programming Context–Planning and Executing a Pilot Survey on Database Access in a Programming Language

Peter Bellström and Nina Kilbrink

Abstract

In this chapter we describe a pilot survey on applying problem-based learning (PBL) in an undergraduate programming course. During the course the students have applied PBL as a complement to traditional teaching and learning techniques. The PBL problem in this survey combines both knowledge about programming and knowledge about databases. We argue that to handle programming the students have to learn programming according to the deep approach to learning in order to be able to apply their knowledge in new programming situations and contexts. The result from this pilot survey indicates from both a tutor and a student perspective that PBL could be one method to reach a deeper understanding on how to access databases in a programming language.

Keywords Problem-based learning (PBL) · Programming · Database access

1. Introduction

Learning how to program is often experienced as a tricky task by students and the failure rates tend to be high [15]. However, in many educations such as in information systems and computer science it is essential that the students actually learn how to program. But what happens when traditional ways of teaching and learning fail? One possible solution to the problem is applying other teaching and learning techniques in an attempt to bridge the problems and shortcomings. In this chapter we describe a pilot survey on applying problem-based learning (PBL) in an undergraduate programming course. We argue that PBL can be used to bridge the shortcomings of traditional teaching and learning techniques. We also argue that to handle programming the students have to learn programming according to the deep approach to learning; otherwise they might never be able to apply their knowledge in new programming situations and contexts.

In the 1970s a distinction between surface and deep approach to learning was made in studies about learning [10]. The surface approach often corresponds to an atomistic view of learning whereas the deep approach often corresponds to a holistic view of learning. In a pedagogical perspective holistic learning, where the learner focuses on understanding and wholeness, is desirable [10]. Studies and experiences have shown that aiming for holistic learning is important when learning computer programming and that not all students do that [2, 8, 17]. Holistic learning is also important for the ability to use the acquired knowledge in new contexts. Therefore, it is important to study how students can reach holistic learning in computer programming, and we discuss PBL as one possible way.

Peter Bellström and Nina Kilbrink • Department of Information Systems, Karlstad University, Karlstad, Sweden.

G.A. Papadopoulos et al. (eds.), *Information Systems Development*, DOI 10.1007/b137171_91,
© Springer Science+Business Media, LLC 2009

As a result, we have applied PBL in our pilot survey as a complement to traditional teaching and learning techniques, such as lectures and projects. Meaning, in our pilot survey we have used PBL as a method and not as an education and study philosophy [6]. Applying PBL as a complement and method is also motivated since learning how to program includes not only learning programming theory but also learning how to program in practice [9].

Finally, we argue that our pilot survey and study are rather unique since students are combining both knowledge about databases and knowledge about programming.

This chapter is structured as follows. In Section 2 we describe the PBL pilot survey including history and related work, planning the PBL pilot survey, executing the PBL pilot survey, and follow-up and evaluation of the PBL pilot survey. In Section 3 we discuss and describe perspectives on the PBL pilot survey and in Section 4 we analyze and discuss the overall picture of the PBL pilot survey. Finally, the chapter closes with a summary and conclusions.

2. The PBL Pilot Survey

In this section we present the overall picture of the PBL pilot survey. This section is for that purpose divided into four subsections starting with *history and related work*, moving on to *planning the PBL pilot survey*, *executing the PBL pilot survey*, and finally ending with a *follow-up and evaluation of the PBL pilot survey*.

2.1. History and Related Work

Applying PBL in education is not a new phenomenon. The characteristics of PBL were already mentioned by Confusius 500 B.C. [13]. The modern version of PBL was first implemented in Canada in the 1960s in the medical education at McMaster University [1]. Thereafter PBL has been applied to different disciplines across the globe.

In comparison to traditional teaching and learning techniques, PBL emphasizes problem solving and group work. In PBL, the problem is first presented to the students in the learning process, they then engage in group work and subsequently define their own learning goals [13, 14]. As a result, students have to take more responsibility for their own learning and at the same time become more critical to what and how they are actually learning.

In the rest of this section, three different studies on how PBL has been applied in three different programming courses are described. Together the three PBL studies provide an idea and overview of how PBL has been applied in other programming courses.

In [9] the authors studied how PBL could be applied to large student groups in an introductory programming course. To be precise, this meant less time with the tutor for the students. In the study the authors wanted "[...] to identify efficiently and inefficiently working tutor less PBL groups and describe their characters." (p. 194). The research methods the authors used were observations of PBL sessions, interviews with the PBL participants, and finally questionnaires that the students were asked to fill out. The observations were coded in a quantitative way. The interviews were used together with questionnaires and students' course grades and course passing percentage to verify the result from the observations. Meaning, the result from the study is classified as quantitative. The authors concluded that tutored PBL groups worked efficiently and that participating students were satisfied. However, in groups which had had less time with the tutor, the result varied more.

In [12] the authors describe how PBL and RoboCode (http://RoboCode.sourceforge.net/) were adopted and combined in a first-year programming course. According to the authors, RoboCode teaches Java (java.sun.com), a programming language, in a fun and rewarding manner and is therefore suitable to use together with PBL. The main idea is to construct a Robot-tank from certain criteria and then compete with it. Students are given the skeleton and some sample code of Robot-tanks and are then free to study, modify, and to construct their own Robot-tanks before entering the competition. The authors argue that their approach fulfils all the characteristics, given by [5], that describe what makes a PBL problem a good problem. In other words, the RoboCode problem should *engage students' interest and motivate them to study for a deeper understanding, include multiple stages, complex enough that all group members are needed and engaged in the problem, open ended*, and finally *incorporate important content objectives of the course*. Finally, the authors argue that their approach has proven to be effective; however, they clearly state that in order to gain the maximum benefit of the RoboCode problem, the students should have some prior group working experience.

In [18] the authors describe a study, in which PBL was incorporated and used in an introductory computer engineering course. The goal was "[...] to develop a more interesting and relevant integrated classroom/laboratory experience for the students." (p. 7). To do so, the authors targeted four things: *classroom learning environment, laboratory experiments, real-world examples*, and the *course web site*. However, in the paper, the connection to PBL is mostly emphasized for the laboratory experiments. Because the authors focus on practical approaches to PBL, the results are also more practical. One example of this is given in connection to the final group assignment that students were to hand in. Since the project was also graded in groups and good solutions measured in code size and code speed were rewarded the project had a competitive nature. According to the authors, the project helped the students to learn things such as teamwork skills, decision making and this aspect motivated the need for assessment. The study reported in [18] is different in one way compared to the studies conducted in [9] and [12]. The students attending the course had already taken at least one programming course and a course in digital logic. In other words, students had some programming knowledge and some knowledge about digital logic when starting the course.

In our pilot survey students have also already taken at least one programming course and a course in database design/technology. However, our pilot survey has at least one distinguishing characteristic compared to the other studies mentioned above. It combines both knowledge about programming and knowledge about databases in a thematic way. Combining knowledge, in a thematic way, has also been mentioned as an appropriate way to work with PBL [13]. Finally, in our pilot survey it was also assumed that the students have some experiences of working in groups since they have already attended other courses at the university.

2.2. Planning the PBL Pilot Survey

Planning the PBL pilot survey was divided into four steps as follows:

1. Planning the time schedule
2. Planning the PBL introduction
3. Planning and developing the problem
4. Planning the follow-up and evaluation

The first step, *planning the time schedule*, was conducted long before the others. The time schedule including lectures, supervision, exercises, project, and examination had to be planned long before actually executing the pilot survey. It was decided to apply the following time schedule:

- Execute workshop 1 (PBL step 1–5, approximately 2 hours)
- Individual independent studies (PBL step 6, approximately 1 week)
- Execute workshop 2 (PBL step 7, approximately 2 hours)

The usage of "PBL step..." refers to the steps in the PBL seven steps method [6, 11, 16]. The seven steps method is one of the most used and adapted methods when applying PBL as a teaching and learning technique [6].

When entering the second step, *planning the PBL introduction*, there already existed an idea of what to present to the students: an adapted and adjusted PBL method or process. Nevertheless, the idea had to be formalized because today there are several PBL methods and processes in existence, e.g., [1, 4, 11, 14, 16]. Apart from that, the method to apply and adjust according to the specific needs for this study also had to be decided upon. Therefore, the focus was put on the seven steps method as described in [6]. However, in [6] the seven steps method is described in a very general and broad manner. Therefore, it becomes necessary to consider how other researchers have described the seven steps method. In this context, there is one particular application of the seven steps method that is interesting in relation to PBL. In [11] the authors use [16] as a basis for an adapted version of the seven steps method useful in a programming situation.

In our version of the seven steps method, the language was simplified in order to give students additional guidance. Everything was presented in Swedish and formulated as follows. *Step 1:* In this step, one of the group members read from the text and afterward the group members individually reflect upon it. The group members then explain concepts, terms, and expressions to each other. *Step 2:* In this step, you should ask yourself what the actual problem/s is/are in the text. *Step 3:* In this step, you are going to analyze the problem and at the same time each group member should express what he/she thinks about in relation to the expressed problem (brainstorming). You could, for instance, ask each other what knowledge you have in relation to the problem and how you could apply it in the problem context. *Step 4:* In this step, you should critically revise, structure, and summarize what the group agreed on in step 3. It should be identified what the group members have to study to be able to solve the problem. *Step 5:* In this step, you should formulate and express the learning goals that the group wants to reach in step 6. The learning goals should be formulated in a way that makes it possible to solve the problem after step 6. For instance, in step 4 you identified a number of areas you have to study. Now you should formulate what learning goals you wish to accomplish during the independent study period. It is important that the learning goals are formulated and expressed in a concrete and precise way. *Step 6:* In this step, the learning takes place in different forms using different sources. Step 6 is the only step in which the group members work and act individually. It should be carried out in such a way that each group member reaches each formulated learning goal in turn. *Step 7:* In this step, you should once again analyze the problem. However, this time you should apply the new knowledge you have acquired in step 6. It is important that group members discuss what knowledge they have acquired in step 6 and explain to each other if anything is experienced as ambiguous. Finally, you should discuss if you have reached the learning goals you formulated in step 5.

In planning the PBL introduction step, it was also natural to decide on what feedback the students were to provide. More precisely, this refers to what the students were to document and hand in for each step in the seven steps method.

When entering the third step, *planning and developing the problem*, once again there existed an idea of its contents, meaning, there already existed an idea about how the actual problem should be formulated. After some thinking, it was decided to use the following problem formulation:

How can you, as a programmer, search and modify data in [the course -specific relational database] applying [the course specific programming language]? In the text handed out to the students, the problem formulation included the names of the specific database management system and the specific programming language in place of the text inside the brackets.

Furthermore, it is important to know that the problem originates from one of the main learning goals in the syllabus stating that students should learn how to construct a program that accesses and modifies data in a relational database. While developing the problem, it was also known that attending students had already taken at least one programming course and one course in database design/technology, i.e., students should already have some prior knowledge about programming and how to handle relational databases. However, the knowledge on how to combine the programming language and relational database was still missing.

In this step, the main inspiration source was [11] and the way the authors, who in a short and concrete way, described their PBL problems in a programming course. For instance, in one task the students were given five lines of text describing the core of the problem of designing a computer file system.

Characteristics of good PBL problems as described in [5] and later on adapted in [12] were also considered. On putting it all together it was decided that a problem description containing a short introduction was to be used followed by the actual problem statement (as described above) and rounding off with a few additional delimitations.

The last step in planning the PBL pilot survey was *planning the follow-up and evaluation*. In this pilot survey, data were gathered from three different sources:

1. Student documentation from workshop 1 and workshop 2
2. Tutors own notes and annotations from workshop 1 and workshop 2
3. Student answers from a questionnaire with open-ended questions

Student documentation was already planned during the second step, planning the PBL introduction, and the tutors own notes and annotations did not include any longer and/or deeper planning. Focus was therefore put on the third and last data source: student answers from a questionnaire with open-ended questions. The questionnaire was planned to be handed out after the students had finished workshop 2. This was motivated, since not only data and feedback about PBL as learning and teaching technique, but also feedback and data regarding used knowledge sources, used time, and so on were of interest. It was decided that the questionnaire should include five questions that were open ended, since the students' apprehensions were of interest.

2.3. Executing the PBL Pilot Survey

Before executing the PBL pilot survey, the students were informed that participating was voluntary. It was pointed out that the PBL survey did not influence the course grade and the students were not judged regarding their participation. Finally, the students were informed that all collected data including course name, course code, and so on were to be given assumed names.

Even though participation was voluntary, all students agreed to participate which was rather important since the class size was very small. Therefore, in workshop 1 (PBL seven steps method step 1–5) one group participated. This group consisted of five students with very different education and background. However, the students had commonality regarding earlier courses: they had already taken at least one programming course and one course in database design/technology. Thereafter, the students were informed that when entering the PBL survey the teacher should instead be seen as a tutor.

The more practical parts of the PBL pilot survey were gone through, meaning, students were first informed about the seven steps method and at the same time also informed about what to write down and document. Finally, the students were informed that after the pilot survey a questionnaire would be handed out. The group was then asked to appoint a chairman and a secretary and to start working with the assigned problem. The introduction took approximately 20 minutes and steps 1–5 in the seven steps method approximately 45 minutes. During workshop 1, the chairman led the group and made sure that all group members participated in the discussion and also that all participants expressed their thoughts and opinions. In addition, for each step in the seven steps method, the secretary wrote down and documented what the group agreed upon.

After the first workshop, the group members had 1 week to study toward the agreed learning goals. When 1 week had passed, the group once again met up to conduct workshop 2. However, this time only four students were able to participate. The group finalized their work by carrying out step 7 in the seven steps method. When the group felt that they had finished their work, they were asked to fill out a questionnaire which all of them agreed to do.

During both workshops, the tutor not only observed the group but also answered questions asked by the group and wrote down important observations.

Finally, in relation to the results reported in [9] and due to the group size it was decided that the tutor should be present at all times during both workshops.

2.4. Follow-Up and Evaluation of the PBL Pilot Survey

As has been mentioned earlier, after the group had finalized step 7 in the seven steps method, the participants were asked to answer a questionnaire. All students that participated in workshop 2 also agreed to fill it out. The questions were formulated in a way that focused on the students' apprehensions regarding the PBL pilot survey. In other words, they were to answer two types of questions: The first type (question 1) dealt with how the students had managed to achieve the learning goals, the sources that had been used, and the amount of time elapsed, expressed in hours and minutes, during step 6. The second type (question 2–5) dealt with the students' apprehension of

- what they had learned during the survey
- what they thought about the problem
- what they thought about the seven steps method in relation to the problem
- what they thought about using PBL: what was good, bad, and interesting?

The students' answers from the questionnaire will be summarized in Section 3.3.

3. Perspectives on the PBL Pilot Survey

In this section, the PBL pilot survey is described and discussed from different perspectives, divided into three sections. First we reflect upon and focus on the notes taken by the tutor and after that we take a closer look at the student perspective. In the student perspective section we focus on one student and her apprehension of the PBL pilot survey. The student perspective in the pilot survey is rather unique since it is actually written by one of the participating students. Having this division was possible, since this student was actually at the time of the pilot survey working part time at the department. In the third section, we summarize the collected data from the student documentation from both workshops and from the students' answers from the questionnaire with open-ended questions.

3.1. The Tutor Perspective

From the tutors' perspective, the PBL pilot survey was a new and very interesting experience. Taking the role of a tutor during a PBL session was somewhat difficult because it is important that the tutor does not act as a teacher [9]. Nevertheless, in workshop 1, five observations were noticed and in workshop 2, two observations were noticed. Yet, all seven were for this survey both important and interesting observations.

The first observation in workshop 1 was made in connection to step 1 in the seven steps method. According to the description of the first step, one of the group members should read from the text and afterward the group members should individually reflect upon it. However, the group members in this survey chose to read it individually and afterward also to individually reflect upon it.

The second observation concerned how the group worked as a team. The appointed chairman made sure that everybody was able to speak and that all participated in the discussions. At the same time, the secretary took notes about what the group agreed upon in connection to all five steps.

The third observation was noticed in connection to one of the questions the tutor was asked to answer. The group asked: Where is the database? In the answer given by the tutor it was pointed out that it was not interesting for the actual problem where the database was located. Although, it was pointed out that a database already existed and that the group should use it and not create a new one.

The fourth observation in workshop 1 was noticed in connection to step 5. After discussing step 5 for a while the group started to think about what knowledge sources to use in step 6. The group then signalled to the tutor that they wanted some hints and guidance. This was done without actually asking the tutor the question. This was possible since the tutor was present all the time during both workshop 1 and workshop 2.

The fifth and last observation in workshop 1 was noticed in connection to how the students discussed and worked with the first five steps in the seven steps method. While listening to the discussions it was not clear what distinguished one step from another and that they therefore seemed to overlap.

Both observations in workshop 2 were noticed in connection to how step 7 was formulated. For the students it was not clear what they should do in step 7. Furthermore, the group was unsure when or even whether they had finalized step 7 or not.

3.2. The Student Perspective

From a student's perspective, this way of working requires a commitment and an ambitious participation. But it is also motivating; it gives you a feeling of as working with a more authentic problem. You have to search for knowledge on your own and combine with earlier knowledge and experiences. The workshop in the beginning is a good starting point where you can discuss your ideas about the problem, and together with your group members find the essence of the problem and what you have to study on your own. This also gives you an understanding about your own knowledge gaps and where you have to fill in.

This is a way of working with programming problem solving that makes you think and reflect about your practical programming and demands you to really try to understand what you are doing. It also adds learning about how to learn programming, i.e., you understand how to find own solutions to new problems. The connection to databases, which was used in this PBL problem, added an extra challenge, while we had to use experiences and knowledge from different areas. Therefore, it was also extra interesting to discuss with the other students in the group, while we had different experiences from programming and databases. Workshop 2 also showed that we had used different methods to find the solution to the problem (books, different web pages, and practical testing), which also made it meaningful to attend this summary discussion, in order to understand that there were different possible solutions to the problem.

3.3. Collected Data

The collected data described in this section, consist of the student documentation from workshop 1 and workshop 2 and of the students' answers from a questionnaire with open-ended questions.

All the students participating in this pilot survey had a positive attitude toward working with PBL in the course. Reflections made in the questionnaire concern that this takes more time than other more traditional ways of working, but also that it is interesting while there is a variation to ordinary ways of working and gives the students possibilities to work in their own way and to focus on what he or she finds interesting. Although, it is also mentioned that there is a risk getting stuck in conceptions and lexicology, rather than focusing on the essence of the problem. The students mention the connection between reading/searching for information and the practical doing as an important ingredient in this learning method. Nevertheless, it is pointed out in the questionnaire that this method could be used as a complement to traditional teaching and learning methods, not only as a replacement.

The students were also asked about the seven steps method in the questionnaire, and they are positive to the method, but it is also mentioned that in this small problem-solving task, the steps could be experienced as overlapping. This is also obvious in the student documentation where the documentation from the different steps in workshop 1 is partly overlapping. The student documentation also partly focuses on the conceptions. Although, the students mention other learning in the questionnaire, for example, they answer that they have learned how to search for information about problems in the programming and database areas.

4. Analyses and Discussion

In this section we analyze and discuss the results presented in Section 3, consisting of the tutors' perspective and the students' perspective on using PBL in this pilot survey. Furthermore, it is complemented by the student documentation from workshop 1 and workshop 2 and of the students' answers from the questionnaire with open-ended questions.

Overall there are many positive outcomes from this pilot survey. However, it has to be considered that all the students had a positive attitude to this PBL exercise, which could have influenced the results. The method has, due to earlier studies [9, 12, 18] and to our pilot survey, a great potential as a complement to traditional teaching and learning techniques when it comes to programming courses. Although, it is pointed out in the student questionnaire, this method should not be used as a replacement, but as complement. This is something worth taking into consideration when planning a PBL exercise.

Experiences from this pilot study point that in a small PBL exercise the seven steps method is overlapping, which means that the method ought to be adapted to the problem used in the PBL method. Another problem that came up with this study is the focus on conceptions and lexicology. The additional limits, mentioned in the formulation of the task, could have been contributing to this problem, which means that we argue that additional limits like this should not be used in this kind of PBL problems.

We want to stress the possibility of using different learning styles as a positive outcome from this study. From a student perspective, this coming together of different experiences and different ways of solving the task added an extra learning through the discussions in the workshops.

In a practical area, like computer programming, the PBL method requires the students to combine theoretical knowledge with a practical doing [9]; it requires the students to both reflect and do something, which earlier studies had pointed out as important in order to reach a holistic learning [3, 8], which indicates that this method can contribute to a deeper learning.

This pilot survey also indicates that the PBL method is a way to learn how to learn, which is pointed out as an important skill in today's society [7]. This would help the learner to reach an understanding, which could be helpful in order to be able to use acquired knowledge in new situations.

5. Summary and Conclusion

In this chapter we have described and discussed a pilot survey on applying PBL as a teaching and learning technique in a programming course. We argue that our pilot survey and study are rather unique at least in one sense since the students had to combine knowledge about programming and about relational databases. To formalize how the group should work and what the group should document and hand in we used an adapted and adjusted version of the seven steps method.

In this survey, it is indicated that the PBL method is a good complement to traditional teaching and learning techniques in programming courses.

The results from this pilot survey indicate that it would be meaningful to go on doing a larger survey on using PBL in programming courses combining knowledge about programming and knowledge about databases.

References

1. Barrett, T. (2005) Understanding Problem-Based Learning, Barrett, T., Mac Labhrainn, I. and Fallon, H. (eds), *Handbook of Enquiry and Problem-Based Learning: Irish Case Studies and International Perspectives*, AISHE and CELT, Galway, pp. 13–25
2. Booth, S. (1992) *Learning to Program: A Phenomenographic Perspective*, PhD thesis, Göte-borgs Universitet, Acta.
3. Dewey, J. (1998) *How We Think*, Houghton Mifflin Company, Boston, MA.
4. Duch, B.J. (2001) Models for Problem-Based Instruction in Undergraduate Courses, Duch, B.J., Groh, S.E. and Allen, D.E. (eds), *The Power of Problem-Based Learning A Practical "How To" for Teaching Undergraduate Courses in Any Discipline*, Stylus, Sterling, Virginia, pp. 39–45
5. Duch, B.J. (2001) Writing Problems for Deeper Understanding, Duch, B.J., Groh, S.E. and Allen, D.E. (eds), *The Power of Problem-Based Learning A Practical "How To" for Teaching Undergraduate Courses in Any Discipline*, Stylus, Sterling, Virginia, pp. 47–53.
6. Egidius, H. (2000) *Problembaserat lärande – en introduktion för lärare och lärande*, Studentlitteratur (in Swedish).
7. The European Parliament and the Council of the European Union (2006) Recommendation of the European Parliament and of the Council of 18 December 2006 on key competences for lifelong learning, *Official Journal of the European Union* (2006/962/EC).
8. Kilbrink, N. (2008) *Legorobotar i skolan: Elevers uppfattningar av lärandeobjekt och pro-blemlösningsstrategier*, Licentiate thesis, Karlstad University Studies, 2008:7 (in Swedish).
9. Kinnunen, P. and Malmi, L. (2005) Problems in Problem-Based Learning – Experiences, Analysis and Lessons Learned on an Introductory Programming Course, *Informatics in Education*, 4: 193–214.
10. Marton, F. and Booth, S. (1997) *Learning and Awareness*, Lawrence Erlbaum, Mahwah, NJ.
11. Nuutila, E., Törmä, S. and Malmi, L. (2005) PBL and Computer Programming – The Seven Steps Method with Adaptations, *Computer Science Education*, 15: 123–142.
12. O'Kelly, J. and Gibson, J.P. (2006) RoboCode & Problem-Based Learning: A Non-prescriptive Approach to Teaching Programming, *Proceedings of the 11th Annual SIGCSE Conference on Innovation and Technology in Computer Science Education*, pp. 217–221.

13. Olstedt, E. (2001) *Critical Thinking? A Study Concerning Learning, Problem Based Learning (PBL) and Information Technology (IT) in Engineering Education*, PhD thesis, Akademitryck AB (in Swedish).

14. Pike, A. and Barber, D. (2003) A Preliminary Investigation of the Role of Problem Based Learning (PBL), *ITB Journal*, 8: 82–91.

15. Robins, A., Rountree, J. and Rountree, N. (2003) Learning and Teaching Programming: A Review and Discussion, *Computer Science Education*, 13: 137–172.

16. Schmidt, H.G. (1983) Problem-based learning: rationale and description, *Medical Education*, 17: 11-16.

17. Segolsson, M. (2006) *Programmeringens intentionala objekt: Nio elevers uppfattningar av programmering*, Licentiate thesis, Karlstad University Studies, 2006:50 (in Swedish).

18. Striegel, A. and Rover, D.T. (2002) Problem-Based Learning in an Introductory Computer-Engineering Course, *Proceedings of the 32nd ASEE/IEEE Frontiers in Education Conference*, Vol. 2, pp. 7–12.

92

"Learning to Research" in a Virtual Learning Environment: A Case Study on the Effectiveness of a Socio-constructivist Learning Design

López-Alonso, C., Fernández-Pampillón, A., de-Miguel, E. and Pita, G.

Abstract

Learning is the basis for research and lifelong training. The implementation of virtual environments for developing this competency requires the use of effective learning models. In this study we present an experiment in positive learning from the virtual campus of the Complutense University of Madrid (UCM). In order to carry it out we have used E-Ling, an e-learning environment that has been developed with an innovative didactic design based on a socio-constructivist learning approach. E-Ling has been used since 2006 to train future teachers and researchers in "learning to research". Some of the results of this experiment have been statistically analysed in order to compare them with other learning models. From the obtained results we have concluded that E-Ling is a more productive proposal for developing competences in learning to research.

Keywords E-learning · Virtual learning environments · Socio-constructivism

1. Introduction

We consider "learning to research" as a key skill not only for future teachers but also to ensure people "lifelong learning". Learning to research means embarking on the process of systematic learning in order to increase our knowledge in a specific area. This involves (i) the selection, organization and processing of existing information; (ii) the choice of adequate analysis strategies; and (iii) the efficient management of information and time, both at individual and in group level. The question of the effectiveness of "learning to research " competency is not new [1], but it is only recently that it has been "officially" acknowledged: in 2005 the European Commission and Parliament published a resolution recommending, for the first time, that this competence should be included in the curricula of EU countries in order to ensure "lifelong learning" [2]. In university education, "learning to research" extends to "learning to learn". "Learning" and "researching" are consecutive inter-related stages of the same process of acquiring and building on knowledge that is developed by every university student.

Following these premises, we have drawn up a learning design for students to learning to research. We have put it into practice within three different learning models: behaviourism, constructivism and socio-constructivism. The methodology is being applied in our under- and post-graduate courses since 2006 as a means of introducing students to certain areas of research during their final years. In the first

López-Alonso, C., Fernández-Pampillón, A., de-Miguel, E. and Pita, G. • Lingüística General, Facultad de Filología, Universidad Complutense de Madrid, Madrid, Spain.

G.A. Papadopoulos et al. (eds.), *Information Systems Development*, DOI 10.1007/b137171_92,

place, it was used in a face-to-face learning environment with satisfactory results. Then, the methodology has been transferred to a virtual learning environment (VLE) in order to achieve more accessibility and effectiveness.

Regardless of the learning model, the results obtained in previous experiences confirm the fact that a VLE improves (i) the student accessibility to the learning process, (ii) the classroom interaction and (iii) their motivation towards the learning [3]. We have also observed a relationship between learning models, learning activities and the learning environment used. For instance, the first stages in the learning process corresponding to the activities of *topic choice* and *bibliographical compilation* are usually easier and faster to perform either individually in any instructional environment or collaboratively in face-to-face environment. However, in the last stages, *construction* and *analysis of a problematic,* the results improve when students work in a virtual environment with a socio-constructivist model. These observations indicate that the learning model in a certain activity would need to be transformed when transferred to an e-learning environment in order to improve the results.

1.1. The Research Question

In spite of the fact that technology is an efficient and effective support for implementing any learning model [4], there is still no answer to whether it is more efficient and effective to some pedagogical models or not. The huge range of technological possibilities [4], pedagogical proposals and learning styles [5], and the few experiments carried out within a well-defined theoretical framework, make this question difficult to answer [6].

In this chapter we present a case study analysing the effectiveness of using a socio-constructivist learning model along with a VLE in knowledge construction activities. Some studies deal with the influence in the students' performance of the learning environment [7] or the influence of the learning model [8] independently.

Our objective is to build up a theoretical framework for the relationship between learning models and learning processes in VLEs. In order to do so, we raise the following research questions: Is a socio-constructivist VLE more effective to "learn to research" than a behaviourist or a constructivist one? Do the students build their knowledge better in socio-constructivist virtual learning scenarios than in behaviourist or constructivist ones? Is there any type of activities better perform using a virtual socio-constructivist environment than using other approaches?

To answer these questions we carry out an experiment based on statistical methodology, using *t-student* and *ANOVA* techniques [9]. We have evaluated three different learning experiences with three groups of university students, using a VLE. Each group of students has been through the same learning activities but in a different learning model: a socio-constructivist approach, a constructivist approach and a behaviourist one.

We present this case study organized in five sections: introduction; the socio-constructivist learning model; the description of the design and implementation of the VLE; the methodology and results of the experiments; and finally, the discussion and conclusions.

2. The Socio-constructivist Learning Model

The behaviourist model is based on the knowledge transmission from the teacher to the student [10], while constructivist approaches [11] and socio-cultural approaches [12–14] are learning theories which postulate that knowledge is not a mimetic copy of reality but rather a reconstruction of this reality; in other words, comprehension develops from the representations constructed by the subject. Two further models applied to learning were developed from this notion: the Piagetian cooperative model and the socio-cultural collaborative model.

Cooperative constructivist models consider that it is the student who should control his or her own learning process using a distributional approach. It implies the division of work among those participating, whereby each student resolves his or her tasks individually, and the results are finally polled with those of the rest of the group [15].

In contrast, socio-constructivist learning is collaborative. It is essentially a social process, in which the students are responsible both for their own learning and for that of the rest of the group. It implies the contribution simultaneous and integrated of each and every one of the members to carry out a task. Numerous specialists have dealt with these two types of learning [16, 17], either to show the differences between them or to attempt to minimize these.

In our case, following Brufee [18], we consider that these are stages that may occur in the pedagogical relationship (learner/teacher/medium) [19], as both types of learning may be presented during the teaching process.

In our case study the learning activities of information selection and organization are basically the responsibility of the teacher. It is a face-to-face learning strategy structured by the teacher and directed towards the students. These activities have an essentially behaviourist and non-social constructivist character. However, in the rest of the activities of the learning process, in the virtual learning environment, the learning responsibility lies in each student's commitment to the rest of the group. In this case the character is collaborative.

Our experiment, therefore, involves social and personal interactive learning. In this learning process there is a harmonious blend of "how we learn" – cooperatively and collaboratively – with "where we learn" – in the classroom or in the VLE.

3. Design and Implementation of the VLE

The influence of ICT in universities has transformed many traditional teaching environments into virtual learning environments (VLE) [20]. A VLE is a web application integrating a set of tools for online teaching and learning that allows both non-face-to-face learning (e-learning) and blended learning (b-learning) in which offline experiences and e-learning are combined [6].

The most commonly used VLEs in universities are learning management systems (LMS) such as WebCT-Blackboard, Moodle [4] or Sakai [21]. Despite criticism of the inflexibility of these systems, [4, 22, 23], our experience at UCM shows that with an appropriate selection and combination of their functionalities, it is possible to support many different models and learning designs [24].

Virtual learning environments are the containers for virtual learning scenarios (VLS), where the learning process takes place [25–27]. Learning scenarios can be created either by the institution or by the teachers themselves. In both cases teachers are the managers and the ultimate responsible for VLS teaching and learning. It has been observed, however, that there is a general lack of theoretical and methodological framework when building these scenarios [20, 25]; this is probably due to a lack of technological competence and good-practice guidelines to provide orientation.

The socio-constructivist model previously presented has been implemented in a VLE named E-Ling. The learning design consists of three different phases comprising eight stages. Each stage has one or more activities (Fig. 92.1). The phases correspond to the three main steps in a scientific project [28] and the stages show the different analytical levels which mark out the consistency and progression of the research.

Stage 1 corresponds to the formulation of the "topic", which is individual at first but which may lead to group discussion.

Stage 2, which is essentially theoretical, involves finding out about other research on the same subject and the analytical methods used.

Stage 3, "Constructing the problematic", corresponds to the theoretical approach to be adopted depending on the subject proposed and justification of the choice.

Stage 4, "Constructing an analysis model" reflects the concepts and hypothesis that will prevail in the task of observation.

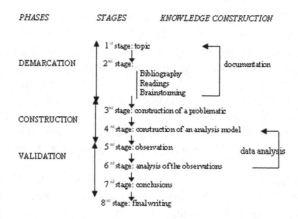

Figure 92.1. Diagram of the phases and stages defining the learning to research procedure.

Stage 5, "Data observation", establishes the hypotheses and the way in which data resulting from the analysis are observed.

Stage 6, "Analysis of the observations", gives the information obtained and compares the results with the hypotheses.

Stage 7, "Conclusions", is a synthesis of the research path taken, the characteristics of the analytical model, the selected field of observation, the method followed, the research results and the future prospects.

The VLE, E-Ling, has been built in WebCT using four learning scenarios: contenidos, actividades, comunicación and biblioteca de apoyo (Fig. 92.2):

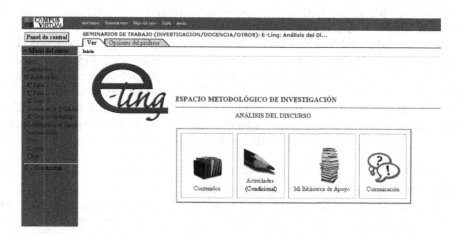

Figure 92.2. The VLE four learning scenarios: contents, activities, communication and support library.

The activities scenario consists of 10 sequential activities: topic choice, bibliography, readings, brainstorming, construction of problematic, model of analysis, observation, analysis of the observations, conclusions and final writing. These activities have been designated as either individual and/or collaborative to implement the three learning models used. The students are supported by using the other three scenarios: contents, communication and support library. These last scenarios are essential from the sixth activity onwards, where the socio-constructivist model is applied.

Next section describes how the VLE E-Ling has been used in the experimentation of our case study.

4. Experiments: Methodology and Results

In order to evaluate the efficiency of our framework, a VLE with a socio-constructivist learning design, we have tested Stage 4 of Phase 2 – the construction of the analysis model – (Fig. 92.1). We have used a statistical method of evaluation. In our method we analyse the results using t-student and ANOVA techniques. These techniques, broadly used in education [9], allow the results' comparison regarding the measuring parameters. The procedure followed is the comparison between the socio-constructivist learning model and the two other models in order to verify the working hypothesis.

4.1. Methodology and Procedure

Our research hypothesis is that the socio-constructivist learning model implemented in a VLE enhances the students' level of learning. Therefore, the null hypothesis (H0) used for testing is "our framework does NOT influence the students' learning results". Taking H0 as a starting point, two experiments were set: Experiment 1, which contrasts ET and T1, and Experiment 2, which contrasts ET and T2, where

ET (Experimental treatment): the socio-constructivist learning experience in the VLE.

T1 (Treatment 1): the individual constructivist learning experience in the VLE.

T2 (Treatment 2): the behaviourist learning experience in the face-to-face learning environment.

The procedure was carried out as follows [29]:

1. Selection of participants:

   Experiment 1: 10 students to whom ET and T1 were applied at two different times (paired sample).

   Experiment 2: two groups of nine students each. The first group, experimental group, is made up of 9 of the 10 students[1] participating in Experiment 1. The second group, the control group, is formed by a student selection, a priori better prepared than the experimental group.[2] This implies that any bias in the resulting data would be expected to favour the control group, which would mean not rejecting H0.

   Due to the small size of the sample data, it is necessary to replicate these experiments in the following academic courses to validate the results [30]. However, working with real students gives us more reliable results than an artificially increased sample with volunteers non-involved in this learning process.

2. Choice of topic:

   Experiment 1: The two topics proposed to the students were similar with regard to the area of knowledge and level required.

   ET: Topic1, "Discourse according to F. Rastier".

   T1: Topic 2, "Discourse according to Beaugrande and Dressler".

   Experiment 2: Topic," Rhetoric".

3. Independent variable:

   Treatment type (ET, T1 and T2).

4. Dependent variable:

   The pooled mark obtained by the students in a post-test held after the learning experiment. The evaluation criteria for each question and the corresponding mark were set a priori.

5. Selection of data analysis techniques.

   In Experiment 1, a t-test hypothesis contrast method for paired samples was used. In Experiment 2, the sample is formed by two independent groups, so an ANOVA is used. The confidence interval for hypothesis testing was set at the standard 95% ($p \leq 0.05$) (for discussion see [31]).

6. Research procedure

---

[1] One of the students did not attend to the experimental session.

[2] Students in this group were in the last year of their degree.

Experiment 1: The students draw up a synthesis file from bibliographic material that they themselves selected and classified. In the ET there was one single file for the group, produced collaboratively and supported by the VLE "Virtual Blackboard" tool. In T1, each student compiles an individual file.

Experiment 2: In the group learning with ET, the students made up a collaborative file on the research topic using the VLE "Virtual Blackboard". There was therefore only one file for all the students. In the group learning with T2, each student compiled a file individually from material provided and explained by the teacher.

Once the experiment was finished, the students took part in a post-test on the knowledge acquired.

4.2. Analysis of Results

Figures 92.3 and 92.4 show the statistical analysis of the post-test results for Experiments 1 and 2, respectively.

H0: average = 0, 0
Alternative. not equal
t-statistic = -5,0565
p-value = **0,000684282**

Figure 92.3. t-Student hypothesis testing for post-test ET–post-test T1.

Sources	+ squares	Gl	M. Square	F- quotient	P-Value
Btwn group	39,0139	1	39,0139	6,05	**0,0256**
Intra-group	103,111	16	6,44444		
Total	142,125	17			

Figure 92.4. ANOVA table for total by treatment (post-test ET–post-test T2).

The mean values of post-test evaluation marks in Experiment 1 differ by 2.5 points, being higher in collaborative than in individual constructivist learning ($\overline{x}_{col} = 6.85$ and $\overline{x}_{ind} = 4.35$). In Experiment 2 the mean results of cooperative behaviourist and collaborative constructivist treatments also differ significantly ($\overline{x}_{col} = 6.05$ and $\overline{x}_{bhv} = 3.11$). Both experiments rendered a p-value indicating that the differences between means are statistically significant (with the significance level for hypothesis testing set at a standard $p \leq 0.05$).

5. Discussion and Conclusions

From the statistical point of view the analysis of the results shows that the activities performed in the socio-constructivist model in a VLE are more effective than the behaviourist and cooperative constructivist ones either in virtual or face-to-face environments.

In particular, these results point out the following: first, learning in a VLE is more successful if it involves a social process of collaborative knowledge construction than if cooperative behaviourist or constructivist strategies are used. Second, learning activities for knowledge building can be more effectively developed in VLEs than in face-to-face environments. We draw a certain dependency among the learning model – socio-constructivist, learning activities, knowledge construction and the learning environment – VLE that improves student learning.

Nevertheless, these results should be considered cautiously. First, because although a double process of experimentation and analysis was carried out, the sample was small. The small number of doctorate students and undergraduates in their final years means that the results will have to be confirmed by repeating the experiments over successive years.

Second, the experiments have taken place, only, in one of the phases within a whole learning design that combines other learning models and environments. However, taking into account that the combination of models and methods is a common practice in real teaching situations [23], establishing the individual usefulness of each model does not seem viable. Therefore, we consider that studies about models, activities and/or environments' efficiency must always refer to a particular learning context and that in real practices it is a blended context.

Whatever the case, we consider that inductive experimentations – as the case study presented – are essential for being able to build a theoretical framework that helps teachers to implement their VLEs. This framework can be established formally analysing the relationships among models, learning activities and VLEs from case studies. These good-practice guidelines are basic tools to guarantee not only lifelong learning but effective lifelong learning.

Acknowledgements

This experiment was carried out within the project framework "Un modelo hipermedia modular para la enseñanza de la Lingüística General" TIN2005-08788-C04-03 funded by DGICYT.

References

1. Brown, A., Campione, J. and Day, D. D. (1981) Learning to learn: on training student to learn from texts. *Educational Researcher*, 10, pp. 14–21.
2. Parlamento Europeo (2006) Recomendación del Parlamento Europeo y del Consejo sobre las competencias clave para el aprendizaje permanente, *Diario Oficial de la Unión Europea* L 394, pp. 10/18. Available online: http://eur-lex.europa.eu/LexUriServ/site/es/oj/2006/l_394/l_39420061230es00100018.pdf
3. López Alonso, C., Fernández-Pampillón, A. and de Miguel, E. (2007) La construcción del conocimiento en el Campus Virtual. Análisis de una experiencia de trabajo colaborativo, *IV Jornada Campus Virtual UCM. Experiencias en el Campus Virtual: Resultados*. Editorial Complutense, Madrid.
4. Britain, S. and Liber, O. (2004) A Framework for the Pedagogical Evaluation of Virtual Learning Environments, *JISC-commissioned report*. Available online: http://www.jisc.ac.uk/uploaded_documents/jtap-041.doc
5. Meyer, A. (1998) Synthesis of learning theories and concepts. Available online: http://hagar.up.ac.za/catts/learner/ameyer/synthesisoftheories.htm
6. Leidner, D. and Jarvenpaa, S. L. (1995) The use of information technology to enhance management school education: a theoretical view. *MIS Q*, 19(3), pp. 265–291
7. Vermetten, Y. J., Vermunt, J. D. and Lodewijks, H. G. (2002) Powerful learning environments? How university students differ in their response to instructional measures. *Learning and Instruction*, 12, pp. 263–284.
8. Joia, L. A. (2002) Assessment of a socio-constructivist model for teacher training: A case study. *Education Policy Analysis Archives*, 10(44) Available online: http://epaa.asu.edu/epaa/v10n44/
9. Jurs, S. G., Wiersma, W. (2004) *Research Methods in Education*, Pears
10. Skinner, B. F. (1969) *Contingencies of Reinforcement: A Theoretical Analysis*. Appleton-Century-Crofts, New York.
11. Piaget, J. (1967) Biologie et connaissance, París, Gallimard
12. Vigotski, L. (1985) Pensée et langage,París, Messidor. Editions Sociales
13. Bourdieu, P. (1982) Ce que parler veut dire, París, Fayard
14. Schütz, A. (1993) La construcción significativa del mundo social. Introducción a la sociología comprensiva, Alexandria, VA.
15. Johnson, D. W., Johnson, R. T. and Holubec, E. J. (1999) *Circles of Learning. Cooperation in the Classroom*, Barcelona, Paidos
16. Dillenbourg, P., Baker, M., Blaye, A. and Malley, C. (1996) The evolution of research on collaborative learning, Spada, E. and Reiman, P. (Eds.) *Learning in Humans Machine: Towards An Interdisciplinary Learning Science*, Elsevier, Oxford, pp. 189–211.
17. Gross, B. (2002) El ordenador invisible, Gedisa, Barcelona
18. Brufee, K. (1995) *Collaborative Learning: Higher Education, Interdependence, and the Authority of Knowledge*, The John Hopkins University Press, Baltimore y Londres

19. López Alonso, C. and Séré, A. (2004) Entornos formativos en el ciberespacio: las plataformas educativa" *Español Actual. Revista de español vivo*, Arco/Libros, Madrid

20. PLS Ramboll (2004) Studies in the Context of the E-learning Initiative: Virtual Models of European Universities, *Management for the European Commission*. Available online: http://www.elearningeuropa.info/extras/pdf/virtual_models.pdf

21. Sakai community map (2008) Available online: http://sakaiproject.org/index.php?option = com_wrapper&Itemid = 588

22. Carliner, S. (2005) Course Management Systems Versus Learning Management Systems, Available online: http://www.learning-circuits.org/2005/nov2005/carliner.htm

23. Conole, G. and Fill, K. (2005) A learning design toolkit to create pedagogically effective learning activities, *Journal of Interactive Media in Education*, Available online: http://www-jime.open.ac.uk/2005/08/conole-2005-08.pdf

24. UCM Virtual Campus (2008) Available online: https://www.ucm.es/info/uatd/CVUCM/index.php

25. López Alonso, C., Fernández-Pampillón, A. and De Miguel, E. (2008) Propuesta de integración de LAMS en el marco conceptual del espacio de aprendizaje socio-constructivista E-ling Actas de la *Conferencia Europea de LAMS 2008*, Cádiz, http://lamsfoundation.org/lams2007/papers.htm

26. Koper, R. and C. Tattersall (eds.) (2005) *Learning Design – A Handbook on Modelling and Delivering Networked Education and Training*. Springer Verlag, Heidelberg

27. Burgos, D. and Corbalán, G. (2006) Modelado y uso de escenarios de aprendizaje en entornos b-learning desde la práctica educativa, *III Jornadas Campus Virtual, Universidad Complutense, Madrid*, Available online: http://dspace.ou.nl/bitstream/1820/716/1/BURGOSandCORBALAN_15June2006_Review.pdf

28. Stengers, I. (1995) L'Invention des sciences modernes, Flammarion, Paris

29. Chen, W. F. (2005) Effect of Web-Browsing Interfaces in Web-Based Instruction: A Quantitative Study, *IEEE Transactions on Education*

30. Yin, R. (1994) *Case Study Research: Design and Methods* (2nd ed.). Sage Publishing, Beverly Hills, CA.

31. Cohen, J. (1994) The earth is round (p<.05), *American Psychologist*.

93

IS Degrees – Sociotechnical or Technosocial?

Jenny Coady and Rob Pooley

Abstract

It is widely agreed that information systems is a field requiring knowledge and competence, spanning business processes, information infrastructure and technical processes, uniting these to deliver information needs of organisations. In designing curricula which will educate new IS professionals appropriately, we are faced with a daunting range and volume of material. Despite attempts to structure and scope this, the problems remain and become worse with time. We revisit such a degree course, noting that many existing courses are based in management and business schools. We, however, are based in a computer science department. We have experience of convincing technologically focused students that understanding organisational and social issues is crucial to successful software engineering and students with an interest in organisations and people that they need technical understanding of information systems. We review some key proposals for IS model curricula and conclude with a proposal suited to the students we recruit.

Keywords Information systems education · Sociotechnical systems · Model curricula

1. Introduction

Modern organisations face continued pressure for change and adaptation in their business environment. Sambamurthy and Kirsh [8] explain that, with increased pressures towards globalisation and competitive advantage, firms are being compelled to re-evaluate their traditional structures and work processes. It is also widely accepted that the quality of an organisation's information system is a key in gaining maximum efficiency. Information systems are complex systems and require both technical and organizational expertise for design, development and management. There has long been agreement that the IS curriculum should be comprised of some combination of technical and sociotechnical subjects. The creation of the IS 2002 report [3], building on the earlier report IS 97, goes some way to addressing this; however, Turner and Lowry [13] show that there is much disagreement as to what the mix of these subjects should be and how best to equip students in this area. BISD 2007 [2] created a business IS design curriculum based on goals and restrictions of the Bologna Declaration and Dublin descriptors, and this led us to question how an IS degree could be implemented effectively within Heriot Watt University.

Abraham et al. [1] suggest that IS programmes derived in business schools are well positioned to equip students with the skills and capabilities desired for information technology (IT) professionals in the IT departments of organizations and that, as such, business schools have an advantage over competing programmes in alternative schools, such as computer science and information studies, since they have the necessary functional area and management skills that IT executives in non-IT organizations need. However, it is our opinion that by working from a computer science school, with the cooperation of the School of Management and Languages within Heriot Watt University, an improved IS programme can be

---

Jenny Coady and Rob Pooley · Department of Computer Science, Heriot Watt University, Edinburgh, Scotland.

G.A. Papadopoulos et al. (eds.), *Information Systems Development*, DOI 10.1007/b137171_93,

developed to ensure students are attracted to the course, despite falling numbers in computer science recruitment, and that this will create IS graduates that will be desired in industry.

2. Some Key Existing Proposals

For decades researchers have worked to improve the effectiveness of information systems in organisations, yet their successful provision, to optimally support organisational information processing, has remained elusive [10]. The prevalence of information systems development (ISD) failures testifies to this. It has been suggested that ISD failures could be attributed to the narrowness of the perspective of the analyst and the need for a more authentic view of the ways in which people in organisations process information and make decisions. These lessons led to the development of many current methodological paradigms which have given rise to the ISD methodologies taught in universities and used in industry [15, 11].

Landry et al. [5] suggest that the graduate of an IS programme should be equipped to function adequately at an entry level position within industry and have a good basis for career development. Gupta and Wachter [4] had earlier suggested that there is a need for academia to monitor industry continually to ensure that graduates can acquire the necessary mix of skills to perform competitively in the jobs market. This has also been backed by industrial speakers who have come to HWU as part of ongoing lectures in the current CS / IT courses.

The influential IS 2002 [3] report defines four characteristics of the IS profession which have been relatively constant over time and have been integrated into the curriculum. These are

- IS professionals must have a broad business and real-world perspective.
- IS professionals must have strong analytical and critical thinking skills.
- IS professionals must have interpersonal communication and team skills and have strong ethical principles.
- IS professionals must design and implement information technology solutions that enhance organisational performance.

Figure 93.1, taken from IS 2002, presents a high-level categorization of the exit characteristics that emphasise the central role of technology-enabled business development at the intersection of the four major areas that were identified in the initial assumptions about the IS profession.

Carlsson et al., in creating the proposal in BISD 2007 [2], justify their approach as diverging from IS 2002 due to a need for emphasis on capabilities of graduates and not merely a course-oriented approach. Abrahams et al. [1] suggest that although IS programmes are well placed in business schools to help to deliver the skills and capabilities desired for professionals, programmes do need to improve in order to attract students to help address shortages in the workplace and deliver evolving skills needed by industry. Snoke et al. [9] note that anecdotal evidence from IS industry interviews suggests that tertiary curricula in IS do not meet the needs of industry. Lynch and Fisher [6] build on this idea to suggest that various studies, including [14] and [12], show that just as information systems practitioners are unhappy with IS graduates' skills, information technology practitioners are not satisfied with current, more technically focused IT graduates, who are often seen to be lacking the aptitude and skills to work effectively in collaborative teams.

It is these soft skills that form a key strand of the curriculum presented in this chapter. We agree strongly with Turner and Lowry's suggestion [13] that a revision of IS curriculum can be put forward to adopt a more student-centred/active learning approach to achieve a better calibre of graduate for the workplace. There is an emerging consensus that the current role of the academic has shifted from knowledge giver to facilitator or guide to active learners, encouraging students to work more on self-directed learning, thus preparing them for more real-world situations and enabling them to develop more of the softer skills that cannot often be taught.

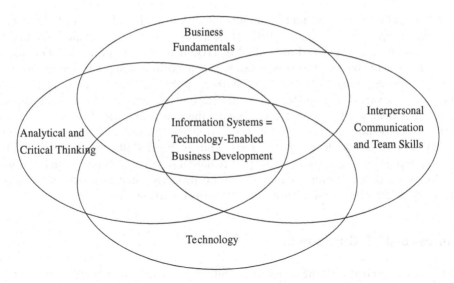

Figure 93.1. High-level categorization of IS graduate exit characteristics.

3. What Is Different in Our Approach

We believe our course, described below, is a satisfactory compromise, given the pragmatic decisions we needed to make, but that the ideal IS course remains elusive. Briefly stated, we would have wanted our course to have the sort of balance shown in Table 93.1. We assume the standard Heriot Watt 8 module, semester-based year/stage leading to a four-stage bachelor's degree.

Table 93.1. Ideal curriculum.

Stage	Semester	Technical	Sociotechnical	Human centred/ generic	Applied/project based
1	1	Programming	Technology and society	Study skills for university	Databases
	2	Computer systems	Management of organisations	Interaction with systems	Emerging technologies – mini projects
2	1	Database management systems	Organisational behaviour	Interaction design	Internet, communications and mobility
	2	Information system design	Operations management	Critical and computational thinking	Creative design project
3	1	Software engineering	Knowledge management	Human-centred design	Group project
	2	Professional development	Sociotechnical and soft systems	Research methods	
4	1	Advanced option	Advanced option	Advanced individual project	
	2	Advanced option	Advanced option		

The first two columns are the underpinning "core" knowledge elements of the degree. In these elements we seek an appropriate balance between learning concerning technical factors affecting IT systems and learning concerning social/individual behaviour within organisations. Our use of the term "organisation" rather than "business" is deliberate. We see a world where organisations are of many types and have widely divergent aims. Governments, charities, public services, even armed forces should be included. Students are aware of and concerned about issues such as organisational and business ethics. We need to address these if we want to attract and motivate the best young people.

The other columns show our concern for student-centred learning and transferable skills. It should not be assumed that we see the learning of generic and practical skills as a separate matter from the acquisition of knowledge, however. Indeed we expect to have a significant emphasis on these in all modules, but we want to ensure that learning is externalised and properly integrated across the curriculum. To achieve that, we include both individual and group projects of various sizes.

4. A "Technosocial" IS Curriculum

In reality, we have ended with the structure for our core 3 years shown in Table 93.2. Stage 4 is made up of advanced options (60%) and an individual project (40%) and is essentially the same as in Table 93.1.

Table 93.2. Actual course structure.

Stage	Semester 1	Basis	Semester 2	Basis
1	Software development	Technical	Introduction to computer systems	Technical
	Emerging technologies	Applied technology	Technology in society	Sociotechnical
	Praxis	Generic	Introduction to databases	Technical
	Interactive systems	Human centred	Management and enterprise	Organisational
2	Interaction design	Human centred	Software design	Technical
	Fundamentals of marketing	Organisational	Creative design (project)	Application
	Internet technology	Applied technology	Database management	Applied technology
	Organisational behaviour	Orga4isational	Operations management	Organisational
3	Software engineering (group project)	Application	Software engineering (group project)	Application
	Knowledge management	Organisational	Research methods	Generic
	Critical thinking	Generic	Soft systems	Sociotechnical
	Business policy	Organisational	International strategic management	Organisational

The modules are categorised by their role in the curriculum or their "basis". However, unlike the four categories of our ideal curriculum, we have ended with seven such categories: generic – three modules, technical – two modules, applied technology – three modules, sociotechnical – two modules, human centred – two modules, organisational – seven modules and application – three modules. If we compare this in detail with the "ideal" structure proposed in Table 93.1, we can see the effects of compromise. There are three sets of constraints which have forced these compromises.

- *Resources*: We have limited teaching resources available for this degree. This is partly due to the need to live within a budget and partly due to a lack of relevant knowledge and background among colleagues in the computer science department. This has tended to push us both towards a more technically based course than many IS and BIS degrees and towards dependence on modules from the School of Management and Languages..
- *Cultural bias*: We have encountered and had to answer the reluctance of some colleagues to accept that some subjects can be taught except from any standpoint other than a technical or a mathematical one. This is both subtle and hard to counter in a computer science department which has grown with such a culture embedded within it.

- *Reciprocal lack of understanding* with business and management-based colleagues. We believe the correct view of information systems incorporates individual, organisational and technical perspectives on system management and development. Within most current business and management programmes, "organisational" views tend to be biased towards commercial entities and their needs. Understanding of individual needs is often catered for only minimally. BIS degrees typically follow these trends and the IS 2002 model curriculum embodies this, with reference to "business" rather than "organisation" and a focus on the individual only in terms of transferrable skills. We are concerned to prevent our degree following suit.

5. Conclusions and Further Work

IS 2002 asserts that good teaching staff are vital to the strength of an IS programme. It further asserts that, in order to maintain successful development and delivery of the curriculum, the interests and qualifications of those staff must allow the course and curriculum not only to be taught but also to be modified and changed. Herein lies our argument for the rationale behind our approach as a team to the programme developed in this chapter.

Technology and the business environment continue to change [1]; this makes it necessary that the IS discipline must also evolve or else run the risk of producing graduates not needed in industry. The very foundation of this course stems from our belief that as organisations change and go global so the skills needed in graduates change. At the same time the beliefs of students change, with the balance between personal gain and altruistic concern for the environment and world development shifting.

In order to keep industry equipped with good workers with relevant skills and ensure greater uptake of courses within the university, by addressing the concerns of the current generation of applicants, our new IS degree programme will consciously pursue both a greater technological emphasis and a wider analysis of the needs of organisations, including those outside the traditional commercial sector. It will be run in a CS department, where, in our context at least, the technological and sociotechnical aspects can be managed in greater detail. At the same time, by working closely with our School of Management, we seek to provide the knowledge of globalised organisations needed to produce graduates that are sought after by employers.

Northedge [7] has argued that traditional teaching and learning strategies no longer accommodate diversity in the student population. The notion of "one size fits all" is no longer acceptable, and disciplines should be obliged to make attempts at alternative ways of facilitating the transfer of knowledge to students. In creating this curriculum we have opted to think of alternative ways and means of being facilitators of knowledge acquisition by engaging through various tools and techniques available to us, such as use of 2nd life, small tutorial groups, lab-based individual and group exercises, seminars, essays and lectures, and in doing so we believe we can incorporate the majority of transferable skills that are sought after by employers, by making them key aspects of our curriculum as opposed to a bolt on.

Our wider, bolder claim is that information systems is a distinct discipline. It takes input, in the form of information and theories, from computer science, management and sociology, but it should arrive at a new synthesis as a consequence of its concerns with effective and humane organisations. It should resist being a sub-discipline and, instead, make explicit its unique viewpoint. We have begun, in the chapter reviewed here and in the new curricula being developed in many places, a debate which will be informed by our successes and failings. As a community we need to continue the debate in a constructive way, leading to new IS professionals with the attributes sought by employers and society.

In the end the words we use, sociotechnical or technosocial, mean little. What is important is that we are successful in these aims.

Acknowledgements

The authors gratefully acknowledge the work and inspiration of the rest of the IS development team at Heriot Watt: Helen Ashton, Sandy Louchart, Brian Palmer and Judy Robertson.

References

1. Abraham, T., Beath, C., Bullen, C., Gallagher, K., Goles, T., Kaiser, K. and Simon, J. (2006). IT workforce trends: Implications for IS programs, *Communications of the Association for Information Systems*, Volume 17, pp. 1147–1170.
2. Carlsson, S. Hedman, J. and Steen, O. (2007) Model curriculum for a bachelor of science Program in Business Information Systems Design (BISD 2007): Organisational impacts. In *Proceedings of the 16th International Conference on Information Systems Development (ISD2007)*, NUI Galway, Ireland.
3. Gorgone, J., Davis, G., Valcich, J.S., Topi, H., Feinstein, D. and Longenecker, H., Jr. (2002). *IS 2002 Model Curriculum and Guidelines for Undedgraduate Degree Programs in Information Systems*, Association for Computing Machinery, Association for Information Systems, Association for Information Technology Professionals.
4. Gupta, J. N. D. and Wachter, R. M. A. (1998). Capstone course in the information systems curriculum, *International Journal of Information Management*, Vol. 18, No. 6, pp. 427–441.
5. Landry, J., Longenecker, H., Haigood, B. and Feinstein, D. (2000). Comparing entry-level skill depths across information systems job types: Perceptions of IS faculty, *Proceedings of Sixth Americas Conference on Information Systems*, Long Beach, CA.
6. Lynch, K. and Fisher, J. Tomorrows workforce today: What is required by information systems graduates to work in a collaborative information systems workplace. (Book Chapter XV) in *Information Systems and Technology Education: From University to the Workplace*. IGI Global, Hershey, PA, pp. 311–326, ISBN-10: 1599041146.
7. Northedge, A. (2003) Rethinking teaching in the context of diversity. *Teaching in Higher Education*, Vol. 8, No. 1, Jan , pp. 17–32 (16 Routledge).
8. Sambamurthy, V. and Kirsch, L. J. (2000). An integrative framework of the information systems development process, *Decision Sciences*, Vol. 31, No. 2, pp. 391–411.
9. Snoke, R., Underwood, A. and Bruce, C. (2002). An Australian view of generic attributes coverage in undergraduate programs of study: An information systems case study. *Proceedings of HERDSA 2002*, 590-598. Retrieved 3rd April 2008 from http://www. ecu.edu.au/conferences/herdsa/main/papers/ref/pdf/Snoke.pdf.
10. Stapleton (2001).
11. Stapleton, L. and Murphy, C. (2002). Examining non-representation in engineering notations: Empirical evidence for the ontological incompleteness of the functionally-rational modelling paradigm, *Proceedings of the IFAC World Congress 2002*, Elsevier: Amsterdam.
12. Toleman, M., Roberts, D. and Ryan, C. (2004) Retrofitting generic graduate attributes: A case-study of IS undergraduate programs, *Informing Science + Information Technology Education Joint Conference – InSITE 2004*, 625–635 (Rockhampton, 25–28 June).
13. Turner, R. and Lowry, G. (2003) Education for a technology-based profession: softening the information systems curriculum. (Book Chapter XIII) in *Issues in Information Systems Education*, T. McGill, Editor, IRMA Press, Hershey, PA, pp. 153–172, ISBN 1-931777-53-5.
14. Von Hellens, L. Wong, S. and Orr, J. (2000). IT skills requirements: Perspective from industry. In *Proceedings 11th Australasian Conference on Information Systems: ACIS 2000*. Brisbane: ACIS. (*ACIS2000 Proceedings*, CD-ROM, 2000).
15. Walters, S. A., Broady, J. E. and Hartley, R. J. (1994). A review of information systems development methodologies, *Library Management*, Vol. 15, No. 6, pp. 5–19.

94

Teaching Medium-Sized ERP Systems –
A Problem-Based Learning Approach

Axel Winkelmann and Martin Matzner

Abstract

In order to increase the diversity in IS education, we discuss an approach for teaching medium-sized ERP systems in master courses. Many of today's IS curricula are biased toward large ERP packages. Nevertheless, these ERP systems are only a part of the ERP market. Hence, this chapter describes a course outline for a course on medium-sized ERP systems. Students had to study, analyze, and compare five different ERP systems during a semester. The chapter introduces a procedure model and scenario for setting up similar courses at other universities. Furthermore, it describes some of the students' outcomes and evaluates the contribution of the course with regard to a practical but also academic IS education.

Keywords Diversity · ERP · Enterprise resource planning · Course outline · Case study · Teaching · IS education · University · Information systems

1. Introduction

Enterprise resource planning (ERP) software has gained much prominence in the IS literature and in IS education. It is a significant phenomenon in practice and hence, an important component of the IS curricula [14, 16, 23]. These kinds of standardized enterprise software systems seek to integrate all functional aspects and business processes of a company with the objective to offer a holistic view on company data and functionality [10, 22]. Although the market for ERP systems is very diverse, the coverage seems to be biased. On the one hand, few big global players such as SAP or Oracle are omnipresent. On the other hand, hundreds of less complex systems offer a good functional coverage for companies of up to 5,000 users but are hardly mentioned in the media. For example, more than 300 ERP systems are on the German market but only few, large systems are well known in public.

ERP education in IS curricula seems to be biased toward large systems as well (e.g., [8, 9, 11, 15, 21]). Many universities offer ERP courses based on large packaged systems, especially SAP systems (e.g., [9, 15]). This is very important for students' education because these systems have very large customer bases and students will most likely work on such a system later on if they start a career in large corporations [14]. Furthermore, many big software development companies offer a good university support, hand out valuable material, and have published many academic and practical books about their ERP systems. For example, SAP, the leading ERP vendor has established the largest ERP university alliance with more than 400 universities worldwide accessing their ERP system [9]. But there is also a downside of this way of teaching ERP. Students only get to know one or two well-known systems. A broad market overview of the

Axel Winkelmann and Martin Matzner • Institute for IS Research, University of Koblenz-Landau, Koblenz, Germany.

G.A. Papadopoulos et al. (eds.), *Information Systems Development*, DOI 10.1007/b137171_94,
© Springer Science+Business Media, LLC 2009

ERP market is not part of their education. This would also foster the personal IS skills such as systemic-thinking and problem-solving skills. The one-sided education might foster the concentration on the ERP market as later on (ex-)students might tend to choose a big standard system for their company as well, because they have not learned about smaller and better fitting alternatives. Furthermore, large systems tend to be very complex. Hence, we noticed many times that students tried to find the right fields, buttons, and screens instead of actually thinking about the processes behind the user interface.

The bias in ERP education is astonishing, because a comprehensive understanding of IS implies a broad, unbiased education in this field. There have been many efforts to match IS education toward industry needs already. For example, [20, 5] describe skills for industry-ready IT graduates in the information systems centric curriculum. Hence, a graduate should possess personal skills such as systemic-thinking and problem-solving skills, interpersonal skills such as communicative and collaborative skills, and technical knowledge such as process management and systems development skills. A broader insight into the ERP market can be a valuable supplement for existing IS education. In this chapter, we describe a course that picks up teaching with technology by dealing with national ERP systems. The course should not be understood as a substitute to courses on large packaged software but it should be understood as a valuable supplement to it. During the course students were asked to become acquainted with five different medium-sized ERP systems by using a scenario that describes different retail processes. It turned out that the students' understanding for ERP systems and business processes strongly improved. Finally, all students were very satisfied with this way of studying.

In the second section, we describe a procedure model as recommendation how to set up a similar course at other universities. The third section deals with exemplary results of the seminar. The results are to be seen as encouragements for possible objectives, outcomes and achievements of similar courses at other universities. Furthermore, in the fourth section the achievements of the course are evaluated in order to estimate the learning effect with regard to industry needs.

2. Procedure Model and Description of the Course

For the implementation of an ERP seminar with various ERP systems a multi-level procedure is reasonable in order to select appropriate ERP systems. First of all, the area that shall be discussed in the seminar needs to be selected (e.g., concentration on production only) and – if appropriate – linked to a domain-oriented framework (Nr. 1 in Fig. 94.1). The identification of appropriate ERP manufacturers is necessary for developing a textual guideline and vice versa (2 and 3a). According to Stewart et al., problem-based learning is a very good way of teaching information systems [20]. It is very challenging because many times documentation and functionality are not aligned. Therefore, a scenario that describes real processes within a company is the starting pointing for the students (3b). After some introductory lessons about the ERP market and software evaluation in general, students will start analyzing the systems (4), which should be presented at the end of the course (5). See Fig. 94.1 for a procedure model that has proved to be very

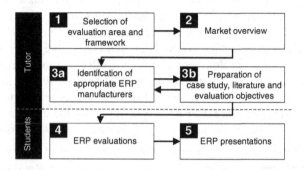

Figure 94.1. Procedure model for the implementation of a course "ERP systems".

valuable for us. It is very helpful to include the course into an information systems master's degree, because students will then be able to understand and use process models and data models. There should not be too many students in order to ensure a proper mentoring and an individual in-depth examination of the systems. In our case, only 10 master students from the second IS master semester ("Wirtschaftsinformatik") attended the course.

2.1. [Step 1] Selection of Evaluation Area and Framework

Today, even medium-sized ERP systems offer complex functionality. Due to their standardization efforts they have to offer solutions to different requirements. To narrow down the evaluation task for students it is reasonable to focus on smaller aspects of each system (e.g., only considering production planning and scheduling). According to the kind of university degree a focus on specific study objectives and domains is reasonable. The discussed course instance was, i.e., based on specific retail processes. Production issues were not part of the course.

Technical and domain-specific frameworks can help selecting appropriate ERP software. They can serve as guidelines and leitmotif for students' evaluations. Technical frameworks such as the ARIS house [11] or the Zachman framework [24] provide formal and highly structured ways of defining an enterprise or its underlying IT. Domain-oriented frameworks provide structured information and data about a domain (see Table 94.1 for some examples).

Table 94.1. Technical and domain-specific reference frameworks for ERP courses.

Framework	Description
Architecture of integrated information systems (ARIS)	The ARIS framework consists of four general views: function view, organization view, data view, and process view. It does not give any recommendations for the development of IS in retail but gives some general advice [11, 17, 18].
ARTS	The Association for Retail Technology Standards offers a best practice data model for retail applications. Action charts and data models allow a comparison between best practice and examined ERP system, see http://www.nrf-arts.org/
Retail application architecture (RAA)	The RAA has been developed by IBM in order to help companies plan and develop their IT systems. It explains best practice activity chains and data models [12, 19].
Retail-H	In accordance with the ARIS framework, the Retail-H describes retail companies with conceptual views of functions, data, and processes [2].
Y-CIM	The Y-CIM model graphically explains the integration of business and technical aspects. It provides interrelations between various sorts of computer-aided systems and production planning systems and can be seen as a procedural model for implementing CIM [10].

We decided for the Retail-H framework as it is known internationally and offers a good insight into retail companies [3, 7, 13]. The framework serves as a reference model and summarizes the tasks of a retailing company. It differs between functions, data, and processes. Each function (e.g., contracting, purchasing) is broken down into sub-functions with best practice process models (modeled with event-driven process chains) and data models (modeled with entity relationship models). The different levels of granularity allow a better classification of parts of the scenario. Furthermore, students are able to gain a good insight into best practice processes. They are able to compare the data models of ERP systems with the Retail-H reference models in order to discuss best ways of translating business requirements into ERP software. The shape of the Retail-H is based on the logical structure of a retail company (see Figs. 94.2 and 94.3 on page XXX.). On the left side, all tasks concerned with the suppliers are placed in logical order (contracting is the first thing to do before actually purchasing and receiving goods, etc.). On the right side, all tasks associated with customers are placed. Logistical functions with goods receipt, warehousing and goods issue are arranged horizontally.

2.2. [Step 2] Market Overview

There are many possibilities for getting a market overview. Unfortunately, most press is only about the top 10 ERP players on the market (SAP, Oracle, Microsoft, Infor, etc.). Small systems are hardly mentioned in articles. A first starting point to identify appropriate ERP systems for a lecture on ERP can be a face-to-face contact at exhibitions such as CEBIT or CES. Many technical or retail journals also discuss different ERP systems. Software evaluation and overview platforms such as IT-Matchmaker or ERP market studies (e.g., [4]) can also help in finding appropriate systems. Table 94.2 gives an overview on different selection methods.

Table 94.2. Methods for identifying appropriate ERP products.

Choice	Examples	Advantages and disadvantages
Face-to-face meeting at conferences or fairs	CEBIT, Hanover, Germany CES, Las Vegas, USA Retail Solution, Birmingham, UK	+ Face-to-face meeting − Mostly wrong contact person at fair − Incomplete market overview
Discussion of ERP systems in technical or retail journals	ERP-Magazine Retail technology journal Computer week	+ Detailed ERP lists + Reviews and background information − Random search for articles − Incomplete market overview
Market overview studies and software evaluation platforms	IT-Matchmaker Gartner studies	+ Detailed ERP lists + In-depth functionality overview

2.3. [Step 3a] Identification of Appropriate ERP Manufacturers

Criteria for the evaluation and selection of ERP systems for university teaching can be "company size" and "customer base" (system importance in the market), a "strategic fit" of the functionality for the objectives of a course, or the "willingness" of ERP manufacturers to support a university course.

In our case, all ERP systems provide retail activities such as ordering, storing, and delivering goods. A strong emphasis was on conditions and prices. All ERP manufacturers were asked for a remote access to their systems. Hence, no effort was necessary for the installation of a system on university servers. Furthermore, manufacturers ensured appropriate master data and user rights. It turned out to be sensible to send each manufacturer a draft of the scenario in order to ensure a proper preparation of the system. In total, five systems were available for evaluation.

Most ERP manufacturers have between 50 and 500 employees. Hence, the identification of an appropriate contact person for a first call is very important. It seems reasonable to get in touch with either the manager or marketing staff of the company at first. CIOs/CTOs turned out to be too busy to get them involved in the first place. Often they fear a technology drain and an abuse of their software at universities. Therefore, they might decline inquiries when asked first.

2.4. [Step 3b] Preparation of Scenario, Evaluation Objectives, and Literature

Selecting appropriate ERP systems and preparing a scenario interact with each other. For example, if the objective of the course is to look at retail processes, an ERP system, that offers PPS functionality only, will not be suitable. A strong emphasize on prices and conditions in the scenario will not be sensible if there are only systems available without any marketing functionality. For our lecture, the scenario should be close to a real situation in a company. Students had to reproduce a general and a specific retail process within each ERP system. The actual scenario consists of 10 pages of process description and examples. In Table 94.3, a compendium is given.

Table 94.3. Scenario for ERP course (compendium).

Generic retail process	Enter a framework contract (1,000 PCs for 299 Euro each)
	Normal purchase price 349 Euro each
	Order 150 PCs for next month for 299 Euro each
	Supplier sends a delivery notification
	Supplier delivers 150 PCs that have to be checked and stored
	A customer asks for an offer on 10 PCs
	The customer orders eight PCs relating to the initial offer
	Take order amount from the warehouse and ship to the customer
Specific retail process	Check for basic price conditions, transaction-based conditions, and subsequent price conditions for purchase and sales (conditions such as basic bonus, market share increase bonus, listing bonus, allowance adjustment bonus, etc. are given in the scenario)
	Check if the system is capable of conditions depending on specific objects such as regions, customer loyalty, etc.
	Check for calculation possibilities in purchase (different brutto and net costs, etc.)
	Evaluate warehouse structures in terms of organization, areas, and attributes such as restrictions in weight or article characters (explosives, chemicals, etc.)
	Check if it is possible to split sales offers into orders
	Check if it is possible to deliver to different stores with different prices but send all bills once a month to one headquarter. If a certain sum is crossed, headquarter shall receive a bonus.

Students should be able to understand the processes mentioned within a scenario. Hence, additional literature is necessary (e.g., for retail literature [5, 2, 6, 7]). Students had to evaluate the ERP systems based on the requirements of the scenario. They had to enter all necessary data in order to properly present the functionality later on and had to model the processes that were possible with the ERP functionality. Furthermore, relevant data aspects should also be modeled. A drawback of the remote access was the lack of direct database access. Therefore, students had to derive data models from functionality and user interface layouts.

2.5. [Step 4] ERP Evaluations

We gave a short introduction on ERP manufacturers and the relevance of their system in the market. Students did not know four of five systems prior to the lesson. There are various ways to introduce users to a new system (e.g., [1, 3]). For example, key user trainings ("train the trainers") or end-user trainings are two ways of introducing a new ERP system to an organization. Within this seminar, it turned out that students did not need any sort of training but were able to understand the systems on their own. Only some discussion sessions and telephone calls with the ERP manufacturers were necessary for the evaluation of the systems.

2.6. [Step 5] ERP Presentations

For the system presentations, a 2-day block seminar is very sensible. Students were asked to present their system for 60 minutes each. They had to answer questions on the system for another 30 minutes. A 2-day seminar gives a compact impression on different ERP systems and allows a good comparison of all five systems. It comes very close to real situations as companies that want to buy ERP software often have a look at various systems in a very short time. Students had to present the scenario within their ERP systems in real time. Furthermore, they presented extra information.

3. System Evaluations and Presentations

3.1. General Comparison

All five systems offer at least a software architecture and graphical user interface that is not older than 10 years. Systems 1–4 are German products that are sold locally only (Germany, Switzerland, Austria). System 5 is an international product that belongs to a large software company. All companies – except number 5 – are small-to medium-sized enterprises that developed their recent system architectures at the end of the 1990s. System 1 is just about to release a new product version with an improved IT architecture. Hence, students were able to get to know the old and the new architectures. All systems have a relevant market share. System 3 is a niche product that is well known but only relevant to food retailers (cf. Table 94.4)

Table 94.4. General information about the systems.

	System 1	System 2	System 3	System 4	System 5
Company size	25	60	60	200	> 70,000
Market entry of recent architecture	1998 / 2007	1998	1996	2000	n. a.
Number of installations	400	350	10	1,000	50,000
Customer size (users)	10–250	20–500	50–5,000	10–5,000	5–5,000

The market for ERP products is very dynamic. In Germany alone, there are still more than 300 software solutions. But many ERP products have been bought up or terminated already. Even various big software producers such as Baan, Peoplesoft, or Retek are not in business anymore. Only few new software producers entered the ERP market in the last years. Hence, existing ERP producers have to find a strategic positioning in order to survive the market concentration. Manufacturer 1 has developed an improved architecture based on the current state of the art. Approved functionality but modern interface possibilities and fast and reliable implementations offer some advantage over other companies. Manufacturer 2 has a solid architecture and good functionality but does not offer any additional advantages at the moment. During the evaluation it turned out that the architecture does not meet all modern demands anymore. Manufacturer 3 has chosen to be a well-known niche player. With 10 installations in the niche, the manufacturer has a broad market range. Furthermore, the manufacturer cooperates with two supplementary software manufacturers in order to build some sort of "best of breed" alliance. System 4 is an add-on, based on System 5 which is a market leader in the SME sector. Architecture changes in Systems 4 and 5 are done at the moment but are not finished yet.

3.2. Functional Comparison

Systems 1 and 3 are specialized trade systems (see Table 94. 5 for a functional comparison). Therefore, students expected them to be very suitable for our scenario. Nevertheless, it turned out that none of the five systems was capable of supporting the whole processes that were demanded by the scenario. Although students gained deep knowledge about all five systems, they were not able to

Table 94.5. Examples of functional characteristics.

	System 1	System 2	System 3	System 4	System 5
Trade level	Wholesale and retail	Wholesale and retail	Wholesale (Food)	Wholesale and retail	Wholesale and retail
Differentiated structures	o	+	+	+	+
Central buying and branch office structures	+	+	+	+	+
Interorganizational processes	o	+	+	+	+
Purchase conditions – number of price scales	>10	>10	–	>10	>10
Purchase contract type					
Amount	+	+	+	+	+
Value	–	–	+	–	+
Delivery schedule	–	+	–	+	–
Units of quantity					
Basic unit	+	–	+	+	+
Sales unit	+	+	+	+	+
Purchase unit	+	+	+	+	+
Storage unit	+	+	+	+	+
Removal unit	–	–	+	–	–
Management of delivery notifications	–	+	+	o	o
Sales bonus based on					
Assortment in total	–	+	–	+	–
Article group	–	+	–	+	–
Single articles	+	+	–	+	–

prefer any system at the end. System 1 was very modern, with broad functional coverage. System 2 offered an even broader functional coverage but also an inferior usability. System 3 was not capable of all processes but offered some sophisticated features from the food area. Systems 4 and 5 covered various but not all requirements.

Although students used all systems via remote access, it was possible to present the systems fluently. The short interval between each presentation allowed a good comparison of functionality, ergonomics, and screen design. In Fig. 94. 2, the same function (purchase order) is displayed in Systems 1, 3, 4, and 5 as an example for comparisons. While System 1 uses tables for the handling of orders, Systems 4 and 5 prefer fields that can be entered while pressing the tab key. System 3 is somewhere in-between.

Direct comparisons of user interfaces offered the chance to compare different usability concepts. For example Fig. 94.3 accentuates the need for a valid style guide during software development. Both screens (nearly) offer identical functionality but do not look the same at all. Fields and buttons are of different sizes and are not at the same place.

3.3. Technical Comparison

All ERP systems have two-tier architectures. Only the new version of System 1 already has a three-tier architecture, System 5 is changing to three-tier at the moment. Most companies except Company 4 used an object-oriented approach for software development. Especially the development with Java and .Net seems to be very popular for all developers. When asked for an estimate on the development effort, two manufacturers estimated it to be between 80 and 150 man-years. Although the estimate is very imprecise, the figure gives an indication that standard software development is very time consuming and

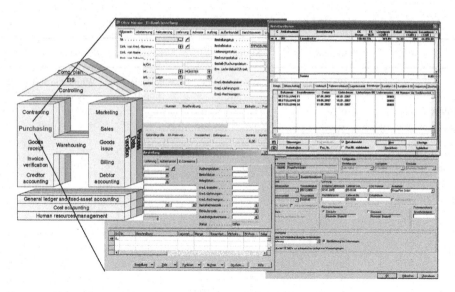

Figure 94.2. Example for different GUI concepts for the same functional task.

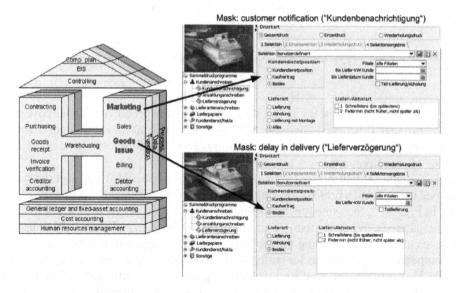

Figure 94.3. Identical screens with different layouts (System 2).

costly. All five systems at least support a windows operating system and an Oracle or MS SQL database (see Table 94.6).

    Students had to describe parts of each system with entity relationship Models (see [1]). For example, students should model the warehouse possibilities of each system. As they did not have access to the actual database tables, they had to assume the table structure from GUI and system behavior. Data models offered another opportunity to discuss certain aspects of each system and the modeling task allowed a recapitulation of data modeling issues within the course. Furthermore, students realized while discussing

Table 94.6. Technical overview.

	System 1	System 2	System 3	System 4	System 5
Programming paradigm	Object oriented	4GL, Object oriented	Object oriented	Procedural	Object oriented
Programming language	C#, .Net	Gupta, C++, Java	Smalltalk, Java	C-Side	.Net
Development (man-years)	n. s.	80	n. s.	150	n. s.
Database support	Gupta, MS SQL, Oracle	Adabas, DB2, Gupta, MaxDB, MS SQL, Oracle	DB2, Oracle	MS SQL	MS SQL
OS support					
Unix	–	+	–	–	–
SOLARIS	–	+	+	–	–
Linux	–	+	+	–	–
Windows	+	+	+	+	+

individual ERMs that a conceptual phase in front of the actual implementation is very sensitive in order to allow flexible functionality.

4. Course Evaluation

4.1. Students' Perspective

An anonymous, final evaluation of the course proved a high interest in the area. All master students were very satisfied although the amount of work for this course was higher than for other courses. Some students mentioned the usage of the framework to be very helpful. The interest for ERP systems has increased during the seminar – although it was already very high before the course. The ERP knowledge has increased considerably and students said they also have gained knowledge about retail processes. The scenario proved to be very useful, although the level of difficulty of the seminar turned out to be very high. See Table 94.7 for an overview of the students' evaluation.

Table 94.7. Students' evaluation of the ERP course.

	Average grade (1 = very high, 5 = very low)	SD
Knowledge before course	2.50	0.71
Interest in ERP issues before course	1.88	0.60
Interest in ERP issues after course	1.63	0.48
Motivation for own thoughts and opinion building	1.63	0.48
Learning atmosphere (1 = very positive, 5 = very negative)	1.50	0.50
ERP knowledge gain in general	2.00	0.87
Knowledge gain on discussed ERP systems	1.00	0.00
Knowledge gain in comparison to other seminars	2.29	1.00
Usefulness of scenario	1.38	0.48
Adequacy of chosen systems for course	1.25	0.43
Level of difficulty (1 = very difficult, 5 = very easy)	1.33	0.47
Effort needed	1.20	0.40
Effort needed in comparison to other courses	1.16	0.37

4.2. Manufacturers' Perspective

At the beginning of the course, the ERP companies were skeptical about the course. Most of them hardly had any experience with university courses. Therefore, they expected a lot of additional work and no benefits at all. Some manufacturers even argued that competitors might steal some ideas. To counter this apprehensibility, we decided only to allow remote access via university IP addresses. Furthermore, ERP presentations were declared internal with no employees of ERP manufacturers allowed.

Once the course started, manufacturers turned out to be very helpful. One manufacturer invited students over to his place for a 2-day introduction to his ERP system. Other manufacturers offered help lines and customized help files in order to ease the familiarization for the students. During the seminar, some manufacturers started questioning me about the progress and how they could help.

The remote access to the ERP systems was helpful for manufacturers as well as universities because it helped keeping the effort for an ERP implementation low. Furthermore, manufacturers did not have to fear an abuse of their software. All five manufacturers were very satisfied with the results of the seminar. All were interested in the evaluation results for their system. Some even asked students for joining them for an internship. So far, all manufacturers are looking forward to repeating the course.

4.3. Lecturer's Perspective

The idea was to establish a counterbalance to a one-sided IS education based on ERP systems of global players. In former courses with very large ERP systems, many students tried to click the right buttons instead of understanding the whole system and processes behind it. Therefore, the scenario did not focus on a specific and detailed company process but served as a story for the examination of different ERP systems. Although the initial effort for the seminar was very high, feedback from students and manufacturers proved it to be a valuable component in IS education. Furthermore, similar courses are a chance for lecturers to gain insight into different ERP systems.

References

1. Aldrich, C. (1999). "Best Practices in End-User Training." Gartner Research Note TU-09-4549.
2. Becker, J., T. Rotthowe, et al. (1998). A Framework for Efficient Information Modeling – Guidelines for Retail Enterprises. International Conference on Information Systems (ICIS).
3. Becker, J., W. Uhr, et al. (2001). Retail Information Systems Based on SAP Products. Springer, Berlin, Heidelberg, New York.
4. Biscotti, F., C. Pang, et al. (2003). ERP Software Market Trends and Forecast: Europe. Gartner, Stamford, CT.
5. Boyle, T. A. and S. E. Strong (2006). "Skill Requirements for ERP Graduates." Journal of Information Systems Education 17(4): 403–412.
6. Brown, C. V. and I. Vessey (2003). "Leveraging the ERP Learnings for the Next Wave of Enterprise Systems Projects." MIS Quarterly Executive 2(1): 65–77.
7. Chen, P. P. (1976). "The Entity Relationship Model – Toward a Unified View of Data." ACM Transactions on Database Systems (TODS) 1(1): 9–36.
8. Gable, G. and M. Rosemann (1999). ERP in University Teaching & Research: An International Survey. 3rd Annual SAP Asia Pacific Institutes of Higher Learning Forum. Maximizing the Synergy between Teaching, Research and Business. 1-2 November 1999, Singapore, North Sidney, SAP Australia Pty Ltd.
9. Hawking, P., B. McCarthy, et al. (2004). "Second Wave ERP Education." Journal of Information Systems Education 15(3): 327–332.
10. Klaus, H., M. Rosemann, et al. (2000). "What is ERP?" IS Frontier 2(2): 141–162.
11. Mahrer, H. (1999). SAP R/3 implementation at the ETH Zurich – a higher education management success story? Americas Conference on Information Systems, August 13–15, Milwaukee, WI.
12. Mason, J. B. and D. J. Burns (1998). Retailing. Houston International Thomson Publishing.
13. Müller-Lankenau, C., S. Klein, et al. (2004). Developing a Framework for Multi Channel Strategies – An Analysis of Cases from the Grocery Retail Industry. Proceedings of the 17th Bled Electronic Commerce Conference, Bled.
14. Noguera, J. H. and E. F. Watson (1999). Effectiveness of Using Enterprise Systems to Teach Process-Centered Concepts in Business Education. AMCIS, August 13–15, Milwaukee, WI.

15. Pellerin, R. and P. Hadaya (2008). "Proposing a New Framework and an Innovative Approach to Teaching Reengineering and ERP Implementation Conceptsq." Journal of Information Systems Education 19(1): 65–74.

16. Peslak, A. R. (2005). "A Twelve-Step, Multiple Course Approach to Teaching Enterprise Resource Planning." Journal of Information Systems Education 16(2): 147–156.

17. Scheer, A-W. (1997). CIM. Computer Integrated Manufacturing. Towards the Factory of the Future. Springer, Berlin, Heidelberg, New York.

18. Scheer, A-W., F. Abolhassan, et al. (2004). Business Process Automation. ARIS in Practice. Springer, Berlin, Heidelberg, New York.

19. Stecher, P. (1993). "Retail Application Architecture." IBM Systems Journal 32(2): 289–306.

20. Sternquist, B. (2007). International Retailing. London Fairchild Books.

21. Stewart, G., M. Rosemann, et al. (2000). Collaborative ERP Curriculum Developing Using Industry Process Models. Proceedings of the 2000 Americas Conference on Information Systems.

22. Victor, F., R. May, et al. (1999). Doing the Right Thing Right: Experiences on an Interdisciplinary SAP R/3 Education Project. 3rd Annual SAP Asia Pacific Institutes of Higher Learning Forum. Maximizing the Synergy Between Teaching, Research and Business, November 1–2, Singapore, North Sidney, SAP Australia Pty Ltd.

23. Winkelmann, A. and K. Klose (2008). Experiences while selecting and implementing ERP systems in SMEs: a case study. Americas Conference on Information Systems, Toronto, Canada.

24. Zachman, J. A. (1987). "A Framework for IS Architecture." IBM Systems Journal 36(3): 277–293.

95

Statistical Analysis for Supporting Inter-Institutional Knowledge Flows in the Context of Educational System

Renate Strazdina, Julija Stecjuka, Ilze Andersone and Marite Kirikova

Abstract

Inter-institutional networks become more and more important for today's organizations. Despite mostly business-oriented organizations recognizing the possibilities that come with these networks, academic and educational systems are a typical example of inter-institutional network, and viewing these institutions as elements of a single network would yield positive results for all the parties. However, there is almost no research on the educational system as an inter-institutional network, especially in information system development education. The purpose of this chapter is to consider the education system as an inter-institutional network and to define the feedbacks existing within it in order to improve the network's overall performance. Besides this the purpose is to find the data sets required for feedbacks analysis and appropriate methods for data analysis.

Keywords Inter-institutional systems · Educational systems · Statistical methods

1. Introduction

During the last decades the importance of inter-institutional networks (inter-organizational networks) has increased in almost all organizations [1]. Many of the researchers argue that such partnerships promote mutual trust, knowledge sharing, and relationship-specific assets that enhance performance [2–5]. However, most of the existing research analyses business-oriented organizations instead of not-for-profit, especially, academic and educational institutions although it was recognized that academic and educational institutions are typical elements of the inter-institutional networks, especially in terms of knowledge sharing.

From the other side there are a lot of problems within the educational inter-institutional networks because different educational institutions use different knowledge models and it is difficult to transfer knowledge between the elements of the network. These problems are particularly pronounced in the field of information systems development education. For example, the tendency of past years shows that the first-year students of the Faculty of Computer Science and Information Technology of the Riga Technical University (the university) have different knowledge levels in the information technology (IT) field despite the fact that all secondary schools in Latvia have to apply the same education standard for computer science curriculum and there is a possibility to take a centralized test for the secondary school students that are interested in IT field. However, only the form and time of the test are predefined by the Ministry of

Renate Strazdina, Julija Stecjuka, Ilze Andersone and Marite Kirikova • Department of Systems Theory and design, Riga Technical University, 1 Kalku, Riga, LV-1658 Latvia.

G.A. Papadopoulos et al. (eds.), *Information Systems Development*, DOI 10.1007/b137171_95,
© Springer Science+Business Media, LLC 2009

Education and Science, the content of the test is defined by the school and the subsequent marking process is performed by the teacher of the same school. Thus different schools can have different approaches to the centralized test and the same result can reflect different knowledge levels of secondary school students. As a result, one group of students may be bored during the studies, while another group might not be able to deal with the content and volume of knowledge that the university can pass to the students and what the students in their first years of higher education are capable of absorbing and processing. Curriculum development and education process organization are time-consuming processes making it difficult for the university to respond to particular students' needs if these are only identified subsequent to the students having been admitted [6]. So, an approach is required to allow the university to be prepared in advance for admitting a specific contingent of students in order to provide high-quality studies to students with different knowledge levels in IT field.

The described situation in the education system shows that the inter-institutional networks and information and knowledge flows between the elements of the networks are not very effective, possibly because of the lack of regular analysis of existing knowledge available in the network.

To eliminate the above-mentioned problems it is necessary to collect information about the elements of the network and relationships between them, in this particular case information about university applicants' potential knowledge in the IT field before they come to the university. However, the volume of the information is considerable (approximately 18,000 secondary schools graduates every year) making it difficult to analyze the entire population. In order to get the results under such conditions statistical methods can be appropriate.

The described approach is developed as part of the scientific project *Development of the prototype for the support of inter-institutional flow of knowledge*. In this chapter we present the results of some of the project's sub-activities related to some statistical data usage in order to provide effective inter-institutional knowledge flows.

The chapter is structured as follows – Section 2 gives an overview of the inter-institutional model developed for the education system in Latvia and existing knowledge flows in the model, Section 3 gives an overview of the data types needed to support statistical analyze, Section 4 describes the data gathering procedure, Section 5 describes the statistical methods used to analyze and produce data for supporting inter-institutional knowledge flows, and Section 6 gives an overview of statistical data usage for supporting the inter-institutional knowledge flows in the context of the educational system. Conclusions and future research directions are defined at the end of the chapter.

2. Inter-Institutional Model for Education System in Latvia

Every inter-institutional network consists of its elements – organizations – and relationships between these elements (resource, knowledge, materials and others) [1]. In order to develop an inter-institutional network for education system in Latvia all elements and relationships between them were defined. This research analyzed computer science-related education only starting from the level of secondary school, so the defined inter-institutional system model consists of the following elements:

- At institutional level: (school level) secondary school student (1), teacher of informatics (3), management of a school (2); (the university level) student (5), lecturer (6), scientist (4).
- At municipality level: board of the schools (9).
- At national level: Ministry of Education and Science (7).

It was recognized that some important knowledge flows influencing education programs come from the industry, namely entrepreneurs working in the information technology industry. So it was decided to include industry (8) as an element of the inter-institutional system. The model of the system is presented in Fig. 95.1.

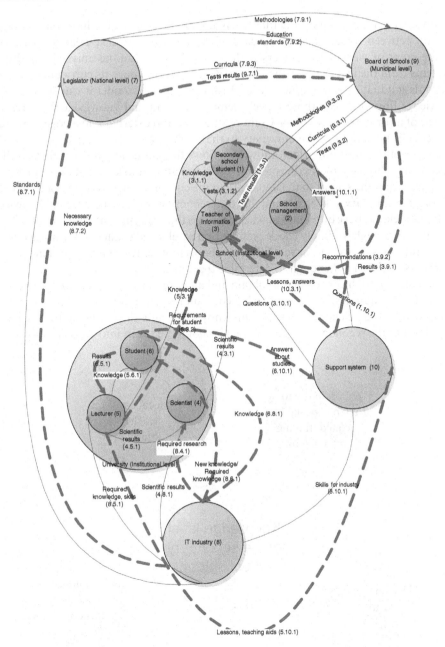

Figure 95.1. Inter-institutional model and knowledge flows (direct relationships are shown in *solid lines* where feedbacks are shown with *dotted lines*).

3. Data Type for supporting Statistical Analysis

As was mentioned before, it could be useful to collect data for analyzing inter-institutional knowledge flows to obtain more detailed knowledge about different elements of the network and to promote mutual trust, knowledge sharing, and relationship-specific assets that enhance performance. For example, data about the knowledge level of potential IT students or data about requirements from the industry would be important to improve the performance of the network.

As it can be seen from Section 2 the inter-institutional model contains many knowledge flows between the elements of the model and it would be challenging and time consuming to regularly obtain data about all existing flows, so it is necessary to define the main elements for the educational system and main knowledge flows between these elements. In case of the computer science-related education system in Latvia from the point of view of the university the main elements are the university and the secondary school. This stems from the fact that it is the University that has to adapt its curriculum depending on the secondary schools graduates' preparedness level. From the defined model it can be seen that there are different knowledge flows between those two elements – both internal knowledge flows (e.g., knowledge from the teacher of informatics to secondary school students) and external knowledge flows (e.g., requirements for students from lecturer of the university to the teacher of informatics).

However, one of the most important knowledge flows that influences the university is the knowledge level of the secondary school graduates (the possible university applicants). Nonetheless, this knowledge flow does not go directly from the school to the university in the current model so there is a need to build such a flow. In addition, it is necessary to keep in mind that different organizations use different knowledge models – in this case different schools have different knowledge models thus causing a situation in the education system where it is not always enough to simply check examination results and evaluate the knowledge level that the university applicants are supposed to have. Different schools have different teaching standards and curriculums so tests results are often not enough to determine these differences.

A possible solution to the problem is to obtain and analyze the information about knowledge level of the secondary school graduates in the context of computer science curriculum standard issued by LR Ministry of Education and Science [7]. Besides this knowledge flow the following parameters influencing the knowledge level of the secondary school graduates should be taken into consideration (Fig. 95.2):

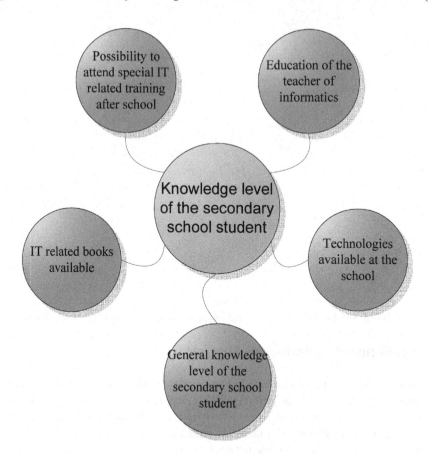

Figure 95.2. The spectrum of factors that influences university applicant knowledge level.

- education of the teacher of informatics;
- technologies available at the school;
- possibility to attend special IT-related training after school;
- IT-related books, journals, etc., available: and
- general knowledge level of the secondary school student.

The defined set of the parameters is not limited to these five parameters in the real world; however this study is at the starting phase, so it could be difficult to analyze all existing factors that can influence knowledge level of secondary schools students.

4. Data-Gathering Procedure

When the required data for inter-institutional knowledge flow analysis are defined the procedures for data gathering must be determined. There are many ways to acquire the needed data such as surveys, documents analysis, interviews, etc. [8–9,10] The main task is to select the most appropriate data gathering procedure or several procedures for each data type in order to acquire appropriate and usable information because some methods are more appropriate for different data sources (documents, people, information systems) and amounts than others. For example, for large volumes of data or respondents it is useful to use surveys, whereas for smaller groups of respondents and specific questions it is better to use interviews. In order to get the necessary information for choosing the most appropriate data-gathering method the following analysis was performed (see Table 95.1). The analysis is built on the basis of the situation at the faculty of computer science and information technology at the university.

In case where the volume of the information is considerable (where the possible units' pool is the total number of secondary school graduates) it is impracticable to analyze every single student so statistical methods for data analysis can be the most appropriate.

5. Statistical Methods Overview for Supporting Inter-Institutional Knowledge Flows

Statistical data analysis methods are used widely in research, however predominantly so in areas that are not directly related to information technologies. Nevertheless, within the context of this study, which views information systems as social systems, it was assumed that statistical data analysis methods would be a suitable tool because "statistics are powerful tools for organizing and understanding data [9]."

Within the context of this study, the possible units' pool is the total number of all secondary school graduates (approximately 18,000 graduates) part of which could potentially choose to study information technologies at the university. In addition to that, computer science teachers (approximately 400 teachers) are also agents that can exert an influence on the university's curriculum. Finally, employers also have an indirect (yet significant) influence over the university's study programs, however at the first phase analysis of employers is not included.

As none of the populations listed above are homogeneous and every individual within each group exerts a unique influence on the university, it is crucial to understand the average effect of each of the three groups.

There are two types of statistical approaches that could be used for data analysis [10]:

- Descriptive statistics – summarize, simplify, and describe a large number of measurements.
- Inferential statistics help researchers to interpret what the data mean by generalizing them.

There are many statistical methods that could be used in research: frequency distributions, graphical representation of data, measures of central tendency, measures of variability, and measures of relationship.

Although statistical methods can contribute toward meaningful research results, they are nevertheless fraught with deficiencies one should be wary of when analyzing the results. For one, looking at the

Table 95.1. Analysis of the data-gathering method.

Data group	Date source	Data amount	Data-gathering method
Knowledge level of each individual student in the context of computer science teaching standard issued	Tests results in paper format (from the secondary schools) Secondary school graduates self-assessment in paper format (the university level) Secondary school graduates assessment in paper format (the university level)	~18,000 secondary school students ~ 500 secondary school graduates (those applying for the faculty of computer science and information technology) ~ 300 secondary school graduates (those starting studies at the faculty of computer science and information technology)	Survey
Education of the teacher of informatics	Specially developed questionnaire for teachers Lectures at institutions providing curricula for teachers of informatics Documents publicly available (curricula information)	~ 400 teachers of informatics Four institutions providing curricula for teachers of informatics	Survey Interviews Document analysis
Technologies available at the school	Specially developed questionnaire for teachers Documents publicly available	~ 400 secondary schools	Survey Document analysis
Possibility to attend special IT-related training after school	Specially developed questionnaire for secondary school students	~18,000 secondary school students	Survey
IT-related books available	Specially developed questionnaire for secondary school students and for libraries Library information systems	~18,000 secondary school students	Survey Information analysis form information system
General knowledge level of the secondary school student	Documents publicly available	~1–2 general studies about knowledge level of secondary school students	Document analysis

averages only does not convey any information on the extremes, which might be very important for the university. For example, a student with inadequate level of pre-acquired knowledge might not be able to meet the requirements of his/her curriculum, while a highly pre-trained student might not find the study program challenging enough and lose the motivation to go on with the education. An analysis of averages might miss these two categories of dissatisfied students.

It is also crucial to note that any statistical result will inevitably contain errors – thus the average level of knowledge conveyed through such methods may be different from the real one. Therefore, any adjustments made to the curriculum based on results obtained through statistical analysis might still not be appropriate for students' pre-acquired knowledge level.

In addition, as the average knowledge level is measured for *all* the secondary school students – while it is a certainty that only some of them will actually choose to study computer science after graduation – this measurement may differ significantly from what would have been obtained were only the pool of those students analyzed that intend to study information systems and technologies after school. The use of averages when analyzing computer science teachers' responses may also be problematic as each such individual will have considerable influence over a significant number of secondary school students.

Negative aspects notwithstanding, the use of statistical analysis data is still beneficial as it provides the university with a clearer picture of what levels of pre-acquired knowledge its students are likely to have in the forthcoming years. This, in turn, allows for timely curriculum adjustments to reflect the expected knowledge level of newly enrolled students and to prepare additional study materials to accommodate the specific needs of either very poorly or exceedingly well-prepared undergraduates.

6. Statistical Data Application

6.1. Forecast Data About First-Year Students' Knowledge Level and Scope in IT Field

The use of forecast data about first-year students' knowledge level in the IT field allows the University lecturers to determine the knowledge level of students that will be joining the university in the next study year. The main purpose of such a forecast is to help the University's lecturers to be prepared for the particular student contingent by modifying the current curriculum and study courses in accordance with identified first-year students' knowledge base and background level.

Secondary school students knowledge level in the field of IT can be gauged by using the standard for informatics curriculum as a baseline. The second factor determining secondary school students' knowledge level is the intersection of the curriculum of the educational establishment training the informatics teacher and the standard for informatics curriculum. As a result the potential students' knowledge schema is defined (Fig. 95.3). Within the study four educational institutions of LR dealing with preparing teachers of informatics were selected. Study program of selected educational institutions is in process of analysis in context of the standard in order to get forecast of the students' knowledge schema. Therefore, four secondary school students' knowledge schemas can be created.

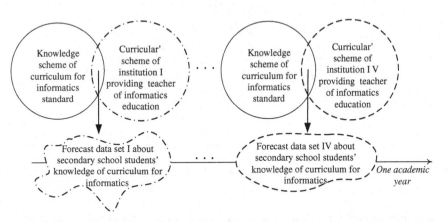

Figure 95.3. Potential students' knowledge schemas.

The above-mentioned scheme demonstrates the ideal case where the teacher has fully mastered his/her curriculum and is following the standard for informatics curriculum. Each intersection corresponds to a secondary school student instructed by a teacher graduated from one of the four educational establishments (I, II, III, or IV).

This type of forecast can be produced as long as there are no changes in the standard's knowledge scheme. Therefore, we can speak about the forecast for one study year only. This means that it is necessary to review the curriculum standards for secondary schools every year and to monitor the changes to ensure that if the standard has been changed, the knowledge scheme of the standard has to be changed as well. Moreover, the forecast data can be changed when any changes are determined in the curriculum of the institutions providing teacher education. Based on any of these changes, the intersection between the curriculum of the educational establishment training the informatics teacher and the standard for informatics curriculum will change as well.

Acquired forecast data sets are retained in the context of one study year. Accumulated historical data will allow exploring the dynamics of secondary school students' knowledge from year to year (Fig. 95.4).

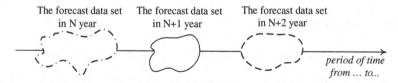

Figure 95.4. The forecast data dynamic in context of period of time.

Based on the results of acquired forecast data, the lecturer can make an intersection between the acquired knowledge set and the knowledge set required for his/her discipline. Moreover, the lecturer can compare his/her subject topics with the knowledge scheme of the standard (Fig. 95.5). This type of comparison allows observing how particular course topics are covered with forecast data. If knowledge schemes differ considerably, then the lecturer may modify particular topics of the course to achieve better conformance between the topic and students ability to comprehend the material.

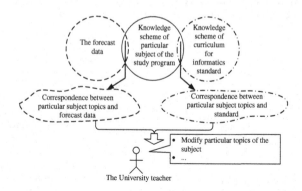

Figure 95.5. The correspondence between forecast data and knowledge scheme in the subject of the study program.

From the implementation point of view, forecast data creation and use in the context of prototype will be carried out in following way: there is the module which supports the knowledge scheme of the standard. With the help of a visualization tool, the lecturer will be able to determine the intersection between the knowledge defined by the standard and the knowledge necessary for his/her course. The result would be an image showing the forecast data. The same procedure has to be repeated for each curricular scheme of institution providing teacher education. The usage of the visualization mechanism allows building different schemes. All acquired images are organized in a layered manner where each layer is the intersection of two schemes:

- The intersection between the curriculum of the educational establishment training the informatics teacher and the standard for informatics curriculum => the shaded segments make the forecast data.

- The intersection between the scheme of the forecast data and the knowledge required for a particular course $=>$ the correspondence between forecast data and course topics.
- The intersection between the knowledge scheme of the standard and the knowledge required for a particular course $=>$ the correspondence between the standard and course topics.

The comparison of different layers is performed using the prototype that represents data as on the screen in the form of colored conceptual schemes and diagrams. However, providing a detailed prototype description is outside the scope of this chapter.

6.2. The Forecast and Real Data to Support Knowledge Flows

The approach to data analysis described in the previous section allows obtaining forecast data on students' knowledge, thus enabling the university to be pro-active in adjusting its curriculum to the specific needs of the student contingents. At the same time, the actual level of knowledge exhibited by newly enrolled students may differ significantly from the forecast. This is explained by the fact that the forecast knowledge level is determined from documents analysis, while actual students' data are obtained from surveys and processed using statistical methods.

Forecast and real data comparison allow analyzing with which knowledge level and scope the university lecturers want to see students and which knowledge level and scope students really have. Actual student data might enable the university to respond more quickly to any deviations from the forecast.

The forecast and real data analysis purpose is to provide feedbacks within the inter-institutional education system. For example, we can observe forecast knowledge in the context of real data and determine what the university can propose to approximate these data to the maximum extent. The actors of feedback are [6].

- University staff – as a result of the forecast and real data approximation, the teachers can see which curriculum parts have to modified in order to be in accordance with defined students' audience;
- Teachers of informatics at schools – they can be informed about the situation in neighboring schools thus providing benchmarking. This kind of information can be generated using the prototype special module.
- Secondary school students – they can get information about the university, its requirements, courses, and study materials to be prepared for studies at the university.
- Employers – they can review the knowledge schemes to understand what kind of knowledge the university students have.

7. Conclusions and Future Work

Research results demonstrate that the educational system does indeed operate like an inter-institutional network and that there is a number of feedbacks between the network elements. The analysis of such feedbacks can provide information that allows the university to adjust, thus providing a positive effect on the entire network. The data required for the analysis can be obtained by using typical data-gathering methods and statistical data analysis. Further research directions relate to analyzing real data sets and improving proposed approach.

Acknowledgments

The research work reflected in the chapter is supported by the Riga Technical University, Project No. ZP-2007/06.

References

1. Hatch, M. J.: Organization Theory: Modern, Symbolic, and Postmodern Perspectives. New York: Oxford University Press Inc (1997)
2. Asanuma, B.: Manufacturer-supplier relationships in Japan and the concept of relation-specific skill, Journal of the Japanese and International Economics, 3: 1–30 (1989)
3. Dyer, J. H., Nobeoka, K.: Creating and managing a high-performance knowledge-sharing network: the Toyota case, Strategic Management Journal, 21: 345–367 (2000)
4. Holmstrom, B., Roberts, J.: The boundaries of the firm revisited, Journal of Economic Perspectives, 12: 73–94 (1998)
5. Nishiguchi, T.: Strategic Industrial Sourcing: The Japanese Advantage. New York: Oxford University Press (1994)
6. Deliverables of project Nr. ZP-2007/06: Development of the prototype for the supporting of inter-institutional flow of knowledge, Riga, RTU, 2007-2008, unpublished.
7. The informatics curricula standard applied by Latvian Republic Ministry of Education, http://informatika.liis.lv/default.aspx?tabID = 1 (in Latvian)
8. Keyes, J.: Knowledge Management, Business Intelligence, and Content Management. The IT Practitioner's Guide. New York: Auerbach Publications, Taylor & Francis Group (2006)
9. Graziano, A. M., Raulin, M. L.: Research Methods: A Process of Inquiry. Needham Heights, MA: Allyn & Bacon 6 edition (2006)
10. Vogt, W. P.: Quantitative Research Methods for Professionals, Upper Saddle River, NJ: Pearson Education, Inc. (2007)

96

Using Agile Methods? – Expected Effects

Stefan Cronholm

Abstract

This chapter focuses on the movement from traditional to agile methods. What are the expected benefits of using agile methods instead of traditional ones? The chapter compares identified benefits in traditional and agile methods and takes a critical attitude in order to reveal possibilities and risks with the expressed benefits in agile methods. The chapter also tries to answer the questions of what benefits are lost and what benefits are preserved when moving to agile methods.

Keywords Agile methods · Traditional information system development methods

1. Introduction

This chapter focuses on the concept of software methods and on the movement from traditional methods to agile methods. This movement is based on a criticism of traditional methods. According to Nandhakumar and Avison [33], traditional methods are too mechanistic to be used in detail. Truex et al. [42] are more dogmatic and claim that traditional methods are merely unattainable ideals and hypothetical 'straw men' that provide normative guidance to utopian situations. Furthermore, methods that are different to grasp will remain unused [44]. Baskerville et al. [4] claim that 'to compete in the digital economy, companies must be able to develop high-quality software systems at "Internet speed"—that is, deliver new systems to customers with more value and at a faster pace than ever before.'

The common understanding of traditional methods is that they require too much of planning activities, are too sequential, and there are too much work with documentation. These experiences could be seen as anomalies that need attention. In this way, development of agile methods could be seen as cumulative, that is, agile methods are built on existing traditional methods where the 'good' parts are kept and the bad parts are omitted or replaced.

On the other hand, the enormous popularity of agile methods does not justify an uncritical review. These methods should be reviewed and criticized in the same way as other types of methods are reviewed. There are provocative statements that motivate a review such as is this popularity to that system developers do not need to care about boring documentation and instead can get an outlet for their creativity? How could scrum be seen as a panacea against delays and increased costs? [29].

The aim of this study is to identify and compare the differences between expressed effects in traditional and agile methods in order to present expected effects. The research question therefore reads: what are the expected effects of using agile methods? An effect is defined as 'a change which is a result or consequence of an action or other cause' [3]. Cambridge Dictionaries [10] provide a similar definition: 'the

---

Stefan Cronholm • Department of Management and Engineering, Linköping University, Linköping, Sweden.

G.A. Papadopoulos et al. (eds.), *Information Systems Development*, DOI 10.1007/b137171_96,

result of a particular influence.' The 'change' or the 'particular influence' is in this case the movement from traditional methods to agile methods.

The concept of traditional methods has been discussed for several decades (i.e., [11, 45, 28, 30, 2, 29]). It is hard to find one common definition of the concept of traditional methodology. According to Jayaratna [28], a methodology provides 'an explicit way of structuring one's thinking and actions.' It is also hard to find a handy definition of the concept of agile method. A broad definition is presented by Cockburn [13] who defines the process of agile development as the 'use-of-light-but-sufficient-rules.' According to Abrahamsson et al. [1], the academic research on the topic of agile methods is still scarce, most of the publications are written by consultants or practitioners.

After this introductory section, a brief description of the research method is presented in Section 2. Section 3 presents identified effects of the traditional, respectively, the agile methods. Finally, in Section 4 the conclusions are presented.

2. Research Approach

The idea is to identify and compare expected effects of using agile methods and of using traditional methods. In order to answer the research question the research has been carried out in three steps: (1) identify and analyze expected effects in traditional methods, (2) identify and analyze expected effects in agile methods, and (3) compare identified effects in order to understand what are the 'added effects,' 'lost effects,' and 'preserved effects.' Expected effects are identified in the literature by searching for statements or utterances about traditional and agile methods. The term 'expected effect' is used since the effects identified are presented in literature. If the effects would have been identified from real development projects the term perceived would have been used. The research approach can be characterized as inductive, but theoretical support is used in order to explain and define the identified effects.

The utterances from the traditional methods have been gathered from familiar and well-known method contributions such as object modeling technique (OMT), [37], structured analysis and structured design (SASD), [45], and soft systems methodology (SSM) [12]. The gathering of utterances from the agile methods has started by reading the principles behind the 'Agile Manifesto' [6]. Important contributions to the concept of agile have then been traced from the Agile Manifesto. Examples of agile methods analyzed are rational unified process (RUP), [34], extreme programming (XP), [5] scrum [38], crystal [13], and adaptive software development (ASD) [24].

Finally, the identified effects are compared by using a Venn diagram where three sets are identified: (1) Effects that only exist among the agile methods – this is an added effect! (2) Effects that only exist among traditional methods – this is lost effect! (3) The intersection between the two method types consists of effects that exist among both the method types – this is a preserved effect (see Fig. 96.1).

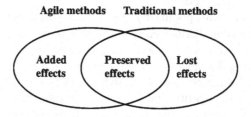

Figure 96.1. The relation between identified effects.

According to Abrahamsson et al. [1], there are no sharp borders between traditional and agile methods. Of course there can be overlapping parts, but all the chosen methods could primarily be categorized as traditional or agile. An effect could be viewed as a benefit, as a drawback, or as both. If an identified effect should be valuated as a benefit or a drawback, is out of the scope of this chapter. Such a judgment has, for example, to consider the actual context where the method will be used, the maturity of the method users, the subjective attitudes of the method users, and the managers' (and other stakeholders) perspective on the development process.

3. Findings

3.1. Expected Effects of Traditional Methods

The identified expected effects of the traditional methods are 'governing,' 'rationality,' 'structure,' 'standardization,' and 'flexibility.' The first identified effect is 'governing.' 'Govern' is defined as 'to have a controlling influence on something' [10]. Goldkuhl and Lyytinen [21] claim that strategies and methods govern peoples' actions in social practices. A method can be viewed as an instrument for action and an instrument governs the action in certain ways [19]. To govern or to steer can be viewed both as something positive and something negative. For example, when method users are confused and do not know what or how to do, there is of course a need for governing. On the other hand, 'governing' can be perceived as negative when the method users want to do something else than the method recommends. That is, when the method users have better action alternatives than the suggested ones. Too much governing can thereby lead to frustration.

The second identified effect is 'rationality.' 'Rationalism' is defined as 'the belief or principle that actions and opinions should be based on reason rather on emotions or religion' [10]. Boland and Pondy [7] claim that historically software development is characterized by rationality and the actions performed are justified on rational grounds. A software method is aiming at a rational process that does not contain any gaps. Weber [43] talks about practical rationality that consists of three types of sub rationalities: instrumental rationality means the appropriateness of the means to given ends, rationality of choice means the setting of ends in relation to values, and normative rationality means the evaluation and application of ethical principles in action. The three rationalities are put together under the label of methodical–rational conduct of life.

The third identified effect is 'structure.' 'Structure' is defined as 'the arrangement of and relations between the parts of something complex' [35]. Jayaratna [28] defines 'method' as 'an explicit way of structuring one's thinking and actions. A methodology should tell you "what" steps to take and "how" to perform those steps but most importantly the reasons "why" those steps should be taken in a particular order.' From this definition we can see that 'structure' is one important concept when discussing methods. Jayaratna [28] tells us that using methods means to act in a structured way. A method informs about what, when, how and, why something should be done.

The fourth identified effect is 'standardization.' 'Standardization' is defined as 'usual rather than special, especially when thought of as being correct or acceptable' [10]. Cronholm [15] claim that organizations adopt methods in order to achieve more standardized way of performance. One important purpose is to formalize actions in order to reduce undesired variation and to control and to anticipate actions [32]. Organizations thereby view methods as an instrument for institutionalizing and are looking for uniform ways of structure the developing process through a wider use of methods. Using methods will also lead to simplified maintenance of documentation. Using method-based and computer-supported tools will also lead to an increased standardization [15]. Examples of such tools are rational rose enterprise [26] and systems architect [36].

The fifth identified statement is 'flexibility.' 'Flexible' is defined as 'able to change or to be changed easily according to the situation' [10]. This means that the way the work will be performed should be able to change according to the nature of the assignment. Since methods per se are instruments for standardization, the room for flexibility will of course decrease. Goldkuhl et al. [20] acknowledge that there are situations when the appropriateness of methods can be challenged. Many methods are developed with the aim of making them generally applicable. However, the differences in development circumstances seem to be extensive and also growing due to the general technological and organizational evolutions. The diversity of development and change situations gives rise to a need to combine and integrate different methods [23]. Method integration means to integrate two or more methods into a new one. The aim of this process is to achieve a method that is more suitable due to the problem that should be solved.

It seems that the expected effects of the traditional methods stem from a management and organizational perspective. The character of the effects is close to concepts as control and method institutionalizing. Traditional methods contain support for 'governing,' 'standardization,' 'rationality,' and 'structure.' At the same time there must be room for 'flexibility' which could be seen as a something opposite or a contrast.

3.2. Expected Effects of Agile Methods

The identified effects of the agile methods are 'rationality,' 'team work,' 'adaptability,' 'structure,' 'less documentation,' 'late changes,' 'simplicity,' 'creativity,' and 'improvisation.' The first identified effect is 'rationality' (see also section 3.1). Rationality is discussed in terms of productivity and effectiveness [1]. An important meaning of 'rationality' is that the project should deliver software early in the process and frequently. The clients should gain value rapidly and therefore an incremental strategy is adopted. At regular intervals, the team reflects on how to become more effective, then tunes and adjusts its behavior accordingly (ibid). These findings are in line with Baskerville et al. [4] who also have experienced that need of releasing features more often.

When most people are thinking of rationality they are thinking of being rational in order to reach the goals. The goals are usually expressed as functions or demands that the IT system should possess. In the dynamic systems development method (DSDM) [17], there is goal rationality but the goals are instead expressed in terms of fixed time and fixed resources. That means that the functionality of IT system can be reduced (or increased) depending on how the process proceeds.

The second identified effect is 'team work.' 'Team work' is defined as 'when a group of people work well together' [10]. A strong encouragement is that business people and developers should work closely to each other. Face-to-face conversations are encouraged and the project should be carried out with a constant pace where there are no delays or no interruptions [1]. Furthermore, there should be self-organizing teams and developers should be trusted.

The third identified effect is 'adaptability.' 'Adapt' is defined as 'to change something to suit different conditions' and 'adaptability' is defined as 'a necessary quality in an ever-changing work environment' [10]. In the agile methods there is an imperative to be adaptive or flexible. One of the fundamental ideas in extreme programming (XP) is that there is no process that fits every project as such, but rather practices should be tailored to suit the needs of individual projects [5]. According to Grenning [22], adoptability means that not all parts of the method are used. Rather, only parts that are needed should be chosen.

The fourth identified effect is 'structure' (see also Section 3.1). Almost every agile method is divided into a sequence of different phases. For example, the methods of the Crystal family contain guidelines of policy standards, work products, 'local matters' tool, and standards and roles [13]. There is also an imperative that methodology users should iterate. ASD is one of the agile methods that do not contain much structure. One of the ideas in ASD is to provide guidance enough to prevent projects from falling into chaos. That means that the absence of structure needs to be replaced by improvisation and creativity.

The fifth identified effect is 'less documentation.' The system developers are encouraged to keep the code simple and straightforward [1]. Related to this effect is the saying that the agile method users should 'travel light.' According to Ambler [2] one of the greatest misunderstandings about agile methods is that this means that you do not have to create any documentation at all. What it means is that the documentation burden should be kept as minimal as possible (ibid). This effect is in line with the effect of 'rationality' since it supports the imperative of early deliverance.

The sixth identified effect is 'allow late changes.' McCauley [31] argues that the underlying philosophy of process-oriented traditional methods is that the requirements are completely locked in and frozen before the succeeding phases. There is a need for flexible and adaptable methods that allow developers to make late changes in specifications. Highsmith and Cockburn [25] mean that changes should be allowed throughout the whole development process. The utterance, it is better that developers are 'responding to change over following a plan' [6], is in line with the previous ones. The use of iterations and prototyping is proposed means in order to allow late changes.

The seventh identified effect is 'simplicity.' The agile method user is encouraged to invent simple solutions (ibid). The reason is that early solutions should be easy to change and that there should be less to change. Program code should be kept as simple as possible in order to support early delivery [41]. Rapid evolution and speed go hand in hand with simplicity.

The eighth identified effect is 'creativity.' 'Creativity' is defined as 'producing or using original and unusual ideas' [10]. A recommendation is that agile methods should not offer too much guidance that suppresses emergence and creativity [1]. According to Stolterman [39], (traditional) method developers should accept that everything could not be governed by rationality since you cannot predict which actions will be successful. This statement is close to the findings by Introna and Whitley [27]. They claim that there is a risk for an exaggerated belief in using methodologies and that those methodologies cannot bring light to all characteristics of the situation that need to be discovered.

The ninth identified effect is 'improvisation.' 'Improvisation' is defined as 'to invent or make something, such as speech or a device, at the time when it is needed without already having planned it' [10]. Stolterman [39] claims that it is impossible to plan for and structure all future situations that can arise in an development project. There is a risk for over structuring work processes and there must be room for improvisation and spontaneity. Too much structure reduces the action possibilities and could also lead to a reduced job satisfaction. This overall message of 'improvisation' is that it is hard (or even impossible) to structure everything in detail. Probably, it is not desirable. Improvisation can be seen as ad hoc work. That means that the development process is not based on a coordinated policy. According to Nandhakumar and Avison [33], developers' work practices have an improvisational character where team members are protective of their professional autonomy.

The analysis has revealed that agile methods are favoring effects such as adaptability, flexibility, and less management control. The utterance 'the clients should gain value rapidly' [1] brings forward the concept of client within a description of an effect. These effects could be seen as a reaction against most of the traditional methods. The followers of agile methods mean there is risk of slavishly following all recommendations in traditional methodologies. You should always ask yourself questions like what methodology parts are needed and why.

3.3. Comparison of Effects

In order to gain an overview of the findings concerning the comparison, the findings are summarized in the following list: the added effects are flexibility (adaptability) less documentation, team work, allow late changes, simplicity, creativity, and improvisation. The lost effects are governing and standardization. Finally the preserved effects are rationality and structure.

3.3.1. Added Effects

The effect of 'flexibility' is identified in both the traditional and in the agile methods. Despite this, 'flexibility' is categorized as effect of the agile methods (see discussion in Section 3.2). The occurrence of flexibility among the traditional methods could be questioned since the possibility to be flexible is quiet reduced. The corresponding effect in the agile methods is 'adaptive.' To be adaptable is one of the foremost recommendations within the agile methods.

The effect of 'less documentation' could be seen as a reaction against traditional methods. Traditional methods are more documentation intensive since there are lots of proposals for how to describe and illustrate analysis results. Those who are in favor of documentation procedures are usually claiming that documentation is not a routine-like work; it is an important analysis step. The main argument for documenting the IT system is that the documentation will support maintenance work. 'Traveling light' is an imperative within the agile methods. It means that only necessary documentation should be produced. The implicit statement is that traditional methods produces unnecessary documentation.

The effect of 'team work' is one of the most highlighted in the agile methods. Of course, it is possible to identify this effect within the traditional methods, but it is not emphasized in the same way. Another added effect is 'late changes.' Late changes are something that is allowed and accepted in the agile methods. Keeping 'things simple' is a condition for the possibility to allow late changes. The ultimate idea in the traditional methods is that late changes should not be needed. Late changes are a sign of an insufficient requirements analysis.

The effect of 'creativity' is another added effect identified. Stolterman [39] means that rationality could be viewed as a contrast to 'creativity.' Furthermore, an open attitude toward the situated nature of development processes is important [8]. These perceptions are also in line with discussions of situated actions [40]. One underlying assumption for bringing forward creativity as a key effect is that the software development process is viewed as an artistic process [18]. Stolterman [39] claims that creativity has not been studied enough and is something that still occurs in the darkened.

Finally, 'improvisation' is seen as an added effect. 'Improvisation' is perceived as an opposite to 'structure.' 'Structure' is one the foremost expected effects among the traditional methods and therefore could 'improvisation' be seen as an added effect among agile methods.. According to Abrahamsson et al. [1] 'improvisation' is one issue that agile methods are dressing explicitly.

3.3.2. Lost Effects

Both traditional and agile methods could be viewed as they are governing the method users since they consist of recommendations of what to do and how to do it. The difference is that traditional methods are governing in a more detailed way than the agile ones. As discussed in Section 3.1, governing could be viewed as something positive and as something negative.

'Standardization' is one effect that is not identified among the agile methods. One main purpose with standardization is to formalize actions on a detailed level in order to reduce undesired variation and to control and to anticipate actions. Agile methods are very much the contradictory. There is a desire for variation! There is an imperative for being adaptive and flexible, to act according to the special conditions that exist in every project, and to tailor projects to suit individual needs.

3.3.3. Preserved Effects

'Rationality' is highlighted both in traditional and agile methods. The concept is in both cases referring to the process; there is an imperative to be rationale. The main difference is that in agile methods the claim of the meaning of 'rationality' is that project should deliver software earlier and more frequent than in traditional methods. But, a too high focus on early delivery could lead to an unnecessary amount of iterations that instead will slow down the development process.

'Structure' is another concept that is common in both agile and traditional methods. Using (traditional) methods is to act in a structured way. A method informs about what, when, how, and why something should be done [28]. There is also structure in the agile methods since there usually is a division into sequential phases. However, the structure is not that detailed and the method users are not encouraged to follow the structure in the same predicted way as in the traditional methods.

4. Conclusions

It is clear that many of the added effects in agile methods could be seen as a reaction of the traditional ones (see Section 3.3.1). New demands, such as fast delivery, could be viewed as a protection against delayed software projects and increased costs. Tight couplings between the client and the development team with face-to-face meetings are another reaction that is done in order to secure quality. The added effects are examples of anomalies from the paradigm of traditional methods. The recommendation 'fast delivery' is one of the most important. There is also a risk of being 'too fast.' According to Cronholm [16], early requirement specifications are not something that always is well formulated or well defined. Requirements need to mature and develop over time and therefore the development process could not be shortened too much. It is important that the quality aspect is preserved.

The effect 'standardization' is identified as a lost effect. Instead of 'standardization,' concepts like variation, flexibility, and adaptability are highlighted. Standardization does not necessarily need to be viewed as something 'bad.' It is a well-known fact that standardization provides advantages in terms of communication between project members and less vulnerability in projects. In addition, a standardized method or process is probably more supportive for novice method user than a non-standardized one.

Another difference identified is that the individual and team aspects are more focused in agile methods. That is, there has been a movement of centralized management or organizational control toward decentralized units as teams or individuals. According to Nandhakumar and Avison [33], traditional methods are used 'as a necessary fiction to present an image of control or to provide a symbolic status.' Furthermore, they report that developers' work practices have an improvisational character where team members are protective of their professional autonomy and where social control has more influence to their practice than the suggested methodologies. This increased attention to the individual and team aspect could be seen as an opposition to institutionalized processes which are viewed as a threat against adaptability and flexibility. One claim considering the team aspect reads: 'Rationalistic and control-oriented design approaches may hamper innovative group design' [8].

On the other hand too much freedom, which is the negative side of 'professional autonomy,' could cause chaos and uncontrollable projects. One example of the agile methods is ASD [24]. ASD seems to contain very vague imperatives or recommendation for *how to do*. According to Abrahamsson et al. [1], ASD is fundamentally about 'balancing on the edge of chaos' and ASD is not providing detailed method support that could 'suppress emergence and creativity.' A general idea of a method is to provide clear recommendations of *how* to proceed. One definition of the concept of method reads 'an approach to performing systems development projects, based on a specific way of thinking, consisting of directions and rules, structured in a systematic way in development activities with corresponding development products. [9]' Based on this definition it seems doubtful if ASD could be classified as a method. Based on the effects identified, it seems like the traditional methods have a focus on the supplier (the developer) and are developed from a management and organizational perspective. The agile methods have focus both on the supplier and on the client (see Section 3.2). That means that the agile methods provide an external focus as well as an internal focus.

Methods are usually based on earlier success stories, that is, they are based on successful experiences from practice. Furthermore, methods are not static 'objects.' New insights of how to develop IT systems are continually experienced. The identified added, preserved, and lost effects are examples of a cumulative method development. Acknowledging that method development is cumulative, another way of understanding the progress of agile methods is to apply the theories about Hegel's method of logic. The theory is based on the concept of advancing contradictory arguments, of thesis and antithesis [14]. First, there existed no formal development methods (the thesis). The emergence of the traditional methods could be seen as a reaction to that no method support was available (the antithesis). Second, the anomalies/dissatisfaction with the traditional methods (the thesis) has worked as a condition/driver for constructing the agile methods (the synthesis). There has been a cumulative method development since there has been a movement from no methods, via traditional method to agile methods.

One message in this chapter is that the agile methods should also be questioned and criticized in the same way as the traditional ones. Outcomes of reviews of agile methods will provide input to the ongoing process of cumulative method development.

References

1. Abrahamsson, P., Salo, O., Ronkainen, J., and Warsta, J. (2002). Agile Software Development Methods. VTT Electronic, Espoo. http://www.vtt.fi/inf/pdf/publications/2002/P478.pdf , site accessed Jan 26. 2008.
2. Ambler, S. (2002). Agile Modeling: Effective Practices for Effective Programming. Wiley & Sons, Inc, New York.

3. AskOxford.com. (2008). http://www.askoxford.com/?view=uk. Site accessed Jan 15, 2008.
4. Baskerville, R., Levine, L., Pries-Heje, J., Ramesh, B., & Slaughter, S. (2003). Is Internet-speed software development different? IEEE Software, 20(6), 70–77.
5. Beck, K. (1999). Extreme Programming Explained: Embrace Change, Addison-Wesley, Reading, MA.
6. Beck, K., Beedle, M., van Bennekum, A., Cockburn, A., Cunningham, W., Fowler, M., Grenning, J., Highsmith, J., Hunt, A., Jeffries, R., Kern, J., Marick, B., Martin, R. C., Mellor, S., Schwaber, K. and Sutherland, J, Thomas, D. (2001). Manifesto for Agile Software Development. http://agilemanifesto.org/, Site accessed Jan 26, 2008.
7. Boland, A. J. and Pondy, L. R. (1983). Accounting in organizations: a Union of natural and rational perspectives, Accounting, Organizations and Society, 8, 223–234.
8. Bratteteig, T. and Stolterman, E. (1997). Design in groups – and all that jazz. In Kyng, M. and Mathiassen, L. (eds.), Computers and Design in Context, The MIT Press, Cambridge, MA.
9. Brinkkemper, S.,Motoshi, S. and Harmsen, F. (1998). Assembly techniques for method engineering. In Pernici, B. and Thanos, C. (eds.), Proceedings of the Tenth International Conference on Advanced Information Systems Engineering (CAiSE*98), Pisa, Italy.
10. Cambridge Dictionaries Online. (2008). http://dictionary.cambridge.org/. Site accessed Jan 15, 2008.
11. Checkland, P. (1981). Systems Thinking, Systems Practice, Wiley, Chichester, UK.
12. Checkland, P. and Scholes, J. (1999). Soft Systems Methodology in Action, Wiley & Sons, Toronto.
13. Cockburn, A. (2002). Agile Software Development, Addison-Wesley, Boston
14. Croce, B. (1985). What is Living and What is Dead of the Philosophy of Hegel, University Press of America, Lanham, MD.
15. Cronholm, S. (1995). Why CASE Tools in Information Systems Development?, In Dahlbom, B., Kämmerer, F., Ljungberg, F., Stage, J. and Sörensen, C. (eds), Proceedings of the 18th Information Systems Research in Scandinavia (IRIS 18), Gjern, Denmark.
16. Cronholm, S. and Goldkuhl, G. (2005). Communication analysis as perspective and method for requirements engineering. In Maté, J. L. and Silva, A. (eds.), Requirements Engineering for Sociotechnical Systems, Idea Group Inc., Hershey, PA.
17. DSDM Consortium. (1997). Dynamic Systems Development Method, Version 3, DSDM Consortium, Ashford.
18. Ehn, P. (1989). Work-Oriented Design of Computer Artifacts, Lawrence Erlbaum, Hillsdale, NJ.
19. Goldkuhl, G. (2005). Socio-instrumental pragmatism: a theoretical synthesis for pragmatic conceptualisation in information systems. In Proceedings of the 3rd Intl Conf on Action in Language, Organisations and Information Systems (ALOIS), University of Limerick, Limerick.
20. Goldkuhl, G., Lind, M. and Seigerroth, U. (1998). Method integration: the need for a learning perspective. IEE Proceedings Software, 145(4): 113–118.
21. Goldkuhl, G. and Lyytinen, K. (1982). A language action view of information systems. SYSLAB report no 14, SYSLAB, University of Stockholm, Stockholm, Sweden.
22. Grenning, J. (2001). Launching 'XP at a Process-Intensive Company', IEEE, 18: 3–9.
23. Harmsen, A. F. (1997). Situational Method Engineering. PhD dissertation. Moret Ernst & Young Management Consultants, Utrecht, The Netherlands.
24. Highsmith, J. A. (2000). Adaptive Software Development: A Collaborative Approach to Managing Complex Systems, Dorset House Publishing, New York.
25. Highsmith, J. and Cockburn, A. (2001). Agile Software Development – The Business of Innovation, Computer 34(9):120–122.
26. IBM Software. (2008). Rational Rose Enterprise. http://www-306.ibm.com/software/awdtools/developer/rose/ enterprise/index. html. Site accessed Jan 26, 2008.
27. Introna, L. D. and Whitley, E. A. (1997). Against method-ism. Information Technology & People, 10(1): 31–45.MCB University Press.
28. Jayaratna, N. (1994). Understanding and Evaluating Methodologies, McGraw-Hill Book Company, London.
29. Juell-Skiels, G. (2007). In Swedish: Irrläror frälser oss inte., Computer Sweden, Oct 29.
30. Kruchten, P. (1999). The Rational Unified Process: An Introduction, Addison Wesley Inc., Reading, MA.
31. McCauley, R. (2001). Agile Development Methods, Poised to Upset Status Quo, SIGCSE Bulletin 33(4): 14–15.
32. Mintzberg, H. (1983), Structure in Fives: Designing Effective Organizations, Prentice-Hall, Engle wood Cliffs, NJ.
33. Nandhakumar, J. and Avison J. (1999). The Fiction of Methodological Development – a Field Study of Information Systems Development, Information Technology & People 12(2): 175–191.
34. Object Management Group. (2008). UML Resource Page. http://www.uml.org/. Site accessed Jan 26, 2008.
35. Oxford English Dictionary. (2008). http://www.askoxford.com/. Site accessed Jan 26, 2008.
36. Popkin Software. (2008). Systems Architect. http://www.telelogic.com/campaigns/popkin/index.cfm. Site accessed Jan 26, 2008.
37. Rumbaugh, J., Blaha, M., Premerlani, W., Eddy, F. and Lorensen, W. (1991). Object-Oriented Modeling and Design, Prentice–Hall, Englewood Cliffs, NJ.
38. Schwaber, K. (1995). Scrum Development Process, OOPSLA 1995 Workshop on Business Object Design and Implementation, Springer-Verlag, Berlin.
39. Stolterman, E. (1991) The Hidden Rationale of Design Work (In Swedish: Designarbetets dolda rationalitet), PhD Thesis. Department of Information Processing, Umeå University, Sweden.
40. Suchman, L. A. (1987). Plans and Situated Actions: The Problem of Human-Machine Communication, Cambridge University Press, New York.

41. Takeuchi, H. and Nonaka, I. (1986). The new product development game, Harvard Business Review, Jan/Feb: 137–146.

42. Truex, D. P., Baskerville, R. and Travis, J. (2000), A methodical systems development: the deferred meaning of systems development methods, Accounting, Management and Information Technologies, 10(1): 53–79.

43. Weber, M. (1978). Economy and Society, University of California Press, Berkeley, CA.

44. Wiegers, K. E. (1998). Read My Lips: No New Models, IEEE Software 15(5): 10–13.

45. Yourdon, E. (1989). Modern Structured Analysis. Prentice-Hall, Englewood Cliffs, NJ.

97

Finding Categories and Keywords in Web Services

Christian Kop, Doris Gälle and Heinrich C. Mayr

Abstract

Nowadays web services are a common way to integrate functionality in an information system, but most of the time it is very difficult to find an appropriate service. If users of web service engines do not exactly know what they want, they often browse through categories and search with keywords. This, however, depends on the knowledge of the web service owner and his/her willingness to assign such keywords. This chapter gives a proposal to provide the user with candidates for keywords and categories which are derived directly from the web service specification itself.

Keywords Web services · Web service search · Web service categorization · Keywords for web services · Web service user roles

1. Introduction

Web services are an interesting domain not only for the web community but also for enterprise applications. For small companies and private users there exist many web services on several search engines and repositories (e.g., RemoteMethods http://www.remotemethods.com/, StrikeIron http://www.strikeiron.com, and WebserviceX.NET http://www.webservicex.net/). The web service retrieval is realized in different ways [2]. Some provide keyword search or ordered lists. A common way is structuring of web services through categories.

All these approaches and techniques are based on the assumption that adequate metainformation (e.g., categories and keywords) is provided for a certain web service. To our knowledge, the web services are indexed with keywords and categorized in one of the following two ways:

- Manually: The creator or the web service provider assigns keywords and categories for a web service according to his/her knowledge of the service. This approach depends on the knowledge of a person and his/her willingness to assign such keywords.
- Automatically: Based on linguistic tools and approaches (e.g., determination of the frequency of words), the necessary keywords and categories are extracted. This approach helps to relieve the user from manually assigning the service with keywords and categories. However, if documentation is not done, no automatic processing of keywords can be performed. In fact, a large amount of documentation is needed to get useful keywords and categories. Fan et al. [4] analyzed many web services. The authors found out that most of the publicly available web services only have little documentation. As an effect, this also decreases the quality of keywords that can be found with linguistic approaches.

To conclude the most important factor of web service search, categorization and retrieval strongly depend on the willingness and documentation skills of a human. Whereas the documentation skills are

Christian Kop, Doris Gälle and Heinrich C. Mayr • Institute of Applied Informatics, Alpen-Adria-Universität, Klagenfurt, Austria.

G.A. Papadopoulos et al. (eds.), *Information Systems Development*, DOI 10.1007/b137171_97,

available, a lack of willingness to document often is the reason that other people cannot find the right web service. Therefore, we propose a third approach to find keywords for web services and to categorize them:

The keywords and categories are directly derived from the tags of a Web service specification.

This has the advantage that the creator only must concentrate on writing the web service specification. Little attention can be paid on additional documentation or manual categorization. Of course this approach also has a basic assumption–namely, that good and meaningful names for tags are used. Nevertheless, such an approach is promising since a meaningful name for tags is a minimal requirement that can be achieved in most cases. Examining examples for web services we found good and meaningful names.

The chapter is structured as follows: in the next section related work to this topic is presented. In Section 3 existing web service languages, in particular OWL-S, are briefly introduced. In the following section we will argue why web service specifications offer more opportunities for our approach than ordinary documents. Section 5 presents and describes a list of possible categories and keywords that can be derived automatically from OWL-S and WSDL documents, and in the following section we discuss the appropriateness of this data for specific user types. In the last section we will give a summary and an outlook of how this kind of categorization extraction can be optimized in practice.

2. Related Work

There is a lot of research activity in the domains of automated and collaborative categorization of documents, but there is less work to find about categorization of web services. Reading the literature in this domain, we mainly found

- literature for classifying web services,
- articles where categorization and assignment of keywords are done manually combined with clustering to relate a web service within a taxonomy, and
- articles which propose categorization from the additional documentation a web service might have.

In the field of service-oriented architectures (SOA), different ways for classifying services exist. Josuttis [7] defined three categories that are based on different SOA layers: (1) basic services in fundamental SOAs, (2) composed services in federated SOAs, and (3) process services in process-enabled SOAs. This classification shows a good overview about the different categories regarding the SOA stages of extension but we think this feature is not useful for most types of users that want to order their web services.

Josuttis presents also other approaches to classify services. A determination criterion is, e.g., the internal or external users of the service and public enterprise services. In practice also the difference between national and international services is used to group the services. Sometimes it can be reasonable to distinguish between reading and writing services. There exist also different categorizations of business services where, e.g., Allen [1] distinguishes between commodity services, territory services, and value-added services.

Since we concentrate our approach mainly on public available web services, we think that the different classification approaches in literature are not practicable for the requirements of the intended users of this kind of services.

Another approach is the community-based web service site WSFinder.com (http://wsfinder.jot.com). Registered users manually assign services to categories. They even have the possibility to add new categories, change and delete existing categories.

The benefits of Wikis, with Wikipedia on the top, are a matter of common knowledge. The use of a Wiki in this context is ambivalent because beside the benefits there exist also problems. An important challenge is the motivation of the users. They must spend their time and knowledge for adding and categorizing new web services. Every registered user can change the site so it is possible that a user cannot find the added web service because another changed the category or even deleted it. Wikipedia, for example, has some functionalities to avoid such problems (e.g., not everyone can delete an entry and an undo functionality), but these functionalities do not solve the problems completely.

To avoid these inconsistencies during manual assignment of categories, Wu et al. [12, 13] propose the use of personal hierarchies for document repositories which are then merged to a so-called "consensus hierarchy." The users are more motivated to concentrate on a hierarchy that cannot be changed from all other users.

In order to provide automatic extraction of categories and keywords, Fan et al. [4] took a snapshot of public available web services. They present their result in a hierarchy of all found services. For this purpose they used descriptions from the registries and documentation tags from the WSDL (web service description language) files. The services get clustered with the hierarchical agglomerative cluster algorithm to get a browsable service hierarchy. The results were not really encouraging because the descriptions often were very short (over 80% of the text descriptions have less then 50 words). Three years later a look at available web services does not show a better documentation situation so we think that a clustering that only base upon words from the textual descriptions cannot be useful. Hence, in addition to these approaches we propose to extract hints for categories and keywords from the different tags within a web service description itself.

3. Existing Web Service Languages

Actually there are three important web service languages available, namely WSDL, OWL-S, and WSML. WSDL is a quite common standard in practices but it focuses on syntactic features of a web service interaction and more on its technical aspects. Therefore, the W3C has developed the language OWL-S. OWL-S (web ontology language for services) [8] is an ontology for describing semantic and syntactic web service information. It builds on the web ontology language and therefore provides a machine readable and interpretable structure.

OWL-S supports the idea of automatic discovery, invocation, composition, and interoperability of web services. OWL-S descriptions consist of three main parts: profile, model, and grounding. The different parts allow a user to concentrate the search of information on specific questions. The service profile should answer the question "What does the service provide for prospective clients?" This part is used to get an overview about the service and its functionality. The service model documents present more details about the functionality of the service. So it answers the subject "How is it used?" The third component is the service grounding that answers the question "How does one interact with it?" and therefore provides syntactic information. This part also covers WSDL specifications.

Besides the OWL-S standard there exist also other description languages. For the description of syntactic information in practice, the web service definition language (WSDL) [3] is used very often. This standard is integrated in the grounding part of OWL-S. The European counterpart of OWL-S working group is the web service modeling ontology (WSMO) initiative [9]. They focus also on the description of semantic web service information. There exist mapping concepts from the web service modeling language (WSML) to OWL [10].

Since OWL-S is a standard that covers WSDL in its service grounding section and describes more than syntactic aspects of services interaction, we will mainly concentrate on OWL-S.

4. Ordinary Documents Versus Web Service Specifications

Although web services can be seen as documents, the previous section showed that they are special documents, with special features. These features can help to find categories and keywords. Table 97.1 shows some differences between usual documents and web services.

4.1. Structure

The structure of documents depends on the specific system. Generally they do not have any restrictions on the structure and contain natural language. For the publication of a web service standardized document structures, mostly based on XML, are used. Some of the tags also contain natural language, but since it is embedded in tags you can find the needed information easily. Web service documents show among other things machine interpretable data. This knowledge can be used to extract information more accurately.

Table 97.1. Differences between documents and web services.

Distinguishing feature	Document	Web service
Structure	Differs – mostly natural language – no machine interpretable data	Standardized structure in (de facto) standard, e.g., OWL-S documents represent machine interpretable semantic information
Domain	Different domains for different purposes	At least one additional default domain (namely software engineering)
Users	Depends on domain and purpose	Different types of (IT) experts who want to find and use a web service

Ordinary documents normally have no requirements on the structure and so the data are in general neither machine readable nor machine interpretable.

4.2. Domain

Like other documents, web services can belong to several different domains (medicine, bank, etc.). However, a web service in addition also belongs to the domain of "software engineering." This can be seen as a good basis for the next distinguishing feature (the users). The potential users/readers of web services can be reduced to a small set of user roles. Knowing the group of users can help to propose the right category and keyword to the right group of users.

4.3. Users

To support users of web service registries it is important to know who they are and what goals they pursue. In general document repositories it is difficult ascertaining the different user roles. In the domain of web services and software engineering, it is possible to reduce the diverse users on a manageable number of roles.

In [6] possible user groups who have dissimilar requirements on web service documentation were presented. Thus, they are also interested in different parts of the documentation. The human users were distinguished between managers, domain experts, requirements engineers, software engineers, and web service architects.

The different interests can be used to propose different keywords and categories from the web service documentation. A web service architect develops services and so he/she will potentially be interested to categorize in technical details. The software engineers integrate services in their applications so they also focus on technical parameters and use these features to organize their services. Although also requirements engineers are IT experts, their interests will not go too deep into the technical details but rather into the functional parts. So the arrangement in functional groups will be a useful strategy for their selected web services. The experts of a domain mainly concentrate on words of the given domain of the services and also use this as an ordering feature. Managers in their role as decision makers probably are more interested in economic features and also in coarse domain information to arrange their subset of web services.

5. Categories and Keywords Derived from Web Services

As has been mentioned above, one problem of categorization is that it has to be done manually by the user. This is difficult if the user is not the creator of the web service. Therefore, providing him/her with any proposals about the intended purpose and domain of the web service would be very helpful. Even if the service has been already categorized by its creator, it is possible that the intended categorization system of the user does not match with the categories of the creator.

Since web service specifications are semi-structured, it might be obvious to derive such categories from the document structure itself. In this chapter we will explain what can be derived. Therefore, we have studied the examples *CongoBuy*, *BravoAir*, *Amazon* (see e.g., http://www.daml.org/services/owl-s/examples.html, http://www.ai.sri.com/daml/services/owl-s/1.1/examples.html, respectively).

5.1. Useful Tag Information Derived from OWL-S Documents

Within the profile, process, and grounding sections of these examples we looked for categorization candidates which could be interested for users. We found out that there are a lot of them. We therefore picked out the most interested ones which we list is Table 97.2.

Table 97.2. OWL-S tag candidates for categorizations.

Keyword /category candidates	OWL-S section	Derived from pattern	Extracted examples
Service name	Profile	<profile:serviceName> **BravoAir_ReservationAgent** </profile:serviceName>	*BravoAir_ReservationAgent*
Service category	Profile	<profile:serviceCategory>... <profile:value **Airline reservation services** </profile:value> </profile:serviceCategory>	*Airline reservation service*; *Travel Agent*
Service process name	Model	<process:CompositeProcess rdf:ID = **"BookFlight"**>	*BravoAir_Process, BookFlight*
Input parameter	Profile, model	<profile:hasInput rdf:resource = "... #**"DepartureAirport"**> <process:hasInput> <process:Input rdf:ID = **"DepartureAirport"**> ... </process:Input> </process:hasInput>	*DepartureAirport, OutboundDate, PreferredFlightItinary_In*
Output parameter	Profile, model	<profile:hasOutput ...> <process:hasOutput ...>	*AcctName_Out ReservationID*
Name of contact person/ institution	Profile	<profile:contactInformation><actor:name>**BravoAir Reservation department** </actor:name> </profile: contactInformation>	*BravoAir Reservation department*
Role of contact person	Profile	<profile:contactInformation> <actor:title>**Sale Representative** </actor:title></profile:contactInformation>	*Sale Representative*
Participant	Model	<process:hasParticipant>	*Client*
Datatype of parameters	Model	e.g. <owl:Class rdf:ID = **"CreditCardType"**>	*CreditCardType*
Process type	Model	<process:CompositeProcess>	*Atomic, Simple, Composite*
Port information	Grounding	<http:binding verb = **"POST"** /> <**soap**:binding transport = " ..."> <http:binding verb = **"GET"** />	*soap, POST, GET*
Quality criteria	Profile	<profile:rating rdf :resource = "&concepts#**GoodRating**"> within <profile:qualityRating>	*GoodRating*
Additional textual information	Profile, model	text description within<profile:textDescription> or<rdf:comment>	
Profile hierarchy	Profile, profile hierachy	<profileHierarchy: **AirlineTicketing**> Classes, Object Properties, subClassOf Specifications in the Profile hierarchy File	*AirlineTicketing Ecommerce, CommercialAirlineTravel, Product*

As can be seen from the examples in Table 97.2, a system that provides the users with categories and keywords from the OWL specification itself has to deal with two main challenges: the information is extracted from a specific OWL-S tag directly or from the values of certain tags or tag parameters. Examples for the first class are *CompositeProcess, soap: http, and profileHierachy:AirlineTicketing*. Examples for the latter are *Airline Reservation Agent, BravoAir_ReservationAgent, and CreditCardType*. Furthermore, it can happen that the extracted candidate for the category has a natural language style (e.g., *Airline Reservation Agent*) or it is artificial (e.g., *CreditCardType*). If it has a natural language style, nothing is left to do. However, if it is artificial, we propose to use the evaluation and verbalization strategy introduced in [5].

Finally, the importance of the examples has to be decided. We therefore propose two kinds of metainformation which were already mentioned (categories and keywords):

- (Domain) categories: help to rank the service within a service taxonomy.
- Keywords: help to index the service according to further "dimensions."

We will briefly now go through the categorization candidates, describe them and relate them to one of the metainformation items. The candidates *Service name* and *Service category* and *Process name* describe the service itself and the context of the service. Thus these values can be classified as categories.

We propose that *input parameter, output parameter, name of contact person/institution, role of contact person, participant, process type, port information, quality criteria, and data type* belong to keywords since they do not specify the semantics of the service itself but dimensions of features to which the descriptions of the service can be refined. The port information can be taken from WSDL description(s) referenced in the grounding.

We also propose to use textual description which can be found in tags like "textDescription," "comment" to get further categorization concepts. Linguistic tools like taggers (e.g., QTAG [11]) must be used to categorize the words appropriately and filter out stop words (e.g., *service, web, string*) Afterward verbs and nouns can be used as candidates for categorization (see also: [4]).

The optional *profile hierarchy* (e.g., "AirlineTicketing" in<profileHierarchy:AirlineTicketing> of Table 97.2) refers to *addition profile hierarchy information* in another document. It was introduced by the W3C consortium in order to relate and position a web service in a broader context of web services (see http://www.daml.org/services/owl-s/1.1/ProfileHierarchy.html). Without any further information "AirlineTicketing" in <profileHierarchy> can already be used as a candidate for a category since it provides a more general notion for the service. Stepping into the profile hierarchy document itself gives more *additional information* that can be used to find further categories and keywords. The profile hierarchies used in the BravoAir as well as in the CongoBuy examples describe top ontologies and taxonomies for commercial domains. Figure 97.1 shows an excerpt.

In this excerpt of the ontology *AirlineTicketing* is a sub class of E-commerce. Once again such a sub class specification can be used to extract the next broader context of the service, namely E-commerce. Furthermore, within the top ontology relationships to other classes can be specified. The object property

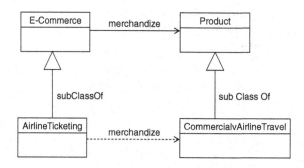

Figure 97.1. Part of the ontology of the profile hierarchy.

specifies a relationship that an E-commerce (service) merchandizes products. Within the sub class airline ticketing, this relationship is bounded to the special product CommercialAirlineTravel. Hence the advantage of looking inside such a profile hierarchy is twofold. The super classes of a given service (e.g., AirlineTicketing and E-commerce) provide a taxonomy of categories. On the other hand, the related classes (*CommercialAirlineTravel, Product*) provide candidates for keywords.

5.2. Information Derived from WSDL Specifications

OWL-S actually covers the WSDL specification in its service grounding section and offers much more information of web service aspects. However, WSDL 1.1 [3] is widely used actually. We think also the recent version 2.0 will get common in practice but we concentrated our research in this case on the more popular version 1.1. Thus it is also important to know if we can get at least some of the information when we have only WSDL specifications. Looking inside the WSDL 1.1 definition, we could identify some tags which could be candidates for keywords and categories. Particularly, the following candidates from Table 97.2 can be also derived from WSDL tags: *Service name, Service Process name, Parameters (Input/Output), Port information, Datatype of parameters, Additional textual information.* The **Service name** (e.g., "*BravoAirReservation_Agent*") can be derived from the tag parameter *name* within the WSDL tag <service> (e.g., <service name = "*BravoAirReservation_Agent*">). The **Service process name** (e.g., "*BravoAir_Process*") can be extracted from <operation name = "*BravoAir_Process*">. The **parameters** (e.g., "*DepartureAirport*") can be found in <part name = "*DepartureAirport*"> within the tag <message>. However, an explicit distinction between input and output parameters is not supported. **Port information** is extracted from the same patterns which were mentioned in Table 97.2. At least simple **data types** (e.g., string, integer) can be extracted. Finally, information within the tag <documentation> can be used to find further keywords and categories.

6. Categories, Keywords, and Types of Users

The web service profile, model, and grounding focus on a certain kind of intention a reader/user might have. Depending on the placement of a certain category in the profile, model, or grounding sections, specific categories should be offered to specific kinds of users. Therefore, the types of user roles will be discussed first. Afterward the appropriateness of each of the categories, listed and motivated in Section 5.1, will be described for these types of users.

A **WS Architect** develops web services, checks how it works, and customizes them. He/she focuses more on the technical details. Hence categories derived from the grounding and model will help him/her a lot.

The **SW Engineer** integrates web services in the existing software of an enterprise. He/she will be more interested in the profile information than the WS architect but only on information related to the functionality. He/she will (must) be certainly interested in the model itself and how the web service works.

Requirements Engineers mainly focus on the question "what a system should provide." Together with the domain expert, he/she must also know if the service fits. He/she might be interested to trace back to the persons listed in the contact information in order to get more background information. He/she must also know something on "how it works," since the change from "what" to "how" is somewhat blurred. Therefore, he/she might be interested in the service profile and the service model but only a little bit in the service grounding.

Domain experts and managers are the typical end users with a minimal or no technical knowledge. There is no doubt that they focus mainly on information from the profile.

The category candidates *Service name, Service category, Profile hierarchy*, additional profile hierarchy information, and *Service process* describe the web service or part of it. Thus they implicitly tell something about the purpose and the semantics of a web service. This information is important for all kinds of users. User specific categories appear in those candidates who belong to the keywords.

Input parameter, output parameter, and *data type* information refine the categorization of a web service. Knowing the input and output parameters as well as their data types is mainly important for the requirements engineer, the software engineer, and the web service architect. On the contrary, the next two candidates for categorization (*role of contact person, contact person*) are mainly interesting for managers and domain experts. Here, we assume that the role of the contact person can tell something about the specific context in which the web service is used. If, e.g., a web service has a contact person whose role is "sales representative," this could be a hint that this service "supports" sales representatives. Of course in that context the role of a person can have another meaning. The contact person "sales representative" can also be named just to inform who has to be contacted if someone wants to use/buy this service. Therefore, it is necessary that the role of the contact person is only provided as candidate for categorization if

(1) it fits to the meaning "service supports this specific kind of user." This can be assured if other terms also refer into this direction.
(2) the person who has to categorize gets the information that the role of contact person can only be used for the context given in (1).

The contact information itself could be only a hint if an enterprise instead of a person is named. Such information might be interested for a manager who wants to know which enterprise is related to this service. Most often users conclude about the quality of a software from the enterprise/provider who has constructed it (e.g., a web service from enterprise X is much more trustworthy than a similar web service from enterprise Y).

The candidates *process type* and *port information* are typical examples for more technical-oriented persons (software engineer and web service architect).

The quality criterion is a subjective measure to categorize a web service according to its value. It says nothing about the meaning, purpose, or context of the web service. However, together with other categories, it can be a decision support particularly for managers but also for other types of users.

No good examples were given for the moment for *participant*. In the examples examined, the most general notions "TheClient" and "TheServer" were used. Nevertheless according to the OWL-S specification [8], participant seems to be a promising keyword candidate if more meaningful names are used. Also for the additional textual information, it is hard to decide which role profits the most. This strongly depends on the content of the additional textual documentation and where it is located within a web service specification (i.e., at the beginning as an overview description or somewhere in the middle of the specification, in the profile, process, or grounding section).

7. Conclusion and Future Work

Today the search for web services is based on keywords and categories that are assigned manually or extracted automatically from a textual documentation. This implies that someone is willing to either document the web service or to create such metainformation like categories and keywords. Since web services are semi-structured documents, a third approach was presented in this chapter. Web service elements (tags, tag parameters, values of tags, and tag parameters) were used as candidates for categories and keywords. Hence the appearance of a Web service does not strongly depend on its good documentation. Instead, a good specification is a good basis for keywords and categories.

As a next step we will combine our category and keyword extraction with social classification. As described in [13] each user can generate his/her personal categorization hierarchy. Hints for categorization will be extracted from the web service specification and offered to the user. Afterward these personal hierarchies are merged to a so-called consensus hierarchy. Applying our role-specific category and keyword extraction approach to these consensus hierarchies should result in role-specific consensus hierarchies

References

1. Allan, P. (2006) Service Orientation: Winning Strategies and Best Practices. Cambridge University Press, Cambridge.
2. Bachlechner, D., Siorpaes, K., Fensel, D., Toma, I. (2006) Web Service Discovery – Reality Check. Technical Report, DERI – Digital Enterprise Research Institute, January 17.
3. Christensen, E., Curbera, F., Meredith, G., Weerawarana, S. (2001) Web Services Description Language (WSDL) 1.1., March 2001, http://www.w3.org/TR/wsdl.
4. Fan, J., Kambhampati, S. (2005) A snapshot of public web services. *SIGMOD Record*, 34(1): 24–32.
5. Fliedl, G., Kop, C., Vöhringer, J. (2007) From OWL class and property labels to human understandable natural language, NLDB, pp. 156–167.
6. Gälle, D. Kop, C., Mayr, H. C. (2008) A uniform web service description representation for different readers, ICDS, pp. 123–128.
7. Josuttis, N. (2007) SOA in Practice. The Art of Distributed System Design. O'Reilly, Sebastopol, CA
8. Martin, D. et al. (2004): Semantic Markup for Web Services W3C Member Submission 22 November 2004, http://www.w3.org/Submission/2004/SUBM-OWL-S-20041122/
9. Roman, D., Keller, U., Lausen, H. de Bruijn, J., Lara, R., Stollberg, M., Polleres, A., Feier, C., Bussler, Ch., Fensel, D. (2005) Web Service Modeling Ontology, *Applied Ontology*, 1(1): 77–106.
10. Steinmetz, N., de Bruijn, J., (2008) WSML/OWL Mapping – WSML Working Draft, January 2008, http://www.wsmo.org/TR/d37/v0.1/20080125/d37v0.1_20080125.pdf
11. Tufis, D., Mason, O. (1998) Tagging Romanian texts: a case study for QTAG, a language independent probabilistic tagger. In Proceedings of the First International Conference on Language Resources & Evaluation (LREC), 589–596.
12. Wu, H., Gordon, M. D., DeMaagd, K. (2004) Document co-organization in an online knowledge community. In CHI '04 Extended Abstracts on Human Factors in Computing Systems (Vienna, Austria, April 24–29, 2004). CHI '04. ACM Press, New York, NY, pp. 1211–1214.
13. Wu, H., Gordon, M. (2007) Collaborative structuring: organizing document repositories effectively and efficiently. *Communications of the ACM*, 50(7), July: 86–91.

98

MEDNET: Telemedicine via Satellite Combining Improved Access to Health-Care Services with Enhanced Social Cohesion in Rural Peru

Dimitrios Panopoulos, Ilias Sachpazidis, Despoina Rizou, Wayne Menary, Jose Cardenas and John Psarras

Abstract

Peru, officially classified as a middle-income country, has benefited from sustained economic growth in recent years. However, the benefits have not been seen by the vast majority of the population, particularly Peru's rural population. Virtually all of the nation's rural health-care centres are cut off from the rest of the country, so access to care for most people is not only difficult but also costly. MEDNET attempts to redress this issue by developing a medical health network with the help of the collaboration medical application based on TeleConsult & @HOME medical database for vital signs. The expected benefits include improved support for medics in the field, reduction of patient referrals, reduction in number of emergency interventions and improved times for medical diagnosis. An important caveat is the emphasis on exploiting the proposed infrastructure for education and social enterprise initiatives. The project has the full support of regional political and health authorities and, importantly, full local community support.

Keywords Telemedicine · TeleConsult · Rural health care · Medical care network

1. Introduction: Clinical and Technical Requirements

Peru is officially classified as a middle-income country. Strong economic growth over nine consecutive years (9% in 2007; 10% in Jan 2008 alone), low inflation and a budget surplus coupled with the growth in reserves have resulted in Fitch Ratings raising Peru's foreign currency debt rating to the investment grade level of BBB in April 2008 [1]. However, despite surging economic growth, large sections of the population remain marginalized with distinct inequalities between those living in urban and rural areas.

The aim of the project MEDNET is to develop a medical health network in Peru targeting these very locations which have been virtually abandoned by the state.

The sites chosen for inclusion in MEDNET are Chongos Alto, Comas, Pariahuanca, Puerto Ocopa, Mazamari, Rio Negro, S.M. de Pangoa (Fig. 98.1).

Dimitrios Panopoulos • Decision Support Systems Laboratory, National Technical University of Athens, Athens, Greece **Ilias Sachpazidis** • Department Cognitive Computing and Medical Imaging, Fraunhofer IGD, Darmstadt, Germany **Despoina Rizou** • Department Cognitive Computing and Medical Imaging, Fraunhofer IGD, Darmstadt, Germany **Wayne Menary** • GeoPac, Coventry, UK **Jose Cardenas** • Department of Informatics, DIRESA Junin, Peru **John Psarras** • Decision Support Systems Laboratory, National Technical University of Athens, Athens, Greece

G.A. Papadopoulos et al. (eds.), *Information Systems Development*, DOI 10.1007/b137171_98,
© Springer Science+Business Media, LLC 2009

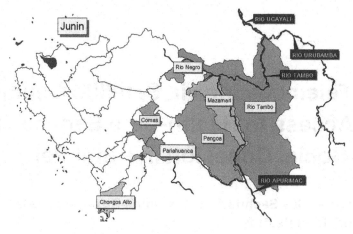

Figure 98.1. Map outline of the sites selected in Junín, Peru, for inclusion in MEDNET.

1.1. Medical Situation

Currently, patients travel long distances just to arrive at the rural health centres chosen for inclusion in MEDNET. Unfortunately, there is a dearth of medical equipment at these health facilities. If the physician is uncertain and decides to refer the patient for further consultation and/or examination, only approximately 5% of patients can afford to attend. Large sections of the community in these regions are effectively disenfranchised from the health service as a result of long distances, high costs associated with travel and lodging, cultural obstacles and endemic poverty. The isolated nature of these sites also impact upon the medical staff with medics feeling isolated and vulnerable with no access to expert second opinion, severe lack of health resources and poor communication between health outposts and the regional health authority – DIRESA Junín.

1.2. Doctors Needs

After studying for the career of medicine in Peru, medical students have to complete a period of time practising medicine in a rural environment (SERUM – abbreviation of medical student undertaking Rural Medical Service). Competition for these posts is very high since, without this experience, a medic is unable to apply for employment at any public hospital in Peru. In addition each rural health care centre has a named medic who is responsible for the site. DIRESA Junín can therefore ensure appropriate cover for the health outposts. However, the SERUM working at any particular site often find themselves working alone and unable to seek a second opinion. This was witnessed first hand in Puerto Ocopa where the medical director was absent and the SERUM was working alone. The danger is that if the SERUM makes a mistake that is not corrected, this particular practise could become embedded throughout their medical career. *The overriding need is therefore to facilitate continual professional development.*

At many of the sites, the medics expressed the fact that many patients were transferred to Huancayo needlessly because of the decision to *err on the side of caution.* This implies a cost which is unacceptable to many patients: both economic and cultural. Patients simply do not have the money to pay travel and lodging costs associated with transfers from the health centres to the main hospitals in Huancayo. Costs average around s/.200 (46) for these transfers and considering daily wages are approximately s/.10 (2.3) per day, many patients find themselves effectively disenfranchised from the national health service (M. Gonzales, 2008, *The average salary is considerably less in satipo*, personal communication).

Additionally, many people, particularly in the jungle region of Rio Negro, Pangoa, Mazamari and Rio Tambo, are native peoples and do not want to travel to the urban regions for cultural reasons. *The overriding need for the medic here is to be able to provide basic medical diagnosis avoiding the need for urgent patient transfers (e.g. provision of pre-natal U/S controls) and receive expert second opinions.*

The lack of reliable and fast communications in all of the MEDNET establishments in Peru has a direct impact on administrative efficiency. Inefficient communications directly impact upon the resources available to the medics at each site. For example, at Puerto Ocopa, DIRESA Junín had no idea that the health centre was unable to access a fund to purchase fuel which is available to support rural outposts with access to vehicles and/or boats. DIRESA Junín also has no way to directly contact these health outposts and vice versa. This can result in delays in receiving basic provisions (syringes, etc.) as well as a failure to accurately record and update vital health statistics. *The overriding need here is to improve communications between rural isolated outposts and other health centres and the main health authority (DIRESA Junín).*

1.3. Health-Care Infrastructure Needs

The main health-care requirement at each establishment is basic diagnostic equipment. Where sites do have microscopes or ultrasound (U/S) machines (microscopes available at Chongos Alto, Puerto Ocopa, Mazamari and S.M. de Pangoa: U/S available at S.M. de Pangoa) they are either not currently functioning (e.g. the U/S at S.M. de Pangoa and the microscopes at Puerto Ocopa) or are not DICOM compatible.

Unstable electrical supplies jeopardize the refrigeration of patient samples and basic reagents whilst many of the sites do not have earthing and/or lightning systems. With high frequency of thunder and lightning activity it will be a basic requirement to implement earthing systems in order to provide appropriate protection to equipment.

None of the sites have access to any kind of Internet access. Where Internet access is available in the local community, it is extremely slow.

Mazamari, Pangoa and Rio Negro are the only sites with a fixed telephone landline. Chongos Alto, Puerto Ocopa, Pariahuanca and Comas can be contacted through a satellite community telephone. Mobile phone coverage is sporadic but CLARO (part of the telecom group América Móvil) provides better coverage, on average, to most of the MEDNET sites in Peru compared to MOVISTAR (owned by Telefónica Móviles).

Radio plays a major part in communications in the more isolated sites, particularly in the jungle region of Satipo.

2. Architecture and Major Components of the System

The network participant will communicate with the help of the collaboration medical application based on TeleConsult & @HOME medical database for vital signs, which has been developed by Fraunhofer IGD and MedCom GmbH, with partial financing of the European Commission.

2.1. TeleConsult

TeleConsult is a stand-alone application running on Windows 2000/XP. The application is able to acquire medical images from any ultrasound device through a video grabber attached to the computer [2]. Furthermore, DICOM-based agents would store medical images from any DICOM-compliant device (DICOM is a worldwide standard for the representation of medical imaging data). TeleConsult application is a combination of a 2D/3D DICOM Viewer, an image grabbing software, medical annotation tools and a medical telecommunication tool [3]. Fig. 98.2 illustrates the user interface of TeleConsult.

The largest part of the user interface is used for the display of the images. On the left side of the software all images, currently loaded into TeleConsult, are listed [4]. In the centre of the user interface, there is place for showing the details of one or more images. All operations, a user of the software can operate, can be assigned to the following eight modules:

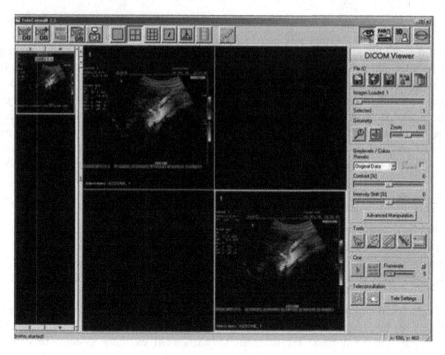

Figure 98.2. TeleConsult user interface.

- The Database Interface menu
- The Image View menu
- The File I/O menu
- The Geometry menu
- The Greylevels/Colors menu
- The Tools menu
- The Cine menu
- The Teleconsultation menu

TeleConsult is currently used in several European locations and provides an excellent, proven communication tool for telemedicine systems. The system also provides easy localization options for Spanish and Portuguese.

2.2. Medical Database/Health-Care Records

There are alternative ways to manage clinical information using paper cards and charts, but for clinical trials, monitoring and analysis of population data and telemedicine, computerization of some sort is generally required. A key challenge is to create sustainable systems that are able to be used widely and can support several of the above tasks, rather than using multiple "stove pipe" applications.

Problem issues with ICTs and Electronic Medical Records:

- Data collection and entry (including data completeness and quality)
- Data standards (common data models and open standards)
- Difficulties in reuse of technology and avoiding re-invention of systems
- Tensions between standard approaches and local requirements
- Safety, security and confidentiality of medical data
- Language and cultural differences
- Short-term quick solutions that do not scale up, especially spreadsheets

Our medical imaging application offers a patient management database with the following possible operations:

- Creation, modification and deletion of patients
- Creation, modification and deletion of studies
- Storing of images, configurations, videos and other (additional) files assigned to a patient and study
- Swapping out data (images) to other storage medias, whereby the purpose is to prohibit the local hard disk of getting full
- Export and import of patients/studies and images to external files, whereby the purpose is the exchange of data between several databases
- Loading of images, configurations and videos into TeleConsult
- Importing of DICOM images into the database
- Sending and receiving of messages, together with patient, study and image information from and to other TeleConsult workstations (offline messaging)
- Importing/exporting of vital signals (ECG, BP, SPO2, Glucose) into the database

The database is based on *open*EHR; the definition of the "electronic health record" corresponds to the "Integrated Care EHR" as defined in ISO/DTR 20514: The Integrated Care EHR is defined as a repository of information regarding the health of a subject of care in computer processable form, stored and transmitted securely and accessible by multiple authorized users. It has a commonly agreed logical information model which is independent of EHR systems. Its primary purpose is the support of continuing, efficient and quality integrated health care and it contains information which is retrospective, concurrent and prospective [5].

The EHR has the following characteristics:

- Patient-centred: one EHR relates to one subject of care, not to an episode of care at an institution.
- Longitudinal: it is a long-term record of care, possibly birth to death.
- Comprehensive: it includes a record of care events from all types of carers and provider institutions tending to a patient, not just one speciality; in other words there are no important care events of any kind not in the HER.
- Prospective: not only are previous events recorded, so is decisional and prospective information such as plans, goals, orders and evaluations.

2.3. Satellite Communication/AmerHis

The selected regions in Amazon have no access to broadband communications. Therefore, AmerHis system is going to be utilized. AmerHis makes use of DVB-RCS bi-direction European standard. Thales Alenia Space España is leading the AMERHIS project within the Hispasat Amazonas satellite. AmerHis is an advanced communication system, supported and co-funded by ESA and the industry to deploy an advanced communications system based on a regenerative payload on board the *Amazonas* satellite [6].

The AMERHIS system integrates a broadcasting multimedia network with an interaction network by combining two standards, the DVB-S and DVB-RCS, into one unique regenerative and multi-spot satellite system. In this manner, the users calling for broadband and interactive services will be able to utilize standard stations (RCSTs) at both transmitting and receiving sides. Next figure illustrates the concept.

In this system, the DVB-RCS return channel standard is applied by all users to access through a standard uplink to the satellite. On board, the regenerative payload (OBP) is in charge of multiplexing that information from diverse sources into one or more DVB-S data streams capable of being received by any standard IRD equipment. The onboard repeater is capable of not only multiplexing signals coming from the same uplink but also cross-connecting and/or broadcasting channels coming from separate uplink coverage areas to different downlink coverage areas.

3. Community Engagement

Through the convocation of medical staff and local community representatives, we managed to obtain a good impression of the needs of not only the health-care establishment but also the wider community.

The recurring themes from the seven sites chosen were the need for (1) basic medical diagnostic equipment (such as u/s: there were no [functioning] ultrasounds or working microscopes at any of the rural health centres); (2) improved communications – for the wider local community and also for essential medical information; (3) expert second opinion; (4) improved institutional efficiency; (5) capacity building programmes and (6) stable electrical supply.

At each site in Peru chosen for inclusion in MEDNET, the local municipality has offered their full support. The actual support provided will depend on the clinical and technical requirements of each site, and also to a certain degree, the funds available at each municipality – though even municipalities with limited funds offered assistance "in-kind". *The question of stable electricity supply will therefore be resolved by the municipalities.*

The additional services the project consortium members plan to provide at each site in an attempt to exploit the MEDNET infrastructure (e.g. Internet, VoIP) are also of particular interest to each municipality and the services could easily be divided between municipality and health-care centre, particularly in Chongos Alto, Mazamari, Rio Negro, Comas and S.M. de Pangoa due to the proximity of both.

In order to assess user needs for the sites chosen in Peru, a clinical requirements audit was undertaken at each site. Additionally, at each site, the local mayor, or their deputy, along with representatives of the local community together and the medical staff responsible for the site were invited to attend a meeting in which an outline of the MEDNET project was presented. Sustainability is a primary objective of MEDNET and involvement of the local community is crucial if sustainability is to be achieved. In total, roundtable meetings were held with in excess of 56 top-level stakeholder representatives from the seven sites and the two referral hospitals in Huancayo.

4. Expected Impacts

Regional workshops involving both public and private institutions delivering health services identified the most urgent health needs as viewed by the population. Based upon these locally perceived priority health concerns, together with statistics and epidemiological results from DIRESA Junín, the following were characterized as priority regional health problems:

- Basic hygiene
- High prevalence of infant malnutrition
- Female health problems: teenage pregnancy; maternal mortality
- High incidence of infectious/contagious diseases
- Family violence

Many of these priority health concerns are highly communicable and can be addressed both clinically and through the design of public health programmes in MEDNET.

Additionally, the Conditional Cash Transfer programme "Juntos" is an antipoverty initiative launched by the Peruvian government in 2005. Eligibility depends on several factors, e.g. a family must have children under the age of 14 and live in a community where at least two basic needs – running water, electricity, schools, health services – are unmet. Families receiving the cash in Peru must enrol their children in schools and ensure that they are vaccinated. Pregnant mothers must take part in pre-natal care programmes and post-natal controls. In addition, the adults must have national identification cards and make sure that their children have birth certificates.

This pilot project proposal in Peru aims to identify opportunities and synergies for co-operation and integration with current health sector reforms and the "Juntos" programme, particularly

- Helping the health services and education operators become involved in a more effective way
- Facilitating capacity building programmes aimed at improving service quality
- Providing a platform that can be exploited to deliver improved standards in education and promote social enterprise in order to alleviate poverty

General benefits accruing from the application of MEDNET in Peru are improved quality of health service to approximately 102,000 located in the pilot project locations; a reduction in the level of inequitable access to medical services; provides scientific and technological assistance to professional health workers – e.g. continuing professional development; facilitates an integrated level of patient attention; optimizes administrative process embedding efficiency within the health system; augments health awareness amongst the general population.

5. Conclusions – Future Work

Health service coverage in rural and isolated communities in Latin America is extremely low. Although the states deliver services, the level of medical attention is characterized by limited infrastructure and resources, in both equipment and professional personnel. With this lack of infrastructure it is difficult to effectively confront the health problems faced by the population. Also, the population of these regions suffer from extreme poverty. The poorest fail to access the health service – for economic reasons. The costs involved, transport and lodging, coupled with cultural barriers, deter approximately 95% of patients from undertaking this referral – patients in rural Peru are therefore essentially disenfranchised from the nation's health-care service. Finally, geographical barrier is another mitigating factor resulting in social exclusion. Often patients have to walk and travel in boat many hours just to reach these health-care outposts only to find that they are referred to more urban centres due to a lack of medical equipment and/or the need of attending medics for expert second opinion.

Today, ICTs permit greater access to health information and thereby allow patients, potential patients and families to learn more about health problems, care options, and prevention strategies. However, for those without computers or even telephones, as is the case for the regions being targeted, access to these information resources is more a promise than a reality. Community clinics may be able to provide some with access to information resources, but funding for such services and for the clinics themselves is vulnerable to retrenchment in public services and budgets. Deficits in literacy and language skills may create further difficulties for disadvantaged populations. The gap in access may actually widen if information services improve only for the more affluent and educated.

MEDNET will develop a medical network that addresses the problems of delivering health care to rural and isolated communities in Latin America. The medical network will be supported by expert physicians located at referral hospitals within urban centres, where the majority of health-care resources are often located. The medical applications will vary from gynaecology, paediatrics, cardiology to typical infectious diseases for the region such as malaria and tuberculosis.

The telemedicine network will enable patients to access ultrasound examination, ECG test, blood test and blood test imaging for automation diagnosis locally, reducing the need to travel long distances.

The project will empower medical doctors to constantly and remotely keep track of their patients with minimum effort, assisted by an intelligent automated infrastructure. A sophisticated Collaboration Model will manage the whole service and will be aware of each patient's medical record, providing an information channel between the medical staff, the patients and their carers (family, friends, etc.).

Electronic health records of each patient, extracted from the examinations, will be stored in a health-care database. Patient's demographic information along with haematological and imaging examinations, ultrasound examinations, electrocardiogram and dermatological images will be stored into the database along with the prescribed medication.

According to predefined limits, the system will be able to alert patients and physicians about increases in risk of patients' condition based on medical data stored into the medical database. Moreover, physicians will be able to share information and request medical advice from expert physicians, thus facilitating rapid and informed patient treatment in these isolated areas, e.g. in Amazonia.

The locations selected for inclusion in MEDNET will be connected over satellite communication based on DVB-RCS protocol via the European AmerHis system which can provide concurrently up to 4/8 Mbits in the upload and download links, respectively. In addition, the medical platform is based on the results of previous European Union-funded telemedicine projects – TeleInViVo, T@LEMED, @HOME project (IST-2000-26083).

The clinical impact and added value of MEDNET will be the following:

- To enable the efficient and cost-effective use of high-level and high-quality medical resources available in large cities for improvement of health services for residents in remote and rural underserved regions
- To help reduce morbidity and mortality in underserved regions by providing a means for early detection and treatment of contagious diseases, such as malaria and tuberculoses, by the use of telematics and e-health technologies
- To improve primary health-care through the use of telematic ultrasound systems transferring expert's "know-how" in large cities to more remote areas
- To contribute to the advancement of medical research, diagnosis and treatment methods, through the efficient collection and sharing of data on treatment outcomes and patient demographics

MEDNET will also offer the possibility to compare two different access technologies (transparent and regenerative satellites) in order to assess the benefits of the mesh connectivity offered by AmerHis and to compare the cost of operation of both alternatives.

Acknowledgement

This project is partially funded under the 7th Framework Programme by the European Commission.

References

1. The Associated Press (2008) *Fitch raises Peru's rating to investment grade,* Retrieved April 03, 2008 from: http://www.iht.com/articles/ap/2008/04/03/business/LA-FIN-Peru-Debt-Rating.php
2. Kontaxakis, G., Walter, S. and Sakas, G. (2000) *EU-TeleInViVo: an integrated portable telemedicine workstation featuring acquisition, processing and transmission over low-bandwidth lines of 3D ultrasound volume images,* Information Technology Applications in Biomedicine: Proceedings of IEEE EMBS International Conference, pp. 158–163
3. TeleInVivo (2008) Retrieved April 03, 2008 from: http://www.igd.fhg.de/teleInViVo
4. Sachpazidis, I. and Hohlfeld, O. (2005) *Instant messaging communication gateway for medical applications,* IASTED International Conference on Telehealth, 19–21 July 2005, Banff, Canada
5. OpenEHR (2008) *OpenEHR future-proof and flexible,* Retrieved April 5, 2008 from: http://www.openehr.org/home.html
6. Alcatel Alenia Space Espana (2006) *AlcatelAmerHis system,* Retrieved January 5, 2008 from: http://www.alcatel.es/espacio/pdf/amerhis.pdf

99

Why Can't We Bet on ISD Outcomes: ISD "Form" as a Predictor of Success

Mike Newman, Shan L. Pan and Gary Pan

Abstract

The record of failure to deliver large-scale information systems (IS) in a timely fashion that offer value to major commercial and public organizations is legendary. Just looking to critical success factors such as top management support and user involvement in order to understand how to deliver better systems can at best be a partial solution. We seem to overlook an obvious area in our organizations: what can we learn from our information system development (ISD) historical patterns? In order to develop this idea we draw on parallels in sport where current performance and behaviour are believed to be closely linked to historical precedents, or "form". In that domain, historical patterns are a fallible but valuable predictor of success. Our thesis is that past negative patterns in ISD will tend to repeat themselves without radical intervention. Put another way, failure begets failure. After examining the game of football as an allegory for ISD, we look briefly at two organizations that have experienced a pattern of failure in the IS area in the past but have transformed the way they build IS, moving from negative patterns to successful ones. This chapter ends with suggestions for managers charged with developing new IS as to how they might use their understanding of ISD "form" to improve their chances of success.

Keywords Information systems development · Success and failure · Historical patterns · Form · Case studies

1. Introduction

> 'Those who cannot remember the past are condemned to repeat it'.
> George Santayana

If you browse some of the multitude of gambling web sites, you will find a plethora of opportunities to bet on sporting outcomes as well as other non-sporting activities (e.g. political outcomes). What you will not find is odds offered on the outcome of major information systems (IS) projects such as the NHS' Connecting for Health or specific components of it such as the "Choose and Book" system. Yet there are many parallels between sporting outcomes and the outcomes of major IS projects. It is strongly believed that a history of success/failure ("form") is a strong predictor of sporting outcomes. Our thesis is that understanding ISD "form" can help IS developers to understand and, predict success and failure and, where necessary, to punctuate the process with more radical strategies.

Much is made in the popular press as well as academic writing of the enigma of building IS that offer value to commercial as well as public organizations. But the spectre of failure haunts organizations as they pile resources on top of resources but produce a failing process of IS development (ISD) akin to a monetary

Mike Newman • Manchester Business School, The University of Manchester, Manchester, UK; Copenhagen Business School, Copenhagen, Denmark. **Shan L. Pan** • Department of Information Systems, National University of Singapore, Singapore. **Gary Pan** • Singapore Management University, Singapore.

G.A. Papadopoulos et al. (eds.), *Information Systems Development*, DOI 10.1007/b137171_99,
© Springer Science+Business Media, LLC 2009

black hole, escalating for years until someone "pulls the plug" [2, 6, 12, 16]. Along with a plethora of IS failures is a multitude of solutions offered. We often look to critical success factors such as top management support and user involvement in order to understand how to deliver better systems but this is clearly subject to the critique of partiality. In looking at critical success factors and concentrating on the present we seem to be ignoring a source of evidence that has much to teach us: an organization's ISD history. If we want to avoid repeating the past failures then organizations must make a realistic assessment of their history and attempt to transcend them if they discover weaknesses. Simple tinkering with the success factors will probably not work (unless you are very lucky). Organizations would do better if they learn from the past in order not to repeat their mistakes [3, 5, 12] and avoid the trap of "learning to fail" [8].

Some simple examples from sport may help to illuminate the point. In competitive sport, pundits try to assess the chances of a team or an individual win by looking to recent patterns of success and/or failure. In horse racing, a horse (and jockey) is assessed for its form. Form is a view of the horse's performance over the last few races: its recent history. The parallels with ISD are obvious: a horse's form becomes the organization's ISD history; the current conditions and the ability of the jockey can be compared with the critical success factors in the ISD process. Interestingly, in the betting industry form is probably more important than all other factors in forming odds. The major difference with ISD is the time horizon: ISD projects last months or years rather than a few minutes. Nonetheless, past patterns are believed to have a strong relationship to current behavior. Without radical change, past negative patterns of ISD tend to be reproduced in current developments [8].

In this chapter, we begin by using football as an allegory for ISD [14]. We deepen our analysis by looking at how two large organizations have experienced a pattern of failure in the ISD in the past but have transformed the way they build IS, moving from negative patterns to successful ones [11, 18]. The chapter ends with suggestions for managers charged with developing new IS as to how they might use ISD form to improve their chances of success.

1.1. Football as an Allegory for ISD

"Allegory: a work in which the characters and events are to be understood as representing other things and symbolically expressing a deeper, often spiritual, moral, or political meaning" (*Encarta UK Dictionary*). In our chapter the allegory is a game of football which is used to represent the way we develop and adopt information systems in organizations. Figure 99.1 represents a picture of a field of play in football with the goals at either end.

Why do we use football as our allegory? Football is a world-wide game and consequently the basic rules and parameters are widely known. But it is also a complex game involving many stakeholders (owners, managers, players, reserves, coaches, scouts, referees, regulatory bodies, media etc). In ISD there are also many stakeholders with competing demands. In football, no matter how strong the side is there is always a risk of losing a particular match. Failure is common in ISD projects even in previously successful project teams. The 90 minute game time in football consists of 11 players per side so it is essentially a team game employing players with different specialisms (goalkeeper, defenders, midfield and attackers). IS project teams also have many specialists: from those who interface with users to back-room technical personnel to telecommunication experts. Also the context(s) of the game is complex. Much can depend on the physical conditions of the pitch, the weather, the referee, and in a wider sense the changing regulations agreed by the football governing bodies (e.g. recent changes to the so-called offside rule; the discussion over the use of goal-line technology). Context in ISD can provide many unexpected perturbations (entry and exit of key persons; new technology emerging, budget crises, etc.). Each football team has "form" or a history of wins, losses and draws and individual players who are constrained or prevented to play by injuries and the totting up process of yellow (a caution) and red (sending off) cards awarded in previous matches for foul or even dangerous play. These injuries and cards can have a significance beyond the current game, of course. Organizations also have "form" when it comes to their history of successful and failed projects [13]. In a general sense, we carry our histories into the future, constraining some events and enabling others.

While there are obvious parallels with ISD, and we shall be elaborating on these parallels later, there are limitations to this allegory. First is the time dimension: a football game is 90 minutes of continuous action whereas an ISD project can take months or years to complete. Second, in a football game we would normally be watching the game live or mediated through the media. In research we normally interview third-party witnesses for their accounts of events. By careful interpretations of their accounts and with additional evidence from documents and observations we build up a story of the IS project [10]. A football game has three possible outcomes for a club: win, loss or draw. In ISD we talk of success, failure or something less well defined but, in contrast to football where outcome is never in doubt, ISD outcomes are often ambiguous and relative.[1] Finally, a football game is essentially competitive and can be conflictual. While we acknowledge this, others have drawn parallels with the "battles" and conflicts that can occur between designers and users in ISD and sometimes even referring to ISD as a "game" [4]. In summary, every allegory has limitations and the author and readers alike should not try to read too much into the story that is told. Used carefully, however, an allegory can reveal deeper insights into the phenomena we are studying, namely ISD.

1.2. Historical Context – "Form" or Antecedent Conditions

In summary, in addition to the critical events, a process model [17] looks at the history or form of the game (Fig. 99.1). In the case of a football game this might include among other issues a side's recent form (wins, losses, draws), injuries to players, the number of games played, cards (yellows and reds) and the entry or exit of players or manager from the club. These issues are believed to be strongly associated with the current game and the side's chance of winning. Indeed, some pundits talk of teams having slumps and winning or losing streaks.[2] We know that the record of failure to deliver large-scale IS in a timely fashion that offer value to major commercial and public organizations is legendary. Our thesis is that past negative patterns (i.e. negative form) in ISD will tend to repeat themselves [13]. In other words, organizations, just

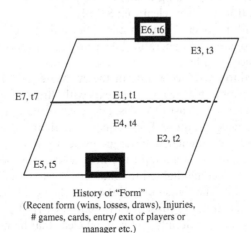

History or "Form"
(Recent form (wins, losses, draws), Injuries,
games, cards, entry/ exit of players or
manager etc.)

Figure 99.1. A Football Allegory: History or "Form"[3]

---

[1] Owing to space considerations, we will not be addressing the complex question as to what constitutes success and failure in ISD in this chapter. Where the matter is not obvious, we will adopt a stakeholder view which may involve multiple and conflicting opinions on the subject.

[2] In the case of football there is often a large amount of money wagered world-wide on a particular game with separate odds for a home win, away win or a draw. Spread betting is a more sophisticated version of this with real-time odds offered on possible events during the game (e.g. next goal scorer).

[3] Figure 99.1 also shows the major, critical events En at time tn. In a previous paper we developed a model that attempted to explain ISD outcomes in terms of history, context and outcomes [14].

like football clubs, can experience slumps in ISD performance, producing and reproducing failure after failure until the organization is mired in a culture of failure [9, 8].

In looking back and learning from our historical ISD form, we can look ahead to more favourable outcomes in the IS we build. Successful processes can then be institutionalized so as to create new, positive histories to build upon [13]. When football clubs appear to be developing losing streaks, the owners often move quickly to change the manager (and consequently the playing system) and/or to bring in new players. In ISD projects the timescale often precludes such speedy reactions even though radical solutions may be required to break the cycle of failure (new project managers and other staff, new IT partners, new methodologies, etc.) [18].

The next few pages illustrate the ideas we have discussed above. We show two major organizations that developed patterns (a "culture") of failure and show how they turned this around by "shocking" the status quo.[4]

2. Case 1: Telecoms Corp

Telecoms Corp (or just Telecoms) is a subsidiary of a US-based conglomerate, herein called Gen-Comm. They employ about 14,000 people in several geographically dispersed locations in North America. Telecoms' annual revenue was about $1.6 billion, on which it earned $118 million in profits. The Supply Division was responsible for centralized purchasing, inventory control, warehousing and distribution from two large central warehouses. Telecoms operated within an industry that was undergoing de-regulation. The pressures to contain costs confirmed the need for more sophisticated IS management, especially in the materials management area. Historically, materials and inventory management at Telecoms suffered from gross inefficiencies and waste. Previously, no attempt to build IS to control inventory costs had been successful. IS at Telecoms had traditionally been developed for Supply by the head office group, Management Information Services (MIS). Responding to ad hoc requests, MIS had built several isolated systems spread over three hardware platforms. It was clear that Supply had a "mish-mash" of eight or nine systems that had been implemented with no overall plan in mind. Several of these systems were quite large and represented high costs of development and operation. At Telecoms there were deep misgivings concerning the ability of MIS to deliver successful IS.

Telecoms Corp attempted to introduce a state-of-the-art Materials Management System (MMS) in their Supply Division. This attempt lasted well over 10 years with three repeated cycles of failure creating a negative history and low expectations ("cast of thousands, cost of millions, delivering nothing"). But at Telecoms there was a high tolerance of failure. For example, the financial penalties of failure were not so great because of the company's semi-regulated state: greater costs were compensated for by higher call charges. Staff had secure jobs and many were in posts whose tenure was measured in decades rather than years. However, growing competition highlighted the financial waste in the Supply area and the ongoing failure of MMS was focussed upon. The transition point came when the long-standing vice president (VP) of Supply was asked to step aside and was subsequently retired early. The new VP removed several key people including the project manager at Supply and made it clear that he was not going to work with the senior managers who had served under the old VP. He had learned of the trouble with MMS and wanted to establish control over the project immediately. Besides the removal of several key project staff, the new VP also terminated the contract with the existing software partner by paying a negotiated percentage for the modules delivered and paying the remaining portion of the software license fee upon acceptance. Under pressure, the software contractor agreed on terms of severance of the contract, getting most of their contracted money out of the deal but losing the lucrative, 5-year maintenance contract. A new project manager was introduced and he formed an alliance with MIS who together successfully re-justified the project and delivered the MMS successfully within time and budget.

---

[4] For details of the interpretive research methods employed, please refer to the original papers [18, 11].

3. Case 2: US Insurance Corporation

The US Insurance Corporation is a large insurance corporation with assets of many billions of dollars. The corporation offers a full range of insurance products both personal and commercial through a nation-wide branch network of 22 offices and several sub-offices. The case focuses on the introduction of new state-of-the-art claims system called Claims Automation Information System or CAIS. Up to the time of introducing CAIS, computer support for the major insurance functions (underwriting and claims) was non-existent. Competitors were developing sophisticated IS, thereby reducing the cost of claims and improving customer service. The history of ISD at US Insurance could be characterized by a large gulf between the branch personnel – traditionally the users and the main data suppliers, and the head office function – the originator of most IS. Needless-to-say, the resulting IS at US Insurance enjoyed a poor acceptance rate among users either because the quality was unacceptable or because they had become irrelevant after the months or often years required to build them: the reputation of the IS group at Headquarters (HQ) was poor. For the proposed CAIS, the radical, user-centred approach to project management adopted was both an acknowledgement of past problems and an attempt to create a discontinuity with the old way of developing ISD projects. The project was predicted to save $10m costs per year for an investment of $16m.

The project proceeded for a year when it became apparent that the user project leader was unable to continue for various reasons. The project group quickly intervened to solve this problem successfully by replacing the user with a key IS person and one of the visionaries on the project. The project was able to proceed rapidly after this intervention but it did not prevent a major problem on the near horizon: the summer pilot tests at two branches produced crucial technical problems. The Management Information Services (MIS) group reasserted its leadership and provided internal programmers to re-write the system "from the screens back-wards". The team was successful and these interventions established the viability of the project system. After this the project enjoyed a period of stability for the next 18 months as the software was developed. Following this a new pilot was re-commissioned at a test branch using the new software. Although 300 errors were detected in the system these flaws were removed incrementally over the next few months until CAIS was ready to be rolled out to the branch network and implemented thereafter at the rate of one installation per month. This challenge was overcome successfully and the system stabilized. As a result the project was completed. After this success the project team then moved on to further development work (i.e. underwriting) using the new methodology, now *institutionalized*, which was codified and labelled Business Systems Engineering.

4. Lessons and Practical Implications

Telecoms Corp exhibited three cycles of failure to deliver an MM system in the Supply Division each exhibiting similar patterns leading to failure. Only after a radical re-organization of the project team and a rapprochement between the project team and the central MIS group was it possible to create the conditions leading to success. There were similarities in the case of US Insurance. The history of developing IS by the HQ was very poor as judged by the users in Claims. Previous IS were judged to be either irrelevant or of poor quality if indeed they were completed at all and as a consequence user expectations for the CAIS project were very low. The new claims system represented a radical break from history in the structure of the project (user-led as opposed to MIS-led); technology (e.g. state-of-the-art IS technology); and people (user support staff). Returning to the original statement, "Those who cannot remember the past are condemned to repeat it" we can begin to see some lessons for IS practitioners and their managers. Ignorance of the past is often accompanied by a strong attachment to old ways of developing systems (old technologies, old methods, old structures) rather like ancients clinging to their idols. If these old ways worked before, well and good, but if they failed before repeatedly, why should they work now? Our thesis is that failing patterns in ISD tend to be reproduced unless discontinuities are introduced [9]. And this has been confirmed in the two cases we have presented.

The cases teach us that we need a realistic and critical assessment of past patterns (ISD form) and if there is a history of failure of ISD outcomes we need to design new and often radical approaches to developing systems.

One promising part of the assessment is to examine the socio-technical (ST) factors in building the system: task, technology, actors and structure [7]. [5] For example, in the case of Telecoms Corp, in response to a crisis unrelated to the project, senior management changed the actors, the technology of ISD and the structure: the project manager was removed and replaced by a senior person with a new approach (actors); the failing development approach was replaced by getting MIS into the process to build the IS (technology); the software partner was bought out and MIS was grafted in as a partner (structure). The task of building a MMS remained the same throughout. Similarly, at US Insurance we saw a new and radical approach to building and delivering a sophisticated claims system in order to avoid the expected failures as evidenced from the past. Again there were changes to traditional ST elements such as actors, the technology of ISD and structure: there were to be new IS staff and one of the visionaries on the project became the project leader (actors); the use of state-of-the-art systems to build systems such as the use of a model office (technology); MIS group leading the project (structure). Interestingly, as with Telecoms Corp, the task (delivering a new claims system) remained a constant need throughout. If we put these elements together and develop an ISD form it suggests a new, radical approach to IS planning, risk assessment and budgeting. This amounts to a procedure that organizations might consider conducting before embarking on major systems projects: a pre-methodology audit. The steps illustrated in Table 99.1 demonstrate how this might be done in practice.

Table 99.1. A summary of the steps involved in developing an ISD form

---

Identifying and Institutionalizing ISD form

The current project manager (PM) or champion needs to assess the recent history of delivering major IS in your organization or division (using up to, say, 5 years of history):

Step 1: Identify Building Approaches

Specifically, the PM should examine the building approaches that were previously used in terms of socio-technical elements and ask some critical questions of IS staff and users (a questionnaire could also be used as a supplement), namely

Actors (e.g. Were the right people in charge of the project? In both cases described above, key people had to be replaced or retired. They were seen as part of the problem and associated with failing patterns).

Technology (e.g. Was the technology workable or too complicated? Was there a package solution available and was it used? Was the development methodology appropriate?).

Structure (e.g. Were all major stakeholders involved and did they buy in to the project?).

Task (e.g. What problems were we solving and were they relevant and important and did they remain so?).

Were there any significant interactions between the above socio-technical elements?

Assess IS that were completed, delivered and accepted by users and those that were not.

Have any major commitments been made in the recent past (technology platforms, software packages, e.g. ERP systems)? These may constrain your current degrees of freedom to make changes.

Step 2: Identify Project Development Patterns

Look for patterns in previous projects and decide where the weaknesses are in those socio-technical elements detailed above.

These patterns and weaknesses constitute your assessment of ISD form in your division or organization (say, on a 5-point scale from excellent to very poor). If there are major failings in the ISD form (e.g. rated as poor or very poor), propose radical changes for your current project that are seen as a discontinuity with the past and get the buy-in for these. You could use the same social-technical factors for this stage (e.g. new methodologies; new leadership; new technologies). For example, in our two cases we would rate their ISD form as very poor. A further refinement would be to assess form for each socio-technical element.

Step 3: Institutionalize the Assessment of ISD Form

Develop a project proposal and business plan that reflect this new, radical approach and present it to senior management.

As appropriate, employ staff and co-opt users who are motivated and sympathetic to the new approach.

Be flexible. ISD is a process and radical changes and large IS take time to build and will produce unplanned side-effects which may affect your ability to deliver the project as specified. You may have to make adjustments and learn from what works and from what does not.

If you cannot get the level of support you need for the new approach, consider a smaller project or abandoning the project altogether.

If the new approach works, consider codifying it and persuading senior management to use it on future projects.

---

[5] We have begun this process and have applied our socio-technical process model to detailed case evidence from a variety of countries and contexts [1, 15].

Individually and collectively in organizations, we carry our histories into the future with us but as we have tried to show is that does not mean we cannot overcome the weaknesses of our past ISD efforts. Our thesis has been that historically failing approaches to ISD, without any radical changes, will tend to be reproduced in current practices. This has been borne out by the two case examples we have presented. It was only when radical steps were taken to change the way they built systems that they could break the cycle of failure and curtail the escalation of resources [8]. A negative ISD form will give you a guide to show you what **not** to do or what you **cannot** do, but the project team still has to manage the current process and overcome the many vicissitudes on the path to delivering a successful IS just as was experienced in the cases presented. A football club may have good form but you still have to win your current game. In looking back and learning from our historical ISD form, we can look ahead to more favourable outcomes in the IS we build. Successful processes can then be institutionalized so as to create new, positive histories to build upon. We may not be able to bet on successful IS outcomes but we can improve our chances of delivering systems that offer value and benefits to stakeholders.

References

1. Bob-Jones, B. Newman, M., and Lyytinen, K. (2008) Picking up the pieces after a "successful" implementation: networks, coalitions and ERP systems, Forthcoming in the Proceedings of AMCIS 2008, Toronto, Canada.
2. Drummond, H. (1996) Escalation in Decision-Making: The Tragedy of Taurus. Oxford University Press, Oxford, U.K.
3. Ewusi-Mensah, K. (1997) Critical issues in abandoned information systems development projects. Communications of the ACM 40 (9), 74–80.
4. Hirschheim, R., and Newman, M. (1991), Information systems development as symbolism: myth, metaphor, and magic. Information Systems Research, 2 (1), 29–62.
5. Iacovou, C., and Dexter, A. (2005) Surviving IT project cancellations. Communications of the ACM 48 (4), 83–86.
6. Keil, M. (1995) Pulling the plug: software project management and the problem of project escalation. MIS Quarterly 19 (4), 421–447.
7. Leavitt, H. (1964) Applied organization change in industry: structural, technical, and human approaches. In New Perspectives in Organizational Research. Chichester: Wiley, 55–71.
8. Lyytinen, K., and Robey, D. (1999) Learning failure in information systems development. Information Systems Journal 9 (2), 85–101.
9. Lyytinen, K., and Newman, M. (2005) Information systems development as punctuated socio-technical change, Working Paper, The University of Manchester.
10. Myers, M., and Newman, M. (2007) The qualitative interview in IS research: examining the craft. Information and Organization, 17 (1), 2–26.
11. Newman, M., and Robey, D., (1992) A social process model of user-analyst relationships, MIS Quarterly, June, pp. 249–266.
12. Newman, M., and Sabherwal, R. (1996) Determinants of commitment to information system development: a longitudinal investigation. MIS Quarterly 20 (1), 23–54.
13. Newman, M., Pan, S., and Pan, G. (2006) Can information systems development "form" teach us anything?, Working paper, The University of Manchester.
14. Newman, M. (2007). Context, Process and outcomes of ISD: an allegorical tale. Proceedings of the Americas Conference on Information Systems, Keystone, Colorado, August 10–12.
15. Newman, M., and Zhao, Y. (2008) The process of ERP implementation and BPR: a tale from two Chinese SMEs. Information Systems Journal. Published electronically April 15.
16. Pan, S., Pan, G., Newman, M., and Flynn, D. (2006) Escalation and de-escalation of commitment to information systems projects: insights from a project evaluation model. European Journal of Operational Research 173 (3), 1139–1160.
17. Pentland, B. T. (1999) Building process theory with narrative: from description to explanation. Academy of Management Review, 24 (4), 711–724.
18. Robey, D., and Newman, M. (1996) Sequential patterns in information systems development: an application of a social process model. ACM Transactions of Information Systems, 14, January, 30–63.

Index

G.A. Papadopoulos et al. (eds.), *Information Systems Development*, DOI 10.1007/b137171,
© Springer Science+Business Media, LLC 2009

Printed in the United States
By Bookmasters